THE YEAR'S WORK IN
MODERN LANGUAGE
STUDIES

THE
YEAR'S WORK IN
MODERN LANGUAGE
STUDIES

GENERAL EDITOR
PETER J. MAYO

SECTION EDITORS

LATIN, ROMANCE LINGUISTICS, FRENCH, OCCITAN
BRIAN J. LEVY, M.A., PH.D.
Reader in French,
University of Hull

SPANISH, CATALAN, PORTUGUESE, GALICIAN, LATIN AMERICAN
STEPHEN PARKINSON, M.A., PH.D.
Lecturer in
Portuguese Language and Linguistics,
University of Oxford

ITALIAN, ROMANIAN, RHETO-ROMANCE
JOHN M. A. LINDON, M.A.
Professor of Italian Studies,
University College London

CELTIC
DAVID A. THORNE, M.A., PH.D.
Reader in Welsh,
University of Wales, Lampeter

GERMANIC
DAVID A. WELLS, M.A., PH.D.
Professor of German,
Birkbeck College, University of London

SLAVONIC
PETER J. MAYO, M.A., PH.D.
Formerly Senior Lecturer in
Russian and Slavonic Studies,
University of Sheffield

VOLUME 58

1996

Published by
W. S. MANEY & SON LTD
for the
MODERN HUMANITIES RESEARCH ASSOCIATION

1997

The Year's Work in Modern Language Studies may be
ordered from the Hon. Treasurer, MHRA, King's
College London, Strand, London WC2R 2LS,
England.

ISBN 0 901286 85 0

ISSN 0084-4152

Printed in Great Britain by
W. S. MANEY & SON LIMITED
HUDSON ROAD   LEEDS LS9 7DL

CONTENTS

ABBREVIATIONS

NAME INDEX

PREFACE

This volume surveys work, published in 1996, unless otherwise stated, in the fields of Romance, Celtic, Germanic, and Slavonic languages and literatures. This is the last volume to be edited by Peter Mayo, who will, however, continue as Slavonic Editor for the time being. As from volume 59 the General Editorship will be taken over by Stephen Parkinson, who will also continue in his role as editor of the Spanish, Catalan, Portuguese, Galician, and Latin American sections.

The attention of users is drawn to the lists of abbreviations at the end of the volume. It should be noted, however, that abbreviations for Acta, *Festschriften*, and other collective and general works that relate only to one section of the volume are sometimes given in the relevant section (usually though not always, in an introductory 'General' subsection) rather than in the list at the end of the volume. An asterisk before a title indicates that the item in question has not been seen by the contributor.

The Editors wish to record with sorrow the death of Dr T. V. Benn, a contributor to the French Studies section of *The Year's Work* for almost a quarter of a century, beginning with Volume 11 (survey years 1940–49), to which he contributed the section on nineteenth- and twentieth-century French literature, and continuing thereafter to contribute, or jointly contribute, the twentieth-century French literature section until Volume 33 (survey year 1971).

Many authors, editors, and publishers supply review copies and offprints of their publications. To these we and our contributors are grateful and we invite others to follow their example, especially in the case of work issuing from an unusual or unexpected source of publication. We would ask that, whenever possible, items for review be sent directly to the appropriate contributor rather than to one of the editors. However, items relating to a number of fields are best sent to one of the editors who will then take appropriate steps.

The compilation of a contribution to the volume, especially in the field of the major languages and periods of literature, is a substantial research task requiring wide-ranging and specialized knowledge of the subject besides a huge reading effort accompanied by the constant exercise of critical judgement. Our thanks are due both to the authors and to the many other individuals and institutions who have contributed in one way or another to the making of this volume. They include, in particular, the compiler of the name index, Peter Mayo, and our printers, W. S. Maney & Son Ltd, amongst whose staff we would single out Derek Brown and Liz Rosindale with whom, as ever, it has been a pleasure to collaborate.

5 December 1997   P.J.M., B.J.L., S.R.P., J.M.A.L., D.A.T., D.A.W

1

LATIN

I. MEDIEVAL LATIN

By Maura K. Lafferty,
Assistant Professor, Intercollegiate Center for Classical Studies in Rome

1. General

Medieval Latin: An Introduction and Bibliographical Guide, ed. F. A. C. Mantello and A. G. Rigg, Washington, DC, Catholic University of America P., xiv + 774 pp., aims at an admirable comprehensiveness, including sections written by a wide variety of specialists with generous bibliography on diverse aspects of Medieval Latin philology, on types of medieval Latinity (ranging from biblical and liturgical to legal and administrative to technical and everyday), as well as on Medieval Latin literature of all kinds. Peter Stotz, *Handbuch zur lateinischen Sprache des Mittelalters*, Munich, Beck, vol. III, xx + 352 pp., the first of five volumes to appear, covers the changing phonetics of Medieval Latin. J. Herman, 'The end of the history of Latin', *RPh*, 49:364–82, argues that Latin ceased to be a mother tongue and was not generally understood by the mid-8th c. in Gaul as the result of phonetic changes in the vernacular, while in Spain and Italy the distinction between the Latin and the vernacular did not occur until the 10th c. M. Banniard, 'Latin tardif et latin mérovingien: communication et modèles langagiers', *REL*, 73:213–30, summarizes the state of research on the movement from Latin to the Romance languages, especially to French, from the 3rd to the 8th c., and proposes a new chronology, based on communication in Latin to the end of the Merovingian period, between literate and non-literate, particularly in preaching the sacred scripture and saints' lives. G. Markus, 'What were Patrick's alphabets?', *CMCS*, 31:1–15, studies the meaning of *abgitorium* and *elementa* when applied by Tirechnan to Patrick's acts of writing. P. Burton, 'Fragmentum Vindobonense 563: another Latin-Gothic bilingual?', *JTS*, 47:141–56, examines a 5th-c. palimpsest from a non-Vulgate Latin version of Matthew's passion, arguing that it was originally a portion of the Latin half of a bilingual text. D. R. Bradley, 'Thrice Blessed Virgin', *MJ*, 31:81–95, re-edits three unrelated Marian lyrics and looks at some common elements. M. Kapp, '*Ardua spes mundi*', *ib.*, 97–102, is a study of a fragment of a processional hymn in a Goslar manuscript. *Studien zur Überlieferung der Flores temporum*, ed. H. Mierau et al. (Monumenta Germaniae Historica, Studien und Texte, 14), Hanover, Hahn, xxx + 141 pp. M. Gorman, 'The commentary on the Pentateuch attributed to Bede in PL 91.189–394: First Part', *RB*, 106:61–108, argues on the basis of the manuscript tradition that this work is not an Irish creation, as long believed, but a pre-existing commentary drawn largely from standard patristic sources, with interpolated passages of a pronounced 'Irish' flavour. A. Bastiaensen, 'La poésie de Venance Fortunat: observations à propos d'une nouvelle édition', *Mnemosyne*, 49:168–81, discusses textual problems in Fortunatus's corpus in connection with M. Reydellet's 1994 edition. B. Bennan, 'Text and image: "reading" the walls of the sixth-century cathedral of Tours', *JMLat*, 6:65–83, studies the verse *tituli*, surviving in the works of Venantius Fortunatus, which provided the key for interpreting the 6th-c. frescoes from the cathedral of Tours, which do not themselves survive. F. Dolbeau, 'Le sermonnaire augustinien de Mayence (Mainz, Stadtbibliothek 1 9): analyse et histoire', *RB*, 106:5–52, catalogues the texts copied in this manuscript, describes their transmission and discusses the motives of the Chartreuse monk who collected these rare texts. P.-I. Fransen, 'Traces de Victor de Capoue dans la chaîne exégétique d'Hélisachar', *ib.*, 53–60, edits the exegetical texts on Paul's letter to the Romans by the 6th-c. Victor of Capua quoted in Hélisachar, and edits several of the texts from Paris, BN, MS lat. 11574. A. de Vogüé, 'L'auteur du commentaire des Rois attribué à Saint Grégoire: un moine de Cava?' *ib.*, 319–31, argues that the commentary contains features that connect it to Cava.

J. Van der Straeten, 'Catalogues de manuscrits latins: inventaire hagiographique: vingtième série', *AB*, 114:139–74, continues his catalogue of manuscripts containing hagiographical material. Girard J. Etzkorn, *Iter Vaticanum franciscanum: A Description of Some One Hundred Manuscripts of the Vaticanus Latinus Collection* (Studien und Texte zur Geistesgeschichte des Mittelalters, 50), Leiden, Brill, xi + 301 pp., describes manuscripts between Vat. lat. 2900 and 9900 dealing primarily with philosophical and theological manuscripts from Franciscan authors. I. Moreira, 'Augustine's three visions and three heavens in some early medieval florilegia', *Vivarium*, 34:1–14, shows how the florilegists' choices make a creative contribution to medieval thought. A. O'Leary, 'An Irish apocryphal apostle: Muirchú's portrayal of Saint Patrick', *Harvard Theological Review*, 89:287–301, argues that the sources for Muirchù's *Vita sancti Patricii* include apocryphal biographies of the apostles.

Meinolf Schumacher, *Sündenschmutz und Herzensreinheit: Studien zur Metaphorik in lateinischer und deutscher Literatur des Mittelalters*, Munich, Fink, 737 pp. A. Rolet, 'L'arcadie chrétienne de Venance Fortunat:

un projet culturel, spirituel et social dans la Gaul mérovingienne', *Médiévales*, 31 : 109–27, argues that Fortunatus's poems combine in his topos of the *locus amœnus* the classical idea of privileged *otium* with the Christian ideal of monastic isolation, creating a model of *Romanitas* for the Frankish aristocracy. W. McCready, 'Isidore, the Antipodeans, and the shape of the earth', *Isis*, 87 : 108–27, discusses the Antipodes and world geography in Isidore's *Etymologiæ* and Bede's *De temporum ratione*. C. Watkins, 'Doctrine, politics and purgation: the Vision of Tnuthgal and the Vision of Owein at St. Patrick's Purgatory', *JMH*, 22 : 225–36, examines two vision-narratives set in Ireland to explore their eschatological beliefs in the context of the development of the idea of purgatory. *Le Clerc au moyen âge* includes: J.-M. Boivin, 'Les Paradoxes des *Clerici regis:* l'exemple, à la cour d'Henri II Plantagenêt, de Giraud de Barri' (47–61), who looks at the functions of a *clericus* at the king's court in the works of Gerald of Wales; D. Buschinger, 'La critique du clergé dans le roman animalier au moyen âge' (81–89), with discussions of the satirical representations of the clergy in *Ecbasis cuiusdam captivi* and Nivard's *Ysengrimus*; and J. Ducos, 'Le clerc et les météores: constitution et évolution d'une culture encyclopédique' (151–64), who examines the use of the inherited tradition in the sections on meteors in the encyclopædic literature of the high Middle Ages. M. E. J. Hughes, 'Medieval parody as literary benefactor: "Furor, Reddo" ', *MH*, n.s. 23 : 67–97, looks at the analogy of thief to author in Vitalis of Blois's *Aulularia*, the *Speculum stultorum* and other Latin and vernacular works of the high Middle Ages. P. Walter, 'Le terrorisme diabolique au Moyen Age: quelques témoignages empruntés à la littérature et aux *exempla*', Glaudes, *Terreur*, 21–35, looks at the function of diabolic imagery in Latin (for example, in visionary and exemplary material), as well as in vernacular literature and art from the 11th c. on. Dina De Rentiis, *Die Zeit der Nachfolge: zur Interdependenz von 'imitatio Christi' und imitatio auctorum im 12.–16. Jahrhundert*, Tübingen, Niemeyer, x + 184 pp., argues that the Renaissance concept of *imitatio* grew out of the religious ideal of *imitatio Christi*; together with vernacular works, it looks at Petrarch's *De vita solitaria, De otio religioso, Familiares*, and instruction in rhetoric and poetry in the 12th and 13th c. J. Leonhardt, 'Classical metrics in medieval and Renaissance poetry: some practical considerations', *CM*, 47 : 305–23, gives practical advice on reading, editing, and commenting on Latin poems written in classical metres in the Middle Ages and the Renaissance.

Criticism and Dissent in the Middle Ages, ed. Rita Copeland, CUP, xii + 332 pp., contains several essays concerning the relationship between Latinity and critical dissent, including her own 'Introduction: dissenting critical practices' (1–23), which discusses the authority and institutional power of Latin grammar. Others are: J. Enders, 'Rhetoric, coercion, and the memory of violence' (24–55), based on discussions of rhetoric from the *Ad Herrenium* to Abelard; M. Irvine, 'Heloise and the gendering of the literate subject' (87–114); M. Camille, 'The dissenting image: a postcard from Matthew Paris' (115–50), which 'interrogates' speaking, reading, and writing in the Middle Ages as pictured by Matthew Paris; and R. Hanna III, ' "Vae octuplex", Lollard socio-textual ideology, and Ricardian–Lancastrian prose translation', (244–63), on the complexity of the ideological relationship for Lollards between authoritative Latin texts and translations of them. Y. Hen, 'The structure and aims of the *Visio Baronti*', *JTS*, 47:477–97, argues that the 7th-c. vision of heaven and hell served to offer instruction on private penance, charity, and monastic conduct to the monks of Longoretus and Millebecus. K. Wolk, 'The legend of Saint Dorothy: medieval vernacular renderings and their Latin sources', *AB*, 114:41–72, surveys the Latin versions of the legend of Dorothy from the second half of the 5th c. (*Martyrologium Hieronymianum*) through to the 15th c., particularly in the various versions of the *Legenda aurea*. The second part of the article surveys the various vernacular versions of the legend. F. Dolbeau, 'Le dossier de Saint Canion d'Atella', *ib.*, 109–23, surveys the passions of the Italian saint and relates them to other hagiographical material in preparation for a larger study. R. Godding, 'Italica Hagiographica (II): chronique d'hagiographie italienne', *ib.*, 411–30, is an annotated bibliography of recent work on Italian saints' lives. B. Effros, 'Symbolic expressions of sanctity: Gertrude of Nivelles in the context of Merovingian mortuary custom', *Viator*, 27:1–10, argues for the spiritual significance of the burial customs depicted at Gertrude's burial in her anonymous *vita*. Thomas Forrest Kelly, *The Exultet in Southern Italy*, OUP, xvi + 352 pp. + 16 pls, examines the non-artistic aspects of the rolls (liturgy, ceremonial, text, music), as well as their making. N. Orchard, 'The medieval masses in honour of St Apollinaris of Ravenna', *RB*, 106:172–84, surveys the masses assigned to St Apollinaris throughout the Middle Ages. *BEC*, 154.1, looks at Clovis in historical writing, including P. Bourgain, 'Clovis et Clothilde chez les historiens médiévaux des temps mérovingiens au premier siècle capétien' (53–85), and C. Beaune, 'Clovis dans les miroirs dominicains du milieu du XIIIᵉ à la fin du XIVᵉ siècle' (113–29), which includes discussions of Clovis in Vincent of Beauvais, Guillaume Peyraut, Thomas Aquinas and Robert Gervais. M. Heinzelmann, 'Clovis dans le discours hagiographique du VIᵉ au IXᵉ siècle', *BEC*, 154:87–112, discusses the relationship between Gregory of Tours's portrait of Clovis in his *Historia Francorum* and other hagiographical writings. M. E. Jones, *The End of Roman Britain*, Ithaca,

Cornell U.P., ix + 323 pp., includes a section on *romanitas* (or rather, the lack of *romanitas*) of St Patrick, Gildas, and 'Nennius's' *Historia Brittonum*. K. McKinley, 'The medieval commentary tradition 1100–1500 on *Metamorphoses* 10', *Viator*, 27:117–49, contrasts the interest in secular and literary aspects of Ovid's poem in the 'vulgate' commentary, Thomas Walsingham and Ralph Regius with the allegoresis of Arnulf of Orleans, John of Garland and Pierre Bersuire. J. D'Amato, 'The *Turris Pharo* at Cape Miseno: a monument of medieval scholarship', *ib.*, 215–64, examines the scholarly tradition on an ancient lighthouse at Misenum arising from a misunderstanding of ancient texts in late antique and medieval commentaries on Vergil, Horace, and Juvenal. *MJ*, 31, contains a series of articles on the history of Medieval Latin scholarship, particularly on the figures behind monumental editorial projects, including L. Ulrich, 'Ein Gelehrtenleben für das Latein des Mittelalters: Norbert Eickermann (Fickermann): ein Beitrag zur Geschichte der Monumenta Germaniae Historica' (3–19); and P. von Moos, 'Muratori und die Anfänge der italienischen Mediävistik' (21–37). S. Timpanaro, 'Franco Munari', *Belfagor*, 51:417–46, reviews the scholarly work of Munari, including his contributions to Medieval Latin scholarship.

2. ANGLO-SAXON ENGLAND

L. Kornexl, 'Ein benediktinischer Funktionsträger und sein Name: linguistische Überlegungen rund um den *circa*', *MJ*, 31:39–60, considers the Benedictine use of words formed from *circum/circa* to describe the overseeing role assigned by the *Regula Benedicti* 48.17–18 to an older monk, particularly as these words are used in the reformed monasteries of Anglo-Saxon England. S. Gwara, 'A record of Anglo-Saxon pedagogy: Aldhelm's *Epistola ad Heahfridum* and its gloss', *JMLat*, 6:84–134, introduces and edits Aldhelm's letter, which, he argues, was composed after the *Carmen de virginitate*. D. Porter, 'Ælfric's *Colloquy* and Ælfric Bata', *Neophilologus*, 80:639–60, argues that Ælfric's student Ælfric Bata, in connection with changing teaching aims, edited the successive versions of the *Colloquy* and perhaps wrote the continuous gloss on it, and may have been influential in making public A.'s pedagogical works. D. Howlett, 'Numerical play in Wulfstan's verse and prose', *MJ*, 31:61–67, examines the elegiac prologue to the *Breviloquium de omnibus sanctis* and the prose preface of the *Life of Æthelwold* and argues that Wulfstan's use of such wordplay can be used to correct and confirm the text of his works. R. J. S. Grant, 'A copied "tremulous" Worcester gloss at Corpus', *NMi*, 97:279–83, argues that the Worcester scribe with the 'tremulous hand' glossed the OE version of Bede's *Historia ecclesiastica* with reference to a C-type Latin text. P. Meyvaert, 'Bede, Cassiodorus, and the Codex Amiatinus', *Speculum*, 71:827–83, examines the relationship between the Codex Amiatinus at Wearmouth Jarrow and the Codex Grandior that Cassiodorus had assembled at Vivarium. H. Hartzell, 'An early Missal fragment in the British Library', *RB*, 106:308–18 + pls, describes British Library, Royal MS 4 A.xiv ff. 1*–2*, a bifolium containing portions of the temporale for Passiontide from the end of the 9th c. Michelle Brown, *The Book of Cerne: Prayer, Patronage, and Power in Ninth-century England*, London, British Library–Toronto U.P., 252 pp. + illus.

J. Pizarro, 'Kings in adversity: a note on Alfred and the cakes', *Neophilologus*, 80:319–26, argues that this anecdote did not originate in the late 10th- or early 11th-c. Latin *Life of Saint Neot*, but draws on Boethian *exempla*, influenced by Germanic folk tales. S. Coates, 'The bishop as pastor and solitary: Bede and the spiritual authority of the monk-bishop', *JEH*, 47:601–19, examines Bede's development of the monastic ideal in his *Historia ecclesiastica* and his two *Vitæ Cuthberti* in the context of earlier hagiography, particularly earlier works about the life of St Martin (e.g. by Sulpicius Severus, Venantius Fortunatus, and Gregory of Tours). P. Sorrell, 'Alcuin's "comb" riddle', *Neophilologus*, 80:311–18, puts Alcuin's thank-you letters, one prose and one verse, for the gift of an ivory comb in the context of Anglo-Saxon Latin and vernacular riddle-form.

3.   THE CAROLINGIAN AND OTTONIAN PERIOD

R. Collins, 'The state of research: the Carolingians and the Ottonians in an Anglophone world', *JMH*, 22:97–114, gives a thoughtful overview of recent bibliography on this period, including many items on Latin literature and literacy, historiography, and palæography. E. Hellgardt, 'Zur Mehrsprachigkeit im Karolingerreich: Bemerkungen aus Anlaß von Rosamond McKittericks Buch "The Carolingians and the Written Word" ', *BGDSL*, 118:1–48, examines the use of Latin side by side with the vernaculars, German and the Romance, in the Carolingian period, arguing against true multilingualism, since Latin was always a learned language. K. Zeichel-Eckes, 'Florus von Lyon, Amalarius von Metz und der Traktat über die Bischofswahl', *RB*, 106:109–33, gives a critical edition of Florus's so-called *Liber de electionibus episcoporum* and puts it into its historical context. A. Albuzzi, 'Pergamene inedite dei secoli X e XI nell'archivio privato Antonia Traversi di Meda', *Ævum*, 70:193–210 + 1 pl., edits a series of Lombard documents preserved in the Benedictine monastery of S. Vittore di Meda. V. von Büren, 'Une edition critique de Solin au

IXe siècle,' *Scriptorium*, 50 : 22–87, looks at the evidence of manuscripts and of citations for Solinus's *Collectanea rerum memorabilium*.

M. Perrin, 'La composition de l'*In honorem sanctae crucis* de Raban Maur: possibilités et limites de l'explication de la structure de l'œuvre', *REL*, 73 : 199–212, argues that the number of poems contained in the work, twenty-eight, is a perfect number, signifying the Law and the Gospel, and that the whole series recounts the sacred history of the world and of humanity. M. Giovini, '*Quod decet ore teri*: Giovenale e il mito delle Eliadi nei *Versus Eporedienses* (XI sec.)', *Maia*, 48 : 39–49, describes the *Versus Eporedienses* from Ivrea, Biblioteca Capitolare, MS LXXXV. Id., 'Il concetto di *humanitas nei Gesta Berengarii imperatoris* (X sec.) e la xv satira di Giovenale', *ib.*, 301–09, describes the Berengar of the poem as a transfiguration of *pius Æneas* and as an antitype of Christ, before showing how the author draws on Juvenal 15 for his concept of *humanitas* in *Gesta Berengarii* 3.

D. Deliyannis, 'Agnellus of Ravenna and iconoclasm: theology and politics in a ninth-century historical text', *Speculum*, 71 : 559–76, explicates oblique references to iconoclasm in Andreas Agnellus's *Liber pontificalis ecclesiae Ravennatis*. J. M. H. Smith, 'A hagiographer at work: Hucbald and the library at Saint-Amand', *RB*, 106 : 151–71, discusses Hucbald's hagiographical work and how it reveals the contents of the library at Saint-Amand in the 10th c. D. Appleby, 'Sight and Church reform in the thought of Jonas of Orleans', *Viator*, 27 : 11–33, looks at the act of seeing holy places, images, and miracles in Jonas's *De cultu imaginum* as a useful devotional practice.

4. THE ELEVENTH CENTURY

New editions include: Benzo of Alba, *Sieben Bücher an Kaiser Heinrich IV*, ed. H. Seyffert (Monumenta Germaniae Historica, Scriptores, 65), Hanover, Hahn, x + 832 pp.; and *Three Eleventh-Century Anglo-Latin Saints' Lives: Vita S. Birini, Vita et miracula S. Kenelmi and Vita S. Rumwoldi*, ed. and trans. Rosalind C. Love, OUP, cxxxix + 149 pp., with a general introduction to 11th-c. Anglo-Latin hagiography, as well as sections on the Latinity, the manuscripts, and the historical and cultic contexts of each of the lives. P. Busonero et al., 'Un sistema di rigatura nei codici cassinesi del secolo XI', *Ævum*, 70 : 213–16, looks at a system of ruling used in Greek and Latin book production in Italy in the 11th c. J.-M. Sansterre, 'Le moine ciseleur, la Vierge Marie et son image: un récit d'Ekkehart IV de Saint-Galle', *RB*, 106 : 185–91, discusses Ekkehard IV's use of the legend of the monk Tuotilo in his *Continuatio casuum sancti Galli*. M. Goullet, '*Planctum describere*: les deux lamentations funèbres de Jotsaud en l'honneur d'Odilon de Cluny', *CCMe*, 39 : 187–208, edits, translates, and comments on two funeral laments for Odilo of Cluny, with an explanation of the Latin musical technology by A. Deschamps (209–20). P. Henriet, 'Chronique de quelques morts annoncées: les saints abbés clunisiens (Xᵉ–XIIᵉ siècles)', *Médiévales*, 31:93–108, studies death scenes in the *vitae* of the abbots of Cluny. I. Resnick, 'Anselm of Besate and humanism in the eleventh century', *JMLat*, 6:1–11, uses Anselm to show the success and failure of classical humanism and the study of the arts in this period.

5. The Twelfth Century

M. Braccini, 'La cantilena di S. Farone: *iuxta rusticitatem = rustica romana lingua*', *CN*, 56:7–43, looks at references to the vernacular in works concerning St Farone, the *Carmen*, *Cantilena*, the *Vita Faronis* and other Latin works. Henry of Huntingdon, **Historia Anglorum: The History of the English People*, ed. Diana Greenway, OUP, clxxii + 899 pp., is a new edition and translation. P. Bakker, 'Syncrat-égorèmes, concepts, équivocité: deux questions anonymes conservées dans le ms Paris, B.N., lat. 16.401', *Vivarium*, 34:76–131, edits two anonymous questions and relates them to the semantics of Pierre d'Ailly's *Conceptus*. J. Santos Paz, 'Nouvelles données sur la tradition du *Liber subtilitatum* d'Hildegarde de Bingen', *JMLat*, 6:197–208, discusses the complex relationship in the manuscripts between the *Liber simplicis medicine* and *Liber composite medicine*, to which H. herself refers as a single book, the *Liber subtilitatum diuersarum naturarum creaturarum*. F. Negri, 'Il lezionario cluniacense a Polirone nel XII secolo', *Ævum*, 70:217–41 + 2 pls, uses Mantova, Biblioteca Communale, MS 132 (A V 2), to illustrate the ties between Cluny and Polirone in the mid-12th c. Walter of Châtillon, *The Alexandreis of Walter of Châtillon: A Twelfth-Century Epic*, trans. David Townsend, Philadelphia, Pennsylvania U.P., xxix + 214 pp., is a translation of the epic into verse, with commentary, including translations of many glosses hitherto unavailable in printed form.

S. Echard, 'Map's metafiction: author, narrator and reader in *De nugis curialium*', *Exemplaria*, 8:287–314, shows how Walter Map makes problematic the relationship between *poeta* and *lector* by thrusting responsibility for understanding on to the reader. N. Adkin, 'Walter of Châtillon, *Alexandreis* 4.254–55: *Preter quos nullus regnavit . . . a crimine mundus*', *Ævum*, 70:257–61, argues that Walter is citing Ecclesiasticus 49.5 in these lines. H. Bayer, '*Parasitus Golias*: Gottfried von Strassburg (Gunther von Pairis) und die zeitkritisch-häretische Schulpoesie der Carmina Burana', *MJ*, 31:39–80, looks at Catharism in a wide range of 12th-c. literature, especially Latin literature. M. Giovini, 'L'insonnia come metafora del *tædium vitae* in Arrigo da Settimello', *Maia*,

48:349–60, shows how Henry of Settimello draws on an image of Boethius in his *Elegia de diversitate fortunae et philosophiae consolatione* (1192–93). R. Fulton, 'Mimetic devotion, Marian exegesis, and the historical sense of the Song of Songs', *Viator*, 27:85–116, argues that commentaries on the Song of Songs by Honorius Augustodonensis, Rupert of Deutz, Philip of Harvengt, Alan of Lille, William of Newburgh and Alexander Neckham use it as a vehicle for a mimetic re-creation of intimate conservation between Mary and Christ. C. Villa, 'Tra *fabula* e *Historia*: Manegoldo di Lautenbach e il "Maestro di Orazio" ', *Ævum*, 70:245–56, looks at the concepts of *historia* and *fabula* in *magister* Mainegaudus's commentary on Horace's *Ars Poetica* in Bern, Burgerbibl. 327 (12th–13th-c.). A. Luzi, 'Il filo: un testo anonimo da riscoprire', *Maia*, 48:57–63, describes a comic poem in leonine hexameters and its manuscript context, dates it, and analyses its metre and diction. K. Jacobi et al., 'From *intellectus verus/falsus* to the *dictum propositionis*', *Vivarium*, 34:15–40, considers the semantics and the development of Abelard's technical terminology.

S. Twyman, 'Papal *Adventus* at Rome in the twelfth century', *Historical Research*, 69:233–53, examines descriptions of the popes' entrances into Rome in the papal *vitae* and other 12th-c. Latin texts. D. Foote, 'Taming monastic advocates and redeeming bishops: the *Triumphale* and episcopal *Vitae* of Reiner of St. Lawrence', *Revue d'histoire ecclésiastique*, 91:5–40, explores the tension between worldly and extra-worldly concerns in Reiner of St Lawrence's *Triumphale Bulonicum*, *Vita Evracli episcopi Leodiensis*, *Vita Wolbodonis*, and *Vita Reginardi*, by placing these works in their literary and historical context as part of the struggle by the monastery of St Lawrence in Liège to protect its property in the 12th c. J. Tolan, 'Anti-hagiography: Embrico of Mainz's *Vita Mahumeti*', *JMH*, 22:25–41, argues that the *Vita Mahumeti*, the first Latin biography of Mohammed in verse (*c.* 1100), is modelled on contemporary verse hagiography and portrays Mohamed as a heresiarch, reflecting an increasing knowledge of Islam and a resurgence of heresy in Europe. F. Gastaldelli, ' "Optimus Prædicator": l'opera oratoria di San Bernardo', *AC*, 51:321–418, examines contemporary descriptions of Bernard's preaching, both in Latin and in the vernacular, and considers the evidence for the historical settings in which Bernard preached. G. then examines first the sermons which have survived in written form, their transmission and themes, then sermons of which only reports survive; and finally the *sententiae* and *parabolae* attributed to the abbot. Robert G. A. Kurvers, *Ad faciendum Peregrinum: A Study of the Liturgical Elements in the Latin Peregrinus Plays in the Middle Ages*, Frankfurt am Main, Lang, xi + 245 pp., examines the geographical, historical, and liturgical contexts of the Latin Peregrinus plays, and analyses their rubrics and liturgical sources. Monika Otter, *Inventiones: Fiction and Referentiality in Twelfth-Century English Historical Writing, Chapel Hill, North Carolina U.P., x + 230 pp., considers the interrelationship between fact and fiction in saints' lives (Goscelin, Flocard) and *historiae* (William of Malmesbury, William of Newburgh, Geoffrey of Monmouth, Walter Map, Gerald of Wales) of the late 11th and 12th c. S. Bagge, 'Ideas and narrative in Otto of Freising's *Gesta Frederici*', *JMH*, 22:345–77, examines the thematic unity based on the allegorical and typological connections between important episodes, using Otto's *Gesta* to illustrate medieval 'modes of perception'. J.-Y. Tilliette, 'Invention du récit: la "Brutiade" de Geoffroy de Monmouth (*Historia regum Brittaniae*, 6–22)', *CCMe*, 39:217–33, argues that the first part of the *Historia* combines 'matters' drawn from classical epic, the French *chanson de geste*, and Celtic mythological material, to create a comprehensive and secular historical narrative. D. C. van Meter, 'An echo of Adso of Montier-en-Der in Herman of Tournai's *Liber de Restauratione S. Martini Tornacensis*', *RB*, 106:192–202, discusses H.'s inclusion of a prophecy on the course of the Flemish succession and its relationship to eschatology (particularly that of Adso of Montier-en-Der) in the 12th c.

W. Purcell, *Ars poetriae: Rhetorical and Grammatical Invention at the Margin of Literacy*, Columbia, South Carolina U.P., vii + 193 pp., examines Matthew Vendôme's *Ars versificatoria*, Geoffrey of Vinsauf's *Poetria nova* and *Documentum de modo et arte dictandi et versificandi*, John of Garland's *Parisiana poetria*, Gervasius of Melkley's *Ars poetica*, and Eberhard the German's *Laborintus* as self-consciously literate works written early in the shift from orality to literacy. Suzanne Reynolds, *Medieval Reading: Grammar, Rhetoric and the Classical Text*, CUP, xvi + 235 pp., uses glosses on Horace's *Satires* in 12th-c. manuscripts from England and northern France as evidence for reading practices and literary theory. B. Roy and H. Shooner, 'Arnulfi Aurelianensis "Glosule de Remediis amoris"', *JMLat*, 6:135–96, is an edition of Arnulf of Orleans's commentary on Ovid's *Remedia amoris*.

6. THE THIRTEENTH CENTURY

M. Kapp, 'Ein Skriptorium im Goslarer Neuwerkkloster? Studien zur Paläographie des Goslarer Evangeliars und verwandter Handschriften', *MJ*, 31:69–81 + pls 1–15, argues for the attribution of the 13th-c. Goslar Evangelary and the manuscripts associated with it to the scriptorium at Neuwerk, the first monastery for nuns at Goslar.

F. Knapp, 'Wirklichkeit und Fiktion in der lateinischen Version des arabischen "Poetik"-Kommentars', *ib.*, 97–103, considers the relationship between reality and fiction in Hermann the German's Latin translation of Averroës's Arabic commentary on Aristotle's *Poetics*. M. Carruthers, 'Boncompagno at the cutting-edge of rhetoric: rhetorical *Memoria* and the craft of memory', *JMLat*, 6:44–64, explores the works of Boncompagno as evidence for the use of the art of memory in theory and in practice, emphasizing the relationship between *memoria* and *inventio*, in the 12th and 13th c. S. Menache and J. Horowitz, 'Quand le rire devient grinçant: la satire politique aux XIIIᵉ et XIVᵉ siècles', *MA*, 102:437–63, examine the theme of laughter in Latin and vernacular political, satirical lyrics from England and France.

J. Fredell, 'Margery Kempe: spectacle and spiritual governance', *PQ*, 75:137–66, argues that the Book of Margery Kempe replaces male images of authority and incorporation within a community with female ones stressing self-governance and corporeal independence. H. Benveniste, 'Joinville et les "autres": les procédés de représentation dans l'*Histoire de saint Louis*', *MA*, 102:27–55, argues that the author of the history compares 'others' (Mongols, Bedouins) to himself, metaphorically and metonymically.

J. Leeker, 'La présence des auteurs classiques dans l'historiographie des pays romans', *CM*, 47:325–57, traces the use of classical authors in Romance and Latin universal histories, national chronicles, and local chronicles, where they are used primarily as sources for 'proofs' to be used in contemporary debates.

7. THE FOURTEENTH AND FIFTEENTH CENTURIES

L. Voigts, 'What's the word? Bilingualism in late-medieval England', *Speculum*, 71:813–26, looks at the simultaneous use of English and Latin and 14th- and 15th-c. scientific and medical works in England. A. Rigg, 'A Latin poem on St. Hilda and Whitby Abbey', *JMLat*, 6:12–43, is an edition of and commentary on this 14th- or 15th-c. poem in leonine verse. G. Barbero, 'La prefazione di Guillaume Fichet all'*Editio princeps* dell'*Orthographia* di Gasparino Barzizza', *Ævum*, 70:507–26, is a study and edition of Fichet's introduction to Barzizza's *Orthographia* printed with the text in 1470–71. E. Reiter, 'The reader as author of the user-produced manuscript: reading and rewriting in popular Latin theology in the late Middle Ages', *Viator*, 27:151–69, examines the creative, almost authorial, role of the reader-scribe in transforming works of theology in the act of copying. C. Pyle, 'The art and science of Renaissance natural history', *ib.*, 265–312, examines Pier Candido Decembrio's *De animantia Naturis* in Vatican Library MS Urb. lat. 276, how it illustrates the changing study of zoological nature, in its use of the medieval encyclopædic tradition of Thomas of Cantimpré's *Liber de natura rerum* and in the illustrations added in the 16th c. by Teodoro Ghisi. M. Pedralli, 'Il medico ducale milanese Antonio Bernareggi e i suoi libri', *Ævum*, 70:307–48 + 2 pls, examines the evidence for the library belonging to the astrologer and doctor Antonio Bernareggi. P. Sverzellati, 'Il libro-archivio di Nicodemo Tranchedini da Pontremoli, ambasciatore sforzesco', *ib.*, 371–91, describes the contents of an archival manuscript which belonged to Nicodemo Tranchedini.

J. D. Mann, 'The devilish pope: Eugenius IV as Lucifer in the later works of Juan de Segovia', *Church History*, 65:184–96, looks at apocalyptic imagery in Juan de Segovia's *History of the Council of Basel*, *Epistola ad Guillielmum de Orliaco*, *Liber de substantia ecclesiae*, and *Liber de magna auctoritate episcoporum*. E. O'Connor, 'Hell's pit and heaven's rose', *MH*, n.s. 23:25–61, examines the typology of female sights and smells in the Italian Humanist Panormita's *Hermaphroditus* and its sources in classical and Christian literature. A. Coldiron, '*Translatio*, translation, and Charles d'Orléan's *parole*d poetics', *Exemplaria*, 8:169–92, includes an examination of the social and political ramifications of *translatio* and translation in Antonio Astesano's translation of Charles d'Orleans's poems *into* Latin as well as in C.'s own *translatio* into French lyric of Sallust's *Bellum civile*.

Gertrud Jaron Lewis, *By Women, For Women, About Women: The Sister-Books of Fourteenth-Century Germany*, Toronto, Pontifical Institute of Mediæval Studies, xiii + 329 pp. + 14 illus + 2 microfiches, examines these Latin and vernacular texts, their literary genre, their use of imagery, and what they tell us about Latin and vernacular literacy and learning, and about women as authors and scribes. C. Kallendorf, 'The historical Petrarch', *AHR*, 101:130–41, discusses P.'s republican sentiments particularly as represented in his *Africa* and his *Secretum*.

C. Zintzen, 'Antike und Renaissance', *MJ*, 31:103–29, looks at the reception of Greek and Roman *Geistesleben*, literature and philosophy by Italian humanists of the 15th c. L. Rossi, 'Presenze di Petrarca in commenti danteschi fra Tre a Quatrocento', *Ævum*, 70:441–76, looks at citations of Petrarch in commentaries on Dante's vernacular and Latin works. 'Lorenzo Valla: a symposium', *JHI*, 57:1–86, includes three studies of Valla's exposure of the Donation of Constantine: S. I. Comporeale, 'Lorenzo Valla's *Oratio* on the Pseudo-Donation of Constantine: dissent and innovation in early Renaissance Humanism' (9–26); R. K. Delph, 'Valla Grammaticus, Agostino Steuco, and the Donation of Constantine' (55–77); and R. Fubini, 'Humanism and truth: Valla writes against the Donation of Constantine' (79–86). D. Coppini, 'Variante de "errori" d'autore nella tradizione di testi umanistici: il caso dell' "Hermaphoditus" del Panormita', *MJ*, 31 : 105–14, considers the 'errors' made in this text in order to show how the medieval tradition of commentaries on classical suthors had a decisive influence on humanistic scholars of the 15th century.

NEO-LATIN

POSTPONED

2

ROMANCE LANGUAGES

I. ROMANCE LINGUISTICS

By John N. Green, *University of Bradford*

1. Acta, Festschriften

The quarter centenary in 1995 of the American Annual Symposia on Romance Languages is greeted this year by two sets of proceedings, catching up the schedule while diverging in editorial style. *Papers* (Los Angeles) assembles 31 items, almost all on syntax and phonology, drawing inspiration from a good range of Romance varieties, but with little overtly comparative material; the editors provide an introduction, useful summaries, and a consolidated list of references, but no index. Editorially spartan by contrast, though neatly produced, *Papers* (Seattle) offers 25 contributions, again concentrating on syntax and phonology, almost a third leavened by comparative insights. *Actas* (Santiago de Compostela), VII, is devoted to medieval and Renaissance philology and textual criticism; the remaining volumes have recently been released and will be surveyed next year.

Scritti di linguistica e dialettologia in onore di Giuseppe Francescato, ed. Silvana Monti, Trieste, Ricerche, 1995, xlviii + 363 pp., includes a bibliography of F.'s writings by E. Fava (xxi–xli) and 42 papers by well-known authors covering traditional dialectological themes of North Italy and Switzerland, together with contact between Romance and adstrate languages. An unusual twin offering, *Studi rumeni e romanzi, omaggio a Florica Dimitrescu e Alexandru Niculescu*, ed. Coman Lupu and Lorenzo Renzi, Padua, Unipress, 1995, 3 vols, xi + 410, 411–746, 747–1086 pp., also includes bibliographies (respectively 3–16, 17–28) and groups its numerous papers into: Balkan linguistics, ethnography, general and Romance linguistics, and theory and history of literature. *Essays in Honor of Josep M. Solà-Solé*, ed. Suzanne S. Hintz, NY–Frankfurt, Lang [vi +] 334 pp., charts the vicissitudes in linguistic and literary relations between Catalan and Castilian. *Evolution and Revolution in Linguistic Theory*, ed. Héctor Campos and Paula Kempchinsky, Washington D.C., Georgetown U.P., 1995, xiv + 418 pp., a thinly veiled festschrift for C.-P. Otero, has contributions by many prominent generative theorists led by Chomsky himself; one item relevant here, J. W. Harris, 'The morphology of

Spanish clitics' (168–97), applies the Halle-Marantz model of distributed morphology to categories of gender and number, seen as 'proprietary' [inherent] in nouns, but 'vicarious' in adjectives.

2. GENERAL ROMANCE AND LATIN

What makes a Romance language? Is there a prototype, and how might we recognize it? Rebecca Posner's thoughtful and sometimes provocative survey of *The Romance Languages*, CUP, xvii + 5 maps + 376 pp., published to coincide with her retirement from the Oxford Chair, responds to the eternal questions in neatly balanced sections on similarities (a 'club' of languages rather than a family, still in awe of Latin, and clustering round the Italian archetype) and on differences (divergent change, creolization, and the struggle for linguistic identity), adumbrating the shift of attitudes that may undermine club membership more rapidly than centuries of linguistic evolution. Klinkenberg's *Des Langues romanes* (*YWMLS*, 57:22), hitherto coolly received, attracts an appreciative review article from M. Iliescu, *TrL*, 32:169–76. Also positive is the rejoinder by G. Skytte, 'A propos de l'article d'Anna Sőrés', *RevR*, 31:282–86 (*YWMLS*, 57:28), pointing to features which could have added hierarchic subtleties to the proposed classification, such as adjective position or the correlation of prepositional accusatives with the absence of partitives.

Lexikon der romanistischen Linguistik. II, 1. Latein und Romanisch, ed. Günter Holtus et al., Tübingen, Niemeyer, xlii + 605 pp., completes coverage of the early period and of comparative grammar, treading a careful path between controversies in over 30 articles penned by a panoply of illustrious scholars. An evaluation by Robert de Dardel of progress in the reconstruction of proto-Romance (90–100) foreshadows his monograph, *A la recherche du protoroman* (supp. to *ZRP*, 275), *ib.*, xviii + 182 pp., detailing his distinctive multi-layered approach to reconstruction, illustrated from main constituent and pronoun orders. Further detail is given in a companion volume co-authored with Ans de Kok, *La Position des pronoms régimes atones — personnels et adverbiaux — en protoroman*, Paris, Champion, 438 pp. D. also contributes an avowedly speculative account of 'Les noms des jours de la semaine en protoroman', *RLiR*, 60:321–34, claiming that the three evident patterns, MARTIS DIES, DIES MARTIS, and MARTIS, disguise a fourth: MD_1 is the oldest and incorporates a functional genitive, M is an ellipsis whose -IS ending was metanalysed as a suffix designating days of the week, DM is appositive having lost its genitive sense, and MD_2 is the most recent and originally a semi-learned form. No wonder the Portuguese preferred a numerical solution! Inspired by Dardel's method, G. Cadorini, 'Quelques hypothèses sur des aspects de la morphologie du frioulan prélittéraire', *RLiR*, 60:463–83, attempts to reconstruct the large north-central area of Ladin, which should have been described in the missing sixth chapter of Ascoli's *Saggi ladini* of 1873, when remnants of the original speech community may still have survived. Meanwhile, a crusty R. Cano Aguilar, 'Problemas metodológicos en sintaxis histórica', *RELing*, 25, 1995:323–46, castigates those who get carried away by procrustean models or their own rhetoric; and E. Pulgram, 'Proto-languages in prehistory', *LSc*, 17, 1995[1996]:223–39, broadly sympathetic to comparative reconstruction, looks loftily beyond proto-Romance to the proto-Latin which may have been spoken in the iron-age village whose vestiges were found on the Palatine Hill.

Studi storico-epigrafici sul Lazio antico, ed. Heikki Solin, Rome, Institutum Romanum Finlandiae, viii + 259 pp., the first part of a project to revise vol. x of the *CIL*, has seven beautifully illustrated studies, including S.'s 'Sul concetto di Lazio nell'antichità' (1–22) and M. Kajava, 'Nuove iscrizioni dal Lazio meridionale' (187–220, with plates). S. and colleagues also edit *Acta colloquii epigraphici latini*, Helsinki, Societas Scientiarum Fennica, 1995, 425 pp., including M. Leiwo, 'The mixed languages in Roman inscriptions' (293–301), a fascinating insight into the sociolinguistics of code-switching and contact between Greek and Latin. Tablets found at Murecina in 1959 reveal the rough-and-tumble life of 1st-c. moneylenders, with smart accounts and scant grammar: J. Andreau, 'Affaires financières à Pouzzoles au 1er siècle ap. J.-C.', *REL*, 72, 1994[1995]:39–55; and P. Flobert, 'Le latin des tablettes de Murécine (Pompéi)', *REL*, 73, 1995[1996]:138–50, which focuses on five tablets with enought text to allow some reconstruction of morphology and syntax, showing disintegrating cases, Romance-type periphrastic perfects and passives, and causal QUOD + subjunctive.

M. Banniard, 'Latin tardif et latin mérovingien', *ib.*, 213–30, spurning diglossia, instead proposes 'vertical communication' as a tool to validate his hypothesis of serious disruption to routine communication in the 8th c. The dating is consistent with that of R. Wright, who rehearses the issues in 'Latin in Spain: early Ibero-romance', *Procs* (Odense), 277–98, and contributes a fine reconstruction of 'Latin and Romance in the Castilian chancery (1180–1230)', *BHS* (Liverpool), 73:115–28, revealing 40 years of intrigue and tussle to get the modern, Toledan, Romance style established in the north (see also *YWMLS*, 57:21). Certain aspects of W.'s work are criticized by E. Alarcos Llorach, 'Estertores latinos y vagidos romances', *BRAE*, 75, 1995:433–45, in a lecture opening an exhibition on the Silos scriptorium, but he does agree with W. that Romance was spoken long before it was written. The last word must go to one who admires W.'s work but cannot accept his dating. J. Herman, 'The end of the history of Latin', *RPh*, 49:364–82, asks the crucial question: when did Latin cease to be the *native* language of ordinary people? Indirect answers can be found in the writings of prelates: in 530 Caesarius thought his Arles congregation could understand the Vulgate when read aloud, in 600 Isidore took understanding for granted, as did Gregory in 602, but in Gaul comprehension started to crumble around 620/630 and by 760 the common people could not even understand the Lord's Prayer. The Latin/Romance distinction was not the *consequence* of the Carolingian reforms, but a fact they reluctantly acknowledged.

3. History of Romance Linguistics

Romanists will find much of absorbing interest and enduring value in two bio-bibliographical dictionaries: Harro Stammerjohann's magnificent *Lexicon Grammaticorum*, Tübingen, Niemeyer, xxviii + 1047 pp., has universal scope and achieves definitive status by excluding the living, deftly complementing Wilfried Kürschner's *Linguisten Handbuch*, Tübingen, Narr, 1994, 2 vols, xxx + 574, 575–1191 pp., which covers only German-speaking scholars alive at the date of compilation. A well-balanced assessment of a gifted Danish Romanist is contributed by Gunver Skytte, *Kr. Sandfeld. Vie et œuvre*, Copenhagen, Museum Tusculanum Press, 1994, 122 pp., trans. from the 1991 Danish original. Among many tributes, full-scale necrological evaluations are offered by A. Niculescu for 'Alf Lombard (Paris, le 8 juillet 1902–Lund, le 1er mars 1996)', *RLiR*, 60:636–40; and by F. Abel for 'Hans Helmut Christmann (1929–1995)', *RF*, 108:194–201, the latter staking a claim for C. as a respected but often rebellious kingmaker within the (West) German Romanist tradition. Insights into the East come, almost fortuitously, from Matthias Perl's *Bibliographie zur romanischen Sprachwissenschaft in der DDR (1949–1990)*, Wilhelmsfeld, Egert Vlg, 1995, ix + 79 pp., which reveals nods of political approbation in its numerous entries for Portuguese and Romanian contrasting with relative neglect or silence elsewhere; a solid body of work on Creoles emanating from Leipzig, where it continued a long tradition, in fact depended on two scholars, Perl himself and P. Thiele. A desperately sad note by P. Matvejević, 'De la romanistique, en cette fin de siècle', *SRAZ*, 39, 1994:199–203, records the loss of irreplaceable Judeo-Spanish MSS in the conflagration of Sarajevo.

Distilling wisdom from a number of influential works, S. Gensini, 'Sul metodo della "storiografia linguistica" ', *LS*, 31 : 547–63, admonishes scholars to strive for a truly disinterested approach, to counteract a natural tendency to overrate the historical significance of the moment they are reconstructing. Duly scrupulous, P. Swiggers and P. Desmet, 'Brachet, Schuchardt et l'étude du latin vulgaire', *Orbis*, 38, 1995:179–88, reproduce a letter in which Brachet, a pupil of Diez, expresses admiration for Schuchardt's *Vokalismus des Vulgärlateins* and asks his advice on the extent of syncope and the use of *ESSERE as an auxiliary. Roles reversed, D. and S., 'Note sur les rapports entre Arsène Darmesteter et Hugo Schuchardt', *ib.*, 189–96, reveal Darmesteter announcing the publication of vol. 2 of his *Morceaux choisis* and commending a bright young pupil Jean Kirste. Tracing two strands of dialectology as practised in France, D. Baggioni, 'De Coquebert de Montbret et Raynouard au duo G. Paris/P. Meyer', *RLaR*, 100:135–62, contrasts expansive 19th-c. movements to rehabilitate patois and capture the national past through the study of dialects, with the treatment meted out to Occitan, centralized out of consciousness by the 1870 decision to adopt standard northern French for universal schooling. Such struggles were not confined to the south, according to G. Bergounioux, 'Aux origines de la société de linguistique de Paris', *BSLP*, 91:1–36, who documents a society of amateurs, after a lacklustre first decade, pushed aside by Americanists and comparativists from the École Pratique des Hautes Études, abetted by Minister of Public Education Victor Duruy, determined to create the premier learned society for language in France.

4. PHONOLOGY

An excellent comparative study by D. Recasens, 'An articulatory-perceptual account of vocalization and elision of dark /l/ in the Romance languages', *LSp*, 39:63–89, identifies the formant transitions responsible for an unconditioned change (favoured by following dento-alveolars) which was widespread in early western Romance and remains live in some central–southern areas. Attacking a belief that has survived since the 1850s, X. Ballester, 'La tipología y el acento prehistórico latino', *Emérita*, 64:59–63, concludes that fixed initial stress is not typologically impossible, but simply cannot be inferred from the intertonic vowel loss adduced in its support. In 'Lenition and optimality theory', *Papers* (Los Angeles), 253–65, H. Jacobs, once an advocate of underspecification phonology, now recants in favour of a hierarchy of constraints in which even fewer underlying features need be specified and modern allophonic lenition can be seamlessly predicted. Similarly for D. E. Holt, 'From Latin to

Hispano-Romance', *PCLS*, 32:111–23, the phonological changes leading to dialect split in Iberia (nasalization, simplification of ambisyllabic sonorants, and mid-vowel diphthongization) can be linked via optimality theory; but for A. C. Quicoli, 'Cyclicity and stress erasure in Portuguese and Spanish', *RivLing*, 7, 1995[1996]:293–331, an almost identical set proves the superiority of the classic Halle-Vergnaud approach to stress, provided that suffixes are precategorized into cyclic or stress-domain. Theory aside, a very practical footnote by V. Noll, 'Computer in der romanischen Sprachwissenschaft: das Problem der Sonderzeichen', *ZRP*, 112:559–603, laments the side-effects of inflexible software and desktop publishing: missing accents and 'phonetic' transcriptions virtually reduced to coded messages.

5. Morphology

On the basis of a careful comparison of an extensive corpus of 422 verbs across Iberoromance, A. Monjour, 'Zum galicischen Verbalsystem', *RJ*, 46:287–313, decides that Galician inflection has subverted many of the historical affinities to Portuguese and is synchronically distinct from both its neighbours. M. Maiden, 'The Romance gerund and "system-dependent naturalness" in morphology', *TPS*, 94:167–201, shows how stem alternations spread analogically from the preterite to the gerund when Romance speakers extrapolated from diachronic trends, even those that were not, in Wurzel's sense, 'natural'. Applying minimalist principles to 'External allomorphy and contradictions in Romance', *Probus*, 8:181–205, J. Mascaró reaches the rather unilluminating conclusion that competing alternants which have not been lexicalized are selected at phrase evaluation level on the basis of least marked syllabic structure. More ingeniously minimalist, L. Silva-Villar, 'Merge and cliticization in Old Romance futures/conditionals', *Papers* (Seattle), 239–50, dispenses with Long Head Movement by treating *aver* as a clitic and the split futures as genetically distinct from their synthetic counterparts, which took over as soon as the parameter banning initial clitics ceased to apply. A contrasting traditional approach to the origins of future and conditional inflections and the suppletive stems of the verb 'to go' can be found in André Lanly, *Deux Problèmes de linguistique française et romane*, Paris, Champion, 64 pp. Defending their template approach against counterclaims by R. A. Mester that there is a direct relationship between their special class and perfect stem allomorphy (*YWMLS*, 52:21, 56:26), S. Davis and D. J. Napoli, 'On root structure and the destiny of the Latin second conjugation', *FLinHist*, 16, 1995:97–113, remain adamant that the best predictor lies in the root: it survives if it is monosyllabic, monomoraic, and has no sonorant in its onset. One might perhaps query the psycholinguistic plausibility of such templates.

Tense Systems in European Languages ii, ed. Rolf Thieroff, Tübingen, Niemeyer, 1995, x + 343 pp. (see *YWMLS*, 57:25), contains essays on French (69–94), Portuguese (95–115), Italian (117–34), and Romanian (135–52), together with an interesting overview by T. focusing on perfectivity and anteriority. Back one stage, *TrL*, 31, 1995, carries two articles which, despite rather specific titles, seek to establish a common terminology for verbal categories: J. M. Brucart and G. Rigau, 'Le système des temps verbaux en espagnol et en catalan' (79–103), advocate a little tidying-up but do not think the differing traditions cause too much confusion, while M. A. Coelho da Mota, 'Les temps et les modes verbaux en portugais' (105–18), draws extensively on C. Blanche Benveniste's proposals for spoken French. A new perspective on AVERE periphrases from D. Jacob, 'Von der *Subjekt*-Relevanz zur Gegenwartsrelevanz', *RJ*, 46:251–86, claims, counter to the orthodox view propounded by Harris and Fleischman, that Romance compound forms mesh with a complex pattern of interpersonal relations radiating around the subject of the sentence. Meanwhile, P. Kempchinsky, 'Perfective auxiliaries, possession and existence in Romance', *Papers* (Seattle), 135–44, is busy rehabilitating the old analysis of HAVE as 'BE WITH' and examining the consequences for modern Romance of diverging choices of auxiliary selection, participial agreement and lexical exponency. From an impressive sample of 19 Romance varieties, which he is right to think puts his analysis some way ahead of its competitors, P. Bessler, 'L'accord du participe passé', *CanJL*, 40, 1995[1996]:269–90, finds concord is obligatory with passives and near-universal with unaccusatives; the participle is adjectival and its agreement merits morphosyntactic treatment on its own terms rather than as an incidental effect of some other process.

6. SYNTAX AND SEMANTICS

Like Cleopatra, it seems, clitics cannot cloy; but they can melt into sets of attractive features. Daniel L. Everett, *Why There Are No Clitics*, Dallas, Summer Institute of Linguistics, xii + 188 pp., draws heavily on Romance data to argue that pronouns, affixes, and clitics can all be derived from the phi-features that exist independently in the lexicon and stack in different hierarchical combinations to form heads of functional categories. Rejecting head-driven syntactic accounts, J. Auger, 'Subject-clitic inversion in Romance', *Papers* (Los Angeles), 23–40, shows how a morphological analysis in which clitics

are affixes can be satisfactorily extended to post-verbal position. No
less controversial is the status of SE. *Pace* Cinque, with whom she
agrees on the distributional facts, C. Dobrovie-Sorin, 'Syntactic
configurations and reference: *se/si* in Romance', *Papers* (Seattle),
73–86, adduces evidence from control clauses to reinterpret what
was formerly considered a nominative *si* as a middle-passive; but
E. Raposo and J. Uriagereka, 'Indefinite *SE*', *NLLT*, 14:749–810,
after grappling with some slippery issues of subject and object
licensing within minimalist theory, come reluctantly to the view that
Romance impersonals with overt objects are active not passive. All
one could wish to know about Wackernagel, in original and modern
manifestations, can be found in *Approaching Second: Second Position
Clitics and Related Phenomena*, ed. Aaron L. Halpern and Arnold M.
Zwicky, Stanford, CSLI Publications, xxiv + 629 pp., which includes
contributions by P. Barbosa on European Portuguese (1–40), by C.
Nishida on Old Spanish (333–73) and by D. Wanner on 'Second
position clitics in Medieval Romance' (537–78). The well-known link
between clitic climbing and infinitival complements is further refined
by A. Terzi, 'Clitic climbing from finite clauses and tense raising',
Probus, 8:273–95. Similar themes recur in a fine series of empirical
studies by M. E. Davies: 'Analyzing syntactic variation with computer-
based corpora', *His(US)*, 78, 1995:370–80; 'A corpus-based approach
to diachronic clitic climbing in Portugese', *HisJ*, 17:93–111; and
'The diachronic interplay of finite and non-finite verbal complements
in Spanish and Portuguese', *BHS* (Glasgow), 73:137–58. Extending
the paradigm, S. A. Montrul, 'Clitic-doubled dative "subjects" in
Spanish', *Papers* (Seattle), 183–95, examines the correlation between
pro-drop and pre-verbal dative experiencers (here treated as pseudo-
subjects), and its interaction with clitic-doubling; taken together, the
two parameters set Spanish aside from most of its Romance
neighbours.

  Parameters and Functional Heads. Essays in Comparative Syntax, ed.
Adriana Belletti and Luigi Rizzi, NY–Oxford, OUP, 300 pp., in
addition to interesting material on subject clitics, V2, N-raising and
complex inversion, carries studies by: R. Zanuttini, 'On the relevance
of tense for sentential negation' (181–207), pointing out that NegP is
parasitic on T[ense]P so that Romance imperatives and small-clause
participles cannot be straightforwardly negated; and M. T. Guasti, 'A
cross-linguistic study of Romance and Arbëresh causatives' (209–38),
using evidence from French, Italian, and two varieties of Albanian,
both to support a verb-incorporation analysis and to identify, for
French only, two distinct causative complements with differing
structural and semantic properties — ideas further refined in her
'Semantic restrictions in Romance causatives', *LI*, 27:294–313.

Weighing into a different debate 'On the controversial status of Romance interrogatives', *Probus*, 8:161–80, G. rejects the attractive IP-analysis which dovetails so well with observed word order, concurring with Rizzi that questions are CPs, though governed in turn by the pro-drop parameter. Complex parameter interactions are tackled by J. Gutiérrez Rexach, 'The scope of universal quantifiers in Spanish interrogatives', *Papers* (Seattle), 87–98, who uses comparative data to determine the possible pair-list readings of *cada* and its Romance cognates; and by E. Torrego, 'On quantifier float in control clauses', *LI*, 27:111–26, who dismisses Sportiche's 1988 analysis as inadequate, unpacks floating into two discrete processes not necessarily connected with quantification, and confesses to admiration for Baltin's proposal to treat floating quantifiers as predicate specifiers of V projections. Other unanchored items include: G. Alexandrova, 'Participial clauses in Bulgarian, Italian and Spanish', *Papers* (Seattle), 1–12, noting the reduced argument structure and the exclusion of unergatives from what Romanists know better as 'ablative absolutes'; and B. Vance, 'Null subjects in Middle French discourse', *Papers* (Los Angeles), 457–74, drawing on Surselvan to buttress a competitive model of grammatical change, and observing that stable discourse coindexing cannot of itself stave off erosion of null-subject status when pitted against the free occurrence of co-referential pronouns.

7. Discourse and Pragmatics

The ambitious EUROTYP project is yielding valuable typological results, but with implications for areal classification mirroring those that once bedevilled Romance. Giuliano Bernini and Paolo Ramat see *Negative Sentences in the Languages of Europe*, Berlin, Mouton de Gruyter, xiv + 274 pp., swirling outwards from the whorl of Romance and validating the concept of a central European core with limited syntactic divergence; yet A. Nocentini, 'Tipologia e genesi dell'articolo nelle lingue europee', *AGI*, 81:3–44, presents the grammaticalization of topic and focus strategies as embryonic and epicyclic in the east, but generally complete in the west, where obligatory morphological marking is possibly allied to the loss of inflection. *La Subordination dans les langues romanes*, ed. Hanne Leth Andersen and Gunver Skytte, Copenhagen, Munksgaard, 1995, 107 pp., assembles 11 papers mainly on French and Italian, celebrating (or perhaps just making the best of) a diversity of theoretical perspectives. Culling examples from a corpus of recent novels, M. Sedano, 'Estructura y forma de las hendidas en cinco lenguas románicas', *HisL*, 8:123–53, finds that cleft relatives (93%) are much more frequent than cleft infinitives (7%), though the ratio is less discrepant in Italian, which she ascribes to the paucity of permissible relativizers in these constructions, as compared with Portuguese, Spanish, Catalan, and French. A.-M. Spanoghe's intriguing 'Mais ou et donc or ni car?', *SN*, 68: 107–21, assesses the relative merits of the extensive and intensive taxonomies proposed by L. Lundqvist for French and M. Casado Velarde for Spanish, as a prelude to plans for a trilingual dictionary of discourse connectors. A. Espunya i Prat, 'The realisation of the semantic operator progressive in English and Romance languages', *LSc*, 18: 295–303, finds that whereas Eng. *be* + V-*ing* and Sp./Cat. *estar* + gerund are stative progressives predicated on a homogeneous stretch of time, *ir*/*anar* + gerund is a dynamic progressive dividing time into consecutive phases. In a typically thorough and widely applicable survey, M. Manoliu-Manea, 'Inalienability and topicality in Romanian: pragma-semantics of syntax', pp. 711–43 of *The Grammar of Inalienability*, ed. Hilary Chappell and William McGregor, Berlin, Mouton de Gruyter, xiv + 931 pp., emphasizes that the crucial relationship in Romance is solidarity rather than possession, though discourse and cognitive factors also play a part.

Reconstructing the pragmatics of a dead language is a hazardous undertaking, but scholars are increasingly willing to make the attempt for Latin. P. M. Suárez Martínez, 'El sistema de la gradación en latín', *Emérita*, 64: 45–58, disputing the traditional view of two clear degrees of comparison, firstly objects that not all adjectives are gradable (a *comparative* reading of DOCTIOR is semantic nonsense) and instead proposes a new scale of what he delightfully labels 'elation'. Also favouring a scalar approach, A. Bertocchi and A. M. Orlandini, 'Quelques aspects de la comparaison en latin', *IF*, 101: 195–232, observe that in comparisons of inequality the comparator can never be a semantic negative (hence *ULLO, *QUOQUAM) and that ablative complements are more frequent in formulaic usage. O. also contributes 'Disjonction et négation en latin', *BSLP*, 91: 147–67, on the pragmatics of AUT and VEL and their interaction with negation, revealing that Latin had wider choice than modern Romance in the expression of subjective disjunction. Identifying a marked shift towards the subjunctive between archaic and classical usage, P. A. Perotti, 'Sulle interrogative indirette in latino', *Latomus*, 55: 329–38, speculates that a true modal nuance of 'suggestivity', present in most of the early examples, was properly rendered by the subjunctive but gradually grammaticalized. The first issue of a new periodical, *Travaux de linguistique* (Luxembourg, not Ghent), reports articles by C. Bodelot, 'L'interrogation indirecte "totale" ou les subordonnées à particule interrogative en latin' (77–92) and by L. Sznajder, 'Que réfléchit le réfléchi latin?' (131–57). A somewhat ponderous piece by

M. Bruña Cuevas, 'Le discours direct introduit par *que*', *FM*, 64:28–50, makes the valid points that such constructions are by no means rare in French or Spanish, are certainly not variants of indirect speech, and can probably trace a direct lineage to parallel complementizer structures in Latin. Lastly, M. J. Echarte Cossío, 'Acusativo y dativo: dinámica sincrónica del latín al castellano', *RELing*, 26:83–107, employs semantic concepts of movement, direction, destination and telicity to juxtapose and contrast the two forms and two misaligned functions of Latin with the three forms and functions of Castilian, concluding that the simple grammatical dichotomy of direct versus indirect object suits neither language.

8. Lexis

Commenting on the upsurge of interest in the influence of Arabic on Romance, F. Corriente, 'Novedades en el estudio de los arabismos en ibero-romance', *RELing*, 26:1–13, is at pains to stress that Romance loans came not from the classical language but via the Andalusian dialect, where a long period of stable bilingualism led to blends and morphologically hybrid forms — a thesis propounded in his well-received book *Árabe andalusí y lenguas romances*, Madrid, Mapfre, 1992, 270 pp., and no doubt to be echoed in his new project to revise, systematically by etymon, all the Arabic loans recorded in the Spanish Academy Dictionary: 'Hacia una revisión de los arabismos y otras voces con étimos del romance andalusí o lenguas medio-orientales en el Diccionario de la RAE', *BRAE*, 76:55–118, 153–95. Meanwhile, Kiesler's *Wörterbuch der Arabismen* (*YWMLS*, 57:30) has received a cautious welcome from M.-D. Glessgen, *RLiR*, 59, 1995:204–09, praising its innovative treatment of phonetic adaptation, but less convinced by the semantics of historical background. The transmission of non-classical Arabisms is neatly illustrated by H. Schwertek's detective work on 'Passer à tabac', *RF*, 108:451–54, whose only etymological connection to 'tobacco' lies in its spelling; the word's ultimate source is Arabic *tabaq*, 'cover, lid' in the classical language, its modern sense of 'beating' having apparently developed from Catalan *tabac* and its related verb *tabacar* 'to cheat, swindle'. Two other Arabic loans, denoting 'begging for mercy' and 'making elaborate greetings' are documented by L. Groza, 'Parallélismes phraséologiques franco-roumains. Le cas des expressions "demander l'aman" et "faire des salamalecs"', *RLiR*, 60:403–12; the matching collocations in semi-jocular registers of both languages suggest a common source, possibly via Turkish.

In a rather thin year for non-Arabic etymology, three studies stand out. In '*Avoir son pain cuit*: huit siècles d'ambiguïté sémantique',

Neophilologus, 80:517–38, E. Dawes scrapes away layers of polysemy to reveal a literal meaning and several metaphors, of which 'sexually satisfied' is the oldest and most widespread (from Plautus on), whereas the antonymy between 'having made one's fortune' and 'being ruined (or dead)', though very persistent, seems confined to French, where ruin was probably an ironic offshoot of fortune. E. Grab-Kempf, 'Zur Etymologie iberoromanischer Bezeichnungen für Vitex agnus-castus L. Verbenaceae', *ZRP*, 112:266–76, traces folk etymologies in numerous dialectal variants, concluding that a typical modern form like *añocasto* blends lambs with years and reinterprets the Greek root (possibly ἄκαστος) as Latin CASTU, no doubt because of the herb's reputed anaphrodisiac properties. According to M. Alinei, 'L'etimologia di *magnano* "calderaio ambulante" et l'inizio dell'articolo nelle parlate neo-latine', *QS*, 17:191–202, not only tinkers but also definite articles trace their origins to the Bronze Age; their name comes not from MANU- but from a 'Germanic' placename La Magna (Germans were apparently good at tinkering), but with loss by metanalysis of the 'article'.

Lexikalische Analyse romanischer Sprachen (LA, 353), ed. Peter Blumenthal et al., Tübingen, Niemeyer, vii + 163 pp., brings together selected contributions to a 1995 conference on post-structural semantic analysis and lexicographic practice. *Namenforschung. Ein internationales Handbuch zur Onomastik* (*YWMLS*, 57:29), has completed publication with a further vol. of specialist articles (II, xxx + 912 pp.) and a comprehensive set of indexes (III, xxxii + 369 pp.), so converting an authoritative survey into an effective work of reference. The appetizing sixth vol. of H. Vernay's *Dictionnaire onomasiologique des langues romanes*, Tübingen, Niemeyer, xiv + 187 pp., covers food, cookery, housing, and clothing (*YWMLS*, 53:20, 54:23, 56:31, 57:30). Drawing on the Romanian core vocabulary project (*YWMLS*, 50:21–22, 56:32), D. Munteanu, 'Estudio comparativo de los vocabularios representativos del español y rumano', *RELing*, 25, 1995:411–26, finds that the two languages have lexical cores of similar size and structure, but fewer shared cognates than in many Romance pairs; so, there can be no justification for postulating a special peripheral area of Romance (collapse of stout Bartolian party and one round to Mańczak; *YWMLS*, 53:14). Two contrastive taxonomies, inspired by the work of M. Gross and intended to facilitate automatic translation, map the types of BE + complement constructions and the distributional constraints which apply in areas with competing copulas: E. Marques Ranchhod, 'Les *VSUP* issus du latin *esse* et *stare* dans les langues romanes', *LInv*, 19, 1995[1996]:265–88, and A.-I. Rădulescu, 'Analyse contrastive des formes *être PRÉP X* en français et en roumain', *ib*, 289–324.

Reinterpreting an old distinction, A.-M. Di Sciullo, 'Prefixes and suffixes', *Papers* (Los Angeles), 177–94, shows how suffixes change categories with consequences for the argument structure of their complement domains whereas aspectual prefixes change the event structure of their stem; variation in Romance prefixation patterns is within expected limits and explained by morphological underspecification. Mindful of Anderson's dictum that morphemes acquire inflectional status from context, F. Rainer, 'Inflection inside derivation', *YM*, 8:83–91, reconsiders Spanish and Portuguese forms like *claramente* or *cãezinhos*, but is inclined to continue treating them as only marginal infractions of Greenberg's 'Universal 28'. Fresh light is cast on a hoary problem in Italian and Romanian by E. Magni, 'Il neutro nelle lingue romanze: tra relitti e prototipi', *SSL*, 35, 1995[1996]: 127–78; the briefest examination of the diverging polysemy of -*a* is enough to dispel any thoughts of continuity or even common innovation, but both languages have independently sought to make full and ingenious use of their inherited morphemes. In a two-part series of 'Notes on some adverbial and prepositional formations in Romance', *Ronshu* (Aoyama Gakuin U.P.), 36, 1995:29–44 and 37:193–207, H. E. Wilkinson explores a neglected lexical set with uncommonly high rates of survival across modern Romance, including forms in ALI + QU/C, those strengthened by ECCE-, interrogative adverbs in U- which lost their original C- by metanalysis, and ending with a range of temporal and spatial expressions in which an original prepositional phrase or loose periphrasis has grammaticalized into a simple Romance adverb; though presented as a historico-etymological study, filling in the gaps of underdocumented 'minor' varieties, W.'s work lends itself to recasting in onomasiological terms, and as such could be even more valuable.

9. DIALECTOLOGY AND SOCIOLINGUISTICS

Surveying models and practice from H. Kloss onwards, Ž. Muljačić, 'Introduzione all'approccio relativistico', *LPr*, no. 2:87–107, believes standardology has entered its postmodern phase and demonstrates the cyclicity of emergence and reabsorption of distinct Romance varieties, calculated at 150–60 around AD 1200 and likely to be reduced to a maximum of 40, counting in the Creoles, by the start of the next millennium. M. also reports briefly on a colloquium held in Skopje in honour of Božidar Nastev, *ZB*, 32:206–07, at which endangered varieties of Romance were among the themes debated. In similar vein, the unequal struggle of Romance languages surrounded by English in North America features prominently in *IJSL*, 121, ed. François Grin, and devoted to 'Economic approaches to language and language planning'. A mini-section of *Lengas*, 40, asks how much trust one should place in attitudinal surveys as a sociolinguistic instrument. A. Kristol, 'Sondages d'opinion à thématique sociolinguistique' (123–37), gives a salutary reminder of 'misreporting' by older speakers with vivid recollections of persecution in their youth, while younger generations have no such inhibitions — though probably far fewer skills in the language. K.'s article is neatly rounded off by J. Wüest, 'Attitudes et représentations' (139–48), and 'Bibliographie des enquêtes sociolinguistiques en domaine occitan' (149–53).

Creolistics continues to grow exponentially; we can do no more than mention major trends here. *Pidgins and Creoles. An Introduction*, ed. Jacques Arends et al., Amsterdam, Benjamins, 1995, xvi + 412 pp., is a substantial collection of 26 articles, giving a fair impression of the whole field, with a rare glimpse of Annobonese. The controversial relexification hypothesis championed by C. Lefebvre and J. Lumsden as an explanation for the distinctive syntax of Haitian Creole is subject to careful historical and ethnolinguistic scrutiny by J. V. Singler, 'Theories of creole genesis', *JPCL*, 11:185–230, who concludes that Bickerton's conditions for the emergence of a radical creole were not met in Haiti and that the predominance of Gbe speakers in the first 50 years of the sugar boom is at least consistent with the Lefebvre-Lumsden hypothesis, though this in turn is so weakly formulated as to be untestable. Needless to add, Lefebvre is unconvinced and her response, 'The tense, mood, and aspect system of Haitian Creole', *ib.*, 231–311, reaffirms her belief in the continuous transmission of grammar (in this case, Fong-Gbe). Nearer home, S. Santoro, 'Lingua franca in Goldoni's *Impresario delle Smirne*', *ib.*, 89–93, rehabilitates some literary fragments previously dismissed as confected; while L. Minervini offers a detailed and very well referenced account of 'La lingua franca mediterranea', *MedRom*, 20:231–301, illustrating the macaronic multilingualism prevalent around the Mediterranean coast when the pidgin emerged, at the cusp of the later medieval and early modern eras.

FRENCH STUDIES*

LANGUAGE

By GLANVILLE PRICE, *University of Wales Aberystwyth*

1. GENERAL AND BIBLIOGRAPHICAL

The following abbreviation is specific to this section: *Espace francophone*, II: pp. 537–964 of *Le Français dans l'espace francophone*, II, ed. Didier de Robillard and Michel Beniamino, Champion (for vol. I, see *YWMLS*, 55:43–44).

Jeanne Ambrose, *Bibliographie des études sur le français parlé*, Didier Érudition, 83 pp., is a follow-up to the bibliography published by Claire Blanche-Benveniste and Colette Jeanjean in their 1987 book, *Le Français parlé* (see *YWMLS*, 49;26); it is selective but nevertheless lists, alphabetically by author, 1078 items.

L. Melis and P. Swiggers, 'Chronique de linguistique générale et française (VII)', *TrL*, 30 (May, 1995):119–44, is devoted to 'Études morphologiques'. As from no. 30, *TrL* devotes its rubric 'Informations' not as in the past to listing Belgian *mémoires de licence* in the field of French linguistics but to presentations of doctoral theses in the field submitted either in Belgium or in a neighbouring country.

Claude Hagège, **Le Français, histoire d'un combat*, EMH, 130 pp. A. Szulmajster-Celnikier, *La Linguistique*, 32.2:35–61, an overview of 'La politique de la langue en France', and seeking to cover the whole period from 842 to the present day, is, though useful, inevitably unoriginal.

Jacqueline Picoche, **Études de lexicologie et dialectologie*, ed. Nelly Andrieux-Reix and Geneviève Hasenohr, CILF, 1995, 394 pp.

Dennis Ager, *'Francophonie' in the 1990s: Problems and Opportunities*, Clevedon, Multilingual Matters, 215 pp., presents a wide-ranging and well-documented survey that will prove useful both for the abundant data it provides and for the insights it offers into the problems facing both the individual and highly diverse territories making up *la Francophonie* and the French-speaking world as a whole. *Espace francophone*, II, includes, in addition to a number of papers mentioned in Sections 11–15 below, the following more general ones, under the overall heading 'Concepts, instruments et problématiques': D. Baggioni, 'Éléments pour une histoire de la francophonie (idéologie, mouvements, institutions)' (789–806); J.-C. Turi, 'L'emploi du

---

* The place of publication of books is Paris unless otherwise stated.

français dans la francophonie du point de vue juridico-constitutionnel' (807–16); R. Ludwig, 'Francophonie et hispanophonie: points de comparaison et hypothèses' (819–33); P. Hawkins, 'Esquisse d'une comparaison des mondes anglophone et francophone' (835–45); R. Breton, 'La démographie des francophones est-elle insaisissable?' (849–54); D. Baggioni and J.-M. Kasbarian, 'La production de l'identité dans les situations de francophonie en contact' (855–69); B. Maurer, '"Continuité" et "convivialite": utiliser le concept de *continuum* pour situer les français d'Afrique' (873–85); D. Baggioni and R. Breton, 'Communauté(s) linguistique(s), espace(s) francophone(s) et réseaux de communication: le problème de la délimitation d'un/des ensemble(s) dans la "francophonie"' (887–901); and A. Bretegnier, 'L'insécurité linguistique: objet insécurisé? Essai de synthèse et perspectives' (903–23). Josseline Bruchet, *Langue française et francophonie: répertoire des organisations et associations œuvrant pour la promotion de la langue française*, CILF, 179 pp.

2. History of Grammar and of Linguistic Theory

Actas (Santiago de Compostela), VIII, includes: W. Ayres-Bennett, '"Tres-estrange & tres-François": l'usage du terme *français* au XVIIᵉ siècle et la tradition de la *latinitas*' (81–90); J.-P. Saint-Gérand, 'Les enjeux d'une "théorie" de la préposition dans les grammaires du début du XIXᵉ siècle' (185–206); P. Desmet and P. Swiggers, 'Gaston Paris: aspects linguistiques d'une œuvre philologique' (207–32); and H. Baat-Zeev Shyldkrot, 'Antoine Meillet devant la norme' (247–56). J. Lago Garabatos, 'L'article. Vie, mort et survie d'une classe', *TrL*, 30 (May 1995): 39–49, commends the modernity of the classification of parts of speech adopted by Nicolas Beauzée and argues for the recognition of a class *détermination nominale* that is to include both determiners and adjectives. L. Rosier, 'La parataxe: heurs et malheurs d'une notion linguistico-littéraire', *ib.*, 51–64, seeks to rehabilitate the concept of parataxis (the unintelligible 'English' abstract on p.154 prompts me to comment that the editors of *TrL* really ought to have all such abstracts vetted by a competent native speaker). F. Neveu, 'La notion d'apposition en linguistique française: perspective historique', *FM*, 64: 1–27, runs from the precursors of Port-Royal to the 1990s. Stefan Gutwin, *Der 'accord du participe passé' als Testfall der französischen Grammatikschreibung* (RA, 40), viii + 140 pp.

Z. Marzys, 'La codification du français à l'époque de la Renaissance', *VR*, 55: 126–42, is a reconsideration of views expressed in 1974 (see *YWMLS*, 36: 33). The contents of *Origins of Language*, ed. Jürgen Trabant, Budapest, Collegium Budapest, vii + 219 pp., are mainly outside the scope of *YWMLS*, but two devote some attention to 18th-c. ideas in France, viz. J. Trabant, 'Thunder, girls, and sheep, and other origins of language' (39–69); and H. Meschonnic, 'Si notre marche dans le langage est une chute depuis l'origine ou si on y va en trébuchant' (116–41).

3. HISTORY OF THE LANGUAGE

Histoire de la langue française: 1914–1945, ed. Gérald Antoine and Robert Martin, CNRS, 1056 pp. R. A. Lodge, 'Stereotypes of vernacular pronunciation in 17th–18th century Paris', *ZRP*, 112:205–31, continues his series of text-based studies of vernacular French in the early modern period (see *YWMLS*, 56:38, 56, and 57:35). *LBer*, Sonderheft 7, entitled *Language Change and Generative Grammar*, ed. Ellen Brandner and Gisella Ferraresi, Opladen, Westdeutscher Vlg, 292 pp., includes G. A. Keiser, 'V2 or not V2? Subject-verb inversion in Old and Modern French' (168–90), arguing that 'interrogatives did *not* undergo syntactic change during the centuries'; and R. Waltereit, 'Zur Diachronie elliptischer Ausdrücke im Französischen' (130–45).

4. TEXTS

Robert-Léon Wagner, *Textes d'étude (ancien et moyen français)*, ed. Olivier Collet (TLF, 460), 1995, xiv + 386 pp., is much more than a new edition of a work first published in 1949; with updated and extensively revised comments and bibliographies and 27 more texts, it is in effect a new work.

J. R. Smeets, *RLiR*, 60:335–402, compares the language of the manuscripts of Gautier de Belleperche's *Chevalerie de Judas Macchabée* (13th c.), concluding that the author was from Ponthieu-Vimeu. T. Matsumura, 'Un mémoire de 1448 (Compiègne), étude lexicographique', *ib.*, 51–72, itemizes and glosses, with references to the *FEW*, Tobler-Lommatzsch, the *TLF* and other works, but little by way of further comment, over 350 words and expressions from the text in question. J.-P. Chambon, *ZRP*, 112:387–400, identifies and comments at length on eleven 'touches régionales' in the farce *Colin qui loue et despite Dieu* [...] (late 15th c. or 16th c.). V. Mecking, *ib.*, 401–08, identifies nearly a hundred culinary terms (some of them not in *FEW*) in M. Lemmer's edition of *Das Allerneueste Pariser Kochbuch* (1752).

5. PHONETICS AND PHONOLOGY

The wide-ranging scope of Françoise Argod-Dutard's well-devised and useful *Éléments de phonétique appliquée*, Armand Colin, 269 pp., emerges less clearly from its title than from its lengthy subtitle, 'Prononciation et orthographe en français moderne et dans l'histoire de la langue. Aspects prosodiques et métriques'; it combines successfully an overview of the phonetic structure of modern French and its relation to orthography with a historical perspective and a section, 'De la parole au plaisir des sons et des rythmes', which covers not merely versification but prose also. **French Generative Phonology: Retrospectives and Perspectives*, ed. Chantal Lyche Salford U.P., 1994, 287 pp. N. Armstrong, 'Variable deletion of French /l/: linguistic, social and stylistic factors', *JFLS*, 6:1–21, is more limited in scope than the title suggests; A. considers the treatment of the definite article, the clitic pronouns *il* and *elle*, and final /l/ after an obstruent (as in *table*), in the speech of schoolchildren in Dieuze (Lorraine). D. C. Walker, 'The new stability of unstable *-e* in French', *ib.*, 211–29, demonstrates that the 'lexical repertory of stable schwas' is much greater than would appear from A. B. Hansen's 1994 study (*ib.*, 4:25–54). R. Desrochers, 'Les liaisons dangereuses: le statut équivoque des erreurs de liaison', *LInv*, 18, 1994[1995]:243–84, analyses the motivations underlying different types of error. *Symposium* (Seattle) includes M. E. Scullen, **'French syllable structure: reconsidering the status of the onset' (229–38); and B. Tranel, **'Exceptionality in optimality theory and final consonants in French' (275–91).

See also Taylor, *Sound Evidence*, under DIALECTS AND REGIONAL FRENCH below.

6. ORTHOGRAPHY

Bernard Cerquiglini, *Le Roman de l'orthographe. Au paradis des mots, avant la faute, 1150–1694*, Hatier, 171 pp. + 16 pls, argues that contemporary advocates of the reform of French spelling 'témoignent d'une inspiration rétrograde', and takes us on an enjoyable tour, enlivened by many a vivid image and striking turn of phrase, which, while duly covering the longer time-span suggested by his title, dwells mainly on the 16th and 17th centuries; Théodore de Bèze and Louis Meigret are contrasted as the 'conservateur moderne et sans nostalgie' and the 'héros solitaire d'un échec admirable' who 'fondent ensemble le débat orthographique, c'est-à-dire une interminable querelle'. M. Mathieu-Colmas considers the 'Syntaxe du trait d'union: structures complexes', *LInv*, 19, 1995:153–71.

7. GRAMMAR

OLD AND MIDDLE FRENCH

C. Buridant, '*Varietas delectat*. Prolégomènes à une grammaire de l'ancien français', *VR*, 55:88–125, draws attention to a range of parameters that a grammar of Old French should take into account. A. Henry, 'Français médiéval *quanqui*: forme-fantôme', *RLiR*, 60:513–21, argues that it really existed. S. Marnette offers 'Réflexions sur le discours indirect libre en français médiéval', *Romania*, 114:1–49.

MODERN FRENCH

Marc Wilmet, *Grammaire critique du Français* [*sic*] (the capital *F*- appears on both the cover and the title-page), Louvain-la-Neuve, Duculot, 670 pp., is — as those who are familiar with the author's earlier work will not be surprised to learn — a volume that abounds in questionings and penetrating insights; it is admirably undogmatic, quoting and commenting on the views of other grammarians, and abundantly illustrated with authentic examples. The fruit of many years profound and original reflection on the structure and functioning of the French language, this is a work that will richly repay the time and careful attention needed to assimilate it. Michael Allan Jones, *Foundations of French Syntax*, CUP, xxvi + 557 pp., is a book to be welcomed with open arms; whereas so many works adopting a transformational-generative approach are virtually unreadable except for devotees, this one assumes no prior knowledge of linguistics and the author is mindful throughout of the needs of those of his potential readers who are students or teachers not of theoretical linguistics but of French; his 'Introduction' explaining lucidly the concepts and terminology to be followed (demystifying, for example, the 'X-bar framework' and 'movement rules') is a model of its kind and can be recommended for its own sake. The coverage of French syntax is virtually all-embracing, taking in: verbs and verb phrases; voice; tense, aspect, and mood; noun phrases (including *inter alia* determiners, constructions with *de*, universal quantifiers); pronouns; adjectives, adverbs, and negation; prepositions; infinitival clauses; and inversion and QU-movement. Roger Hawkins and Richard Towell, *French Grammar and Usage*, London, Arnold, xx + 425 pp., defines its coverage on the basis of two media of communication, written French and spoken French, and two broad registers, the formal and the informal; where there is variability or hesitation in the use of a grammatical phenomenon, or a change in progress that has not yet been fully accepted, prescriptive norms are followed. Margaret Lang and Isabelle Perez, *Modern French Grammar: A Practical Guide*, London, Routledge, ix + 357 pp., is a well-devised two-part work for intermediate and advanced learners in which a section on 'Structures' is followed by one (counting for well over half the volume) on 'Functions', classified under the headings

'Exposition', 'Attitude' and 'Argumentation'; there is an accompany-ing *Modern French Grammar Workbook*, ix + 82 pp. Herwig Krenn, **Französische Syntax*, Berlin, Schmidt, 1995, 246 pp.

K. Nymansson, 'Le genre grammatical des anglicismes con-temporains en français', *CLe*, 66.1, 1995:95–113, seeks to identify factors operative in assigning gender to Anglicisms. Observing the hesitation shown by grammars as to whether *français*, etc., should be capitalized or not in utterances of the type *Son père est F/français*, A. Bochnakowa, 'Remarques sur l'ethnique attribut français', *RRL*, 40, 1995 [1996]: 191–99, applies a variety of tests and concludes that, in the construction in question, 'les ethniques attributs désignant la nationalité [...] sont bel et bien des substantifs' and that they should therefore be capitalized. Ph. Barbaud, 'La nominalisation d'un participe passé: la suppléance *mettre/mise* en composition lexicale', *CanJL*, 40, 1995:127–64, is a general study of the substantivization of past participles, arguing that an analysis in generative terms is inadequate and proposing one 'en termes de structure syntaxique exocentrique'. K. George, '"De la belle ouvrage": cross-gendering in unconventional French', *JFLS*, 6:163–75, identifies a range of different factors giving rise to the phenomenon under discussion. J. Lamarche, **'Gender agreement and suppletion in French', *Sympo-sium* (Seattle), 145–57.

Alan Huffman, *The Categories of Grammar: French 'lui' and 'le'*, Amsterdam, Benjamins, xiv + 378 pp., has the great merit of being both theoretically significant and readily accessible. Claiming (with ample justification) that 'no grammar has ever completely succeeded in explicating the choice between *lui* and *le* [used as shorthand forms for "indirect object" and "direct object" respectively]', and high-lighting numerous constructions in which the traditional categories of 'dative' and 'accusative' 'provide little understanding' (*je le prie/lui demande de venir* to quote an example of but one), H. sets himself the task of solving the problem 'in terms of categories which are deductively appropriate'. This he does within a framework for linguistic analysis elaborated by William Diver and his pupils at Columbia and adopting what he terms 'an instrumental view of meaning'. It is quite impossible within the confines of a necessarily brief review to do justice either to the theoretical approach in general or to this particular application of it. I will merely amplify my opening remark by commenting not only that this is a book that *should* be read but that it *can* be read without the risk of incurring the sense of frustration that inflicts one when one attempts to grapple with all too many other theoretically important works that have appeared within the last forty years and which make no concessions to the needs of those to whom they are apparently addressed. Julia Herschensohn,

Case Suspension and Binary Complement Structure in French, Amsterdam, Benjamins, xi + 200 pp., argues, within the framework of Chomsky's 'minimalist program', that 'internal argument structure and Case assignment in French are binary in nature' and that this is 'responsible for determining the syntax of typical transitive verbs as well as a number of constructions involving nonthematic subjects'. Ulrich Detges, **Nominalprädikate: eine valenztheoretische Untersuchung der französischen Funktionsverbgefüge des Paradigmas 'être Präposition Nomen' und verwandter Konstruktionen*, Tübingen, Niemeyer, xiv + 290 pp. L. Kister, 'Accessibilité pronominale des *dét. N1 de (dét.) N2*: le rôle de la détermination', *LInv*, 19, 1995:107–21, and A. Poncet-Montange, 'Trois classes de groups nominaux *N à N*', *ib.*, 173–204, both relate specifically to French. The latest addition to the 'Langue et culture' series (see *YWMLS*, 54:36 and 37), is no. 30, Reidar Veland, *Les Marqueurs référentiels 'celui-ci' et 'celui-là': structure interne et déploiement dans le discours direct littéraire*, Geneva, Droz, 457 pp., a typically thorough thesis in the Scandinavian tradition, based on a corpus consisting of the passages in direct speech from a hundred works of narrative prose from the period 1953–88; the author surveys recent work in the field and appreciates in particular that of G. Kleiber. Id., 'Les constructions tripartites en *celui*', *RLiR*, 60:111–46, develops an interpretation put forward by M. Gross in his *Grammaire transformationnelle du français: syntaxe du nom* (1977). A. Carlier, *JFLS* 6:133–62, discusses the generic interpretation of *ce, ça*, in dislocated constructions of the type *Les gosses, ça se lève tôt le matin*. G. Kleiber, 'Sur les (in)définis en général et les SN (in)définis en particulier', *BSLP*, 90, 1995:21–51, seeks to 'mettre en relief "quelques" tenants et "quelques" aboutissants définitoires de l'opposition *défini/indéfini*'. C. Schapira, **'De la grammaire au texte littéraire: valeurs grammaticales, sémantiques, stylistiques et pragmatiques de *on* en français classique', *Neophilologus*, 79, 1995:555–71.

Christian Touratier, *Le Système verbal français*, Armand Colin, 253 pp., is a most welcome work. Though some of the diagrams presenting schematically the morphology of verbs may not perhaps be very helpful, the commentary they are designed to illustrate is rigorous and lucid and, more importantly, the discussion of the values and uses of tenses, moods, voices, and aspect is subtle, insightful, and thought-provoking. There is also comment on the analyses proposed by other scholars (among them, A. Burger, J. Dubois, G. Guillaume, R. Jakobson, J. Pinchon, M. Riegel, H. Sten, R.-L. Wagner). Laurent Gosselin, *Sémantique de la temporalité en français. Un modèle calculatoire et cognitif du temps et de l'aspect*, Louvain-la-Neuve, Duculot, 291 pp., is a difficult and demanding book but one that could prove richly rewarding for those who have adequate preparation in such fields as philosophy, logic, and psycholinguistics to master it. Lars-Erik Wiberg, *Le Passé simple: son emploi dans le discours journalistique*, Stockholm, Almqvist & Wiksell, 1995, 254 pp. D. M. Engel has three good articles on the use of tense: 'Plus-que-parfait: past anterior or past punctual?', *LInv*, 18, 1994 [1995]: 223–42, looks at the role of the pluperfect in modern journalistic texts; 'Le passé du passé', *Word*, 47: 41–62, studies the role of the past anterior, the pluperfect, and the *passé surcomposé* on the basis of a questionnaire-based survey; 'L'expression du temps et la variation linguistique', *RevR*, 31: 215–33, the most wide-ranging of the three, examines 'les mélanges non-classiques, l'occurrence de temps verbaux différents, qui ne sont pas condifiés dans les livres de grammaire', especially in journalistic usage. Stefan Gutwin, *Der 'accord du participe passé' als Testfall der französischen Grammatikschreibung*, Tübingen, Niemeyer, viii + 140 pp. A.-R. Delbart, *RLiR*, 60: 485–512, studies Brassens's use of the past historic. Anca Gheorghiu-Gaţă, 'Le futur français. Questions de morphologie et de sémantisme', *RRL*, 39, 1994[1996]: 217–24, concludes that 'les effets de sens du futur sont de nature phrastique, mais aussi de nature discursive et pragmatique'.

Aidan Coveney, *Variability in Spoken French. A Sociolinguistic Study of Interrogation and Negation*, Exeter, Elm Bank, v + 271 pp., is a well-documented and clearly thought out study, based on a corpus consisting of interviews with a fairly but not excessively homogeneous group of informants from the *département* of the Somme, while also taking due account of wider historical, geographical, and sociological contexts and of previous work in the field. This is an original and significant work that offers valuable insights for future research. P. Larrivée, '*Pas* explétif', *RevR*, 31: 19–28, argues that, both in standard French and in Quebec French, *pas* can have functions analogous to those of expletive *ne*.

M. Bruña Cuevas, 'Le discours direct introduit par *que*', *FM*, 64: 28–50, contrasts Old French and Modern French. Elena Negoiţă-Soare, 'Un modèle syntaxique de la concession en français contemporain', *RRL*, 39, 1994[1996]: 225–35, seeks to propose 'un modèle syntaxique cohérent de la concession en français, en éliminant tous les autres tours recensés par les grammaires traditionnelles sous le nom de concessives sans autre raison que des effets de sens concessif [*sic*]'. N. Franken, 'Pour une nouvelle description de *puisque*', *RevR*, 31: 3–18, is a well-argued article claiming that *puisque* does not express a causal link but that it has four possible uses all deriving from its role as a 'connecteur permettant de justifier un acte par référence à une règle conditionnelle'. The stated aim of Claude Muller's interesting book, *La Subordination en français: le schème corrélatif*, Armand Colin, 256 pp., is to investigate not all subordinate clauses but those, namely consecutives, comparatives, interrogatives, and certain types of concessives, which 'échappent aux schémas simplistes: relative ou conjonctive, complétive ou circonstancielle'. Whether or not these do, as M. claims, reveal 'les vestiges modernes du vieux système indo-européen des corrélatifs', this wide-ranging and well thought out volume constitutes a significant contribution to our understanding of French syntax. Id., 'Quand *où* sert de *quand*', *ZFSL*, 106:6–21, sheds light on a familiar but curiously understudied feature of syntax. N. Furukawa, '*Il n'y a que toi qui puisses le faire!* — à propos de l'emploi thématique d'un type de proposition subordonnée', *RevR*, 31:271–82, ponders the semantic status of relative clauses such as *qui puisses [...]* in the example quoted in the title. A.-M. Perrin-Naffakh discusses '*Aussi* adjonctif: de la syntaxe à la sémantique', *FM*, 64:136–54. A. Borillo, 'Le déroulement temporel et sa représentation spatiale en français', *CPr*, 27:109–28, looks at contexts in which *devant/derrière* and other essentially spatial expressions, when seen from the point of view of the 'progression inverse du temps et de ego en direction l'un de l'autre', can metaphorically represent temporal relationships. R. J. Marquis, *'The distribution of *à* and *de* in Tough constructions in French', *Symposium* (Seattle), 35–46. C. Schwarzee, 'Die farblosen Präpositionen des Französischen: vage Prädikate oder Kasus-marker?', *RF*, 108:1–22, analyses the prepositions *à*, *de*, and others within the framework of functional lexical grammar and argues that in some functions they are pure case markers while in others they represent a predicate.

TrL, 29 (December 1994), a thematic issue, 'La cohérence textuelle: cohésion et rupture', ed. Walter De Mulder and Liliane Tasmowski-De Ryck, includes the following papers, illustrated mainly and in most cases exclusively from French: Co Vet and R. Landeweerd, 'Locuteur externe et protagoniste interne: le cas du discours reporté' (9–19), comparing the descriptions of the *sujet parlant* given by O. Ducrot and P. Sells; N. Furakawa, '*Ce que je crois, c'est que ...*: séquence thématique et ses deux aspects, cohésion et rupture' (21–37); S. Vogeleer, 'Le point de vue et les valeurs des temps verbaux' (39–58); A.-M. Berthonneau and G. Kleiber, 'Imparfaits de politesse: rupture ou cohésion?' (59–92); W. De Mulder, 'Déterminants, cohérence et raisonnement par défaut' (93–105); F. Hallyn, 'De la métaphore filée au modèle analogique: cohérence et pertinence' (107–23); and M. Charolles, 'Cohésion. cohérence et pertinence du discours' (125–51). M. Barra-Jover, 'Quantification et relation interphrastique: à propos du sens oppositif de *tout en* + gérondif, *tout de même*, *après tout* et autres', *TrL*, 30 (May 1995):5–38, is defined as the problem of the 'rapport entre un groupe d'énoncés (concessifs ou adversatifs) et la quantifica-tion du type *tout*'. S. Porhiel, 'Marqueurs de catégorisation', *CLe*,

66.1, 1995:77–93, deals with words or expressions such as *touchant, dans le cadre de, espèce de*. J. Vlemings, 'Il y a un *mais*, mais il n'y en a qu'un seul', *RevR*, 61:51–64, takes issue with those who claim that *mais* constitutes two linguistic entities, corresponding to Spanish *pero/ sino*, German *aber/sondern*, and argues for a monosemic description of *mais*. M. Achard, 'Perspective and syntactic realization: French sentential complements', *Linguistics*, 34:1159–98, is a cognitive grammar investigation. H. Nølke, 'Les adverbes paradigmatiques révisés: non sur tout mais surtout sur *surtout*', *Rask*, 4:3–33, is a follow-up both to his own 1983 article (see *YWMLS*, 47:44) and to work by others on 'focus particles' in English and German. A. Blank, '*Tyson est aux anges*:zur Semantik französischer Funktionsverbgefüge', *ZFSL*, 106:113–30, argues for the creation of a 'phraseological semantics'.

8. Lexicography

Emmanuèle Baumgartner and Philippe Ménard, *Dictionnaire étymologique et historique de la langue française*, LGF, 848 pp. T. R. Woodridge, 'Les graphies du *Thresor de la langue françoyse*', *CLe*, 66.1, 1995:55–66, is on J. Nicot's 1606 dictionary. J. Picoche, 'Définitions actancielles', *ib.*, 67–76, cogently argues the case for defining verbs in dictionaries on the basis of their behaviour in personal forms rather than on that of the infinitive. V. Tolédano, 'Traitement lexicographique des sigles', *ib.*, 67, 1995:55–70, analyses discrepancies between and within the *TLF*, the *Grand Robert* and the *Grand Larousse* in their treatment of *sigles*, and has suggestions for tidying up the treatment thereof. J. S. Jensen, 'A propos de Maurice Grevisse: *Le bon usage* (treizième édition par André Goosse [...]), — et de quelques autres livres de grammaire française', *RevR*, 61:115–29, is a review article based on the work that, by a typographical horror, he refers to throughout as *Le bon Usage*, and also surveying many of the generally excellent Scandinavian studies of French grammar that have appeared in recent decades. *Actas* (Santiago de Compostela), VIII, includes É. Brunet, 'L'exploitation des données de l'Institut National de la langue française' (703–20), and É. Martin, 'La place d'une base de données textuelle dans la recherche linguistique. L'exemple de FRANTEXT' (721–28). *Lexicographie et informatique: autour de l'informatisation du Trésor de la langue française: actes du colloque international de Nancy (29, 30, 31 mai 1995)*, ed. David Piotrowski, Didier-Érudition, 388 pp.

Marc Baratin and Marianne Baratin-Lorenzi, *Dictionnaire des synonymes*, Hachette, xiii + 829 pp. Pierre Merle, *Le Dico de l'argot fin de siècle*, Seuil, 431 pp., is a mine of surprising information with quantities of examples *saisis sur le vif* and often dated and localized with astonishing precision (e.g. 'entendu rue Saint-Denis, le 6 janvier

1996, dans la bouche d'une fille lasse'); this will prove to be an invaluable source for future lexicologists. Catherine Rouayrenc, *Les Gros Mots*, PUF (Que sais-je? 1597), provides an extensive classified repertoire of religious, sexual, and excremental terms, followed by lexical and semantic, morphological and syntactical, and pragmatic analyses. Lorédan Larchey, **Dictionnaire de l'argot parisien,* Éd. de Paris, 240 pp.

With only a couple of exceptions, the contributions to *Les Dictionnaires bilingues*, ed. Henri Béjoint and Philippe Thoiron (Champs linguistiques), Louvain-la-Neuve, Duculot, 256 pp., deal either specifically to a greater or less extent with French or with general matters that those interested in the field of French lexicology should be aware of. Among the latter are: C. Marello, 'Les différents types de dictionnaires bilingues' (31–52); B. Lépinette, 'Le rôle de la syntaxe dans la lexicographie bilingue' (53–69); and M. Lemmens, 'La grammaire dans les dictionnaires bilingues' (71–102). Most of the language-specific items take aspects of French-English lexicography: V. Grundy, 'L'utilisation d'un corpus dans la rédaction du dictionnaire bilingue' (127–49), and F. Knowles, 'L'informatisation de la fabrication des dictionnaires bilingues' (151–68), both discuss the *Oxford-Hachette French Dictionary*, while K. also considers the computerization of dictionaries, as does E. Macklovitch, 'Les dictionnaires bilingues en-ligne et le poste de travail du traducteur' (169–97), the latter mainly on the basis of his experience at Laval University; R. P. Roberts, 'Le traitement des collocations et des expressions idiomatiques dans les dictionnaires bilingues' (181–97), deals more generally with French and English dictionaries; and three contributors bring in French and languages other than English: X. Blanco, 'Élaboration et réutilisation des exemples dans la lexicographie bilingue' (103–10), on French and Spanish; T. Szende, 'Problèmes d'équivalence dans les dictionnaires bilingues' (111–26), on French and Hungarian; and A. Class, 'Problèmes de préparation rédactionnelle de dictionnaires bilingues spécialisés: quelques réflexions' (199–211), on French and German.

9. Lexicology

While standing on its own as a thought-provoking contribution to both lexicological and lexicographical studies, Igor A. Mel′čuk, André Clas and Alain Polguère, *Introduction à la lexicologie explicative et combinatoire*, Louvain-la-Neuve, Duculot, viii + 256 pp., is also a helpful adjunct to Mel′čuk's *Dictionnaire explicatif et combinatoire du français contemporain: recherches lexico-sémantiques* (3 vols, Montreal Univ. Press, 1984–1992); theoretical discussion is illustrated throughout by examples and commentary. C. Le Clerc, *Die verbale Erfassung von Lichteindrücken im Französischen. Eine Betrachtung aus lexematischer und prototypensemantischer Sicht*, Geneva, Droz, 300 pp. Jean Bouffartigue, Anne-Marie Delrieu and René Garrus, *Étymologies du français*, Belin, consists of three vols: *Les Racines latines*, 384 pp., by J. B and A.-M. D, is devoted mainly to studies of families of words that can be traced to the same root or semantically related roots (e.g. *bucca* and *os, campus* and *rus*), but also discusses, *inter alia*, suffixes, prefixes, the replacement of Latin roots by Germanic ones, doublets, Latin elements that have passed into French via other languages, etc., etc.; *Les Racines grecques*, 336 pp, also by J. B and A.-M. D, proceeds mainly by a thematic classification of Greek roots and their derivatives but also covers prefixes and suffixes and various other aspects of the Greek contribution to French; *Les Curiosités étymologiques*, 429 pp., by R. G., highlights the multifarious ways in which apparently unrelated words can be traced to common origins (e.g. *gaine* and *vanilla, pieu* and *travail*). These three volumes combine erudition and entertainment value in a most pleasing way. Alain Rey, *Le Réveille-mots: une saison d'élection*, Seuil, 238 pp., is a series of broadcast talks on lexical matters prompted by words that came to the fore during the French electoral period of 1994–95 (*ministre, candidat, scandale, corruption, responsabilité, indécis*, to quote a few that seem particularly relevant at the time, during the month before the British general election of 1997, when these lines are being written); the author succeeds in the aim, implied in his title, of waking us up to the origins, echoes, and implications of words. Sylvie Brunet, *Les Mots de la fin du siècle* (Coll. Le français retrouvé), Belin, 254 pp. Jacqueline Authier-Revuz, *Ces mots qui ne vont pas de soi: boucles réflexives et non-coïncidences du dire*, Larousse, 1995, 2 vols, iv + 864 pp. A. Henry, 'Ancien français *doi(s)ne*', *Romania*, 114:225–30, reviews all known examples of *doine, doisne*, concludes that we are dealing with two different words, but is at a loss to propose etymologies. R. Arveiller, *TLP*, 33–34:21–30, offers 48 'Notes de lexique' on words beginning with C-. Id., 'Addenda au *FEW*, XIX (Orientalia), 24ᵉ article', *ZRP*, 112:1–38, covers etyma from *ulaq* to *yasamīn*, while the 25th and final article, *ib.*, 232–65, covers those from *yāgmūrluq* to *Zwāwa*. Id., 'Le français *vaciet* et sa famille', *RLaR*, 100:211–22, corrects and completes the *FEW* article, VACCINIUM. Michael D. Picone, *Anglicisms, Neologisms and Dynamic French*, Amsterdam, Benjamins, xii + 462 pp., is an important volume; P. defines seven categories of Anglicisms and a variety of other concepts with which he operates (e.g. lexical versus syntactic borrowing and 'the analyticity-syntheticity axis'), and sets the period with which he is specifically concerned (the mid-80s) within 'the larger neological context'; he then provides, under the headings 'Juxtapositional neology', 'Binomial constructions' and 'Neological diversity', a richly documented and perspicacious analysis that will surely come to be regarded as a major contribution to the study of this already much studied field. The scope of Philip Thody, *Le Franglais: Forbidden English, Forbidden American*, London, Athlone, 1995, 300 pp., is clearly defined by its double subtitle, 'Law, politics and language in contemporary France. A study in loan words and national identity'. Three chapters of 'Arguments', ranging widely, informatively and entertainingly over the (somewhat neurotic? — my word, not Thody's) preoccupation of French intellectuals and politicians with the imagined threat to their language, are followed by four chapters classifying and commenting on Anglicisms in various spheres of life and a list of some hundreds of words and expressions used in English in what is easily recognizable as a French form (*adieu, force majeure, ménage à trois*, and the like). Marion Cypionka, **Französische 'Pseudoanglizismen': Lehnformationen zwischen Entlehnung, Wortbildung, Form- und Bedeutungswandel*, Tübingen, Narr, 1994, 288 pp. B. Benhamouda, **L'Origine arabe de la langue française*, Dialogues, 133 pp., discusses words of Arabic origin. Claudine Brécourt-Villars, **Mots de table, mots de bouche. Dictionnaire étymologique et historique du vocabulaire classique de la cuisine et de la gastronomie*, Stock, 431 pp.   K. Baldinger has fun with French and a few Spanish and German 'Jeux de mots avec des noms de lieux réels ou fictifs', *TLP*, 33–34:31–38. C. Caws presents a historical analysis of *entre chien et loup*, *ib.*, 67–80; and Id., *ZRP*, 112:409–23, takes *peur bleue* as an example of how to set about the descriptive analysis of a 'locution'.   O. Naudeau, *Romania*, 114:517–21, discusses the origin and meaning of OFr *aigroi* (in *de tel aigroi*, OProv. *de tal agrei*) and concludes that it is French (i.e. not Occitan) in origin and a back-formation meaning 'poids' from *agregier* 'alourdir, accabler'. A. Lodge, '"Haggis" and the medieval French connection', Smith, *Essays*, 7–10, argues that it is not impossible that the word is a derivative of *hacher*. On more recent culinary dishes, M. Höfler, *TLP*, 173–78, traces the history of *paella, pizza, moussaka* and *muesli* in French. F. Rainier, *ZRP*, 112:486–88, argues that *accompagnateur* 'accompanist' is a concealed Italianism. M. Nerlich, offering annotations to the history of the word *adventura — *aventure*, *ib.*, 347–64, claims that not only the history of the word but, with it, 'en partie l'histoire de la littérature du moyen âge' is in need of revision. G. Roques, 'Mes *bottes* secrètes', *ib.*, 427–37, comments on a number of idioms involving the word *botte* and on related expressions. E. Dawes, '*Avoir son pain cuit*: huit siècles d'ambiguïté sémantique', *Neophilologus*, 80:517–38, argues that this is a pan-European idiom and that the meaning 'to be financially ruined, or dying' derives by irony from the meaning 'to have made a fortune'. C. Beaumont-James proposes an 'Analyse sémantique du mot *chanson*',

CLe, 67, 1995: 163–92. H. Bäckvall, 'Néologismes nodiériens', *RevR*, 31: 163–93, studies the aims (which include the ridiculing of pretentious neologisms) of Charles Nodier's *Notions élémentaires de linguistique* (1834), and identifies the neologisms in it that have survived. K. George, '*Le monde et le demi-monde* — half-measures in French', *FSB*, 61: 1–3, identifies words and expressions incorporating *moitié*, *demi-*, or *mi* plus a few comparable ones. C. Tourniaire, Smith, *Essays*, 345–52, examines the use of the *pied* in French idioms as defined in the *Robert électronique*. A. Vercruysse's study, *TrL*, 30 (May, 1995): 65–81, of the use of *liquide* and *liquidité* in the technical language of economics is presented as an 'illustration d'une perspective cognitive de la métaphore'. Jean-Philippe Bouchard, **Les Mots du sport: la tête dans le guidon*, Seuil, 236 pp. J. Labelle, 'Le traitement automatique des variantes linguistiques en français: l'exemple des "concrets"', *LInv*, 19, 1995: 137–52, proposes a method for disambiguating instances of nouns such as *bleuet* (fruit, flower), *canard* ('duck', 'newspaper', [in Canada] 'kettle'). Gaston Gross, **Les Expressions figées en français: noms composés et autres locutions*, Gap, Orphrys, 160 pp. *RLFRU*, 15, includes F. Drijkoningen, 'On the antisymmetry of words: category changing prefixation in French' (33–45); and W. Zwanenburg, 'French adverb formation: derivation versus inflection and word structure levels' (59–71), the latter (arguing that the formation of adverbs in -*ment* belongs to inflexion rather than to derivation) also found in *ALH*, 43: 277–92.

10. ONOMASTICS

M.-T. Morlet, 'Les noms de personne dans la région de Langres (Haute-Marne) au XIVe siècle', *TLP*, 33–34: 313–32, is based on an account-book of a religious order. C. Schmitt, *ib.*, 469–82, examines the importance of place-name evidence for the study of the Romanization of the valley of the Moselle. G. Taverdet, 'De quelques nasalisations surprenantes', *ib.*, 499–506, comments on a few place names in Burgundy.

11. DIALECTS AND REGIONAL FRENCH

Jean-Pierre Chambon, Claude Michel, and Pierre Rézeau, **Mélanges sur les variétés du français en France, d'hier et d'aujourd'hui*, vol. 1, Klincksieck, 1994, 259 pp. Claudine Fréchet, **Le Français parlé à Annonay (Ardèche)*, Klincksieck, 1995, vi + 252 pp. Pierre-Valentin Berthier, **Glossaire de la Champagne berrichonne*, B. Royer, 297 pp. Jill Taylor, *Sound Evidence: Speech Communities and Social Accents in Aix-en-Provence*, Berne, Lang, 333 pp., identifies, on the basis of an impressively detailed phonetic description, the characteristic features of the pronunciation of French in Aix and, in the words of Henriette Walter in her Preface, shows 'just how speech varieties and social variables interact inside a regionally homogeneous group'. M. Francard evaluates 'Un instrument pour l'étude de la variation linguistique en Belgique francophone: la banque de données VALIBEL', *Actas* (Santiago de Compostela), VIII, 729–36. *Espace francophone*, 2, includes P. Knecht, 'La Suisse romande: aspects d'un paysage francophone conservateur' (759–70); and J.-P. Goudaillier, 'La situation luxembourgeoise: vers un changement de statut de la langue française?' (771–83). J. R. Klein and B. Lamiroy, 'Lexique-grammaire du français de Belgique: les expressions figées', *LInv*, 1994 [1995]: 285–320, analyse some 400 expressions on the basis of a model proposed by M. Gross. W. Müller, 'La langue en Suisse romande à la fin du moyen âge', *TLP*, 33–34: 333–45, identifies words, forms, and proper names in 12th–14th-c. charters. M. Auzanneau, 'Paroles de marché', *Linguistique*, 31.2: 47–62, finds the principle of 'dialectal bilingualism' helpful in studying the sociolinguistic situation in rural markets in Poitou. René Lepelley, **Paroles de Normands: textes dialectaux du XIIe au XXe siècle*, Caen U.P., 1995, 168 pp.

12. ANGLO-NORMAN

Procs (Odense) contains authoritative studies by two of the editors of the *Anglo-Norman Dictionary*, viz. D. A. Trotter, 'Language contact and lexicography' (21–39), and W. Rothwell, 'Adding insult to injury: the English who curse in borrowed French' (41–54). There are also contributions by D. A. Kibbee, 'Emigrant languages and acculturation: the case of Anglo-French' (1–39); and T. de Jong, 'Anglo-French in the 13th and 14th centuries: continental or insular dialect?' (55–70). W. Rothwell, 'Playing "follow my leader" in Anglo-Norman studies', *JFLS*, 6: 177–210, vigorously exposes the uncritical acceptance by one scholar after another of demonstrably erroneous 19th-c. views as to the 'degeneracy' of Anglo-Norman.

13. FRENCH IN NORTH AMERICA

Jean Forest, **Anatomie du québécois*, Montreal, Triptyque, 339 pp. **Français du Canada, français de France*, IV: *Actes du quatrième colloque international*, ed. Thomas Lavoie, Tübingen, Niemeyer, vi + 406 pp. C. Verreault and T. Lavoie, 'Genèse et formation du français au Canada: l'éclairage de la géographie linguistique', *RLiR*, 60: 413–62, is a well-documented account (with 24 maps) of a major ongoing study. Y.-Ch. Morin, 'The origin and development of the pronunciation of French in Quebec', *Procs* (Odense), 243–75, argues that any consideration of the origins of Quebec French 'must carefully distinguish the specific evolution of its lexicon, its syntax, its morphology, and its pronunciation — which may be relatively independent from one another' and notes that 'a large and difficult [research] program' still lies ahead. *BFF*, no. 7, 'Spécial Canada', is mainly devoted to literary matters, but also includes W. Sarcher, 'Le Québec et la France: aspects et problèmes linguistiques de la francophonie' (31–40); and B. Bagola, '*Danger anglicismes*: la défense de la langue française en France et au Québec' (41–55).

P. Martin studies the 'Durée acoustique des semi-consonnes et de leur voyelle correspondante en français du Québec', *Phonetica*, 53:33–54, and, 'L'opposition entre /ɛ/ (bref) et /ɛ:/ (long) en français actuel du Québec', *Linguistique*, 31.2:33–45, shows that the phonemic opposition is still widely observed. M.-Th. Vinet, 'On certain adverbs of quantification in Quebec French', *Probus*, 8:207–21, discusses the status of *benben, trop trop* and *le diable* and the ways in which they differ from standard French *beaucoup*. T. Nadashi, 'Subject NP doubling, matching, and minority French', *LVC*, 7, 1995:1–14, is on the French of adolescent speakers in predominantly Anglophone communities in Ontario. A. Lapierre, 'A propos du discours lexicographique québécois', *TLP*, 33–34:233–46, analyses reactions to various dictionaries of Quebec French. L. Meney, 'Origines et caractéristiques du français québécois', *CLe*, 67, 1995:5–36, investigates borrowings from western French dialects, archaisms, borrowings from native American languages, and Anglicisms.

Espace francophone, 2, includes: A. Valdman, 'Le français en Louisiane' (633–50); R. Breton, 'Crépuscule ou survivance des *Francos* et de la franco-américanie? (Une communauté bien vivante mais qui ne pouvait pas *être un pays*)' (651–64); and G. and M.-C. Hazaël, 'Quel français parle-t-on aux Antilles?' (665–87).

Cynthia K. Stäbler, *Entwicklung mündlicher romanischer Syntax: das français cadien in Louisiana*, Tübingen, Narr, 1995, xiv + 222 pp. C. Lyche, 'Genèse et traits caractéristiques du français cadien: un aperçu phonologique', *RevR*, 61:29–49, has both diachronic and synchronic dimensions.

14. FRENCH OUTSIDE EUROPE AND NORTH AMERICA

Espace francophone, 2, includes: G. Prignitz, 'Contraintes et paradoxes du Burkina Faso, pays essentiellement multilingue et résolument francophone' (547–64); M. Daff, 'Présentation de quelques caractéristiques du français parlé et écrit au Sénégal' (565–75); A. M. Igué, 'La situation du français au Bénin' (577–885); S. Lafage, 'La Côte d'Ivoire: une appropriation nationale du français?' (587–602); A. Moussirou-Mouyama and T. de Samie, 'La situation sociolinguistique au Gabon' (603–13); É. Kouba-Fila, 'Image et réalité du français au Congo' (615–29); A. Boukous, 'La francophonie au Maroc: situation sociolinguistique' (691–703); and F. Laroussi, 'Le français en Tunisie aujourd'hui' (705–21). Sélim Abou, Choghig Kasparian and Katia Haddad, *Anatomie de la francophonie libanaise*, Ottawa, AUPELF, 318 pp. J. Taylor studies 'Code switching in Dakar', *Linguistique*, 31.2:63–78.

15. French in India and the Pacific Area

Espace francophone, 2, includes: R. Breton, 'Le français à Pondichéry: des réalités au mythe' (725–31); and C. Lombardini, 'La francophonie polynésienne: entre français popa'a... et "mélange"' (735–56).

16. French Creoles

Alleyne Mervyn, *Syntaxe historique créole*, Karthala, 208 pp. Sibylle Kriegel, *Diathesen im Mauritius- und Seychellenkreol*, Tübingen, Narr, 232 pp. Ralph Ludwig, *Kreolsprachen zwischen Mündlichkeit und Schriftlichkeit: Zur Syntax und Pragmatik atlantischer Kreolsprachen auf französischer Basis*, Tübingen, Narr, 424 pp. Charmant Theodore, *Haitian Creole–English English–Haitian Creole Dictionary*, NY, Hippocrene, 1995, 291 pp. Maurice Barbotin, *Dictionnaire du créole de Marie-Galante*, Hamburg, Buske, 234 pp. Benjamin Moïse and Marie-Noëlle Recocque, *Dictionnaire d'expressions créoles par mots*, Desormeaux, 1995, 319 pp., and *Dictionnaire d'expressions créoles par thèmes*, Desormeaux, 1995, 234 pp. M. Milfort de Ariza examines the position of 'L'haïtien face à la valeur sociale et aux domaines d'emploi du créole et du français', *Procs* (Brasília), 653–60, referring to the periods both before and after 'l'instrumentalisation officielle du créole en Haïti à partir de 1979'.

17. Sociolinguistics

It emerges from F. Gadet's survey of the treatment of linguistic variation in a number of recent works, 'Variabilité, variation, variété: le français d'Europe', *JFLS*, 6:75–98, that French sociolinguistics still has some catching up to do. See also Coveney, p. 36 above.

18. Pragmatics

CLF, 16 and 17 (1995), 'Les différents plans d'organisation du dialogue et leurs interrelations', publish the *Actes* of the VIᵉ Colloque de pragmatique de Genève (June 1995), with a number of contributions relating specifically to or illustrated from French. In vol. 16: R. Bouchard, 'Des praxéogrammes aux discours écrits: analyse des interactions, analyse de discours et pertinence' (9–51); D. Vincent, 'Du dialogue au soliloque: des interactions plus ou moins conversationnelles' (53–68); C. Kerbrat-Orecchioni, 'La construction de la relation interpersonnelle: quelques remarques sur cette dimension du dialogue' (69–88); D. Luzzati, 'De l'erreur en dialogue homme-machine' (175–92); C. Rossari, 'Du monologique au dialogique, du narratif au discursif: continuum ou rupture?' (193–210); L. Perrin, 'Du dialogue rapporté aux reprises diaphoniques' (211–40); and É. Miche, 'Les formes de diaphonie dans un débat parlementaire' (241–65). In vol. 17: M. Burger, 'L'identité négociée: rapports de place(s) dans un entretien télédiffusé' (9–33); A. Ferrari and A. Auchlin, 'Le point: un signe de ponctualisation' (35–56); J.-M. Luscher, E. Roos and C. Rubattel, 'Prises de parole et interventions dans l'organisation de la conversation' (57–98); E. Roulet, 'Étude des plans d'organisation syntaxique, hiérarchique et référentiel du dialogue: autonomie et interrelations modulaires' (123–40); R. Vion, 'La gestion pluridimensionnelle du dialogue' (179–203); A.-C. Berthoud and L. Mondada, 'Traitement du topic, processus énonciatifs et séquences conversationnelles' (205–28); and A. Reboul and J. Moeschler, 'Le dialogue n'est pas une catégorie naturelle scientifiquement pertinente' (229–48). *Ib.*, 18, 'Approches modulaire, pragmatique et expérientielle du discours et des énoncés', publishes the interim results of research carried out by three teams at the Unité de linguistique française of the University of Geneva; the following papers relate to or are illustrated from French: L. Filliettaz, 'Vers une approche interactionniste de la dimension référentielle du discours' (33–67); A. Grobet, 'Phénomènes de continuité: anaphoriques et traces de points d'ancrage' (69–93); É. Miche, 'Approche modulaire de l'organisation polyphonique dans un discours parlementaire genevois' (95–128); L. Perrin, 'De la structure énonciative et de l'organisation polyphonique d'un échange épistolaire' (129–56); C. Rossari, 'Identification d'unités discursives: les actes et les connecteurs' (157–77); J.-M. Luscher and B. Sthioul, 'Emplois et interprétations du Passé composé' (187–217); L. de Saussure, 'Encapsulation et référence temporelle d'énoncés négatifs au Passé Composé et au Passé Simple' (219–42); M. Kozlowska, '*Ensuite* et l'ordre temporel' (243–74); J. Jayez, 'Référence et aspectualité. Le problème des verbes dits "aspectuels"' (275–98); J. Moeschler, 'Ordre temporel, narration et analyse du discours' (299–328); K. Stroumza, 'Intégrité des formes de l'écrit' (357–80); and D. Firget, 'Figures et espaces mentaux: la prétérition' (383–411).

19. SPECIAL REGISTERS

S. Verlinde, 'La combinatoire du vocabulaire des fluctuations dans le discours économique', *CLe*, 66, 1995:137–76, looks at nouns and verbs expressing increase or decrease in French business texts.

20. CONTRASTIVE STUDIES

Luc Ostiguy, Robert Sarrasin, and Glenwood Irons, *Introduction à la phonétique comparée: les sons: le français et l'anglais nord-américains*, Quebec, Laval U. P., 200 pp. Judith Berman and Anette Frank, *Deutsche und französische Syntax im Formalismus der LFG*, Tübingen, Niemeyer, ix + 247 pp. (LFG = Lexical-Functional Grammar). Rhéa Delveroudi, *La Notion de sujet et sa réalisation dans l'énoncé en grec moderne et en français*, Gap, Ophrys, 297 pp. M.-H. Côté, 'Concurrence structurale, conditions d'appréhensibilité et changement syntaxique: la chute de la structure V2 en français', *CanJL*, 40, 1995:165–200, starts with OF and brings in detailed comparison with Germanic languages, especially Icelandic and Yiddish. F. Cornish, '"Antecedentless" anaphors: deixis, anaphora, or what? Some evidence from English and French', *JL*, 32:19–41, shows that such anaphors are 'interesting for an understanding of how anaphora works generally'. L. Cornips and A. Hulk compare 'Ergative reflexive reflexes in Heerlen French and Dutch', *SL*, 50:1–21. R. Washio, 'Does French agree or not?', 18, 1994 [1995]:377–414, may not be fully accessible to those who are not familiar both with GB theory and with Japanese. Mohamed Hairet, *Fonctionnement du système verbal en arabe et en français*, Gap, Ophrys, 232 pp.

EARLY MEDIEVAL LITERATURE

By A. E. COBBY, *University of Cambridge*, and FINN E. SINCLAIR

The following abbreviations have been used as particular to this section:
Sturm-Maddox, *Transtextualities*, for *Transtextualities of Cycles and Cyclicity in Medieval French Literature*, ed. Sara Sturm-Maddox and Donald Maddox (MRTS, 149), 1996, vi + 203 pp.; and Kelly, *Medieval Opus*, for Douglas Kelly, *The Medieval Opus: Imitation, Rewriting, and Transmission in the French Tradition*, Amsterdam, Rodopi, xv + 427 pp.

I. GENERAL

Richard Barber, *The Knight and Chivalry*, rev. edn, Woodbridge, Boydell, 1995, xvi + 415 pp., is a much expanded and updated revision of the 1970 work (*YWMLS*, 32:210), taking new research into account. Also expanded since the previous (1990) edition is the *Répertoire international des médiévistes (International Directory of Medievalists)*, 8th edn, Turnhout, Brepols, 1995, xxiii + 670 pp., whose coverage, theoretically of medievalists working in all countries and disciplines, continues to be somewhat eclectic. Michel Zink, *Medieval French Literature: An Introduction*, trans. Jeff Rider (MRTS, 110), 1995, xii + 171 pp., is a translation of *Le Moyen Age: littérature française*, 1990 (*YWMLS*, 53:52), with a conclusion taken from the longer, 1992 edition; the translation offers additional notes and an expanded bibliography and chronology. *Medieval France: An Encyclopedia* (GRLH, 932: Garland Encyclopedias of the Middle Ages, 2), ed. William W. Kibler and Grover A. Zinn, 1995, xxvi + 1047 pp., is a welcome new reference work, which devotes much space to literature in its mixture of short reference items and substantive articles, written by international authorities. Rita Copeland, *Rhetoric, Hermeneutics, and Translation in the Middle Ages: Academic Traditions and Vernacular Texts*, CUP, 1995, xiv + 295 pp., examines the relationship between rhetoric and hermeneutics, positing this as the nexus within which the character of medieval vernacular translation is defined. Jean Flori, *La Chevalerie en France au moyen âge* (Que sais-je?, 972), PUF, 1995, 128 pp., replaces *La Chevalerie* by P. du Puy de Clinchamps in the same series. F. outlines the history and nature of knighthood and chivalry, together with its social and literary manifestations, its ritual, chivalric myths, the religious role of chivalry, and its links with courtesy, courtly love and the epic. D. R. Howlett, *The English Origins of Old French Literature*, Dublin, Four Courts Press, x + 180 pp., maintains that the maturity of the oldest extant French literature, and the abundance of insular manuscripts, are to be explained by the literature's being not of continental but of insular, specifically Anglo-Latin, origin. He uses patterns of repetition as evidence that the repetitivity characteristic of Old French literature derives from its Latin origins; much weight is placed on line-, word-, syllable-, and letter-counts. Burt Kimmelman, *The Poetics of Authorship in the Later Middle Ages: The Emergence of the Modern Literary Persona*, NY, Lang, 288 pp., examines the development of literary autocitation from the early to the late Middle Ages and the changing relationship of individual to text. The increase in authorial involvement, from the textual inclusion of signatory anagrams through the use of the character-narrator, is seen as leading to the evolution of the modern literary persona. Sarah Spence, *Texts and the Self in the Twelfth Century*, CUP, xi + 167 pp., argues that the development of a notion of selfhood parallels the rise of vernacular literature. The 12th-c. 'self' is defined in spatial and visual terms, relating body and vernacular text in a way which transcends the perceived temporality and self-sufficiency of Latin literature, and allows for the intrusion of partiality and difference. Jacques Stiennon, *L'Ecriture* (Typologie des sources du moyen âge occidental, 72), Turnhout, Brepols, 1995, 132 pp. + 5 pls, studies medieval writing from the points of view of physiology, materials, scribal skills, and training (including the identification of hands), and in relation to medieval mentalities. There is considerable discussion of the role of the written word in medieval society, and both Latin and vernacular literature are cited in evidence for the use of and attitude to the written and the scribe. Theresa Tinkle, *Medieval Venuses and Cupids: Sexuality, Hermeneutics, and English Poetry*, Stanford U.P., 294 pp., examines the multiple representations and transformations of Venus and Cupid in response to varying codes of sexual morality reflected in Latin, French, and English poetry. Cupid is linked with the Ovidian tradition in French literature, a culturally specific use of mythography which is read as displaced in favour of Venus by the nationalistic and classicizing trends of Chaucerian poetry. Jean Verdon, *Le Plaisir au moyen âge*, Perrin, 200 pp., uses literary sources liberally in investigation of sexual and other pleasures, and discusses the relationship between the literary representations and reality. Nigel Wilkins, *Catalogue des manuscrits français de la bibliothèque Parker (Parker Library), Corpus Christi College, Cambridge*, Cambridge, Corpus Christi College, 1995, 189 pp., describes 65 MSS containing medieval French in this rich collection. K. Ciggaar, 'La dame combattante: thème épique et thème courtois au temps des croisades', *Actes* (Groningen), 121–30, looks for fighting women in literature and history, finding them in Eastern and Western crusade sources, in romances and, later, in *chansons de geste*, where they remain courtly figures. M. A. Jubb, 'Enemies in the Holy War, but brothers in chivalry: the Crusaders' view of their Saracen opponents', *ib.*, 251–59, argues that the reality of Muslim behaviour, as seen in the East in the later 12th c., and as exemplified especially by Saladin, led to a change of spirit in the portrayal of some of the enemy in *chansons de geste* and chronicles composed after 1180. These show a climate of mutual respect and the figure of the good Saracen; it is not essential in them to be a Christian in order to be a knight, though Christianity is a *sine qua* non for salvation. S. Marnette, 'Réflexions sur le discours indirect libre en français médiéval', *Romania*, 114:1–2, considers a range of medieval texts in order to define the characteristics of 'discours indirect libre'. Ambiguity and polyvalence are seen as key traits in its use. E. J. Mickel, 'Les germes de la culpabilité au moyen âge', *TLit*, 8, 1995:25–41, mines a variety of early French literary texts for instances of the greatest crimes (impiety and its results, treachery and betrayal), and finds their origin in the ancient world. J.-C. Mühle-thaler, 'Mourir à table: contextualisation et enjeux d'une séquence narrative au XIIe siècle (de la *Chanson de Guillaume* à *Erec et Enide*)', *Banquets*, 217–33, finds that death at table has negative connotations, always being associated with loss of self-control; one so killed is either guilty (a traitor or a tyrant) or, if innocent, has to have his death justified. D. Staines, 'The medieval cycle: mapping a trope', Sturm-Maddox, *Transtextualities*, 15–37, is a wide-ranging essay which traces the history of the term 'cycle' from the 9th c. to the present day. M. Zink, 'Trente ans avec la littérature médiévale: note brève sur de longues années', *CCMe*, 39:27–40, sums up trends and reflects on the development of the field over the last 30 years.

2. EPIC

GENERAL. C. Blons-Pierre, 'L'expression de la rapidité dans *La Chanson de Roland* et dans *La Chanson de Guillaume*: une manière d'établir une distinction entre Francs et Sarrasins', *Actes* (Groningen), 111–20, shows how the poets use the verbs *saillir*, *curre*, *fuir* and *brochier* of individuals and groups and so reveal their vision of the two sides. The author of *Guillaume* may mock Franks as individuals but shows only Saracens fleeing *en masse*, the *Roland* poet never mocks Franks or shows them fleeing but praises them through the use of *brochier*. B. Finet-van der Schaaf, 'L'image de la Frise et des Frisons dans la littérature en ancien et en moyen français et dans quelques chroniques en moyen néerlandais', *ib.*, 441–50, finds that in 12th-c. and 13th-c. epic texts the image of Frisians is positive, before becoming predominantly negative in later French texts as in Middle Dutch. M. Gosman,

'"Rex Franciae, Rex Francorum": la chanson de geste et la propagande de la royauté', *ib.*, 451–60, links language and power in
Capetian history and the *chanson de geste*, seeing epic poets as royalists
helping the kings of Paris to build the kingdom of France. He studies
the way in which the Capetians used language to underpin their
authority, the *chanson de geste* as a propaganda vehicle (by considering
the language used of France, the French and Charlemagne), and
finally the role of Saint-Denis both in the consolidation of Capetian
power and in literature. S. Kay, 'Le problème de l'ennemi dans les
chansons de geste', *ib.*, 261–68, discovers a change of attitude in the
12th c., as the enemy changes from being the outsider to being
perceived also within one's own society. She focuses on the opposition
between external and internal, showing how the early *chanson de geste*
projects evil outwards while later texts, in reaction against the
romance and courtly culture, increasingly find it within, rejecting
individuality and the interior life and the traitors who manifest these.
A. V. Murray, '*Coroscane*: homeland of the Saracens in the *chansons de
geste* and the historiography of the Crusades', *ib.*, 177–84, studies the
origins and connotations of this place name, showing how Latin
historiography and eschatological traditions combine to influence the
vernacular epic. F. Suard, 'Les héros chrétiens face au monde
sarrasin', *ib.*, 187–208, examines the links between the two religious
worlds as ensembles, taking examples from a wide range of epic texts
and finding that none is altogether lacking in Saracen presence. S.
describes the Saracen world, which is huge, monstrous, marvellous,
splendid, characterized by violence, medicine and beautiful women,
and the complex, paradoxical attitude of Christian heroes to it.
Though it is a hostile, demoniac world it needs to be worthy of the
Christians, and it informs not only the narrative but also the poetics
of the texts. T. Venckeleer, 'Les valeurs chevaleresques et leur
expression dans l'épopée', *ib.*, 517–22, looks at the epithets expressing
conformity of characters or actions to the approved code of chivalry
or to valued characteristics, asking whether (and implicitly showing
that) this vocabulary develops semantically as the fixation of formulaic
collocations leads to fusions and transfers of sense. P. Verelst, 'L'art
de Tolède ou le huitième des arts libéraux: une approche du
merveilleux épique', *ib.*, 3–41, uses a wide range of *chansons de geste* to
find examples of the (non-Christian) marvellous and magic, in people
and in many different objects. D. Collomp, 'Le motif du pape
combattant dans l'épopée', *Colloque* (Aix-en-Provence), 91–112,
shows that the figure of the pope is rare in early *chansons de geste*, and
that where present he is a function, representing church values and
authority, rather than an individual. In later medieval texts fighting
clerics are more common, and with them the fighting pope,

reflecting reality. S. Kay, 'The life of the dead body: death and the sacred in the *chansons de geste*', *YFS*, 86, 1994:94–108, uses Freud and Girard's work on the primitive sacred to identify the primitive beliefs showing through epic deaths. She illustrates the spiritual (but not uniquely Christian) qualities of deaths in several *chansons de geste*, then interprets and illuminates these deaths with the aid of Freud and Girard, ending with a close reading of the death of Bernier in *Raoul de Cambrai*. J.-P. Martin, 'Histoire ou mythes: l'exemple de la chanson de geste', *Littérales*, 19:5–20, starts from the discrepancy between history and *chanson de geste*. In a brief history of *chanson de geste* criticism he reviews the stances and problems of the traditionalist and individualist positions, showing that what is important is not how history is deformed but how it is reformed. He discusses the role of invention, adaptation, ideology, folklore, and myth, concluding that we can no longer study the *chanson de geste* without considering its links with Indo-European myths and their Carolingian manifestations. F. Suard, 'L'eau dans les chansons de geste', *Colloque* (Orléans), 132–47, analyses examples of four roles of water: drinking, a perilous frontier, an incentive to daring which enables the demonstration of power, and baptism.

ROLAND AND CHARLEMAGNE.   *Song of Roland*, trans. with an introd. by Janet Shirley, Felinfach, Llanerch, xvi + [162] pp., has a brief introduction for the general reader and a translation into blank verse, with some paraphrase, based upon all the modern editions. R. Middleton and K. Pratt, 'A fragment of an unknown "Roland" epic', Pratt, *Roland and Charlemagne*, 205–13, is a photographic reproduction and edition of a fragment of 120 lines or part-lines of a text of *c*. 1200, in decasyllabic, monorhymed *laisses*, mentioning Roland and Oliver along with other names known from other texts but hitherto found together in no one text. H. Legros, 'Entre Chrétiens et Sarrasins, des amitiés paradoxales: liberté de l'imaginaire ou rêve d'un monde réconcilié', *Actes* (Groningen), 269–78, examines the nature of the friendship between Naîme and Balan in *Aspremont* and that between Ogier and Karæus in *La Chevalerie d'Ogier de Danemarche*. The first shows up the strength and uniqueness of the bond between Naîme and Charles, the second shows the values of the individual triumphing over society. The contrast reflects the changing mentality between the Third Crusade and the period after the sack of Constantinople. M.-L. Ollier, 'Le discours collectif dans le *Roland*', *ib.*, 491–99, shows how group speech expresses what the group has in common and is linked to a certain political vision of society and of the relations between individuals and society. Collective discourse by the pagans in *Roland* (and in the romance), is contrasted with that of the Franks. Y. Otaka, 'La langue du *Voyage de Charlemagne à Jérusalem et à*

Constantinople: assonances', *ib.*, 279–89, exhaustively lists the assonances, with remarks on phonetics, graphy, Anglo-Norman and
southern characteristics, and anomalies, finding 12th-c. and 13th-c.
traits together with one from the 14th century. M. C. Vos, 'Saragossa
once more: the fortress on a height', *ib.*, 225–32, draws out the
Biblical symbolism and overtones of Saragossa's being placed on a
mountain by the *Roland* poet. J. B. Williamson, 'The figure of the
griffin in the *Chanson d'Aspremont*', *ib.*, 83–89, links the griffin to
Saracens and to a morally reprehensible attitude to wealth, contrasting this with Charlemagne's Christian largesse. S. L. Burch,
'Bramimunde: her name, her nature', Pratt, *Roland and Charlemagne*,
67–81, discusses the problematical etymology of this name. She
concludes that 'munde', with its Germanic ring and use (as '-monde')
for other heroines, may have overtones of 'noble (foreign) lady';
'bram' she relates to *brame, embramir* 'impassion, inflame', with
Bramimunde's ardent desire being in the form of anger and grief at
women's impotence and men's incompetence, 'passionate desire for
effective action'. J. Simpson, 'The gifts of the *Roland*: the Old French
Gui de Bourgogne', *ib.*, 31–65, applies the theory of the gift to *Gui de
Bourgogne*, concentrating on monetary terminology and on father-son
tension, and arguing that economic and genealogical metaphors
reflect inter- and intratextual relationships, the later text paying a
'poisonous tribute' to the *Roland*. W. G. van Emden, in a pair of
articles, 'The reception of Roland in some Old French epics', *ib.*,
1–30, and 'La réception du personnage de Roland dans quelques
œuvres plus ou moins épiques des 12ᵉ, 13ᵉ et 14ᵉ siècles', *Actes*
(Groningen), 353–62, studies the presentation of Roland in many
texts, paying particular attention to the question of his *démesure*, which
van E. finds to be significant for contemporaries as for modern critics.
While the reception in some texts is entirely positive, others show him
as guilty of overweening pride, add a religious dimension perceived
to be lacking in the *Chanson de Roland*, or criticize him indirectly
through another hero. M. de Combarieu du Grès, 'Ysoré "*ber*" et
"*clerc*" dans *Aiquin* (fin XIIᵉ-début XIIIᵉ siècle)', *Colloque* (Aix-en-
Provence), 605–18, draws out the character of Ysoré as a fighting
cleric and a representative and guarantor of local liberty. Y. Foehr-
Janssens, 'La mort en fleurs: violence et poésie dans *Ami et Amile*',
CCMe, 39:263–74, shows how the flowered meadow where heroes
meet is also a battlefield, so that the floral décor helps the expression
of all aspects of interpersonal relationships, while also linking the epic
and romance sides of this inter-generic text. J. H. Grisward, '*Ami et
Amile* et les trois péchés du guerrier', *Littérales*, 19:21–32, links
Lubias's three lying accusations with the Dumézilian concept of the
warrior's three sins, sacrilege, cowardice, and lust or venality. He

suggests that this expression of the trifunctional system was integrated into the pre-existing story of *Ami et Amile* because it offered a ready series of sins, fitted the repetitive nature of the *chanson de geste* and usefully structured the tale, which is notable for threesomes and may have been delivered in three sessions. J. Kjær, 'La réception scandinave de la littérature courtoise et l'exemple de la *Chanson de Roland / Af Rúnzivals bardaga*: une épopée féodale transformée en roman courtois?', *Romania*, 114:50–69, compares *Roland* with its more courtly Old Norse translation, and finds that the changes are in matters very close to the heart of French feudal society but antipathetic to Hákon Hákonarson, the translator's patron; while the style remains epic the ideology undergoes a thorough renewal and becomes courtly. A. Roncaglia, 'Geografia storica di leggende e fiabe: da *Roland* a *Auberon*', *CN*, 56:45–99, studies the problematical place names in the *Roland*, then considers similarly problematical names in the *Roman d'Auberon* and finds them surprisingly realistic. C. Segre, 'Comment présenter la *Chanson de Roland* à l'université', *RLiR*, 60:5–23, compares in detail the editions and translations of Short (*YWMLS*, 52:49) and Jean Dufournet, **La Chanson de Roland* (Collection bilingue), Flammarion, 1993, 450 pp. S. reflects on the principles which should inform student editions, finds both of these lacking in justification and explanation for editorial decisions, and fears they may mislead students by hiding problems.

GUILLAUME D'ORANGE AND THE GARIN CYCLE. *Le Cycle de Guillaume d'Orange: anthologie*, ed. Dominique Boutet (Lettres gothiques, 23), Livre de Poche, 672 pp., publishes excerpts from standard editions of ten texts in the cycle and of the *Chanson de Guillaume*, with facing translations, notes, introduction and bibliography. E. A. Heinemann, 'Existe-t-il une chanson de geste aussi brillante que le *Charroi de Nîmes*?', *Actes* (Groningen), 461–69, continues H.'s work on complex internal and external repetition, showing how they produce in this text a range of effects founded on echo and rhythm, and how subtle detail produces comic and other results. J.-P. Martin, 'De la *Chanson de Guillaume* à *Aliscans*: l'emploi des motifs rhétoriques', *ib.*, 471–79, considers examples of amplification in *Aliscans* and finds not simple inflation but real æsthetic value. He concludes that *Aliscans* is the work of a master not only of traditional methods but of late 12th-c. innovations, in whose hands repetition is not gratuitous, stereotypes not sterile. A. Moisan, 'L'abbé Henri et ses moines dans le *Moniage Guillaume* et le *Moniage Rainouart*, ou la perfidie dans l'état monastique', *Colloque* (Aix-en-Provence), 435–47, analyses the entry of Guillaume and of Rainouart into monastic life, and the monastery's reactions. He finds satire, not of monastic life as such but of possible abuses, expressed through a picture of a fossilized community of silly, greedy, treacherous, cowardly monks with no understanding of their new brethren. Id., 'De la cuisine à la chevalerie et à la vie monastique, ou les trois "fonctions" chez le Rainouart épique', *Banquets*, 337–52, approaches the character of Rainouart as *laborator* turned first *bellator* and then *orator*, who sums up in himself the social ascent through the three estates (these being the medieval manifestation of the primitive division of functions in the Dumézilian sense). M. de Combarieu du Grès, 'Bonnes et mauvaises manières de table dans *La Chanson de Guillaume* et *Aliscans*', *ib.*, 281–301, considers banquets, meals, and food in general in these poems and shows how they manifest *mesure* or *démesure, folie* or *sens*, with abundant examples and detail. L. H. Frey, '"Monday in the evening": refrain and formulism in *La Chanson de Guillaume*', *FSB*, 60:1–4, looks at the content of the *laisses* with a refrain in the light of the limitations imposed a century earlier in northern France by the *Treuga Dei*. L. Schøsler, 'New methods in textual criticism: the case of the *Charroi de Nîmes*', pp. 225–76 of *Medieval Dialectology*, ed. Jacek Fisiak (Trends in Linguistics Studies and Monographs, 79), Berlin–NY, Mouton de Gruyter, 1995, xviii + 331 pp., is a dialect-based discussion of the text's stemma, which gives a result similar to the traditional one but obtained in a new way. S. groups the MSS in three independent families and dates the *A* family later than hitherto. She localizes the MSS and the archetypes according to Dees's method, concluding that the original was from eastern France. An edition of the *F* fragment is included. S.'s methods are discussed at length, and unfavourably, in a posthumous article by D. McMillan, 'Le *Charroi de Nîmes*: stemmatis-ation et délocalisation des manuscrits', *CN*, 56:411–33, who calls S.'s contribution 'science-fiction'. A. Soutou, 'Le vrai emblème de saint Guillem: le cor noir, et non le court nez ou le nez courbe', *RLaR*, 100.1:131–34, follows A. Colby-Hall's interpretation of William's emblem, using evidence from Occitan and heraldry.

THE EPIC OF REVOLT. *Raoul de Cambrai: chanson de geste du XIIᵉ siècle*, introd. and trans. William Kibler (Lettres gothiques, 20), Livre de Poche, 540 pp., uses Kay's 1992 text (*YWMLS*, 54:54) and adds facing translation and editorial matter. W. Calin, 'Évolution de la chanson de geste: merveilleux et mélodrame dans *Renaut de Montau-ban*', *Actes* (Groningen), 43–48, reads *Renaut de Montauban* as an intertext whose most powerful scenes are melodramatic, seeing it as a new kind of *chanson de geste* which marginalizes the previous model. F. Denis, 'Le héros et son double: Bernier face aux Sarrasins dans *Raoul de Cambrai*', *ib.*, 233–39, shows how Bernier's behaviour reflects the more complex approach to Saracens which appears in the late 12th-c. epic, when negative stereotypes are tempered by good qualities. The same oscillation is found in clerical texts, and the literary tensions probably reflect the contemporary climate, contact having generated inconsistent attitudes. B. Duijvestijn, 'Maugis aux Pays-Bas', *ib.*, 49–56, studies the relationship between *Maugis d'Aigremont* and its two Dutch versions. P. Noble, 'Maugis and the role of magic', *ib.*, 71–75, describes the role of Maugis and the importance of magic in *Renaut de Montauban*. Maugis (and the poet) recognize the conflict between magic and Christianity, but the threat is neutralized by Maugis's rejection of his past life. M. de Combarieu du Grès and A. Labbé, 'Figures de clercs dans *Girart de Roussillon*', *Colloque* (Aix-en-Provence), 113–32, survey and classify clerics in this text, finding it to be unusually positive in its attitude, as it uses the topoi of epic clerics but sets itself in opposition to them, stressing their role as peacemakers rather than fighters. A. Labbé, 'Un repas ridicule dans *Renaut de Montauban*: Maugis servi par Charlemagne', *Banquets*, 319–35, finds that disturbed meals indicate grave institutional dysfunction. This particular meal, though comic, also demythifies, for it undermines Charlemagne's authority. L. tentatively outlines a possible Dumézilian approach, in which this episode attacks Charlemagne's sustaining function after the thefts of his crown and his arms have attacked his warrior and sacral functions. M. Tyssens, '*Espaciun* (*Gormont et Isembart*, v. 269)', *CN*, 55, 1995:137–47, surveys the interpretations of this hapax offered by editors and lexicographers, and concludes that it is an error for *esparnison* (Anglo-Norman *esparnisun*).

CRUSADE CYCLE.   R. F. Cook, 'Les épopées de la croisade', *Actes* (Groningen), 93–110, offers an overview of crusade epics and of the problems they pose, especially the questions of cyclical development and the relations between *chanson de geste*, history and ideologies. He identifies the link between crusade epics as ideological: they are propaganda works, inspiring respect for crusading ancestors, while their relationship with history is complex. G. H. M. Classens, 'Some notes on the proto-*Saladin*', *ib.*, 131–40, uses comparison with the Middle Dutch *Roman van Saladin*, *Roman van Cassant* and especially *Dystorie van Saladine* to discover features of the proto-*Saladin*, the lost source of all the known *Saladin*-texts. H. Diament, 'Place names and personal names in medieval French and Provençal crusade epics', *ib.*, 151–58, focuses on the *Chanson d'Antioche* and the *Chanson de la croisade albigeoise*, studying a selection of names in each and calling for further work. P. R. Grillo, 'The Saladin material in the Continuations of the First Crusade Cycle', *ib.*, 159–64, examines the presentation of the figure of Saladin in the 'short' and 'long' Continuations, and the influence of the Chronicle of Ernoul and the *Estoires d'Outremer*. F. Suard, 'La découverte du monde païen dans les chansons de geste de la croisade', *Procs* (Oporto), 107–18, shows that in spite of similarities with chronicle material, the crusade epic is seeking to do something different, as revealed by its method of conveying the novelty of the East less by topographical details than by the role of the marvellous. In addition to fantastic elements derived from romance, there is a new form of Christian marvellous, in which eastern saints help the crusaders.

OTHER EPICS. K. A. Campbell has two essays on *Hervis de Metz*. 'A note on crusade and bourgeois in *Hervis de Mes*', *Actes* (Groningen), 217–23, argues that the text reflects the growing social conflict of its era and the need of the nobility for the wealth of the bourgeois, while going further than this context inasmuch as crusade validates the *mésalliance* of the duke's daughter. C. sees the crusades as a focus for the expression of a certain ideal social order, in which the merchant is as necessary as the knight and the moral rhetoric of crusade justifies social mobility. 'The reiterated self: cyclical temporality and ritual renewal in *Hervis de Metz*', Sturm-Maddox, *Transtextualities*, 157–77, examines cyclicity in the *Geste des Lorrains* as a whole and *Hervis de Metz* in particular. Cyclic temporality links the individual narratives to form one 'mega-narrative', in which the repetition of heroic deeds affirms collective identity. J.-C. Herbin, 'Les enfances "romanesques" de Hervis de Metz', *PRIS-MA*, 12:27–37, shows how the first half of the poem fits Gautier's definition of *enfances* as the time which precedes the elevation to knightly status, but in an original way on account of Hervis's non-aristocratic background; only when he is dubbed do he and the poem become epic. D. Ion compares *Garin le Lorrain* and *Gerbert de Metz* in two articles. In 'Banquet, conflit et fidélité dans *Garin le Lorrain* et *Gerbert de Metz*', *Banquets*, 303–18, she views banquets as a focus for social relations, and shows how they act as a meeting-point and play on the relations established between lineages. In 'Remarques sur les relations de parenté dans *Garin le Lorrain* et *Gerbert de Metz*', *Littérales*, 19:133–51, she considers two variations on the theme of kinship. Different forms of lineage appear in the two poems: in *Garin* the Lorrain clan, limited at the beginning, grows in strength and wealth while the Bordelais are left in shadow; in *Gerbert*, the few Lorrains keep their position while the numerous Bordelais move towards extinction as a group. I. sees the contrast as manifesting the poets' skill but also the rise in importance of the individual. P. Le Rider, 'Le rire dans *Aiol*', *PRIS-MA*, 12:57–74, draws out the comedy of several episodes and features in the early, decasyllabic part of *Aiol*. The poet uses verbal comedy widely, with Aiol being mocked in the text but not by the audience. S. C. Obergfell, 'The role of manuscript illumination in the chanson de geste *Aiol*', *Romania*, 114:316–34, offers a codicological review and finds evidence of a planned programme of illumination. She proposes several functions: to fix the subject of the poem in the memory, to mark major divisions and to act as the visual equivalent of rhetorical topoi and narrative amplification.

3. ROMANCE

GENERAL. E. Baumgartner, 'Sur quelques "marines" médiévales', *Colloque* (Orléans), 11–22, considers the seashore as a rhetorical space, often with a symbolic dimension. F. Dubost, 'Merveilleux et fantastique au Moyen Age: positions et prepositions', *RLaR*, 100:1–35, links the entry of the 'merveilleux' into literature with the birth of romance. The layering of Christian and pre-Christian myth is seen to create a double dynamic generating a duality and ambiguity where 'senefiance' is superimposed on 'semblance'. C. S. Jaeger, 'Patrons and the beginnings of courtly romance', Kelly, *Medieval Opus*, 45–58, questions the influence of patronage on the 'origins of romance'. A. Planche, 'Enfance et ressemblance: regards sur quelques textes médiévaux', *PRIS-MA*, 12:95–103, examines three types of 'twinship': twins separated at birth and reunited; resemblance between children of different sexes raised together; physical doubles. The double is read as acting as intermediary between the self and the external world, being simultaneously same and other. Wolfzettel, *Arthurian Romance*, provides an introductory overview of the importance of Gender Studies to the study of Arthurian romance. The notion of sex/gender as a social construct and semiotic sign is related to the collective unconscious or 'imaginaire', manifested in artistic and literary production. A systematic study across the genre uses a variety of methods to examine the ideological problems linked with gender and the status of women, and their relation to the evolution of Arthurianism. The volume contains several articles relevant to OF studies: A. Putter, 'Arthurian literature and the rhetoric of "effeminacy"' (34–49), traces the changes in the cultural perception of male heroism in the 12th c.; R. Deist, 'Sun and moon: constellations of character in Gottfried's *Tristan* and Chrétien's *Yvain*' (50–65), examines the triangular relationship between the lady, her companion, and the lover, relating this to the myth of sun and moon as principles determining character; A. Rieger, 'Balade des demoiselles du temps jadis. Essai sur l'entrée en scène des personnages féminins dans les romans de Chrétien de Troyes' (79–103), analyses the meetings of the male protagonists with other characters. The lack of individuality ascribed to women marks them as narrative elements, rather than as fully-fledged characters; C. Blons-Pierre, 'Discours féminin et discours masculin dans les romans de Chrétien de Troyes' (104–18), distinguishes between two types of discourse: the rigid social code which marks gender and social rank, and the code of courtly literature which projects a fictional and idealised image of the romance protagonists; D. Kullmann, 'Hommes amoureux et femmes raisonnables. *Erec et Enide* et la doctrine ecclésiastique du mariage' (119–29), considers the relation of Chrétien's attitude towards love within marriage to contemporary ecclesiastical doctrine; J. Nightingale, 'Erec in the mirror: the feminization of the self and the reinvention of the chivalric hero in Chrétien's first romance' (130–46), draws a parallel between *Erec et Enide* and the *Song of Songs*, linking Enide to the image of the Bride. The 'femme-image' constructed by the poet acts as idealized mirror and instrument of self-revelation, allowing the hero to be remodelled according to the 'exemplum' presented by his feminine 'alter ego'; P. Ihring, 'Die überlistete Laudine. Korrektur eines antihöfischen Weiblichkeitskonzepts in Chrétien's *Yvain*' (147–59), views Laudine as possessing a double identity, her romance persona overlying an original connection with the mythical 'fairy of the fountain'; A. Saly, 'Masculin-Féminin dans le *Conte du Graal*' (160–64), measures the balance of male/female relations in the text against the Perceval/Gauvain relationship, concluding there exists a symmetrical correspondence between the two; J.-G. Gouttebroze, 'Un phénomène d'intertextualité biblique dans le *Conte du Graal*: "Qu'il soient une char andui"' (165–75), suggests that the problem of incest is symbolically present in the first section of the narrative. Only a reciprocal silence regarding the identity of future marriage partners neutralizes its potential to develop openly in the second section; and L. de Looze, 'Feminine "contre diction" of the masculine in *Le Chevalier à l'épée*' (183–95), uses neo-Freudian, particularly Lacanian, theory to explore the narrative paradoxes which are expressed in terms of gender and genre. The heroic nature of Gauvain is questioned by this romance, while the author contradicts its generic 'givens' through a *fabliau*-type conclusion.

CHRÉTIEN DE TROYES. M. T. Bruckner, 'Rewriting Chrétien's *Conte du Graal* — mothers and sons: questions, contradictions, and connections', Kelly, *Medieval Opus*, 213–44, posits the mother as the site of contradictions and oppositions in the 'mother text' of *Perceval* and in the *Continuations*. Brigitte Cazelles, *The Unholy Grail: A Social Reading of Chrétien de Troyes's 'Conte du Graal'*, California, Stanford U.P., 325 pp., attests to the political factionalism and strife inherent in the *Conte*. The division between Grail lineage and Arthurian society is represented by the characters of Perceval and Gauvain, their parallel quest for power indicating the lack of coherency and stability of the chivalric world and the failure of traditional chivalry. C. argues convincingly for a reading which grounds the romance in its 12th-c. socio-historical context. *La Copie de Guiot: fol. 79v-105r du manuscrit f.fr.*

794 de la Bibliothèque Nationale 'li chevaliers au lyeon' de Crestien de Troyes, ed. Kajsa Meyer, Amsterdam, Rodopi, 1995, 345 pp., is the first published facsimile of the Guiot MS, containing what is probably the clearest version of Chrétien's text. Particular interest lies in the relatively simple form of orthography which appears to correspond closely to the phonetic reality of the period. The edition contains a transcription of the text, together with notes on variants, a full description of the MS and its transcription, classification of MSS and notes on previous editions. J. Flori, 'La notion de chevalerie dans les romans de Chrétien de Troyes', *Romania*, 114:289–315, views Chrétien's romances as reflections and instigators of a chivalric ideal in which the 'chevalier' is primarily a warrior, a conception which links more closely with the 12th-c. epic than with the 13th-c. romance. The vocabulary pertaining to chivalry provides a particular focus of study. J.-G. Gouttebroze, 'À quoi sert le repas du Graal? Remarques sur la liturgie du Graal dans *Le Conte du Graal*', *Banquets*, 467–78, gives an anthropological reading of the *Conte* which links the motif of feasting to both Celtic and Oedipal myth. J. Helm, 'Deus si beles ymages, une molt bele conjointure', *AUMLA*, 84:85–110, is a numerological and mythological reading of *Erec et Enide*. Emphasis lies on the harmonious nature of the medieval universe, where truth transcends through allegory, and on the disparity between modern and medieval frames of reference. Sandra Hindman, *Sealed in Parchment: Rereadings of Knighthood in the Illuminated Manuscripts of Chrétien de Troyes*, Chicago U.P., xiv + 225 pp., divides the depiction of the knight into five categories: 'Clerc', 'Bachelor', 'Seignor', 'Combateur', and 'Roi'. Each aspect provides comment on the sociopolitical background of Northern France in the 13th c., and the political crisis of the aristocracy under a newly-centralised monarchy. The study also focuses on the manuscripts as evidence of the uneasy transition from oral to written culture. E. Kennedy, 'Who is to be believed? Conflicting presentations of events in the *Lancelot-Grail* cycle', Kelly, *Medieval Opus*, 169–80, sets Perceval against Galahad as Grailwinner, a substitution which marks the conflicting nature of the voice of authority across the pre-cyclical and cyclical narrative tradition. N. J. Lacy, 'Motif transfer in Arthurian romance', *ib.*, 157–68, suggests motif transfer is significant to the study of reader reception theory, as well as to an intertextual analysis of the Arthurian corpus conceived as a whole. D. Maddox, 'Cyclicity, transtextual coherence, and the romances of Chrétien de Troyes', Sturm-Maddox, *Transtextualities*, 39–52, discerns two criteria, genealogy and customs, whose elements recur throughout the corpus of Chrétien's romances, giving them a 'protocyclic coherence'. This becomes significant in relation to the cyclifying tendencies of later Arthurian romance. B. Marache, 'Arthur

entre coutume et aventure', *PRIS-MA*, 11:165–73, views the depiction of Arthur in *Erec et Enide* as the beginning of his metamorphosis
from historical personage (as in Monmouth and Wace) to ambiguous
symbol. Later romances continue this progression, opposing the
feudal ideal of kingship to an exploration of the individual conscience.
Per Nykrog, *Chrétien de Troyes: romancier discutable*, Geneva, Droz,
230 pp., provides a critical discussion of commentaries on, and
interpretations of, Chrétien's romances, from the Middle Ages to the
present, advocating a return to critical study based on the texts
themselves. L. Oliver, 'Spilled wine and lost sovereignty in Chrétien's
Perceval', *NMi*, 97:91–102, presents an examination of the 'spilled
wine episode' in *Perceval* and in the Welsh *Peredur*. Specific differences
regarding the recipient of the insult appear between the two versions
when the incident is related back to Celtic sources. A. Saly, 'Les
Enfances Perceval', *PRIS-MA*, 12:221–35, considers the topos of
vengeance in relation to Chrétien's *Perceval* and the variants *Parzival*,
Perlesvaus, *Peredur*, and *Percyvell*. Since vengeance does not form a
primary source of intrigue in *Perceval* or *Parzival*, but is present in the
other three variants, S. concludes that the theme is not derived from
Chrétien. Claudia Seebass-Linggi, *Lecture d'Erec: traces épiques et
troubadouresques dans le conte de Chrétien de Troyes*, Bern, Lang, 295 pp.,
analyses intergeneric influences to claim that *Erec*'s 'contamination'
by epic and Provençal 'cansos' in its depiction of chivalry and love
marks the birth of a new literary form, that of courtly romance. J.-J.
Vincensini, 'Échange de mets, échange de mots, échange de corps
dans *Le Conte du Graal*', *Banquets*, 493–509, examines the geometric
balance between the four episodes in which Perceval shares a meal.
Excess is opposed to frugality, speech to silence, men to women, in an
attempt to illustrate Perceval's alienation from society in three
different spheres: sexual relations, language, and gastronomy.

OTHER ARTHURIAN. *Three Arthurian Romances: Poems from Medieval
France — 'Caradoc'; 'The Knight with the Sword'; 'The Perilous Graveyard'*,
trans. Ross G. Arthur, with introd. and notes, NY–London, Dent,
xviii + 216 pp. *ArLit*, 14, ed. James P. Carley and Felicity Riddy,
Woodbridge, Brewer, 160 pp. R. Baudry, 'La Vertu nourricière du
Graal', *Banquets*, 433–50, considers the image of the Grail as a source
of nourishment across a wide range of Arthurian texts, concluding
with a brief glance at its modern image. Although the form and
context of the nourishing Grail is seen to be in constant flux, the
durability of this primary attribute is read as evidence of the
fundamental laws of human imagination. A. Berthelot, 'Le Graal
nourricier', *ib.*, 451–66, suggests that the ambiguity of Chrétien's
Grail is replaced in the *Continuations* by a dual focus on the Grail as
magical artefact and as Christian symbol. F. Brandsma, 'The

presentation of direct discourse in Arthurian romance: changing modes of performance and reception?', Kelly, *Medieval Opus*, 245–60, demonstrates the alteration in the presentation of direct discourse from verse to prose, as one aspect of medieval stylistics. M.-L. Chênerie, 'Vengeance et chevalerie dans le *Tristan en Prose*', *Romania*, 113, 1992–95 [1996]: 194–226, links the theme of vengeance to pagan prehistory and to the 'chanson de geste'. Its presence in the romance destabilises the notion of the courtly ideal. R. Colliot, 'Arthur, roi de la chevalerie terrienne dans le *Roman de Laurin*', *PRIS-MA*, 11: 211–20, points to the simplification and impoverishment inherent in Arthur's depiction, despite his noble attributes. Two pieces by M. de Combarieu [du Grès]: 'Enfantines (étude sur les enfances de Lionel et Bohort dans le *Lancelot* en prose)', *ib.*, 12: 133–55, which relates the depiction of the two cousins to that of Lancelot, with emphasis on their dominant 'humour' and temperament; and 'Les quêteurs de merveilles: étude sur la *Queste del Saint Graal*', *RLaR*, 100: 63–90, associating 'semblance' and 'senefiance' in the *Queste* with 'merveilles' and their meaning. The capacity to discover the 'merveilleux' is ultimately linked to the quester's capacity to appreciate and to interpret, a concept which is carried over into the area of reader response theory. A. Combes, 'L'âtre périlleux. Cénotaphe d'un héros retrouvé', *Romania*, 113, 1992–95 [1996]: 140–74, focuses on the text's haunting by death on the levels of content, metaphor, and allegory. G. D'Amours, 'Merlin et le Tao', *DFS*, 35: 3–18, posits the notion that the spiritual themes of Merlin literature form fundamental 'mythemes' which connect with Taoism. Parallels are drawn between the Grail and the Tao, and between the mythical oriental beast the Ky-Lin and the unicorn, while Merlin is presented as an atemporal figure allowing Western access to Oriental spiritualism. J. R. Doner, 'Scribal whim and miniature allocation in the illustrated manuscripts of the *Continuation-Gauvain*', *MAe*, 65: 72–95, discerns an evolution in the historiated initials and miniatures of this collection of MSS. Although there appear to be no direct links between them, they do apparently share common trends and ascribe to discernible patterns of illustration. L. Gowans, 'The Grail in the West: prose, verse and geography in the *Joseph* of Robert de Boron', *NFS*, 35: 1–17, studies the relationship between the one extant verse MS, Paris BN fr.20047, and the 15 prose versions of *Joseph*, concluding that Robert composed in prose and that the narratorial voice of the verse version is therefore supplied by the redactor. *Lancelot-Grail: The Old French Arthurian Vulgate and Post-Vulgate in Translation*, vol. 5, ed. Norris J. Lacy, NY, Garland, xi + 438 pp. M. Mikhaïlova, 'Le Clerc: personnage de la fiction/ personnage-fiction. Le clerc écrivant dans la littérature arthurienne',

Colloque (Aix-en-Provence), 417–34, studies the polyvalent nature of the role of the *clerc*/hermit in the *Queste del Saint Graal*. His tripartite function, as narrator, reader and character, posits him as mimetic double of the author, an ambiguous producer of rhetoric and signification. L. Morin, 'De la souveraineté dans le *Roman d'Yder*: la déloyauté d'Arthur et l'excellence d'Yder', *PRIS-MA*, 11:185–98, examines the opposition between Yder and Arthur as ideal and anti-type of sovereignty. K. Pratt, 'The Cistercians and the *Queste del Saint Graal*', *RMS*, 21:69–96, suggests that the cumulative effect of themes and motifs in the *Queste* does indicate that the author had a particular connection with, or interest in, the Cistercian order. Moral and religious didacticism is, however, ultimately seen to cede to a secular focus, as the romance exalts an elite group of fighting men, rather than a religious order or calling. Ad Putter, **'Sir Gawain and the Green Knight' and the French Arthurian Romance*, OUP, 1995, 292 pp. A. Saly, 'Le Roi Arthur dans le *Perlesvaus*: le mauvais roi et la chauve au bras bandé', *PRIS-MA*, 11:199–209, examines the symbolic and mythical value of the mutilated maiden as allegory of the king's deficiencies. *The Formation of Culture in Medieval Britain: Celtic, Latin, and Norman Influences on English Music, Literature, History, and Art*, ed. Françoise H. M. Le Saux, Lampeter, Mellen, 1995, xiv + 197 pp., provides an overview of intercultural influences. Of particular interest to OF studies is N. Thomas, 'The politics of romance: some observations on the political content of the *Roman d'Yder*' (171–81). This considers the anti-Arthurian stance of the romance, concluding that *Yder* is concerned with the 'renovatio' of the courtly ideal from within, rather than with an unmitigated assault on the chivalric ethos. P. Simons, 'The "Bel Sanblant": reading *Le Bel Inconnu*', *FS*, 50:257–74, examines the use of 'sanbler' and 'sanblant' as ambiguous signs in a textual frame of reference which is itself marked as unstable. The generic codes of romance and lay are deconstructed and subverted by an author who consistently blurs the boundaries between fiction and 'reality', highlighting the unreliability of meaning generated through text. Richard Trachsler, *Clôtures du cycle arthurien: étude et textes*, Geneva, Droz, 570 pp., studies the closure of the Arthurian cycles and the solutions offered by a range of texts and MSS, focusing in particular on the death of Arthur. The romance tradition is related to the chronicle: while the latter traces a historical continuum, the romance envisages no possibility of a narrative extending beyond the death of Arthur. The Arthurian cycle thus exists in a self-perpetuating spatial and temporal vortex. The principal aim of the study is to provide an intertextual analysis of the themes which serve to link and to differentiate between the corpus of selected texts. M. Seguy, 'L'ordre du discours dans le désordre du monde. La recherche de la transparence dans la *Quatrième Continuation*', *Romania*, 113, 1992–95 [1996]: 175–93, considers Perceval as the means of reducing the ambiguity of linguistic signs in a world depicted as torn between the forces of good and evil. R. S. Sturges, 'Desire, allegory, and the structure of the Prose *Lancelot*', *DFS*, 34:3–15, concentrates in particular on the structure of the *Queste*. Allegorical interpretation of the Grail is divided into four categories: historical; allegorical; topological; anagogical, which apply to the different experiences of each of the questing knights, according with their differing spiritual states. *La Suite du Roman de Merlin*, ed. Gilles Roussineau, 2 vols, Geneva, Droz, cxlv + 326, 327–804 pp., is a continuation of the prose *Merlin* attributed to Robert de Boron. This is the first full edition to take account of Cambridge University Library, Additional 7071 (MS *B*), unknown to previous editors. The relation of MS *B* to the other MS versions of the text is examined in the Introduction, which also provides a critical and linguistic analysis. J.-R. Valette, 'La merveille et son interprétation: l'exemple du *Lancelot* propre', *RLaR*, 100:163–208, is a semiotic reading of the 'merveille' and the 'merveilleux'. The reader's capacity to comprehend and interpret literary allegory is dependent on knowledge of its particular system of signs. I. Weill, 'Le clerc et "l'hermite preudome" dans le *Lancelot-Graal*', *Colloque* (Aix-en-Provence), 579–89, divides the religious world into a tripartite structure in which each type of cleric/holy man fulfils a different function. This Christian ethos overlies the idealized Celtic world of the text and points the way to a greater 'senefiance'. F. Wolfzettel, 'Les "Enfances" de Lancelot du Lac. Pour une approche générique du thème', *PRIS-MA*, 12:105–16, draws an opposition between the model of the 'enfances' narrative in epic and in romance. In the romance the hero's search for self and identity replaces the father with the Lacanian 'nom-du-père', typifying the rejection of lineage and prolonging the 'espace d'enfance'. M. Zink, 'Traduire saint Bernard: quand la parabole devient roman', Kelly, *Medieval Opus*, 29–42, focuses on the influence of Cistercian spirituality on Arthurian romance, particularly the *Quête du Graal*. Rather than the narrative being impoverished through the addition of allegory, the contrary occurs, with religious spirituality becoming absorbed by romance literature.

TRISTAN AND ISEUT. G. J. Brault, * "Entre ces quatre ot estrange amor". Thomas' analysis of the tangled relationships of Mark, Isolt, Tristan and Isolt of the White Hands', *Romania*, 114:70–95, examines Thomas's discourse on the universal nature of anguish in love with reference to the 'La Salle aux Images' episode, contained only in the Turin manuscript. J. Chocheyras, 'Le personnage d'Arthur dans le *Tristan* de Béroul', *PRIS-MA*, 11:159–63, considers the chronological relationship of *Tristan* and Chrétien's *Cligès*, proposing that the former's depiction of Arthur as powerful sovereign and 'romance hero' provides a counterpoint to the criticism of the king in *Cligès*. C.R. Dover, 'From non-cyclic to cyclic *Lancelot*: recycling the heart', Sturm-Maddox, *Transtextualities*, 53–70, traces the narrative strategies by which an earlier 'non-cyclic' version is incorporated into the *Lancelot*. The theme of the heart provides a key element in this adaptation. Y. Foehr-Janssens, 'Lit d'amour, dit de mort. Thomas d'Angleterre et l'esthétique romanesque', *MA*, 102:403–17, considers the introspective nature of discourse in *Tristan*, the distinction drawn between 'voleir' and 'desir', and death as the last resort of love (beyond the pleasure principal). A. Gross and J. Thibault-Schaefer, 'Sémiotique de la tonsure de l'"insipiens" à Tristan et aux fous de Dieu', *Colloque* (Aix-en-Provence), 243–75, remark on the semiotic complexity inherent in the interpretation of the tonsure: sign of madness, sign of a cleric. The image of the tonsured Tristan which appears in several MS illuminations signals his marginalization and assimilates lay madness to sacred or expiatory madness. Christiane Marchello-Nizia, **Tristan et Yseut: les premières versions européennes*, Gallimard, 1995, lx + 1728 pp. Roger Pensom, *Reading Béroul's Tristan: A Poetic Narrative and the Anthropology of its Reception*, Bern, Lang, 116 pp., studies two problematic areas: the text's æsthetic unity, and the set of relations which link text and society. A stylistic and semantic analysis examines the text in terms of its paradoxes and discontinuities, relating these to the influence of two distinct schemes of social ordering, Germanic and Celtic. This 'liminality' and confusion of a world in transition is balanced against the text's poetic form, which gives æsthetic order and coherence. P. V. Rockwell, ' "Je ne suiz mie soffisanz": insufficiency and cyclicity in the Lancelot-Grail Cycle', Sturm-Maddox, *Transtextualities*, 71–91, assesses the cyclical connection among the texts of this cycle, concentrating on the continuous deferral of a notion of heroic sufficiency which propels the narrative onward from text to text without its gaining closure. *Le Roman de Tristan en prose*, vol. 8, ed. P. Ménard, B. Guidot, and J. Subrenat (TLF, 462), 1995, 405 pp., is the penultimate volume in this edition of the Vulgate. As previously, the text is preceded by an analysis of the MSS, together with a critical appreciation of the text. A section on 'literary problems' considers the implications of the romance's focus on Galahad at this point and the introduction of a predominant religious ethos. This is influential on both literary and ideological levels of analysis, juxtaposing the themes of secular and holy knighthood to produce a thematically 'complete' narrative and emphasising the function of Galahad as metaphor of the chivalric ideal. J. R. Scheidegger, 'Flux et reflux de la marée et du désir dans

Tristan et Iseut, *Colloque* (Orléans), 111–31, links the image of the tide with desire. The fluctuation and instability of both is further linked with the ambiguity of a discourse which confounds its signifiers; 'la mer', 'l'amer' (aimer), and 'l'amer' (amer); 'l'amur' and 'la mort'. B. Schlyter, 'Le *Roman de Tristan* en prose: une édition longtemps attendue', *NMi*, 97:113–20, describes the content of each of the seven published volumes, relating this to their style, particularly the increasing use of 'entrelacement'.

LAIS.   P. F. Ainsworth, ' "The letter killeth": law and spirit in Marie de France's lay of *La Fresne*', *FS*, 50:1–14, delineates and explores the spiritual allegory underlying the lay, and the implicit contrast between law and grace. The twin 'merveille' is here æsthetic and spiritual; Marie weaves her tale through a skilful and provocative rewriting of Biblical themes, provoking questions on the nature of grace and man's place in the divine scheme. Margaret M. Boland, *Architectural Structure in the 'Lais' of Marie de France*, NY, Lang, 1995, x + 226 pp., analyses the order and structure of the *lais* as they appear in Harley MS 978, concluding that they form a coherent and balanced unity. Analogy is drawn with the structure of the medieval cathedral, balance and harmony being glossed as allegorical reference to the Christian universe. J. Brumlik, 'The lyric "malmariée": Marie's subtext in *Guigemar*', *RoQ*, 43:67–80, points to *Guigemar*'s synthesis of the fey mistress and the lyric *malmariée*, evoking an image which problematizes literary models of women. Marie de France, **Lais*, ed. A. Ewert, Bristol Classic Press, 1995, lxxii + 223 pp. B. A. Masters, 'Involution of meaning in the Harley *Cheuerefoil*', *Parergon*, 13:81–115, views the polyphonic form of the text (as in Harley MS 978) as a visual inscription of its content. This symbiotic relationship mirrors that of the *lai*'s two lovers, and signals the necessary complicity of narrator and reader in a process which produces meaning through the manipulation of known formulæ. J.-L. Picherit, 'Le châtiment des amants dans le lai d'*Equitan* de Marie de France', *MA*, 102:419–24, considers the punishment of the 'amants' in the light of 12th-c. law, linking adultery and treason, and playing on the semantic duality of the Latin 'adulter': adultery and counterfeiting. B. Semple, 'The male psyche and the female sacred body in Marie de France and Christine de Pisan', *YFS*, 86:164–86, examines the status of the male/female body in regard to sanctity and desire. The traditional denial of female accession to the 'logos' (Christian teaching) is overturned in the work of Marie and Christine, creating the paradox of a body at once sexual and sacred. M. Stanesco, 'Du démon du midi à l'Éros mélancolique: topologie du féerique dans le lai narratif breton', *Poétique*, 106:131–59, links the hour of midday with both fairy encounters and death/passage to the 'Otherworld'. The importance of the 'fée' in the

Breton *lai* is a manifestation of the human desire for contact with the unknown in a world increasingly influenced by medieval rationalism.

ROMANS D'ANTIQUITÉ. E. Baumgartner, 'Benoît de Sainte-Maure et "l'uevre de Troie"', Kelly, *Medieval Opus*, 15–28, discusses the complex relation between Benoît and his sources, the subsequent work appearing a mosaic drawn from diverse models. C. Croizy-Naquet, 'La description de Troie et ses avatars dans le *Roman de Troie* en prose du XIIIᵉ siècle', *CCMe*, 39:305–20, contrasts the description of the city in Benoît's verse romance and in its later prose adaptation. From an accumulation of verbal elements emphasizing the supernatural, unquantifiable, and inaccessible nature of Troie, its prose image is reduced to one which is historical, accessible, and spatially specific. L. Harf-Lancner, 'De la biographie au roman d'Alexandre: Alexandre de Paris et l'art de la conjointure', Kelly, *Medieval Opus*, 59–74, examines the diverse intertextual themes, motifs and 'senefiances' which reveal Alexandre as an 'author-architect' of romance.

OTHER ROMANCES. Alexandre du Pont, *Le Roman de Mahomet*, ed. and trans. Yvan G. Lepage, Leuven, Peeters, ix + 173 pp., replaces the 1977 edition, providing a modern French translation of the OF text in place of the Latin version of the poem, as previously. The introductory analysis does, however, make much comparison between the Latin and OF poems. A. Eskénazi, ' "Variantes graphiques" dans *Guillaume de Dole*', *RLiR*, 60:147–83, is a philological study of the Lecoy edition of the text. E. Gauchier, 'Enfances diaboliques: *Robert le Diable*', *PRIS-MA*, 12:17–26, relates *Robert* to the motif of 'enfances' as it appears in 13th-c. prose cycles. The nature/nurture debate which these present is here overshadowed by the concept of 'anti-nature', while the linear progression towards identity is replaced by a cyclical return to a state of infancy and madness. *Gautier d'Arras*, *'Ille et Galeron'*, ed. and trans. Penny Eley, London, King's College, liii + 228 pp., provides a full literary analysis, comparing the interrelation of MSS *P* and *W*, and considering intertextual influences on the romance. A new translation into English is added. J.-L. Leclanche, 'Le clerc et la clergie à travers les *Dolopathos* de Jean de Haute-Seille et d'Herbert', *Colloque* (Aix-en-Provence), 363–84, considers the emphasis on Christian sanctity which appears in both the Latin and French versions of the *Dolopathos*. D. Maddox, 'Inventing the unknown: rewriting in *Le Bel Inconnu*', Kelly, *Medieval Opus*, 101–23, analyses the theme of 'costumes' as a specific type of structuring discourse in Renaut de Bâgé's rewriting of Chrétien. D. Rieger, 'Fiction littéraire et violence. Le cas de la *Fille du comte de Pontieu*', *Romania*, 113, 1992–95 [1996]:92–117, treats the rapport between literary and historically real violence. The text verges on a realism which can only be denied through a return to the fictional model. **Robert le Diable: roman du XIIe siècle*, ed. A. Micha (GF, 878) Flammarion, 125 pp. P. Simons, 'The squire, the dwarf, and the damsel in distress: minor characters in the *Bel Inconnu*?', *FMLS*, 32:27–36, examines the 'metatextual' nature of the romance which juxtaposes elements from different forms of medieval narrative. Conventional generic codes are subverted through the ambiguity of the minor characters. M. B. Speer, ' "Translatio" as "inventio": Gaston Paris and the "Treasure of Rhampsinitus" (Gaza) in the *Dolopathos* romance', Sturm-Maddox, *Transtextualities*, 125–55, demonstrates how autonomous brief narratives can be assimilated to a larger narrative coherence through an examination of the transtextual 'mouvance' of three sections of the Seven Sages cycle. N. Thomas, 'The Old French *Durmart le Galois*: a demystified version of the Perceval story?', *Parergon*, 13:117–28, notes how *Durmart* opposes the Grail tradition of the 'chevalier-messianique' through its relocation of the quest to a recognizable and unequivocal moral universe, that of the Crusades. R. Trachsler, 'Parler d'amour. Les stratégies de séduction dans *Joufroi de Poitiers*', *Romania*, 113, 1992–95 [1996]:118–39, traces the way in which the text exploits the possibilities offered by the Occitan tradition, focusing attention on the declaration and expression of love.

4.   Religious Writings

Two editions treat the work of Pierre d'Abernon of Fetcham: *La Lumere as Lais*, vol. i, ed. Glynn Hesketh, London, ANTS, 212 pp., is the first of three volumes presenting what is probably the earliest of P.'s three works, using as base Oxford, Bodleian Library, Bodl. 399 (MS *B*). Vol. ii will conclude the text and give variant readings; vol. iii will provide the Introduction, Glossary, and Notes. Id., *La Vie seint Richard*, ed. D. W. Russell, London, ANTS, 1995, xiii + 175 pp., is the Anglo-Norman translation of an earlier Latin 'vita' by Ralph of Bocking. This is the first edition of the complete text, including both 'le premier livre' (the 'Vie') and 'le secund livre' (the Miracles section). *The Medieval Translator*, vol. v, ed. Roger Ellis and René Tixier, Turnhout, Brepols, xvi + 488 pp., is the latest volume in an ongoing series which covers a wide variety of texts, genres and languages. Of particular interest are the studies by K. Ashley and P. Sheingorn, 'The translation of Foy: bodies, texts and places' (29–49), who consider the different implications of translation/'translatio' in the context of the dissemination and reformulation of the cult of St. Faith; and by F. Bourgne, 'Translating Saints' Lives into the vernacular: "Translatio Studii" and "Furta Sacra" (translation as theft)' (50–63), who takes a different slant, considering the implications of vernacular translation and cultural contextualization as theft. *The Legend of Mary of Egypt in Medieval Insular Hagiography*, ed. Erich Poppe and Bianca Ross, Dublin, Four Courts Press, vii + 299 pp., traces the reception of a single 9th-c. Latin source in insular vernaculars during the Early and Late Middle Ages; of particular relevance is J. Weiss, 'The metaphor of madness in the Anglo-Norman Lives of St. Mary the Egyptian' (161–73), which compares the three versions of the text as 'exempla'. Robert le Chapelain, *'Corset': A Rhymed Commentary on the Seven Sacraments*, ed. K. V. Sinclair, London, ANTS, 1995, x + 150 pp., is the earliest known account of the Seven Sacraments in Anglo-Norman, providing previously undocumented evidence of early 13th-c. religious practices.

5. Other Genres

LYRIC. M. Gérard, 'Quand la lèpre fleurit . . . Corps et écriture dans les *Congés* de Jean Bodel et Baude Fastoul', *Littérature*, 102:14–28, reflects on the language used of leprosy by the two poets.

DRAMA. *Le Jeu d'Adam*, ed. and trans. Wolfgang van Emden (British Rencesvals Publications, 1), Edinburgh, Société Rencesvals British Branch, xviii + 83 pp., opens a new series of student texts. The edition is conservative, the English translation is free, being designed for acting, the introduction, bibliography, notes, and glossary are aimed at students. A. Cowell, 'Feminine semiotics and masculine desires: *Courtois d'Arras* and the proper male reader in the Middle Ages', *Symposium*, 50:16–27, examines the links between usury, prostitution, and transgressive poetics in contemporary philosophy and in the *jeu*. M. Infurna, 'Esotismo e teatro medievale: Jean Bodel', *MedRom*, 20:45–55, relates the *Jeu de saint Nicolas* to contemporary tales of and attitudes to the Orient, focusing particularly on the *arbre sec*. He finds a blend of contemporary Arras, anti-Muslim propaganda and eastern exoticism.

HISTORICAL. E. Baumgartner, 'Brut et les ancêtres d'Arthur', *PRIS-MA*, 11:139–48, considers the retrospective importance attached to the figure of Arthur in the modern reading of Wace's *Brut*, a perspective influenced by his significance in the medieval romance. P. E. Bennett, 'L'épique dans l'historiographie anglo-normande: Gaimar, Wace, Jordan Fantosme', *Actes* (Groningen), 321–30, examines the vernacular influence evident in early chronicles. The study thus forges a link between chronicle and epic in addition to the clear influence exerted on the chronicle by Latin poetry (both medieval and ancient). P. Eley, 'Epic elements in the *Chronique des Ducs de Normandie*', *ib.*, 345–51, points to the greater use of formulaic language in Benoît's *Chronique* than in his earlier *Roman de Troie*. This shift towards epic mode serves to signal the historical aim of the work, written for the English king, as well as to imbue the somewhat obscure source material with a borrowed glory. The political context obviates a more emphatic linkage between epic and chronicle, avoiding uncomfortable parallels being drawn between English royal ancestors and French heroes. E. Freeman, 'Geffrai Gaimar, vernacular historiography, and the assertion of authority', *SP*, 93 : 188–206, analyses the methods used by the *Estoire des Engleis* to assert and facilitate its own acceptance as an authoritative version of the past. J.-G. Gouttebroze, 'Entre les historiographes d'expression latine et les jongleurs, le clerc lisant', *Colloque* (Aix-en-Provence), 215–30, seeks to define the term 'clerc lisant' with reference to Gaimar's *Estoire des Engleis*, Wace, and the *chanson de geste*. The 'clerc' functions as mediator at the politically powerful juncture between the written Latin corpus and its vernacular interpretation/adaptation. V. B. Jordan, 'The multiple narratives of Matthew Paris' *Estoire de seint Aedward le rei*: Cambridge University Library MS Ee.iii.59', *Parergon*, 13 : 77–92, studies the tripartite structure of the MS which presents three separate, but interconnected pictorial or narrative versions of the 'estoire'. L. Löfstedt, '*Li quatre livre des reis* et la traduction en ancien français du décret de Gratien', *NMi*, 97 : 315–28, examines the differing aim and audience of the French translations of each of the above texts, considering the interrelation of the two translators. *A Partial Edition of 'Les Fais des Rommains', with a Study of its Style and Syntax*, ed. Thomas J. McCormick, Jr, Lampeter, Mellen, 1995, 252 pp., studies the stylistic and syntactical changes which took place between the 13th-c. OF version of the text and the 15th-c. MS copy (British Museum Old Royal 20 C 1). It is the 15th-c. version which is edited here, with accompanying notes of changes from the original. Gabrielle M. Spiegel, **Romancing the Past: The Rise of Vernacular Prose Historiography in Thirteenth-Century France*, Berkeley, California, U.P., 1995, 440 pp.

MORAL, DIDACTIC, AND ALLEGORICAL WORKS. L. Evdokimova, 'Dispositions des lettrines dans les manuscrits du *Bestiaire d'amour* et sa composition: des lectures possibles de l'œuvre (1ère partie)', *MA*, 102 : 465–78, considers the arrangement of the illuminated initials in the different MS versions as marking different forms of textual interpretation. M.-R. Jung, '*Ovide, texte, translateur* et gloses dans les manuscrits de l'*Ovide moralisé*', Kelly, *Medieval Opus*, 75–98, remarks on the importance attached to the French author/translator of the *Metamorphoses*. This, together with his multi-faceted role, is revealed by textual glosses, illuminations and rubrics. C. Lucken, 'Richard de Fournival, ou le clerc de l'amour', *Colloque* (Aix-en-Provence), 399–416, places the *clerc* in the context of a discourse on love which relates both to lyric tradition and to the emblematic code of the bestiary. M. Perugi, 'Le centaure poursuivi. Esquisse d'une recherche littéraire et figurative à propos des Sagittaires dans la *Mort Aymeri* et d'une figure marginale au f°5 du chansonnier provençal *R*', *Compar(a)ison*, 1:21–56, compares marginalia and marginalisation. The centaur is read as symbolizing 'wild men', or pagans, the 'otherness' of both placing them beyond the borders of Christian society and the medieval text.

ROMAN DE RENART. J. R. Simpson, *Animal Body, Literary Corpus: The Old French 'Roman de Renart'* (Faux Titre, 110), Amsterdam–Atlanta, Rodopi, [v] + 242 pp., argues that the narrative of the *Renart* and its thematic concerns can be viewed as both historically determined and as a self-generating literary system, and that it offers an important insight into the changing relations between power and writing in the emerging Capetian state. S. uses different branches to explore ideas of imitation and tradition, of literacy and performance, the treatment of lineage, the representation of change and transition, conversion and epiphany, royal ambitions and their failure, commemoration and forgetting. He concludes that the branches of the *Renart* are 'in part shaped by a reaction to a project to control' on the part of 12th-c. Capetian Paris. R. Bellon, 'Lévi-Strauss en Renardie: manières de table, cru et cuit dans *Le Roman de Renart*', *Banquets*, 393–405, views eating habits and table manners as a social marker, but above all as a point of comparison in the play of anthropomorphism and zoomorphism in the *Renart*; they express the shifting identities and metamorphoses in the text. M. Bonafin, 'Le nom du loup et le trickster-renard: la discussion sur les stratifications ethniques dans le *Roman de Renart*', *Reinardus*, 9:3–13, approaches animal names and animal nature from a folklore point of view, arguing that they represent the remains of totemic beliefs and seeking traces of such extra-textual ethnic connections in the text. N. Harano, 'Le texte γ de la Branche IV du *Roman de Renart*', *ib.*, 51–58, asks whether the γ family represents a third version or an amplification of α and β, without coming to a definitive decision. C. de Saulnier, 'Le clerc auteur et personnage dans *Renart le Contrefait*', *Colloque* (Aix-en-Provence), 515–28, finds that the author (an ex-priest) is confused with the clerical characters in the text, who not only represent stereotypes of wealth and sensuality but also reflect the author's personal situation of being denounced and unfrocked for bigamy. The character of Renart completes his anthropomorphism by becoming a clerk, and the author takes his revenge by identifying with him and perverting the traditional faults of the clerical character. P. Wunderli, 'Ehe, Ehebruch und Aventüre: zu einigen Verschiebungen des höfischen Wertsystems im *Roman de Renart*', *RZLG*, 20:275–97, looks at marriage, adultery, and adventure in *Renart* in the light of courtly romance; what in the latter is ennobling is far from so in *Renart*. C. Zemmour, 'Perception de la verticalité végétale par les animaux dans le *Roman de Renart*: chesne: signifiant, signifié et valeurs symboliques', *Reinardus*, 9:189–204, is a lexicological and hermeneutic study of the meaning of the oak tree.

FABLIAUX. *Medieval Comic Tales*, ed. Derek Brewer, 2nd edn, Woodbridge, Brewer, xxxiv + 190 pp., is a revised and expanded edition, with a completely new introduction, of the 1973 collection (*YWMLS*, 35:217). It includes ten French *fabliaux*, and the non-French sections contain some useful analogues. The introduction discusses humour in general and medieval humour in particular, relating the medieval comic tale to other traditional literary forms and to parallels in folklore, before presenting the various corpora featured in the anthology, with particular attention being paid to *fabliaux* (including recent scholarship) and trickster tales. Two new volumes of the *Nouveau recueil complet des fabliaux (NRCF)*, ed. Willem Noomen, Assen, van Gorcum, vol. VIII, 1994, xxvi + 438 pp., vol. IX, xxvi + 366 pp., add a further 31 *fabliaux* to this definitive new edition, leaving only one more volume to come. Like their predecessors they contain a general introduction, inventory of MSS, index of proper names and glossary, and give for each text diplomatic editions of all MSS, a critical edition, an introduction and notes. Each contains a list of errata in previous volumes. L. C. Brook, 'The moral of *La Housse partie*', *RF*, 107, 1995:396–401, shows how the text can be read both from a worldly and from an anagogical viewpoint, and must be so read if its meaning is to be discerned. The moral, which at first seems superficial in relation to the tale, covers a dual deeper significance, a description of the world as cynical and self-seeking, and a parallel with the life of Christ. The hero is like the Christian man who acknowledges the richness of God's gift and responds with the gift of himself. K. Busby, 'The respectable *fabliau*: Jean Bodel, Rutebeuf, and Jean de Condé', *Reinardus*, 9:17–31, approaches these three accomplished writers from the point of view of non-parodic intertextuality, and shows by study of the stylistic, rhetorical and structural features which their work shares with the rest of OF literature that it belongs to a far from marginal genre, and that it is less scandalous and more respectable than tends to be thought. B. J. Levy, '"Tant va la cruche à l'eau…": parodies et périls hydriques dans les fabliaux français', *Colloque* (Orléans), 41–60, mines a wide variety of *fabliaux* for occurrences of water as a source of laughter or disaster, finding it in the form of river, spring, and bath, and drawing out its parodic exploitation, its dangers and its relation to obscenity. M.-T. Lorcin, 'Le statut de l'objet dans les fabliaux français',

Reinardus, 9:75–85, counts and classifies objects (other than food, places or animals), and shows that they are not a mere background but contribute to the tales: they may show class or wealth, they contribute to theatricality by making the action more visual, they may play a central narrative role. She concludes that they deserve further study, and draws attention to the value placed by the characters upon such objects. J.-B. Renard, '"Out of the mouth of babes": the child who unwittingly betrays its mother's adultery', *Folklore*, 106, 1995:77–83, adduces medieval and modern manifestations of this *fabliau* theme. In modern instances there tends to be a suggestion of incest, in the *fabliaux* a kind of spiritual incest since the parish priest is involved, so that the adultery is aggravated. R. ends with a psychoanalytical interpretation of the theme. P. Sosso, '*Le Vilain de Bailleul* et la nouvelle de Ferondo', *SFr*, 39, 1995:201–12, compares the *fabliau* with *Decameron* III, 8 and finds in Boccaccio's version greater complexity and motivation, greater depth of character and a more sophisticated style. J. M. Ziolkowski, 'The erotic *pater noster*, redux', *NMi*, 97:329–32, is a reply to Löfstedt's 1988 reply (*NMi*, 89:212–14) to Z.'s 1987 article (*NMi*, 88:31–34) on erotic meaning in medieval Latin, French, and English. He brings new evidence from literature and canon law to indicate that 'a cele aprist sa patrenostre' in *Frère Denise* means 'had sexual intercourse with her'.

MISCELLANEOUS. T. Hunt, 'A burlesque tale of adventure', *FMLS*, 31, 1995:117–27, publishes a formerly unedited *dit* from MS B.N. fr. 837, in four-line rhyming stanzas of 176 Franco-Picard alexandrines (no date is proposed). H. warns against the dangers of too lightly attributing parody, and calls this *dit* neither parody nor satire but an entertaining skit.

LATE MEDIEVAL LITERATURE

By LESLIE C. BROOK, *University of Birmingham*

1. NARRATIVE GENRES

EPIC. R. Colliot, 'Le personnage de Renier dans les *Enfances Renier*: romanesque et conformisme', *PRIS-MA*, 12:117–32, demonstrates how the poem reflects and recasts commonplace epic themes, with an overriding desire by the hero throughout to discover his proper lineage and be worthy of it. M.-F. Notz, 'Nature et surnaturel dans *Tristan de Nanteuil*', *Actes* (Groningen), 77–82, analyses the effect of the mixture of epic and romance *motifs* in this lengthy, complex poem. L. Crist, '*Baudouin de Flandres* et le "Deuxième Cycle de la Croisade"', *ib.*, 141–50, re-examines the evidence for connecting the fragment of this lost poem to the cycle, and reverts to his earlier opinion that there is no connection. M. Malfait-Dohet, 'La fonction de la bâtardise dans la définition du héros épique du Deuxième Cycle de la Croisade', *ib.*, 167–76, selects two *chansons* within the cycle, *Baudouin de Sebourc* and the *Bâtard de Bouillon*, and analyses the differing reactions to their condition by the two heroes, raising the question of the social, political, and moral issues involved. L. Brook, 'Roland devant le monde sarrasin dans l'*Entrée d'Espagne*', *ib.*, 209–16, concentrates on an analysis of Roland's fight against Ferragu and his journey to the Near East, which mark two distinct stages in the presentation of R. as a hero. L. Zarker Morgan, 'The "narrator" in Italian epic: Franco-Italian tradition', *ib.*, 481–90, examines the different roles of the narrator in five texts (*Geste Francor*, *Aliscans*, *Gui de Nanteuil*, *Entrée d'Espagne*, and its continuation), and links her findings with later Italian developments as typified by Ariosto. H.-E. Keller, 'La chanson de geste en prose et l'amour courtois', *ib.*, 375–82, looks at the attitudes towards love in the various parts of the *Geste de Garin de Monglane en prose*, and observes that courtly love was still flourishing in a developed form at the Burgundian court in the late 15th c., most notably in the section of text which traces the growth of the love of Roland and Aude. A. Moisan, 'Les traditions rolandienne et turpinienne dans les *Croniques et conquestes de Charlemagne* de David Aubert', *ib.*, 399–408, shows that this 15th-c. prose adaptation mixes the poetic tradition of the later versions of the *Roland* with that of the Turpin chronicle, with adjustments by A. to make the story coherent and in conformity with the tastes of his day. *The Old French Crusade Cycle, Vol. X: Godefroi de Buillon*, ed. Jan Boyd Roberts, [Tuscaloosa], Alabama U.P., xxvi + 147 pp., is the final volume in the series, and consists of an abbreviated prose version of the cycle; the introduction places the text within the context of the cycle and examines the Franco-Picard language.

ROMANCE. Alexandre du Pont, *Le Roman de Mahomet*, ed. Yvan G. Lepage, Leuven-Paris, Peeters, ix + 173 pp., is an update of L.'s earlier edition (1977), with the Latin text on which the French version is based replaced by a modern French translation, together with a good introduction and detailed notes on the text. M. Simó, 'Las inserciones líricas en el *Meliacin* de Girart d'Amiens', *CN*, 55:211–32, compares the lyric insertions with those of *Guillaume de Dole* and the *Roman de la Violette* and finds that in *Meliacin* they form part of the narrative structure itself, as the romance is largely a commentary on lyric poetry, whereas in the other two romances the insertions were of a more decorative, literary nature. P. Dembowski, '*Meliador* de Jean Froissart, son importance littéraire: le vrai dans la fiction', *EF*, 32.1:7–19, defends this last Arthurian verse romance against Longnon's view of its incoherence by demonstrating its overall structure and the author's desire to present a European view of chivalry, upholding the old standards, and thereby producing a real reflection of the aspirations of the nobility of the late 14th c.; while M. Stanesco, 'Les lieux de l'aventure dans le roman français du moyen âge flamboyant', *ib.*, 21–34, finds that with rare exceptions, such as the *Histoire des Seigneurs de Gavre*, the late medieval romance, from *Perceforest* onwards, tends to retain a poetic, abstract geography rather than one which reflects reality, despite a growing awareness and knowledge of the real world. J. Taylor, 'Courtly patronage subverted: *Lancelot en prose, Petit Jehan de Saintré*', *MedRom*, 19, 1994[1996]:277–92, shows, by a close comparison between Lancelot's treatment by Guinevere and Saintré's by the Dame des Belles Cousines, how La Sale brings romance more into the real world and explores Saintré's need to emancipate himself from the woman's influence and assume a masculine chivalric identity. S. Carden, '"Forment pensifz ou lit me mis": le songe dans le *Livre du Cuer d'Amours espris*', *LR*, 49, 1995[1996]:21–36, examines the overall dream structure and the interior dreams and their effects, concluding that René d'Anjou's purpose was to fix his personal experience for all time through literary composition.

2. POETRY

R. O'Gorman, 'Le *Dit de la Rose*: dit allégorique en forme de prière en l'honneur de la Vierge', *MA*, 102:57–71, 217–27, provides an analysis and edition of this 168-line poem, which contains an *incipit* of a Latin hymn as the last line of each stanza. S. Bliggenstorfer, 'Eustache Deschamps et la satire du ventre plein', *Banquets*, 357–70, is a brief stylistic analysis of the widespread references to food and eating in D.'s poems; and M. Butet, 'De la tempête aux retenues: l'eau dans la poésie d'Eustache Deschamps', *Colloque* (Orléans), 23–40, traces the frequency of references to water in its various manifestations, and the allegorical or medicinal significance it has for the poet. N. Bordessoule, 'Rhétorique de la chasse, rhétorique du désir dans "La Prise amoureuse" de Jehan Accart de Hesdin', *MoyFr*, 34:7–18, examines the effect of the imagery in this early 14th-c. allegorical poem, which alternates narrative with lyric insertions. S. Taylor, 'Les vices de vilenie: la métamorphose des péchés capitaux et des vertus chez Alain Chartier', *MA*, 102:73–79, is a brief analysis of the vices and virtues which are given a political as well as a religious and moral stamp in the *Bréviaire des Nobles*. R. Giannasi, 'Chartier's deceptive narrator: *La Belle Dame sans Mercy* as delusion', *Romania*, 114:362–84, writing in a rather familiar style, analyses the role of the narrator, who uses the feigned death of his mistress to cover his rejection by her, while the story of the *débat* which he pretends to have overheard is a covert means of expressing his anger and frustration. C. Galderisi, 'Personnifications, réifications et métaphores créatives dans le système rhétorique de Charles d'Orléans', *ib.*, 385–412, is a largely Zumthor-inspired analysis of C.'s metaphorical language and its effects. J.-C. Mühlethaler, '"J'ayme qui m'ayme": intertextualité, polyphonie et subjectivité dans les rondeaux de Charles d'Orléans', *ib.*, 413–44, sees C.'s use of the first person as an attempt to explore how to express the self, but, because of the poet's awareness of his poetic inheritance, this should not be too closely read as autobiography. Tony Hunt, *Villon's Last Will: Language and Authority in the 'Testament'*, Oxford, Clarendon Press, 166 pp., explores through a close reading V.'s various ironic strategies for undermining authority and meaning, and demonstrates the dissolution of identity through the vehicle of language. B. Sargent-Baur, 'Persuasion and (special) pleading in François Villon', *FCS*, 22:1–18, deals with the *Poésies diverses* and the *Testament*, analysing V.'s rhetorical prowess and strategies, either in pleading for a favour or money or, in the case of the *Testament*, in presenting himself as victim, in order to elicit from his reader a favourable view of his life and actions and sympathy for the unjust treatment he had received. K. Uitti, 'Villon's *Le Grand Testament* and the poetics of marginality', *MP*, 93:139–60, is valuable as a reminder of the reactions to V. from Sainte-Beuve onwards, for an interesting comparison with the narrative stance of the *Roman de la Rose*, and for some thought-provoking analysis of parts of the *Testament* and its lyric insertions. R. Pensom, 'La magie de la métrique dans le *Testament* de Villon', *Romania*, 114:182–202, builds on the work of Frappier, analysing stanzas XXXIX and XL and the *Ballade des Dames* to demonstrate various rhythmic patterns which underlie the sense and underpin our intuitive response to the verse. R. Van Deyck, 'François Villon ou la virtuosité verbale', *MoyFr*, 34:205–15, is a brief examination of V.'s syntax and its relationship to possible interpretations of the text. P. Verhuyck, 'L'oral et le livresque dans les *Repues franches*', *Neophilologus*, 80:359–75, analyses the complex nature of the work, which appears to reflect a reading aloud to encourage listeners to purchase the book. C. Kiening, 'Inszenierte Tode, ritualisierte Texte: die Totenklagen um Isabella von Bourbon (†1465) und Maria von Burgund (†1482)', *Acta* (Seeon), 455–93, examines in some detail the style and attitudes to death in a range of poems written on the deaths in different circumstances of Isabella and her daughter. *George Chastelain: Le Miroir de la Mort*, ed. Tania Van Hemelryck, Louvain, Université Catholique, 1995, 187 pp., is the first full critical edition, with a detailed introduction, using Bruxelles, Bibliothèque Royale MS 21530 as base, of this moralizing poem, which contains traditional motifs concerning death. A. Collet, 'Dix-neuf strophes inconnues des *Vigiles des Morts* de Pierre de Nesson', *Romania*, 114:535–48, consists of an analysis of the extra stanzas contained in a recently discovered MS. E. Caron, 'Grande rhétorique et productions satiriques populaires: correspondances?', *MoyFr*, 34:19–29, compares some 15th-c. satirical verse, particularly that of Meschinot, with the *sottie*. G. Gros, 'Guillaume Alecis et Jean Bouchet: pour un style français de l'oraison mariale', *MA*, 102:81–92, provides a close comparison between two poems written some thirty years apart in honour of the Virgin. D. Desrosiers-Bonin, 'Le temple des grands rhétoriqueurs', *MoyFr*, 34:43–52, is a brief analysis of the symbol of the temple in poetry from Chastelain into the 16th century. M. Randall, 'L'étymologie rhétorique dans le *Chappelet des dames* de Jean Molinet', *ib.*, 135–44, explores the problems of understanding the rhetorical strategy used by M. to praise his patroness, Marie de Bourgogne, comparing his use of language with that of some religious writing of his day. F. Suard, 'Les Épîtres de Guillaume Crétin', *ib.*, 175–88, analyses the style of the 30 verse epistles.

3. Drama

Les Fragments du mystère auvergnat de Sainte Agathe, ed. Graham A. Runnalls (Inedita & Rara, 9), Montreal, CERES, 1994, 68 pp., consists of an edition of two fragments from the late 15th c., later used as the cover of a 16th-c. tax register; accompanied by a detailed and thorough literary and linguistic study. Id., 'Les mystères de la Passion en langue française: tentative de classement', *Romania*,

114:468–516, provides an important contribution to the understanding of the relationship between the various surviving versions of the
Passion play, of which nine distinct groups are discernible. Id., 'La
circulation des textes des mystères à la fin du moyen âge: les éditions
de la *Passion* de Jean Michel', *BHR*, 58:7–33, develops the work of
Jodogne and Chocheyras, examining the sixteen known published
editions of the play between 1486 and 1542, and tracing the family or
commercial relationships between the various Parisian printers and
publishers responsible for this text; R. goes on to suggest that the
editions produced were firstly for readers, but also for producers and
actors. B. Roy, 'Quand les Pathelin achètent du drap', *Médiévales*, 29,
1995[1996]:9–22, analyses the passages concerning clothes and
fabrics in *Pathelin*, concentrating on the clothes of Triboulet, René
d'Anjou's fool at court and player in the farce. André Tissier, *Recueil
de farces (1450–1550)*, vol. x (TLF, 471), 436 pp., contains seven
farces: *Le pet*; *Tarabin, Tarabas et Triboulle-Ménage*; *Mahuet, natif de
Bagnolet, qui va à Paris au marché pour vendre ses oeufs et sa crème*; *Le
gentilhomme et son page*; *Le pauvre Jouhan*; *Les femmes qui aiment mieux suivre
et croire Folconduit, et vivre a leur plaisir*; and *La cornette* by Jehan
d'Abondance. O. Dull, 'The rhetoric of space and Aquinas's theory
of analogy in late Medieval French drama', *MoyFr*, 34:53–65, looks
briefly at the symbolic use of space, particularly in the morality play
and the *sottie*, in which she discerns an influence of Thomist
epistemology.

4. HISTORICAL LITERATURE

H. Benveniste, 'Joinville et les "autres": les procédés de représentation dans l'*Histoire de saint Louis*', *MA*, 102:27–55, examines a series of
specific episodes to demonstrate the different ways in which J. projects
alterity, depending on whether the peoples involved — Jews,
Bedouins, Mongols — are capable of assimilation into Christianity or
not. E. Gaucher, 'Les joutes de Saint-Inglevert: perception et écriture
d'un événement historique pendant la guerre de Cent Ans', *ib.*,
229–43, compares the perspective of five different accounts of the
thirty-day joust that took place in 1390, whilst English and French
diplomats negotiated a truce in the war. G. Melville, 'Der Held — in
Szene gesetzt: einige Bilder und Gedanken zu Jacques de Lalaing
und seinem Pas d'armes de Fontaine des Pleurs', *Acta* (Seeon),
253–86, discusses the 15th-c. accounts of an exemplary knight and
chivalric ideals in changing times for the conduct of warfare, with
particular attention to the splendour and staging of the tournament
organized by Lalaing in 1450, some three years before he was killed
in battle by cannon fire.

5. RELIGIOUS, MORAL, AND DIDACTIC LITERATURE

C. Lucken, 'Richard de Fournival, ou le clerc de l'amour', *Colloque* (Aix-en-Provence), 399–416, sees the *Bestiaire d'Amours* as differing from earlier love-treatises by projecting an image of the lover as a *fol hardi*, using rhetoric in his cause. Sarah Kay, *The Romance of the Rose* (Critical Guides to French Texts, 110), London, Grant & Cutler, 1995, 125 pp., provides a lively and stimulating analysis of the poem, which makes it accessible to the reader while demonstrating its challenging and elusive nature. Douglas Kelly, *Internal Difference and Meanings in the 'Roman de la Rose'*, Madison, Wisconsin U.P., 1995, ix + 228 pp., concentrates on Jean de Meun's section of the poem and tackles the enigma of interpretation via a perceptive analysis of medieval modes of composition, showing how J. forces the reader to consider for himself the moral implications of the text. S. Huot, 'Drama and exemplarity in the narrative text: reader responses to a passage in the *Roman de la Rose*', *Acta* (Seeon), 494–507, takes the passage in which Genius discusses the relationship between husband and wife to show how some MSS separate it from the original discourse and turn it into an *exemplum* by the narrator. M. McMunn, 'Animal imagery in the text and illustrations of the *Roman de la Rose*', *Reinardus*, 9:87–108, indicates, with the aid of detailed lists, the differences between the two authors of the *Rose* in the range of animal references, and suggests that in some MSS the animal imagery may reflect the tastes of patrons. G. Cropp, 'The Ulysses and Circe episode in *Le Livre de Boèce de Consolacion* and the tradition of the French translations', *AUMLA*, 85:1–13, offers a close comparison between the version of this episode in Book IV, metre iii in this 14th-c. verse–prose version, which incorporates an element of translated commentary, and the other French versions and Boethius's Latin. R. Blumenfeld-Kosinski, 'The scandal of Pasiphae: narration and interpretation in the *Ovide moralisé*', *MP*, 93:307–26, examines the way the poet deals with the sexual taboo of bestiality, concluding that whereas the story itself can be related in considerable detail, its extreme form of perversion allows for little interpretative moralizing. M. Possamaï-Perez, 'Nourriture et ivresse dans l'*Ovide moralisé*', *Banquets*, 237–54, demonstrates that food and drink may have either positive or negative effects, but that the author develops Ovid's text allegorically to transform gluttony into spiritual food, and drunkenness into a love of God. D. Lagorgette, 'Le discours du banquet dans *Les Cent Nouvelles Nouvelles*, *Les Evangiles des Quenouilles* et *Le Livre de la Deablerie*', *ib.*, 199–214, shows in all instances a rather negative attitude to popular feasts, which lead either to sin or animality and lack of dignity, whilst women on their own merely imitate robust male communal eating; and Y. Roguet, 'Gloutonnerie, gourmandise et caquets', *ib.*, 257–77, surveys references and attitudes to gluttony and its effects in a wide range of texts.

CHRISTINE DE PIZAN (DIDACTIC AND POETIC WORKS). Dulac, *de Pizan*, includes the following essays: L. Dulac, 'L'autorité dans les traités en prose de Christine de Pizan: discours d'écrivain, parole de prince' (15–24), highlights the variety of ways C. uses to establish her credibility and reliability as a writer in these treatises; C. Reno, 'Le *Livre de Prudence/Livre de la Prod'hommie de l'homme*: nouvelles perspectives' (25–37), brings fresh arguments to bear to support the view that the *Livre de la Prod'hommie de l'homme* dates from 1405 or 1406 (Solente's view), and that the *Livre de Prudence* is a late version of it, which was in circulation before the death of Louis d'Orléans in November 1407; S. Pagot, 'Du bon usage de la compilation et du discours didactique: analyse du thème "Guerre et paix" chez Christine de Pizan' (39–50), illustrates how C. chooses *exempla* not for their historical interest but because they had significance for contemporary events, and indicates that illustrative material borrowed from elsewhere is always given her own emphasis or slant; E. Hicks, 'Situation du débat sur le *Roman de la Rose*' (51–67), sees the quarrel as essentially about the image of woman, with the most serious attitude being taken by Gerson, while the positions adopted by the adversaries of the quarrel have parallels in modern interpretations of the *Rose*; K. Brownlee, 'Hector and Penthesilea in the *Livre de la Mutacion de Fortune*: Christine de Pizan and the politics of myth' (69–82), points out that exceptionally in this poem C. as author shares the Trojans' grief at the death of Hector, because of his mythical connection with the Valois monarchy, while with Penthesilea there is some personal identity in her condition as widow and writer; J. Cerquiglini-Toulet, 'Sexualité et politique: le mythe d'Actéon chez Christine de Pizan' (83–90), sees, as have others, the transformation of Actaeon into a stag by Diana as a symbol of the English king's betrayal of Charles VI; but it is also used by C. to represent her own transformation, as a writer, into a man; F. Autrand, 'Mémoires et cérémonial: la visite de l'empereur Charles IV à Paris en 1378 d'après les *Grandes Chroniques de France* et Christine de Pizan' (91–103), argues that the relation of events by C. in the *Livre des Fais et bonnes meurs du sage roy Charles V*, adapted from the *Grandes Chroniques*, served as a message to the English in current peace negotiations that French sovereignty must be maintained; C. Gauvard, 'Christine de Pizan et ses contemporains: l'engagement politique des écrivains dans le royaume de France aux XIVe et XVe siècles' (105–28), describes in some detail the political and literary climate in which writers became increasingly aware of their independence and power to comment on and influence events; C. Laennec,

'Prophétie, interprétation et écriture dans *L'Avision Christine*' (131–38), indicates C.'s concern to establish immortality through her writings, while recognizing that whether or not her works relate truth will depend on interpretation by future readers; M.-T. Lorcin, 'Le *Livre des trois vertus* et le *Sermo ad Status*' (139–49), draws attention to the originality of C. in the distinctions she makes between different groups of women, as well as to the changes in style and approach for the different categories; A. Tarnowski, 'Autobiography and advice in *Le Livre des trois vertus*' (151–60), examines C.'s role in this text, in which she projects herself as both receiver and giver of advice, which would apply as much to herself as to those she advises; K. Varty, 'Autour du *Livre des trois vertus*, ou si Rayson, Droicture et Justice faisaient des cours d'introduction à la civilisation française du moyen âge' (161–71), reviews the many issues concerning life and social attitudes reflected in this text which make it so appropriate as an introduction to medieval culture for undergraduate students; C. Clarke-Evans, 'Christine de Pizan's feminist strategies: the defense of the African and Asian ladies in the *Book of the City of the Ladies*' (177–93), offers a feminist analysis of the significance of C.'s inclusion of pagan women in her *Cité*; G. Cropp, 'Les personnages féminins tirés de l'histoire de la France dans le *Livre de la Cité des Dames*' (195–208), provides biographical details concerning the women who cover a thousand years of French history, though most of them are recent or contemporary with C., and shows that C. omits details concerning them that do not suit her argument; J.-C. Mühlethaler, 'Problèmes de récriture: amour et mort de la princesse de Salerne dans le *Décaméron* (IV, 1) et dans la *Cité des Dames* (II, 59)' (209–20), shows that by eliminating certain details from the story of Ghismonda, C. reduces her to an *exemplum* with a predetermined significance, inviting pity and not admiration; A. Slerca, 'Dante, Boccace, et le *Livre de la Cité des Dames* de Christine de Pizan' (221–30), is a brief comparison between C.'s text and its suggested sources; J.-L. Picherit, 'Les références pathologiques et thérapeutiques dans l'œuvre de Christine de Pizan' (233–44), reviews the metaphorical uses to which C. puts medical analogies and their remedies to social and political situations, reflecting a contemporary preoccupation with medicine; B. Ribémont, 'Christine de Pizan: entre espace scientifique et espace imaginé (*Le Livre du Chemin de long estude*)' (245–61), demonstrates how C. superimposes her poetic imagination on established encyclopaedic knowledge of geography and cosmography in order to produce a didactic and not a scientific work; C. Brucker, 'Le monde, la foi et le savoir dans quelques œuvres de Christine de Pizan: une quête' (265–80), explores C.'s attitude towards learning, which inspires precepts for living, but these need to be allied to faith based on a love of God to provide one with a true moral framework; E. Richards, 'In search of a feminist patrology: Christine de Pizan and "Les glorieux dotteurs"' (281–95), shows that C.'s knowledge of patristic texts is greater than she is often given credit for, and that the preciseness of her knowledge allows her to argue effectively on the nature of woman against Aquinas's view; N. Margolis, 'La progression polémique, spirituelle et personnelle dans les écrits religieux de Christine de Pizan' (297–316), traces an evolution in the religious writing throughout the various stages of C.'s literary career, with a growing importance accorded to the Virgin Mary; C. Willard, 'Christine de Pizan's allegorized psalms' (317–24), suggests that the summary execution of Montagu in October 1409 provided the historical and political crisis which inspired the King of Navarre to commission C.'s commentary on the penitential psalms; B. Altmann, 'L'art de l'autoportrait littéraire dans les *Cent Ballades*' (327–36), stresses the importance of the development noted in *ballades* 1, 50 and 100 in projecting an image of C. as a writer; M. Zimmerman, 'Les *Cent Balades d'amant et de dame*: une réécriture de *L'Elegia di Madonna Fiammetta* de Boccace?' (337–46), decides that the similarities and differences between the two works do not allow one to conclude with any degree of certainty that C.'s work is a deliberate rewriting of the Italian one; J. Beer, 'Christine et les conventions dans le *Livre de la Mutacion de Fortune*: "abriger en parolles voires"' (349–56), illustrates that, following convention, C. makes frequent assurances of the truth of her statements in verse which are not necessary in the prose section; A. Strubel, 'Le style allégorique de Christine' (357–72), points out that C. tends to reserve allegory for those works in which she speaks of herself, and that the personifications she uses are almost exclusively feminine, forming a convenient way of developing argument and debate; M. Weil, '"Je suis comme toy": dialogue de Christine de Pizan' (373–81), explores how C. constructs a literary self through the various voices of dialogue and in response to her husband's death; G. Zink, 'La phrase de Christine de Pizan dans le *Livre du Corps de Policie*' (383–95), offers a sympathetic analysis of C.'s syntax which conveys her complex and searching arguments; R. Brown-Grant, '*Des hommes et des femmes illustres*: modalités narratives et transfomations génériques chez Pétrarque, Boccace et Christine de Pizan' (469–80), shows how C.'s approach and intention differ from her Italian predecessors; and T. Fenster, '*Simplece* et sagesse: Christine de Pizan et Isotta Nogarola sur la culpabilité d'Eve' (481–93), draws attention to C.'s view of Eve expressed in the *Epistre au dieu d'Amours*, as trusting in her dealings with the serpent in comparison with male interpretations which portray her as weak. Chance, *Gender*, contains the following relevant essays: E. Richards, 'Rejecting essentialism and gendered writing: the case of Christine de Pizan' (96–131), explores C.'s use of the *Ovide moralisé* and of allegory as a means of modifying prevailing views of woman as essentially different from men, so that the *Cité des Dames* is seen as an allegory of the City of God; C. Nouvet, 'Writing (in) fear' (279–305), examines the voice of Cupid in the *Epistre au dieu d'Amours* and the significance of the signature 'Creintis' at the end of the poem as an expression of the female condition; and K. Brownlee, 'Rewriting romance: courtly discourse and auto-citation in Christine de Pizan' (172–94), analyses the use of the letter of Dame Sebille, borrowed from the *Duc des vrais amans*, in the *Livre des trois vertus* as an effective critique of courtly discourse. X. Zhang, 'Du miroir des Princes au miroir des Princesses: rapport intertextuel entre deux livres de Christine de Pizan', *FCS*, 22, 1995:55–67, sees the same re-use as a warning to all women of the potentially evil effects and damage to their reputations of yielding to 'fin'amors'. L. Walters, 'Boethius and the triple ending of the *Cent Balades*', *FS*, 59:129–37, looks at the final four ballads and sees C. as presenting herself as the new female Boethius, at the same time displacing Jean de Meun as a commentator on him and on Aristotle. B. Altman, 'Last words: reflections on a "lay mortel" and the poetics of lyric sequences', *ib.*, 385–99, analyses the structure and themes of the 'Lay de Dame' at the end of the *Cent Balades d'amant et de dame*, and finds that it functions as an *envoi* to the preceding *balades* and that it has thematic echoes with other poems by C., which make it an appropriate last word by her on love. K. Brownlee, 'Widowhood, sexuality, and gender in Christine de Pizan', *RR*, 86, 1995:339–53, explores the literary strategies employed by C. to avoid presenting herself as an object of sexual desire. H. Solterer, 'Flaming words: verbal violence and gender in pre-modern Paris', *ib.*, 355–78, examines C.'s use of aggressive and polemical language in the Rose quarrel and in her later *Lamentacion sur les maux de la guerre civile* and *Ditié sur Jehanne d'Arc*. R. Blumenfeld-Kosinski, '"Femme du corps et femme par sens"', *ib.*, 87:157–75, concentrates on the saints in the final part of the *Cité des Dames*, stating that C. uses the hagiographical tradition as part of her polemic against male misogyny, by demonstrating the positive qualities of the women in question. M. Donovan, 'Rewriting hagiography: the *Livre de la Cité des Dames*', *WIFS*, 4:14–26, demonstrates that C. always chose saints whose martyrdom occurred in society as a result of male oppression, as distinct from self-isolating ascetics, in order to provide positive role-models. C. Webb, 'La mythologie révisionniste chez Christine de Pizan', *ib.*, 27–38, compares specific portrayals in the *Cité des Dames* with Boccaccio, to illustrate how C. subverts masculine literary authority, and then goes further in the *Ditié de Jehanne d'Arc* by independently creating a feminine myth.

6. MISCELLANEOUS

S. Bazin-Tacchella, 'Un chirurgien-clerc: Guy de Chauliac', *Colloque* (Aix-en-Provence), 31–44, is an analysis of the French version of the *Chirurgia*, contained in B.N. MS fr. 24249. C. Deluz, 'Quelques aspects de la nouvelle clergie dans la société des XIVe et XVe siècles', *ib.*, 133–47, reviews through library inventories and works translated the scope of intellectual interest in the later Middle Ages. D. Lagorgette, 'Images du clerc obscur dans quelques textes en moyen français', *ib.*, 345–62, treats principally the *Cent Nouvelles Nouvelles*, *Pathelin*, the *Evangiles des Quenouilles*, and the *Quinze Joyes de Mariage*, to show the variety of images projected of the clerk; while C. Ferlampin-Acher, 'Grandeur et décadence du clerc Estiene dans *Artus de Bretagne*', *ib.*, 165–95, traces the change from a portrayal of a clerk displaying encyclopædic learning in the 14th-c. version to that of an enchanter practising black magic in the 15th-c. one in B.N. MS fr. 12549. *Les Demandes d'Amour*, ed. Margaret Felberg-Levitt (Inedita & Rara, 10), Montreal-Quebec, CERES, 1995, 499 pp., represents a welcome complete edition which updates the work of Klein and is based on all known MSS containing *demandes d'amour*, and many *incunabula*; appends variants for each *demande*; and has a good introduction which includes details of each MS. H. Millet and M. Hanly, 'Les batailles d'Honorat Bovet: essai de biographie', *Romania*, 114:135–81, is a lengthy analysis of the life of this 14th-c. Benedictine monk, jurist, and diplomat, known particularly for his *Arbre des batailles* and *L'Apparicion maistre Jehan de Meun*, which reflect the political and religious issues of his day.

THE SIXTEENTH CENTURY

By SARAH ALYN-STACEY, *Trinity College, Dublin*

1. GENERAL

Abbreviations for publications mentioned in this chapter are as follows: *Claude Le Jeune et son temps en France et dans les états de Savoie 1530–1600. Musique, littérature et histoire. Actes du colloque international de Chambéry 4–7 novembre 1991*, ed. Marie-Thérèse Bouquet-Boyer and Pierre Bonniffet, Berne, Lang, 412 pp., is referred to as *Actes* (Chambéry); *Humanism and Letters in the Age of François Ier: Proceedings of the Fourth Cambridge French Renaissance Colloquium 19–21 September 1994*, ed. Philip Ford and Gillian Jondorf, Cambridge, Cambridge French Colloquia, xii + 200 pp., as *Procs* (Cambridge); *Marguerite de Navarre 1492–1992. Actes du colloque international de Pau (1992)*, ed. Nicole Cazauran and James Dauphiné, Éditions Interuniversitaires, 1995, 746 pp., as *Actes* (Pau); and *Amour sacré, amour mondain: poésie 1574–1610*, (Cahiers V.-L. Saulnier, 12), Presses de l'École Normale Supérieure, 1995, 151 pp., as *Amour sacré, amour mondain*.

Actes (Chambéry) is an important publication divided into three parts: 'Musique' (1–176); 'Littérature' (177–333); 'Histoire' (334–85). Although it takes as its focal point the French composer Claude Le Jeune, it offers insights into a variety of important and often relatively obscure Renaissance figures, and throws light on the cultural activities at the court of Marguerite de France and Emmanuel-Philibert, a relatively neglected area of French Renaissance studies. Papers on specific authors will be found under the heading appropriate to them, and we shall mention here only those of a more general nature. M.-T. Bouquet-Boyer, 'Une seconde messe de Claude Le Jeune?' (1–4), looks at Le J. in the context of the influx of French (particularly Picard) and Flemish influences on the music and Chapel of Turin, and gives a full description of one of his recently found MSS, the *Missa ad placitum*; H. M. Brown, 'Le Jeune et ses chansons' (35–45), highlights the need for a study which would both locate the *chanson* repertoires in their broader intellectual context and analyse changes in *chanson* style in the 1550s and 1560s, and focuses on the stylistic development attested by each of Le J.'s 14 *chanson* settings; J.-M. Noailly, 'Claude Le Jeune et le Psautier des églises réformées' (70–81), examines the four collections of psalms (1564, 1598, 1618) which Le J. set to music for the Reformed Church, the circumstances in which they were published, the textual variants they present, and characterizing the 125 settings used for the 152 texts, calls for an edition of the whole of the composer's corpus; I. His, 'Le "Livre de

Melanges" de Claude Le Jeune (Anvers, Plantin, 1585). Au cœur du débat modal de la seconde moitié du XVIᵉ siècle' (82–92), throws light on Le J.'s *Livre de Melanges*, arguing that it forms an important component of his output and exposing the systems from which its innovative modal lay-out is derived; F. Dobbins, 'The Canzonette of Claude Le Jeune' (93–101), looks at Le J.'s relatively neglected *villanelle*, drawing attention to his adaptation of Italian models and setting the genre in the context of the time; J. Feuillie, 'De Josquin à la "musique mesurée": à la recherche de points de repère pour l'exécution des œuvres de Claude Le Jeune' (102–17), considers the difficulty facing modern performers of 16th-c. polyphony; J.-P. Ouvrard, 'François Regnard. Motets et chansons' (116–28), offers a brief survey of the works of R., showing his polyphonic settings to be typical of ecclesiastic and Flemish musical culture; B. Gagnepain, 'Réforme et humanisme dans l'œuvre de Jean Servin' (129–36), offers insights into the works of this obscure Protestant composer who set to music works by, among others, Marot, Bèze, Guéroult and Buchanan; G. Durosoir, 'La première décennie de l'air de cour et la postérité de la musique mesurée (1602–1612)' (153–60), reviews divergent opinions on the influence of French Renaissance measured music and, drawing attention to the work of Guédron and the anonymous pieces in two books of airs (P. Ballard, 1606, 1610), concludes that whether they were conscious of it or not, composers continued to be greatly influenced by it and only found their own voice when they asserted their independence from its rigidity; D. Paquette, 'Les formes musicales à l'époque de la Renaissance' (161–68), briefly surveys the changes in musical performance during the reign of Henri IV, examining the new instruments used, the rise of choreographed dance, *ballet de cour*, the *air de cour*, and Protestant music; R. Moffa, 'Musica, poesia e spettacolo alla corte di Torino tra la fine del XVI° secolo a l'inizio del XVII°' (169–76), covers the period 1570–1620 and identifies some of the poets and musicians who performed at the Savoy court in Turin; J. Balsamo, 'La musique dans l'éducation aristocratique au XVIᵉ siècle' (190–97), analyses the fundamentally Aristotelian sources of the reticence of French nobility and educational theorists to embrace music as anything but a solitary, entertaining pastime, in marked contrast to the Italians who saw it as the mark of an aristocrat. An interesting counterpoint to this is F. Roulier, 'L'importance de la musique dans la formation de l'homme de cour d'après le "Livre du courtisan" de B. Castiglione' (198–218). E. G. Rossi, 'Savoiardi e Piemontesi alle corti di Emanuele Filiberto e Carlo Emanuele I° (1560–1600)' (334–38), briefly, and in very general terms, characterizes the Savoy Court 1560–1600; I. Soffietti, 'Il Piemonte nella seconda metà del XVI° secolo:

legislazione e politica ecclesiastica' (339–44), examines the reforms which Emmanuel Philibert introduced concerning law and religion; B. Signorelli, 'Per una ricerca sistematica sugli stranieri presenti nel ducato di Savoia nella seconda metà del XVI° secolo' (345–56), refers to book-keepers' documents and attendance lists to show the influx of Hebrew, Spanish and Portugese communities into Savoy 1560–1600.

D. Ménager, *La Renaissance et le rire*, PUF, 1995, 235 pp., analyses what humour meant to the Renaissance, showing how it was conditioned by the changing socio-political and religious climate to articulate a contradictory mixture of pleasure and pain, and although focused on France, the work makes useful reference to Italy, Spain, and Britain, so facilitating comparison. M. challenges what he sees as a misconception of Renaissance humour ensuing from Bakhtin's negative appraisal of 'official culture' and praise of 'popular culture', showing that it was in fact the cultured classes which produced some of the most comic texts of the time. R.J. Knecht, *The Rise and Fall of Renaissance France 1483–1610*, London, Fontana, xx + 668 pp., is a useful reference work which traces chronologically, and seeks to account for, the shift from order and economic boom established in the first half of the 16th c. to chaos and economic depression. It provides a wealth of information on the administrative and socio-economic structures of the time. O. Pot, 'François ou rommant? Une variante originale du mythe de la langue maternelle', *BHR*, 58:381–404, takes the example of *Suisse roman* to support his argument that the concept of a single French language in the 16th c. is invalid and utopic, and that the language was, in fact, translinguistic. P. Cifarelli, 'Le Corbeau reine des oiseaux? Les versions françaises de la fable du Renard et du Corbeau au seizième siècle', *Reinardus*, 9:33–50, explores how the treatment of this fable perpetuates medieval tradition primarily by its sustained dependence on Latin sources, although an evolution is apparent at a stylistic level. T. Cave, 'Suspense and the pre-history of the novel', *RLC*, 280:507–516, argues that Amyot's preface to his translation of Heliodorus' *Aethiopica* (1547) signals an important development in the approach to reading narrative. A.'s focus on synoptic suspense generated by *ordo artificialis* is examined in the light of 17th-c. reading and gradually placed in the broader context of the modern narrative, C. concluding that A.'s preface is best considered as an 'exceptional variant' of the time, each period's reading of narrative and attitude to suspense largely being a reflection of the wide-ranging changes of social/political organization, sensibility, and epistemology. *Emblemata: Lyons 1550*, ed. Betty I. Knott, introd. John Manning, Hants–Brookfield (VT), Scolar Press, xxx + 238 pp., is worthy of mention because it makes available for the first time a facsimile of the

1550 edition of Andrea Alciati's *Emblematum Liber* (Lyon, Bonhomme), thought to be the most authorative version of this text which exercized such a great influence on French Renaissance Emblem books. Each emblem is accompanied by an English translation of the Latin text and a commentary.

BIBLIOGRAPHICAL

Sybille von Gültingen, **Répertoire bibliographique des livres imprimés en France au seizième siècle, fasc. hors série. Bibliographie des livres imprimés à Lyon au seizième siècle*, vol. III (Bibliotheca Bibliographica Aureliana,147), 239 pp., 1995, and vol. IV (Bibliotheca Bibliographica Aureliana, 154), 227 pp., Baden-Baden–Bouxwiller, Koerner, are two very useful research tools. Louis Desgraves offers two works worthy of note: *Dictionnaires des imprimeurs, libraires et relieurs de Bordeaux et de la Gironde (XVᵉ–XVIIIᵉ siècles)* (Bibliotheca Bibliografica Aureliana, 145), Baden-Baden–Bouxwiller, Koerner, 1995, 325 pp., which provides a very clearly set out index of printers, a historical and biographical note accompanying each entry. *Inventaire des fonds Montaigne conservés à Bordeaux* (Études Montaignistes, 21), Champion, 1995, 169 pp., is a comprehensive bibliography locating the MSS and printed editions (both old and new) of M.'s works conserved in the various archives and libraries of Bordeaux, a full bibliographical description (including the history of each copy where possible) accompanying each entry; it is particularly useful because it also lists works from M.'s library and original documents concerning his life and family. J.Veyrin-Ferrer, 'Les œuvres de Clément Marot', *Procs* (Cambridge), 151–69, challenges G. Defaux's assertion that the first collective 1538 edition of M.'s works was printed by Jean Barbou, arguing that it was more likely to have been François Juste. Jean-Paul Barbier offers two works of bibliographical interest: *Bibliographie des discours politiques de Ronsard* (THR, 205), 211 pp., is a revised version of the 1984 bibliography, includes significant details on new editions found in the intervening twelve years since its first publication; and 'Une curiosité bibliographique: la première édition des *Homilies* de Pontus de Tyard', *BHR*, 58:427–35, corrects earlier datings of de T.'s three books of *Homilies*, dating the *editio princeps* of the first book to 1585 and the publication of the third book and first collective edition of all three books to 1586. G. Banderier offers two bibliographical notes on Du Bartas: 'Notes sur deux éditions anciennes de Du Bartas (éléments pour une bibliographie à venir)', *ib.*, 437–38, providing what is claimed to be the first precise bibliographical description of two works by Du B. conserved at the Bibliothèque Publique et Universitaire of Geneva and at the Universitätsbibliothek at Basle: *La Sepmaine* (1582) and *Les Œuvres* (1583); and 'Une édition inconnue de la première *Sepmaine*', *ib.*, 681–83, drawing attention to two different editions of the work both published in Nîmes in 1581, a copy of one being conserved at the Bibliothèque Municipale of Besançon, a copy of the other being held at the Bibliothèque Municipale of Nîmes. R. Bodenmann, 'Le Manifeste retrouvé de Théodore de Bèze et de ses collègues contre la Formule de concorde (1578)', *BSHPF*, 142:345–87, draws attention to an important document, de B.'s *De corporis Christi omnipraesentia* (1578) conserved at the Bibliothèque Publique et Universitaire, Geneva. Mary Beth Winn, 'Treasures for the Queen: Anne de Bretagne's books from Anthoine Vérard', *BHR*, 58:667–80, revises research done to date on the printed books offered to the Queen by the typographer, focusing attention primarily on the significance of his dedication to her of works by Christine de Pisan and translations of Boccaccio, and concluding that her patronage of V. was generally modest. C. Lemaire, 'La Bibliothèque des imprimés de la reine Marie de Hongrie régente des Pays-Bas, 1505–1558', *ib.*,119–39, provides a few insights into the dissemination of many works by French writers, although the bibliography it presents is regrettably arbitrary, being restricted to printed works not mentioned in the catalogue of the Bibliothèque Nationale, and to manuscripts which are by contemporary authors and which are unknown elsewhere; it highlights the need for a complete inventory to be published. A number of bibliographical articles have appeared concerning Marguerite de Navarre: M. D. Orth, 'Manuscrits pour Marguerite', *Actes* (Pau), 85–105, discusses some of the illuminated MSS at M. de N.'s disposal in the Royal Library of Blois, deeming of major importance the *Initiatoire Instruction en la religion chrestienne pour les enffans*, and arguing that this MS probably dates from after 1530 but before the 'Affaire des Placards' of 1534, and is probably a translation into French of a catechism by Johann Brenz. This article gives food for thought to D. Venard, 'Un catéchisme offert à Marguerite de Navarre', *ib.*, 107–08, who concedes that O. is correct in her identification of the catechism as a translation of Brenz, and that it is not, as he thought, the work of Gérard Roussel and Guillaume Farel. Id., 'Un catéchisme offert à Marguerite de Navarre', *BSHPF*, 142:5–32, elaborates on this revision, proposing that the catechism was written in 1526 in Strasbourg, was based on a work by Brenz, and was copied by Roussel and Farel who offered it to Marguerite d'Angoulême on her marriage to the King of Navarre; the catechism is reproduced. F. Giacone, 'Le premier ouvrage de Marguerite de Navarre: *Dialogue en forme de vision nocturne* ou *Pater noster?*', *Actes* (Pau), 261–89, is particularly worthy of note as it argues that, contrary to general opinion, the work to which M. de N. refers in her penultimate letter to Briçonnet is not the *Dialogue* but the *Pater noster*, a third MS of which G. has located at the Arsenal and reproduces in the appendix, together with the variants of the first and second MSS. Also worthy of mention are: B. Ardura, 'Le Livre et la Réforme catholique à Verdun sous l'épiscopat du prémontré Nicolas Psaume (1548–1575)', *RFHL*, 90–91:7–47; C. Teisseyre, 'Réseaux et pratiques du négoce de libraire en Europe du XVIe au XIXe siècle', *ib.*, 92–93:347–60; A. Jammes, 'Un bibliophile à découvrir, Jean de Gagny', *BBib*, 35–81; D. Hillard, 'La Destruction de Jérusalem en bande dessinée (Paris, vers 1515)', *ib.*, 302–40; D. Vannijnsberghe, 'Quelque documents pour servir à l'histoire de la reliure à Tournai (XVe-début XVIe siècle)', *ib.*, 363–78; and T. Peach, 'Une œuvre charitable de Louis de Gonzague et d'Henriette de Clèves: la fondation dotale de 1588', *RHDFE*, 73, 1995:41–58, and *ib.*, 74:425–26.

HUMANISM, THOUGHT

Procs (Cambridge) commemorates the birth of François Ier by offering ten papers which provide insights into various aspects of the King's patronage of humanism in the early 16th c. Papers on specific writers are mentioned under the appropriate section, and we will deal here only with those concerned with humanism in the broader sense. S. Bamforth, 'A forgotten humanist tribute to François Ier: the *Geographia* of Paolo Pietrasanta' (17–40), examines the Franco-Milanese connection in François Ier's reign, revealing, through the examination of a little known work dedicated to the King, P.'s *Geographia*, the profound Milanese loyalty to him, his eclectic literary tastes, and the persistence of Neo-Latin humanist panegyric well into the 1530s. M. Heath, 'The education of a Christian prince: Erasmus, Budé, Rabelais — and Ogier le Danois' (41–54), analyses the dichotomy inherent in the education of a Renaissance prince: the apparent incompatibilty between the careers of arms and letters, and the attitude towards chivalric practice as expressed in humanist writings (notably treatises on kingship) with which François Ier would have been familiar. F. Lestringant, 'Le mythe de François Ier, de Clément Marot à André Thevet' (55–72), examines the myth which was perpetuated in literature after F.'s death, and, with particularly detailed reference to Thevet's *Cosmographie universelle* (1575), argues that it was the monarch's reconciliation of a career in arms and letters which particularly led writers to consider his reign nostalgically as a lost Golden Age. J. Dupèbe, 'Un chancelier humaniste sous François Ier: François Olivier (1497–1560)' (87–114), considers the patronage afforded by this relatively neglected figure who had sympathies with the Reform and sought to promote religious tolerance.

The revised second edition of Marie-Madeleine de La Garanderie's *Christianisme et lettres profanes: essai sur l'humanisme français (1515–1535) et sur la pensée de Guillaume Budé*, Champion, 1995, 443 pp., first published in 1976, deserves mention. It has been considerably expanded, offering further insights into the assimilation and promotion of classical influences, new or enlarged sections of particular interest bearing for example on Budé, Erasmus, Nicolas Bérault and Germaine de Brie. Guy Poirier, *L'Homosexualité dans l'imaginaire de la Renaissance*, Champion, 1996, offers a clear and interesting study of attitudes towards homosexuality through the analysis of a range of theological, medical, legal, political, literary, and travel documents. T. Tolley, 'States of independence: woman regents as patrons of the visual arts in Renaissance France', *RenS*, 10:237–58, highlights the importance of various female members of the French royal family in promoting the visual arts, concluding that their involvement was usually, if not always, politically motivated. M. Wolfe, 'The strange afterlife of Henri III: dynastic distortions in early Bourbon France', *ib.*, 474–89, considers the contrasting attitudes towards Henri III and Henri IV, highlighting the political significance of the former's unceremonious burial. Béatrice Nicollier-De Weck, *Hubert Languet (1518–1581). Un réseau politique international de Melanchthon à Guillaume d'Orange* (THR, 293), 1995, xx + 678 pp., draws largely on L.'s highly prolific correspondence (no less than 1057 letters spanning the period 1550–81) with 114 people scattered throughout Europe, to present not so much a personal as a political biography of this man. This work provides important insights not just into the political profile of L., situating him clearly in the struggle against the Papacy for a moderate Reformation in Europe, but into the major political concerns of the time, such as the religious conflict in France, and the wars in the Netherlands. Detailed notes and an appendix deal with the as yet unresolved question of whether L. is the author of the *Vindicæ contra tyrannos* (1581), N.-De W. offering the plausible hypothesis that he is not, even though he probably shared its views. A second appendix merits mention as it gives a very useful, comprehensive inventory of L.'s correspondence. Franck Collard, *Un historien au travail à la fin du XVe siècle: Robert Gaguin* (THR, 301), 368 pp., is a very full and scholarly study of this often forgotten figure whose works were so frequently published in the 16th c., and who marked a crossroads in historiography, fusing as he did traditional medieval and new humanist approaches. M.Yardeni, 'Hotman et la naissance de l'histoire-propagande en France', *Actes* (Chambéry), 377–85, traces the career of H., examining the fusion of history, religion, ideology, and propaganda in his writings.

Several important works on the Reformation have appeared. Frank Lestringant offers *L'Expérience huguenote au Nouveau Monde (XVIe siècle)* (THR, 300), 400 pp., a collection of 21 articles already published 1978–1994 and in unrevised form, yet despite a certain duplication, the work is adequately homogenous and provides valuable information on the Huguenot corpus of texts on the New World, in the epilogue tracing their legacy into the 18th c. Divided into three parts, 'La France Antarctique du Brésil', 'La Floride au cœur des ténèbres', 'Vers la Nouvelle-France', it covers such key figures as Villegagnon, Thevet, Pierre Richer, Marc Lescarbot, d'Aubigné, Du Bartas, and Du Plessis-Mornay. Judith Pugh Meyer, *Reformation in La Rochelle. Tradition and Change in Early Modern Europe, 1500–1568* (THR, 298), 182 pp., breaks new ground as hitherto studies have paid little attention to the city's early development. P.M. focuses on the growth of Protestantism in La Rochelle from its origins through to the commitment to the national Protestant movement in 1568, paying particular attention to the role of social, economic and political factors in the Reformation's attraction for the *Rochelais*, the extent to which the city's experience may be said to be exemplary of the Reformation's success elsewhere in France, and finally seeking to explain why the Reformation ultimately failed. Her findings are supported by a wealth of archival references, making this a highly scholarly and commendable work. Thomas A. Lambert et al., *Registres du Consistoire de Genève au temps de Calvin (1542–1544)*, vol. 1 (THR, 305), xlii + 446 pp., is a useful research tool, particularly for biographical research, as it provides much information on the history of discipline in the Reformed Church, and goes far beyond Frédéric-Auguste Cramer's transcription of the registers which scholars have tended to rely on. It is carefully annotated with useful glossary, geographical glossary, and *index locorum* and *nominum*. Mention should also be made of W. Monter, 'Les exécutés pour hérésie par arrêt du Parlement de Paris (1523–1560)', *BSHPF*, 142: 191–224, another useful research tool, giving as it does the names of those executed by the greatest secular court in Renaissance Europe for heresy (excluding those accused of *non sacramentatina* blasphemy), and also setting this procedure in France in the European context and in Paris in its broader national context, and heresy in the context of other 16th-c. crimes. R. Devos, 'Entre catholiques et réformés: l'existence d'un tiers parti dans la Savoie du XVIe siècle', *Actes* (Chambéry), 368–76, argues plausibly, with reference to documents concerning Marc-Claude de Buttet and his cousin, Jehan Piochet de Salins, that despite the unequivocally hostile attitude of the Savoy Senate to the Reform, there was an informal third faction of sceptical, or at least broad-minded, Catholics in the duchy. Christian Belin, *L'Oeuvre de Pierre Charon, 1541–1603: littérature et théologie de Montaigne à Port-Royal*, Champion, 1995, 362 pp., is an in-depth, very clear and scholarly analysis of the theological ideas articulated in the work of C., and their reception in and influence on the 17th c.

Actes (Pau) offers insights into various aspects of the social and religious thought of Marguerite de Navarre and her close associates. F. Michaud-Fréjaville, 'Marguerite d'Angoulême, reine de Navarre, duchesse de Berry, "laquelle a fort humainement traité ses sujets de Berry"' (45–57), concludes that M. de N. chose to intervene hardly at all in the administration of the duchy of Berry because of her preoccupation with the broader issues of rulership. L. Ripart, 'Les mariages de Marguerite' (59–83), analyses the political motivation and repercussions of M. de N.'s marriages to the Duc d'Alençon and to Henri d'Albret. N. Lemaître and M. Veissière, 'Lefèvre d'Étaples, Marguerite de France et les évêques de leur temps' (109–134), focuses on L. d' E.'s links with bishops during his time in Paris, Meaux, Strasbourg, Blois and Nérac, and the influence he exerted on them through his writings and teachings. V. Mellinghoff-Bourgerie, 'L'échange épistolaire entre Marguerite d'Angoulême et Guillaume Briçonnet: discours mystiques ou direction spirituelle?' (135–57), examines the nature of the correspondence between M. de N. and B. 1521–24 in the light of Lucien Febvre's assertion that it is not an intimate dialogue, and concludes that the letters were written in a Pauline and ecclesiastic spirit, reflective of sympathies for the Reform. R. Cooper, 'Marguerite de Navarre et la réforme italienne' (159–88), explores the relatively neglected subject of M. de N.'s links with several Italian groups of Reformers. C. Desplat, 'Ordres et "estats": les représentations sociales dans l'œuvre de Marguerite de Navarre' (205–34), argues that the portrayal of social hierarchy in M. de N.'s works highlights the social tensions of the day.

INDIVIDUAL WORKS OR WRITERS

1995–96 saw the important publication of two further volumes of Théodore de Bèze's correspondence, edited by Alain Dufour et al.: *Correspondance de Théodore de Bèze*, vol. 18 (THR, 292), 1995, xiv + 270 pp., covers 1577; vol. 19 (THR, 304), xxxii + 280 pp., covers 1578. Also on de B. is R. Bodenmann, 'Le manifeste retrouvé de Théodore de Bèze et de ses collègues contre la Formule de concorde (1578)' (see *supra*, BIBLIOGRAPHICAL). Still on the epistolary front, E. Viennot offers two articles on the letters of Marguerite de Valois which highlight the need for them to be published in their entirety. The first, 'A propos de la Saint-Barthélemy et des Mémoires de Marguerite de Valois: authenticité du texte et réception au XVIIe siècle', *RHLF*, 40:894–917, challenges the view that M. de V.'s letters are apocryphal and refers to them to correct what V. considers to be popular misconceptions about the Saint-Barthélemy massacre; no doubt a response from sceptics will follow. The second, 'Autour d'un "démarriage" célèbre: dix lettres inédites de Marguerite de Valois', *RHR*, 43:5–24, edits ten letters written by M. de V. 1593–99, the period of the annulling of her marriage to Henri IV; each letter is clearly contextualized and provides important insights into the Queen's character, correcting several misconceptions about her role in this significant political event.

Particularly important is *Béroalde de Verville 1556–1626* (Cahiers V.-L. Saulnier, 13), Presses de l'École Normale Supérieure, 227 pp., which comprises a dozen enlightening articles. N. Kenny, '"Car le nom mesme de libéralité sonne liberté": les contextes sociaux et économiques du savoir chez Béroalde de Verville' (7–24), argues that the socio-economic developments of the day leave their imprint on the works of de V., and traces the related concepts of *liberté* and *libéralité* as they emerge in his works, concluding that if at first he seems to defend these values, refusing to trade his works for commercial gain, he nevertheless ends up questioning their validity, so indicating the changing relations between the writer and his public. I. Zinguer, 'Verville médecin' (25–39), focuses on the medical career of de V., examining both the way in which it informs his work and his attitudes towards the medical practices of the day. S. Bamforth, 'Autour du manuscrit 516 du Wellcome Institute de Londres — quelques réflexions sur Béroalde de Verville, médecin et alchimiste' (41–56), offers important new evidence attesting the extent of de V.'s involvement with alchemy, the influence of which on his work is often deemed modest. The remainder of the article traces de V.'s medical training, practice and philosophy, emphasizing his sustained links with alchemy and arguing that his reputation amongst his contemporaries was largely founded on his activities in that field. J.-R. Fanlo, 'Image édifiante et poisson soluble: la *Pietà* du *Cabinet de Minerve*' (57–82), analyses the apparent textual discontinuity in 'Rencontre IV' of this work, concluding that it is a deliberate narrative effect, articulating the principle that the world, like the text, is unstable and in perpetual transformation. S. Bokdam, 'Le désir et ses objets: de l'art au songe dans *Le Cabinet de Minerve*' (83–97), looks at the same piece, attributing the text's structural coherence to its sustained and central exploration of the theme of desire; three aspects of this theme, art, dream and love, are examined as they emerge in the work and in relation to the text's preoccupation with perpetual movement.

M. Renaud, '*L'Histoire des vers qui filent la soye* de Béroalde de Verville: "Vray stille d'ange" ou vers de Mirliton?' (99–110), re-evaluates this rare work which has to date received little critical attention. Situating it in relation to both contemporary works of the same didactic/ scientific genre and the rest of de V.'s corpus, R. argues that it does not have a mere didactic function to encourage sericulture in the Touraine but articulates broader philosophical concerns. In a most enlightening article, G. Polizzi, 'Les *Riches inventions* de Béroalde de Verville' (111–40), draws attention to the rich and complex intertextual links between de V.'s works and Francesco Colonna's *Hypnerotomachia*. Simultaneously revealing much about the editorial practice of the day, P. examines de V.'s translation of this work (*Tableau des riches inventions* . . ., Paris, Guillemot, 1600), arguing that it owes little to C.'s text, being essentially a paraphrase of Jean Martin's 1546 translation; he concludes that the deviations from the Italian hypotext derive from a fundamental redefinition of the work: de V. no longer sees the dream as allegorical but as a dream in the modern sense of the term, that is, as a reflection of the dreamer's psyche and his desire for what is forbidden. D. Mauri, '*La Pucelle d'Orléans* et *Le Voyage des princes fortunez*: deux miroirs à facettes' (141–55), shows that although these two works by de V. treat different subjects, significant structural and thematic parallels exist between them. T. Cave, '*Le Voyage des princes fortunez*: un cas particulier de l'*ordo artificialis*' (157–67), analyses de V.'s preference for *ordo artificialis* over *ordo naturalis*, situates it in the context of the time (it was a recent technique in France, being first exploited by Amyot in 1547) and points to parallels to be drawn between the use and effect of first person narration by de V., Rabelais and Montaigne. H. Moreau, 'L'intelligence des écritures dans le *Moyen de parvenir*' (169–78), argues that the language and themes in this work reflect a considerable concern with hermeneutics, and that de V. is articulating an important statement on the difficulty of interpretation and of arriving at absolute comprehension. Also concerned with interpretation is M.-L. Demonet, 'La valeur des *notes* chez Béroalde de Verville' (179–200), who situates de V.'s preoccupation with linguistic questions in a philosophical framework, notably that of his evolution towards a more pronounced scepticism, which reinforced his belief that, given their variability, words alone have no intrinsic value; D. concludes that, given its variability and depth of meaning, *Le Moyen de parvenir* constitutes the fulfilment of de V.'s declared intention to write a work praising the word. In an epilogue to these eleven articles, A. Tournon, 'Des puzzles à pièces erratiques' (201–12), insists on the importance of de V. as a writer worthy of recognition, yet accepts that the text presents considerable difficulties in terms of interpretation, as the author deliberately cultivates ambiguity through calculated incoherence and polysemic expression so that there is no univocal meaning. On de V.'s scientic poetry, see S. Bamforth 'Béroalde de Verville, poète de la connaissance' (*infra*, AFTER THE PLÉIADE).

Several important editions have appeared. *Pierre de L'Estoile: Registre-journal du règne d'Henri III*, vol. II, ed. Madeleine Lazard and Gilbert Schrenk (TLF, 465), 289 pp., covers 1576–78, and is a valuable source of information on the period. *Bonaventure Des Periers: Le Cymbalum mundi, avec un dossier et des textes d'accompagnement*, ed. Yves Delègue, Champion, 1995, 159 pp., is an excellent, very comprehensive edition; in the introduction, D. considers the variety of interpretations which this enigmatic work has received, and plausibly argues that the work is deliberately subversive in that it suggests that the word is an abuse of power. Interestingly, he does not enter into the debate concerning authorship of the work, and just accepts that it is uncertain. Especially useful are the accompanying texts, comprising various documents in which Des P. is quoted and also the history of the trial of the *Cymbalum mundi*. Particularly welcome is *Barthélemy Aneau: Alector ou le coq. Histoire fabuleuse*, ed. Marie Madeleine Fontaine, 2 vols (TLF, 469), cxxvii + 1008, the first edition of this unusual work to be published since 1560. The introduction is very scholarly, exploring in detail the text's symbolism and sources and situating it in the context of Renaissance philosophy and literary trends. A useful biographical section throws new light on A. and his links with other writers of the day. The editorial practice used is particularly judicious given the numerous orthographical inconsistencies of the 1560 edition: these are reproduced, although a few (clearly signalled) have been modified for the purpose of clarity. However, one quibble: F. offers no conclusive evidence to support her view that these inconsistencies may be directly attributed to the author. *Bénigne Poissenot: Nouvelles histoires tragiques*, ed. Jean-Claude Arnould and Richard A. Carr (TLF, 470), 329 pp., makes available an important text which will do much to inform us about P.'s contribution to the development of the narrative genre. If the 'Introduction' is rather summary, the footnotes to the text are very detailed.

Three works have appeared on Helisenne de Crenne: *Helisenne de Crenne: les epistres familieres et invectives*, ed. Jerry C. Nash, Champion, 232 pp., presents the 1539 edition with a clear introduction, providing a summary profile of the author and situating the work in relation to various strands of current critical theory. J. Incardona, 'Les Angoysses douloureuses qui procedent d'amours, une vision ambiguë de l'amour', *RHR*, 42 : 7–28, offers a particularly interesting article, adopting the welcome recent approach to de C.'s novel whereby not just the first part but the whole of the text is taken into account; rejecting the view that the novel is simply a didactic and moralizing condemnation of love, and examining the emotion in relation to the diverse focalizations offered by the various narrators, I. concludes that the text permits of two diametrically opposed interpretations: one whereby love emerges explicitly as negative, another whereby it emerges implicitly as positive. Complementing this is E. Guild, '"Suyvant le naturel du sexe foeminin": the representation of the feminine in *Les Angoisses douloureuses qui procedent d'amours*', *Procs* (Cambridge), 73–85, who does, however, consider only the first book; taking the body as a site of representation and construction of identity, G examines how de C. unsettles the prevailing discourses of the female body (notably those of Arthurian romance), and how the differences in function and representation of the female body depend upon whether a text is male-authored or female-authored.

Two works look at the question of textual borrowing: V. Wakerley, 'Heloys ou Andreas? A problem of authorship in MS Royal 116F II in the British Museum Library', *NFS*, 35.2:18–26, demonstrates that *Les Epistres de l'Abesse Heloys* (1500), attributed to Bernard André, is an adaptation, and in parts even a translation, of Andreas Capellanus's *Tractatus de Amore*, and that the MS's importance resides precisely in its intertextual links with its source and in the fact that it signals the sustained popularity of works of its kind into the early 16th century. N. Hester, 'Textes volés? *L'estat, description et gouvernement des royaumes et republiques du monde* de Gabriel Chappuys', *BHR*, 58:651–65, reveals that contrary to general opinion this is not an original work by C. but a deliberate and skilfully disguised plagiarism of a work by Francesco Sansovino, *Del governo e amministrazione di diversi regni e republiche* (1583). Turning to another translator, D. Dalla Valle offers 'Rolland Brisset, premier traducteur du *Pastor fido*', *Actes* (Chambéry), 326–33, a brief biographical survey of B., tracing his career as a translator and writer of prose verse, and speculating as to why he should have chosen to translate Guarini's *Pastor fido*.

The question of authorship has given rise to two articles worthy of mention: A.-M. Cocula, 'Pourquoi La Boétie ne peut être l'auteur du *mémoire* touchant l'édit de janvier 1562', *BSAM*, no. 4:51–56, analyses the divergent arguments of Paul Bonnefon, Malcolm Smith and the author, and argues, not always convincingly, that the mémoire is not by La B. but is probably the work of a highly-placed French ecclesiast. B. Chevignard, 'Jean-Aimé de Chavigny: son identité, ses origines familiales', *BHR*, 58:419–25, offers new information on the identity of Nostradamus's first commentator, arguing that Jean de Chevigny and Jean-Aimé de Chavigny are, in fact, the same person, being pseudonyms employed by a certain Jean Chevignard; this highlights the need for a biography on C.

The following are worthy of note: G. Banderier, 'Un texte inédit de Constant d'Aubigné', *ib.*, 97–104, reproduces a hitherto unpublished MS by Agrippa d'Aubigné's son, entitled *Harangue du fils ainé de Monsieur d'Aubigné à l'anterrement de Monsieur de Rohan*; J.-L. Bourgeon, 'Les *Mémoires* de Tavanes et la Saint-Barthélemy: mode d'emploi', *BSHPF*, 42:33–54, draws attention to a neglected document which provides interesting insights into the Saint-Barthélemy massacre, its political aftermath, and the historical perspective in which it was viewed in the 17th c.; M. Veissière, 'Dédicace d'une édition de Raymond Jordan à Guillaume Briçonnet', *BHR*, 58:141–49; A. Legros, 'La vie et l'œuvre d'un médecin contemporain de Montaigne, Pierre Pichot', *RFHL*, 92–93:361–74; R. Bodenmann and M. Schwarz Lausten, 'Une lettre oubliée de François Lambert d'Avignon', *BSHPF*, 142:155–74, which provides a useful bibliography of L.'s works.

MULTIPLE WORKS OR WRITERS

Edmund J. Campion, *Montaigne, Rabelais, and Marot as Readers of Erasmus*, Lampeter, Mellen, 1995, 166 pp., sets out to examine the imitation of specific works of Erasmus by Montaigne, Rabelais, and Marot. The work is useful in that it summarizes recent scholarship on E.'s influence on these three writers and indicates parallels between them, but it cannot be said to break new ground, falling short of its stated intention largely because of its failure to analyse the intertextual operations determining the appropriation of the hypotext. Two aspects of the approach are particularly problematic, being highly speculative in nature. Firstly, the decision to analyse the three writers in reverse chronological order, taking Montaigne first 'because his creative imitation of Erasmus was the least obvious to sixteenth-century readers'; how can we be sure of this? Secondly, the rejection of 'modern critical theories' on the grounds that they generate anachronistic interpretations, and an attempt to show how 16th-c. readers would understand the texts by analysing them in the light of Renaissance theory. This naively suggests that it is possible to recuperate the past in an absolute sense. Moreover, quotation practice is inconsistent: quotations from works in French and Latin are given in English in the body of the text and in the original language only in the footnotes, whilst in chapter five (on Marot's imitation of E.) French and Latin texts are given in the body of the text so that, according to C., the reader will be better able to appreciate the process of adaptation. But surely such an appreciation is also the aim of the earlier chapters?

2. RABELAIS AND THE CONTEURS

Two important publications have appeared on Rabelais. The first, *CTex*, no. 15, 'Rabelais: Actes de la journée d'étude du 20 octobre 1995', comprises eight articles, concerned largely with the *Tiers Livre*. T. Cave, '"Je pareillement …": instances de la première personne chez Rabelais' (7–18), shows, through an essentially philological analysis of certain passages of the *Tiers* and *Quart Livres*, how the narrator figure frequently blurs the demarcation between reality and fiction by inserting himself intermittently into the text, so signalling extra-textual experience; situating this fictional-factual figure in the broader historical context, C. argues that R. marks an important stage in narrative development and particularly as a forerunner of Montaigne. C.-G. Dubois, '"La Chanson de Ricochet": fonction de la réitération dans le *Tiers Livre* de Rabelais' (19–32), examines the philosophical significance of the allusion to the 'Chanson de Ricochet' (*Tiers Livre*, chapter ten), discussing it in relation to the question of judgement and will. E. Kotler, 'La question du mariage de Panurge: une enquête sur les limites du dialogue' (33–47), offers an interesting analysis of the use of dialogue in the *Tiers Livre*, concluding that the book is tantamount to a parody of dialogue's ability to resolve contradiction and arrive at truth. J. Céard, 'Le Jugement de Bridoye' (49–62), proposes a new interpretation of the enigmatic passage of Bridoye's judgement, suggesting that it is an apologue. M. Renaud, 'Le Livre/le monde — notes sur l'idée de nature chez Rabelais' (63–75), exposes very clearly how R.'s declining use of natural imagery, and his shift to increasingly abstruse allegory in his later works, lead away from an exploration of the material world towards a virtual world. A. Tournon, 'Un silence signé Rabelais' (77–87), is a dense but stimulating article which examines the concept of the unfaithful wife and the questions it raises concerning, for example, responsibility and free-will. J.-Y. Pouilloux, 'De l'interprétation: déraison des raisons' (89–95), considers various aspects of logic in the *Tiers Livre*. M.-L. Demonet, 'Le "signe mental" dans l'œuvre de Rabelais' (97–111), is a particularly interesting article which analyses R.'s definition of the 'signe mental' as it emerges in the concept of Pantagruelism and the Papimane episode in the *Quart Livre*, concluding that his signs are not fixed and do not refer the reader to one single absolute meaning.

The second, *ERab*, 31, offers seven papers followed by R. Fivaz-Silbermann's 'Table et index' of *ERab* publications 1956–96 (117–30). The first five papers, given at five conferences in 1994, offer useful insights into R.'s treatment of various facets of nature. G. Demerson, 'Rabelais et la nature de l'eau' (11–29), examines R.'s attitude to water as one of the four elements composing the universe in order to discern whether he viewed nature as a coherent or incoherent construct; D. concludes that despite man's vulnerability, R. considered him as capable of working within nature's framework to avoid chaos and to promote harmony and order. D. Desrosiers-Bonin, 'Rabelais et la nature féminine' (31–47), challenges the view that R. was a misogynist, arguing that his presentation of women is so varied that it eludes such narrow categorization, and is in fact reflective of an evolving, more indulgent attitude towards women characteristic of the period. A. Gendre, '"A ceste heure parle-tu naturellement". Réflexions sur le langage naturel chez Rabelais' (49–63), analyses what it means in R.'s view to speak naturally as opposed to conventionally, and perceives a condemnation of artifice. B. Bowen, 'Les géants et la nature des trippes' (65–73), examines the broad comic significance of the tripe leitmotif in R.'s works, concluding that it is essentially exploited to lend realism to his portrayal of the giants. J. C. Nash, 'Rabelais et l'environnement moral: une étude sur le bien et le mal fictifs' (75–97), examines R.'s text in the light of Wittgenstein's view that ethics and æsthetics are one, arguing that the systematic Manichæan juxtaposition of examples of good and evil and the triumphs of the former over the latter attest the narrative's moral motivation. J. C. Persels, '"Straitened in the bowels", or concerning the Rabelaisian trope of defecation' (101–12), analyses R.'s scatological references in the light of similar contemporary discursive practice, demonstrating what has been known for a long time, that is, that they serve a greater purpose than to provide mere humour, being part of a well-contextualized, recognizable, rhetorical design. J. E. G. Dixon, 'Concordance des œuvres de François Rabelais' (113–15), revises some of the entries in the 1992 concordance of R.'s works.

A. Tournon, '*En sens agile': les acrobaties de l'esprit selon Rabelais*, Champion, 1995, 193 pp., is a very clear study which, through close analysis of specific passages, draws attention to the explicit and implicit levels of meaning inherent in the *Tiers Livre*. The *index locorum* and *index notionum* are particularly useful. M. J. Freeman, 'Bringing up (big) baby: Gargantua's childhood', *RoS*, 28:29–43, argues the importance of situating in the context of the 16th c. what R. tells us about the education and childhood of Gargantua, and suggests that the exposition of a happy childhood is intrinsic to Pantagruelism and to R.'s underlying didactic motivation. G. Defaux, '"Hoc est porcus meus": Rabelais et les monstres du *Quart Livre*', *Adirel*, 9:37–50, is an interesting article because it returns to the question of how the *Quart Livre* should be read. Rejecting a 'lecture topographique' in favour of a broader approach, a 'lecture cosmographique', which takes into account the biographical and historical circumstances in which the book was written, he challenges the view that the *Quart Livre* is merely a succession of adventures pieced together in an arbitrary fashion, arguing that it is in fact very precisely structured, and that it (and particularly the monsters) are important instruments of R.'s mordant satire against the Roman Catholic Church. T. Glon, '*Pantagruel* et l'invention de la fiction', *RHR*, 42 : 29–48, examines the way in which R. circumspectly fuses the real with the fantastic in *Pantagruel* to articulate complex questions, but the analysis does not really offer any new insights. More interesting is M. Marrache, 'Les "fascheries" de Panurge', *ib.*, 49–61, which examines in detail the articulation of Panurge's 'fascheries' prompted by his dilemma as to whether or not he should marry, and concludes that if they are a fundamental trait of his character, it is because R. deliberately endows the character with multiple functions: to embody scepticism about the validity of interpretation, personal choice and desire, as a counterpoint to the cunning exposed in *Pantagruel*, and in anticipation of the *Quart Livre*.

On Marguerite de Navarre, the most significant new publication is *Actes* (Pau). Divided into four parts: 'Marguerite et son temps' (13–258), 'Poèmes et théâtre' (259–422), 'Heptaméron 1: le texte et son écriture' (423–591), and 'Heptaméron 2: nouvelles en perspective' (593–730), it offers perspectives on many aspects of M. de N.'s output. Each genre will be dealt with in the appropriate section, mentioning here only those articles of relevance to her narrative production. N. Cazauran and J. Dauphiné, 'Avant-propos' (7–11), point out that if M. de N.'s narrative output has tended to eclipse the importance of her drama and poetry, only a comprehensive consideration of her works in their entirety will inform us about her æsthetic. S. Arredondo, 'La réception de l'*Heptaméron* en Espagne: raisons d'une absence' (189–204), attributes Spanish hostility to the *Heptaméron* (which persisted well into the 17th c.) to negative political attitudes ·towards France, stimulated largely by the conflict over Navarre and the Battle of Pavia, and which led the Spanish to view M. de N. as one of the enemy; in contrast, the attitudes towards the Spanish articulated in the *Heptaméron* suggest a neutrality on M. de N.'s part. R. Aulotte, 'L'inspiration satirique dans l'*Heptaméron* et dans le *Théâtre profane*' (235–43), concentrates on social satire in the *Heptaméron*, unfortunately touching only fleetingly on M. de N.'s drama; A. argues that the satire is often undermined by what he terms the Queen's 'impatience' which leads her to articulate her moral in a very explicit and direct fashion. P. Pelckmans, 'Pour un profil thanatologique de l'*Heptaméron*' (245–58), analyses the concept of death as it emerges in its various forms in the *Heptaméron*, concluding (not surprisingly) that its prevalence makes the work representative of the time. In section three, eight articles deal with the textual genetics of the *Heptaméron*. R. Salminen, 'Une nouvelle lecture de l'*Heptaméron*: le manuscrit 2155 de la Bibliothèque Nationale de Paris' (425–35), highlights the problematic question of establishing a base text for an edition of the *Heptaméron*; S. explains her reasons for basing her forthcoming edition not on MS 1512 (as Michel François did) but on MS 2155, arguing that it appears to represent the last version M. de N. revised. L. Fontanella, 'Petites considérations à propos de la tradition manuscrite des *Nouvelles*' (437–44), argues that certain features (notably the number of *nouvelles*, their position in the text, the presence or absence of dialogue between the *devisants*), expose certain phases of the *Heptaméron*'s composition and developments; F. also considers the differences between the four MSS of the text. S. Lefèvre, '*L'Heptaméron* entre éditions et manuscrits' (445–82), examines M. de N.'s links with the *Heptaméron*'s original two editors, Pierre Boaistau and Claude Gruget, and concludes that they probably used Adrien de Thou's transcription of the text and at least one other MS; the attached bibliography of all known MSS of the *Heptaméron* is particularly useful. N. Cazauran, 'Post-scriptum à propos d'un manuscrit: New York, Pierpont Morgan Library 242' (483–90), draws attention to the intertextual divergences which this MS presents in relation to the others, noting in particular a certain flippancy and licence which considerably modifies the *nouvelles*, although the reasons for such modification may only be guessed at. E. Kotler, 'L'implicite narratif ou la morale incidente de l'*Heptaméron*' (491–509), examines what K. defines as the subjective, incidental moralizing which informs the opinions of the *devisants*, and concludes that their morality is undoubtedly representative of M. de N.'s own essentially Pauline moral outlook, based on faith, hope and charity. J. Lecointe, 'Les lieux rhétoriques de la personne dans les récits de l'*Heptaméron*' (511–25), situates M. de N.'s characterization in the context of the classically-inspired rhetorical tradition enjoying favour at the beginning of the Renaissance, and concludes that she is working very much in an Augustinian tradition, the characters being defined not by *a priori* nature but by their acts. S. Perrier, 'Des "choses qui sont si plaisantes à la chair": l'art de l'allusion dans l'*Heptaméron*' (527–36), draws attention to the paradoxical coexistence in the *Heptaméron* of the spiritual and the profane, arguing that it reflects M. de N.'s concern with Man in his entirety, and going on to examine how she uses allusion to articulate subtly ideas on essentially worldly pleasures. N. Cazauran, 'Un nouveau "genre d'écrire": les débuts du dialogue mondain' (537–91), offers some new insights into the *devisants* through a close analysis of the language used in their dialogues. Section four begins with P. de Lajarte, 'Autour d'un

paradoxe: les nouvelles de Marguerite de Navarre et sa correspondance avec Briçonnet' (595–634), a very interesting article which sets
out to explain the 'worldly versus the religious' paradox in the
Heptaméron's prologue, through an intertextual reading which takes
into account M. de N.'s correspondence with Briçonnet, and which
reveals that Oisille's discourse has very close lexico-semantic affinities
with B.'s letters. E. Vaucheret, 'De la réalité historique à la fiction
narrative: la xxie nouvelle de l'*Heptaméron*' (635–44), analyses the
way in which M. de N. transforms the story of Rolandine, and argues
that her choice of story reflects her preoccupation with the psychology
of love, social problems of the time, and her feminist sympathies.
F. Charpentier, 'La guérison par la parole. A propos de la xxxiie
nouvelle de l'*Heptaméron*' (645–55), focuses on the characters in the
stories related by the *devisants*, drawing particular attention to the
antithetical significance of the word and silence in the *Heptaméron*: the
word brings happiness because through it the truth is revealed,
whereas silence brings negativity, because it conceals the truth; C.
provides a clear analysis of the centrality of this antithesis to *nouvelle*
32. M. D. Vivero Garcia, 'La Fonction argumentative du discours
narratif dans l'*Heptaméron*. L'exemple de la lviie nouvelle' (657–67),
uses the narrative theories of J. M. Adam to define the argumentative
processes deployed in the *Heptaméron*; through a close decoding of
nouvelle 57, V. G. reveals how the pragmatico-argumentative efficiency
of the story is assured because the narrative contains within itself the
necessary signs for its interpretation. A. González Alcaraz, 'La
structure spéculaire dans la lxiie nouvelle de l'*Heptaméron*' (669–75),
draws attention to the specular structure of the *nouvelles*, showing how
no. 62 exemplifies a particularly coherent and sustained use of the
effect. C. Martineau-Génieys, 'Les secrets de la dame du Vergier'
(677–94), is a particularly interesting article, not only analysing
nouvelle 70 in relation to its hypotext, *La Châtelaine de Vergy*, and
showing that M. de N. injects greater realism into it, but also
examining why it should have attracted the Queen's attention, and
arguing that there are grounds for believing that she had access to an
old MS and considered it a true story. M. Bideaux, 'Dieu acteur dans
les récits de l'*Heptaméron*' (695–718), examines the references to God
in the *Heptaméron*, indicating the diverse actantial roles He assumes
and the repercussions that the resultant variable figure has on the
narrative and particularly on its realism. G. Mathieu-Castellani,
'Rien nouveau sous le soleil ...' (719–29), discusses the problematic
question of novelty as it is debated in the *Heptaméron*. N. Cazauran,
'Les devisants de l'Heptaméron et leurs "nouvelles"', *RHLF*,
5:879–93, looks at the language used by the *devisants* at the end of

each *nouvelle* to comment on the one just completed and to introduce the following one.

3. POETRY

Amour sacré, amour mondain offers a selection of papers on the paradoxical coexistence of spiritual and profane love in Renaissance poetry. Papers on specific poets will be found in the appropriate section, and we mention here only those items of a more general nature. A. Gendre, 'Ouverture' (7–8), briefly outlines the paradox. C.-G. Dubois, 'L'amour médecin, l'amour sorcier: quelques récurrences de la lyrique amoureuse au début du règne de Henri III' (113–24), examines the repercussions of a 'lecture analogique' and a 'lecture syllogique' on a decoding of metaphors evoking amatory pain, taking examples from various poems written 1570–80; A. Mantero, 'Ingéniosité et herméneutique: une poésie du chiffre et de la figure' (125–39), considers the use of the sonnet to articulate both worldly and religious themes, noting certain parallels in meaning; T. Cave, 'Conclusions' (141–46), argues that there is a contamination between the two sorts of love.

A number of publications on scientific poetry have appeared. I. Pantin, *La Poésie du ciel en France dans la seconde moitié du seizième siècle* (THR, 297), 1995, 555 pp., is a very dense, scholarly work offering a commendably clear perspective on the development of scientific poetry in the 16th century. Divided into three sections, the first part, 'Contexte et topique', enlightens us in detail about the scientific climate of the time and how it is reflected in the writings (both philosophical and literary) of the day; the second part, 'Renaissance d'une poésie du ciel', analyses how these themes emerge in poetry, notably in the works of the Pléiade; the third part, 'l'âge didascalique', looks at the shift in the treatment of scientific themes in the last third of the 16th c., with particular reference to Jean Edouard du Monin. *NRSS*, 14, includes: J. Dauphiné, 'Poésie, connaissance, sacré' (9–13), a short article which discusses what the sacred meant to the scientific poets writing 1575–1615, and concludes that they saw themselves as divinely chosen instruments to interpret the divinely created cosmos; M. Jacquemier, 'Babel dans la tradition scientifique' (63–76), who demonstrates the duality of the myth of Babel in scientific poetry, indicating that it was exploited for both its negative and its positive associations; and J. Miernowski, 'La littérature anti-scientifique à la Renaissance comme réflexion sur les limites d'une culture' (91–100), who draws attention to the way scientific poetry's exaltation of knowledge coexisted with a counter-current of anti-scientific poetry emphasizing the limits of Man's knowledge.

E. Weber, 'Le Prototype de la strophe sapphique: son exploitation musicale au XVIe siècle (textes latins, néo-latins, français, allemands)', *Actes* (Chambéry), 16–34, examines the fortunes of the Sapphic stanza in Latin, Neo-Latin, French, and German poetry. Two complementary articles appear in *RLC*, 280: F. Charpentier, 'Le désir d'épopée' (417–26), traces the ambiguous emergence of the epic genre in French Renaissance poetry, showing how and attempting to explain why the poets of the time would write in the epic style yet never officially labelled their works 'epic'; and O. Rosenthal, 'Aux frontières de l'épique et du lyrique' (457–67), argues that for French Renaissance poets the epic represented an ideal and was a catalyst for invention rather than a model to be adhered to precisely. R. also offers 'Présences du lecteur dans la poésie lyrique du XVIe siècle', *Poétique*, 105:71–85, which addresses the question of the reader's role in the constitution of a poem's meaning through an analysis of the reader figure in the poetry of a number of poets (Ronsard, Du Bellay, Sponde, Du Bartas). S. Lafont, 'Rose, femme, événement: parcours d'un poncif', *ib.*, 106:179–97, offers interesting transhistorical insights into the rose cliché in amatory poetry through a decoding of three particular uses of it, one of these being in Ronsard's ode 'Mignonne, allon voir . . .', the other two being by Hugo and Rilke. L. Sozzi, '"Coeli cupidine tractus": note sul mito di Icaro nella poesia del rinascimento', *Mélanges Terreaux*, 175–203, examines the myth of Icarus in Italian and French Renaissance poetry, showing how it was endowed with both positive and negative connotations. M. McGowan, 'Réjouissances de mariage: 1559. France-Savoie', *Actes* (Chambéry), 177–89, analyses the themes articulated in the poems written in French to celebrate the marriage of Emmanuel Philibert and Marguerite de France, arguing that they were common to both the French and the Savoy Courts for many years.

PRE-PLÉIADE

Particularly welcome are a number of publications on Marguerite de Navarre's relatively neglected poetry. *Actes* (Pau) offers the following: S. de Reyff, '*Le Triomphe de l'agneau* ou la vision différée' (291–308), who presents a reading of the *Triomphe de l'agneau* which highlights the coherence underlying the text's apparent disparate irregularity; R. D. Cottrell, 'Figures emblèmatiques dans *La Coche* de Marguerite de Navarre' (309–25), a close decoding of *La Coche* which reveals its political significance as an apology for absolute monarchy and for divine royal right; M.-M. Fontaine, 'Les Deux Amours, ou l'arithmétique de Marguerite de Navarre. *La Coche*' (327–49), taking the same text as an example of the very precise arithmetic which informs M. de

N.'s works, and examining the emergence in *La Coche* of the Trinity and its bearing on the poem's meaning; and P. Sommers, '*La Navire et Le Dialogue en forme de vision nocturne*: dilemmes corporels' (351–64), who examines these two works in relation to the dichotomy whereby a choice must be made between the human body and the mystical body of Christ, and concludes that what interests M. de N. above all is the body which suffers and which prefers imperfect human beauty to divine perfection. Robert D. Cottrell, *La Grammaire du silence: une lecture de la poésie de Marguerite de Navarre*, Champion, 1995, 312 pp., attempts to analyse how M. de N.'s poems generate meaning, but the approach is rather arbitrary and the findings inconclusive. In the first part, C. surveys the correspondence between Briçonnet and M. de N. (1521–24) on the grounds that the bishop's views inform to a large degree her poetry; however, the intertextual repercussions are only explored in relation to the *Dialogue*, the *Petit Œuvre*, the *Oraison de l'âme fidèle* and the *Oraison à nostre Seigneur Jesus Christ*, and even then not in the depth one would have expected or hoped. The second part analyses the *Miroir de l'âme pécheresse* and an arbitrary selection of poems, most of which were published in the *Marguerites*, and in the third part C. examines poems written after 1547. Although no general and far-reaching conclusions are reached, the work does provide a useful decoding of the specific texts selected. M. Brothwood, 'Marguerite de Navarre: the *via crucis* and "Rhéno-Flamand" influences', *BHR*, 58:597–610, examines how the influence of the Netherlands and the Rhineland informs M. de N.'s treatment of the *via crucis* in her poetry.

Three particularly interesting articles on Marot in *Procs* (Cambridge) merit mention. G. Jondorf, 'Marot's Première Eglogue de Virgile: good, bad, or interesting?', (115–32), analyses and tries to account for some of the apparent mistranslations in M.'s rendition of V.'s first eclogue, arguing that in some respects his version is superior to Servius's commentary and to Guillaume Michel's attempt. P. M. Smith, 'Clément Marot and humanism' (133–50), challenges the view that M.'s links with humanism have been overestimated and that more attention should be given to his links with his vernacular predecessors; this is a highly scholarly paper, demonstrating through a clear analysis of M.'s tributes to acknowledged humanists of the day and his activities in areas traditionally associated with humanism, that his highly eclectic work was, in fact, consciously informed and motivated by humanism. G. H. Tucker, 'Clément Marot, Ferrara, and the paradoxes of exile' (171–93), takes as a starting point M.'s paradoxical attitude towards exile and discusses it in a broader context, notably how it emerges in the work of Ortensio Landi, and the resultant interplay of existential and literary strategies of identity to which it gives rise.

L.Youens, 'Alice's toothache and the God of Love: editorial emendations in the poetry of Thomas Crecquillon's *Chansons*', *BHR*, 58: 81–95, draws attention to an important area of intertextuality often relegated solely to the field of musicology. It analyses the frequently substantial reworkings of various French poems by the prominent Franco-Flemish composer Crecquillon (*c.* 1515–*c.*1557), and in a very useful appendix provides a list of poems which he set to music and which are only extant in their musical form. D. Cowling, '"Saint" François and his temple in 1508: BN MS français 1680', *Procs* (Cambridge), 1–16, in a close reading of metaphor and allegory in the *Livre de la dédicace du temple*, examines the emergent image of François Ier, and shows thereby the important role which the *Rhétoriqueurs* played in fashioning political ideology of the early 16th century. A. Saunders, 'How emblematic is Scève's *Délie*?', *BHR*, 58:405–17, offers an important article which highlights the extent to which the *Délie* is not a conventional emblem book, and indicates that a possible source is Guillaume de la Perrière's *Cent considérations de l'amour* (1543). F. Rigolot, 'Quand Laure retrouve sa voix française: Louise Labé anti-pétrarquiste?', *Adirel*, 9: 51–64, examines the way in which L. subtly and ironically adapts the Petrarchan voice to the female perspective. L. Terreaux, 'A propos de Nicolas Martin (Saint-Jean de Maurienne, 15...–1571)', *Actes* (Chambéry), 299–311, enlightens us about this little-known musician-poet from the Maurienne, analysing and explaining his *Noelz*, and situating them in the context of the time. R. Cooper, 'Antoine du Saix, poète, diplomate et transfuge savoyard', *Mélanges Terreaux*, 441–63, offers interesting insights into the life and poetry of another neglected Savoyard.

RONSARD AND THE PLÉIADE

On the Pléiade in general, Malcolm C. Smith, *Ronsard and Du Bellay versus Bèze: Allusiveness in Renaissance Literary Texts*, Geneva, Droz, 1995, has twofold aims: firstly, to trace in detail the long-running feud between the Pléiade and de B. on pagan versus Biblical inspiration, and secondly, to exemplify the technique of allusive attack so common in Renaissance invective. S. usefully draws attention to less well-known texts inspired by the polemic, and shows just how closely linked the theological and literary issues of the time were. F. Rouget, 'L'esthétique de l'ode et de la chanson de la Pléiade (1550–1560)', *RR*, 87:455–64, adequately refines the stylistic distinction between the *ode* and the *chanson* (*style élevé/style bas*), and highlights their dissimilarities by an analysis of their respective thematic, rhetorical, and prosodic features.

A number of important articles have appeared on Ronsard, not least the following, unfortunately omitted from earlier years, and which appear in the first section of *Mélanges Terreaux*: E. Kushner, 'Orphée, chantre de lui-même' (39–50), who examines the Orphique mission which R. bestows upon himself as expressed in his poetry; M. C. Smith, 'Italianisms in the work of Ronsard' (51–67), who reviews italianisms in R.'s works and usefully revises a number of Hope's datings; C. Demaizière, 'Quelques avatars de la création lexicale dans la *Franciade*' (69–85), analysing in detail the language in the various editions of the *Franciade*; H. Weber, 'La description dans la *Franciade*' (87–95), a complementary piece looking at the various stylistic devices used by R. in descriptive passages in the same work; and J.-C. Moisan, 'Le "logos" dans les *Amours de Cassandre* de 1584' (97–118), who borrows the concept of *logos* from the Groupe μ, and offers a highly theoretical article which exposes the isotopic structure of these sonnets. Y. Bellenger, 'Ronsard et la fin des amours: les *Sonets pour Hélène* ou l'anti-Desportes', *Amour sacré, Amour profane*, 9–23, offers a few new insights into the importance of this collection, focusing particularly on the importance of the depiction of Hélène, whom B. sees as a forerunner of female characters in 17th-c. theatre. C. Perry, 'La double face du désir dans les "métamorphoses" de Ronsard: rêve d'intimité et quête de l'origine', *RR*, 87:1–19, is a very clear article which, through a close decoding of some of the liminary pieces of the 1553 edition of the *Amours* and sonnet 20 (including its 1587 variants), examines the complex dichotomy inherent in R.'s intention to write poetry which is both accessible and yet also characterized by a certain hermetism. G. Fasano, 'La déconstruction du matériau épique dans la poésie encomiastique de P. de Ronsard', *RLC*, 280:427–44, demonstrates how R.'s views on inspiration and what constitutes worthy poetry inform his encomiastic epic poetry, which reveals a conscious and careful reworking of classical sources. J. Brooks, 'Ronsard, Bertrand, Boni and the process of revision', *Actes* (Chambéry),137–52, argues that a number of the latter two poets' *chansons* were written on texts subsequently updated to take into account their revisions, and looks at the particular example of their settings for R., for which dates are proposed which suggest they existed at least a decade before publication. H. Moreau, 'Claude Le Jeune interprète de Ronsard ou de la difficulté de la concurrence des arts', *ib.*, 234–39, tries to account for the surprising infrequency with which Le J. set to music R.'s poetry which was, however, so popular with other musicians of the day. D. Gilman, 'L'empreinte de Bacchus: Ronsard,

Ficin, et la musique de la lyre', *ib.*, 240–52, is a dense, philosophical article which analyses how some of F.'s views inform R.'s concept of invention, particularly as expressed in 'A Monsieur de Belot' (1569).

The following are specifically on Du Bellay: Y. Bellenger, 'Les dernières années de Du Bellay: poésie et politique', *Mélanges Terreaux*, 205–23, analysing the moral didacticism in Du B.'s political poetry; P. Blanc, 'Les raisins verts du Pétrarquisme: sur la douceur, et sur son cheminement de Pétrarque à Du Bellay. Essai de critique différentielle', *ib.*, 225–37, using the example of Du B. to analyse the reception of Petrarch in France, focusing particularly on the transposition of the concept of *douceur*; Josiane Rieu, *L'Esthétique de Du Bellay*, SEDES, 1995, 279 pp., which is primarily intended for undergraduates but is worthy of mention here as it provides a useful synthesis of the evolution of Du B.'s æsthetic principles and an anthology of pertinent texts; and *Joachim Du Bellay: divers jeux rustiques*, ed. Ghislain Chaufour, Gallimard, 333 pp., adhering to the editions of Chamard and Saulnier, but providing notes that are particularly detailed and commendably innovative as they give a broad range of transhistorical intertextual references.

On Belleau, G. Demerson, 'Paradigmes épiques et collision des genres. A propos du *De Bello Huguenotico* de Remy Belleau', *RLC*, 280:443–56, offers an interesting analysis of how B.'s anti-Huguenot poem exploits the epic genre in an original way, essentially by fusing it for satirical ends with the macaronic tradition. D. Ménager, 'Ronsard, Belleau et les blasons de 1554–1556', *NRSS*, 14:29–41, challenges the notion that B.'s scientific *hymne-blasons* are largely either directly imitated from R. or have been corrected by him, and argues that they do in fact reflect greater originality than they have hitherto been credited with.

In *Actes* (Chambéry), three articles deal to a greater or lesser degree with Baïf: I. Fenelon, 'Claude Le Jeune and the Greeks' (5–15), focuses on the theories of B.'s *Académie de poésie et de musique*, notably its aspiration to fuse poetry and music and to revive Greek genera, and argues that Le J.'s *Dodécacorde* (1598) is the most important monument to the *Académie*'s concept of Greek mode; P. Bonnifet, 'La musique mesurée profane de Claude Le Jeune: des voix et des pas' (46–63), is particularly interesting because it examines the transposition of Baïf's metrical verse into musical form by Le J.; G. Demerson, 'Un thème lyrique de J.-A. de Baïf: la métamorphose' (219–33), gives a profound analysis of B.'s sustained interest in and poetical expresssion of the theme of metamorphosis, and attempts to define thereby his individual lyrical personality and style.

On associates and contemporaries of the Pléiade, a number of articles have appeared. On Dorat, Geneviève Demerson, 'Dorat sur le tombeau de Ronsard', *Mélanges Terreaux*, 119–31, gives an interesting analysis of four poems written by D. to commemorate R.'s death. The Savoyard poet Marc-Claude de Buttet is the subject of three articles, two by S. Alyn-Stacey: 'Marc-Claude de Buttet et sa "trouppe fidelle" savoisienne', *Actes* (Chambéry), 312–25, an examination of de B.'s links with various literary groups and individuals in Savoy; and 'A la recherche d'un style poétique: quelques résonances de Ronsard dans l'*Amalthée* de Marc-Claude de Buttet', *Mélanges Terreaux*, 133–50, an intertextual analysis which argues that although de B. worked very much in the tradition of R., his imitation is never servile; and the third by G. Demerson, '"Des éléphants mitrés": remarques sur l'esprit satirique de M.-C. de Buttet', *ib.*, 239–61, who discusses various aspects of satire, illustrating general observations by specific reference to de B.'s poetry. De B. is also referred to at length by R. Devos, 'Entre catholiques et réformés: l'existence d'un tiers parti dans la Savoie du XVIe siècle' (see *supra*, HUMANISM, THOUGHT). M.-Th. Courtial, 'George Buchanan et la Saint-Barthélemy: la *Satyra in carolum lotharingum cardinalem*', *BHR*, 58:151–63, offers no surprises by attributing the marked change in B.'s poetry after 1573 to the grave political situation in France. C. usefully reproduces this satirical work against the Cardinale de Lorraine (together with variants and a French translation), but says little that Philip Ford has not already said in his article 'George Buchanan and the *Satyra in carolum lotharingum cardinalem*', MRTS, 1986, 43–50. An important publication is *Nostradamus. Les Premières Centuries ou prophéties (édition Macé Bonhomme de 1555). Édition et commentaire de l'Épître à César et des 353 premiers quatrains*, ed. Pierre Brind'Amour, Geneva, Droz, lxii + 600 pp. This is undoubtedly the most scholarly edition to date of N.'s *Prophéties* and it does much to enlighten us about this legendary figure. The great merit of this edition is its clarity, each verse being followed by its own specific critical apparatus offering textual variants, details on prosody (reminding us of what scholars often forget, that this is poetry, and that the meaning may be distorted if this is not acknowledged), a lexicon, a paraphrase into modern French, an analysis indicating sources and historical allusions. The introduction situates N. in relation to other Renaissance poets, highlighting the esteem in which the Pléiade held him and the (minor) influence which he exerted upon the group. However, the details B.d'A. provides about Jean de Chevigny are contradicted by B. Chevignard, 'Jean-Aimé de Chavigny: son identité, ses origines familiales' (see *supra*, INDIVIDUAL AUTHORS OR WRITERS).

AFTER THE PLÉIADE

On metrical verse, D. R. Lamothe, 'Claude Le Jeune: les *Pseaumes en vers mesurés*', *Actes* (Chambéry), 64–81, examines the way in which Baïf's psalms in metrical verse were reworked by d'Aubigné et de la Noue before Le J. set them to music in 1606. This is complemented by J. Brunel, 'La poésie mesurée française après Jean-Antoine de Baïf', *ib.*, 264–78, which examines the metrical verse produced 1575–1620, notably by Rapin, d'Aubigné and de la Noue, exposing their attempts to make it less austere, and also the eventual indifference with which the genre met. More specifically on d'Aubigné, two publications deserve mention. F. Lestringant, 'Agrippa d'Aubigné et Le Tasse: de la *Jérusalem délivrée* aux *Tragiques*', *Mélanges Terreaux*, 289–315, is an intertextual study examining the parallels between T.'s cosmos and d'A.'s in these two key works. *Agrippa d'Aubigné: Les Tragiques*, ed. Jean-Raymond Fanlo, 2 vols, Champion, 1995, x + 1024 pp., offers the hitherto unedited Geneva MS, the last version corrected by d'A. Despite the absence of a glossary, the critical apparatus is commendable, not least for its detailed intertextual references to other contemporaries, so situating the work clearly in the broader context of the time. The appendices include an important section which challenges the dating and therefore the political-historical significance of the final version, F. arguing that it is a poetical reconstruction of history rather than a 'pamphlet jailli au feu de l'événement'. *Clovis Hesteau de Nuysement. Les Oeuvres poétiques. Livre III et dernier*, ed. Roland Guillot, TLF, 464, 229 pp., is the welcome final volume in this series. The notes are particularly detailed, giving useful intertextual references. Three interesting articles on Sponde have appeared: B. Petey-Girard, 'Méditation psalmique et quête de la parole chez Jean de Sponde', *RHR*, 43:25–43, which explores the figure of the *méditant* in the *Méditations* and its rhetorical implications; M. Richter, 'Calvinisme et amour mondain: peut-on dater les sonnets d'amour de Sponde?', *Amour sacré, amour mondain*, 73–90, attempting to define both the circumstances in which S. wrote his collection of 26 love poems and his underlying motivation, by analysing the poems in a poetico-ideological perspective and showing how they are informed by Calvinism; and G. Mathieu-Castellani, 'Eros et Thanatos dans la poétique de Sponde', *ib.*, 91–100, who demonstrates how these two conflicting poles of desire are central to S.'s poetry. I. Laban, 'L'image inconsistante, remarques sur deux textes de Théophile de Viau', *RHR*, 42:63–80, shows how, despite de V.'s apparent disdain for order and rules in poetry, two of his works, *La Solitude* (1620) and *La Maison de Sylvie* (1624), signal a highly coherent, albeit complex and original, æsthetic vision. *Blaise de Vigenère: Le Psaultier de David torné en prose mesurée ou vers libre, édition de 1588*, vol. 2, ed. Pascale Blum-Cuny, Le Miroir Volant, 575 pp., is a welcome publication, the first volume having appeared in 1991. This second volume provides a detailed critical apparatus for the *Psaultier*, and, most usefully, the complete text of the *Pseaumes penitentiels de David* (1587) and the *Prières et oraisons* (1595). G. Banderier, 'L'Image du paon (*Sepmaine*, IV, 171–184) chez les continuateurs de Du Bartas', *NRSS*, 14:77–89, examines the re-emergence of the peacock metaphor in the work of two of Du B.'s disciples, Christofle de Gamon and Jean Edouard Du Monin. S. Bamforth, 'Béroalde de Verville, poète de la connaissance', *ib.*, 43–55, draws attention to the often negative reception of de V.'s scientific poetry, attributing this to a misdirected reading which focuses on the relationship between poet and text instead of on the relationship between text and reader. Useful insights are offered into this relatively unknown side of de V.'s output and the close links between his scientific poetry and other areas of his thought. F. Mauger, 'Antoine de Chandieu et Etienne Delaune: les *Octonaires sur la vanité et inconstance du monde*. Un recueil d'emblèmes?', *BHR*, 58:611–29, examines this relatively neglected work by de C., offering a close analysis of the only known copy of the 1580 edition, and locating its important place in the emblematic tradition. Complementing this is F. Bonali-Fiquet, 'Engagement spirituel et procédés stylistiques dans les *Octonaires sur l'inconstance et vanité du monde* d'Antoine de La Roche-Chandieu', *Amour sacré, amour mondain*, 25–36, which examines this work's spiritual themes and stylistic techniques, arguing that they reflect the poet's early baroque tendencies. On Desportes, two articles are worthy of note: L.Willett, 'Le *clair-obscur* dans une chanson de Desportes mise en musique par Claude Le Jeune (1585), *Actes* (Chambéry*)*, 279–87, which examines the figure of *enargeia* to evoke chiaroscural images, illustrating its particularly sophisticated exploitation in the late 16th c. through an analysis of D.'s *chanson* "Blessé d'une playe inhumaine" (*Les Amours d'Hippolyte*, 1573) and Le J.'s setting for this text, showing how the trope articulates the notion of an unpredictable, unstable universe; and J. Rieu, 'Sur les Sonnets et poèmes spirituels de Philippe Desportes', *Amour sacré, amour profane*, 37–58, who situates D.'s spiritual poems written 1575–87 in relation to the religious poetry of the period, showing how they are counter to the popular tormented *sermonnaire* style. M.-M. Fragonard, 'Dialogue d'âmes auprès d'un corps perdu', *ib.*, 59–72, examines the theme of the final farewell to a loved one as articulated in Du Perron's ambiguous poem on the death of the Amiral de Joyeuse. M. Clément, '*Le Miroir de l'amour divin* ou l'enjeu de la conversion du discours amoureux', *ib.*, 101–11, considers the theme of love in this little-known work by Pierre de la Croix. J. Brunel, 'D'un siècle à l'autre: remarques sur quelques variantes dans l'œuvre de Scévole de Sainte-Marthe', *Mélanges Terreaux*, 263–87, draws attention to the relatively neglected poetical output of S.-M. and, through a survey of textual variants, traces his literary evolution. M. Bideaux, 'La poétique de J.-B. Chassignet: "ni plus ni moins que la vois contrainte dans l'estroit canal d'une trompette"?', *ib.*, 347–70, examines the poetic theories expounded by C. in the *Mespris de la vie et consolation contre la mort* (1594). Y. Giraud, 'La Poésie amoureuse d'Antoine de Nervèze', *ib.*, 371–94, offers a useful survey of de N.'s little-known love poetry.

4. DRAMA

Recueil de Farces 1450–1550, vol. x, ed. André Tissier (TLF, 471), 440 pp., offers the texts of the following seven plays: *Le Pet* (21–63); *Tarabin, Tarabas et Triboulle-Ménage* (65–116); *Mahuet Badin, natif de Bagnolet, qui va à Paris au marché* (117–81); *Le Gentilhomme et son page* (183–223); *Le Pauvre Jouhan* (225–96); *Les Femmes qui aiment mieux suivre et croire folconduit* (297–322); *La Cornette* (323–88). Like the other volumes in the series, the critical apparatus is particularly commendable, making this a valuable contribution to Renaissance studies.

On Marguerite de Navarre's drama, the following have appeared: G. Hasenohr, 'Représentations et lectures de la nativité à l'aube de la Renaissance', *Actes* (Pau), 365–401, who provides useful insights into the tradition to which M. de N.'s *Comédie de la Nativité* belongs by offering an analysis of the place, role and function that religious discourse attributed to the Nativity theme at the beginning of the Renaissance in a variety of genres, eg. Mystery plays, sermons, *noëls*, etc.; and B. Marczuk-Szwed, 'Les motifs mystiques dans le théâtre biblique de Marguerite de Navarre', *ib.*, 403–21, who examines the religious ideas expressed in the *Comédies*, particularly those concerning a mystical life.

G. A. Runnalls, 'La circulation des textes des mystères à la fin du moyen âge: les éditions de la *Passion* de Jean Michel', *BHR*, 58:7–33, is a very scholarly, useful article which offers a wealth of information on a relatively neglected area, namely the circulation of printed and MS versions of Mystery and Miracle plays. Particularly important is the revised chronology which R. presents of the *Passion*'s 16 editions. O. A. Dull, 'Late medieval French Morality plays; from allegory to "mimesis"', *SFr*, 116:17–27, uses the example of André de la Vigne's *Sotise a huit personnaiges* (1507) to demonstrate how the didactic aims of the late Morality plays were actually undermined through the use of allegory, which had become a mere source of entertainment devoid of moral substance. C. Mazouer offers two articles: 'La Moralité au XVIe siècle en France', *BHR*, 58:351–65, examining the survival of the *moralité* well into the 16th c., despite the Pléiade's opposition to it, and attributing this primarily to *contaminatio* by other genres; and 'La figure de David dans les tragédies de la Renaissance', *Actes* (Chambéry), 253–63, analysing the contradictory, multi-faceted and generally idealized Biblical figure of David in 16th-c. tragedy. D. Cecchetti, 'La nozione di *tragédie sainte* in Francia tra rinascimento e barocco', *Mélanges Terreaux*, 395–413, usefully analyses some of the theoretical French texts on Biblical tragedy published in the second half of the 16th c., notably by Théodore de Bèze, Louis Des Masures, André de Rivaudeau, Jean de la Taille, and Jean Vauquelin de la Fresnaye, demonstrating that all advocated the supremacy of Christian truth over pagan myth.

5. MONTAIGNE

Two enlightening sets of conference proceedings have appeared. *La Problématique du sujet chez Montaigne*, ed. E. Kushner, Champion, 1995, 196 pp., is a collection of papers (given in 1992 at a conference in Toronto) which explore the portrayal of the self in the *Essais*. R. Aulotte, 'Au sujet du sujet' (3–8), offers an introductory article, examining whether or not it is valid to talk of a subject when the author himself knows full well, and declares in no uncertain terms, that the *moi* speaking has only a precarious identity. There then follows a first section, 'Indices textuels de la subjectivité', which comprises the following: L. M. Heller, 'Montaigne conteur: "je" dans "De l'exercitation"' (11–21), an interesting narratological description of the riding accident anecdote which, adopting Benveniste's dichotomy of two types of text but one subject, attempts to define the status of the *je énonciateur* and the *je narrateur*; Y. Bellenger, 'Montaigne commentaire de lui-même dans les premiers chapîtres des *Essais*' (23–40), challenging Samuel de Sacy's view that the *Essais* do not portray a man but 'déballe un fichier', arguing that the tone is, in fact, highly personal and gives rise to an equally personal portrait of Montaigne; J. Brody, 'Montaigne et le sujet mixte' (41–54), examining M.'s use of Latin quotations, pointing out that he rarely cites *stricto sensu*, but modifies for his own ends. Whilst this use of classical quotation reflects M.'s humanist orientation, it is also responsible for making his text less accessible to modern readers. The second section, 'Le sujet, l'autre, le monde', offers the following: I. Zinguer, 'Autoconstitution, aspect de la subjectivité chez Montaigne' (57–72), who argues that M. is aware that the individual is in a continual process of self-construction, and examines the essentially ascetic programme for this construction advocated in the *Essais*; E. Limbrick, 'La relation du scepticisme avec la subjectivité' (73–85), who begins by pointing out that classical scepticism does not disdain subjectivity, then proceeds to analyse how this positive side of scepticism informs M.'s *Apologie de Raimond Sebond*; and R. Melançon, 'L'entretien avec soi' (87–102), who argues that the *Essais* represent an internal dialogue with M.'s self, and function as a substitute for discussion with an *alter ego*. The third section, 'Montaigne et nous', includes the following: F. Paré, 'Rencontre de deux Michel: Michel Serres et Michel de Montaigne. Le sujet sporadique' (103–18), who draws attention to the common concerns of M. and S., concluding that contemporary critical thought tends not to declare its debt to the Renaissance and particularly to M., preferring to acknowledge Descartes; G. Defaux, 'Subjectivité, écriture et essai chez Montaigne: l'exemple "Des coches" (III, 6)' (121–48), who argues the prevalence of the 'self' as the key subject of the *Essais*, and after reviewing various critical approaches (Structuralist, Post-Structuralist, Modernist, Post-Modernist) in the light of this, offers an analysis of M.'s 'self' as it emerges in "Des Coches"; and F. Rigolot, 'Perspectives modernes sur la subjectivité montaignienne' (149–70), who offers important reflections on critical approaches of relevance not just to M. but to the Renaissance in general. R. argues that if critics tend to be more interested in the text than in the historical veracity of facts, this does not mean the death of the subject and biography is still important. Drawing attention to the interest M.'s melancholy has attracted from psychological approaches, R. concludes that the text must have primacy because it is the word which articulates M.'s 'self', his essence. *BSAM*, nos 1–3, 'Marie de Gournay et l'édition de 1595 des *Essais* de Montaigne: actes du colloque organisé par la Société Internationale des Amis de Montaigne les 9 et 10 juin 1995, en Sorbonne', is a useful collection of articles which does much to inform us about de G.'s personality, her role in editing the *Essais*, and various broader textual issues. G. Nakam, 'Marie Le Jars de Gournay, "Fille d'alliance" de Montaigne (1565–1645)' (11–21), offers a profile of de G., giving insights into how her contemporaries viewed her, what her writings reveal about her moral and political views and her relationship with Montaigne. C. Blum, 'Les principes et les pratiques: Marie de Gornay éditrice des *Essais*' (25–37), rejects the usual approach of comparing the 1588 Bordeaux MS with the posthumous 1595 edition of the *Essais*, comparing instead the editions which de G. edited between 1595 and 1635, and attempting thereby to expose her editorial practice, notably the motivation behind her corrections to M.'s text. He makes a justified appeal for a critical edition of the 1595 text. A. Tournon, 'Le "bon ange" et le bon usage: Montaigne au purgatoire' (39–50), examines the 1595 edition in the light of M.'s MS emendations to the punctuation of the 1588 Bordeaux copy, and reveals how it differs from the norms of the day. I. Konstantinovic, 'A propos de certaines leçons de l'édition de 1595' (55–67), questions what is understood by the definitive text of the *Essais*, particularly the authenticity in this respect of the 1595 edition, and argues that all the variant editions contribute to the 'établissement vivant du texte'. This is complemented by J. Casals, 'Amphibologie et défauts théoriques dans le débat sur l'édition des *Essais* de Montaigne' (69–78), who argues that the problematic question of what constitutes the definitive edition of the *Essais* is actually irrelevant because it relies upon the answer to an equally irrelevant question: what were M.'s last wishes? What should interest critics is the text itself, not the vain attempt to establish M.'s last wishes. O. Millet, 'Les préfaces et le rôle de Marie de Gournay dans la première réception des *Essais*' (79–91), examines de G.'s preface to the 1595 edition of the *Essais* in relation to its later variants, concluding that she remains consistently stoical about the reception which she expected the *Essais* to have (they would only be understood by an elite). N. Dauvois-Lavialle, 'Le Montaigne de Marie de Gournay, auteur-auctor' (95–107), considers de G.'s appropriation of the *Essais*, signalling that she progressively comes to dissociate the author of the *Essais* from the author that she herself has become in her capacity as editor. Inevitably, this raises questions about the authenticity of the text. M. Ishigami-Iagolnitzer, 'Réflexion sur le rapport entre Michel de Montaigne et Marie de Gournay' (109–20), is an inconclusive article which attempts to explain the relationship between M. and de G., comparing it in an absurdly irrelevant way to other relationships between famous male writers and their young female admirers in Europe and the Far East. K. Csüros, 'Pierre de Brach, ami et éditeur de Montaigne' (121–34), offers an enlightening profile of this *bordelais* poet, arguing that his literary output deserves more attention than it has received to date, interest being focused for the most part on his relations with other writers of the day, notably Montaigne. K. Keffer, 'La textomachie: la protection des *Essais* de Montaigne' (135–43), is a rather summary article which examines the spirit in which de G. and M. edited the *Essais*, concluding that they adhered to the same essentially 'protect-ive' ethic. D. N. Losse, 'Triple contexture: La Boétie, Montaigne, Marie de Gournay et l'amitié pré-texte, texte et édition de 1595' (145–51), looks at the way in which de G., in her 1595 preface, seeks to validate her status as female editor by exploiting explicit intertex-tual links which establish parallels between her friendship with M. and his friendship with La Boétie. E. Berriot-Salvadore, 'L'héritage de Montaigne ou les voies de l'émancipation de Marie de Gournay'

(153–60), examines the duality of de G.'s voice which is, on the one hand, assimilated by M.'s voice, yet, on the other hand, dissociates itself from him and asserts itself in an individual way, in part because of her female status. M. Clément, 'Les éléments épars d'un art poétique dans *L'Ombre de la Damoiselle de Gournay*' (163–73), argues that the poetic theories expressed in this work represent an amalgamation of Du Bellay's *Deffence et Illustration* and some of M.'s ideas, therefore indicating that de G. aligned herself with the partisans of free invention against the rigour advocated by Malherbe. M.-C. Bichard-Thomine, 'Des métaphores chez Marie de Gournay: réflexion linguistique et pratique littéraire' (175–92), considers, and situates in the climate of the time, de G.'s anti-Malherbien theories on metaphor, but after examining the use of metaphor in her works, concludes that the transposition from theory to practice is not consistent. V. Worth-Stylianou, 'Marie de Gournay et la traduction: défense et illustration d'un style' (193–206), analyses de G.'s translation of the some 1200 quotations of the *Essais* in relation to the period's hostility to linguistic elitism, highlighting her conservative views on the French language, her positive attitude towards translation, and her actual translation practice. W.-S. concludes that de G. was not only linguistically highly competent, but was generally very sensitive to the stylistic effect which M. intended the original quotation to produce. J.-C. Arnould, 'L'histoire du "Proumenoir de Monsieur de Montaigne": fondation de l'œuvre et naissance de l'écrivain' (207–17), examines the ambiguity concerning various aspects of this work, notably authorship, date of composition and sources, and argues that the variants are reflective of de G.'s evolving ideological, moral, linguistic and æsthetic views. A. L. Franchetti, 'L'ombre et le monument: Marie de Gournay éditrice de ses propres œuvres' (219–32), offers a rapid review of the various modifications to which de G. subjected her works, concluding that she was working very much in a spirit of contradiction, on the one hand trying to establish a monument, a 'livre-ombre à la manière des *Essais*', on the other hand constantly demolishing and rebuilding it out of a profound sense of disatisfaction.

A very scholarly and clear work is Jean-Yves Pouilloux, *Montaigne: l'éveil de la pensée* (Études Montaignistes, 19), Champion, 1995, 243 pp., which comprises a number of previously published articles on various facets of the *Essais*, generally emphasizing the instability inherent in both writing and reading processes. Olivier Millet, *La Première Réception des Essais de Montaigne* (Études Montaignistes, 23), Champion, 1995, 249 pp., revises previous work on the impact of the *Essais* by presenting in chronological order a series of French and Neo-Latin texts (accompanied by English translations) written 1576–1639, and which give a critical appraisal of the *Essais*. Although the selection is rather arbitrary, the work does at least provide a useful insight into the reception of the *Essais* in France, and makes us all the more impatient for the forthcoming volume on their reception in other European countries. Particularly interesting is Edward Benson, *Money and Magic in Montaigne: the Historicity of the Essais* (THR, 295), 1995, 199 pp. Arguing that money and magic were, for M. and his contemporaries, related concerns (both, for example, providing access to power), B. examines these two themes as they emerge in five of the *Essais* and situates them in the context of the time. Mary B. McKinley, *Les Terrains vagues des Essais: itinéraires et intertextes* (Études Montaignistes, 25), Champion, 191 pp., offers seven articles published 1989–93 but presented here in revised form; the opening chapter is new. This work examines M.'s use of spatial metaphors to evoke the text, and highlights a general tendency to evoke a journey towards an uncertain territory of ideas and expression. It is in this uncertain territory that an intertextual network of references stretching from antiquity to M.'s contemporaries or near contemporaries (notably La Boétie, Sebond, Erasmus, Ariosto) may be discerned. Pointing out that these more modern writers are not exploited in the same way as the classical ones, this study focuses on the way in which M. inserts them into the textual space of the *Essais*. Jean Lacouture, *Montaigne à cheval*, Seuil, 332 pp., is superficial and tells us nothing new. Ian Maclean, *Montaigne philosophe*, PUF, 127 pp., is a useful work, aimed primarily at undergraduates. It reviews in a very clear manner the various aspects of M.'s philosophy, situating him in his time and highlighting his originality. Richard Regosin, *Montaigne's Unruly Brood: Textual Engendering and the Challenge to Paternal Authority*, Berkeley–Los Angeles–London, California U.P., ix + 254 pp., is a commendably clear work which examines the complex topos of textual progeny in the *Essais*, analysing both its broad significance for literary conception and its repercussions on our reading of the text. Similarly, but adopting a different perspective, T. Peach, '"Les enfantemens de nostre esprit." The *enfant/essai* topos in Montaigne's *Essais*', *RoS*, 27:7–14, reviews M.'s attitude towards children, then proceeds to compare the notion of text as offspring as it emerges in the *Essais*, perceiving a deliberate break with Christian tradition, M. entrusting any chance of immortality to his writings rather than to real live children. R. Calder, 'Suum cuique pulchrum: fatherhood, authorship and self-love in Montaigne's "De l'affection des peres aux enfans"', *BHR*, 58:367–79, is a very clear, enlightening article which demonstrates how Terence's *Adelphi* and parts of Aristotle's *Nicomachean Ethics* inform this *essai* (II, 8), and particularly its views on *philautia*, more profoundly than is generally thought. A. Legros, '"Comme une autre histoire . . ." Montaigne et Jésus-Christ', *ib*., 577–96, offers a particularly interesting article. Arguing that the figure of J.-C. is more prevalent in the *Essais* than is often thought, being frequently signalled indirectly (through allusion, metonymy, scriptural intertextuality etc.), L. analyses the significance of these references, concluding that, far from indicating a clear evolution towards deism, they are symptomatic of M.'s meditation upon death. A. Eyquem, 'La mort de Montaigne, ses causes rediscutées par la consultation posthume de médecins spécialistes de notre temps: M. Daudon, J. Thomas, P. Trotot, R. Bernouilli, P. Albou, A. Eyquem et F. Pottiée-Sperry', *BSAM*, no. 4:7–16, is a curious article, summarizing the conclusions of a round-table discussion and speculating on the cause of M.'s death on the basis of various details provided in a letter by Estienne Pasquier and the *Journal de voyage*. S. W. Farquhar, 'Montaigne et la théologie naturelle: herméneutique, religion et politique', *ib*., 17–28, examines M.'s sceptical redefinition of hermeneutics in the *Apologie de Raimond Sebond*, pointing out that this scepticism informs not just his theological views but also his broader ideological perspective. S. Statius-Oliveau, 'La ponctuation de Montaigne: jeu sophistique', *ib*., 29–40, considers the repercussions of M.'s punctuation on the articulation of his scepticism in the Bordeaux copy of the *Essais*, and takes for particular analysis 'Du jeune Caton' (I, 37). K. Sellevold, 'La doute implicite: une lecture pragmatique de l'essai "De la vanité" (III, 9)', *ib*., 41–49, demonstrates how M. exploits the reflexive functions of language so that doubt permeates the text, thereby reinforcing the philosophical (and essentially sceptical) orientation of the *Essais*. G. Defaux, 'Ut mus in pice: Brody, Montaigne et la "lecture philologique"', *MLN*, 111:647–70, is a highly virulent (and at times very personal) attack criticizing B.'s philological approach to decoding M., arguing that it imposes a methodological straitjacket on the text which leads to very partial and generally incoherent conclusions. No doubt a reply will be issued. I. R. Morrison, 'Montaigne and torture in criminal justice', *FSB*, 58:9–10, examines M.'s divergent views on the merits and demerits of torture.

THE SEVENTEENTH CENTURY

By ELFRIEDA DUBOIS, *sometime Reader in French,*
University of Newcastle upon Tyne

1. GENERAL

LitC, 28, is devoted to 'Le style au XVIIe siècle'. G. Molinié,
'Presentation' (7–9); D. Dalla Valle, 'Style maniériste, style baroque'
(13–22), analyses the relationship of the two styles in historical
perspective; F. Berlan, 'Lexique et genre: Boileau et la candeur'
(22–41), investigates the semantics of 'candeur' from Latin to French
and shows Boileau's uses, mainly satirical; A. Desprechins, 'Ecriture
et tapisserie au XVIIe siècle' (43–57), shows the link between verbal
and plastic expression with references to *L'Astrée*; M. Le Guern, 'Le
style dans les Rhétoriques de Caussin et de Vossius' (61–68),
comments on the differences of *De eloquentia sacra et humana* (1619) and
Commentariorum rhetoricorum sive oratoriorum institutionum libri sex (1630);
G. Molinié, 'Style et littérarité' (69–74), shows the link between style
and variety of literary expressions; F. Dumora-Mabille, 'Entre clarté
et illusion: l'*energeia* au XVIIe siècle' (75–94), examines descriptive
methods, pictorially and verbally; G. Conesa, 'Le style de la comédie'
(95–109), discusses rhetorical use and its development from early to
later comedy; D. Denis-Delendo, 'Réflexions sur le "style galant":
une théorisation floue' (147–58), examines the æsthetics of mundane
conversation and writing; P.-J. Salazar, 'Voix d'oraison féminine: sur
le style de l'éloquence d'extase' (158–69), comments on Mme
Guyon's writing on *Cantique des Cantiques*; G. Declercq, 'Usage et bel
usage: l'éloge de la langue dans les *Entretiens d'Ariste et d'Eugène du Père
Bouhours*' (113–36), is centred on the *Deuxième Entretien*, in praise of the
French language; J. Dejean, 'L'écriture féminine: sexe, genre, et nom
d'auteur au dix-septième siècle' (137–46), comments on Choisy and
the criticism by Donneau de Visé; A. Kibédi Varga, 'Le Dialogue de
l'honnête homme au philosophe' (173–80), looks at two forms:
'dialogue dialectique' and 'dialogue didactique'; A. Pricipato, 'La
position du dialogue littéraire dans quelques traités du XVIIe siècle'
(181–93), deals with theories by Lamy, La Mesnardière, d'Aubignac,
and Corneille; B. Bray, 'Le style épistolaire: la leçon de Madame de
Sévigné' (197–209), discusses theoretical manuals and Sévigné's 'style
naturel'; N. Doiron, 'Le style obscur. 'Enigme 1' (211–38), comments
on various forms: enigmatic, ambiguous, mysterious, with examples;
F. Hallyn, 'L'anagramme et ses styles au XVIIe siècle' (239–54),
considers the anagram as belonging to baroque æsthetics; P. Zoberman, 'L'éloquence d'apparat et le style' (255–71), with a complex

discussion on 'elocutio', relates it to 'cérémonies d'apparat'; E. Bury, 'Style et période' (275–83), comments, from Vaugelas and d'Ablancourt, on 'périodes simple et composée'; I. Landy-Houillon, 'L'ellipse: une figure de Madame de Sévigné' (285–94), discusses Sévigné's personal use of ellipsis; R. Garrette, 'Contraintes métriques et alchimie du style: enquête sur la phrase-quatrain dans les tragédies de Racine' (295–310), looks at the relation between sentence and verse and distinguishes between 'phrase grammaticale' and 'stylistique'; and N. Fournier, 'Style et syntaxe: l'exemple de la place du sujet dans la phrase classique' (311–41), investigates style in relation to grammatical rules, ante- and post-position of the subject and their stylistic effects. Claude-Gilbert Dubois, *Le Baroque en Europe et en France*, PUF, 195, 312 pp., makes distinctions and similarities between the development of baroque writing in France and elsewhere in Europe over a prolonged period. *Dom Juan* and *Phèdre* are seen as baroque plays, and classicism is considered an offshoot of the baroque; some questionable suggestions.

Bernard Beugnot, *Le Discours de la retraite au XVIIe siècle*, PUF, 297 pp., traces the theme to the classical 'otium', the *Georgics*, through the New Testament; he discusses the location, gardens, 'cabinets de curiosité', alcoves or any 'locus amœnis', he includes religious poetry, pastoral novels, praise of country life (away from the 'embarras de Paris'), retreat into a religious community, hermits, and finally advantages of private life.

Wolfgang Leiner Etudes sur la littérature française du XVIIe siècle (*PFSCL*, 95), ed. V. Schröder and Rainer Zaiser, 399 pp., a collection of Leiner's articles, written between 1956–83, reprinted on the occasion of his seventieth birthday. A. Kibédi Varga, 'Réflexions sur le classicisme français: littérature et société au XVIIe siècle' *RHLF*, 96:1063–68, confined to the second half of the century, considers the artist as part of society, and two centres of artistic activity, 'la Cour' and 'la Ville', Versailles and Paris. W. Howarth, 'The *Agréables Conférences*: a question of genre', Smith, *Essays*, 35–39, analyses from a linguistic aspect the text (in the Deloffre edition of 1961) of *Agréables Conférences de deux paysans de Saint-Ouen et de Montmorency sur les affaires du temps*, and notes the piece's sociological significance. A. Calder, 'Images of the peasantry in classical French literature', *ib.*, 41–44, quotes examples from Molière's plays, La Fontaine, and of course the bleak passage from La Bruyère, and concludes that these are views of human nature generally. *DSS*, 191, contains the following: C. Allen, 'Enfants et serpents: la religion de Poussin' (229–40), who discusses Poussin's approach to religious mythology; J. Deprun 'A propos du Jugement de Salomon de Poussin' (241–45), interpreting the religious significance of the painting; D. Dalla Valle, 'La Généreuse Allemande de Mareschal: aspects thématiques, dramatiques et théoriques' (247–57), commenting on the baroque play of 1631 with its abundance of action; V. Carraud, 'Arnauld théologien cartésien? Toute-puissance, liberté d'indifférence et création des vérités éternelles' (259–76), noting Arnauld's criticism of Malebranche and his position between Descartes and Augustine; J.-N. Laurenti, 'Un exemple de perfidie racinienne: le retournement des matériaux d'opéra dans *Phèdre*' (277–87), on the basis of IV/6 'Où me cacher . . .', shows the different handling of the scene in the Quinault-Lulli opera; P. Zoberman, 'Eloquence et notabilité: le cas de Barrême de Manville' (289–95), studying the rhetoric used by this 'robin' in late 17th-c. Arles as a 'prédication parlementaire'; S. Allaire, 'Ecriture épistolaire et pouvoirs du style: les lettres d'amour de Marie-Catherine Desjardins (1668)' (297–316), studies these authentic love letters, of one voice in a disappointed passion, and their literary quality. *Ib.*, 192, is devoted to 'Les Usages du Manuscrit'. B. Beugnot, 'Introduction' (445–50); H. Bots, 'Une source importante pour l'étude de la République des Lettres: les Fonds néerlandais' (451–59), accounts for university, royal and private collections; J. Lesaulnier, 'Les manuscrits Port-Royalistes et Jansénistes' (461–76), points to the rich, but dispersed collections; D. Muzerelle, 'Le Recueil Conrart à la Bibliothèque de l'Arsenal' (477–87), accounts for the original and later reintegrated collection; C. Bustaret, 'Le Papier "Ecriture" et ses usages au XVIIe siècle' (489–511), discusses, with illustrations, the varieties of paper and watermarks; M. Couvreur, 'La Petite Académie et la tradition des manuscrits à peinture' (513–21), discusses *estampes* and illustrated manuscripts as precious objects; A. McKenna, 'Les manuscrits philosophiques clandestins à l'Age classique' (523–35), traces the history of their discovery, from 1912 to the present, and raises the question of their impact at the time; F. Charbonneau, 'Le bavardage du manuscrit: Les *Mémoires* du jeune Brienne' (537–45), discusses the manuscript and its publication, seeing it as a 'manuscrit de travail'; N. Doiron, 'Un poète galant méconnu "Diereville du Pontlevesque"' (547–59), from archival sources, establishes a detailed biography; P. A. Fabre, 'Les "saintes ratures" d'Ignace de Loyola' (561–74), discusses the autograph manuscript of the 'Journal des motions intérieures' of Ignatius and its hagiographical use in the 17th c.; J.-R. Fanlo, 'Autoportrait d'Agrippa d'Aubigné en Jésuite régicide: un manuscrit inédit du Fonds Tronchin' (575–89): Tronchin, as literary executor, held d'Aubigné's papers; this controversial manuscript is here introduced and published; V. Maigne, 'Le manuscrit comme absolu' (591–99), comments on the documentary status of the manuscript in the 17th c.; N. O'Connor, 'Sources manuscrites et histoire des femmes: une marquise en Arles au XVIIe siècle' (601–17), discusses and publishes from the marquise de Robiac's manuscript (now in the States), mainly concerning family archives; and B. Beugnot, 'Pistes bibliographiques' (619–22), offers an enlarged bibliography from the articles.

Philippe-Joseph Salazar, *Le Culte de la voix au XVIIe siècle. Formes esthétiques de la parole à l'âge de l'imprimé*, Champion, 1995, 400 pp., extending the century, 1590–1720, studies the change from oral to printed culture, beginning with treatises on voice and sound (Kircher, Gassendi, Mersenne), voice production as part of rhetoric, based on Bary (*Méthode pour bien prononcer*), Lamy (*L'Art de parler*), and including music; a chapter on the inspired voice in sacred poetry and mysticism, with reference to François de Sales and Surin, and later quietism; finally 'vox regis' (as 'vox Dei'), and royal triumph, until the voice becomes secularized (cf. *DSS*, 132). *SCFS*, 18, includes: F. Boitano, 'Naudé's *Advis pour dresser une bibliothèque*, a window into the past' (5–19), recounts N.'s career as a librarian in Rome and then in Mazarin's service; he saw a library as storing universal knowledge; S. James, 'Descartes: the shape of a life' (21–31), discusses Gaukroger's recent biography and stresses his initiative in epistemology; M. Bernos, 'Conversion ou apostasie? Comment les chrétiens voyaient ceux qui quittaient leur église pour l' "église adverse" ' (33–48), comments on the 'change of heart', its motives and the adverse reaction of the churches; P. Parker, 'Définir la passion: correlation et dynamique' (49–58), lists definitions and interpretations of passion in Senault, Coeffeteau, and Descartes; T. Worcester, 'Defending women and Jesuits: Marie de Gournay' (59–72), points to the correlation between misogyny and anti-Jesuit attitudes and comments on de G.'s writings in defence of both; W. Brooks, 'The significance of engravings as examples of the personal iconography of the second Madame, Duchess of Orléans, 1671–1722' (72–89), comments, alongside illustrations, on the successive often flattering portraits from youth to the 'symbol of French dignity'; M. Slater, 'La Fontaine's hidden images' (91–101), uncovers camouflaged images of human beings and animals in a number of fables; D. Clarke, ' "User des droits d'un souverain pouvoir": sexual violence on the tragic stage (1635–40)' (103–20), refers to scenes of rape (*Scédase*, *Crisante*, and *Lucrèce*), assessing the political significance; M.-C. Canova-Green, 'Le roi, l'astrologue, le bouffon et le poète, figures de la création dans *Les Amants Magnifiques* de Molière' (121–31), interprets the play as a triumph of the poet in the character of Clitidas, over the king as 'machiniste'; M. Reilly, 'Racine's hall of mirrors' (133–44), interprets some plays in Sartrean terms of characters being prisoners of the 'Other'; A. Soare, 'Néron et Narcisse ou le mauvais mauvais conseiller' (145–57), in a close reading, considers Narcisse as having been made the evil counseller by Nero; V. Desnain, 'At the altar: marriage and/or sacrifice in Racine' (159–66), discusses the ambiguous nature of the altar in *Iphigénie* and the sacrificial character of marriage for women; J. Trethewey, 'Anti-judaism in Racine's *Athalie*' (167–75), interprets the 'local colour' of bloodshed as a charnel Jewish ideology Christians cannot accept; and W. Ayres-Bennett, 'Enfin D'Urfé vint?' (177–80), based on Sancier-Chateau's investigation of d'Urfe's corrections of editions of *L'Astrée*, suggests that he could be considered as having done for prose what Malherbe did for poetry.

Art de la lettre Art de la Conversation à l'époque classique en France, ed. Bernard Bray and Christoph Strosetzki, Klincksieck, 1995, 372 pp., is an important thematic volume. D. Schmitz, 'La théorie de l'art épistolaire et de la conversation dans la tradition latine et néo-latine' (11–23), discusses Cicero, Seneca, Pliny, Christian letters in the Middle Ages and humanists (Erasmus and Vives); M. Fumaroli, 'De l'âge de l'éloquence à l'âge de la conversation: la conversion de la rhétorique humaniste dans la France du XVIIe siècle' (25–45), considers rhetoric in historical perspective, and points to Italian research into the art of conversation as a basis for its development in France: rhetoric changes in register from eloquence to conversation; B. Beugnot, 'Les voix de l'autre: typologie et historiographie épistolaires' (47–59), considers this 'dialogue des absents', separated by time and space, and includes the relationship in spiritual directions; A. Montondon, 'Les bienséances de la conversation' (61–79), in a sociological approach, investigates formalities, subjects and language in polite society; I. Landy-Houillon, 'Lettre et oralité' (81–91), discusses the relationship between written and spoken language, and would keep them distinct; R. Duchêne, 'Lettre et conversation' (93–102), rejects the conclusion of the previous paper, seeing conversation as an underlying element in the letter; R. Morabito, 'Lettres et civil coversazione dans l'Italie du XVIIe siècle' (103–31), stresses the social function of the letter and the important role of secretaries in Italy; V. Kapp, 'L'art de la conversation dans les manuels oratoires de la fin du XVIIe siècle' (115–29), discusses manuals (Bary, Méré, Vaumorière) as well as conversation in novels and its æsthetic function; J. Altman, 'La politique de l'art épistolaire au XVIIe siècle' (131–44), lists manuals from the 16th c. to *Le Secrétaire des Républicains*, of 1793; C. Strosetzki, 'La place de la théorie de la conversation au XVIIIe siècle' (145–63), explains that less emphasis on rhetoric made conversation freer; C. Wentzloff-Eggebert, 'La conversation et le roman. A propos de l'oralité dans la littérature narrative au XVIe et au XVIIe siècles' (167–78), examines the use of dialogue in *Amadis de Gaule*, *Heptaméron*, *Astrée*, and the

Scudéry novels; V. Mellinghoff-Boergarie, 'Un entretien sans dialogue? De la correspondance de François de Sales aux *Lettres spirituelles* de Jean-Pierre Caussade' (179–200), gives a narrow view of letters of spiritual direction as lacking in subjects and theological substance; many were indeed written to women; U. Michalowski, 'Malherbe épistolier' (201–16), comments that M. links letters and conversation and in his letters from Paris shows himself as a critical chronicler; Y. Giraud, 'De la lettre à l'entretien: Puget de La Serre et l'art de la conversation' (217–31), comments on the *manuels*, mainly *Le Secrétaire à la mode* and the changes of taste and style; M. Albert, 'Du paraître à l'être: les avatars de la conversation féminine dans *La Prétieuse*' (233–44), discusses it as oral literature and a source for the study of conversation among women; B. Bray, 'L'écrire ou le dire: l'expression de l'amour dans l'*Histoire amoureuse des Gaules* de Bussy-Rabutin' (245–55), comments on the satirical writing and distinguishes three forms of love: 'l'amour se déclare, s'écrit, se fait'; G. Malquori Fondi, 'Conversations d'amour par lettres: un recueil méconnu de Le Pays, un roman inconnu de Pradon' (257–70), introduces Pays's *Amitiés, Amours et Amourettes* (1664) and Pradon's *Le Commerce galant ou Lettres tendres et galantes de la jeune Iris et de Timandre* (1682); J. Grimm, ' "Comme nous sommes gens à profiter de tous nos malheurs . . ." Les bienfaits de l'exil: la genèse d'une poétique dans la *Relation d'un voyage de Paris en Limousin*' (271–88), comments on the letter form and the information supplied; G. Bonacorso, 'Une correspondance familiale: les lettres de Racine à sa sœur' (289–303), analyses the stylistic and linguistic aspects of the letters, as they reflect R.'s career; Y. Bellenger, 'Le récit de voyage par lettres dans le *Nouveau Voyage d'Italie* de Misson' (305–23), accounts for the *Voyage* (1692) of a Huguenot émigré who takes his pupil from Britain to Italy on the Grand Tour; P. Hourcade, 'Bons mots et entretiens chez Saint-Simon (325–39), examines passages of conversation in the narrative; G. Harodie-Bouzinal, ' "Billets font conversation." De la théorie à la pratique: l'exemple de Voltaire' (341–54), states that the 'billet' stands between oral and written forms and became fashionable in the 18th c., much used by Voltaire.

B. Melançon, 'Diderot et l'autre de la lettre. Conversation et correspondance' (355–67), explains D.'s view that letters convey the voice of the writer. François Lagarde, *La Persuasion et ses effets. Essai sur la réception en France au dix-septième siècle*, PFSCL, 91, 1995, 203 pp., analyses, in seven chapters, the nature of persuasion, its procedures and the ways it is received; language is to insinuate itself into the heart, indeed 'toucher le cœur'. Two chapters are devoted to the 'persuasion' exercised by the theatre. Having examined various dramatic forms, the effect of their 'persuasion' appears to be that comedy makes the spectator feel he would not like to be the ridiculous character presented, whereas in tragedy he would wish to be the admired character; discussing the Church's hostility to the theatre, this can be ascribed to rivalry. The role and influence of language and rhetoric are analysed in the relevant texts (Balzac, Naudé, La Mothe le Vayer, Boileau). The chapter on Pascal deals mainly with the *Provinciales* and suggests that P. presents a 'persuasion purifiée' against a 'persuasion corrompue'. Under 'une persuasion essentielle', Descartes is mentioned as being against persuasion: 'penser seul' and the *Logique* aiming at a pure, inner, transcendant persuasion. Persuasion is of a fragile nature, as it is used for diverse purposes in the 17th c., and will, from its mimetic nature, move towards the individual and the original. *DSS*, 193, is a special issue on Desmarets de Saint-Sorlin. M. Laugaa, 'La réception de Desmarets de Saint-Sorlin dans la *Biographie* Michaud et *Les Visionnaires* de Nicole' (719–33), discusses Michaud's article and the controversy around the *Visionnaires* and the *Imaginaires*; M.-M. Fragonard, 'L'affaire Morin' (735–52), discusses M.'s somewhat unbalanced religious positions in relation to Desmarets's; H. Stenzel, 'Epopée chrétienne et modernité: le cas de Desmarets' (753–65), assesses D.'s changing approach to the use of 'fable', i.e. mythology; R. Briand, 'Les Lettres spirituelles de Desmarets de Saint-Sorlin' (767–78), describes the spiritual direction, mainly addressed to women, as based on personal experience; B. Chedozeau, 'Pierre Nicole lecteur des œuvres de spiritualité de Jean Desmarets de Saint-Sorlin: un conflit d'anthropologies' (779–88), assesses the conflict in terms of a 'doctrine néantiste' against N.'s moralizing humanism and an eventual rejection of mysticism; S. Houdard, 'Des rêveries au sommeil des puissances. Les modèles de l'intériorité chez Desmarets de Saint-Sorlin' (789–97), analyses the *Délices de l'esprit* in its ambiguity of dream, vision, and 'anéantissement'; H. Merlin, 'Desmarets et quelques figures du "moi"' (799–812), traces attitudes to 'moi' and 'amour-propre', and shows from 'épîtres dédicatoires' (to Richelieu) its use in flattery of a patron; O. Rosenthal, 'Que pour juger en maistre de la Langue et de la Poésie françoise, il faut estre bon Orateur et bon Poète François' (813–24), is centred on *La Comparaison de la Langue et de la Poésie Françoise avec la Grecque & la latine* . . . (1670), discusses the 'Ancients and Moderns', and gives Desmarets the role of a 'mask' as critic and poet; G. Mathieu-Castellani, 'L'amour modeste de Desmarets de Saint-Sorlin' (825–37), shows in *Amours* and other poems two tendencies, the older from Petrarch and the classical from Malherbe; G. Molinié, 'L'*Ariane* et le plaisir littéraire' (839–43), comments on the 'baroque' novel and its erotic character; S. de Baecque, 'La dévotion du Bel Esprit: fragments d'une poétique du récit dans l'œuvre de Desmarets de Saint-Sorlin' (845–57), comments on D.'s investigation of fable, its fictitious validity, set against revealed truth and the multiple meanings of 'Esprit'; C. Jouhaud, 'Desmarets, Richelieu, Roxane et Alexandre: sur le service de plume' (859–74), discusses the theme of Alexander in *Roxane*, in its treatment reflecting D.'s relation with Richelieu; and A. Viala, 'La guerre des institutions et la modernité' (875–90), looks at D. as belonging to the establishment and yet fights for modernity, in later years, a 'moderne vieillard'

2. POETRY

E. Safty, 'La déchéance physique et ses conséquences dans la poésie baroque en France' *DFS*, 34:17–34, with references to classical models and examples from early 17th-c. poetry, discusses the themes of old age and repentance, and concludes on a 'christianisation du Parnasse'. Marie Le Jars de Gournay, *Bouquet de Pinde, composé de fleurs diverses*, ed. Maddalena Bertela, Ravenna, Longo Editore, 1995, 311 pp.

LA FONTAINE. J. Grimm, *Le 'dire sans dire' et le dit. Etudes lafontaini-ennes II*, *PFSCL*, 93, vii + 305 pp., contains 16 articles: 'L'Adone de Marino et l'Adonis de La Fontaine: une comparaison structurale' (1–11), sets M.'s 'baroquisme' against La F.'s classicism; ' "Comme nous sommes gens à profiter de tous nos malheurs . . ." Les bienfaits de l'exil: la genèse d'une poétique dans la *Relation d'un voyage de Paris en Limousin*' (12–25), analyses the letter form as classically 'utile et agréable'; ' "Je m'écarte un peu trop". L'épître "A M. Simon de Troyes": épître, conte, satire' (26–43), comments on the letter in verse form and its satirical story; 'Les Épîtres en vers de La Fontaine' (44–63), further discusses La F.'s letters as they evoke the social reality of his time; ' "Le faucon". La Fontaine et Boccace: proximité ou distance' (64–73), considers the 14th-c. and 17th-c. tales in their structure as 'nouvelles'; 'L'amour sans corps ou l'art du "dire sans dire" dans les *Contes et nouvelles* de La Fontaine' (74–93), is centred on the writings of the mid-seventies, and comments on the non-representation of physical love, using metaphors; ' "On ne vit donc si cruelle aventure". A propos du Conte d'un paysan qui avait offensé son Seigneur' (94–106), reflects on the social and linguistic aspect of the *conte*, the Foucquet affair in disguise; ' "Comment on traite les pervers". La satire anticléricale dans les *Contes*' (107–20), comments on the anticlericalism of the time, pointing to 'paillardise et tart-ufferie'; ' "Mais quant aux noms, il faut au moins les taire". Réflexions socio-critiques sur les *Nouveaux Contes de Monsieur de La*

Fontaine' (121–35), discusses the 1674 edition and places their anti-clerical satire against the background of the *Provinciales* and *Tartuffe*; 'La Fontaine — être de papier? Des insuffisances d'une analyse structuraliste du récit s'érigeant en absolu' (136–57), takes H. Lindner's structuralist analysis to task, as directed against his own edition; ' "Proprement toute notre vie ..." Evasion utopique, "rentrée en soi" et fol emportement dans les Fables' (158–64), analyses the theme of dream as utopia in *La laitière et le pot au lait* and *Le curé et le mort*; ' "Et la terre chemine". La Fontaine — précurseur des Lumières' (165–80), stresses. La F.'s socio-critical approach as a 'Frühaufklärung'; ' "Le sens et la raison y règlent toute chose". Contribution à une anthropologie des Fables' (181–98), develops the notion of a 'homo classicus', and La F.'s own tension between an optimistic utopian spirit and a pessimistic view of his time; ' "Qui t'engage à cette entreprise?" Les engagements de La Fontaine' (199–221), shows in a thematic reading of the fables a socio-critical attitude within a personal independence; 'Portraits d'Alexandre le Grand à l'époque de Louis XIV' (222–53), lists the use of the figure of Alexander for Louis XIII and Louis XIV, by writers and painters (La F. creates a negative image of Alexander); finally ' "Enfans, soyez bons, Jupiter le veut". Initiation au Théâtre rétivien à propos de la "Fable dramatique" *La Cigale et la Fourmi*' (254–69), considers the play by Rétif de la Bretonne (1771–72), based on the fable. In *La Fontaine et l'Orient (Actes du colloque de Tunis)*, ed. Alia Baccar, *PFSCL*, 98, 170 pp., Z. Benaissa, 'Le traitement lexical des ethnies orientales dans les *Fables* de La Fontaine' (11–15), discusses references to oriental expressions and their sound value in poetry; H. Akkari, 'Le vocabulaire de l'Orient chez La Fontaine' (17–33), lists the limited vocabulary (with a concordance at the end) which gives a superficial and ambiguous picture; M. Ali Drissa, 'Fantasmes et fantaisie de l'orient dans les *Fables* de La Fontaine' (34–45), discusses French 'engouement' with a romanticized Orient; J. Grimm, ' "Deux vrais amis vivaient au Monomotapa ..." Evasion orientale, "rentrée en soi" et fol emportement dans les *Fables*' (47–55), links the themes of travel and dream and builds an antithetical structure between utopia and reality; M. R. Rahmouni, '*Joconde* de La Fontaine et Préambule des *Mille et une nuits*' (57–63), suggests as intermediary between the two texts, part of the *Orlando furioso*, of oriental origin; J. Azzouna, 'Boccace, La Fontaine et l'Orient ou "la Culture et le Plaisir" ' (65–83), shows parallels and differences between the treatment of the Orient in the 14th c. and the 17th c.; R. Marzouki, 'De l'utilisation des *Fables* de La Fontaine comme source d'écriture dans la littérature arabe (poétique et politique)' (85–91), discusses translations from foreign writers, including the *Fables* and their influence on modern

Arabic literature; A. Guellouz, 'Une religion des fabulistes? La religion dans la vie et dans l'œuvre de Ibn al-Muqaffa' et de La Fontaine' (93–107), discusses the religious positions of the Islamic and the Christian *fabulistes* and the apologies in their writings; A. Niderst, 'Y a-t-il une sagesse orientale dans les *Fables* de La Fontaine?' (109–16), argues that La F.'s ideas on the Orient are of bookish origin and hardly more than a 'voile coloré'; H. El Annabi, 'L'Orient et les affaires européennes à l'époque de La Fontaine: les *Fables* et les faits' (117–25), gives a historico-critical account of some fables which refer to relations between Europe and the Orient at the time; A. Baccar, 'Figures de l'Orient dans le *Poème de la captivité de Saint Malc*' (127–33), analyses the different aspects of an imaginary oriental setting, some hostile, others edifying; H. Hemaidi, 'Microlecture du théâtre de La Fontaine: l'Orient occulté?' (135–41), attempts to show the theatricality of some fables with an imaginary oriental setting; F. Pelisson-Karro, '*L'Ane vêtu de la peau du Lion*, Fable et histoire de porcelaine' (143–62), traces, with illustrations, Dagoty's work in a neo-classical style; and H. Skik, 'L'Orient dans les *Fables*, les *Fables* en Orient: quelques repères' (163–68), indicates a widespread interest in fables in Arabic literature, and interest in French literature which dates from Bonaparte's campaign in Egypt. M.-O. Sweetser, 'Pleasures and pains, lessons and revelations of travel in La Fontaine', *DFS*, 36:23–37, discusses the *Voyage de Paris en Limousin* as positive reply to Grimm's article and the topos of 'homo viator'; B. Croquette, 'Les héros de l'épopée à l'aune de la fable: La Fontaine et Homère' *RLC*, 70:469–73, compares the humble characters of the *Fables* to the heroes in Homer. O. Leplatre, 'Le pouvoir absolu de la haine, la passion du politique dans les *Fables* de La Fontaine', *RR*, 87:195–208, comments, along some fables, on the expression of contempt and sarcasm. E. Keller, 'Psyché découvrant Cupidon: portées symboliques d'un épisode. De La Roque à La Fontaine', *RHLF*, 96:1069–83, centres on the main scene and compares the different versions, Pujet de la Serre's and considers La F.'s as an original contribution. Herbert De Ley, *Fixing Up Reality. La Fontaine and Lévi-Strauss*, *PFSCL*, 97, 109 pp., attempts to interpret the fables and the animal kingdom along Lévi-Strauss's structuralist mythologies, under various headings, including sex and food, structure and meaning of exchange, Jupiter and the Lion, the notion of power; in conclusion it is suggested that perhaps La F. could be considered as the founder of structural anthropology.

Anne Mantero, *La Muse théologienne. Poésie et théologie de 1630 à 1680*, Berlin, Duncker und Humboldt, 1995, 529 pp., gives a detailed account of theological positions, assesses critically the theological vocabulary used by the poets, various forms of rhetoric in the service of dogma; deals with the poets of the early century, usually referred to as baroque, then Godeau, Corneille's translation of the *Imitation*, and Surin.

3. Drama

LitC, 27, is devoted to 'L'esthétique de la comédie', ed. Gabriel Conesa, who provides an 'Introduction' (7–10). A. Tissier, 'Sur la notion de "genre" dans les pièces comiques. De la farce de *Pathelin* à la comédie de *L'Eugène* de Jodelle' (13–24), surveys plays in their structure from the 15th to the 16th c.; H. Baby-Litot, 'Réflexions sur l'esthétique de la comédie héroïque de Corneille à Molière' (25–34), traces a development from one dramatist to the other; A. Arcellaschi, 'Plaute entre le tragique et le comique: la comédie humaine ou la divine comédie?' (35–42), writes in defence of Plautus's plays and their mixed genre; D. Gambelli, 'Le *Dom Juan* de Molière et les machines de la tragédie' (43–52), draws a comparison with the *Commedia dell'Arte*: the ending is not tragic but a confluence of word and gesture; J. Serroy, 'De *L'École des femmes* à *Britannicus*. Il faut qu'une porte soit ouverte ou fermée' (53–65), explains the symbolic theatrical use of the door, closed in the comedy, a palace with two doors in the tragedy; J.-M. Civardi, 'La dissertation de Heinsius sur le jugement d'Horace au sujet de Plaute et de Térence' (67–116), discusses the texts of 1618 and 1629, with an annotated edition of Latin text and French translation; J.-P. Néraudau, 'La personne sous le masque: réflexions sur la dramaturgie de Térence d'après l'*Heauton-timouremenos*' (117–24), discusses the lighthearted treatment of a serious subject with the insight into a human character; E. Bury, 'Comédie et science des mœurs: le modèle de Térence aux XVIe et XVIIe siècles; (125–35), comments on translation, influence, and appreciation of the playwright; G. Degen, 'Le rire de Bergson et l'esthétique de la comédie' (139–59), dismisses B.'s theory and proposes laughter in a play as a means of denouncing ideologies; D. Bertrand, 'De la légitimité du rire comme critère de la comédie' (161–70), argues that 'faire rire les honnêtes gens' is a revolutionary statement, laughter belonging to farce, introduced into comedy; J. Emelina, 'L'esthétique du plaisant' (171–82), quotes 'castigat ridendo mores' and distinguishes between laughing at someone (comic), and laughing with someone, the 'plaisant'; P. Stewart, 'De la *catharsis* comique' (183–93), sees catharsis in comedy as different from tragedy with two categories: 'ridicule' and 'distanciation', since we do not sympathize with the character; A. Blanc, 'La *catharsis* du désir dans le théâtre de Marivaux' (195–203), discusses two aspects of love in the plays, the emotional and the physical; V. Sternberg, 'Rhétorique et esthétique comique dans le théâtre de Scarron' (205–18), analyses S.'s various rhetorical devices in his plays; G. Conesa, 'Le personnage et le discours de son temps' (219–29), discusses the use of 'sentences' in plays, at first intercalated, and later integrated; N. Fournier, 'Dire et redire: formes et fonctions du rapport des paroles dans les comédies de Marivaux' (231–42), distinguishes three forms: direct, indirect, indirect free speech; G. Forestier, 'Structure de la comédie française classique' (243–57), analyses intrigue, obstacles, and the denouement, sometimes with a ballet; J.-C. Ranger, 'La comédie, ou l'esthétique de la rupture' (259–79), comments on laughter as a sign of discontinuity: the characters in comedy are linked neither to past nor future; R. Guich-emerre, 'Gratuité et développement ludique dans les comédies de Scarron et de Molière' (281–89), comments on gratuitous tirades and ballet scenes, building up playful fantasy; C. Mazouer, 'Colombine ou l'esprit de l'ancien théâtre italien' (291–303), discusses C. as 'suivante', but showing penetrating views on social justice in a satirical vein; she represents the spirit of the Italian theatre; J. Guilhembet, 'Les fonctions d'Arlequin dans cinq comédies de Marivaux' (305–20), points to the important role of Arlequin in many plays when Arlequin eventually drops his mask and becomes a 'personnage'; J.-M. Jacques, 'La figure de l'étranger dans la Comédie Nouvelle à propos du *Bouclier* de Ménandre' (323–32), discusses Attic comedy and the encounter between Greek and Barbarian; T. Mala-chy, 'Du droit à la folie à la folie du droit: la comédie de *Tartuffe*' (335–37), opposes group and individual, and sees Tartuffe as a marginalized stranger; J. Morel, 'Les Plaideurs, réécriture et provoca-tion' (229–41), refers to pleading in *Georges Dandin* and Racine who wanted to compete; P. Robinson, 'L'imaginaire et la distanciation comique chez Marivaux et Beaumarchais' (343–51), compares the 'esprit ludique' of the two authors and a changing classical tradition; M.-C. Canova-Green, 'La comédie anglaise aux XVIIe et XVIIIe siècles: modèle ou anti-modèle?' (353–65), accounts for reactions in France or by those who had a direct knowledge, to comedies of humour (Ben Jonson) and of manners (Restoration plays); and J. Mallinson, 'Vision comique, voix morale: la réception du *Misan-thrope* au XVIIIe siècle' (367–77), comments that the play was admired in the 18th c. and critics pointed to the moral and also æsthetic aspects.

Christian Delmas, *La Tragédie de l'âge classique (1553–1770)*, Seuil, 1995, 266 pp., accounts for this extended period of different forms of classicism, centred on the 'spectacle' of tragedy, productions, and stage sets, theatres in the capital, actors and audience; under the heading of 'la fabrique d'une tragédie', D. deals with playwrights from Hardy to Voltaire, with some references to critical writings, in an illustrated volume.

CORNEILLE. *DSS*, 190, is a special issue, introd. A. Niderst, 'Corneille parmi nous' (7–13). M. Margitic, 'Le pouvoir de la vue chez Corneille: *Mélite* et au-delà' (15–23), shows how characters see or do not see each other, and stresses the physical aspects in the plays; R. Guichemerre, 'La cruauté dans les premières comédies de Corneille' (25–31), observes the cynical cruelty behind the 'badinage galant' and refers to a 'théâtre de la cruauté'; C. Biet, 'Clarice, veuve et femme libre, un moment' (33–41), comments, from the play, on the social freedom in widowhood; L. Piccola, 'De la tragédie sénéquienne à la tragédie de machines: permanence de Médée' (43–52), compares *La Toison d'or* and *Médée*; the representation of her character in both plays is in the tradition of Seneca; A. Couprié, 'Le corps dans le théâtre de Corneille: du Cid à Pertharite' (53–59), analyses the two aspects of the body, to be dominated or linked to physical strength; J. Deprun, 'Questions théologiques sur *Polyeucte*' (61–66), discusses Lemaître's verdict on personal heroism as 'gloutonnerie mystique'; P. Tomlinson, 'Le personnage de Cléopâtre chez Mairet et Corneille' (67–75), compares M.'s attempt to whitewash Cleopatra with C.'s political interpretation; A. Blanc, 'L'écriture du temps dans *Rodogune* et *Nicomède*" (77–83), shows the handling of time between 'empty' scenes and those crowded with action; J. Morel, 'A propos de *Sophonisbe*' (85–87), relates Corneille's preface to his play as a disguised criticism of Mairet's; D. Dalla Valle,' 'Le mythe d'Oedipe et la suggestion de Sénèque: les tragédies de Prévost et de Corneille' (89–101), elaborates on the versions of the myth and its Christianizing by Corneille; P. Alexandre, 'Honneur mondain et honneur intime dans *Oedipe, Othon, Tite et Bérénice* et *Suréna*' (103–10), compares the personal honour of the inner voice to the mundane form in society; and J.-C. Guizennec, ' "Moi, Pierre Corneille" ' (111–13), accounts for his film, ahowing the young C. as pupil of the Collège de Bourbon. Georges Forestier, *Essai de génétique théâtrale, Corneille à l'œuvre*', Klincksieck, 387 pp., with the intention of 'saisir Corneille à l'œuvre', studies the creative process, its mystique, and poetics and rhetorical embellishments through all its stages: choice of subject, building up of the action, working out the themes of love and politics (with an increasing emphasis on the latter). Corneille's own comments in the *Discours* are analysed as is his coming to terms with 'vraisemblance' and 'bienséances'; F. ends on a discussion on heroic tragedy. A. Georges, 'L'appel de Polyeucte et de Néarque au martyre', *RHT*, 96:192–211, investigates the attitudes to martyrdom from early christian times, the warning against 'rushing' into it, its inspired character; argues against any interpretation as self-glorification. C. B. Kerr, '*La Veuve* de Corneille', *ib.*, 321–36, discusses the production by Christian Rist, on his own text, *La Veuve ou le traître trahi*, (1990), as a modern handling of a 'chef-d'œuvre inconnu'.

DONNEAU DE VISÉ. M. Vincent, *L'Amour échappé*, une revue de la société observée par Donneau de Visé', *TLit*, 9:87–103, analyses the piece, set in a mythological background, with its portraits of people from 'Cour, Ville, Province', noting their real identity and their stories of 'relations galantes'.

DU RYER. *Saül. Tragédie (1642)*, ed. Maria Miller, Toulouse, Société de Littératures Classiques, 91 pp., an annotated text with a detailed introduction on the playwright, the choice of a Biblical text, other treatments of the subject, and performances.

MOLIÈRE. *Le Nouveau Moliériste*, II, ed. Robert McBride and Noël Peacock, Glasgow and Ulster U.P., 1995[1996], 351 pp. E. Dubois, 'L'éducation de Molière au collège de Clermont' (21–35), accounts for the educational system, syllabus, activities and masters at the time of Pocquelin and Conti; F. Mallet, 'La religion de Molière' (35–55), assesses the circles M. frequented, as 'humanistes chrétiens'; C. Mazouer, 'Les Défenseurs ecclésiastiques de Molière au XVIIe siècle' (57–68), shows those in the Church who showed understanding of the theatre, Le Moyne, Ménestrier, Rapin, as Jesuits who used plays as part of their teaching, as against the rigorist views of Bossuet and Jansenist circles; H. Phillips, 'Molière: la querelle du *Tartuffe* et la querelle du théâtre', (69–88), accounts for M.'s own defence of *Tartuffe* and the theatre, mentions a parallel in Racine's reply to Nicole, and concludes on M.'s secularism; J. Dubu, 'La sépulture religieuse de Molière' (89–93), gives a detailed account of the Church's ruling, and the burial at night as without 'pompe', but by the Church; J. Truchet, '*Tartuffe, Les Femmes savantes, Le Malade imaginaire*: trois drames de l'imposture' (95–105), discusses the meaning of imposture, seen by the 18th c. as anticlericalism, false philosophical positions, and imposture of the medical profession; C. Lambot, 'Le *Tartuffe* de Molière, un coup de théâtre' (107–22), points to two 'coups de théâtre' (lines 1557, 1901–02, when Orgon is told that he has to leave his home, and Tartuffe is arrested), and concludes on our assenting belief in the 'jeu de théâtre'; R. Albanese, Jr, 'Hypocrisie et dramaturgie dans *Dom Juan*' (123–44), analyses the different aspects of hypocrisy, with regard to women, father, and religion; Dom Juan is unmasked before the Statue, but does not cheat, and the end is a 'spectacle creux'; R. McBride, 'Une philosophie du rire (suite)' (145–61), examines the role of the *raisonneur*, often more ready to listen, with a clear sense of the ridiculous side of the monomanic hero, who takes himself seriously, concludes on a general feeling for the amusing aspects of life; M. Bacholle, 'Fragments d'un discours atrabilaire et amoureux: Alceste aux miroirs de Bergson et Barthes' (163–69), rejects Bergson's assessment with regard to Alceste, points to Barthes's view on jealousy, the end a social suicide; N. Akiyama, 'La musique dans les comédies-ballets de Molière' (171–87), studies the role of music and its importance in the plays, as it is integrated; R. Kenny, 'Molière et ses Egyptiens' (189–209), having accounted for the role of the 'Bohémien' at the time, lists their role in various plays, including ballets; J.-P. Collinet, 'Molière épistolier' (211–27), analyses the use of letters and 'billets' in the plays, and concludes on Molière as 'épistolier comique'; M. Gutwirth, 'Insaisissable Alcmène' (229–46), traces the story of Alcmene to ancient mythology, refers to modern treatment by Kleist and Giraudoux, to Sosie (Rotrou, *Les Sosies*), and concludes on the radicalization of comedy; J. Clarke, 'Les théâtres de Molière à Paris' (247–72), lists and describes the theatres used, the 'jeux de paume', 'Petit Bourbon', 'Palais Cardinal', and their structure; D. Whitton, '*Le Misanthrope*, 1975–1995. Vingt ans de mise en scène en France' (275–96), comments on various and radical interpretations as 'Classiques du peuple', at Vincennes, and others, classical performances at, among others, the TN Strasbourg, the Marais, and, in 1989 the Comédie Française; N. Peacock, 'Molière en Angleterre' (297–304), accounts for translations and adaptations and their popularity; G. Snaith, '*Tartuffe* à Manchester' (305–07), comments on the Christopher Hampton translation performed in 1995: N. Peacock, '*Tartuffe* en Ecosse' (308–09), and mentions the adaptation by Liz Lochhead, performed in 1995 in Edinburgh and Glasgow; B. Madinier, 'Le Japon à notre porte' (310–12), accounts for a performance by a Japanese company at Avignon in 1995; and N. Peacock, 'Deux *Malades* carnavalesques' (313–15), refers to a performance in Helsinki, 1994–95, and at Avignon, 1994. *EsC*, 36.1, is an issue on 'Molière', pref. R. Albanese Jr. L. W. Riggs, 'Dom Juan: the subject of modernity' (7–20), examines the play from a semiotic angle with emphasis on the desacralization of the world; J. F. Gaines, 'Molière and Marx' (21–30), takes a critical view of former 'marxisant' interpretations of Molière: Cairncross, the *Annales* school, *Editions Sociales*, and others; M. S. Koppisch, ' "Til Death do them part": love, greed and rivalry in Molière's *L'Avare*' (32–49), looks at the play from those themes and stresses the contagious influence of avarice which remains unchanged at the end; R. Albanese, Jr, 'Dynamisme social et jeu individuel dans *Dom Juan*' (50–62), reflects on Dom Juan's cynical unmasking of those he meets, his mimicking others and his narcissism; F. Nepote-Desmerres, 'Y a-t-il des dénouements bâclés dans les comédies de Molière?' (63–72), examines the variety of endings, some artificial, close to 'machines', some containing logical conclusions, others fortuitous; V. Krause, 'Bâtardise et cocuage dans *L'Ecole des Femmes*' (73–81), comments on Arnolphe as illegitimate son and on the cuckoldry which links the play to popular tradition; B. Weltman-Aron, '*Le Misanthrope* mis en tropes: Molière, Marmontel et Rousseau' (82–90), points to the 18th c.'s partly critical, partly admiring attitudes to Molière, which insists more on ridiculing than correcting behaviour. Jean-Baptiste Molière, *Le Misanthrope*, ed. Jonathan Mallinson, Bristol Classical Press, lxi + 130 pp., has a text based on the Blackwell edition and the *Grands Ecrivains*; the Introduction deals with the ambiguity of the characters, their relationship to society, the different forms of comedy within the play and its anti-traditional ending. The commentary follows the text closely. Bernadette Rey-Flaud, *Molière et la Farce*, Droz, 267 pp., continues an earlier study on medieval farce with its own æsthetic principles, comments on Molière's early farces which show French and Italian influences, on *Amphitryon* as a 'farce travestie', and on *George Dandin* as a 'farce tragique'; with *Les Fourberies de Scapin* the old genre is renewed. W. S. Brooks, 'Louis XIV's dismissal of the Italian actors: the episode of the *Fausse Prude*', *MLR*, 91 : 840–47, comments on the performance of the play, considered a satirical attack on Mme de Maintenon; the Italians not heeding advice were dismissed. William Brooks and Philip Yarrow, *The Dramatic Contribution of Elisabeth Charlotte duchesse d'Orléans*, Lampeter, Mellen, 366 pp. M. S. Koppisch, 'Désordre et sacrifice dans *George Dandin*', *TLit*, 9 : 75–86, quotes the similar attacks on the play by Bourdaloue and Rousseau, analyses questions of language and legal justice in the play, qualifying it as a black comedy. N. Peacock, 'Molière's handling of rhyme: the translator's perspective', Smith, *Essays*, 45–50, comments on modern English verse translations (with their difficulties), and concludes that through them a new appraisal of M.'s handling of verse is indicated.

RACINE. *Les Tragédies romaines de Racine: 'Britannicus', 'Bérénice', 'Mithridate' (Actes des colloques de Marseille 1995, et de la Sorbonne 1996)*, ed. and introd. P. Ronzeau and A. Viala, Klincksieck, 234 pp. G. Forestier, 'Dramaturgie racinienne (petit essai de génétique théâtrale)' (13–38), discusses the Roman themes in parallel with Corneille's treatment and sees C.'s technique as extraordinary and R.'s as natural; C. Delmas, 'Stratégie de l'invention chez Racine' (39–50), explores the rivalry of the characters in the plays and stresses the political themes and the poetic imagination as double aspects; J. Rohou, 'Structure et signification dans *Britannicus, Bérénice et Mithridate*' (51–72), stresses the moral aspects, particularly the Augustinian–Christian, in the period 1660–80, and argues for some of R.'s personal experience; J.-P. Néraudau, 'Mais où sont ces Romains que fait parler Racine?' (73–90), examines the plays alongside Roman history, as interpreted by Racine and ends on the question: 'des Romaines perruqués ou des contemporains romanisés?'; A. Viala, 'Péril, conseil et secret d'Etat dans les tragédies romaines de Racine: Racine et Machiavel' (91–113), studies the political dimension of the plays against *The Prince* which in Racine becomes 'littérarisé'; B. Croquette, 'Racine et l'éblouissement cornélien' (115–21), analyses the 'regard' in the plays of both authors and contrasts Corneille's 'gloire' with R.'s 'blessure'; J. Emelina, 'L'espace dans les tragédies romaines de Racine' (125–38), comments on space according to the stage, the near surrounding and the distant places; G. Declercq, ' "Alchimie de la douleur"': l'élégiaque dans *Bérénice* ou la tragédie éthique' (139–65), restates the elegiac character of the play in a double tragedy; C. Bret, 'La passion des larmes' (167–83), examines the vocabulary of tenderness and tears and stresses their cathartic character; P. Fievre, 'Traitement des textes, *Britannicus*, *Mithridate*, *Bérénice* de Jean Racine' (189–216), comments on the computer studies of the texts; finally, G. Forestier, 'Jean Racine. Approche bibliographique' (217–34), gives a bibliography of the exceptionally numerous publications over the last ten years. *Le Mythe de Phèdre. Les Hippolyte français du dix-septième siècle. Textes des éditions originales de La Pinelière, de Gilbert, et de Bidar*, ed. Allen G. Wood, Champion, 384 pp., examines the treatment of Hippolytos in *Hippolyte* (1635), *Hypolite ou le Garçon insensible* (1647), and *Hippolyte* (1675), with annotated texts, and biographical notes on the authors. René Pommier, *Etudes sur Britannicus*, Sedes, 1995, 164 pp., sets out to reject certain interpretations of the play, by Goldmann, Mauron, and Barthes, by a close reading, in particular, of two important scenes: I/I (Agrippine), and IV/4 (Narcisse encouraging the murder); the fiercest attack is directed against Goldmann's interpretations, which the author disproves 'à coup de citations'. Jean Racine, *Phèdre*, ed. Richard Parish, Bristol Classical texts, xlii + 123 pp. The text is the 1697 modernized edition; the Introduction covers literary, linguistic, stylistic, and poetic aspects, all thoroughly and subtly argued; there are accounts of performances and a Commentary, rigorously and thoughtfully presented.

4. PROSE

Georges Molinié, *Du Roman Grec au Roman Baroque*, Toulouse-Le Mirail U.P., 1995, 456 pp., presents a comparative study of narrative techniques in the Greek novel of the first and second centuries, with the baroque novels of Spain and France in the sixteenth and seventeenth centuries; there are the different narrative forms: first or third person, retrospective accounts; 'in medias res' beginnings, symmetric or antithetical structures; various forms of description, negative, comparative, hyperbolic, euphemism in some human relationships; a parallel is always established between the Greek and the baroque novels. The section on the French novel deals with several early 17th-c. authors, among whom are Audiguier, Camus, Des Marets, Gombauld, Gomberville, and then, later in the century, La Calprenède, and La Serre. *L'Astrée* receives detailed analysis under various headings and there are references to theoretical writings. In the period of Louis XIII the model of Heliodorus was still very much alive. Günter Berger, *Pour et contre le roman. Anthologie du discours théorique sur la fiction narrative du XVIIe siècle*, PFSCL, 92, 234 pp., discusses the development of the genre of the Preface, patronage and standing of the novelist, criticism and defence of the novel; there is an anthology of prefaces from D'Audiguier (1616), to Letters to and from the abbé de Bellegarde (1702).

BOSSUET. C. Smith, 'Bossuet's self-improvement. Reading the variants in the *Oraison Funèbre d'Yolande de Monterby*', Smith, *Essays*, 51–56, discusses some of the changes made by Bossuet, in the direction of 'raison' prevailing over 'pompe' without losing any of its rhetorical quality.

CHALLE. Robert Challe, *Mémoires, Correspondance Complète, Rapports sur l'Académie et autres pièces* (TLF), ed. Frédéric Deloffre and Jacques Popin, 764 pp., is the first complete annotated edition with commentaries on contemporary events, and on the letters from Quebec (1683), with various documents in the appendices.

LA BRUYÈRE. Louis van Delft, *La Bruyère ou du Spectateur*, PFSCL, 96, 43 pp., interprets La Bruyère's anthropological perspective on society, as spectator and judge, and, within the limitations of 'la cour' and 'la ville', examines style and language. M. Escola, 'Ce que peut un fragment. Une note en marge des *Caractères*', TLit, 9:105–26, discusses the elements of the *Fragment* (eighth edition of the *Caractères*), as the first of its kind in French literature, earlier interpretations, and concludes on a 'texte possible'.

LA ROCHEFOUCAULD. Richard C. Hodgson, *Falsehood Disguised: Unmasking the Truth in La Rochefoucauld*, West Lafayette, Purdue U.P., 1995, xiii + 176 pp., examines the relationship between falsehood and truth in the 'Baroque', i.e. the fluid role of 'amour-propre'; and shows the modernity of the *Maximes*, with references to Lautréamont, Nietzsche, and Lacan. E. Moles, 'Form and paradox in La Rochefoucauld', Smith, *Essays*, 29–34, examines some 'tournures' in the *Maximes*, comparing them to the dislocated blocks of Cubist painters, and pointing to some of their poetic qualities.

MME DE SÉVIGNÉ. *RHLF*, 96.3, is a special no., 'Images de Madame de Sévigné (Colloque de Paris 1995)', introd. R. Duchêne. B. Bray, 'Premier lecteur, premier admirateur: le Cousin Rabutin' (366–77), comments on this less studied part of her correspondence, and on 'Rabutinage' as a family term; M.-C. Grassi, 'Naissance d'un nouveau modèle: l'apparition de Madame de Sévigné dans les traités d'art épistolaire' (378–93), lists and comments on 18th-c. manuals and anthologies of 'model' letters; G. Haroche-Bouzinac, 'Voltaire et Madame de Sévigné, Un éloge en contrepoint' (394–403), notes how Voltaire's early praise gave way to the criticism that her contents lacked philosophy; J.-Y. Huet, 'Madame de Sévigné en Angleterre: Horace Walpole et Madame Du Deffand' (404–35), from their correspondence looks at the admiring references to Mme de S.'s letters, and mentions the *Sevigniana* at Strawberry Hill; P. Placella Soumella, 'Madame de Sévigné en Italie' (436–45), explains that interest began in the later 19th c. with the early 20th-c. translations and critical studies began to appear; E. Bury, 'Madame de Sévigné face aux critiques du XIXe siècle: Sainte-Beuve et consorts' (446–60), discusses articles of 1829, 1849, and 1861: for the Romantic era she was seen as an individualist; also mentions Lanson and Faguet; R. Duchêne, 'Madame de Sévigné, Personage de roman dans l'œuvre de Proust' (461–74), points to the novelistic, fictitious presentation in *A la recherche* (there are very few actual quotations). Jacqueline Queneau Jean-Yves Patte, *L'Art de vivre au temps de Madame de Sévigné*, ed. Dominique Missika, Nil, 224 pp., describes, through the well-known biography, features of everyday and society life and social habits among upper-class people. Marie-Hélène Sabard, *Madame de Sévigné vue par des écrivains de Bussy-Rabutin à Philippe Sollers*, École des lettres, 251 pp., is a collection of judgements on letters with comments.

D'URFÉ. Anne Sancier-Chateau, *Une Esthétique nouvelle: Honoré d'Urfé Correcteur de L'Astrée (1607–1625)*, Geneva, Droz, 1995, 444 pp., is set in the history of printing and publications, examines the variants and corrections (linguistic, grammatical, stylistic) that D'U. made in successive editions, and argues that D'U. thus helped to bring about the change from 16th-c. to 17th-c. French and would hold a place in the development of prose similar to that of Malherbe in poetry.

5. THOUGHT

ARNAULD. *Interpreting Arnauld*, ed. Eleanor J. Kremer, Toronto U.P., x + 183 pp., publishes the Proceedings of a 1994 colloquium, on the tercentenary of Arnauld's death. J. Vance Buroker, 'Arnauld on judging the will' (3–12), deals with logic, in the light of Descartes's and with linguistic and semantic problems related to it; A. Nelson, 'The falsity of sensory ideas: Descartes and Arnauld' (13–32), examines A.'s *Objections* to Descartes's *Méditations* and attempts to show that, in fact, there was some agreement between the two positions; P. A. Schouls, 'Arnauld and the modern mind (the *Fourth Objection* as indicative of both Arnauld's openness to and his distance from Descartes)', (35–50), shows Arnauld bound by pre-modern Augustinian thought, and holding Descartes's position as compatible with Christian faith although he was on the Index; T. M. Lennon, 'Arnauld and scepticism: *questions de fait* and *questions de droit*' (51–63), reviews the problems, emphasizing the point of papal infallibility, and concludes that the distinction between 'fait' and 'droit' led to A.'s scepticism; A.-R. Ndiaye, 'The status of the eternal truths in the philosophy of Antoine Arnauld' (64–75), discusses Arnauld's position in relation to Descartes and Malebranche: he did not follow, but considered philosophy as useful to religion, with an emphasis on pastoral care; E. J. Kremer, 'Arnauld's interpretation of Descartes as a Christian philosopher' (76–90), comments that A., in defence of Descartes, saw him in the tradition of medieval theology; V. Carraud, 'Arnauld a Cartesian theologian? Omnipotence, freedom of indifference, and the creation of eternal truths' (91–110), argues that whereas Descartes faces theology from his philosophy, A., as a theologian, looks at philosophy, which accounts for their different positions; G. Hunter, 'Arnauld's defence of miracles and its context' (111–26), explains A.'s position in defence of the Church's teaching, à propos of 'La Sainte Epine'; J.-L. Solève, 'Arnauld versus Nicole. A medieval dispute?' (127–44), states that A. argues against the Augustinian position on divine illumination, using Aquinas's argument of truth in the intellect: as a theologian A. is Augustinian, as a philosopher he tends towards Aquinas; S. Nadler, ' "Tange montes et fumigabunt": Arnauld on the theodicies of Malebranche and Leibniz' (145–63), comments that A. criticized Malebranche for holding that all would be saved, and Leibniz for not accepting a full omnipotence of God; R. C. Sleigh, Jr, 'Arnauld on efficacious grace and free choice' (164–75), shows A.'s change of position from his defence of Jansen and his later turn to Aquinas, refers to his *Instruction sur l'accord de la grâce avec la liberté* and its uneasy argument.

BAYLE. *De l'Humanisme aux Lumières: Bayle et le protestantisme. Mélanges en l'honneur d'Elisabeth Labrousse*, ed. Michelle Magdelaine et al., Universitas–Oxford, Voltaire Foundation, xvi + 742 pp., includes a 'Notice biographique' (ix–xvi), and W. Rex, 'Introduction' (1–8); J. A. Vazquez, 'Recuerdos de Elisabeth en la Argentina' (9–14); B. Armstrong, 'Pierre du Moulin and James I: the Anglo-French programme' (17–29), examines the possible link of the French

Protestant and Anglican churches; B. Dompnier, 'Pierre du Moulin, les capucins et la règle de saint François. Autour des controverses de Sedan, 1640–41' (31–44), analyses Bayle's articles on the controversies as they reflect mentalities; L. Bergon, 'L'installation de la Réforme à Millau (Aveyron). Etat de la recherche' (45–52), concerns assemblies 1572–76 and their religious and political impact; J. Poujol, 'Une fille du pasteur au couvent à l'époque de Mazarin' (53–65), accounts for the forced placement of a protestant girl in a convent and her eventual release; Y. Keumenacker, 'Un de mes amis catholique romain . . . "Catholiques et protestants au temps des dragonnades"' (67–75), based on the journal of J. Migault, relates some limited peaceful coexistence between the two communities; J. Woodbridge, 'An eighteenth-century fronde? The conspiracy of the prince de Conti against Louis XV, 1755–57' (77–93), gives a detailed account of the events; J. Baubérot, 'La crise et le renouveau de l'éthique dans la société française' (95–109), follows the attitudes to 'éthique' or 'morale', from the Revolution to the present; A. Encrevé, 'Félix Pécaut et le miracle' (111–36), discusses *Le Christianisme libéral et le miracle*, 1869; F. Higman, 'Calvin et l'*imago Dei*' (139–48), points to the rhetorical side of Calvin's writing; O. Fatio, 'Prêcher à Genève en 1669' (149–55), discusses controversial sermons on the question of universal grace; G. H. M. Posthumus Meyjes, 'Les années de Jacques Gaillard aux Pays-Bas et son sermon sur *L'Echole saincte des femmes*, 1667' (157–68), discusses the French pastor's sermon as a guideline for young women; B. Roussel, 'La discipline des Eglises réformées de France en 1559: un royaume sans clergé' (169–91), analyses the structuring of the reformed churches through their synods; M. Carbonnier-Burkard, 'Larmes réformées' (193–206), comments on the spiritual significance of tears, as seen by the reform; R. Zuber, 'Madame Des Loges devant son Dieu' (207–17), discusses *Le Mémoire*, her spiritual diary; C. Berkvens-Stevelinck, 'La tentation de l'arminianisme' (219–29), publishes and discusses Prosper Marchand's *Confession de foi*, from a Leyden MS; M. Chevallier, 'L'Education chrétienne des enfants de Pierre Poiret, source du catéchisme de John Wesley' (231–42), discusses the controversial text and its adaptation; C. Secrétan, 'L'étranger dans les Pays-Bas au siècle d'or' (245–53), gives an account of the various nations having taken up residence and their reception; J.-D. Candaux, 'Genève au temps de Pierre Bayle: la relation de Hieronymus Brückner' (255–71), discusses Brückner's account as a background to B.'s stay in 1670; M. Magdelaine, 'L'Irlande huguenote: utopie ou réalité?' (273–87), comments on establishing a refuge which did not come off; R. Whelan, ' "The foolishness of preaching": rhetoric and truth in Huguenot pulpit oratory' (289–300), discusses J. Abadie's effort to make Huguenots conform to Anglicanism; J. Delumeau, 'L'Amérique du Nord, terre de toutes les promesses (XVIIe–XVIIIe siècle)' (301–07), comments on the short-lived millenarian dream of the Puritans, prefiguring the Independence of 1776; G. Bedouelle O.P., 'Catherine Par une reine luthérienne?' (311–22), discusses the *Lamentacion of a Sinner* as a document of Protestant humanism; G. Audisio, 'Un Provençal hérétique et obstiné: Turin 1594–96' (323–41), discusses Jean Dupuy's conversions and condemnation by the Inquisition; P. Denis, 'Edmond Richer, protestant malgré lui?' (343–58), shows the Catholic theologian, ultramontane at first, then with gallican and Protestant sympathies; B. Cotteret, 'Cromwell, un roi sans couronne?' (359–63), agrees with V. Hugo on Cromwell's royal aspirations; P.-E. Leroy, ' "Au nom du père . . ." Le testament de Claude Sorreau et la vocation de pasteur de son fils Isaac' (365–80): the father's wish was briefly fulfilled, then the pastor renounced his position; S. Deyon, 'S'il est nécessaire que les filles soient sçavantes", un manifeste féministe au dix-septième siècle' (381–94), discusses the position of Anna-Maria Schurman; M.-C. Pitassi, 'Etre femme et théologienne au XVIIe siècle, le cas de Marie Huber' (395–409), discusses the theological and pietist positions in her writings; O. Millet, 'Calvin en mélange: ses quelques chapitres des *Diverses leçons* de Louis Guyon empruntés au Réformateur français' (413–28), characterizes the *Leçons* as a disguised presentation of Calvin; J.-P. Pittion, 'Notre maître à tous: Aristote et la pensée réformée française au XVIIe siècle' (429–43), comments on the teaching of Aristotelian philosophy in Protestant academies, but no scholasticism; E. Van der Wall, 'Cartesianism and Coccéianism: a natural alliance?' (445–55), explains J. Cocceius's liberal Protestantism and rationalist features; F. Lebrun, 'Protestantisme et protestants français vers 1680 à travers le *Dictionnaire* de Furetière' (457–61), lists RPR words with an underlying hostility to Protestantism; J. Le Brun, 'Un jugement protestant inédit sur le débat entre Richard Simon et Jean LeClerc' (463–73), refers to an anonymous BL manuscript of Protestant origin in favour of Simon; J. Solé, 'Les débuts de la collaboration entre Adriaan van Paets, protecteur de Pierre Bayle à Rotterdam, et le gouvernement de Louis XIV (1679–1680)' (477–94), relates the diplomatic relationship with d'Avaux, French ambassador to The Hague; G. Cerny, 'Jacques Basnage and Pierre Bayle: an intimate collaboration in refugee library circles and in the affairs of the Republic of Letters (1655–1705)' (496–507), describes a personal literary friendship; E. R. Briggs, 'Bayle ou Larroque? De qui est l'*Avis important aux réfugiés* de 1690 et de 1692?' (509–24), argues for a joint authorship and outlines de Larroque's career; R. Howells, 'Jurieu in dialogue: *La Politique du clergé* and Pascal's *Lettres provinciales*' (525–33), discusses the use of fictional dialogue in polemical writings; F. Laplanche, 'Basnage critique de Richard Simon' (535–45), comments on B.'s inept criticism of S.'s scholarship; H. Bots, 'Le plaidoyer des journalistes de Hollande pour la tolérance (1684–1750)' (547–59), discusses the writings of Bayle, Locke, and Leclerc on tolerance; M. Yardeni, 'Pierre Bayle et l'histoire de France' (563–70), examines B.'s approach to the history of France in preceding centuries; P.-F. Moreau, 'La foi, la raison, l'expérience dans les *Pensées diverses*' (571–79), rejects an opposition between reason and faith and argues for belief and experience; J. Lagrée, 'La critique du stoïcisme dans le *Dictionnaire* de Bayle' (581–93), examines the article 'Chrysippe' in its implied stoicism; G. Mori, ' "athée spéculatif" selon Bayle: permanence et développement d'une idée' (595–609), discusses B.'s position with regard to atheism, emphasizing his rationalism; L. Bianchi, 'Libre pensée et tolérance: Pierre Bayle et Guy Patin' (611–21), refers to B.'s admiration for P.'s subversive ideas; W. H. Barber, 'Pierre Bayle, Benjamin Furly and Quakerism' (623–33), accounts for the cultured businessman in Rotterdam, anticlerical in his views, who became a Quaker, and had contacts with Bayle; R. H. Popkin, 'Pierre Bayle and the conversion of the Jews' (635–43), discusses conversions, with examples, as a personal process rather than a divine purpose; A. McKenna, 'Pierre Bayle et Port-Royal' (645–63), analyses B.'s writings on Port-Royal: in his article on Pascal, he approves of the refusal of natural and metaphysical proofs in religion; H. Bost, 'L'écriture ironique et critique d'un contre-révocationnaire' (665–78), comments on controversial writings around the Revocation; S. O'Cathasaigh, 'Bayle and Locke on toleration' (679–92), compares L.'s more limited and B.'s unlimited toleration; E. James, 'Schism and the spirit of toleration in Bernard Mandeville's *Free Thoughts on Religion*' (693–700), shows different forms of intolerance and M.'s own cynical but humane tolerance; G. Paganini, 'Hume et Bayle: conjonction locale et immatérialité de l'âme' (701–13), investigates B.'s impact on the *Treatise of Human Nature*; finally, H. Mason, 'Voltaire and Elie Bertrand' (715–26), examines the correspondence with the Swiss pastor and shows their common interests.

DESCARTES. René Descartes, *Le Monde, L'Homme*, ed. Annie Bitbol-Hesperiès and Jean-Pierre Verdet, Seuil, liii + 225 pp., is the first edition of the two texts in one volume: *De l'homme* of 1662 is chapter xviii of *Le Monde ou Traité de la lumière*. The volume also reproduces the *Théâtre anatomique*, with its plates that Descartes had consulted for his work.

PASCAL. *RSH*, 244, is devoted to 'Pascal, l'exercice de l'esprit', ed. C. Meurillon. H. Michon, 'Y a-t-il une science de l'homme?' (11–29), comments on P.'s distinction between 'science de l'homme'

and 'science de Dieu', and knowledge 'par le cœur'; T. M. Harring-
ton, 'Dieu comme objet de connaissance chez Pascal' (31–51),
examines the ways of knowing God, pointing to the limitations of
philosophy or Bible alone: they are given by special grace, transforming the heart; D. Descotes, 'Arithmétique et littérature' (53–79),
examines the *Potestatum numerarum Summa*, later integrated into the
Traité du Triangle, and further developed in *De l'esprit géométrique*;
L. Thirouin, 'Montaigne "demi-habile"? Fonction du recours à
Montaigne dans les *Pensées*' (81–102), from the 'liasse: raison des
effets', follows P. in his reading and criticism of Montaigne until he
has integrated the thoughts; A. McKenna, 'Deux termes-clefs du
vocabulaire pascalien: idée et fantaisie' (103–16), is a rewritten paper
1994, analysing 'idée' (*Pensées* 164 and 25 (S)), the idea of truth and
happiness, and 'fantaisie' from 455 (S), and showing influence from
Descartes and Gassendi; H. Bouchilloux, 'La méthode démonstrative
comme résidu de l'art de persuader' (117–37), studies 'De l'esprit
géométrique' and 'De l'art de persuader', linked to 'netteté', and to
will and heart in persuasion; C. Meurillon, 'Mémoire et vérité:
itinéraire pascalien' (139–57), examines forms of memory, individual
and collective, of images and truth, of things human and divine;
T. Shiokawa, '*Justus ex fide vivit* et *fides ex auditu*: deux aspects de la foi
dans l'apologétique pascalienne' (159–78), is based on *Pensée* S39,
Provinciale xviii, and the preface to the *Traité du Vide*, examining the
relation between faith and reason, and faith and knowledge; J. Plaine-
maison, 'Le combat pour la vérité: du "désir de la connaître et de la
défendre" à l'assurance de la victoire' (179–84), explains from some
Provinciales (xii, xviii) the fighting for truth with the certainty of
victory; J. R. Cole, 'Pascal's plans for the Apology: two successive
conceptions in the Two-Column Table' (15–32), based on the
authenticity of the Pascalian order of the *liasses*, examines the columns
separately and argues that they represent two successive conceptions,
the first the Augustinian 'la nature est corrompue', and the second,
'misère de l'homme sans Dieu' for the more worldly readers, pointing
to the two meanings of 'misère': unhappiness and sinfulness'; a gap
remains between the two columns. Pol Ernst, *Les Pensées de Pascal.
Géologie et stratigraphie*, Universitas–Oxford, Voltaire Foundation,
479 pp., presents a genetic and chronological assessment of the text,
having examined watermarks on the different papers used, including
cut and repasted pieces, and from there establishes a chronological
order of the stages in the apologetic project. J. A. Gallucci, 'Entre
copie et autographe: le texte des *Pensées* de Pascal', *TLit*, 9:65–74,
discusses the two copies of the text, with emphasis on *Pyrrhonisme*, and
suggests that the reader would benefit from having the *texte authentique*
as well as the copies available together. A. Krailsheimer, 'Some

thoughts on translating the *Pensées* again thirty years on', Smith, *Essays*, 25–28, reflects on the differences Pascal scholarship has made since his first translation in 1966, and on the quotations from Biblical texts, his choice being the Authorised Version.

THE EIGHTEENTH CENTURY

By D. A. Desserud, *Associate Professor of Politics,*
University of New Brunswick at Saint John,
and J. E. Fowler, *French Section, University of Kent, Canterbury*

1. General

CULTURE AND THOUGHT. D. Bates, 'The epistemology of error in late Enlightenment France', *ECS*, 29:307–27. The Enlightenment meant to remove error from science and society, but did it dispel or expel that which contradicted its understanding of truth? J. DeJean, 'Did the seventeenth century invent our *Fin de Siècle*? Or, the creation of the Enlightenment that we may at last be leaving behind', *CI*, 22:790–816. M. Delon, 'Réhabilitation des préjuges et crise des Lumières', *RGI*, 1995, no. 1:143–56, looks at the treatment of prejudice in the 18th c.

A. Fraysse and P. Fraysse, 'Entre psychiatrie et histoire des mentalités: le cas d'Antoine Bois, médecin pendu à Toulouse en 1780', *AMid*, 108:189–200. E. A. Williams, 'Medicine in the civic life of eighteenth-century Montpellier', *Bulletin of the History of Medicine*, 70:205–32, argues that Montpellier was a 'medical town': that is, medicine and its institutions created a sense of communal solidarity as did similar traditions and institutions of religious life in other communities. But the analogy is more profound than this, for the medical profession helped overcome some of the bitter divisions between Catholics and Protestants, and even rich versus poor. This helped mitigate the violence that tore apart other communities during the Revolution. J. Merrick, 'Impotence in court and at court', *SECC*, 25:187–202. notes that impotence was more than a medical curiosity for Enlightenment figures: it had profound impact on the administration of ecclesiastic law (annulments could be granted if impotence was 'proven', often in open court), and for court politics and intrigue. Was Louis XVI impotent or not? C. Adams, 'A choice not to wed? Unmarried women in eighteenth-century France', *Journal of Social History*, 29:883–94. C. Jones, 'The great chain of buying: medical advertisement, the bourgeois public sphere, and the origins of the French Revolution', *AHR*, 101:13–40. James S. Pritchard, *Anatomy of a Naval Disaster: The 1746 French Naval Expedition to North America*, Montreal, McGill–Queen's U.P., 1995, xvi + 322 pp., provides a rare insight both into the 18th-c. world of transatlantic travel, and Louis XV's court politics (particularly Maurepas and his desire for family advancement) which launched and were ultimately responsible for the failure of the d'Enville expedition, the 'largest French naval expedition mounted during the War of the Austrian Succession'. D. M. McMahon, 'The birthplace of the Revolution: public space and political community in the Palais-Royal of Louis-Philippe-Joseph d'Orléans, 1781–1789', *French History*, 10:1–29. S. M. Peterson, 'The social origins of Royalist political violence in directorial Bordeaux', *ib.*, 56–85.

T. M. Luckett, 'Crises financières dans la France du XVIIIe siècle', *RHMC*, 43:266–92, examines the *disette d'argent*, a sort of financial crisis that occurred periodically throughout the *ancien régime*. But the term has created some confusion. L. provides a detailed history, with chronology, and an economic explanation for what these mini-crises were, what caused them, and what effect they had. This article certainly contributes to our understanding of the context in which contemporary writers were writing on economic matters, but nevertheless it provides few surprises. Steven L. Kaplan, *The Bakers of Paris and the Bread Question, 1700–1775*, Durham, Duke U.P., xviii + 761 pp. There is much more to this book than its (nevertheless fascinating) title might indicate. K. discusses bread in 18th-c. France from every conceivable angle: agriculture and technology, but most importantly, politics, culture, and mythology. This well-researched and weighty book provides context and insights to much more than the Flour War. Pierre Saint-Amand, **The Laws of Hostility: Politics, Violence, and the Enlightenment*, Minneapolis, Minnesota U.P., xi + 180 pp. John D. Woodbridge, **Revolt in Prerevolutionary France: The Prince de Conti's Conspiracy Against Louis XV, 1755–1757*, Baltimore, Johns Hopkins U.P., 1995, xvii + 242 pp. Vesna C. Petrovich, **Connaissance et rêve(rie) dans le discours des Lumières*, NY–Bern, Lang, xii + 222 pp.

R. A. Lodge, 'Stereotypes of vernacular pronunciation in 17th–18th-century Paris', *ZRP*, 112:205–31. Bernard Cerquiglini, *L'accent du souvenir*, Minuit, 1995, 165 pp., is a fascinating discussion of the introduction of *l'accent circonflexe* in 1740 by the Académie française.

D. G. Thompson, 'The Lavalette Affair and the Jesuit Superiors', *FH*, 10:206–39. J. de Viguerie, 'Les catéchismes enseignés en France au XVIIIe siècle. Première approche', *RHEF*, 82:85–108, examines a curious contradiction: the 18th c. was the *grande époque de la catéchisation*, but also a time of tremendous growth in irreligiousness.

M. Hyde, 'Confounding conventions: gender ambiguity and François Boucher's painted pastorals', *ECS*, 30:25–57, examines B.'s paintings of pastoral romance and sees in them the context of the anti-rococo reaction of Rousseau and Diderot, among others, who regarded his 'effeminate' portraits as examples of corruption and of the loss of virile virtue. H. argues that this 'very ambiguity indicates that the categories of gender operative at this historical moment were not unilaterally fixed, not the same in all contexts, but rather, were fluid, contingent and in flux' (48). Mary D. Sheriff, *The Exceptional Woman. Elisabeth Vigée-Lebrun and the Cultural Politics of Art*, Chicago U.P., xiv + 353 pp. R. Rand, 'Civil and natural contract in Greuze's *L'Accordée de village*', *GBA*:221–34. M. Oppenheimer, 'Nisa Villers, née Lemoine (1774–1821)', *ib.*, 165–80. J. Baillio, 'Vie et œuvre de Marie Victoire Lemoine (1754–1820)', *ib.*, 125–64. M. Wolff, 'An early painting by Greuze and its literary associations', *Burlington Magazine*, 580–85. P. Stein, 'Boucher's chinoiseries: some new sources', *ib.*, 598–604. C. Clements, 'The Duc d'Antin, the royal administration of pictures, and the painting competition of 1727', *Art Bulletin*, 78:647–62. L. Walsh, 'The expressive face: manifestations of sensibility in eighteenth-century French art', *Art History*, 19:523–50. JoLynn Edwards, **Alexandre-Joseph Paillet: expert et marchand de tableaux à la fin du XVIIIe siècle*, Arthéna, 376 pp.

Geoffrey V. Sutton, *Science for a Polite Society: Gender, Culture, and the Demonstration of Enlightenment*, Boulder, Colorado, Westview Press, 1995, xiii + 391 pp. The clever subtitle refers to the popular parlour-room displays of electricity and other things that flash and go bang. These had a profound effect, S. argues, on the fascination and acceptance of new science in polite society. The salons, then, become important venues for the nurturing of Enlightenment science. There is a particularly interesting chapter on Émilie du Châtelet. P. F. Rice, ***'Stamitz and Rameau: a possible musical influence', pp. 59–74 of *TransAtlantic Crossings: Eighteenth-Century Explorations*, ed. Donald Nichol, St John's, Newfoundland, Memorial U.P., 1995, 117 pp.

LITERARY HISTORY, PUBLISHING, AND JOURNALISM. *Going Public: Women and Publishing in Early Modern France*, ed. Elizabeth C. Goldsmith and Dena Goodman, Ithaca, Cornell U.P., 1995, viii + 249 pp., is a collection of essays looking at the ways and means by which women in the 17th and 18th c. distributed their writings. U. Schuttler-Rudolph, ***'Französische Russlandpublizistik zur Zeit der Aufklärung (1754–1789): Eine Bibliographie', *Das Achtzehnte Jahrhundert*, 19, 1995:118–28, looks at the treatment of Russia in French periodicals during the thirty years before the Revolution.

2. NON-FICTION
INDIVIDUAL AUTHORS

MME DE CAMPIN. C. R. Monfort and J. T. Quintana, 'Madame Campin's *Institution d'Education*: a revolution in the education of women', *AJFS*, 33:30–44.

CHALLE. F. Deloffre and W. Trapnell, 'The identity of the "Militare philosophe": further evidence', *StV*, 341:27–60, present C. as the one and only author of the *Difficultés sur la religion proposées au père Malebranche*, 'the most intimate, moving and significant testimony to the "crise de conscience européenne"' (p. 27). Will this careful and well constructed argument resolve once and for all an intriguing debate that has puzzled for 85 years?

MME DE CHARRIÈRE. Medha N. Karmarkar, *Madame de Charrière et la révolution des idées*, NY, Lang, 241 pp.

CONDILLAC. F. Crispini, 'Intellectual history, history of ideas, history of linguistic ideas. The case of Condillac', pp. 141–50 of *Historical Roots of Linguistic Theories*, ed. Lia Formigari and Daniele Gambarara, Philadelphia–Amsterdam, Benjamins, 1995, viii + 309 pp.

CONDORCET. L. Gillard, 'Condorcet, deux autres paradoxes?' *AESC*, 51:201–14.

MME DU COUDRAY. N. R. Gelbart, 'The monarchy's midwife who left no memoirs', *FHS*, 19:997–1023. Considerable, albeit informed, speculation is required to fill in the many gaps in our knowledge of du C., the remarkably progressive midwife and author of the textbook, *Abrégé de l'art des accouchements*. Some of this speculation is distracting and of questionable importance, but otherwise G. provides a fascinating study which is less a history of medical science than it is a history of medical education, and so best understood in Enlightenment terms.

MME DUPIN. S. Dangeville, 'Deux "articles" inédits de l'*Ouvrage sur les femmes* de Madame Dupin', *Études Jean-Jacques Rousseau*, 7, 1995:183–204.

ESTÈVE. G. Delpierre, 'Chardin Péruvien: *Les Dialogues sur les arts entre un artiste américain et un amateur français* de Pierre Estève', *RHLF*, 95, 1995:294–305.

MME DE GRAFFIGNY. E. Showalter, 'Graffigny at Cirey: a fraud exposed', *FrF*, 21:29–44. D. W. Smith, 'La composition et la publication des contes de Mme de Graffigny', *FS*, 50:275–84. J. Sgard, 'Françoise de Graffigny lectrice de Prévost', *TLit*, 9:127–36. V. L. Grayson, 'The genesis and reception of Mme de Graffigny's *Lettres d'une Péruvienne* and *Cénie*', *StV*, 336:1–135, is a well-documented and scholarly study which charts the differing reputations of the works in question. J.-A. McEachern and D. Smith, 'Mme de Graffigny's *Lettres d'une péruvienne*: identifying the first edition', *ECentF*, 9:21–35.

LA HARPE. H. Nakagawa, 'Une conclusion sur le temps des philosophes: La Harpe', *ELLF*, 66, 1995:61–74.

LA METTRIE.   *Machine Man and Other Writings*, trans. Ann Thomson, CUP, xxx + 179 pp.

LAVOISIER.   B. Bensaude-Vincent, 'Between history and memory: centennial and bicentennial images of Lavoisier', *Isis*, 87:481–99.

LESPINASSE.   B. Melançon, 'Du corps épistolaire. Les correspondances de Julie de Lespinasse', *OL*, 51:321–33.

MAISTRE.   G. Garrard, 'Joseph de Maistre's civilization and its discontents', *JHI*, 57:429–46, argues that the reactionary M., more royalist than the King, more Catholic than the Pope, displayed remarkable prescience of Freudian psychology; but it is not clear why Freud is a valuable point of comparison, since the Freud connection, which is soon dropped in any case, is tenuous at best. Far better is G.'s analysis of M.'s rejection of Rousseau, of Voltaire, and his affinity to Hobbes, less anachronistic comparisons to be sure.

MORELLET.   D. Medlin, 'André Morellet's library', *Libraries and Culture*, 31:574–602.

PIRON.   P. Verèb, 'Alexis Piron défenseur des Modernes ou un épisode inédit de la querelle des Anciens et des Modernes', *RHLF*, 95, 1995:282–93.

POTIER.   R. Toupin, *Les Écrits de Pierre Potier*, Ottawa U.P., xxi + 1329 pp.

SAINT-SIMON.   P. Bayley, 'Saint-Simon and the coronation at Rheims: ritual, ideology and writing', *StV*, 341:1–26, notes how S.-S.'s meticulous presentations of the coronation at Rheims, a memoir 'at the cross-roads of prose genres', convince and establish trust. Does this particular care serve, however, as a rhetorical device, and so convince and even deceive? M. Stefanovska, 'A monumental triptych: Saint-Simon's *Parallèle des trois premiers rois Bourbons*', *FHS*, 19:927–42, seeks to look less at the 'exactitude' of the work and more at the 'ideological and conceptual' issues influencing S.-S.

MME DE STAËL.   B. G. Smith, 'History and genius: the narcotic, erotic, and baroque life of Germaine de Staël', *FHS*, 19:1059–82.

DIDEROT AND THE ENCYCLOPÉDIE

WORKS.   *Œuvres, Tome IV. Esthétique-Théâtre*, ed. L. Versini, Laffont, 1663 pp., is now available: a scholarly and affordable edition covering the *Salons* and the drama. *Paradoxe sur le comédien*, ed. Jane Marsh Dieckmann, Hermann, 126 pp., puts at the disposal of a wider readership the scholarly work devoted to the publication of the *Paradoxe* by Hermann in the definitive *Œuvres complètes*. The volume also includes *Observations sur Garrick* and *Observations sur un ouvrage intitulé: Traité du mélodrame*.   The editor draws on a previously unpublished MS of the *Observations sur Garrick* which may have been corrected by D. himself, arguing that 'l'intérêt majeur de ce manuscrit est de présenter un texte intermédiaire entre les *Observations sur Garrick* et le premier état du *Paradoxe*' (119).

THOUGHT, INFLUENCE, INTELLECTUAL RELATIONSHIPS. Frank A. Kafker, *The Encyclopedists as a Group: A Collective Biography of the Authors of the Encyclopédie*, Oxford, Voltaire Foundation, 215 pp. Peter H. Kaufman, *The Solidarity of a Philosophe: Diderot, Russia and the Soviet Union*, NY, Lang, 198 pp. Béatrice Didier, *Alphabet et raison: Le paradoxe des dictionnaires au XVIIIe siècle*, PUF, 283 pp., examines the tension between the irrational, alphabetic organization of Enlightenment dictionaries and the rationalistic aspirations of the period. Paying detailed attention to Bayle, Voltaire, and the *encyclopédistes*, the study raises issues of the broadest relevance for understanding the contradictions of the Enlightenment. Y. Bénot, 'L'esclavagisme dans la 4e édition de l'*Histoire des deux Indes* (1820–1821)', *DhS*, 28:325–35, effects a comparison between the 1780 text and the posthumous edition in order to reveal extensive modifications of the passages on slavery contained in Book XI, modifications which tend to soften the position adopted by Diderot. A. Strugnell, 'Postmodernism versus Enlightenment and the problem of the Other in Raynal's *Histoire des deux Indes*', *StV*, 341:169–82, is an excellent piece which argues that D.'s contributions to the work, whilst showing that Enlightenment critique can imply a certain imperialist appropriation of alterity, nevertheless ultimately subvert postmodernism in advance by showing that certain universal values are vital to the political empowerment of the Other. This involves a nuanced consideration of the treatment of two different types of alterity — Eastern and British — in the *Histoire*. J. Lough, 'Did the *philosophes* take over the Académie française?', *ib.*, 336:153–94, reviews Lucien Brunel's thesis that there was a 'conquête de l'Académie' on the part of the *philosophes* in order to conclude that it is somewhat overstated. Whilst D.'s case is deliberately excluded, the piece nevertheless helps to adjust the specialist's perspective on an aspect of the social and intellectual climate in which the *encyclopédistes* and the *philosophes* moved. Benoît Melançon, *Diderot Epistolier*, Quebec, Fides, 509 pp., systematically examines D.'s letters both for their treatment of themes such as absence, time, self-representation, and triangularization, and in order to move towards a poetics of private correspondence. The author also raises interesting questions concerning the relationship between the spheres of private and public and the kinship of letter-writing to the emergence of autobiography and the *journal intime*. This is a study which well deserves to be read and opens up important avenues for future research.

THOUGHT AND PROSE FICTION. N. Cronk, 'Reading expectations: the narration of Hume in *Jacques le fataliste*', *MLR*, 91:330–41, puts forward an interesting argument according to which D.'s novel, no less than Hume's *Enquiry concerning Human Understanding*, suggests that free will and determinism can be reconciled by shifting the analysis from the world to the individual's perception of it. In D.'s case it is the implied reader who is 'freely compelled' (p. 341) to question the world of fiction. Thus Humean compatibilism is presented as a vital part of the intellectual context of *Jacques le fataliste*. J. E. Fowler, 'Competing causalities: family and convent in Diderot's *La Religieuse*', *ECent*, 37:75–93, raises the question of whether the novel's anti-conventual thesis is undercut by its exploration of family relationships, actual and metaphorical.

ÆSTHETICS. Julie Wegner Arnold, **Art Criticism as Narrative*, NY, Lang, 161 pp., deals with Diderot's 1767 *Salon*. J. C. Hayes, 'Sequence and simultaneity in Diderot's *Promenade Vernet* and *Leçons de clavecin*', *ECS*, 29:291–305, is an interesting reading which argues that the two texts examined offer us 'a way to go beyond the confining, dichotomizing logic that the bleaker critics of Enlightenment thought have focused on' by undoing the conceptual distinction between 'sequential discursivity and panoptic systematicity' (p. 302).

MONTESQUIEU

S. M. Mason, 'Montesquieu's vision of Europe and its European context', *StV*, 341:61–87, continues her series on M. and commerce. In this perceptive and tightly argued piece, she demonstrates how a wider reading of M. on international (and in particular imperial) commerce transforms the 'one dimensional profile of M. as a herald of commercial republicanism' (p. 66). Instead, M. emerges as one who understood and linked commerce to Enlightenment. In this way, M.'s theories of commerce and its effects on the citizen fit perfectly with his theory of commerce and its effects on the nation.

Claude Morilhat, *Montesquieu: politique et richesses*, PUF, 122 pp.; and Gérard Bergeron, *Tout était dans Montesquieu: Une relecture de 'L'Esprit des lois'*, Harmattan, 266 pp., are two books designed for the general reader, but both of interest to the specialist as well. While neither will astound M. scholars, both serve to demonstrate the profundity of M. and the utility of reading or re-reading him in these interesting political times.

Rebecca Kingston, *Montesquieu and the Parlement of Bordeaux*, Geneva, Droz, 329 pp., is a reworking of the author's doctoral thesis into an intelligent and well-crafted study which fills a significant gap in M. studies. K. integrates M.'s *parlement* experience and the 'new insights in the field of criminal justice to his understanding of the dynamics of human association' that came with it, with his political philosophy, specifically his treatment of diversity. An important contribution. D. Casajus, 'Montesquieu, Tocqueville, Durkheim: variations autour d'une typologie', *L'Homme*, 140:7–24. B. Binoche, *'Montesquieu et la crise de la rationalité historique', *RGI*, 1995, no. 1:31–53.

ROUSSEAU

CORRESPONDENCE, WORKS, BIOGRAPHY. Clare Elmquist, *Rousseau: père et fils*, Odense U.P., 277 pp.

THOUGHT AND INTELLECTUAL RELATIONSHIPS. The winter issue of *NLH* (no. 27) is dedicated to Todorov and, primarily, his reading of Rousseau. T. Todorov, 'Living alone together' (1–14), discusses R.'s introduction of a new and revolutionary concept of 'a man as a being who *needs others*' (p. 2). T.'s reading is engaging and challenging, and in places delightfully controversial. He is rejoined by: P. H. Werhane, 'Community and individuality' (15–24); F. Ferguson, 'A reply to Tzvetan Todorov's "Living alone together"' (25–34); and S. A. Mitchell, '"Living together alone or together": commentary on Tzvetan Todorov's "Living alone together"' (35–42). Also responding are: R. Wokler, 'Todorov's otherness' (43–47), who quite sharply challenges T.'s reading of R., disputing several key sections in T.'s argument; G. S. Morson, 'Misanthropology' (57–72); and S. Justman, 'Regarding others' (83–94). T. replies in 'The gaze and the fray' (95–106). A lively and refreshingly stimulating debate. R. A. Jones, 'Durkheim, realism, and Rousseau', *Journal of the History of the Behavioural Sciences*, 32:330–53, and M. S. Cladis, 'What can we hope for? Rousseau and Durkheim on human nature', *ib.*, 456–72, note the importance of R. in the development of Durkheim's sociology. C. Kelly, 'Rousseau's philosophic dream', *Interpretation*, 23:417–44, argues that R. scholars fail to appreciate the diversity of his works, concentrating instead, for example, on his political writings at the expense of his writings on music. One such neglected work is R.'s 'Fiction or allegorical fragment on revelation'. Claude Wacjman, *Les Jugements de la critique sur la 'folie' de J.-J. Rousseau: représentations et interprétations 1760–1990*, StV, 337, viii + 248 pp. A. O. Rorty, 'The two faces of stoicism: Rousseau and Freud', *JHP*, 34:335–56, looks at how both R. and F. adapted stoicism for quite different therapeutic purposes. Frederick W. Dame, *Jean-Jacques Rousseau and Political Literature in Colonial America*, Lewiston–Lampeter, Mellen, ix + 127 pp. A. M. Melzer, 'The origin of the counter-Enlightenment: Rousseau and the new religion of sincerity', *American Political Science Review*,

90:344–60. Paul Audi, *De la veritable philosophie: Rousseau au commencement*, Le Nouveau Commerce, 1994, 158 pp. Roger Barny, *Le Droit naturel à l'épreuve de l'histoire: Jean-Jacques Rousseau dans la Révolution (débats politiques et sociaux)*, Les Belles Lettres, 1995, 352 pp.

Études Jean-Jacques Rousseau, 7, is titled 'Politique de Rousseau' and contains papers by: R. Polin, 'Jean-Jacques Rousseau, philosophe de l'histoire de la culture' (9–26); G. Lafrance, 'L'interprétation éthico-juridique du *Contrat social*' (27–44); S. Goyard-Fabre, 'La guerre et le droit international dans la philosophie de Rousseau' (45–78); J. Ferrari, 'De la religion civile dans la pensée politique de J.-J. Rousseau' (79–100); A. Philonenko, 'Rousseau et le roi de Pologne' (101–16); G. Allard, 'La pensée politique des *Dialogues*: le juste, l'injuste et le juge' (117–42); J.-M Beyssade, '"*Sophie et mon champ*" ou *La Politique des modernes*' (143–60); and J.-P. Marcos, 'La question de la "loi naturelle" selon Rousseau', (161–82). Also included is D. Marie, 'Correspondance et autobiographie. Genèse réelle et genèse imaginaire de l'idée de *complot* dans deux lettres de J.-J. Rousseau' (205–67). M. Evans, 'Freedom in modern society: Rousseau's challenge', *Inquiry*, 38, 1995:233–55, argues that the puzzling paradox contained in *Social Contract*, that the 'individual can be free and yet obligated to obey the state' can be reconciled when we stop trying to impose a model of individuality and hope on R.'s theory. In other words, the paradox is ours, not R.'s.

A. D'Atri, 'The theory of interjections in Vico and Rousseau', trans. C. Dodd, pp.115–28 of *Historical Roots of Linguistic Theories*, ed Lia Formigari and Daniele Gambarara, Philadelphia–Amsterdam, Benjamins, 1995, viii + 309 pp. Raymond Trousson and Frédéric S. Eigeldinger, *Dictionnaire de Jean-Jacques Rousseau*, Geneva, Slatkine, 961 pp. M. Cladis, *'Rousseau's soteriology: deliverance at the crossroads', *Religious Studies*, 32:79–91.

LITERARY. N. Graap, 'Das Gemeinwesen von Clarens: Zum Verhältnis zwischen Utopie, "Vertu" und "Amour" in Jean-Jacques Rousseau's *Julie ou la Nouvelle Héloïse*', *LJb*, 36, 1995:63–81. Two pieces by J. Still: 'Questioning commerce: the case of Rousseau's *Du contrat social*', *BJECS*, 19:33–46; and 'Rousseau's La Nouvelle Héloïse: passion, reserve, and the gift', *MLR*, 91:40–52, which examines inequality in both its economic and sexual sense; the first is unacceptable to R., apparently the second is not. The author presents the work as a dynamic political utopia; an interesting thesis, but she spends far too much time justifying this choice, and her justifications distract from her central argument. Despite this quibble, S. presents a strong and interesting argument. T. M. Scanlan, 'The portrayal of Christopher Columbus and the natives of San Salvador in Rousseau's *La Découverte du Nouveau Monde*', *OL*, 51:257–66, observes how R.'s libretto for his 1739 opera gets little attention from critics; but a study of the way R. uses the Noble Savage theme in this work reveals interesting connections between the libretto and R.'s later works. V. Reinking, 'Rousseau's bliss: jouissances', *StV*, 1995, 332:335–48. W. A. Ulmer, 'Rousseau's *Emile* and Wordsworth's Drowned Man of Esthwaite', *ELN*, 1995, 33:15–19. Yves Vargas, *Introduction à l'"Emile" de Jean-Jacques Rousseau*, PUF, 1995, vii + 343 pp.

VOLTAIRE

WORKS. The new critical edition of V.'s works is still in progress. This year sees the publication of *The English Essays of 1727*, ed. R. A. Waller, 614 pp., and *Histoire de Charles XII*, ed. Gunnar von Proschwitz, Oxford, The Voltaire Foundation, 701 pp. Aimed at a wider public is *L'Ingénu*, ed. Édouard Guitton, LGF, 282pp. This convenient edition also includes: *La Bastille, Épître à Uranie, Entretiens d'un sauvage et d'un bachelier, Relation de la mort du Chevalier de La Barre*, and extracts from the correspondence of 1762–67.

THOUGHT AND INFLUENCE. *Voltaire, The Enlightenment and The Comic Mode: Essays in Honor of Jean Sareil*, ed. Maxine G. Cutler, NY, Lang, 284 pp. M. Mervaud, 'Les *Anecdotes sur le czar Pierre le Grand* de Voltaire: genèse, sources, forme littéraire', *StV*, 341:89–126, examines V.'s increasingly idealized representation of Peter, and suggests that the *Anecdotes* might be viewed as narrative rather than history. A number of critics have been interested in pursuing connections between V. and less well-known figures. P. de Gain, 'L'influence de Las Casas dans l'*Essai sur les mœurs* de Voltaire', *ib.*, 139–49, shows that L.C.'s scathing account of the European conquest of South America is treated by V. as a reliable source. G. Haroche-Bouzinac, 'Voltaire et Mme de Sévigné: un éloge en contrepoint', *RHLF*, 96:394–403, examines V.'s guarded appreciation of Mme de Sévigné's letters, arguing that his comments betray above all his expectations of Frenchness on the one hand and femininity on the other. G. Gargett, 'Religion, journalism and the struggle against *philosophie*: Trublet at the *Journal chrétien* (1758–1760)', *StV*, 336:195–331, brings out Trublet's surprisingly conciliatory attitude to the *philosophes* and to V. in particular. M. S. Rivière, 'Voltaire and La Beaumelle: a detrimental, yet mutually beneficial, literary duel', *AJFS*, 33:10–29, explores the effects on V. of the lesser writer's 1753 edition of *Le Siècle de Louis XIV*, which expressed criticism as well as appreciation of V.'s skill as historian. J. Vercruysse, 'D'Astier, une bonne étoile, filante, de Voltaire: une correspondance inédite de décembre 1764–janvier 1765', *StV*, 341:159–64, shows how d'A. who was briefly French consul in Amsterdam, helped V. deny

authorship of the *Dictionnaire philosophique* and the *Evangile de la Raison*.
A. Owen Aldridge, 'Voltaire and Wesley', *ib.*, 151–57, discusses how
Wesley attacked a 1778 English edition of the works of V., who was
then satirically defended in a piece whose author claimed to be the
French writer's ghost. It throws light on the reception of V. in
England. Interest in V.'s correspondence also continues. Deirdre
Dawson, **Voltaire's Correspondence: An Epistolary Novel*, NY, Lang,
190 pp. M.-H. Cotoni, 'Une lettre oubliée de Voltaire à Frédéric II',
StV, 341:165–67, presents a previously unpublished letter of 1777,
especially significant for specialists as this is a year for which only
three of V.'s letters to Frederick were previously available.

LITERARY. Jean-Marie Roulin, 'Le grand siècle au futur: Voltaire,
de la prophétie épique à l'écriture de l'Histoire', *RHLF*, 96:918–33,
examines the tension between prophecy and history in *La Henriade*,
and suggests consequences for reading V.'s historical writings.
D. Lévy, 'L'ironie de Voltaire dans le chapitre 16 de *L'Ingénu*', *StV*,
341:127–38, analyses in detail the chapter indicated in order to
disengage four structures of irony; this is a useful close reading with
broader relevance for V.'s narrative. *RTr*, 51, contains several pieces
on Voltaire. J.Sgard, 'De Cunégonde à Julie' (121–30), explores the
implications of V.'s vitriolic attack on *La Nouvelle Héloïse*, suggesting
especially that he sees in Julie a defiant heroine or anti-establishment
figure who shocks his conservative side, whilst Cunégonde is a
'victime résignée' (130); N. Fournier, '*Zaïre*: Voltaire et l'intertexte
racinien' (11–36), circumscribes the full extent of Racine's influence
on V.'s style in *Zaïre*, whilst presenting the play as particularly unusual
and revealing in this connection given the speed with which it was
composed; and M. Lombardi, 'Beaumarchais et la "méthode de
Zadig"' (39–53), compares chapter 3 of V.'s *conte* with Beaumarchais's *La Gaîté de l'Amour français* in order to suggest that both authors
are occupied in different ways with the possibility of deducing truth
from visual clues.

3. PROSE FICTION

GENERAL

**Tradition in Transition: Women Writers, Marginal Texts and the Eighteenth-
Century Canon*, ed. Alvaro Ribeiro and James G. Basker, OUP, 350 pp.
John W. Howland, **The Letter Form and the French Enlightenment: The
Epistolary Paradox*, NY–Bern, Lang, 197 pp. **Romans de femmes du
XVIIIe siècle*, ed. Raymond Trousson, Laffont, 1180 pp.

INDIVIDUAL AUTHORS

BERNARD. N. Ekstein, 'Appropriation and gender; the case of Catherine Bernard and Bernard de Fontenelle', *ECS*, 30:59–80, discusses the attribution of Catherine Bernard's tragedy *Brutus* to Fontenelle, and generalizes the issue in terms of the appropriation by men of texts written by women.

BERNARDIN DE SAINT-PIERRE. M. Cook, 'Childhood in the works of Bernardin de Saint-Pierre', *RoS*, 28:17–27.

CHALLE. Two excellent scholarly editions with introductions and notes will help meet the continuing renewal of interest in C. These are: *Mémoires, Correspondance complète, Rapports sur l'Acadie et autres pièces*, ed. Frédéric Deloffre and Jacques Popin, Geneva, Droz, 764 pp.; and *Les Illustres Françaises*, ed. Jacques Cormier and Frédéric Deloffre, Librairie Générale Française, 710 pp. Anne de Sola, 'Dialogue et mimésis dans *Les Illustres Françaises*', *StV*, 341:183–223, is a very useful piece which explores C.'s literary techniques in a narratological manner and shows his pivotal role in integrating French novelistic tradition with a use of *sensibilité* which heralds the practice of later writers.

CRÉBILLON FILS. The resurgence of interest in C. continues. *Le Sopha*, ed. Raymond Trousson, Paris–Geneva, Slatkine, 362 pp., is a very affordable edition with a sound if brief introduction, but lacks notes. *RHLF*, 96.1, is devoted to C. and contains contributions of a generally high quality informed by a wide range of approaches. J. Sgard, 'Catalogue des œuvres de Claude Crébillon' (3–20), draws on the recent publication of the correspondence of Mme de Graffigny in order to undertake the task of drawing up a more reliable corpus of C.'s works than has yet been available; A. Feinsilber and E. Corp, 'Crébillon fils et Marie-Henriette Stafford, histoire anglaise. Avec un lettre inédite' (21–44), help fill in gaps in C.'s biography; M.-H. Cotoni, 'Les *égarements* de deux néophytes dans le monde: La Vallée et Meilcour' (45–70), which compares C.'s *roman d'apprentissage* with Marivaux's *Paysan parvenu*, throws new light on both texts; P. Hartmann, 'Education et aliénation dans *Les Égarements du cœur et de l'esprit*' (71–97), is a rich analysis which situates C.'s best-known work in relation to chapter 4 of Montesquieu's *L'Esprit des lois*, Lord Chesterfield's letters to his son, and several typical *manuels de civilité* of the time, and which concludes that in the case of C.'s hero/narrator the writing of narrative is the only education which does not lead to alienation; F. Juranville, 'Un roman d'apprentissage au XVIIIe siècle: écriture et gai savoir dans *Les Égarements du cœur et de l'esprit*' (98–110), argues the existence of an ironic distance in C.'s text between Meilcour the narrator and Meilcour the hero, a distance which betokens a certain optimism; and T. Viart, 'Le Sylphe, ou les lumières d'une allégorie' (111–21), suggests that the allegorization of desire in *Le Sylphe* is significant for the evolution of C.'s later writing. Similarly, *RTr*, 51, contains a cluster of pieces on Crébillon. Françoise Gevrey, 'Le ridicule dans *Les Égarements du cœur et de l'esprit* (55–69), argues that C.'s representation of the ridiculous develops from that of La Bruyère, though C. introduces new distinctions and exploits the dramatic and æsthetic potential of the theme; J.-P. Seguin, 'Variation des styles et choix lexicaux dans les *Égarements du cœur et de l'esprit*' (71–85), is an important discussion which demonstrates C.'s construction of a 'registre lexical' (p. 72) through which he attributes a distinct style of speaking to different characters, whilst maintaining a distance between on the one hand the characters and on the other the narratorial voice and perspective; V. Géraud, 'La "parlure" de Versac', (87–103), examines Versac's jargon in order to demonstrate its theatricality and its potential to confer power. Versac transforms the hyperbole of the *petit-maître* into trenchant irony — and yet sentiment survives intact, in the *non-dit* of such discourse; and R. Jomand-Baudry, 'Lectures du récit dans *Ah quel conte!* de Crébillon fils' (105–19) examines the self-reflexive aspects of the work, in order to show that C. incites the reader to construct meaning as multiple and fluctuating.

CRÉBILLON PÈRE. M. Soulatges, 'Idoménée de Fénelon à Crébillon père. Du statut ambigu donné à l'expérience tragique', *DhS*, 28:385–96, compares Fénelon's representation of the infanticide king in *Les Aventures de Télémaque* with C.'s characterization of the same figure in his first tragedy. In contrast to F.'s Idomeneus, that of C. achieves transcendance in the face of absurdity.

MME D'ÉPINAY. *Les Conversations d'Émilie*, ed. Rosena Davison, Geneva, Voltaire Foundation, 528 pp. C. Cazenobe, 'L'Histoire de madame de Montbrillant: un laboratoire des formes romanesques', *RHLF*, 96.2:229–45, asserts that it is time to recognize Mme d'E.'s novelistic art: the text in question is not a disguised memoir but an experimentation in genre and literary technique.

LACLOS. *Les Liaisons dangereuses*, ed. René Pomeau, Flammarion, 549 pp. J. Vanpée, 'Dangerous Liaisons 2: the Riccoboni-Laclos sequel', *ECentF*, 9:51–70, examines the 1782 exchange of letters between L. and Mme Riccoboni, which L. attached to the 1787 Nantes edition. L.'s editorial decision proves interesting in more than one way: we can observe Riccoboni insisting on reading L.'s portrayal of the sexes as a woman, and the double preface of the original novel is mirrored by a double postface composed of the letters.

PRÉVOST. *Manon Lescaut*, ed. Mireille Cornud-Peyron, Hachette, 287 pp., is a convenient edition which includes notes and a summary of themes.

RESTIF DE LA BRETONNE. Daniel Baruch, **Restif de la Bretonne*, Fayard, 341 pp., is a biographical study. Peter Wagstaff, *Memory and Desire: Rétif de la Bretonne, Autobiography and Utopia*, Amsterdam–Atlanta, Rodopi, 177 pp., is a largely psychological reading which takes us through themes such as exile, utopia and family romance. The author amply demonstrates his thesis that R. is driven back from an unstable dynamic world into an excessively closed, rural utopia. Moreover, a connection is established between familial and utopian themes on the one hand and style and structure on the other. Hence the 'endlessly reiterative layering of time and tense, memory and foresight' characteristic of *Monsieur Nicolas* allows the creation of 'a self-referential utopian space' (p. 153). F. Bassani, 'Jean-Jacques Rousseau et Rétif de la Bretonne, ou sensibilité et mémoire dans les *Confessions* et *Monsieur Nicolas*', *RTr*, 51 : 227–38. M. Björkman, 'Rétif de la Bretonne en Suède', *DhS*, 28 : 455–70, explores the circumstances within which a Swedish readership gained access to R. in translation.

MME RICCOBONI. F. Berger Sturzer, 'Literary portraits and cultural critique in the novels of Marie-Jeanne Riccoboni', *FS*, 50 : 400–12, suggests that the author's use of portraits grounds a critique both feminist and cultural, and thereby anticipates the changes of the Revolution.

SADE. Colette V. Michael, **Sade: His Ethics and Rhetoric*, NY, Lang, 249 pp. Jean-Pierre Mourey, *Philosophies et pratiques du détail: Hegel, Ingres, Sade, et quelques autres*, Seyssel, Champ Vallon, 174 pp., contains far less reference to S. than the title suggests, but may be of interest to those who wish to see his obsession for the corporeal part over the whole briefly discussed in terms of the history of æsthetics and the ambiguous function of the detail (sometimes docile, sometimes disruptive) within that history.

SOUZA. M. Karmarkar, 'Narrative transvestism and male/female friendship in Adélaïde de Souza's *Adèle de Sénange*', *WIFS*, 4 : 40–49 investigates how the use by Souza of a male narrative voice sets up a subversion of the narrating 'I' and complicates the question of closure.

4. THEATRE

GENERAL

P. Robinson is author of two articles which are of wide scope 'Remarques sur les valets de comédie et la Foire', *RHLF*, 96 : 934–42 uses historical and theoretical arguments to challenge the view that the *valet de comédie* develops progressively into a figure of pre-Revolutionary emancipation in the period 1740–80. 'Les vaudevilles, un médium théâtral', *DhS*, 28:431–49, follows two airs through a number of plays from the period 1740–70 in order to show how *vaudevilles* became an integral part of the whole, exercising an influence on dialogue and mood. Others concentrate on the theatre-going public. Y. Jubinville, 'Théâtre et cafés à Paris', *ib.*, 415–30, refers to Diderot's *Le Neveu de Rameau* and Voltaire's *L'Écossaise* to support the view that 18th-c. cafés and theatres were a place where unofficial discourse was generated. Jeffrey S. Ravel, '*La Reine Boit!* Print, Performance, and Theater Publics in France, 1724–1725', *ECS*, 29:391–411, whilst historical in orientation, includes a discussion of Voltaire's preface to *Hérode et Mariamne*.

INDIVIDUAL AUTHORS

BEAUMARCHAIS.   Two editions by Françoise Bagot and Michel Kail: **Le Barbier de Séville*, Gallimard, 204 pp.; and **Le Mariage de Figaro*, Gallimard, 313 pp. Jean-Pierre de Beaumarchais, **Beaumarchais, le voltigeur des Lumières*, Gallimard, 128 pp.

DORVIGNY.   R. Wrigley, 'From Ancien Régime fall-guy to Revolutionary hero: changing interpretations of Janot and Dorvigny's *Les Battus paient l'amende* in later eighteenth-century France', *BJECS*, 9:125–40, reviews the success of D.'s play in the period 1779–80 and during the Revolution in order to conclude that 'the viability and versatility of Janot as a commentator on the Revolution depends on the scope that he offered for parodic inversion' (p. 125).

MARIVAUX.   C. Cavillac, 'L'ingénuité dans *Arlequin poli par l'amour* et *La Dispute*', *RHLF*, 96:1084–1105, is a psychological reading which contends that in the texts discussed Marivaux disavows his masculine narcissism by representing it as a quintessentially feminine attribute.

5.   POETRY

See VOLTAIRE: LITERARY (*La Henriade*).

THE ROMANTIC ERA

By JOHN WHITTAKER, *University of Southampton*

1. GENERAL

R. Dineen, '"Nulle part le bonheur ne m'attend": cruelty in the *fantastique*', *AUMLA*, 84, 1995: 1–19, compares negative elements in the work of three writers: Balzac's *L'Elixir de la longue vie* and *La Peau de Chagrin* illustrate the Romantic desire for the unobtainable; Gautier seeks refuge from the human condition in the concept of beauty; Villiers de l'Isle-Adam gives his characters acts of specific malevolence as a means of escaping alienation, his representation of cruelty prefiguring the Absurd. H. F. Majewski, 'Reading melancholy: French Romantic interpretations of Dürer's engravings', *NCFS*, 25: 13–29, shows that the engravings 'The Knight, Death and the Devil' and 'Melancholia I' are icons of the French Romantic imagination, and elements from them are transposed into texts by Hugo, Gautier, Michelet and Nerval to represent the confrontation of creativity with the limitations of the chosen art. Massimo Colesanti, *La Disdetta di Nerval*, Ro, Edizioni di storia e letteratura, 1995, xi + 315 pp., is a collection of essays dealing with a number of authors. From the Romantic period, in addition to Nerval, attention is given to Lamartine, Mérimée, Sainte-Beuve, and Stendhal. Mathilde Fournier, *Les Romantiques*, Toulouse, Editions Milan, 64 pp., is a slim volume for beginners, which provides a worthwhile introduction to the main features of Romanticism. There are restrictions in a format which permits a maximum of two pages per author or topic, and the major Romantics are inevitably casualties, though there is probably enough to encourage students to read their works. Maija Lehtonen, *Etudes sur le romantisme français*, Helsinki, Suomalainen Tiedeakatemia, 1995, 197 pp., contains articles mainly on Chateaubriand, but also on Sainte-Beuve, Musset, and Madame de Staël, all of which have previously been published over a period from 1969 to 1990. All are in a slightly modified form, and some bibliographical references have been added. Claude Pichois and Max Milner, **De Chateaubriand à Baudelaire: 1820–1869*, Flammarion, 448 pp., is a new revised edition.

2. CONSULATE WRITERS

CHATEAUBRIAND.   P. Mosley, 'Chateaubriand and Charlotte: was it love?', Smith, *Essays*, 77–81, considers C.'s relationship with Charlotte Ives, the daughter of the vicar of Ilketshall St Margarets, though it leaves the question unresolved, for lack of conclusive evidence. A. Sanderson, 'Chateaubriand's Alps: The use of negative vocabulary', *ib.*, 83–89, examines the language used by C. to describe mountains in general and the Alps in particular, and concludes that their negative portrayal reflects his preference for more southern vistas, except in his later years, when public admiration for mountains had become so widespread that he felt obliged to make concessions. F. Bassan, 'Chateaubriand au tribunal de Stendhal', *NCFS*, 25 : 1–12, suggests that Stendhal's apparent dislike of C., and frequent criticism of his exuberant style, may be attributed to a desire to measure himself against the most famous French writer for two generations, in order to establish his own originality. C. Mouchard, 'Chateaubriand, Milton, l'épopée et la prose', *RLC*, 70 : 497–505, traces the numerous allusions to Milton in C.'s writing, and concludes that his prose is at the same time very close to that of Milton and very different. His prose translations of *Paradise Lost* were not so much attempt to emulate Milton as to understand him from a 19th-c. perspective. B. Chaouat, 'Restaurer les *Mémoires d'outre-tombe*: une fiction éditoriale', *Romantisme*, 91 : 99–110, gives an account of the uneasy relationship which a succession of 'éditeurs-apôtres' have pursued with the text, and which has diverted their attention from C.'s purpose in writing it. P. Hubner, 'Solitude et Mémoires: la plénitude du vide ou le désert paradoxal de l'Extrême-Occident', Siganos, *Solitudes*, 55–65, finds that, for the C. of the *Mémoires d'outre-tombe*, North America becomes a stage setting for a typically Romantic representation of solitude, the writer portraying himself as a unique individual in isolation from the rest of humanity. W. Troubetzkoy, 'De quelques monstres et de quelques châteaux ou l'éclosion du poète', *ib.*, 91–98, shows how, although it has sometimes been argued that C. had an influence on Byron, there is more evidence of influence in the opposite direction: the *Mémoires* have a distinctly Byronic tone, and the mythology which he attaches to the Château de Combourg has a great deal in common with that surrounding Newstead Abbey. J. F. Hamilton, 'The gendering of space in Chateaubriand's Combourg: archetypal architecture and patriarchal object', *Symposium*, 50 : 101–13, shows that Combourg is the psychic centre of the *Mémoires d'outre tombe*, becoming C.'s inner reality and referent for a number of structures and motifs. Colin Smethurst, *Chateaubriand: 'Atala' and 'Rene'*, London, Grant and Cutler, 1995, 91 pp., seeks 'to rescue them from the catalogue of literary works whose interest seems to have faded', largely as a result of their association with generalized notions of Romanticism, by drawing attention to the complexity which lies behind their apparent simplicity.

CONSTANT. R. Dineen, 'Love and absurdity in Constant's *Adolphe*', *AUMLA*, 86:1–16, examines the portrayal of Adolphe's painful experience of love with reference to the fundamental Romantic attitudes to the emotions, and ends by comparing him to Meursault in *L'Etranger*.

MADAME DE KRÜDENER. F. Ley, 'Le Roman *Valérie* jugé par Gœthe, Jean-Paul et Sophie Laroche', *RHLF*, 96:313–16, shows that G. thought it very bad, in the first instance, though he revised his judgement in later years; Jean-Paul Richter liked it, mentioning it three times in his *Vorschule der Aesthetik*; Sophie Laroche valued it highly, and stated that it was the most beautiful text she had read.

MADAME DE STAËL. B. G. Smith, 'History and genius: the narcotic, erotic and Baroque life of Germaine de Staël', *FHS*, 19:1059–81, is mainly concerned with the view of history in *Corinne*, and finds that S.'s genius rested on a bio-epistemology which was incompatible with modern forms of knowledge, leading to the conclusion that her life should be read in terms of irreducible multiplicity. J. Isbell, 'The painful birth of the Romantic heroine: Staël as political animal, 1786–1818', *RR*, 87:59–67, argues that S. turned to literature only as an alternative to politics, from which she had been excluded by Napoleon, in an attempt to retain her political voice through the medium of coded fiction. During the Restoration years, she began to reinvent herself as the heroine of one of her novels. Y. Schlick, 'Beyond the boundaries: Staël, Genlis and the impossible femme célèbre', *Symposium*, 50:50–63, compares evidence of the conflict between feminine modesty and renown, in Mme de Genlis's *De L'Influence des femmes sur la littérature* and S.'s *De la littérature*, then in the three short stories by de Genlis, 'La Femme auteur', 'La Nouvelle Politique' and 'La Femme philosophe', and in S.'s *Corinne*. Beate Maeder-Metcalf, *Germaine de Staël Romancière: Ein Betrag zur Geschichte des frühromantischen Romans*, Frankfurt am Main, Lang, 1995, 197 pp., compares the reception of S.'s novels *Delphine* and *Corinne* in France and in Germany, and suggests that this is indicative of the different theoretical approaches in the two countries in the early years of the century.

3. POETRY

BERTRAND. M. N. Richards, 'Famous readers of an infamous book: the fortunes of *Gaspard de la Nuit*', *FR*, 69:543–55, shows how the first collection of prose poems published in France was considered an important reference by authors including Baudelaire, Mallarmé, Villiers de l'Isle-Adam, Huysmans, Max Jacob, and André Breton. R. Sauvé, 'L'Ecole flamande de *Gaspard de la Nuit* ou la solidifacio du texte', *NCFS*, 24:279–86, examines the structure and the thematic of the paratext and the *Premier Livre*, and indicates that the prose poems are rich in intra- and intertextuality, and may gain in depth and significance when cross-read with the other pieces in the same *Livre*.

HUGO. D. Chauvin, 'Victor Hugo: Babel et le clairon. L'histoire et l'eschatologie', Glaudes, *Terreur*, 37–45, compares and contrasts the two kinds of fear portrayed in the poems from *La Légende des siècles*, 'La Vision d'où est sorti ce livre' and 'La Trompette du jugement'. Albert W. Halsall, **Victor Hugo et l'art de convaincre*, Montréal, Editions Balsac, 1995, 496 pp. Victor Hugo, **L'Art d'être grand-père*, Mille et une nuits, 184 pp., includes a postface by Philippe Di Meo.

LAMARTINE. N. Ruwet, 'Lamartine: la musique du "Lac"', *LaF*, 110:86–102, is a detailed examination of the language of the poem and the techniques employed therein, laying stress on its universality and features which are said to be reminiscent of the finale of an opera or symphony. *Correspondance de Lamartine avec Charles Dupin et documents épistolaires*, ed. Marie-Renée Morin, Clermont-Ferrand, Centre de recherches révolutionnaires et romantiques de l'université Blaise-Pascal (Clermont 1), 1995, xv + 179 pp., is a collection of letters from a number of sources, in particular the manuscripts of the Institut. The letters are presented as follows: 'Correspondance de Lamartine et de Charles Dupin (1834–1862)', between L. and the mathematician and naval engineer whom he had first met in 1827; 'Lamartine et son entourage, étapes épistolaires (1819–1866)'; 'Lamartine vu par Louis de Vignet dans sa correspondance avec Aymon de Virieu (1821–1837)'; 'Les deux voyages en Orient. Lettres de Marianne de Lamartine à Cécile de Cessiat (1832 et 1850)', all providing interesting insights into the poet's personality.

MUSSET. P. Jousset, 'L'art poétique de Musset dans les Poésies Nouvelles: principes et pratique', *IL*, 48.2:10–18, notes that M. refused to exploit empty eloquence, thereby dissociating himself from the fashions attributed to Romanticism, and sought to attach his art to well-established poetic traditions and rules of prosody, while claiming the modernity of his poetry from the heart. **Alfred de Musset, poésies: Faire une perle d'une larme. Actes du colloque d'agrégation du 2 décembre 1995*, ed. José-Luis Diaz, SEDES, 1995, 148 pp. Alain Heyvaert, **L'Esthétique de Musset*, SEDES, 1995, 342 pp. Thomas G. Masaryk, *Polemiken und Essays zur russischen und europäischen Literatur- und Geistesge-schichte*, Vienna–Cologne–Weimar, Böhlau, 1995, 402 pp., contains a chapter on 'Musset, Gœthe, (Lenau)', which portrays M. as the poetic representative of the France of his time, and gives particular attention to the *Confession d'un enfant du siècle*.

VIGNY. N. Rinsler, 'Vigny's caravan: more than a vehicle', Smith, *Essays*, 91–95, defends the integrity of 'La Maison du berger' against the tendency to gloss over, or even omit, the central section. Attention is drawn to a number of lines which appear to offer a direct response to Lamartine.

4. The Novel

BALZAC

ABa, n.s. 16, 512 pp., has its first section devoted to 'Lectures et relectures', and including: M. Andréoli, 'A propos d'une lecture d'*Eugénie Grandet*: science et intuition' (9–38), comparing a personal reading with the semiotic reading of R. Le Huénen and P. Perron; P. Dufour, 'Les avatars du langage dans *Eugénie Grandet*' (39–62), which demonstrates that language is part of the characters which B. creates, and that he creates language through the characters; E. Roy-Reverzy, '*La Duchesse de Langeais*: un romanesque de la séparation' (63–81); L. de Laguérenne, 'Des variations religieuses pour orgue de *La Duchesse de Langeais* à la sonate de Vinteuil' (83–97), on a possible link between B. and Proust; P. Petitier, 'Balzac et la "signifiance"' (99–115), on his use of the word; and A. Vaillant, 'Balzac: la poétique de l'outrance' (117–31), on his style, and critical reactions to it. The second section, 'Autour des *Contes drolatiques*', brings together papers given at the Journée de Saché in October 1994, including: R. Chollet, 'La jouvence de l'archaïsme: libre causerie en Indre-et-Loire' (135–50), on a predilection shared by B. and Nodier for reviving elements of outdated language; M.-C. Bichard-Thomine, 'Le projet des *Contes drolatiques* d'après leurs prologues' (151–64), on pastiche and rewriting; and A. Hammouti, 'La moralité dans les *Contes drolatiques* de Balzac' (165–78), suggesting that the stories are fables with an explicit moral at the end, though this represents a licentious parody of classical morality. The third section, 'Sources et documents', includes: J.-L. Dega, 'Le conventionnel protecteur de Bernard-François Balzac: Jean-Pierre Lacombe Saint-Michel' (181–91), identifying the unnamed benefactor as the father-in-law of his second son; R. Tranchida, 'Inventaire des impressions balzaciennes' (193–239), giving detailed evidence of B.'s work as a printer; H. Maruyama, 'Aux Sources du "Centenaire" II' (241–65), continuing the investigation into the sources of this early work; and A. Kleinert, 'Du *Journal des dames et des modes* au "petit journal" d'*Illusions perdues*' (267–80), on the models for the portrayal of Lucien de Rubempré's work as a journalist. The fourth section, 'Points de vue et perspectives', contains: M. Pinel, 'Significations spirituelles de la mer dans *La Comédie humaine*' (283–309), on the association of images of the sea with a particular vision of Man and of society; A.-M. Lefebvre, 'Bianchon, un astre du cosmos balzacien' (311–30), which identifies Bianchon as the key figure in the hierarchical pyramid of characters in *La Comédie humaine*; C. Eades, '*Le Colonel Chabert*: récit romanesque et récits filmiques' (331–48), comparing the narrative perspective of the novel with that of the films by René Le Hénaff and Yves Angelo; S. Vachon, 'L'œuvre au comptoir: la moitié de *La Comédie humaine* a paru en feuilletons' (349–61), on the statistics and the importance of serial publication; C. Dédéyan, 'Balzac et Béranger' (363–91), on the close links between the two, and B.'s references to Béranger in the novels; and A. Mikhailov and M. Aucouturier, 'Balzac dans l'œuvre de Pasternak' (393–408), showing how Pasternak's reading of B. influenced his development as a writer. The final section, 'Notes', contains: J. Boudard, 'Les lacs de la Campagne romaine ont-ils inspiré Balzac' (409–16), on the Auvergne lake in *Illusions perdues*; and T. Farrant, 'Au Chevet de Coralie' (417–26), on an episode from the same novel. *Ib.*, n.s. 17, 490 pp., is dedicated to the memory of the celebrated B. specialist Pierre-Georges Castex (who died during the course of the year), and opens with M. Ambrière, 'Hommage à Pierre-Georges Castex (5–12). It contains: M. Andreoli, 'Lecture et cinéma: à propos du film "Le Colonel Chabert"' (13–22), which considers how far the success of Yves Angelo's film was due to B. and how far to Depardieu; A.-M. Baron, 'Artifices de mise en scène et art de l'illusion' (23–36), on the use of dramatic scenes in *La Comédie humaine* magically to transform reality; C. Becker, 'Zola et Balzac' (37–48), showing how Z.'s career as a novelist was guided by his admiration for B.; P. Berthier, 'La présence de l'Espagne dans la presse des années 1830' (49–72), on the sources of B.'s Spanish references; P. Brunel, 'Variations balzaciennes sur Don Juan' (73–94), on his treatment of the theme in *L'Elixir de longue vie*; R. Chollet, 'La "Vie de Molière": analyse d'un texte apocryphe' (95–116), suggesting that this text, which has served as an introduction to a number of editions, was not by B., but was a patchwork of borrowings from other writers, assembled by an unknown hand; L. Chotard, 'L'ombre de Balzac dans la querelle réaliste. Une biographie de Champfleury par Nadar' (117–27), identifying the nature of the links between the two writers; R.-A. Courteix, 'L'éloquence politique dans *La Comédie humaine*' (129–41), on B.'s ambivalent attitude to political oratory; C. Dédéyan, 'Guy de Pourtalès et Balzac' (143–53), on the influence of B. on the life and work of this 20th-c. writer of Swiss origin; R. Fortassier, 'Les *Etudes analytiques*: du rejet à une pleine reconnaissance' (155–65), on the unfinished section of *La Comédie humaine*; J. Guichardet, '"Réserves": quelques exemples de suspens du texte balzacien' (167–80), which focuses on the years 1830–35; P. Havard de la Montagne, 'Sous le signe de quelques clochers dionysiens et parisiens: les ancêtres maternels de Balzac' (181–210), on members of the Sallembier or Sallambier family; M. Labouret, 'Méphistophélès et l'androgyne: les figures du pacte dans *Illusions perdues*' (211–30), on Lucien de Rubempré's search for an *alter ego*; A. Lascar, '*Le Curé de village*, étude en rouges' (231–43), on the symbolism of colour; A.-M. Lefebvre, 'De Séraphîta à Spirite: le génie et l'ange' (245–67), showing how an image was conveyed by B. from Swedenborg to Gautier; M. Lichtlé, 'Crimes et châtiments de la vie privée dans *Le Lys dans la vallée*' (269–86), which shows that legal imagery is by no means absent from the novel; A. Lorant, 'Balzac et le plaisir' (287–304), on his description of female sexuality; M. Ménard, 'Le style de la surcharge chez Balzac: l'enseignement des variantes' (305–20), on the lessons which may be learned from the variants of the Pléiade edition; A. Michel, 'A propos d'un paysage: présence de la beauté dans le roman balzacien' (321–34), on poetic and visionary landscapes in the novels; M. Milner, 'Balzac et les paradis artificiels' (335–45), on his use of opium and hashish; R. Pierrot, 'Aux marges de l'œuvre: la *Correspondance*' (347–53), suggesting the need for a CD-ROM edition; N. Preiss, 'Les *Scènes de la vie privée*: scènes originaires? Autour du lexique de la vie privée' (355–66), which shows that B.'s use of language enables interpretation on a number of levels; A. Raitt, 'L'art de la narration dans *Ferragus*' (367–75), in praise of a work which has tended to be neglected; J.-L. Tritter, 'Questions de grammaire dans Balzac' (377–87), on his solution of grammatical problems by reasoned logic; J. Tulard, 'Les adaptations cinématographiques des romans de Balzac entre 1940 et 1944' (389–94), drawing attention to the frequency of films based on B.'s novels during these years, by comparison with those before and after; and S. Vachon, 'Balzac, Rousseau, Louis Protat' (395–422), on the true origin of the anecdote which Rastignac recounts in *Le Père Goriot*, concerning the death of the Mandarin. C. Mossman, '*Sotto voce* — opera in the novel: the case of *Le Père Goriot*', *FR*, 69:387–93, observes that more has been written about the transformation of novels into libretto than about the introduction of opera into the novel. It shows how the denouement of *Le Père Goriot* is executed as an opera, with Vautrin as the lead singer. E. Bordas, 'Scénographie du dialogue balzacien', *MLN*, 111:722–33, identifies two main functions of dialogue in *La Comédie humaine*: On the one hand, an opportunity for the dramatic interaction of two characters; on the other, when one of the characters delivers a monologue with only occasional interventions revealing the presence of his interlocutor, an opportunity to introduce new ideas and areas of meaning. O. Heathcote, 'From cannibal to carnival: orality and violence in Balzac's Gobseck', *MLR*, 91:53–64, differs from the traditional view of the novel as a narrative of stasis and order, finding instead a portrayal of a society which is both ecstatic and diseased, as well as being violent. Particular evidence is found in the past and present of Gobseck, Anastasie, and Maxime. D. W. P. Lewis, 'Between the sheets: the perils of courtship by correspondence in Balzac's *La Femme abandonné*', *NCFS*, 24:296–305, shows how the protagonists unwittingly mislead each other by the letters they write at crucial moments in the story, hiding their true feelings and triggering unforeseen consequences. M. D. Garval, 'Balzac's *La Comédie humaine*: the archival rival', *ib.*, 25:30–40, finds a reflection in such works as *Le Colonel Chabert* of the development of official registers of births, marriages and deaths, leading to a situation in which human existence could be predicated upon bureaucratic documentation. A.-M. Smith-Di Biasio, '"Le Texte de la vie des femmes": female melancholia in *Eugénie Grandet*', *NFS*, 35.2:52–59, sets out to analyse the text of Eugénie's life in terms of the melancholia described by Freud, and reaches the conclusion that the melancholic texture of this text remains as a nostalgic reminder of a libidinal position which must be relinquished, albeit symbolically, in order to accede to a place in culture. F. Vernier, 'Le corps créateur ou l'artiste contre la nature', *Romantisme*, 91:5–17, suggests that the novella *Sarrasine* merits greater attention as an attempt by the author to investigate the nature of artistic creation. C. Foucart, 'Le sida: l'actuelle peau de chagrin', Glaudes, *Terreur*, 341–51, shows that B.'s novel, by providing a means of magically suspending the normal rules of human life and death, has served as a model for contemporary novelists dealing with the problem of AIDS. Lucien Dällenbach, *La Canne de Balzac*, José Corti, 219 pp., takes the famous walking stick as a central symbol around which is constructed a reassessment of B.'s position at the end of the 20th century. Emphasis is laid on his contemporary relevance, and on his ability to qualify as both modernist and postmodernist. The stick is clearly the sceptre of the King of the Novel, and the conclusion calls for new research activity based on *La Comédie humaine*. Ingrid Ulrike Lange, *Der Selbstmord in Honoré de Balzac's 'Comédie Humaine'*, Bonn, Romanistischer Vlg, 1995, 249 pp., examines the motif of suicide, and attempts at suicide, as well as the contemplations preceding suicide. B. appears to blame society, for suicide in *La Comédie Humaine* is not only the consequence of predisposition, but also of environmental influences such as the isolation of people in large cities. Pierre-François Mourier, *Balzac: L'Injustice de la loi*, Michalon, 1995, 120 pp., is concerned with the 58 lawyers of *La Comédie humaine*, the nature of crime and of errors of justice as represented in the novels, B.'s authoritarian leanings and his portrayal of a corrupt society. Having started to train as a lawyer, B. had become disenchanted with the law. *La Comédie humaine* drew attention to the failings of the Code Civil, and B. took on the role of examining magistrate in dealing with the weaknesses of the society of his time. *Balzac*, ed. Michael Tilby, London–NY, Longman, 1995, x + 361 pp., provides extracts from the full range of critical writing on B., from Sainte-Beuve to psychoanalytical, feminist, structuralist, formalist, and post-structuralist readings, though it does not contain any new material. Henri Troyat, *Balzac*, Flammarion, 1995, 548 pp., is a biography which is aimed at the general public and, though thorough and readable, is not really innovative. Jean Broyer, *Le Père Goriot: 40 questions, 40 réponses, 4 études*, Ellipses-Marketing, 62 pp. Alain Schaffner, *Balzac: La Peau de chagrin*, PUF, 128 pp.

EDITIONS. *Contes bruns*, ed. Marcel Bouteron, L'Harmattan, 164 pp. *Eugénie Grandet*, ed. Véronique Anglard, Alleur, Marabout, 275 pp. *La Femme de trente ans*, ed. Gérard Gengembre, Flammarion, 318 pp. A number of editions by Nadine Satiat have appeared: *La Maison du chat qui pelote*, Flammarion, 120 + xxvi pp.; *La Peau de chagrin*, Flammarion, 416 pp.; and *Vendetta*, Flammarion, 136 + xx pp. *Œuvres diverses, II*, ed. Pierre-Georges Castex, Roland Chollet and René Guise, Gallimard, 1852 pp., covers a period of intense creative activity from 1824 to 1834, bringing together a range of different texts written by B., other than those which were to form part of *La Comédie humaine*. The high standards that we associate with the Pléiade editions of B. are amply maintained, and the critical apparatus is thorough and informative. One can only regret that this is the last edition on which Castex and Guise left their distinctive mark, for neither lived to see it published.

STENDHAL

K. Golsan, 'History's Waterloo: prediction in *La Chartreuse de Parme*', *NCFS*, 24:332–46, suggests that the predictions in the novel of Napoleon's campaign in Italy and of Fabrice's fate constitute reflections on the status of history, which was subject to major changes in the years after Waterloo. B. Vibert, 'Du Code civil au Code pénal: une réécriture villérienne de Stendhal', *RHLF*, 96.6:1137–143, continues the investigation begun by Del Litto and Raitt into S.'s influence on Villiers de l'Isle Adam, focusing on the textual common ground shared by the two writers, and attempting to define the use which Villiers made of his source. S. Moussa, 'La tradition de l'amour courtois dans *De l'Amour* et dans *La Chartreuse de Parme* de Stendhal', *Romantisme*, 91:53–65, shows how S. derives certain motifs which appear in the Chartreuse, such as the sufferings which love entails and the submission of the lover to his lady, from the Provençal tradition of courtly love. *Campagnes en Russie: Sur les traces de Henri Beyle dit Stendhal*, Maisonneuve et Larose, 1995, 310 pp., contains the proceedings of a conference on 'Stendhal et la Russie' held by the Société des Rencontres Stendhaliennes Franco-Russes in Moscow and St Petersburg in September 1994. The volume includes some unpublished material written by S., and 27 papers: M. Cadot, 'L'eau et la glace, ou la Russie de Michelet' (74–85); N. Balachov, 'Le Principe lyrique dans le contrepoint des romans de Stendhal' (86–91); B. Didier, 'Le Journal du Voyage en Russie' (92–100); P. Laforgue, 'Hugo, la campagne de Russie et le progrès de l'histoire' (101–08); R. G. Bezzola, 'Stendhal, biographie: la vie de Napoléon' (109–28); A. Stroïev, 'La Russie vue par Stendhal: les transformations des topoï' (129–35); O. Printseva, 'Stendhal et Moscou', (136–37); E. Dmitrieva, 'Stendhal dans les revues russes des années 1830' (138–45); V. Troubetskoi, 'Folie et bonheur' (146–54); T. Sokolova, 'Boris Reizov, spécialiste de l'œuvre de Stendhal' (155–61); G. Nivat, 'Réflexion sur le bonheur stendhalien et le "bonheur russe"' (162–67); O. Smolitskaia, 'Quelques paradoxes de l'interprétation de l'œuvre stendhalienne chez les critiques soviétiques' (168–69); V. Miltchina, 'Stendhal et Alexandre Tourgeniev' (170–74); A. Mikhailov, 'Stendhal et Gogol' (175–81); I. Staf, 'Stendhal et Agrippa d'Aubigné' (182–84); E. Grétchanaia, 'Le Salon de Madame de Krüdener à Paris en 1802–1803' (185–89); S. Zenkine, 'Stendhal touriste et le problème de la culture' (190–95); C. de Grève, 'L'image de la Russie en France au moment du départ de Stendhal' (196–209); L. Volpert, 'Stendhal et Pouchkine' (210–22); M. R. Guinard, 'Stendhal et la Russie: figures d'ailleurs' (223–28); J.-L. Darcel, 'Les Soirées de Saint-Petersbourg et Joseph de Maistre' (229–39); E. Etkind, 'Stendhal et Lermontov' (240–45); A.-M. Delocque-Fourcaud, 'L'administration impériale en campagne'(246–51); G. Friedlander on Russian heroes (252–56); P. Zaborov, 'Le Baron de Damas' (257–62); M. Di Maio, 'Russie, mélancolie, prémonitions' (263–71); and M. Crouzet, 'La retraite de Russie considérée comme expérience romantique' (272–77). Margherita Leoni, *Stendhal, la peinture à l'œuvre*, L'Harmattan, 255 pp, is a shortened version of her doctoral thesis, *L'Inscription du pictural chez Stendhal*, examined at the University of Paris in 1994. It is a detailed investigation of the numerous links between the visual arts, visual perceptions and S.'s text. Particular attention is given to his *Histoire de la peinture en Italie*, *Les Chroniques italiennes* and *La Chartreuse de Parme*.

EDITIONS. *La Chartreuse de Parme*, ed. Pierre-Louis Rey, Klincksieck, 184 pp. *Stendhal et la Hollande*, ed. Elaine Williamson, London, Institute of Romance Studies, lxxii + 596 pp., presents about 200 unpublished administrative documents written by S. during the years 1810–13, when he was serving as auditeur au Conseil d'Etat with responsibility for Crown lands in Holland. This is intended to be the first of two volumes consisting of documents in S.'s hand, discovered by the editor in the Archives nationales and covering a range of administrative matters. What is of particular interest to the reader of the novels is the clear indication that administration served as a proving ground for S.'s developing style. *Notes d'un dilettante*, ed. Jean-Baptiste Gouraud, Table ronde, 224 pp.

OTHER WRITERS

BOREL. *Champavert, le lycanthrope*, ed. Irénée D. Lastelle, Aix-en-Provence, Sulliver, 128 pp.

GAUTIER. M. Meilly, 'Madeleine séductrice/Théodore séducteur: rupture et réconciliation dans *Mademoiselle de Maupin*', *NCFS*, 25:50–59, concentrates on the character of Madeleine de Maupin, whereas modern criticism treating the subject of androgyny has tended to focus on d'Albert. She is ultimately reconciled to her fundamental bisexuality through a reversal of sexual roles which enables a complete rupture of the established social norms.

HUGO. D. Peyrache-Leborgne, 'Roman historique et roman-idylle chez Dickens et Hugo: *A Tale of Two Cities* et *Quatrevingt-treize*', *DFS*, 36:52–67, compares the portrayal of the Revolution in the two novels, both of which demonstrate the long-term effects of the Terror on the Romantic sensibility. Neither is faithful to historical reality, and both lay greater emphasis on the idyllic and the poetic. Myriam Roman and Marie-Christine Bellosta, *Les Misérables, roman pensif*, Belin, 1995, 346 pp., present the novel as a combination of the forms previously used by the author: historical novel, novel of contemporary reality, first person narrative, *fait divers*, social and political novel. This total novel is created from the melodrama of the popular novel, with the addition of a complex plot, the interruption of the narrative for digressive reflection and the exploitation of the poetic resources of imagination and mythology. It portrays sentiments and adventures which escape from reality, as well as providing a cultural and historical representation of society. Not least, it creates a reality from signs and symbols which need to be decoded and, as such, it is addressed to the thinking reader.

NERVAL. M. Brix, 'Grandeurs et servitudes d'"une profession qui n'en est pas une": Nerval, *Lorely* et le métier d'écrivain', *AJFS*, 33:86–106, shows how N.'s journeys along the Rhine influenced his development and his vocation as a writer. Roger Mazelier, *Gérard de Nerval et l'humour divin*, Saint-Quentin-en-Yvelines, Les Trois R, 1995, 235 pp., begins with an account of N.'s rehabilitation during the first half of the 19th c., and leads us through the complex procedure of decoding his writing in a further 23 'notes'. The subjects vary from his use of 'indigestible' words to his reading of Dickens, and a link between his coded messages and the paintings of Hieronymous Bosch. Henri Bonnet, **Sylvie de Gérard de Nerval. Etude de l'œuvre*, Hachette Education, 96 pp.

SAINTE-BEUVE. J.-F. Perrin, 'Romantisme et mémoire involontaire: le cas de *Volupté*', *Romantisme*, 91:43–52, identifies S.-B.'s originality in making memory a vital weapon in the battle fought in the narrator's soul between Sin and Grace, preparing the ground for the distinctively Romantic approach to reminiscence.

SAND. K. Wren, 'Halfway to paradise: failed utopia in the early fiction of George Sand', *AJFS*, 33:73–85, is concerned with the four works of 1832: *Indiana, Melchior, Valentine* and *La Marquise*. The prevailing sense of disillusionment, which will permeate *Lélia*, is attributed to the recognition that sexual incompatibility can be more injurious to personal happiness than social opprobrium. N. E. Rogers, 'Sand's peasant heroines: from victim to entrepreneur, from "connaissance" to "idée", from *Jeanne* to *Nanon*', *NCFS*, 24:347–60, traces the evolution in ways of perceiving the world in the three heroines of *Jeanne, La Petite Fadette* and *Nanon*. S. L. F. Richards, 'Une Jeanne d'Arc ignorée: George Sand's *Jeanne*', *ib.*, 361–69, shows S. setting up a subversive, counter-cultural discourse in a figurative space where conceptions of gender, sexuality and religion are suspended. A. Guidette-Georis, 'George Sand et le troisième sexe', *ib.*, 25:41–49, considers the problem that S.'s *Indiana*, though it contains many references to Shakespeare's Ophelia, indicates that S. identified more strongly with Hamlet when pleading the cause of oppressed women. C. Dale, 'The mirror of Romanticism: images of music, religion and art criticism in George Sand's eleventh *Lettre d'un voyageur* to Giacomo Meyerbeer', *RR*, 87:83–112, suggests that S. used the letter to raise the consciousness, not only of Meyerbeer but also of the whole of her generation, to issues which were close to her heart. In so doing, she enabled her own experience to serve as a mirror for that of her contemporaries. J. Hatem, 'Scission du cœur et désordre du corps dans *Lélia* de Sand', *Romantisme*, 91:19–34, makes it clear that this is not a libertine novel and, though it contains elements which are reminiscent of Sade, this is in no way an imitation, but rather an indication of a common starting point, from which S. pursues the inevitable consequences of depravity to their logical conclusion. *George Sand lue à l'étranger: Recherches nouvelles 3*, ed. Suzan van Dijk, Amsterdam–Atlanta, Rodopi, 1995, 150 pp., contains the Proceedings of the conference on 'George Sand hors de France', held in Amsterdam in June 1994. The first section, 'George Sand romancier français', includes: S. van Dijk, 'Introduction: un contexte à la réception sandienne aux Pays-Bas'(7–22); J.-L. Diaz, 'Inventer George Sand (1812–1828)' (25–35), on her early development as a writer; and C. Planté, '"Elle n'eut d'ailleurs rien de la femme auteur"' (36–48), on her use of writing as a means to escape the restrictions imposed by her gender. The second section, 'L'étranger: aperçus et témoignages', contains: K. J. Crecelius, 'George Sand en Allemagne: la réception de son œuvre' (51–59), followed by a list of articles on S. appearing in the German press; P. Sebe-Madácsy, 'George Sand en Hongrie: admirations et censures' (61–66); I. Miháilá, 'George Sand en Roumanie: le rôle des idées politiques pour la réception de son œuvre' (68–77), which shows that S., though her novels were read by many, came too early to influence the development of the Romanian novel; and G. Logger-Martel, 'George Sand aux Pays-Bas: préférences pour son théâtre' (79–89), showing that her dramatic works were better received by the Dutch than her novels. The third section, 'Les Pays-Bas: cadres commerciaux et culturels', includes: B. Luger, 'Les écrivains étrangers aux Pays-Bas: le rôle des intermédiaires entre livre et lecteurs' (93–99), on translation, printing and book distribution; A. Jourdan, 'L'image du Français aux Pays-Bas: d'un tyran à l'autre' (100–12), which does not deal specifically with S., though it provides a background to the reception of her work; J. Leerssen, 'Imagerie et distance culturelles: une sociopolitique du goût' (113–20), on the evidence in the novels *Historie van Mejuffrouw Sara Burgerhart* and *Camera Obscura* of Dutch attitudes to French culture during the Romantic era; W. van den Berg, 'Les horreurs du romantisme français' (121–28), on the gradual acceptance by the Dutch of the work of French Romantic authors including S.; and E. van Boven, 'George Sand et l'image de la femme auteur aux Pays-Bas' (129–40), on the slow progress in Holland towards the emancipation of women writers, for whom S. served as a significant model. The volume ends with an appendix: J. Castricum, C. Kruikemeier and S. van Dijk, 'George Sand en traduction' (143–49). *Marie d'Agoult, George Sand, Correspondance*, ed. Charles F. Dupêchez, Bartillat, 1995, 301 pp., contains the letters of a short, noisy and notorious friendship. S. and d'Agoult, the mother of Cosima Liszt and later to be known as the writer Daniel Stern, were considered to be the most intelligent and the most liberated females of their time. After Marie's departure from Nohant, they became enemies, and she was the target of attacks by S. in the novels.

VIGNY. M.-C. Cambien, '*Servitude et grandeur militaires*: l'autoconsultation du Docteur Noir', *NCFS*, 24:319–33, focuses on V.'s hesitation, in 1832–33, between the historical novel and the 'consultation', and shows that *Servitude et grandeur* is a combination of the two genres.

5. DRAMA

DUMAS, *père*. P. Campion, '*Antony* d'Alexandre Dumas ou la scène de l'évidence', *RHT*, 48:407–30, examines the play's striking success from the point of view of staging, the use of space and the management of its impact upon the audience. It shows that the Romantic stage is a meeting point for the physical, the imaginary and the psychological, with the potential at the same time to reveal and to hide.

HUGO. F. Bassan, 'La création de *Marion de Lorme*', *ib.*, 431–46, tells the story of the composition, public readings and early performances of the play and of its success, re-examining dated documents which help to clarify the account of its reception, and explain different versions of the story such as that in *Victor Hugo Raconté*. **Hernani*, ed. Claude Eterstein, Flammarion, 192 pp.

6. WRITERS IN OTHER GENRES

M.-P. Le Hir, 'The Société des Gens de Lettres and French Socialism: association as resistance to the industrialization and censorship of the press', *NCFS*, 24:306–18, indicates the importance of the *Acte Notarié d'Association* of the Société des Gens de Lettres, a document which reveals the support given by a significant number of well-known writers, as well as similarities with the statutes of workers' associations.

BALLANCHE. **Lettres de Ballanche à Madame Récamier, 1812–1845*, ed. Agnès Kettler, Champion, 984 pp.

COMTE. Juliette Grange, *La Philosophie d'Auguste Comte*, PUF, 448 pp., is a detailed and effective reintroduction to C.'s thinking, drawing attention to its contemporary relevance as a model for a post-philosophical philosophy. C. is a worthy philosopher for the late 20th c. in that he proposed a metareligion which would be shared by many, yet also private, and a vision of humanity as a moral community united in its diversity. He envisaged politics dissolving its classical forms in favour of a clear relationship between philosophical and scientific truth.

LAMARTINE. *Histoire de Charlotte Corday*, Seyssel, 1995, 119 pp., presents the text of the 'Livre 44e' of the *Histoire des Girondins*, with a preface by Roger Parisot, 'L'Ange de l'assassinat ou Lamartine et Charlotte Corday'. This describes the work as 'parfaite en son genre', indicates L.'s strong admiration for his subject, and assesses the religious, moral and political context of Marat's murder.

LEROUX. B. Viard, 'Pierre Leroux: une critique "socialiste" de la Terreur', *Romantisme*, 91:79–87, shows that L. was a seer rather than a Utopian, to the extent that he inveighed not only against individualism and capitalism, but also against the totalitarian features of the Terror; his definition of socialism changes after 1845, as it becomes associated with republican principles.

MICHELET. L. Gossman, 'Jules Michelet: histoire nationale, biographie, autobiographie', *Littérature*, 102 : 29–54, notes that, though it is by no means uncommon for the work of historians to contain echoes of their personal life, M.'s invention of the individual nation as a subject of history is particularly striking, in so far as it reflects his personal, affective and quasi-erotic stake in that history. Laurence Richer, *La Cathédrale de feu: Le Moyen Age de Michelet, de l'histoire au mythe*, Editions Palam, 1995, 330 pp., goes meticulously through the first six volumes of the *Histoire de France* and shows how M.'s Middle Ages continue well beyond any conventional date ascribed to their ending, and constitute an opposition to modern emancipation. *Cours au Collège de France*, ed. Paul Viallaneix, 2 vols, Gallimard, 1995, 706, 750 pp., is the first complete and chronologically arranged edition of the lectures. Some were published during M.'s lifetime, but most were previously unpublished, and it was necessary to establish the text from the manuscript holdings of the Fonds Michelet in the Bibliothèque historique de la Ville de Paris.

MONTEIL. C. Warne, 'Amateurs and collectors: Amans-Alexis Monteil and the emergence of a professional archive culture in nineteenth-century France', *AJFS*, 33 : 45–72, is an evaluation of the work of an innovative historian who rescued manuscripts from neglect and built up an extensive collection, while playing an important mediating role at a time when the state was seeking to establish a 'professional' system, which would eventually supersede and exclude the 'amateur' antiquarian culture.

NODIER. M. Rice-Defossé, 'Nodier's post-Revolutionary poetics of terror: *Thérèse Aubert*', *NCFS*, 24 : 287–95, examines the disintegration of conventional gender distinctions in this short story of 1814, and suggests that the inscription of radical difference into narrative sequence results in a new poetics.

SAINT-SIMON. Dagmar Pietz, *Zur literarischen Rezeption des Comte de Saint-Simon*, Bonn, Romanistischer Verlag, 265 pp., begins by underlining the specific character and energy of the first four decades of the 19th century. From S.'s original concepts of 'pouvoir spirituel' and 'pouvoir temporel' and his particular use of the word 'industriel', we move to the way in which his pupils defined more clearly their master's thinking, and made his ideas popular, using new media such as newspapers. Attention is then given to the historical and sociocultural background of literary 'producteurs', 'récepteurs', and 'distributeurs'. We are shown how Stendhal's *Armance* represents a society characterized by Saint-Simonian tendencies. Balzac had not read S.-S.'s work, but he had personal contact with several of his followers, and it is shown that his writings on the nature of society owe a debt to Saint-Simon.

THE NINETEENTH CENTURY
(POST-ROMANTIC)

By EMILY SALINES, *Middlesex University*

1. GENERAL

The following abbreviations have been used for titles specific to this section: Perron, *Itinéraires*, for *Itinéraires du XIXème siècle*, ed. P. Perron et al., Toronto, Centre d'Études Romantiques Joseph Sablé, 346 pp.; Falconer, *Kaleidoscope*, for *Kaleidoscope*, ed. G. Falconer and M. Donaldson-Evans, Toronto, Centre d'Etudes Romantiques Joseph Sablé, 228 pp; and Smethurst, *Romantic Geographies*, for *Romantic Geographies*, ed. Colin Smethurst, UGFGP, 305 pp.

N. Arambasin, *La Conception du sacré dans la critique d'art en Europe entre 1880 et 1914*, Geneva, Droz, 446 pp. C. Bernard, *Le Passé recomposé. Le roman historique français du dix-neuvième siècle*, Hachette, 320 pp. * *Twelve Views of Manet's 'Bar'*, ed. B. R. Collins, Princeton U.P., xxi + 318 pp. N. Daneshvar-Malevergne, 'Narcissisme et solitude dans la littérature fin de siècle française et anglaise', Siganos, *Solitudes*, 79–89, looks at the creation and the interrelation of narcissism and solitude and shows how they illustrate a dual tendency towards destruction and regeneration. E. Darragon, 'Kirkeby-Delacroix: l'art-histoire', *Critique*, 52: 151–62, establishes a parallel between the two, as artists who write on art. I. Daunais, *L'Art de la mesure ou l'invention de l'espace dans les récits d'Orient (XIXe siècle)*, Saint-Denis, Vincennes U.P., 218 pp. M. Drouin, 'Le commandant Forzinetti: autour d'une correspondance inédite', *CNat*, 70:342–47. *EF*, 32. 3, is a special issue on 'Québec, une autre fin de siècle' which comprises the following: M.-A. Beaudet and D. Saint-Jacques, 'Lectures et critiques de la littérature française contemporaine au Québec à la fin du XIXe siècle' (7–20); M. Pierssens and R. Benardi, '*L'Écho des jeunes:* une avant-garde inachevée' (21–50); D. Chartier, 'Hector Fabre et le *Paris-Canada* au cœur de la rencontre culturelle France-Québec de la fin du XIXe siècle' (51–60); R. Beaudoin, 'Réception critique de la littérature québécoise au Canada anglais (1867–1901)' (61–76); L. Robert 'Patriots-on-Broadway. *Denis le patriote* de Louis Guyon' (77–93); P. Rajotte, 'La représentation de l'Autre dans les récits de voyage en Terre sainte à la fin du XIXe siècle' (95–113); and A. Compagnon, 'Brunetière au Québec' (155–26). M. Freeman, 'L'image Villon sous le Second Empire', Cameron, *Champ*, 149–60, emphasizes Villon's popularity in the 19th c., and the evolution of the perception of the poet. D. Gamboni, *The Destruction of Art. Iconoclasm and Vandalism since the French Revolution*,

London, Reaktion Books, 410 pp. W. A. Guentner, '"Enfin Daguerre vint": photography, travel and nineteenth-century French narrative', *RLMC*, 49:175–202, explores the passage from a culture of words to a culture of images as an explanation for the difference between 19th-c. and 20th-c. travel literature. M. Hannoosh, **Painting and the Journal of Eugène Delacroix*, Princeton U.P., 1995, 221 pp. R. Hobbs, 'L'apparition du peintre-écrivain', Cameron, *Champs*, 127–37, emphasizes the phenomenon as anchored in the 19th c., and particularly in the *fin-de-siècle*. Holmes, *Women's Writing*, has a good introduction and a fascinating chapter on 'Women in French Society, 1848–1914' (3–25), which gives an overview of the evolution of women in relation to society, politics and culture. See also THE NOVEL, RACHILDE. S. Kern, *Eyes of Love. The Gaze in English and French Paintings and Novels 1840–1900*, London, Reaktion Books, 283 pp., analyses what he calls the 'proposal composition' in paintings and literature and reassesses the interpretation of women as objectified victims of the male gaze by focusing on the subjectivity of women's eyes. H. Kramer, 'Degas in Chicago', *NC*, 15.3:19–22, concerns the 'Degas: beyond impressionism' exhibition; and B. Lambert, 'Cézanne le Grand', *RDM*, March:157–64, deals with the 1996 Cézanne exhibition. R. Le Huenen, 'L'inscription du quotidien dans le récit de voyage au XIXème siècle', Perron, *Itinéraires*, 193–203, looks at the conditions of the inclusion of the *quotidien* and its status within the text, emphasizing the evolution of the genre, which is subverted in Flaubert's *Voyage en Orient*. M. Losch, 'The iconography of sleep and the life-cycle: the influence of theosophical literature and the art of Paul Gauguin on Georges Lacombes' *Le Lit*', *NCFS*, 24:447–60, examines for the first time Lacombe's symbolist bed as a whole. M.-F. Melmoux-Montaubin, 'L'esthète fin-de-siècle: l'œuvre interdite', *Romantisme*, 91:88–98, looks at the æsthete's logic of non-creation as opposed to the logic of the artist in *fin-de-siècle* novels. E. J. Mickel, 'Transmission and transformation, uses of textual expression', Falconer, *Kaleidoscope*, 111–30, reminds us of the evolving attitude to originality in the 19th century. F. Monneyron, *L'Androgyne décadent. Mythe, figure, fantasmes*, Grenoble, ELLUG, 180 pp., looks at the degradation of a myth in France and England. The aspects considered are: 'Du mythe à la figure' (13–52), which studies the difference of perception of male and female androgyny; 'Esthétisme et androgyne' (53–72); 'Sexualité et androgyne' (73–128); and 'Occultisme et androgyne' (129–60). J. Newton, 'Rodin and the installation of "L'Homme qui Marche" at the Palais Farnese', Smith, *Essays*, 187–93, retraces the episode. J. Newton, 'Auguste Rodin and Arsène Alexandre', Cameron, *Champs*, 113–25, outlines the relationship between the two. P. O'Donovan, 'Style and autonomy: literature and the question of a public sphere', *ib.*, 3–11, takes Bourdieu as theoretical framework in his study of the role of autonomy in French culture, focusing in particular on the 19th century. *Parisian Fields*, ed. Michael Sheringham, London, Reaktion Books, 200 pp., has a chapter by R. Clark, 'Threading the maze: nineteenth-century guides for British travellers to Paris' (8–29). D. Smith, *Transvaluations: Nietzsche in France 1872–1972*, Oxford, Clarendon Press, xiii + 250 pp. R. Squadrelli, 'Entre le peintre et l'homme de lettres, Camille Lemonnier', *CNat*, 70:139–50, looks at the phenomenon of the 'peintre-écrivain' and retraces Lemonnier's artistic career. *StLM*, 29.1, is devoted to (English) 'Nineteenth-century realism, theory and practice'. D. Trotter, 'Modernity and its discontents: Manet, Flaubert, Cézanne, Zola', *Paragraph*, 19:251–71, centres round the motif of the *flâneur*, as central to the reading of modern literary or visual texts. J. Voisine, 'La magie de la peinture: variations sur le motif du portrait au XIXe siècle', *RLMC*, 49:63–82. S. Vachon, 'Le catalogue Delalain des imprimeurs parisiens brevetés au dix-neuvième siècle', Perron, *Itinéraires*, 305–45. K. Wilkin, 'Monsieur Pellerin's collection: a footnote to "Cézanne"', *NC*, 14.8:18–23, presents the collector (born in 1852), focusing in particular on his Cézannes, considered the painter's most ambitious paintings. B. Wright, 'East meets West: the Suez Canal as portrayed by its official artist, Narcisse Berchère', Smethurst, *Romantic Geographies*, 264–76, looks at the propagandist exercise in Berchère's *Le Désert de Suez*.

2. DRAMA

M. Dubar, 'Solitudes à la scène, solitude de la scène', Siganos, *Solitudes*, 205–15, argues that contrary to the received idea that drama is a destruction of solitude, solitude is central to dramatic writing, basing herself on *fin de siècle* European drama. P. McGuinness, 'Le théâtre symboliste: entre *Le Livre* et *La Scène*', Cameron, *Champ*, 309–19, analyses the Symbolists' distrust of the theatre.

FIGUIER. M. Pierssens, 'L. Figuier et l'échec du "théâtre scientifique"', Perron, *Itinéraires*, 205–15, retraces F.'s project of scientific vulgarization through drama.

3. POETRY

M. Blaise, 'Le poète et la solitude: étude d'un cliché (Dickinson, Mallarmé, Rilke)', Siganos, *Solitudes*, 99–111. L. Forestier, 'Du Bon Usage des coffrets: à propos de Coppée, Cros et Huysmans', Cameron, *Champs*, 161–69, studies the evolution of the image of the 'coffret' in Coppée's *Le Reliquaire*, Cros's *Le Coffret de santal*, and

Huysmans's *Le Drageoir aux épices*. H.-J. Frey, *Studies in Poetic Discourse: Mallarmé, Baudelaire, Rimbaud, Hölderlin, trans. W. Whobrey, Stanford U.P., 198 pp. R. Killick, 'Le concours de sonnets de "La Plume" (1890)', Cameron, *Champ*, 203–18, offers an appraisal of the situation of the sonnet at the end of the 19th century. J.-J. Lefèvre, 'Un duel au temps du symbolisme: la rencontre Darzens-Moréas', *ib.*, 293–308, retraces the event. Y. Tardy, 'From *Flânerie* to *Dérive*', *NCo*, 21 : 41–51, looks at the transformations of the *flâneur* from Baudelaire to the Lettrists and Situationists.

BAUDELAIRE. M. Bercot, 'Baudelaire, le diable et le fou', *TLit*, 8, 1995 : 269–85, looks at Baudelaire within the context of the debate about the nature of *mélancolie* and shows that Baudelaire embraces the notion of evil in opposition to positivism and ideals of man's inherent goodness. *Bulletin Baudelairien*, 31.1, gives the bibliographical *recensement* for 1995 with supplements for years 1994 and 1993. *Ib.*, 31.2, contains: J.-C. Susini, 'L'empreinte de Tite-Live dans *Les Fleurs du mal*' (41–50), which looks in particular at 'La cloche fêlée', 'Duellum', and 'Portraits de maîtresses'; J.-C. Le Boulay, 'Baudelaire lecteur de Nerciat' (51–74), who shows the link between N.'s *Felicia* and *Monros* and some of the *Fleurs du mal;* M. Zimmerman, 'Video Meliora, bis' (75–76), which is a follow-up to J. Deprun's article 'Un souvenir d'Ovide dans une lettre à Madame Aupick' (*ib.*, 30: 56–58); J. Pellegrin, 'La tyrannie des faibles' (77–82), on Baudelaire and Karr; F. Desbuissons, 'Antoine Fauchery, peintre, graveur, écrivain' (83–99), on the possible engraver of Courbet's drawing for the *Salut Public;* and Y. Mortelette, 'Les bons chiens, Macbeth, et "L'œuvre sans nom"' (100–05), who reassesses the meaning of *les bons chiens* in the light of two intertexts: the quotation from *Macbeth* and the painting by Stevens, arguing against Jerôme Thélot's view of the poem as a *badinage*. O. Classe, 'Baudelaire's "Le Cygne": rêverie d'un passant à propos d'une reine', Smith, *Essays*, 119–23, compares B.'s poem with Hugo's 'Rêverie à propos d'un roi' as a manifestation of shared material between the two poets. A. Czerniawski, 'Norwid, Baudelaire and a puzzle', *ib.*, 133–37, is a study of Cyprian Norwid's possible link with Baudelaire. G. Gasarian, *De Loin tendrement: Études sur Baudelaire, Champion, 269 pp. K. Golsan, 'The beholder as flâneur: structures of perception in Baudelaire and Manet', *FrF*, 21 : 165–82, shows the links between the two and concludes with the fact that Manet's spectator is a *prince des flâneurs*. J. Hiddleston, 'From Boudin to Guys, from landscape to the painting of modern life', Cameron, *Champ*, 65–70, considers Baudelaire's views of landscape painting. B. Howells, *Baudelaire, Individualism, Dandyism and the Philosophy of History*, Oxford, European Humanities Research Centre, 207 pp., looks at B.'s attitude to individualism and individuality through eight previously published — but revised — essays, situating him within the broader contexts of 19th-c. historical, cultural, and artistic speculation. The first part concentrates on *La Fanfarlo, Salon de 1846* and *Journaux Intimes*, while the second looks at Baudelaire in relation to Emerson, Carlyle, Maistre, Ferrari and Chevreul. P. Laforgue, 'Baudelaire, Hugo, et la royauté du poète: le romantisme en 1860, *RHLF*, 5:966–82, looks at Hugo as part of Baudelairean poetics. F. Leakey, '*Les Fleurs du mal:* a chronological view', *MLR*, 91:578–81, presents a new view, based on documentary and textual evidence, of the chronology and composition of the *Fleurs du mal*. S. Murphy, 'La scène parisienne: lecture *d'Une Mort héroïque* de Baudelaire', Cameron, *Champ*, 49–61, explores the socio-cultural background to the prose poem, concentrating on theatre and ideology. F. Ponikwer, '"L'homme des foules": the vampiric "flâneur"', Smith, *Essays*, 139–42, is a study of the figure of the *flâneur*. V. K. Ramazani, 'Writing in pain: Baudelaire, Benjamin, Haussman', *Boundary2*, 23.2:199–224, focuses on the modern city as sublimation of the body in *Le Spleen de Paris*. E. Salines, 'The opium landscape in translation: Baudelaire's *Un Mangeur d'opium* and De Quincey's autobiographical writings', *NCo*, 21:22–39, explores Baudelaire's amalgam æsthetics. C. Scott, 'Seascapes of sound: Baudelaire's "Parfum exotique"', Smith, *Essays*, 113–17, analyses the poem's acoustic patterning. S. Stephens, 'L'expérience urbaine et l'évolution d'un genre: le cas du poème en prose baudelairien', Cameron, *Champ*, 39–47, explores B.'s search for a form to match the experience of the city. G. M. Sutherland, 'Baudelaire "Pluviose, irrité …"', Smith, *Essays*, 125–31, revolves round an analysis of the word 'pluviôse'. F. Vatan, 'La mélancolie sans miroir: une lecture de "Brumes et pluies"', *FR*, 70:219–30, argues for Poe's influence on B., basing herself on a comparison of the poem with Poe's 'Raven' and 'Philosophy of Composition'. A. K. Wettlaufer, 'Paradise Regained: the *flâneur*, the *badaud*, and the æsthetics of artistic reception in *Le Poème du haschisch*', *NCFS*, 24:388–97, looks at the tensions between the poetic and the narcotic, and their links with reader's reception. C. A. P. Willsdon, 'Baudelaire's "Le Voyage"and Maxime Du Camp's Middle Eastern photography', Smethurst, *Romantic Geographies*, 247–63, emphasizes Baudelaire's ambivalence to photography in general and to Du Camp's *Egypte, Nubie, Palestine et Syrie. Dessins photographiques* in particular.

DESNOYERS. L. Abelès, 'Fernand Desnoyers, "le dernier bohème"', Cameron, *Champ*, 141–47, looks at the poet as exemplary of the *bohème* through his life and friends and literary choices.

LAFORGUE. 'Two poems by Jules Laforgue translated and with an introduction by Louis Simpson', *NC*, 15.1:81–89. The two poems in question are 'Autre complainte de Lord Pierrot' and 'Légende'. J.-L. Debauve, 'La publication des "Œuvres complètes" de Jules Laforgue', Cameron, *Champ*, 249–61, retraces the history of the publication of Laforgue's works in the 20th century. A. Holmes, 'Finding a language: Verlaine and Laforgue', *FS*, 50:285–98, details the parallel stages which led both poets to self-expression.

LECONTE DE LISLE. R. Lloyd, 'Bijoux de Bloomington ou des marguerites dans le champ littéraire', Cameron, *Champ*, 219–26, presents *Les Bijoux de Marguerite*, published in 1899.

MALLARMÉ. M. Bowie, 'Pierre Ménard, author of "La Musique et les Lettres": towards a poetic of Mallarmé's late prose', Smith, *Essays*, 175–85, looks at the ways in which 'the arts of the verse-poet are indeed transferred by Mallarmé to the structure of prose' (p. 184). M. Breatnach, *Boulez and Mallarmé. A Study in Poetic Influence*, Aldershot, Scolar Press, 160 pp., considers the relationship between poetry and music in Boulez's *Pli selon pli. Portrait de Mallarmé*. C. Chadwick, *The Meaning of Mallarmé. A Bilingual Edition of his 'Poésies' and 'Un Coup de dés'*, Aberdeen, Scottish Cultural Press, 177 pp. D. Degener, '"Votre nom se mêle au sien": la première lettre connue de Stéphane Mallarmé à Sarah Helen Whitman', *RHLF*, 96:1166–75, presents Sarah Helen Whitman and reproduces the letter. P. A. Genova, 'Word, image, chord: Stéphane Mallarmé and the interrelationship of the arts in late nineteenth-century Symbolist literary reviews', *DFS*, 36:81–101, starts with a summary of M.'s place within the Symbolist movement, before concentrating on his reviews and studying the nature of his defence of modern painting, the æsthetic importance of the link between music and poetry, and the general significance of the reviews. P. Hambly, 'Pastiche et parodie chez Mallarmé', Cameron, *Champ*, 177–202, explores the humoristic aspect of *A un poète immoral* and *Chansons bas*. B. Marchal, 'La correspondance de Stéphane Mallarmé: compléments et suppléments, VII', *FS*, 50:35–53, continues L. J. Austin's work on Mallarmé's correspondence. J. McCann, 'To what is Mallarmé referring?', *Neophilologus*, 80:385–98. J. M. Mitchell, 'Une étude de l'ironie dans *plaisir sacré* de Mallarmé', *RHLF*, 96:1144–65. M. C. Olds, 'Mallarmé and internationalism', Falconer, *Kaleidoscope*, 157–67, looks at *La Musique et les lettres* as part of 19th-c. international political utopianism, emphasizing the mix of politics and poetics. R. Pearson, **Unfolding Mallarmé: The Development of a Poetic Art*, Oxford, Clarendon Press, xii + 316 pp. G. Robb, *Unlocking Mallarmé*, New Haven–London, Yale U.P., 251 pp., aims, as the title suggests, to provide strategies for understanding Mallarmé. In addition, this excellent book demonstrates the auto-referential character of Mallarmé's poetry. The first section of the book concentrates on a historical-prosodic perspective on the poems (Chapters 1–5).

The second section gives selective analyses of some poems treated as manifestations of a prosody which is central to the poems (Chapters 6–10). A. Rosenblithe, 'Moving space: Mallarmé's "jeux circonvolutoires" in Rilke's *Sonette an Orpheus*', *CLS*, 33:141–60. R. Saunders, 'Shaking down the pillars: lamentation, purity, and Mallarmé's "Hommage" to Wagner', *PMLA*, 111:1106–20, analyses the significance of ritual and philosophical defilement which creates Mallarmé's poetic purity.

RIMBAUD. A. Borer, 'La découverte de la "maison Rimbaud"', *NRF*, 519: 4–17, gives a fascinating account of R.'s constant escape from place. F. Caradec, '*La Lanterne de Boquillon* éclairant Charleville', in Cameron, *Champ*, explores the childhood readings of the poet. R. D. J. Duvick, '"Rouler aux blessures": feminine figures in Rimbaud's *Illuminations*', *NCFS*, 24:406–16, shows how feminine figures are both essential and threatening to R.'s poetic project. G. M. Macklin, 'The disinherited child in the poetry of Arthur Rimbaud', *RoS*, 28: 45–59, looks at childhood as a 'key thematic and structural component of R.'s work across all his collections' (p. 58) and as part of R.'s quest for a new poetic style echoing the private language of the children of 'Les Effarés' and 'Les Poètes de sept ans'. Id., 'The reinvention of time and space in Rimbaud's *Illuminations*', *NFS*, 35: 60–75, analyses the proclivity in details of space and time in R.'s prose poetry through the close study of key texts from *Illuminations*. Id., 'Rimbaud's "Barbare": the floating and reverberating text', *Neophilologus*, 80:41–52, explores the semantic and linguistic properties of 'Barbare' and concludes that this poem is very representative of the Rimbaldian desire for upheaval both visionary and linguistic. Id., '"Finding the formula": perspectives on the one-liner in Arthur Rimbaud's *Illuminations*', *FMLS*, 32:329–42, gives a classification of one-liners, insisting on their diversity and the extent to which R. uses the device.

VERLAINE. See LAFORGUE above.

3. PROSE

N. Bachleitner, 'Un "Zola allemand"? Les romans sociaux de Marx Kretzer et le naturalisme français', *CNat*, 70:115–37, looks at the influence of naturalism on 'Jüngstdeutsche' at the end of the 19th century. J.-P. Bertrand, M. Biron, J. Dubois, and J. Paque, **Le Roman célibataire d'*À Rebours' à 'Paludes'*, Corti, 241 pp. A. Fonyi, 'La solitude du narrateur dans le récit fantastique', Siganos, *Solitudes*, 199–204, reads solitude as the literary expression of epistemological torments. D. Holmes, 'Feminism, romance and the popular novel: Colette Yver (1874–1953), Gabrielle Reval (1870–1938) and Marcelle Tinayre (1871–1948)', pp. 47–62 of Holmes, *Women's Writing*, looks at the feminist dimension of turn-of-the-century novels. J.-M. Lecaudé, 'Le naturalisme, ennemi de tout sentiment religieux dans le roman?', *NZJFS*, 17.1:5–22, considers Naturalism's attitude towards religion and Naturalists' treatment of questions related to God and Grace. B. Overton, **The Novel of Female Adultery: Love and Gender in Continental European Fiction, 1830–1900*, London, Macmillan–NY, St Martin's Press, xiii + 284 pp. J. Stubbs, 'Hypnotisme et automatisme dans la fiction "fin-de-siècle"', Cameron, *Champs*, 275–83, emphasizes the theme of hypnosis as a challenge of the real and realism. P. M. Wetherill, 'Flaubert, Zola, Proust and Paris: an evolving city in a shifting text', *FMLS*, 32: 228–39, looks at the interaction of city and narrative. Id., 'Visions conflictuelles: le Paris de Flaubert, Zola, Monet, Degas, Caillebotte', Cameron, *Champ*, 27–38, studies the instability of the city and the manifestation of such instability in art and literature.

BANVILLE. P. Andrès, 'Banville et l'art du conte', *NCFS*, 24: 381–87, argues for more critical interest towards B.'s short stories.

BARBEY D'AUREVILLY. L. Fraisse, '*Le rideau cramoisi:* Marcel Proust lecteur de Barbey d'Aurevilly', *TLit*, 8, 1995: 319–40. A. H. Pasco, 'Kaleidoscopic reading in Barbey's *Les Diaboliques*', Falconer, *Kaleidoscope*, 99–110, argues against the generally held critical views that the volume of stories lacks unity, and emphasizes instead the intimate relationship between all the stories of the volume and the unity created by the reader's perceptions of these stories.

BARRÈS. A. Pütz, 'Ernst Jünger und Maurice Barrès, Begegnungen im Raum der Fiktion', *WB*, 42: 188–206.

FLAUBERT. 'Gustave Flaubert: 11 letters newly translated from the French by Geoffrey Wall', *Cambridge Quarterly*, 25: 212–42. L. Adert, **Les Mots des autres: lieu commun et création romanesque dans les œuvres de Gustave Flaubert*, Lille, Presses Universitaires du Septentrion, 304 pp. L. M. Birden, 'Power and discourse in nineteenth-century sexuality as presented in *L'Éducation Sentimentale*', *NCFS*, 24: 398–405, reads the novel as 'a normative work for its century' in relation to sexual attitudes. H. Boenisch, 'Heine, Arnold, Flaubert and the cross-Channel link: implicit connections textual and technological', Smith, *Essays*, 143–47, is about the impact of telegraphy in the second half of the 19th century. L. Bouilhet, **Lettres à Gustave Flaubert*, ed. and ann. Maria Luisa Cappello, CNRS, 780 pp. A. Brown, '"un assez vague spinozisme": Flaubert and Spinoza', *MLR*, 91: 848–65, looks at F.'s recurrent interest in Spinoza as a case history of the relationship between literature and philosophy. R. D. E. Burton, 'The death of politics: the significance of Dambreuse's funeral in *L'Éducation Sentimentale*', *FS*, 50: 157–69, sees this event as a double pastiche of Goriot's funeral and political funerals of the French liberal-republican tradition, Dambreuse's death symbolizing the failure of all politicians to counter Louis-Napoleon. E. L. Constable, 'Critical departures: *Salammbô*'s orientalism', *MLN*, 111:625–46, argues that the hyperbolic use of detail in the novel both represents and critiques orientalist strategies. J. Deppman, 'History with style: the impassible writing of Flaubert', *Style*, 30:28–49, examines Flaubert's celebrated style. J. Gassin, 'Flaubert plagiaire de Flaubert dans *Madame Bovary*', *AJFS*, 333.1:107–19, uses a psychoanalytical approach to study the repetitions in the novel. A. Green, 'Flaubert's myth of civilisation and Orient', Smethurst, *Romantic Geographies*, 215–25, looks at the evolution of Flaubert's idealization of the Orient, from Romantic fantasy to disappointment at the Western perversion of Orient towards the end of his life. H. Heep, 'Degendering the other: object of desire in Flaubert's "Un cœur simple"', *DFS*, 36:69–77, shows convincingly how Félicité achieves self-realization outside of social gender norms by degendering social relationships. A.-V. Lambros, **Culture and the Literary Text: The Case of Flaubert's Madame Bovary*, NY, Lang, 85 pp. M. J. De Lancastre, '"Ó sino da minha aldeia" di Fernando Pessoa: una poesia flaubertiana?', *RLMC*, 49:103–05. E. Le Calvez, 'Description, construction: l'espace du texte (l'exemple de *l'Éducation sentimentale*)', *ib.*, 83–102, establishes a theory of description, emphasizing in conclusion the interdependence of mimesis and semiosis. H. Mason, 'Flaubert on Voltaire', Smith, *Essays*, 101–05, looks at Flaubert's ambivalent attitude to the philosopher, concluding with the idea of his enduring admiration. M. Orr, 'Reflections on "bovarysme": the Bovarys at Vaubyessard', *FSB*, 61:6–8, is a fascinating analysis of the Vaubyessard episode which emphasizes the paradox of sameness between two superficially different social worlds. A.-M. Paillet-Guth, 'Flaubert et l'adverbe *alors:* cohésion et dérision', *FM*, 64:51–62, looks at the subjectivity of the adverb and its narrative function. L. M. Porter, 'Emma Bovary's narcissism revisited', Falconer, *Kaleidoscope*, 85–97, argues for an interpretation of Emma Bovary as pathologically narcissistic. A. Raitt, 'Flaubert off-stage and on stage', Smith, *Essays*, 107–12, looks at Flaubert's attitude to the idea of his novels being adapted for the stage. P.-L. Rey, **'Madame Bovary' de Gustave Flaubert*, Gallimard, 194 pp. J. M. Reynolds, 'Flaubert's *Un Cœur simple*', *Explicator*, 55.1:26–29. P. A. Tipper, 'Frédéric's "pre-coital" cigarette: causal indeterminacy in *L'Éducation sentimentale*', *Neophilologus*, 80:225–41, analyses the internal logic subtending narrative fiction as the main purveyor of meaning to the reader and tests this theory with the study of the tobacco motif at the end of *L'Éducation sentimentale*. T. Unwin, 'Æsthetic capital? Parisian seductions in *L'Éducation sentimentale*', Cameron, *Champ*, 13–25, follows Bourdieu's analysis of the novel and concentrates on the integration of literary and æsthetic fields of experience into Flaubert's text. A. Weber-Caflisch, 'La place de la culpabilité dans *L'Éducation sentimentale* et "La Légende de saint Julien l'Hospitalier"', *TLit*, 8, 1995:288–317, looks at the Œdipal dimension of guilt in both works. P. Willemart, *Dans la chambre noire de l'écriture, 'Hérodias' de Flaubert*, Toronto, Paratexte, 132 pp., is a second version of a study in Portuguese published in 1993 (Sao Paulo, EDUSP). It concentrates on the creative process, as revealed by the manuscript of the text, adopting a psychoanalytical outlook. G. A. Willenbrink and G. Bonaccorso, 'Nouvelles remarques sur "Corpus I"', *SFr*, 118:76–84, is part of a debate between the two authors on F.'s 'avant texte'.

GONCOURT. D. Baguley, 'A fresh look at the Goncourt *Journal* (intime)', Falconer, *Kaleidoscope*, 169–78, emphasizes the diary dimension of the text, of which the introspective side is often overlooked by critics. See also ZOLA.

HENNIQUE. N. White, 'Dining out with Léon Hennique', *EFL*, 32–33:41–63, is a fascinating analysis of *Un accident de Monsieur Hébert*, a little known Naturalist novel of adultery.

HUYSMANS. D. Grojnowski, ***À Rebours' de J.-K. Huysmans*, Gallimard, 89 pp. *En Route*, ed. Dominique Millet, Gallimard, 659 pp. B. L. Knapp, 'Huysmans and the monstrous imagination of Odilon Redon', Falconer, *Kaleidoscope*, 201–11, looks at Redon's impact on H. as revealed in Des Esseintes's fascination with the painter. C. Nunby, 'Huysmans and the æsthetics of solitude in *Croquis parisiens*', *FrF*, 21:187–206. M. Tilby, 'Le monde vu de (trop?) près: le Degas de J.-K. Huysmans', Cameron, *Champ*, 91–103, explores the tensions and contradictions in H.'s perception of Degas. N. White, *À Rebours* et la "Préface écrite vingt ans après le roman": écoles, influences, intertextes', *ib.*, 105–11, looks at the 1903 edition of the novel as a oasis for an exploration of its intertextual dimension.

JARRY. T. Bridgeman, 'On the *Like*ness of similes and metaphors with special reference to Alfred Jarry's *Les Jours et les nuits*)', *MLR*, 91:65–77, reconsiders the functioning of simile and metaphor, using J.'s text to test existing theories.

LOTI. M. Lerner, 'Pierre Loti on Broadway', Smith, *Essays*, 215–19, refers to *La Fille du ciel*, first performed in New York in 1912. F. Salaün, 'La fin d'un monde. La pelote basque dans *Ramuntcho* de Pierre Loti', *Europe*, 806–07:113–26, presents the sport as central to L.'s presentation of the Basque community and his contrasting of the traditional and the new.

LOUŸS. J.-P. Goujon, 'José-Maria de Heredia et Pierre Louÿs l'après leur Correspondance inédite', Cameron, *Champ*, 239–48, outlines the relationship between the two writers, concentrating on their correspondence between 1890 and 1905.

MAUPASSANT. P. Bayard, 'Maupassant et l'éclipse', Glaudes. *Terreur*, 215–28, identifies as an eclipse motif the themes of disappearance, denial and madness in Maupassant's works, concluding that the fear of madness is central to the act of writing. P. W. M. Cogman 'De Meilhac à Maupassant: signes curieux', Cameron, *Champ* 265–74, looks at the intertextual links between Maupassant's *Le Sign* and Meilhac's *Les Curieuses*. S. Leabhart, 'No free rides: descriptive frame as ideology in Maupassant's "L'Aveu"', *Symposium*, 50:40–49, shows the narrative importance of metaphors in Maupassant's text J. Malrieu, **'Le Horla' de Guy de Maupassant*, Gallimard, 196 pp M. Sillam, '*Bel-Ami*, héros de la transgression', *CNat*, 70:83–92, looks at Georges Duroy as 'le type même de l'arriviste', and details the forms transgression takes (work, private life), showing this transgression to be the basis of Duroy's success.

MIRBEAU. C. Lloyd, **Mirbeau's Fictions*, Durham U.P. ix + 115 pp. C. Lloyd, 'Octave Mirbeau et la caricature', Cameron *Champ*, 285–92, emphasizes Mirbeau's black humour. R. Ziegler 'Birth and the book: the incunabulum in Octave Mirbeau's *L'Abb Jules*', *DFS*, 36:103–12, shows how *L'Abbé Jules* is an archetypal decadent text in its distortion of the natural reality it evokes, and the manipulation of its textual ancestors.

PHILIPPE. M. Puget, 'De Zola à Charles-Louis Philippe: *Bubu d Montparnasse*', *CNat*, 70:169–77, explores the link between Philippe and naturalism through a study of Parisian spaces. D. Roe, 'Une vocation avortée? Charles-Louis Philippe, poète, 1893–6', Cameron *Champ*, 227–37, presents unpublished poems of Philippe's youth.

RACHILDE. Two pieces by D. Holmes: 'Rachilde (1860–1953) decadence, misogyny and the woman writer', pp. 63–82 of Holmes *Women's Writing*, looks at Rachilde's use of the forms and convention of the decadent text and explores the contradiction of an explicitly misogynistic woman writer working within masculine forms and ye questioning and subverting gender roles; and 'Monstrous women Rachilde's erotic fiction', Hughes, *Erotic*, 27–48, replaces R.'s work within the context of decadence and outlines the specificity o eroticism as written by a woman, focusing in particular on the reversal of familiar sexual scenarios, but stressing also R.'s ambivalence to her characters, described by herself as 'monstrous'. G. Tegyey **L'Inscription du personnage dans les romans de Rachilde et de Marguerit Audoux* (Studia Romanica de Debrecen, Series Litteraria, 19) Debrecen, Université Lajos-Kossuth, 1995, 142 pp.

RENAN. A. Coule, 'Ernest Renan et l'École française d'Athènes' *Bulletin de correspondance hellénique*, 120:255–59. G. Séginger, 'Renan la recherche d'un *Surdieu*', *Romantisme*, 91:67–77. G. Séginger 'Renan et l'exigence du fragmentaire: les *Souvenirs d'enfance et d jeunesse*', *FS*, 50:412–24, looks at the combination of reason and poetry, unity and fragmentation within R.'s autobiographical text.

ROSNY. *CNat*, 70, has a section devoted to J. H. Rosny, which comprises an introduction (181–84), a chronobibliography (185–209), 'L'ombre du manifeste. Autour d'une lettre d'Alexandrine Emile-Zola' (211–63), and J. B. Sanders, 'Une lettre inédite de J.-K. Huysmans à Rosny aîné' (265–67).

ROSTAND. *Cyrano de Bergerac*, trans. Christopher Fry, with introd. and notes by Nicholas Cronk, OUP, 154 pp.

SAINTE-BEUVE. E. Bury, 'Madame de Sévigné face aux critiques du XIXe siècle: Sainte Beuve et Consorts', *RHLF*, 96:446–60. J. Malavié, 'La conscience pécheresse dans *Volupté*', *TLit*, 8, 1995:241–52, looks at the religious inspiration in S.-B.'s novel.

SCHWOB. R. Ziegler, 'Escaping the mortal web of time in Marcel Schwob's "Arachné"', *NCFS*, 24: 440–46, argues that 'Arachné' prefigures S.'s view of time as seen in *Le Livre de Monelle*.

TAINE. **Taine au carrefour des cultures du XIXe siècle. Colloque organisé par la Bibliothèque Nationale et la Société des Études romantiques et dix-neuvièmistes, 3 décembre 1993*, ed. S. Michaud, Bibliothèque Nationale de France, 181 pp.

VALLÈS. P. M. Moores, 'L'enfance chez Jules Vallès et Romain Gary: révolte et renaissance', Cameron, *Champ*, 331–41, looks at the similarities between *L'Enfant* and G.'s *La Vie devant soi*. M. Van Zuylen, 'Pour une esthétique du comique: *L'Enfant* de Jules Vallès', *EF*, 32:141–63, argues that V. embodies Baudelaire's ideal of 'comique pur' through an analysis of his strategies.

VERHAEREN. D. Gullentops (trans. Peter Read), 'Verhaeren and Marinetti', *FMLS*, 32:107–118, explores the poet's relationship to Futurism. Id., **Inventaire de la bibliothèque d'Émile Verhaeren à Saint-Cloud*, Lettres Modernes, 147 pp. J. Marx ,'Verhaeren en France', *RHLF*, 96: 246–65, looks at Verhaeren's relationship with late 19th-c. French authors and his role in the elaboration of Flemish originality. Id., **Verhaeren: Bibliographie d'une œuvre*, Brussels, Académie Royale de langue et de littérature françaises, 675 pp.

VERNE. R. Chambers, 'Phileas Fogg's colonial policy', Falconer, *Kaleidoscope*, 131–44, is an excellent and entertaining study of the dialectics of assimilationist and exoticizing tendencies as symbolized by Phileas Fogg and Passepartout. A. E. Hudson, 'Discover Paris with Jules Verne and "Paris au XXe siècle"', *FR*, 70:245–58.

VILLIERS DE L'ISLE-ADAM. *RSH*, 242, is a special issue, 'Villiers de l'Isle-Adam: Poète de la contradiction', ed. B. Vibert, and containing: D. Oster, 'Totem et tabou (d'une figure imaginaire)' (11–28); D. Bilous, 'Signes de te(s)te (la dédicace chez Villiers)' (29–39); P. Berthier, '"*Gare*, dessous!..." (épigraphes cruelles)' (41–51);

P. Glaudes, 'L'ironie de Narcisse (lecture du "Désir d'être un homme")' (53–74); M. Viegnes, 'Le retour de la "chère morte": variation sur un thème orphique chez Villiers et Mallarmé' (75–87); A. Raitt, 'L'Angleterre et les Anglais dans l'œuvre de Villiers de l'Isle-Adam' (89–118); B. Vibert, 'La proie et l'ombre: le chasseur mélancolique' (119–35); and B. Sarrazin, 'Un rire bizarre, bizarre ... De Saturne à Janus: Villiers et Bloy' (137–59). I. Rosi, 'La "nonpareille des Florides": Chateaubriand, Villiers e le meraviglie del "nuevo mondo"', *RLMC*, 49:311–54. B. Vibert, 'Du code civil au code pénal: une réécriture villérienne de Stendhal', *RHLF*, 96:1137–43, revolves round 'Le Convive des dernières fêtes'. M.-A. Voisin-Fougère, **'Contes cruels' de Villiers de l'Isle-Adam*, Gallimard, 206 pp. R. Ziegler, 'Mourning incorporation and creativity in Villiers' "Véra"', *FrF*, 21:319–33, argues that the decadent text distinguishes between melancholy and mourning in that the madness of the hero is remedied by the æsthetic practice of the writer.

ZOLA. L. Besse, '"Le feu aux graisses": la chair sarcastique dans *Le Ventre de Paris*', *Romantisme*, 91:35–42, shows *Le Ventre de Paris* as describing sarcastic flesh rather than lavish flesh — an attack of abundance. *CNat*, 70, has a thematic section devoted to 'Espaces, désirs, transgressions': I. Chessid, 'Au seuil du désir: le dévoilement de la transgression chez Zola' (7–17), looks at the image of the veil as symbolic of the theme of transgression in the Rougon Macquart; B. Nelson, 'Désir et consommation dans *Au Bonheur des Dames*' (19–34), uses Benjamin's *Book of Passages* to explore the novel's subversive presentation of the sociey of consumption, looking in particular at the emblematic function of the Grand Magasin, seen as social and cultural space; M.-A. Voisin-Fougère, 'Ironie et intertextualité dans *Pot-Bouille*. Désirs, tendresses et haines zoliennes' (35–44), looks at intertextuality as a tool of irony; A. Fernandez-Zoila, '*Le Docteur Pascal* et *Lourdes:* une transvaluation des imaginaires' (45–66), explores the forms of subjectivity in the two novels; M. Wetherill, 'Transgressions. Topographie et narration dans *La Bête humaine*' (67–82), looks at the narrative mechanisms of topography. *Ib.* also contains: C. Daudin, 'Pour une éthique de l'œuvre: Péguy lecteur de Zola' (337–41); and M. Domange, 'Les Zola et les Fasquelle' (320–25). M. Louâpre, 'La bête et la machine', Perron, *Itinéraires*, 257–87, takes *La Bête humaine* as emblematic of a paradigm of the Beast and the Machine which reveals a redefinition of humanity at the end of the 19th c. at the outset of what Perron sees as the century of violence. R. Lethbridge, '"Le Delacroix de la musique": Zola's critical conflations', Cameron, *Champ*, 81–90, emphasizes the rivalry between art and literature for Zola. H. Markland Harder, 'The woman beneath: the *Femme de marbre* in Zola's *La Faute de l'abbé Mouret*', *NCFS*, 24:426–39, looks at the marble statue as erasing the apparent dichotomy between chaste and erotic figures and calling into question the notion of gender by its mixture of feminine and masculine qualities. P. Oriol, 'Émile Zola et Bernard Lazarre', *CNat*, 70:326–36. J. Przybos, 'The æsthetics of dirty laundry', Falconer, *Kaleidoscope*, 179–91, looks at the body and its functions in *L'Assommoir*. C. Rauseo, 'Zola et Goncourt: vérité et vraisemblance dans *L'Œuvre:* la scène de la pose', *CNat*, 70: 151–68, looks at Edmond de Goncourt's criticism of *l'Œuvre*, and the conscious rejection by Z. of verisimilitude as betraying truth. S. Saillard, 'La première traduction espagnole de *Nana*', *ib.*, 95–114, is a detailed presentation of the context, the reception for the translation, as well as an overview of the translation choices made by Tomás Fernández Tuero. M. Sachs, 'Émile Zola and the Dreyfus Affair, the writer in the public arena', Falconer, *Kaleidoscope*, 213–28, retraces the episode. R. M. Viti, 'Vizetelly's translation of Zola's *Fécondité*: the master in an English dress', *NCFS*, 24:417–25, shows how Vizetelly's cutting and cloaking the text in generality transform Z. into a pornographer rather than a reformer.

THE TWENTIETH CENTURY, 1900–1945

By ANGELA M. KIMYONGÜR, *Lecturer in French, University of Hull*

1. ESSAYS AND STUDIES

C. Coquio, 'Les derniers des Apaches ou qui a peur à Paris vers 1900', Glaudes, *Terreur*, 121–48, is an interesting account of the vogue for novels about Red Indians, 'romans d'Apaches', at the turn of the century in France. It is argued that the appeal of stories about savages (this is naturally how the 'Apaches' were seen) terrorizing honest folk is clearly linked to bourgeois fear of and need to demonize the *classes laborieuses* and the threat which the latter represented of an uprising such as that of the Commune. The mythology of the 'Apache' is also linked to contemporary fears of rising crime, anarchism, and the resentment of the Jews. Marilène Patten Henry, *Monumental Accusations. The 'Monuments aux morts' as Expressions of Popular Resentment*, NY–Bern, Lang, xii + 242 pp., is a sympathetic and very readable contribution to the cultural history of the First World War in France. It begins by attempting to establish certain truths about the war: the level of unnecessary mortalities and the injustices committed in the name of patriotism. The resentment generated by this experience of war within the *poilus* and their families was exorcized not by official attempts to commemorate the dead, such as the consecration of the tomb of the unknown warrior, deemed inadequate to acknowledge the suffering of the individual dead, but only by the construction of the 'monuments aux morts' in towns and villages throughout the land. These monuments finally allowed the expression of the grief and guilt of individual communities. The distinction between the fictional and factual sources used to establish this thesis is sometimes blurred by slipping frequently from one to another, in a way which gives them equal weight. It is a pity that more attention is not given to the monuments which give their name to the study, since much of the analysis does cover familiar territory: the nature of the suffering of the *poilus* and their rapidly blunted patriotic illusions. C. O'Brien. 'Beyond the can[n]on: French women's response to the First World War', *FrCS*, 7:201–13, challenges the myth promoted by the literary canon that the literature of the First World War was written exclusively by men. O'B. unearths and analyses a number of largely forgotten novels by women writers which deal with the experience of war and offer a new perspective on that experience. It is argued that these novels were not forgotten because they were badly written, but because 'their ideological responses to the conflict were muffled after the armistice'. J. Kaempfer, 'Métaphores de l'horreur. Le baptême du feu', Glaudes, *Terreur*, 315–28, considers the tendency of modern French novels to convey the reality of the battlefield not by showing heroic figures accomplishing heroic deeds, but rather by depicting 'des héros sans grandeur' who have only a confused notion of the events in which they are participating. Authors referred to include Giono, Céline, Romains, and Drieu la Rochelle. Martha Hanna, **Mobilisation of Intellect: French Scholars and Writers during the Great War,* Cambridge, MA, Harvard U.P, 320 pp. **Ecritures franco-allemandes de la Grande Guerre,* ed. Jean-Jacques Pollet and Anne-Marie Saint-Gille, Arras, Artois U.P., 261 pp. Surrealism continues to be a favoured area of study with a number of substantial publications both on the movement in general and on artists associated with it. Carole Reynaud-Paligot, *Parcours politique des surréalistes 1919–1969,* CNRS Editions, v + 339 pp., is a thorough and informative study which sees itself as filling a gap in surrealist studies by concentrating specifically on the political aspect of the movement. (Helena Lewis's *Dada Turns Red. The Politics of Surrealism* had already looked at surrealism from the political perspective in 1988, but it is much less detailed on the postwar period). This volume follows the politics of the movement from the end of World War I to its official demise in 1969. The work is well-documented, making use of recently available correspondence (notably that of Breton). It traces the political identity of surrealism from its anarchic beginnings to its association with the French Communist Party and the subsequent divergence of paths, with Aragon remaining in the communist fold while Breton and others moved on to new, but always political destinations. While dedicated to seeing surrealism as a political movement, the study also includes a useful chapter on the complex relationship between surrealism as a literary and artistic movement and its political identity. An interest in surrealism and in cultural studies are brought together in Marja Warehime, *Brassaï. Images of Culture and the Surrealist Observer,* Baton Rouge–London, Louisiana State U.P., xviii + 193 pp., which is not simply a critical analysis of B.'s development as a photographer, but also, as the title suggests, attempts to place him in a much wider framework. The cultural climate of the 1930s and B.'s sometimes complicated relations with surrealism are central to the analysis, which sees B. as a transitional figure, taking inspiration from Baudelaire's 'peintre de la vie moderne', situated between realism and surrealism, and yet looking ahead to modern media culture. The wide frame of cultural reference, including B.'s own literary work as well as his photography, together with the detailed analysis of individual photographs, combine to make this a valuable contribution to both surrealist and cultural studies. Katharine Conley, *Automatic Woman. The Representation of Woman in Surrealism,* Lincoln–London,

Nebraska U.P., xvi + 179 pp., begins by exploring the fascination which surrealism has exercised over women, both as creative artists and as critics, despite its perceived misogyny, a perception which C. seeks to refine. C. then discusses early representation of what she terms 'automatic woman', the ambiguous muse figure of male surrealists, at once potentially demeaning to the woman, and yet powerful and creative. This tension is pursued through a juxtaposed study of Breton ('the emblematic male surrealist') and his early representations of woman, and the work of two women surrealists, Leonora Carrington and Unica Zürn, who went beyond the role of muse to become creators themselves. This is a lucid and perceptive study of both the movement in general and of these two artists in particular. *Pensée mythique et surréalisme*, ed. Jacqueline Chénieux-Gendron and Yves Vadé, (Pleine Marge, 7), Lachenal et Ritter, 284 pp., is a collection of papers from a conference held at Cerisy-la-Salle in 1994 and is divided into three sections: 'Le Mythe introuvable', 'Tours et détours de la pensée mythique' and 'L'inéluctable mythe du surréalisme'. Contributions include: J. Chénieux-Gendron on the notion of surrealist rhetoric (25–48); M. Suzuki on Breton's use of masks (49–60); M. Asari on the theme of ecstasy and the search for myth in Breton (61–74); N. Piégay on 'sens mythique' in Aragon's *Le Paysan de Paris* (75–86); D. Carlat on Breton's concept of myth (87–104); and D. Rabaté on automatic writing as the founding mythology of surrealism (105–16). In the second section: Y. Vadé on myth as an interface between fantasy and reality (119–31); J. de Serment on mythic aspects of the poetry of Leiris (133–46); R. Amossy on Dali's interpretation of traditional myths (147–61); M. Watthee-Delmotte on Dali's reinterpretation of the myth of Saturn (168–81); and R. Golan on the relationships between myth and history, politics and myth in interwar France (183–206). In the final section: A. Russo on the elaboration of a myth around André Masson (209–28); R. Navarri on the myth which the surrealists created around themselves in order to justify their place in society (229–44); G. Colvile on the surrealist mythification of woman (245–62); and D. Viart on the representation in the literary criticism of the 1940s of the relationship between surrealism and myth. Jean-Paul Clébert, **Dictionnaire du surréalisme*, Seuil, 608 pp. A. Balakian, '*Littérature*/lits et ratures/Erutarettil: a retrospective on an avant-garde journal', *FMLS*, 32: 182–92, in a special number on 'The International Avant-Garde', provides a survey of the journal *Littérature* (1919–24) which gives an insight into the state of the avant-garde between these years. J. Stubbs, 'Surrealism's Book of Revelation: Isidore Ducasse's *Poésies*, *Détournement* and automatic writing', *RR*, 87: 493–509, argues that while *Les Chants de Maldoror* have always been seen as central to the development of surrealism, the importance of Ducasse's *Poésies* has not always been fully recognized. The links between *Poésies* and automatic writing are particularly explored. Frédéric Lefèvre, *Une Heure avec M. Barrès, J. Cocteau, G. Courteline, R. Dorgelès, J. Giraudoux, Mme. J. London, P. MacOrlan, J. Maritain, F. Mauriac, H. de Montherlant etc.*, ed. Nicole Villeroux, Laval, Siloë, 335 pp., contains a re-edited selection of L.'s long-running 'Une Heure avec' interviews with prominent literary figures in *Les Nouvelles Littéraires*. The choice of interviews is deliberately arbitrary, but concentrates primarily on the major figures of the interwar right wing, plus a number of writers seen as unjustly forgotten. Each interview is preceded by biographical notes on the interviewee. Two articles by J.-F. Sirinelli confront accepted views of the 1930s. 'Le mystère français', *FrCS*, 7 : 121–24, characterizes the 1930s as a period of opposing cultural tendencies: on the one hand, it was a time of cultural stagnancy, and on the other it possessed the dynamism of a culture in transition. 'Le temps des intellectuels?', *ib.*, 125–29, challenges the perception of the 1930s as a time of the commitment of left-wing intellectuals. The author sees the right-wing intellectuals of the time as being equally active and wonders whether the role of the intellectuals has not been over-stated. Jeannine Verdès-Leroux, *Refus et violence: politique et littérature à l'extrême droite des années trente aux retombées de la Libération*, Gallimard, 514 pp. *Critique*, 594 : 1–916, is devoted to 'Le Fascisme et la France'. Francine Muel-Dreyfus, *Vichy et l'éternel féminin. Contribution à une sociologie politique de l'ordre des corps*, Seuil, 384 pp.*Créer pour survivre. Actes du colloque international Ecritures et pratiques dans les prisons et les camps de concentration nazis, Reims 20–22 septembre 1995*, FNDIR, 264 pp. D. Boak, 'Four Frenchwomen's narratives of World War II', *JES*, 25, 1995 : 381–97, attempts to rescue from critical oblivion some of the memoirs and fictionalized accounts of World War II which have been largely forgotten. Works discussed include: Beatrix Beck, *Une Mort irrégulière* (1950); Dominique Arban, *La Cité d'injustice* (1945); Micheline Mauvel, *Un Camp très ordinaire* (1957), and Yvonne Pagniez, *Scènes de la vie du bagne* (1947). V. Engel, 'L'image de la nuit dans la littérature de la guerre. Lueurs et clartés sur un motif emblématique de Brasillach à Wiesel', *LR* (special issue), 'La littérature des camps', 1995 : 41–50, sees the image of night as central to an understanding of the different ways in which French and German writers perceived the Second World War. Examples of the image are traced through a variety of authors and texts. For the Nazis and those who supported them, night is seen in a positive way as 'le symbole exaltant d'une force sombre et mystique', while for the 'résistants' and 'combattants' it represents 'le lieu d'un combat librement choisi' and finally for the 'déportés' it takes on a nightmarish quality. Elaine Marks, *Marrano as Metaphor.*

The Jewish Presence in French Writing, NY, Columbia U.P., 187 pp. Yvonne Y. Hsieh, *From Occupation to Revolution. China through the Eyes of Loti, Claudel, Segalen and Malraux (1895–1933)*, Birmingham, AL, Summa, x + 202 pp., examines the representation of China by four writers associated with the country in various ways, in an attempt to identify some of the dangers, in particular of misrepresentation and distortion, facing the writer attempting to convey the otherness of a foreign country. Each writer's response to China is set firmly in the context of his own historical moment and its tendency towards sinophilia or sinophobia. This lucid and clearly structured analysis also brings a particular sensitivity to the potential contradictions inherent in the fascination of French writers with the Orient. Henri Copin, **L'Indochine dans la littérature française des années vingt à 1954: exotisme et altérité*, L'Harmattan, 320 pp. In John M. Dunaway, *The Double Vocation. Christian Presence in Twentieth-Century French Fiction*, Birmingham, AL, Summa, xi + 196 pp., the double vocation in question is that of Christian and novelist. D. seeks to establish whether these vocations are compatible or mutually exclusive through an analysis of the work of writers of the 'Renouveau catholique' (Bernanos, Mauriac, and Green, together with their precursor Bloy). This tradition is seen as being continued in the present day by the writer Vladimir Volkoff. The study highlights interesting parallels between the established Catholic writers and Volkoff. The final chapter on 'The Novel and Christian Belief' ranges quite widely on the problems and challenges which confront a Christian writing fiction on spiritual topics and yet attempting to avoid a narrowly didactic work. I. Husson-Casta, 'Les trois solitudes du roman de détection', Siganos, *Solitudes*, 171–77, identifies the 'trois solitudes' as the three central figures in any detective story: the victim, the perpetrator and the detective. This analysis is tested with reference to works by Gaston Leroux and Agatha Christie. Henri Mitterand, *La Littérature française du XXe siècle* (Coll. 128), Nathan, 128 pp., is a celebratory 128th title in this series, in which M. gives a concise and readable overview of the century's literary movements and personalities, ending with an optimistic anticipation of the 21st century. This is a useful reference work for students. Philip Thody, *Twentieth Century Literature. Critical Issues and Themes*, London, Macmillan, xi + 301 pp., is a conceptually more ambitious attempt to give an account of the century's literature. An erudite, yet personal view, this volume makes thoughtful reading for the specialist and non-specialist. It ranges across British, European, and American literature, covering themes such as religious faith, political commitment and realism. Specific to this period are discussions of Alain-Fournier and Proust in 'Visions of childhood 1: the child unhappy on its own account' (48–67), and

'Moral dilemmas 1: religion, ethics and some incidental truths' (157–69), which includes some discussion of Claudel and Mauriac. Neal Oxenhandler, *Looking for Heroes in Postwar France. Albert Camus, Max Jacob and Simone Weil*, Hanover, New England U.P., 234 pp., is not so much a work of literary criticism as an intensely personal account of a literary and philosophical journey, in the course of which the author finds travelling companions in Camus and his search for morality, in Jacob with his complex sexuality and spirituality and in Weil, whose rejection of her own Jewishness and her difficult relationship with her body, particularly expressed in her migraines, find echoes in the author's own life. It is also the story of a francophile's long relationship with France and French culture. **Mythologies de l'écriture et roman*, ed. Jean Bessière (Etudes romanesques, 3) Les Belles Lettres, 242 pp. Gisèle Mathieu-Castellani, *La Scène judiciaire et l'autobiographie* (Ecriture), PUF, 229 pp., considers, in a wide-ranging work, the similarities between the genre of autobiography and the criminal trial. Autobiography is seen as a genre in which the author plays a variety of roles: accused and accuser, lawyer and judge, moving from one to another as the moment requires, but always with the aim of 'proclamer sur soi la vérité'. Authors of this period referred to in the study are Gide and Leiris. *Ecritures de femmes. Nouvelles cartographies*, ed. Mary Ann Caws, Mary Jean Green, Marianne Hirsch, and Ronnie Scharfmann, New Haven–London, Yale U.P., ix + 413 pp., is an anthology of women's writing in French. The subtitle indicates the editors' ambition to redraw the cultural map, not only by including both French and francophone writers, together rather than separately, but also by establishing new and more complex literary affiliations which go beyond the traditional male-centred groupings of 20th-c. literature (modernism, surrealism, existentialism, etc.). A series of thematic subsections, 'Parentés', 'Violences', 'Se dire', and 'Imaginer', group together writers from different periods and countries. Each extract is preceded by a short biographical introduction. The bibliography would have benefited from a listing of preliminary critical reading on each writer.

2. POETRY

Ian Higgins, *Anthology of First World War French Poetry*, Glasgow, UGFGP, xxxii + 144 pp., renders the same valuable service to the French poetry of the First World War as he did for the poetry of World War Two with his *Anthology of Second World War French Poetry* (1982). He has rescued from 'collective amnesia' and has made accessible to the reader poems which, as he points out, are little read even in France. The anthology provides a representative sample of the work of the well-known (Apollinaire, Aragon and Romains), but also of the forgotten war poets, and includes not only the poetry of former soldiers, but, just as importantly, the work of some of the women left behind at home. With its useful introduction and notes on individual poems, this collection is an invaluable resource for students both at school and at undergraduate level. J. H. King, 'Gabriel Péri and the poetry of commemoration', *JES*, 26:17–35, examines the nature of the commemorative poetry which a number of poets were inspired to write about this communist martyr of the Second World War. Given the relative obscurity of P. as a public figure, this poetry did not so much celebrate a well-known figure as create a powerful myth of resistance and martyrdom. The author offers a thoughtful comparative analysis of the form and imagery of poems by Aragon, Eluard, Scheler, Masson, Emmanuel, and Guil-levic. J. Le Cornec, 'Le télégramme-poème. D'un motif de la modernité à un modèle d'écriture', *Poétique*, 107:301–20, considers the influence of the technological developments of the early years of the century on the poetry of the period, not simply as a 'motif de la modernité', but also in terms of its impact on poetic discourse and form. Marie-Claire Bancquart, **La Poésie en France du surréalisme à nos jours*, Ellipses-Marketing, 117 pp.

3. AUTHORS

ALAIN-FOURNIER. D. James, 'Decay and social disruption in *Le Grand Meaulnes*', Smith, *Essays*, 231–36, challenges traditional approaches to the novel 'as a documentary or nostalgic celebration of the past', and looks beyond this to identify the ways in which it represents some of the significant social tensions of the time.

ALBERT-BIROT. D. Kelly, 'From painter to poet: the visual poetry of Pierre Albert-Birot in *La Lune ou le livre des poèmes*', *FMLS*, 32:37–54, attempts to remedy the critical neglect of A.-B., an artist in his own right as well as a poet, through an analysis of his visual poetry and a convincing demonstration that it is a significant part of his poetic output and not simply ornamental.

APOLLINAIRE. Laurence Campa, *L'Esthétique d'Apollinaire*, SEDES, 240 pp., is a useful work which is part criticism and part anthology. It treads a delicate path in attempting to synthesize A.'s æsthetic vision, whilst at the same time acknowledging that, as an artist for whom movement and ambivalence were all important, and for whom theory and practice were inseparable, he never formally elaborated an *art poétique*. Drawing on writings as various as articles, lectures, corres-pondence, the poetry itself, C. none the less detects an artistic discourse, a discourse she defines as essentially protean and subversive, distinct from that of the avant-garde. P. Por, 'Apollinaire durant la guerre: reprise d'une controverse', *Littératures*, 34:121–44, is a closely argued analysis of A.'s writings on war, concentrating on what he refers to as their problematic elements, to which A.'s poetic greatness should not blind us. P. refers specifically to the poet's 'discours haineux et militariste'. *Guillaume Apollinaire 2: 1963, cinquantenaire d'Alcools*, ed. Michel Décaudin, *RLMod*, Minard, 198 pp. Catherine Moore, *Apollinaire en 1908, la poétique de l'enchantement: une lecture d'Onirocritique*, *ALM*, Minard, 100 pp. Peter Read, *Picasso et Apollinaire: les métamorphoses de la mémoire 1905–1973*, J.-M. Place, 1995, 316 pp.

ARAGON.   J.-Y. Debreuille, 'Quand le sens glisse sur le son. *Les Yeux d'Elsa* d'Aragon', *Poétique*, 106:199–211, explores *Les Yeux d'Elsa* through an analysis of rhyme, an important element in A.'s resistance poetry, and the centrality of rhyme both in deciphering the codes of *poésie de contrebande* and, equally, in rendering them indecipherable for the enemy. R. Short, 'The sense of the peasant in Aragon's *Le Paysan de Paris*', Smith, *Essays*, 257–61, is a lively exploration of the ever provocative and fertile associations or, more obviously, dissociations inherent in the collocation *paysan/Paris*. Valère Staraselski, *Aragon. La Liaison délibérée*, L'Harmattan, 1995, 367 pp.

ARTAUD.   Camille Dumoulié, *Antonin Artaud*, Seuil, 176 pp., is an eminently readable and lucid literary biography. A much more densely argued and allusive account is to be found in Evelyne Grossman, *Artaud/Joyce le corps et le texte*, Nathan, 240 pp. In this study A. and Joyce are grouped together as notoriously difficult writers, linked not so much by biography — there is no question of a mutual literary influence or their belonging to a common school of thought — as by what are seen as their similar conceptions of the activity of writing. Joyce and A. are seen as subject to a modern crisis of identity which has a profound impact upon the relationship between the body and the psyche. Writing fulfils the function of reconstructing, through the text, the body from which each writer is alienated. Florence de Mèredieu, *Sur l'électrochoc: le cas Antonin Artaud*, Blusson, 256 pp., is very much an interdisciplinary study with a long section given over to a technical discussion of the development of electro-convulsive therapy as a psychiatric treatment, with details of its use and its impact on the patient. In the second half, A.'s writings, in particular the *Cahiers de Rodez*, are seen to give a privileged insight into the effects of this therapy upon a particular individual who resisted its use. M. uses these texts to analyse the impact of ECT on A.'s writing through a study of recurrent themes and his use of language. I. Poutier, '"La vraie culture": art et anthropologie dans l'œuvre d'Artaud', *FR*,

69:726–38, concentrates on A.'s writings on art and his particular interest in non-Western cultures and anthropology. Already evident in *Le Théâtre et son double*, this interest develops in later writing and helps define his understanding of 'la vraie culture'. L.-A. Boldt-Irons, 'Anarchy and androgyny in Artaud's *Héliogabale ou l'anarchiste couronné*', *MLR*, 91:866–77, traces A.'s fascination with 'le double', which is represented in *Héliogabale* in the existence of male and female principles at once at war with each other (in a state of anarchy) and yet aspiring to a state of unity (androgyny). She explores the tensions created in the shifting patterns between the Double and the One. **Antonin Artaud: figures et portraits vertigineux*, ed. Simon Harel, Montréal, XYZ, 1995, 295 pp. André Roumieux, **Artaud et l'asile 1. Au-delà des murs, la mémoire; récit*, Séguier, 179 pp. **Artaud et l'asile 2. Le cabinet du docteur Ferdière: correspondance et entretiens*, ed. Laurent Danchin, Séguier, 348 pp. Alain and Odette Virmaux, **Antonin Artaud*, Lyon, La Manufacture, 278 pp.

BARBUSSE. J. E. Flower, *'Laodamie* by Henri Barbusse', Smith, *Essays*, 221–30, contains the text of a short 'acte en verse', written by B. in 1891, published here for the first time with brief introductory notes.

BERNANOS. Mary Frances Catherine Dorschell, *Georges Bernanos' Debt to Thérèse of Lisieux*, Lewiston–Queenston–Lampeter, Mellen, xxi + 267 pp., acknowledges that the influence of Thérèse of Lisieux on B. has long been recognized by scholars, though in a random way. Here it is studied for the first time in a systematic and detailed way. The saint's influence is traced through the whole of B.'s work, by looking not only at explicit references to her, but also at the extent to which her spiritual influence permeates the fabric of B.'s writing, culminating in *Dialogues des Carmélites*, seen by D. as his 'spiritual testament'. Louis Muron, *Bernanos*, Flammarion, 316 pp., is a sympathetic and very readable biography which aims to dispel some of the popular misconceptions about the writer. What emerges here is not the arch conservative and doctrinaire Catholic whom some see, but a writer whose preoccupations (his fear of the consequences of materialism and his rejection of totalitarianism) still speak to us today. M. is also keen to defend B. from accusations of anti-Semitism, referring to newspaper articles from the war years in which B. condemns anti-Semitism, showing that he had renounced his earlier views. P. Renard, 'Bernanos et la terreur dans l'histoire de la modernité', Glaudes, *Terreur*, 109–18, contains an analysis of 'l'esprit de Terreur' in *Dialogues des Carmélites*, comparing and contrasting this work with *Les Grands cimetières sous la lune* with its evocation of terror during the Spanish Civil War. **Bernanos et l'interprétation*, ed. Philippe le Touzé and Max Milner (Coll. Actes et Colloques, 37), Klincksieck, 250 pp.

BRASILLACH. R. Griffiths, 'Politics and literature; an intertextual relationship between Brasillach and Claudel', *FrCS*, 7:95–110, probes the intertextual echoes of C. to be found in *Les Sept Couleurs*, finding in this link between the writers evidence that B. was not so much a fascist in the German Nazi tradition, as commentators have frequently seen him, but founded rather in the Mediterranean tradition of Catholic fascism.

BRETON. The year commemorating B.'s birth has prompted a large number of publications, including a special number of *EsC*, 34:5–95, with contributions from: J. Gracq, 'Back to Breton' (5–9); T. Aubert, 'André Breton' (10–20); Anna Balakian, 'Reminiscences and reflections on André Breton' (21–31); S. Metzidakis, 'Breton's structuralism' (32–42); W. Bohn, 'Where dream becomes reality' (43–51); D. Schilling, 'Les retours du procédé: Breton lecteur de Raymond Roussel' (52–63); M. Rosello, '*Martinique, charmeuse de serpents*: "Changer la vue" sous les Tropiques' (64–75); H. Finkelstein, 'Breton and Dali – the utopian Eros in exile' (76–86); and B. Zavatsky, 'Translating André Breton' (87–95). Mathieu Bénézet, *André Breton. Rêveur définitif*, Monaco, Editions du Rocher, 234 pp., is a combination of two texts. The first, briefer text, *Portrait d'André Breton*, written in 1984, is judged by the author to be somewhat unsatisfactory since it approaches B. 'de façon extérieure au texte', something he tries to compensate for in the remainder of the book by concentrating on what is called 'la présence primordiale de l'écriture'. This is done in an abstruse, abstract language which makes few concessions to the reader. Jean-Claude Blachère, *Les Totems d'André Breton. Surréalisme et primitivisme littéraire*, L'Harmattan, 315 pp., is a detailed and thoroughly documented study of the important relationship between primitive art and culture, and surrealism. The volume is divided into four sections, the first dealing with the question of definition. A clear opposition is made between pejorative connotations of 'le primitif' and B.'s more complex understanding of the term. The second section looks at encounters between surrealism and primitive cultures, the third at the translation of experience of the primitive into literature, and the final section attempts an evaluation. *André Breton en perspective cavalière: avec des inédits d'André Breton*, ed. Marie-Claire Dumas, Gallimard, 108 pp., is a collection of 'témoignages' intended as a corrective to what D. sees as the 'dilution abâtardie du surréalisme' which is increasingly current. The work also contains three previously unpublished pieces by B., chosen to characterize his post-1945 interests. Alain and Odette Virmaux, *André Breton*, Lyon, La Manufacture, 162 pp., is a re-edition of this useful introductory guide, containing an updated bibliography which includes the numerous works on B. which have appreared since its first publication in 1987. N. Gardini, 'A metaphysical reading of Breton's theory of the *Image*', *FrF*, 21:61–77, discusses B.'s understanding of poetic imagery in the light of Derrida's definition of surrealism as a 'paradigmatic *system* of metaphors or images', seeing in B.'s theory not a system but a lack of formal coherence. Mark Polizzotti, **Revolution of the Mind: The Life of André Breton*, London, Bloomsbury, 1995, ix + 754 pp. Michel Ballabriga, **Sémiotique du surréalisme: André Breton ou la cohérence*', Toulouse, Mirail U.P, 1995, 368 pp. Gérard Legrand, *André Breton en son temps*, Méréal, 224 pp. Marie-Thérèse Ligot, **Marie-Thérèse Ligot présente 'L'Amour fou' d'André Breton* (Foliothèque, 59), Gallimard, 194 pp.

BOUSQUET. *RSH*, 241:1–243, is a special number on B. which includes a diversity of articles, on B. as art critic and collector, amongst others. There is also a substantial bibliography and extracts from the correspondence between B. and Jean Paulhan.

CÉLINE. The two book-length studies of C. to appear this year both consider him in conjunction with Proust. Pascal A. Ifri, *Céline et Proust. Correspondances proustiennes dans l'œuvre de L.-F. Céline*, Birmingham, AL, Summa, ix + 272 pp., is the more scholarly of the two volumes. Despite the obvious divergences between the two writers' work on the level both of content and language, I. finds ample evidence for the comparisons between C. and Proust which commentators have made since the publication of *Voyage au bout de la nuit* in 1932, and in this study he responds to Vitoux's 1978 invitation to undertake 'l'analyse parallèle des deux plus grands romanciers français de ce siècle', proposing a richly detailed reading of C.'s novels through the optic of *A la recherche*. The work is organized on a thematic basis and helps enrich the reader's perception of both writers. Jean-Louis Cornille, *La Haine des lettres: Céline et Proust*, Arles, Actes Sud, 155 pp., uses a much less orthodox approach. The author focuses on the correspondence between Proust and Gallimard, Céline and the NRF in order to trace C.'s alleged jealousy of Proust's star status at Gallimard and his determination also to be published in the Pléiade collection. S. Silk, 'Céline's *Voyage au bout de la nuit*: the nation constructed through storytelling', *RR*, 87:391–403, looks at the way in which, while apparently unconnected with C.'s later fascist diatribes, there are none the less elements of proto-fascist ideology in the novel, particularly in Bardamu's stories of the French nation. Henri Godard, **Henri Godard commente 'Mort à crédit' de Louis-Ferdinand Céline* (Foliothèque, 51), Gallimard, 224 pp. C. Halsberghe, 'Céline et l'extermination: quelques remarques préliminaires à une (re)lecture des pamphlets', *LR* (special issue), 'La littérature des camps',1995: 167–78, maintains that, in attempting to evaluate C.'s responsibility in the extermination of the Jews, the pamphlets need careful re-examination. Without wishing to exculpate C., something he sees as naïve, he none the less points out that it is as well to reflect on the very ambivalent reception of the pamphlets by the extreme right in France, and highlights their literary effects. Both of these points suggest to him that there is more to them than simple anti-Semitic propaganda.

CENDRARS. Claude Leroy, *La Main de Cendrars*, Villeneuve d'Ascq, Presses Universitaires du Septentrion, 360 pp., is a substantial analysis of C.'s second literary career following the 'double coupure' of the loss of his hand during the war and of his decision to abandon poetry. Evaluating his prose, L. concludes that the latter, while on a par with the poetry in terms of quality, is more subversive and therefore more modern than the poetry. *CCend*, 8–9, 1993–94, is a double issue which contains a number of articles on the theme of C. and music. These include: B. Cendrars, 'Musique en Espagne' (7–13); J.-C. Flückiger, 'Un art de la fugue: Blaise Cendrars et son professeur d'orgue, Carl Hess-Rüetschi' (14–54); F. Pagès, 'La musicalité Cendrars' (55–58); C. Le Quellec, 'Cendrars et la musique: une logique du réel' (59–67); J. Trachsel, 'le plan d'une aiguille' (68–79); J.-C. Vian, 'Les pianos en miroir' (80–95); M.Cendrars, 'Pour saluer Nicole Lachartre' (96–113); and N. Lachartre, 'Croquis figurant les objets de *L'Eubage*' (114–120). *CCend*, 10, 1–277, is a *numéro brésilien* with a number of articles on C. and his discovery of Brazil and its modernist poetry. Also included are a number of hitherto unpublished texts by C., including *Lampion*, an unfinished novel, and correspondence. These are followed by two lectures delivered at the Centre d'Etudes Blaise Cendrars in 1995. Miriam Cendrars, *Blaise Cendrars, l'or d'un poète, Gallimard, 128 pp. Georgiana Colvile, *Blaise Cendrars 4. Cendrars, la Provence et la séduction du Sud, RLMod, Minard, 246 pp. *Blaise Cendrars, La Carissima: genèse et transformation, ed. Anna Maibach, Champion, 336 pp. A. Leaman, 'Eclipsing the self: sexuality and the color black in Blaise Cendrars' prose fiction', *FrF*, 21 : 331–48, traces the symbolism of the colour black, most usually associated with dominant women who threaten to engulf the men they seduce.

CHAR. Serge Velay, *René Char*, Lyon, La Manufacture, 161 pp., is a new edition of this useful introductory guide, first published in 1987. It contains some new material, largely bibliographical, updated since the poet's death in 1988. *NAS*, 44–45, is a special number on C. which contains: S. Persegol, 'Recatégorisations discursives dans la poésie de René Char' (1–33), a semiotic analysis of discourse in C.'s poetry; and J. Fontanille, 'Interstice et résistance dans *Feuillets d'Hypnos*: une forme de vie chez René Char' (34–61), on the discourse of temporality. Jean-Michel Maulpoix, **Jean-Michel Maulpoix présente Fureur et mystère de René Char* (Foliothèque, 52), Gallimard, 196 pp.

CLAUDEL.   Albert Loranquin, *Invitation à Claudel. Autour de la Cantate à trois voix*, Le Roc Saint-Michel, Pierre Téqui, 199 pp., admits the difficulty of getting to grips with C.'s work and proposes an analysis of *Cantate* as a succinct introduction to the themes and preoccupations which characterize C.'s work as a whole. This is a sympathetic and clearly written attempt to make more accessible the work of a writer who is for L. 'un méconnu'. M.-T. Killiam, 'Claudel, l'Amérique et autres vues postmodernes', *FR*, 70:35–43, discusses Claudel as 'ethnologue de l'Amérique', drawing upon his essays on the United States which demonstrate C's belief in his civilizing mission as diplomat, a view dictated by C.'s conviction of his own cultural and spiritual superiority as a Frenchman in America.

COLETTE.   Growing interest in gay and lesbian studies seems to have given a boost to interest in C. as is evidenced by the number of items looking at her writing from this perspective. Elisabeth Ladenson, 'Colette for export only', *YFS*, 90:25–46, in a number entitled 'Same sex, different text, gay and lesbian writing in French', is a study of the ambivalence of C.'s status in the field of literary lesbianism, contrasting her acceptance in the United States as 'the foremother of French literary lesbianism' and the writer's own 'willfully obscure' depiction of lesbians. M. Callander, 'Colette and the hidden woman: sexuality, silence and subversion', Hughes, *Erotic*, 49–68, is a chapter from a volume on women's erotic fiction in France, a subject which is attracting increasing critical attention. Callander traces the complex and frequently contradictory nature of C.'s erotic discourse, which is seen as ranging from the traditional, invoking conventional patterns of compliant female and aggressive male, to the more subversive, both in terms of the reversal of gender roles in heterosexual behaviour and in C.'s exploration of female homosexuality. Other authors explore more broadly-based feminist interpretations of C., as in Corbin, *Mother Mirror*, 11–45 ('Mourning and Jealousy in *La Maison de Claudine*, *La Naissance du jour* and *Sido*'), which examines a number of her autobiographical works. The analysis views the complexity of relations with the mother in the light of feminist psychoanalytical theory, notably that of Irigaray, in order to articulate some of those aspects of the mother-daughter relationship which are absent from traditional cultural representations. The motifs of mourning and jealousy form the focus of the analysis: the confrontation with mourning is seen to help resolve problems of identity of self, while the exploration of jealousy is seen to be more problematical since it opens up areas of tension which are not so easily overcome. A final chapter draws the threads of the analysis together, showing how each author (the volume also has chapters on Beauvoir and Duras) contributes to an understanding of 'difference' in women's autobiographical writing. A. Ryan, 'The construction of the female subject: Belghoul and Colette', Knight, *Women*, 92–105, compares the problematical construction of the self for two female characters who are equally alienated from their environment. The heroine of B.'s *Georgette* is torn between the culture of her Arabic family and that of her French school, while in *Claudine à Paris*, the central character is divided between her rural upbringing and the rigidly codified Parisian society which she has just entered. D. Holmes, 'Everyday adventures, or what makes Colette a feminine writer', Holmes, *Women's Writing*, 125–46, draws instructive parallels between Cixous and C., who, like Cixous, gives importance to female bodily experience. J. M. Rogers, 'The "counter-public sphere": Colette's gendered collective', *MLN*, 111:734–45, argues that well-meaning attempts to place C.'s work in the patriarchal canon give her a status which is at best marginal, and maintains that a greater understanding of her texts can be gained through the optic of feminist cultural studies, particularly from the perspective of community and gender. The construction of gendered communities such as the girls' school in *Claudine à l'école* and the implied bond this creates with female readers prefigures the attempts of later feminist writers to construct a similar bond with their female readers. E. R. Viti, 'Colette's Renée Néré: Simone de Beauvoir's existential heroine?', *FrF*, 21:79–94, provides an analysis of the central characters of *La Vagabonde* and *L'Entrave* as example and counterexample respectively of the existentialist heroine envisaged by Beauvoir in *Le Deuxième sexe*. André Parinaud, *Colette par elle-même: entretiens avec André Parinaud, Ecriture, 1995, 250 pp. F. Giraudet, 'Willy et Colette dans les salons parisiens, *CCol*, no.18:155–66, provides details of the couple's participation in literary salons, a participation not particularly appreciated by Colette. A. Saura, 'Une traduction espagnole de "La Dame qui chante" en 1907', *ib.*,167–71, records the publication of a translation of this extract from *Les Vrilles de la vigne* in a Spanish literary review, and evokes more generally the influence of French literary culture in Spain at the turn of the century.

DELTEIL. *Les Aventures du récit chez Joseph Delteil. Rencontres de Cerisy-la-Salle 2–11 juillet 1994*, ed. Robert Briatte, Montpellier, Editions de la Jonque, 1995, 253 pp., contains a wide range of papers from the Cerisy colloquium, grouped together round the different manifestations of the 'récit' in D.'s works, which he labelled variously 'roman', 'demi-roman', 'biographie passionnée', 'mystère', and 'nouvelle'. Contributions explore topics including the influence of Occitan culture and language on D., animal imagery, the study of the *avant-textes*, D.'s relation to surrealism and the figure of the narrator.

DESNOS. C. Giardina, 'Les jeux de mots dans *Fortunes* de Robert Desnos', *LR*, 50:87–100, is a study of the humour of the word play in *Fortunes* in the context of D.'s interest in freedom and the role language can play in obtaining freedom.

DRIEU LA ROCHELLE. *Drieu la Rochelle écrivain et intellectuel. Actes du colloque international organisé par le centre de recherche 'Etudes sur Nimier', Sorbonne nouvelle — 9 et 10 décembre 1993*, ed. Marc Dambre, Presses de la Sorbonne Nouvelle, 1995, 287 pp., provides evidence, if evidence were needed, of the extent of sensitivities still surrounding discussion of colloboration or collaborators in the editor's need to point out that this volume is in no way a tribute to or an attempted rehabilitation of Drieu. Despite this caution, the collection represents a significant addition to D. scholarship. Contributions include: J. Jurt, on D.'s political commitment and the limits of that commitment in the context of the *entre-deux-guerres* (15–38); G. Leroy, on D.'s work as a journalist during the Occupation (39–51); J.-P. Morel, on D.'s attitude to communism (53–64); R. J. Golsan, on the critical reception of D. in the United States (65–75); J.-Y. Guérin, analysing the friendship of D. and Audiberti through their correspondence (77–88); P. Renard, tracing literary depictions of D. in a number of contemporary novels (89–103); M. Dambre, on D. as seen by the *Hussards* (106–16); M. Hanrez ,discussing the early poetry (119–27); C. Moatti, considering D. as a literary critic (129–47); L. Rasson, exploring the significance of 'désinvolture' in D.'s political and literary texts between 1934 and 1937 (149–62); R. D. Reck, identifying the *Journal* as a 'roman entre-genre' (163–71); J. E. Flower, offering a reading of *La Comédie de Charleroi* as a fascist text (173–81); J. Lecarme, detecting in D.'s *nouvelles* a version of his unwritten autobiography (183–96); F. Dugast-Portes, on *Rêveuse bourgeoisie* (197–210); and in a final article, J. Hervier, proposing an overview of the novels (211–22). The volume also contains a previously unpublished letter from D. to Jean Bayer.

GIDE. Michael Lucey, *Gide's Bent. Sexuality, Politics, Writing*, OUP, 1995, ix + 238 pp., is a densely argued and thought-provoking analysis of G.'s writing from the period when he both became more publicly outspoken about his homosexuality and also turned to left-wing politics. Taking into account the whole range of genres used by G. in this period (*c.* 1920–40) the author offers a complex analysis of the imbrication of sexuality and politics, of private and public, and casts new light upon works where the impact of G.'s homosexuality has not been fully explored: a re-reading of *Les Faux-monnayeurs* is a case in point. This volume is a valuable contribution both to G.

scholarship and to gay studies. Pamela Antonia Genova, *André Gide dans le labyrinthe de la mythotextualité*, West Lafayette, IN, Purdue U.P., xiii + 212 pp., approaches G. through the familiar route of the polarities and creative tensions at work in his writing, here seeing G. as both a writer in the classical tradition and, at the same time, a precursor of modernism. Concentrating on four texts: *Le Traité du Narcisse*, *Le Prométhée mal enchaîné*, *Œdipe* and *Thésée*, the author explores G.'s use of myth, in particular Græco-Roman mythology. This at once associates G. with the classical tradition and, by virtue of his use of myth to explore personal concerns (notably his homosexuality), prefigures modern writers such as Barthes and Tournier. *André Gide*, ed. David Walker (Modern Literatures in Perspectives), London–NY, Longman, viii + 239 pp., is part of a series intended to provide a critical introduction to major writers of the 20th c., and apart from a lack of material published after 1990, it fulfils this rather specific objective well. The volume assembles a wide range of critical approaches to G. by a number of specialists in the field, and as such provides a useful starting point for the non-specialist. Each extract is prefaced by a brief contextualizing introduction to the work from which it is taken. L. Cairns, 'Gide's *Corydon*: the politics of sexuality and sexual politics', *MLR*, 91:582–96, is a closely argued analysis of *Corydon* and its place in contemporary debates on sexual and gender politics. André Gide and Pierre Herbart, **Le Scénario d'Isabelle*, ed. C. D. E. Tolton (Archives André Gide, 7), *ALM*, Minard, 117 pp. H. Hutchinson, 'André Gide and the importance of being influenced', *AUMLA*, 85:55–68, proposes four theories on influence which, H. argues, are central to G.'s writing. M. M. Willen, 'The morality of revolt in Gide's *L'Immoraliste* and Camus' *La Mort heureuse*', *DFS*, 34:77–90, identifies crucial ethical differences between the attitudes of the two writers to the concept of revolt in these two works, this despite their apparent resemblances. While Michel's revolt remains on an individualistic level, Meursault is endowed with a sense of purpose which goes beyond personal happiness. J. Van Tuyl, 'All roads lead to Rome: the parodic pilgrimage in *Les Caves du Vatican*', *RR*, 87:531–40, analyses the motif of the journey in G.'s *sotie*, seeing in the disruption of travel a thematic parallel of G.'s intent to subvert traditional expectations of narrative in *Les Caves du Vatican* as he does in *Les Faux Monnayeurs*. C. D. E. Tolton, 'Symbolism and irony: a new reading of Gide's *Traité du Narcisse*', *SFr*, 40:271–84, identifies the ludic qualities of this text which are often forgotten when dealing with 'this highly cerebral work', and allow a more accurate placing of the text within G.'s work. Thus the *Traité du Narcisse* is more closely affiliated with later ironical and satirical works such as *Le Voyage d'Urien, La Tentative amoureuse* and *Paludes* than with chronologically closer works.

GIONO . *Giono L'Enchanteur. Colloque international de Paris, Bibliothèque Nationale de France (2, 3 et 4 octobre 1995)*, ed. Mireille Sacotte, (Centenaire de Giono), Grasset, 291 pp., contains a collection of papers given at the first international Giono conference held to celebrate the centenary of the novelist's birth. Contributions include: B. Clavel, on G.'s pacifism (13–19); D. Labouret, on G.'s polemical writings (20–33); P. Citron, on G.'s unexpected use of 'le rire' (34–43); W.D. Redfern, on G.'s humour (44–50); M. Cournot, on *Dragoon* (51–52); A.B. Bantel-Cnyrim, on misconceptions of works such as *Regain*, which was particularly popular in Nazi Germany, misconceptions which still mark perceptions of G. (55–64); F. T. Perduca, on G. studies in Italy (65–80); H. Godard on Giono and Faulkner (81–93); C. Baroche, on the theme of 'ennui' (97–103), M. Neveux, on the attempt to go beyond appearances (104–10); M.-A. Arnaud-Toulouse, on the imagery of the garden (111–22); J. Le Gall, on four typical forms of opening in the novels (125–38); J. Chabot, on *Le Hussard sur le toit* (139–52); L. Fourcaut, on the structure of G.'s imaginary world (153–69); J. Bellemin-Noël, on the symbolic importance of blood (170–83); C. Morzewski, on *Batailles dans la montagne* (187–201); P. Arnaud, on G.'s preface to his translation of Moby Dick (202–10); J.-Y. Laurichesse, on the baroque in *Un roi sans divertissement* (211–25); L. Brown, on the structure of *Noë* (226–38); A. Landes, on the importance of *Les Noces* in G.'s work (239–49); A.-A. Morello, on the image of Machiavelli which emerges from G.'s writings about him (250–62); M. Sacotte, on G.'s use of a *fait divers* as the basis for *Ennemonde* (263–73); and J. Meny, on G.'s film script of *Platero et moi* (274–86). Béatrice Bonhomme, *La Mort grotesque chez Jean Giono*, Nizet, 1995, 192 pp., is a detailed stylistic analysis of the language and thematics of death in G.'s work, seeing in the grotesque elements of the depiction of death a defence mechanism against the realization of the truth of the human condition. Christian Morzewski, **La Lampe et la plaie: le mythe du guérisseur dans 'Jean le Bleu' de Giono*, Lille, Presses Universitaires du Septentrion, 1995, 218 pp. **'Le Hussard sur le toit' de Jean Giono, actes du colloque d'Arras des 16 & 17 novembre 1995*, ed. Id., Arras, Artois U.P., 145 pp. Sylvie Giono and André Martin, **Le Goût du bonheur: la Provence gourmande de Jean Giono*, Albin Michel, 202 pp. Laurent Fourcaut, **Laurent Fourcaut commente 'Le Chant du monde' de Jean Giono* (Foliothèque), Gallimard, 240 pp.

GIRAUDOUX. *CJG*, no. 24: 1–195, 'La Folle de Chaillot 1945–1995. Dossier du cinquantenaire', ed. Guy Tessier and Pierre d'Almeida, forms the first part of an intended systematic study of the play and contains a number of articles on aspects of the play's reception and on different productions throughout the world, as well as a dossier of documents related to it. E. Scheele, 'La Guerre et la paix de Pierre-Joseph Proudhon et *La Guerre de Troie n'aura pas lieu* de Jean Giraudoux', *LR*, 50:101–17, sees parallels in the depiction of war and peace by the two writers, parallels presented mainly by a long series of quotations rather than by sustained analysis. A. Struve-Debaux, 'Giraudoux et les jeux du paradis terrestre', *Europe*, 806–07:151–56, in a special number on 'Sport et Littérature' analyses G.'s enthusiasm for sport in the context of his political and patriotic views.

GRACQ. C. Hubner-Bayle, 'La dialectique cruelle de l'amour et de la solitude dans *Hyperion* de Hölderlin et *Au Château d'Argol* de Gracq', Siganos, *Solitudes*, 67–77, traces the conflict between love and solitude and the 'incapacité à aimer un autre que soi-même' in these two works. J.-C. Pleau, 'Gracq et les signes: le problème du sens dans *Le Rivage des Syrtes*', *FR*, 69:453–63, argues that the system of signs in *Le Rivage des Syrtes* directs the reader towards another system of signs in Breton's *Nadja*. P. guides us through the parallelisms between the two works, both of which are based, he argues, on 'l'attente et la reconnaissance des signes'.

GREEN. M. O'Dwyer, 'Léviathan — a forgotten nouvelle by Julien Green', *FSB*, no.58:3–5, offers a brief analysis of this work, which is seen to contain in microcosm many of the themes of G.'s later works.

GUÉRIN. Bruno Curatolo, *Raymond Guérin, une écriture de la dérision*, L'Harmattan, 172 pp. R. Godenne, 'Les Poulpes (1953) de Raymond Guérin', *LR*, 1995 (special issue), 'La littérature des camps':65–70, offers an analysis of the thematics of a novel on the experience of deportation and imprisonment.

GUILBEAUX. N. S. Goldberg, 'From Whitmarsh to Mussolini: modernism in the life and works of a French intellectual', *JES*, 26:153–73, is a detailed and informative exposition of G.'s development from communism to support for Mussolini. The author suggests that despite the seemingly contradictory nature of this political evolution, there is in G.'s æsthetic values a continuity represented by his attachment to modernism.

JAMMES. *Francis Jammes, Oeuvre Poétique complète*, ed. Michel Décaudin, 2 vols, Biarritz, J & D, 1995, 807, 776 pp.

JARRY. T. Bridgeman, 'On the likeness of similes and metaphors (with special reference to Alfred Jarry's *Les Jours et les nuits*)', *MLR*, 91:65–77, is a closely argued analysis of simile and metaphor which challenges common assumptions about the relative value of each: typically the simile is seen as literal and trivial, while metaphor is non-literal, complex and creative. These assumptions are reached, it is argued, by evaluating simile and metaphor out of context. B. rectifies this by discussing them in the context of a specific literary work and concludes that similes may be just as poetic and forceful as metaphors. Claude Launay, *Avez-vous lu? Alfred Jarry l'unique*, Laval, Siloë, 48 pp.

LARBAUD. A. Blasi, 'Valéry Larbaud y las letras uruguyanas', *Symposium*, 49:243–49, sees L. not as a scholar but as a mediator with knowledge of a wide range of cultures, and with a particularly strong affinity with Uruguyan culture, a theme which recurs in his writing. This interest is traced through L.'s correspondence with Supervielle, amongst others.

MALRAUX. The year in which M.'s ashes were transferred to the Panthéon has seen the appearance of a number of substantial studies of the author. Geoffrey T. Harris, *André Malraux. A Reassessment*, London, Macmillan, xvi + 252 pp., appears therefore at a particularly appropriate moment for a reassessment. This detailed yet wide-ranging study attempts to come to terms with the apparent contradictions in M.'s career. Dismissing the simplistic dichotomy between M. 'homme de gauche' and M. 'homme de droite', between the novelist and the art critic, H. identifies continuity rather than change as the key to understanding Malraux. He argues that it was the political climate, and particularly the nature of communism which changed, and not M.'s views, while on the cultural front suggesting that the metaphysical preoccupations underpinning the novels are also present in the art criticism. H. offers a persuasive argument for viewing M.'s career as being more unified than is generally accepted. Jean-Claude Larrat, *Malraux, théoricien de la littérature. 1920–1951* (Ecrivains), PUF, 336 pp., is a lucid and detailed account of M.'s ideas on literature, based on an analysis of a wide range of texts, some of them little known. The volume is organized thematically, covering topics which include surrealism, symbolism, the novel form, myth, character, socialist realism, and proletarian literature. Roger Stéphane, *Malraux, premier dans le siècle*, Gallimard, 120 pp., is an intellectual, literary biography of M., starting from the beginning of his working life, exploring his confrontation with colonialism in Indochina and his first involvement in politics, the disorienting return in 1926 to a Paris where the surrealists had been displaced by Proust, and covers the early novels. The study was interrupted, after discussion of *Les Conquérants*, by the author's death. Philippe Le Guillou, *L'Inventeur de royaumes. Pour célébrer Malraux*, Gallimard, 177 pp., is less a biography than a series of more or less discrete essays, a homage to Malraux. A wide range of different aspects of M.'s life are covered in this volume including his experience of war; the adventures in Indochina, seen particularly through the optic of *La Voie royale*; his relationships with the various women in his life; and his work as Minister for Culture under De Gaulle. A much more precisely focused study is to be found in Hubert de Phalèse, *Les Voix de 'La Condition humaine'. 'La Condition humaine' d'André Malraux à travers les nouvelles technologies* (Coll. Cap'Agreg, 7), Nizet, 1995, 158 pp.. This is another volume in this useful series, which is published by a group of scholars under the collective name Hubert de Phalèse and whose remit is to bring the resources of information technology to bear on the detailed textual analysis of well-known works. The book identifies key themes, such as 'Chine', 'révolution', 'homme', 'mort', etc. and the frequency with which they appear in the novel, as well as offering an analysis of lexis and of the main characters in terms of their appearances in the novel and their individual discourse. Michel Cool, **André Malraux, l'aventure de la fraternité*, Desclée de Brouwer, 120 pp. François de Saint-Chéron, **L'Esthétique de Malraux*, CDU-SEDES, 212 pp. Jean-François Lyotard, **Signé Malraux*, Grasset, 420 pp. A. Greenfeld, 'Wives, mothers and the mirror stage in *La Condition humaine* and *Le Temps du mépris*', *FrF*, 21:231–43, fuels the growing interest in M.'s (rare) female characters by applying the Lacanian theory of the mirror stage of infancy to the relationships between Kyo and May, Kassner and Anna. G.T. Harris, 'Malraux and the psychology of the artist', *FrCS*, 7:77–94, is a fascinating account of M.'s complex psychological make-up, discussing in particular his construction of a personality 'Malraux' behind which 'André' was able, to a large extent, to conceal himself. Maternal absence is identified as the determining factor behind this 'concealment of the "True Self"', and this hypothesis is followed up by an analysis of mother figures in two scenes from *La Condition humaine* and *Les Noyers de l'Altenburg*. **André Malraux*, special issue (Littératures contemporaines, 1), Klincksieck, 103 pp.

MARTIN DU GARD. *Roger Martin du Gard. L'écrivain et son journal*, ed. Christiane Blot-Labarrère (Cahiers Roger Martin du Gard, 5), Gallimard, 230 pp., is a collection of papers from a conference in 1994 of the Centre international de recherche sur Roger Martin du Gard. The contributions which it brings together range more widely than the title might suggest, covering not only aspects of the *Journal*, published in 1992–93, but also, more generally, aspects of the writer's political and moral thought. On this more general level, there are articles by: F. Serusclat, on M. du G. and Rostand (15–29); J.-C. Airal, on his political detachment (30–39); A. Alessandi, on the constancy of moral preoccupations in his work (40–53); C. Andrieux, on the use of political documenton in his fiction (54–65); and J.-Y. Chung, on narrative perspective in *La Mort du père* (66–74). On the subject of the *Journal*, contributions include: H. Emeis, on M. du G.'s representation of André and Clara Malraux (75–87); P. Fawcett, on the motif of 'le voyage' (88–98); H.-S. Kim, on the depiction of World War I (99–112); S. Pandelescu on poetic aspects of the *Journal* (113–26); M. Parra I. Alba, exploring M. du G.'s view of Nazism (127–38); B. Pocknell, who evaluates M. du G. as a dramatist (139–51); A. Santa, who discusses the influence of Zola, *Les Rougon-Macquart* and the realist-naturalist tradition on *Les Thibault* (152–67); F. Tézénas de Montcel, who analyses the rhythm of the *Journal* (168–85); M. Touret, who shows how *Les Mémoires de Maumort* are not merely a 'récit', but also 'une œuvre d'interrogation sur soi-même' (186–97); and F. Zoghaib, who explores the question of sincerity in the *Journal* (198–217). P. Ruter, 'L'apparition des personnages dans *Les Thibault*', *Littératures*, 34: 101–20, attempts to go beyond traditional perceptions of M. du G. simply as an avatar of naturalist literary techniques, detecting in *Les Thibault* a more experimental technique in the presentation of characters, who appear not through the eyes of the omniscient author, but refracted through the subjectivity of other characters.

MAURIAC. Richard Griffiths, *Le Singe de Dieu. François Mauriac entre le 'roman catholique' et la littérature contemporaine, 1913–1930*, (Coll. Malagar), L'Esprit du Temps, 170 pp., invites us to view M. as an author caught in the tension between two literary currents: that of the Catholic novel, essentially didactic and stylistically conservative, and that of the modern novel, increasingly resistant to the constraints of realism and of the omnisicient narrator. The changes of approach identified in M.'s fiction are seen not so much as the result of personal or religious conflicts, but rather as the consequence of M.'s hesitation between these two literary currents. This lucid and perceptive study covers the period to 1930, encompassing the early novels which are firmly rooted in the Catholic tradition, moving on to *Thérèse Desqueroux* which is seen as a novel more psychological than Catholic, and tracing a gradual return to an explicitly Catholic standpoint in *Ce qui était perdu*. A further study is envisaged to investigate the later period of M.'s literary development. Nozomi Takenaka, **Le Sacrifice et la communion des saints dans les romans de François Mauriac* (Coll. Thèmes et mythes), Les Lettres Modernes, 151 pp. P. Cooke, 'Problems of establishing an autobiographical identity: the case of François Mauriac', pp. 17–30 of *Locating Identity. Essays on Nation, Community and the Self*, ed. Paul Cooke, David Sadler, and Nicholas Zurbrugg, DMRPH, provides insights into M.'s ambivalence towards autobiography as a form: at once fearful of what it might reveal, and yet desiring continued interest in himself and his work, an interest which would be encouraged by the revelation of autobiographical details M.'s careful construction of an autobiographical self is considered in the light of this ambivalence and in the specific context of the autobiographical texts which M. wrote. P. Cooke, 'The paternal reverie in Mauriac's "mémoires imaginaires"', *FS*, 50:299–310, argues that while M.'s most memorable fictional characters are usually female, and while critical attention has focused predominantly on these characters, father-figures have an important role to play in the 'mémoires imaginaires', those works which are based on M.'s personal experience. The role of these figures is characterized by absence and loss. This is read as a means of dealing with the premature death of M.'s own father. R. Kanawati, 'Un roman, un film. L'exemple de *Thérèse Desqueroux*', *NZJFS*, 17:23–31, compares M.'s novel and Georges Franju's 1962 film adaptation which, while lacking the spiritual dimension of the novel, nonetheless proposes a valid interpretation of its central character. François Mitterand and François Mauriac, **Mauriac par Mitterand*, Editions de l'Herne, 109 pp.

MICHAUX.   Claude Fintz, **Expérience esthétique et spirituelle chez Henri Michaux: la quête d'un savoir et d'une posture*, L'Harmattan, 336 pp. P. Bonnefis, 'Visage se dit', *RSH*, 243:9–27, contains an analysis of the motif of the face in the work of M. who is described here as a 'visagiste'. **Quelques Orients d'Henri Michaux*, ed. Anne-Elisabeth Halpern and Véra Mihailovich-Dickmann, Findakly, 238 pp.

NIZAN.   M.-P. Arpin, 'Discours social, texte et paratexte: les aléas de la fortune d'*Aden-Arabie*', *FR*, 70:206–18, discusses the social and literary significance of *Aden-Arabie* at different stages in its literary life: its initial publication, its republication in 1960 and again in 1990. In 1931 it was seen as a political pamphlet, in 1960, with its preface by Sartre, the work of a dissident communist, and in 1990 as an important re-evaluation of a past moment.

PAULHAN.   Laurent Jenny, 'Terreur et lieu commun', Glaudes, *Terreur*, 189–201, is a study of P.'s political ideas in the light of his dialectical opposition of 'terreur' and 'rhétorique' in *Les Fleurs de Tarbe ou la Terreur dans les lettres*. Jean-Yves Lacroix, **Bibliographie 1903–1995 des écrits de Jean Paulhan*, IMEC, 268 pp.

PÉGUY.   **Péguy tel qu'on l'ignore*, ed. Jean Bastaire, Gallimard, 464 pp. **Péguy-Senghor, la parole et le monde*, ed. Jean-François Durand, L'Harmattan, 238 pp.

PERSE.   Lucien Clergue, *Saint-John Perse. Poète devant la mer*, Biarritz, J & D, 99 pp., is a beautifully illustrated tribute to P., combining photographs and portraits of the poet taken by C., extracts from a number of his poems, letters, documents and accompanied by texts from a number of writers and critics. **Saint-John Perse, les années de formation: actes du colloque de Bordeaux 17–19 mars*, ed. Jack Corzani, L'Harmattan, 299 pp.

PIEYRE DE MANDIARGUES. P. Berthier, 'Glissements progressifs de la terreur. André Pieyre de Mandiargues, *Le Passage Pommeraye*', Glaudes, *Terreur*, 241–53, analyses M.'s evocation of *Le Passage Pommeraye*, highlighting parallels with Aragon's fictional representations of the *passage* in *Le Paysan de Paris*.

PONGE. Gérard Farasse, *L'Ane musicien. Sur Francis Ponge*, Gallimard, 187 pp., is a thoughtful analysis which renounces the ambition to synthesize and compartmentalize the poetic work of P. in a controlled fashion. The author argues that the poetry discourages the development of a clear, balanced overview, accepting the discrepancies and imbalances rather than trying to iron them out, seeing this approach as a truer reflection of P.'s work. There are separate chapters on metaphor, P.'s drafts, flowers and *L'Abricot*. F. Schverewegen, '*Le Nouveau Coquillage. Francis Ponge, Oeuvres Complètes*', *Poétique*, 108:431–38, proposes an analysis of *Le Nouveau Coquillage*, a text in which S. sees a parallel between the symbolic value of Proust's *madeleine* and that of the *coquillage*, 'une figure de l'origine indécidable et insituable'.

PRÉVERT. Alain Rustenholz, *Prévert, inventaire*, Seuil, 344 pp., is a substantial and informative biography which will be useful not only for those with a specific interest in P., but also for those interested in surrealism, the social and political climate of the 1930s and 1940s, and in the film and music of the time.

PROUST. The opening assertion of Pierre Bayard, *Le hors sujet, Proust et la digression* (Coll. Paradoxe), Minuit, 188 pp., 'Proust est trop long', and the proposition that the length of *A la recherche* could be reduced by eliminating the digressions, suggest a flippancy not borne out by the remainder of this lucid study, which begins by reflecting on the nature of digression as a rhetorical device. In the search for ways of cutting the work, a distinction is made between summary as a reductive technique (recalling Genette's summary of *A la recherche* as 'Marcel devient écrivain'), and that of 'amputation', the removal of certain passages deemed to be 'hors sujet'. The intention of providing the reluctant reader of *A la recherche* with the means to 'amputate' it is, of course, self-defeating, since after an attempt to identify just what is 'hors sujet', where digression begins and ends, B. concludes that the whole of *A la recherche* is a series of digressions, and therefore that the task is impossible. Mario Lavagetto, *Chambre 43: un lapsus de Marcel Proust* (L'Extrême contemporain), Belin, 126 pp., explores the narrative contract underpinning *A la recherche*, a contract which stresses the 'je qui n'est pas moi', and emphasizes that this is not a 'roman à clé'. L. analyses the implications of this contract and the ways in which it is transgressed, particularly in the context of the question of homosexuality in the novel. He focuses on a specific incident, the *lapsus* of the title, where, he maintains, the contract lies in ruins. *Marcel Proust. Ecrire sans fin*, ed. Rainer Warning and Jean Milly (Textes et Manuscrits), CNRS Editions, 215 pp., is a collection of genetic critical studies, focusing particularly on *Albertine disparue*. Contributions are mainly from those already working in the area of genetic, textual studies, but there is also a smaller number of essays from those who, while not normally involved in genetic criticism, are nonetheless equally interested in the impact of the *avant-textes* on our appreciation of *A la recherche*. The intention is to create a dialogue between genetic criticism and more traditional forms of literary criticism. Contributions include: R. Warning, 'Ecrire sans fin. *La Recherche* à la lumiere de la critique textuelle' (13–32); L. Keller, 'Approche d'Albertine' (33–49); J. Milly, 'Problèmes génétiques et éditoriaux à propos d'*Albertine disparue*' (51–77); A. Gresillon, 'Proust ou l'écriture vagabonde. A propos de la genèse de la "matinée" dans *La Prisonnière*' (99–124); W. Nitsch, 'Fantasmes d'essence. Les automobiles de Proust à travers l'histoire du texte' (125–41); K. Holz, 'Le motif de l'"aéroplane" chez Marcel Proust. La transformation narrative d'un avant-texte en con-texte' (143–59); U. Sprenger, 'Genèse et genèse textuelle. Abraham à Combray' (161–80); and K. Stierle, 'Marcel à la chapelle de l'Aréna' (181–204). A genetic approach is also taken by M. A. Schmid, 'Swann's marriage in text and *avant-texte*: a genetic and narratological study', *ZFSL*, 106:40–50, which contains a lucid analysis of the narrative discontinuity between *Un Amour de Swann* and *Noms de pays: le nom*, a discontinuity which makes problematical the reader's understanding of Swann's marriage. The analysis focuses upon the effect of this narrative blank on the reader, on the ways in which P. fills in the blank, and finally traces the development of the blank in the *avant-texte*. Gilles Deleuze, *Proust et les signes* (Quadrige, 219), PUF, 220 pp., is a new edition of this work. The second part has been divided into chapters in an effort to make this section clearer and a reworked version of an article which appeared in 1973 has been added. The first half of Jean-François Kremer, *Les Préludes de Claude Debussy en correspondance avec 'A la recherche du temps perdu' de Marcel Proust. Analyse musicale des vingt-quatre Préludes par Marcel Bitsch*, Editions Kimé, 129 pp., comprises a purely musical analysis of Debussy's *Préludes pour piano*, with the comparative half of the study occupying the remainder of the volume. The impact of symbolism on Debussy and P. and the notion of 'narrativité récurrente' form the focus of the comparative analysis. This work is essentially aimed at musicians, but does nevertheless contains some interesting insights for readers of Proust. Christian Péchenard, *Proust et Céleste*, La Table Ronde, 285 pp., is a personalized, evocative and almost novelistic treatment of the complex relationship between P. and his housekeeper and confidante Céleste. Jean-Yves Tadié, *Marcel Proust*, Gallimard, 952 pp., is a monumental new biography which could not be more different in its scrupulously detailed documentation. It begins by asking the obvious question, 'Pourquoi une nouvelle biographie de Proust?'. The question is answered explicitly by T., who points out that the biography of a writer is never complete, since it is not merely the story of a life, but also of a life's work. The questions posed by the author and the significant gaps which still exist in the documentation indicate with some certainty that this will not be the last new biography. The question is also answered implicitly in the quality of the writing and of its insights. Isabelle Ottaviani and Philippe Poulain, *Le Paris de Marcel Proust*, Editions des musées de la Ville de Paris, 100 pp., is a beautifully illustrated evocation of Paris at the time of P. It contains a largely biographical text and, more interestingly, paintings and contemporary photographs of Parisian interiors and exteriors, as well as of P. and others, together with illustrations of the Paris immortalized in *A la recherche*. A similar subject is approached, but from a much more scholarly perspective in Shinichi Saiki, *Paris dans le roman de Proust*, SEDES, viii + 254 pp. Paris is seen not merely as a decorative backdrop to *A la recherche*, but as a significant entity within the work. The study traces the steps of the hero through Paris in a systematic way in order to identify the ways in which the capital functions within and structures the novel and interacts with other elements of the narrative. Jean-Claude Dumoncel, *Philosophie deleuzienne et roman proustien*, Orléans, Xyz, 128 pp. * *Le grand livre de Proust*, ed. Charles Dantzig, Les Belles Lettres, 272 pp. Thierry Lage, *Marcel Proust*, Toulouse, Milan, 1995, 64 pp. C. Walsh, 'Re-reading Swann's narrative', *RR*, 87:377–89, provides a narratological analysis of one of the rare episodes in *A la recherche* (the pivotal episode recounting the conversion of the Prince de Guermantes to the Dreyfus cause) where a character (Swann) takes over narrative authority from the narrator Marcel. Martine Reid, 'Exécution (Proust)', Glaudes, *Terreur*, 229–39, is a complex analysis of the scene of the public humiliation of Charlus, a scene in which a revolutionary intertext is identified. Charlus, as representative of the pre-Revolutionary aristocracy, is subjected to a social execution by Madame de Verdurin, identified as a 'Robespierre en jupon'. A. Schulte-Nordholt, 'Le dormeur éveillé comme figure du moi proustien', *Neophilologus*, 80:539–54, offers an analysis of the 'dormeur éveillé', that is to say, the narrator not yet in full possession of his working faculties, but in an intermediate zone between sleep and full consciousness. This state, it is argued, allows the narrator an awareness of 'la nuit originelle dont il est issu' and therefore permits him to relive his own genesis. Jean Rousset, 'La Voix de Charlus', *Poétique*, 108:387–93, argues that P.'s characters are distinguished more meaningfully by their voice and language than they are by their appearance. The article examines in particular the variations in tone and volume of the voice of Charlus and the ways in which this reflects the development of his character. E.R. Viti, 'Le Mot de Cambronne: an excremental exclamation and its implications in *A la recherche du temps perdu*', *RoN*, 36:139–44, is a study of P.'s use of homophony, with particular reference to the associations between the words Cambremer, Combray-mère and *merde*, elaborating on the echoes here of an association between the maternal and the excremental, and the implications of this for Proust. C. Rhodes, 'Dialogism or domination? Language use in Proust's *A la recherche du temps perdu*', *MLN*, 111:760–774, uses Bakhtin's theories of language and the novel in order to propose an analysis of the social and political dimensions of the language of servants in *A la recherche*, against the background of the ascendancy of standard French, the decline of *patois* and the social changes of the turn of the century. M.R. Finn, 'Proust et le roman du neurasthénique', *RHLF*, 96:266–89, is a thoroughly documented study of *A la recherche* as a therapeutic exercise, conceived originally by P. as 'l'autobiographie d'un neurasthénique', an analysis suggested by the widespread interest in neurasthenia at the turn of the century, but more particularly by P.'s own exposure to the condition through his father's book on the subject. This conception of the novel is seen as being partly motivated by P.'s desire as a 'narrateur nerveux' to create out of the figure of the *neurasthénique* something infinitely more complex than his father's rather humiliating version. J.-J. Lépine, 'Swann aux derniers salons où l'on cause: les stratégies de la dis-simulation dans *Un Amour de Swann*', *DFS*, 35:33–44, traces underlying similarities between the apparently dissimilar 'salon des Verdurin' and its more aristocratic counterparts. A. Clerc, 'Des chambres de Proust aux cellules de Genet', *Europe*, 808–09:99–102, explores the influence of the experience of imprisonment — self-imposed in P.'s case, externally imposed upon G. — on their respective writing.

QUENEAU. G. Pestureau, 'Raymond Queneau, le moi et l'histoire', *FrCS*, 7:131–39, traces Q.'s political, intellectual and emotional journey through the 1930s.

REBATET. P. A. Ifri, 'The epitexts and allotexts of Lucien Rebatet's *Les Deux Etendards*', *RR*, 87:113–30, is a convincing attempt to rehabilitate a novel which has been excluded from the canon (unjustly according to Ifri) because of R.'s wartime collaboration. The article contains a paratextual analysis of the novel with particular reference to R.'s *Etude sur la composition des Deux Etendards*, a work he compares to *Gide's Journal des Faux Monnayeurs*, R.'s diary (the epitexts) and a series of allotexts, all of which provide fruitful insights into the process of R.'s literary creation.

ROMAINS. *Jules Romains et les écritures de la simultanéité. Galsworthy, Musil, Döblin, Dos Passos, Valéry, Simon, Butor, Peeters, Plissart*, Villeneuve d'Ascq, Presses Universitaires du Septentrion, 305 pp., comprises a collection of papers presented at a conference in 1994 on the theme of 'simultanéité narrative'. R. is seen as a central figure in this literary development, his unanimist vision one specific elaboration of 'simultanéité'. The volume is divided into two halves: the first focusing on R. and unanimism, particularly in *Les Hommes de bonne volonté*. The second section places R. firmly in the wider European context, acknowledging the development of 'simultanéité narrative' across Europe in the early part of the 20th c., when it was associated with the avant-garde, as well as its continuation into the latter half of the century and its association with the *nouveau roman*. The contributions are largely comparative, examining a range of European writers in the light of R. and *Les Hommes de bonne volonté*.

SAINT-EXUPÉRY. Pierre Nguyen-Van-Huy, *Le Devenir et la conscience cosmique chez Saint-Exupéry*, Lewiston–Queenston–Lampeter, Mellen, 1995, 179 pp., offers an alternative to the view of S. as man of action, seeing his philosophy not as one of action, but as a philosophy of being. Central to this philosophy are the concepts of 'devenir', seen as a process of transformation to a superior level of being; and of 'conscience cosmique', an awareness of self as part of a greater mystical body. These themes are traced chronologically through S.'s works, with a chapter devoted to each work. Unfortunately, the study is seriously marred by extremely poor proof-reading. James E. Higgins, *The Little Prince: A Reverie of Substance*, TWAS, xiii + 119 pp.

SEGALEN. Y. Schlick, 'Re-writing the exotic: Mille, Segalen and the emergence of *Littérature Coloniale*', *DFS*, 35 : 123–34, traces the rise at the beginning of the century of colonial literature, as distinct from exotic literature, but which none the less retained an interest in the exotic, while seeking to incorporate it into the literary work in a different way. Writers such as Mille and S. moved away from the romanticism of writers such as Loti, espousing a form of realism which aimed to address colonial issues in a serious way. The tensions which resulted in the failure of the enterprise are then discussed. C. Forsdick, 'Fin-de-siecle exoticism: reading Victor Segalen in the 1990s', *FSB*, no.60 : 13–16, places recent editions of S.'s works in the context of growing interest both in the writer and in the importance for a late 20th-c. audience of the issues he raised, issues such as cultural displacement and representations of the other. Noël Cordonier, *Victor Segalen: l'expérience de l'œuvre*, Champion, 264 pp.

SERGE. N. Visser, 'Authors, narrators, and the poetics of radical fiction', *OL*, 51 : 131–47, argues that the narratological insistence on the distinction between author and narrator is not particularly helpful in the case of radical fiction, where the boundaries between author and narrator are frequently transgressed. V. uses the examples of S. and Silone to demonstrate the possibility of successful radical fiction which is able to move 'beyond modernist impersonal narration'.

THOMAS. Edith Thomas, *Pages de Journal 1939–44, suivies de Journal intime de Monsieur Celestin Costedet*, Hamy, 1995, 333 pp., and *Le Temoin compromis*, Hamy, 1995, 235 pp., both ed. Dorothy Kaufmann, are important first-time publications of T.'s war-time *Journal*, her fictional journal of a *Pétainiste* during the Occupation, and the account of her political evolution during the post-war years. These editions will be useful for those interested in T., in the role played by women during the war, and in the Left, specifically in the Communist Party and the intellectual Resistance during the Occupation.

TRIOLET. Diana Holmes, 'Elsa Triolet: stories of exile and resistance', Holmes, *Women's Writing*, 167–89, proposes a persuasive gendered reading of T.'s pre- and postwar fiction in which she sees the recurrent themes of exile and alienation not merely in terms of the individual's experience, but as metaphors for the postwar experience of women who, having acquired a sense of identity and status in the Resistance, find themselves after the Liberation once more deprived of any social role other than those of wife and mother.

TZARA. *Dada est tatou. Tout est Dada*, ed. Henri Béhar, GF-Flammarion, 382 pp., is a new collection of T.'s Dadaist texts and poems which also includes a useful introduction, notes, chronology of T.'s career and brief details of each name cited in the text.

VALÉRY. William Kluback, *Paul Valéry. Illusions of Civilisation*, NY–Bern, Lang, xii + 147 pp., contains a series of eleven essays on aspects of V.'s thought. Written by a philosopher rather than a literary critic, they are not typical essays in criticism, lacking, as is pointed out in the preface, the apparatus of literary criticism. They are rather thoughtful encounters with V., showing a profound engagement with his ideas from the standpoint of the later 20th c. Florence de Lussy, **'Charmes' d'après les manuscrits de Paul Valéry: histoire d'une métamorphose. 2*, and *'Charmes' d'après les manuscrits de Paul Valéry: histoire d'une métamorphose: mise à jour des pages 357–393*, Les Lettres Modernes, 806 pp. **Paul Valéry, la page, l'écriture*, ed. Robert Pickering, Association des publications de la faculté des lettres et sciences humaines de Clermont-Ferrand, xii + 496 pp. V. Kaufmann, 'Valéry's garbage can', *YFS*, 89 : 67–81, is one of a collection of articles on aspects of genetic criticism in a number entitled 'Drafts'. It presents V. as a writer in thrall to a 'genetic *passion*', for whom the published work and the reader's gaze constitute an interruption of its infinite development. In this he is opposed to Ponge for whom the finished work and the implied gaze of the reader ensure the continuity of the poetic experience. M. Watroba, 'Désir est plaisir. Un poème de Paul Valéry', *Poétique*, 106:213–21, offers a detailed reading of 'Les Pas' in the light of Lacan's ideas on 'désir'.

VERCORS. A. Farchadi, '*Le Silence de la mer* ou l'injonction assourdie', *RHLF*, 96:983–89, considers the text as an example of Suleiman's exemplary ideological narrative, but one which lacks the clear rule of action addressed to the reader which Suleiman sees as being characteristic of the genre. V. Engel, 'Silence sur l'horreur: Vercors ou le songe d'une nuit d'hiver', *LR*, 1995, special issue, 'La littérature des camps': 107–12, analyses V.'s collection of stories *Le Silence de la mer* and in particular the story called 'Le Songe' (which, significantly, was not published during the war) for the light which it casts on the real extent of public knowledge of the concentration camps in 1942, a knowledge which many were later to disclaim.

VERHAEREN. *FMLS*, 32, is a special number on 'The International Avant-Garde 1905–1924', ed. Peter Read. David Gullentops, 'Verhaeren and Marinetti' (107–17), is an attempt to achieve a more balanced perspective than that which has obtained before on the relationship between between V. and M., seeing in the former not a precursor of futurism, but nonetheless active in its development. J. Marx, 'Verhaeren en France', *RHLF*, 96:246–65, discusses the awkward status of the poet, at once part of the French literary landscape and yet very much a 'poète flamand'. M. considers the role V. played in both French and Flemish literary life.

WEIL. Marina Cedronio, **Modernité, démocratie, et totalitarisme. Simone Weil et Hannah Arendt* (Coll. Actes et Colloques, 47), Klincksieck, 149 pp.

THE TWENTIETH CENTURY SINCE 1945

By H. G. McIntyre, *Lecturer in French at the University of Strathclyde*

1. GENERAL

N. Hewitt, *Literature and the Right in Post-war France: The Story of the 'Hussards'*, Oxford, Berg 217 pp., is a balanced study of right-wing literary culture in the period 1944–60, focusing particularly on three major figures of the 'Hussards' group: Nimier, Blondin and Laurent. The first three chapters provide a detailed and comprehensive overview offering a historical and sociocultural framework for the remaining three chapters on individual writers. This approach achieves the dual aim of reassessing these individual writers, each a colourful and interesting figure in his own right, while setting them within the context of the various, sometimes conflicting, right-wing ideologies they inherited. M. Atack, 'Posing the limits of modernity: the æsthetics of commitment in the 1960s', *JIRS*, 4:229–39, looks at the argument which dominated the 1960s between *littérature engagée* and the *nouveau roman*. It takes as its focus the confrontation organized by the Communist journal *Clarté* in 1964 between Sartre, de Beauvoir and Semprun on the one hand and Ricardou, Faye and Berger on the other. Comparing *Les Belles Images* and *La deuxième mort de Ramón Mercader*, A. argues that any crisis of meaning in modernity must inevitably extend to the act of writing and problematize narrative form. 'A questionnaire: French lesbian writers? Answers from Monique Wittig, Jocelyne François and Mireille Best', *YFS*, 90:235–41, reproduces the responses of these three writers to a brief series of questions circulated to five women writers associated with lesbian issues. B. is the only one, in fact, to respond specifically to the questions asked. W., who preferred to rewrite her own questions, speaks of her move to America and adolescent literary influences; while F. provides a general statement about her path into literature and her aims as a writer. Y. A. Guillemin-Young, 'Perspective quadrifide sur la poésie féminine bretonne', *DFS*, 35:109–22, looks at the work of four contemporary 'regional' poets: A. Vannier, H. Cadou, D. Collobert and A. Duval (who writes in Breton in fact), asking in what respect they may be considered 'Breton'. These poets, feeling Breton but largely dispossessed of language and culture, share a common sense of exile and solitude, a 'sens tragique d'absence', and for them the act of writing becomes an attempt at cultural self-definition. There are three chapters of interest for present purposes in Holmes, *Women's Writing*: 'Women in French Society'(193–215) sketches in the background to the expansion in women's writing in

the postwar period by charting progress in female liberation and the
growth of feminism, and includes a few pages of reference to specific
writers; '*Ecriture féminine:* the theory of a feminine writing' (216–30
considers Cixous's concept of *écriture féminine* in its intellectual and
theoretical contexts. There is some discussion of A. Leclerc, but it i
intended primarily as a general overview of what constitutes feminine
writing in the period; 'An open conclusion: women's writing now
(266–78) is a wide-ranging final chapter which combines genera
considerations on female biology and feminist æsthetics, as well as the
predominance of myth and fairytale in much modern women'
writing, with more detailed analysis of two *beurette* novels by Farida
Belghoul and Soraya Nini. A. Elbon, 'Spoonerism as a literary device
in Desnos, Leiris and Roubaud', *RR*, 87.2: 285–95, compares and
contrasts these three practitioners of the art form, with reference to
L.'s *Glossaire j'y serre mes gloses* and R.'s *Autobiographie, chapitre dix.* The
main emphasis, however, is on D.'s *Prose Sélavy* in the context of
Surrealist thinking and theorizing on language, and E. acknowledges
his debt to M. C. Dumas for details of this analysis. A. Hughes and
K. Ince, 'Reading the erotic', Hughes, *Erotic*, 1–25, as well a
presenting and justifying their study in general, discuss issues related
to French women's erotic writing in 20th-c. France. The discussion i
open-minded enough to make no assumptions, asking whether an
identifiable genre of women's erotic writing can be said to b
emerging and, if so, in what distinct generic terms it may be defined
The authors sketch the historico-cultural background from the time
of Rachilde and Colette, and speculate on the socio-political implica
tions of the existence of such a genre.

2. AUTHORS

BAROCHE.   G. Rye, 'Reading identities with Kristeva and Cixous in
C. Baroche's *L'Hiver de beauté*', *Paragraph*, 19.2:98–113, focuses on th
interaction between reading and identity, with particular interest i
female identity, in an attempt to answer basic questions such as: ca
fictional writing change the reader's (self)perception)? In a balance
article, R. draws on the thinking of Kristeva and Cixous on individua
and group identity to provide a theoretical basis for the exploratio
of identity in *L'Hiver en beauté.* The latter seems an ideal test-bed fo
this purpose since it is structured around the concept of dynami
identity ('identité en procès') and Queria can be seen as a reade
reading the life of Isabelle and (re)constructing her own identit
accordingly.

BARTHES.   See CIXOUS.

BEAUVOIR. D. Holmes, 'Simone de Beauvoir (1908–86) and *The Second Sex*', pp. 147–66 of Holmes, *Women's Writing* (see GENERAL), begins with a brief description of the existentialist premises on which B.'s analysis is based before concentrating on two aspects in particular of this analysis: female sexuality and reproduction and woman's role as man's 'Other'. L. Corbin, 'Complicity and silence in *Mémoires d'une jeune fille rangée* and *Une mort très douce*', Corbin, *Mother Mirror*, 45–70, looks at the ambiguity of the mother-daughter relationship in two of B.'s autobiographical texts, in particular the difficulty of differentiating self from mother. Using the motifs of complicity and silence, C. elaborates on the implications of B.'s ambivalent portrayal of her mother for B.'s own sense of selfhood. The discussion is clear and readable in an area where much is not. E. Fallaize, 'Reception problems for women writers: the case of Simone de Beauvoir', Knight, *Women*, 43–56, with its roots in reception theory, explores the reception accorded to B.'s work by her first readers: how B.'s reaction to this affected her attitude to her own work, and finally how this reception has been reflected in the attention accorded to B. by academic critics.

BECKETT. J. Long, 'The reading of *Company*: Beckett and the bi-textual work', *FMLS*, 32:314–28, analyses a series of parallel extracts from French and English versions of *Company*, illustrating the comparatively greater discursive complexity of the English text in the process. This is attributed in the main to its intra- and intertextual references. J. Pilling, 'Beckett's Stendhal: Nimrod of novelists', *FS*, 60:311–17, deals with a 'temporary affiliation' between B. and S. Despite initially modest disclaimers, evidence is found of a passing interest in S. in some of B.'s early writing (*Dream of Fair to Middling Women*), his letters to MacGreevy and in his lecture notes to undergraduates in Trinity. M. O'Reilly, 'Ni prose ni vers: *Comment c'est* de Samuel Beckett', *DFS*, 35:46–53, tackles the thorny problem of whether *Comment c'est* is novel or prose poem. She may not provide a definitive answer but a look at some of B.'s manuscript revisions, dispensing with punctuation and syntax, provides an interesting behind-the-scenes glimpse at how B. strove to create in his readers an experience of uncertainty and disorientation analogous to that felt by his principal character. J. M. Jeffers, 'The image of thought: chromatics in O'Keefe and Beckett', *Mosaic*, 29.4:59–78, draws on the ideas of Gilles Deleuze. There is a general discussion of chromatic theory in the history of ideas and of the implications of the concept of 'image of thought', as well as discussion of O'K.'s painting. B. is relegated to a few pages at the end with two examples of his short fiction, *Ping* and *Ill Seen, Ill Said*. M. Bryden, 'No stars without stripes: Beckett and Dante', *RR*, 87:541–56, compares their ideas of the purgatorial journey, contrasting D.'s Purgatory — a stage on the pilgrim's journey to Paradise — with B.'s world where any beatific vision is a much more remote possibility, unobtainable and perhaps even undesirable. L. M. Roesler, 'Beckett lecteur de Descartes: vers une métaphysique parodique', *ib.*, 557–74, attempts to extend the already considerable corpus of B. and D. comparative analysis to B.'s more recent work, in this instance *Compagnie*, driven by the conviction that *Compagnie* is a 'lecture parodique' of the *Discours de la Méthode* and of D.'s 'effort philosophique vers la certitude'. Two major new biographies add to our understanding of Beckett. A. Cronin, *Samuel Beckett: The Last Modernist*, London, HarperCollins, vi + 600 pp., is possibly the more readable of the two; but J. Knowlson, *Damned to Fame: The Life of Samuel Beckett*, London, Bloomsbury, xxiv + 872 pp., as well as being the more substantial, must also be regarded, thanks to the author's privileged access to B. sources, as the more authoritative. D. D. Green, 'Literature without presence: Beckett, Rorty and Derrida', *Paragraph*, 19.2:83–98, evaluates B.'s literary investigation of the metaphysics of presence as a contribution to contemporary theory in this area. The balance of the discussion is probably more towards metaphysics than literature but B. is kept in sight throughout and repeated comparisons of his position with those of Rorty — who may not have read B. — and Derrida — who confesses to an uneasy proximity to B. — make for profitable and informative reading.

BELGHOUL. A. Ryan, 'The construction of the female subject: Belghoul and Colette', Knight, *Women*, 92–105, develops an initially unlikely parallel between B.'s *Georgette* and C.'s *Claudine à Paris* in terms of the process of self-construction or determination which the respective heroines undergo. Despite the considerable cultural divergences between the two writers, more than enough valid comparisons are found to justify the exercise.

BONNEFOY. *EsC*, 36.3 is a special number devoted to B. There are two contributions from B. himself.: 'Ut pictura poesis' (9–26) a general essay on the relationship of poetry to painting which becomes a three-way comparison with the inclusion of photography. Apart from some initial comments on his own early exposure to painting(s), however, B. remains concerned with general issues; 'Remarques sur l'enseignement de la poésie au lycée'(106–19) recalls B.'s schooldays and adolescence. Of most interest to students of B. will be the section in which he describes the lack of cultural stimulation at home and in his surroundings and records his debt to his secondary education for awakening his sense of vocation. J. R. Lawler, 'Aux mots patients et sauveurs' (27–33), offers a close reading of one poem, *Le mot 'ronce dis-tu?...* from *Ce qui fut sans lumière*, before moving on to a more general consideration of B.'s fascination with Baudelaire — poet and art criticism — and the latter's influence on Bonnefoy. A. V. Williams, 'Yves Bonnefoy: art historian' (34–40), argues that B.'s *L'Arrière-pays* moves beyond a study of Quattrocentro painting to become a poetic and personal meditation on the history of art, combining scholarship with poetic sensibility. G. Gasarian, 'Ecriture de l'errance/errance de l'écriture chez Bonnefoy' (41–51), also deals with *L'Arrière-pays*, leading us through its 'complex labyrinth' by means of a common thread, the twin recurring motif, revealed by B.'s interest in the Ulysses story, of the rejection of the father-figure and the return to the bosom of the mother. E. Grosholsz, 'The Valsaintes poems of Yves Bonnefoy' (52–64), tries to uncover the 'indefinable and inescapable' presence of B.'s old house at Valsaintes in his work. She does so by examining a number of specific texts but, in fact, exceeds her initial remit by broaching much deeper issues related to the human consciousness, such as our sense of location in space and time. R. Stamelman, 'The presence of memory' (65–79), looks at the relationship between a feeling for place and a feeling for the memory of place in B., as well as the passage from memory to dream or illusion. It is a subtle analysis of the complex functioning of oneiric and mnemonic experience. S. ends by listing seven aspects of his subject which would merit further investigation but which space precludes here. E. Glissant, 'Du corps de Douve' (80–83), is a brief but grateful and affectionate homage to B., recalling the effect on him and other poets of his generation of the publication of *Du mouvement et de l'immobilité de Douve*. M. A. Caws, 'Yves Bonnefoy's *Sostenuto*: on sustaining the long poem' (84–93), takes *Dans le leurre du seuil* as her text, a detailed examination of which raises the issue, which she regards as not just æsthetic but moral, of what sustains the long poem. In the process, she emphasizes the 'intensely moral concerns' which underpin B.'s work and elucidates complex links with other texts and writers. R. W. Greene, 'When Apollinaire, Malraux and Bonnefoy write about art' (94–105), assesses three contributions to art criticism, concluding that B. not only surpasses his two notable predecessors but also synthesizes in his own criticism their respective, individual interests in the present and the past.

CAMUS, ALBERT. J. Sarrochi, *Le Dernier Camus ou Le Premier Homme*, Nizet, 1995, 317 pp., is an extensive and painstaking search for the *image paternelle*, based on the premise that C. is an 'artiste inspiré par une herméneutique du père'. Detailed but not restrictive, this study develops into a wideranging, allusive (Tolstoy, Melville, Faulkner) and thought-provoking discussion of *Le Premier Homme* from a variety of angles which sometimes requires, but always repays, careful reading. J.-M. Laclaventine, 'Albert Camus — La Crise de l'homme', *NRF*, 516:8–21, is a translation back into French by L. of a speech delivered by C. at Columbia University in 1946 and only published subsequently in English in a local university magazine, *Twice a Year* P. Dunwoodie, *Une Histoire ambivalente: le dialogue Camus-Dostoievski* Nizet, 240 pp., is a thorough and extensive examination of the 'présence obsédante' of D. in C.'s work: the sweep is broad and all-inclusive (novels, stories, plays and *carnets*), there is ample detailed cross-textual illustration, and the analysis is everywhere as informative as it is clear-sighted. J. Malrieu, *L'Etranger (dossier)* (Folio Plus) Gallimard, 177 pp. M. Morize, *L'Etranger de Camus: étude de l'œuvre* (Repères), Hachette, 96 pp. Y. Ansel, *La Peste (dossier)* (Folio Plus) Gallimard, 406 pp. J. Lévi-Valensi, *La Chute* (Foliothèque), Gallimard, 221 pp.

CAMUS, RENAUD. B. Vercier, 'An interview with Renaud Camus' *YFS*, 90:7–21, is an English translation of an original interview with a writer whose considerable and growing corpus of work deserves more critical attention. The interview ranges over such topics as C.'s idea of the ideal reader, the reception of his work and his definition of what it means to be a homosexual writer.

CHAWAF. D. Holmes, 'Defining a feminine writing: Chantal Chawaf and Marguerite Duras', pp. 231–45 of Holmes, *Women's Writing* (see GENERAL), cites C. as a precursor of Cixous's theorizing but discussion is confined to a straightforward analysis of *Blé et semence*. There is the suggestion, however, that C.'s writing does ironically undermine the superficially clear demarcation between male and female spheres. See also LECLERC.

CIXOUS. A. Aneja, 'Translating backwards: Hélène Cixous's *L'Indiade*', *StH*, 22:50–63, uses C.'s transcultural play to test W. Benjamin's and P. de Man's contention that the translator fails if he or she does not capture the 'originariness' of the original language. A. argues that a text like *L'Indiade* blurs notions such as 'original' and 'derivational' and she finds that Benjamin's and de Man's assumptions do not square easily with the complexities of this post-modern multi-cultural text which is itself both poem and translation. C. Oboussier, 'Synæsthesia in Cixous and Barthes', Knight, *Women* 115–31, considers this phenomenon in both writers not just as a poetic effect but also for its wider epistemological implications. B. does not, in fact, figure prominently but the discussion remains wide-ranging, touching on neuroscience before turning to C. on Clarice Lispector, Kantian taxonomy and rhythm. E. Wilson, 'Hélène Cixous: an erotics of the feminine', Hughes, *Erotic*, 121–46, consists of a reading of two texts, *Le Livre de Promethea* and *La Bataille d'Arcachon*. There are interesting comments on the details of both texts but the article does not lose sight of the more general issue it sets out to address: that C.'s undermining of the notions of identity and subjectivity is best understood in the context of her writing of the erotic relations between women. E. Brown, 'The lake of seduction: body, acting and voice in Hélène Cixous's *Portrait de Dora*', *ModD*, 39:626–49, takes as its premise that for C. the theatre is a metaphor for the feminine position in our culture and interprets C. as undermining Freud's application of the Oedipal model to the Ida Bauer case by challenging the phallocratic origins of both psychoanalysis and classical theatre. M. Bryden, 'Hélène Cixous and Maria Chevska', Knight, *Women*, 106–14, is mostly concerned with a 1992 exhibition by Chevska and her homage to C. but it does contain some comment on C. thoughts on the *œuvre d'être* as opposed to the *œuvre d'art*. See also BAROCHE.

COLETTE. See BELGHOUL.

DES FORÊTS. J. Peterson, 'Lucien-René des Forêts: "Face à l'immémorable"', *MLN*, 111:747–59, takes the publication of the latest instalment in Des F.'s long-running *Ostinato*, in progress since 1983, as the opportunity for a wide-ranging retrospective on Des F.'s work, going back principally to the 1960s but also with some reference to the novels of the 1940s.

DUBOUCHET. G. W. Fetzer, 'André Dubouchet: imagining the real, seeing the unseeable', *NFS*, 35:76–83, examines visual perception as a means of escaping the inner self and discovering that elusive homogeneity of *le réel* that lies outwith man. This perception is defined as bi-directional in nature and F. studies the interplay of two perspectives — that of the poet on the world and the world's point of view as recorded by the poet.

DURAS. J. S. Williams, 'All her sons: Marguerite Duras, antiliterature and the outside', *YFS*, 90:40–70, underlines the growing importance of D.'s work in the area of gay studies. It is an informative chronicle of her contacts with various practitioners and theorists of gay writing and contains some analysis of her own post-1980s writing. C. A. Lindenlaub, '*Un Barrage contre le Pacifique*: autoportrait et lieu mnémonique', *WIFS*, 4:88–99, considers three mnemonic functions of the idea of locus in D.'s novel, emphasizing the spatial and visual or cinematic qualities of her writing. D.'s use of the *lieu mnémonique* indicates the abandonment of narration, the erasure of the autobiographical and her critique of colonialism. L. Corbin, 'Orality and specularity in *Un Barrage contre le Pacifique*, *L'Eden Cinéma*, *L'Amant* and *L'Amant de la Chine du Nord*', Corbin, *Mother Mirror*, 71–113, sees each of the four texts as a transformation of the same ontogenetic tale of D.'s childhood in Indochina, with each subsequent retelling accentuating the shift from autobiography to fiction to legend. The theories of Kristeva and Irigaray inform the subsequent discussion of orality and specularity in the formative mother-daughter relationship.

P. Saint-Amand, 'The sorrows of Lol V. Stein', *Paragraph*, 19.1:21–35, rejects what he sees as Lacan's mistakenly phallocentric and logocentric analysis of the book which he sees as inappropriate to a work which illustrates the impossibility of describing Lol's malady in words. Instead, he prefers to examine the relationship between fiction and psychology from the perspective of D.'s interest in the therapeutic power of trance, hypnosis and the occult. K. Ince, 'L'amour la mort; the eroticism of Marguerite Duras', Hughes, *Erotic*, 147–73, deals with three texts: *L'Homme assis dans le couloir*, *La maladie de la mort*, and *Les Yeux bleus cheveux noirs*. She rejects D.'s own disclaimers and defines her as an obsessively and, in the 1980s, increasingly, erotic writer, with particular reference to her exploration of the tensions between erotic love and western social structures. Y. Y. Hsieh, 'L'évolution du discours (anti-)colonialiste dans *Un Barrage contre le Pacifique*, *L'Amant* and *L'Amant de la Chine du Nord* de Marguerite Duras', *DFS*, 35:56–65, sets out to compare D.'s 'discours (anti-) colonialiste' in the three books in question but, as her judicious use of brackets indicates, she finds it no easier to define D.'s position on colonialism than on her much debated feminism. However, one can at least point safely to an evolution away from the relatively simple anti-colonial feeling of *Un Barrage contre le Pacifique* towards greater plurivocity in her subsequent writing. L. Vickroy, 'The politics of abuse: the traumatised child in Toni Morrison and Marguerite Duras', *Mosaic*, 29.2:91–110, is intended as a detailed analysis of the relationship of trauma to social oppression and demonstrates how this relationship is dramatized in the critiques of colonialism contained in M.'s *The Bheest Eye* and D.'s *The Vice-Consul*.

ERNAUX. S. McIlvanney, 'Recuperating romance: literary paradigms in the works of Annie Ernaux', *FMLS*, 32:240–50, focuses on an unusual aspect of E.'s intertextuality; the ambivalent relationship of her characters to that most 'unfeminist' of genres, romantic fiction. Luckily, this relationship is not pernicious since E.'s female protagonists see the difference between this fiction and their real-life experiences. The discussion, which is clear and informative, draws on a range of feminist theories and manages to encompass a broad spectrum of E.'s writing. M. Bacholle, '*Passion simple* d'Annie Ernaux: vers une désacralisation de la société française?', *DFS*, 36:123–33, ponders the interplay of sacred and profane in *Passion simple*, but in a sociological rather than a religious sense, against the background of changes in social standards in modern France. B. finds that the tension between sexual liberation and the retention of some older, deeply-rooted taboos is paralleled by the *valeurs sacrées* of the mother and the *passion profane* of the narrator. Nothing is that simple, however,

and the narrator's 'profanity' can be construed as containing a
vestigial respect for the sacred. See also ROCHEFORT.

GENET.   D. F. Connon, 'Confused? You will be: Genet's *Les Nègres*
and the art of upsetting the audience', *FS*, 50 : 425–38, points out that
Les Nègres is not so much a play for blacks as for whites and that,
consequently, the relationship between stage and audience is meant
to be an antagonistic one. The article examines the various ways in
which G. sets out to offend, frighten or provoke the racist instincts of
his audience. Principal among these is the confusion generated by the
play's multi-layered complexity which leaves its audience feeling
equally confused and threatened. T. Saulnier, 'Genet encore et
toujours', *NRF*, 524 : 32–49, makes grandiose claims for G.'s reputation which has grown since his death thanks to posthumous publications. Only Chateaubriand is his equal in terms of *splendeur*. There are
comparisons with a variety of modern figures, even Foucault, and
some passing reference to G.'s politics. S.-D. Ménager, 'Vertige du
sentiment de l'altitude comme principe fondateur du théâtre de
Genet', *RHT*, 447–54, wonders why G. was unwilling ever to publish
his 1948 play *Splendid's*. Seemingly, this discarded manuscript contains
manifestations of the 'sentiment d'altitude' which is a primordial
element of G.'s theatre and hence forms an intermediate stage, a
missing link, in the evolution from the bedroom window and balcony
of *Les Bonnes* to the balcony of *Le Balcon* and the *gradins* of *Les Nègres*.
C. Lavery, 'Racism and alienation effects in *Les Nègres*', Smith, *Essays,*
313–17, takes issue with the view that the play is necessarily flawed as
committed theatre because of G.'s penchant for threatricalism. On
the contrary, by rejecting realism and reasoned argument, G. arouses
anger and anxiety in his audience, forcing them to experience directly
their own racist tendencies.

GUIBERT.   R. Sarkonak, 'Traces and shadows: fragments of Hervé
Guibert', *YFS*, 90 : 172–204, deals mainly with the photographic
talents of this protean figure and is, appropriately, amply illustrated.
It does stray into other areas, however; his writing, his friendships
with Foucault and Barthes, and homosexual politics. It may provide
some useful background for students of his writing.

IONESCO.   *NFS*, 35.1, is a special issue devoted to I.'s theatre.
V. Barry, 'Vous avez dit "bizarre"? ou Ionesco de l'anormal au supra-
normal' (1–10), begins from dictionary definitions of bizarre and
normal and proceeds to demonstrate how I. subverts normality in his
plays. The most interesting sections are those on I.'s ideas on the *anti-
monde* of the supra-normal. D. Bradby, '*Voyages chez les morts*: Ionesco's
role in the development of the new theatre æsthetic'(11–20), offers an
interestingly broad sweep, setting I.'s work against the background of
modern 20th-c. developments and making comparisons with Sartre,

Beckett, Vaclav Havel, Vinaver et al. I. C. Chafee, 'Moving day in the cosmos: from Eliade's conservation of the house to Ionesco's *Le Nouveau Locataire*' (21–29), brings the ideas of I.'s friend Eliade to bear on *Le Nouveau Locataire* and interprets the play in a triple perspective; as a parody of rituals for consecrating new structures, as an imitation of ancient burial ceremonies and as a metaphor for the conservation of a new type of theatre — 'a housewarming for the anti-theatre'. C. E. J. Dolamore, 'Evil and ideal in *Macbett*' (30–38), assesses the forces of evil and its ramifications in *Macbett*. Evil is considered mainly from a political standpoint to emphasize I.'s contempt for political action and his view of how man's propensity for evil thwarts his efforts or impulse towards self-improvement. In addition to an extended comparison with Shakespeare, the influence of Jarry and Jan Kott is also noted. G. Féal, 'Euphorie et dépression: la double vision de la sexualité dans *Le Piéton de l'air*' (39–52), uses an imaginative and psychological approach to look behind the 'obvious Message' of *Le Piéton de l'air* and the usual metaphysical interpretations of the play, laying bare instead the subconscious and oneiric dimension of the play and identifying various sexual symbols which give the play its underlying coherence and true meaning. M. Holland, 'Ionesco and tradition' (53–66), maintains a broad, general and theoretical approach, eschewing detailed analysis of specific work and preferring to explore and define I.'s 'modernity' in terms of the traditions of his time. He concludes that I.'s search for originality is not necessarily in conflict with tradition. M. Issacharoff, 'Ionesco's names' (67–73), reviews I.'s practice of choosing misleading or subversive titles when naming his plays as well as the naming or rather non-naming of characters within the plays. Principal reference is to *Délire à deux*. E. Jacquart, 'Ionesco and the creative drive' (74–86), examines the theory and practice of creativity in I.'s theatre, comparing and contrasting I.'s general statements on the creative act with his actual practice of theory on the stage. R. C. Lamont, 'Ionesco en pantoufles' (87–95), regards I.'s meditative and confessional writings and his non-journalistic writings as an art form in themselves. She emphasizes two salient features: the meandering structure and achronological presentation of I.'s reminiscences, and the significance and lasting effects of his childhood memories. J. Long, 'From *The Killer* to *The King*: representation of space in the Béranger cycle' (96–107), examines what the four Béranger plays have in common, with particular reference to the dramaturgical function of space. He cites I.'s increasingly elaborate and ambitious use of stage space, the introduction of outdoor sets etc. P. McGuinness, 'Ionesco and symbolist theatre: revolution and restitution in the avant-garde' (108–19), is basically a comparison of Maeterlinck and Ionesco.

Apart from some brief discussion of M.'s early plays, the bulk of the article is devoted to a comparison of the two writers' dramatic theories. E. Rozik, 'Multiple metaphorical characterization in *Le Roi se meurt*' (120–31), rejects as too simplistic the usual view of language in the Theatre of the Absurd as a vehicle for miscommunication. By way of demonstration, he argues that the apparent difficulties of the dialogue in the play are in fact a reflection of a new mode of characterization, multiple and metaphorical in nature. Once this is realized and accepted, surface absurdity vanishes and intelligibility ensues. S. Smith, 'Signs of emptiness in *Les Chaises*' (132–41), provides an interesting psychological approach to the play, from a variety of angles, which defines it as allegorical dramatization of I.'s anxieties about the reception and interpretation of his work. D. Whitton, 'Interpreting *Les Chaises*: the play in production 1952–1988' (142–52), reviews the various factors determining the interpretation and reception of the play in performance. A comparison of notable French productions from the 1952 premiere onwards reveals no obviously 'correct' way of interpreting it. M. Issacharof and L. Madrid, 'Between myth and reference: Puig and Ionesco', *RR.*, 87:419–30, is a comparison of P.'s *Under a Mantle of Stars* and I.'s *La Cantatrice chauve*, highlighting the undermining of identity, individuality and the idea of character by the use of popular myth and stereotypes in P. and repetition in I.'s theatre. M. Lioure, *Les Chaises* (Folio Théâtre), Gallimard, 146 pp.

JACCOTTET. D. Rochat, '"Cahiers de verdure" ou "les méandres de la rêverie": remarques sur les proses de Philippe Jaccottet', *SF*, 118:29–37, calls attention to the importance of the prose passages in J.'s work and the predominance of the *verger* image. While acknowledging the place of the *Cahiers de verdure* within the thematic and stylistic continuum of J.'s work, Rochat detects none the less a slight but significant shift in his inspiration, exemplified by the alternation of verse and prose passages and the association of the *verger* image with the latter.

LAINÉ. L. Ashdown-Lecointre, 'Le rêve est une seconde vie ou la victoire de l'amour imaginé sur l'amour réel dans *Dîner d'adieu* et *Sylvie*', *NZJFS*, 17.2:14–22, is a comparative, thematic study of L.'s 1991 novel and the Nerval novella with a view to answering the question whether L. was attempting to write a modern-day *Sylvie*. Despite the predominance of the common theme of lost love and the undeniable influence of N., the answer is no.

LECLERC. E. Fallaize, 'A feminine form: Annie Leclerc and Chantal Chawaf', *JIRS*, 4:241–49, looks at the relationship between feminist commitment and formal experimentation in L.'s *Parole de femme* and C.'s *Elwina, le roman fée*, finding that, despite differences, they both embody narratives of female becoming and share a common interest in language and generic questions, satire and parody and a common commitment to a radically feminine future.

LE CLÉZIO. A. Siganos, 'La solitude du violent: trois moments-clefs chez Dostoievski, Le C. et Lispector', Siganos, *Solitudes*, 123–30, uses a narratological approach, and a degree of ingenuity, to discover common mechanisms in three disparate texts (*Crime and Punishment, Le Procès-verbal, A Paixao Segundo G.H.*) which reveal deeper and unsuspected similarities. M. Martiarena, *Mondo et autres histoires (dossier)* (Folio Plus), Gallimard, 384 pp.

LEDUC. A. Hughes, 'Desire and its discontents: Violette Leduc, *La Bâtarde*, the failure of love', Hughes, *Erotic*, 69–92, rejects criticism of *La Bâtarde* as a salacious text, arguing instead that desire for L. is a negation of mutuality and a matter of self-preservation and the destruction of the other. This is illustrated by a subsequent detailed analysis of the book which identifies patterns of domination and subjugation in L.s relationships.

LEJEUNE. K. Bouwer, 'Claire Lejeune: of poetic citizenship', *WIFS*, 4:70–78, addresses L.'s sense of double marginalization, both as woman and poet, and her struggle for acceptance and 'creative citizenship'. B. identifies the importance of spatial imagery, circularity and spirals in L.s work and provides an interesting introduction to a lesser-known figure.

MALRAUX. J. Hartweg, 'De l'esthétique à la poétique: perspectives sur quatre romans de Malraux' *IL*, no.5:19–29, is a methodical study of four novels; *Les Conquérants, La Voie royale, La Condition humaine* and *L'Espoir*. It treats three aspects of M.'s æsthetic — *le farfelu, l'expressionisme* and *la tragédie classique* — before moving on to consider ethical aspects of each of the novels in turn (e.g. the question of suicide in *Les Conquérants*) and finally M.'s poetics. F. de Saint-Cheron, 'Les romans d'André Malraux', *ib.*, no.4:30–32, offers some brief general reflections on M.'s writings as 'œuvres engagées' and 'épopées métaphysiques'. J. Semprun, 'Je me souviens. Je ne me souviens que trop...', *NRF*, 526:24–33, affirms M.'s abiding interest in Spain which, despite the absence of any reference in the *Antimémoires*, never ceased to preoccupy him even long after the Civil War and the writing of *L'Espoir*. S.'s title is a quotation from M. to illustrate that this preoccupation was one of the 'vérités essentielles' of his life and work. Y. Ansel, *La Condition humaine (dossier)* (Folio Plus), Gallimard, 414 pp. G. Soubigou, *L'Espoir (dossier)* (Folio Plus), Gallimard, 663 pp.

MODIANO. A. Morris, *Patrick Modiano*, Oxford, Berg, 228 pp., provides the only comprehensive introduction to M.'s major prose fiction to date in English. After tracing M.'s creative impulse to his childhood unhappiness and rootlessness, Morris treats each of the novels in turn, identifying recurrent themes and gradually building up a comprehensive overview of M.'s work. The analysis is commendably clear, readable and cogent throughout. R. Smadja, 'La solitude dans *Livret de famille* de Modiano et *L'Invention de la solitude* d'Auster', Siganos, *Solitudes*, 137–43, deals not with the present solitude of M.'s and A.'s heroes but the structural void which has always lain at the centre of their lives. This is related to the absence of a father-figure in M. and to the death of the father in A. and is manifested in their similarly neutral, colourless style of writing.

PEREC. C. Andrews, 'Puzzles and lists: Georges Perec's *Un Homme qui dort*', *MLN*, 111:775–96, uses this particular text as a test case to assess how appropriate a metaphor the idea of 'puzzle' is to P.'s work.

QUENEAU. M. Girard, 'Solitudes et solitaires chez Queneau et Calvino' Siganos, *Solitudes*, 131–35, considers, by means of a four-way comparison between *Les Fleurs bleues*, *Le Chiendent*, *Il Cavaliere inesistente* and *Il Visconte dimezzato*, the figure of the *solitaire* in these two authors and their common interest in solitude

REBATET. P. Ifri, 'The epitexts and allotexts of Lucien Rebatet's *Les Deux Etendards*', *RR*, 87:113–30, contains a useful account of the content and writing of the novel for those unfamiliar with it, and attributes its critical neglect to political bias and prejudice. I.'s main interest, however, is a consideration of the unusual number and variety of paratexts associated with this novel, e.g. *Le Journal des Deux Etendards*, R.'s personal diaries, the writings of François Vanillon and Simone Chevallier who served as models for the characters in R. and how these various sources shed light on the composition of *Les Deux Etendards*. Despite the title, the discussion is refreshingly jargon-free.

RICARDOU. M. Sirvent, 'Représentation de l'espace, espace de la représentation (sur l'incipit de *L'Observatoire de Cannes* de Jean Ricardou)', *DFS*, 35:96–107.

ROBBE-GRILLET. R. Ramsay, 'Writing on the ruins in *Les Derniers jours de Corinthe*: from reassemblage to reassessment in Robbe-Grillet', *FR*, 70:231–44, details R.-G.'s attempts to deconstruct the conventions of traditional autobiography by a variety of ludic and intertextual means, the latter chiefly a re-collection of his own earlier texts, motifs, emblems etc. N. M. Frelick, 'Hydre-miroir: *Les Romanesques* de Robbe-Grillet et le pacte fantasmatique', *ib.*, 44–55, tackles the difficult issue of whether the *Romanesques* trilogy should be considered as autobiography or fiction. It develops into an interesting analysis of the complex relationship between the two genres and how this is complicated by the presence in the trilogy of an 'élément imaginaire' and the existence of a 'pacte fantasmatique' between writer and reader. J. Duffy, 'Cinema, modernity and Robbe-Grillet: an analysis of *L'Immortelle* and *Trans-Europe Express*', *FMLS*, 32:55–69, spurred on by the omission of R.-G. from John Orr's *Cinema and Modernity*, sets out to explore R.-G.'s film work and directorial activities and to relate them to the practices of other major directors of the period. Despite her initial strictures, this analysis of R.-G.'s two films is conciliatory. It substantiates Orr's observations on other prominent directors and, in the process, makes points of relevance for R.-G. the novelist.

ROCHEFORT. D. Holmes, 'Feminism and realism: Christiane Rochefort (born 1917) and Annie Ernaux (born 1940)', pp. 246–65 of Holmes, *Women's Writing* (see GENERAL), contrasts two novels by the more overt R. (*Les Petits Enfants du siècle, Les Stances à Sophie)* with E.'s *La Femme gelée* in order to highlight those feminist and social concerns they in fact share (e.g. language and sexuality, female consumerism) and their common use of realism in feminine writing.

SARRAUTE. *EsC*, 36.2, is a special issue devoted to S.'s work. M. Wittig, 'Le déambulatoire: entretien avec Nathalie Sarraute' (3–8), concentrates on S.'s creative writing and elicits a number of interesting comments on the novels and plays. F. Asso, 'La forme du dialogue' (9–20), looks at repetition with reference to dialogic form and 'Le morceau narratif', distinguishing three periods in S.'s work and concluding that repetition does not necessarily signal a lack of evolution. S. M. Bell, 'Endings in autobiography: the example of *Enfances*' (21–36), considers the imposition of shape, in the form of a beginning and ending, on a fragmentary text like *Enfances*, rejecting the idea that *Enfances* is only a collection of fragments, and preferring to emphasize the correspondence between substance and form in the closing episodes of the book and how these combine to create in the reader a sense of completion and ending. G. Brée, 'Le "for intérieur" et la traversée du siècle' (337–43), cites two more recent works, *L'Usage de la parole* (1980) and *Tu ne t'aimes pas* (1989), both written long after *Tropismes* and *L'Ere du soupçon* as evidence of how S.'s 'for intérieur' has expanded over the years. In the process, she discusses S.'s preoccupations with several of the 'grandes questions' of novel writing in the 20th c.: narratological issues , the nature of the subject, the *Moi* versus the Other, etc. A. Jefferson, 'Nathalie Sarraute — criticism and the "terrible desire to establish contact"' (44–62), shifts the focus in *L'Ere du soupçon* from what the essays say to what they do, i.e. what kind of function they fulfil rather than what kind of argument they contain. The purpose is to assess S.'s criticism in the context of her work as a whole and more specifically its role in relation to the novels. J. Lasalle, 'Le théâtre de Nathalie Sarraute ou la scène renversée' (63–74), is a readable assortment of general reflections on S.'s drama, interspersed with reminiscences of his personal conversations with her at Chérence and during rehearsals of *Elle est là*. V. Minogue, 'Nathalie Sarraute, anti-terrorist: a reading of *disent les imbéciles*' (75–88), is a detailed but clear exegesis of a complex text. The 'terrorism' in question is that inherent in the language of description and characterization which is likened to a process of imprisonment. reducing and confining individuals to fixed categories. A. S. Newman, 'Le sentiment de culpabilité: domaine tropismique par excellence?' (89–101), sets out to examine the theme of guilt as one of S.'s fundamental intuitions only to find his presupposition ill-founded. He records his surprise, contrasting the 'sentiment de culpabilité' he did find in S. with the actual guilt he expected to. The outcome is not entirely clear. There is no guilt in *Tropismes* or *Les Fruits d'or*, whereas that in *Tu ne t'aimes pas* may be an ironic attempt to exorcize the feeling of guilt implicit in the accusatory title. J.-L. Rivière, 'L'opération du théâtre' (103–16), deals with J. Lasalle's 1993 production of *Elle est là* but, despite this, proves to be less concerned with this *mise en scène* than with the general issues raised by how any production inevitably imposes an interpretation on the dramatic text, a problem aggravated in this case by the open nature of much of S.'s text. V. Minogue, 'The hand of the child: a basic figure in the work of Nathalie Sarraute', *RoS*, 27:73–83, views this motif from the outset as a dual image, a metaphor for constraint and liberation. The discussion concentrates on *Enfances* and *Tu ne t'aimes pas*. This motif is an element of the 'algebraic logic' binding the autonomous fragments of *Enfances* together while, in the later text, it contributes to the dismantling of the self and individual identity. M. Gosselin, *Nathalie Sarraute. Enfance* (Foliothèque), Gallimard, 257 pp.

SARTRE. B. O'Donohoe, 'Fraternity: liberty or inequality? Incest in Sartre's drama', *FS*, 50:54–65, searches *Les Mouches* and *Les Séquestrés d'Altona* for an answer to the enigma posed by *Les Mots*: why the young S. should transform his relationship with his widowed mother into an imaginary sibling relationship. It is debatable that the exercise provides an answer but the question is interesting. R. Davison, 'Sartre and the ithyphallic: an interpretation of *Erostrate*', Hunter, *Short Story*, 87–102, attempts to elucidate S.'s thinking on a wide range of aspects of human sexuality. A close reading of *Erostrate* aims to demonstrate that S. is debunking Freudian theories and suggesting alternative ontological perspectives. J. Walling, 'Repression and denial: the absent childhood self in Sartre's *Les Mots*', *RoS*, 27:49–62, contests the definition of *Les Mots* as a 'brilliant study in child psychology', arguing instead that S. demonstrates a remarkable lack of empathy with his childhood self. It is not just a case of the mature, later S. distancing himself from his earlier beliefs and values; he is unconsciously identifying with the child he was and repressing and denying the same experiences he did as a child. R. Turcanu, 'Le désir d'être auteur', *DFS*, 35:79–94, considers the relationship between author, narrator and reader in autofiction, in a comparison of Doubrovsky's *Le Livre brisé* and *Les Mots*. The main emphasis is on D. rather than S. but comparisons are always instructive. J. P. Boulé, 'L'envergure du personnage de Jessica dans *Les Mains sales*', *EFL*, 32–33:132–46, takes issue with the way in which critical emphasis on Hugo and Hoederer has overshadowed the female characters and, to right this wrong, examines the character and role of Jessica. Her removal or suppression by S. is seen as an indication of S's general attitude to women. L. Giraudo, *Jean-Paul Sartre. 'Les Mots'* (Balises), Nathan, 128 pp. J. Villani, *Leçon littéraire sur 'Les Mots' de Jean-Paul Sartre* (Major), PUF, 115 pp.

TOURNIER.   S. L. Beckett, 'Entretien avec Michel Tournier', *DFS*, 35:67–78. There is hopefully something of interest to be gleaned from talking directly to an author; this interview manages to touch on a variety of topics related to T.'s work but the questioning could be more insistent and probing. Matters are not helped by T. being less than forthcoming on occasion in several of his replies ('Je ne sais pas', 'Je n'en sais rien'). D. Gascoigne, *Michel Tournier*, Oxford, Berg, 234 pp., gives a welcome overview of all T.'s creative writing to date. The study is thematically based and thoughtfully organized. At its core is a series of clearly written and informative chapters, each focusing on a major theme or aspect of T.'s work. There are also clearly delineated sections within these chapters dealing with individual texts, thus making it easy to dip into the study with profit. The whole is rounded off with general chapters at beginning and end, on T. the craftsman and on his apparent aversion to history, making the book a comprehensive, readable and useful introduction to an author who is not always among the most accessible. A. Bouloumié, *Vendredi ou les limbes du Pacifique (dossier)* (Folio Plus), Gallimard, 379 pp. W. Redfern, *Michel Tournier: Le Coq de bruyère*, Rutherford, Fairleigh Dickinson U.P., 138 pp. J. B. Vray, *Le Roi des Aulnes (dossier)* (Folio Plus), Gallimard, 559 pp.

VANNIER.   M. Bacholle, 'Angèle Vannier: le zodiac comme nouvel ordre féminin/iste', *WIFS*, 4:60–66, elucidates poem by poem the structure and development of V.'s tightly organized twelve-poem sequence *Chambres bleues*, each poem of which is placed under a sign of the zodiac. Whether or not one believes that V.'s use of the zodiacal year is an attempt to subvert the male calendar year, the article offers an interesting glimpse into the work of a writer who, despite ten collections and a novel, remains a less familiar figure.

WITTIG.   J. Birkett, '*Sophie Ménade*: the writing of Monique Wittig', Hughes, *Erotic*, 93–119, offers a close reading of three texts, *L'Opoponax*, *Les Guérillères*, and *Le Corps lesbien*, inspired principally by

Marcuse's views on eros and society. Each text is dealt with separately but the emphasis on intertextuality and the references to Marcuse et al. ensure a more comprehensive picture.

YOURCENAR. J. H. Sarnecki, 'When our gender is a lie: Marguerite Yourcenar's *Achille ou le mensonge (Achilles or the Lie)*', *WIFS*, 4:80–87, concentrates on an early short work of prose poems *Feux*. This collection was inspired by unrequited love but S. argues that behind the series of classical masks or personae adopted by Y. lies a form of 'sexual anarchy' which breaks down barriers of traditional gender representation and emphasizes the fluidity of sexual identity and desire.

FRENCH CANADIAN LITERATURE

By CHRISTOPHER ROLFE, *Lecturer in French, University of Leicester*

(This survey covers the years 1995 and 1996)

1. ESSAYS, GENERAL STUDIES, ANTHOLOGIES

The abbreviation Mathieu, *Mémoire*, is given to the following volume specific to this section: *La Mémoire dans la culture*, ed. Jacques Mathieu, Sainte-Foy, Laval U.P., 1995, xiii + 344 pp. Jacques Pelletier, *Le Poids de l'histoire: littérature, idéologies, société du Québec moderne*, Quebec, Nuit blanche, 1995, 346 pp., is a consummate attempt to bring out the links between literature, ideology and society between the 1930s and the end of the 1980s. P. presents a vigorous, coherent analysis that insists on the dynamics between literature and specific events (the October Crisis, for example). *Les Ecrivains du Québec. Actes du Quatrième Colloque international francophone du Canton de Payrac (Lot)*, ed. Simone Dreyfus, Edmond Jouve, and Gilbert Pileul, Paris, ADELF, 471 pp., contains much that is of value on Québécois writing, writing and identity, and the reception of Québécois writing in France. Of particular value perhaps is the second of its seven sections which consists for the most part of essays on specific writers: for example, E. Jouve, 'Emile Nelligan, poète pour notre temps' (123–38); M.-L. Piccione, 'Entre l'Europe et l'Amérique, la difficile quête identitaire d'Yves Beauchemin' (151–57); N. Chabot, 'Hubert Aquin, un écrivain hors-père' (159–67); and P. Loiseleur des Longchamps, 'Maurice Constantin-Weyer, trappeur, romancier et écrivain' (169–86). *Mythes et mythologies des origines dans la littérature québécoise*, ed. Franca Marcato-Falzoni, Bologna, CLUEB, 1994, 292 pp., consists of 12 essays on the 'founding myths' of Quebec literature. A wide range of authors is discussed, including A. Grandbois, J. Ferron, H. Aquin, A. Hébert, and R. Lalonde. Jean Royer, **Interviews to Literature*, Toronto, Guernica, 196 pp., consists of interviews conducted by one of Quebec's best-known literary critics. Authors interviewed include A. Hébert, J. Ferron, Y. Thériault, M.-C. Blais, M. Tremblay, R. Carrier, F. Théoret, and N. Brossard. Belinda Jack, *Francophone Literatures: An Introductory Survey*, OUP, 305 pp., has a chapter on 'Quebec and French Canada' (57–99). This is generally competent, occasionally very sharp, but — in terms of chronology and emphases — ill-balanced. The derisory guide to further reading somehow fails to mention key studies. J. Melançon, 'Une mémoire totalisante: usages et fonctions du passé en littérature québécoise', Mathieu, *Mémoire*, 79–91. P. Klaus, 'Universalisation de la littérature québécoise contemporaine: métissage et métamorphose littéraires de la belle province', *BFF*, 7 : 115–28.

Daniel Mativat, *Le Métier d'écrivain au Québec (1840–1900). Pionniers, nègres ou épiciers des lettres?*, Montreal, Triptyque, 510 pp., is, in spite of its crass sub-title, a serious and revealing study. *La Vie littéraire au Québec*, vol. III *(1840–1869)*, ed. Maurice Lemire and Denis Saint-Jacques, Sainte-Foy, Laval U.P., xxiv + 671 pp., is, like its preceding volumes, a masterly survey of the circumstances conditioning literary output and its reception, this time during the crucial period leading up to Confederation. P. Hébert and J. Cotnam, 'La *Gazette littéraire* (1778–1779): notre premier œuvre de fiction?', *VI*, 20, 1995:294–312, suggests that, rather than providing a forum for contemporary intellectuals, the *Gazette* was an organ that allowed Fleury Mesplet and Valentine Jautard, writing under pseudonyms, to air their own views and dictate the direction taken by the paper.

Jean Morency, *Le Mythe américain dans les fictions d'Amérique: de Washington Irving à Jacques Poulin*, Quebec, Nuit blanche, 1994, 258 pp., is a comparative study of American and Quebec literature. Jean-François Chassay, *L'Ambiguïté américain. Le roman québécois face aux Etats-Unis*, Montreal, XYZ, 1995, 197 pp., is a collection of essays that tackle an old theme — the Americanness of Quebec literature — from a new angle, namely recent theories of communication. Much of this is interesting but there are far too many digressions and a certain smugness grates. René Lapierre, *Ecrire l'Amérique*, Montreal, Les Herbes rouges, 1995, 161 pp., is a stimulating essay — bereft of any scholarly apparatus — on what America and Americanness mean to Quebec writers. *QuF*, 98, 1995, has a dossier on 'L'Influence américaine sur la culture québécoise' (61–88).

Two articles on how Québécois literature has been received in English Canada are worth checking out: R. Beaudoin, 'Réception critique de la littérature québécoise au Canada anglais', *EF*, 32.3:61–76, and C. Perkes, 'Le pays incertain en traduction anglaise, 1960–1990: seuils et écueils de l'identité littéraire au Canada', *ECan*, 41:41–56.

R. Grutman, 'Effets hétérolingues dans le roman québécois du XIXe siècle', *Littérature*, 101:40–52, discusses the issue of textual plurilinguism, heterolinguism and verisimilitude. See also his 'Hétérolinguisme et tics britanniques dans la littérature québécoise du XIXe siècle', *BFF*, 7:57–63. J. Kwaterko, 'Le roman québécois de 1900 à 1960: démystifications, médiation urbaine et nouveaux courants', *ib.*, 21–29, is a perfectly competent, albeit unoriginal, overview. Etienne Gérard, **La Question raciale et raciste dans le roman québécois: essai d'anthroposémiologie*, Montreal, Balzac, 1995, 216 pp. **Le Roman québécois au féminin (1980–95)*, ed. Gabrielle Pascal, Montreal, Triptyque,

1995, 193 pp. E. Dansereau, 'Lieu de plaisir, lieu de pouvoir: le bavardage comme contre-discours dans le roman féministe québécois', *VI*, 21:429–51, demonstrates how in novels by M.-C. Blais, L. Bersianik, F. Théoret, and F. Noël chatter becomes a means to construct a voice for the historically marginalized voices of women. Patrick Cady, *Quelques arpents de lecture: abécédaire romanesque québécois*, Montreal, L'Hexagone, 1995, 316 pp.

Essays on Modern Quebec Theater, ed. Joseph Donohue and Jonathan M. Weiss, East Lansing, Michigan State U.P., 1995, 254 pp., sets out to explore, from various perspectives, Quebec's theatrical revolution. A short introduction provides an historical overview. This is followed by a first group of essays examining the efforts to define a national identity, a second group dealing with language and translation, and a third set situating Quebec's theatre in a contemporary context. The volume is rounded off by two interpretative essays, and is recommended. P. Groulx, 'Onze pièces sur Dollard', Mathieu, *Mémoire*, 303–29, is an altogether fascinating essay on the (mostly forgotten and forgettable) plays inspired by that suspect hero. J.-C. Godin, 'Théâtre québécois contemporain: du réalisme identitaire au texte scénique', *BFF*, 7:65–73, maps the reorientation in Quebec theatre since the 1980 referendum.

C. Mata Barreiro, 'La traduction du matériel sémiotique des communications interculturelles dans les relations de voyage en Nouvelle-France', *EtCan*, 41:9–24, is a rewarding discussion of how early travel accounts in New France were rendered problematic by the tendency to impose a European pattern of analysis. On the other hand, P. Rajotte, 'La représentation de l'Autre dans les récits de voyage en Terre sainte à la fin du XIXe siècle', *EF*, 32.3:95–113, furthers our understanding of the vogue for travel accounts that bears witness to Quebec's gradual opening out to the world at large.

Three slim volumes by Monique Lafortune deserve mention: *Réalisme et réalité dans la littérature québécoise*, Laval, Mondia, 1994, 130 pp.; *La Littérature du terroir: une littérature identitaire*, Laval, Mondia, 1994, 86 pp.; and *Les Romans québécois du XIXe siècle: le roman historique et le roman d'aventures*, Laval, Mondia, 1995, 68 pp. Although of only limited value to the specialist, these volumes of well chosen and annotated extracts illustrating various key aspects of Quebec literature would be ideal for undergraduates and as general reference tools. A similar judgement might be passed on *Littérature québécoise. Des origines à nos jours*, ed. Heinz Weinmann, Roger Chamberland et al., LaSalle (Quebec), HMH, 349 pp., another excellent anthology/ *manuel* aimed primarily at Quebec *collégiens*. Gilles Pellerin, *Dix ans de nouvelles. Une anthologie québécoise*, Quebec, L'Instant même, 257 pp., brings together 26 stories published by L'Instant même over the last ten years. The anthology celebrates then not only an important genre in Quebec but also the indefatigable efforts of this modest *maison d'édition*. Liana Nissim and Caterina Ricciardi, *Parole sull'acqua. Poesie dal Canada anglofono e francofono*, Rome, Empirìa, 299 pp., is a delightful anthology of poems on the theme of water that throws up some unexpected gems in both languages. *Les Meilleurs Romans québécois du XIXe siècle*, ed. Gilles Dorion, Montreal, Fides, 2 vols, 1096, 1144 pp., anthologizes eleven famous novels. Vol. I contains *L'Influence d'un livre*, *Les Fiancés de 1812*, *La Fille du brigand*, *La Terre paternelle*, *Une de perdue*, *deux de trouvées*, and *Charles Guérin*; vol. II *Jean Rivard*, *Les Anciens Canadiens*, *Jacques et Marie*, *L'Intendant Bigot*, and *Angéline de Monbrun*. Each novel is ably introduced and contextualized. The set constitutes an excellent way of acquiring these key texts.

2. INDIVIDUAL AUTHORS

AQUIN. A. Wall, '*Trou de mémoire*: pour une poétique du recommencement', *VI*, 21:452–77, studies 'literary chatter' in this celebrated novel.

BÉLAND. V.-L. Tremblay, 'La réception critique d'un "mauvais livre"': *Orage sur mon corps* d'André Béland', *QuS*, 22:177–88, suggests that B.'s novel was dismissed as an affront to bourgeois morals rather than because it was poorly written.

BESSETTE. Gérard Bessette and Gilbert La Rocque, *Correspondance*, ed. Sébastien La Rocque and Donald Smith, Montreal, Québec/Amérique, 1994, 164 pp., sheds surprising light on these two novelists and on the small world of Quebec letters. It is perhaps particularly fascinating to encounter La R.'s 'esprit gaulois' and black humour which so rarely penetrate his novels. C. D. Rolfe, 'Of brawls and riots: (pre)figuring social change in three Québécois novels of the fifties', *JIRS*, 3, 1995:305–16, discusses B.'s *La Bagarre*, Jean-Jules Richard's *Le Feu dans l'amiante*, and Pierre Gélinas's *Les Vivants, les morts et les autres*. R. argues that the brawl and the riot are vital literary tropes in these novels that 'helped to move Quebec into a more open, freer realm, not least by helping to move the Québécois novel itself into a more open, freer realm'. L. Hamelin, 'Dans le ventre du récit (lecture de Gérard Bessette)', *VI*, 20, 1995:440–50, is an engagingly personal, and mildly provocative, response to B.'s work.

BLAIS. Mary Jean Green, *Marie-Claire Blais*, NY, Twayne, 1995, 153 pp., provides an excellent introduction to B. for undergraduates whilst also offering much valuable insight (into B.'s evolving attitude to art and her developing feminism, for example) to those already steeped in her novels.

BOMBARDIER. D. Perron, 'Denise Bombardier, pamphlétaire', *VI*, 20, 1995:630–48, analyses B.'s polemical essay *La Déroute des sexes* and discovers a mystical backlash against feminism.

BOURGEOYS. P. M. St Pierre, 'Marguerite Bourgeoys and Abbé Henri-Raymond Casgrain, founders of Canadian historical letters', *BJCS*, 11:42–52, is solid but offers little that is new.

BROCHU. *VI*, 20.1, 1995, has a dossier on the critic, teacher, and writer. Two articles on his output as a novelist are likely to prove of most interest: A. Mercier, '*Adéodat I* d'André Brochu ou comment écrire pour tous' (556–70); and P. Riendeau, 'Le champ existentiel ou les avatars d'une construction identitaire. Sur *La Vie aux trousses* d'André Brochu' (571–86).

BROSSARD. C. Sturgess, '*Le Désert mauve* de Nicole Brossard: polysémie de l'écriture, engagement politique, voyage au féminin', *ECan*, 38, 1995:77–83. K. J. Anderson, 'Revealing the body bilingual: Quebec feminists and recent translation theory', *StH*, 22:66–75, demonstrates how B.'s *Le Désert mauve* and her translator Suzanne Lotbinière-Harwood's treatise *Re-belle et infidèle/The Body bilingual* are two approaches to mastering the problems confronting women as writers and translators. K. Conley, 'The spiral as möbius strip: inside/ outside *Le Désert mauve*', *QuS*, 19, 1995:143–53, argues that B.'s novel 'extends the project of automatism initiated by Breton'.

BROUILLET. C. D. Rolfe, 'Detecting change: women crime writers in Quebec', *BJCS*, 10, 1995:127–38, discusses the way *polars* by B. and Monique Lepage reflect some of the ideological changes that have transformed Quebec society and culture over the last thirty years or so. Monique LaRue's *Copies conformes* is also discussed by way of an epilogue.

CARPENTIER. M. Lord, 'L'ekphrasis fantastique. Descriptif d'étrangeté et modalités du savoir dans "La Bouquinerie d'Outre-Temps" d'André Carpentier', *VI*, 21, 1995:124–37, deals, in the unnecessarily abstruse fashion that seems to be the house-style of *VI*, with the complex forms of descriptive discourse in C.'s fantastic story.

CARRIER. A. Boivin, '*La Guerre, yes sir!* ou la guerre des autres', *QuF*, 96, 1995:85–88.

DESSAULLES. A. Cantin, 'Le *Journal* d'Henriette Dessaulles: la contre-aventure', *VI*, 21:312–23, proposes an alternative — and rather unwieldy — explanation for the notorious shift in the diary's discourse.

DUCHARME. Hélène Amrit, *Les Stratégies paratextuelles dans l'œuvre de Réjean Ducharme*, Les Belles Lettres, 1995, 251 pp., is a dense, at times overwhelming study that emphatically brings out the importance of *ludisme* in D. and in the contemporary Québécois novel in general. Not for the faint-hearted. Giles McMillan, **L'Ode et le désode: essai de* *sociocritique sur 'Les Enfantômes' de Réjean Ducharme*, Montreal, L'Hexagone, 1995, 194 pp. J. Valenti, 'L'épreuve du *Nez qui voque*: des savoirs partagés au ludisme verbal', *VI*, 20, 1995:400–23, is an interesting attempt to grapple with the very qualities that make the novel a 'difficult' read. J.-F. Chassay, 'La tension vers l'absolu total', *ib.*, 21:478–89, reconsiders the negative dimension of everything André Ferron says in *L'Hiver de force* in relation to the endless *chatter* that marks the novel.

FERRON. *L'Autre Ferron*, ed. Ginette Michaud and Patrick Poirier, Montreal, Fides, 1995, 468 pp., consists of a number of articles by established Ferron critics such as Betty Bednarski, 'De l'anglicité chez Ferron: retours et prolongements' (199–220); Jean-Pierre Boucher, 'Ouvertures ferroniennes: "Retour à Val-d'Or" et "Ulysse"' (47–67); and Pierre L'Hérault, '*Le Saint-Elias*: sauver l'enfant' (89–116), together with pieces by relative unknowns. It also includes hitherto unpublished pieces by F., extracts from elements of correspondence, and a series of interviews recorded in 1982. Required reading. J. R. Côté, 'Jacques Ferron, écrivain: l'arrière-boutique', *VI*, 20, 1995:424–37, presents another unpublished text by F., a seemingly insignificant dedication to Jean Marcel in a copy of *Cazou ou le Prix de la virginité* that sheds surprising light on F.'s literary ambitions.

FRÉCHETTE. Louis Fréchette, *La Maison hantée et autres contes fantastiques*, ed. Luc Bouvier, Anjou (Quebec), CEC, 200 pp., is a very competent annotated edition of eleven of F.'s tales, including seven which were to have been published in the writer's projected collection *Masques et fantômes*.

GARNEAU, FRANÇOIS-XAVIER. *EF*, 30.3, 1995, is given over to a series of articles on 'François-Xavier Garneau et son histoire'.

GARNEAU, HECTOR DE SAINT-DENYS. Hector de Saint-Denys Garneau, *Œuvres en prose (Œuvres complètes, vol. II)*, ed. Giselle Huot, Montreal, Fides, 1995, 1183 pp., is an excellent critical edition. There are two main sections: first, manuscripts published by G. between 1927 and 1938; second, divided into six parts, those works published posthumously and including the text of the *Journal*. Hector de Saint-Denys Garneau, *Regards et jeux dans l'espace*, ed. François Hébert, Anjou (Quebec), CEC, 159 pp., conforms to the original 1937 edition of this famous volume. André Prévost, *De Saint-Denys Garneau, l'enfant piégé*, Montreal, Boréal, 1994, 239 pp., is not without interest. However, described as a *récit biographique*, it is a somewhat disconcerting mix of memories (Prévost is a cousin of G.), facts, and the speculative, all written in a cloying, self-consciously poetic style. *Saint-Denys Garneau et 'La Relève'*, *Actes du colloque tenu à Montréal le 12 novembre 1993*, ed. Benoît Melançon and Pierre Popovic, Montreal, Fides, 1995, 133 pp., brings together eight papers which deal with the poet's output, its reception and, especially, the links between G. and the review founded by several of his friends in 1934.

GAUVREAU. Claude Gauvreau, *Ecrits sur l'art*, ed. Gilles Lapointe, Montreal, L'Hexagone, 412 pp., is a compilation of some 60 of G.'s 200 or so pieces on art. This is a most welcome edition since many of these texts, which not only reveal the development of G.'s reflections on art but also shed light on the arts in Quebec between 1946 and 1969, have become very difficult to find. J. Cardinal, 'L'oreille enchantée. Le corps imaginaire de la parole chez Claude Gauvreau', *VI*, 21:520–43, is an analysis of G.'s poetics according to a psychoanalytical theory of language and name.

GÉLINAS. Anne-Marie Sicotte, *Gratien Gélinas. La ferveur et le doute*, Montreal, Québec/Amérique, 2 vols, 334, 296 pp. This biography by G.'s granddaughter does justice to the cultural icon that was G. whilst largely avoiding the pitfalls of obsequiousness. It benefits from access to G.'s papers.

GÉRIN-LAJOIE. V.-L. Tremblay, 'L'Art masculin de réussir dans *Jean Rivard*', *CanL*, 151:47–63, argues that the novel 'correspond à la romance homosociale typique', that is to say war novels, spy novels, westerns, etc. where 'les principales relations sont habituellement avec d'autres hommes'.

GODBOUT. Hilligje Van't Land, *La Fonction idéologique de l'espace et de l'écriture dans les romans de Jacques Godbout*, Casteilla, 1994, 258 pp., is largely given over to a chronological socio-semiotic analysis of G.'s first seven novels. Although it is all too obviously a reworked PhD thesis, this is an interesting, stimulating study. Donald Smith, *Jacques Godbout, du roman au cinéma: voyage dans l'imaginaire québécois*, Montreal, Québec/Amérique, 1995, 255 pp., is a very readable study of G. both as author and *cinéaste*. It comes with a videocassette containing an interview with G. and extracts from several of his films. G. Thérien, '*Memoria* et imaginaire dans la culture québécoise', Mathieu, *Mémoire*, 331–40, proposes *Le Temps des Galarneau* as a paradigm of what he considers to be key elements in the Québécois collective imagination, and more specifically those linked to 'l'indien imaginaire'. P. G. Socken, 'The power of myth and language in *L'Isle au dragon*', *QuS*, 20, 1995:34–41, argues that it is the mythic embodiment of the polemical that makes the novel so accessible and stimulating. R. Mane, 'Marges et frontières dans un roman de Jacques Godbout: *Le Couteau sur la table* (1965)', *ECan*, 39, 1995:171–78. E. J. Talbot, 'Reading ambiguity: violence, character, and change in Jacques Godbout's *Une Histoire américaine*', *DFS*, 36:136–43, discusses Gregory Francœur's reaction to violence in the USA and what might be inferred from this with regard to the issue of political change. On a similar tack but more generalized is D. Chartier, 'Interprétation politique et réception littéraire: les romans de Jacques Godbout dans le courant de la *Révolution tranquille*', *BFF*, 7:75–83. B. Seyfrid, 'Polyphonie, plurilinguisme et vision carnavalesque du monde dans *D'Amour, P.Q.* de Jacques Godbout', *VI*, 21:544–59, seeks to identify the work's æsthetics of shock and dispersion in the light of Bakhtinian theory.

GRANDBOIS. Yves Bolduc, *L'Etoile mythique. Lecture de 'L'Etoile pourpre' d'Alain Grandbois*, Montreal, L'Hexagone, 1994, 210 pp., is an insightful, if at times slightly laborious, reading of G.'s third volume of poetry. It certainly succeeds in bringing out both the richness of G.'s cultural allusions and the stylistic diversity of the poems. Denise Pérusse, **L'Homme sans rivages. Portrait d'Alain Grandbois*, Montreal, L'Hexagone, 1994, 214 pp. Marcel Fortin, *Histoire d'une célébration. La réception critique immédiate des livres d'Alain Grandbois, 1933–1963*, Montreal, L'Hexagone, 1994, 419 pp. P. C. Malenfant, 'De l'œuvre, de la vie, de la vie de l'œuvre: à propos d'Alain Grandbois', *VI*, 21:372–80, revisits G.'s work via a critique of the three aforementioned studies. Nicole Deschamps and Jean-Cléo Godin, *Livres et pays d'Alain Grandbois*, Montreal, Fides, 1995, 151 pp., is a collection of already published articles that constitute a synthesis of the two authors' research on the genesis of G.'s work.

GROULX. Pierre Hébert, *Lionel Groulx et 'L'Appel de la race'*, Montreal, Fides, 204 pp., discusses in depth not only G.'s central work but also his first literary venture, *Les Rapaillages*, and his role within L'Action française.

GUEVREMONT. D. Trudel, 'Ces étrangers d'ici et d'ailleurs', *QuF*, 97, 1995:77–80, discusses *Le Survenant* as part of a dossier on 'L'Errance en littérature', an important topic in the French Canadian context. (Also included are: D. Kanaté, 'Le départ dans le roman du XIXe siécle' (75–76) and J. Morency, 'L'Errance dans le roman québécois' (81–84).) A. Boivin, '*Le Survenant* ou la fin de la société rurale d'ancien régime', *QuF*, 99, 1995:90–94.

GUYON. L. Robert, 'Patriots-on-Broadway. *Denis le patriote* de Louis Guyon', *EF*, 32.3:77–93.

HÉBERT. Peter Noble, *Anne Hébert: Les Fous de Bassan*, GFGP, 1995, 68 pp., is an undergraduate *manuel* that certainly spoon-feeds the dullard but could well spur on the intellectually inquisitive. L. Saint-Martin, 'Les premières mères, *Le Premier jardin*', *VI*, 20, 1995:667–81, discusses the novel in the light of Freud's theory of female development and feminist re-readings thereof. C. Zecher, 'Elisabeth-*sainte* and Aurélie-*sorcière*. The mistress of Kamouraska and her double', *QuS*, 20, 1995:11–18, delves into the complicity of Elisabeth d'Aulnières and her servant Aurélie Caron. Fascinating stuff. R. L. Dufault, 'Traditions et transformations in Anne Hébert's *L'Enfant chargé de songes*', *ib.*, 66–72. L. Harlin, 'Unreliable views of the feminine in Anne Hébert's *Les Fous de Bassan*', *ib.*, 22:127–36, tackles the question of ironic inversion and its role in the novel. A. Boivin, 'Anne Hébert, un intérêt marqué pour l'histoire', *Québec français*, 101:73–76. L. Morin, '*De la nouvelle fantastique au roman fantastique*', *ECan*, 40:17–28, examines two texts, H.'s novel *Héloïse* and Marie José Thériault's *Le Livre de Mafteh Haller*, and brings out how the fantastic æsthetic varies from genre to genre. A. C. Degrange, 'Ecriture et transgression: un réveil de la féminité dans les récits d'Anne Hébert', *BFF*, 7:129–40, is thoughtful enough but adds little that is fresh.

HÉMON. Louis Hémon, *Œuvres complètes*, vol. III, ed. Aurélien Boivin, Montreal, Guérin, 1995, 622 pp., is made up of *Lettres à sa famille*, *Itinéraire*, *Maria Chapdelaine*, and *Nouvelles inédites*. The critical apparatus includes a long and very useful introduction. Id. has also published 'Le roman québécois contemporain: l'opposition entre les espaces masculin et féminin', *ECan*, 39, 1995:179–91, in which he discusses the opposition between male and female space in H.'s *Maria Chapdelaine*, Félix-Antoine Savard's *Les Enragés du grand portage*, Bertrand Vacand's *Louise Genest*, and Jean-Yves Soucy's *Un Dieu chasseur*.

HÉNAULT. *VI*, 21.1, 1995, is largely given over to a dossier on H. The articles amount very much to a mixed bag, though P. Chamberland, 'La longue phrase de *Voyage au pays de mémoire*' (26–52), and L. Bourassa, 'Transports du signe: rime et allégorie dans "Sémaphore"' (74–91) — which analyses the richness of H.'s poetry in terms of its value in the organization of meaning — certainly repay careful reading. A. Spacagna, 'Dé-lire les 'délires' de *A l'inconnue nue* de Gilles Hénault', *ib.*, 300–11, offers a close analysis of the typography, phonetics, and semantic games of H.'s poetry.

JACOB. *VI*, 21.2, includes a major dossier on J. There are six articles plus an interview with the author and a valuable bibliography. Particularly recommended are: P. Nepveu, 'Suzanne Jacob: poèmes de la femme piégée' (243–49); L. Lequin, 'L'éloge du fortuit dans *Les Aventures de Pomme Douly*' (258–65); and L. Joubert, 'Suzanne Jacob et *La Gazette des femmes*: le "beau risque" de la rhétorique et de la subversion' (266–74).

LABERGE. M. Tremblay, 'Analyse de l'oubli dans *Oublier* de Marie Laberge', Mathieu, *Mémoire*, 255–69, takes the play as a starting-point for an interesting discussion about collective memory and imagination in Quebec. D. Perron, 'Dire ce que l'on sait: la "docte ignorance" dans le théâtre de Marie Laberge', *VI*, 21:490–506, examines the role of chatter in several of L.'s plays and its effect on her characters.

LAFERRIÈRE. M. Naudin, 'Dany Laferrière: être noir à Montréal', *ECan*, 38, 1995:47–55, analyses L.'s work in the light of Gilles

Lipovetsky's *L'Ere du vide*. (Articles on other, less well-known immigrant voices include: L. Lequin, 'Mona Latif Ghattas: une mélopée orientale dans un espace blanc', *QuS*, 19, 1995:133–41; and P. G. Klaus, 'Une parabole du colonialisme à l'envers: *Un Ambassadeur macoute à Montréal* de Gérard Etienne', *ib.*, 20, 1995:27–33. See also: U. Mathis, '"Speak what?" Observations à propos de la littérature immigrée au Québec', *BFF*, 7:101–14.)

LALONDE.   L. Gauvin, 'De "Speak white" à "Speak what?": à propos de quelques manifestes québécois', *QuS*, 20, 1995:19–26, analyses L.'s famous poem and its rewriting by M. Marcone as an example of palimpsest and cultural transfer. D. E. Sears, '*Défense de parler*: language on trial in Michèle Lalonde's "La Déffense et illustration de la langue québecquoyse" and "Outrage au tribunal"', *FR*, 68, 1995:1015–21, demonstrates how L.'s use of pastiche, parody, and puns enable her manifestos to propose a radical new language in terms drawn from established discourse.

LANGEVIN.   T. Chadwick and V. Harger-Grinling, 'Frontières linguistiques, culturelles et psychologiques: *L'Elan d'Amérique*', *ECan*, 39, 1995:165–70, discuss the woodsman Antoine as a paradigm of the way former ways of perceiving the world survive into the contemporary period only to provide a source of conflict.

LARUE.   S. Ireland, 'American stories by Monique LaRue and Jacques Godbout', *QuS*, 20, 1995:47–55, ventures, to good effect, into what is fast becoming well mapped territory, i.e. the USA as perceived by Quebec's novelists. D. Canty, 'Le jeu d'imitation dans *Copies conformes* de Monique LaRue', *VI*, 21:324–36, discusses the ontological dilemmas present in the novel.

LEBLANC.   R. Boudreau and A. M. Robichaud, 'Frontières de langues dans une littérature marginale: l'exemple de Gérald Leblanc', *ECan*, 1995:153–63, examine the linguistic plurality in the Acadian poet's work and demonstrates that such a linguistic blend offers a particularly illuminating example of the idea of exclusion inherent in all literature.

LECLERC.   Marcel Brouillard, *Félix Leclerc. L'homme derrière la légende*, Montreal, Québec/Amérique, 361 pp., is a biography in the popular mode: detailed, comprehensive but — understandably, since B. and L. were close friends — something of a hagiography.

LORANGER.   P. Coleman, 'Grounds for comparison: the geography of identity in Françoise Loranger and Gwethalyn Graham', *QuS*, 22:161–76, ventures into the troubled waters of comparative studies in Canadian literature. This discussion of Loranger's *Mathieu* and Graham's *Earth and High Heaven* not only sheds light on these two contemporary novels but also on the complex cultural landscape they shared.

MAHEUX-FORCIER. K. L. Kellett-Bestos, 'Maddening doubles in the novels of Louise Maheux-Forcier', *QuS*, 22:114–26, argues that the double in M.-F.'s fiction exists on 'the same diegetic level as the narrator but also exists as a projection of the narrator's psyche' and that doubles 'are created as a reaction to a societal bias in favour of heterosexuality'.

MAILLET. A. F. Farnell, 'Le monologue splénétique de *La Sagouine*', *QuS*, 19, 1995:113–21, is a compelling analysis of the spleen-filled soliloquy of the old washerwoman who, it is argued, belongs to the ancient tradition of the wise crone.

MIRON. P. Popovic, 'Note provisoire sur une loquèle inachevée (*L'Homme rapaillé* de Gaston Miron)', *VI*, 21:507–17, is a close analysis of the fragments that make up 'L'amour et le militant'.

MONTPETIT. Pamela Sing, *Villages imaginaires. Edouard Montpetit, Jacques Ferron et Jacques Poulin*, Montreal, Fides, 1995, 275 pp., examines how the notion of the village, and more specifically the *experience* of the village, persist in literary form at least into the late 20th c. This immensely rewarding study consists largely of three separate essays: 'Le village traditionnel d'Edouard Montpetit et son contexte littéraire' (31–80), 'Le village carnavalisé de Jacques Ferron' (81–147), and 'Le village postmoderne de Jacques Poulin' (149–244).

MORIN. R. Lahaise, 'Morin l'olympien', *VI*, 21:576–82, is a brief celebration of this most authentic of the 'exotiques'.

NELLIGAN. M. Richards, 'Poet, hero, icon, can we still read Nelligan?', *QuS*, 19, 1995:143–53, confronts the fact that N. is more often dealt with as a way into questions about contemporary Quebec than as a poet in his own right.

POULIN. L. Gauvin, 'Glissements de langues et poétiques romanesques: Poulin, Ducharme, Chamoiseau', *Littérature*, 101:5–24, offers analyses of the three novelists that illuminate Gauvin's contention that 'le roman tel qu'il s'écrit aujourd'hui en espace francophone est une traversée des langues et une interrogation sur la fonction du langage'.

QUESNEL. J. Hare, 'Aperçus de la correspondance de Joseph Quesnel', *VI*, 20, 1995:348–61, whets our appetite for the edition of Q.'s correspondence that he is currently working on. L. Robert, 'Monsieur Quesnel ou le bourgeois anglomane', *ib.*, 362–87, discusses *L'Anglomanie ou le Diner à l'angloise* — 'un des textes fondateurs de la tradition littéraire du Québec' — and speculates on the role played by literary salons in the dissemination of the play.

RIEL. A. Braz, 'The vengeful prophet: revenge in Louis Riel's writings', *DFS*, 35:19–31, examines the extent to which revenge shaped R.'s imagination and argues that it sprung from his own powerlessness together with that of the Métis.

RIOUX. P. R. Gilbert, ' "The killer awoke before dawn": the multiple mirrors of Hélène Rioux's Eléonore', *QuS*, 20, 1995:56–66, discusses intertextuality and its effects in *Les Miroirs d'Eléonore*.

ROY, A. F. Caucci, 'La poésie d'André Roy: anatomie du désir homoérotique', *QuS*, 22:106–13, construes R.'s poetry as a diptych in which the persona's several quests are articulated through homoerotic desire.

ROY, G. *Portes de communications. Etudes discursives et stylistiques de l'œuvre de Gabrielle Roy*, ed. Claude Romney and Estelle Dansereau, Sainte-Foy, Laval U.P., 1995, 213 pp., is a collection of 11 essays which attempt, with some success, to tackle an aspect of R.'s work which for a variety of reasons has been relatively untouched: her language and style. The essays, by the likes of Lori Saint-Martin, Pierre-Yves Mocquais and Romney and Dansereau themselves, range over all R.'s work and are required reading. *Colloque international 'Gabrielle Roy'. Actes du colloque soulignant le cinquantième anniversaire de 'Bonheur d'Occasion'*, ed. André Fauchon, Winnipeg, Saint-Boniface U.P., 756 pp., contains much that is of value, but not a little that will only be of less immediate or passing interest. C. Robinson, 'Gabrielle Roy: entre réalité et fiction', *QuS*, 20, 1995:97–105, examines the boundaries between reality and fiction in R.'s Manitoban cycle, the complementary nature of fictional and autobiographical texts, and the modes of narration. L. Saint-Martin, 'Gabrielle Roy et la critique au féminin', *VI*, 20, 1995:463–66, makes some interesting comments but contains several factual errors regarding publishing rights. F. Théoret, 'Ce que parler veut dire', *ib.*, 684–91, presents some slight reflections prompted by *La Détresse et l'enchantement*. C. Hahn, 'Disappearing horizons: closural strategies in Gabrielle Roy's short-story sequences', *FR*, 70:280–91, discusses the open closure that characterizes R.'s stories and concludes, neatly, that it points to her desire for 'textual immortality while recognizing the utility of textual ending'. C. D. Rolfe, 'Evoking childhood: Gabrielle Roy's *Rue Deschambault* and Jean-Marie Poupart's *Bourru mouillé: pour ceux qui savent parler aux enfants*', *RoS*, 27:63–72, compares and contrasts R.'s gently ironic view of childhood with P.'s celebration of all its mischievousness, disorder, fantasy, and irreverence.

SAINT-LUC DE LA CORNE. P. Lespérance, 'La fortune littéraire du *Journal de voyage* de Saint-Luc de la Corne', *VI*, 20, 1995:329–41, discusses how the work, which constitutes an early milestone in Quebec literary history, was used by later writers to fuel their own ideological arguments. R. Derome, 'Notes sur le pictural et le littéraire aux XVIIIe et XIXe siècles: le cas de Saint-Luc de la Corne', *ib.*, 342–47, briefly analyses two paintings connected with the writer and demonstrates their interaction with the literary.

TREMBLAY. Richard Duchaine, *Ecriture d'une naissance/Naissance d'une écriture: 'La Grosse femme d'à côté est enceinte' de Michel Tremblay*, Quebec, Nuit blanche, 1994, 97 pp., provides an interesting analysis of the narrative discourse. Christopher Robinson, *Scandal in the Ink: Male and Female Homosexuality in Twentieth-Century French Literature*, London, Cassell, 1995, xi + 272 pp., has some important pages on T. and also on other gay and lesbian Québécois writers such as Louky Bersianik. J. Fouchereaux, 'Traduire/trahir *Le Vrai monde?* de Michel Tremblay: *The Real World?/The Real Wurld?*', *QuS*, 20, 1995:86–96, raises questions of translation but is more broadly illuminating too. J. Cardinal, 'L'épreuve de la France. Langue et féminité dans *Des Nouvelles d'Edouard* de Michel Tremblay', *EF*, 31, 1995:109–27. R. Usmiani, 'The bingocentric worlds of Michel Tremblay and Tomson Highway: *Les Belles-sœurs* vs *The Retz Sisters*', *CanL*, 144, 1995:126–40, is an interesting comparison of two plays which have much in common, but which differ essentially in spirit. T.'s echoes postmodern nihilism, the Native playwright's suggests a society in which humanistic values still prevail. A.-M. Rocheleau, 'La folie de Marcel: étude d'un personnage de Michel Tremblay', *VI*, 21:337–50, considers the character's hallucinations as, amongst other things, a defence against an environment over which he has no control.

CARIBBEAN LITERATURE

By BRIDGET JONES, *Roehampton Institute, London*

1. GENERAL

An addition to bibliographical resources noted: Graziano Benelli, **La Negritudine in Italia. A. Césaire, L.-G. Damas, L.S. Senghor (1950–1994)*, Rome, Bulzoni, 1995, 324 pp. As the debate on the nature of *négritude*, *antillanité*, and *créolité* and their connections continues to flourish, if not rage (cf. Burton), well-documented comparative or historical contributions are particularly welcome. The collection *Poétiques et imaginaires. Franco*polyphonie *des Amériques*, ed. Pierre Laurette and Hans-George Ruprecht, L'Harmattan, 399 pp. (hereafter *Poétiques et imaginaires*), is enhanced by Canadian perspectives, notably on Haitian writing and linguistic issues, for example R. Fournier's critical scrutiny of 'Questions de créolité, de créolisation et de diglossie' (149–71). Michael Richardson and Krzysztof Fijalkowski, *Refusal of the Shadow: Surrealism and the Caribbean*, London–NY, Verso, 287 pp., is a volume of new translations with introductions from *Légitime défense* (1932), *Tropiques* (1941–45), and Haitian sources, illuminating the Surrealist enterprise to establish communication while refusing to elide cultural difference, and exploring the specific quality of the Haitian experience. Françoise Lionnet, *Postcolonial Representations: Women, Literature, Identity*, Ithaca–London, Cornell U.P., 1995, 196 pp., aims for 'a truly comparative feminist criticism', reworking her analysis of authors such as Maryse Condé, Myriam Warner-Vieyra and Suzanne Dracius-Pinalie in a broader context of deconstructing hierarchies and increasing cross-cultural understanding. Debra L. Anderson, *Decolonizing the Text: Glissantian Readings in Caribbean and African-American Literatures*, NY, Lang, 1995, 118 pp., also aims to locate her selected novels (Glissant and Chamoiseau) in terms of non-hierarchical and intertextual relationships. Colette Maximin, *Littératures caribéennes comparées*, Pointe-à-Pitre, Jasor–Paris, Karthala, 423 pp., draws on a wealth of examples in French, English and Spanish for a persuasive demonstration of 'l'influence déterminante, sur l'écrivain de la région, de l'héritage folklorique', both in choosing to focus on such domains as the carnivalesque, the sacred and the supernatural, the picaresque hero, and in techniques of presentation. A meditation by E.Sellin, 'A congruence of landscape and the mind. Or, the cartography of the colonialized psyche', *LitR*, 39:492–502, turns especially on Roumain, Glissant, Maximin and others, perceiving Caribbean island landscapes as a 'mode of thought'. C. Britton,

'Eating their words: the consumption of French Caribbean Literature', *ASCALF Yearbook*, 1:15–23, links the gastronomic presentation of Caribbean writers to their status as commodity for the French consumer.

SPECIAL ISSUES OF PERIODICALS. *NLi*, 127, 'Cinq ans de littératures. 1991–1995. Caraïbes.', offers useful surveys and reviews, including judicious viewpoints on 'esthétiques créoles' (P. Degras, 6–16), on the evolution of writing in Creole (M.-C. Hazaël-Massieux, 18–28), a dossier on Glissant, and further discussion of 'créolité'. *Ib.*, 128, 'Haïti. Océan Indien.', contains L.-F. Hoffman on recent Haitian literature (6–13), in particular the novels of Emile Ollivier (15–24).

2. NOVEL AND PROSE WRITING

Hervé Vignes, **Guyane à fleur de mots*, Vitry-sur-Seine, Aguer, 1995, 99 pp., is a short study of the representation of the 'milieu naturel guyanais' in the novels of Jean Galmot, René Jadfard and Micheline Hermine.

3. INDIVIDUAL AUTHORS

CÉSAIRE. Another poetic selection from this canonical 'œuvre', with presentation and notes by R. Toumson, *Anthologie poétique*, Imprimerie nationale, 274 pp. Gloria Saravaya, *Le Thème du retour dans le 'Cahier d'un retour au pays natal' (Aimé Césaire)*, L'Harmattan, 188 pp., somewhat unexpectedly, given her title, provides a detailed textual analysis, inspired by Marcel Jousse's research on techniques of recitation. R. D. E. Burton, 'Two views of Césaire: *négritude* and *créolité*', *DFS*, 35:135–52, deconstructs with zest and clarity the opposing critical discourses on C. of R. Confiant (1993) and R. Toumson and S. Henry-Valmore (also 1993). S. E. D. Littlewood, 'Symbolisme et sexualité; le symbolisme de la féminité dans la quête d'identité d'Aimé Césaire', *ASCALF Yearbook*, 1:46–63, traces the resolution of a sexualized dialogue through the poetic act, and the androgynous figure of Ariel (*Une Tempête*).

CHAMOISEAU. C. Chivallon, '"Eloge de la spatialité": conceptions des relations à l'espace et identité créole chez Patrick Chamoiseau', *ASCALF Yearbook*, 1:24–45, charts the meaning of spatial relations in *Texaco*. (Also printed *NLi*, 127:88–108).

CHARLES. J. Jonassaint, 'La traversée des langues américaines dans *Sainte dérive des cochons*', *Poétiques et Imaginaires*, 255–65, seeks to compensate for critical neglect of Jean-Claude Charles by a close reading of this 1977 'texte pluriel'.

CHAUVET. R. Scharfman, 'Violence discursive, violence psychosociale dans *Amour/Colère/Folie* de Marie Chauvet', pp. 97–115 of *Violence, Théorie, Surréalisme*, ed. Jacqueline Chénieux-Gendron and Timothy Mathews, Lachenal et Ritter, 1994, is a telling account of the almost intolerable violence of C.'s textual resistance to the Duvalier regime.

CONDÉ. D. Y. Kadish and F. Massardier-Kenney, 'Traduire Maryse Condé: entretien avec Richard Philcox', *FR*, 69:749–61, offer a lively insight into this translator's role, and into questions of lexical choice and editorial bias. C. Duffey, 'Tituba and Hester in the intertextual jail cell: New World feminisms in Maryse Condé's *Moi, Tituba, sorcière ... Noire de Salem*', *WIFS*, 4:100–10, analyses the 'postmodern irony' deployed in C.'s mocking but still powerful indictment of racism, and her assertion of the right to *jouissance* for the colonized female body. Two volumes of Robert Jouanny's writings, collected as 'Mélanges' in his honour, *Espaces littéraires d'Afrique et d'Amérique*, L'Harmattan, 304, 318 pp., include some Caribbean topics, such as 'Lecture de *Pension les Alizés* (1988) de Maryse Condé' (I, 251–59).

CONFIANT. The first volume has appeared of *Portulan*, a lavish new literary review, ed. R. Toumson. D.-H. Pageaux, 'Raphaël Confiant ou la traversée paradoxale d'une décennie' (35–58), comments on the fictional treatment of history, sexuality, and on techniques of linguistic invention, in what is viewed as 'ce moment de négativité polémique qu'est la créolité'.

FRANKÉTIENNE. *Poétiques et Imaginaires* contains an instructive interview (47–68), and a discussion by R. Berrouët-Oriol and R. Fournier, 'Poétique, langage et schizophonie: Frankétienne' (83–101).

GLISSANT. C. Britton, '"A certain linguistic homelessness": relations to language in Edouard Glissant's *Malemort*', *MLR*, 91:597–609, is a precise and stimulating commentary on some of the discourses which 'enact their speakers' diverse relations to the language of the European Other'.

GRATIANT. The collected work of Gilbert Gratiant (1895–1985), *Fables créoles et autres écrits*, ed. I. Gratiant, R. Gratiant and J.-L. Joubert, Stock, 744 pp., is a rich source of social commentary, supporting the proposition that 'Le créole peut tout dire'. In addition to the *Fab' Compè Zicaque*, political and autobiographical texts, and some unpublished verse in Creole are presented, with French translation (by P. Pinalie) where appropriate.

HYVRARD. (Not an actual Caribbean author, but most relevant in this section.) A. J. Arnold, 'French national identity and the literary politics of exclusion: the Jeanne Hyvrard case', *AJFS*, 33.2:157–65, offers a warning to critics by demonstrating how that 'absolute Other of Frenchness', a neurotic black French West Indian woman writer, was constructed without any basis in reality.

JEANNE. H.-R. Ruprecht, 'Pour une poétique du simulacre: le ciné-poème de Max Jeanne', *Poétiques et imaginaires*, 239–51, gives some points on J.'s choice of genre for his witty *WESTERN*.

JUMINER. E. Le Carvennec, 'Poétique, éthique, écriture dans les romans de Bertène Juminer', *Poétiques et Imaginaires*, 301–12, stresses the moral lessons to be drawn from J.'s novels.

MORRISSEAU-LEROY. J. Métellus, 'Théâtre et poésie', *Poétiques et Imaginaires*, 69–82, pays tribute to the work of M.-L. as an inspirational 'figure tutélaire', together with Césaire.

PARÉPOU. A. Emera, 'French Guiana introduced to Paris in Creole 110 years ago', *CarQ* 41.3–4, 1995:85–91, ascribes *Atipa*, the earliest known Creole novel, to M. Méteyrand, and comments on the status of 'regional' literatures.

WARNER-VIEYRA. J. M. Rogers, 'Reading, writing, and recovering: creating a women's creole identity in Myriam Warner-Vieyra's *Juletane*', *FR*, 69:595–604, demonstrates the paradigmatic quality of this novelist's work for certain feminist readings.

AFRICAN AND MAGHREB LITERATURE

By MARYSE BRAY, ALINE COOK, HELENE GILL, DEBRA KELLY,
SAMANTHA NEATH, ETHEL TOLANSKY, *University of Westminster,*
and MARGARET MAJUMDAR, *University of Glamorgan*

I. FRANCOPHONE MAGHREB: GENERAL

Several works have appeared dealing with problems and issues arising
in Francophonie at large, particularly questions relating to identity
and culture associated with French, as in Dennis Ager, *Francophonie in
the 1990's: Problems and Opportunities,* Clevedon, UK – Philadelphia –
Adelaide, Multilingual Matters, 215 pp. As for civil-war-torn Algeria,
after the obsession with scrutiny of the political struggles in 1995, the
focus has shifted, perhaps temporarily, to broader cultural issues, less
dependent on current affairs reporting. Nevertheless, the latter still
attracts comment, as in: Hassan (pseudonym), *L'Algérie, histoire d'un
naufrage,* Seuil, 302 pp.; M. Duteil, *Les Martyrs de Tibhirine,* Turnhout,
Brepols, 206 pp.; L. Provost, *La Seconde Guerre d'Algérie,* Flammarion,
199 pp.; S. Labat, *Les Islamistes algériens: entre les urnes et le maquis,* Seuil,
1995, 343 pp.; and Sami Naïr, 'Algérie, Egypte, Turquie: violence
religieuse, violence politique', *TM,* 51 : 145–72. *Maghreb-Machrek,* 154,
'Algérie, la fin de l'unanimisme', has articles by F. Colonna,
M. Vergès, and M. Hocine Benkheira on the conflicts of the last
twenty years. There is also great eagerness to debate related politico-
cultural issues: François Burgat, *L'Islamisme en face,* La Découverte,
264 pp., presses on with his controversial plea for a less dismissive
look at radical Islam; Louisa Hanoune, *Une autre Voix pour l'Algérie,* La
Découverte, 257 pp., seeks another path to real democracy; whilst
O. Roy, 'Le Néo-fondamentalisme islamique ou l'imaginaire de
l'Oummah', *Esprit,* 220 : 80–107, differentiates between Islamism and
Islamic fundamentalism. A more reflective view is given in a
posthumous text by M. Khaïr-Eddine: 'Testament d'un moribond',
ib., 28–39, a metaphor on the decrepit condition of African statehood;
by M. Kacimi 'Je ne reviendrai pas à Tipasa', *TM,* 51 : 173–83; and
again by Pierre Claverie, *Lettres et Messages d'Algérie,* revised and
extended version, Karthala, 280 pp. In a more strictly political vein,
Abdelmoughit Benmessouad-Tredano, *Démocratie, culture politique et
alternances au Maroc,* Casablanca, Editions Maghrebines, 195 pp.,
analyses the rigidity of Morocco's political system. Furthermore, the
new review *Algérie-Littérature/Action* devotes some of its 'dossiers-
débats' to Algerian politico-cultural dilemmas, such as no. 5 on
language, with pieces by J. Derrida, R. Boudjedra, and D. Saadi, and
no. 6 on the religious.

There has been specific interest in spatial, territorial and strategic issues: by Daniel Nordman, *Profils du Maghreb: frontières, figures et territoires (XVIIIe-XXe siècles)*, Faculté des Lettres et Sciences Humaines, Rabat, 258 pp.; by M. Blunden, 'Euro-Mediterranean relations: the conditions for partnership in the Maghreb', *BFA*, 10:15–25; and by J. Samuel, 'Euro-Mediterranean partnership: the case of Tunisia', *ib.*, 26–34. Moreover, *Les Cahiers de l'Orient*, 43, 'La Tunisie en mutation', includes articles on Tunisia as geopolitical and cultural crossroads by E. Weber, J. Lacouture, O. Carré, H. Ben Hammouda, etc.

Cultural, national, and linguistic identity is never absent from the field, as in M. Majumdar, 'National, cultural and literary identity in the *Beur* novel', *FSSA*, 25:72–84. A section of *The European Legacy: Towards New Paradigms*, MIT Press, 1996, 153 pp., includes: S. A. Arab, 'The Conradian inheritance in the African novel' (101–08); F. Vergès, 'A contested legacy: Republican language, *métissage* and emancipation' (137–42); H. Gill, 'Cultural and linguistic dilemmas of middle-class women in post-colonial Tunisia' (114–20); and A. L. Herman, Jr, 'Empire as decline: notes on the cultural critique of imperialism' (121–25), who explores the long-term imperialist legacy, as does Cathy Lloyd, 'Antiracist ideas in France: myths of origin' (126–31). This theme is further developed by A. Stafford, 'Work, racism and writing in 1950's France', *ASCALF Bulletin*, 12:3–13. A. Meddeb, 'Art et transe', *Esprit*, 220:72–79, provides a reflection on artistic creation, on the mutual relationship between Orient and Occident, in a context of *globalisation de l'art*. Yves and Christine Gauthier et al., *L'Art du Sahara*, La Découverte, 140 pp., offer a more specific reflection on the cave paintings from the times before desertification. On film, David Nicolls, 'Louis Malle's "Ascenseur pour l'Echafaud" and the presence of colonial wars in French cinema', *FrCS*, 7:271–82, sees the Algerian conflict as a haunting spectre behind an era of cultural change in France.

Gender issues have inspired a rich crop of feminist writing by authors based in France. Monique Gadant, *Le Nationalisme algérien et les femmes*, L'Harmattan, 1995 [1996], 285 pp., pref. Mohammed Harbi, is a compilation of papers debunking the use of patriotism and religion to legitimize patriarchal oppression. Camille Lacoste-Dujardin, *Des Mères contre les femmes; maternité et patriarcat au Maghreb*, La Découverte, 356 pp., significantly updates this author's investigative work of the 1970s and 1980s, while Julette Minces, *Le Coran et les femmes*, Hachette, 182 pp., attempts to set the record straight about the Koranic basis for female subordination. *BFA*, 9:1–70, publishes papers from a conference held the previous year in London, and assessing women's status as a political issue, by A. Touati, F. Lalami-Fatès, S. Belhassen, etc. A. Bouabaci, 'Entre la reconnaissance par le clan et l'adhésion aux valeurs de l'universalité', *ib.*,10: 1–14, makes the woman writer's claim to be recognized as subject. Françoise Germain-Robin, *Femmes rebelles d'Algérie*, Editions de l'Atelier/Editions Ouvrières, 128 pp, gives a more political angle on Maghrebian women's assertiveness. Yasmina Benguigui, *Femmes d'Islam*, Albin Michel, 185 pp., provides a broader political perspective. Monia Hejaiej, *Behind Closed Doors, Women's Oral Narratives in Tunis*, London, Quartet Books, 369 pp., offers an original glimpse of female subversion through oral tale-telling. Souad Bakalti, *La Femme tunisienne au temps de la colonisation 1881–1956*, L'Harmattan, 307 pp., examines the gender question in Tunisia during colonial times. Daniela Merolla, *Gender and Community in the Kabyle Literary Space. Cultural Strategies in the Kabyle Literary Space*, Leiden, Research School CNWS, 278 pp., examines how categories of gender and community affect each other in the field of literary narratives, i.e. oral narratives in the Kabyle genre *tamacahut* and novels written in French by women writers whose mother tongue is Kabyle.

2. FRANCOPHONE MAGHREB LITERATURE

This year has seen the publication of a number of useful overviews to Francophone writing in which literature from the Maghreb continues to play a prominent part, especially with reference to Algeria. Going beyond the purpose of providing an introduction to writers and their works, many of these surveys also allow an assessment of the major themes and preoccupations of recent years, such as exile, gender, identity, and new approaches to writing, and point the way forward to future developments in critical research. While established writers such as Mohammed Dib, Albert Memmi, Rachid Boudjedra, Driss Chraïbi, Tahar Ben Jelloun, and Assia Djebar continue to predominate in particular studies in articles and books, there is evidence of the emergence of new writers.

There are three new general reference books. The Institut du Monde Arabe's collective work, *Ecrivains arabes d'hier et d'aujourd'hui*, Sindbad, 144 pp., includes a wide range of North African writers. Benjamin Stora, *Le Dictionnaire des livres de la guerre d'Algérie*, L'Harmattan, 350 pp., charts the production of books inspired by the Algerian War from 1955 to 1995, covering fiction, essays, autobiographies, poetry, history and '*témoignages*' by both North African, mainly Algerian, and metropolitan French writers. Salem Chakir and Abdellah Bounfour, *Langues et littératures berbères: Chronique des études* XIII *(1994–1995)*, L'Harmattan, 141 pp., include works in French on

Berber writers in Algeria and Morocco. In addition, several general surveys on Francophone literature include extremely useful and well-researched material. Belinda Jack, *Francophone Literatures: An Introductory Survey*, OUP, 305 pp., provides a thought-provoking introduction and conclusion, reviewing the general issues of each of the Maghreb countries and genres, and highlighting differences and the multicultural richness of Francophone writing. J. has also written the chapter (Nine) on Francophone literatures, pp.199–225 of *The Cassell Guide to Literature in French*, ed. Valerie Worth-Stylianou, London, Cassell. *African Francophone Writing. A Critical Introduction*, ed. Laïla Ibnlfassi and Nicki Hitchcott, Oxford, Berg, 215 pp., contains contributions from a wide range of critics, again with a useful introduction setting the literature in its context. All these last three works include a political and literary chronology. From France appears *Littérature maghrébine d'expression française*, ed. Charles Bonn, Naget Khadda and Abdallah Maahri-Alaoui, Edicef-Aupelf, 272 pp., a general panorama of Maghrebian literature in French by contributors researching and teaching in North Africa. In addition to this general survey, a chapter is devoted to established writers such as Kateb Yacine, Albert Memmi, Mohammed Dib and Tahar Ben Jelloun among others. Bonn, the leading French specialist in the area, has also written a general article, 'Deux ans de littérature maghrébine de langue française', *Migrations*, 1197:46–52.

Women continue to be a central focus. Rachida Titah, *La Galerie des absentes*, La Tour d'Aigues, L'Aube, 165 pp., is an essay on the place of Algerian women in literature and painting. Hafid Gafaiti, *Les Femmes dans le roman algérien*, L'Harmattan, 350 pp., shows women in confrontation with society, exploring the inherent contradictions that exist in the portrayal of women, with particular reference to Assia Djebar, Rachid Boudjedra, Abdelhamid Benhedouga and Aïcha Lemsine. *Francophone Women Writers*, ed. Mary Jean Green et al., Minneapolis, Minnesota U.P., 336 pp., is a collection of essays on women writing in French from diverse Francophone cultures and countries, drawing attention mainly to the condition of women, but also covering more general cultural and linguistic concerns. L. G. Lunt, 'La quête d'identité: la femme dans le roman tunisien contemporain', *IBLA*, 177:55–86 provides a welcome focus on a less well-known literature. P. Geesey, 'Collective autobiography: Algerian women and history in Assia Djebar's *L'Amour, la fantasia*,' *DFS*, 35:153–57, in addition to the reading of the work provides well-researched references to autobiography in a post-colonial context. Two further articles worth noting are: B. Chikhi, 'Algériades: d'Assia Djebar à Nina Bouraoui', *BFA* 9:27–40; and S. Heiler, 'Le "Miroir du Silence" de Aïcha Bouabaci: une poétique silencieuse, chantée et réfléchie', *ib.*, 57–70.

Books on individual authors and the challenges of individual expression include: Bachir Adjil, *Espace et écriture chez Mohammed Dib: la trilogie nordique*, pref. Denise Brahimi, L'Harmattan, 210 pp.; Robert Elbaz, *Tahar Ben Jelloun ou l'inassouvissement du désir narratif*, L'Harmattan, 117 pp.; and Nelly Lindenhauf, *Tahar Ben Jelloun: les yeux baissés*, Brussels, Labor, 158 pp. Also on the subject of B. J. is N. Redouane, 'Marques sociales dans "L'Homme rompu" de Tahar Ben Jelloun', *BFA*, 9:78–95. Two articles from Tunisian journals are: J.-Y. Debreuille, 'Resurgir et agir: le poète au milieu du monde', *Le Livre des Questions* (Tunis), Spring 1996:23–31, on Lorand Gaspar; and A. Mahfoudh, 'Mélancolie, désordre de la mémoire et nouvel ordre du récit dans *Timmimoun* de R. Boudjedra', *IBLA*, 178:271–84. Other journal contributions include H. Wahbi, 'Hommage à Abdelkébir Khatibi', *Etudes Littéraires Maghrébins CICLIM* (Coordination Internationale des Chercheurs sur les Littératures Maghrébines) 11–12:21–28. A special mention should be made of a new journal, *Algérie Littérature/Action*, published by Marsa, whose first number includes an interview with Assia Djebar (1:183–87), and reproduces an interview with Tahar Djaout given in 1991 (1:205–12); a special section devoted to Taos Amrouche (3–4:179–200); and an interview with Mohammed Kacimi (6:109–23). This monthly review publishes a wide variety of material, including unpublished notes by Algerian writers, debates, extracts and essays. *Ib.*, 2:183–221, includes a dossier put together by A. Khelladi on 'Le théâtre algérien'; and *ib.*, 5:171–75, has an interview with the Algerian dramatist Hamida Aït el Hadj.

Three other works to be signalled are: Beïda Chikhi, *Maghreb en textes. Ecriture, histoire, savoirs et symboliques*, L'Harmattan, 248 pp., which questions the status of modernity in contemporary Maghrebian fiction; *The Marabout and the Muse. New Approaches to Islam in African Literature*, ed. Kenneth W. Harrow, Portsmouth, NH, Heinemann – London, James Currie, 238 pp., which devotes its second section exclusively to Maghrebian literature and especially focuses on Assia Djebar and Driss Chraïbi; and *La Traversée du français dans les signes littéraires marocains*, ed. Bénayoun-Szmidt, Bouraoui and Redouane, Toronto, La Source, 251 pp., which is a volume of conference proceedings stressing the particularity of Moroccan literature in French, including the judæo-arab dialogue.

Other new journals this year specially devoted to Francophone questions are *The ASCALF Yearbook*, ed. Peter Hawkins, Bristol, 179 pp., which includes P. Dunwoodie, 'Forging an identity: Algerian writers of the Twenties and Thirties' (65–79); and *JAS*, ed. Hugh

Roberts, which also has an article looking to the pre-independence era, M. Brett, 'Dad's Algeria: Jacques Berque and Albert Camus on the land of their fathers' (84–102). Two very different books on the relationship between West and East are: Nourredine Lamouchi, *Jean-Paul Sartre et le tiers monde*, L'Harmattan, 346 pp., which looks from West to East; and Sophie Noguès, *Guide de l'Orient à Paris*, Parigramme, 252 pp., which focuses on the manifestations of the Orient in Paris with a useful glossary.

3. FRANCOPHONE SUB-SAHARAN AFRICA

Two major works contribute to a wider and deeper understanding of the region's literary output through history: Belinda Jack, *Négritude and Literary Criticism*, Greenwood Press, Westport, Connecticut, 208 pp.; and Ambroise Kom, *Le Dictionnaire des œuvres littéraires de langue française en Afrique du sud du Sahara*, San Francisco, International Scholars Publications, I, *Des origines à 1978*, 668 pp., and II, *1979–1989*, 629 pp. Gérard Albert, *Afrique Plurielle*, Amsterdam, Rodopi, 199 pp., deals with the complex ethnic and literary links in Senegal, the specificity of Zaire and the linguistic problems of African writers. Robert Jouanny, *Tracées francophones*, I. *Espaces littéraires d'Afrique et d'Amérique*, L'Harmattan, 310 pp., shares with the reader his personal taste for the poetry and literature of Black Africa. *The ASCALF Yearbook* has several important contributions to the field: J. Chevrier, 'Présence du mythe dans la littérature africaine' (81–94); R. Little, 'Escaping Othello's shadow: "Un homme pareil aux autres", "O pays mon beau peuple" and "Un chant écarlate"' (95–112); G. O. Midiohouan, 'Problématique d'une définition de la nouvelle dans la littérature négro-africaine d'expression française' (113–25); and P. Hawkins, 'Modernism and post-modernism in some recent African novels in French' (126–36). A. Ridehalgh, 'Khadi Fall's "Senteurs d'hivernage": exile as metaphor?' (137–44), offers two readings of the work, one of which proposes a different way of approaching women's identity in the African novel.

L. Kesteloot, 'Turning point in the Francophone African novel: the Eighties and the Nineties', *ALT*, 20:4–13, highlights the principal trends in recent years, stressing the writers' more personal preoccupations reflected in style and in narrative structure. Josias Semujunga, *De Paroles en figures: essais sur les littératures africaines et antillaises*, L'Harmattan, 178 pp., attempts to highlight some of the particularisms of such writings. *NLi*, 125, 'Cinq ans de littérature', reflects many of the areas of interest to scholars this year, with a section on the literature of Zaire (8–43), a dossier on Calixthe Beyala (62–79), and one on the late Congolese writer Sony Labou Tansi (100–33). G. K.

Fonkou, 'Phénomène d'alternance de code dans quelques romans négro-africains', *EtF*, 11.1:39–51, contains a study on language issues, mainly based on Ferdinand Oyono, with the mention of a few other West African writers. J. Ouédraogo, 'Défis de traduction et délits d'interprète dans deux romans africains', *ib.*, 53–69, is also centred on Oyono, and on Ahmadou Kourouma. A. Kom, 'Écriture, francophonie et identité en Afrique subsaharienne', *DFS*, 35: 169–77, considers the necessity for Africa to extricate itself from cultural dependency on France. Odile Cazenave, *Femmes rebelles: naissance d'un nouveau roman africain au féminin*, L'Harmattan, 349 pp., covers the striking evolution in women's writing in the last ten years. On the same theme Senegalese works evoke much interest, notably Susan Stringer, *The Senegalese Novel by Women: Through Their Own Eyes*, NY, Lang, viii + 201 pp. D. G. Plant, 'Mythic dimensions in the novels of Mariama Bâ', *RAfL*, 27.2:102–11, highlights and develops B.'s clarion call for a depiction of woman's role beyond the one-dimensional. J. Treiber, 'Feminism and identity politics: Mariama Bâ's "Un Chant écarlate"', *ib.*, 27.4:109–23, sees B.'s feminism as integral to the project of African cultural recovery. K. Anyinefa, 'Hello and goodbye to *négritude*: Senghor, Dadié, Dongala and America', *ib.*, 27.2:51–69, addresses the representation of America in the works of the three writers. J. Riesz, 'The *Tirailleur sénégalais* who did not want to be a "Grand enfant": Bakary Diallo's Force Bonté (1926) reconsidered', *ib.*, 157–79, provides a reassessment of D.'s reflections, away from his image of a simpleton or a naïve panegyrist of the French colonial system. Théophile Obenga , *Cheikh Anta Diop, Volney et le sphinx*, Présence Africaine, 516 pp., acknowledges the contribution of D. to African history and sees this as the basis for a positive future. A. Pondopoulo, 'La construction de l'altérité ethnique peule dans l'œuvre de Faidherbe', *CEA*, 3:421–41, defines Faidherbe's view of race and his creation of the 'Fulani' stereotype, a product of the æsthetic and philosophical styles of his time. A. Teko-Agbo, 'Nature et littérature: sensibilité écologique et vision du monde dans "Amkoullel, l'enfant peul de Amadou Hampâté Bâ"', *EtF*, 9.1:21–37, shows how ecology was a concern for this African writer before it became fashionable in the West. *NLi* 126, 'Cinq ans de littératures, 1991–1995: Afrique Noire II', has a section on the literature of Djibouti and two dossiers on Guinean writers: T. Monénembo (80–115), and William Sassine (124–37). Y.Ch. Elenga, 'Désordre et langage de dérision', *Zaïre-Afrique*, 36:459–70, analyses Calixthe Beyala's *Assèze l'Africaine* (1994) and her presentation of women fighting against adversity. A number of works pay tribute to the Congolese writer Sony Labou Tansi following his untimely death in 1995: Anatole Mbanga, *Les procédés de création dans l'œuvre de Sony Labou Tansi: systèmes d'interactions dans l'écriture*, L'Harmattan, 282 pp.; and Jean-Michel Devésa, *Sony Labou Tansi: écrivain de la honte et des rives magiques du Kongo*, L'Harmattan, 379 pp. Josias Semujunga, 'De l'absurde comme style de vie et procès esthétique: "Shaba Deux" de Y. V. Mudimbe', *EtF*, 9.1:5–20, develops the various readings of this work. *Dits de la nuit, anthologie de contes et légendes de l'Afrique centrale* (1994) is analysed in K. Kavwahirehi, 'L'Afrique centrale entre oralité et écriture', *Zaïre-Afrique*, 28:221–28.

· There are very few recent publications on the theatre, so the issue entitled 'Théâtres d'Afrique noire' of *Alternatives Théâtre*, Brussels, June 1995, 96 pp., is particularly useful in this field.

Works from the Indian Ocean are studied by Moradewun Adejunmobi and Jean-Joseph Rabearivelo, *Literature and Lingua Franca in Colonial Madagascar*, NY, Lang, 346 pp.; and in *NLi*, 128, 'Haïti, Océan Indien', which presents studies of the literature of Réunion (40–48), Mauritius (48–75) and Madagascar (76–99).

III. OCCITAN STUDIES

LANGUAGE

POSTPONED

LITERATURE

By RUTH E. HARVEY, *Senior Lecturer in French,*
Royal Holloway University of London

1. MEDIEVAL PERIOD

Specific to this section, *Les Troubadours et l'état toulousain avant la Croisade (1209). Actes du colloque de Toulouse (9 et 10 décembre 1988)*, ed. A. Krispin (Annales de Littérature Occitane, 1), Bordes, CELO and William Blake and Co., 1995, 244 pp. (henceforth *Colloque* (Toulouse)), contains several overview papers. P. Bec, 'La poésie des troubadours et la genèse de la lyrique européenne' (15–27), surveys troubadour activity outside Occitania and foreign imitators of the troubadour lyric. J. Gourc, 'Les troubadours, négociateurs et entremetteurs' (29–43), considers the performers' relations with each other and their public as signalled by their use of 'je–vous' markers. S. Kay, 'The contradictions of courtly love and the origins of courtly poetry. The evidence of the *lauzengiers*', *Journal of Medieval and Early Modern Studies*, 26:209–53, is a masterly re-examination of the problems 'Why love?' and 'Why then?' in the light of two schools of interpretation: the socio-historical and the psychoanalytical. K. argues that the contradictions stem from, and articulate the divided and divisive nature of, court life, while the *lauzengiers*' role as competitors and scapegoats of the lover point to the lyric's underlying narcissistic libidinal economy. S. Spence, '*Lo cop mortal*: the evil eye and the origins of courtly love', *RR*, 87:307–18, explores the role of a growing interest in the visual and in envy, to which the arrows of the evil eye and those of love were complementary cultural responses. Sarah Spence, *Texts and the Self in the Twelfth Century*, CUP, 1996, xi + 167 pp., devotes a chapter to 'Text of the self: Guilhem IX and Jaufre Rudel, Bernart de Ventadorn and Raimbaut d'Aurenga' as part of a wider, complex study of an evolving awareness of the self articulated in Latin and vernacular texts. This development involves interplay between inherited traditions and textual creation, and a differentiation of the latter from the former which depends in part upon spatialization, distance and the visual and upon the relationship between signifier and signified. Guilhem IX's works are viewed as an assertion of autonomy (although he is treated implicitly as literally the first troubadour, which is rather a risky assumption), while Rudel's represent the first steps in vernacular intertextuality, imitation and hence differentiation; Bernart de Ventadorn highlights the rupture between subjective and objective worlds, and Raimbaut emphasizes the distance of the objectified self from the world. M.-R. Bonnet, 'Le clerc et le troubadour dans les *vidas* provençales', *Colloque* (Aix-en-Provence), 65–78, reviews the clerical status and education of the troubadours through a study of the vocabulary of the *vidas* and *razos*. W. D. Paden, 'The troubadours and the Albigensian Crusade', *RPh*, 49, 1995:168–91, enumerates and documents the flaws in the received idea that the crusade sounded the death-knell for the troubadour lyric in Occitania and suggests that the success and tenacity of this notion can be explained by the intellectual climate of the Provençal regionalist revival at the turn of the 20th c.: for influential figures such as Mistral, the crusade was a war of conquest which foreshadowed the hated centralization of the French state.

M. Careri, 'Per la ricostruzione del *Libre* di Miquel de la Tor. Studio e presentazione delle fonti', *CN*, 56:251–408, is but the first part of an extremely detailed study. The conclusions concerning the sources are summarized in a schema on p.320, and this is followed by a diplomatic edition of MS M^{h2} (Madrid, Real Academia de la Historia, Fondo San Román, 2 Ms 26). S. Vatteroni, 'Fragments of Provençal lyric manuscripts: a bibliography', *Tenso*, 12.1:14–30, is a valuable updated and indexed list, of 'notices', diplomatic editions and other relevant publications. L. Borghi Cedrini, 'Una recente acquisizione trobadorica e il problema delle attribuzioni', *MedRom*, 20:3–44, discusses the fragment *z*' and re-examines the *unicum Si faz bona canson*, the last of four poems ascribed there to Ademar lo Negre.

Editions include *Songs of the Women Troubadours*, ed. and trans. Mathilda Tomaryn Bruckner, Laurie Shepard, and Sarah White (GLML, 97A), 1995, lxxvii + 194 pp. The introduction presents some of the problems associated with the place of the *trobairitz* within the tradition of the masculine lyric, and with identifying the *trobairitz* and their corpus. It is not intended to be a full critical edition: critical apparatus is included in the notes only where necessary to explain aspects of the translation. MSS have been consulted again for the 36 pieces selected here and, as the editors acknowledge, they are heavily indebted to Angelika Rieger's monumental edition (*YWMLS*, 53:260). Within these limitations, it will be a useful introduction for non-specialists and a welcome, accessible resource for students unable to cope with the German edition. *Paulet de Marselha: un provençal a la cort dels reis d'Aragó*, ed. Isabel de Riquer, trans. Jordi Cerdà, Barcelona, Columna Edicions, 155 pp., includes revised versions of the critical editions printed in *BRABLB*, 38, with critical notes and translations into Catalan. *Les cançons de l'amor de lluny de Jaufre Rudel*, ed. Victoria Cirlot, trans. Eduard Vilella, Barcelona, Columna Edicions, 113 pp., presents Chiarini's 1985 edition for a Catalan readership. S. Vatteroni, 'Le poesie di Peire Cardenal (IV)', *SMV*, 41, 1995:165–212, continues the project with editions of five more songs: PC 335, 60, 3, 5, 7, and 6. P. Squillacioti, '*Senher Dieu[s], que fezist Adam* di Folchetto di Marsiglia e due versione catalane', *ib.*, 127–64, gives a new edition of PC 156, 12a, together with a diplomatic edition of two later Catalan versions. L. Spetia, 'Riccardo Cuor di Leone tra oc e oïl (*BdT* 420, 2)', *CN*, 56:101–56, revisits the question of which language the *rotrouenge* was originally composed in. A critical edition based on the French *chansonnier C* is followed by a linguistic analysis and a substantial discussion of the development of the 'legend' of the king as an Occitan troubadour; S. concludes that the song was composed in the *langue d'oïl* and that Richard really belongs among the *trouvères*. L. Badia and A. J. Soberanas, '*La Ventura del cavaller N'Huc e de Madona*. Un nouveau roman occitano-catalan en vers du XIVe siècle', *R*, 114:96–134, present a plot summary of the surviving 685 lines, a codicological and palæographical analysis and an edition of the fragment, with notes.

M.-A. Bossy and N. A. Jones, 'Gender and compilational patterns in troubadour lyric: the case of MS *N*', *FrF*, 21:261–80, suggest that the arrangement of six *trobairitz* songs, sandwiched between repeated songs by the 'rakish master', William IX, was deliberate, and sets up a metadialogue between male and female voices. M. Spampinato Beretta, 'Les *trobairitz*: la voix féminine au moyen âge', *RLr*, 100:17–48, is an updated version of an essay published in 1980. A. A. Macdonald, 'A refusal to be silenced or to rejoice in any joy that love may bring: the anonymous Old Occitan *canso Per ioi que d'amor m'avegna*,' *DFS*, 36:3–13, accepts PC 461, 191 as the work of a *trobairitz* (if not Castelloza herself) and discusses its use of the woman's voice, largely in terms of an unproblematic biographical narrative subtending the song. A. Rieger, 'Alamanda de Castelnau: une *trobairitz* dans l'entourage des comtes de Toulouse?', *Colloque* (Toulouse), 183–92, is a slightly revised version of the article in *ZrP*, 107 (*YWMLS*, 53:262). Carol Jane Nappholz, *Unsung Women. The Anonymous Female Voice in Troubadour Poetry*, NY, Lang, 1994, 140 pp, brings together 26 such songs with a brief introduction and no textual notes. The texts, including male-female dialogue pieces in which only the man is named, are reprinted from existing editions, the translations are new. The second issue of *Tenso*, 11, is again devoted to Guiraut Riquier (see *YWMLS*, 56:298–99), and includes: R. Cholakian, 'Riquier's *Letras*: an epistemology of self' (129–47); W. Pfeffer, 'Guiraut Riquier and the study of proverbs' (148–62); and C. Phan, 'Structures poético-musicales du chant mélismatique chez Guiraut Riquier et Alphonse le Sage' (163–78). G. Gouiran, 'Du bon usage de l'hérésie en *fin'amor* chez Bernart de Ventadorn', *RLr*, 100 : 1–16, demonstrates that the *dompna* is the object of criticism in over half the surviving works of this supposedly exemplary proponent of love. L. Paterson, 'L'obscénité du clerc: le troubadour Marcabru et la sculpture ecclésiastique au XIIe siècle en Aquitaine et dans l'Espagne du nord', *Colloque* (Aix-en-Provence), 473–87, suggests that some of the more problematic passages of this difficult poet can be illuminated by reference to contemporary corbel sculptures which proliferate along the pilgrimage route through western France and northern Spain and whose obscenity, like that of the troubadour's songs, had a moralizing purpose. R. E. Harvey, 'Marcabru et la *fals'amor*', *RLr*, 100 : 49–80, examines extracts from the poet's surviving songs in a similar light and argues that this interpretation was dependent on a contemporary knowledge of the troubadour and his milieu: without such awareness, the troubadour could easily be seen by later generations as a *lauzengier*. A. Krispin, 'Espace féodale et espace poétique: Raimbaut d'Aurenga entre Toulouse et Aragon', *Colloque* (Toulouse), 177–82, summarizes what is known of Raimbaut's political situation, places it in the context of the struggle between these two major powers and (less convincingly) examines Raimbaut's works for traces of this conflict. A. Brenon, 'Sur les marges de l'état toulousain, *fin'amor* et catharisme: Peire Vidal et Raimon de Miraval entre Laurac et Cabaret', *ib.*, 139–54, observes that the courts most praised by these poets for their *fin'amor* and *cortezia* were also those where heresy was most firmly implanted and concludes that both phenomena stem from the same aspiration towards the spiritual. G. Gouiran, 'Le poète et le prince: le cas Bertran de Born', *ib.*, 211–18, surveys the connections between Bertran's *sirventes* and the conflicts between the great lords of his time. R. Rosenstein, 'Guiraudo lo Ros ou le conventionnalisme exemplaire', *ib.*, 193–210, presents a study of the context and literary features of this poet's work. M. G. Capusso, 'Contacts franco-ibériques dans la "nouvelle" allégorique de Peire Guilhem (ms provençal *R*)', *RLr*, 100 : 223–45, re-examines the question of attribution and, in greater detail in the context of the literary climate and lyric influences on the work, the identification of the king 'Alphonse' and the *rei Navar* (Alphonse VIII of Castile and Sancho VII, or Alphonse X and Thibaut de Champagne). G. Gouiran, '*Car tu es cavalliers e clers* (*Flamenca*, v. 1899): Guilhem, ou le chevalier parfait', *Colloque* (Aix-en-Provence), 199–214, examines the hybrid depiction of this character as an example of the courtly ideal. K. Busby, 'The Occitan *fabliau* and the linguistic distribution of genres', *N*, 80 : 11–23, looks at the features of *Castia gilos* and the *Novas del papagay* in the light of the paucity of *fabliaux* in Occitan. J.-C. Huchet, 'L'apparition des *novas* au tournant des XIIe et XIIIe siècles', *Colloque* (Toulouse), 45–53, discusses the narrative works of Raimon Vidal de Besalù, arguing that they show a progressive evolution away from any 'support lyrique' and evidence of a 'crise du *trobar*' which antedated the Albigensian Crusade. X. Ravier, 'La topographie dans la *Chanson de Sainte Foy d'Agen*', *ib.*, 29–38, studies the referential and emblematic roles of some places names in this text. M. R. Harris, 'Observations on language and text in an Old Occitan version of Bonaventure's *Miracula*', *RPh*, 49:429–49, offers corrections and supplementary comment on the edition of the *Miracles* of Saint Francis. R. Lafont, 'Guilhem de Tudela, ses origines, les origines de son art', *Colloque* (Toulouse), 219–28, sees Guilhem as Navarrese and his work as part of a school of epic and historical composition which brings together the *Chanson de Sainte Foy*, the *Roland*, the *Canso d'Antioca* and the first part of the *Chanson de la Croisade albigeoise*.

2. FROM 1500 ONWARDS

F.-P. Kirsch, 'Sus l'eroïsme de la Mirèlha mistralenca', *RLr*, 100:247–64, studies the construction and implications of Mirèlha as myth in the context of the ideological climate which produced the Maid of Orleans as a national icon. D. Streight, 'Restoring authenticity and naiveté to Aubanel and Zani', *Tenso*, 12.1:1–13, argues that the love poems of the first part of *La Mióugrano entre-duberto* were indeed an accurate reflection of the poet's inspiration and feelings for the real Jenny Manivet. P. Martel, '*Vox clamans in deserto*: l'Indigène, éditeur de textes occitans médiévaux à Toulouse sous le Second Empire', *Colloque* (Toulouse), 155–76, studies the inflammatory anonymous prefaces to editions of medieval texts published in the 'Bibliothèque romane' collection and attempts to identify the influences on their 'nationalisme occitan'. Mitu Grosu, *Mistral, poète de l'amour*, Jerusalem, HaMakor, 1995, 104 pp., is a short study of the mystery and purity of love in the light of the literary influences of folklore, the troubadour lyric and the works of the Félibres.

IV. SPANISH STUDIES

LANGUAGE

POSTPONED

MEDIEVAL LITERATURE

By JANE E. CONNOLLY, *University of Miami*,
and NOEL FALLOWS, *The University of Georgia*

The following abbreviation is used in this section only: *Smith Vol.* =
*Al que en buen hora naçio: Essays on the Spanish Epic and Ballad in Honour of
Colin Smith*, ed. Brian Powell and Geoffrey West (Hispanic Studies
Textual Research and Criticism 12), Liverpool U.P.–MHRA,
viii + 207 pp.

1. GENERAL

Louise Mirrer, *Women, Jews, and Muslims in the Texts of Reconquest Castile*,
Ann Arbor, Michigan U.P., x + 190 pp., claims that the struggle
between the dominant male Christian culture and the 'other'
indicated by the title is the 'most appropriate paradigm for discussing
literary texts produced during the last centuries of reconquest'. M.
employs multiple approaches (among these, Foucault's theory of
power, linguistic models of 'men's' vs 'women's' language, feminist
theory) to elucidate a vast body of texts (ballads, *Poema de Mio Cid*,
Milagros de Nuestra Señora, *Libro de buen amor*, the *Memorias* of Leonor
López de Córdoba, a poem by Florencia Pinar), arguing that, in
order to strengthen male Christian control, Jewish and Muslim men
are ridiculed and feminized, their female co-religionists are presented
as sexual objects (willing or unwilling), and powerful Christian
women are represented as lustful and threats to social and political
order. Some analyses are thorough and compelling (notably those
related to the *romances*) while others seem superficial and forced (for
example, M. associates the Virgin in *milagro* 21 with the queens in the
ballads *Landarico* and *Doña Blanca*, saying that her power is 'linked to
lawlessness, and her authority, represented chiefly in the context of
weakening male domination, is characterized by a frightening
excess'). Fernando Gómez Redondo, *Poesía española 1. Edad Media:
juglaría, clerecía y romancero*, B, Crítica, 720 pp., offers an exhaustive
anthology of the poetry from the 12th c. to the 14th c. Each selection
is accompanied by an introduction including the historical background for and major characteristics of the poem, and often an
evaluation of the state of scholarship; some of these introductions are

too brief and uninformative, and occasionally misleading (e.g., G. R. makes no mention of the uniqueness of *Santa Oria* within Berceo's hagiographic project, and states as a given the existence of a source, *Vita beatae Aurea*, without mentioning evidence to the contrary). The texts, which are numerous, well-selected, and annotated in footnotes and endnotes, have been 'transcribed' by G. R., although it is unclear if these transcriptions are based on the manuscripts themselves or are conflations of existing editions. The anthology includes an introductory essay (9–43) offering an overview of the poetic developments of the period and an ample bibliography (687–715). Despite its minor drawbacks, this anthology will prove a useful tool for teachers and students of medieval Spanish poetry. M. Á. Pérez Priego, 'Formación del canon literario medieval castellano', *Ínsula*, 600:7–9, offers an overview of the varying constructions of the canon by literary figures throughout the centuries, from the Marqués de Santillana and Antonio de Nebrija to Carlos Bousoño and José Hierro. M. R. Menocal, 'An Andalusianist's last sigh', *La Corónica*, 24.2:179–89, explores the controversies initially provoked by the work of Miguel Asín Palacios (especially *La escatología musulmana en la Divina Comedia*), the subsequent waning of attention paid to his research, and his current 'rehabilitation' reflected in the re-publication of his studies, explaining the fate of A. and his work through comparison of his vision to those of Edward Said and Harold Bloom in the critical realm and Juan Goytisolo and Salman Rushdie in the literary sphere. P. Linehan, 'The court historiographer of Francoism?: *la leyenda oscura* of Ramón Menéndez Pidal', *BHS(G)*, 73:437–50, reviews M. E. Lacarra's and J. Pérez Villanueva's evaluations of don Ramón, and concludes that he never embraced Franco or fascism. R. Wright, 'Latin and Romance in the Castilian chancery (1180–1230)', *BHS(L)*, 73:115–28, discusses the reforming movement to make Romance the language for chancery documents, examining in detail the roles played by various figures in the struggle (notably Martín López de Pisuerga, Diego García, and Rodrigo Ximénez de Rada) and the significance of the Treaty of Cabreros, and considering possible connections with the poetry of the period (*Poema de Mio Cid*, *Libro de Alexandre*, Berceo). A. Deyermond, 'Evidence for lost literature by Jews and *conversos* in medieval Castile and Aragon', *Donaire*, 6:19–30, continues his examination of lost literature, weighing the evidence related to possible works written in Spanish by Jews and *conversos*, from the tenuous (e.g. intermediate vernacular draft translations produced by the Toledo 'school' of translators, love songs by medieval Jewish women) to the probable (e.g. the *Juego de axedrez*, a commentary on the *Proverbios morales*, 15th-c. texts produced by the Santa María/ Cartagena family and the Díaz de Toledo family), and considering the reasons for their loss. E. Bertola, 'Il problema dell'eternità del mondo nel pensiero di Mosè Maimonide', *Sefarad*, 56 : 19–42, analyses the philosopher's view concerning the question of the eternity/non-eternity of the world and its subsequent influence on Aquinas. M. Zavala Gómez del Campo, 'Temas y motivos medievales en cuentos y leyendas de la tradición oral moderna de México', *Actas* (Mexico), 99–121, studies the influence of European folklore on modern Mexican tales and legends. P. Barrette, 'Poemas hagiográficos españoles y el contexto europeo', *ib.*, 169–81, examines the proliferation of hagiographic poems written in medieval English, French and German, versus the paucity of poems written in Castilian, Catalan, Italian and Provençal, and claims that this is due to the fact that, just as Galician-Portuguese was the preferred language for writing *cantigas*, so English, French, and German were the preferred languages for writing lives of saints. C. J. Alejos-Grau, 'Filosofía bajomedieval en fray Juan de Zumárraga', *ib.*, 387–94, is a brief analysis of the medieval sources of the *Regla cristiana breve* (1547), by Juan de Zumárraga, the first archbishop of Mexico. H. L. Sharrer, 'Spain and Portugal', pp. 401–49 of *Medieval Arthurian Literature. A Guide to Recent Research*, ed. Norris J. Lacy, NY, Garland, provides a thorough overview of recent scholarship on Arthurian literature in Spain and Portugal, and suggests possibilities for further research. M. Masera, '"Una vieja con un diente/ que llama a toda la gente": análisis diacrónico del personaje de la vieja en el cancionero popular hispánico', *RevLM*, 8 : 105–10, gives a brief sketch of the figure of the old woman in refrains and songs. M. T. Herrera and M. N. Sánchez, 'Dificultades de la interpretación conceptual en textos científicos medievales', *Dutton Vol.*, 333–41, discuss some lexicographic problems faced by an editor of medieval scientific texts. F. López Estrada, 'Consideraciones sobre el gótico literario', *ib.*, 443–48, compares the literary Gothic to the plastic arts in order to define its characteristics. A few items of interest related to St James and Compostela are: Thomas F. Coffey, Linda Kay Davidson, and Maryjane Dunn, **The Miracles of Saint James: Translations from the 'Liber sancti Jacobi'*, NY, Italica, lxxviii + 169 pp.; Maryjane Dunn and Linda Kay Davidson, **The Pilgrimage to Compostela in the Middle Ages: A Book of Essays*, NY, Garland, xlviii + 188 pp.; the same authors, **The Pilgrimage to Santiago de Compostela: A Comprehensive, Annotated Bibliography*, NY, Garland, 1994, xv + 546 pp.

2. Early Lyric Poetry, Epic, Ballads

KHARJAS, LYRIC POETRY

C. J. McDonald, 'Judah ha-Levi's *Kuzari*: proto-Zionism, the paradox of post-colonial prosody, and the ridiculous rabbi', *BHS(L)*,

73:339–49, rejects the interpretation of Norman Roth that *Kuzari* is a 'manifesto of Zionist ideals', proposing instead that the portrayal of the character of the rabbi as a fool suggests that we are meant to discredit his assertions.

EPIC

V. Castro Lingel, 'The count's wife in *La condesa traidora*, the *Poema de Fernán González*, and the *Romanz del infant Garçía*: how many Sanchas?', *BHS(G)*, 73:371–78, gives a series of inconclusive but suggestive observations regarding the Sancha figure in the Counts of Castile cycle. A. Deyermond, 'The problem of lost epics: evidence and criteria', *Smith Vol.*, 27–43, considers the strength of 11 criteria (ranging from a 'surviving verse fragment' to 'composition by motif in chronicle prose') used to evaluate the existence of a lost Spanish epic, and applies them to various of over 60 proposed candidates. (See also BALLADS.)

POEMA DE MIO CID

J. Gornall, '"¡Fabla, Pero Mudo...!"–"¡Dirévos, Çid...!"': address in the *Poema de mio Cid*', *Smith Vol.*, 45–53, reviews the use of *vos* and *tu* in the *PMC*, suggesting that a 'flexible and sophisticated' system of address is at play in the poem. M. E. Lacarra, 'Sobre las dobles bodas en el *Poema de mio Cid*', *ib.*, 73–90, examines several aspects related to the dissolution of the first marriages of the Cid's daughters and the contracting of the second, and concludes that the treatment of the dual marriages offers more evidence of the poet's legal knowledge. D. G. Pattison, '"¡Dios, que buen vasallo! ¡Si oviese buen señor!"': the theme of the loyal vassal in the *Poema de mio Cid*', *ib.*, 107–13, reviews briefly the legal relationship of vassalage between the Cid and his king. M. N. Pavlovi and R. M. Walker, '"Asil creçe la ondra a mio Çid el Campeador": the role of Minaya Álvar Fáñez in the *Poema de mio Cid*', *ib.*, 115–28, consider why the poet so closely linked the Cid and Minaya, in clear disregard for historical fact; they conclude that, like many other aspects of the poem, this relationship reflects a period of transition in which the Cid, aided by his 'synchronic kindred' headed by Minaya, moves towards the more widespread 'descent system...of which the Infantes have proved to be such unworthy members'. C. J. Pountain, 'Attributive adjective position in the *Poema de mio Cid*', *ib.*, 129–46, examines the factors at play in determining adjective position in the poem. B. Powell, 'The *Cantar del rey don Sancho y cerco de Zamora* and the *Poema de mio Cid*', *ib.*, 147–60, asserts that neither poem influenced the other. G. West, 'The Cid and Alfonso

VI re-visited: characterization in the *Poema de mio Cid*', *ib.*, 161–69, argues that the application of the 20th-c. concept of consistency of character must be limited if not entirely discarded in order to understand the *PMC* as a medieval work. I. J. Rivera, 'Marriage and the exchange of power in the *Poema de Mio Cid*', *JHispP*, 17, 1993 : 129–50, sees marriage in the *PMC* as a strategy with a view to solidifying power relationships with other men. C. Smith, '"Miran Valençia commo yaze la çibdad"', *La Corónica*, 24.2 : 154–65, discusses *PMC* vv. 1610–17 and entertains the possibility that the poet had personal knowledge of the city of Valencia. Id., 'On the bastardy of the literary Cid', *Dutton Vol.*, 645–54, reviews at length the evidence related to the Cid's alleged illegitimacy and rejects the views of J. Duggan and S. Armistead that the *PMC* alludes to the hero's bastardy; S. concludes that the rumour of illegitimacy began relatively late, certainly after the *PMC*. J. Gornall, 'Two more cases of double narration in the *Cantar de Mio Cid*', *La Corónica*, 25.1 : 85–92, analyses the phenomenon of double narration which he defines succinctly as 'recounting aspects which are later described again, often with variations of detail' in *tiradas* 20–22, and *tirada* 126. (See also LIBRO DE ALEXANDRE.)

BALLADS

Alan Deyermond, *Point of View in the Ballad: 'The Prisoner', 'The Lady and the Shepherd', and Others*, London, Dept. of Hispanic Studies, Queen Mary and Westfield College, 95 pp., is an important examination of narrative voice and audience reception in ten ballads and their variants. *Spanish Ballads*, ed. Colin Smith, London, Bristol Classical Press, li + 143 pp., is an updated version, with extensive revisions to the introduction and notes, of an edition originally published in 1964. The introduction is, characteristically, full of substance, and the book will be of special use to teachers and students, as opposed to advanced scholars in the field. S. G. Armistead, 'Ballad hunting in Zamora', *Smith Vol.*, 13–26, publishes eight rare ballads collected in Uña de Quintana in 1980. D. Hook, 'Marksmanship and meaning in "Alora la bien cercada"', *ib.*, 55–72, considers the possibility that the death of the *adelantado* in the ballad might suggest that the attack on Alora was viewed as a 'threat to frontier *convivencia*'. I. Michael, 'Factitious flowers or fictitious fossils? The *romances viejos* re-viewed', *ib.*, 91–105, examines and rejects the tenets of (neo)traditionalism, asserting that there is no relation between the epic and the ballad, and proposes that ballad scholars would better invest their efforts by concentrating on the 'rapidly fading oral tradition', its interaction with learned literature, and its 'great aesthetic effects'. J. Whetnall, 'A question of genre: *Roncesvalles* and the *Siete Infantes* connection', *ib.*, 171–87, disputes the fragmentation theory and, through an examination of parallels of diction and motif between the *Chanson de Roland*, *Roncesvalles*, and the chronicle accounts of *Siete Infantes*, posits a 'generic distinction between ballad and epic', with *Roncesvalles* belonging to the former. M. Altamirano, '*La doncella guerrera*, ¿romance paralelístico?', *Actas* (Mexico), 33–46, focuses on two Leonese versions of the ballad in an attempt to demonstrate that this ballad is atypical of the ballad genre. A. González, 'La complejidad del romance de *La muerte del Maestre de Santiago*', *ib.*, 47–55, analyses the use of symbols in the ballad as a means of creating complex political propaganda. R. Bazán Bonfil, 'Algunas variantes peninsulares y sefarditas del romance de *Amnón y Tamar*', *ib.*, 57–74, shows how two communities interpreted the same biblical episode, and observes that the Sephardic versions of the ballad dwell on the development of the characters, whereas in the Christian versions actions are more important than characters. G. B. Chicote, 'Jimena, de la pica al Romancero: definición del personaje y convenciones genéricas', *ib.*, 75–86, is a study of the female characters in epic poetry and ballads with particular emphasis on Jimena. A. Higashi, 'Una nota a propósito de los cantos noticieros en el ciclo cidiano', *ib.*, 87–97, studies the supposed influence of the *canto noticiero* — a term invented by R. Menéndez Pidal — on the *Carmen campidoctoris*. S. G. Armistead, '"Eyebrows like leeches": Balkan elements in a Judeo-Spanish song', *La Corónica*, 24.2:18–30, investigates the influence on the Judeo-Spanish *cancionero* of cultures among whom Sephardim settled after their expulsion from Spain in 1492. M. T. Cáceres Lorenzo, 'El uso verbal en las fórmulas del romancero de tradición oral. El ejemplo de Gran Canaria — Parte II', *ib.*, 75–77, is a list of tables that complements the author's article on formulas (see *YWMLS*, 57:304). G. Caravaggi, 'Glosas de romances del siglo XVI', *Dutton Vol.*, 137–48, edits and briefly studies seven *glosas*. (See also *CANCIONEROS*.)

4. THIRTEENTH AND FOURTEENTH CENTURIES

POETRY

C. Alvar, 'Épica y lírica románicas en el último cuarto del siglo XIII', *Actas* (Alcalá), 13–24, views the final years of the 13th c. as a period of prime interest for the literary historian owing to the development of new genres and the decline of traditional ones, and offers an overview of these changes as reflected in the epic and the lyric in Iberia, France, and Italy.

J. Trueba Lawand, 'El *Libro de Apolonio*, modelo del caballero virtuoso', *RoN*, 36 : 261–64, states briefly that Apolonius's character is a fusion of *sapientia* and *fortitudo*. C. Real Ramos, 'Nacer en el espino (los *Proverbios morales* de Santob y la paremiología castellana en el siglo XIV)', *Dutton Vol.*, 531–42, reviews the use of proverbs and refrains in the Middle Ages and Golden Age, focusing especially on Don Juan Manuel, Juan Ruiz, and Santob; R. R. argues that Santob is the first to use apothegmatic material as the 'ingrediente principal de materia literaria' and the last to differentiate clearly between the two genres. J. Fradejas Lebrero, 'Una nota al *Rimado de Palacio*', *ib.*, 255–57, suggests that strophe 521 refers not to John 14 : 17 but to a lost apocryphal *Testamento de Cristo*.

F. A. Marcos-Marín, 'Establecimiento de la fecha del *Libro de Alexandre*', *ZRP*, 112 : 424–37, argues for an early date of composition, *c.* 1202–07. According to this theory, Gonzalo de Berceo could not possibly be the author of the *Libro de Alexandre*. C. Alvar, 'Consideraciones a propósito de una cronología temprana del *Libro de Alexandre*', *Dutton Vol.*, 35–44, is a provocative discussion of the implications of an early dating of the *Alexandre* for our views of literary history; A. shows that an early chronology would force us to revise radically many of our notions, most notably those related to audience (i.e. that there existed a diverse and sophisticated public willing to receive the *Poema del Cid*, troubadour song, and a narrative of distant monarchs and wars), influence (especially as related to *PMC* and Berceo), and the development of *clerecía*. S. Baldwin, 'Thunder and lightning: violence in Walter of Châtillon's *Alexandreis* and the *Libro de Alexandre*', *ib.*, 77–106, considers the use of a variety of motifs in both poems in order to evaluate the relation of style to authorial intent in each. I. Michael, '*De situ Indiae*: las maravillas de Oriente en la literatura medieval española', *ib.*, 507–16, examines medieval and modern definitions of the marvellous and its literary manifestations, focusing especially on the *Libro de Alexandre* and Chaucer.

J. S. Geary, 'The "Pitas Payas" episode of the *Libro de Buen Amor*: its structure and comic climax', *RPh*, 49 : 245–61, analyses the morphological structure of the 'Pitas Payas' episode and emphasizes the relationship between this episode and the Old French *fabliaux* corpus.

R. P. Kinkade, 'A thirteenth-century precursor of the *Libro de buen amor*: the *Art d'amors*', *La Corónica*, 24.2 : 122–39, does not propose the late 13th to early 14th-c. French text as a direct source for the *LBA*, but does suggest it as an historical antecedent representing the 'French clerical tradition of didactic eroticism from which the Arcipreste freely drew'. (See also CUADERNA VÍA VERSE.)

OTHER POETRY

Louise M. Haywood, *The Lyrics of the 'Historia troyana polimétrica'* (PMHRS, 3), 83 pp., explores the origin and nature of the *Historia*, comparing it to Benoît de Sainte-Maure's *Roman de Troie* and considering the function of the verse passages in the text. R. Brann, Á. Sáenz-Badillos, and J. Targarona, 'Šěmu'el Ibn Šašón y su poesía hebrea en la Castilla del siglo XIV', *La Corónica*, 24.2 : 56–74, consider Šěmu'el Ibn Šašón, who wrote his poetry in Hebrew and maintained his connections (generic, thematic, prosodic, metrical) with Hebrew and Andalusian traditions, a representative of the intellectual life characteristic of the Jewish communities in northern Castile.

PROSE

ALFONSO X EL SABIO. M. Bailey, 'Las últimas hazañas del conde Fernán González en la *Estoria de España*: la contribución alfonsí', *La Corónica*, 24.2 : 31–40, establishes that the wise and obedient Fernán González seen in the episode of the summoning to Court contrasts radically with the rebel figure in *Poema de Fernán González* and is the result of the conflation of multiple sources, both oral and written. A. A. Biglieri, 'Jerusalén en la obra de Alfonso X', *ib.*, 41–55, considers the representation of Jerusalem as the geographic and symbolic centre of the world in various medieval texts, primarily the *General Estoria* and the *Primera crónica general*. Id., 'Godos, hunos y amazonas y los extremos del mundo en la obra de Alfonso X', *Actas* (Mexico), 455–65, offers a thorough study of the alfonsine conception of geographical frontiers, and the correlation between geographical frontiers and cultural frontiers. P. Linehan, 'From chronicle to history: concerning the *Estoria de España* and its principal sources', Deyermond, *Iberia*, 7–33, examines the sources and ideological concerns that shaped the composition/revision of the *General Estoria* and the *Estoria de España*, drawing on the work of many scholars (notably, Georges Martin, Diego Catalán, Francisco Rico). M. Alvar, 'Alfonso X contemplado por don Juan Manuel', *Actas* (Alcalá), 91–106, shows that Don Juan Manuel found in his uncle the exemplary wise man, admirable both for his intellectual undertakings and his manner of being. A. M. Contreras Martín, 'La imagen del *miles christi* en la cronística castellana de finales del siglo XIII: Gedeón, Josué y David', *ib.*, 343–53, examines the portrayal of these three biblical figures in the *General Estoria* and the manner in which they conform to the chivalric precepts laid out in the *Siete Partidas*.

DIDACTIC LITERATURE. Margaret R. Parker, *The Story of a Story across Cultures: The Case of the 'Doncella Teodor'*, London, Támesis, x + 153 pp., presents a good introduction to the tale of Doncella Teodor in its various cultural and linguistic contexts. In Part I P. offers summaries of the tale (1–14) as it appears in Arabic, in 15th-c. Spain, in the Maya 'Chilam Balam' books, and in 18th-c. Brazilian verse, as well as a review of the history of criticism (14–31) related to each version. Part II (33–101) includes an edition of Biblioteca Nacional, Madrid MS 17853 and of the Zaragoza 1540 printing (Biblioteca Nacional, Madrid R-10688), and a transcription of the Brazilian *cordel* version by Leandro Gomes de Barros; P. has translated each text into English. Part III (103–38) considers the reception of the tale and its defining characteristics, and compares the heroine with her European analogues. Marta Haro Cortés, *La imagen del poder real a través de los compendios de castigos castellanos del siglo XIII* (PMHRS, 4), 77 pp., examines *Libro de los doze sabios*, *Flores de filosofía*, *Libro de los cien capítulos*, and *Castigos de Sancho IV* within the tradition of the *specula principum*, and traces the evolution of political ideology reflected in these compendia from Fernando III to Sancho IV. H. O. Bizzarri, 'La idea de la Reconquista en el *Libro de los doze sabios*', *RFE*, 76:5–29, connects the text to the Order of Santiago and discusses it in terms of a military manual on Reconquest. B. concludes that the text originally consisted of 45 chapters (chs 21–65 of the text as we now know it); to these chapters an introduction was added in the form of a mirror of princes (chs 1–20), and an encomium of Fernando III of Castile (ch. 66). B. argues persuasively that the 12 sages in the text are not a mere narrative device but very real commanders of the Order of Santiago. C. E. Armijo, 'El bestiario medieval: una clave para la interpretación del *Libro de los gatos*', *Actas* (Mexico), 205–19, discusses the iconographical relationship between the *Libro de los gatos* and the medieval bestiary tradition, as one of many possible keys to a complete understanding of the work. R. Beltrán, 'El valor del consejo en los *Castigos e documentos* del rey don Sancho', *Actas* (Alcalá), 107–20, traces the MS history of the *Castigos* and its reception in the 14th–15th c., and offers a detailed analysis of its structure and content. J. M. Cacho Blecua, 'El título de los *Castigos y documentos* de Sancho IV', *ib.*, 153–68, reviews the meaning of *castigos* and *documentos*, asserting that while the former most probably formed part of the original title, the latter is an anachronism imposed in the 17th c.; he suggests *Castigos consejos* as a possible title. M. J. Lacarra, 'Los *exempla* en los *Castigos de Sancho IV*: divergencias en la transmisión manuscrita', *ib.*, 201–12, traces the transformation of *exempla* from the late 13th c. to the late 15th c., showing that the changes are due to the influence of other readings and to a desire to adapt the tales to specific forms of thought. M. Á. Pérez Priego, 'Imágenes literarias en torno a la condición del príncipe en el *Libro de los castigos*', *ib.*, 257–65, examines symbolic language in the *Castigos*, concluding that imagery not only holds political and idealogical significance but reveals considerable literary ability on the part of the author. C. Moreno, 'La inserción de los *exempla* en *Castigos e documentos* de Sancho IV. La retórica del sermón en pro de una empresa de estado', *ib.*, 469–77, summarizes the types of *exempla* included in the *Castigos* and the various techniques used to incorporate them. C. Parrilla, 'En torno al *Libro de Séneca contra la ira e la saña*', *ib.*, 246–55, considers the relationship of the translations contained in three 15th-c. manuscripts to the Latin *De Ira* and to a common vernacular translation dating to the reign of Sancho IV. E. Blanco, 'La enseñanza en la época de Sancho IV: escritos pedagógicos', *ib.*, 313–22, surveys a variety of educational treatises, from Ramón Llull's *Doctrina pueril* to Eciclio Romano's *De Regimine*. M. J. Gómez Sánchez-Romate, 'Los castigos y los premios: infierno, purgatorio y paraíso en el *Lucidario*', *ib.*, 367–77, explores the manner in which Purgatory dominates the representation of the other world in the *Lucidario*. M. Haro, 'Función y contexto del diálogo en el *Lucidario*', *ib.*, 379–97, finds that the *Lucidario* incorporates various dialogic models (e.g. those of Cicero and Petrarch) rather than adhering to more inflexible traditional patterns. F. Magán, 'El *exiemplo* del unicornio en el *Lucidario* de Sancho IV', *ib.*, 453–67, compares the unicorn *exemplum* in the *Lucidario* to the tale in *Libro de los gatos*, *Calila e Dimna*, Odo of Cheriton's *Fabulae*, *Barlaam y Josefat*, and *Speculum Historiale*, and concludes that the variants are principally due to oral tradition. M. Haro Cortés, 'Un nuevo testimonio fragmentario de los *Bocados de oro*', *RevLM*, 8:9–25, edits a fragment held in Biblioteca Menéndez y Pelayo, MS 53.

DON JUAN MANUEL. P. N. Dunn, 'Framing the story, framing the reader: two Spanish masters', *MLR*, 91:94–106, is an enlightening discussion of the narrative structure of Juan Manuel's *El conde Lucanor* and Cervantes's *El casamiento engañoso y coloquio de los perros*. B. Taylor, '¿Emblema o anécdota en *El Conde Lucanor*, exemplo 50?', *RevLM*, 8:223–27, suggests that the weakness of the *consejero* reflects the folklore motif 'el más bajo es el mayor', and that the father and son are allegories of wise worldliness. (See CUADERNA VÍA VERSE, ALFONSO X EL SABIO.)

HISTORIOGRAPHY. F. Gómez Redondo, 'Tradiciones literarias en la historiografía sobre Sancho IV', *Actas* (Alcalá), 181–99, considers the reasons for and process of incorporating literary sources in royal chronicles. G. Orduna, 'Tradición cronística y crítica textual', *Actas* (Mexico), 13–28, comments on the virtual impossiblity of reconstituting the 'original' in the context of critical editions of Castilian chronicles, especially when confronted with a 'versión regia' and a 'versión vulgar' of the same chronicle. The essay focuses primarily on the problems faced by editors of the chronicles of Pero López de Ayala.

OTHER PROSE WRITERS. G. R. de Brevedán, 'Sobre el género de *Barlaam e Josafat*', *Actas* (Mexico), 183–93, classifies *Barlaam e Josafat* as a hagiographic text based on the text's intended meaning and purpose. M. Díaz y Díaz, 'Tres compiladores latinos en el ambiente de Sancho IV', *Actas* (Alcalá), 35–52, compares the lives and work of three compilers from the 1270s to the 1280s (Bernardo de Brihuega, Rodrigo de Cerrato, and Gil de Zamora), focusing on their intellectual formation, their adaptation of sources, and their respect for rhetorical tradition. G. Orduna, 'La elite intelectual de la escuela catedralicia de Toledo y la literatura en época de Sancho IV', *ib.*, 53–62, examines the membership and work of the Cathedral School of Toledo, arguing that all literary work from the early 14th c. was formed in one way or another by this intellectual circle. A. Sáenz-Badillos, 'Literatura hebrea en la época de Sancho IV', *ib.*, 63–77, concludes that Jewish literary production from this period addressed the needs of the Jewish community and was thus destined primarily for internal consumption. M. J. Viguera Molins, 'La literatura en al-Andalus en la última parte del siglo XIII', *ib.*, 79–87, gives a brief sketch of literary figures in al-Andalus and in exile following the loss of power by the Almohads. C. Salinas Espinosa, 'La clasificación y selección de las ciencias en el *Libro del tesoro* de Brunetto Latini', *ib.*, 501–10, concludes that the system of classification of the sciences employed in the *Libro del tesoro* conforms neither to the work's general structure nor to its selection of subjects. T. D. Spaccarelli, 'Recovering the lost folios of the *Noble cuento del enperador Carlos Maynes*: the restoration of a medieval anthology', *RoQ*, 43:217–33, demonstrates the necessity of restoring material missing in the Escorial MS, and edits the corresponding passage in an early Toledo incunable. J. M. Cacho Blecua, 'Los "castigos" y la educación de Garfín y Roboán en *El libro del Cavallero Zifar*', *Dutton Vol.*, 117–35, asserts that editorial intervention (i.e. the subdivisions of the work) by Jacobo Cromberger (1512) and later by Charles Wagner skew our interpretation of the *Zifar*, as the author intended it to be read as a 'continuum narrativo'. C. Soriano, 'El episodio de Baldovín y la sierpe en *La Gran Conquista de Ultramar'*, *Actas* (Alcalá), 511–20, offers a detailed analysis of the title episode.

4. Fifteenth Century

GENERAL, BIBLIOGRAPHY, EARLY PRINTING

Water Lilies / Flores del agua: An Anthology of Spanish Women Writers from the Fifteenth through the Nineteenth Century, ed. Amy Katz Kaminsky, Minneapolis, Minnesota U.P., xix + 494 pp., offers bilingual editions of the *Memorias* of Leonor López de Córdoba, the three *canciones* attributed to Florencia Pinar, and an excerpt from the *Admiración operum Dey* by Teresa de Cartagena. A. M. López Álvarez, Y. Álvarez Delgado, and S. Palomero Plaza, 'Un documento inédito de 1494 sobre Abraham Seneor y Rabí Meir Melamed', *Sefarad*, 56:173–88, is a study and edition of a legal document connected with two 15th-c. *conversos*. D. Seidenspinner-Núñez, 'Inflecting the *converso* voice: a commentary on recent theories', *La Corónica*, 25.1:6–18, offers a useful overview of theories regarding *conversos* and crypto-Judaism in the 15th and 16th c., arguing that Colbert Nepaulsingh's claim the *Lazarillo* was written for and by crypto-Jews is faulty and suggesting that the term '*converso* texts' not be used exclusively for coded texts. J. Casas Rigall, '*Ad grammacticos pertinent*. La teoría de los vicios, figuras y tropos en diez gramáticas hispanas del s. XV', *ib*., 24.2:78–102, examines ten 15th-c. grammars and finds that Aelius Donatus is the principal source. M. V. Amasuno, 'Saber médico, literatura loimológica y la Universidad de Salamanca durante el siglo XV', *Dutton Vol*., 45–70, discusses plague manuals produced at Salamanca. Á. Gómez Moreno, 'An unknown Jewish-Christian controversy in fifteenth-century Talavera de la Reina: towards the end of Spanish Jewry', *ib*., 285–92, considers an intriguing 15th-c. case involving the three religions in which a young Muslim woman's conversion to Judaism resulted in dire consequences; G. M. finds in the legal arguments presented by representatives for Jews and Christians a reflection of contemporary social and religious concerns. N. F. Marino, 'The creation of a contemporary exemplar: Álvaro de Luna', *ib*., 489–94, examines the 15th-c. concept of historical memory and Luna's exemplarification/vilification in chronicles and by Mena, Manrique, and Pérez de Guzmán, among others.

POETRY

CANCIONEROS. M. D. Johnston, 'Poetry and courtliness in Baena's prologue', *La Corónica*, 25.1:93–105, finds that the prologue represents poetic discourse as a form of courtly action. P. Botta, 'El bilingüismo en la poesía cancioneril (*Cancionero de Baena, Cancioneiro de Resende*)', *BHS(L)*, 73:351–59, considers not only the lexical presence of Galician in *Baena* and Castilian in *Cancioneiro Geral*, but the influence of the two languages on the metre and the content of the poetry in the two collections. V. Beltrán, 'Tipología y génesis de los cancioneros: Juan Fernández de Híjar y los cancioneros por adición', *RPh*, 50:1–19, is a thorough study of the complex textual transmission of the *Cancionero de Juan Fernández de Híjar* (15th-16th c.), as contained in Biblioteca Nacional, Madrid, MS 2882. J. C. Conde López and V. Infantes, 'Nuevos datos sobre una vieja historia: *El Cancionero de Oñate-Castañeda* y sus propietarios', *Dutton Vol.*, 163–76, trace the provenance of the *cancionero* to the library of Pedro Núñez de Guzmán. F. Crosas, 'Materia clásica, oscuridad y "culteranismo" cuatrocentista', *ib.*, 177–87, shows that much seemingly obscure 15th-c. poetry becomes perfectly comprehensible once the classical references are identified; C. argues that Mena, Santillana, and Imperial, like Góngora in the 17th c., wrote for an elite audience who had the necessary formation to appreciate the challenge posed by these poets. G. Di Stefano, 'Romances en el Cancionero de la British Library, Ms. Add. 10431', *ib.*, 239–53, examines the organizational criteria for three thematic groupings of poems which include *romances*. M. Frenk, 'Fija, ¿quiéreste casar?', *ib.*, 259–74, discusses dialogue poems in which hypothetical husbands for a young woman are enumerated within the European and Hispanic traditions; F. concludes that the version held in *Cancionero musical de Colombina* and a 12th–13th-c. Latin version differ from others in that they both parody the Three Estates. M. García-Bermejo Giner, 'Algunos aspectos de la definición de amor en la poesía cancioneril castellana del siglo XV', *ib.*, 275–84, surveys the panorama of poems presented by their authors as 'definitions of love', focusing especially on the practice of defining. R. Harris-Northall, 'Linguistic aspects of the *Cancionero de Baena*', *ib.*, 321–31, shows that *Baena* provides additional proof that the Spanish spoken in Andalusia in the second half of the 15th c. was markedly different from standard Castilian. J. J. Labrador Herráiz and R. A. Difranco, 'Del XV al XVII: doscientos poemas', *ib.*, 367–418, is a catalogue of poems which appear both in the *Cancionero del siglo XV* and in other collections. A. Menéndez Collera, 'La figura del galán y la poesía de entretenimiento de finales del siglo XV', *ib.*, 494–505, examines *poemas citadores* (as Brian Dutton terms them), *juegos*, and *justas*, not merely as poetic creations but as reflections of courtly life. C. Parrilla, 'De coplas decimonónicas de cancionero', *ib.*, 517–30, outlines the history of a 19th-c. copy of a *cancionero* (Biblioteca Nacional, Madrid, MS 3777) and discusses its varied contents: a number of compositions by Garcí Sánchez de Badajoz, a group of

'canciones diversas' by a number of 15th-c. notables, *romances*, 301
cuadernas of the *Poema de Yuçuf*. L. Romero Tobar, 'Algunas fuentes
secundarias para la poesía cancioneril', *ib.*, 561–65, edits a handful of
poems discovered by the author in a chronicle and a legal text.
E. Scoles and I. Ravasini, 'Intertestualità e interpretazione nel genere
lirico della *glosa*', *ib.*, 605–14, review the *glosa* from the 15th c. to the
17th c., and conclude that the two defining elements of the genre are
intertextuality and exegesis. A. Chas Aguión, 'Humor y amor. Del
componente humorístico en las *Demandas e respuestas* amatorias',
Salina, 9, 1995:26–36, examines ten *preguntas* related to love from five
cancioneros in order to broaden our view of the use of humour in the
treatment of love in 15th-c. poetry, and shows that humour serves
multiple purposes in sentimental poetry.

SANTILLANA. L. R. Bass, 'Crossing borders: gender, geography
and class relations in three *serranillas* of the Marqués de Santillana',
La Corónica, 25.1:69–84, views the *serranillas* as 'poetic explorations of
aristocratic masculine identity'. P. M. Cátedra, 'El sentido involu-
crado y la poesía del siglo XV. Lecturas virgilianas de Santillana, con
Villena', *Dutton Vol.*, 149–61, considers the reception, interpretation,
and interiorization of the classics in the 15th c., focusing on the
example of Virgil's *Aeneid*; C. shows that Villena's glossing on the
Aeneid is a process of digging out and creating 'sentidos involucrados',
and that Santillana depended on Villena's gloss for his own reading
of Virgil in the *Coronación de mosén Jordi*. (See also CANCIONEROS.)

JUAN DE MENA. Julia Santibáñez Escobar, *El 'Laberinto de Fortuna'.
Una alegoría política del siglo XV. Claves de lectura del poema de Juan de Mena*,
Mexico, JGH Editores, 175 pp., is a study of the labyrinth as symbol.
The author provides an overview of recent scholarship on the poem,
followed by her own analysis of Mena's conscious use of the labyrinth
as a symbol of the political turbulence that plagued 15th-c. Castile.
M. P. A. M. Kerkhof, 'El manuscrito UCB 161 de la Bancroft Library
(Universidad de Berkeley, California): un nuevo códice del *Laberinto
de Fortuna* de Juan de Mena', *Neophilologus*, 80:243–57, gives a
description of the manuscript, which was copied in 1515 from the
first edition of the *Laberinto*, printed in Seville by Hernán Núñez in
1499. G. S. Hutcheson, 'Cracks in the labyrinth: Juan de Mena,
converso experience, and the rise of the Spanish nation', *La Corónica*,
25.1:37–52, views Mena not as a transitional poet from the Middle
Ages to the Renaissance but as one who reflects the *converso* experience
of ambivalence living in Trastamaran Spain; H. argues that the
Laberinto must be read multi-directionally, taking into account both
this ambivalence and the poem's call for national unity.

DIEGO DE VALERA. E. M. Gerli, 'Performing nobility: Mosén
Diego de Valera and the poetics of *converso* identity', *La Corónica*,

25.1:19–36, shows that, in Valera's concept of nobility, public performance and official acceptance are more essential than ethical attributes or genealogy; G. further argues that figures such as Valera complicate the 'question of the *converso* voice', revealing that there was no homogeneous *converso* type sharing social, moral, and political agenda with fellow converts. G. B. Kaplan, 'Toward the establishment of a Christian identity: the *conversos* and early Castilian humanism', *ib.*, 25.1:53–68, examines the 'moral and national currents of humanistic thought' which characterize the *converso* voice, focusing on Alfonso de Cartagena, Diego de Valera, and the poets in Alfonso Carrillo's circle. O. Di Camillo, 'Las teorías de la nobleza en el pensamiento ético de Mosén Diego de Valera', *Dutton Vol.*, 223–37, shows that Valera, whom he views as a perfect model of Castilian Humanism, was most especially concerned with matters relating to civic life and individual behaviour. D.C. pays special attention to the *Espejo de verdadera nobleza* in which V. assumes a radical and 'progressive' position, maintaining that virtue and not birth is the foundation of nobility, and thus rejects the concept of natural inequality between social classes; in this treatise V. introduces ethical concepts (honour, 'limpieza de sangre') which will be of central concern in the Golden Age.

OTHER POETS. A. M. Beresford, 'Theme, style, and structure in the *Disputa del cuerpo e del ánima*', *RevLM*, 8:73–90, finds that the *Disputa* merits more consideration than it has received, arguing that it compares favourably with other late medieval poems on death and salvation and noting that the author masterfully manipulates two genres, the debate and the dream vision. M. Morreale, '*La dança general de la muerte* (II)', *ib.*, 111–77, follows her 1991 article with a miscellany of observations regarding MS witnesses, metrics, phonetics, etc. J.-A. Cid, 'Don Álvaro de Luna y el "águila ballestera": Romancero y poesía estrófica en la tradición oral sefardí', *RPh*, 50:20–45, explores the enduring attraction of Álvaro de Luna (executed in 1453) in balladry and drama, from the 15th c. to the present. Á. Alonso, 'Gómez Manrique, Narváez y Castillejo: ¿poesía obscena?', *Dutton Vol.*, 27–33, discovers a comical-sexual interpretation hidden in several poems 'de caballerías' by the three poets. A. Deyermond, 'Lust in Babel: bilingual man-woman dialogues in the Medieval lyric', *ib.*, 199–221, examines the characteristics of ten bilingual dialogues found in Iberian and non-Iberian poems; D. suggests that the man-woman dialogue-encounters in *Libro de buen amor*, two 15th-c. poems by Carvajal and Imperial, a poem by the Welsh Tudur Penllyn, and one by the Flemish poet Josquin Desprez, may have been inspired, directly or indirectly, by a *tenso* of Raimbaut de Vaqueiras. A. Rodado Ruiz, 'El refrán en la poesía de Pedro de

Cartagena', *ib.*, 547–60, analyses the differences between proverbs and refrains, and finds that C. uses the refrain as a subtle tool to facilitate complex semantic manipulations. V. Roncero López, 'Algunos temas de la poesía humorística de Antón de Montoro', *ib.*, 567–80, examines various types of humour in M.'s poetry: a bitter and self-denigrating humour related to his position as a *converso* and to his situation as an impoverished poet dependent on the generosity of noble sponsors; satirical-burlesque humour directed toward fellow poets; satirical critiques of customs and vices; waggish religious parodies; erotic-comic presentations of women. M. I. Toro Pascua, '*La Sepultura de Amor* de Guevara. Edición crítica', *ib.*, 663–89, is a critical edition of the poem held in British Library Add. 100 and Biblioteca Nacional, Madrid MS 4114; variants, errors, and 'innovations' are given in footnotes. C. Parrilla, 'A propósito de las corresponsales femeninas de Fernando de la Torre. Notas sobre la cultura femenina en el siglo XV', *Salina*, 9, 1995:19–23, uses the *Libro de las veynte cartas e quistiones*, compiled by Fernando de la Torre at the request of Leonor de Foix, to examine the literary tastes and activities of Castilian, Aragonese, and Navarrese women of the first half of the 15th c., revealing a particular proclivity for the epistolary and intellectual debate.

PROSE

CHIVALRESQUE AND SENTIMENTAL FICTION.   J. D. Rodríguez Velasco, *El debate sobre la caballería en el siglo XV. La tratadística caballeresca castellana en su marco europeo*, M, Junta de Castilla y León, 482 pp., is a definitive study of medieval Spanish theoretical manuals on chivalry, with particular emphasis on the life and works of Diego de Valera. R.V.'s biography of Valera supersedes all previous biographies of this author. The bibliography alone is an invaluable research tool, in that it includes a list of all the known treatises on chivalry in medieval Spain, along with the current location of manuscripts. L. Ferrario de Orduna, 'El *Belianís de Grecia* frente a la tradición de los libros de caballerías castellanos', *Actas* (Mexico), 114–21, reviews the literary merits of *Belianís de Grecia*, a text admired by Cervantes in *Don Quijote*, 6; she attributes the success of *Belianís* to the fusion of medieval and renaissance ideas in the text. C. Rubio Pacho, 'Aproximación a los temas amoroso y caballeresco en el *Cuento de Tristán de Leonís*', *ib.*, 23–31, is a study of the text contained in Vatican Library MS 6428, with emphasis on Tristan's role as knight and lover.

CABALLERO DEL CISNE.   M. L. Cuesta Torre, 'Lo sobrenatural en la *Leyenda del Caballero del Cisne*', *Actas* (Alcalá), 355–65, concludes that the use of the supernatural allows for both literal and allegorical readings and that thus Godofredo de Bouillon is both earthly and celestial saviour. J. M. Lucía Megías, 'Dos caballeros en combate: batallas y lides singulares en *La leyenda del Cavallero del Cisne* y el *Libro del cavallero Zifar*', *ib.*, 427–52, is a detailed study which highlights the uniqueness of the *Zifar* for its treatment of battle. R. Ramos, 'Folclore e historiografía en *El caballero del Cisne*', *ib.*, 479–86, suggests that the first chapters of the *Caballero del Cisne* do not derive from a lost French source but are instead a re-elaboration of the existing *Béatrix* with incorporations from other versions of the tale.

DIEGO DE SAN PEDRO. M. Ihrie, 'Rhetoric, didactic intent, and the *Cárcel de amor*', *Hispanófila*, 116 : 1–14, suggests that the *Cárcel* is a book about the effectiveness of rhetoric in two different realms (its success in the world of the allegorical prison, its failure in the politically-charged sphere of the court), which invites the reader to evaluate its proper use and power.

JUAN DE FLORES. M. Roffé, *La cuestión del género en 'Grisel y Mirabella' de Juan de Flores*, Newark, Juan de la Cuesta, 228 pp., is an excellent study of the notion of 'género' — both genre and gender — in *Grisel y Mirabella*. The author situates the text within the tradition of medieval debate poetry, as well as focusing on the relationship between *Grisel y Mirabella* and contemporary medical and legal treatises. J. J. Gwara, 'A new epithalamial allegory by Juan de Flores: *La coronación de la señora Gracisla (1475)*', *REH*, 30 : 227–57, questions Keith Whinnom's dating and identification of historical sources for *Gracisla*, identifying Juan de Flores as the author; G. argues convincingly that the piece was written on the occasion of the betrothal of Leonor de Acuña and Pedro Álvarez Osorio and that *Gracisla* is an example of juvenile literature, a marionette entertainment for the child Leonor. C. Bayardi, 'El infierno de Fiometa y el Purgatorio de Pánfilo', *Acta* (Mexico), 537–48, studies the relationship between the two characters in Juan de Flores's *Grimalte y Gradissa*.

ENRIQUE DE VILLENA. A. Castaño, 'Primeros comentarios a Dante hechos en la Península Ibérica y su relación con las traducciones', *Actas* (Mexico), 263–73, discusses the glosses on Dante's *Commedia* by Enrique de Villena (1428), Andreu Febrer (1429) and Jaime Ferrer de Blanes (1490–1500). R. Recio, '"Por la orden que mejor suena": traducción y Enrique de Villena', *La Corónica*, 24.2 : 140–53, concludes that the primary guiding principle for V. as translator was clarity. (See also SANTILLANA.)

LEONOR LÓPEZ DE CÓRDOBA. M. V. Amasuno, 'Apuntaciones histórico-médicas al escrito autobiográfico de Leonor López de Córdoba (1362–1430)', *RevLM*, 8 : 29–71, claims that López de Córdoba's writing was a petition for justice presented to Enrique III and Catharine of Lancaster during the first week of June 1396; A believes that the monarchs are represented allegorically by the figure of God and the Virgin Mother, and that López de Córdoba was rewarded for her efforts with the bestowal of an *almona* (soap-manufactory). D. S. Severin, 'A letter of complaint from Fernando de Antequera about Leonor López de Córdoba in PN2', *Dutton Vol.*, 633–44, edits a letter addressed to the nobles of Vizcaya related to the discord which arose between Juan II's co-regents, Fernando and Catharine of Lancaster, in which the former places the blame for many problems squarely on the shoulders of López de Córdoba, who he also accuses of corruption and bribery; although not mentioned by S., a strikingly similar letter directed to the nobility of Murcia was edited by J. Torres Fontes in 1964.

OTHER PROSE WRITERS. **Hernando del Pulgar, Los claros varones de España (ca. 1483): A Semi-Paleographic Edition*, ed. Joseph Abraham Levi, NY, Lang, 118 pp. R. E. Surtz, 'Las *Oras de los clavos* de Constanza de Castilla', *Actas* (Mexico), 157–67, discusses the life and works of Constanza de Castilla (d. 1478), granddaughter of Pedro I of Castile, with emphasis on the *Oras de los clavos*, a liturgical treatise. J. A. Valverde, 'Sobre la autoría del *Tratado de montería* del siglo XV', *RevLM*, 8:229–37, offers evidence to support A. de Mariátegui's identification of Fernando de Irango as the author. F. Gómez Redondo, 'Lucena, *Repetición de amores*: sentido y estructura', *Dutton Vol.*, 293–304, finds that Lucena parodies the structure of academic *repetitiones*, thus endowing his work with multiple interpretations as a piece of sentimental fiction, a doctrinal treatise, and a humorous academic parody. R. C. Gonzalo García, 'Notas sobre la difusión y la composición de la *Qüistión de amor*', *ib.*, 305–19, considers the inclusion of two genres (sentimental fiction, history) in the *Qüistión* the result of the work being composed in distinct stages; she believes that the sentimental material was written 'a trozos' and then assembled as a unit, and that the historical material was added at a second, later stage. M. P. A. M. Kerkhof, 'Sobre lapidarios medievales. Edición de un lapidario español desconocido (fols. 16v–20r del códice II-1341 de la Biblioteca de Palacio, Madrid)', *ib.*, 343–58, discusses the medieval tradition of lapidaries and edits one held in a 15th-c. MS which probably derived from a compendium based on Albertus Magnus. M. J. Lacarra, 'Un nuevo manuscrito del *Libro del conosçimiento*', *ib.*, 35–41, offers a description of a hitherto lost version of the *Libro del conosçimiento* held in the Bayerische Staatsbibliothek, Munich, Cod. Hisp. 150. M. A. Sánchez, 'La *Definición de nobleza* de un nuevo Per Afán y otras obritas', *ib.*, 589–604, discusses possible identifications of the author of *Definición de nobleza* (Biblioteca de Palacio MS 1341) and edits the text.

THEATRE

Charlotte Stern, *The Medieval Theater in Castile* (MRTS, 156), ix + 321 pp. The deceptively simple title of this book conceals a work of great scope and erudition. In Part I (1–52), S. discusses Castile's medieval theatre heritage in terms of a lost genre which has been unduly neglected by scholars. Part II considers medieval definitions of theatre (53–70), as well as the influence of civil and canon law (71–91), chronicles and travelogues (92–108), church and municipal minutes (109–28), and the plastic arts (129–43) on theatrical activity in medieval Castile. Part III (145–200) is a thorough study of the notion of literature as performance. A wide variety of texts are discussed, including the *Poema de Mio Cid*, the works of Berceo, the *Libro de Buen Amor, cancionero* poetry, and *Celestina*. Part IV examines the medieval heritage in 16th- and 17th-c. texts, including plays, picaresque novels, travelogues and chronicles, and synodal and ecclesiastical decrees (201–21), as well as modern survivals of medieval theatre (222–42). Part V includes a chronology of theatre in medieval Castile (243–63), and the author calls for a holistic approach to the formulation of a new poetics of medieval theatre which takes into account the dynamic, hybrid nature of the genre (264–78). J. Leyva, 'El *Auto de la Pasión* y su adaptación de la *Pasión trovada* y las *Siete angustias* desde el punto de vista de las circunstancias de su representación', *Actas* (Mexico), 231–49, attempts to elucidate how Alonso del Campos's *Auto de la Pasión* would have been staged in the Middle Ages. He observes that medieval theatre was improvisational and suggests that it is possible that del Campo attempted to revitalize the play by culling ideas from the works of Diego de San Pedro, which were fashionable at the time. C. Stern, 'The medieval theater: replacing the Darwinian model', *La Corónica*, 24.2:166–78, questions what she calls the Darwinian theory on the origins of medieval theatre, according to which the evolution of medieval theatre can be traced to a single source, the 10th-c. *Quem quaeritis in sepulchro*. After providing an overview of scholarship on the subject, S. suggests much more sensible, alternative hypotheses for the poetics of theatre in medieval Castile. J. Maire Bobes, 'Hipocresía y superstición en el teatro castellano primitivo', *Sefarad*, 56:311–32, analyses the role of the *villano* in medieval and early renaissance drama. While professing Christianity the *villano* also advocates the persecution of Jews and *conversos*, and this attitude, symptomatic of the epoch, is condemned by many dramatists.

ALJAMIADO LITERATURE
POSTPONED

LITERATURE, 1490–1700
(PROSE AND POETRY)

By J. A. JONES, *Senior Lecturer in Hispanic Studies in the University of Hull*

1. GENERAL

Luisa López Grigera, *La retórica en la España del Siglo de Oro. Teoría y práctica*, Salamanca U.P., 1994, 189 pp., studies fundamental principles. Javier González Rovira, *La novela bizantina de la Edad de Oro*, M, Gredos, 423 pp., focuses on the reception and development of this genre. Useful contributions on the short story are J. Barella Vigal, 'Heliodoro y la novela corta del siglo XVII', *CHA*, 529–30, 1994:203–22; G. Martínez Camino, 'La novela corta del Barroco español y la formación de una subjetividad señorial', *BHS(L)*, 73:33–47. Rainer H. Goetz, *Spanish Golden Age Autobiography in its Context*, AUS, 1994, xv + 208 pp., is a welcome contribution on a little-studied field. Varied aspects of Golden Age literature are illustrated in P. Mas i Usó, 'Academias ficticias valencianas durante el Barroco', *Criticón*, 61, 1994:47–56; C. Clavería, 'Quintiliano, Virgilio y Horacio no son negocio. La imprenta española en el siglo XVI', *ib.*, 65, 1995:5–15; J. M. Díez Borque, 'Literatura en la calle. Prosa y poesía en las paredes: pasquines del Siglo de Oro español (I)', *BHS(L)*, 72, 1995:365–83. F. Layna Ranz, 'La disputa burlesca. Origen y trayectoria', *Criticón*, 64, 1995:7–160, provides an extensive study of rhetorical practices. O. Di Camillo, 'Interpretations of the Renaissance in Spanish historical thought: the last thirty years', *RQ*, 49:360–83, provokes thinking on fundamental aspects. Empire and literature are highlighted in Brownlee, *Cultural Authority* which contains: W. Cohen, 'The discourse of empire in the Renaissance' (260–83); J. R. Resina, 'The role of discontinuity in the formation of national culture' (284–303); H. U. Gumbrecht, 'Cosmological time and the impossibility of closure. A structural element in Spanish Golden Age narratives' (304–21).

2. THOUGHT

A. Bustamante García, *La octava maravilla del mundo. Estudio histórico sobre El Escorial de Felipe II*, M, Editorial Alpuerto, 1994, 887 pp., is a fittingly monumental work. A. G. Kinder, 'The Protestant pastor as intelligencer: Cassiodoro de Reina's letters to Wilhelm IV, Landgrave of Hesse-Cassel', *BHR*, 58:105–18, furnishes valuable material. Garau Amengual, 'Apuntes para un estudio de la vida y obra de

Juan Bautista Escardó (Palma de Mallorca, [1581]–1652)', *Criticón*, 61, 1994:57–68, updates us on this Jesuit preacher and writer. *Olin Vol.* includes: J. Bilinkoff, 'Teresa of Avila and Carmelite reform' (165–86); J. W. O'Malley, 'The Society of Jesus' (138–63). Female spirituality is lucidly discussed in R. Cueto, 'Connexions and interests on the path of virtue: Mauricia Pérez de Velasco (c.1598–1674) and the expansion of the Augustinian recollection in Spain', *Fryde Vol.*, 351–74; and M. A. Rees, 'Doña María Vela y Cueto and infused knowledge', Wing, *Belief*, 1–7. Terence O'Reilly, *From Ignatius Loyola to John of the Cross: Spirituality and Literature in Sixteenth-century Spain*, Aldershot-Brookfield, Variorum, 1995, x + 271 pp., is a useful collection. Aspects of two closely related humanists are brought out in J. A. Jones, 'Faith and rationalism in late Spanish Humanism: the contribution of Pedro de Valencia', Wing, *Belief*, 170–77; J. Pascual Barea, 'Un epitafio inédito de Benito Arias Montano a su maestro Pedro Mexía', *ExP*, 4–5, 1994–95:301–06. Aviva, *Heritage*, includes: J. S. Gerber, 'Towards an understanding of the term: "The Golden Age" as an historical reality' (15–22); N. Kramer Hellinx, 'El aspecto de la Inquisición en la obra de Antonio Enrique Gómez (1600–1663)' (169–84). Jewish influence is also highlighted in D. Reyre, 'Topónimos hebreos y memoria de la España judía en el Siglo de Oro', *Criticón*, 65, 1995:31–53. M. Zuili, 'Algunas observaciones acerca de un moralista toledano del siglo XVII: Alejo Venegas de Busto', *ib.*, 17–29, pinpoints Erasmian influence. J. M. W. Robbins, 'Spiritual pain: Ribera and the visual representation of suffering', Wing, *Belief*, 178–85, makes psychological/aesthetic connections. García de la Concha, *Fray Luis*, includes: M. Fernández Alvarez, 'Fray Luis de León desde la historia' (29–42); S. Alvarez Turienzo, 'Fray Luis de León en el laberinto renacentista de idearios' (43–62); A. Alcalá, 'Peculiaridad de las acusaciones a fray Luis en el marco del proceso a sus colegas salmantinos' (65–80); J. Barrientos García, 'Fray Luis de León profesor de la Universidad de Salamanca' (81–118); J. L. González Novalín, 'Inquisición y censura de Biblias en el Siglo de Oro. La *Biblia de Vatablo* y el proceso de fray Luis de León' (125–44); K. Hölz, 'Exégesis bíblica y erudición filológica en el humanismo español' (145–58); J. López Gajate, 'El emblema de fray Luis de León' (159–72); G. Morocho Gayo et al, 'Cipriano de la Huerga maestro de humanistas' (173–93); R. Reyes Cano, 'El retrato de fray Luis de León por Francisco Pacheco: fijación retórica y verdad histórica' (195–206); T. Viñas, 'El Convento de San Agustín y fray Luis de León' (207–21); M. Andrés Martín, 'La espiritualidad de fray Luis de León' (223–39); F. Garrote Pérez, 'Mito y sentido en fray Luis de León' (253–72); A. Guy, 'El eclecticismo de fray Luis de León' (273–86); A. Márquez, 'De mística luisiana: ser o no ser

(287–98); C. Morón Arroyo, 'Espesor de la letra. La hermenéutica de fray Luis de León' (299–312); C. C. Swietlicki, 'Fray Luis de León: el humanista más humano' (313–22); J. M. Becerra, 'Las Exposiciones del *salmo 26* y del *Libro de Job*, de fray Luis de León. Vocabulario común' (323–30); G. Hinojo Andrés, 'La *recusatio* horaciana en Luis de León' (331–40); J. Maristany del Rayo, *'Reportatum De Angelis.* Alcance, noticia y paralelismo con el *corpus* luisiano (Salamanca, curso 1570–1571)' (341–55); C. Cuevas, 'Fray Luis de León y la visión renacentista de la naturaleza: estética y apologética' (367–80); A. Rallo Gruss, 'El diálogo como exégesis: función filológica y función catequística en *De los nombres de Cristo* de fray Luis de León' (451–69); K. Reinhardt, 'Una exposición castellana del *Cantar de los Cantares*, hasta ahora desconocida, atribuida a Fray Luis de León' (471–83); L. Schwartz, 'Las traducciones de textos griegos de fray Luis y su contexto humanista' (527–48); R. Cao Martínez, 'El estilo de fray Luis de León a la luz de un cuadernillo autógrafo de la "Exposición del Cantar de Cantares"' (571–608); F. J. Fuente Fernández, 'La imagen del "Buen Pastor" en fray Cipriano de la Huerga y fray Luis de León' (629–37); F. Layna Ranz, 'La tradición de las burlas estudiantiles en la Universidad de Fray Luis de León' (649–54); A. López Castro, 'La armonía en fray Luis de León' (655–75); J. J. Sendín Vinagre, 'Las *Exposiciones* del Maestro León, o cómo se hace literatura a propósito de las Letras Sagradas' (701–07). *Jaime Juan Falcó. Obras completas. Volúmen 1. Obra poética,* ed. Daniel López-Cañete Quiles, León U.P., clxxxi + 328 pp., and *Cristóbal Méndez. Libro del ejercicio corporal y de sus provechos,* ed. Eduardo Alvarez del Palacio, León U.P., 414 pp., are valuable additions to the León series on Spanish humanists. F. Fortuny Previ, 'Los humanistas y el *libro de Espectáculos* de Marcial', *BHR,* 58:631–42, focuses on Classical influence and Lorenzo Ramírez de Prado. *Actas* (León) includes: N. Fernández Marcos, 'La exégesis bíblica de Cipriano de la Huerga' (29–46); E. Fernández Tejero, 'Del amor y la mujer en Cipriano de la Huerga y Luis de León' (87–103); A. Feliz Carbajal, 'Comentario al Cantar de los Cantares de Cipriano de la Huerga' (105–18); J. Llanos García, 'El reflejo humanista en los predicadores españoles del siglo XVI', (127–34); J. F. Domínguez Domínguez, 'Tradición clásica y ciceronianismo en Cipriano de la Huerga (1509/10–1560). Primer acercamiento' (151–97); J. González Vázquez, 'Humanismo y Clasicismo en la obra latina de Fray Luis de Granada' (199–205); C. Miguélez Baños, 'Figuras retóricas en Cipriano de la Huerga y el *Tractatus de figuris rhetoricis* atribuido a B. Arias Montano' (207–23); J. A. Jones, 'El humanismo en la segunda mitad del siglo XVI. Arias Montano y Pedro de Valencia' (225–35); J.Fernández Fernández, *Apología por las letras humanas* (1604) de Lorenzo de Zamora' (263–76);

J. Paradinas Fuentes, 'Corrientes filosóficas del humanismo en los escritos de Cipriano de la Huerga' (291–309); E. Alvarez del Palacio, 'El ejercicio físico en la obra de Cristóbal Méndez, médico y humanista: referencia a la mujer y a las monjas' (311–28); V. Moreno Gallego, 'Sobre humanismo y fe en el siglo XVI: *De veritate fidei christianae* de Luis Vives y sus impresiones' (329–53); P. Celada Perandones, 'Humanismo y educación popular en la España del siglo XVI: el caso de León' (355–77); J. L. Ocásar Ariza, 'Un humanista del siglo XVI: Juan de Arce de Otálora' (379–87); D. Yáñez, 'Los estudios en la congregación de Castilla en el s. XVI' (489–508); V. Bécares Botas, 'Los libros del cisterciense. Fondos localizados de los monasterios zamoranos de Moreruela, Valparaíso y San Martín de Castañeda' (509–17); A. Linaje Conde, 'Los escritores cistercienses en la Europa del humanismo' (519–29); J. M. Nieto Ibáñez and A. M. Martín Rodríguez, 'Humanismo y literatura monacal antigua: la traducción de San Macario por Pedro de Valencia' (531–38); F. R. de Pascual, 'La espiritualidad cisterciense en el siglo XVI' (679–711).

3. LYRICAL AND NARRATIVE POETRY

GENERAL. S. Fernández Mosquera, '"El cancionero": una estructura dispositiva para la lírica del siglo de oro', *BH*, 97, 1995:465–92, underlines Petrarchan influence. Relatively unknown collections are examined in A. Luis Iglesias, 'Notas a un cancionero poco conocido del museo Lázaro Galdiano. Van añadidas en este artículo algunas precisiones sobre *Henares de agua clara enriquecido*: soneto en memoria de Cipriano de la Huerga', *Actas* (León), 249–61; D. Devoto, 'Un millar de cantares exportados', *BH*, 96, 1994:5–115; K. Brown, 'Doscientas cuarenta seguidillas antiguas', *Criticón*, 63, 1995:7–27. J. Arribas, 'Lexical notes of "Amor", "Tiempo" and "Fortuna" in the poems of the Spanish pastoral romances', *RoN*, 37:75–88, is a computer-aided study. A. Ramajo Caño, 'Huellas clásicas en la poesía funeral española (en latín y romance) en los Siglos de Oro', *RFE*, 73, 1994:313–28, looks for sombre Classical traces. A lengthy contribution is J.L. Herrero Ingelmo, 'Cultismos renacentistas (cultismos léxicos y semánticos en la poesía del siglo XVI)', *BRAE*, 74, 1994:13–192, 237–402, 523–610; *ib.*, 75, 1995:173–223, 293–393.

LUIS DE LEÓN. C. Codoñer, 'Fray Luis: "interpretación", traducción poética e *imitatio*', *Criticón*, 61, 1994:31–46, brings out varied aspects of translation. García de la Concha, *Fray Luis*, includes: E. de Bustos, 'Ritmo semántico en Fray Luis de León' (357–66); H. Ettinghausen, 'Horacionismo vs. neoestoicismo en la poesía de fray Luis de León' (241–52); L. Iglesias Feijoo, 'La *Dispositio* de la "Oda a Salinas"' (395–411); F. Márquez Villanueva, 'Trasfondos de

"La profecía del Tajo". Goticismo y profetismo' (423–40); C. Maurer, 'La "figura" en fray Luis: poesía y traducción' (441–50); E. L. Rivers, 'La elegía de fray Luis de León y sus antecedentes genéricos' (485–95); F. Bartolomé Benito and G. Bodelón Velasco, 'Alegoría y emblema en la Oda IX "Las Serenas"' (559–69); A. Correa Ramón, 'La flora renacentista en la "Oda a Todos los Santos" de fray Luis de León (en el espejo de fray Luis de Granada)' (609–14); I. Elizalde, 'Fray Luis de León en la poesía de Miguel de Unamuno' (615–28); F. Gómez Redondo, 'Armonía y diseño formal en la *Oda a la vida retirada*' (639–47); A. Lozano y de Castro and F. Labajos Briones, 'La "Oda a Salinas" desde la estética originaria' (677–81); R. Medina, 'Eroticismo e imitación-emulación en los cinco sonetos de fray Luis de León' (683–700). T. O'Reilly, 'The image of the garden in *La vida retirada*', Wing, *Belief*, 9–18, perceptively traces literary and biblical associations. R. ter Horst, 'Poetics and economics in the "Vida retirada" of Fray Luis de León', *HR*, 64: 149–69, points to interesting dualities. S. Pérez-Abadín Barro, 'El "genus natalis" en la Oda IV de Fray Luis de León', *BH*, 97, 1995:493–501, examines the use of Classical sources. R. Archer, '*De tres soy la segunda hermosura* de fray Luis de León', *RFE*, 73, 1994:405–15, looks at authorship.

SAN JUAN. R. Ros García, 'El poema "Que bien sé yo la fonte": la plegaria eucarística de un místico', *RE*, 54, 1995:75–113, explores dates and sources. I. Bengoechea, 'Nuevos manuscritos sanjuanistas todavía', *ib.*, 175–83, provides new documentary sources. J. V. Rodríguez, 'Experiencia colmante de Dios en San Juan de la Cruz', *ib.*, 293–325, looks at the nature of mystical plenitude. E. Díaz, 'Un colectivo sumergido en la noche oscura', *ib.*, 357–73, links San Juan and liberation theology. M. C. Sillato, 'Juan Gelman, San Juan de la Cruz y el espíritu de la Cábala', *RCEH*, 20:505–17, makes interesting associations. M. T. Gómez-Avila, 'Amor humano y divino en el poema *¡Oh llama de amor viva!*', *CH*, 16, 1994:287–96, analyses the nature of love.

GÓNGORA. M. M. Gaylord, 'Góngora and the footprints of the voice', Brownlee, *Cultural Authority*, 79–106, follows poetic utterance as a physical itinerary. K. Krabbenhoft, 'Góngora's stoic pilgrim', *BHS(L)*, 73: 1–12, detects Stoic influence. N. Ly, 'Tradición, memoria, literalidad. El caso de Góngora', *BH*, 97, 1995:347–59, highlights G.'s innovative approach. E. H. Friedman, '*Creative Space*. Ideologies of discourse in Góngora's *Polifemo*', Brownlee, *Cultural Authority*, 51–78, emphasizes competitive aspects. T. E. Peterson, 'The generation of mythic language in the "Polifemo"', *JHispP*, 17, 1993[1994]: 191–212, relates myth to linguistic and structural patterns. J. Roses Lozano, *Una poética de la oscuridad. La recepción crítica de las "Soledades" en el siglo XVII*, M-London, Tamesis, 1994, xviii + 213 pp., usefully reviews opinions. A. Carreira, 'Entre la huerta de don Marcos y *Les Roches Fleuries*. Las *Soledades* de Góngora editadas por Robert Jammes', *Criticón*, 61, 1994:113–20, contains valuable ideas on editing Golden Age works. Id., 'Pedro Espinosa y Góngora', *RFE*, 74, 1994:167–79, assesses G.'s influence. P. Ruiz Pérez, 'Una proyección de las *Soledades* en un poema inédito de Trillo y Figueroa (con edición del prólogo y libro 8 del *Poema heroico del Gran Capitán*)', *Criticón*, 65, 1995:101–77, is a scholarly study and edition.

OTHERS. R. Recio, 'El concepto *intérprete tan fiel* de Antonio de Obregón', *BHS(L)*, 73:225–37, links Petrarchan influence and principles of translation. D. L. Heiple, *Garcilaso de la Vega and the Italian Renaissance*, Pennsylvania State U.P., 1994, xv + 428 pp., re-reads in a Renaissance context. R. H. Chinchilla, 'Garcilaso de la Vega senior, patron of humanists in Rome: classical myths and the new nation', *BHS(G)*, 73:379–93, points to the propagation of ideas about the emerging Spanish empire. P. J. Smith, 'Homographesis in Salicio's song', Brownlee, *Cultural Authority*, 131–42, uncovers male relationships. L. M. Bernstein, 'Francisco de Aldana's epistle to Galanio: a poem of synthesis', *Hispanófila*, 117:1–10, focuses on ambiguity. S. Pérez-Abadín Barro, 'La influencia de Bernardo Tasso en Francisco de la Torre', *BHS(L)*, 73:13–18, adds to our knowledge of Italian influences. Id., 'Las odas de Baltasar de Alcázar: elementos clásicos y configuración retórica', *Neophilologus*, 80:61–74, studies moral/satirical Classical influence. A. Masoliver, 'Un monje original y gran poeta: Cristóbal de Castillejo (1490?-1550)', *Actas* (León), 237–48, offers a sound overview. M. A. Candelas Colodrón, 'La *compositio* en las silvas de Quevedo', *Criticón*, 65, 1995:65–86, stresses important rhetorical devices. F. Bravo, 'El saber del escritor. Por una teoría de la cita', *BH*, 97, 1995:361–74, raises intertextuality in a Quevedo sonnet. A. Ramajo Caño, 'Para la filiación literaria de un soneto de Quevedo ("Miré los muros de la patria mía")', *ib.*, 529–44, contextualizes the poem. L. Schwartz Lerner, 'Tradition and authority in Lope de Vega's *La Dorotea*', Brownlee, *Cultural Authority*, 3–27, analyses imitation in the light of new theories. E. García Santo-Tomás, 'Creación/recreación: Lope de Vega y las bofetadas a Elena Osorio', *Criticón*, 65, 1995:55–63, sees reflections of a love affair in *Rimas de Tomé Burguillos*. D. McGrady, 'Merlín y sus mentiras: el pasaje más oscuro de *La gatomaquia*', *BHS(L)*, 73:239–43, analyses verses 130–44. F.J. Díez de Revenga, 'Cervantes poeta y su recepción por los poetas de nuestro siglo', *BBMP*, 71, 1995:25–47, discusses neglected aspects. R. Schmidt, 'Maps, figures, and canons in the *Viaje del Parnaso*', *Cervantes*, 16.2:29–46, reflects on literary tensions. P. Ontañón de Lope, 'Dos estudios sobre Sor Juana', *BH*, 97, 1995:545–64, establishes targets for psychoanalytic interpretation.

J. Estruch Tobella, 'Cuarenta sonetos manuscritos de Francisco Manuel de Melo', *Criticón*, 61, 1994:7–30, provides a valuable edition. J. M. Oliver, 'Los matrimonios de José Pellicer. (Noticias de su vida familiar y descendencia.)', *ib.*, 63, 1995:47–88, describes marital details, whilst Id., '*Poesías de D. José Pellice*r: un manuscrito poético reencontrado', *ib.*, 65, 1995:87–100, reveals a major documentary source.

4. PROSE AND THE NOVEL

PICARESQUE. H. Sieber, 'Literary continuity, social order and the invention of the picaresque', Brownlee, *Cultural Authority*, 143–64, places the genre in a dialogic context. María de los Reyes Coll-Telletxea, 'Subjetividad, mujer y novela picaresca: el caso de las pícaras', *JILS*, 6, 1994:131–49, studies the construction of the female subject. C. Clark and A. Rodríguez, 'Posible impacto paródico del título: *La vida de Lazarillo de Tormes, y de sus fortunas y adversidades*', *RFE*, 73, 1994:399–403, discuss the impact of the title. C. R. Rabell, 'La confesión en jerigonza del *Lazarillo de Tormes*', *BHS(L)* 73:19–32, uncovers fascinating linguistic aspects. R. El Saffar, 'The prodigal "I": *Lazarillo de Tormes* as cultural analyst', Millington, *Hispanisms*, 14–35, is a Freudian-Lacanian re-reading. F. Cabo Aseguinolaza, 'El caso admirable de Lázaro de Tormes: el prólogo del *Lazarillo* como *insinuatio*', *BH*, 97, 1995:455–64, uses rhetoric to resolve problems of the prologue. R.G. Moore, 'No death, no closure: the open ending of Quevedo's *Buscón*', *RLA*, 6, 1994:539–45, unearths yet more ugliness in Pablos's life. M.S. Arredondo, 'De Lazarillo a Estebanillo: novedades picarescas del *Estebanillo González*', *RFE*, 75, 1995:255–79, points to deviations from the picaresque norm.

OTHERS. J. Edwards, 'Spanish Jews and *conversos* in Renaissance Rome: *La lozana andaluza*', *Donaire*, 6:31–36, gives important contextual material. L. Imperiale, 'Entre el altar y el lupanar: confesiones extra-oficiales de un vicario andaluz en Roma', *QIA*, 75, 1994:49–63, explains the marginalization of this work. Id., 'Discurso autorial y anti-lenguaje en *La lozana andaluza*', *CH*, 16, 1994:321–32, discusses narrative point of view. E. Blanco, 'Notas crítico-textuales al *Relox de príncipes*', *BRAE*, 75, 1995:477–522, illuminates publishing in the Golden Age. J. Weiner, 'Sebastián de Horozco (1510–1580) y un cuento anticlerical suyo', *RFE*, 76:31–45, is a scholarly contribution. D. Reyre, 'La voz *judío* en el *Tesoro de la Lengua Castellana o Española* de Sebastián de Covarrubias y en su *Suplemento*', *Criticón*, 61, 1994:81–94, reflects views on Jews. R. El Saffar, 'The "I" of the beholder. Self and other in some Golden Age texts', Brownlee, *Cultural Authority*, 178–205, discusses gender relations. García de la

Concha, *Fray Luis*, includes: F. Lázaro Carreter, 'Fray Luis de León y la clasicidad' (15–27); V. García de la Concha, '*De los Nombres de Cristo*, comentario al Cantar de los Cantares' (381–94); J. A. Jones, 'Imitación y sabiduría en *La perfecta casada* de Luis de León' (413–21); J. San José Lera, 'De estética y retórica luisianas. Algunas consideraciones sobre el número en la prosa de fray Luis de León' (497–513); A. Sánchez Zamareño, '*De los nombres de Cristo* y la instalación en la utopía' (515–25); C. P. Thompson, 'La teoría de los nombres y la metáfora en la poesía de fray Luis de León' (549–55). R. Krauel, 'El esquema heroico de la historia de Abindarráez', *RoN*, 37:39–47, underlines incomplete heroism. J. M. Lucía Megías, 'Dos folios recuperados de un libro de caballerías manuscrito: *Don Clarís de Trapisonda* (Biblioteca de Palacio: II. 2504)', *RFE*, 76:47–69, is a valuable textual study. H. Ettinghausen, 'Quevedo 350 years on', *BHS(L)*, 73:91–103, perceptively reviews major critical works. K. Budor, 'Quevedo y la *Guerra de los Uscoques*: sus fuentes documentales', *RFE*, 75, 1995:333–44, sheds light on Quevedo's stay in Italy. C. D. Presberg, 'Deliverance in the prison-house: paradoxes of self, culture, and language in the writings of Quevedo', *His(US)*, 78, 1995:25–32, raises issues of confinement and liberation. M. S. Brownlee, 'Postmodernism and the baroque in María de Zayas', Brownlee, *Cultural Authority*, 107–27, indicates foreshadowings of the modern. A. R. Williamsen, '"Death becomes her": fatal beauty in María de Zayas's "Mal presagio casar lejos"', *RLA*, 6, 1994:619–23, explores contrasting elements. L. Vollendorf, 'Reading the body imperiled: violence against women in María de Zayas', *His(US)*, 78, 1995:272–82, attacks patriarchy. L. J. Gorfkle, 'Seduction and hysteria in María de Zayas's *Desengaños amorosos*', *Hispanófila*, 115, 1995:11–28, considers conflictive sexual/gender attitudes. M. S. Arredondo, 'Avisos sobre la capital del orbe en 1646: *Los Peligros de Madrid*', *Criticón*, 63, 1995:89–101, portrays aspects of a little-known work by Baptista Remiro de Navarra.

CERVANTES

GENERAL. R. ter Horst, 'Cervantes and the paternity of the English novel', Brownlee, *Cultural Authority*, 165–77, shows C.'s contribution to the rise of the novel. D. Finello, *Pastoral Themes and Forms in Cervantes's Fiction*, Lewisburg, Bucknell U.P.–London–Toronto, Associated U.P., 1994, 299 pp., establishes the importance of the genre for Cervantes. C. Colahan, 'Sigismunda, Mary and Athene: Cervantes and Neoplatonic hieroglyphics', *RoN*, 37:17–22, makes Classical/Christian connections. D. Eisenberg, 'Cervantes, autor de la *Topografía e historia general de Argel* publicado por Diego de Haedo',

Cervantes, 16.1 : 32–53, detects self-praise by C. *Cervantes,* ed. Harold Bloom, NY, Chelsea House Publishers, 1994, 200 pp., makes accessible excellent articles in English. *Cervantes and the Modernists. The Question of Influence,* ed. Edwin Williamson, London-M, Tamesis, 1994, x + 148 pp., contains: E. Williamson, 'Introduction: the question of influence' (1–8); N. G. Round, 'Towards a typology of quixotisms' (9–28); M. Woods, 'Invisible works: Cervantes reads Borges and Nabokov' (29–41); P. J. Smith, 'Cervantes, Goytisolo and the sodomitical scene' (43–54); E. J. Hughes, 'Prisons and pleasures of the mind: a comparative reading of Cervantes and Proust' (55–72); E. C. Riley, 'Whatever happened to heroes? *Don Quixote* and some major European novels of the twentieth century' (73–84); M. Bell, 'Novel, story, and the foreign: Cervantes, Thomas Mann and Primo Levi' (85–102); E. Williamson, 'The quixotic roots of magic realism: history and fiction from Alejo Carpentier to Gabriel García Márquez' (103–20); P. Swanson, 'Writing the present, reading the past: Cervantes, Güiraldes, Fuentes' (121–33); D. Scheunemann, 'The problem of the book: *Don Quixote* in the age of mechanical reproduction' (135–48). D. de Armas Wilson, '"The matter of America". Cervantes romances Inca Garcilaso de la Vega', Brownlee, *Cultural Authority,* 234–59, focuses on the idea of empire. J. P. Gabriele and L. L. Kenreich, 'De Dulcinea del Toboso a Melania de Salignac: el arquetipo cervantino en *El concierto de San Ovidio*', *Neophilologus,* 80:417–24, evaluates C.'s influence on Buero. C. Manso, 'José Martínez Ruiz, Azorín, de cara a Cervantes', *BH,* 96, 1994:521–28, portrays Azorín's attempts to understand C.

DON QUIXOTE. P. N. Dunn, 'Framing the story, framing the reader: two Spanish masters', *MLR,* 91 : 94–106, compares C. and J. Manuel. D. O. Mosquera, '*Don Quijote* and the quixotics of translation', *RLA,* 6, 1994:546–50, indicates how C. anticipates modern theorists. J. R. Resina, 'Cervantes's confidence games and the refashioning of totality', *MLN,* 111 : 218–53, seeks to reconcile burlesque and philosophical aspects. E. M. Anderson, 'His pen's Christian profession: Cide Hamete writes the end of *Don Quixote*', *RLA,* 6, 1994:406–12, concentrates on Cide Hamete's apostrophe to his pen. E. Baker, 'Breaking the frame: Don Quixote's entertaining books', *Cervantes,* 16.1 : 12–31, reflects on reading. A. Rodríguez and M. Ramírez, 'Whistling in the dark: chapters 19 and 20 of Part One of *Don Quijote*', *ib.,* 16.2 : 107–13, discovers a change in narrative patterns. J. G. Weiger, 'On the "Autores" of *Don Quijote*', *BHS(G),* 73:263–69, discusses authorship in fiction and reality. R. M. Flores, 'Estructura estilística en el *Quijote*', *Cervantes,* 16.2 : 47–70, establishes the structural importance of the prologues. A. J. Cascardi, 'History and modernity in the Spanish Golden Age. Secularization and

literary self-assertion in *Don Quijote*', Brownlee, *Cultural Authority*,
209–33, reveals tensions of past and present. B. Fuchs, 'Border
crossings: transvestism and "passing" in *Don Quijote*', *Cervantes*,
16.2:4–28, explains the blurring of orthodoxy. P. Ruiz Pérez, 'Los
enemigos del caballero: Micomicona, Trifaldi y el de la Blanca Luna',
BH, 97, 1995:503–28, analyses ternary patterns. E. H. Friedman,
'Sancho's mid-section: mind and matter in the Sierra Morena', *RLA*,
6, 1994:465–71, points to changes in Sancho's character. M. S.
Carrasco Urgoite, 'Don Alvaro Tarfe: el personaje morisco de
Avellaneda y su variante cervantina', *RFE*, 73, 1994:275–93, evaluates the respective presentation of characters. F. Rico, 'El primer
pliego del "Quijote"', *HR*, 64:313–36, illustrates the pressures of the
publishing world. C. M. Andrés Gil, 'El libro de Avellaneda como
purgante de la locura quijotesca', *Cervantes*, 16.1:3–11, underlines
the central role of the apocryphal book in *DQ*. J. Aladro-Font and R.
Ramos-Tremolada, 'Ausencia y presencia de Garcilaso en el *Quijote*',
ib., 16.2:89–106, explain facets of a Garcilasian subtext in Part II. G.
Montserrat, 'Don Quixote in Yoknapatawpha: Faulkner's champions
of dames', *SLRev*, 27, 1995:23–42, picks up echoes of *DQ*.

OTHER WORKS. N. Cox Davis, 'Marriage and investment in *El
celoso extremeño*', *RR*, 86, 1995:638–55, reassesses the work in the light
of monetary terminology. M. A. Encinar, 'La formación de personajes
en tres novelas ejemplares: *El licenciado Vidriera*, *El celoso extremeño* y *La
fuerza de la sangre*', *Cervantes*, 15.1, 1995:70–81, deals with the
interaction of the individual and society. M. S. Collins, 'Transgression
and transfiguration in Cervantes's *La española inglesa*', *ib.*, 16.1:54–73,
highlights an Erasmian challenge. S. L. Parker Aronson, 'La "tex-
tualización" de Leocadia y su defensa en *La fuerza de la sangre*', *ib.*,
16.2:71–88, criticizes 17th-c. attitudes to women. P. Lewis-Smith,
'Fictionalizing God: providence, nature, and the significance of rape
in *La fuerza de la sangre*', *MLR*, 91:886–97, considers C.'s handling of
providence. R. Hitchcock, 'A heterodox reading of Cervantes's
Rinconete y Cortadillo', Hunter, *Short Story*, 29–37, brings out the
challenge of *morisco*/Christian tensions. S. Boyd, 'Cervantes and the
art of re-creation', Wing, *Belief*, 19–24, shows how *La gitanilla* affirms
and questions belief structures.

LITERATURE, 1490–1700
(DRAMA)

By CHARLES GANELIN, *Associate Professor of Spanish, Purdue University*
(This survey covers the years 1995 and 1996)

1. *CELESTINA*

J. T. Snow and R. Garza, 'Celestina' de Fernando de Rojas: documento bibliográfico (décimonono suplemento)', *Celestinesca*, 19:125–43, continue to supply the literary world with the most complete *Celestina* bibliographic tool, which here encompasses entries 723–802. I. J. Rivera, 'Visual structures and verbal representation in the *Comedia de Calisto y Melibea* (Burgos, 1499?)', *ib.*, 3–30, details, in a solid and well-constructed essay, the interaction of the verbal and pictorial text and woodcuts of the Burgos edition — which forces the reader to link diegesis of the *argumento* to the mimesis of the woodcuts to produce mutually enriching readings. F. Cantalapiedra, 'El refranero celestinesco', *ib.*, 31–56, replies to critics of his earlier article on *refranes* and their relation to the question of *Celestina*'s authorship; C.'s partial conclusion indicates fewer and poorer *refranes* in the last four acts than in the first act and ensuing development. F. Maurizi, 'El auto IX y la destronización de Melibea', *ib.*, 57–69, employs Bakhtinian semiotics of carnival to explain why Elicia and Areúsa draw a repellent picture of Melibea's beauty precisely in Auto IX; the topos of the ugly woman and the focus on breasts and stomach occur in the banquet scene, an ideal Bakhtinian context for parodic commentary on the grotesque body. In an elegant and provocative essay, P. Cocozella, 'From lyricism to drama: the evolution of Fernando de Rojas' egocentric subtext', *ib.*, 71–92, takes the reader from Rojas to Rodrigo Cota and Juan de Mena, to Ausiàs March, to describe the 'egocentric subtext' of 15th-c. Hispanic letters that develops from the lyrical to the dramatic to a theatrical phenomenon; the psychological illumination of the *Celestina*'s monologues are a 'dialogue of self to self'. L. M. Brocate, 'Cutting commentary: *Celestina*, spectacular discourse, and the treacherous gloss', *ib.*, 20:103–28, focuses on overheard dialogues and asides, readers and reading to make the asides a metaphorical index and gloss of the text itself for the benefit of spectators within and without the text. F. J. Sánchez, 'Negocio y contemplación: el discurso erótico como capital simbólico en *La Celestina*', pp. 19–27 of *Brave New Words: Studies in Spanish Golden Age Literature*, ed. E. H. Friedman and C. Larson, U.P. of the South, xvii + 279 pp. (hereinafter referred to as Friedman,

Brave New Words), contextualizes Calisto and Melibea's love within fiscal and personal negotiations, especially Celestina's. Social relationships as well as the metaphorical world of courtly love are placed within an emerging class consciousness. *M. T. Narváez, 'El Mancebo de Arévalo, lector morisco de *La Celestina*', BHS(L), 72, 1995:255–72. E. M. Gerli, 'Complicitous laughter: hilarity and seduction in *Celestina*', HR, 63:1995, 19–38, reasserts the adage that comedy is serious business by defining the various registers of laughter as an important component of dialogue and how it functions 'as the counterdiscourse of virtue'. One case in point, according to G., is Alisa whose laughter may very well signal a more complex character than heretofore has been ascribed to her.

2. GENERAL

M. D. Stroud, *The Play in the Mirror: Lacanian Perspectives on Spanish Baroque Theater*, Bucknell U.P., 242 pp., draws from his previous Lacanian studies of the *comedia* and expands them considerably in order to apply one kind of psychoanalytic criticism to the *comedia* 'in a more direct and comprehensive way' than has been carried out to date. Five of his seven chapters present concise and informative introductions to important aspects of often difficult and elusive Lacanian thought (subject, desire, ethics, phallic signification, and the like) with concomitant analyses of specific *comedias*: *La vida es sueño*, *La dama boba*, *El caballero de Olmedo*, *El castigo sin venganza*, *A secreto agravio, secreta venganza*, *El burlador de Sevilla*, *La dama duende*, *Don Gil de las calzas verdes*, *El príncipe constante*, and *La Santa Juana*. While one may take issue with a Lacanian approach to literature and therefore question S.'s theoretical stance, the book is well-researched and well-written, though greater attention could have been paid to Anglo-American feminist readings of several of these plays. Nonetheless, S. rightly concludes that both psychoanalysis and literary criticism seek 'to deal as directly as possible with the otherness, the gaps, the loose ends, the problematic of desire'. Though these terms function within both a Lacanian and, for example, an Iserian system, S.'s summarizing remark is accurate and helps to formulate the context of the author's (literary) analyses. W. Egginton, 'An epistemology of the stage: theatricality and subjectivity in Early Modern Spain', NLH, 27:391–413, supports Maravall's contention that *comedia* worked as an ideological tool of the monarchy, by positing that theatre formed a new mode of subjectivity in which subjects enter into 'an inherently conflictual relation with the social order'. J. M. Regueiro, 'Textual discontinuities and the problems of closure in the Spanish drama of the Golden Age', Brownlee, *Cultural Authority*, 28–50, reinforces the impossibility of closure (the movement from 'order disturbed to order restored') in a genre rife with textual discontinuities; to continue to analyse the *comedia* as a homogenous enterprise runs 'the risk of distorting a cultural reality'. G. McKim-Smith and M. L. Welles, 'Portrait of a lady: the violence of vision', Friedman, *Brave New Words*, 221–46, propose, via a subtle understanding of scopophilia and feminism, a fascinating correspondence between the representation of women in the *comedia* and 20th-c. vandalism against female subjects in painting. I. Arellano, 'Valores visuales de la palabra en el espacio escénico del siglo de oro', *RCEH* 19:411–43, details how stage objects are brought to life by their mention and elaboration; A. discusses the problems with gestures and letters, emblems, and *ut pictora poesis*. Id., 'La edición de textos teatrales', *La Comedia*, 13–50, precedes, due to the collection's delay in appearing, the author's other informative statements on critical editions. A. outlines the fundamental aspects to be included in them, signals that much teamwork is needed to bring out minor theatrical pieces, and urges rigour and honesty in all editions. M. V. Diago, 'La mujer en el teatro profesional del Renacimiento: entre la sumisión y la astucia (A propósito de *Las tres comedias* de Juan de Timoneda)', *Criticón*, 63, 1995:103–17, notes the development of passive female characters who take on greater relief to become, in Timoneda, increasingly complex subjects of the action. M. de los A. Villalba García, 'Gestualidad escénica en la comedia barroca de capa y espada', *Gestos*, 20, 1995:19–38, at times belabours the obvious with a catalogue of gestures and their possible relationship to social models. G. V. García-Luengos, 'Treinta comedias desconocidas de Ruiz de Alarcón, Mira de Amescua, Vélez de Guevara, Rojas Zorrilla y otros de los mejores ingenios de España', *Criticón*, 62, 1994:57–78, publishes additional titles and precise descriptions of *sueltas* disinterred from the inner recesses of Madrid's Biblioteca Nacional; G.-L. promises future individual studies on the plays. R. Serrano-Deza, 'Un protocolo de análisis infoasistido aplicado al teatro de los Siglos de Oro. Del tratamiento del texto a la construcción de hipótesis', *ib.*, 79–98, demystifies computer-aided analyses to focus on the Golden Age theatre text as a sequential model with three branches ('localización, polarización y resultado') especially applicable to 'oppositional' characers; a detailed bibliography and two diagrams accompany the essay. This somewhat technical article should be read in conjunction with A. Moll's (see TIRSO DE MOLINA). C. Oriel, 'The play of presence and absence: writing and supplementarity in the *comedias de privanza*', pp. 36–51 of *El arte nuevo de estudiar comedias: Literary Theory and Spanish Golden Age Drama*, ed. B. Simerka, Bucknell U.P, 260 pp. (hereinafter cited as Simerka, *Arte nuevo*), revisits the Derridean postulation of writing as supplement as a constitutive element of the important transition in Spain from an oral to a written culture; O. is especially refreshing in his insistence on the 'pre-eminence of the literary text itself', a position all too often compromised in the postmodern world. H. W. Sullivan, 'Jacques Lacan and the Golden Age drama', *ib.*, 105–24, has chosen Calderón's *La vida es sueño* as a platform for a wider discussion on the Lacanian subject and language. S., who over the years has been the prime mover behind Lacanian studies of the *comedia*, here begins with Basilio's 'signified-less' astrological prediction as a basis for a better acquaintance of the premodern concept of the subject. A. R. Lauer, 'The *comedia* and its modes', *HR*, 63:157–78, attempts to tame the hybridity of the *comedia* through a taxonomy composed of 'Heraclitean mode' (tragic or exemplary plays), 'Democritean mode' ('comic' and 'sublime' plays), and 'Socratic mode' ('debates', 'dialogues', and plays of mystic contemplation). L. recognizes the dangers with any system of classification and welcomes the possibility of further modifications with new data.

3. Calderón de la Barca

J. M. W. Robbins, 'Male dynamics in Calderón's *A secreto agravio, secreta venganza*', *Hispanófila*, 39:11–24, utilizes a Ciceronian ideal of 'specular friendship' as well as E. Sedgwick's Queer Theory to define the 'honour panic' that forces Lope de Almeida to seek vengeance against his sullied honour; R. finds two alternative kinds of relationships between men that arise out of honour's effects. M. L. Thomas, 'Conversions of the woman monarch in the drama of Calderón de la Barca', pp. 143–56 of *Spanish Women in the Golden Age: Images and Realities*, ed. M. S. Sánchez and A. Saint-Saëns, Greenwood, x + 299 pp., primarily describes Calderón's characterization of the historical Queen Christina of Sweden in *Afectos de odio y amor* and *La protestación de la fe* and how the fictionalized protagonist subjugates herself either to natural law or to Roman Catholicism. C. Morrow, 'Gender anxiety in *El alcalde de Zalamea*', *Gestos*, 20, 1995:39–54, holds that anxiety over gender roles and freedom is portrayed through the gaze (Isabel) and conduct (La Chispa) which are punished through confinement (Isabel) and removal from the public sphere (Chispa) in order to re-establish patriarchal order and authority in accordance with prescribed behaviour by 16th-c. moralists. Calderón dowses the spark and blinds the gaze. E. Friedman, 'The *comedia* and focalization: the case of *La vida es sueño*', Friedman, *Brave New Words*, 246–57, uses narratology as a frame for approaching Golden Age theatre; through generic recasting, F. maintains that the absent narrator in C.'s play becomes a key structuring agent and a crucial marker of presence. D. Reyre, 'Escenificación del deicidio en los autos sacramentales de Calderón (elementos teatrales del antijudaísmo español)', *Criticón*, 63, 1995:139–62, examines in nine *autos* Calderón's staging of Jesus's Passion and a demonization of Judaism; Calderón's emphasis may have arisen out of Olivares's political openings to Jewish financiers, with the 1643 fall of the Count-Duke giving free reign to dramatic disapproval. I. Arellano, 'Para el repertorio de loas sacramentales de Calderón. Un autógrafo inédito de Calderón: la loa auténtica de *El año santo de Roma*', *ib.*, 62, 1994:7–32, continues his important contributions to Golden Age textual studies and reasons convincingly for this *loa*'s authenticity. S. Hernández Araico, 'El mito de Veturia y Coriolano en Calderón: *Las armas de la hermosura* como Matronalia reales', *ib.*, 99–110, weaves an intelligent thesis to re-date and to link C.'s development of myth to three important late 17th-c. queens important to the Spanish political orientation in Mesina. D. Fox, 'The literary use of history: *El médico de su honra* in contexts', Simerka, *Arte nuevo*, 206–32, carries the play's implications beyond its classification as an 'honour play'. Through a detailed understanding of historical context and of the need to combine literature and history for a more accurate cultural depiction, F. sees the staging of degeneration into farce because of the king's unconscionable actions; finally Calderón opts for passive resistance as the alternative to violence in removing the monarch. M. Greer, '"La vida es sueño — ¿o risa?": Calderón parodies the *auto*', *BHS(L)*, 72:313–25, encourages a reading of a playful Calderón in *entremeses* and *mojigangas*. G. studies the *Mojiganga de las visiones de la muerte*, written for performance with the *auto La vida es sueño*, which celebrates life, as a companion piece to the more sombre *desengaño* pictured in the *auto*; just as the *auto* elevates the host for spiritual pleasure, so the *mojiganga* passes the *bota* to drink in human pleasure. J. B. Hall, 'Madness and sanity in Calderón's *El alcalde de Zalamea*', *Iberoromania*, 43:52–67, reasons that Captain Alvaro is not evil but suffers from insanity occasioned by Isabel's astonishing beauty; his subsequent actions, therefore, are the product of an unbalanced mind. In the end, H. states, perhaps Pedro Crespo's death penalty is unwarranted, though it does call into question the limits of human knowledge in learning all possible facts to act appropriately. In a refreshingly 'different' perspective †R. Carter, 'Liberty, comedy and irony in *La vida es sueño*', *FMLS*, 32:354–71, begins with a reference to the 1980 *Superman* movie and its opening scene, and compares its implausibility to that of the first encounter among Rosaura, Clarín, Clotaldo, and Segismundo. C.'s ensuing theological orientation questions Clotaldo's teaching and the nature of Segismundo's freedom, to deduce that equivocal language used comically evokes self-serving and self-deceiving attitudes that we of the (post)modern world find around us and that allow us to understand Calderón.

4. ANA CARO

C. Larson, 'Valor judgments, or women writers and the *comedia*', Friedman, *Brave New Words*, 259–70, cleverly examines 'the state of the sexual union' by continued exploration of the Golden Age canon and the need to expand it through the addition of women writers, L. pays particular attention to aesthetic value, citing *Valor, agravio y mujer* as a representative example of Golden Age women's writing. T. S. Soufas, 'A feminist approach to a Golden Age *dramaturga*'s play', Simerka, *Arte nuevo*, 127–42, places Ana Caro's *Valor, agravio y mujer* within the contexts of the *comedia* and of 17th-c. theatre in general. In a solid feminist reading accompanied by an extensive and helpful bibliography, S. attributes to Leonor's use of speech the ability to carry out her manipulation of disguise to shift blame 'away from the objectified victim of passion'; the protagonist successfully displaces responsibility from a man's moral behaviour away from the female. †L. Luna, 'Ana Caro, una escritora 'de oficio' del siglo de oro', *BHS(L)*, 72:11–16, gives a fundamental 'life and works' in order to understand C.'s literary production in its context. In addition to documentary evidence about the author's life, L. finds that it is 'errado' to focus on Caro only from a feminist position or from a monolithic ideological standpoint; rather, critics need to see an historical feminine subject 'en estrecha conexión con el poder'.

5. MIGUEL DE CERVANTES

E. Anderson, 'The gentility and genius of Pedro de Urdemalas, engendered by Lope de Vega and Cervantes', Friedman, *Brave New Words*, 175–89, delineates, with her accustomed grace and insight, differences in rank and gender between the two plays, concluding that acting in Lope's play is a question of transgression with a concomitant negative valuation of marriage, while in Cervantes's Pedro de Urdemalas a more feminine reading of the world is evinced. F. A. de Armas, 'Painting and graffiti: (sub)versions of history in Golden Age theater. (Notes on Cervantes and Claramonte.)', *Gestos*, 21:83–101, equates painting and the foundation of the state's power as well as graffiti and the subversion of history. The Duero prophecy and both a portrait and a blank canvas in Cervantes's *comedia* call into question assumed beliefs in the *comedia*'s use as a tool for the state's power. Graffiti on Raphael's painting, placed by Imperial soldiers during the sack of Rome, find their way to Cervantes's tragedy as a cautionary tale: neither pope nor emperor have acted in exemplary fashion. In Claramonte, it is lovers who subvert normal discourse and channels of communication, and who act through forgery, who are successful in being married; ultimately, the *comedia* undercuts the lofty values of the state it purports to reflect and uphold. Id., 'The necromancy of imitation: Lucan and Cervantes's *La Numancia*', Simerka, *Arte nuevo*, 246–55, reveals the central importance of Lucan's *Pharsalia* to an understanding of Cervantes's play. A. focuses on necromancy, its close relation with imitation, and the ensuing dialogues in the text between C. and Lucan, and between Virgil and Lucan; finally, C. foregrounds necromancy 'as a metaphor for the very process of imitation' which serves as the ending of one stage of Cervantine poetics and the beginning of a more 'quixotic enterprise'. C. Larson, 'The visible and the hidden: Speech act theory and Cervantes's *El retablo de las maravillas*', *ib.*, 52–65, offers a felicitous blend, on the one hand, of Searle, Austin, and Grice, and solid literary analysis on the other, in a reconsideration of language's power to create worlds and its limitations. Of particular note, according to L., is the lie and its social and moral implications as well as the response it elicits from the *entremes*'s onstage listeners. W. Egginton and D. R. Castillo, 'The rules of Chanfalla's game', *RLA*, 6, 1994:444–49, take Maravall's studies of Golden Age society as their ideological starting point and review the standard semiotic codes of Baroque Spanish theatre to foreground Cervantes's subversion of the typical *comedia* 'galán'; Chanfalla's rules in *El retablo de las maravillas* equate theatrical and social conventions, allowing Cervantine satire its full effectiveness against the propagation of state ideology in theatre. An interesting addition to the re-evaluation of Cervantes's 'historical' *comedia* is B. N. Stiegler, 'The coming of the new Jerusalem: apocalyptic vision in Cervantes' *La Numancia*', *Neophilologus*, 80:569–81, who takes the position that images of the Apocalypse, read in accordance with Klaus Koch's theological formulations, allowed Cervantes to fashion Numantia as a microcosm of the world; the destruction of evil (Romans) and the redemption of the just (Numantians), together with the enthronement of Philip II, add up to a pro-Spanish Imperial attitude as Spain is predicted to live a golden age as if it were the kingdom of God.

6. *La Estrella de Sevilla*

Heavenly Bodies: The Realms of 'La estrella de Sevilla', ed. F. A. de Armas, Bucknell U.P., 294 pp., brings together essays, most of which were first presented at a Penn State conference on this *comedia*. F. A. de Armas, 'The mysteries of canonicity' (15–28), studies the reception accorded *La estrella de Sevilla*, its canonical status deriving in large measure from its link to historical events. J. A. Parr, 'Toward contextualization: canonicity, current criticism, contemporary culture' (29–42), draws on his previous work on the *comedia* canon to focus on literary commentary and its 20th-c. move to 'theory'; in particular, P. takes up this movement in a discussion of male reaction to female beauty in *Estrella*. G. M. Burton, 'The mirror crack'd: the politics of resemblance' (45–63), takes Estrella's broken mirror to be a metaphor for 'resemblance' as a primary tenor of the play's action; the breaking of the mirror shatters the basis of order/resemblance in feudal society. F. P. Casa, 'The centrality and function of King Sancho' (64–75), revisits the king's two bodies and assigns Sancho's failure as a monarch to his inability to function properly as a man; only with his recognition of wrongdoing can he repair the damage he has wrought. M. McKendrick, 'In the wake of Machiavelli—*Razón de estado*, morality, and the individual' (76–91), finds Machiavelli imbued in the text through the tension arising out of the conflict between justice and the state; 'tacitismo', she contends, is a clear indicator of the Italian ruler's presence. H. Sturm, 'Historical and textual underpinnings' (92–101), returns to *Estrella* for a look at its ethics: a mirror of princes that instructs monarchy in the exercise of power. C. Connor, 'The Moor's ghost: the orientalist subtext at play in the play' (105–18), is a superb reading, informed by Said's work, of the monarch's attempted seduction of Estrella as a metaphor for the Reconquest's Moorish/Christian conflicts. A. J. Cruz, 'Star gazing: text, performance, and the female gaze' (119–34), brings a well-informed Lacanian reading to elucidate the 'seamless relation of text to performance' that posits a male spectator; C.'s focus on Estrella allows the reader/spectator to recognize the effect of the female gaze. D. L. Heiple, 'Madness as philosophical insight' (135–45), considers Sancho Ortiz and his 'mad scene' to place at least this aspect of the *comedia* within a tradition of the wise madman; the resulting 'infernal vision' indicates a troubled world represented in the play. J. Mandrell, 'Of material girls and celestial women, or, honor and exchange' (146–60), relies on Madonna to point out an important paradox in *Estrella*: Estrella is the protagonist, yet is limited in her agency because she also incarnates exchange value. The servant Natilde's attempt at freedom, M. rightly attests, ends in death and signals the impossibility of escape for a woman from being the culturally-determined signifier that she is. S. L. Fischer, 'The authority of the text' (163–80), employs a well-honed Iserian reader-response approach to suggest that true textual authority resides in the reader, the one responsible for filling in 'gaps' and 'indeterminacies' of that text through subject experience or, as F. states, 'the artistic pole'. C. Hernández Valcárcel, 'Intertextuality in the theater of Lope de Vega' (181–94), firmly rooting herself in a traditional analysis of the many intertextualities of plot, characterization and theme throughout Lope's dramatic output, strongly leans toward Lope's authorship of *Estrella*. On the same question, A. Rodríguez López-Vázquez (195–205) compiles classical references from Claramonte and other authors associated at one time or another with *Estrella* to affirm that all evidence points to Claramonte as author of a 1617–18 short version of the *comedia* as well as of a 1623 re-elaboration. A. K. Stoll, 'Staging and polymetry' (206–17), carries her insightful interest in *comedia* performance to the area of metre where imagery and meaning are conveyed in an 'autotextual' mise-en-scène; such a staging would be a first step to a full intertextual one in which both text as written and its various subtexts would be presented. For E. L. Bergmann, 'Acts of reading, acts of writing' (221–34), speech acts and the often-described 'papeles' act as agents that exclude Estrella from language and thus enable her losses; only when she reaffirms traditional values of honour do her actions and words take on value, and then only to 'constitute her renunciation'. J. F. Burke, 'Writing the *saturnalia*' (235–44), offers a suggestive reading in which a *Saturnalia* is 'inscribed' within the play to instruct the audience in proper action that the king's 'personal Carnival' threatens to destroy. C. Oriel, 'Shame, writing, and morality' (245–57), lucidly highlights the fundamental tension between inscription and orality in *Estrella* that is indicative of the many conflicts within the play; presence and absence, in particular, is a key duality that posits a question of metaphysics and being. E. L. Rivers, 'The shame of writing' (258–76), here reprints his ground-breaking essay first published in 1980; R. updates in an introductory paragraph additional references on speech act theory and its application. The entire volume's 'Works cited' (277–89), containing the bibliographical references from the essays here collected, yields a delightfully eclectic as well as a fundamental bibliography on theoretical approaches and on *La Estrella de Sevilla* itself. S. L. Fischer, 'Reader response, Iser, and *La estrella de Sevilla*', Simerka, *Arte nuevo*, 86–104, builds on her companion piece (listed above) to hold that Iser's concept of 'blanks' are not meant to impede meaning but to find a path to its creation; she trains much of the spotlight on the spaces created by Sancho Ortiz's refusal to speak and King Sancho's much-studied order, 'hablad', and its consequences for the monarch.

7. TIRSO DE MOLINA

C. Ganelin, 'Who was that masked woman? Female identity in Tirso de Molina's *La mujer por fuerza*', *IJHL*, 6–7:103–21, posits, in a feminist reading, the creation of a female subjectivity and highlights Tirso's subversion of traditional gender roles. G. maintains that this *comedia* has remained unstudied in part because of its strong female character and in part because questions remain concerning its authorship. J. Cull, ' "Hablan poco y dicen mucho": the function of discovery scenes in the drama of Tirso de Molina', *MLR*, 91:619–34, adroitly addresses the popularity of emblems as part and parcel of *comedia* production, appearing generally at the end of a play and predominantly in a central niche of the stage; emblems are heralded by music, interpreted by actors, and serve to prefigure, summarize or indoctrinate. The article, though applied to Tirso only, carries serious import for numerous *comedias* whose value will be enhanced with emblems in mind. †E. W. Hesse, 'Gender and the discourse of decay in *El burlador de Sevilla*', *BC*, 47:155–63, focuses on the kinds of speech used for perverse purposes to highlight the moral decay of the epoch. S. Pendzik, 'Female presence in Tirso's *El burlador de Sevilla*', *ib.*, 165–81, illuminates women's function as a subversive force against the established order in order to expose its flaws; 'invisible' women and peculiar silences, particularly Anfriso's at the play's close, leave many ends untied. L. Vázquez, '*El burlador de Sevilla*: claramente de Tirso, y no de Claramonte (breve anotación crítica)', *ib.*, 183–90, yet again takes up the gauntlet to refute the attribution of the play to Claramonte; V. chooses not to reiterate Rodríguez López-Vázquez's 'laberínticos análisis', relies on Casalduero's studies, restates old and often-refuted attacks against Claramonte's poetic abilities, and finally questions why Cátedra substituted Casalduero's edition for R.L.-V.'s. I. Benabu, 'Reading the opening of a play: Tirso's *El burlador de Sevilla*', *ib.*, 191–200, reads the first scenes, from a director's perspective, to signal Don Juan as the instigator of all stage-business and to explain how Tirso manipulates the scene to ensnare the audience in Don Juan's web. B. Mujica, 'The end: modern productions of *El burlador de Sevilla*, with special attention to closings', *ib.*, 201–22, offers a companion piece to Benabu's and examines five productions of the play and the differences in their closings; though the productions are of unequal and uneven quality, three re-establish the social order, and two create a sense of disequilibrium with a deliberate lack of resolution. C. D. Presberg, '*El condenado por presumido*: the rhetoric of death and damnation in *El burlador de Sevilla y convidado de piedra*', *ib.*, 223–43, reads the play, in somewhat turgid prose, as a dramatized homily on God's justice seen in both the natural and supernatural arenas. A. Moll, 'Don Juan in cyberspace: editing a *comedia* on the information superhighway', *ib.*, 245–66, takes the reader on a fascinating investigation of creating an electronic edition, but only after outlining important areas of consideration in textual criticism and their application to computer work. M.'s essay should be standard reading for anyone undertaking an electronic text project. J. W. Thacker, 'Comedy's social compromise: Tirso's *Marta la piadosa* and the refashioning of role', *ib.*, 267–89, affirms the play's comicity and its position as a debate between youthful expressions of self and more conservative notions of role-playing with carnivalesque elements clearly laid out. T.'s position is certainly valid but could go farther in delineating the subversive nature of the play. C. B. Weimer, 'The oedipal drama of Tirso's *La república al revés*', *ib.*, 291–309, underscores the infrequent treatment of this classical theme in the *comedia*; the play's debt to Oedipus and the resolution of its own kind of riddle allow W. to re-evaluate yet another understudied Tirso playtext. B. Simerka, 'The *indiano* as liminal figure in the drama of Tirso and his contemporaries', *ib.*, 311–20, employs Said's paradigms for addressing the effects of minority discourses; here, S. sees the *indiano* as the dangerous Other and as a Spaniard by birth, a double identity that precludes consistent characterization in the *comedia*. J. T. Cull, 'Purging humor(s): medical and scatological imagery in Tirso de Molina', *ib.*, 321–39, with his own humour intact, suggests that Tirso followed conventions on the use of scatological humour and documented what daily life continually paraded before its observers. M. L. Welles, 'The anxiety of gender: transformation of Tamar in Tirso's *La venganza de Tamar* and Calderón's *Los cabellos de Absalón*', *ib.*, 341–72, brings her usual clarity and conciseness to bear as she emphasizes that gender anxiety reflects a crisis of political power, and that this anxiety is projected in both Tirso's and Calderón's distortions of the Biblical narrative. J. T. Abraham, 'The other speaks: Tirso de Molina's *Amazonas en las Indias*', Simerka, *Arte nuevo*, 143–61, sees in the play an attempt to erase the 'other' in dealings with the inhabitants of America; the actions of the Pizarros, regardless of historical 'accuracy', become prime examples of exploitation in the so-called New World. J. A. Parr, 'On canonization and canonicity: *El burlador de Sevilla y convidado de piedra* (Or, A rake's progress and pride of place)', *ib.*, 235–45, addresses the problems of delineating the 'appropriate' canon(s) for this or other *comedias* as well, and gives the reader a concise overview on the Protean nature of the *comedia* canon. R. ter Horst, 'Epic descent: the filiations of Don Juan', *MLN*, 111 : 255–74, relies on 'propagation' and a theory of *pietas* to fascinate the reader with new vistas on the relationship between the *Burlador* and Zorrilla's *Don Juan Tenorio*, including a speculative and highly interesting surmisal of the subject of D. Pedro Tenorio's secret talks with the King of Naples in the earlier play. T. H. brings to bear the very different lineage from the later play (another kind of propagation) as well as the differing importance of parentage within the text. *Tirso de*

Molina: His Originality Then and Now, ed. Henry W. Sullivan and R. A. Gallope, Ottawa, Dovehouse, 225 pp., collects papers from a 1990 conference on Tirso held at the University of Missouri-Columbia. In a simply-titled essay that belies its import, J. M. Ruano de la Haza, 'Tirso's stagecraft' (15–39), enlivens for the contemporary reader/ viewer the truly spectacular nature of stagings of Tirso's plays. Mountains, paintings, gardens were carefully simulated not only for the spectacle itself but also to convey precise locations of scenic action; in this regard, R. pointedly signals that the *comedia* far outdistanced Shakespearian productions where a bare stage was more the rule. Bringing us to the 20th-c. stage, C. Larson, 'The uniqueness of Tirso in contemporary stagings: modern audiences meet the master' (40–56), elucidates the afterlife of *Marta la piadosa* as a result of a meeting between the production and reception of a playtext, given a contemporary audience's decidedly distinct horizons of expectations. The audience's reception of an openly sexualized performance, documented by L., attests to Tirso's understanding of the human condition and ability to be translated into a modern staging idiom. A. K. Stoll, 'Metadrama and "quimeras pastoriles": Tirso's *La fingida Arcadia*' (57–70), sees the eponymous play as a satire of the *comedia*. S. relies on Hornby and Brecht for theoretical underpinnings that serve her well, as the play's world is itself a fluid stage. In development of his work on Madrid *comedias* of the 1620s, W. R. Blue, 'A sense of space in five comedies by Tirso' (71–79), observes how characters configure space which, in turn, influences their world outlook; this relationship, B. cogently proposes, permits the reader a more concise understanding of the historico-cultural conditions of the city. D. L. Smith, '*El vergonzoso en palacio*: a play for actors' (80–101), begins with an affirmation that this Tirsian master-piece is about acting. S. deftly combines a reading of the *Cigarrales* and a critique of the play's 1990 Madrid performance to remind the reader/spectator of the fascination produced by theatre/life similarit-ies and to speculate on the actor-audience relationship in 17th-c. Spain. M. L. Stoutz, 'On the significance of the title of Tirso's *El vergonzoso en palacio*' (102–12), explores the varied semantic field elicited by the word 'vergonzoso', the carnival nature of *comedia*, as well as the Dionysian and its relation to pagan ritual. In a clever and provocative essay, V. H. Oakey, 'Chaotic nights on a sunlit stage: four night scenes by Tirso' (113–32), reads darkness in *El vergonzoso en palacio*, *La villana de la Sagra*, *Marta la piadosa*, and *Don Gil de las calzas verdes*, as a way to highlight the 'chaos repressed by cultural norms', exposing them in the light of day in afternoon performances. L. C. Johnson, 'The (ab)uses of characterization in *Don Gil de las calzas verdes*' (133–43), reveals the ties between power, love, and money to show how Tirso tackles the question of identity and character in a very 'post-Modern' reading well ahead of its time. Further applying a Lacanian approach, M. D. Stroud, 'Sainthood and psychoanalysis: Tirso's *Santa Juana*' (144–61), critically binds together hysteria, masochism, and sainthood to reveal how Tirso, in his dramatic trilogy could intuit truths about the human condition that Lacan came to elucidate through a reading of Freud. H. W. Sullivan, 'Sibling symmetry and the incest taboo in Tirso's *Habladme en entrando*' (162–86), continues the tradition of his Lacanian readings of Tirso of yet another unheralded but extraordinary Tirsian *comedia* whose dénouement consists of mixed-sibling marriage. The other Tirsian trilogy is studied by L. Fothergill-Payne, 'The Pizarro trilogy and the question of history: from *ars historica* to New Historicism and beyond' (187–205), who adroitly takes on the history/poetry debate to approach the role played by theatre on a stage where 'historical monologic sources' are never sufficient. F.-P. believes that New Historicists tend to flatten the literary text leaving no room for *admiratio* in Tirso's artful 'blending' of literary and historical readings. J. A. Parr, 'On the authorship, text, and transmission of *El burlador de Sevilla y convidado de piedra*' (206–25), summarizes the seemingly endless debate between pro-Tirso forces (incarnated in L. Vázquez) and the pro-Claramonte ones (protagonized almost single-handedly by Rodríguez López-Vázquez) to attempt to impose closure in this 'authorship war', adducing nicely elaborated philosophical tenets on the 'death of the author', that Tirso is indeed the likely author of the first Don Juan play.

8. Juan Ruiz de Alarcón

B. Simerka, 'Dramatic and discursive genres: *La verdad sospechosa* as problem comedy and marriage treatise', Simerka, *Arte nuevo*, 187–205, divides her essay into six parts in order to offer the reader a well-grounded and wide-ranging synthesis of genre theory to flesh out the multiple discourses that inform Alarcón's 'problem play'. S. rightly sees in this *comedia* the commingling of the literary and the social; an understanding of these discourses, especially *vis-à-vis* marriage, are indispensable to tackling the play.

9. Lope de Vega

F. de Armas, 'The allure of the oriental other: Titan's *Rossa Sultana* and Lope de Vega's *La santa liga*', Friedman, *Brave New Words*, 191–208, further elucidates the relationship between Renaissance painting and the *comedia*, as de Armas has done superbly on other occasions as well, here revealing Lope's comments on Titian, his competition with Cervantes (*La batalla naval*), and his modification of pictorial and emblematic traditions to urge a repositioning of Spain from the margins to the centre of conflict with respect to the question of Islam; the Orient is 'feminized' and not permitted to coexist with the West. A. Robert Lauer, 'A neo-historical reading of *Fuenteovejuna*', *ib.*, 209–19, investigates another aspect of Lope's reading of history and creation of poetry in order to defend the Catholic Kings' centralization of power by weakening the military orders and orchestrating subservience of the people; historical distortions yield a poetically 'true' account of an historical event. R. Castells, '*El caballero de Olmedo* de Lope de Vega: "aojado estás"', *RoN*, 36: 101–10, proffers yet another contribution to further refine the meaning of 'aojado estás'. J. C. de Miguel y Canuto, 'Casi un siglo de crítica sobre el teatro de Lope: de la *Poética* de Luzán (1737) a la de Martínez de la Rosa (1827)', *Criticón*, 62, 1994:33–56, produces an important summary of poetics, concluding that a Neo-Aristotelian orientation predominates; Lope's attempts at tragedy are severely criticized, and his poetic language is praised except for the 'excesses'. Contradictions arise among Lope's later commentators because they critique his plays piecemeal without a reading of the entire corpus. G. M. Burton, 'Deconstruction and the *comedia*: the case for *Peribáñez*', *ib.*, 21–35, examines the concept of resemblance in Derrida's critique of metaphysics in a smooth blending of theory and practice applied to Lope's concept of divine and terrestrial justice. E. H. Friedman, 'Theater semiotics and Lope de Vega's *El caballero de Olmedo*', *ib.*, 66–85, expands work on contemporary *comedia* performance which deny a single, unified 'interpretation' of the text in favour of general questioning of textual 'authority'. Theatre semiotics, for F., forces a look at signs within a 'performance continuum' that begins with a reading and proceeds to performance often in order to take us back to the written text. C. B. Weimer, 'Desire, crisis, and violence in *Fuenteovejuna*: a Girardian perspective', *ib.*, 162–86, successfully applies Girard's theory of mimetic desire that perforce leads to violence and to crisis; ritual sacrifice through the death of Fernán Gómez — which acts, too, as a Derridean *pharmakon* — cleanses both Castile and Fuenteovejuna of destructive desire. T. A. Sears, 'Like father, like son: the paternal perverse in Lope's *El castigo sin venganza*', *BHS(L)*, 73:129–42, reduces Ferraran society to the Duke, whose body politic encloses spectators as well as immediate family members far from being an ideal father, the Duke's exclusion of the maternal leads to a 'devouring father' who ultimately stands alone. J. de José Prades, 'Dignificación de "los peores" de la comedia clásica en e teatro de Lope de Vega', *RLit*, 114:419–32, discusses how Lope too the 'bobo' and 'villano' and dignified him in the figure of the 'gracioso', especially in *El villano en su rincón*, in which Juan Labrador becomes the prototype of 'dignificación'.

10. FRANCISCO DE LA CUEVA Y SILVA

M. Kidd, 'Triangular desire and sensory deception in Francisco de la Cueva y Silva's *Trajedia de Narciso*', *MLN*, 110:271–82, employs Girard's theory of mimetic desire to ascertain that the *Trajedia*, with its dual triangulations of desire and the Narcissus theme, may anticipate both honour and mythological plays of the *comedia nueva*. The esteem in which Cueva y Silva was held by both Cervantes and Lope, according to K., may well have translated into the latter's imitation of his theatre.

11. LUCAS FERNÁNDEZ

F. Maurizi, *'La teatralización del soldado a fines siglo XV', *Criticón*, 66–67:287–305.

12. DIEGO SÁNCHEZ DE BADAJOZ

Criticón, 66–67, dedicates a special issue to 'Diego Sánchez de Badajoz y el teatro de su tiempo'. M. A. Pérez Priego, 'La tradición representacional de la Sibila y la *Farsa del juego de cañas* de Diego Sánchez' (5–15), studies the originality of S.'s play through the tradition of the Sybilian prophecy and the *Ordo Prophetaron*; P.P. tracks their early appearances in Catalonian and Western Peninsular drama in the 15th and 16th centuries. M. Débax and M. Martínez Thomas, 'Las didascalias en la obra teatral de Diego Sánchez de Badajoz' (17–42), focus on stage directions, taking in all parts of the texts, including those concerning authorship and even the contexts of artistic creation; they generate classifications for stage directions and their functions within the dramatic texts. C. Nácher Escriche, 'La retórica de la mezcla en las *Farsas* de Diego Sánchez de Badajoz' (43–56), offers an interesting reading with a theoretical reliance upon both Lacan and Barthes; the very practice of 'mixing' his ingredients, N. explains, is the key to S.'s ability to teach not only Sacred History but also how to see the theatre. A. Iglesias Ovejero, 'Nombres de personajes y figuras tradicionales o tradicionalizadas en la *Recopilación* (1554) de Diego Sánchez de Badajoz' (57–74), employs a semiotic approach to the onomastics of this poetic text, with three principal and five secondary categories. F. Cazal, 'Reglas de escritura en el teatro de Diego Sánchez' (75–104), successfully classifies the generic traits of the 'pastor' in S.'s theatre in an effort to outline a syntax of the character's speech, an important technical aspect of farce. Idem., 'La riña en el teatro de Diego Sánchez de Badajoz' (105–34), gives the reader a companion piece to his previously cited article, here framing the quarrel ('riña') as an important constituting factor in S.'s farce. A. Hermenegildo, 'El control de la fantasía: usos catequísticos en el teatro de Diego Sánchez de Badajoz' (135–45), describes the network of signs employed by S. in his *Farsa teologal*; here the writer reorganizes the traditional order of example followed by religious instructions, to present doctrine followed by a farce, a kind of theatre-within-theatre. C. Sancho, 'Lo cómico y lo devoto en la *Recopilación en metro*' (147–55), applies a well-worn Bakhtinian model to refute critics who see in the *Farsa theologal* and the *Farsa del colmenero* an ambivalent attitude toward doctrinal instruction; the partial carnavalesque structures are introduced as a humoristic element to further those teachings. T. Rodríguez, 'El discurso religioso en el teatro de Diego Sánchez de Badajoz' (157–70), sees in S.'s theatre a strong convergence between religious instruction and a 'voluntad teatral' that produces a catechism fully integrated into the dramatic text. J. García-Varela, 'Para una ideología de la exclusión: el discurso del 'moro' en Sánchez de Badajoz' (171–77), briefly treats an Other within Spanish society, here the *morisco*, first in a Renaissance context and then within the theatre of S; the playwright's discourse concerning the Moor, Jew, and *morisco* is one of exclusion within texts which seek to consolidate one, true religious identity. J. C. Garrot, 'El problema converso en la *Recopilación en metro*' (179–94), summarizes the pro- and anti-*converso* identity issue concerning S., and after careful analysis of the society as well as of S.'s *farsas*, decides that a division among Christians 'de distinto origen' is not a principal factor in the *Recopilación*. G. presents a solid premise in favour of a 'paciencia catequizadora' in S. With fine critical acumen B. F. Weissberger, 'El 'voyeurismo' en el teatro de Diego Sánchez de Badajoz' (195–215), shows how feminist psychoanalytical theories of theatre and film can successfully be brought to bear on an early Renaissance playwright. Through a detailed analysis of the *Farsa de Santa Susaña* and the *Farsa de Tamar*, W. concludes that the 'pastor' becomes a voyeuristic 'double' of the spectator as he beholds the women protagonists of the farces, and that S. thus saw the possibilities that such a character could lend to theatre. A. Molinié-Bertrand, 'Diego Sánchez de Badajoz y los alimentos terrenales' (217–23), lists the foods present in two farces and notes the obvious that bread and wine are recurring themes with symbolic meaning. M. J. Martínez, 'Las farsas profanas de Diego Sánchez de Badajoz' (225–42), comments on two non-religious farces, the *Farsa de la hechicera* and the *Farsa de la ventera*, suggesting possible dates of composition and noting the parodic function of the first and the social commentary made in a comic vein of the second; however, the first of these farces, in M.'s eyes, is unique in S.'s work for the admixture of literary conventions employed. F. Cazal, 'Notas sobre la *Farsa de Moysén* y la *Farsa del Molinero*' (243–86), compiles explanatory notes as well as the texts of the two farces in a laudable effort to facilitate their reading and comprehension by students, thus widening the readership of pre-Lopean theatre texts.

13. ANTONIO DE SOLÍS

F. Serralta, 'Una loa "particular" de Solís y su refundición palaciega', *Criticón*, 62, 1994: 111–44, comments on two versions of a Solís *loa*, in particular the reasons for their creation and the circumstances of their publication, and publishes an edition of both versions that may help to illustrate both the technique of dramatized adulation and Solís' practice of self-recasting.

14. ANONYMOUS

E. Canonica, 'Del pecado plurilingüe a la absolución monolingüe. La *Farsa del sacramento, llamada de los lenguajes*', *Criticón*, 66–67:369–82, explains, in the first study on this anonymous farce, the presence of multiple linguistic registers in a doctrinal work; the 'plurilingualism' of the sinners contrasts with the monolingualism of the allegorical characters, which illustrates in the first a parting from the ways of truth. M. de los Reyes Peña, 'El "Aucto de Thamar" del Ms. B2476 de la Biblioteca de "The Hispanic Society of America": estudio y edición', *ib.* 83–414, traces the *romance* and early theatrical tradition of the Tamar theme, describes the anonymous 'aucto' — which is not the *Farsa de Tamar* of Sánchez de Badajoz — and presents an edition with notes.

LITERATURE, 1700–1823

By GABRIEL SÁNCHEZ ESPINOSA, *Lecturer in Hispanic Studies, The Queen's University of Belfast*

(This survey covers the years 1990–96)

I. BIBLIOGRAPHY AND PRINTING

BIBLIOGRAPHY. F. Aguilar Piñal, *Bibliografía de autores españoles del siglo XVIII*. VII, *R–S*, VIII, *T–Z*, M, CSIC, 1993–95, 926, 706 pp., includes authors like Rodríguez de Campomanes, Samaniego and Sempere y Guarinos, Torres Villarroel, Trigueros, Viera y Clavijo, and the Villanuevas, adding 700 bibliographical references to the previous volumes. Two volumes dedicated to anonymous works, to be published within the next few years, will see the completion of this bibliography. *Short-title Catalogue of Eighteenth-Century Spanish Books in The British Library*, 3 vols, London, British Library, 1994. The first two volumes of the catalogue list in alphabetical order of authors' names, and significant words from the title in the case of anonymous works, something in excess of 6000 different entries: those contained in the voluminous general catalogue of the British Library, to which have been added new items acquired since the end of 1992. The denomination 'Spanish books' covers all the books printed in Spain in any language and those printed in Spanish in Europe — the inclusion of Sephardic texts is particularly welcome. Works printed in Spanish America and the Philippines are not included. The third volume is entirely taken up by four indexes: a subject index; a fascinating index of engravers and artists, evidence of the important function of the visual image and of the quality achieved by the engravings in 18th-c. books; an extremely useful chronological index of works listed according to their printers; and finally an index of places where they were printed.

BOOKS AND PRINTING. G. de Andrés, 'El hispanista Obadiah Rich y la almoneda de libros españoles en Londres en 1824', *BRAH*, 190, 1993:283–311, concerns the auction of books and manuscripts which belonged to the arabist José Antonio Conde. Rich was also involved in the sale of the libraries belonging to Juan de Iriarte and the marqués de Astorga. J. Catalá Sanz and J. Boigues Palomares, *La biblioteca del primer marqués de Dos Aguas. 1707*, Valencia U.P., 1992, 365 pp., is a significant inventory of aristocratic taste at the beginning of the 18th century. G. Lamarca Langa, *La cultura del libro en la época de la Ilustración. Valencia, 1740–1808*, Valencia, Edicions Alfons e Magnànim, 1994, 214 pp., studies 256 library catalogues obtained from 1302 *post mortem* inventories. F. Patier, *La biblioteca de Tomás López*, M, El Museo Universal, 1992, 273 pp., reconstitutes the inventory of the library of the principal map maker of the Spanish Enlightenment. López is one of the best examples of those specialists sent to study abroad on a royal grant. J. Carrete Parrondo, 'La ilustración de los libros. Siglos XV al XVIII', pp. 271–359 of J. Carrete Parrondo et al., *Historia ilustrada del libro español. De los incunables al siglo XVIII* (Biblioteca del Libro, 60), M, Fundación Sánchez Ruipérez, 1994, 586 pp. F. Lopez, 'Antonio Sanz, imprimeur du roi et l'édition populaire sous l'Ancien Régime', *BH*, 95, 1993:349–78, chronicles the confrontation between Curiel, the printing commissioner known for his strictness, and Antonio Sanz, the royal printer, between 1757 and 1766, brought about by the unlicenced printing of pamphlets of popular literature. From the centres of government there is an attempt to increase the legal and ideological controls over this type of popular publication. Broadsides and chap-books, as can be observed in the case of Antonio Sanz, turn out to be, on the other hand, fundamental for the economic survival of printing houses until the last decades of the 18th century. J. Moll Roqueta, *De la imprenta al lector. Estudios sobre el libro español de los siglos XVI al XVIII*, M, Arco Libros, 1994, 174 pp., contains two articles of special interest: 'Tres notas sobre la Imprenta Real' (133–58) and 'Dos inventarios de la imprenta de Joaquín Ibarra' (159–74).

2. THOUGHT AND THE ENLIGHTENMENT

El mundo hispánico en el Siglo de las Luces, 2 vols, M, Editorial Complutense, 1355 pp., gathers together the papers delivered at the first conference of the *Sociedad Española de Estudios del siglo XVIII*, celebrated in Salamanca in June 1994. F. Aguilar Piñal, *Introducción al siglo XVIII* (Historia de la Literatura Española, 25), B, Ediciones Júcar, 1991, 240 pp. *El siglo que llaman ilustrado. Homenaje a Francisco Aguilar Piñal*, ed. J. Álvarez Barrientos and J. Checa Beltrán, M, CSIC, 889 pp. P. Álvarez de Miranda, *Palabras e ideas: el léxico de la Ilustración temprana en España (1680–1760)*, M, RAE, 1992, 743 pp. Id., 'Un relato inédito e inacabado del P. Andrés Merino: la *Monarquía de los Leones*', *Dieciocho*, 16, 1993:13–24. L. Domergue, *La censure des livres en Espagne à la fin de l'Ancien Régime* (Bibliothèque de la Casa de Velázquez 13), M, Casa de Velázquez, 354 pp., makes a series of attempts to examine the phenomenon of civil censorship in 18th-c. Spain. Aspects covered include the legal context of book production; the variety of criteria in the reformist establishment concerning how civil censorship should act — Campillo, Andrés Piquer, Real Academia de la Historia; the personality and practices of the different kinds of censors and reviewers (those attached to the Vicaría eclesiástica de Madrid and those from the Academia de la Historia, with special emphasis on Jovellanos); the criteria used by reformist censors to recommend non-publication or revision of specific works; the dilemmas of the 18th-c. Spanish intellectual confronted by the choice between censorship or self-censorship, with special emphasis on the cases of Cadalso and Arroyal; finally, the various ways in which the main literary genres cohabited with censorship are reviewed. After reading this work one feels the need for a future comparison of the varieties and concrete application of the Spanish case with those of other European government censorships.

J. Gutiérrez, 'Carlo Denina y su defensa de España. Introducción, notas y edición de textos', *Dieciocho*, 15, 1992: 1–82, is a timely edition of a text more often referred to than read. G. edits and situates in its context the translation by the diplomat Manuel de Urcullu on the basis of the Barcelona edition (1786?); also included are the *Cartas críticas para servir de suplemento al discurso*, translated by Urcullu himself (Madrid, 1788). P. Ilie, 'El templo de Minerva en la España del XVIII', *HR*, 59, 1991: 1–23, points to the importance of the polysemous motif of Minerva for the Spanish Enlightenment: crystallization of the hopes and frustrated expectations of the *ilustrados*. S. Jüttner, 'El historiador filósofo: un mito político del Absolutismo Ilustrado', pp. 113–27 of *La secularización de la cultura española en el Siglo de las Luces*, ed. M. Tietz and D. Briesemeister (Wolfenbütteler Forschungen, 53), Wiesbaden, Harrassowitz, 1992, 311 pp. (hereafter Tietz, *Secularización*). I. L. McClelland, *Ideological Hesitancy in Spain 1700–1750*, Liverpool U.P., 1991, 152 pp., highlights the context of the ideological confrontation between scientific experimentalism and scepticism, with particular focus on the publication of *Medicina scéptica* (1725) by Martín Martínez, and distinguishes an ideologically hesitant middle way between *ilustrados* and *anti-ilustrados*; Torres Villarroel is given as the perfect example of such a position. F. Sánchez Blanco, *Europa y el pensamiento español del siglo XVIII*, M, Alianza Editorial, 1991, 414 pp.

3. LITERARY HISTORY

GENERAL. *Historia de la literatura española. Siglo XVIII*, ed. G. Carnero (Historia de la Literatura Española, 6–7), 2 vols, M, Espasa Calpe 1074 pp., produced by a list of 23 collaborators among the mos outstanding in their field, bears witness to the great critical stride made in the study of 18th-c. literature as a result of the intens research activities carried out in the last 15 years. Constant reference are made to the European literary context, within which the case o

Spain is given its rightful place. The pages devoted to the framework and modes of the literary life (education, cultural institutions, the book and the periodical press) are somewhat brief. Chapter 2 brings into focus the starting point of the Spanish Enlightenment without reducing it to the isolated figure of Feijoo and giving Mayans, Sarmiento, Pérez Bayer and Cerdá y Rico the attention they deserve. Chapter 3, written by Sebold in characteristic vein, is devoted to neoclassical doctrine and precepts and to the birth from its midst — Cadalso — of Romanticism. Chapters 4 and 9 deal with poetry, devoting sections to the survival of the Baroque (Gies), to the Rococo in poetry (Gies), to enlightened poetry (Deacon), longer poems (Deacon and Carnero), sensibility (Polt), the *Noches lúgubres* by Cadalso (Sebold), Jovellanos (Polt), Meléndez (Polt), Cienfuegos (Polt) and the poets whose careers spanned both centuries (Carnero and Polt). The variety of critical approaches allows the same author to be dealt with in different sections and avoids the danger of rigid classification and compartmentalization. Furthermore, the attention devoted to authors of the first rank does not exclude the sketching in of minor figures. Four chapters (5, 6, 7 and 10) deal with the theatre, the most important literary genre of the century in the editor's opinion. Obviously it is the genre which is studied in most detail throughout the work. Sufficient attention is given to such aspects as the functioning of *coliseos* and acting companies, the preferences and attitudes of the public, the musical theatre — a genre whose inclusion is welcome, the campaigns for the reform of the theatre, neoclassical aesthetics and theatrical practice, the figures of Tomás de Iriarte and Leandro Fernández de Moratín, the new theatre of sensibility, Jovellanos and Romantic drama (Sebold), the popular dramatists of the end of the century — Rodríguez de Arellano, Valladares de Sotomayor, Comella, and Zavala y Zamora, and finally political theatre during the period of the Guerra de la Independencia. The great prose figures of the second half of the 18th c. are dealt with by leading specialists: Cadalso (Glendinning), Jovellanos (Caso González), Forner (Lopez); the rest of chapter 8 is a swift survey of travel literature which deserves to be treated at greater length. Without a doubt this chapter devoted principally to reformist and ideological prose will leave more than one reader dissatisfied given the absence of certain significant secondary — and also primary — figures of the Spanish Enlightenment and the omission of some subgenres. The final chapter, devoted to narrative and the novel, after an adequate introduction to the genre which situates the Spanish case in a European context, balances the major figures — Torres Villarroel, Isla — with the attention given to the novelists of the final third of the

century, who until a few years ago remained unknown or underval-
ued, seeking to correct the widespread fallacy about the virtual
nonexistence of the novel in 18th-c. Spain. What stands out in this
history is both the fact that it reflects the latest state of the debate and
its usefulness as a working tool. *Historia literaria de España en el siglo
XVIII*, ed. F. Aguilar Piñal, M, Editorial Trotta-CSIC, 1158 pp.,
follows the broad 18th-c. concept of the term 'literature', in other
words, everything that is expressed by means of writing, not limiting
itself to the study of creative works and including both the realms of
letters and of science. It aims to be a history of the written culture of
Spain during the 18th c., and only concerns itself with published texts
of the period. There are two main divisions: literature of erudition
(literary theory and history, philology, philosophy, religion, historiography, antiquarian literature, economics, politics and law, the
sciences, art and music) and literature of creation (poetry, theatre,
novel, essay, popular literature, *costumbrista* and travel literature).
Basically the panorama is chronological within each section and
subgenre. J. Álvarez Barrientos, F. Lopez, and I. Urzainqui, *La
República de las Letras en el siglo XVIII*, M, CSIC, 1995, 226 pp., bring
together three studies not included in the preceding volume: J. Álvarez
Barrientos, 'Los hombres de letras' (19–61) is a good synthesis of his
many recent articles on the situation of the 18th-c. Spanish writer,
the pages devoted to the economic aspects of the writer's career being
of special interest; F. Lopez, 'El libro y su mundo' (63–124) adopts a
consistently European perspective, constituting an excellent introduction to the new ways of approaching the study of the Spanish
Enlightenment provided by the various dimensions of the book world,
with particularly thought-provoking notes (107–09) on a possible
quantitative study of the writing community in 18th-c. Spain based
on F. Aguilar Piñal's *Bibliografía*; I. Urzainqui, 'Un nuevo instrumento
cultural: la prensa periódica' (125–216) undertakes a panoramic
survey of the presence and role of the periodical press during the
Spanish 18th c., a topic lacking or insufficiently dealt with in the
recent histories of 18th-c. Spanish literature published by Aguilar
Piñal and Carnero. J. Álvarez Barrientos, 'El escritor según Tomás
de Iriarte: su plan de una Academia de Ciencias y Buenas Letras'
ALE, 10, 1994:9–35, continues his reconstruction of what the
Spanish 18th-c. intellectual was and wanted to be, in other words the
status of the writer. In this case he refers to the frustrated hopes of the
reformist intellectuals regarding their desire to have an institution
that would protect sciences and letters during the different administra-
tions of Floridablanca; Sarmiento's *Reflexiones literarias* (1743) contain
the seed of Iriarte's plan, an effort to dignify the writer's profession
Godoy shelves the project once and for all in September 179

P. Álvarez de Miranda, 'Las academias de los novatores', pp. 265–300 of *De las Academias a la Enciclopedia: el discurso del saber en la modernidad*, ed. E. Rodríguez Cuadrados, V, Edicions Alfons el Magnànim, 1993, 428 pp. J. Cebrián, 'La Historia literaria de España de los Mohedano: concepto, finalidad y primeros reparos', *Cuadernos de Estudios del Siglo XVIII*, 2, 1992:57–71. A. Gil Novales et al., *Diccionario biográfico del Trienio Liberal*, M, Ediciones El Museo Universal, 1991, 737 pp., is an invaluable tool which should not be ignored despite having ended up all too soon on the reduced counters of department stores. *Ilustración y Neoclasicismo. Primer suplemento*, ed. D. T. Gies and R. P. Sebold (Historia y Crítica de la Literatura Española, 4.1), B, Crítica, 1992.

PROSE. J. Álvarez Barrientos, *La novela en el siglo XVIII* (Historia de la Literatura Española, 28), B, Ediciones Júcar, 1991, 449 pp. J. Álvarez Barrientos, 'Fernando Gutiérrez de Vegas y su novela *Los enredos de un lugar* (1778–1781)', pp. 35–45 of *Art and Literature in Spain: 1600–1800. Studies in honour of Nigel Glendinning*, ed. C. Davis and P. J. Smith, London-Madrid, Tamesis, 1993, 247 pp. (hereafter, *Glendinning Vol.*). J. Álvarez Barrientos, 'El modelo femenino en la novela española del siglo XVIII', *HR*, 63, 1995:1–18. G. Carnero, 'La novela española del siglo XVIII: estado de la cuestión (1985–1995)', *ALE*, 11, 1995:11–35. R. M. Pérez Estévez and R. M. González Martínez, *Pretendientes y pícaros españoles en Roma* (Estudios y Documentos, 50), Valladolid U.P., 1992, 140 pp., is an edition of the text *El passeo de Roma concluido en Nápoles*, an anonymous manuscript of 1736 written in Rome by a Spaniard in search of preferment. M. Tietz, 'El proceso de secularización y la problemática de la novela en el siglo XVIII', Tietz, *Secularización*, 227–46. I. Urzainqui, 'Hacia una tipología de la traducción en el siglo XVIII: los horizontes del traductor', pp. 633–38 of *Traducción y adaptación cultural España-Francia*, ed. M.-L. Donaire and F. Lafarga, Oviedo U.P., 1991, 655 pp. (hereafter Donaire, *Traducción*).

DRAMA. F. Aguilar Piñal, 'Las refundiciones en el siglo XVIII', *CTC*, 5, 1990:33–41. J. Álvarez Barrientos, 'Público y creencia en la comedia de magia', *Homenaje a Alberto Navarro González*, Kassel, Reichenberger, 1990, 5–16. G. Carnero, 'Los dogmas neoclásicos en el ámbito teatral', *ALE*, 10, 1994:37–67. *Teatro politico spagnolo del primo Ottocento*, ed. E. Caldera, Roma, Bulzoni, 1991, 251 pp., covers the period 1808–40, including G. Carnero on Gaspar Zavala y Zamora (19–41) and E. Larraz on Francisco de Paula Martí (105–24); F. Lafarga, 'Teatro político español (1805–1840): ensayo de un catálogo' (167–251). J. Cañas Murillo, 'Una nota sobre la polémica del teatro en el siglo XVIII: el *Manifiesto por los teatros españoles y sus actores* de Manuel García de Villanueva', *AEF*, 15, 1992:27–38. Checa Beltrán, 'Los clásicos en la preceptiva del siglo XVIII', *CTC*,

5, 1990:13–31. P. Deacon, 'The removal of Louis Reynaud as director of the Madrid theatres in 1776', *BHS(L)*, 68, 1991:163–72. M.-J. García Garrosa, *La retórica de las lágrimas. La comedia sentimental española, 1751–1802*, Valladolid U.P., 1990, 272 pp., centres on Spanish translations of French sentimental comedies, from *La razón contra la moda* to the parody *El gusto del día*, emphasizing the thematic analysis of these productions. P. B. Goldman, 'Dramatic works and their readership in eighteenth-century Spain: social stratification and the middle-classes', *BHS(L)*, 66, 1989:129–40. J. Herrera Navarro, *Catálogo de autores teatrales del siglo XVIII*, M, Fundación Universitaria Española, 1993. F. Lafarga, 'El teatro ilustrado en España, entre tradición y modernidad', pp. 143–56 of *Spanien und Europa im Zeichen der Aufklärung*, ed. S. Jüttner, Frankfurt, Lang, 1991, 376 pp. E. Palacios Fernández, 'El teatro barroco en una carta de Bernardo de Iriarte al conde de Aranda (1767)', *CTC*, 5, 1990:43–64. J. Pérez Teijón, *Literatura popular y burlesca del siglo XVIII (léxico y fraseología)*, Salamanca, 1990, 120 pp., studies the literary recreation of popular vocabulary and phraseology in the *sainetes* of Torres Villarroel, González del Castillo, Ramón de la Cruz and the *tonadillas* of the second half of the 18th century. J. M. Sala Valldaura, *El sainete de la segunda mitad del siglo XVIII. La mueca de Talía*, Lérida, Lleida U.P., 1994. J. Vellón Lahoz, 'Lope de Vega y Trigueros: poética y nacionalismo en la dramaturgia española dieciochesca', *Dieciocho*, 19:275–283, deals with the activities of Trigueros in his reworkings of plays by Lope de Vega, within the framework of an attempt at the end of the century to adjust the imagination to the neoclassical unities. At the same time as he participates in the growing tendency to defend Golden Age theatre, he reproduces the sentimental schema of the *comedia lacrimosa*.

PERIODICAL LITERATURE. F. Aguilar Piñal, '*Las Guías de forastero. de Madrid* en el siglo XVIII', *AIEM*, 35, 1995:451–73, traces a panoramic picture of the emergence and development of the *Kalendario particular y Guía de forasteros en la Corte de Madrid*, from its first documented appearance in 1722, but does not discount the possibility of *Guías* for the years immediately before that, of which no trace has been found. These publications are associated between 1722 and 1769 with the Sanz printing family. He situates in Ensenada's period of office a definitive subordination of the *Guía* to government directives. The bibliographical list for this publication between the years 1722 and 1800 (457–73) has extremely useful indications of copies located in Spanish public libraries. J. Álvarez Barrientos, 'E periodista español del siglo XVIII y la profesionalización del escritor', *EHS*, 52–53, 1990:29–40. J. E. de Graef, *Discursos mercurial*

Económico-políticos, ed. and introd. F. Sánchez Blanco, Seville, Fundación El Monte, 251 pp., is an annotated anthology of *discursos*. Sánchez Blanco, who reproduces the scant data known about this foreigner who had settled in the Spain of Fernando VI, sees in him someone actively involved in propagating the principles of the Enlightenment. He contrasts his independent approach to what he defines as the purely technocratic reforming tendencies of Wall, Campomanes and Floridablanca. S.B. presents the hypothesis that the first two issues corresponding to the year 1752, may have appeared after the fall of Ensenada, which occurred in 1754, and suspects behind the façade of Graef the existence of a pro-Ensenada faction, anxious to remain in the shadows. He sees in the pro-Ensenada tendency of the periodical the cause of its suppression by Wall in November 1756. *La Pensadora Gaditana*, ed. C. Canterla, Cadiz U.P., 275 pp., is an anthology of 17 of the 52 *pensamientos* which appeared in this periodical printed in Cadiz in 1763–64. The editor comes out in favour of the real existence of Beatriz Cienfuegos. 'Periodismo e Ilustración en España', *EHS*, 52–53, 1991, is a special issue which brings together papers given at the international conference on Spanish periodical literature of the 18th c., organized by the Instituto de Filología of the CSIC and held in Madrid in November 1989. I. Urzainqui, 'Crítica teatral y secularización: *El Memorial Literario* (1784–1797)', *BH*, 94, 1992:203–43, situates drama criticism from the viewpoint of a civil ethic based on a reformist ideology.

VERSE. R. P. Sebold, 'Periodización y cronología de la poesía setecentista española', *ALE*, 8, 1992:175–92. J.-M. Sala Valldaura, 'La poesía contrarrevolucionaria (1793–1795): Forner, el conde de Noroña y González del Castillo', *RLit*, 57, 1995:83–107.

4. INDIVIDUAL AUTHORS

ÁLVAREZ DE TOLEDO. J. Garau Amengual, 'La poesía solemne de Gabriel Álvarez de Toledo', *AH*, 225, 1991:147–79.

ÁLVAREZ DE CIENFUEGOS. R. Froldi, 'La tragedia *Idomeneo* de Álvarez de Cienfuegos', *Entresiglos*, 2, 1993:145–55. Á. G. Loureiro, 'La poesía de la muerte de Álvarez de Cienfuegos: el deseo de la razón produce monstruos', *HR*, 60, 1992:435–56, analyses his poem 'La escuela del sepulcro' in the tradition of *Night Thoughts* by Edward Young.

AMAR Y BORBÓN, J. *Discurso sobre la educación física y moral de las mujeres*, ed. M.-V. López Cordón, M, Cátedra-Instituto de la Mujer, 1994, 270 pp. C. Sullivan, 'Josefa Amar y Borbón and the Royal Aragonese Economic Society', *Dieciocho*, 15, 1992:95–148.

ARROYAL. J. Pallarés Moreno, *León de Arroyal o la aventura intelectual de un ilustrado*, Granada U.P.–Oviedo, Instituto Feijoo de Estudios del siglo XVIII, 1993, 295 pp.

AZARA. G. Sánchez Espinosa, *Las memorias de José Nicolás de Azara (ms. 20121 de la BNM)*, Frankfurt, Lang, 1994, 529 pp., is a doctoral thesis which edits for the first time the complete text of the diplomat's memoirs (315–519).

BLANCO WHITE, J. *Obra poética completa*, ed. A. Garnica and J. Díaz García, M, Visor, 1994, 448 pp. M. Murphy, *Blanco White: Self-Banished Spaniard*, New Haven–London, Yale U.P., 1989, 270 pp.

CAMPILLO, J. *Dos escritos políticos: Lo que hay de más y menos en España. España despierta.*, ed. and introd. D. Mateos Dorado (Clásicos Asturianos del Pensamiento Político, 3), Oviedo, Junta General del Principado de Asturias, 1993, lxx + 233 pp.

COMELLA. F. Huerta Viñas, 'Un cambio ideológico en el teatro, visto a través de tres obras de Comella', *Entresiglos*, 2, 1993:171–82. I. L. McClelland, 'The Comellan conception of stage-realism', *Dieciocho*, 16, 1993:111–18.

CRUZ. M. Coulon, **Le sainete à Madrid à l'époque de don Ramón de la Cruz*, Pau U.P., 1993. J. M. Sala Valldaura, 'Bases y tópicos morales de los sainetes de Ramón de la Cruz', *ALE*, 8, 1992:157–74. Ramón de la Cruz, *Sainetes*, ed. J. M. Sala Valldaura, B, Crítica, 470 pp, includes as an appendix C.'s prologue to the 1786–91 edition of his *Teatro*.

FEIJOO Y MONTENEGRO. R. Alarcón Sierra, 'La prensa en el siglo XVIII. El Padre Feijoo y Luis de Cueto: una polémica sobre la *Gaceta de Zaragoza*', *Cuadernos de Estudios del Siglo XVIII*, 2, 1992:3–28. R. Haidt, 'How should medicine know the body: Feijoo's *El médico de sí mismo*', *Dieciocho*, 19:7–26, compares Feijoo's *discurso*, José Gazola's *El mundo engañado de los falsos médicos* (1729), and Francisco Arias Carrillo's *El médico de sí mismo u el arte de conservarse la salud por el instinto* (1733), within the context of the polemic between empiristas and galenistas.

FERNÁNDEZ DE MORATÍN, L. *Apuntaciones sueltas de Inglaterra*, ed. A. Rodríguez Fischer, B, PPU, 1992. Id., *La comedia nueva. El sí de las niñas*, ed. J. Pérez Magallón, B, Crítica, 1994, 355 pp., includes a splendid collection of footnotes. Id., *Poesías completas*, ed. J. Pérez Magallón, B, Sirmio, 1995, 628 pp., is a magnificently annotated edition based on the section *Poesías sueltas* from *Obras dramáticas y líricas* (1825) to which are added the poems that the author did not want to include in his Paris edition. The introduction situates Moratín's poetics in their context, as well as providing an excellent biographical summary. J. Dowling, 'El comerciante gaditano: el Don Roque de Moratín', *Dieciocho*, 16, 1993:67–76.

FERNÁNDEZ DE MORATÍN, N. *Arte de putear*, ed. I. Colón Calderón and G. Garrote Bernal, Málaga, Ediciones Aljibe, 1995, 239 pp. Id., *La Petimetra. Desengaños al teatro español. Sátiras*, ed. D. T. Gies and M.-Á. Lama, M, Castalia-Comunidad de Madrid, 219 pp. P. Deacon, '¿Quién fue la Dorisa de Nicolás Fernández de Moratín?', *Dieciocho*, 16, 1993 : 49–65, rejects her identification with Francisca Ladvenant, the actress's sister and with his wife Isidora Cabo Conde. A character more literary than real in the tradition of the love elegy in Roman literature.

FORNER. F. Aguilar Piñal, 'Los *Discursos filosóficos* de Forner', *REE*, 48, 1992 : 95–106.

GALLEGO. L.-F. Díaz Larios, 'Juan Nicasio Gallego: un poeta entre siglos', *Entresiglos*, 2, 1993 : 99–108.

GARCÍA DE LA HUERTA. R. Andioc, 'De estornudos, flatos y otros modos de "dispersar". (Huerta y los fabulistas: un nuevo poema satírico)', *Dieciocho*, 16, 1993 : 25–48. P. Deacon, 'Vicente García de la Huerta y el círculo de Montiano: la amistad entre Huerta y Margarita Hickey', *REE*, 44, 1988 : 395–421. M.-Á. Lama, *La poesía de Vicente García de la Huerta*, Cáceres, Universidad de Extremadura, 1993.

GARCÍA MALO. G. Carnero, '*Doña María Pacheco* y las normas de la tragedia neoclásica', *Dieciocho*, 17, 1994 : 107–27. I. García Malo, *Doña María Pacheco, mujer de Padilla*, ed. G. Carnero, M, Cátedra, 172 pp., situates the conservative message of this neoclassical tragedy, first performed in 1789 and hostile to rebellion against royal authority, in the political context of the period between the beginning of the French Revolution and Fernando VII's return from France, a context in which the character of María Pacheco and the episode of the rebellion of the Comuneros are transformed into the political symbol which they would become for the literary and political liberalism of the first half of the 19th century. Id., *Voz de la naturaleza*, ed. and introd. G. Carnero, M, Támesis, 1995, 393 pp., reconstructs the biography and work of this forgotten writer, with an edition of eight of the 12 novels in the collection that appeared between 1787 and 1803. The novel *El benéfico Eduardo* (1803) provides a model of enlightened philanthropy.

GÓMEZ ORTEGA. F.-J. Puerto Sarmiento, *Ciencia de Cámara. Casimiro Gómez Ortega (1741–1818). El científico cortesano* (Estudios sobre la Ciencia, 17), M, CSIC, 1992, 369 pp.

GONZÁLEZ DEL CASTILLO. J. M. Sala Valldaura, '*Hannibal* de González del Castillo, en los inicios del melólogo', *AF*, 14, 1991 : 49–76.

ISLA, J.-F. DE *Historia del famoso predicador fray Gerundio de Campazas, alias Zotes*, ed. and introd. J. Álvarez Barrientos, B, Planeta, 1991, has an introduction summarizing the varied and changing response to this novel and situates it in relation to the broad perspective of renewal of this genre in Europe around the middle of the 18th century. Id., *Historia del famoso predicador fray Gerundio de Campazas, alias Zotes*, ed. and introd. J. Jurado, M, Gredos, 1992, 975 pp. R. Haidt, 'Fray Gerundio and luxury: the rococo aesthetics of feminized form', *Dieciocho*, 17, 1994:143–63.

JOVELLANOS, G.-M. *Obras Completas. Tomo IV: Correspondencia 3 (Abril, 1801–Setiembre, 1808). Tomo V: Correspondencia 4 (Octubre, 1808–1811)*, ed. and introd. J.-M. Caso González, Oviedo, Instituto Feijoo de Estudios del Siglo XVIII, 1988–90, 594, 638 pp., bring together the complete letters of Jovellanos and his correspondents in a collection of 2091 documents perfectly annotated and ordered in chronological sequence. Id., *Memoria en defensa de la Junta Central. Tomo I. Memoria. Tomo II. Apéndices*, ed. and introd. J.-M. Caso González (Clásicos Asturianos del Pensamiento Político, 1), 2 vols, Oviedo, Junta General del Principado de Asturias, 1992. Id., *Obras Completas. Tomo VI: Diario 1 (Cuadernos I a V, hasta 30 de agosto de 1794)*, ed. and introd. J.-M. Caso González and J. González Santos, Oviedo, Instituto Feijoo de Estudios del Siglo XVIII, 1994, 653 pp., is the latest instalment, so far, of one of the most important and successful achievements in contemporary 18th-c. studies. Let us hope that the death of Professor Caso will not mean the abandonment of this project which is as fundamental for our field as it is for Hispanism in general. J.-M. Caso González, 'La experiencia de un editor de cartas dieciochistas', *Cuadernos de Estudios del Siglo XVIII*, 2, 1992:45–56, gives a summary of the criteria used in his editions based on his experience with the correspondance and diaries of Jovellanos. As far as the translation of 18th-c. texts is concerned, his general rule is to modernize spelling, accentuation and punctuation. He favours writing out abbreviations in full. His criteria regarding footnotes are explained. Id., 'Jovellanos y su tiempo', *BHS(L)*, 68, 1991:91–105.

LEÓN Y MANSILLA. N. Glendinning, 'La Soledad tercera de José León y Mansilla (1718)', *BHS(L)*, 68, 1991:13–24, associates the survival of gongorism in the early decades of the 18th c. with the desire of the upper echelons to maintain traditional Spanish values, given their sense of insecurity *vis-à-vis* the new Bourbon regime.

LOBO. I. Arellano, 'Notas sobre poesía dieciochesca: las obras festivas de Eugenio Gerardo Lobo', *Notas y Estudios Filológicos*, 7, 1992:12–31. Id., '*El triunfo de las mujeres*, loa mariana y sacra del poeta dieciochesco Eugenio Gerardo Lobo (materiales para el estudio del género y su evolución)', *Criticón*, 55, 1992:141–61.

LUZÁN, I. DE. *Obras raras y desconocidas*, ed. and introd. G. Carnero, Zaragoza, IFC, 1990, 220 pp., includes among other items the *Carta latina de Ignacio Philalethes* (1743) and the *Plan de una Academia de Ciencias y Artes* (1750–51). Id., *Arte de hablar, o sea, Retórica de las conversaciones. Se añaden los Avisos de Isócrates a Demónico, traducidos del griego,* ed. and introd. M. Béjar Hurtado, M, Gredos, 1991, 230 pp. Id., *La virtud coronada,* ed. and introd. F. Jarque Andrés (Ottawa Hispanic Studies, 9), Ottawa, Dovehouse, 1992, 222 pp. C. Barbolani, 'La razón contra la moda: reflexiones sobre Luzán traductor', Donaire, *Traducción,* 551–59. M.-A. Figueras, 'Para "mi Poética basta lo dicho"'. Luzán, Montiano, Llaguno y la segunda edición de la Poética', *Tropelías,* 2, 1991:23–40.

MARCHENA, J.   Marchena, *Obra española en prosa (historia, política y literatura),* ed. and introd. J.-F. Fuentes, M, Centro de Estudios Constitucionales, 1990, 281 pp., is an annotated anthology. It includes the speeches published in *El Observador* (1787) and his *Discurso sobre la literatura española* (1819).

MAYANS Y SISCAR, G.   *Escritos literarios,* ed. and introd. J. Pérez Magallón, M, Taurus, 1994, 418 pp., is an annotated anthology for university students, representative of Mayans's writings on literary themes during his long career.

MELÉNDEZ VALDÉS.   J. H. R. Polt, 'Juan Meléndez Valdés's translations from the Latin', *Dieciocho,* 16, 1993:119–30. R. Haidt, '*Los besos de amor* and *La maja desnuda*: the fascination of the senses in the Ilustración', *REH,* 29, 1995:477–503, sees the cycle of anacreontic poems *Los besos de amor* by Meléndez and the *Maja desnuda* by Goya as an illustration of the new sensibility regarding the erotic among the Spanish enlightened minorities.

MONTENGÓN Y PARET, P.   *El Rodrígo. Eudoxia. Selección de Odas,* ed. and introd. G. Carnero, 2 vols, Alicante, Instituto Juan Gil Albert, 1990. G. Carnero, *Pedro Montengón y Paret,* Alicante, Caja de Ahorros Provincial de Alicante, 1991. Id., 'Pedro Montengón (1745–1824): un poeta entre dos siglos', *HR,* 59, 1991:125–41, addresses the question of self-censorship in his compositions on American and reformist themes in the editions published in Ferrara (1778–79) and Madrid (1794) of the *Odas de Filópatro.*

MOR DE FUENTES.   E. Quintana Pareja, 'José Mor de Fuentes y la escritura autobiográfica de su tiempo', pp. 333–42 of *Escritura autobiográfica,* ed. J. Romera Castillo et al., M, Visor, 1993, 505 pp.

MUÑOZ.   M.-T. Nava Rodríguez, 'Robertson, Juan Bautista Muñoz y la Academia de la Historia', *BRAH,* 187, 1990:435–55.

NASARRE, B.   **Disertación o prólogo sobre las comedias de España,* ed. J. Cañas Murillo, Cáceres, Universidad de Extremadura, 1992.

PÉREZ BAYER, F.   *Por la libertad de la literatura española,* ed. A. Mestre, Alicante, Instituto Juan Gil Albert, 1991, 597 pp.

QUINTANA, M.-J. *Memoria del Cádiz de las Cortes*, ed. F. Durán López, Cádiz U.P., 214 pp.

RODRÍGUEZ CAMPOMANES. V. Llombart, *Campomanes, economista y político de Carlos III*, M, Alianza Editorial, 1992, 407 pp. C. de Castro, *Campomanes, estado y reformismo ilustrado*, M, Alianza Editorial, 540 pp.

TORRES VILLARROEL. E. Martínez Mata, *Los 'Sueños' de Torres Villarroel*, Salamanca U.P., 1990, 179 pp. E. Martínez Mata, 'La predicción de la muerte del rey Luis I en un almanaque de Diego de Torres Villarroel', *BH*, 92, 1990:837–45, reveals that the controversial almanach of 1724 has not been lost, as was thought. A copy has survived in the library of Bartolomé March in Madrid, under the title *Melodrama astrológico*. Torres included it in subsequent anthologies of his works as corresponding to the year 1726. Torres wanted to hide the actual text of his partly successful prediction, once its accuracy had made him famous.

MARQUÉS DE UREÑA (G. MOLINA Y ZALDÍVAR). *El viaje europeo del marqués de Ureña*, ed. with commentary M. Pemán Medina, Cadiz, Unicaja, 1992, 687 pp., is an edition of the manuscript of the memoirs of his travels through France, England and the Low Countries. An enlightened journey: U. is interested in arts, institutions, industry, sciences and customs. He leaves Cadiz in the Spring of 1787 and is back in Spain in October 1788. Of particular interest are his reflections about the economies of France and England and his notes about music.

VELÁZQUEZ. P. Deacon, 'Portrait of an eighteenth-century Spanish intellectual: Luis Joseph Velázquez', *Glendinning Vol.*, 105–16.

ZAVALA Y ZAMORA. R. Fernández Cabezón, *Lances y batallas: Gaspar Zavala y Zamora y la comedia heroica*, Valladolid, Aceña, 1990. G. Zavala y Zamora, *Obras narrativas*, ed. G. Carnero, B, Sirmio, 1992, 269 pp., has editions of *La Eumenia, o la Madrileña* (1805), his original novel, and *Oderay* (1804), a translation from the French.

LITERATURE, 1823–1898

By DEREK FLITTER, *Senior Lecturer in Modern Spanish Language and Literature, University of Birmingham.*

1. GENERAL

David S. Zubatsky, *Spanish, Catalan, and Galician Literary Authors of the Eighteenth and Nineteenth Centuries: An Annotated Guide to Bibliographies*, Metuchen–NY, 1995, 156 pp., includes essayists, journalists, linguists, and literary critics among his authors in a valuable reference guide. Tomás Rodríguez Sánchez, *Catálogo de dramaturgos españoles del XIX, M, Fundación Universitaria Española, 1994, 685 pp. *Poesía española del siglo XIX*, ed. Jorge Urrutia, M, Cátedra, 1995, 558 pp., has a balanced, informed and closely argued introduction that is profusely documented — especially that section dealing with the first half of the century — and intellectually stimulating. The selection inclines towards breadth, rather than depth, of coverage, a sensible option when even the non-specialist reader will already be familiar with poets like Espronceda and Zorrilla (nine and seven poems respectively) but unlikely to know even Ruiz Aguilera and Selgas. David Thatcher Gies, *The Theatre in Nineteenth-Century Spain*, CUP, 1994, 392 pp., is an authoritative contribution to what is a dauntingly broad field, one that goes well beyond the canonical texts in its indefatigable and perceptive coverage of all aspects of the theatre. The study is predominantly chronological, but shrewdly and seamlessly establishes a thematic direction in each of its major chapters — theatre and dictatorship for the first third of the century and a substantive chapter centred on women and the theatre are two examples, the end result being a stimulating survey volume that is meticulously documented, internally coherent and remarkably lucid, from the initial overview to the conflicting visions of neo-Romanticism and Realism that conclude the volume. A Spanish version, *El teatro en la España del siglo XIX*, 546 pp., appeared under the same imprint in 1995. Charles Ganelin, *Rewriting Theatre: The Comedia and Nineteenth-Century Refundición*, Lewisburg, Bucknell U.P., 1994, 272 pp., considers the role of the *refundición* in the evolutionary processes of literary history, with major chapters on *La estrella de Sevilla* (versions by Trigueros and Hartzenbusch); *Marta la piadosa* and *El alcalde de Zalamea* (as reworked by López de Ayala). The principal thrust of G.'s argument considers the dialogue between each successive *refundición* and the original text, contending that in this creative interaction the canon is progressively critiqued and an amended legacy transmitted. Lou Charnon-Deutsch, *Narratives of Desire: Nineteenth-Century Spanish Fiction by Women*,

Pennsylvania State U.P., 1994, 223 pp., deals impressively with issues of female subjectivity, desire and bourgeois domestic ideology in challenging the sexual ideology of traditional canon formation. Chapters on the prominent Cecilia Böhl de Faber, Rosalía de Castro, and Pardo Bazán are complemented by substantial material on the much lesser known María del Pilar Sinués de Marco. In a sensitive discussion, the author illuminates competing desires and ideologies in their problematic relationship to the existing patriarchal system of social order. N. Santiáñez-Tió, 'El héroe decadente en la novela española moderna (1842–1912)', *BBMP*, 71, 1995:179–216, surveys 23 novels from Romanticism to the 'Generation of 1898', including works by Alarcón, Galdós, Valera, Pardo Bazán, and Alas. Carlos Moreno Hernández, *Literatura y cursilería*, Valladolid U.P., 1995, 199 pp., is an adventurous study — M.H. describes his book as an exploratory journey — that maps out conceptually and contextually the history of *lo cursi* as indissolubly associated with the appearance and uneven consolidation of the Spanish bourgeoisie. Specific chapters are dedicated to Zorrilla, Bécquer, Campoamor, and Clarín, in a book that valuably complements existing studies of the aesthetic and intellectual currents prominent in 19th-c. Spain. D. Gies, 'Lost jewels and absent women: toward a history of the theatre in nineteenth-century Spain', *CH*, 17, 1995:81–93, sets out several of the larger issues detailed in his volume on the theatre, of which this essay was originally a foretaste. J. B. Monleón, 'Vampiros y donjuanes (sobre la figura del seductor en el siglo XIX)', *RHM*, 48, 1995:19–30, relates a variety of literary material — from Zorrilla to Galdós and Pardo Bazán — to the structures, tensions, and intimate contradictions of bourgeois patriarchy. A. Ezama, *'Cuentos locos y literatura fantástica. Aproximación a su historia entre 1868 y 1910', *Anthropos*, 154–55, 1994:77–82. L. Litvak, *'Entre lo fantástico y la ciencia ficción. El cuento espiritista en el siglo XIX', *ib.*, 83–88. J. Rubio Jiménez, 'Teatro y política: *Las aleluyas vivientes* de José María Gutiérrez de Alba', *CH*, 17, 1995:127–41, helps to fill a gap in our knowledge of 19th-c. Spanish theatre. C. García Antón, 'Temas cervantinos en el teatro español del siglo XIX: "El licenciado Vidriera"', *RLit*, 57, 1995:529–42, regards the *refundiciones* by Romero Larrañaga and González Elipe as closer to Cervantes than Moreto's much earlier text. E. Lewis, 'Riquísimos mosaicos de perlas desechadas: una versión modernista del *Tenorio*', *CH*, 17, 1995:52–64, analyses the creative dialogue between Careta y Vidal's *El audaz don Juan Tenorio* of 1897 and the broader Don Juan Tradition. A. Andreu, 'María Guerrero: ficción y mito', *ib.*, 9–21, revises the image of the actress communicated by early biographies.

2. ROMANTICISM

Derek Flitter, *Teoría y crítica del romanticismo español*, CUP, 1995, 322 pp., a revisionist study of the reception of Romantic ideas in Spain in the first half of the 19th c., is a Spanish version of the author's *Spanish Romantic Literary Theory and Criticism*, CUP, 1992 (see *YWMLS*, 55 : 384). Celia Romea Castro, *Barcelona romántica y revolucionaria. Una imagen literaria de la ciudad, década de 1833 a 1843*, B, Universitat de Barcelona, 1994, 407 pp., is an ambitious volume covering local topography, social structures, and political organization as well as developments in literature and aesthetics; it is thus inevitably somewhat schematic, but none the less an invaluable point of reference. The selection of literary 'Anexos' and extensive 'Bibliografía' are enlightening, as is the detailed information on figures such as the elusive Monlau or 'Covert-Spring'.

The first part of *CH*, 18.1, headed 'The Romantic Movement in Spain', reproduces papers from the Symposium that formed part of the 1994 Kentucky Foreign Language Conference. P. Bly, 'Mesonero Romanos and the pleasures of the imagination' (7–14), stresses that M.R.'s *costumbrista* writings are more than just facsimile copies of contemporary reality, rephrasing Larra in stating that Mesonero 'mira, y si no ve, imagina muy bien'. B. Dendle, '*Las ruinas de mi convento*, a Romantic novel by Fernando Patxot' (15–24), sees his chosen text as a fully fledged example of Spain's broadly conservative Romanticism and as a novel of some originality that fully merited its contemporary fame. D. Flitter, 'The Romantic theology of *Los amantes de Teruel*' (25–34), delineates an intertextual relationship according to which Hartzenbusch's play is seen effectively to counter Rivas's *Don Alvaro*, and in so doing to initiate the move towards those more traditionalist prescriptions of later Romantic drama. S. García Castañeda, 'Eugenio de Tapia, escritor de costumbres' (35–41), takes an expansive view of life and work, locating his author as 'uno de aquellos españoles liberales en política y conservadores en literatura' whose work manifested broader tensions between the influx of foreign ideas and a *casticista* sense of national identity. G. Gullón, 'Notas sobre un nuevo contexto para el estudio del romanticismo' (42–49), indicates the urgency of a fresh consensus regarding Spanish Romanticism, underlining the importance of passion in the Romantic text. M. Iarocci, 'Enrique Gil y Carrasco en la evolución del sentimiento lírico postromántico' (50–58), identifies in Gil's verse an essential Romantic metaphysics, a poetic cosmology anchored in the apprehension of a supernatural world, rooted in the eighteenth century but culminating only in Bécquer and Rosalía de Castro. S. Miller, 'From the "Introducción sinfónica" to "Madrid moderno":

ideas concerning the post-canonical Bécquer' (59–66), detects the seeds of a 'post-exalted', more realistic writer in pieces as early as 'El rayo de luna', 'Tres fechas' and the 'Cartas literarias', more prominent in the post-1868 writings and suggestive of a radically different approach that an older Bécquer might have followed. R. Sebold, 'Poética de la duda religiosa en el verso de Bermúdez de Castro' (67–74), locates the entirety of Bermúdez's poetic production within a sceptical informing tradition — roving from Cadalso to Bécquer, with some quotes misleadingly stripped of a proper context — in a densely textured survey. P. Silver, 'The politics of Spanish Romanticism' (75–80), in an iconoclastic essay, points to the shortcomings of ideologically loaded perspectives that project a 'dogmatic link between Spanish romanticism and Liberalism' and proposes instead a view of the Spanish movement as essentially a *Biedermeier* one. T. Vilarós, 'La Renaixença catalana: romanticismo y construcción nacional' (81–89), argues that a Romantic framework facilitated the integration of Catalan regionalist sentiment into a progressive Europeanism, regarding Romanticism as a means of recuperation and reconstruction.

The *Centro Internacional de Estudios sobre el Romanticismo Hispánico* has produced the proceedings of two of its triennial conferences: *Romanticismo 5. Actas del V Congreso (Nápoles, 1–3 de Abril de 1993): La sonrisa romántica (sobre lo lúdico en el Romanticismo hispánico)*, Rome, Bulzoni, 1995; and, with admirable promptness, *Romanticismo 6. Actas del VI Congreso (Nápoles, 27–30 de Marzo de 1996): El costumbrismo romántico*, Rome, Bulzoni, 303 pp. The latter collected papers bear out Leonardo Romero's reference to a multifaceted *costumbrismo* containing 'semillas de contradicción y de complejidad', although most contributors employ the phrase 'costumbrismo romántico' without regarding it as an oxymoron. J. Alvarez Barrientos, 'Costumbrismo y ambiente literario en *Los españoles pintados por sí mismos*' (21–27), looks at the perceived status of the profession of writer in the early part of the 19th c.; L. Basalisco, 'Los artículos costumbristas de E. Gil y Carrasco (1815–46) en el *Semanario Pintoresco Español*' (29–34), takes a brief and schematic look at three of the articles; E. Caldera, 'La vocación costumbrista de los románticos' (45–52), sees a 'clave costumbrista' at the heart of contemporary interpretations of Romanticism; M. Cantos Casenave, ' "Gitanofilia": de algunos rasgos costumbristas del "género andaluz" ' (65–70), details part of the fashionable recovery of 'lo andaluz'; M. Cattaneo, 'Del costumbrismo de Larra a la "visión alucinada" de Nieva: *Sombra y quimera de Larra*' (71–79), appraises the 1976 'adaptation' of *No más mostrador*; T. Cirillo Sirri, 'Notas costumbristas del Duque de Rivas en Nápoles' (81–88), introduces some epistolary material as well as R.'s account of his trip to the ruins of Paestum; M. Comellas Aguirrezábal, 'La reacción antirromántica de Mesonero Romanos' (89–101), would have benefited from a consideration of Mesonero's literary articles in the *Semanario Pintoresco Español*, which contradict much of the thrust of a piece based on too selective a use of material; F. Crespo Giménez, 'El costumbrismo exótico de Mariano Fortuny' (103–08), illustrates — with plates and commentary — Fortuny's artistic concerns; L. Díaz Larios, 'Los viajeros costumbristas' (109–16), looks at a broad selection of travellers' tales, their changing emphases and sources of inspiration; J. Escobar, 'Costumbrismo: estado de la cuestión' (117–26), views *costumbrismo* as rooted in 18th-c. aesthetics and as alien to Romanticism, although the absence of reference to Fernán Caballero at least partly disables the thesis; M. P. Espín Templado, 'El costumbrismo como materia teatral durante el período romántico' (127–34), in exploring a neglected facet of *costumbrismo* emphasises the dramatic potential of the 'cuadro'; H. Felten and K. Weingärtner, '¿Costumbrismo romántico? Observaciones en torno a la estructura intertextual de *El estudiante de Salamanca*' (135–42), reinterpret *costumbrismo* by positing Espronceda's use of Romantic motifs as a series of 'costumbres textuales'; A. Ferraz Martínez, 'Pintar, retratar, daguerreotipar' (143–54), carefully documents Spanish interest in the pioneering work of Daguerre and its direct and indirect implications for *costumbrismo*; D. Flitter, 'Historia y pueblo en el costumbrismo romántico: Fernán Caballero y la capilla de Valme' (155–61), drawing chiefly on *La familia de Alvareda*, reinforces Javier Herrero's view of Fernán Caballero's *costumbrismo* as firmly anchored in Romantic traditionalism; R. Froldi, 'Anticipaciones dieciochescas del costumbrismo romántico' (163–69), revisits a series of 18th-c. texts felt to have paved the way for a fully fledged *costumbrismo* that F. considers 'creación del Romanticismo'; S. García Castañeda, 'El pintoresco mundo de la calle o las costumbres del día en aleluyas' (171–76), takes an amusing and illuminating look at some enduring satirical motifs; P. Garelli, 'Aspectos del costumbrismo periodístico de Manuel Bretón de los Herreros' (179–87), surveys some long-neglected articles as a foretaste of her forthcoming critical edition; D. Gies, 'Costumbrismo y magia: un curioso manual sobre *La mágica blanca* de 1833' (189–97), effectively links his subject with contemporary preference for the *comedia de magia*; J. Gómez Montero, 'Los límites de la representación en la lírica costumbrista' (199–207), traces a contradictory pattern of convergence and ludic divergence binding and severing *costumbrista* verse and Romantic lyric; A. González Troyano, 'Los espacios privilegiados de la Andalucía de Estébanez' (209–12), examines Estébanez's tavern settings as *casticista* examples of a seamless and stable society; L. de Llera, 'Tertulias románticas y modernistas en el Madrid castizo' (213–21), in a rather disjointed essay, locates *costumbrismo* as effective bridge between Romantic *Parnasillo* and *modernista* literary circles; F. J. Martín, 'El problema de España y el proyecto ilustrado en el costumbrismo de Larra' (223–29), feels that Larra's concerns transcend those of contemporary *costumbrismo* and should thus be considered within a much broader historical picture running from Enlightenment to *Desastre*; D. Montalto Cessi, 'El epígrafe espejo de los costumbristas' (231–37), takes up Correa Calderón's invitation to examine these citations; M. P. Palomo, 'Texto e imagen en el *Semanario Pintoresco*: Mesonero y Alenza' (239–47), elucidates the historical development of the 'grabado costumbrista' with close attention to Mesonero's *Semanario Pintoresco*, examining the relationship between illustration and text and emphasizing the increasingly independent stature of the former; G. Pozzi, 'Imágenes de la mujer en el costumbrismo' (249–57), reveals the insistent presence of the paradigms of woman-hood favoured by patriarchal control; A. Ramos Santana, 'Las tabernas, escenarios costumbristas' (259–63), surveys examples of a familiar setting which encouraged the broad brush-strokes of *costumbrista* description to be supplemented by a degree of detail supplied by the reader's experience; A. Reina Palazón, 'El costumbrismo en la pintura sevillana del siglo XIX' (265–73), ascribes the pre-eminence of *costumbrista* painting in Seville to Romantic 'populist' theories of nationhood, difference and cultural identity; A. Romero Ferrer, 'La proyección teatral y romántica de Andalucía: "El género andaluz"' (275–84), examines the idealized vision of Andalucía contained in this comic theatre, viewing it as entirely representative of Romantic *costumbrismo*; L. Romero Tobar, 'La descripción costumbrista en los viajes aéreos' (285–98), considers the potential of ascent by balloon for creating a new descriptive technique, one available to but not adopted by *costumbrista* writers; D. Shaw. 'La pintura... festiva, satírica y moral de las costumbres' (299–303), examines *costumbrismo* as a 'reconceptualization' of national history and cultural identity motivated by an ideologically loaded contemplation of reality.

P. Menarini, '*Zelmiro*, de José Andrew de Covert-Spring: la primera traducción española de *Antony*', *CH*, 17, 1995:94–103, takes a fascinating look at a previously unknown Spanish version antedating that of Eugenio de Ochoa. L. Romero Tobar, 'Drama romántico y relato corto, un caso de poéticas fronterizas', *ib.*, 117–26, explores the symbiotic relationship between the two genres, specifying connections between Rivas's *Don Alvaro* and an anonymous tale entitled 'El ermitaño' appearing days after the play's première. C. Moreno Hernández, 'Lo cursi y lo grotesco: algunos aspectos del romanticismo español', *RHM*, 48, 1995:7–18, sees the two discrete elements as pertaining respectively to a triumphant traditionalist Romanticism exemplified by Zorrilla and a radical 'esproncediano' variant, with *El estudiante de Salamanca* 'tamed' by *Don Juan Tenorio*; moving into the later part of the century, M.H. sees the feminine principle (Doña Inés, or Gabriela de la Guardia of *El escándalo*) as instrumental in the 'domestication' of radical high Romanticism, while *La desheredada* functions within the established schema as parody of the *novela folletinesca*. E. Penas Varela, 'Poética de la novela histórica romántica', *RLit*, 58:373–85, breaks no new ground, but is well documented and maps out the essential features.

3. REALISM AND NATURALISM

The indefatigable Juan Luis Alborg has published the latest volume in his *Historia de la literatura española. V: Realismo y naturalismo. La novela. Parte primera: Introducción, Fernán Caballero, Alarcón, Pereda*, M, Gredos, 772 pp. It differs enormously from A.'s previous volume (1980) on Spanish Romanticism in that approximately half of this one is a general — if thoroughgoing and shrewd — introduction that covers not just European countries individually, but the United States as well. One therefore wonders whether A. has struck a suitable balance between, for example, Naturalism in Belgium (25 pages) and the work of Fernán Caballero (18). This reader at least regrets the absence of the kind of detailed and specific argument found in the earlier volume; the documentation is still there, but this time it seems unduly concentrated and cluttered. Pura Fernández, **Eduardo López Bago y el naturalismo radical. La novela y el mercado literario en el siglo XIX*, Amsterdam, Rodopi, 1995, 257 pp. C. Servén Díez, 'De "La dama de las camelias" a la codorniz romántica: sobre la mujer liviana en la novelística de la Restauración', *RLit*, 58:83–105, considers how Galdós (*Rosalía*), Palacio Valdés (*Riverita*), Valera (*Genio y figura*) and Alas (*La Regenta*) rejected Dumas's prescription for the redemption of a fallen woman by erotic love. P. Fernández, 'Orígenes y difusión del Naturalismo: la especificidad de la práctica hispana', *ib.*, 107–20, documents tensions between those 'accommodating' Naturalism to Spain and more radical exponents of Zola's doctrine.

4. INDIVIDUAL AUTHORS

ALARCÓN. *El sombrero de tres picos*, ed. Eva F. Florensa, introd. Sergio Beser, B, Crítica, 1993, 224 pp., exemplifies the high academic quality normally found in the *Biblioteca Clásica* series. B.'s 'estudio preliminar' provides a telling commentary, admirably informed and both discerning and incisive in its framing and pinpointing of A.'s work. F.'s more extensive prologue is strong on the traditions informing the text and on its 'marco espaciotemporal', in sections that powerfully elucidate its meaning. K. Larsen, 'La conflagración romántica y la termodinámica realista: *El niño de la bola*', *Actas* (Irvine), V, 245–51, considers the presence of fire imagery in the metaphorical dimensions of the characters and in the impulses that intimately condition them.

ALAS. **Obras completas. Tomo I: La Regenta*, ed. with prologue by Santos Sanz Villanueva, M, Turner, Biblioteca Castro, 1995, 900 pp. D. Pratt, 'Frígilis and decorative science in *La Regenta*', *AG*, 27–28, 1992–93[1996]:131–43, drawing on Bakhtin, looks at Crespo as an artistic image of scientific language and contemporary scientific concerns, ironizing the words and actions of the Vetustans and therefore functioning as a ratifier of the narrator's critique. H. Gold, 'Literature in a paralytic mode: digression as transgression in *La Regenta*', *RHM*, 48, 1995:54–68, argues that digression, in deconstructing the text's structures and hierarchies, covertly challenges unitary aspirations to cohesiveness of narrative and social control. B. Epps, 'Traces of the flesh: land, body and art in Clarín's *Doña Berta*', *ib.*, 69–91, views the text as marked with the 'permanent impermanence' or relentless brevity of human existence, in which the foregrounded sites of personal traces are landscape, works of art, and the maternal body. B. Wietelmann Bauer, 'Something lost: translation, transaction, and travesty in Clarín's *Su único hijo*', *ib.*, 92–105, relating the text to Vico's *Scienza Nuova*, points to the debasement of marriage, the use of money, and the use of language — three principal contracts governing social life — as an essential part of A.'s satirical vision. R. Pope, 'Las sirenas de Vario y la visión de Clarín', *ib.*, 106–13, universalizes the classical poet's problematic relationship with writing and letters as evoked by A.'s tale. I. J. López, 'Clarín y la imaginación literaria romántica', *ib.*, 274–85, is based on A.'s critique of Galdós's *Tormento* and specifically on his assessment of Pedro Polo and the connexions with his own depiction of Fermín de Pas. L. detects a stripping away of 'mistificación romántica' in the new literary language of Realism. A. Coletes Blanco, 'Ironía y sátira antiinglesa en la narrativa breve de Clarín: "Snob", "El Torso" y otros relatos', *BHS(L)*, 73:245–54, looks at English references in A.'s work before and after his reading of Carlyle, broadly confirming Rutherford's view that A. 'digería bastante mal el mundo ánglico'. C. Martínez-Carazo, 'La huella del romanticismo en la novelística de Clarín', *RoQ*, 43:176–83, locates in *La Regenta* and *Su único hijo* a characteristic survival of Romantic elements in late-century Realism, and argues that despite A.'s preference for innovation he did not entirely renounce past traditions. A. Ezama, **'La erótica de la muerte

en un personaje clariniano: Angel Cuervo. Estudio de una pasión',
ALE, 10, 1994:69–80.

BÉCQUER. *Rimas. Leyendas. Cartas desde mi celda*, ed., introd. and
notes by María del Pilar Palomo, B, Planeta, 1996, 220 pp., is an
inevitably limited selection accompanied by a helpful, if brief,
introduction and even more sparse 'bibliografía fundamental'. The
reading order of the *Rimas* unusually respects the *Libro de los gorriones*
manuscript. A. Risco, *'Fantasías orientales de Bécquer', *Anthropos*,
154–55, 1994:89–95. J. Estruch Tobella, *'Transgresión y fantasía
en las leyendas de Bécquer', *ib.*, 95–99. L. M. Fernández, *'De la
"poética de los muertos" al paisaje trascendente. Una aproximación
a las relaciones entre Chateaubriand y Bécquer', *ALE*, 10,
1994:81–100. E. Hastings, *'El enigma de "La mujer de piedra" de
Bécquer', *El Gnomo*, 3, 1994:35–47. I. Mizrhai, *'El fragmento de
Bécquer', *ib.*, 49–63. J. Rubio Jiménez, *'En torno a la autoría y la
primera difusión de "Los Borbones en pelota"', *ib.*, 65–91. J. Rubio
Jiménez and E. Ortes, *'Bibliografía', *ib.*, 163–211. A. Rodríguez
and M. Pflug, 'Las imágenes clásicas de la Rima XLI de Bécquer',
RLit, 57, 1995:167–70, identifies Virgilian elements in the poem.
A. Alatorre, 'De nuevo sobre el texto de las *Rimas* de Bécquer', *NRFH*,
44:149–54, takes up — against Sebold's criteria for his recent
edition — the issue of the corrections to the *Libro de los gorriones*
manuscript.

BRETÓN DE LOS HERREROS. J. Vellón Lahoz, 'Moralidad y censura
en las refundiciones del teatro barroco: *No hay cosa como callar*, de
Bretón de los Herreros', *RLit*, 58:159–68, takes a detailed look at this
adaptation of Calderón from the evidence of B.'s manuscript and the
changes inserted in it prior to its performance in 1827.

CABALLERO. *Genio e ingenio del pueblo andaluz*, ed. Antonio A.
Gómez Yebra, M, Castalia, 1994, 668 pp., gathers together under a
single cover F.C.'s collections of popular verse including the important *Cuentos y poesías populares andaluzas* of 1859. G.Y. provides a
perceptive introduction, and reproduces also the prose prefaces to
the different collections. This is an opportune volume that makes a
lot of the author's lesser-known work more accessible. J. Herrero,
'The castrated bull in *La gaviota*', *RCEH*, 21:155–65, makes an
original reading of the novel's characterization and setting based on
programmatic symbolism. The traditionalist world-view of the conscious author, H. argues, is subverted by a contradictory unconscious
text whose images of castration erode conservatism and patriarchy,
the conflicting discourses meanwhile revealing the author as divided
between her social group and her personal independence.

CASTRO. *El caballero de las botas azules*, ed. Ana Rodríguez-Fisher,
M, Cátedra, 1995, 344 pp., is a timely new critical edition with a well

documented introduction that emphasises the Protean nature of Rosalía's text. C. Davies, 'The return to mother cathedral, a stranger in no man's land: Rosalía de Castro through Julia Kristeva', *Neophilologus*, 79, 1995:63–81, makes a psychoanalytical study of five religious and non-religious poems — from *Follas novas* and *En las orillas del Sar* — each relating a journey to a sacred place.

DURÁN.   D.L. Shaw's edition of the *Discurso*, with its perceptive commentary and notes, has made an appearance in Spanish translation, Málaga, Agora, 1994, 117 pp.

ECHEGARAY.   J. Dowling, 'La recepción del teatro de Echegaray en México, 1875–1878', *CH*, 17, 1995:36–51, locates performances of E.'s drama within a specific ideological context and as a necessary focus of moral desiring for cultivated sectors of Mexican society.

ESPRONCEDA.   A. Sherman, Jr, 'Espronceda, androgyny and the quest for the Romantic self', *CH*, 18:111–23, focuses on the interplay of male and female *personae* in E.'s verse, arguing that they project in their combinations a divided self and eventually an androgynous totality that erodes patriarchal distinctions in favour of a more egalitarian social construct. R. Sebold, 'Lágrimas y héroes en *Sancho Saldaña*', *HR*, 64:507–26, contrasts Usdróbal ('héroe moral') with Sancho ('héroe artístico' calculatedly fitted to the text's literary strategies). A. Selim Selimov, 'La historia de dos Adanes: La estructura integral de *El diablo mundo*', *His(US)*, 78, 1995:773–79, sees in E.'s poem two parallel texts — one concerning Adán, Salada, and Lucía, the other E. himself and Teresa — that are formally independent but conceptually and metaphorically united.

GIL Y CARRASCO.   F. López Criado, 'Las estructuras psico-míticas de Enrique Gil en *El señor de Bembibre*', *RLit*, 57, 1995:77–107, is a confused and disjointed scrutiny of levels or dimensions of crisis in the novel. R. Sebold, 'Tuberculosis y misticismo en *El señor de Bembibre*', *HR*, 64:237–57, in an insightful and original piece, identifies the pathological and clinical history of Beatriz, her two illnesses — one psychological, the other physical — as prompting the novel's negation of human ties.

GÓMEZ DE AVELLANEDA.   L. Hernández, *'On the double: "Tres amores" and the postponement of love in Avellaneda's theater', *LF*, 1994:39–47.

LARRA.   D. Nordlund, 'Larra: theatrical criticism and social revolution', *RHM*, 48, 1995:233–49, charts L.'s changing approach to the theatre in a piece that is discerning in its detail but unduly sparing in essential contextualization. A. Sherman, Jr, 'Larra and satire: the question of Don Carlos and the Spanish monarchy', *CH*, 17, 1995:211–23, briefly maps out the 'reformative activity' of L.'s satire. J. Rae Krato, 'Eighteenth-century attitudes towards women and Larra's "El casarse pronto y mal"', *Hispanófila*, 116:29–34, views L.'s piece as a commentary on the radical change in female roles occurring in the Enlightenment, contending that the roots of L.'s vision of woman as the embodiment of Romantic ideals were embedded in the previous century.

MENÉNDEZ PELAYO. A special issue of *BBMP*, 1994, is dedicated to M.P. under the title *Estudios sobre Menéndez Pelayo. Número extraordinario en Homenaje a don Manuel Revuelta Sañudo*. The three main sections are devoted to 'obra', 'epistolario', and 'biblioteca', and contain contributions from noted specialists such as Santoveña Setién, Madariaga de la Campa, Morón Arroyo, and González Herrán. Topics covered include M.P. and Krausism and his role in the conflict between Liberalism and traditionalism.

PALACIO VALDÉS. B. Dendle, 'Los artículos no recogidos de Armando Palacio Valdés en *El Día*, 1880–1881', *BBMP*, 72:199–237, briefly introduces — with details of publishing history — a cluster of pieces. J. A. Marrero Cabrera, 'Una campaña de prensa en el otoño de 1904. José de Betancourt (Angel Guerra) y la candidatura de Armando Palacio Valdés para la Real Academia Española', *AG*, 27–28, 1992–93[1996]:185–98, is fascinatingly documented, reprinting contributions from a variety of writers including Galdós, Rueda, Blasco Ibáñez, Baroja, Unamuno, and Maeztu.

PARDO BAZÁN. L. Otis, 'Science and signification in the early writings of Emilia Pardo Bazán', *REH*, 29, 1995:73–106, closely contextualizes ideas contained in 'La ciencia amena', relating them to *Pascual López*. J. Pérez, 'Subversion of Victorian values and idea types: Pardo Bazán and the "Angel del hogar"', *Hispanófila*, 113, 1995:31–44, examines a group of short stories from the 1890s, arguing that they are illuminated and enriched by our reading them as ironic and subversive reactions to ideal types. C. Patiño Eirín, 'Aproximación a los prólogos de Emilia Pardo Bazán', *BBMP*, 71, 1995:137–67, with a helpful appendix, illustrates how authors' prefaces typically responded to processes of continuity or rupture in literary construction.

PEREDA. A. Clarke, 'Pereda's *Pedro Sánchez*: the Dickens connection', *Lomax Vol.*, 187–208, makes a good case for P.'s modelling his novel on *David Copperfield*. M. Aguinaga Alfonso, 'Los títulos en los artículos de costumbres y en los relatos breves de Pereda', *BBMP*, 71, 1995:169–77, reflects on the titles found in P.'s first four collections.

PÉREZ GALDÓS. *Trafalgar. la Corte de Carlos IV*, ed. Dolores Troncoso with preliminary study by Geoffrey Ribbans, B, Crítica, 1995, xxiii + 561 pp., contains a discerning general introduction to the *Episodios* (ix–xxiii) that uses G.'s own — often neglected — comments on his creation as a starting point. T.'s prologue, as is the practice in this collection, addresses the texts with greater specificity, and provides an informed and uncluttered preview. Arguably, more space might have been dedicated to the location of these first *episodios* within the 19th-c. tradition of the historical novel, although the edition is illuminating and rigorous, a point reinforced by the extensive 'notas complementarias' that complete the volume. *Cuentos fantásticos*, ed. Alan E. Smith, M, Cátedra, 298 pp., following on from S.'s critical study of the 'cuentos inverosímiles' (see *YWMLS*, 55 : 394), gathers together for the first time 12 tales covering the period 1865–97; 'Rompecabezas' makes its first appearance in a published volume, while 'Una industria que vive de la muerte' and 'El pórtico de la gloria' are extremely rare: none of the three is to be found, for example, in the Aguilar *Obras completas*. Previous editions of all twelve are documented. While those familiar with S.'s recent study will find little that is new in the introduction, the collection is a welcome one for *galdosistas* and others. Pedro Ortiz Ormengol, *Vida y obra de Galdós*, B, Crítica, 924 pp., as an immensely and sensitively detailed critical biography, is a monumental contribution to Galdós studies, proceeding majestically through the life and work and admirably annotated and indexed. An academic 'must-have' and a fine example of scholarship. Geoffrey Ribbans, *History and Fiction in Galdós's Narratives*, Oxford, Clarendon Press, 1993, 310 pp., holds up to thoroughgoing scrutiny the broad historical dimensions of G.'s work, novels and *Episodios* alike, elucidating the processes by which the perception and treatment of history informed G.'s creative task. Effective contrasts are made with writers like Valle-Inclán, Baroja, and Unamuno, while the entire study is seamlessly readable and commendably free of jargon. Catherine Jagoe, *Ambiguous Angels: Gender in the Novels of Galdós*, Berkeley, UC Press, 1994, 239 pp., is fundamentally concerned with the thesis novels of the 1870s and the later *novelas contemporáneas*. While it is unfortunate that the *Episodios* are left out of the equation, this penetrating analysis does not in any way disappoint. The reconstruction of the 'ángel del hogar' motif is followed by a chapter on G. and the 'Women question'. Subsequently considered are: the tragic end of women in the early novels — *Gloria*, for example, is seen to recoil from its own subversion of conventional femininity; the transition from religious fanaticism to compulsive consumerism; and a striking reading of *Tristana*. This book is an indispensable contribution to work in the broader 19th-c. field as well as to the more specialized one. *La desheredada* and *Tormento* respectively are considered in two of the major chapters of Stephanie Sieburth, *Inventing High and Low: Literature, Mass Culture, and Uneven Modernity in Spain*, Durham, Duke U.P., 1994, 280 pp. The former is viewed as an allegory for the role of art in modern times, while the latter, while parodying the *folletín*, is felt consciously to adopt that genre's utopian qualities and revolutionary thrust.

Textos y contextos de Galdós, ed. John W. Kronik and Harriet S. Turner, M, Castalia, 1994, 209 pp., publishes the proceedings of the *Fortunata y Jacinta* Centenary Symposium. The editors' 'Introducción' (9–14) charts the peaks and troughs of G.'s historical reputation. Under the heading 'Galdós y el realismo europeo' is J. Stern's '*Fortunata y Jacinta* in the context of European Realism' (17–36), underlining G.'s challenging of social and moral convention in his exploration of individuals in their relationships with institutions and in the essential ironies and ambiguities that problematize his vision. Under the twin heading 'La narrativa del primer Galdós. Galdós cuentista' are: M. P. Palomo, 'El artículo costumbrista y *La fontana de oro*' (39–54), a piece of literary detective work that unearths a forgotten Galdosian text, the journalistic piece 'La Carrera de San Jerónimo en 1821' — reproduced in an appendix, in order to clarify the issue of the ending(s) of G.'s novel; L. Bonet, 'Don Elías Orejón, el espía que surgió de la sombra (*La fontana de oro*)' (55–65), a close examination of G.'s early-established preference for caricature and the grotesque as a source of both humour and dynamic tension; E. Rubio Cremades, 'Los relatos breves de Galdós' (67–78), broadly surveys the multiple possibilities and directions of the short fiction. 'Lecturas de *Fortunata y Jacinta*' comprises: D. Estébanez Calderón, 'Naturaleza y sociedad: claves para una interpretación de *Fortunata y Jacinta*' (81–90), which scrutinizes the rhetorical figures used to articulate the novel's fundamental binary opposition; F. Caudet, '*Fortunata y Jacinta*: el "naturalismo espiritual"' (91–104), which, concerned with the impact of French Naturalism in Spain, opts for a view of G.'s novel as demonstrative of a socio-historical, rather than biological, determinism; C. Menéndez Onrubia, 'Historia y familia en *Fortunata y Jacinta*' (105–14), which takes up the relationship between history and fiction in linking the novel's representation of family history and contemporary political and economic history; J. Rodríguez Puértolas, '"Quien manda, manda": la ley y el orden en *Fortunata y Jacinta*' (115–25), similarly immersed in the historical processes of the *Restauración*, considers the ineluctable authoritarian power-structures viewed as essential characteristics of bourgeois society; J. M. Navarro Adriaensens, 'Registros sociolingüísticos en la caracterización de personajes en *Fortunata y Jacinta*' (127–34), investigates the distinctive lexical choices of G.'s characters, relating them to their respective personalities and social status; P. Ortiz Ormengol, 'La opinión de Unamuno sobre *Fortunata y Jacinta*' (135–40), considers the philosopher's comments on the novel as contained in a 1920 letter to Azaña and Rivas Cherif; F. Márquez Villanueva, 'Notas sobre el manuscrito de *Fortunata y Jacinta*' (141–45), dealing with the manuscript belonging to the Harvard University library and its variance with other versions. The section of 'Notas' is unified by the memory of Stephen Gilman. R. Cardona's introductory 'Homenaje' (149–50) is followed by contributions from former pupils: C. Wright, ' "Un millón de ojos": visión, vigilancia y encierro en *Doña Perfecta*' (151–56), makes a programmatic symbolic reading of confined spaces and cautionary vigilance; M. Krow-Lucal, 'El personaje recurrente en la obra de Galdós' (157–61), from a structural perspective, turns to a characteristic Galdosian feature of what Gilman himself called the 'vast nether warehouse of narrative possibilities'; A. Smith, 'La imaginación galdosiana y la cervantina' (163–67), is based on a distinction between negative and creative aspects of imagination and between allegory and myth; F. González Arias, 'Diario de un viaje: las cartas de Emilia Pardo Bazán a Benito Pérez Galdós' (169–75), reviews the multi-faceted dialogue between the two authors, reconstructed from some of the 93 letters to G. from Pardo Bazán. 'Coloquio: la originalidad de Galdós', includes three contributions to the various round-table discussions: C. Blanco Aguinaga, 'La "originalidad" de Galdós' (179–83), concludes that the 'originality' of any European Realist can only reside in the specificity of their character's socio-historical context; B. Ciplijauskaité, 'El lenguaje de la rebeldía' (185–88), argues that the disjunctive histories of 19th-c. Spanish literature and society condition G.'s moral, thematic and linguistic emphasis on *libertad*; J. Sinnigen, '*Fortunata y Jacinta* y la novela realista: transformación social e identidad individual' (189–92), looks at G.'s subversive incorporation of discourses of feminism into his fiction. G. Gullón offers the *conferencia de clausura* with his '*Fortunata y Jacinta* en el vértice de la modernidad' (195–209), placing G. on the threshold of modernity not so much on account of his formal innovation as on that of his sensitive communication of interiority in individuals confronting new realities.

A double issue of *AG*, 27–28, 1992–93[1996], is dedicated to the memory of Ricardo Gullón, with personal tributes from G. Gullón, 'Carácter de la trayectoria crítica de Ricardo Gullón' (15–19) and from P. Ortiz Ormengol, 'Homenaje a Ricardo Gullón' (21–29). Many of the articles that follow carry dedications to the *maestro*. R. Cardona, 'Más sobre Kafka y Galdós' (31–40), with reference to *Miau* and to recent work linking it with Kafka's *The Trial*, underlines essential differences between the two authors' novelistic worlds. H. Turner, 'Metaphors of what's unfinished in *Miau*' (41–50), continuing T.'s broader and ongoing analysis of Galdós's metaphorical thinking, looks at the novel within Bakhtinian terms of polyphony and liminality. B. Dendle, 'Orbajosa revisited, or the complexities of interpretation' (51–67), schematizing opposed critical opinion and fixing on textual details often given only cursory attention, makes fresh claims for the complexity and maturity of the novel. G. Ribbans, '*La desheredada*, novela por entregas: apuntes sobre su primera publicación' (69–75), combines literary detective-work with persuasive interpretation of material in contextualizing and dating the discrete processes of writing and publication and synthesizing their implications for the nature of the finished product. J. Whiston, 'Heroes and villains in Galdós: *Lo prohibido* and *Macbeth*' (77–91), drawing on G.'s documented preference for Shakespeare, pursues an unexpected density of parallels between the two texts. M. López-Baralt, '*Fortunata y Jacinta* según televisión española: la lectura cinematográfica del clásico galdosiano por Mario Camus' (93–107), considers the 'readerly' emphases of the film director in popularizing the literary text. J. Grimbert, 'Galdós's *Tristana* as a subversion of the Tristan legend' (109–23), scrutinizes a salient example of the novel's network of literary and cultural allusions, and suggests G.'s knowledge of at least one of the medieval versions of the legend. J. Lowe, 'Cigars, slippers and nightcaps: attitudes and actions in *La Regenta* and *Tristana*' (125–29), casts an interesting sidelight on connections between the two novels. Y. Arencibia, 'Tanteos de estilo. *Nazarín* de Pérez Galdós' (145–56), is a detailed stylistic examination of the different stages of gestation of G.'s novel. D. Urey, 'Desire and death in *El 19 de marzo y el 2 de mayo*' (157–75), views the narrative of Gabriel's odyssey as illustrative of the fundamental connection between discourse and representation, in which the search for ultimate meaning or truth is destined to end in 'nada'. In the 'Documentos' section is L. Willem, 'Moreno-Isla's unpublished scene from the *Fortunata y Jacinta* galleys' (179–83), reviewing one scene deleted in its entirety (and, unlike several others, not reprinted in the footnotes to Francisco Caudet's current Cátedra edition).

Rumbos, 13–14, 1995, is dedicated to *Realidad e imaginación en la obra de Pérez Galdós*. The theme is introduced by J. Peñate Rivero (5–8) and subsequently examined in a series of significant contributions by: V. Fuentes, 'Galdós en la encrucijada noventayochista: de *Misericordia* a *Electra*' (9–23), assessing G.'s conscious reaction to the end-of-century crisis and highlighting his anticipation of the work of salient 20th-c. thinkers including Bakhtin and Walter Benjamin; S. Miller, 'Galdós en su tiempo y en el nuestro' (25–39), contrasting G.'s interpretation of history with that of Ortega y Gasset and considering G.'s authorial perspective on his contemporary world, its view of him, and our own retrospective and often imperfect historical judgements of each; J. Avila Arellano, 'El realismo/naturalismo de Galdós en el equilibrio entre la exactitud y la belleza de la expresión' (41–59), examining the multiple functions of referentiality within G.'s texts; P. Bly, 'Cómo pintar en la novela la verdad del estío madrileño, según Picón y Galdós' (61–74), based on *La de Bringas* and Picón's *La hijastra del amor*, underlining G.'s superior integration of narrative description into the text's dramatic tensions; V. Chamberlin, 'Eroticizing Isidora's traffic jam in Fortunata's dream' (III, 7, 4)' (75–86), emphasizing an evolution in style as well as G.'s capacity to adopt circumstantial detail to situation and personality; M. Yáñez, 'Una *incógnita* elevada al cuadrado y una *realidad* cuestionable' (87–102), specifying a multiplicity of *incógnitas* in contending that Manolo Infante's investigations are a fictional representation of the impossibility of uncovering truth; R. Cardona, '*La campaña del Maestrazgo*: palimpsesto romántico' (103–15), stressing the serious motives underlying G.'s parodic and/or ludic employment of Romantic strategies and motifs; L. Behiels, 'Los retratos en la cuarta serie de los *Episodios Nacionales* de Benito Pérez Galdós' (117–26), constructing a typology of portraiture that is instrumental to G.'s processes of characterization; C. Menéndez Onrubia, 'El carácter cinematográfico del teatro de Benito Pérez Galdós' (127–38), exploring the visual dimension of G.'s theatre in its stage directions and in its attention to setting, costume, gesture and perspective; T. Sackett,'Metadrama, modernismo y noventayochismo en *Bárbara* de Pérez Galdós' (139–51), elucidating a variety of elements — decorative and discursive — pertaining to G.'s responses to interrelated contemporary movements, to his text's consciousness of its own theatricality and to G.'s critique of Restoration society; J. Peñate Rivero, 'Ironía, instancias narrativas y significación en *Necrología de un prototipo*, de Pérez Galdós' (153–77), mainly concerned with the ironic configurations of G.'s piece.

W. de Ràfols, 'Lies, irony, satire, and the parody of ideology in *Doña Perfecta*', *HR*, 64:467–89, considers claims for and against the text's designation as a *roman à thèse*, concluding that it can equally justifiably be seen as an 'antithesis novel'. F. J. Higuero, 'Tensiones dialécticas del narrador-personaje en *El amigo manso* de Benito Pérez Galdós', *HisJ*, 16, 1995:387–98, identifies a stream of structural and thematic antagonisms present in the text. L. Delgado, ' "Más estragos que las revoluciones": detallando lo femenino en *La de Bringas*', *RHM*, 48, 1995:31–42, makes an incisive structural reading of 'lo accesorio' as feminine principle at work in G.'s text and its multiplicity of implications. T. Franz, 'Don Francisco as fate: the construction of the cenotaph in *La de Bringas*', *Neophilologus*, 80:259–67, sees Bringas's weaving as a writing into being of the 1868 Revolution that would bring down the class to which he belongs. P. Ontañón de Lope B., 'Simbolismo en *Lo prohibido* de Galdós', *Actas* (Irvine), v, 264–71, deals with the perceived central motifs of the text: sex, motherhood, and money. M. Yáñez, 'Autores y lectores de un texto llamado Fortunata', *ib.*, 252–63, assesses the character of Fortunata as a metaphor for the processes of reading. T. Fuentes Pevis, 'Drink and social stability: discourses of power in Galdós' *Fortunata y Jacinta*', *BHS(L)*, 73:63–77, starting from Foucault and examining bourgeois strategies of discipline and control emblematized in discourses on drink in late 19th-c. Spain, reveals how the views of G.'s bourgeois characters are calculatedly subverted; Mauricia, the rebel who resists discipline, therefore stands outside bourgeois control. L. Delgado, 'Pliegos de (des)cargo: las paradojas discursivas de *La incógnita*', *MLN*, 111:275–98, fixes on the Bakhtinian idea of heteroglossia as exemplified by Galdosian texts perceived as scenes of confrontation between a multiplicity of belief systems. The co-existence of various possible meanings solves, D. claims, the apparently paradoxical elements of Manuel Infante's narration. N. Santiáñez-Tió, 'Poéticas de modernismo. Espíritu lúdico y juegos de lenguaje en *La incógnita* (1889)', *ib.*, 299–326, contends that the multiple functions of *juego* in G.'s novel help us to comprehend its most innovative features and to locate it within Spanish and European *modernismo*. W. Raabe, 'Isidora: Galdós's depiction of a prostitute', *RHM*, 49:20–33, focuses on 'prostitute discourse': that is, on common social and linguistic codes defining prostitution. T. Bordóns, 'Releyendo *Tristana*', *NRFH*, 41, 1993:471–87, analyses the novel's ideological constructions, particularly the 'Angel del hogar'. J. Hoffman, 'Not so happily ever after: rewriting the courtship script in *Tristana*', *RHM*, 48, 1995:43–53, examines the complication and subversion of bourgeois demarcations of courtship and marriage in the novel, highlighting G.'s sardonic undermining of readerly assurance. R. Quirk, 'Levels of intertextuality in Galdós's *Tristana*', *RoQ*, 43:25–30, views the text as an encyclopaedic summary of literary themes, contending that it thus becomes a critique of life's imitation of art. J. Torrecilla, 'Los enemigos del *Halma* (Identidad cultural y canon literario)', *NRFH*, 41, 1993:489–504, contends that G. 'nationalized' Zola's Naturalism through conscious reintepretation. V. Chamberlin, *"Deleitar enseñando": humor and the didactic in Galdós's *Misericordia*', *Symposium*, 48, 1994:174–83. P. Bly, 'La máscara del lenguaje erótico-financiero en tres novelas sociales de Pérez Galdós', *RLit*, 58:387–97, dealing with *La de Bringas*, *Lo prohibido* and *La familia de León Roch*, shows how *amour propre* is a fundamental character weakness of Rosalía and Eloísa in their attempted mimicry of the phallocentric male code. B. fixes on the uses of financial and erotic language at key points in the texts. L. Pasto-Crosby, 'La autoridad del narrador y la dialéctica de las alianzas: el experimento de la serie *Torquemada*',

BBMP, 72:143–62, looks at putative relationships and alliances between implied reader, narrator, author, and characters.

D. Urey, '"Immaculate Conceptions" and other mysteries in Galdós's *Cádiz*', *BHS(L)*, 72, 1995:41–72, as well as emphasizing the literary value of the often disparaged early *episodios*, makes a detailed case for their exposition of the repression of women in Spanish culture through their undermining of stereotypes of the feminine. G. Ribbans, 'Una creación galdosiana — Teresa Villaescusa — entre la historia y la ficción', *Actas* (Irvine), ii, 113–24, views this character as a key figure in the feminist elements of the second period of the *Episodios*, embodying the interaction between 'official' collective history and individual experience. The same author's 'The novelist interprets history: Galdós's *La de los tristes destinos*', *Lomax Vol.*, 225–40, considers G.'s depiction of the June 1866 insurrection, the 1868 Revolution, and the figure of Isabel II. L. Condé, 'Womanpower in Galdós's *Voluntad (1895)*', *ib.*, 209–23, argues that G.'s concession of power to Isidora (and María Guerrero) emblematized his concept of 'una sociedad nueva'.

M. D. Gómez Molleda, 'Masonería y revolución liberal en Galdós', *RCEH*, 21:143–53, regards G.'s largely negative attitude towards freemasonry in the *Episodios nacionales* as a product both of the evolution of his own political ideals and of his superimposition of present concerns onto the historical past. G. Cabrejas, 'Los niños de Galdós', *NRFH*, 41, 1993:333–51, examines G.'s depiction of children and their psychology as just one element in his reconstruction of social reality. A. Smith, 'Galdós, Kafka y Rosa Montero: contra el discurso patriarcal', *RHM*, 48, 1995:265–73, links *Miau* with Kafka and with Rosa Montero's *Amado amo* with a focus on discourses of power and their articulation.

RIVAS. E. Caldera, 'La polémica sobre el *Don Alvaro*', *CH*, 17, 1995:22–35, draws together the diverse critical responses appearing at the time of its first performance in a balanced appraisal that underlines the interface between literature and ideology in reviews of the play. F. LaRubia Prado, '*Don Alvaro* y la retórica de la ausencia', *RHM*, 49:5–19, is a jargon-laden muddle brimming with phallic symbols and castration fantasies that renders the play unrecognizable.

VALERA. M. Loud, 'El amor platónico en *Pepita Jiménez*', *His(US)*, 79:400–10, traces parallels between V.'s novel and the *Phaedrus*, specifically concerning the ennobling of erotic love. L. views the text as a response to Catholic traditionalists but also as a critique of the Krausist *racionalismo armónico* that V. at first sight appears to defend. J. R. Resina, '*Pepita Jiménez*: del idilio a la Restauración', *BHS(L)*, 72, 1995:175–93, connects the conflicts found in V.'s novel, albeit confusedly, with contemporary political events. J. Castillo, 'El viaje como epistemología en *Morsamor* y el *Persiles*', *REH*, 30:297–314, sees V.'s text, like that of Cervantes, as a metaphor for human experience describing a metaphysical journey towards knowledge. Ultimately, C. feels *Morsamor* to subvert the established pattern by renouncing transcendence and acknowledging the limitations of language and of life. C. DeCoster, 'Bibliografía anotada de la correspondencia de Juan Valera', *BBMP*, 71, 1995:227–53, is well documented. M. A. Ayala, 'Valera y la novela de la segunda mitad del siglo xix', *ib.*, 72:87–98, shows how detail culled from V.'s personal correspondence might confirm or amend judgements publicly expressed in his literary criticism.

ZORRILLA. *El molino de Guadalajara. Drama en cuatro actos*, Guadalajara, Patronato Municipal de Cultura, 1994, 144 pp. *Traidor, inconfeso y mártir*, ed. José Luis Gómez, B, 1994, 288 pp. Ignacio Vallejo González and Pedro Ojeda Escudero, *José Zorrilla. Bibliografía con motivo de un Centenario (1893–1993)*, Valladolid, Ayuntamiento, 1994, 167 pp.

The published *Actas del Congreso sobre José Zorrilla: Una nueva lectura*, ed. Javier Blasco Pascual, Ricardo de la Fuente Ballesteros, and Alfredo Mateos Paramio, Valladolid U.P.–Fundación Jorge Guillén, 1995, 574 pp., is a splendid homage volume of outstanding quality. Included are: G. Gullón, 'Presentación' (5–9), underlining the centrality of Z.'s presence in a Romanticism that articulated a conscious and fundamental break with the prescriptions of the 18th c.; E. Caldera, 'El amor y el tiempo en el *Don Juan Tenorio*' (13–23), integrates Z.'s treatment of love *a lo humano* and *a lo divino* into the parallel temporal structures of the text, and confirms the originality and topicality of the play within the wider Don Juan tradition; R. Cardwell, 'Espec(ular)ización en la otra mujer: la Inés de *Don Juan Tenorio*' (25–43), using Foucault and Luce Irigaray, examines Z.'s characterization of Inés according to theories of specularization and discourses of power; L. Fernández Cifuentes, 'Zorrilla y la ética de la autobiografía' (45–55), provides some insightful commentary on the circumstances and implications of Z.'s unreliable narration of his own past in the *Recuerdos del tiempo viejo*; R. de la Fuente Ballesteros, 'Lectura unamuniana del *Don Juan Tenorio*' (57–70), posits a reading of the *Tenorio* as '*Don Juan* trascendentalista' owing much to Schopenhauer that came to define Unamuno's *El hermano Juan*; S. García Castañeda, 'Amor, celos y venganza en las leyendas de Zorrilla' (71–80), identifies Z.'s consistent thematic concerns as evidenced by a cluster of verse tales; D. Gies, 'Todos los fuegos el fuego: Zorrilla, Don Juan y el amor romántico' (81–95), takes a detailed look at the prevalence of flame imagery in the *Tenorio* and its diverse functions and implications; G. Gullón, 'El papel de la pasión en la obra de

Zorrilla (un nuevo contexto para el estudio de la literatura romántica)'
(97–108), examines Z.'s textual articulation of interiority, most
specifically in *Margarita la tornera* and *El puñal del godo*, as a paradigm
for Romantic practice; C. Hernández Alonso, 'Recepción de Zorrilla
en la prensa de la época' (109–24), documents the critical acclaim
and popular appeal enjoyed by Z. over several generations;
M. Mayoral, 'El concepto de la feminidad en Zorrilla' (125–40),
surveys the spontaneity of expression and emotional independence of
a range of dramatic heroines, contrasting Z.'s depictions with his
equivocal attitude towards Gertrudis Gómez de Avellaneda as woman
and poet; R. Navas Ruiz, 'El primer Zorrilla' (141–49), takes a brief
look at the early poetry; J.-L. Picoche, 'Las creencias y la religión de
Zorrilla según sus obras en prosa' (151–63), views Z.'s literary
commitment to Catholic traditionalism as profoundly and sincerely
inspired rather than as a calculated commercial strategy; L. Romero
Tobar, 'Zorrilla: el imaginario de la tradición' (165–84), delineates
Z.'s adherence to a *tradicionalismo estético*; E. Rubio Cremades, '*El
puñal del godo*: un drama de técnica romántica pura' (185–202), is
closely concerned with sources and influences before briefly relating
Z.'s play to earlier Romantic drama; R. Sebold, 'Zorrilla en sus
leyendas fantásticas a lo divino' (203–18), features a consideration of
El cantar del romero as an original contribution to interpretations of the
supernatural and an examination of Z.'s preference for the *deus ex
machina* as a form of resolution in the *leyendas*. The volume contains a
further 35 *comunicaciones*.

R. de la Fuente Ballesteros and F. Gutiérrez Flores, 'La "teatrali-
dad" en el *Don Juan Tenorio* de Zorrilla', *CH*, 17, 1995:65–80, analyse
the convergence of textual and extratextual dramatic rhythms in a
piece that stresses the multiplicity but also the essential coherence of
theatrical effects. J.-L. Picoche, 'De Moreto a Zorrilla. Un estudio
sobre la refundición de las travesuras de Pantoja con el título de *La
mejor razón, la espada*', *ib.*, 104–16, appraises Z.'s modifications for the
better and suggests that the *refundición* contains in embryonic form
some of the emphases found in his *Tenorio* of the following year. R. ter
Horst, 'Epic descent: the filiations of Don Juan', *MLN*, 111:255–74,
argues that rivalry with *El burlador* is built into Z.'s play from the
beginning, basing his case on binary oppositions between father and
son and on the text's ambivalent attitude regarding deference towards
forebears.

The second part of *CH*, 18.1, is dedicated to '*Don Juan Tenorio*:
Spanish Romanticism, the play, the legacy', and includes papers
delivered at the Sesquicentennial Conference held at Michigan State
University. The preface by G. Mansour (93–98) crystallizes the major
issues considered. Directly related to Z.'s play are: D. Schurlknight,

'Zorrilla, Espronceda and Romanticism(s): considerations on two stories of Don Juan' (99–110), where *El estudiante de Salamanca* and *Don Juan Tenorio* are viewed as respectively subverting and supporting the status quo in constructs emblematic of their essential bases, one radical the other traditionalist; N. Mayberry, '*Don Juan Tenorio* as the end-marker of Spanish Romanticism' (124–33), concentrating on the concept of fate or fortune, regards the play as a new form of expression catering for bourgeois values and as a text which provides a foretaste of later dramatic production while foreclosing on Romanticism proper; P. Ullman, 'Another fivefold polysemous approach to *Don Juan Tenorio*' (134–40), makes a whimsical application of contrapuntal method, specifically to the character of Doña Inés; J. Matallana-Abril, 'La herencia del *Don Juan Tenorio* en el mundo galdosiano de las novelas contemporáneas' (141–48), is principally concerned with the characterization of Joaquín Pez in *La desheredada*, tracing patently theatrical recourses that mirror the extravagantly self-conscious theatrical procedures of Z.'s text. D. Gies, '*Don Juan Tenorio*: una bibliografía en el aniversario de su estreno (1844–1994)' (186–97), is invaluable in its gathering of critical editions and secondary material.

A. Dorca, 'Juegos retóricos e invención de una identidad en la escritura autobiográfica: los *Recuerdos del tiempo viejo* de José Zorrilla', *HR*, 64:359–72, examines narratological strategies and intimate motivation in the poet's memoir.

LITERATURE, 1898–1936

By K. M. SIBBALD, *McGill University*

1. GENERAL

BIBLIOGRAPHY. A useful summation covering 1993–95 is contained in M. C. Simón Palmer, 'Información bibliográfica', *RLit*, 58:221–342, see particularly references to the 20th c. (302–40) for reviews, theses, items from the general press about our period, and specific criticism on Antonio Machado, Ramón Sender and Antonio Espina not covered here.

PERIODICAL HISTORY. José María López Ruiz, *La vida alegre. Historia de las revistas humorísticas, festivas y satíricas publicadas en la villa y corte de Madrid*, M, Compañía Literaria, 1995, 345 pp., documents more than 400 publications from the chronological span 1735–1990, highlighting satirical writing from Larra to *La Cordoniz* with useful bio-bibliographical sketches. F. Caudet, '*Octubre* en su contexto político-cultural', *Iberoromania*, 43:68–87, points up the general politicization of the 1930s and indicates a royal company of European predecessors including *Die Linkscurve* (Berlin) and *Commune* (Paris), alongside such magazines in Spain as *Sin Dios, Orto, Mujer, Frente Literario, Hechos, Diablo Mundo, El Tiempo Presente, Después* and many others that never achieved the mythic status of *Octubre*. Of marginal interest here, J. Domingo, 'Periodismo de los españoles exiliados en Cuba', *CHA*, 547:101–10, gives the context for the right-wing *Diario de la Marina* and, more specifically, for the leftist *España Nueva*, that includes information on *Claridad* and *¡Ayuda!* (1937), *Nuestra España* and *Alma Gallega* (1939) and Manuel Altolaguirre's celebrated, if short-lived, review *La Verónica* (1942).

LITERARY AND CULTURAL HISTORY. Describing the long, wide boulevard through the Spanish Montmartre with its unparalleled choice in entertainment from *zarzuela* to high drama, vaudeville and pantomime to light opera and whodunits, S. Salaün, 'El paralelo barcelonés (1894–1936)', *ALEC*, 21:329–50, considers this the ideal vantage point, at the juncture between bazaar and Tower of Babel, from which to observe turn-of-the-century cultural activity and the triumph of modernity. M. Palenque, '*El poema del trabajo* (1898): un libro temprano de Gregorio Martínez Sierra', *Salina* (U. de Tarragona), 10:155–60, analyses the curious mixture of revolutionary ideas held by the very young middle class liberals, Gregorio and María Martínez Sierra, then still only *novios*. C. Heydl-Cortínez, 'Giner de los Ríos: el maestro en unos poemas de Unamuno, Antonio Machado y en la prosa de Juan Ramón Jiménez', *HisJ*, 16,

1995:339–49, notes general admiration, an obvious continuing of the line in Unamuno and Machado and even in Jiménez's shared predilection for Krausist idealism, plus some lightweight speculation about a common understanding that in the perfection of Nature is to be found the presage of God's presence. As typical of the anti-*modernista* satires published by Manuel del Palacio, Agustín Bonnat, José de Laserna, Félix Cuquerella, Emilio Taboada and Juan Pérez Zuñiga, among others, in, particularly, *Madrid Cómico* and *Gedeón*, J. Serrano, 'La parodia del modernismo: el *Tenorio modernista* de Pablo Parellada (1906)', *ALEC*, 21: 365–84, brings forward the model by 'Melitón González' that takes aim at the 'faunos patizambos, siringas hipoginas, libélulas verdescantes, féminas cloróticas y nenúfares sitibundos' of the period. Less facetiously, M. D. Dobón, '*Sociólogos* contra *estetas*: prehistoria del conflicto entre modernismo y 98', *HR*, 64:52–72, is a rebuttal of John Butt's 1980 attack on the 'critical fallacy' of focusing on the Generation of 1898 as a literary movement separate from modernism (see *YWMLS*, 42:344), as she reaffirms two clearly opposing views held by 'el partido estético', scathingly defined by Unamuno, and the 'sociólogos', so named by Azorín, as opinions clashed over the wisdom of María Guerrero's plan to stage Gabriele D'Anunzio's *La città morta* in 1898. In a forward projection, T. R. Franz, '*Tiempo de silencio* and its Cela-like resonances of the Generation of 1898', *His(US)*, 79:429–38, constructs a palimpsest in which a single paradigm is progressively reshaped in *El árbol*, *Troteras y andanzas*, *La colmena* and *Tiempo de silencio*, while similarities between Martín Santos and Azorín's *La voluntad* (1902), José Gutiérrez Solano's *Madrid callejero* (1923) and Valle-Inclán's *Luces de Bohemia* (1924) and *Tirano Banderas* (1926) are also explored to show how such recycling is an integral part of the contemporary Spanish narrative. Various aspects of cultural life are emphasized as the 19th c. turns into the 20th c.: starting with the cliché that all Spanish intellectuals have some 'gotas de sangre jacobina' in their make-up, P. Aubert, 'La Révolution française: relecture en Espagne d'un événement fondateur (1889–1936)', *Homenaje Ouimette*, 35–56, argues that the French Revolution forms part of the civic education of such diverse writers as Unamuno, Ortega, Antonio Machado, Pérez de Ayala, Azaña, Araquistain, Marcelino Domingo, Álvaro de Albornoz and Julio Besteiro, while E. I. Fox, 'El "hombre nuevo": la tutela del pueblo y el liberalismo español', *ib.*, 117–30, traces the tutorship notion back to Joaquín Costa in 1895, identifying its initial popularity with Rafael Altamira, Ángel Ganivet, José Nakens and Azorín, and explains a second round with Ortega and Salvador de Madariaga, who at first hoped for a renewed liberalism from Primo de Rivera's dictatorship; R. Johnson, 'Gender and nation in Spanish fiction between the wars

(1898–1936)', *ib.*, 167–79, privileges the women's writing that also formed part of the national consciousness during the period to illustrate, by way of Margarita Nelken's *La trampa del arenal* (1923) and Federica Montseny's *La indomable* (1928), an active idealism very different from the usual male paralysis and *aboulia*; while N. Dennis, 'Culture in the Second Republic: the *Comités de Cooperación Intelectual*', *ib.*, 87–99, sheds some light on the plans of Arturo Soria y Espinosa to involve leading figures of varying political stripe, writers like García Lorca, Gómez de la Serna, Gerardo Diego, Regino Sáinz, and musicians like Gustavo Pittaluga and Rodolfo Halffter, in the on-going cultural life of the new Republic in the provinces, although the particular reconstruction here of José Bergamín's participation in 1932 in Galicia gives useful details of his lectures but concedes the tour's lack of success. M. M. Ferreyra, 'El debate crítico en torno a la problemática del surrealismo español', *HisJ*, 17 : 141–49, merely rehearses the standard critical positions but, if exhaustive, adds nothing new to the debate. *The Spanish Avant-garde*, ed. Derek Harris, MUP, 1995, 223 pp., presents an image of the Spanish avant-garde as a multi-faceted artistic phenomenon in 16 short articles that range over the poetry, fiction, painting, film and theatre of the period; not designed as a history, this is a helpful introduction to major trends in Spanish vanguardism for, particularly, the English-speaker, and it contains: D. Harris, 'Squared horizons: the hybridization of the avant-garde in Spain' (1–14); A. Soria Olmedo, 'Ramón Gómez de la Serna's oxymoronic historiography of the Spanish avant-garde' (15–26); J. E. Serrano, 'The theory of the novel in Ramón Gómez de la Serna's *The Novelist*' (27–38); N. Dennis, 'Writers in the bathroom: readings in the Spanish avant-garde' (39–53); W. Bohn, 'Visual poetry in Catalonia: Carles Sindreu i Pons' (54–69); G. Morelli, 'The ludic element in the Spanish avant-garde: Gerardo Diedo's *jinojepa*' (70–83); J. Brihuega, 'The language of avant-garde art in Spain: a collage on the margin' (84–96); E. Carmona, 'From Picasso to Dalí: "Arte Nuevo" and the Spanish masters of European avant-garde painting' (97–109); A. Sánchez Vidal, 'Góngora, Buñuel, the Spanish avant-garde and the centenary of Goya's death' (110–22); J. B. Monleón, 'Metropolis and utopia: Francisco Ayala's *Hunter in the Dawn*' (123–35); H. T. Young, 'Bridges to romance: nostalgia in Eliot, Salinas and Lorca' (136–48); G. Gullón, 'Sociocultural context and the Spanish avant-grade: theory and practice' (149–64); E. O'Hara, 'Exercises in the dark: Rafael Albert's cinema poems' (165–77); A. Sinclair, '*Concerning the Angels*: a representation of alchemical process' (178–89); C. B. Morris, 'The oblique language of Luis Cernuda: creative ruin or fragments shored?' (190–203); and P. McDermott, 'Subversions of the sacred: the sign of the fish' (204–17).

New approaches provide enlightenment: J. P. Duffey, 'Montage in Hispanic vanguard prose, 1926–1934: neurasthenia, back projection, and chase scenes', *Hispanófila*, 118:29–38, elucidates well how Sergei Eisenstein's cinematographic techniques run over into much prose written in the 1920s and 1930s by Francisco Ayala, Pedro Salinas and Antonio Espina in Spain, by *contemporáneos* like Jaime Torres Bodet and Xavier Villaurrutia in Mexico, and by Vicente Huidobro in his *novela-film*; Rosemary Geisdorfer Feal and Carlos Feal, *Painting on the Page: Interartistic Approaches to Modern Hispanic Texts*, Albany, NY, SUNY U.P., 1995, 341 pp., have chapters on Valle-Inclán's *Sonata de primavera*, Salinas's *Víspera del gozo*, and Ayala's *El jardín de las delicias*, providing new, often feminist, readings that, through recourse to philosophy, semiotics, pyschoanalysis, narratology and pop culture, mediate relations between literature and the visual arts in what is certainly a revamping of the 'critical' canon; while David William Foster and Roberto Reis edit with critical apparatus a mammoth commentary *Bodies and Biases: Sexualities in Hispanic Cultures and Literature*, Minneapolis, Minnesota U.P., xxxii + 440 pp. Willis Barnstone, *Sunday Morning in Fascist Spain. A European Memoir 1948–1953*, Carbondale–Edwardsville, IL, South Illinois U.P., 1995, 280 pp., has a somewhat misleading title that, in fact, belongs to Chapter 7 (166–241), where brief mention is made of Antonio Machado, Federico García Lorca, Jorge Guillén, and Vicente Aleixandre, in some very personal memories that range from England and France to Greece and Italy, from Beijing and Buenos Aires to Tibet and Turkey. Taking good care of the seventh art form, Peter William Evans, *The Films of Luis Buñuel. Subjectivity and Desire*, OUP, 1995, xii + 202 pp., focuses current film theory on male and female images in nine films in order to re-evaluate particularly work carried out in Mexico.

2. POETRY

I. López-Calvo, 'Las muertes de Rubén Darío en la poesía española', *La Torre*, 10:1–7, rides his hobby-horse to a lather adducing examples in Jiménez, both Machados and Guillén of various poetic debts, including the use of Darío's favourite *alejandrinos* and *endecasílabos*; D. Romero López, 'Los *topoi* de la poesía modernista', *Hispanófila*, 118:39–48, distils from the usual critical sources nine binary oppositions to explain, in convincing fashion, the harmonious dichotomy found in poetry by both Machados, Valle-Inclán, Jiménez, Salvador Rueda and others of the turn of the century; while, at the other end of the modernist scale, Monique Allain-Castrillo, *Paul Valéry y el mundo hispánico*, M, Gredos, 1995, 395 pp., is a serious examination, buttressed by a prologue by Carlos Bousoño and an epilogue by José Hierro. Rosa María Martín Casamitjana, *El humor en la poesía española de vanguardia*, M, Gredos, 467 pp. C. G. Bellver, 'Game-playing and reading "ultraísta" poetry', *Hispanófila*, 118:17–27, uses Roger Caillois's four categories of play to map the minefield and, incidentally, to prove her point that there is no clear victory for either writer or reader in *ultraísta* fun and games. With no suggestion of either anxiety or influence, F. Ruiz Soriano, 'La impronta elotiana en *Hijos de la ira* de Dámaso Alonso', *RLit*, 58:168–76, finds similar *topoi* and images of loss and decline from two members of the same literary tradition in poetic diaries that reflect personal crisis and profound analysis of the decadence of Western culture (see also *YWMLS*, 55:408). J. Valender, 'En torno a la estancia de Manuel Altolaguirre en Cuba (1939–1943)', *RCEH*, 20:556–66, recounts the circumstances of the fortuitous landing in Cuba which delayed for four difficult, if productive, years Altolaguirre's intention of taking up residence in Mexico, both to give details of editorial ventures like *Atentamente* (1940), *La Verónica* (1942), and the printing of nearly 200 titles including Lezama Lima's *Espuela de plata*, as well as to slate roundly poor scholarship in Gonzalo Santonja, *Un poeta español en Cuba: Manuel Altolaguirre. Sueños y realidades del primer impresor del exilio*, B, Círculo de lectores, 1994. Nigel Dennis edits and introduces *En torno a la poesía de José Bergamín*, Lleida, Pages, 1995, 266 pp. Francis Komla Aggor, *Eros en la poesía de Miguel Hernández*, York, SC, Spanish Literary Publications, 1994, 142 pp., is a compact monograph that explores the range of erotic expression from the early 'vergel, sensualismo, sexo' of *Perito en lunas*, through the sublimation in 'un barroquismo de Dios' of the *auto sacramental*, poems and prose of 1933–34, to the expression of true love in *El rayo no cesa*, and beyond into a glorification of sexuality in the war poetry. L. Dolfi, 'Epistolario inédito de Juan Larrea a Vittorio Bodini', *BFFGL*, 18, 1995:119–27, transcribes 11 letters and several postcards written between 1966 and 1967 to Bodini and publisher Giulio Einaudi, which are concerned with surrealism, Larrea's conception of poetry and the editorial history of *Versión celeste* (see also *YWMLS*, 55:413). Luisa Cotoner Cerdó edits with critical apparatus Manuel Machado, *El mal poema (1909–1924)*, B, Montesinos, 227 pp. James Valender continues his fascination with the dynamic duo of Altolaguirre and wife, and introduces his selection of Concha Méndez Cuesta, *Poemas (1926–1986)*, M, Hiperión, 1995, 219 pp., and thereby corrects critical neglect in good faith but with a very restricted anthology that includes all *Vida a vida* (1932) and *Niño y sombras* (1936), some 30 poems from *Poemas. Sombras y sueños* (1944), but only three poems from each of the five additional books published between 1926 and 1981 plus others rescued from various scattered literary journals and another three from the still unedited 'Con el alma en vilo', for all of which is provided a useful bibliography. Ignacio Javier López edits Emilio Prados, *Jardín cerrado (Nostalgias, sueños, presencias) 1940–46*, Málaga, Centro Cultural de la Generación del 27, 1995, 411 pp., with an insightful 'Introducción' (11–56) that refers closely to the earlier editorial work of Id. and Patricio Hernández, in a bio-bibliographical commentary that situates Prados within his own generational context and informs the reader of the latest critical views, all topped off with a useful bibliography (57–66), followed by the carefully annotated text (see also *YWMLS*, 51:360, and 52:371–71).

INDIVIDUAL POETS

ALBERTI. María Asunción Mateo gathers the material together for A.'s autobiographical **De lo vivo y lejano*, M, Espasa Calpe, 274 pp., whilst C. Feal, 'Rafael Alberti, de la nostalgia a la esperanza', *Salina*, 9, 1995:75–77, elucidates the apparent contradiction between nostalgia and combat by showing how A. jibes personal and collective testimony in his poetry of exile. With help from Freud and Bruno Bettelheim, H. Laurenson, 'Consolation in purity: fairy-tale in the early lyrics of Rafael Alberti', *BHS(L)*, 73:153–63, takes a hard look at the de-sexed composite of Sophia, the Virgin Mary and Little Red Riding Hood to find the prelude to the discord between *id* and *ego* in the projection of desire that caused the breakdown in *Sobre los ángeles*. R. G. Havard, 'Rafael Alberti *De un momento a otro*: the matter of poetry, politics and war', *BHS(G)*, 73:81–126, draws parallels with Wilfred Owen, Dylan Thomas, and W. H. Auden in arguing for recognition against the critical tide that the volume is a major work in its own right which develops organically from the earlier poetry.

CERNUDA. A familiar point of view reappears, *Antología poética*, ed. Philip Silver, M, Alianza, 187 pp., where the text is taken from the 1974 (Barral) *Poesías completas*, and the 'Introducción' (7–18), a revised version of a 1974 paper, pushes C. as a moral force in Francoist Spain and makes very general remarks on Eros and Thanatos, Andrew Marvell and Paul de Man, C. and T. S. Eliot. In similar vein, and to be read together with profit: Bernard Sicot, *Quête de Luis Cernuda. 'Primeras poesías', 'Ocnos' et 'Variaciones sobre tema mexicano'*, Paris, L'Harmattan, 1995, 365 pp., uses Freudian analysis to explore convincingly the binary system *otredad-exilio* foregrounded in C.'s conflictive, confrontational journey of self-discovery; while K. J. Bruton, '"La mirada" in the poetry of Luis Cernuda — the 'hedgehog on the prowl"', *ALEC*, 21:27–40, takes his cue from

Roger Cardinal's 1981 study on the poetic imagination, and seizes on this obsessive, self-conscious, endlessly shifting, and very revealing concept, present in all four chronological phases of C.'s poetic odyssey. H. Pato, 'After a title: Cernuda, Goethe, Ocnos, and the ass', *REH*, 30:315–26, indulges in some textual archeology for the select few who, like her, boast a Greek lexicon and the time to read C.'s difficult poetry.

DIEGO. *CHA*, 553–54:7–69, is an uncritical *homenaje* commemorating the centenary of Diego's birth that contains: A. del Villar, 'La palabra según Gerardo Digo' (7–22), celebrating D. as the organizer in chief of the Spanish vanguard and intersperses a reading of 'Ultima palabra' with a very personal account of D.'s historical achievements; A. López Castro, 'Gerardo Diego, músico y poeta' (23–58), a timely reminder of the great importance of music in D.'s life and work; and F. Ruiz Soriano, 'Hidalgo and Hierro bajo el magisterio de Gerardo Diego' (59–69), documenting the first meeting on 29 March 1938 between D. and José Luis Hidalgo and José Hierro to estimate the importance of *Versos humanos* and *Alondra de verdad* on the younger men's postwar poetry.

GARCÍA LORCA. A flurry of editorial activity of rather mixed value: *Viaje a la luna. (Guión cinematográfico)*, ed. Antonio Monegal, V, PreTextos, 1995, 128 pp., is an important addition to the extant *obra* that both reproduces in facsimile and transcribes the text (56–76), and provides an excellent 'Introducción' (7–55) that tells how the MS was unearthed in Oklahoma in 1989 and gives valuable information about the curious publishing history in English and Spanish of this common project of G.L. and Emilio Amero, all with reference to the early Spanish cinema, surrealism and G.L.'s own brand of frustration, violence and sexual transgression; *Así que pasen cinco años. Leyenda de tiempo*, M, Cátedra, 1995, 361 pp., follows the 1933 text typed by Pura Ucelay for the Club Teatral Anfistora, with an 'Introducción' (9–175) that contextualizes title and subtitle, and explicates at some length plot, characters and themes, with special emphasis on children's songs, stage sets, colours, music and the ballet (see also *YWMLS*, 52:364 and 47:378–79); *Bodas de sangre*, ed. Allen Joseph and Juan Caballero, M, Cátedra, 1995, 167 pp., attempts to produce the definitive text by privileging the 1938 Losada version over those published in 1954 by Aguilar and in 1984 by Alianza while noting discrepancies and alternative readings; the long 'Introducción' (11–90) depends heavily upon Angel Alvarez de Miranda's 1963 study on metaphor and myth to define the drama as modern tragedy and G.L. as a modern Euripides, while the bibliography (89–90) is only of limited value, slanted towards tragedy and composed of items published before 1985; *La casa de Bernarda Alba*, ed. Allen Joseph and

Juan Caballero, M, Cátedra, 1995, 199 pp., seizes the opportunity to correct the usual critical alignment of the 'three tragedies' by defining the work as a 'drama poético andaluz' deriving from an Andalusia set somewhere on a par with other legendary toponyms like La Mancha, Yoknopatawpha and Macondo, but little has been done to update the pre-1975 bibliography (105–14); and P. Menarini, '*El público* y *Comedia sin título*: dos enmiendas posibles y un reportaje olvidado', *Salina*, 9, 1995:67–74, who argues both that the 'Solo de Pastor Bobo' is really a *captatio benevolentiae*, *loa* or prologue like others by G.L. and, therefore, does not belong between *cuadros* 5 and 6 but should begin the work, and also that the real title of *Comedia sin título* is, in fact, 'El sueño de la vida', reproducing one of G.L.'s last interviews on 29 May 1936 with the *Heraldo de Madrid* to support his theory. More of the correspondence sheds autobiographical light on G.L.'s circle: J. Valender, 'Cartas de Salvador Novo a Federico García Lorca', *CHA*, 548:7–20, reproduces three letters dated 11 and 25 December 1933 and January 1935, respectively, to explain the identity of 'Adela' and the real, or ardently desired, relationship between G.L. and the 'indiecito que llevas debajo de la tetilla izquierda', together with a useful commentary on the 'Romance de Angelillo y Adela' (1934), Novo's version of the few short days of intense friendship in Buenos Aires in 1933; while, in a 'Homenaje a Manuel Angeles Ortiz en el centenario de su nacimiento (1885–1995)', 'Cuatro dibujos y una carta inédita de Federico García Lorca', *BFFGL*, 18, 1995:9–15, handsomely reproduces the family portraits of Federico (1924), Francisco (1925), Concha (1925) and Isabel (1927), and a letter referring to the 'goma elástica, que es la amistad' between painter and poet. Cecilia J. Cavanaugh, SSJ, *Lorca's Drawings and Poems. Forming the Eye of the Reader*, Lewisburg, PA, Bucknell U.P., 1995, 202 pp., rights a perceived lack of critical interest: Chapter 1 outlines G.L.'s own view of the intrinsic connections between the two art forms; Chapter 2 focuses on the 1927–28 drawings and poems and the influence of Sebastià Gasch's *totalisme* and friend Salvador Dalì; Chapter 3 analyses G.L.'s presentation of space and place where the setting (New York) relates to his portrayal of the human figure; and Chapter 4 studies the phenomenon of the arabesque, starting with G.L.'s own signature, and its corresponding poetic metaphors in the *Diván del Tamarit*. A. A. Anderson, 'Bibliografía lorquiana reciente XVIII (1984–1995)', *BFFGL*, 18, 1995:151–56, is the usual useful round-up with details of editions, unpublished theses and reviews not found here. Candelas Newton, *Understanding Federico García Lorca*, South Carolina U.P., 1995, 190 pp., is very standard criticism forming part of the new series of guides destined for such a diverse public that it is bound not to satisfy anyone. Sumner Greenfield, *Lorca, Valle-Inclán y las estéticas de la disidencia*, SSSAS, 219 pp., contains some 19 previously published essays from 1955 to 1994, with eight on G.L., six on Valle-Inclán, and one apiece on Unamuno and the Generation of 1898, and is the distinguished scholar's own monument. S. Wahnón, 'La recepción de García Lorca en la España de la posguerra', *NRFH*, 43, 1995: 409–31, astutely contrasts the quick recuperation of Antonio Machado, due mainly to Dionisio Ridruejo's intelligent intervention, with G.L.'s protracted literary exile because of the falangists' poor opinion of 'las aguas turbias y cenagosas de un marxismo judío' surrounding G.L.'s adaptation of *Fuenteovejuna*, his championship of gypsy, Jew and black, and political advocacy of the poor and disadvantaged, all of which prove the brave attempts in the 1940s by Dámaso Alonso, Guillermo Díaz Plaja, Laín Entralgo, Vivanco and Charles David Ley to be the exception not the rule until G.L.'s return to the Spanish canon in the mid-1950s. S. Handley, 'Federico García Lorca and the 98 Generation: the *andalucismo* debate', *ALEC*, 21:41–58, examines how the *hecho andalusí* was used and abused between 1840 and 1927, resulting all too often in the familiar clichés of *la Andalucía de pandereta*, and argues that G.L.'s *Romancero gitano* formed part of the spirited *andalucista* movement in Granada which offered a better alternative than either a degenerate *flamenquismo* or an obdurate *castellanismo*. The poetry receives some useful critical attention: J. Valender, 'García Maroto y el *Libro de poemas* de García Lorca', *NRFH*, 44:155–65, hunts down a shadowy figure and finds in García Maroto's 1958 memoirs corroboration that the initiative for the publication of *Libro de poemas* came from Imprenta Maroto, that G.L.'s reluctance to publish was deep-seated and long-standing, that G.L. considered his poetic apprenticeship over when he gave García Maroto 'aquel caos juvenil y poético' to order, interpret and decipher, and, as a result, his collaboration was 'arbitrario e infantil' in editing the volume; F. Graffiedi, 'El macrotexto del *Romancero gitano* de Federico García Lorca', *La Torre*, 10:55–83, hammers away to show the symmetry, structure and composition at thematic and semantic levels, complete with graphs and illustrations; J. Salazar Rincón, '"Arbolé, arbolé", o las paradojas del amor lorquiano', *RLit*, 48:121–48, is a close reading with detailed references to both variants and previous criticism; and T. McMullan, 'Federico García Lorca's *Poeta en Nueva York* and the city of tomorrow', *BHS(G)*, 73:65–79, reads G.L. through *Urbanisme* (1925), and documents intelligently an implicit dialogue with Charles Edouard Jeanneret-Gris to trace their common enthusiasm for 'esta Babilonia trepidante y enloquecedora'. On the theatre: C. Christopher Soufas, *Audience and Authority in the Modernist Theatre of Federico García Lorca*, Tuscaloosa, AL, Alabama U.P., 190 pp., contends that

G.L.'s theatre should be set in the context of the artistic paradigms of European modernism between the wars, arguing for a move away from the traditional Lorcan criticism that has highlighted Spanish thematic and social issues in order to consider better G.L.'s metadramatic approach with its typically modernist rejection of empirico-mimeticism and acceptance of an 'outside' authority; G. Edwards, 'The way things are: toward a definition of Lorcan tragedy', *ALEC*, 21:271–90, meanders through a wealth of platitudes and defines very little; A. Gago Rodó, 'Los ejemplares de cuatro estrenos de García Lorca (1927–1934)', *BFFGL*, 18, 1995:97–118, usefully notes the history and context of the *libretos apógrafos* of *Mariana Pineda* (13 October 1927), *La zapatera prodigiosa* (24 December 1930), *Bodas de sangre* (7 March 1933) and *Yerma* (28 December 1934), and, in a valuable if not exhaustive appendix (109–18), notes the variants in what are probably the earliest known acting versions of these texts; to be read together with profit, D. E. C. Norlund, *HisJ*, 16, 1995:421–31, explicates G.L.'s 'social pathology and Juan's twisted authority in *Yerma*', while M. C. C. Mabrey, *Hispanófila*, 116:35–45, uses Foucault to interpret Yerma's growing frustration as her sexuality conflicts with the power structure depicted in G.L.'s 'tragic poem' and suggests that this mirrors G.L.'s own experience as a homosexual, while J. Albert Galera, '*Yerma* o el juego de los contrarios: semiosis y sentido', *Salina*, 9, 1995:99–110, arrives at much the same conclusion after a painstaking semiotic analysis of the play's isotopes; J. Hoeg, 'Steps to an ecology of *La casa de Bernardo Alba*', *REH*, 30:81–101, is so burdened with critical jargon that some valid points about female suicide, material resources and power struggles are, unfortunately, obscured; J. A. Giménez Micó, 'Lorca: teatro posible e imposible', *ALEC*, 20, 1995:351–64, follows G.L.'s own division and compares one of each, *La zapatera prodigiosa* and *Comedia sin título*, to explain how G.L. planned to re-educate public taste. Paul Julian Smith, *García Lorca/Almodóvar: Gender, Nationality, and the Limits of the Visible*, CUP, 1995, 25 pp., fastens upon the tyrannical mothers in both Mario Camus's, not entirely successful, film version of *La casa de Bernarda Alba* of 1987 and Almodóvar's *Entre tinieblas* of 1983 to explicate how this mythical, phallic mother-image, so typical of the tradition of Spanish misogyny, is actually a projection of the omnipotent, historical, father-fascist element in postwar Spain.

GUILLÉN. The 1993 centenary finally spills over into print (see also *YWMLS*, 56:390–93). From G.'s birth-place, *Jorge Guillén, el hombre y la obra. Actas del I simposium internacional sobre Jorge Guillén. Valladolid, 18–21 de octubre de 1993*, ed. Antonio Piedra and Javier Blasco Pascual, Valladolid U.P.–Fundación Jorge Guillén, 1995, 518 pp., is an important collection that will inevitably become the *guillenista vademecum* for some time to come; the elegant volume, with Rafael Alberti's original poster on the cover, is divided into three parts, the official conference papers, the round table-discussions and a series of shorter articles: thus, in alphabetical order, E. Alarcos Llorach, 'La forma como salvación en la poesía de Jorge Guillén' (11–23), takes up a familiar stance and reiterates the continuity of G.'s point of view and the unity of his poetic product to illustrate G.'s enduring belief in form as man's salvation; J. M. Blecua, 'Al margen de *Homenaje*' (25–40), shows himself the most informed of readers; B. Ciplijauskaité, 'Las raíces castellanas de *Cántico*' (41–54), celebrates Valladolid in G.'s poetry; C. Couffon, 'Jorge Guillén en París' (55–65), is an account of G. at the Institut d'Etudes Hispaniques in the Sorbonne, with ample quotation from G.'s letters between 1961 and 1983; E. Dehennin, 'La poética de Jorge Guillén vista desde *El poeta ante su obra* (1975)' (67–79), defines G. as a 'lector clásico', seduced in the week by classicism and by the baroque on Sunday, in Eugenio d'Ors's words; F. J. Díaz de Castro, '"Quedan los nombres": el arte del retrato en la poesía de Jorge Guillén' (81–104), lists the literary portraits from *Hacia 'Cántico'* to *Aire nuestro*; F. J. Díez de Revenga, 'Jorge Guillén y 1927' (105–18), gives details of the tricentenary, finishing *Cántico* and Murcia; A. García Berrio, 'Jorge Guillén: figuras de la imaginación' (119–26), highlights the association 'cathedral' and 'universe' in G.'s poetic world; V. García de la Concha, 'El espacio imaginario castellano en la poesía de Jorge Guillén' (127–40), muses on Jiménez's title of 'Reino' for *Cántico* and finds G. typical of the 1914 Generation; A. A. Gómez Yebra, 'Al *Final*, el amor' (141–60), explicates at length what love means for this fundamentally uxorious poet; F. Lázaro Carreter, 'Jorge Guillén: el fin de la poesía pura (de *Cántico* a *Clamor*)' (161–78), makes a hard and fast division according to his own preferences; J. L. López Araguren, 'Relectura de Jorge Guillén hoy, desde el punto de vista filosófico-religioso' (179–80), briefly defends G.'s 'integrismo' against Ortega's 'dehumanization' or Corpus Barga's 'denaturalización'; E. Lledó, 'Consciencia y luz en Jorge Guillén' (181–93), reads *Cántico* from an ethical point of view; J. M. Pozuelo Yvancos, 'La poética y la crítica literaria de Jorge Guillén' (195–219), finds another 'verdadero Jano intelectual' like Pound, Eliot and W. H. Auden in the criticism; F. Quintana Docio, 'Réplicas intertextuales elocutivas en la poesía de Jorge Guillén' (221–43), is clear and well-structured; K. M. Sibbald, '*Desde París*: crónicas y ocio' (245–55), characterizes G. as a Baudelairian 'flâneur' *à la* Benjamin in the chronicles written for *La Libertad* and *El Norte de Castilla*; A. Soria Olmedo, 'Jorge Guillén y la joven literatura' (257–78), reads *Hacia 'Cántico'* to contextualize G. and his generation; friends and fellow poets and writers like Angel Crespo,

Rosa Chacel, Antonio Gamoneda and Francisco Pino, María Victoria Atencia, Antonio Carvajal, Luis García Montero and Claudio Rodríguez record comments that are never dull and are often amusing and informative, as are the 'reviviscencias' of Claudio and Ángel Guillén, Antonio Rubio Sacristán, Emilio Gómez Orbaneja, Miguel Delibes and Rafael Lozano; all topped up with short pieces by Francisco Abad (349–58), José María Barrera López (359–64), José María Bascells (365–72), Antonio Carvajal (373–84), Andrew Debicki (385–94), Monserrat Escartín (395–404), David Ferry (405–10), Eugenio Florit (411–16), Elena Gascón Vera (427–38), Francisco Giner de los Ríos (427–38), Joaquín González Muela (439–442), Gabriel Jackson (443–46), Denah Lida (447–54), Oreste Macrí (455–68), Juan Montero (469–78), Rogelio Reyes (479–88), Bernard Sesé (489–98), Margarita Smerdou Altolaguirre (499–504), and Wai-Lim Yip (505–14). From the other side of the Atlantic, K. M. Sibbald edits and introduces the collection *Guillén at McGill: Essays for a Centenary Celebration*, Ottawa, Dovehouse, 197 pp.: K. M. Sibbald, 'Jorge Guillén at McGill: "una marcha al Canadá, conforme, sino alegre"' (13–38), documents the circumstances surrounding G.'s one-year appointment at the Canadian university and his poetic activity while in Montreal; B. Ciplijauskaité, 'Atisbos de Góngora en *Cántico*' (39–57), contains revealing passages from the still unpublished correspondence between G. and his first wife, Germaine Cahen, that shed much light on the simultaneous writing of G.'s doctoral thesis on the *Polifemo* and the composition of poems like 'Los amantes', 'Bella adrede' and, particularly, 'Salvación de la primavera', which contain G.'s mature, gongorine and wonderfully erotic reflections on the act of love; J. C. Wilcox, 'The nightingale the rose the ass: Jorge Guillén's intertextualization of Juan Ramón Jiménez. (A transtextual analysis)' (58–92), is an exemplary Bloomian analysis of the much-touted influence of Juan Ramón on G. which argues cogently that the amity and enemity between the poets was Oedipal in nature, and it should be read together with H. T. Young, 'Rereading and rewriting the poem: Juan Ramón Jiménez and Jorge Guillén' (155–73), which explores each poet's process of revision, self-allusion and recreation through their somewhat protracted lyrical autobiographies; J. Barroso Castro, 'Jorge Guillén and Vicente Aleixandre: dos ventanas frente a frente' (93–111), adduces some novel parallels between G., Le Corbusier, Freud and Aleixandre to illustrate similarities and important differences in both poets' reconstruction of reality; D. Odartey-Wellington, 'Epistolary narrative as literary form: the correspondence of Pedro Salinas and Jorge Guillén' (112–19), emphasizes the multi-layered narrativity that makes it possible to read this exchange of letters as a classic epistolary novel of

exile; I. Soldevila-Durante, 'Prosa poética guilleniana en su generación: los años de la vanguardia (1920–1928)' (120–34), takes a hard
look at some neglected material; J. Cano Ballesta, 'Jorge Guillén and
the young poets of the twenties and thirties' (135–54), documents,
with reference to the periodical literature of the period, the admiration for G. of such contemporaries as Domenchina, Francisco Pino,
José María Luelmo, Pedro Pérez Clotet and Cernuda, as well as the
special relationship between G. and Miguel Hernández; and, topping
off this homage, F. J. Díez de Revenga (174–94), examines G.'s own
Homenaje to find the beat of modern life rather than the usual literary
reflections (see also *YWMLS*, 55:412). And, finally, with an Aristotelian impulse to gloss the gloss *ad infinitum*, L. Dolfi, 'Omaggio a Guillén:
una poesía di Mario Hernández', *QIA*, 78, 1995:84–86, reproduces
the original, together with a translation into Italian, of a 1993
celebratory poem glossing G.'s 'Naturaleza viva' and his thoughts on
viewing Juan Sánchez Cotán's 'Bodegón con membrillo, repollo,
melón y pepino' in the San Diego Museum of Art, as Hernández
viewed 'Bodegón con cerdo y zanahorias' in the 1992–93 Prado
exhibition. More of G.'s correspondence gets into print: D. Pineda
Novo, 'Correspondencia inédita entre Jorge Guillén y Juan Ruiz
Peña (1934–1983)', *CHA*, 553–54:73–103, is a selection of some 145
letters exchanged between G. and his sometime student at the
University of Seville that gives news of *Cántico* and its various editions,
Dámaso Alonso and Pedro Salinas, the '"flameante" realismo
histórico' of the 1960s, G.'s return to Spain, and the intimacies of
family life; while E. González Mas, '14 cartas inéditas de Jorge
Guillén', *Salina*, 10:174–78, annotates G.'s travel plans, nostalgia for
Puerto Rico, and dislike for Richard M. Nixon in the years between
March 1964 and July 1974. A. Carreira, 'Jorge Guillén y la unicidad
de su lenguaje', *RLit*, 57:543–64, is a finely honed piece arguing,
with some merit, that *Cántico* was G.'s real work of genius never
matched by the subsequent books, metaphorically speaking the *allegro
molto* of a modern concerto followed by the slow movement (*Clamor*),
the final *rondeau* (*Homenaje*) and the variations on a theme (*Y otros
poemas* and *Final*). (See also JIMÉNEZ and SALINAS.)

JIMÉNEZ.   B. Ciplijauskaité, 'Apostilla a una polémica: J. R.
Jiménez y los poetas del 27', *Homenaje Ouimette*, 77–85, quotes from
the unedited correspondence between Jorge Guillén and Germaine
Cahen to point up certain details in the feud between Guillén and J.
that confirm that if their animosity was bitter and personal, both were
professionals with regard to each other's poetry (see also *YWMLS*,
56:392). Teresa Gómez Trueba, '*Estampas líricas*' en la prosa de Juan
Ramón Jiménez, Valladolid U.P., 1995, 222 pp., distinguishes three
modalities in J.'s lyric prose, *retratos*, *paisajes* and *recuerdos*, through

which to consider the influence of Ortega's *perceptivismo*, J.'s Madrid as opposed to his contemporaries' Castile, and the themes treated in J.'s autobiographic prose. Using much the same material but with exemplary clarity, J. Forrest and C. Jaffe, 'Figuring modernity: Juan Ramón Jiménez and the Baudelairian tradition of the prose poem', *CL*, 48:265–93, press Walter Benjamin into service in an effective comparison of 'La negra y la rosa' and 'La Belle Dorothée'. A. del Villar, 'El primer encuentro de Juan Ramón Jiménez con su Dios deseado', *CHA*, 557:99–109, is a great rigmarole involving the yearly solstices, St. John's Eve and an identification with God of the anonymous male figure in 'Mar ideal' dated 19 June 1911. (See GUILLÉN and MACHADO, A.)

MACHADO, A.   *Poesía*, ed. José Carlos Mainer, B, Ediciones Vicens Vives, 1995, xlvii + 24 pp., is designed for use in Spanish schools and colleges and to this end the introduction, which presents a masterly synthesis of M.'s poetry with some discerning comments on the poet's life, unsystematic reading habits, eye for landscape, his key poetic symbols, use of pseudonyms, and subtle use of colour, complements well the final quiz section compiled by José Enrique Serrano, while the judicious selection, practical rather than complete, makes this a most serviceable reader. J. Torrecilla, '¿Modernidad o autenticidad? La originalidad de Antonio Machado', *BHS(G)*, 73:45–63, explains M.'s anti-French bias rather as a battle fought out of his very real anxiety of influence than as a struggle against the Spanish cultural tradition *per se*. S. J. Joly, 'The dream and the imagination in Antonio Machado's poetry', *Hispanófila*, 117:25–43, uses Jungian psychoanalysis to interpret M.'s search for self-knowledge in his confrontation with the unconscious. Important findings are to be had in James Whiston, *Antonio Machado's Writings and the Spanish Civil War*, Liverpool U.P., 261 pp., who identifies more with Octavio Paz than E. Allison Peers in his positive assessment of M.'s last writings: wandering over this 'uncultivated hillside' leads to a solid appreciation of how well placed M. was to carry on the work of culture in the difficult circumstances of war-torn Spain by promoting an enlarged consciousness of that conflict as his part in the defence of the values and domain of the Spanish Republic, while M.'s views on pacifism, militarism and pluralism, the place of the intellectual in society, and his conviction as to the worth of critical consciousness all emerge from six chapters dealing with *Juan de Mairena* (1936) (13–48), *La guerra* (1937) (49–84), M.'s writings in *Hora de España* (85–105 and 107–48), his Civil War sonnets (149–91), and his contributions to *La Vanguardia* (1938–39) (193–239).

SALINAS.   Badly needed scholarly editions of Salinas's love poetry are forthcoming: *La voz a ti debida. Razón de amor. Largo lamento*, ed.

Montserrat Escartín, M, Cátedra, 1995, 567 pp., has a generally very reliable text of the first cycle with an introduction good on cross-references between S.'s poetry, essays and letters, although the nucleus of *Largo lamento*, the poetic rendition of S.'s final break with Katherine Reding, still has to be definitively constructed, and 'Amor, mundo en peligro' has wrongly been added here while 'La falsa compañera' certainly does belong to the collection; and *El contemplado. Todo más claro y otros poemas*, ed. Francisco Javier Díez de Revenga, M, Castalia, 205 pp., uses a clean version of the 1981 *Poesías completas* text and edits the two works in traditional fashion, according to their respective 1946 and 1949 publication dates, in preference to Soledad Salinas de Marichal's recent re-ordering according to the earlier gestation of *Todo más claro y otros poemas*, which includes poems written between 1936 and 1949; the 'Introducción biográfica y crítica' (9–50) situates well the poetry in the context of Salinas's life and recent criticism, and is complemented by an up-dated bibliography (51–64). Stephanie L. Orringer, *Pedro Salinas's Theatre of Self-Authentication*, NY, Lang, 1995, ix + 137 pp., explores with clarity and many useful connections to S.'s poetry the central preoccupations and quest for authenticity in his dramatic constructs. Vialla Hartfield-Méndez, *Woman and the Infinite. Epiphanic Moments in Pedro Salinas's Art*, Lewisburg, PA, Bucknell U.P., 185 pp., adduces parallels with Walt Whitman, Juan Ramón, Marcel Proust, the French Symbolists and Rubén Darío, all favourite authors of S., to show woman as the source of those transcendental 'spots of time' in human experience; the four chapters deal with modern literary epiphanies (13–35), woman in memory and myth (36–97), time, space and the epiphanic moment (98–153), and woman and the emanent in memory (154–68). (See GUILLÉN and JIMÉNEZ.)

3. PROSE

Francisco Ayala crafts a masterly essay on 'Creación imaginaria', *Homenaje Ouimette*, 5–11, that serves as a summation of his own art and the prologue to the homage volume. C. Alonso, 'Admiración y recepción literaria. (Epistolario de Eduardo Ranch y Pío Baroja)', *ECon*, 9:51–70, documents 20 years of assiduous friendship between February 1933 and December 1955, with generous quotation from the 95 letters exchanged by B. and the 'amigo' of *Las memorias*, E. Ranch Fuster (1897–1967). (See also AZORÍN below.) J. Kirkpatrick, 'Concha Espina: giros ideológicos y la novela de mujer', *HisJ*, 17:129–39, traces the line from feminism to fascism, using Rachel Blau DuPlessis to indicate the victory of traditionalism in *La flor de ayer* (1944) after the creative experimentalism of the earlier *La virgen prudente* (1929). J. Labanyi, 'Women, Asian hordes and the threat to the self in Giménez Caballero's *Genio de España*', *BHS(L)*, 73:377–87, reads the sexual politics in this hybrid tract and/or avant-garde text via German fascism, Nancy Chodorow and Jessica Benjamin to discern amid the highly charged sexual vocabulary and imagery Giménez Caballero's advocacy of fascism as the antidote to male fears of the annihilation of their *ego*. J. M. Salguero Rodríguez, 'El primer Sender (1916–1939) y sus textos teatrales', *ALEC*, 21:351–64, collates information from theatre reviews and critical essays published in *La Libertad* to attest to Sender's evident knowledge of vanguard techniques of the Russian and German theatre put into practice in *El secreto*, the lost text of *La llave* and the post-war novels. R. Johnson, 'María Zambrano's theory of literature as knowledge and contingency', *His(US)*, 79:215–21, draws parallels with Ortega, Sartre and Derrida but finds Zambrano less reductive, especially when focusing on female characters like Benigna in *Misericordia* as most suited to her theorizing about literature as the true *locus* of poetic reason.

INDIVIDUAL WRITERS

AZORIN. M. D. Dobón, 'Correspondencia inédito del encuentro y amistad entre Azorín y Baroja', *BH*, 97, 1995:605–29, reproduces 18 letters that prove that the two writers knew each other by 1897 or at the very latest 1898, as well as documenting a common dislike for violence, plans to publish a Spanish equivalent of *L'Aurore*, squabbles with Unamuno, and lots of literary gossip to support the opinion that 'los intelectuales somos así crueles y terribles'. Proof of that particular pudding is digested in 'Azorín falsificador: una violenta polémica literaria fin de siglo', *BHS(G)*, 73:171–85, when D. goes on to analyse the mischief-making in A.'s supposed 'interviews' with Jacinto Benavente and Eugenio Sellés that were designed to bring A. into the limelight by sniping at María Guerrero and the *modernistas*. G. Jurkevich, 'Azorín's magic circle: the subversion of time and space in *Doña Inés*', *BHS(G)*, 73:29–44 and *BHS(L)*, 73:49–61, employs Marianna Torgovnick's parameters to reveal A.'s view of time as circular and human life as an inescapable, uroboric circle, thus prefiguring many philosophical points of view that would later dominate European thought and letters. M. Martín Rodríguez, 'Azorín, adaptador teatral: el caso de *Maya*, de Simon Gantillon', *ALEC*, 20, 1995:393–408, recounts the uproar that followed the Madrid staging of this French play about prostitution, even in A.'s version decorously minus the swearing, comparison of bust sizes, hints of lesbianism, work-load and general 'odeur de femelle', but claims that the moral backlash obscured A.'s real aim of attempting to stage a modern *auto sacramental* or anti-naturalist piece of *superrealidad*.

GANIVET. Anticipating centenary interest and the first in the projected complete *obras completas* comes *Granada la bella*, ed. Fernando García Lara, Granada, Diputación Provincial–Fundación Caja de Granada, 161 pp., which takes due note of the variants of this prelude to *Idearium español* written in Helsingfors in February 1896 by the then Spanish consul, later recognized as the 'urbanista precursor de la ortodoxia urbanológica española' by the Sociedad Central de Arquitectos no less, as Ángel Isac explains in an informative preliminary study 'Ganivet y la crítica de la cuidad moderna' (11–52). From the same collection with the curious dating 1898–1995, also come: Nil Santiáñez-Tió, *Ángel Ganivet: una bibliografía anotada 1892–1995*, Granada, Diputación Provincial–Fundación Caja de Granada, 265 pp., an essential tool that will also promote further research; and Raúl Fernández Sánchez-Alarcos, *La novela modernista de Ángel Ganivet*, Granada, Diputación Provincial–Fundación Caja de Granada, 329 pp., a thorough revindication of G.'s extraordinarily suggestive novels using recent hermeneutical studies.

GÓMEZ DE LA SERNA. *Teatro muerto. (Antología)*, ed. Agustín Muñoz-Alonso López and Jesús Rubio Jiménez, M, Cátedra, 1995, 583 pp., brings together the original 'Teatro muerto' collection prepared by G.S. in 1956 and other minor texts: from *Prometeo* the experimental pieces *La utopia (I)*, *Beatriz*, *El drama del palacio deshabitado*, *Los sonámbulos*, *La utopia (II)*, *Los unánimes*, *El teatro de la soledad*, and *El lunático*, as well as the 'pantomimas y danzas' *La bailarina*, *Acesos al silencio*, *Las rosas rojas*, *El nuevo amor*, *Los dos espejos*, *Las danzas de pasión*, *El garrotín*, *La danza de los apaches*, *La danza oriental*, *Los otros bailes* and *Fiesta de dolores*; the long 'Introducción' (9–136) contextualizes well the state of the art in 1908–12 and explicates this 'síntesis gráfica de sus ideas' that attests G. S.'s deep involvement and keen interest in the renovation of the Spanish theatre as 'Vice Presidente de Teatro de Ensayo' and regular contributor to *Prometeo*. D. Serrano-Dolader, '*La viuda blanca y negra* o la teatralización de la novela en Gómez de la Serna', *ALEC*, 21:119–41, defines G.S.'s first long novel as 'una nivola teatralizada'.

ORTEGA. In good company with Charles Peirce, Max Weber, Saussure, Marinetti, Wittgenstein, Le Corbusier, Freud and Edmund Husserl, O.'s essay on 'The crowd phenomenon' appears in *From Modernism to Postmodernism: An Anthology*, Cambridge, MA, Blackwell, xiv + 731 pp., a mammoth compendium from Descartes and Rousseau to Sandra Harding and David Hall. Zeroing in on particular facets of O.'s work: P. Cerezo Galán, '*Meditaciones del Quijote* o el estilo del héroe', *Homenaje Ouimette*, 57–75, posits O.'s programme of action

for a discredited nation as directly opposed to that of Unamuno;
while M. Durán, 'Ortega y von Uexküll: de la biología a la razón
vital', *ib.*, 101–16, traces a debt to the German biologist, particularly
in *Ensimismamiento y alteración* and *La rebelión de las masas*; and
T. Mermall, 'Abstracto/concreto: clave retórica para la comprensión
de Ortega', *ib.*, 181–90, highlights a fundamental trope in the
'Prólogo a los franceses' of *La rebelión de las masas*, whereby O.
defended concrete historical values and individual life experience
over revolutionary utopias and impersonal, homogeneous abstract
values as a defence against the fascism he once found attractive. B.
Matamoro, 'La cocina de Ortega', *CHA*, 548:33–44, dishes up quite
a menu of ideas on O. as a modern *clerc*, his method of writing
philosophy, and his indebtedness to Heidegger; while R. García
Alonso, 'De lo uno a lo otro. De Antonio Machado a José Ortega y
Gasset', *ib.*, 45–55, follows through with a new critical alignment.

UNAMUNO. *Prensa de juventud*, ed. Elías Amézaga, M, 1995, Compañía literaria, 372 pp., contains unedited articles published by a very
young U. in *El Noticiero Bilbaíno* under such pseudonyms as 'baserritar-
bat' and 'Peru el aldeano'. *La agonía el cristianismo*, ed. †Victor
Ouimette, M, Espasa Calpe, 188 pp., usefully corrects the errata in
previous Spanish versions of the text by reference to the first edition
published in Madrid in 1931, as well as the excellent translations by
Jean Cassou into French in 1925 and by Anthony Kerrigan into
English of 1974, and, in an exemplary 'Introducción' (9–62),
contextualizes both the genesis in Paris and the European ramifications of this essay viewed as part of U.'s battle against any 'dogma
que mata la fe'. Some more of the voluminous correspondence gets
into print: *Cartas de Ciro Bayo a Unamuno. Un diálogo difícil, ed. J. A.
Ereño Altuna, Salamanca, Diputación de Salamanca, 150 pp.; and
*Epistolario americano (1890–1936), ed. Laureano Robles, Salamanca
U.P., 579 pp. M. Tasende and L. T. González-del-Valle, '"La mística
española": un ensayo rescatado de Unamuno', *BHS(G)*, 73:5–28,
reproduce the text (16–28), which appeared as an introduction to
Volume VIII of the *Antología universal ilustrada*, suggest a date of
composition between 1909 and 1912, and point out differences in an
earlier piece on the same theme 'De mística y humanismo' (1895) and
clear similarities with *Del sentimiento trágico de la vida* (1912). Francisco
La Rubia Prado, *Alegorías de la voluntad, pensamiento, pensamiento orgánico,
retórica y desconstrucción en la obra de Miguel de Unamuno*, Madrid,
Libertarias-Prodhufi, 286 pp., presses Jonathan Culler, Paul de Man,
Hillis Miller and Meyer Abrams into service in an ambitious study
divided into two sections that evaluates and critiques U.'s problematic
of organicism, examining, first, the *Völkerpsychologie* and U.'s *organicismo
positivo* in order to consider, secondly, U.'s eventual rejection of

mimetic representation. M. M. Landa Sopena, 'La literatura vasca en la obra de Unamuno', *HisJ*, 16, 1995:317–37, once again documents U.'s opinions of Antonio de Trueba, José María de Salaverría, Vicente de Arana, Timoteo Orbe, and Francisco de Iturribarria to no great purpose (see also *YWMLS*, 56:399). M. J. Valdés, 'La intrahistoria de Unamuno y la nueva historia', *Homenaje Ouimette*, 237–50, looks at *En torno al casticismo*, the articles in *Las Noticias* and *Paz en la guerra* in order to adduce parallels with Fernand Braudel and bring U. in line with most recent historiographical theorizing. On the novels: L. Hynes, '*La tía Tula*: forerunner of radical feminism', *Hispanófila*, 117:45–54, lines up contemporary feminists like Alison Jagger, Shulamite Firestone, Jeffner Allen, Ann Oakley, and Andrea Dworkin to argue that U.'s novel does, indeed, preview the rejection of oppressive marriage systems, support for woman-centred religious fervour, a radical attack on traditional male–female roles and biological motherhood, and the need for a new model of society but, following the practice of radical feminism, then deconstructs the same theorizing in thought-provoking fashion to show that Tula's cult of the Virgin Mary is merely a residual exercise of patriarchal catholicism, that the strength of her radical aversion to motherhood is counter-balanced by her sexless doll play, that her matriarchal beehive model is doomed to failure, and, consequently, that U.'s character is only a non-effective precursor in the battle yet to be won; while T. R. Franz, 'Unamuno's contribution to the stream of consciousness narrative', *ib.*, 55–62, revises the usual nomenclature to begin with Edouard Dujardin's *Les Lauriers sont coupés* (1887), and cites Pérez Galdós and Leopoldo Alas to clarify U.'s position. In comparative vein: F. La Rubia Prado, 'Unamuno contra Croce', *RoN*, 36:305–13, reads again the prologue to the 1911 Spanish translation of *Estetica come scienza dell'espresione e linguistica generale* to underline U.'s profound rejection of Croce's idealism; N. R. Orringer, 'Unamuno and St. José Martí, the good', *Homenaje Ouimette*, 191–201, contends that the apostle of Cuban freedom served as the major model for U.'s Manuel Bueno and indicates two literary dress rehearsals in the articles 'Cartas de poeta' and 'Sobre el estilo de José Martí' of 1919; while, moving on, T. R. Franz, 'Envidia y existencia en Millás y Unamuno', *ib.*, 131–42, tracks down intertextualities on the Cain and Abel theme in *Volver a casa* (1990), and H. Cazorla, 'Breve juego unamuniano: *Una noche con Clark Gable*, de Jaime Salom', *Estreno*, 12.2:11–12, notes the *première* at the Theatre Thalia in New York in 1994, and pencils in a Unamunian background for the dual role of Flora and Dora. G. Ribbans, '"Indigesto, mezquino, pedestre, confuso": a hostile contemporary critique of Unamuno's *Poesías* (1907)', *Homenaje Ouimette*, 203–16, weakly defends U. against the unfavourable review in *Revista Latina* on 1 September 1907 by Augusto Vivero, who slated the 'puro plomo' of the poetry and accused U. of plagiarizing Jean-Marie Guyau; and N. G. Round, 'Some preliminary thoughts on the Unamunian speech act', *ib.*, 217–36, explains in convoluted fashion why 'Del dicho al hecho no hay trecho' in that same poetry. C. Feal, 'Cómo se hace teatro una novela: *Sombras de sueño* de Unamuno', *ALEC*, 20, 1995:315–49, highlights the usual Unamunian mosaic of binary inter-relationships to suggest that his equally divided and contradictory female figures present a possible solution to the male rivalries played out within the self.

VALLE-INCLÁN. Following on an earlier study, Jesús Rubio Jiménez edits with full critical apparatus *Retablo de la avaricia, la lujuria y la muerte*, M, Espasa Calpe, 493 pp., and comments fully on both the overall meaning of the collection and the connections between the five independent plays (see also *YWMLS*, 56:402). Despite some high-handed opinions about 'el insoportable' Charlie Chaplin, the 'mundo cursi y pavitonto' that swooned over Rudolf Valentino, and Yankee bad taste, J. Barreiro, 'Las opiniones de Valle-Inclán sobre el cine: una entrevista desconocida', *ALEC*, 20, 1995:503–55, cites fragments from V.-I.'s interview with *El Cine* of December 1927 attesting to high hopes about what the cinema might achieve. Javier Serrano Alonso and Amparo de Juan Bolufer, *Bibliografía general de Ramón del Valle-Inclán*, Santiago de Compostela U.P., 1995, will obviously further critical interest. A. Zamora Vicente, 'Los años difíciles: Valle-Inclán y la Fundación San Gaspar', *BRAE*, 75, 1995:455–75, examines the record to find that this charitable fund for 'socorros de literatos pobres' awarded V.-I. the sum of 400 pesetas in February 1902 in view of what he described as his 'situación angustiosa'. Javier Serrano Alonso, *Los cuentos de Valle-Inclán: estrategia de la escritura y genética textual*, Santiago de Compostela U.P., 315 pp. I. J. López, 'Bradomín y la estatua de piedra en *Sonata de otoño*', *HR*, 64:73–88, shows hows the *Sonatas* are characterized by a rewriting in an ironic key of the themes common to Symbolism, European decadence and Spanish *fin de siècle*, and adduces a long line of parallels to this ironic example of *donjuanismo* from Baudelaire to Paul de Man. Enrique Torner, *Geografía esperpéntica: el espacio literario en los esperpentos de Valle-Inclán*, Lanham, MD, Univ. P. of America, xviii + 144 pp. S. I. Cardona, 'El enemigo necesario: don Latino de Hispalis, el gracioso de *Luces de Bohemia* de Ramón María del Valle-Inclán', *ALEC*, 21:423–30, documents the 'juego de escarnio' in V.-I.'s paradoxical nod to tradition *via* satire and parody.

4. THEATRE

Critical work on the drama of the period is also noted above under GARCÍA LORCA, SALINAS, GÓMEZ DE LA SERNA, SENDER, UNAMUNO and VALLE-INCLÁN. Items not recorded here on García Lorca and Unamuno may be found in L. M. Pottie, R. Cameron, and C. Costello, 'Modern drama studies: an annual bibliography', *MoD*, 39:247–330, see particularly section E: Hispanic (284–89). David George, *The History of the 'commedia dell'arte' in Modern Hispanic Literature with Special Attention to the Work of García Lorca*, Lewiston-Queenstown-Lampeter, Mellen, 1995, 186 pp., is a brief introduction to the reappearance in the 20th c. of the art form as the paradigmatic symbol of the modernist concern to make sense of life's absurdity, with wide-ranging chapters on the theoretical views of Adrià Gual, Benavente, Pérez de Ayala, Rivas Cherif and Valle-Inclán; García Lorca and the eternal comic spirit of the *commedia*; Benavente and the circus, carnival, and the move towards Eduardo Zamacois's tragic portraiture of Pierrot; the irony, disillusion and ultimate destruction of the 'poor Pierrot' myth by Manuel Machado, Leopoldo Lugones and Valle-Inclán; and the renewal of the mask by García Lorca. Catherine Arturi Parilla, *A Theory of Reading Dramatic Texts. Selected Plays by Pirandello and García Lorca*, NY, Lang, 1995, ix + 185 pp., is anchored in the work of Iser, Ingarden and Jauss, with reference to Peter Szondi and Mario Valdés; the readings of García Lorca's drama add few new insights. M. A. Gómez, 'La (trans)posición de una ideología: de *La Señorita de Trevélez* a *Calle Mayor*', *Estreno*, 22.2:45–50, 58, considers the moral and ideological bridge between the adaptation by Gabriel Ibáñez for Radio TVE and the performance directed by Edgar Neville in 1935 of the former work, and Juan Antonio Bardem's memorable film version of *Calle Mayor*, clearly influenced by Fellini's *I vitelloni*, finding in both works severe criticism of Spanish society in the first half of this century. Particular attention is paid to dramatic theorizing: V. García Plata, 'Primeras teorías españolas de la puesta en escena: Adrià Gual', *ALEC*, 21:291–312, documents Gual's innovative ideas on decoration and scene sets, particularly his use of colour to order scenic effects, in his contributions on scenic theory to *Teatre intim* (1898–1905), and in two essays, 'Blanch y negre' and 'Noctum'; J. Martori, 'Guimerà en Madrid', *ib.*, 313–28, uses the Catalan dramatist's private correspondence with María Guerrero and Pedro Díaz de Mendoza and over 300 of his articles in the Madrid press to record the dynamic at work between Barcelona and Madrid in the theatre world; B. A. González, 'La teoría de la crítica teatral durante la Segunda República: el caso de Juan Chabás', *ib.*, 365–92, quotes extensively from theatre criticism written for *Luz* in

1933–34 to show the doctrinal coherence and clear understanding of the historical context that informed Chabás's belief in the compatibility of both a socio-political stand and aesthetic renewal in the theatre, and adds a useful bibliography of essays, reviews and other periodistical writings in *Luz, España, El País, El Sol, La Gaceta Literaria, La Voz* and *Ahora*; G. Rey Faraldos, 'Antonio Espina: teoría y creación en el teatro de vanguardia', *ib.*, 409–437, sheds light on a neglected figure who brought his own mixture of the absurd and the comically paradoxical both to the experimental pieces of the 1920s *Su Excelencia Don Capirote. Boxiganga en tres pedazos y un pico, S. W. film G.3* and *Fatum*, and the constructive reviews written for *Luz, Crisol* and *El Sol* in the 1930s; whilst D. Vela Cervera, 'El estreno en Madrid de *El señor de Pigmalión* de Jacinto Grau (18-V-1928): la plástica escénica de Salvador Bartolozzi', *ib.*, 439–61, explains why, after prestigious *estrenos* in Charles Dullin's *Théâtre de l'Atelier* in Paris and Joseph Čapek's National Theatre in Prague, the first performance in Madrid in 1928 marked a watershed moment in the introduction of innovative scenery that would later enhance performances of work by Valle-Inclán and García Lorca. Alberto Romero Ferrer and Marieta Cantos Casenave edit with critical apparatus, Pedro Muñoz Seca, **Entrada general y Los morenos o Estreno del episodio dramático, en verso, original de Don Ananías Gómez titulado ¡Ay de mí!*, Cadiz, Fundación Pedro Muñoz Seca, 1995, 211 pp. A. Fernández Insuela, 'En la senda del teatro social de preguerra: *Los semidioses* (1914), de Federico Oliver', *Salina*, 9, 1995: 116–25, comments at length on the three hot topics of 1914, the anti-bullfight lobby, emigration and the need for agrarian reform, that are woven into the dense fabric of this recreation of contemporary society, and adds as an appendix some interesting quotations from the reviews published in *ABC, La Correspondencia de España, El Globo, Nuevo Mundo* and *La Esfera*.

LITERATURE, 1936 TO THE PRESENT DAY

By ABIGAIL LEE SIX and OMAR A. GARCÍA, *Queen Mary and Westfield College, University of London.*

1. GENERAL

F. Carrasco Heredia et al., *Los andaluces del siglo XX*, Córdoba, Ateneo de Córdoba, 246 pp., is a useful work of reference; all listings appear in alphabetical order, and there is an index (237) by field, which makes it easy to find those included in the literature section, which includes Caballero Bonald, Gala, García Baena, Martín Recuerda, among others; its limitation lies on its omission of contemporary Andalusian writers such as Ana Rossetti, Luis García Montero, and Juana Castro, amongst others. A. Lee Six has written the chapter on Spain in Sturrock, *Guide*, 377–90; the period spanned is from 1960 to the present day and the approach informative, rather than polemical. I. Michael, 'The Spanish Civil War and the care of books in Madrid', *BHS(G)*, 73 : 285–97, is an excellent, well-documented article on the methods used to safeguard books during the Civil War; of relevance to us is that it sheds light on the Lázaro [Galdiano] Collection of MSS, and indicates the need for further research.

2. POETRY

GENERAL. The predominant tendency for this end of the millennium continues to be an emphasis on realism, but as will be pointed out below, other tendencies do exist, and just as strong, even if they do not enjoy the privileges of some publishers. Unfortunately, it is worth pointing out that *Ínsula*, one of the journals with the longest tradition in this field, is limiting itself (and the readers) more and more by constraining itself to mere book reviews of the latest collections, published by the mainstream houses of Spain, and offering the critic more over-the-top reviews than necessary, where all poets and their latest arrivals are presented not with an objective critical eye, but with that of a friend trying to promote the work. Let us hope that in the future, *Ínsula* leaves room for some serious studies as well. *Poesía y exilio. Los poetas del exilio español en México*, ed. Rose Corral, Arturo Souto, and James Valender, Mexico, El Colegio de México, 1995, 468 pp., is a collection of papers from a 1993 conference on the self-explanatory title, including poets such as José Moreno Villa, José Bergamín, Concha Méndez, Emilio Prados, Pedro Garfias, Juan Rejano, Ernestina de Champourcin, León Felipe, Luis Cernuda, Juan Larrea, Max Aub, and Agustí Bartra; it is introduced by José

Ángel Valente, and it also includes a section of *testimonios*. J. Fradejas Lebrero, 'La forma litánica en la poesía del siglo XX', *RLit*, 58:399–425; the relevant part for this section (416–) includes Otero, Gala, Pedro Álvarez, Gloria Fuertes, Jorge Semprún, and Manuel Mantero; it is mainly a selection of poems, some of which appear in works of other genres, displaying the *forma litánica*, defined as the repetition of the refrain after each line. F. Ruiz Soriano, 'Hidalgo y Hierro, bajo el magisterio de Gerardo Diego', *CHA*, 553–54:59–69, documents the importance of D.'s poetry, where his *creacionismo* mainly influenced Hidalgo, whilst his move towards existential and social poetry serves as reference to both Hierro and Hidalgo. M. B. Ferrari, 'Postismo/novísimos: ¿La tradición de la ruptura?', *LetD*, 72:95–108, could be seen as polemic; it claims there is a continuum between the *postismo* of the 1940s and the *novísimos* (though it only deals with the works of Carnero and Gimferrer at any length), indicating their similarities in the importance they give to language over referent, the presence of fragmentation, and the breaking away from other established forms. *Mundo abreviado. Lectura de poetas españoles contemporáneos*, ed. Pilar Celma et al., Valladolid, Ámbito, 1995, 479 pp., is divided into four sections to cover from the so-called 1936 generation to the seventies, offering an analysis of the poetry of Miguel Hernández, Luis Rosales, Juan Gil-Albert, Gabriel Celaya, Blas de Otero, José Hierro, Francisco Brines, Claudio Rodríguez, José Ángel Valente, Pedro Gimferrer, Luis Antonio de Villena, and Antonio Carvajal, while at the same time contextualizing the poetic period; its deficiency lies in the fact that not all citations are properly identified. Catherine Ruth Christie, *Poetry and Doubt in the Work of José Ángel Valente and Guillermo Carnero*, Lewiston-Queenston-Lampeter, Mellen, 283 pp., offers a comparative approach of C. and V. on remembering, perception, metapoetry, and intertextuality, while the first two parts of the book provide the relevant literary background of the period; it covers V.'s first four poetry collections of the anthology *Punto cero*, and C.'s work up until 1990; at the centre of the argument is the preoccupation or doubt of both writers with the connection between word and world. *La nueva poesía (1975–1992)* (Poesía española, 10), ed. Miguel García-Posada, B, Crítica, 266 pp., is a welcome edition which takes into account the different tendencies in contemporary poetry, which the critic defines as *neopurismo*, *poesía de la experiencia*, and *impresionismo*, while highlighting other trends; (9–30) traces the evolution of this field during the 17 years concerned, claiming there have been no abrupt ruptures, and giving special attention to some common elements in today's poetry, such as: writing urban poetry, fictionalizing the subject, employing narrative poetry, expressing disenchantment, resorting to traditional metrics, organizing the collection in a symmetrical fashion as a whole, re-reading the tradition and imitating other poets such as Gil de Biedma, returning to realism with its contemporary frame, finding their literary models mainly in the generations of 1898, 1927, and 1950; (31–242) is an anthology with a brief introduction preceding a selection from each of the following poets: Miguel d'Ors, Fernando Ortiz, Rosa Romojaro, Eloy Sánchez Rosillo, Luis Alberto de Cuenca, Ana Rossetti, Javier Salvago, Jon Juaristi, Abelardo Linares, Andrés Sánchez Robayna, Juan Manuel Bonet, Justo Navarro, Andrés Trapiello, Julio Martínez Mesanza, Juan Lamillar, Luis García Montero, Blanca Andreu, Álvaro Valverde, Felipe Benítez Reyes, Carlos Marzal, Roger Wolfe, José Antonio Mesa Toré, Almudena Guzmán, and Álvaro García. Nigel Glendinning, *Painting and Poetry in Contemporary Spanish Women Writers*, London, Queen Mary & Westfield College, 33 pp., explores the connection between the poetic word and the different aspects of the visual arts in Amparo Amorós, Blanca Andreu, María Victoria Atencia, Ángela Figuera Aymerich, Luisa Castro, Isla Correyero, Gloria Fuertes, Emilia González Fernández, Carmen González Marín, Menchu Gutiérrez, Almudena Guzmán, Amalia Iturbide, María del Carmen Pallarés, Marta Pérez Novales, Ana Rossetti, Fanny Rubio, María Sanz, Concha Zardoya, at the same time that it takes into account the work of Alberti, Carnero, Cernuda, Machado, Salinas, and Valente, for a comparative approach.

ALEGRE HEITZMAN. G. Guerrero, '*Sombra y materia*, de Alfonso Alegre Heitzmann: la capacidad expresiva del lenguaje', *Ínsula*, 595–96:27–28, presents A.H.'s poetry as a dialogue of opposites, resident in the hyphen between the two poles, a poetry 'vinculada al mito' that tries to transcend linguistic limitations.

ÁLVAREZ PIÑER. C. Aurtenetxe, 'De esta palabra que ya es nuestra (Luis Álvarez Piñer al fin entre nosotros)', *Ínsula*, 595–96:23–25, is on *Poesía*, the anthology of A.P.'s complete works, a writer who was practically unknown until he received the *Premio Nacional de Poesía* in 1991; in a rather impressionistic analysis, his poetry is seen as having clarity and precision to express the obscure, a work of reflection.

BRINES. L. Martínez de Mingo, 'La acendrada despedida de Francisco Brines', *Ínsula*, 591:20–21, is personal and anecdotal, then highlights B.'s *La última costa* and his book on poets *Escritos sobre poesía española*.

CAMPOS PÁMPANO. M. A. Lama, 'La línea de sombra de Ángel Campos en *Siquiera este refugio*', *Ínsula*, 594:24–25, is on this poet's fifth collection, which includes poems dating as far back as 1982.

where paradoxically unity is expressed through a writing that groups different motives.

COLINAS. J. L. Puerto, 'Antonio Colinas: la poesía como itinerario de purificación', *CHA*, 556:59–84, is an overview of key elements in C.'s work; the poet is portrayed as a loner before the predominant aesthetics of today; his poetry is achieved through the fusion of pre-Socratic opposites, and a continued process of discovery and revelation.

CONDE. D. Gilliam, 'The dilemma of the divided self in three poems by Carmen Conde', *Hispanófila*, 118:49–63, is a good article on C.'s poems 'Encuentro conmigo', 'Límite', and 'Dominio' from *Iluminada tierra* (1951), which seem to respond by rejecting the calmness and emptiness raised in 'La otra experiencia'; it examines the duality of the self in the representation of her female subject, a dichotomy of inner self and outer woman brought about by society's (mis)representation of women, yet the poet cannot visualize the two selves as one in the world, which is left for the reader to do.

CRESPO. María Teresa Bertelloni, *El mundo poético de Ángel Crespo*, M, Huerga y Fierro, 171 pp., is a revised second edition that analyses the different aspects of C.'s poetry, relying on a philosophical approach.

CUENCA. L. Martínez de Mingo, 'La difícil facilidad de un poeta sobrado', *Ínsula*, 595–96: 25–26, is a bit over the top on *Por Fuertes y Fronteras*, full of praise for Cuenca's poetry.

DUQUE AMUSCO. A. Ramoneda, 'La palabra, carne iluminada', *Ínsula*, 591:25–27, is on *Donde rompe la noche*, and it indicates that the text is able to interpret reality and in doing so, it creates another one, just as authentic, in what the critic calls 'juanramoniana salvación'.

FIGUERA AYMERICH. Jo Evans, *Moving Reflections. Gender, Faith and Aesthetics in the Work of Ángela Figuera Aymerich*, London, Támesis, 162 pp., is an important work that rescues F.A., who belonged — according to some — to the generation of 1927, while others include her in the generation of 1936, although her publications clearly place her with the group of post-Civil War writers; Evans examines her work in the context of marginalized women's writing, and current theory in the field, presenting her as a precursor of those women writing post-Franco, such as Rossetti; she also highlights in the process the patronizing patriarchal discourse that has dominated criticism on F.A., and other women writers, due in part to gender expectations sometimes even unconsciously assumed by the poet herself.

GARCÍA MONTERO. F. J. Díaz de Castro, '*Habitaciones separadas*, de Luis García Montero', *Ínsula*, 594:22–24, highlights love, solitude, and freedom in G.M.'s collection indicated in the title, and looks at the structure of the book, which is tied with his temporal reality, the quotidian, and finally the socio-political element.

GONZÁLEZ. Emilio Alarcos Llorach, *La poesía de Ángel González*, Oviedo, Ediciones Nobel, 332 pp., is a collection of works on G., dating as far back as 1969 and as recent as 1996 when the poet was admitted to the Academy; (7–190) was published in 1969 by the University of Oviedo, and covers G.'s work up to *Tratado de urbanismo* (1967); (191–292) reproduces conversations with G. which took place in 1985, and which were published in pp. 51–94 of *Ángel González verso a verso*, Oviedo, Caja de Ahorro de Asturias, 1987; 'Recato y elegía' (293–307) was published in 1990; (309–30) includes: an article of 1985 when the poet received the Príncipe de Asturias Prize; another one for the presentation of the book *Angel González verso a verso*; and finally the *laudatio* when the poet aspired to a seat in the *Real Academia*. Overall, the relevance of this volume is that it makes accessible to the reader separate works on G.

LASA. J. Kruz Igerabide Sarasola, 'Mikel Lasa: La letra y el silencio de un poeta moderno', *Ínsula*, 591 : 22–23, is on *Memory Dump*, a many-sided work presented in a chronological sequence of production, stressing the themes of the impossibility of love and poetry, and the uselessness of the latter albeit its vital necessity.

MARTÍN. J. J. Lanz, 'La poesía de Sabas Martín', *CHA*, 551 : 152–59, briefly covers M.'s poetry collections *Títere sin cabeza*, *Pa(i)saje*, *Indiana sones*, *Peligro intacto*, and *Navegaciones al margen*, presented as poetic evolution of his constant preoccupation with the inauguration of space through the word.

NÚÑEZ. A. L. Prieto de Paula, 'Aníbal Núñez: una epifanía', *Ínsula*, 591 : 23–25, indicates that N. is a marginalized writer whose work is beginning to be valued posthumously; it concentrates on the role of ruins as a space in his work, especially post-1974.

ORTEGA. T. Sánchez Santiago, 'El resplandor del reposo', *Ínsula*, 595–96 : 26–27, is on two collections, *Mudanza* and *Hilo solo*, where language is seen as an instrument to translate reality.

PANERO. A. López Castro, 'Leopoldo Panero ante la naturaleza', *LetD*, 72 : 31–56, mainly presents P.'s poetic vision of the universe based on the complementary relationship of subject and object as parts of a whole, where at times they change places.

PROVENCIO. I. Rodríguez, 'La grieta luminosa del sentido', *Ínsula*, 594 : 19–21, is on *Deslinde*, presented as a poetry of limits, under the influence of music, 'una poesía que lee su tradición poniéndola en crisis'.

RODRÍGUEZ. J. J. Lanz, 'Claudio Rodríguez en la generación del 50: del conocimiento como participación al lenguaje como celebración y leyenda', *LetD*, 70 : 89–125, is a very good article that starts by questioning the classification by Castellet and others of the so-called generation of 1950; it delves into the polemic between poetry of discovery and poetry of communication, and examines the role of Francisco Ribes's anthologies; it then goes on to analyse R.'s approach to the use of language, memory, and history and legend, in his poetry, indicating a progressive distrust in language as a means of discovery albeit being the only space where poetic knowledge is possible.

RODRÍGUEZ. A. Ortega, 'La especie y el mundo', *Ínsula*, 591:27–28, is on *Mis animales obligatorios*, which expresses a fragmented individual perception, which breaks away from logical, traditional syntax, presenting the reader with a multiplicity of images for him or her to actively establish the semantic connections which create the entire web in his poetry.

ROSSETTI. C. García, '*Punto umbrío*: claroscuro para la pérdida', *Ínsula*, 594:21–22, is on *Punto umbrío*, considered as an isolated link when compared to her previous production of erotic poetry; the critic considered it a 'discurso de soledad' yet indicates that 'el amor se convierte para ella en religión'. R. Sarabia, 'Ana Rossetti y el placer de la mirada', *RCEH*, 20:341–59, is on R.'s 'sexualization' of everything, where touch and sight prevail over all the other senses, even defying psychoanalytic theories on women's gaze; it indicates that R. goes beyond the conventional antinomy of masculine and feminine.

VALENTE. *El silencio y la escucha: José Ángel Valente*, ed. Teresa Hernández Fernández, M, Cátedra-Ministerio de Cultura, 1995, 286 pp., is divided into two parts: the first deals primarily with general aspects of V.'s production (memory, aesthetics, language, subjectivity, mysticism), while the second concentrates on specific issues and texts; then it concludes with a previously unpublished epilogue written by the poet. V. Cervera Salinas, 'César Vallejo y José Lezama Lima en la poética de José Ángel Valente. (Un dualismo americano)', pp. 177–86 of *La palabra en el espejo. Estudios de literatura hispanoamericana comparada*, Murcia U.P., examines the presence of Vallejo's sense of abandonment in V.'s earlier works, and then explores the connection with the topics of religion and *thanatos* from Lezama's work. Jacques Ancet et al., *En torno a la obra de José Ángel Valente*, M, Alianza, is a collection of papers presented at the *Residencia de Estudiantes* in 1992 that has kept the conversational tone of the papers, with a wide-ranging approach that portrays the evolution of the poet's creation.

VALVERDE. C. J. Morales, 'José María Valverde: cincuenta años de poesía', *RHM*, 49:165–71, is a celebration of the collection *Hombre de Dios*, which is presented as the key to all his future collections, where V. bears witness through his poetry, questioning a God in which he believes and for whom he hungers, despite His apparent absence.

3. PROSE

GENERAL. Scarlett, *Body*, is a sophisticated and wide-ranging investigation of the elaboration of the physical in 19th- and 20th-c. Spanish fiction, only parts of which fall within the ambit of this section. Within a chapter on Rosa Chacel is a study of *Memorias de Leticia Valle* (1945) (77–98), a fictional autobiography in confessional mode that prefigures — so S. argues — works like Martín-Santos's *Tiempo de silencio* and Goytisolo's *Señas de identidad*. *La sinrazón* (1960) and *Barrio de Maravillas* (1976) are more briefly covered here too. Another chapter (140–65) explores sample novels of the Franco regime: Cela's *La familia de Pascual Duarte*, Martín Gaite's *Entre visillos*, and Martín-Santos's *Tiempo de silencio*. Here S. argues that under dictatorship, 'the subterranean channeling of protest into textual bodies is also the key reason why male- and female-authored narratives of this epoch share more common ground in their representations of the body as *vivencia*' (141). The final chapter (166–85) deals with the post-Franco era, studying Garcia Morales's *El silencio de las sirenas* (1985), Llamazares's *Luna de lobos* (1985), Puértolas's *Queda la noche* (1989), and Muñoz Molina's *Beltenebros* (1989), seeing these novels as engaged in a common battle against 'the banalization of the human body that we confront in the society of spectacle' (185). O. Barrero Pérez, 'Novela española de los años cuarenta y cincuenta: los vínculos del realismo', *Salina*, 9, 1995:96–98, posits a kinship between the *tremendismo*, that characterizes the 1940s and the social realism of the 1950s, concluding that both focus on symptoms rather than causes of social ills. M. Bertrand de Muñoz, 'Dos novelas de la Guerra Civil en Madrid: *Campo del moro* de Max Aub y *Las últimas banderas* de Ángel María de Lera', *Actas* (Valencia), 471–80, compares and contrasts the portrayal of the same event from the same (losing) side, concluding that A.'s account is more varied, more complex, and overall a better piece of writing, but that both share a powerful and pervasive sense of betrayal.

ALÓS. Genaro J. Pérez, *La narrativa de Concha Alós: texto, pretexto y contexto*, M–London, Támesis, 1993, 95 pp., devotes a chapter to each of nine of A.'s works published between 1962 and 1986, situating this under-studied writer between the first postwar women writers such as Laforet and Matute, and the post-Franco ones like Tusquets. P. focuses on certain recurrent themes and preoccupations in A.'s writings, including the alienation of women in patriarchal society, as well as the perception of the woman as predatory, the Civil War, and the environment; and formal features based around polarities such as inside/outside and reality/fantasy.

AUB. *Actas* (Valencia) contains sections dealing with A.'s life and general stature, his theatre and his essays, poetry, journalism, and cinema, as well as his production post-1936. J. A. Pérez Bowie, 'Max Aub: los límites de la ficción' (367–82), studies A.'s metafictional techniques in *La vida y obra de Luis Álvarez Petreña, Páginas azules* in *Campo de los almendros*, and *Jusep Torres Campalans*. C. Alonso, 'Reflexiones sobre la evolución narrativa de Max Aub' (383–93), discerns a change of direction in A.'s literary career marked by the publication in 1945 of his *Discurso de la novela española contemporánea*. J. L. Guereña, 'Max Aub, sueños y realidad de sus campos' (433–42), deals with the narrative series *El laberinto español* in a lyrical and eulogistic vein. M. Quiroga Clérigo, '*El laberinto mágico* de Max Aub. (Aquella guerra incivil)' (443–70), deals with the same series under a different name, admiring the sensitivity with which A. portrays the pain of the Civil War. J. Quiñones, 'Los relatos perdidos en el laberinto: la narrativa breve de Max Aub en torno a la Guerra Civil' (481–87), studies 34 pieces, of which only 16 have been published in Spain. The article classifies them by their subject matter and point of view. P. Sáenz, 'Ambigüedad, ficción y metaficción en *Jusep Torres Campalans*' (488–94) and V. Tortosa, 'En un lugar del tiempo llamado siglo XX: *Jusep Torres Campalans*, entre el biografismo y la historia' (495–511), both deal with this work's generic ambiguity and collage structure, as well as A.'s use of parody. G. Sobejano, '*La calle de Valverde* en el linaje de las novelas de la vida literaria' (514–32), places this novel of 1961 in a literary historical context ranging back as far as Galdós and forward to Luis Martín-Santos, with many interesting stops in between. J. Rodríguez, 'El realismo trascendente de *Las buenas intenciones*' (533–43), attempts to account for and remedy the critical neglect of this novel of 1954, via a parallel with Galdós's novels. D. Cuenca Tudela, '*La verdadera historia de la muerte de Francisco Franco* o la ficción y la realidad en la obra de Max Aub' (545–57), pleads for balance between readings that depend excessively on historical contextualization and those that are too quick to ignore this. V. de Marco, '*Historia de Jacobo*: la imposibilidad de narrar' (559–65), studies the way in which this text demonstrates the inadequacy of narrative to express human barbarism. D. Fernández Martínez, 'La leyenda de *Jusep Torres Campalans*' (825–58), provides the publishing history of this work, including the illustrations and photographs, and considers its reception as well as A.'s responses to his reviewers and critics.

BENET. I. Estrada, '"Sopla y adivina": *En la penumbra* como parodia del deseo', *RHM*, 49: 121–35, analyses how desire and its frustration within the novel are mirrored by the reader's own experience, but argues that humour offsets this aspect of the text.

CELA. J. Pérez, 'Text, context and subtext of the unreliable narrative: Cela's *El asesinato del perdedor*', *ALEC*, 21:103–18, is a critical survey of this novel of 1994, which compares and contrasts it with C.'s earlier fiction.

CUNQUEIRO. N. Salvador Miguel, 'La tradición medieval en la novelística de Álvaro Cunqueiro', *Dutton Vol.*, 581–87, pinpoints the study of the projection and pertinence of the medieval period to later centuries as a neglected area of study and proceeds to consider this with reference to *Merlín y familia* and arthurian tradition on the one hand, and on the other, *Cuando el viejo Sinbad vuelva a las islas* and the *Thousand and One Nights*. The approach here is a traditional one of cataloguing what are termed medieval echoes.

DELIBES. Y. Agawu-Kakraba has two articles on D.: 'Miguel Delibes and the politics of two women: *Cinco horas con Mario* and *Señora de rojo sobre fondo gris*', *Hispanófila*, 117:63–77, compares the female protagonists of these novels in the light of Cixous and Irigaray, coming to the conclusion that despite the differences between Carmen and Ana, they are both victims of D.'s own patriarchal discourse; 'Speech, writing, and the confession of unfulfilled desire: Miguel Delibes' *Cartas de amor de un sexagenario voluptuoso*', *BHS(L)*, 73:389–400, considers the epistolary status of this work and argues — with partial success — that D. uses this mode both to operate a gender reversal (giving the male protagonist the role traditionally associated with a female character) and to interrogate the features of speech versus writing. J. Highfill, 'Reading at variance: icon, index, and symbol in *Cinco horas con Mario*', *ALEC*, 21:59–83, takes as its methodological framework Charles Sanders Peirce's typology of signs and discusses the consequences of their contradictory implications for D.'s novel. G. Wogatzke-Luckow, 'Des Soliloquium als Verfahren der Selbstzerstörung und der Selbstverteidigung: *Señora de rojo sobre fondo gris*', *Iberoromania*, 43:88–102, reads the novel as a psychoanalytical exploration of its male protagonist, suggesting an autobiographical link between Antonio and his creator.

DÍAZ-MAS. C. G. Bellver, 'Humor and the resistance to meaning in *El rapto del Santo Grial*', *RR*, 87:145–55, studies the deconstructive implications of the brand of humour found in this novel of 1984, in the light of its postmodernist credentials.

ESPINA. Y. Agawu-Kakraba, 'Reinventing identity: class, gender, and nationalism in Concha Espina's *Retaguardia*', *RoN*, 36:167–79, studies this novel of the Civil War, published in the heat of the conflict, and considers its relationship with the Nationalist propaganda machine, paying particular attention to the problematic implications of E.'s portrayal of female characters.

DE FOXÁ. L. Hickey, 'Presupposition and implicature in *Madrid de corte a checa*', *BHS(G)*, 73:419–35, studies this Nationalist novel published in 1938, in the light of pragmatic theory, successfully accounting by this means for a significant area of the narrative strategy and its value as right-wing propaganda.

GOYTISOLO, JUAN. The critical industry generated by this writer never loses momentum. Brad Epps, *Significant Violence: Oppression and Resistance in the Narratives of Juan Goytisolo. 1970–1990*, Oxford, Clarendon Press, xiv + 513 pp., is a critical tour de force, with a substantial chapter on each of the texts it covers: *Reivindicación del conde don Julián, Juan sin tierra, Makbara, Paisajes después de la batalla*, and *Las virtudes del pájaro solitario*. Grounded in an impressively eclectic theoretical range, E. constructs complex and subtle readings of these novels, which confront some of the most problematic aspects of G.'s writing without, however, taking refuge in facile solutions. Abigail Lee Six, *Goytisolo: 'Campos de Níjar'*, London, Grant and Cutler, 92 pp., conforms to the style and approach of the CGST series. Randolph D. Pope, *Understanding Juan Goytisolo*, Columbia, South Carolina U.P., 1995, xv + 182 pp., is part of a similar series, but this time author-rather than text-based. The stated purpose of this series is to provide judicious literary assessment in compact form. P. certainly achieves this, no mean feat in the case of a writer as complex as G. Following a chronology and an introduction covering biography and general literary evolution in cultural context, there are chapters on *Juegos de manos* and *Duelo en el Paraíso*, on *Campos de Níjar* and *La Chanca*, on the *Mañana efímero* trilogy, on the Mendiola trilogy, and on G.'s latest writings, up to and including *La saga de los Marx*. E. Cibreiro, 'La literatura como delincuencia: la agresión al lector en *Makbara* y *Paisajes después de la batalla*', *RCEH*, 20:433–48, analyses the transgressive and aggressive features of these two novels, asserting that among the consequences of their presence in *Makbara* is the reader's inability to identify with the protagonists and that this in turn leads to a coldly cerebral engagement with the text, whereas in *Paisajes*, the technique is developed further, for it entails constant humiliation of the reader through trickery on the narrator's part. Thus for C., the reading process with respect to these texts is both a threat and a challenge issued by Goytisolo. C. Moreiras Menor, 'Juan Goytisolo, F.F.B. y la fundación fantasmal del proyecto autobiográfico contemporáneo español', *MLN*, 111:327–45, considers the relationship between Franco's death and a boom in autobiographical texts by Spanish writers, using G.'s two-volume work, *Coto vedado* and *En los reinos de*

Taifa as a paradigm. I. Nolting-Hauff, 'Romanexperiment und Regimekritik in *Señas de identidad* von Juan Goytisolo', *RF*, 108:89–111, makes the extraordinary claim that *Señas* can be considered the first really experimental Spanish novel this century and then goes on to find it not so experimental after all, in view of its political commitment. J. S. Squires, '(De)mystification in Juan Goytisolo's early novels, from *Juegos de manos* to *La resaca*', *MLR*, 91:393–405, studies G.'s first five novels, arguing that the traitor-figures in them do not banish myth, but harness it in order to effect some kind of psychological release for themselves. Although insightful in places, this reviewer found the article ultimately unconvincing.

LAFORET. V. de Marco, '*Nada*: el espacio transparente y opaco a la vez', *RHM*, 49:59–75, studies the juxtaposition of the public outside space of the city with the private interior space of the flat in c/ Aribau, setting this against the temporal divide between time of writing and time of action and asserting that it is this dual contrast that sets up the narrative tension of the novel.

MARTÍN GAITE. F. J. Higuero, 'La exploración de la diferencia en *Nubosidad variable* de Carmen Martín Gaite', *BHS(L)*, 73:401–14, is a critical appreciation of the novel, concentrating on its deconstructive and fragmentary qualities.

MERINO. V. R. Holloway, 'La circunscripción del sujeto: meta-ficción, mito e identidad en la narrativa de José María Merino', *ALEC*, 21:85–101, studies the dialectical relationship between myth and metafiction in *Novela de Andrés Choz*, *El caldero de oro*, *La orilla oscura*, *El centro de aire*, and *Los trenes de verano*.

MILLÁS. H. Vélez Quiñones, 'Juan, José, and Millás: memory, desire and literary identity in Juan José Millás's *Volver a casa*', *RHM*, 49:149–64, is a critical appreciation of this novel, informed by Barthesian theory.

MUÑOZ MOLINA. M.M. is interviewed by E. Scarlett, *ECon*, 7, 1994:69–82. The conversation is introduced by a brief survey of M.M.'s career to date and then the author talks, *inter alia*, of the relationship between his fictional and non-fictional writings, his mentors (including Salinas and Borges), his attitude towards the postmodern, and his future plans.

RUIZ. M. Juliá, 'Nuevas propuestas para la historia: la fantasía "ucrónica" de Raúl Ruiz', *BHS(L)*, 73:415–25, studies R.'s historical tetralogy, consisting of *El tirano de Taormina* (1980), *Sixto VI: la relación inverosímil de un papado indefinido* (1981), *La peregrina y prestigiosa historia de Arnaldo de Montferrat* (1984), and *Los papeles de Flavio Alvisi* (1985), highlighting the importance R. accords to love as the only way of making sense of the past and discussing his parody of the postmodern crisis of trust in historiography.

SÁNCHEZ FERLOSIO. F. González Castro, 'La diferencia fantástica en *Industrias y andanzas de Alfanhuí*', *His(US)*, 79:20–27, refutes the widespread characterization of this novel as standing alone, without precedent in recent Spanish literary history, forging links with pre-Civil War writing, such as that of Ramón Gómez de la Serna and the Surrealists, and in the postwar period, with Azorín's writings of the 1940s and with the *nouveau roman* in France. The article concludes by attributing the fantastic quality of S.F.'s novel to the prevalence of metaphor and oxymoron, in contrast to the dominant social realist style of its time. J. Pérez-Magallón, '*Alfanhuí*: marginalidad y reescritura de la picaresca', *BHS(L)*, 73:165–77, argues for a link between the particular type of marginality associated with this novel and its exploitation of the picaresque tradition, concluding that in spite of its acknowledged defects, it is more deserving of a place in the canon than S.F.'s more famous and less flawed *El Jarama*.

TUSQUETS. A. Lee Six, 'Protean prose: fluidity of character and genre in Esther Tusquets's *Siete miradas en un mismo paisaje*', Harris, *Culture*, 177–86, perceives a link between the generic ambiguity of this work and what it argues is a palimpsestic portrayal of its protagonist.

4. DRAMA

GENERAL. Theatre seems to move away more from the academic stance of viewing it as any of the other genres, in a tour de force to accept it more as a media production, with the possibility of a collective script, which is what the *Teatro Independiente* has done since the end of the 1960s. Some, such as Nel Diago, listed below, claim that the text is coming back to coexist with other scenic forms, acknowledging that some texts resemble mere scripts, as part of the alternative forms of the 1990s. M. F. Vilches de Frutos, 'La temporada teatral española 1993–94', *ALEC*, 21:385–422, is an informative collection of brief reviews of those plays staged during the period indicated in the title; it gives an overview of the stage, presenting an increase in the number of collective plays, many times by independent groups, some of which involve audience participation in their approach; it mentions works staged in Madrid (including foreign, Spanish classics, postwar theatre, contemporary, and independent groups), Catalonia, and the different autonomous communities; it stresses the point of budget cuts for public theatres, and it mentions the drastic news that the *Centro Nacional de Nuevas Tendencias Escénicas*, created in 1984 and directed by Guillermo Heras, has been shut down. Candyce Leonard and John P. Gabriele, *Panorámica del teatro español actual*, M, Fundamentos, 206 pp., start by briefly evaluating the situation of theatre post-Franco, paying particular attention to younger writers born in the 1950s and 60s; then it includes interviews with five of those playwrights: Lluïsa Cunillé, Juan Mayorga, Antonio Onetti, Itziar Pascual, and Margarita Sánchez Roldán (25–56); and it concludes with a section dedicated to a play by each of the five authors concerned (59–206). Carles Alberola et al., *Islas* (Colección Teatro Siglo XX-Serie Textos, 1), Valencia U.P., 167 pp., is the first text of what promises to be a series to give voice to new dramatists, in this case seven of the eight authors of the Valencian group 'Ínsula dramataria': Carles Alberola, Chema Cardeña, Roberto García, Alejandro A. Jornet, Ximo Llorens, Carles Pons, and Paco Zarzoso; the one whose work is not included is Pascual Alapont, who, unlike the others, does not form part of the group of *dramaturgos solitarios del teatro alternativo*, as defined by Nel Diago (18); the latter (11–24) tries to define the directions of Spanish drama today, paying particular attention to writers of the *Comunidad Valenciana*, regardless of the language chosen by them; this group in particular he places as followers of postmodern aesthetics in their dramas; the rest of the book is dedicated to a play by each of the seven authors mentioned above, two in Catalan, and the others in Spanish. *The Cambridge Guide to Theatre*, ed. Martin Banham, CUP, 1995, 1233 pp., is an updated edition, which covers theatre from all over the world; of special interest for this section are pp. 1018–19, as well as individual entries for Miguel Mihura, Enrique Jardiel Poncela, José López Rubio, Antonio Buero Vallejo, Alfonso Sastre, Jaime Salom, Francisco Nieva, Antonio Gala, and José Luis Alonso de Santos. Its purpose is to serve as a reference work; perhaps a drawback is that the listing is in alphabetical order, and it would be more useful if authors were listed following the countries which they represent.

AUB. Of particular interest for this section are: C. Ortego Sanmartín, 'Lugares y espacios del destierro en el teatro del exilio de Max Aub', *Actas* (Valencia), 299–310, which studies that the vicissitudes projected in A.'s works are partly autobiographical, in so far as the experience of exile is concerned, thus at times re-interpreting postwar Europe from America; P. Pedraza Jiménez, 'Los personajes femeninos en el teatro político escrito desde el exilio', *ib.*, 311–18, which explores the major role women play in his dramas, and claims they are the ones who best exemplify the dichotomy of before and after the war in his works; and D. Shaw, 'La búsqueda de la autenticidad en *Morir por cerrar los ojos*', *ib.*, 319–24, which indicates that the search for authenticity is intrinsic to this particular play framed in the historical reality of France.

BUERO VALLEJO. A. J. Ridley, 'Goya's rediscovery of reason and hope: the dialectic of art and artist in Buero Vallejo's *El sueño de la razón*', *BHS(G)*,73 : 105–15, is a good article that analyses the dialectic of Goya and his art based on three stages that the critic identifies as: catalytic — when Goya interprets his art, parasitic — when art seems to have a life of its own and serves the purpose of making him question his sanity, and symbiotic — when art and artist reach a state of peaceful coexistence; it is a Goya that needs the parasitic stage where the monsters of his imagination can pave the way to the reconciliation with his dormant reason, pinpointing the importance of hope complemented by doubt in B.'s theatre. *El teatro de Buero Vallejo: homenaje del hispanismo británico e irlandés*, ed. Victor Dixon and David Johnston, Liverpool U.P., 200 pp., is a collection of ten articles, seven of which are dedicated to *El concierto de San Ovidio, Las Meninas, Jueces en la noche, Las cartas boca abajo, La fundación*, and *El tragaluz*, respectively; one article (13–28) explores the Platonic interpretation of insanity present in B.'s works; another one (85–110) deals with Unamuno's 'mito cainita' present in B.'s plays; and (127–39) concentrates on the topic of violence.

QUILES. J. P. Gabriele, 'Una charla con Eduardo Quiles', *ALEC*, 21 : 431–39, interviews Q., perhaps the best known, together with José Ruibal, of the underground dramatists; it indicates who influenced his theatre and his evolution as a playwright, contextualizing his theatre in general.

RIAZA. P. Ruiz Pérez, 'El drama del terrorismo en *La emperatriz de los helados* de Luis Riaza', *RLit*, 58 : 451–76, has a somewhat misleading title; it starts by questioning the apparent apathy with respect to contemporary dramatists and their works, then it includes (451–56) his views on theatre, and finally moves on to concentrate on the work expressed in the title, indicating that although this is an atypical play in R.'s production, there is the recurrent theme of the mechanisms of power, albeit the fact that the selected motive of terrorism has been absent from the Spanish stage; it overall places this play in the context of R.'s theatre and the stage today.

SASTRE. U. Aszyk, 'Observaciones sobre la reconstrucción y transfiguración artística de la biografía del científico, teólogo, hereje y mártir, Miguel Servet, en dos obras de Alfonso Sastre *Flores rojas para Miguel Servet* y *La sangre y la ceniza*', *Ometeca*, 3–4:166–90, is a well-documented comparative study of the re-creation of Servet in both works cited in the title.

V. CATALAN STUDIES*

LANGUAGE

By VICENT DE MELCHOR, *Universitat Autònoma de Barcelona,*
PEP SERRA, *Universitat de Girona,* and
BERNAT JOAN I MARÍ, *Universitat de les Illes Balears*
(This survey covers the years 1995 and 1996)

The following abbreviations are exclusive to this section: Goenaga, *Grammatica: De grammatica generativa,* ed. Patxi Goenaga, Guipúzcoa, Euskal Herriko Unibertsitatea–Gipuzkoako Foru Aldundia, 1995, 207 pp.; *Variació: La sociolingüística de la variació,* ed. M. Teresa Turell Julià, PPU, 1995, 296 pp.; *Misc. Colón: Miscel·lània Germà Colón,* ed. Josep Massot, vols 3–6 *(ELLC,* 30–33) PAM, 1995–96, 304, 316, 312, 380 pp.

1. GENERAL

Institut d'Estudis Catalans: *Diccionari de la llengua catalana,* B, Enciclopèdia Catalana–Edicions 62, 1995, xl + 1908 pp., establishes a bridge between the earlier *Diccionari general de la llengua catalana* by Pompeu Fabra (1932) and the future dictionary by the Institut, and gathers about 80,000 entries — 30,000 more than Fabra's. Unlike the later it is a collective, institutional product elaborated by a group of several dozens of specialists. This new dictionary 'seeks to be a normative work, interdialectal, modern, and useful to communication': normative or official, as the Institut is the legal linguistic authority for Catalan; interdialectal as it gathers dialectal varieties — geographical or social — that now are not specially marked; modern as it includes certain terminological and encyclopaedical uses but also common words not recognized before (*escindir, rerefons, fregidora, màfia, fonoteca, anorac, misto, verdader, quadro*), including colloquialisms (*pirar, guipar, cangueli, fer un riu*), and taboo words (*cony, fotre, titola*). The authors have thoroughly reviewed Fabra's dictionary (unification of materials, gender), but some parts (e.g. verbs) are still widely dependent on Fabra's definitions, grammar features, sub-entries, and examples. *Qüern,* 1, 1995, 112 pp., is a specialized bibliographical bulletin on Catalan language and literature, published biennially, from the Middle Ages to *c.* 1830; this first issue collects 713 entries.

---

* The editor once more wishes to thank Dr Núria Martí i Girbau for co-ordinating and translating the sections on Language and Nineteenth- and Twentieth-Century Literature.

Catalan Dictionary. Catalan–English, English–Catalan, London, Routledge, 1994, xxxix + 339 + iii + 269 pp., may be added to other new bilingual Catalan dictionaries, such as Ann Duez and Bob De Nijs, *Diccionari català–neerlandès*, B, Enciclopèdia Catalana, 1993, 936 pp.; Dan Nosell, *Diccionari català-suec*, B, Enciclopèdia Catalana, 1994, lvi + 656 pp., and Antoni Seva (dir.), *Diccionari llatí–català*, B, Enciclopèdia Catalana, 1994, 701 pp.

2. HISTORICAL AND DIALECTOLOGY

Josep M. Nadal and Modest Prats, *Història de la llengua catalana*, vol. II: *El segle XV*, B, Edicions 62, 606 pp., is a long-awaited comprehensive survey of the social history of the Catalan language during the 15th century This dense work, which may be also regarded as a reference book, is divided into two chapters (1412–79 and 1479–1519), with shared structure: the historical background is followed by social and cultural comments, Catalan relationships with other languages (Latin, Spanish, and Italian), and the study of the literary prose and poetry, including special subjects such as the names given to Catalan, the changing concept of 'Spain', and the relevance of the introduction of printing. As the authors remark, the 15th c. was as crucial to Catalan as to many other European languages, since it is the transition from Middle Ages to Renaissance. Attempts were made to arrive at a standard Catalan through the two available models of the time, in which the centre of the world shifted from the Mediterranean to the Atlantic, and Castile started as an imperial power, i.e., letters (the Italian model) or arms (the Castilian model); and through printing. But the challenge proved to be impossible from the 16th c., in spite of the 15th c. being the Catalan Golden Age for literature, and the still long-retained hegemony of Catalan in Catalonia, Valencia, the Balearic Islands, and even in southern and insular Italy. *Política lingüística de l'Església catalana. Segles XVI–XVII*, ed. Modest Prats, Vic, Eumo, 1995, 198 pp., edits various papers on linguistic affairs issued by the Roman Catholic councils of the *provintia Tarraconensis* (Catalonia and adjacent territories) held in 1591, 1636, and 1637. *La llengua catalana al segle XVIII*, ed. Pep Balsalobre and Joan Gratacós, B, Quaderns Crema, 1995, 89 pp., is the edited version, with notes and references, of the ten papers presented in the conference with the same title (Banyoles, 11/12-XII-1993) to which three more works have been added, including a very useful bibliographic repertory of some 430 titles on the topic. In spite of not being a work of synthesis, a complete state of affairs may be obtained from its reading. The book is divided into four parts: an introduction and three sections, following the thematic division of the conference: grammarians and grammars, linguistic usages, and regional approaches. As a whole, the papers present a significant set of new hypotheses and methods of analysis as well as some little known or unpublished materials; furthermore, they are mutually enriching, helping to make the lacunae in one or other fields noticeable. The book should help to shed light on the linguistic and cultural situation prior to the *Renaixença*. *Llengües en contacte als regnes de València i de Múrcia: segles XIII–XV*, ed. Jordi Colomina i Castanyer, Alacant U.P., 1995, 292 pp., is a helpful introduction to the understanding of the complex sociolinguistic situation in Valencia and Murcia in the Low Middle. Ages. 12 specialists — linguists and historians — study topics such as as: the language of Valencian Moors and Jews (Carme Barceló, Dolors Bramon), the Mozarabic language of Valencia (Joan Domingues), the linguistic interferences of Aragonese on the Catalan of the early Valencian documents in Romance (Lluís Gimeno, Ricard Bañó, Joan J. Ponsoda), the influence of Catalan on the Murcian Spanish (Pilar Díez de Revenga, Jordi Colomina), the linguistic usages in the Catalan-Aragonese Chancery (Joan Manuel del Estal), the linguistic border in the northern Valencian (Vicent García Edo), the origin of the Spanish dialects in Valencia (Pere D. Garzón), and the Italian influences on the early lexicographers from Valencia and Tortosa (Germà Colón). Joan J. Ponsoda, *El català i l'aragonès en els inicis del Regne de València segons el Llibre de Cort de Justícia de Cocentaina (1269–1295)*, Alcoi, Marfil, 363 pp., edits in the second part 639 entries of the local court registers in the early Kingdom of Valencia, i.e., at the time in which the Christian newcomers (especially Catalans and Aragonese) and the old Muslim settlers coexisted, with their own languages — Catalan, Aragonese, and Arabic. Each entry has an average 75 words often reflecting the actual Catalan (or better, Catalans) of the colonists (and the scribes). Their speech is studied in the third part according to the usual levels of linguistic analysis, and includes a lexicon of more than 450 items. The first part of the book provides an historical account, describes the manuscript and identifies its scribes, finally sketching the background of population and languages used in Cocentaina by the end of the 13th c. — according to the author, at this time the ratio between Catalan-speaking people and Castilian-Aragonese-speaking people should be fifty-fifty, with some Occitans and others, and about 70 per cent of Catalans came from Western Catalonia and spoke Western Catalan, i.e, the language and dialect that finally succeeded and remained in the kingdom of Valencia. Joan Bastardas, *La llengua catalana mil anys enrere*, B, Curial, 1995, 348 pp., edits and reviews 11 articles already published on the early Catalan language history, among them three on the passage from Latin to Catalan (39–145).

3. Phonetics and Phonology

B. Palmada, 'En defensa de labiodental', Goenaga, *Grammatica*, 11–24, provides conclusive evidence in favour of the existence of the feature labiodental, showing that the feature is empirically justified and that simplicity can not be maintained out of that evidence. M. À. Pradilla, 'El desàfricament prepalatal intervocàlic al català de transició nord-occidental/valencià', *Variació*, 53–116, describes and explains a linguistic change in progress in the prepalatal order, in Benicarló. The change is identified as the diachronic process of deaffrication, which affects the phonological variable /ʒ/ in intervocalic position, in the north-eastern Catalan of transition/Valencian. C. Plaza Arqué, 'Lleialtat lingüística, edat i nivell educatiu: la *e* postònica a la Conca de Barberà', *ib.*, 117–38, deals with a dialectal phonetic change in la Conca de Barberà, the replacement of the dialect variant [i] by an intermediate variant [e]: the consolidation of the former variant is due to a factor of local prestige, although the youngest generation shows a tendency to adopt the standard form [ə]. J. Pla Fulquet, 'L'obertura de la [ə] a Barcelona: el xava i altres varietats', *ib.*, 139–64, studies the vowel [ə] in the speech of the metropolitan area of Barcelona. An acoustic analysis shows that although the dispersion field of [ə] is close to that of [a], a clear distinction is still kept between these two vowels; increased formality in style has no influence on the behaviour of the vowel. B. Montoya Abad, 'L'observació del canvi fonològic en el català balear', *ib.*, 165–220, follows the development of five variable rules which apply or have applied in the phonology of Balearic Catalan in the last two centuries. The only one of these five rules still in progress is the change of ['ə] to ['ɛ]. The other four rules analysed have all been contrary to the evolution of the rest of variants of the domain. E. Clua, 'Weak prepositions in Tortosan Catalan: alternation of prepositions, allomorphy or phonological process', *CWPL*, 5.1 : 29–66, and 'Les preposicions febles *a* i *en* en els complements locatius i direccionals: justificacions des de la fonologia generativa no lineal', *Actes* (Frankfurt), III, 157–68, describe the behaviour of the prepositions in the dialect of Tortosa, explaining [ən] corresponding to *a* in certain contexts as the result of a process of consonantal epenthesis. S. Oliva, 'El sintagma fonològic: interaccions entre eurítmia i sintaxi', *ib.*, 141–56, shows how phonological phrases are restructured into longer units because of the interaction of two types of rules: those that follow syntactic structure and those caused by eurythmia. M. R. Lloret, 'Dissimilació de sonants i representació autosegmental', *ib.*, 169–83, argues that the dissimilation of sonants shows a regularity and a scope that allow a general formal analysis.

M. R. Lloret and J. Viaplana, 'Els clítics pronominals singulars del català oriental: una aproximació interdialectal', *Misc. Colón*, v, 273–309, is a general description of the phonological behaviour of clitic pronouns which shows the connections between the dialectal systems. T. Cabré i Monné, 'Fenòmens lingüístics dependents de l'estructura prosòdica', *Actes* (Frankfurt), iii, 185–94, and 'Condicions prosòdiques i minimitat en el tipus reduplicatiu *puput*', *Caplletra*, 19, 187–94, deal in more detail with aspects already discussed by the author in an earlier study (*YWMLS*, 56:420). J. Colomina i Castanyer, 'La simplificació dels grups consonàntics finals en català', *Actes* (Frankfurt), iii, 195–224, offers a detailed and explanatory description of the simplification of final consonantal groups in Catalan making use of the concept of sonicity. J. Jiménez Martínez, 'Aproximació als grups de consonants en posició final de mot en català des de la teoria de l'Optimitat', *ib.*, 225–58, uses Optimality Theory to study the differences in the behaviour of word-final -*nt* in general Valencian and in the Catalan of Catalonia; the different dialectal options are explained through the different ordering of some of the phonological principles that are involved in these processes. D. Recasens, 'Coarticulació i assimilació en fonologia. Dades de moviment lingual sobre els grups consonàntics amb C2 = /d/ en català', *Caplletra*, 19:11–26, proves completely that the fricative consonants, emitted with high lingual requirements, have the same place of articulation preceding /d/ and in intervocalic position. An inverse relation is thus observed between resistance to coarticulatorial effects and the required articulatory control. B. Palmada, 'La representació de les palatals', *ib.*, 27–42, justifies the complex character of the palatal segments through the phonological analysis of their behaviour. The most relevant explanatory contribution is related to the fact that vocalization processes only take place in complex segments, but do not necessarily affect all of these segments in a particular system. L. Romera and A.M. Fernández, 'Nasal palatal: segment complex', *ib.*, 43–50, deal with the characterization of the palatal nasal from a perspective which they call Articulatory Phonology. The complex character of this segment is taken as an assimilation, a superimposition of gestures. R. and F. claim that the advantage of this model over previous models is based on its elimination of empty categories (a simplification of the theory) and on the possibility of establishing different degrees of assimilation. N. Dols and M. Wheeler, 'El consonantisme final del mallorquí i el "llicenciament d'obertures"', *ib.*, 51–64, propose a new interpretation of the coda position in Majorcan, using a special mechanism, aperture licensing, which allows the appearance of aperture not associated to any syllable. The extension of this analysis to all the forms of the language accounts for the behaviour of final consonants in assimilation processes. J. I. Hualde, 'Sobre el concepte de derivació fonològica: alguns fenòmens vocàlics en basc i en català', *ib.*, 65–80, examines a series of vocalic phenomena in Basque and Catalan dialects which traditionally required extrinsic ordering of the phonological rules and analyses them following Lakoff's 1993 model. J. Jiménez, 'Els aplecs *ts* i *dz* en valencià. Una anàlisi de la teoria de l'optimitat', *ib.*, 81–112, aims to prove that in Valencian /ts/ and /dz/ behave as a group of phonemes and not as a phonematic unit, in contrast with the phonemes /tʃ/ and /dʒ/. P. Serra, 'L'estructura prosòdica i l'accent', *ib.*, 113–44, establishes the phonological and morphological bases of the lexical accentuation of Catalan, within the theoretical framework of Optimality Theory, and shows the existence of a regular process of accent assignment. P. Prieto, 'Aproximació als contorns tonals del català central', *ib.*, 161–86, is a first inventory of tonal variations of Catalan. P. starts from Bonet's 1984 work and applies Pierrehumbert, Beckman, and Hirschberg's models to Catalan. C. Lleó, 'Processos reduplicatius en català i ritme prosòdic: de l'adquisició fonològica a la formació de mots', *ib.*, 195–214, describes the morphological process of partial reduplication which has formed a group of words in Catalan, gathered under what is called *puput* type. L. makes an interesting distinction between syllable reduplication (phonological reduplication) and foot reduplication (morphological reduplication). J. Harris, 'La projecció sintaxi-fonologia en els clítics del català i de l'espanyol', *ib.*, 229–58, studies the behaviour of clitics and of groups of clitics in Spanish and in the Catalan of Barcelona, within the Distributed Morphology framework, concluding that the modifications of terminal elements corresponding to clitics in S-Structure result basically from the familiar Adjunction operation and, in particular, from the impoverishment that takes place in the component of Morphological Structure. P. Serra, 'Sobre l'enduriment prematur dels conceptes: a propòsit de les erres', *RCat*, 107 : 9–31, studies the connections between syllabic positions and the types of /r/ and concludes that a position in the melodic skeleton associated to /ɾ/ geminates in an open syllable.

4. LEXIS AND MORPHOLOGY

J. Corbera, 'L'alguerès al Diccionari Etimològic i Complementari de Joan Coromines', *Misc. Colón*, III, 247–53, analyses in detail the references to the Catalan of Alguero made by Joan Coromines in the DECLC and states that the attention paid by this author to that Catalan dialect is slight and partly inaccurate. K. Morvay, 'A la recerca del material fraseològic als diccionaris', *ib.*, 287–301, highlights the little attention which Catalan dictionaries have devoted to

phraseological units. T. Cabré i Castellví, 'Terminologia i diccionaris', *ib.*, IV, 277–305, contains three sections: the first one deals
with the role of the terminology in general dictionaries, the second
one presents the criteria followed for the inclusion of terminology in
the DIEC updating and the third tackles problematic cases related to
terms. L. Gràcia, 'Los nombres agentivos en -DOR y la noción de
herencia en morfología', Goenaga, *Grammatica*, 51–66, applies Levin
and Rappaport's analyses to non eventive constructions with nouns
ending in *-dor* in Catalan (instrumentals and occupations). O. Fullana,
'Why nominal infinitives express manner', *CWPL*, 4.2, 1995 : 211–27,
assumes that the normal meaning of nominal infinitives in Catalan is
a manner reading, which is due to a Conceptual Lexical Structure
specific to phrases headed by nominal infinitives. X. Luna, 'Alguns
mots dialectals empordanesos', *Misc. Colón*, VI, 235–44, is on the
Catalan traditional lexicon of the Empordà region, although it
contains some elements that are not exclusive to it. L. Rabassa,
'Morfologia verbal: estudi del parlar de dos informadors andorrans
originaris de la localitat d'Andorra', *ib.*, 245–90, highlights the
similarities and differences, in verbal morphology, between two
idiolects of Andorra. J.-A. Mesquida i Cantallops, 'Actualitat dels
estudis sobre el llenguatge científic català', *Actes* (Frankfurt), III,
275–95, reviews the different organisms and institutions that have
contributed to solving the shortages in scientific Catalan, from the
perspective of the 'Prada Manifesto' of August 1973, which reported
the need for social normalization of scientific Catalan and internal
normativization of that specialized language. M. Lorente Casafont,
'La teoria de l'estructura argumental i la representació del lèxic', *ib.*,
323–35, concentrates on the syntactic information contained in
verbal lexical units and proposes a representation of the grammatical
information of verbs based only on syntactic criteria. Institut d'Estudis
Catalans, 'L'elaboració del *Diccionari de la llengua catalana*. Criteris
aprovats per la Secció Filològica', pp. 11–54 of *Documents de la secció
filològica III* (Biblioteca Filològica, 30), IEC, 117 pp., explain many
linguistic aspects (morphological, phonological, syntactic) of the
general criteria adopted by the IEC for the elaboration of the
Diccionari de la llengua catalana, a very useful document for Catalan
language scholars. M. R. Lloret, 'El tractament de les formes
nominals "invariables" quant a nombre', *Caplletra*, 19 : 215–28, deals
separately with the cases in which *s* does not belong to the root. For
the first group she maintains Lloret and Viaplana's 1992 proposal,
because it can account for the grammatical treatment that has to be
given to final vowels of nominals which do not belong to the root
neither are gender or derivative morphemes. In the other cases, L.
proposes a lexical marker which blocks the assignment of the regular

marker. J. Calvo Pérez, 'El tamp en valencià', *ib.*, 259–78, is a classification of the Valencian verbal system which combines phonological, morphological and syntactic aspects. M. Pérez Saldanya, 'Analogia i canvi morfològic: a propòsit de les formes verbals velaritzades', *ib.*, 279–306, concludes that the velarization process in verbal forms is very heterogeneous both because of the variety of factors that come together in it and because of the variety of dialectal results; the study nevertheless clarifies the explanation of the general application of this process in a notable way. M. Sifre, 'Reflexions sobre la vocal temàtica', *ib.*, 307–32, accounts for the different functions which the thematic vowel fulfils in the language, both at a phonic level and at a semantic and morphological level, reflecting on the rigidity of the inflection-derivation division in relation to the fact that the thematic vowel shows features characteristic of these two morphological processes. J. Viaplana, 'Sobre la irregularitat verbal', *ib.*, 333–48, notes that in the area of verbal irregularity, atypicities are frequent and irregularities are few. V. proposes that all variations must be included, in an adequate way, in the lexicon of the language. P. Sancho, 'Aspectes formals de les preposicions en català', *ib.*, 349–64, is a good example of the interaction between the different grammar components. S. observes that, in relation to the phonic aspects of prepositions in Catalan, many of the phonological rules show strong syntactic, morphological and semantic restrictions.

5. SYNTAX, SEMANTICS AND PRAGMATICS

G. Rigau, 'Propiedades de FLEX en las construcciones temporales de infinitivo: la legitimación del sujeto', Goenaga, *Grammatica*, 173–84, provides a characterization of infinitive tense constructions in Catalan and Spanish, providing a simple explanation of the most relevant properties of these structures: the possible presence of a lexical subject, the postverbal position of that subject and the absence of negation. M.T. Espinal, 'La condición de absorción lógica', *ib.*, 151–60, claims that the licensing of the structures which show the phenomenon of 'expletive negation' requires a logical absorption operation, a well-formedness condition on logical forms which cancels any projection from a syntactic constituent Neg into an independent conceptual constituent. N. Arturo Monné, 'La variació d'*haver* auxiliar al català nord-occidental', *Variació*, 221–58, accounts for the change from an initial system of two auxiliaries, *ser* and *haver*, to a final stage in which *haver* is the only auxiliary in all contexts. S. Oliva, 'Els complements adverbials adjunts', *EMarg*, 54, 1995:5–19, provides phonological evidence of the difference that holds between governed adjuncts, predicate adjuncts and sentential adjuncts. N. Martí, '*De* in Catalan elliptical nominals: a partitive Case marker', *CWPL*, 4.2, 1995:243–65, studies the appearence of *de* in elliptical indefinite nominals in Catalan, in relation to the phenomena of *en* pronominalization and dislocation. M.'s proposal is that *de* is the head of a Case functional projection which receives partitive Case from the head of QP; the elements *en* and *de* of dislocated elements are morphological realizations of the assigned partitive Case. M. Batllori, C. Sánchez, and A. Suñer, 'The incidence of interpolation on the word order of Romance languages', *ib.*, 185–209, is a syntactic explanation of the problem of interpolation structures in Romance, with examples from medieval Catalan, Spanish, Portuguese and Galician; the conclusion is that interpolation is a kind of stylistic construction related to the syntactic projection FocusP. V. M. Longa, G. Lorenzo, and G. Rigau, 'Expressing modality by recycling clitics', *ib.*, 5.1:67–79, show Catalan to be an example of a language that has no modality clitics, compared with languages such as Fiorentino, Polesano and in a certain way Spanish, which have elements specifically designed by the modal orientation of the sentence, and other languages, such as Asturian or Galician, which use the strategy of recycling, which enables the Accusative clitics to express modality. I. Muixí, 'Optional participial agreement with direct object clitics in Catalan', *ib.*, 127–45, deals with the optional agreement showed by third person direct object clitics with the participle in the Catalan dialect of Barcelona, which is quite peculiar in comparison with the behaviour of other Romance languages. M.'s analysis proposes that clitics are an example of XP movement, which, together with the evidence of a close connection between participial agreement, A-movement of the clitic DP and the alternation of auxiliary verbs, can explain the obligatoriness or the impossibility of participial agreement, as well as the described optionality in the Catalan of Barcelona. A. Bel, 'Early negation in Catalan and Spanish', *ib.*, 5–28, deals with the acquisition of the negative marker *no* in Catalan and Castilian in relation to the verb. The acquisition of the notion of tense is described and the functional category responsible for the fixation of the Neg parameter is analysed. B. concludes that functional categories are already present in the first syntactic realizations. A. Rossich, 'Un tipus de frase negativa del nord-est català', *EMarg*, 56:109–15, is a brilliant and well-documented work on the negative construction *poc que/poca*. R. concludes that the form of this dialectal construction that must be used in writing is *poca* and not *poc* nor *poc que*. M. Pérez Saldanya, 'Gramaticalització i reanàlisi: el cas del perfet perifràstic en català', *Actes* (Frankfurt), III, 71–107, shows that the grammaticalization process of the periphrastic past follows a diachronic itinerary which starts from the cognitive domain of space to the one of tense and is also related to the domain of aspectual relations. This explains why the verb *anar* (to go) progressively loses its lexical meaning and adopts a more and more grammatical meaning. T. Badia, 'La lingüística computacional i la descripció del català', *ib.*, 307–22, is a first approach to the computer treatment of Catalan, in the field of computational linguistics. J. V. Calatayud Cuenca, 'L'experiència espacial del cos en les unitats fraseològiques catalanes: més enllà de la imatge creativa', *ib.*, 337–54, using the tools of cognitive linguistics to observe that phraseological units are built from image-schema with a capacity to structure experience coherently. V. Salvador, 'Fraseologia del *com*', *ib.*, 355–80, uses the framework of cognitive linguistics, to start the study of *com* from the ideative or propositional function; he continues the argumentation referring to the textual function and ends with expressive or interpersonal values showed by certain phrases incorporating *com*. M. J. Cuenca, 'Aproximació sintàctico-pragmàtica a les *question-tags* en català', *ib.*, 397–408, studies the question tags of Catalan not with respect to theoretical problems, already dealt with in previous works of the author, but in their use in an oral text of argumentative character. A. Saragossà Alba, 'Una introducció al concepte "pronom"', *ib.*, 409–39, comments on what are the most important problems of the concept of pronoun, and on how a definition can be elaborated which can be applied not only to replacing personal pronouns, but also to other personal pronouns. J. Todolí, 'Doblament i represa pronominal en català', *ib.*, 441–64, is the study of pronoun doubling and of the factors involved in the application of this process. T. shows that it is a complex phenomenon involving different factors such as the animacity of the constituent, the thematic relation between it and the verb, and the informative-discursive status; doubling also depends on the type of grammatical subject.

6. Sociolinguistics

LANGUAGE PLANNING

Isidor Marí, *Plurilingüisme europeu i llengua catalana*, Valencia U.P., 1995, sees a place for Catalan as a language of day-to-day use in the Catalan countries, and supports a model for Europe based on plurality of languages and diversity as one of the main values of our culture. Miguel Siguan, *L'Europa de les llengües*, B, Edicions 62, 218 pp., on the other hand, suggests an organization of language planning in order to avoid contradictions between the recognition of language plurality within the different states and the maintenance of some *interlinguae* (not only one, as some scholars suggest). Bernat Joan, *Les normalitzacions reeixides*, B, Oikos-Tair, 224 pp., studies how some

European minority languages have become national languages during the 20th c., to look for possibilities in language planning for Catalan. Without conflict there is no change, hence the studies of language conflictivity. Albert Bastardas, *Fer el futur: sociolingüística, planificació i normalització del català*, B, Empúries, 107 pp., gives rules about how to improve the future of the Catalan language. Lluís Flaquer, *El català, llengua pública o privada?*, B, Empúries, 376 pp., provides an intersection between sociolinguistics, law and language planning, to discuss the health of Catalan as a private language (because of the reduction of the percentage of Catalan speakers , by migration and population movement) and as a public language (much more better nowadays than a few years ago, especially in Catalonia). Vicent Pitarch, *Control lingüístic o caos*, Alzira, Bromera, 1995, 248 pp., is on conflict in Valencia, not only because the status of the two languages (Catalan and Spanish), but because of the model of 'Valencian'. There is a temptation to make a specific grammar for colloquial Valencian, trying to differentiate it from the Catalan standard language. For this reason, many citizens of Valencia are not clear as to what model of formal/standard language they should use: a secessionist one, or the Catalan standard. For the Valencian scholar, there are only two options: language control or chaos. Brauli Montoya, *Alacant: la llengua interrompuda*, V, Denes, analyses the process of language substitution in Alacant, and makes a map of zones where 'language desertion' (language shift) is strong, zones with a moderate degree of language shift and zones with a low language shift.

ANALYSIS OF SPEECH

Amparo Tusón, *Anàlisi de la conversa*, B, Empúries, 1995, 104 pp., follows Hudson's sociolinguistic approach.

MEDIEVAL LITERATURE

By LOLA BADIA, *Professor of Catalan Literature at the Universitat de Girona*

I. GENERAL

BIBLIOGRAPHY. *BAHLM*, 9:1–52, includes information on Catalan for the year 1995. R. Alemany Ferrer, *Guia bibliogràfica de la literatura catalana medieval*, Alicante U.P., 1995, 184 pp., is a survey for beginners. G. Avenoza, 'La bibliografia dels antics textos catalans. Accés informàtic als materials', *CatR*, 8, 1994[1996]:9–25, describes the computerized archive of medieval Catalan texts known as BITECA. (See also R. Beltran under TIRANT LO BLANC AND OTHER NARRATIVE TEXTS.)

COLLECTED ESSAYS AND HISTORICAL CONTEXT. Two anthologies of 'classical' essays: J. Rubió Balaguer, *Estudis literaris*, B, Edicions 62, 263 pp., and F. Soldevila, *Cronistes, joglars i poetes*, ed. J. Molas and J. Massot Muntaner, B, BAO, 469 pp. G. Tavani, *Per una història de la cultura catalana medieval*, B, Curial, 225 pp., and J. Vidal Alcover, *Estudis de literatura medieval i moderna*, ed. P. Anguera and M. Sunyer, Palma de Mallorca, Moll, 570 pp., also collect old studies. J. Aurell, *Els mercaders catalans al Quatre-cents. Mutació de valors i procés d'aristocratització a Barcelona (1370–1470)*, Lleida, Pagès, 428 pp., supplies new data to the understanding of merchants' cultural background. A. Hauf writes a rich introduction to the reprint of J. Pou Martí, OFM, *Visionarios, beguinos y fraticelos catalanes (siglos XIII–XV)*, Alacant, Instituto de Cultura Juan Gil-Albert, 745 pp. J. M. Nadal and M. Prats, *Història de la Llengua Catalana. 2. El segle XV*, B, Edicions 62, 601 pp., is the second issue of a history of the Catalan language begun in 1982. M. Peña, *Cataluña en el Renacimiento: libros y lenguas (Barcelona, 1473–1600)*, Lleida, Milenio, 372 pp., is an essay on book production. J. Ponsoda, *El català i l'aragonès en els inicis del Regne de València segons el Llibre de Cort de Cocentaina (1269–1295)*, Alcoi, Marfil, 393 pp., studies early linguistic interferences. A. Rubio Vela, *L'escrivania municipal de València als segles XIV i XV: burocràcia, política i cultura*, V, Generalitat Valenciana–Consell Valencià de Cultura, 1995, 142 pp., is on Valencian scribes' cultural background.

2. LYRIC AND NARRATIVE VERSE

AUSIÀS MARCH

R. Archer, *Aproximació a Ausiàs March*, B, Empúries, Barcelona, 200 pp., analyses poems 92–97 and 105, updates studies on allegory and metaphor and suggests new Marchean sources; in his 'El llegat ausiasmarquià d'Amedée Pagès', *LlLi*, 7:291–316, A. discusses Pagès's works. L. Cabré, 'Aristotle for the layman: sense perception in the poetry of Ausiàs March', *JWCI*, 56:48–60, relates poems 119 and 120 to Aristotle's *De anima* and explains how a knight could assimilate theology, natural and moral philosophy through lessons for laymen held by Dominican friars in Valencia. M. A. Coronel Ramos, 'La fuente de la traducción latina de Ausiàs March realizada por Vicente Mariner (Turnoni, 1633)', *BSCC*, 71.1, 1995:5–80, shows that Mariner used editions *c* and *d*. V. Fàbrega Escatllar, 'Ausiàs March i les expectatives de la Catalunya medieval: un comentari al cant 72', *EMarg*, 54, 1995:98–103, envisages M.'s apocalyptic ideas. J. Farré Capdevila and A. Moix Capdevila, 'L'amor espiritual en el poema 45 d'Ausiàs March', *ELLC*, 31, 1995:55–78, insist on the gap between flesh and soul in love. Two contributions on M.'s use of classical tradition: C. Garriga, '*Volgra sser nat cent anys ho pus atràs*', *Actes* (Andorra), 385–91, and J. Redondo, 'Hipòcrates líric a l'Humanisme català', *Faventia*, 18.1:89–103.

OTHER POETS

M. de Riquer, *Les poesies del trobador Guillem de Berguedà*, B, Quaderns Crema, 428 pp., edits the Catalan troubadour, with translation and notes. R. Archer, 'Aproximació al maldit', *Actes* (Berkeley), 21–35, investigates Catalan specimens of that troubadouresque genre. An edition of Sant Jordi with Italian translation and notes: J. de Sant Jordi, *Poesia*, ed. D. Siviero, Milan, Luni, 127 pp. J. Turró publishes his critical edition of Romeu Llull's *Obra Completa*, B, ENC, 322 pp., with rich biographical and literary studies. J. Pujol, '*Psallite sapienter*: la gaia ciència en els sermons de Felip de Malla de 1413 (Estudi i edició)', *CN*, 56.1–2:177–250, is a commented edition. A. Ferrando, 'El concepte d'escola valenciana aplicat als poetes valencians de l'època de Fenollar: consideracions sobre el seu bilingüisme', *Solà-Solé Vol.*, 199–217, and J. V. Saval, 'Les líriques tradicionals catalana i castellana: Punts de connexió i diferències', *ib.*, 171–86, are essays on comparative literature.

NARRATIVE VERSE AND JAUME ROIG'S *ESPILL*

Three new editions of *novas rimadas*: L. Badia and A. J. Soberanas, '*La ventura del cavaller N'Huc e de Madona*. Un nouveau roman occitano-catalan en vers du XIVe siècle', *Romania*, 114:96–134; S. Thiolier-Méjean, *Une Belle au Bois Dormant médiévale. Frayre de Joy er Sor de Plaser. Nouvelle d'oc du XIVe siècle. Text, traduction, notes et commentaires*, Paris, Université Paris IV, 239 pp., and A. Giannetti, *Llibre dels set savis de*

Roma, Bari, Adriatica, 239 pp. A. Carré and J. Solervicens, *Dos assaigs sobre cultura i literatura dels segles XV i XVI*, B–Vic, Universitat de Barcelona–Eumo, 118 pp., contains a survey of R.'s medical knowledge found in his *E*, by A. Carré (7–71). Also on R.: M. Puig Rodríguez-Escalona, 'Un episodi d'Apuleu a Jaume Roig', *Actes* (Andorra), 563–66; J. Guia, 'Corella també en menjava, d'olives', *RCat*, 105:83–114, unconvincingly proposes Roís de Corella as author of *Lo procés de les olives*.

3. DOCTRINAL AND RELIGIOUS PROSE

RAMON LLULL AND LULLISM

A critical edition of three Catalan works by L.: *Llibre dels articles de la fe, Llibre què deu hom creure de Déu, Llibre contra Anticrist. Nova Edició de les Obres de R.L.*, III, ed. A. J. Pons, J. Gayà, and G. Schib, Palma de Mallorca, 166 pp. A reprint of a 17th-c. anthology with a study by A. Bonner: Raimundus Lullus, *Opera (Strasbourg, 1651)*, Stuttgart–Bad Cannstatt, Frommann and Holzboog, 1109 pp., and a contribution on 16th-c. Lullism: A. Soler, 'Joan Bonllavi, lul·lista i editor eximi', *ELLC*, 31, 1995:125–50. Two interpretative books on literary aspects of Llull: R. J. González-Casanova, *The Apostolic Hero and Community in Ramon Llull's 'Blanquerna'. A Literary Study of a Medieval Utopia*, NY–Bern, Lang, 1995, 161 pp., and M. D. Johnston, *The Evangelical Rhetoric of Ramon Llull. Lay Learning and Piety in the Christian West around 1300*, OUP, 274 pp. Some contributions to philosophical problems: A. Bonner, 'Més sobre el mot i el concepte de 'dignitats' en Ramon Llull', *ELLC*, 32:5–14, and 'Ramon Llull: relació, acció, combinatòria i lògica moderna', *SLu*, 34, 1994[1996]:51–74; F. Domínguez, '*Principia philosophiae [complexa]* y Thomas Le Myésier', *ib.*, 93–102; J. Gayà, '*Ascensio, virtus*: dos conceptos del contexto original del sistema luliano', *ib.*, 3–49; H. Hames, 'Elijah and a shepherd: the authority of revelation', *ib.*, 93–102; and three articles by J. E. Rubio: 'La figura S de l'Art lul·liana i el *Llibre de contemplació en Déu*', *LlLi*, 7:61–90; 'El "coneixement per la negativa" com a conseqüència epistemològica de l'oposició bé-mal al *Llibre de contemplació*', *Randa*, 36, 1995:5–15 and 'L'estètica en Ramon Llull: una qüestió epistemològica', *Tesserae*, 2:73–80. P. Villalba, 'Ramon Llull: *Arbor scientiae* o *Arbre de sciència*', *Faventia*, 17.2, 1995:69–76, suggests a Latin first redaction for *Arbor scientiae. Constantes y fragmentos del pensamiento luliano. Actas del simposio sobre Ramon Llull en Trujillo, 1994*, ed. F. Domínguez and J. de Salas, Tübingen, Niemeyer, 172 pp., has 12 contributions; two of them approach literary questions: L. Badia, 'La ficción luliana en los orígenes de las letras catalanas' (59–76), and F. Domínguez, 'El proyecto luliano de predicación cristiana' (117–32).

RELIGIOUS AND MEDICAL WRITERS

Two contributions on Eiximenis: X. Renedo, 'Totes artificials laqueries ... Dietètica i moral en un capítol del *Terç del Crestià* de Francesc Eiximenis', pp. 921–31 of *Actes del Ier Col·loqui d'Història de l'Alimentació a la Corona d'Aragó. Edat Mitjana*, ii, Lleida, Institut d'Estudis Ilerdencs, 1995, 000 pp., and D. Rogers, 'A *stemma codicum* for Francesc Eiximenis' *Dotzè del Crestià*', pp. 321–34 of *Iberia and the Mediterranean World of the Middle Ages. Studies in Honour of Robert I. Burns, S.J*, i, Leiden–NY–Cologne, Brill, 1995, 348 pp. M. Pérez, *La vida de sant Vicent Ferrer*, ed. A. Ferrando, V, Valencia U.P.–Vicent Garcia, 194 pp. Also on Ferrer: D. Viera and J. Piqué, 'Vicent Ferrer i el sermó del dia de Sant Jordi', *Actes* (Berkeley), 275–85. A. Hauf publishes an anthology from I. de Villena, *Vita Christi*, B, Edicions 62, 1995, 352 pp., with a useful introduction, and J. Guia, 'Passions paral·leles. Concordances estilístiques en la literatura catalana del segle XV', *RCat*, 111 : 137–64, verifies that I. de Villena's account of Christ's Passion is very similar to the *Passi en cobles* by Gassull. C. Wittlin describes two incunabula with devotional works: 'L'*Escala de Paradís* del metge tortosí Antoni Boteller', *ELLC*, 31, 1995 : 79–93, and 'El *Psaltiri* del 1480 i altres restes de la *Bíblia valenciana* dels cartoixans de Portaceli', *Actes* (Berkeley), 287–301. L. Garcia Ballester, M. McVaugh, and P. Gil-Sostres publish the critical edition of Arnau de Vilanova's *Regimen sanitatis ad regem Aragonum*, *Arnaldi de Villanova Opera Medica Omnia*, x,1, B, 933 pp., with a very rich essay on the genre 'regimen sanitatis'. Still on Vilanova: A. Trias, 'El català en el llatí del *Regimen sanitatis ad Regem Aragonum*', *ELLC*, 32 : 33–52. G. Avenoza, 'Del calaix de l'apotecari i de l'especier', pp. 781–804 of *Scripta philologica in memoriam Manuel Taboada Cid*, ii, Corunna U.P., studies medical texts from Biblioteca Nacional Madrid MS. 10.162.

4. HISTORICAL AND ARTISTIC PROSE, NOVEL

HISTORIOGRAPHY

A. Ferrando, 'Fortuna catalana d'una llegenda germànica: el tema de l'emperadriu d'Alemanya falsament acusada d'adulteri', *Actes* (Frankfurt), ii, 197–216, studies the diffusion of a Carolingian legend in Catalan chronicles. J. D. Garrido Valls, 'L'aliança entre l'emperador Enric VII de Luxemburg i Frederic III de Sicília segons una crònica anònima catalana del segle XV', *ib.*, 217–30, publishes a small chronicle from a Biblioteca Nacional Madrid MS. R. J. González-Casanova, 'Western narratives of Eastern adventures: the cultural poetics and politics of Catalan expansion, 1300–1500', *CatR*, 8, 1994[1996] : 211–27, relates Muntaner's ideology to Martorell's.

J. M. Pujol Sanmartín, 'The *Llibre del rei En Jaume*: a matter of style', Deyermond, *Iberia*, 35–65, is a major contribution on the *Llibre dels feits*; R. B. Tate, 'The rewriting of the historical past: *Hispania et Europa*', *ib.*, 85–103, refers to Catalan writers.

TIRANT LO BLANC AND OTHER NARRATIVE TEXTS

J. Villalmanzo, *Joanot Martorell. Biografia ilustrada y diplomatario*, V, Ajuntament de València, 581 pp., compiles all information available about M. and his family. R. Beltran and J. Izquierdo, 'Bibliografia d'estudis sobre *Tirant lo Blanc*', *LlLi*, 7:345–406, list 372 items published between 1737 and 1995. Two contributions by J. Perujo: *La coherència estructural del 'Tirant lo Blanch'*, V–Alacant, Generalitat Valenciana–Institut de Cultura Joan Gil-Albert, 1995, 287 pp., and 'El *Tirant lo Blanch* i la *Història del rei Omar An-Numan*', *ELLC*, 31, 1995:107–23. (See also DRAMA.) J. Guia, 'L'autoria del *Tirant* de Martorell a Corella', *SdO*, 434:57–59, and *De Martorell a Corella. Descobrint l'autor del 'Tirant lo Blanc'*, B–Catarroja, Afers, 301 pp., wrongly claims that Joan Roís de Corella wrote *T*. Two contributions of M. Piera on *Curial e Güelfa*: 'L'elaboració de conceptes humanistes a *Curial e Güelfa*', *Actes* (Berkeley), 211–20, and *'Aquells qui ho voldran saber, lligen maestre Guido de Columpnis*: una lectura de *Curial e Güelfa*', *CatR*, 9.1, 1995[1996], 113–24. A. Annicchiarico, *Varianti corelliane e 'plagi' del 'Tirant': Achille e Polissena*, Fasano di Brindisi, Schena, 101 pp., studies the textual variants of a mythological remake by R.C. in connection with its presence in *T*. Other minor contributions on R.C.: L. Lucero, 'La tradició ovidiana en l'obra de Joan Roís de Corella: una aproximació parcial', *Actes* (Andorra), 437–42; E. Trilla and V. Cristobal, 'Las *Heroidas* de Ovidio en Joan Roís de Corella', *ib.*, 693–97.

5. TRANSLATIONS AND OTHER GENRES AND TEXTS

T. Martínez, 'Coluccio Salutati i una expositio catalana', *LlLi*, 7:273–90, studies a *glossa* in a Catalan translation of Seneca. J. Kiviharju, *Las glosas del mestre Aleix de Barcelona en su edición catalana del 'De Regimine Principum' de Egidio Romano y su versión navarroaragonesa*, Helsinki, AASF, 1995, 138 pp., publishes some scholastic *glossae* on moral and natural philosophy both in Catalan and Aragonese. L. Badia, *Textos catalans tardomedievals i ciència de natures*, B, Reial Acadèmia de Bones Lletres de Barcelona, 101 pp, discusses the influence of natural philosophy on literary texts. M. Barceló and G. Ensenyat, *Ferrando Valentí i la seva família*, Palma de Mallorca, Universitat de les Illes Balears–PAM, 101 pp., enrich the biography of the translator into Catalan of Cicero's *Paradoxa*. V. Martines Peres, 'Tiempo y espacio en la versión catalana de la *Queste del saint Graal*', *HR*, 63: 373–90, analyses some literary features of that translation. T. Martínez, 'Antoni Canals, Alonso de Cartagena i unes notes de literatura comparada', *MedRom*, 20:116–42, investigates the reception of Seneca. L. Martín Pascual, 'El tigre transformat en serp i la tigressa emmirallada. Algunes notes sobre la configuració dels bestiaris catalans', *ELLC*, 32:15–32, and E. J. Neugaard, 'Spanish and Castilian Aesopica', *Solà-Solé Vol.*, 161–70, deal with Catalan *exempla*. Two contributions on epistolography and folklore: D. Prince, 'A reappraisal of the correspondence of Violant de Bar (1365–1431)', *CatR*, 8, 1994[1996]: 295–308, and M. P. Janer, 'Introducció al tema de la metamorfosi als contes meravellosos catalans', *ib.*, 239–44. Three works on paremiology by M. Conca and J. Guia: *Els primers reculls de proverbis catalans*, B, PAM, 326 pp.; 'Sentències i proverbis en la *Disputa de l'ase*', *ELLC*, 32:53–76, and 'Estudi paremiològic del *Llibre de Tres*', *Randa*, 37, 1995:17–41.

6. DRAMA

Formes teatrals de la Tradició Medieval. Actes del VII Col·loqui de la Société Internationale pour l'Étude du Théâtre Médiéval, ed. F. Massip, B, Institut del Teatre, 524 pp., the proceedings of a conference held at Girona in 1992, includes: F. Huerta, 'Una mostra del teatre nadalenc de transició: la "representació" de la nit de Nadal' (433–36); F. Massip, 'El món de l'espectacle en *Tirant lo Blanc*' (151–62); L. Quirante, 'Notas sobre *Lo fet de la Sibil·la e de l'emperador Sésar*' (453–59); X. Renedo, '*Turpia feminarum incesta lascivarum* (El joc teatral en el capítol 283 del *Tirant lo Blanc*)' (209–16); and P. Vila, 'Joglars i ministrils al Rosselló a través de la documentació d'arxiu' (231–36). Also on liturgical drama, M. Rodríguez Macià, 'La processó de la Mare de Déu, un acte clau de la Festa d'Elx', *CatR*, 8, 1994[1996]: 313–21; P. Vila, 'El drama litúrgic a Sant Joan de les Abadesses als segles XIV i XV', *RCat*, 111:91–109, and J. Mas Vives, 'El gènere de la "moralitat" en el teatre català antic', *LlLi*, 7:91–104.

LITERATURE (NINETEENTH AND TWENTIETH CENTURIES)

By MARGARIDA CASACUBERTA, *Lecturer in Catalan Literature at the Universitat de Girona*, and MARINA GUSTÀ, *Lecturer in Catalan Literature at the Universitat de Barcelona*

1. GENERAL

P. Gimferrer, *L'obrador del poeta (1970–1996)*, B, La Magrana, 172 pp., and J. Romeu, *Assaigs i altres indagacions crítiques*, RABLB-Quaderns Crema, 200 pp., collect, respectively, textes on theory and practice of poetic creation. Two contributions of a miscellaneous character with materials on several contemporary authors: *De Rusiñol a Monzó: Humor i literatura*, B, PAM, 128 pp., with articles, also, on J. Carner, F. Trabal, P. Calders, and J. Pla; and J. Massot i Muntaner, *Escriptors i erudits contemporanis*, B, PAM, 334 pp., with texts on J. Estelrich, M. Batllori, L. Villalonga, J. Rubió i Balaguer, among others. J. Aulet, 'Estudis recents de literatura catalana contemporània', *SdO*:605–07, 773–76, gives a complete and documented report on the new erudite and critical contributions to the study of Catalan literature in the 19th and 20th c.; and A. Lonzà, 'Aproximació bibliogràfica a Joan Fuster d'ençà de la seva mort', *SdO*:268–70, brings the state of studies on J. Fuster up to date.

2. RENAIXENÇA

I. Cònsul, 'L'any del Segle Romàntic. Balanç provisional', *SdO*:402–04, is a first review of the historiographical production which has been generated by the four colloquia celebrated in 1995. While awaiting the publication of the corresponding proceedings, some of these materials have appeared as articles in several publications. This is the case of J. M. Benet i Jornet, 'Aspectes de la passió amorosa en l'obra de Guimerà', *ib.*, 59–61. However, the inertia of the *Segle Romàntic* has favoured the appearance of several studies on the authors and the most relevant aspects of Romanticism in Catalonia. At last the first volume of the complete work of J. Verdaguer, *Dos màrtirs de ma pàtria, o siga Llucià i Marcià*, Vic, Eumo Editorial-Societat Verdaguer, 286 pp., has appeared. The extensive study (13–128) and the careful and exemplary edition are by Ricard Torrents. Narcís Garolera has published an edition of *Flors del calvari*, B, Columna, 202 pp., with an introduction, '*Flors del calvari*, un tombant en la poesia de Verdaguer' (7–26). By the same author, *Sobre Verdaguer. Biografia, literatura, llengua*, B, Empúries, 224 pp. The

mythical figure of Verdaguer has been the object of study in
L. Soldevila, *Jacint Verdaguer. Formació i dimensió d'un mite*, Argentona,
L'Aixernador, 1995, 192 pp. On the important literary figure of
Àngel Guimerà, J. Martori, 'El teatre de Guimerà a Madrid. Un
punt d'arrencada en la seva projecció internacional', *SdO*:62–63, and
C. Duran Tort, 'Els inicis d'una amistat perdurable. Primeres cartes
de Pere Aldavert a Àngel Guimerà', *LlLi*, 7 : 331–44, are noteworthy.
N. Oliveras, *He mort el llop! Introducció a l'obra d'Àngel Guimerà*,
Argentona, L'Aixernador, 1995, 174 pp., provides a global approach
to the trajectory of Guimerà. The other great author of the Catalan
19th c. has had, in Valls in 1996, his colloquium. A tasting of the
materials presented have appeared in the dossier 'En el centenari de
Narcís Oller', *SdO*:922–33, with contributions from A. Yates, 'Narcís
Oller, començaments i finals' (922–25); E. Cassany, 'Narcís Oller en
la tradició realista' (927–29); M. Aritzeta, 'El cicle de Vilaniu,
conflictes d'una poètica realista' (931–33). M. Vidal Tibbits, for his
part, devotes an article to 'Ironia i paròdia a *L'escanyapobres*, de Narcís
Oller', *Actes* (Berkeley), 267–73. A. Maseras, *Vida de Narcís Oller*, ed.
M. Corretger, Tarragona, El Mèdol, 118 pp., provides a useful
document to understand the reception of Oller's narrative. With
respect to the 19th-c. novel, J. M. Domingo, *Josep Pin i Soler i la novel·la
1869–1892. El cicle dels Garriga*, B, Curial-PAM, 291 pp., establishes
the dimensions of an author not very well known until now.
M. Serrahima and M. T. Boada, *La novel·la històrica en la literatura
catalana*, B, PAM, 215 pp., exhumes an unpublished text which had
become mythical. One of the authors studied by S. is the object of the
attention of *Sis estudis sobre Antoni de Bofarull*, Reus, Centre de Lectura,
168 pp., with contributions by P. Anguera, M. Tomàs, J. Ginebra,
X. Vall, and J. Tiñena. The history of literary ideas is further enriched
with J. M. Quadrado, *Assaigs literaris*, ed. A. Tayadella, B, PAM, xxix
+ 253 pp., and especially with the editor's prologue. The Valencian
dramatic tradition has in the figure of E. Escalante one of its decisive
mainstays. The appearance of the *Teatre original complet*, 2 vols., ed.
and introd. J.-L. and R. Sirera, V, Alfons El Magnànim, 1995,
testifies it from now. Popular literature, so unknown in the mechanisms of its creation and diffusion, is the object of a suggestive article:
A. Serrà Campins, 'Aproximació al poeta oral de llengua catalana',
LlLi, 7:7–59. J. Castellanos: 'Mercat del llibre i cultura nacional
(1882–1925)', *Els Marges*, 56:5–38, analyses the proverbial balance
of the author-editor-reader-audience relation between two mythical
dates in the history of the contemporary novel from the point of view
of the relations between the publishing industry and the Catalan
language, in an article which will undoubtly become a historiographical point of reference.

3. MODERNISME

The interest in *Modernisme* seems to suffer a certain decrease, probably temporary. During the last year, only two studies devoted to two central figures of this movement, Joan Maragall and Santiago Rusiñol; a study on a marginal figure, Diego Ruiz; and a study of reception, have appeared. L. Quintana i Trias, *La veu misteriosa. La teoria literària de Joan Maragall*, B, PAM, 513 pp., studies the *Elogis* by Maragall and establishes its text critically. M. Casacuberta, 'Santiago Rusiñol a Mallorca. La interpretació artística del paisatge illenc entre els jardins abandonats i *L'illa de la calma*', *Randa*, 38:5–42, reviews the significance of the different stays of Rusiñol in Mallorca. R. Anglada Bou, 'Notes per a una lectura dels contes de Diego Ruiz des de l'imaginari decadentista', *EMarg*, 55:79–87, presents part of the literary production of the 'metge filòsof'. On the figure of Gabriele D'Annunzio, attractive as well as ambiguous, A. Camps i Olivé, *La recepció de Gabriele D'Annunzio a Catalunya*, Curial-PAM, 261 pp., and 'Darrere les petges de D'Annunzio: Ambrosi Carrion i el debat sobre la qüestió teatral a començaments del segle XX', *SdO*:593–95.

4. NOUCENTISME

The 1994 exhibition on *Noucentisme* is in the origin of V. Panyella, *Cronologia del Noucentisme*, B, PAM, 149 pp., which comes from the catalogue published on that occasion. E. Serra i Casals, 'La revista *Teatràlia* com a plataforma noucentista', *EMarg*, 55:7–28, is valuable because of its contribution to uncovering the connections between *Noucentisme* and theatrical genres. This year, several collections of letters or fragments of collections of letters between relevant figures of that cultural period have seen the light: E. Bou and J. Murgades, 'Correspondència d'Eugeni d'Ors a Jaume Bofill i Matas (Guerau de Liost)', *ib.*, 56:99–108; C. Bastons, 'La correspondència de mallorquins amb Unamuno (I)', *Randa*, 39:61–88, with important correspondents such as J. Estelrich, G. Alomar, J. Alcover, and M. S. Oliver; and M. L. Julià, 'Tast d'un ric epistolari. Vint cartes entre Maria Antònia Salvà i Mateu Obrador', *ib.*, 39:29–60. This year the Majorcan poet has been recovered by M. L. Julià, *Lectures de Maria Antònia Salvà*, B, PAM, 228 pp., and 'L'*Antologia* carneriana de Maria Antònia Salvà', *SdO*:570–71. The first period of Riba criticism is clarified by J. Malé, *Carles Riba i el Noucentisme. Les idees literàries (1913–1920)*, B, La Magrana, 330 pp. The rigorous study by M. Ortín, *La prosa literària de Josep Carner*, B, Quaderns Crema, 535 pp., concentrates on the C.'s narrative prose, especially that published in books up to 1930; V. Martínez-Gil, 'Txèkhov i Carner:

del realisme al realisme màgic', *EMarg*, 56:115–21, focuses on a
Carnerian story to point out the feasibility of a study of comparatistics.
Carner's prose is precisely one of the negative arguments which are
put forward by X. Pericay and F. Toutain, *El malentès del Noucentisme.
Tradició i plagi a la prosa catalana moderna*, B, Proa, 315 pp., who —
misunderstanding the meaning of literary history and imitating its
methods — question the validity and the effectiveness of the
contributions of *Noucentisme* to the configuration of the modern
literary prose. They are probably trying to be the last — and
ahistorical and, therefore, anachronistic — link with the tradition of
antinoucentisme, which began in parallel to the movement. This
tradition is reviewed with perspicacity and full awareness by J. Murgades, 'Sinopsi de l'antinoucentisme històric', *LlLi*, 7:61–127.

5. The Twentieth Century

The historiographical scene period in Catalan literature in the 20s
and 30s is characterized by variety and wandering. A. Obiols, *Buirac*,
Sabadell, Fundació La Mirada, a collection of critical articles
exhumed from *L'Opinió*, is important because of the ignorance which
the present audience still have of a decisive figure in the cultural and
literary life in those years. The shrewd, well-documented, suggestive
study by J. M. Balaguer published as a 'Pròleg' (9–56), reveals O.'s
full importance. For similar reasons, J. Crexells, *Obra Completa I. De
Plató a Carles Riba*, ed. A. Schrem, prol. J. Molas, B, La Magrana, 700
pp., is to be celebrated. The collection of letters between J. Rubió i
Balaguer and M. Rubió i Lois, *Cartes de la guerra, maig 1938-gener 1939*,
ed., notes and introd. J. Galofré, B, PAM, 140 pp., is a document of
the first magnitude to understand the role of the literature daily on
the front and the rearguard, despite its condition of personal
documents. The whole dimension of the figure of Lluís Nicolau
d'Olwer is gradually getting known, beyond his academic production
and even his public political role, for instance in M. Vilà i Bayerri
and J. Molar i Navarra, 'Bibliografia sobre Lluís Nicolau d'Olwer',
LlLi, 7:407–25, and M. Vilà i Bayerri, 'Mallorca en la vida i l'obra
de Lluís Nicolau d'Olwer', *Randa*, 39:89–103. A similar case is
J. Estelrich, who is the object of attention this year in his centenary
by I. Graña, 'Joan Estelrich cent anys després. Contra l'oblit i la
dispersió?', *SdO*:315–18, and, id., 'Joan Estelrich (1896–1958):
presència, acció i intervenció en la cultura catalana del segle xx',
pp. v-xxvii of J. Estelrich, *Entre la vida i els llibres*, PAM, xxvii + 340 pp.
R. Mosquera, 'Presència catalana en *La Gaceta Literària* (1927–1932)',
Randa, 38:43–98, is an important piece of the study of the relationships between Catalan and Castilian intellectuals. However, the

literary genres and authors have received comparatively less attention. On the avantgarde, the proceedings of the colloquium *Les avant-*
gardes en Catalogne, dir. S. Salaün and E. Trenc, París, Presse de la
Sorbonne Nouvelle, 1995, and M. Subiràs i Pugibet, 'Relectura de
l'obra poètica catalana de Sebastià Sánchez-Juan, 1924–1939',
Reduccions, 64, 1994–95:69–91. On theatre, two contributions:
F. Sureda Font, 'El teatre a Manacor en temps de la Segona
República', *Randa*, 37:171–82; and, especially, M. M. Gibert, 'Dues
comèdies inèdites de Joan Oliver', *LlLi*, 7:129–66. On the novel,
J. Nogué i Font et al., 'Orientalisme, colonialisme i gènere. *El Marroc*
sensual i fanàtic, d'Aurora Bertrana', *Documents d'Anàlisi Geogràfica*,
29:87–107, is an interdisciplinary article on the subject of travel
narratives. Finally, S. Cabolleria Ferrer and M. C. Codina Contijoch,
'La col·lecció Els poetes d'ara', *SdO*:826–27, is on editorial aspects of
poetry.

The postwar scene is, however, very different. This year 50 years
of a mythical underground publication are celebrated in the dossier
'Fa cinquanta anys, "Ariel"', *SdO*:727–33, with contributions by
J. Triadú, J. Perucho, J. Romeu, and J. Sarsanedas. The immediate
postwar period is analysed from the Majorcan point of view by
J. Massot i Muntaner, *El primer franquisme a Mallorca. Guerra civil,*
repressió, exili i represa cultural, B, PAM, 486 pp. Two authors made in
exile are studied in: A. Pi i Murugó and A. Vilà i Serret, 'L'obra
mexicana d'Agustí Bartra', *SdO*:315–18; M. Bacardí, 'Les "relacions"
de Xavier Benguerel', *ib.*, 568–69; and M. A. Cerdà Surroca, 'Xavier
Benguerel: Icària, Arcàdia', *Actes* (Berkeley), 118–30. With respect to
poetry, D. Keown, *Sobre la poesia catalana contemporània*, V, Eliseu
Climent, 208 pp., is a collection of reading material of some of the
central poets of the contemporary tradition. J. Ballester, *La poesia*
catalana de postguerra al País Valencià, V, 3 i 4, 1995, is a valuable survey;
M. Guerrero, *J. V. Foix, investigador en poesia*, B, Empúries, 482 pp., is
particularly useful. Other noteworthy studies on poets born before
the war are: J. Julià, 'La palimpsestació a la poesia de Gabriel
Ferrater', *EMarg*, 55:96–108, and P. Ballart, 'Poesia i modernitat:
una lectura de *Coral romput*', *ib.*, 39–71. With respect, particularly, to
the globality of the figure of Espriu, the following contributions are of
very great interest: P. Cocozzella, 'Salvador Espriu between 1898
and 1936', *Actes* (Berkeley), 45–62, and 'Aspectes de la persona tràgica
en Salvador Espriu', *ZfK*, 8, 1995:74–103; also: V. Berger, 'Salvador
Espriu und *Primera història d'Esther: improvisació per a titelles*', *ib.*, 104–17,
and M. Trambaioli, 'La presencia del teatro de Salvador Espriu en
La pell de brau', *Actes* (Berkeley), 249–66. Finally, I. Cònsul, 'Perfil d'un
poeta. Narcís Comadira', *SdO*:46–48. There is a small trickle of
studies on narrative, with an exception caused by the imminent

celebration of the centenary of Josep Pla's birth. Mercè Rodoreda's work has merited the interest of C. Cortés i Orts, *Els protagonistes i el medi en la narrativa de Mercè Rodoreda*, Alacant, Institut de Cultura Juan Gil Albert, 140 pp., and M. I. Mencos, 'Mercè Rodoreda i la mirada transgressora (en *La meva Cristina i altres contes*)', *Actes* (Berkeley), 167–74. On the procedures of Pere Calders' brief narrative, M. Duran, 'Humor, ironia i fantasia irracional en alguns contes de Pere Calders', *ib.*, 63–69. J.-V. Garcia, 'Ferran de Pol. L'escriptura i la vida (1911–1995)', *SdO*:34–37, approaches the literary figure of Lluís Ferran de Pol. The possible specificity of the contemporary island narrative is suggested by S. Alzamora in 'Narrar a Mallorca, narrar Mallorca', *ib.*, 571–73. There are several individual contributions on some Majorcan authors: Baltasar Porcel is studied by M. Subiràs i Puigibet, 'Concepció del món i actitud vital a *Les pomes d'or*, de Baltasar Porcel', *Randa*, 39:105–18, and by R. Cabré, 'Els contes de *Molts paradisos perduts*', *ib.*, 119–45; P. Rosselló Bover 'Miquel Àngel Riera: aproximació biogràfica a l'home que va crear bellesa', *SdO*:804–07, and 'Aproximació a Joaquim Verdaguer a través dels seus articles: "La vida humorística"', *Randa*, 36, 1995:81–105; finally M. Alcover, *Llorenç Villalonga i les belles arts. Un ideari estètic noucentista*, prol. M. C. Bosch, Edicions Documenta Balear, is on a marginal and, somewhat poorly focused aspect of Llorenç Villalonga's work. The critical production on Josep Pla has benefited from the chronological incentive, and is basically of biographical interest: C. Badosa, *Josep Pla. Biografia del solitari*, B, Edicions 62, 376 pp., has an ambitious as well as dubious approach due to the apriorisms from which it starts; J. Pla, *Cartes a Pere*, ed. X. Pla, B, Destino, 256 pp., has material of interest that goes beyond biography; J. Martinell, *Josep Pla vist per un amic de Palafrugell*, B, Destino, 248 pp., for his part, offers a product of a memorialistical line; *Josep Pla vist per Eugeni Forcano*, Sabadell, Ausa, 1995, 220 pp., has basically the incentive of the photographic material; finally, M. Pairolí, *La geografia íntima de Josep Pla*, B, La Campana, 204 pp., reviews some of the most significative scenes in Pla's literature, and C. Casajuana, *Pla i Nietzsche: afinitats i coincidències*, B, Edicions 62, 124 pp., tries out some comparative approaches. A. Viana, 'La batalla dels llibres de Josep Pla', *SdO*:319–22, proposes a suggestive reading of some of the influences which P. states. *Homenatge a Xavier Fàbregas*, B, PAM, 88 pp., is the proceedings of a colloquium held in 1993 in the Université de Paris-Sorbonne (Centre d'Études Catalanes) with speeches by M. C. Zimmermann, M. Badiou, E. Gallén, F. Formosa, and J.-L. Sirera. G.-J. Graells, 'La "generació dels 70" vint-i-cinc anys després', *SdO*:652–54, gives a global view of the 'generació dels 70', and J. Vilà i Folch, 'Gent de teatre', *ib.*, 655–56, analyses it from the point of

view of theatre creators. The latest works of J. M. Benet i Jornet are
the object of readings by C. Batlle, 'Postfaci. *E. R.*, notes de lectura',
pp. 81–110 of J. M. Benet i Jornet, *E. R.*, B, Edicions 62, 1994,
110 pp., and C. Morell, 'Sobre el teatre de Josep Maria Benet i Jornet
i les darreres tendències de la dramatúrgia catalana', *Actes* (Frankfurt),
II, 57–76. Other interesting contributions are A. Nadal, 'Aproximació
a l'obra dramàtica de Marià Villangómez', *Randa*, 37:183–92;
R. Pérez González, 'Rodolf Sirera, vint-i-cinc anys després',
SdO:595–97, and M. Vallverdú, 'Del *strip-tease* al teatre irregular.
O com despullar el teatre a la manera de Joan Brossa', *EMarg*,
55:88–96. The field of literary translation, in which J. M. Boix i
Selva stands out, is the principal centre of the attention of J. Faulí,
'Josep M. Boix i Selva: traductor, editor i poeta', *SdO*:367–68, and of
R. Flotats Crespí, 'Josep M. Boix i Selva i *El paradís perdut*. Un
anostrament del poema èpic de John Milton', *ib.*, 369–71. Literary
criticism and historiography, through the work and figure of some of
the most important critics, is focused by X. Pla i Barbero, 'Maurici
Serrahima, crític i teòric de la literatura', *ib.*, 26–28, and J. Rubió i
Balaguer, *Estudis literaris. Trames culturals i individualitats creadores*, prol.
J. Molas, B, Edicions 62-La Caixa, 268 pp. J. Molas, for his part, sees
his teaching, critical, historiographic and publishing work examined
in the volume in his honor, *A Joaquim Molas*, B, PAM, 158 pp., with
contributions by M. Jorba, J. Castellanos, J. M. Benet i Jornet,
P. Gimferrer, M. Gustà, J. M. Balaguer, J. Aulet, J. Murgades, J. M.
Castellet, T. Rovira, among others. M. Casacuberta, 'Joaquim Molas,
un clàssic', *SdO*:427–28; I. Cònsul, 'Joaquim Molas, el mestre', *ib.*,
743–44, and J. Fontana, 'Homenatge a un home coherent', *ib.*, 850,
also discuss M.'s work. The work of J. M. Castellet has also received
aknowledgment in 'Josep Maria Castellet, setanta anys', *ib.*, 888–97,
with articles by J. Molas, P. Gimferrer, A. Broch, J. F. Yvars, and
D. Jou.

VI.   PORTUGUESE STUDIES

LANGUAGE

By STEPHEN PARKINSON, *Lecturer in Portuguese Language and Linguistics,
University of Oxford*

(This survey covers the years 1995 and 1996)

1.   GENERAL

The following abbreviations will be used extensively in this section:
APL 9: *Actas do IX Encontro Nacional da Associação Portuguesa da Linguística
(Coimbra, 1993)*, L, APL, 1994, 478 pp.; *APL 10*: *Actas do X Encontro
Nacional da Associação Portuguesa da Linguística (Évora, 1994)*, L, APL,
1995, 627 pp.; *APL 11,*: *Actas do XI Encontro Nacional da Associação
Portuguesa da Linguística (Lisboa, 1995)*, 3 vols, I, *Corpora*, ed. Maria
Fernanda Bacelar do Nascimento, Maria Celeste Rodrigues, and José
Bettencourt Rodrigues, II, *Dicionários*, ed. Isabel Hub Faria and
Margarida Correia, III, *Gramática e varia*, ed. Inês Duarte and Matilde
Miguel, L, APL, 456, 330, 601 pp.; *Cong. Int.*; *Actas do Congresso
Internacional sobre o Português (Lisboa, 1994)*, 3 vols, ed. Inês Duarte and
Isabel Leiria, L, APL–Colibri, 363, 517, 570 pp.; *Actas* (Hamburg):
*Actas do 4 Congresso da Associação Internacional de Lusitanistas (Universidade
de Hamburgo, 6 a 11 de Setembro de 1993)* ed. M. Fátima Brauer-
Figueiredo, L–Op–Coimbra, Lidel-AIL, 1115 pp.; *Workshop*: *Actas do
Workshop sobre Fonologia (Coimbra 27–28 setembro, 1993)*, L, APL, 1994,
125 pp.; *Carvalho Vol.*: *Semiótica e linguística portuguesa e românica.
Homenagem a José Gonçalo Herculano de Carvalho*, ed. Jürgen Schmidt-
Radefeld, Tübingen, Narr, 1993, xxxii + 353 pp.; *Tarallo Vol.*: *Português
brasileiro. Uma viagem diacrônica. Homenagem a Fernando Tarallo*, ed.
Ian Roberts and Mary A. Kato, Campinas, UNICAMP, 1993,
425 pp. Brazilian Portuguese and European Portuguese are abbreviated BP and EP respectively.

Isabel Hub Faria et al., *Introdução à linguística geral e portuguesa*, L,
Caminho, 630 pp., is an uneasy compromise between introductory
textbook and collective survey. P. Teyssier, 'Especifidade do português', *Cong. Int.*, II, 191–207, follows Coseriu in placing Portuguese in
a Southern Romance group: lexically close to Castilian, phonologically close to Catalan, morphosyntactically more conservative than
either. M. H. M. Mateus, 'O português: caminhos de investigação',
ib., I, 7–22, reflects on the lack of projection of research published in
Portuguese. E. Bechara, 'A tradição gramatical luso-brasileira', *ib.*,
175–88, surveys grammatical writers up to Said Ali. I. Duarte,

'Gramáticas do Português', *APL 11*, III, 13–18, is a survey complemented by a bibliography, *ib.*, 143–49, and critical comments from G. Matos, 'Morfo-sintaxe e sintaxe nas gramáticas descritivas do século XX', *ib.*, 105–21. R. A. Lawton, 'As palavras, diversamente colocadas (uma gramática sistemática)', *Actas* (Hamburg), 167–75, introduces his still unpublished grammar focusing on *linguística da posição*, and based on a literary corpus. L. H. Wittmann, T. R. Pêgo, and D. Santos, 'Português brasileiro e português de Portugal: algumas observações', *APL 11*, III, 465–87, explore corpus-based resources for identifying morphological and lexical divergences between EP and BP; prefigured by L. H. Wittmann and M. J. Pereira, 'Português europeu e português brasileiro: alguns contrastes', *APL 10*, 613–27, on the omission of definite articles in BP. A. T. Castilho, 'Para uma gramática do português falado', *Cunha Vol.*, 79–101, discusses the appropriate framework for a grammar of spoken Portuguese based on NURC materials. Id., 'O português do Brasil', *Actas* (Santiago de Compostela), VI, 869–75. M. F. Brauer-Figueiredo, 'O português falado. Descrição sistemática dos seus aspectos', *APL 11*, I, 323–47, and 'Aspectos do português falado em Portugal e na Alemanha', *Actas* (Hamburg), 35–54, gives samples of unmonitored speech.

ORTHOGRAPHY. A. M. Araújo, 'Breve notícia da ortografia portuguesa', *Cunha Vol.*, 431–48 , summarizes eight centuries of orthographic uncertainty. F. Gonçalves, 'A ortografia na antiga gramatografia portuguesa', *APL 11*, III, 39–52. E. Gonzalez, 'Algumas considerações sobre a ortografia e as suas reformas', *ib.*, 315–24, is a mixed bag of questionable facts and principles, on Portuguese and French orthographic reform. José Victor Adragão et al., *Novo Acordo Ortográfico*, L. Texto, 1995, 94 pp., includes a list of words whose orthography would change if the *Acordo* were to be implemented. P. M. Garcez, *'The debatable 1990 Luso-Brazilian orthographic accord', *LPLP*, 19, 1995:151–78.

GRAMMARIANS. A. Torres, 'Fernão de Oliveira e a sua Gramática em edição crítica', *Actas* (Santiago de Compostela), VI, 211–19. M. C. Fonseca, 'Os monemas funcionais em gramáticas e obras afins do século XVII. Algumas considerações', *APL 10*, 209–19, finds more concern with prepositions than conjunctions. T. Marayama, 'Padre João Rodriguez; testemunha auricular da língua japonesa medieval', *Cunha Vol.*, 657–65, interprets R.'s comparisons of Japanese and Portuguese sibilants. M. F. Menéndez, 'Alguns aspectos da evolução do discurso de D. Raphael Bluteau', *APL 11*, II, 137–50, compares two *dedicatórias*, showing B. reducing his personal prominence. L. L. Fávero, 'As concepções linguísticas no século XVIII em Portugal: *Arte da Gramática Portugueza* de Antônio José dos Reis Lobato', *ib.*, III, 333–50, is a brief introduction to a 1770 grammar dedicated to the

Marquês de Pombal and prescribed by him for use in schools. Bernardo de Lima e Mello Bacelar, **Gramática filosófica da língua portuguesa. Reprodução fac-similada da edição de 1783*, introd. Amadeu Torres, L, Academia Portuguesa da História, xvi + 242 pp. Maria Filomena Gonçalves, *Madureira Feijó, Ortografista do século* XVIII. *Para uma história da ortografia portuguesa*, L, ICALP, 1992, 142 pp., is a brief account of a latinizing 18th-c. authority. M. F. Gonçalves, 'O "artigo" e "as partes do discurso" na antiga gramaticografia portuguesa', *Actas* (Hamburg), 117–29, traces differences in criteria for identifying parts of speech, as exemplified by the changing status of the article. José Tavares de Macedo, *Obras Inéditas: Ensaio sobre o estudo histórico das línguas. Elementos de Gramática Portugueza*, ed. Ivo Castro, L, APL, 148 pp., is a newly-discovered, and ultimately derivative 19th-c. work of historical grammar. On more recent figures, *Cunha Vol.* contains: E. Bechara, 'O estudo da fraseologia na obra de João Ribeiro' (483–90); R. B. Neto, 'Pensamento e ação de Rocha Lima no território da língua portuguesa', (463–82).

CORPORA. *APL 11*, I, is devoted to linguistic corpora with a list of Portuguese corpora (421–47) and a 'Mesa redonda sobre Corpora linguísticos' (19–263), including: A. T. Castilho, G. M. O. Silva, and D. Lucchesi, 'Informatização de acervos da língua portuguesa' (113–28); M. T. C. Biderman, 'Desenho e análise de um corpus do português contemporâneo' (129–41); M. F. B. Nascimento and J. B. Gonçalves, 'Corpus de referência do Português Contemporâneo (CRPC) — desenvolvimento e aplicações' (143–49); I. H. Faria, 'Corpus de Aquisição do português europeu: a primeira fase' (165–71); M. C. Viana, 'Corpora de fala em P. E. Constituição, segmentação e etiquetagem' (189–216); D. Santos, 'On the use of parallel texts in the comparison of languages' (217–39); other relevant items are: D. E. A. Callou, 'Análise comparativa dos corpora. Conclusões gerais' (417–19); A. I. Mata, 'Apresentação preliminar do CPE FACES: um Corpus de Português Europeu Falado por Adolescentes em Contexto Escolar para o estudo da prosódia dos estilos da fala' (349–58).

2. HISTORICAL

Clarinda de Azevedo Maia, *História da Língua Portuguesa. Guia de estudo*, Coimbra U.P., 1995, 106 pp., is a useful bibliographical guide. P. Teyssier, 'La koiné portugaise', Holtus, *Lexikon*, II/2, 679–92, gives a brief history of the language to the 16th c. A. M. Martins 'Gramáticas históricas do português', *APL 11*, III, 53–71, is a critical survey. M. F. Xavier, 'Dos problemas de constituição às potencialidades de utilização de corpora: o caso do CIPM', *ib.*, I, 159–69 discusses the exploitation of a corpus previously presented in M. F. Xavier, M. T. Brocardo, and M. G. Vicente, 'CIPM — um corpus informatizado do português medieval', *APL 10*, 599–612. C. A. Maia, 'O galego-português medieval: sua especifidade no contexto dos romances peninsulares e futura diferenciação do galego e do português', *Cong. Int.*, I, 33–51, surveys studies of the divergence of Galician and Portuguese. A. Emiliano, 'Considerações sobre o estudo da documentação notarial anterior ao século XIII', *APL 9*, 195–210, highlights grapho-lexemic conversions from notarial Latin to Romance. S. Parkinson, 'Os tabeliães de 1290 e a dialectologia medieval portuguesa', *Cunha Vol.*, 667–76, uncovers a series of parallel documents generated by a general levy on notaries, and draws conclusions for late 13th-c. dialects. C. Rodrigues, 'Proposta de datação de três manuscritos medievais', *APL 9*, 363–76, assigns a mid-14th-c. date to versions of the *Costumes de Santarém*. J. A. Ferreira, '*Terceira Partida* de Afonso X: subsídios para a sua edição e estudo linguístico', *Actas* (Santiago de Compostela), VII, 187–204, and 'Um fragmento reencontrado da *Terceira Partida* de Afonso X', *Cunha Vol.*, 573–96. Simona Chándana Schlede, *Untersuchungen zur Graphematik portugiesischer Texte des 16. Jahrhunderts*, Geneva, Droz, 1995, 287 pp., is a detailed graphemic study of a 50,000-word corpus. I. Castro, 'Para uma história do português clássico', *Cong. Int.*, II, 135–50, uncovers problems for editors and linguists failing to recognize that 18th-c. Portuguese is close but not identical to 20th-c. varieties. T. Anderson, 'Sobre o desenvolvimento histórico da diferenciação das línguas portuguesa e brasileira', *Iberoromania*, 42, 1995:1–7, draws on a corpus of 19th- and 20th-c. journalistic texts to show the emergence of distinctive Brazilian features (wider use of *esse*, possessives without articles) after 1850, and the appearance of *estar + a +* infinitive in European Portuguese only in the 20th c. D. Messner, 'O "Dicionário dos dicionários portugueses" e o "Corpus da Gaceta de Lisboa"', *APL 11*, II, 173–79, reports on his lexicographical project (*YWMLS*, 56:461), and on studies of a 1700–1850 journal, showing the preservation of article + possessive (*contra* BP) and the decline of *mui* after 1785; similarly, T. Anderson and D. Messner, 'The Portuguese language between 1700 and 1850', *PortSt*, 10, 1994:65–71, adding some data on the frequency of the *perfeito composto*.

PHONOLOGY. A. Monjour, 'Galegische und portugiesische Skriptae', Holtus, *Lexikon*, II/2, 692–720, is a dense account of phonological and graphemic developments, with useful cartography but sadly preserving the now-discredited 1192–93 'earliest texts'. F. Peixoto da Fonseca, 'Phonétique synchronique de l'ancien portugais', *Orbis*, 37, 1994:54–86, gives an annotated list of grapheme-phoneme equivalences. J. S. Jensen, 'Comment un -s peut devenir un -r', *Cunha Vol.*,

187–203, finds Brazilian counterparts (intrusive i, loss of final -s) to Italian *as* > *e*. H. Lüdtke, 'As origens do -*i* final do português antigo', *Carvalho Vol.*, 281–84, reflects on the preservation of final atonic /i/. A. M. Martins, 'A evolução das vogais nasais finais [ã], [õ], [ẽ], no português', *Cunha Vol.*, 617–46, uses dialect data to show that paragogy and diphthongization are totally distinct, and to suggest that the generalized diphthongization of final nasals was a precondition for the merger of nasal endings.

MORPHOLOGY AND SYNTAX. Rosa Virgínia Mattos e Silva, *O português arcaico. Morfologia e sintaxe*, SPo, Contexto, 1994, 138 pp., provides a much-needed concise manual. C. Lyons, 'Old Portuguese possessives in a Romance perspective', *Willis Vol.*, 3–10, argues that Old Portuguese *ma/ta/sa* are relics of a pan-Romance series of weak possessives, rather than reduced forms of *mia/tua/sua*. N. Nunes, 'Os valores aspectuo-temporais dos verbos *haver* e *ter* na Crónica de D. João I de Fernão Lopes', *APL 10*, 397–405, associates *haver* (auxiliary or full verb 'to acquire') with perfective aspect and *ter* (usually full verb, 'to hold'; occasionally auxiliary) with imperfectivity. R. V. M. Silva, 'Variação e mudança no português arcaico: *ter* e *haver* em estruturas de posse', *Cunha Vol.*, 299–311, gives a more subtle analysis of types of possession. I. Ribeiro, 'A formação dos tempos compostos: a evolução histórica das formas ter, haver e ser', *Tarallo Vol.*, 343–86. T. Riiho, 'Sobre la yuxtaposición de los pronombres personales tónico y átono en el gallego-portugués antiguo', *Actas* (Santiago de Compostela), VI, 239–45, lists cases of pronoun duplication.

F. Tarallo, 'Diagnosticando uma gramática brasileira: o português d'aquém e d'além mar ao final do século XIX', *Tarallo Vol.*, 69–105, traces typical BP features such as null objects and full subjects back in time. M. A. G. L. Rossi, 'Estudo diacrônico sobre as interrogativas do português do Brasil', *ib.*, 307–42, gives a GB analysis of the decline of S-V inversion. M. Davies, 'A corpus-based approach to diachronic clitic climbing in Portuguese', *HisJ*, 17:93–111, finds a general decrease in clitic climbing, and its virtual elimination in BP. Id., *'The evolution of causative structures in Spanish and Portuguese', *Papers* (El Paso), 105–22. A.M. Martins, *'Clitic placement from Old to Modern Portuguese', *Acta* (Los Angeles), 295–307 (see also SYNTAX: CLITICS).

ETYMOLOGY. Maria Helena de Teves Costa Ureña Prieto et al., *Do grego e do latim ao português*, L. FCG–JNICT, 1995, 224 pp. J. M. Piel, 'Apontamentos e sugestões etimológicas de toponímia mirandesa (hipóteses e certezas)', *Carvalho Vol.*, 285–89; À. Galmés de Fuentes, 'La "mallatia" en León y Portugal (Etimología y origen de una institución jurídica mozárabe)', *ib.*, 295–99. A. B. Veiga, 'Considerações em torno de *Antônio Chimango*', *Cunha Vol.*, 501–10, gives an etymology for *Chimango/Ximango*. R. A. Cunha-Henkel, 'Empréstimos lexicais bantos no português do Brasil', *Actas* (Hamburg), 55–62.

3. PHONETICS AND PHONOLOGY

GENERAL. S.-H. Lee, 'Fonologia lexical do português', *CEL*, 23, 1992 : 103–20, represents a first attempt at a complete plan of Lexical Phonology for Portuguese: four levels of morphological processes are identified, but almost all phonological rules are concentrated in level 4 and the postlexical component. Stress rules are located at four different levels. M. A. Freitas, 'Empréstimos, teoria auto-segmental e abertura vocálica', *ib.*, 71–81, shows BP loans to be subject to normal lexical and postlexical rules. M. J. Marçalo, 'A flutuação de fonemas em português: uma questão de morfologia?', *APL 10*, 255–68, lists cases of free variation, but fails to find criteria for distinguishing morphological and phonological factors. M. C. Viana et al., 'Sobre a pronúncia de nomes próprios, siglas e acrónimos em português europeu', *Cong. Int.*, III, 481–519, show that proper names do not require different rules of pronunciation from common nouns; acronyms are also predictable. Rule-based and neural net models of text-to-speech synthesis are equally viable. I. Trancoso, M. C. Viana, and I. Mascarenhas, 'Léxicos de pronúncia: a experiência do projecto ONOMASTICA', *APL 11*, I, 241–63. M. Yavas, *'Phonological selectivity in the first fifty words of a bilingual child', *LSp*, 38, 1995 : 189–202.

SYLLABLE STRUCTURE. M. H. M. Mateus, 'A silabificação de base em português', *APL 10*, 289–300, proposes a nuclei-first syllabifica-tion algorithm, with a proliferation of empty onsets and nuclei. M. Vigário and I. Falé, 'A sílaba do português fundamental: uma descrição e algumas considerações de ordem teórica', *APL 9*, 465–78, calculate the frequency of different syllable types and discuss the application of the Sonority Sequencing Principle and a Dissimilarity Condition. M. H. M. Mateus, 'Onset of Portuguese syllables and rising diphthongs', *Workshop*, 93–104, assigns /j w/ in rising diph-thongs to the onset, to preserve a putative restriction of the rhyme to three segments. M. J. Freitas, 'Uma questão de ataque silábico nas primeiras palavras', *APL 11*, III, 283–95. E. d'Andrade and M. C. Viana, 'Sinérese, diérese e estrutura silábica', *APL 9*, 31–42, discuss syllabic analyses of diphthongs and /w/. M. A. C. Miguel, 'Heavy diphthongs: a phonological view', *Workshop*, 105–14, runs through well-known cases of underlying and surface diphthongs. A. Andrade, 'Percepção de C ou CC oclusivas por ouvintes nativos de português europeu', *APL 11*, III, 153–86, finds no consistency in cues used by speakers to distinguish multiple consonants in underlying and derived clusters, having shown in 'Estudo acústico de sequências de oclusivas em português europeu', *APL 9*, 1–15, that they are produced distinctly.

CONSONANTS. A. Andrade and I. Mascarenhas, 'Para um estudo do vozeamento em início de vogal diante de consoante oclusiva', *Cong. Int.*, III, 529–46, show that high VOT reflects affrication, with great inter-subject differences. L. Bisol and D. Hora, 'Palatalização da oclusiva dental e fonologia lexical', *APL 9*, 61–80, confirm its postlexical status. M. S. Demasi, 'O -L pós-vocálico na fala culta do Rio de Janeiro', *Cunha Vol.*, 115–43, finds many diphthongs resulting from l-vocalization.

VOWELS. J. A. Moraes, D. Callou, and Y. Leite, 'Vocalismo tônico do português do Brasil: descrição acústica', *Cong. Int.*, III, 369–77, give basic F1/F2 measurements, showing the BP vowel system to be more compact than that of EP. M. L. Wetzels, 'Mid-vowel alternations in the Brazilian Portuguese verb', *Phonology*, 12, 1995:281–304 (Id. 'Mid vowel neutralization in Brazilian Portuguese', *CEL*, 23, 1992:19–55), uses the latest vowel quality features in an elegant analysis of the large number of rules neutralizing mid-vowel distinctions. A. Andrade, 'Reflexões sobre o "e mudo" em portugués europeu', *Cong. Int.*, II, 303–44, gives a lengthy survey of research on unstressed vowels, and tests a range of claims on the basis of an investigation of pretonic /e/; the presence or absence of the vowel is inseparable from the modification of its consonantal context. S. Parkinson, 'Phonetics and phonology of Portuguese "closèd a"', *Willis Vol.*, 27–36, argues that nasalized and atonic variants are phonetically and phonologically distinct. A. Avram, 'A propos du statut phonologique des voyelles nasales portugaises', *Carvalho Vol.*, 87–91, criticizes Tlaskal for not being Praguean enough. M. M. Machado, 'Aspectos da nasalidade vocálica do português culto do Rio de Janeiro: estudo cine-radiográfico', *Cunha Vol.*, 239–54, gives detailed measurements; length and pharyngal constriction are important factors while /õ/ and /ã/ are distinguished by lip-rounding. J. A. Moraes and W. L. Wetzels, 'Sobre a duração dos segmentos vocálicos nasais e nasalizados em português. Um exercício de fonologia experimental', *CEL*, 23, 1992:153–66, show that nasal /ã/ is systematically longer than oral or nasalized /a/, particularly in pretonic position, pointing to biphonemic status, though other length effects complicate the picture. M. Drenska, 'Os ditongos do português europeu e as correspondentes combinações vocálicas do búlgaro. Análise auditiva', *APL 10*, 167–76, compares /ai au oi/ in the two languages. On atonic vowels, D. Callou et al., 'Um problema na fonologia do português: variação das vogais pretônicas', *Cunha Vol.*, 59–70, show considerable variability of raising and lowering o pretonic mid vowels in S. Paulo; for Rio de Janeiro, E. V. Silva, 'Uma contribuição para o conhecimento do português no Brasil: as pretônicas fluminenses', *ib.*, 391–97, traces the complex conditioning of raising (sensitive to vocalic and consonantal context) and a limited (harmonic) lowering. Similarly, Y. Leite, D. Callou, and J. Moraes, 'Neutralização e realização fonética: a harmonia vocálica no português do Brasil', *Cong. Int.*, III, 395–404, claim that raising of atonic mid vowels is harmony, phonological not phonetic, with no significant sociolinguistic conditioning. F. Seraine, 'Importância de uma visão diacrônica', *Cunha Vol.*, 383–89, sees raising in the North East as a relic. M. R. Delgado-Martins, B. Harmegnies, and D. Poch, 'Changement phonétique en cours du portugais européen', *APL 11*, III, 249–59, find great variability in the realization of high vowels in initial unstressed /Vs/ sequences, suggesting that their elimination is in progress. A. Andrade and I. Mascarenhas, 'Sobre a variação fonética de /i/ — uma primeira abordagem', *APL 10*, 25–43.

SUPRASEGMENTALS. E. d'Andrade, 'Na onda do acento', *Cong. Int.*, I, 157–74, surveys accent studies, with notes on the small number of EP-BP accent divergences. J. Brandão de Carvalho, 'La quantité en portugais: reformulation d'une vieille hypothèse', *Cunha Vol.*, 103–14, outlines a quantity-based account of stress, which he traces back to Oliveira. In the unmarked case, stress falls on a final heavy syllable or on the penult if the final is light. Unstressed vowel reduction only affects light syllables. G. Massini-Cagliari, 'Sobre o lugar do acento de palavra em uma teoria fonológica', *CEL*, 23, 1992:121–36, favours lexical rules. L. Bisol, 'The stress in Portuguese', *Workshop*, 19–32, makes extensive use of extrametricality and abstract underlying consonants. I. Pereira, 'Grid-only vs. constituency in the study of stress in Portuguese', *ib.*, 115–25, is inconclusive. On stress cues, J. A. Moraes, 'Sobre as marcas prosódicas do acento em português', *Cunha Vol.*, 323–35. On suprasegmentals, S. Frota, 'On the prosody of focus in European Portuguese', *Workshop*, 45–66, claims that focus in EP is purely phonological; L. C. Cagliari, 'Prosódia: algumas funções dos suprasegmentos', *CEL*, 23, 1992:137–51, makes exploratory comments on intonation, rhythm, voice quality, etc. M. H. Mateus, 'Factos prosódicos nas gramáticas portuguesas', *APL 11*, III, 123–42.

PHRASAL PHONOLOGY. L. Bisol, 'Sandi vocálico externo: degeminação e elisão', *CEL*, 23, 1992:83–101, gives valuable data on interverbal fusion and elision of /a/ in BP, both identified as prosodic restructuring, blocked by stress on the second vowel. M. Ellison and M. C. Viana, 'Antagonismo e elisão de vogais átonas finais em português europeu', *APL 11*, III, 261–81, show the complementarity of elision, fusion and diphthong formation in interverbal vowel sequences, and correctly eliminate stress clash but unconvincingly invoke a ranked set of alignment restrictions. M. R. Delgado-Martins, 'Relação fonética/fonologia: a propósito do sistema vocálico do português', *Cong. Int.*, I, 311–25, reviews analyses of syllable structure in fast speech, and queries the usefulness of such data for purposes of abstract phonological theory. S. Frota, 'Os domínios prosódicos e o português europeu: fenómenos de sandhi', *APL 10*, 221–37, claims applicability of the prosodic hierarchy to *crase*, sibilant sandhi and haplology.

MORPHOPHONEMICS.   M. A. C. Miguel, 'Interpretação fonológica de alguns plurais em português', *APL 10*, 331–39, reanalyses plural alternations in terms of Government and Charm phonology; metaphony is harmony with final /u/, and the plural allomorph *-es* represents the filling of an empty nucleus. P. R. Petrucci, 'Fatos de estabilidade no português brasileiro', *CEL*, 23, 1992:57–71, analyses vowel harmony as the reassignment of features left floating by Theme Vowel truncation.

4. SYNTAX AND MORPHOLOGY

GENERAL.   Mário Vilela, *Gramática da Língua Portuguesa*, C, Almedina, 1995, 381 pp., provides an elementary and conservative approach to grammatical analysis. R. Meyer-Hermann, 'Alguns dados sobre a ordem de palavras no português falado culto na cidade de S. Paulo', *Actas* (Hamburg), 185–202, taps NURC transcripts for data on SV and VS order.

G. A. Matos, 'Estruturas binárias e monocêntricas em sintaxe: algumas observações sobre a coordenação de projecções máximas', *APL 10*, 301–15, finds arguments for analysing the first of two coordinated elements as Specifier to the second. M. Colaço and A. Gonçalves, 'A concordância do objecto com o particípio passado e a categoria AgrO', *APL 10*, 117–32, analyse *ter o livro lido* as non-auxiliary *ter* with a small clause, and not a case of past participle agreement; the order of constituents in the small clause reflects the status of the AgrO constituent. V. Bianchi and M. C. F. Silva, 'On some properties of Agreement-Object in Italian and Brazilian Portuguese', pp. 181–97 of *Issues and Theory in Romance Linguistics: Selected Papers from the Linguistic Symposium on the Romance Languages XXIII*, ed. Michael L. Mazzola, Georgetown U.P., 1994, xiv + 546 pp. (hereafter Mazzola, *Issues*) see strong AgrO behind null objects and clitic placement. I. Roberts, 'O português brasileiro no contexto das línguas românicas', *Tarallo Vol.*, 409–25, outlines the interest of the combination of the (weakened) null subject, null objects and clitic position; detailed studies are provided by M. E. L. Duarte

'Do pronome nulo ao pronome pleno: a trajetória do sujeito no português do Brasil', *ib.*, 107–28; M. A. Morais, 'Aspectos diacrônicos do movimento do verbo, estrutura da frase e caso nominativo no português do Brasil', *ib.*, 263–306; C. C. Galves, 'O enfraquecimento da concordância no português brasileiro', *ib.*, 387–408; J. M. Nunes, 'Direção de cliticização, objeto nulo e pronome tônico na posição de objeto em português brasileiro', *ib.*, 207–22; S. M. L. Cyrino, 'Observações sobre a mudança diacrônica no português do Brasil: objeto nulo e clíticos', *ib.*, 163–84; V. C. Cerqueira, 'A forma genitiva "dele" e a categoria de concordância (AGR) no português brasileiro', *ib.*, 129–61; E. G. Pagotto, 'Clíticos, mudança e seleção natural', *ib.*, 185–206. I. Duarte, 'A topicalização em português europeu: uma análise comparativa', *Cong. Int.*, I, 327–60, equates EP Topicalization with Scrambling rather than Wh-movement or Clitic Left Dislocation. N. Maier, 'Causative constructions in French and Portuguese', Mazzola, *Issues*, 355–65, studies inflected infinitives as complements of causative verbs. A. S. Silva, 'Estruturas causativas no português: ordem das palavras e atribuição de caso em fazer, mandar, deixar + inf. Perspectiva cognitiva', *APL 10*, 541–55, attempts to relate word order choices to the semantics of the *fonte de energia* of the action. On ellipsis, I. Mascarenhas and M. B. Mendes, 'As estruturas do escoamento (sluicing) em português', *APL 10*, 277–88, analyse ellipses of the form '... mas não sei quem'; G. A. Matos, 'A distribuição do despojamento', *Cong. Int.*, II, 275–300, is on 'stripping' (e.g. *João vai hoje ao cinema mas ao restaurante não*); by the same author, 'Estrutura-P, transformações, predicados elípticos e pronominais', *APL 9*, 305–19. E. Gärtner, 'Sobre a posição das orações comparativas no sistema gramatical português', *Actas* (Hamburg), 103–15.

TENSE AND ASPECT. F. Oliveira, 'Algumas particularidades do aspecto em português', *Cong. Int.*, II, 151–90, explores the relationship between progressivity (implying lack of conclusion to an event or state), perfectivity, and event typology. F. Oliveira and A. Lopes, 'Tense and aspect in Portuguese', Thieroff, *Tense*, II, 95–117. J. A. Peres, 'Sobre a semântica das construções perfectivas em português', *Cong. Int.*, II, 33–58, reorganizes the tense system in terms of absolute and relative tense to give the past participle full value as a marker of anterior relative tense; both preterite and perfect are labelled present anterior. J. M. Barbosa, 'Sistemas verbais portuguesas e dinâmica linguística', *APL 10*, 57–67, uses a similar scheme, distinguished by a distinction between *cantara* (past anterior) and *tinha cantado* (past perfect), to focus on reduced systems in which relative tense contrasts are lost. B. Lohse, 'Alguns parâmetros constitutivos da estrutura semântica do sistema verbal português', *Cong. Int.*, III, 415–34, highlights the increasing interchangeability of perfect and imperfect subjunctives, confirming the different temporal structure of indicative and subjunctive forms. By the same author, 'Aspecto e tempo relativo', *Actas* (Hamburg), 177–84. D. Santos, 'Integrating tense, aspect and genericity', *APL 9*, 391–405, is on habituals. M. H. C. Campos, 'Para uma reinterpretação de alguns fenómenos aspectuais', *Cong. Int.*, II, 77–93, applies Culioli's *discreto-denso-compacto* classification to Portuguese. D. Santos, 'Imperfeito: a broad-coverage study', *APL 10*, 523–39, uses an annotated corpus to identify a range of alternative or concurrent values (aspectual, stylistic, discourse-related). A. C. M. Lopes, 'Tempo, aspecto e coesão discursiva', *APL 11*, III, 351–71, studies the interaction of tense and aspect in establishing sequences of events. Similarly, A. C. S. Rodrigues and P. T. Galembeck, 'Formas de pretéritos perfeito e imperfeito do indicativo no plano textual-discursivo', *ib.*, 439–53, find GPF data show (unsurprisingly) the preterite associated with foregrounding, sequencing and factuality, and the imperfect with backgrounding, simultaneity and unreality. A. Gonçalves and M. J. Freitas, 'Estatuto de *a* em construções aspectuais do português. Evidências da aquisição na interacção fonologia/sintaxe', *ib.*, 297–313, provide data on the absence of *a* in continuous constructions in child language, but shed little light on phonology or syntax. F. Irmen, 'A temporalidade dos tempos verbais em português: o futuro', *Carvalho Vol.*, 151–61, sees the synthetic future as modal, future tense being expressed periphrastically. T. Móia, 'Aspectos da semântica das expressões temporais com *desde* e *até* — questões de Aktionsart', *APL 10*, 341–59, explores how achievements and accomplishments can combine with *desde* (rarely) and *até* (regularly), making them the inverse of their apparent English counterparts *since* and *until*. N. V. Soares, 'Começar a Vinf e pôr-se a Vinf: marcadores de que fronteiras?', *ib.*, 557–67, uses a Culiolian framework. B. Pottier, 'Estar como modalisateur de ser', *Cunha Vol.*, 369–72, has an alternative view of copula selection.

MOOD AND MODALS. On the subjunctive, M. J. Vieira dos Santos, 'Para uma gramática dos usos: talvez + conjuntivo', *APL 11*, III, 455–63, notes differences of meaning between *talvez* + subjunctive and corresponding indicative + *talvez*. The former suspends truth judgements (the main function of the subjunctive) while the latter casts doubt. K. Böckle, 'L'"infinito pessoal" portugais et le problème du subjonctif "illoqique" dans la complétive préposée introduit par (*le fait*) *que* dans les langues romanes', *Carvalho Vol.*, 105–22, argues that the strength of modal meaning of the Portuguese subjunctive is protected by the use of the personal infinitive in amodal contexts. B. Schäfer, 'O futuro do conjuntivo — um conjuntivo?', *Actas* (Hamburg), 233–42. On modal verbs, M. H. C. Campos, 'Para a caracterização do marcador modal *dever*', *APL 10*, 93–104, rejects syntactic criteria for distinguishing epistemic and deontic values; the deontic reading requires a temporal gap between the time of utterance and the modalized predicate. C. Augusto and F. Melka, 'A contrastive study of two modal verbs CAN and MUST in two Romance languages (French and Portuguese) and two Germanic languages (Dutch and English)', pp. 59–70 of *Translation and Meaning part 3. Proceedings of the Maastricht Session of the 2nd International Maastricht-Lodz Duo Colloquium on Translation and Meaning (Maastricht 19–22 April 1995)*, ed. M. Thelen and B. Lewandowska-Tomaszczyk, Maastricht U.P., explore a limited corpus, showing that Portuguese uses *ter de* as complementary to *dever*. M. C. L. Augusto, 'Quando saber é poder. Contribuição para uma análise contrastiva português-holandês dos verbos: poder/kunnen, querer/willen e saber/weten', pp. 153–72 of *Actas del Congreso Internacional Luso-Español de Lenguaje y Cultura en la Frontera (Cáceres, 1 al 3 de diciembre de 1994)*, ed. J. M. C. González and A. V. Camarasa, Cáceres, Extremadura U.P., covers a wide range of modal meanings of *saber* and *poder*. A. Gonçalves, 'Aspectos da reestruturação sintáctica em português europeu: as construções com verbos modais', *APL 9*, 235–50, proposes that modals are not genuine auxiliaries but become them as a result of restructuring.

VERBS. C. Pountain, 'Infinitives with overt subjects: a pragmatic approach', *Willis Vol.*, 11–25, places the personal infinitive in the broader Romance context of overt subject marking in infinitives, insisting that the selection of personal or impersonal infinitive is motivated by the pragmatics of subject identification. L. Semenova, 'Características semântico-funcionais do infinitivo gerundial', *Actas* (Hamburg), 253–56. J. G. H. Carvalho, 'As orações de gerúndio no galego e no português. Ensaio de linguística contrastiva', *Actas* (Santiago de Compostela), VI, 317–25, uncovers widespread ambiguity of function. T. M. Chaby Nascimento, 'Disposição para a passiva e disposição passiva', *APL 11*, III, 209–24, groups obvious examples of lexical restrictions on passivization. H. M. Silva, 'Do agente da passiva e da sua ocultação', *APL 9*, 421–35, presents the *ser*-passive as a device for concealing agents. M. H. Moura Neves, 'Estudo das construções com verbo-suporte em português', *APL 11*, III, 383–99, explains the BP preference for support verb constructions in terms of preferred argument structure and the greater communicative potential of nominal constructions. E. M. Ranchhod, 'Les VSup issus du latin *esse* et *stare* dans les langues romanes', *LInv*, 19, 1995:265–88, focuses on *ser de, estar em* etc.

NOUNS. G. Silva and D. Callou, 'O uso do artigo definido diante de possessivo', *Cong. Int.*, III, 115–25, show higher frequency of articles with possessives (69%) in educated speech, particularly in

Brazilian regions colonized relatively late; contraction with prepositions, inalienable possession and singular number are factors
favouring use of the article. A.-M. Spanoghe, 'Elementos para uma
interpretação discursiva do possessivo português', *Verba*, 23:67–82,
compares three possessive constructions (*o meu livro, meu livro, o livro*) in
terms of their discourse function of presenting the referent as
identifiable; see also her **La syntaxe de l'appartenance inaliénable en
français, en espagnol et en portugais*, Frankfurt, Lang, 1995, 263 pp.
D. Woll, '"Na França" e "em França", mas só "na Alemanha" —
porquê?', *Carvalho Vol.*, 163–76, documents considerable variation in
usage, seeing it as a gradual erosion of traditional Romance resistance
to incorporating articles in place names. P. Santos, 'Duas espécies de
genéricas', *APL 9*, 407–20. A. M. Brito, 'A ordem de palavras no SN
em português numa perspectiva de sintaxe comparada — um caso
particular: os Ns deverbais eventivos', *Cong. Int.*, I, 81–106, proposes
various functional heads in the NP, to explain nominalization
structures. C. N. Correia, 'Determinação nominal e diátese', *APL 10*,
133–48, highlights the relationship between nominalization and
passivization. M. Gonçalves, '"Ah! Está a estudar gramática!"
Reconsiderações sobre o género', *APL 11*, III, 547–61, attempts to
rescue gender from relegation to a purely formal category.

PRONOUNS. C. Ferreira et al., 'A pessoa e a não-pessoa em
discursos de informantes no projecto NURC/Salvador', *Cunha Vol.*,
145–53, apply Benveniste's terms to Brazilian subject pronouns,
covering similar ground to J. Freitas, '*Nós* e *a gente* em elocuções
formais', *ib.*, 155–63, and 'Os pronomes pessoais sujeito na norma
urbana culta de Salvador. Resultados parciais', *Actas* (Santiago de
Compostela), VI, 701–11. M. I. Aldinhas-Ferreira, 'Quando -*se* é
parte inalienável de X: um aspecto particular da construção reflexa',
Cong. Int., III, 39–56, identifies and lists verbs whose reflexive use is
equivalent to a transitive construction with an inalienably possessed
object such as parts of the body or emotions. A. H. Branco,
'Reciprocal sentences are zoom constructions', *APL 9*, 81–93.
R. Kuttert and J. F. Silva, 'A diferença sintáctica e semântica entre
duas construções com *se* não reflexo', *Carvalho Vol.*, 123–50, go over
familiar ground on passive and impersonal *se*.

CLITICS. I. Duarte and G. Matos, 'A colocação dos clíticos em
português europeu e a hipótese minimalista', *APL 10*, 177–93, analyse
enclisis as movement of the verb into the constituent containing the
clitic, as compared to proclisis (the rule of last resort) where the clitic
moves to the verb. A. M. Martins, 'A colocação dos clíticos e a
relevância da categoria sigma', *Cong. Int.*, II, 95–134, extends this,
invoking the category Sigma carrying specifications of propositional
affirmation or negation: echo answers are a case of verb movement

to Sigma; enclisis results from movement of the verb to Sigma in S-structure, and proclisis occurs where Sigma has other content, and verb movement takes place in LF. See also A. M. Cortez-Gomes, 'Contextos aparentados e os pronomes clíticos no português europeu', *APL 9*, 145–54. A. Endruschat, 'A colocação do pronome clítico no português actual: gramaticalização vs pragmatização', *Cong. Int.*, III, 23–57, simplistically claims that enclisis (and mesoclisis) with fusion are grammaticalizations, while proclisis is a question of pragmatic emphasis rather than pure syntax; her 'Acerca da colocação dos pronomes clíticos no português de angolanos e moçambicanos', *Actas* (Hamburg), 95–102, points to variation from the norm, as does J. L. Monteiro, 'A sínclise na fala urbana culta do Rio de Janeiro', *Cunha Vol.*, 313–21. M. Miguel, 'Os clíticos dativos possessivos *lhe* do português e *lui* do francês', *APL 9*, 321–34, links possessive *lhe* with Small Clauses.

ADVERBS. R. Ilari, 'A categoria advérbio na gramática do português falado', *Cong. Int.*, I, 107–39, expounds *Quadro-Q*, a detailed classification of adverbs by function (predicative vs non-predicative) and constituency; adverb position is very regular inside individual classes. (The table is unfortunately missing.) J. Roche, 'Observations sur l'adverbe chez quelques poètes bresiliens', *Cunha Vol.*, 373–81, piles on the statistics. R. Rodrigues, 'Os advérbios *durante* Q N *de* T e *por* N *de* T. Duas formas de quantificar a duração', *APL 10*, 497–508, compares *durante* (continuous or iterative, included in period of reference) with *por* (non-iterative, end point potentially outside period of reference). E. M. Ranchhod, 'Comparative Romance syntax. Frozen adverbs in Italian and Portuguese', *LInv*, 20 : 33–85, lists idiom chunks incorporating *como* and discusses their compositionality.

NEGATION. F. R. Gonçalves, 'Sobre a negação frásica em português europeu: propriedades e estrutura sintáctica', *APL 9*, 251–71, is on the NegP constituent. J. A. Peres, 'Concordância negativa através de fronteiras frásicas', *APL 10*, 435–51, looks at negative concord in complex sentences (*Não acredito que o Paulo vá fazer nada . . .*).

COMPLEMENTATION. E. Chimbutane, 'A estratégia do pronome resumptivo na formação de orações relativas restritivas de OD e OBL do português de Moçambique', *APL 11*, III, 224–48, exemplifies and analyses Mozambican resumptive pronouns: well-formedness is guaranteed by analysing *que* as a complementizer (in Comp) and not a relative (in SpecComp). M. A. Kato, 'Recontando a história das relativas em uma perspectiva paramétrica', *Tarallo Vol.*, 223–61. I. Duarte, 'Propriedades de COMP em construções completivas', *APL 9*, 181–94, ranges over wh-extraction and the personal infinitive. M. H. D. Marques, 'Subordinação e complexidade sintática', *Cunha Vol.*, 277–87, gives statistics for journalism and Economics.

DISCOURSE.　Corpus-based studies include S. F. Brandão, 'Estratégias argumentativas no Corpus APERJ', *APL 11*, I, 397–406; G. M.
O. Silva, 'Estratégias argumentativas no corpus PEUL', *ib.*, 407–15,
D. Callou and M. C. R. Costa, 'Estratégias discursivas na fala do Rio
de Janeiro', *ib.*, 381–95; L. L. Fávero, M. L. C. V. O. Andrade, and
Z. G. O. Aquino, 'Correcção: uma estratégia de reformulação
textual', *ib.*, 267–80. O. Lopes, 'Partículas de agulhagem discursiva
n' *O Crime do Padre Amaro*', *Cong. Int.*, I, 189–202, identifies a range of
discourse particles. J. Schmidt-Radefeld, 'Partículas discursivas e
interaccionais no português e no espanhol em contraste com o
alemão', *Carvalho Vol.*, 63–78, highlights the use of direct address for
discourse purposes. R. Meyer-Hermann, 'Processos de topicalização
e focalização no português falado', *ib.*, 25–42, looks at the discourse
function of a range of constructions. I. G. V. Koch, 'O papel da
organização textual na construção de sentido', *Cong. Int.*, III, 341–51,
illustrates backward linking. H. Weinrich, 'Análise textual dos
demonstrativos em português', *Carvalho Vol.*, 15–23, makes obvious
comments on cohesion. B. Moreira, 'Para a constituição de um
conjunto de marcadores enunciativos intermodais', *APL 10*, 359–73,
analyses *mal*. H. M. V. P. Trigo, 'Do estudo problemático dos
conectores', *APL 11*, III, 585–93.

STYLISTICS.　R. Lima, 'Dois matizes estilísticos do *E* inicial de
frase', *Cunha Vol.*, 721–29, exemplifies *tonalidade afectiva* and *efeito
surpresa*. M. L. G. Marques, 'Os bordões da língua falada e variação',
APL 11, I, 309–22. M. F. B. Nascimento, 'Aspectos da sintaxe do
Português falado (repetições lexicais e de estruturas sintácticas em
produções orais: fenómenos de deslocação)', *Cong. Int.*, I, 203–223,
argues that repetition in spoken Portuguese is based on discourse
processes involving units smaller than the sentence. E. M. Wolf, 'O
enunciado apreciativo (semântica e pragmática)', *Carvalho Vol.*, 55–62,
explores Gricean principles in expressions of value judgement. On
political and legal language, H. M. S. Nunes, 'Para uma caracterização da linguagem jurídica. A função dos advérbios na Constituição
da república Portuguesa', *APL 10*, 381–96; M. H. Sandaia, 'O
encontro com a palavra do outro', *ib.*, 509–23; I. R. Warner,
'Discurso reproduzido e técnicas de persuasão num exemplo de
discurso eleitoral (eleições presidenciais 1991)', *Actas* (Hamburg),
265–72. On weather forecasts, J. M. Parker and R. L. Coimbra,
'Para uma estilística metereológica', *APL 10*, 419–33.

MORPHOLOGY.　Maria Nazaré de Carvalho Laroca, *Manual de
morfologia do português*, Campinas, Pontes–UFJF, 1994, 98 pp., is
unadventurous on basic inflection and derivation. D. Santos, 'Português computacional', *Cong. Int.*, III, 167–84, discusses problems raised
by a morphological analysis program. A. Villalva, 'Configurações

não-binárias em morfologia', *APL 10*, 583–97, accepts ternary branching for *autor-compositor-intérprete* or *um bate-escova-aspira*, as distinct from recursive binary structures as in *limpa-para-brisas*.

5. SEMANTICS AND LEXICON

I. H. Faria, 'Os dicionários que temos e os que deveríamos ter', *APL 11*, II, 13–116, is a round table on dictionaries, electronic dictionaries and spellcheckers, including observations by M. L. C. Buescu (27–32), M. L. C. Biderman (55–61) and H. Batoréo (101–16) on the content of entries, M. F. B Nascimento (43–54) on collocations, G. L. Silva (63–66) and M. T. R. F. Lino (67–71) on technical terminology. M. Correia et al. (275–317) provide a list of dictionaries. M. Vilela, 'O dicionário na aula de português', *Cong. Int.*, II, 239–59, is on the microstructure of entries, focusing on textual functions. E. M. Ranchhod, 'Construção de dicionários electrónicos do português: problemas teóricos e metodológicos', *ib.*, I, 265–81, explains the DIGRAMA system of incorporating morphological and syntactic information into electronic dictionary entries, as do S. Eleuterio et al., 'A system of electronic discionaries of Portuguese', *LInv*, 19, 1995:57–82. M. T. F. Lino, 'Neologia, terminologia e novas técnicas de informação', *ib.*, 23–32, reports on a terminology database. I. M. Desmet, 'Terminologia e vocabulários científicos e técnicos do português. Princípios teóricos e metodológicos', *Actas* (Hamburg), 63–74. M. H. M. Neves, 'A tarefa de investigação das ocorrências dos nomes comuns', *Cong. Int.*, III, 259–74, identifies a range of key properties of nouns, including abstract-concrete, countable-uncountable. L. A. Pereira, 'Para um dicionário de combinatórias do português', *ib.*, 197–206, gives a sample of collocations of *certo*. A. M. P. P. Oliveira, 'A questão dos brasileirismos: uma proposta de sistematização', *APL 11*, II, 207–18, applies Gladstone Chaves de Melo's classification to some putative *brasileirismos*. D. Messner, *'Methodologische Überlungen zur Erforschung von Lusismen', *Lusorama*, 27, 1995:28–39. J. A. S. Pinilla, 'Para um vocabulário de hispanismos em português', *APL 10*, 453–61. On the history of lexicography: D. Messner, *'Sobre dicionários portugueses antigos: uma inventariação I', *Lusorama*, 28, 1995:45–64; C. A. A. Murakawa, 'A lexicografia praticada por António Morais da Silva', *APL 11*, II, 151–58, claims modernity for M., in his use of a range of forms of definition, and his provision of stylistic and register information. M. T. C. Biderman, 'Vocabulário fundamental: cultura e sociedade', *Cong. Int.*, III, 215–37, compares the 2217 items of *Português Fundamental* with her own 2469-word *Vocabulário Básico de Português Brasileiro*. A. Soares da Silva, 'Sobre a estrutura da variação lexical. Elementos de lexicologia cognitiva', _APL 11_, III, 413–23. M. T. Hundertmark-Santos Martins, *Die falschen Freunde. Os falsos amigos_, Tübingen, Niemeyer, 1995, xii + 372 pp.

SEMANTICS. H. J. Batoréo and M. Correia, 'Conhecimento semântico e informação lexicográfica', _APL 11_, II, 101–16, discuss the meanings of _a_ and _em_ as a purely lexical problem of polysemy. H. J. Batoréo and I. H. Faria, 'Estudo sobre a variação de referência nominal nas narrativas em português europeu: "A vaca é o boi ou o touro?"', _APL 10_, 69–91, study acquisition of marked and unmarked terms. A. C. M. Lopes, 'Semântica lexical e interpretação textual', _Cong. Int._, II, 445–70, shows the need for prototype semantics to explain proverbs, while R. Rodrigues and M. Baptista, 'A polissemia de "linha" — da teoria do protótipo à parecença de família', _APL 11_, III, 195–207, reject informants' perceived prototype (_linha=fio_). J. S. Teixeira, '"Branco é, galinha o põe"', _APL 11_, II, 229–35.

DERIVATION. L. Lobato, 'A derivação regressiva em português: conceituação e tratamento gerativo', _Cunha Vol._, 205–30, proposes a category-neutral base for related verbs and nouns. M. M. Basílio, 'Verbos em a(r) em português: afixação ou conversão?', _Delta_, 9, 1993:295–304. M. C. Augusto, 'Contributo para um estudo da relação forma-significado nos compostos do tipo V+C', _RLRFU_, 15:1–17, finds various productive, semantically or syntactically opaque verb + noun compounds, used especially in the creation of nicknames. D. Messner, 'Os compostos "verbo + substantivo" em português', _Carvalho Vol._, 99–104, sorts a corpus of 400 compounds by a variety of criteria. J. R. F. Bessa, 'A (in)variação flexional de certos vocábulos compostos do português e seu tratamento lexicográfico', _Cunha Vol._, 35–48, argues that all compound colour terms (e.g. _azul-marinho_) are adjectives which may function as (singular) nouns, and that dictionaries should pay less attention to their nominal or adjectival functions and more to their complex patterns of inflection. J. Schmidt-Radefeld and J. A. do Campo, 'Análise contrastiva dos compostos nominais em alemão e português', _Actas_ (Hamburg), 243–52. C. Caetano, 'Formação de palavras em português. Os sufixóides e a vulgarização dos formantes eruditos', _APL 11_, III, 517–28, claims that _-base, -piloto, -chave_ and _pirata_ function as suffixes, and traces the increasing productivity of learned affixes such as _-mania, -logia_. M. Correia, 'As palavras derivadas: objectivos e modos de tratamento em bases de dados lexicais', _APL 10_, 149–66, describes the derivational component of the GENELEX lexical database. A. M. M. Martinho and F. Soares, 'Siglas e acrósticos', _APL 10_, 269–76. U. Pinto and J. J. D. Almeida, 'Tratamento automático de lexias compostas', *APL 11*, II, 261–73. G. M. Rio-Torto, 'Processos e paradigmas de formação de palavras em português', *Cong. Int.*, III, 275–91, gives an overview of derivational types and word-formation rules: see also her 'Formação de verbos em português: parassíntese, circunfixação e/ou derivação', *APL 9*, 351–62. J. A. S. Pinilla, 'O sufixo diminutivo *-inho* e a sua tradução para o espanhol', *ib.*, 377–90, takes diminutives from four Spanish translations of *O Mandarim*. T. Johnen, *'Zur pragmatik von portugiesisch *-inho* und Partikelentsprechung im Deutschen', *Lusorama*, 27, 1995:40–57.

REGÊNCIA. O. G. L. A. S. Campos, 'Os verbos *esquecer, lembrar* e *recordar* na língua portuguesa escrita do Brasil', *APL 11*, III, 425–37, tabulates corpus data on the ocurrence of constructions involving *esquecer* and *lembrar* according to textual type. For the former, *esquecer* + SN is more used than *esquecer(-se) de* SN; for the latter, *lembrar-se de/que* is the only high-frequency construction. M. I. A. Ferreira, 'Fenómenos de alternância na estrutura argumental de predicadores verbais: um problema na descrição lexicográfica', *ib.*, II, 237–45. P. Gonçalves, 'Uma hipótese sobre estratégias de aprendizagem do Léxico do Português/L2 em Moçambique', *Cong. Int.*, II, 471–90, finds simplification of the range of verb matrices, with agentive verbs always transitive. M. E. Macedo, 'Análise de regências fixas ("dar com", "dar por", etc.) a partir de listas de concordâncias', *APL 11*, III, 373–82, identifies a class of fixed expressions with argument structure distinct from that of the base verb, exemplified by structures incorporating *dar* (*dar conta de, dar de* (*comer*), *dar para, dar lugar a*) taken from concordance data.

PHRASEOLOGY. G. Funk, 'Os adagiários que temos e os que deveríamos ter', *APL 11*, II, 219–27, reviews dictionaries of proverbs; her 'A definição do conceito proverbial', *Insulana*, 1995:75–100, reviews definitions and criteria, with Portuguese materials. H. Kröll, 'O numeral sete na língua portuguesa', *Carvalho Vol.*, 177–86, gives extensive examples of *sete* as an intensifier or superlative. Id., *'Die Bezeichnungen für männliche Homosexuelle im Portugiesichen', *Lusorama*, 27, 1995:82–97, and *'Zum Wortschatz für virgindade und de(s)floração im Portugiesischen', *ib.*, 28, 1995:65–73. M. F. B. Nascimento and A. Carvalho, 'Preto e branco ou Branco e preto? (Como se combinam os nomes de cores)', *APL 11*, I, 367–80. C. Hundt, 'Expressões idiomáticas: estáveis e variáveis' *Actas* (Hamburg), 157–66, shows that set phrases have lexical and dialectal variants. M. E. B. Silva, 'A criação figurativa na linguagem do pescador artesanal', *Cunha Vol.*, 399–407, gives a conventional sorting of figures of speech.

REGISTER. J. B. Gonçalves, 'Um exemplo de vocabulário temático observado em diferentes tipo de corpora', *Cong. Int.*, III, 185–95, studies meteorological vocabulary in the different corpora making up the *Português Fundamental. APL 11*, I, contains P. M. Neto, 'Combinatórias lexicais num corpus linguístico especializado' (359–66); M. E. B. Silva, 'Estudo lexical de uma sociovariante profissional' (297–308); M. L. Pretto, 'Vocabulário jurídico: um estudo sociolingüístico na área do direito de trabalho' (181–89). I. M. Alves, 'O vocabulário do carnaval brasileiro', *Actas* (Santiago de Compostela), VI, 727–35.

GLOSSARIES. M. H. M. Mateus, 'Elaboração de glossários: problemas, métodos e técnicas', *Cunha Vol.*, 289–98, reflects on general principles for glossaries of medieval texts. M. C. M. Leonel, 'Glossário do *Grande Sertão: Veredas*: campos lexicais', *APL 11*, II, 129–36, explores the field of knives. E. M. S. Nascimento, 'Formações verbais hipotéticas do glossário do *Grande Sertão: Veredas*', *ib.*, 119–27, gives entries for 20 otherwise unattested verbs (e.g. *dalalar, espetacular, mimelar, retentear*). N. S. A. Martins, 'Arcaísmos de Guimarães Rosa e sua abonação em textos medievais', *Actas* (Santiago de Compostela), VI, 737–48, finds archaic features of lexicon and syntax.

HISTORICAL. Antônio Geraldo da Cunha, *Os verbos dar, dizer, estar e fazer no Vocabulário do Português Medieval*, RJ, Fundação Casa de Rui Barbosa, 1995, 82 pp., gives extended entries and brief notes on frequency. P. Teyssier, 'A propos des mots *mano* et *mana* dans Gil Vicente', *Cunha Vol.*, 731–41, tries several explanations for their distinct semantic and phonological development. C. Rocha, 'Saber e conhecer em fórmulas e expressões fixas num corpus de textos notariais dos sec.s XIII a XV', *APL 10*, 481–95, finds cases of interchangeability of these usually contrasting verbs.

6. SOCIOLINGUISTICS AND DIALECTOLOGY

SOCIOLINGUISTICS

GENERAL. M. H. A. Carreira, 'Pedido de desculpa e delicadeza: para o estudo dos seus processos linguísticos em português', *APL 10*, 105–16, places requests on a scale from orders to wishes.

BRAZIL. More NURC data are released in **A linguagem falada culta na cidade do Rio de Janeiro. Materiais para o seu estudo*, II *Diálogo entre informante e documentador*, ed. D. Callou and C. R. Lopes , RJ, UFRJ, 1993; **Análise de textos orais*, ed. D. Preti, SPo, Projecto NURC/SP USP-FFLCH, 1993. Emanoel dos Santos, *Certo ou Errado? Atitudes e crenças no ensino da língua portuguesa*, RJ, Graphia, 117 pp., gives data on the perception and evaluation of phonological variables used by the Brazilian educational system as markers of correctness. Similarly,

M. A. Kato, 'Português brasileiro falado: aquisição em contexto de mudança linguística', *Cong. Int.*, II, 209–37, shows that key features of BP pronominal syntax (null object, no pro-drop) are reversed by educational norms insisting on clitics and inversion. R. V. M. Silva, 'O português são dois (variação, mudança, norma e a questão do ensino do português no Brasil)', *ib.*, 375–401, reviews variation in article use and relative clause formation, to reassert the need for awareness in first-language teaching. M. M. Azevedo, 'Linguistic features in the literary representation of vernacular Brazilian Portuguese', *HisL*, 6–7, 1995:449–73, lists salient features exploited in fiction: the data are interesting if not surprising. M. E. B. Silva, 'Traços fonéticos como identificadores grupais', *Actas* (Santiago de Compostela), VI, 681–90, finds correlation of social prestige and linguistic conservatism. On creolization as a factor in Brazilian Portuguese, J. Holm, 'O português vernáculo do Brasil: evidência de contacto de línguas nas expressões idiomáticas', *Cong. Int.*, II, 359–74, gives unconvincing examples of Brazilian phrases with African or creole counterparts, and H. R. Mello, 'Contato linguístico na formação do português vernáculo do Brasil', *ib.*, III, 353–67, emphasizes the historical influence of Cabo Verde and São Tomé creoles on BP, with an extensive but uncritical list of common features (e.g. double negation, *ter* as an existential). This approach is broadly contested by F. Tarallo, 'Sobre a alegada origem crioula do português brasileiro: mudanças sintáticas aleatórias', *Tarallo Vol.*, 35–68. A. N. Isquerdo, 'Léxico regional e conservadorismo lingüístico', *APL 11*, II, 191–206, discusses 25 verbs in the lexicon of Amazonian rubber-tappers, confusing register-specificity with conservatism.

PORTUGAL. J. N. P. C. Cardoso, 'Estudo sociolinguístico de uma freguesia rural portuguesa', *APL 9*, 113–29, gives a non-quantitative account of variation in dialect features. S. M. Oliveira, 'Mudança e continuidade nas formas de tratamento em Évora', *Actas* (Hamburg), 203–14, compares 1983 and 1993 survey results: *colega* is out of fashion, *Sr* + title is more acceptable. F. Sousa-Möckel, 'O comportamento linguístico dos portugueses residentes na Alemanha', *ib.*, 257–64, charts interference and language shift.

AFRICA. Perpétua Gonçalves, *Português de Moçambique. Uma variedade em formação*, Maputo, Eduardo Mondlane U.P., 91 pp., contains published and unpublished conference papers. P. Vázquez Cuesta, 'Observações sobre o português de Moçambique', *Actas* (Santiago de Compostela), VI, 631–47, lists syntactic and lexical features of *crónicas* by Mia Couto. (See also SYNTAX: CLITICS, COMPLEMENTATION, REGÊNCIA.)

DIALECTOLOGY

BRAZIL. C. C. Pereira, 'A evolução dos estudos dialectológicos no Brasil', *Cunha Vol.*, 349–68, gives a historical survey. B. Head, 'Os parâmetros da variação dialectal no português do Brasil', *Cong. Int.*, III, 141–65, argues for a more complex view of regional and social differentiation of BP dialects, from Bahian data. D. Callou, J. Moraes, and Y. Leite, 'Para uma nova dialectologia: a realização do S e R posvocálicos no português do Brasil', *ib.*, 405–13, shorn of diagrams, shows *r*-weakening dividing a northern area (Rio, Salvador, Recife) from a southern one; *s*-palatalization appears only in Rio and Recife; in 'Aspectos fonéticos do português do Brasil: pluralidade de normas', *APL 11*, III, 187–94, they add summary data on postvocalic *l* and post-tonic vowels in the five cities covered by NURC: Porto Alegre has lower levels of *l*-vocalization. J. Mota and V. Rollemberg, 'Constritivas implosivas na norma culta brasileira: alveolares ou palatais', *Actas* (Santiago de Compostela), VI, 671–79, find variable levels of palatalization on Salvador. S. F. Brandão, 'O /R/ implosivo no norte do Estado de Rio do Janeiro', *Cunha Vol.*, 49–58, studies postvocalic *r* in 13 locations and 3 age groups. Final deletion is frequent in all groups, particularly infinitives and *qualquer*, less so in nouns, adjectives, and monosyllables; medially, deletion is found only in *porque*, otherwise vibrants are predominant in older speakers and isolated areas, and velar or glottal fricatives in younger speakers; S. F. Brandão, 'A vibrante retroflexa: um traço distintivo do falar dos pescadores campistas', *Actas* (Santiago de Compostela), VI, 649–70. O. A. Furlan, 'Aspectos da influência açoriana no português do Brasil em Santa Catarina', *Cunha Vol.*, 165–86, finds few unambiguous Azorean features resulting from the mass immigration of 1748. B. F. Head, 'A alternância entre "b" e "v" em palavras de origem indígena no português do Brasil', *APL 10*, 239–53, identifies dialectal patterns in *b/v* alternations in words of Amerindian origin; the (Northern) dialect origin of colonizers is a factor reinforcing the lack of a *b/v* contrast in Tupi. E. V. Silva, 'Conservadorismo e inovação em um falar do norte fluminense', *Actas* (Santiago de Compostela), VI, 691–99. S. A. M. Cardoso, 'Sobre a presença de empréstimos em falares rurais brasileiros', *ib.*, VI, 713–26, and 'Língua e cultura: sobre empréstimos documentados nos falares rurais', *Cunha Vol.*, 71–78, studies terms of French origin for spectacles and clothing.

PORTUGAL. M. L. S. Cruz, 'Os corpora dialectais do CLUL: sua caracterização e objectivos', *APL 10*, I, 151–58, gives an overview; G. Hammermüller, 'O ILB à margem dum atlas linguístico de Portugal', *Actas* (Hamburg), 131–44, laments the underuse of ILB materials and the slow progress of the ALEPG. L. S. Cruz, 'Aspectos fonéticos do barlavento do Algarve: as vogais finais acentuadas', *Cong. Int.*, III, 345–58, links lack of paragogy and diphthongization of front vowels to a more general lowering of front vowels and raising of back vowels. E. d'Andrade, 'Algumas particularidades do português falado do Funchal', *APL 9*, 17–29, studies the variability of /l/-palatalization, as does M. Gonçalves, 'Para um estudo da palatalização do L e da ditongação do I no dialecto madeirense', *Actas* (Santiago de Compostela), VI, 611–30. M. C. R. Bernardo, 'Variação e ensino do português: aspectos da situação na Ilha de São Miguel', *Cong. Int.*, III, 521–27, comments on dialect features still stigmatized by teachers. G. Hammermüller, 'O tratamento de vós em Rio de Onor', *Carvalho Vol.*, 43–54, finds different address forms for insiders and outsiders, an important factor in communal identity. M. V. Navas Sánchez-Elez, 'Español y portugués en la frontera luso-española (formas intransitivas acompañadas del pronombre reflexivo en Barranqueño)', *Cong. Int.*, III, 453–79, suggests that the higher number of pseudo-reflexives in Barranquenho is a throwback from Old Portuguese rather than being influenced by Spanish. J. Carrasco González, 'A língua portuguesa na Extremadura espanhola: o caso de Valencia de Alcântara', *ib.*, 57–73, gives notes on the state of Portuguese, with brief samples, in a less studied border area; M. C. Vilhena, 'Falares portugueses em território castelhano: Herrera de Alcântara', *Cunha Vol.*, 417–28, gives phonetic details.

7.   PORTUGUESE-BASED CREOLES

GENERAL.   A. Bartens, 'Considerações preliminares sobre os sistemas verbais dos crioulos de base portuguesa e sobre os contínuos dialectais', *Actas* (Hamburg), 21–28. By the same author, **Die iberoromanisch-basierten Kreolsprachen: Ansätze der linguistischen Beschreibung*, Frankfurt, Lang, 1995, vii + 345 pp. G. A. Lorenzino, 'Uma avaliação socio-linguística sobre São Tomé e Príncipe', *Cong. Int.*, III, 435–51, highlights the interplay between three creoles — Lungwa Santomé, Lungwa Ié (Principense), Lunga Ngolá (angolar).

ANNOBON.   G. de Granda, 'Las retenciones léxicas africanas en el criollo português de Annobón y sus implicaciones sociohistóricas', *Carvalho Vol.*, 199–208, finds equal proportions of Kwa and Bantu compared with a majority of Bantu terms in Santomense. Id., **Sociolinguística de un microespacio criollo-portugués de África (Annobón)'*, *Orbis*, 38, 1995:130–48.

CABO VERDE.   D. Pereira, 'O ensino da língua portuguesa e minorias linguísticas de origem caboverdiana', *Cong. Int.*, I, 53–80, points to features of Cabo Verde creole which cause problems in the

Portuguese educational system (lack of articles, verb inflection, tense markers).

GUINÉ-BISSAU. W. Bal, 'Pa papiá di pekador na Kriyôl', *Carvalho Vol.*, 189–97, ranges widely over lexical items to do with people. H. H. Couto, 'National identity and ethnic identity in Guinea-Bissau', *Procs* (Brasília), 661–68, finds the unifying value of Kriol threatened by decreolization.

SÃO TOMÉ. Philippe Maurer, **L'angolar: un créoloe afro-portugais parlé à São Tomé*, Hamburg, Buske, viii + 288 pp.

PAPIAMENTO. Silvia Kouwenberg and Eric Mirra, **Papiamentu*, Munich, Lincom, 1994, ii + 57 pp. P. Maurer, 'L'influence des languages africaines sur la signification des lexèmes du papiamento de Curaçao', *Actas* (Santiago de Compostela), VI, 771–79, shows Romance lexical items taking on the semantic range of their African counterparts.

ASIAN CREOLES. A. N. Baxter, 'Um importante sincretismo no Português crioulo de Malaca: a preposição multifuncional ku', *Cunha Vol.*, 15–33, shows *ku* in Kristang to combine the functions of 16th-c. Portuguese *com* and *a*, conditioned by the widespread prepositional marking of direct and indirect objects in its S. Asian substrate. P. Teyssier, 'Avoir au sens d'être dans les créoles portugais d'Asie', *Carvalho Vol.*, 209–18, charts the extension of *ter* to take over the role of non-copular *ser*, combined with the loss of copulas and in Malaccan and the loss of possessive *haver* in Ceylon creole.

MEDIEVAL LITERATURE

POSTPONED

LITERATURE, 1500 TO THE PRESENT

POSTPONED

VII. GALICIAN STUDIES

LANGUAGE

By DAVID MACKENZIE, *Professor of Spanish, National University of Ireland, Cork*
and HENRIQUE MONTEAGUDO, *Lecturer in Galician Philology,*
University of Santiago de Compostela

1. BIBLIOGRAPHICAL AND GENERAL

X. L. Regueira Fernández, *Guía bibliográfica de lingüística galega*, Vigo, Edicións Xerais de Galicia, 249 pp., covers the same ground as García Gondar's *Repertorio* (*YWMLS*, 57:398), but is more selective and better organized, the introductory paragraphs to each section pointing to the most useful works therein. Id., 'Os estudios de lingüística galega', *Vázquez Vol.*, 47–67, is an overview of Galician linguistics from its hesistant beginnings in the 19th c. through the lean years to the blossoming of the post-Franco period. C. Noia Campos, 'O galego escrito no Portugal do século xv', *ib.*, 69–76, publishes the Portuguese and Galician texts of a constitution approved in the Viana do Castelo synod of 1486, with a contrastive linguistic study. She concludes that there were probably two scribes, and that there is contamination in both texts; her claim that the Portuguese text shows evidence of a written culture, while the Galician seems to represent an oral one needs more support than she provides. F. Tato Plaza, 'Comentario a unha receta medieval para a preparación de tinta', *ib.*, 335–50, provides a detailed linguistic commentary to this short 15th-c. text. H. Monteagudo Romero, 'Noticia dun texto prosístico en galego do século XVII: *Memoria da fundación da Confraría de Cambeadores*', *ib.*, 351–75, provides a contrastive linguistic study of both MSS of this 17th-c. forgery, important because of the paucity of documents in Galician of this period, and fascinating because the dialect features present, roughly coincident with modern ones, allow M. to posit the Santiago area as that of the dialect of the forger.

2. GRAMMAR

F. Dubert García, 'Algúns aspectos da morfoloxía verbal e da estructura da sílaba en galego: as vocais temáticas postónicas da C-II e da C-III en hiato', *Verba*, 22 1995[1996]:125–55, analyses the variant forms, with either hiatus or diphthong, of the type *traes/trais, trae/trai, traen/train*, in P2, P3 and P6 of the present indicative of a group of verbs, relating them to the complex historical development of vowel hiatus in Galician, especially in word-final position, and goes on to justify the adoption of forms without diphthong in standard Galician. C. Silva Domínguez, 'É meu amigo/ é o meu amigo/ é amigo meu', *CadL*, 14:5–20, attempts to explain the presence or absence of the article in phrases combining possessive and personal noun where the latter functions as attribute. The approach is interesting, but the treatment is shallow. X. M. Pérez Sardiña, 'Os adverbios absolutos de lugar. Achega semántica e dialectal', *ib.*, 13:89–104, uses an oral corpus to study absolute adverbs of place (*aquí-aí-alí*; *acó-aló*; *acá-alá*), concluding that their true semantic coordinates are inclusion/punctuality on one axis, proximity/distance on the other, with a further opposition within the distance feature of separation/non-separation. E. Guerbek and E. Zernova, 'Algunhas peculiaridades do uso das preposicións e frases prepositivas con significado prelocativo e poslocativo no galego (comparado co castelán)', *ib.*, 105–14, point to the vitality in Galician of prepositions and prepositional phrases which are obsolescent in Castilian (*alén/alén de*, *tras/tras de*) by means of an ingenious experiment using Galician-speaking and Castilian-speaking children, and then deal with constructions such as *detrás miña* (equivalent to *detrás de min*) compared with *detrás mío* (equivalent to *detrás de mí*), which have both greater vitality and higher status in Galician. Their explanation of the difference in gender in this construction between Galician and Castilian does not, however, convince.

3. Semantics, Lexis, Etymology, and Onomastics

C. García, *Glosas da lingua*, Vigo, Xerais, 292 pp., investigates in a somewhat superficial fashion from a lexicographical or semantic angle some 250 Galician lexical items, prinicipally from literary sources. M. González González, 'O Diccionario da Lingua Galega da Real Academia Galega', *Actas* (Santiago–Corunna), 111–19, explains the format of this projected dictionary, which will contain 30,000 entries, selected from the *Tesouro lexicográfico* of the Instituto da Lingua Galega. The most controversial feature will surely be the proposed inclusion of Castilian words, which, together with dialectal and sub-standard forms, will carry an asterisk. This looks to be another run-of-the-mill medium-sized dictionary, rather than the extensive citation-based lexicon that the Galician-speaking world is waiting for. I. González Fernández, 'Diccionario italiano-galego', *ib.*, 121–29, and 'Diccionario castelán-galego da Real Academia Galega', *ib.*, 131–39, announces two more imminent productions: both will contain illustrative citations, translated into the target language, and the usual grammatical and morphological information. The Italian volume, produced by the staff of the Italian Section at the University of Santiago de Compostela, will have 10,000 entries, and the Castilian, 12,000. X. A. Rodríguez Río, 'Os traballos terminolóxicos en lingua galega: unha aproximación á súa situación e necesidades', *CadL*, 13:35–74, studies the pattern of the introduction of neologisms in Galician, concentrating particularly on the recent past, indicates what in his opinion are the principal problems, and suggests ways of dealing with them. A. M. Lorenzo Suárez and J. Gómez Guinovart, 'Terminoloxía, informática e lingua galega', *ib.*, 5–33, present and describe their trilingual English-Castilian-Galician vocabulary of computer terminology, available on a Web site, and provide a brief discussion of the problems surrounding the introduction of neologisms into Galician. M. A. Conde Teira, 'Acerca dos nomes dos anfibios e réptiles galegos', *ib.*, 75–88, using in the main data extracted from the *Atlas Lingüístico de Galicia*, discusses the problem of deciding on agreed common names for these animals, going on to provide an organized list of species found in Galicia, and proposing common generic names and names for the most common varieties. E. Montero Cartelle, 'La interdicción sexual en el gallego medieval: la expresión de los órganos sexuales femeninos', *Verba*, 22, 1995[1996]:429–47, takes his examples, principally of euphemisms for *vulva*, from the *Cantigas d'escarnho* in this short study which its author announces as the first instalment of a larger enterprise. A. I. Boullón Agrelo, 'Descendentes galegos de *Iohannes*', *Vázquez Vol.*, 377–92, examines the use of the name in Galicia from the medieval period to the present day, finding it as a forename — *Xoán, Xoanna*, a surname — *Eanes* (and variants), and a toponym, with the addition of *San — Seoane*; in 'Cronoloxía e variación das fórmulas patronímicas na Galicia medieval', *Verba*, 22, 1995[1996]:449–75, B.A. uses a corpus of seven collections of documents, mostly of the early Middle Ages, in this detailed survey of Galician patronyms, the majority of which end rather disappointingly in *-z*. R. Mariño Paz, 'Consideracións sobre a historia dos sufixos *-ancia/-anza, -encia/-enza, -icia/-iza, -icio/-izo* e as terminacións *-cia/-za* e *-cio/-zo* en galego', *ib.*, 157–89, examines a large corpus of texts from the medieval period to the 19th c. and confirms the general impression that the endings apparently preserving the *yod* correspond to lexical items introduced into Galician after the 15th c., except in the east of Galicia, where they are found also in the earlier period. The thesis is somewhat vitiated by a failure to acknowledge that there might be a difference between orthography and pronunciation, especially where there is a difference of register.

4. DIALECTOLOGY

F. Fernández Rei and C. Hermida Gulías, *A nosa fala. Bloques e áreas lingüísticas do galego*, Santiago de Compostela, Consello da Cultura

Galega, 149 pp. + 3 cassettes, provide a rich selection of the dialectal
varieties of Galician, with audio tapes of 43 interviews and their
corresponding transcriptions, a useful accompaniment to F.'s now-
standard *Dialectoloxía galega* (Vigo, Xerais, 1990). However, although
great care has been taken in the selection and presentation of the
interviews, some aspects of the transcriptional criteria are questionable. F. Boller, 'Paradigmas interferenciais no galego exterior zamo-
rano', *Verba*, 22, 1995[1996]:31–71, announces an *Atlas lingüístico
regional da zona de contacto galego-português-espanhola*, and studies certain
verb forms in this region using data collected for the atlas, concluding
that, rather than a 'bundle', he has an 'enmaranhado' of isoglosses,
betraying an extremely complex dialect mix. He provides 23 maps
for 12 verbs. D. Míguez Iglesias, 'Seseo e gheada en Viceso (Brión)',
CadL, 14:39–57, studies the survival of these two dialectal phenomena
in a small rural community by means of a comparison between three
generations, showing that, although both are in retreat, the *gheada* is
much more resistant than *seseo*. Nevertheless, the explanation given
appears less than convincing, the author neglecting for example to
mention the fact that the area chosen for study is very close to the
seseo/non-*seseo* isogloss. X. Soto Andión, 'Algúns trazos fonéticos do
galego da Terra de Montes (Concello de Forcarei)', *ib.*, 59–84, studies
various elements that characterize the speech of this community in
the area of central Galician, such as the fall of intervocalic [d], the
vitality of the *gheada* in its various realizations, aspiration and
rhotacism of implosive [s], and the phonetic adaptation of neologisms.
F. Dubert García, 'Algúns fenómenos fonéticos e fonolóxicos da fala
de Santiago de Compostela', *Vázquez Vol.*, 133–55, in a cogent and
persuasive article illustrated with transcriptions, examines certain
features — vowel harmony, epenthetic and paragogic vowels, *gheada*,
seseo, and rhotacism — of the speech of the capital, concluding that
the latter's influence on the surrounding region is gradually increasing, but that this increase is recent, given the unevenness of the
diffusion of the features in question. R. Álvarez, 'Na estrema do
galego: a lingua do Bierzo Baixo trasmitida por Fernández y Morales',
ib., 157–202, undertakes a detailed linguistic study of F.'s *Ensayos
poéticos en dialecto berciano* (León, 1861), showing that he appears to
have recorded the peculiarities of the Galician spoken in this part of
León with reasonable accuracy, and that the variety shares many
features with large areas of E. Galician. R. Mariño Paz, 'Aproximación ó mapa dialectal galego dos séculos xviii e xix', *ib.*, 77–105,
notes that *grosso modo* the dialectal observations of Sobreira,
Sarmiento and others generally correspond to the results of modern
surveys.

5. SOCIOLINGUISTICS AND PSYCHOLINGUISTICS

J. Kabatek, *Die Sprecher als Linguisten. Interferenz- und Sprachwandelphänomene dargestellt am Galicischen der Gegenwart*, Tübingen, Niemeyer, 434 pp., in an important book which publishes his doctoral thesis, deals with interference and linguistic change in modern Galician, using questionnaires and interviews with university students and radio and television announcers to show the ways in which they influence perceptions of the language metalinguistically. M. A. Fernández Rodríguez and M. A. Rodríguez Neira, *Actitudes lingüísticas en Galicia*, Corunna, Real Academia Galega, Seminario de Sociolingüística, 562 pp. + 9 maps, present the third volume bringing together the results of their huge *Mapa sociolingüístico de Galicia*. As with the previous volumes, one is struck by the huge size of the sample — nearly 39,000 informants were interviewed — and by the scope of the questionnaire. The refined and rigorous use of statistical methods allowed the team both to arrive at global conclusions for the whole sample, and also to fine-slice the corpus to make very precise evaluations by sector (geographical, age, profession, etc.). However, if the principal problem in the previous volume on usage was the impossibility of comparing claimed and actual performance, in this volume it is the concept of attitude and the measurement of it. Nevertheless, one of the most significant results brought forth here is the more positive attitude of the young towards the language (though this is found also in the population as a whole and in all groups) in contrast to the results of the first two volumes, on first language and usage respectively, in which this group was depressingly negative by and large. On the whole, these three volumes of the *Mapa Sociolingüístico de Galicia* may be said to constitute a landmark in Galician language studies, and will be an indispensable reference tool for further work in this area. M. López Morales, 'Características da evolución do léxico dunha nena bilingüe galego-castelán', *CadL*, 13:115–32, shows how, in a bilingual context, children begin by mixing items from both languages indiscriminately, without incorporating them into their active vocabulary in either language. Subsequently a reduced number of items is incorporated in both languages, and, finally, the two languages are differentiated. M. Pérez Pereira et al., 'Comparanza da adquisición das formas de posesión do galego e o castelán en nenos bilingües', *ib.*, 14:21–38, show that the Galician possessives are incorporated later than the Castilian ones, and explain this by pointing to the fact that in Galician the pronominal and adjectival forms are identical, making the Galician scheme easier to master (cast. *mi libro / es mío*, gal. *o meu libro / é meu*). C. Hermida Gulías, 'Galego e portugués durante o século XIX

(1840–1891)', *Vázquez Vol.*, 107–19, looks at the frequent reference to its relationship with Portuguese as a means of raising the status of Galician by polemicists of the period, while noting a relative paucity of advocates of a Portuguesist orthography. This line of investigation is carried into the 1890s by E. X. González Seoane, 'O debate sobre a independencia do galego na última década do século XIX', *ib.*, 121–31, who comes to a similar conclusion, namely that there were few borrowings from Portuguese in the period he reviews, and that those that did occur represent an attempt to escape from a Castilian form rather than a positive Portuguesist bent. F. Fernández Rei, 'A posición do galego, lingua románica reemerxente', *ib.*, 15–46, brings up to date and publishes in Galician his cogent and well-documented discussion in French (*YWMLS*, 46:469), of the status of Galician, concluding that, however close it may be to Portuguese from a strictly linguistic viewpoint, when sociolinguistic factors are taken into consideration, it must be considered a separate language. R. Lorenzo, 'A situación actual do galego', pp. 283–309 of vol. I of *Actas do Congresso Internacional sobre o Português (Lisboa, 1994)*, 3 vols, ed. Inês Duarte and Isabel Leiria, Lisbon, APL–Colibri, 363, 517, 570 pp., after a brief historical account, provides an overview of recent work on the status of Galician in various domains, with the benefit of his own deeply-felt and trenchantly expressed commentary. The tone is generally pessimistic, as L. laments what he sees as the wasting of a unique opportunity to reinforce the position of the language against the inroads of Castilian after the death of Franco in education, the media, publishing and spheres of official activity such as administration and the law.

LITERATURE

By Dolores Vilavedra, *Department of Galician Philology,*
Universidade de Santiago de Compostela
and Derek Flitter, *Senior Lecturer in Modern Spanish Language and Literature,*
University of Birmingham

1. General

A. Figueroa, *Lecturas alleas*, Santiago, Sotelo, 155 pp., is a rigorous analysis of Galician literature as a designated 'weak' system in its relations with other, stronger, systems, a study founded on the French writer and critic Philéas Lebesgue's similar work on the 'Xeración *Nós*'. Xesús Alonso Montero, *Lingua e literatura galegas na Galicia emigrante*, Corunna, Xunta de Galicia, 258 pp., coming from one of the leading experts in the field, is an indispensable study, particularly for the specialist reader, of an area still lacking in critical definition and requiring considerable historical research. Claudio Rodríguez Fer, *Acometida atlántica (por un comparatismo integral)*, Sada, O Castro, 315 pp., is a comparative study dealing with Ánxel Fole, Novoneyra, Tovar, Valente, López-Casanova, Vicente Risco, Otero Pedrayo, Álvaro Cunqueiro, and Pimentel, based on a diversity of connections — thematic, structural, ideological, historical, and biographical, to name but a few — existing not just between those authors named but also between their own life and work and the broader Hispanic background. A. Tarrío, 'A crítica literaria', *ColL*, 137–38:212–15, provides a lightning survey and historical synthesis of the principal perspectives of Galician literary criticism from 1916, taken as the starting point of the 'Xeración *Nós*', to the present day. X. L. Barreiro, 'O ensaio filosófico en Galicia', *ib.*, 202–06, deals with the question of definition as well as with that of the genre's historical emergence and its informing conditions. R. Fonte, 'Panorámica de ensaio', *AELG*, 1995:139–42, is a brief but insightful overview of the year's most important pieces. H. Monteagudo, 'Nación/creación. Estética e política no agromar do ensaio galego', *ib.*, 63–110, studies the ideological as well as linguistic parameters influencing and facilitating the prose essay in *galego*.

2. Contemporary Literature

X. M. Salgado, 'O grupo Nós. O Seminario de Estudios Galegos', *ColL*, 137–38:93–114, is an excellent synthesis of the period and its creative beginnings. H. González and D. Vilavedra, 'Contra vento e marea: a recuperación do discurso literario na posguerra', *ib.*, 149–62, take a panoramic look at works appearing immediately after

the Civil War. V. Freixanes, 'A narrativa galega dos últimos anos: a
nova fronteira', *ib.*, 177–96, sees one of the most noted exponents of
contemporary narrative survey. the wider field. X. L. Axeitos, 'A
poesía galega dos últimos 30 anos', *ib.*, 163–76, provides a similar
overview of recent poetry. M. C. Ríos Panisse, 'Dos escritores do
Rexurdimento ás Irmandades da Fala', *ib.*, 65–80, reviews this
extensive period's major authors. X. Alonso Montero, 'O *Soneto Neo-
Latino* (Vila Nova de Famalicão, 1929–1933): estudio dunha revista
poética singular, especialmente das colaboracións galegas', *AELG*,
1995:11–38, examines a curious Portuguese magazine dedicated to
stimulating the cultivation of the sonnet in Romance languages.
H. González, '1995: unha bandexa chea de bos poemarios', *ib.*,
167–74, makes an optimistic assessment of the year's poetry. R. Raña,
A noite nas palabras, Santiago, Sotelo, 242 pp., analyses Galician poetry
appearing between 1947 and 1962, the objective being to elucidate
its key components and hence to delineate a putative generational
grouping. X. González-Millán, *A narrativa galega actual (1975–84).
Unha historia social*, Vigo, Xerais, 390 pp., makes an exhaustive study
of the decade after Franco from an avowedly — and rigorously
argued — socio-critical perspective. D. Vilavedra, 'O bilingüismo
como estratexia narratolóxica nos albores da prosa galega de ficción
(1880–1930)', pp. 483–95 of *Actas del X Simposio de la Sociedad Española
de Literatura General y Comparada*, Santiago de Compostela U.P.,
495 pp., scrutinizes literary enunciation as a possible sociolinguistic
tool. M. Angeles Rodríguez, *Poética da novela de autoformación: o
Bildungsroman galego no contexto narrativo hispánico*, Santiago, Xunta–
CILLRP, 311 pp., studies a genre occupying a privileged place in
Galician narrative, framing it within the larger Hispanic context.
S. Gaspar, 'Dez anos de narrativa galega (cen anos de cine)', *AELG*,
1995:111–25, illustrates the close relationship between Galician
detective fiction and the North-American *film noir* by elucidating the
cinematographic techniques commonly found in this form of prose
narrative. The same author's 'E nisto, un *impasse*', *ib.*, 161–65, rather
pessimistically contemplates the year's new prose fiction. M. F.
Vieites, 'Camiño dunha difícil normalización', *AELG*, 1995:175–81,
surveys the year's new drama. The same author's 'Notas arredor da
peza breve na literatura dramática galega. A brevidade como
imposición e como elección', *Grial*, 131:361–78, examines the factors
that led to the increasing protagonism of shorter pieces in Galician
theatre.

3. Individual Authors

BLANCO AMOR. X. Castro, 'O tecido simbólico en *A esmorga*', *Grial*,
129:5–14, is a shrewd analysis of the novel's symbolic procedures.

D. Manera, 'Note sui romanzi galeghi di E. Blanco Amor', *Vázquez Vol.*, 669–80, looks fairly cursorily at critical evaluations of B.A.'s narrative work.

CABANA. T. Araújo, 'Primeiros intentos narrativos de D. X. Cabana', *BGL*, 14:107–12, is intended to shed some light on C.'s little-known early narrative work.

CASTELAO. C. Rodríguez Fer, 'Castelao, artista e político que fixo literatura', *ColL*, 137–38:115–32, provides a broad critical synthesis of C.'s multi-faceted production.

CASTRO. Joanna Courteau, *The Poetics of Rosalía de Castro's Negra Sombra*, Lewiston, Mellen, 1995, 119 pp., is a disappointment: intellectually flimsy, whimsical and superficial, it is burdened by internal contradictions, while the extensive use of long quotations only summarily examined tends to exacerbate these problems. X. Alonso Montero, 'Azorín, lector de Rosalía', *Anales Azorinianos*, 5:13–26, appraises Azorín's articles on Rosalía's poetry (helpfully documented in the form of an appendix). V. Álvarez, 'Sobre a *demisión* de Rosalía: unha carta inédita de M. Murguía', *Grial*, 131:389–94, attempts to clarify this vexed question with reference to a previously unpublished letter. C. Blanco, 'Rosalía de Castro: a estranxeira na súa patria', *ColL*, 137–38:81–92, examines issues of marginalization extracted from Rosalía's life and work. L. Fontoira, 'Algúns problemas textuais de *Follas novas*', *Vázquez Vol.*, 401–06, seeks to resolve specific linguistic questions arising from editions of the text. A. López and A. Pociña, 'Ricardo Carballo Calero na historia do rosalianismo. Unha aproximación bibliográfica', *BGL*, 15–16:179–91, document, with commentary, the contributions to Rosalía studies by an eminent specialist. K. March, 'Rosalía de Castro, novelista do seu tempo', *Unión Libre*, 1:37–44, considers Rosalía's image as 'escritora' in the light of contemporary paradigms.

CUNQUEIRO. T. López, '"Algún día...", poema de Álvaro Cunqueiro', *BGL*, 14:113–18, salvages a poem that has remained unpublished since its first appearance in a Buenos Aires magazine in 1930. M. X. Nogueira, 'O país das naves e das flotas. Achegamento á presencia da cultura portuguesa na obra de Cunqueiro', *Vázquez Vol.*, 681–700, pays serious attention, for the first time, to Cunqueiro's interest in specific aspects of Portuguese culture.

DÍAZ CASTRO. A. Blanco Torrado, *A ascensión dun poeta. X.M. Díaz Castro*, Lugo, Caixa Galicia, 95 pp., is a modest, principally thematic, study of the poetry.

DIESTE. A highlight here is the volume *Congreso Rafael Dieste*, ed. X. L. Axeitos, Santiago, Xunta, 318 pp., which reproduces papers delivered at the 1995 Corunna conference. The collection includes: X. Alonso, 'A palabra e o silencio na obra de R. Dieste' (123–35), on

D.'s conception of committed literature; M. Aznar, 'Farsas y guiñol en el teatro de R. Dieste' (199–236), seeks to insert D.'s theatre into an identifiable popular tradition; C. Gurméndez, 'R. Dieste y su horizonte filosófico europeo' (15–28), locates D.'s essays within a contemporary European context; E. Irizarry, 'Del realismo mágico al realismo mitopoético. Félix Muriel' (279–96), looks at the evolution of D.'s realism from *Dos arquivos do trasno* to *Historias e invenciones de Félix Muriel*; R. Nicolás, 'Entre dúas literaturas' (55–66), ponders the problematic question of the place accorded to D. in generationally determined histories of Galician and Spanish literature, while the same author's 'R. Dieste: bibliografía en 1995' (149–71), surveys the critical interest produced by the dedication to D. of the *Día das Letras Galegas* in 1995; L. Pozo, 'R. Dieste: diálogo estético coa Xeración do 27' (267–78), considers the collection *Rojo farol amante* within a Spanish context; E. Ruibal, 'Breve aproximación á poética teatral de Dieste' (245–56), examines the philosophical and aesthetic positions underlying D.'s own drama and his writing on the theatre; L. Suñén, 'La conciencia de estilo en los artículos del joven Dieste' (101–08), takes a schematic look at D.'s journalistic prose; A. Tarrío, 'R. Dieste: periodismo y literatura' (67–82), establishes a thematic nucleus around which D.'s journalistic writing is felt to have turned; D. Villanueva, 'R. Dieste, narrador' (297–318), looks at the publishing history of D.'s novels and seeks to establish their most characteristic features with regard to content.

FOLE. A. Requeixo, *Ánxel Fole. Aproximación temática á súa obra narrativa en galego*, Vigo, Cumio, 143 pp., is a rigorously argued and ground-breaking new study of F.'s work.

IGLESIAS ARAÚXO. A. M. Spitzmesser, 'Ritos da pasaxe: a búsqueda de identidade en *Vento de seda* de Bieito Iglesias', *Grial*, 129:15–23, analyses the novel as *Bildungsroman*.

MANUEL ANTONIO. X. R. Pena, *Manuel Antonio e a vangarda*, Santiago, Sotelo, 202 pp., is an indispensable new study at the heart of which is the debate concerning the existence — or non-existence — of a Galician avant-garde and the essential parameters defining such a movement.

MENDEZ FERRÍN. *Retorno a Tagen Ata*, introd. A. Capelán, Vigo, Xerais, 123 pp., has in its introduction, from the pen of a noted specialist, a piece of fundamental importance conceived as an approach to the biographical, literary and ideological determinants informing the gestation of the work.

NEIRA VILAS. D. Vilavedra, '*Chiquinho* e *Memorias dun neno labrego*: dous casos de recorrencias temáticas nas literaturas colonizadas', *Vázquez Vol.*, 715–24, provides a comparative analysis of thematic procedures employed in two novels from the Cape Verde Islands and Galicia respectively.

OTERO ÁLVAREZ. 'A tradición romancística galega: a figura de Aníbal Otero', *BGL*, 15–16:47–76, rapidly surveys studies of the *Romancero* appearing in Galicia by way of introduction to the anthology made by O.A. that is offered in the article.

OTERO PEDRAYO. *O señorito da Reboraina*, introd. X. M. Salgado, Vigo, Xerais, 287 pp., provides a solid introduction (7–61) to the new, normalized and annotated edition of O.P.'s novel.

QUEIZÁN. S. Reisz, '"Daquelas que cantan"... sen miramentos', *AELG*, 1995:127–37, is an extended commentary on Q.'s poetic production that links the evolution of the writer's poetics with contemporary processes of feminist linguistic renovation within a broader Hispanic context.

RISCO. A feature here is the appearance of the proceedings of the 1995 Ourense conference, *Congreso Vicente Risco*, ed. Carlos Casares, Santiago, Xunta, 426 pp. X. M. Castro, 'Literatura e mensaxe ideolóxica no derradeiro V. Risco' (145–56), is a revisionary piece that views R.'s post-Civil War production as consistent with earlier stages of his writing, thus challenging the prevailing view that R.'s late work was reactionary in tone and outlook; F. García, 'Formas da fantasía na obra narrativa de V. Risco' (201–12), makes a symbolist reading of R.'s Castilian narrative; M. X. Lama, 'Alemaña e *Mitteleuropa*' (269–82), elucidates the sources informing R.'s vision of Germany and his means and objectives in employing them; B. Losada, 'V. Risco na cultura galega' (321–30), evaluates R.'s role in various spheres of Galician cultural life; J. Ribera and O. Rodríguez, 'Relacións entre Risco e Joan Maragall' (331–51), effects a comparativist study of the two writers; F. Serrano, 'Risco e as referencias a Irlanda e o irlandés' (55–66), is a well documented examination of R.'s knowledge of and interest in Ireland; A. Tarrío, 'Introducción á obra literaria de V. Risco' (187–200), analyses the narrative from the point of view of readerly experience and the model reader; M. Valcárcel, 'Risco na prensa ourensá' (213–34), is a stylistic and thematic study of these texts; X. L. Varela, 'Sociedade e cultura xermanas en Risco' (255–68), surveys the image of Germany projected in R.'s work and specifically in *Mitteleuropa*; D. Vilavedra, 'Enunciación e parodia en *O porco de pé*' (39–54), examines parodic strategies and how they are articulated; D. Villalaín, 'Risco e o teatro' (371–94), scrutinizes R.'s interest, creative and critical, in the theatre as a vehicle for experimentation.

RODRÍGUEZ MOURULLO. M. T. Bermúdez, 'Gonzalo R. Mourullo na narrativa galega', *AELG*, 1995:39–61, is a rare study of a neglected figure of the Galician 'Nova Narrativa'.

TORRES. O. Novo, 'A voz interna, conmovida, última. Análise temática da obra de X. Torres', *Unión Libre*, 1 : 131–47, effects a thematic analysis of T.'s poetry.

VÁZQUEZ. *Festa da palabra silenciada*, 12, is dedicated to the sisters Dora and Pura Vázquez. The issue includes: C. Panero, 'A poeta Dora Vázquez' (17–19); M. X. Queizán, 'A sonoridade na poesía de Dora Vázquez' (25–27); C. Blanco, 'Pura Vázquez ou o pulo do desacougo' (13–16); V. Sanjurjo, 'Pura Vázquez: unha poética da "galeguidade"' (22–24).

VILLAR PONTE. M. F. Vieites, 'De John Millington Synge a Antón Villar Ponte. Teatro, literatura dramática e construcción nacional na periferia atlántica. Anotacións para un estudio preliminar', pp. 51–167 of *Como en Irlanda*, Santiago, IGAEM, 256 pp., is an extensive study of V.P.'s drama as part of the cultural project undertaken by the *Irmandades da Fala* in their construction of national identity, one that establishes connections with the evolution of an Irish national theatre.

VIII. LATIN AMERICAN STUDIES

SPANISH AMERICAN LITERATURE
THE COLONIAL PERIOD

POSTPONED

THE NINETEENTH CENTURY

By ANNELLA McDERMOTT, *Department of Hispanic, Portuguese and Latin American Studies, University of Bristol*

1. GENERAL

M. Goloboff, 'Gauchos eran los de antes', *Hispamérica*, 74:57–61, is a short note on the different attitudes taken to the gaucho in Argentinian texts, particularly from the 19th c. G. Gómez Ocampo, 'Historia, leyenda y representación literaria en dos cronistas decimonónicos: Ricardo Palma y José María Cordovez Moure', *Procs* (Brasília), 1167–73, examines how the factual and the fictional are treated in these writers, their presentation of 'photographic' material in words, and their nostalgia for the old colonial cities, which was to influence significantly subsequent costumbrists. Beatriz González Stephan et al., **Esplendores y miserias del siglo XIX. Cultura y sociedad en América Latina*, Venezuela, Monte Ávila, 1995, 531 pp. B. González Stephan, 'De fobias y compulsiones: la regulación de la barbarie', *Hispamérica*, 74:3–20, examines the concept of 'cleanliness', physical, moral and linguistic, in the discourse on modernity in early 19th-c. Latin America. R. Gutiérrez Girardot, 'Modernismo', *CAm*, 205:23–29, concentrates on the significance for *modernismo* of the movement of population from the countryside to the city. L. Íñigo-Madrigal, 'Las abuelitas de los modernistas', *ib.* 30–35, explores the importance of childhood memories, representing nostalgia for an irrecoverable past, for a number of *modernista* poets. William H. Katra, **The Argentine Generation of 1837: Echeverría, Alberdi, Sarmiento, Mitre*, Rutherford, Farleigh Dickinson U.P., 368 pp. Eva Löfquist, **La novela histórica chilena dentro del marco de la novelística chilena 1843–1879*, Gothenburg U.P., 1995, 359 pp. F. Masiello, 'Melodrama, sex and nation in Latin America's *fin de siglo*', *MLQ*, 57:269–78, looks at the treatment of delinquency and perversion in newspaper crime reports and gossip columns, and in literature. Adolfo Prieto,**Los viajeros ingleses y la emergencia de la literatura argentina*, Argentina, Sudamericana, 189 pp. N. Vogeley, 'Italian opera in early national Mexico', *MLQ*, 57:279–88, focuses on the usefulness of opera, both in performance and through libretti published with translations, in providing a terminology that enabled the new social elite to define itself as 'civilized' in contrast to the 'barbaric' indigenous or uneducated populace.

INDIVIDUAL AUTHORS

BELLO, ANDRÉS. J. Concha,'Bello y su gestión superestructural en Chile', *RCLL*, 43–44:139–61, is concerned with B.'s studies in grammar and jurisprudence in the years 1830–55, and the contribution these made to the creation of a Chilean identity.

BORRERO, JUANA. I.A. Schulman, 'Una voz moderna: la poesía de Juana Borrero', *CAm*, 205:36–41, points to links between the poems of this youthful writer, dead by the age of 18, and those of the *modernistas*.

CASTILLO DE GONZÁLEZ, AURELIA. L. Campuzano, 'Cuando salí de La Habana. *Cartas de México* (1893) de Aurelia Castillo de González', *CAm*, 205:70–79, emphasizes C. de G.'s predisposition to see Mexico as an example of a progressive independent Republic, potentially a model for a future independent Cuba.

DARÍO, RUBÉN. S. Abate, 'Elementos hagiográficos en la obra de Rubén Darío', *His(US)*, 79:411–18, looks at elements taken by D. from the lives of saints, particularly in poems and short stories of the period 1896–1905. E. Espina, 'Rubén Darío: la timidez del cisne y el cuerpo ausente', *La Torre*, 9, 1995:201–20, examines the presentation of erotic desire in D.'s verse, drawing attention to the absence of transgressive subversion. J.M. Martínez, 'Nuevas luces para las fuentes de *Azul*', *HR*, 64:199–215, proposes Henri Murger and Shelley as possible influences on three of the short stories and one poem.

ECHEVERRÍA, ESTEBAN. J.C. Mercado, 'La propuesta estética en las *Rimas* de Esteban Echeverría', *Procs* (Brasília), 1368–73, points to the nationalist, as opposed to the universalist, tenor of E.'s Romanticism. J.C. Mercado, **Building a Nation: the case of Echeverría*, Lanham, MD–London, University Press of America, 1995, vi + 244 pp. K. Silva Gruesz, 'Facing the nation: the organic life of *La cautiva*', *REH*, 30:3–22, questions the view that the poem shows barbarism triumphing over civilization.

FERNÁNDEZ DE LIZARDI, JOSÉ JOAQUÍN. A. Benítez-Rojo, 'José Joaquín Fernández de Lizardi and the emergence of the Spanish American novel as a national project', *MLQ*, 57:325–39, discusses the particular form of Mexicanness that his works proposed. N. Shumway, '*Don Catrín de la Fachenda* and Lizardi's crisis of moral authority', *REH*, 30:361–74, argues that the work is ambiguous, reflecting both the contemporary debate between traditional authority and modernity, and L.'s internal conflict between the cautious reformist and the radical.

GÓMEZ CARRILLO, ENRIQUE. A. Kanzepolsky, 'Fábulas de un viajero', *CAm*, 205:53–61, explores the theme of travel in the writings of G.C.

GÓMEZ DE AVELLANEDA, GERTRUDIS. S. Banusch, '*Baltasar* de la Avellaneda', *CHA*, 548:121–29, relates G. de A.'s biography, briefly, and posits a connection between the figure of the tyrant Baltasar in the novel and the novelist's stepfather. B. Pastor, *'Simbolismo autobiográfico en la novela *Sab* de Gertudis Gómez de Avellaneda', *Aldaba*, 28:389–403.

GORRITI, JUANA MANUELA. T. Barrera, 'La fantasía de Juana Manuela Gorriti', *Hispamérica*, 74:103–11, examines the role of supernatural elements in G.'s short stories. G. Batticuore, 'Itinerarios culturales. Dos modelos de mujer intelectual en la Argentina del siglo XIX', *RCLL*, 43–44:163–80, examines the contrasting significance of journeys made by G. (within Latin America) and Eduarda Mansilla (to Europe).

HOSTOS, EUGENIO MARÍA DE. A. A. Rivera, '*La tela de araña* de Eugenio María de Hostos: mujer, muchedumbre y modernidad', *REH*, 30:41–65, looks at this recently-discovered novel in terms of its author's attitudes to women, popular culture, writing, and politics.

ISAACS, JORGE. J. Cantavella, 'Miradas y lágrimas en *María* de Jorge Isaacs', *CHA*, 552:85–99, accuses I. of manipulating reader response.

LUGONES, LEOPOLDO. H.M. Fraser, 'Apocalyptic vision and Modernism's dismantling of scientific discourse: Lugones' *Yzur*', *His(US)*, 79:8–19, examines this short piece of fiction as an examples of Lugones' and by extension Modernism's scepticism concerning the claims of experimental science.

MANZANO, JUAN FRANCISCO. S. Labrador-Rodríguez, 'La intelectualidad negra en Cuba en el siglo XIX: el caso de Manzano', *RevIb*, 62:13–25, sets out to correct the picture of Manzano as a poorly-educated slave, producing a spontaneous text, by showing that he had intellectual concerns, which he consciously expressed in his autobiography.

MARTÍ, JOSÉ. Alfonso Herrera Franyutti, *'Martí en México: recuerdos de una época*. Mexico, Consejo Nacional para la Cultura y las Artes, 339 pp. Y. Martínez-San Miguel, 'Sujetos femeninos en *Amistad funesta* y *Blanco sol:* el lugar de la mujer en dos novelas latinoamericanas de fin del siglo XIX', *RevIb*, 62: 27–45, examines in these novels, by Martí and Mercedes Cabello de Carbonera respectively, the theme of the changing role of women as urbanization and modernization advance. S. Molloy, 'His America, our America: José Martí reads Walt Whitman', *MLQ* 57 : 369–79, takes a rather sceptical look at the significance M. assigns to Whitman in the continental programme M. is proposing. J. Ramos, 'The repose of heroes', *ib.* 355–67, examines the terms of the discourse whereby M. legitimates the sacrifice a soldier makes of his life for the good of the community. B. Subercaseaux, 'Martí: modernización y cultura', *CHA*, 552 : 47–54, stresses the relevance for today's cicumstances of M.'s thought on the conflict between modernity and traditional cultural forms, with particular reference to *Nuestra América*. A. Vera-León, 'José María Heredia, José Martí: Imaginación de la tierra', *REH,* 30 : 23–40, investigates M.'s use and re-elaboration of certain key metaphors in Heredia, in particular those relating to land and water.

PALMA, CLEMENTE. G. Mora, '*La granja blanca* de Clemente Palma: relaciones con el decadentismo y Edgar Allan Poe', *CAm*, 205 : 62–69.

RODRÍGUEZ, SIMÓN. S. Rotker, 'Nation and mockery: the oppositional writings of Simón Rodríguez', *MLQ,* 57 : 253–67, stresses R.'s heterodox stance.

SARMIENTO, DOMINGO FAUSTINO. G. Areta Marigó, 'Sarmiento a vueltas con la barbarie', *CHA*, 551 : 7–17, is concerned mainly with *Facundo*. Diana Sorensen Goodrich, **Facundo and the Construction of Argentine Culture*, Texas U.P., 248 pp. G. Verdevieso, 'Memoria colectiva y ciudad letrada en *Recuerdos de provincia*', *REH,* 30 : 375–91, concentrates on S.'s treatment of the foundation of his native city of San Juan, for which he had to rely on oral testimony, rather than written documents.

SILVA, JOSÉ ASUNCIÓN. J. L. Arcos, 'Silva y la poesía cubana. Relaciones', *CAm*, 205 : 42–52, refers to ties of friendship, correspondence, affinities and similarities between S. and the Cuban poets Zenea, Martí, Del Casal, and Poveda. P. Elmore, 'Bienes suntuarios: el problema de la obra de arte en *De sobremesa* de José Asunción Silva', *RCLL,* 43–44 : 201–10, concentrates on the theme of the nature and limitations of art in this posthumously published novel by S.

XIMENO Y CRUZ, DOLORES MARÍA. N. Araújo, 'Voz y voces de *Aquellos tiempos . . . Memorias de Lola María*', *CAm*, 205 : 80–90, looks at the importance of notions of gender for both the writer and the reader of these memoirs.

THE TWENTIETH CENTURY

By D. L. SHAW, *Brown-Forman Professor of Spanish American Literature in the University of Virginia*

1. GENERAL

See, as always, the annual Bibliographic Supplements to *BHS(G)*, the 'Recent Articles' section in *RIAB* and the *ModD* annual bibliography for items not included here. For information on periodicals, see the *MLA Directory of Periodicals*, recently in its 8th edition.

GENERAL WORKS. *The Cambridge History of Latin American Literature*, ed. R. González Echevarría and E. Pupo Walker, 3 vols, CUP, xx + 670, 619, 864 pp. (vol. II: *The Twentieth Century*, 619 pp., vol III, 383–739, bibliographies). *Encyclopedia of Latin American Literature*, ed. V. Smith London, Fitzroy Dearborn, 900 pp., a superb handbook. L. Bethell, **Ideas and Ideologies in Latin America since 1870*, CUP, 600 pp. I. Jaksic, 'Anti-technological humanism in 20th century Latin America', *REH*, 30:179–201, tracing it from Alberdi to Enrique Molina. J. Ortega, 'Identidad y postmodernidad en América Latina', *La Torre*, 35, 1995:429–44, seems to be about the need to redefine Latin American identity. F. and A. de Toro, **Borders and Margins. Post-Colonialism and Post-Modernism*, Frankfurt, Vervuert, 1995. P. Hulme, 'La teoría poscolonial', *CAm*, 202:3–8, is vague. S. Colás, 'Of creole symptoms, Cuban fantasies and other Latin American postcolonial ideologies', *PMLA*, 110, 1995:382–96, seeks to understand the term 'postcolonial'. J. Poblete, 'Homogeneización y heterogeneización en el debate sobre la modernidad', *RCLL*, 42, 1995:115–30, applies Kant, Hegel and Habermas to Latin American literature. R. Giesdorfer Feal and Carlos Feal, **Painting on the Page: Interartistic Approaches to Modern Hispanic Texts*, Albany, SUNY U.P., 1995, xxii + 341 pp..

THE AVANT-GARDE. *Palavra, literatura e cultura*, vol. III, *Vanguarda e Modernidade*, ed. A. Pizarro, Campinas, Fundação Memorial, 1995, 750 pp., has articles by major critics. J. Schwartz, **Vanguardas latino-Americanas, polémicas, manifestos e textos críticos*, São Paulo, EDUSPH. 1995. G. Gliemmo, 'Las vanguardias latinoamericanos', *Cuadernos de Marcha*, 109, 1995:71–75, relates the 20s to the 60s.

POETRY. M. Crow, 'El surrealismo latinoamericano', *La Torre*, 34, 1995:193–200, is too slight. G. Yudice, 'Latin American Poetry and Postmodernity', *JILS*, 7, 1995:157–80, is on its departure from vanguardism. R. Sarabia, **Poetas de la palabra hablada: poesía his-panoamericana contemporánea*, London, Támesis, 190 pp. R. Xirau, **Poesía iberoamericana contemporánea*, Mexico D.F., 1995. J. Siles, *La *poesía nueva en el mundo hispánico*, M, Visor, 1994. T. Running, **The Critical Poem: Borges, Paz and Other Language-Centered Poets*, Lewisburg, Bucknell U.P., 192 pp. J. Iffland, **La poesía revolucionaria de Centro-américa*, San José, C.R., Editorial Universitaria, 1994, 309 pp. On FICTION: L. Parkinson Zamora and W. Faris, **Magical Realism*, Durham, Duke U.P., 1995, 592 pp. M. E. Angulo, **Magic Realism*, NY, Garland, 1995, 144 pp. D. K. Danow, **Magical Realism and the Grotesque*, Lexington, Kentucky U.P., 1995, 183 pp. S. Juan-Navarro, 'La ambigua postmodernidad de los novelistas del Boom', *JILS*, 7, 1995:181–205, is on Fuentes and Cortázar. L. A. Griffo González, **Espacio social e ideología del Boom*, M, Universidad Autónoma, 1995. F. Aínsa, 'Nueva novela histórica y relativización del saber historio-gráfico', *CAm*, 202:9–18, relates the two. A. Pulgarín, *La novela histórica en la narrativa hispánica posmodernista*, M, Fundamentos, 1995, 230 pp., has essays on García Márquez and Posse. L. Baer Barr, **Isaac Unbound: Patriarchal Traditions in the Latin American Jewish Novel*, Tempe, Arizona State U.P., 1995, 201 pp. N. García Canclini, 'Narrar la multiculturalidad', *RCLL*, 42, 1995:9–20, applies his theory to contemporary narrative. D. Lagmanovich, 'El microrrelato hispanoamericano', *Chasqui*, 23.1, 1994:29–43, offers a typology.

GENDERED WRITING. **Bodies and Biases, Sexualities in Hispanic Cultures*, ed. D. W. Foster and R. Riess, Minneapolis, Minnesota U.P., 424 pp. (hereafter Foster, *Bodies*). A. Jones and C. Davies, **Latin American Women's Writing*, OUP, 224 pp. M. B. Tierney-Tello, **Experimental Fiction by Women Writing under Dictatorship*, Albany, SUNY U.P., 286 pp. *STLC*, 20.1 is on contemporary women writers including V. Ocampo, Castellanos, Poniatowska, Gambaro, other women dramatists, Giannina Braschi, Morejón, T. Kamenszain, Esquivel, S. Plager, and the feminine fantastic. *La nueva mujer en la escritura de autoras hispánicas*, ed. J. Alcira Arancibia and Y. Rosas, Montevideo, Instituto Literario, 1995, 222 pp., includes 12 essays on Latin American women writers. *ETL*, 24.1–2, is a special number on Hispanic women writers including Cuza Malé, Allende, Lugo Filippi, Morejón, Castellanos, and Cuban and Salvadoran women's poetry. E. M. Martínez, *Lesbian Voices from Latin America*, NY, Garland, 223 pp., discusses M. Alabau, N. Cárdenas, S. Molloy, R. Roffiel, and L. M. Umpierre. A. Gladhart, 'Playing gender', *LALR*, 47:59–89, is on feminism, transvestism etc. in plays by R. Castellanos, S. Berman, and S. Torres Molina.

THEATRE. **Variaciones sobre el teatro latinoamericano*, ed. A. de Torc and K. Pörtl, Frankfurt, Vervuert, 247 pp., another volume in the series. O. Pellettieri and E. Rovner, **La puesta en escena en Latinoamérica* BA, Galerna, 143 pp., seven essays. M. A. Giella, *De dramaturgos: teatr latinoamericano actual*, BA, Corregidor, 1994, 238 pp., has importan interviews with five dramatists and essays on Gambaro, Díaz, Pavlovski and others. I. Watson and S. Epstein, *"Theatre after the dictatorships: developments in Chile and Argentina', *New Theatre Review*, 41, 1995:40–54.

ON MORE THAN ONE COUNTRY/AUTHOR. C. M. Zlotchew, *Voices of the River Plate*, San Bernadino, Evans, 1995, 200 pp., has interviews with Argentine and Uruguayan writers. K. Kohut ed., *Literatura del Río de la Plata hoy*, Frankfurt, Vervuert, 268 pp. has 20 essays on Argentine and Uruguayan literature in the last 20 years. *Culturas del Río de la Plata 1973–95*, ed. R. Spiller, Frankfurt, Vervuert, 1995, 605 pp., has 37 essays on the same. E. G. Kantaris, *Contemporary Women's Narrative from Argentina and Uruguay*, OUP, 264 pp., has chapters on Peri Rossi, Valenzuela, A. Somers, S. Molloy, Roffé, and M. Traba. R. J. Friis, 'Vision of the muse in *Canción de la verdad sencilla* and *Veinte poemas de amor*', *Chasqui*, 23.1, 1994:10–17, sees Julia de Burgos (Puerto Rico) as expanding on Neruda's themes. D. L. Shaw 'Three post-Boom writers and the Boom', *LALR*, 47:5–22, examines the ideas about the Boom of Skármeta, R. Ferré, and G. Sainz. R. García Castro, '*Santa materia* (1954) de B. Subercaseaux [Chile] y *Vida ejemplar del esclavo y el señor* de M. Ramos Otero [Puerto Rico]', *RevIb*, 174:149–61, is on their vision of the male body. J. A. Jaffe, 'Las Casas's *Brevísima relación* and Cortázar's *Apocalipsis en Solentiname*', *Chasqui*, 23.1, 1994:18–28, is on both writers' 'millenary vision'. B. Heller, 'Landscape, femininity and Caribbean discourse', *MLN*, 111:391–416, ranges over L. S. Pedrera, Lezama Lima, Glissant, and R. Ferré on Caribbean landscape. K. Ellis, 'Azúcar y lenguaje en la poesía caribeña', *CAm*, 199, 1995:3–15, a wide survey. M. Pérez de Mendiola, *Bridging the Atlantic: Toward a Reassessment of Iberian and Latin American Cultural Ties*, Albany, SUNY U.P., vi + 227 pp. C. Ruiz Barrionuevo and C. Real Ramos, *La modernidad literaria en España e Hispanoamérica*, Salamanca U.P., 255 pp. *Antipodas* 6–7, 1994–95 [1996], has an interview and five articles on Allende, five articles on Peri Rossi and seven on Valenzuela. P. G. Earle, 'Martínez Estrada y Sábato', *CHA*, 547:51–59, is too discursive. M. E. de Valdés, 'Testimonio and fiction of the Maya', *BHS(L)*, 73:79–90, is on Castellanos and Menchú. M. Manzar Coats, *Borges, Escher, Sarduy*, M, Pliegos, 208 pp. B. Kaiserskern, *Fuentes, García Márques und der Film*, Frankfurt, Vervuert, 1995, 249 pp. *Estudios sobre la narrativa en Francia, España y América Latina*, ed. E. Hofner and K. Schole, Frankfurt, Vervuert, 318 pp., has essays on Cortázar, Borges, Asturias, and others. V. Leñero, *Lotería*, Mexico D.F., Mortiz, 1995, 135 pp., has essays on Arreola, Donoso, Puig, Usigli, Agustín, and others. H. Lavín Cerda, *Ensayos casi ficticios*, Mexico D.F., UNAM, 1995, has essays on Vallejo, Rulfo, García Márquez, Borges, Paz, Neruda, and others.

R. Gutiérrez Girardot, *Cuestiones*, Mexico D.F., FCE, 1994, has essays on Vallejo and A. Reyes. J. Ortega, *Arte de innovar*, Mexico D.F., UNAM, 1994, 487 pp., has essays on Arreola, Rulfo, Boullosa, and Cortázar. S. Spitta, *Narratives of Transculturation in Latin America*, Houston, Rice U.P., 280 pp., includes essays on Arguedas and Garro. *Río de la Plata*, 15–16, is an *Actas*, with more than 50 items on authors including, Posse, Murena, Cortázar, Tizón, Peri Rossi, Sábato, Saer, Borges/Bioy Casares, S. Ocampo, Reyles and many others. *¿Entiendes? Queer Readings, Hispanic Writings*, ed. E. L. Bergman and P. J. Smith, Durham, Duke U.P., 1995, (hereafter Bergman, *Queer Readings*) includes 'queer research' on Pizarnik, Lugo Fillippi, L. R. Sánchez, Piñera, and Mistral.

CRITICISM. J. Beverley, '¿Hay vida más allá de la literatura?', *CAm*, 199, 1995:25–32, same old attack on standard criticism. M.-L. Pratt, 'La heterogeneidad y el pánico de la teoría', *RCLL*, 42, 1995:21–28, is on the challenge of subalternity for literary criticism. A. Brooksbank Jones, 'Towards reciprocity', *JHR*, 3, 1994–95 [1996]:425–40, discusses Latin American feminist criticism, especially that of Debra Castillo. P. D'Allemand, 'A. Losada y la crítica histórico-cultural en Latinoamérica', *ib.*, 353–66, is not nearly critical enough.

2. INDIVIDUAL COUNTRIES

ARGENTINA

D. Viñas, **Literatura argentina y política*, BA, Sudamericana, vol. 2: *De Lugones a Walsh*, 222 pp. H. M. Frazer, 'Lugones' *Yzur*', *His(US)*, 79:8–19, is on the decay of referential language. D. Pardue, 'Lugones y el haikú', *Chasqui*, 23.2, 1944:86–94, is on scarce similarities. J. Schwartz, 'La trayectoria masmedular de O. Girondo', *CHA*, 553–54:217–30, is on his 'vindicación de la palabra'. J. Boccanera, **Viaje por la poesía de J. Gelman*, BA, Sudamericana, 1994, 252 pp. M. del C. Sillato, 'Com/posiciones de J. Gelman', *Hispamérica*, 72, 1995:3–14, comments on his 'translations' and Jewishness. See too her 'Juan Gelman, San Juan de la Cruz y el espíritu de la Cábala', *RCEH*, 20:505–17, on exile and mystical experience in *Citas y comentarios* (1982). J. S. Kuhnheim, 'Una entrevista con Olga Orozco', *NTC*, 16–17, 1995–96:239–68, has a long introduction. Her *Gender Politics and Poetry in 20th Century Argentina*, Gainesville, Florida U.P., x + 201 pp., is chiefly on Orozco and Pizarnik. A. M. Fagundo, *Literatura femenina de España y las Américas*, M. Fundamentos, 1995, 267 pp., has a chapter (209–29) also on Orozco and Pizarnik. L. Evangelista, 'La poesía de A. Pizarnik', *Atenea*, 473:41–51, is too bellelettristic.

FICTION.   G. Marín, '*Olimpio pitango de Monalia* de E. Holmberg', *RevIb*, 174:85–102, introduces this hitherto unpublished vanguardist novel. D. L. Hernández, *Roberto Arlt, B, Montesinos, 1995, 366 pp. See too his **Los Cuentos de Roberto Arlt*, Sta Cruz de Tenerife, Universidad de la Laguna, 1995, 160 pp. *Quimera*, 144, has a 'dossier Roberto Arlt' with a chronology and eight brief articles. J. Riera, 'La novela urbana de Arlt', *QIA*, 78, 1995:44–57, is too introductory. H. Brioso Santos, 'Macedonio Fernández a destiempo', *CAm*, 58:175–89, is obvious on his attack on logic. A. M. Zubieta, **A. Cancela y L. Marechal*, Rosario, Viterbo, 1995.

BORGES.   M. R. Barnatán, **Borges, biografía total*, M, Temas de Hoy, 1995, 519 pp. J. Woodhall, **A Life of J. L. Borges*, London, Hodder, 208 pp. M. E. Vásquez, *Borges, esplendor y derrota*, B, Tusquets, 355 pp., is biographical and gossipy. C. Meneses, 'Presencia de Borges en Mallorca', *QIA*, 78, 1995:20–32, is excellent on his early outlook. *Variaciones Borges* (Aarhus, Denmark), 1 and 2, have seven and 19 articles respectively, a significant journal. E. Ripetto, **Relato y sociedad*, BA, Centro Editor de América Latina, 1994, 107 pp. C. Caeque, **Conversaciones sobre Borges*, B, Destino, 1995, is a symposium. M. Couture, 'Borges in *Orígenes*', *REH*, 30:203–19, describes three essays. R. Ramos Tremolada, 'La morada del poeta', *La Torre*, 34, 1995:349–65, is more on authorship than on Borges. C. Magris, 'Dos aproximaciones a Borges', *CHA*, 548:59–69, is too bellelettristic. L. M. Madrid, 'Borges: el significado versus la referencia', *RevIb*, 174:163–74, nothing new on his view of reality and writing. R. Gutiérrez Girardot, 'La literatura como parodia en Borges', *Hispamérica*, 73:3–13, is discursive and uncritical. T. Ambrose, 'Borges, Foucault, Derrida, una interpretación védica', *La Torre*, 34, 1995:147–66, calls on the Upanishads. R. Zuleta, 'La superación del pesimismo en Borges', *Iberoromania*, 43:139–44, argues that scepticism excludes pessimism. D. Balderston, *'The fecal dialectic' is one of the 'queer readings' in Bergman, *Queer Readings*, 29–45. F. Aínsa, 'Los sueños de Borges y Calvino', *CHA*, 553–54:105–09, is really on Calvino. On his poetry see especially L. Maier, *Borges and the European Avant-Garde*, NY, Lang, 186 pp., a major contribution, and Id., 'Borges's early love poetry', *Chasqui*, 23.2, 1994:48–53, on its relationship to his affair with Concepción Guerrero. L. Madrid, 'Entre los nombres y la repetición: la vanguardia', *JHR*, 3, 1994–95[1996]:339–51, relates Borges' thought to vanguardist aspirations to transcend space, time and language. G. Videla, 'Borges, juez de Góngora', *CHA*, 552:63–70, excellent on his underlying poetic outlook. M. F. Varela, 'Borges entre la palabra y el silencio', *Iberoromania*, 43:126–38, is on his anti-rhetorical stance and view of metaphor. On his prose: R. A. Borello, 'La prosa de Borges', *CHA*,

551:51–60, is too cursory on its development. J. M. Cueta Abad, *Ficciones de una crisis*, M, Gredos, 1995, 270 pp. E. Aizenberg, *Borges, el tejedor del Aleph*, M, Iberoamericana, 168 pp., is on his Jewish affinities. D. Nouhaud, *Examen de la Bibliothèque de Borges, Ficciones, El Aleph*, Limoges U.P., 1995. J. Browitt, 'Borges and Romantic individualism', *Imprévue*, 1995, no.2:81–102, is social criticism of 'El Sur'. H. J. Brant, 'Homoerotic desire in 'La forma de la espada'', *Chasqui*, 25.1:25–38, is another 'queer' reading. N. E. Alvarez, '"El muerto" de Borges', *RevIb*, 174:137–48, obvious on its technique. D. Balderston, 'Borges, Averroes, Aristotle', *His(US)*, 79:201–06, nothing new on 'La busca de Averroes'. N. E. Alvarez, 'Unas acotaciones al texto borgeano', *CH*, 17, 1995:276–85, complains rightly about the state of texts, editions and criticism.

OTHER WRITERS. J. de Navascués, *La narrativa de Bioy Casares*, Pamplona, Emsa, 1995, 139 pp. R. Pellicer, 'La trama fantástica en los últimos cuentos de Bioy Casares', *La Torre*, 35, 1995:445–64, is on its (and his) evolution. G. Tomassini, *La obra cuentística de S. Ocampo*, BA, Plus Ultra, 1995, 137 pp. J. Sanjinés, *Fronteras semióticas en los relatos de Cortázar*, NY, Lang, 1994, xi + 261 pp., long on theory, light on the stories. E. Cedola, *Cortázar*, BA, Edicial, 1994, 98 pp. C. Ortiz, *Cortázar*, BA. Almagesto, 1994, 133 pp. I. Stavans, *Cortázar: A Study of the Short Fiction*, Boston, Twayne, 160 pp. P. Ontañón, *En torno a Cortázar*, Mexico D.F., UNAM, 1995. L. Parkinson Zamora, 'Descifrar las heridas', *NTC*, 16–17:153–75, is on the theme of torture in Cortázar. M. E. Schwartz, 'Cortázar's plural parole', *RoN*, 36:131–37, is on 'metaphysical interstices' in three stories. M. Mosher, 'Los "desespacios" y los "destiempos" en los "Wormholes" de Cortázar', *Hispanófila*, 116:69–82, compares theories from modern physics. S. Aboul-Hosa, 'La Maga as the "central" character in *Rayuela*', *HisJ*, 16, 1995:307–16, is on her deeper vision. J. García Méndez, '*Los premios* de Cortázar', *LNL*, 297:9–18, is on its experimentalism. M. I. Filinisch, 'Continuidad de los parques', *Hispamérica*, 73:113–19, applies Genette. C. Ruiz, 'Fin de etapa', *RCL*, 48:113–19, examines this tale from *Deshoras*. P. J. O'Connor, 'A Benjaminian reading of "El examen"', *LALR*, 46, 1995:5–32, is on its melancholy tone of dissatisfaction. M. S. Fernández Utrera, 'Cortázar y *Libro de Manuel*', *RCEH*, 20:225–40, is on its renovation of the revolutionary novel. N. Riley, *Cannibalism and homage in Cortázar's *The Meneads* and *We Love Glenda so Much*', Hunter, *Short Story*, 145–58. P. Piglia, 'Homenaje a Cortázar', *CAm*, 200, 1995:97–102, is chatty. P. Sánchez López, 'La recepción española de la narrativa de Sábato', *CHA*, 553–54:145–59, gives factual details. S. I. Stein, 'Polysemous perversity and male hysteria in *El túnel*', *BHS(L)*, 73:427–55, is on Castel's mother's responsibility.

C. Basette, **La familia de Pascual Duarte and El túnel [...] the Exercise of Craft*, Lanham, U.P. of America, 1994, 170 pp. M. E. Llorente, 'El "Informe sobre ciegos"', *CHA*, 551:71–94, is very insightful. H. Brant, 'Homoeroticism and homophobia in Denevi's "Michel"', *RLA*, 7, 1995:379–84, is on the story as symbolic of machismo. See too his 'Camilo's closet: sexual camouflage in Denevi's *Rosaura a las diez*', Foster, *Bodies*, 203–16, on Camilo's probable homosexuality. P. Paez, **M. Puig*, BA, Almagesta, 1995, 171 pp. M. Kunz, **La novelística de M. Puig*, Lausanne, SSEH, 1994, 214 pp., apparently works backwards from *Cae la noche tropical*. K. Kulin, **M. Puig*, Budapest, Akademiai, 1995, 154 pp., in Hungarian. B. L. Lewis, 'The reader and Puig', *CH*, 17, 1995:286–92, is on reader-response to *Sangre de amor correspondido*. R. L. Gómez-Lara, **Intertextualidad generativa en El beso de la mujer araña*, Miami, Universal, 170 pp. M. Issacharoff and L. Madrid, 'Puig and Ionesco', *RR*, 87:419–30, is debatable on absence of characterization. G. Riera, 'La ficción de Saer', *MLN*, 111:368–90, is complex on *El entenado* as allegory. R. Gnutzman, 'Bibliografía de y sobre Saer', *Iris*:39–50, most helpful. M. Yáñez, 'Piglia, la inclusión perenne', *CAm*, 201, 1995:90–95, is too general. M. Grzegovczyk, 'Gombrowicz, Piglia y la estética del basurero', *Hispamérica*, 73:15–33, puts *Respiración artificial* into a different context. J. A. Madrazo, 'Entrevista a R. Piglia', *Atenea*, 473:95–107, with handy declarations. S. Regazzoni, 'Il circo grottesco di Haroldo Conti', *RI*, 57: 17–25, is on the creative *compromiso* of *Mascaró* (1975). M. Lemaître, '*Arráncame la vida* de A. Mastretta', *RevIb*, 174:185–97, examines the narrator. M. Giardinelli, '¿Qué se escribe en la Argentina de hoy?', *RO*, 179:134–40, is on his own work and the return to the historical novel. K. V. Stone, 'Mempo Giardinelli and the anxiety of Borges's influence', *Chasqui*, 23.1, 1994:83–90, is chiefly on 'La entrevista' in his *Antología personal*. N. Girona, 'La novela argentina de los 80', *CAm*, 202:19–23, is vague on Eloy Martínez, Piglia, and recent history. M. L. Bastos, 'La ficción de la violencia', *La Torre*, 35, 1995:373–82, describes a handful of examples mostly from the 80s. 'Encuentro', *RO*, 179:79–133 has personal declarations by A. Diaconú, R. Rabanal, and H. Tizón. S. Lorenzano, '*La casa y el viento* de Tizón', *Hispamérica*, 72, 1995:91–99, is on the search for identity. C. Ferreira Pinto, 'La figura materna en *En breve cárcel* de S. Molloy', *RoN*, 36:155–62, is on reconciliation. N. Cristophe, 'The female grotesque in *Cola de lagartija*', *RHM*, 48, 1995:365–80, is on its use to symbolize Argentinian atrocities. D. E. Marting, 'Valenzuela and new realities: *Realidad nacional desde la cama*', *LF*, 22:107–20, is on its sceptical satire. C. R. Perricone, 'Valenzuela's *Novela negra con argentinos*: a metaphysical game', *RoN*, 36: 237–42, sees its theme as literary creativity. V. Martínez, 'In search of the word:

performance in *Novela negra con argentinos*', *Chasqui*, 23.2, 1994:54–64, is on the novel's theatrical elements. A. B. Dellepiane, 'The short stories and novels of Vlady Kociancich', *LF*, 22:77–89, is introductory.

THEATRE. O. Pellettieri edits **De Brecht a Monti: teatro en lengua alemana y teatro argentino*, BA, Galerna, 1995, 136 pp., and, with G. Woodyard, *De O'Neill al 'Happening': teatro norteamericano y teatro argentino*, BA, Galerna, 123 pp., with ten essays by major critics. See too O. Pellettieri, 'El teatro paródico [...] en Buenos Aires, 1970–72', *LATR*, 30.1:33–42, examining three types. N. Glickman and V. Cox, 'Poder inglés en el teatro argentino de principios del siglo xx', *BHS(L)*, 73:255–67. A disguised version of the same has appeared in *HisJ*, 16, 1995, 269–83. M. A. Salgado, 'Las "farsas pirotécnicas" de Alfonsina Storni', *LATR*, 30.1:21–32, is on her feminist re-writes of plays by Euripides and Shakespeare. O. Pellettieri weighs in again with 'El teatro de O. Dragún', *LATR*, 29.2:5–14, on Brechtian influence. M. Contreras, *Griselda Gambaro: teatro de la descomposición*, Concepción U.P., 1994, on family and social decay in her work. N. L. Molmaro, 'Panoptic theatre and Gambaro's *El campo*', *LATR*, 29.2:29–41, applies Foucault. E. J. Neutzel, 'Psychosexual fascism in Gambaro's *Bad Blood*', *ModD*, 39:457–64, is on sexism and sexual abuse. J. Graham-Jones, 'Two productions of *Telarañas* by E. Pavlovsky', *LATR*, 29.2:61–70, examines significant changes. M. Castelví interviews Beatriz Mosquera, *ib.*, 30.1:105–10, on her work and on recent Argentine theatre. A. Pagni, '*Punto de Vista*: Revista de Cultura 1978–93', *NTC*, 16–17:177–89, discusses the evolution of this left-wing review. E. G. Kantoris, 'Argentine cinema after the "Process"', *BHS(G)*, 73:219–44, examines some late 80s films.

BOLIVIA

M. A. Salgado, 'Una lectura maquiavélica de Pedro Shimose', *RHM*, 48, 1995:349–64 comments on his *Reflexiones maquiavélicas* (1980). J. Beverley, 'The real thing', *MLQ*, 57:129–39, is on R. Menchú and *testimonio*. K. Richards, 'Sexuality and death [...] in [...] N. Taboada's *Manchay Puytu*', *JHR*, 3, 1994–95[1996]: 377–85, is on *mestizaje* in this 1977 novel.

CHILE

P. Rubio, *Gabriela Mistral ante la crítica: bibliografía anotada*, Santiago de Chile, Dirección de Bibliotecas, 1995, 437 pp.. covers 1905–95. A. Canseco Jerez, **L'avant-garde chilienne et ses précurseurs: Emar et Huidobro*, Paris, L'Harmattan, 1994, 123 pp. L. A. Perdigo, **The

Origins of Huidobro's Creacionismo, Lewiston, Mellen, 1995, 360 pp.
M. Rodríguez Santibáñez, 'El creacionismo de Huidobro', *CHA*,
556:93–105, is on the role of poetic delirium. A. R. Domenella,
'Huidobro 1934: tres dispares novelas', *CAm*, 58:163–74, comments
descriptively on *Cagliostro*, *Papá* and *La próxima*. M. Jofre, 'El último
poema de P. de Rokha', *Atenea*, 47, 1995:215–18, it is to his daughter
Sandra. P. Martínez, *ib.*, 157–75, presents an interview with
E. Lafourcade and two letters which contribute to Neruda's bio-
graphy. D. Russell, 'Reflections on Neruda's posthumous poems',
RCEH, 20:327–40, on their themes of love and death. J. M. Mount,
'El sobreviviente en las últimas obras de Neruda', *La Torre*, 34,
1995:295–311, is on 'El sobreviviente saluda a los pájaros'. D. G.
Anderson, 'La *Elegía* de Neruda'. *ib.*, 167–74, is on his last poetic
work. M. Gottlieb, 'Parra o el método del discurso', *Atenea*,
473:71–94, is superficial. J. Zapata, **Enrique Lihn*, Curicó (Chile), La
Noria, 1994. O. Sarmiento, 'Entrevista: Jorge Teillier', *Hispamérica*,
73:59–68, has useful material. S. Mansilla, 'Clemente Riedemann y
la temporalidad histórica', *RCL*, 48:39–62, is a political reading.
H. Castellano Girón, 'Fuentes de la poesía de Rosamel del Valle',
Atenea, 473:53–69, shows they were chiefly English, American, and
French.

FICTION. J. Román-Lagunas, *Chilean Novel: Secondary Sources and a
Bibliography*, Metuchen, Scarecrow, 1995, 578 pp. M. J. Orozco, **La
narrativa femenina chilena, 1923–80*, Saragossa, Amibar, 1995, 293 pp.
M. Martin, '*Alsino* y la novela modernista', *RevIb*, 174:71–84, is on its
prophetic vision. M. Rodríguez Fernández, '*El lugar sin límites*', *RCL*,
48:97–100, contains only banal generalities. V. Cortínez, '*Historia
personal del Boom* de Donoso', *RCL*, 48:13–22, emphasizes its universalist approach. J. Olivares, '"Paseo" de Donoso', *MLN*, 37:97–107,
is on the theme of repression. J. Joset, 'Espacio urbano en la trilogía
española de Donoso', *La Torre*, 35, 1995:407–27, is on its illusoriness.
J. M. Hemogodeuc, 'Exilio en *El jardín de al lado*', *Imprévue*, no. 1:57–75,
is on the loss of identity and the search for values. P. Meléndez-Páez,
'El desgaste del exilio en *La desesperanza* de José Donoso', *Chasqui*,
23.2, 1994:66–73, is on the novel's three stages. R. Castillo and
M. L. Fischer, 'Una conversación con Donoso', *RCL*, 48:135–43,
with very important and sad details. B. Schultz-Cruz, **Las inquisiciones
de J. Edwards*, M, Pliegos, 1994, 224 pp.; see too his 'Bibliografía
sobre Jorge Edwards', *Chasqui*, 23.1, 1994:91–107, going up to
December 1982. F. Noguerol, 'La última narrativa de J. Edwards',
QIA, 76, 1994:51–62, is thematic on *Fantasmas de carne y hueso*.
L. Guerra Cunningham, 'Historia y memoria en la narrativa de F.
Alegría', *RCL*, 48:23–38, is on time and imagination. I. Dulfano,
'Polymorphous narrators and kaleidoscopic procedures in *La Casa de*

los Espíritus', *Chasqui*, 23.1, 1994:3–9, examines fragmentation and varied narrative voices. S. Serafín, '*De amor y de sombra*', *RI*, 57:3–15, is rather general on self-masking versus *testimonio*. L. V. Braun, 'Narrative strategies in *La última cancion de Manuel Sendero*', *RCEH*, 20:409–32, is on Dorfman's use of unreality. S. Garabano, '*Vaca sagrada* de Eltit', *Hispamérica*, 73:121–27, is on its dialogue with history. J. Maloof, 'Alienation, incest and metafictional discourse in Eltit's *El cuarto mundo*', *RHM*, 49:107–20, is on its political and feminist defiance. G. Novat, 'El cuarto mundo de Diamela Eltit y *Cristóbal Nonato* de Carlos Fuentes', *Chasqui*, 23.2, 1994:74–85, is really on her feminism. M. L. Pratt, 'Overwriting Pinochet', *MLQ*, 57:151–63, is chiefly on Eltit.

THEATRE. H. A. Ovitt Dabel, 'Trends in contemporary Chilean theatre 1941–88', *SELA*, 39.1, 1995:1–12, deals with both coded and open protest. O. A. Díaz-Ortiz, 'M.A. de la Parra: *Matatangos*', *LATR*, 29.2:43–60, is on its debunking of Gardel. P. Bravo-Elizondo interviews Inés Margarita Stranger on her recent work in *ib.*, 30.1:89–95.

COLOMBIA

J. G. Cobo-Borda, *Historia portátil de la poesía colombiana*, Bogotá, Tercer Mundo, 1995, 315 pp., up to date and informative.

GARCÍA MÁRQUEZ. J. García Usta, *Como aprendió a escribir García Márquez, Medellín, Lealon, 1995, 372 pp. L. F. García Nuñez, *Repertorio crítico sobre García Márquez, Bogotá, Instituto Caro y Cuervo, 1995. R. Fiddian, *Gabriel García Márquez*, London, Longman, 1995, ix + 244 pp., very competent. J. G. Cobo Borda, 'García Márquez: contar cantando', *CHA*, 552:55–61, is on Venezuelan popular music in his work. G. Dopico Black, 'Leyendo las cartas de García Márquez', *BHS(G)*, 73:187–217, is on letters in *El coronel* and *Crónica*. R. K. Anderson, 'La realidad y la destrucción de la línea en *Cien años de soledad*', *ETL*, 25:71–85, is on its subversion of cognition. E. Rahoun and S. Siebarth, 'Critics' responses to incest in *Crónica de una muerte anunciada*', *REH*, 30:433–59, is on Angela's father as the villain. D. M. Koeninger, 'Escape from the Time of the Cholera', *HisJ*, 16, 1995:297–305, is descriptive on love and death. R. A. Kerr, '*Del amor y otros demonios*', *His(US)*, 79:772–80, is on symbolic spaces and related images in the novel.

THEATRE. J. S. Kuhnheim, 'Construction and race in [E. Buenaventura's] *Historia de una bala de plata*', *LATR* 29.2:95–109, is on its use of slavery and racism as metaphors.

CUBA

C. López, 'Poesía cubana actual', *LNL*, 297:51–62, is not very informative. B. Heller, *Contrapuntal Readings in the Poetry of J. Lezama Lima*, Lewisburg, Bucknell U.P., 208 pp. B. Levinson, *Mimesis, History and Revolution in Lezama Lima's American Expression*, Lewisburg, Bucknell U.P., 208 pp. C. Ruiz Barrionuevo, '*Paradiso* de Lezama Lima', *La Torre*, 35, 1995:465–83, is too introductory. L. Rensoli, 'Notas sobre *Paradiso*', *CHA*, 558:29–47, is on Aristotelian influence. L. Campuzano, 'Ultimos textos de una dama', *CAm*, 201, 1995:46–53, is on late works by Dulce María Loynaz. L. O. Collman, '*Juego de dama* de B. Cuza Malé', *La Torre*, 34, 1995:313–27, is on her dissidence. J. Maloof, 'Entrevista: Nancy Morejón', *Hispamérica*, 73:47–58, with useful material. C. Davies, 'National Feminism in Cuba 1900–1935', *MLR*, 91:107–23, examines womens' writing in the period. S. Montero, 'La narrativa femenina cubana 1923–58', *CHA*, 544, 1995:19–42, is also a useful survey. B. Stawicka-Pirecka, 'Carpentier y el diálogo entre vanguardias europeas y barroco latinoamericano', *CAm*, 59:92–99, is on his relation with the painter Wilfredo Lam. R. Richard, 'El tiempo recobrado en *Viaje a la semilla*', *Iris*:133–52, is too elementary. C. Vásquez, 'La Habana en *El acoso*', *CAm*, 202:30–35, is on it as symbolic space. L. Acosta, 'De vuelta sobre *Los pasos perdidos*', *ib.*, 201, 1995:32–45, is too discursive. M. Millington, 'Gender monologue in *Los pasos perdidos*', *MLN*, 111:346–67, castigates it for male-centred discourse. A. Langenhorst, '*La aprendiz de bruja*', *Iberoromania*, 42, 1995:102–16, analyses this 1956 play by Carpentier. A. Cacheiro, '*El mundo alucinante*', *His(US)*, 79:762–71, is on its critique of the Cuban Revolution. R. D. Souza, *G. Cabrera Infante*, Austin, Texas U.P., 200 pp. J. Machover, *G. Cabrera Infante*, Miami, Universal, 151 pp. *Poética de la frialdad: la narrativa de V. Piñera*, ed. F. Valerio-Holguín, Lanham, U.P. of America, 128 pp. G. Guerrero, 'Sarduy o la religión del vacío', *CHA*, 552:33–46, is on his view of nothingness as the basis of the real. J. I. Gutiérrez, '*Gallego* de Barnet', *QIA*, 75, 1994:15–29, is on its synthesis of ethnology, poetry and fiction. A. Pereira, *Novela de la revolución Cubana 1960–90*, Mexico D.F., UNAM, 1995, 292 pp., a survey. R. Fernández-Fernández, *El teatro del absurdo de J. Triana*, SSSAS, 1995, 94 pp. L. Seda, '*Timeball* de Joel Cano', *LATR*, 30.1:5–19, postulates its use of chaos theory. L. Campuzano, 'La revista *Casa de las Américas* 1966–95', *NTC*, 16–17:215–37, is on its consistency.

DOMINICAN REPUBLIC

E. Gimbernat González, 'Poetas dominicanas de hoy', *LF*, 22:143–63, examines a handful of them.

ECUADOR

J. J. Chica, *La novela ecuatoriana 1970–85*, NY, Lang, 1995, x + 193 pp. O.Caro, 'Du réalisme au réalisme social en Equateur', LNL, 297:89–99, too quick a survey. I. Eguez, 'Mestizaje y novela histórica en Ecuador', *CAm*, 199, 1995:16–24, is a survey from the 50s to the 90s. D. V. Galván, 'A. Yañez Cossío en ciencia ficción', *LF*, 22:65–75, is on her 'committed' science-fiction.

GUATEMALA

R. J. Callan, 'Archetypes in stories by Arévalo Martínez', *CH*, 17, 1995:293–301, is Jungian. *RI*, 54, 1995, is a tribute to Asturias with eight articles on lesser-known works. M. Zapata, 'Hibridización y ruptura', *LNL*, 297:117–28, is on Asturias's *El Señor Presidente* as a crossroads novel. F. Noguerol Jiménez, *Satira en A. Monterroso*, Seville U.P., 1995, 252 pp. W.H. Corral, *Monterroso ante la crítica*, Mexico D.F., Era, 1995, 235 pp. M. Fernández Molina, 'La actividad teatral en Guatemala en la primera mitad del siglo xx', *LATR*, 29.2:131–45, is a chapter of literary history. W. Feliciano, *El teatro mítico de C. Solórzano*, Mexico D.F., UNAM, 1995, 257 pp., contains close readings of his plays.

HONDURAS

J. N. Gold, *Clementina Suárez, Her Life and Poetry*, Gainesville, Florida U.P., 1995, 305 pp. E. M. de Costa, 'Teatro La Fragua's liberating Honduran theatre', *LATR*, 29.2:111–30, examines this popular theatre group.

MEXICO

J. L. Martínez and M. Domínguez, *La literatura mexicana del siglo xx*, Mexico D.F., Consejo Nacional, 1995, 285 pp. J. J. Blanco, *Un siglo de escritores mexicanos*, Mexico, Cal y Arena. *CHA*, 549–50, is on modern Mexican culture, with essays on recent fiction, poetry, theatre, cinema, etc. D. J. Anderson, 'Cultural studies and reading culture in 20th century Mexico', *IJHL*, 6–7, 1995:207–35, proposes a 'new' emphasis. A. López González, *Sin imágenes falsas*, Mexico D.F., Colegio de Mexico, 1995, essays on 20th-c. Mexican writers. G. de Beer, *Contemporary Mexican Women Writers*, Austin, Texas U.P., 304 pp. L. Leral, *Breve historia del cuento mexicano*, Puebla U.P., 1995. I. Stavans, *Antiheroes: Mexico and its Detective Novel*, Rutherford, Fairleigh Dickinson U.P., 180 pp., the translation of his 1993 book.

M. del M. Paúl, 'Contemporáneos: la narrativa de un grupo de poetas', *CHA*, 553–54:255–69, is on their renovation of prose in the late 20s. M. K. Long, 'Salvador Novo's *Continente vacío*', *LALR*, 47:91–114, is on this odd, debunking, travel book. R. Medina, 'Paz poeta y Paz ensayista', *RHM*, 49:92–106, is on his self-defences. C. Román-Odio, 'El sujeto dividido de *Piedra de Sol*', *His(US)*, 79:28–35, is on its erotic ambiguity. J. Quiroga, '*Blanco*: una poética del espacio', *La Torre*, 35, 1995:329–47, is on the poem as an 'escenificación del tantrismo'. C. Lafer and H. de Campos, 'Conversación sobre O. Paz', *CHA*, 558:7–27, discuss his reflections on modernity. M. Oliveras Williams, 'El monólogo dramático en la poesía de J. E. Pacheco', *RevIb*, 174:175–84, brings out its Anglo-Saxon origin. R. T. Conn, 'Americanismo andante: Alfonso Reyes and the 30s', *LALR*, 46, 1995:83–98, criticizes his eurocentrism. B. Matamoro, 'La Argentina de A. Reyes', *Atenea*, 472, 1995:69–75, is on his idealistic vision of Latin America. A. Rangel Guerra, 'A. Reyes, teórico de la literatura', *His(US)*, 79:208–14, comments on *El deslinde*. A. Zamora, 'A. Reyes: el intelectual', *HR*, 64:217–36, is too uncritical on *Visión de Anáhuac*. M. Glantz, '*La sombra del caudillo* de M.L. Guzmán', *NRFH*, 43, 1995:163–75, is on its still relevant political metaphor. E. Negrín, **La narrativa de J. Revueltas*, Mexico D.F., Colegio de Mexico, 1995, 310 pp. J.M. Lassus, '*Los días terrenales* de Revueltas', *LNL*, 297:101–16, is on its 'mutilated' central characters. C. Harris, 'A. Yáñez's international image', *BHS(L)*, 73:277–87, calls for a more inclusive perspective. J. Espinosa, **La focalización inconsciente en Pedro Páramo*, M, Pliegos, 172 pp. G. Fares, 'Juan Rulfo: cuestión de fechas', *RevIb*, 174:237–39, establishes his birthdate as 1917. M. S. Jordan, 'Noise and communication in Juan Rulfo', *LALR*, 47:115–30, is on his theme of absence of communication.

FUENTES. R. Sauter, **Del silencio a la palabra*, Frankfurt, Vervuert, 1995, 373 pp. R.L. Williams, **The Writings of Carlos Fuentes*, Austin, Texas U.P., 208 pp., said to be especially good on *Terra Nostra*. See too his 'Fuentes: the reader and the critic', *His(US)*, 79:222–33, on the broad lines of his critical outlook. **Carlos Fuentes*, ed. G. García Gutiérrez, Mexico D.F., Colegio Nacional, 1995, said to be on *Los días enmascarados* and *Cantar de ciegos*. A. Echevarría, 'América y Europa en *Una familia lejana*', *La Torre*, 35, 1995:383–405, is on their interrelationship. S. Juan Navarro, 'La reescritura de la conquista en 'El mundo nuevo' de Fuentes', *RevIb*, 174:103–28, discusses Part II of *Terra Nostra*. M. J. Lemaître, '"La desdichada" de Fuentes', *ETL*, 25:3–11, relates it to Nerval's 'El desdichado'. A. Rivero-Potter, 'Columbus's Legacy in *Cristóbal Nonato*', *RCEH*, 20:306–25, is on the novel as polyphonic and revisionist. W. H. Corral, 'Fuentes's non-fictional prose', *WLT*, 70:267–76, is discursive on his criticism.

OTHER FICTION. T.M. Hertz, 'Carnivalizing the Mexican ethos', *RoQ*, 43:31–44, is on the prose of J. Ibargüengoitia. D. Shaw, 'Jesusa [... in ...] Poniatowska's *Hasta no verte Jesús mío*', *BHS(L)*, 73:191–204, is on her complexity. M. Vargas, 'Power and resistance in *De noche vienes*', *HisJ*, 16.2, 1995:285–96, is too descriptive. A. González, 'Entrevista con Ignacio Solares', *Chasqui*, 23.2, 1994: 112–24, has useful declarations. K. A. Nance, 'The riddle-contest in Paulo de Carvalho-Neto's *Mi tío Atahualpa*', *ib.*, 23.1, 1994: 60–67, is on deconstruction of *indigenismo* in this 1972 novel. R. Etchegoyen, '*Como agua para chocolate*', *CHA*, 547:119–25, is (again) on cooking. J. F. Cammarata, '*Como agua para chocolate*', *ETL*, 25:87–103, is too descriptive on plot. C. Ortiz, '*Como agua para chocolate*, manera de hacerse', *LF*, 22:121–30, is on its complex feminism. K. M. Glenn, 'Postmodern parody and culinary narrative art in *Como agua para chocolate*', *Chasqui*, 23.2, 1994:39–47, is on its parody of pop-fiction. P. Bacarisse, 'The two novels of Josefina' Vicens', *LF*, 22:91–106, is on their theme of ontological insecurity. D. A. Castillo, 'Reading loose women reading', *MLQ*, 57:289–303, is on prostitution in Antonia Mura's *Del oficio* (1972). S. M. Smith 'Reflexiones sobre la identidad en *Las posibilidades del odio*', *Chasqui*, 23.1, 1994:75–82, is on national and personal identity in M. L. Puga's 1978 novel.

THEATRE. I. Pertusa, 'Las realidades mágicas en el teatro de Elena Garro', *ETL*, 25:105–15, is on the characters' sense of the marvellous. H. Ceballos, *Hugo Arguelles, Mexico D.F., Gaceta, 1994. P. Beardsell, 'Three plays by Hugo Salcedo', *LATR*, 29.2:71–84 is on real and symbolic migration. S. Magnarelli, 'S. Berman's *Entre Villa y una mujer desnuda (1943)*', *LATR*, 30.1:55–74, is on gender-identity in the play.

NICARAGUA

E. Waters Hood and C. Ojeda, 'Entrevista con Gioconda Belli', *Chasqui*, 23.2, 1994:125–32, contains comments on the Nicaraguan literary scene. S. Daydí-Tolson, 'Correspondencia entre Cardenal y Thomas Merton', *REH*, 30:393–432, prints interesting letters by Cardenal 1959–68. A. Kaminski, 'Intertextuality and defiance in M. Najlis's *Cantos de Ifigenia*', *LALR*, 46, 1995:48–65. R. McCallister, 'El jaguar y la luna', *La Torre*, 34, 1995:273–93, examines this poem by P. A. Cuadra.

PANAMA

E. Birmingham-Pokorny, *Critical Perspectives in E. Jaramillo-Levi's Work*, Miami, Universal.

PARAGUAY

R. Cornejo-Parriego, '*Vigilia del almirante* de A. Roa Bastos', *RCEH*, 20:449–62, is on history versus fiction. A. Albónico, '*Contravida* de Roa Bastos', *RI*, 57: 27–35, is destructive on Roa's new novel (1995). B. Partyka, 'La silenciosa voz femenina en la literatura paraguaya', *Hispamérica*, 73:35–45, surveys its emergence. G. da Cunha-Giabbai, 'Ecofeminismo latinoamericano', *LF*, 22:51–63, introduces R. Ferrer's *Desde el encendido corazón del monte* (1994).

PERU

L. F. Alarco, *Tres autores: Mariátegui, Arguedas, Adán*, Lima, Amauta, 1995, 121 pp. J. Flo, 'Acerca de algunos borradores de Vallejo', *NTC*, 16–17:93–127, verbose but with interesting material. G. Brotherston and N. Gómez, '"Telúrica y magnética" de Vallejo', *CHA*, 548: 109–19, comment on this late poem. M. Miller, 'Vallejo: the poetics of dissent', *BHS(G)*, 73:299–321, tries for a 'new' critical position. J. Coaguilera, *J. R. Ribeyro*, Lima, Campodonico, 1995, 132 pp. C. Arroyo Reyes, 'Valdelomar y el movimiento colonialista', *CHA*, 557:83–95, is on their foundational role. P. Archibald, 'Orality and literacy in Arguedas', *JILS*, 6, 1994:49–72, is on his unthinkable thoughts about Peruvian culture. S. Spitta, 'El mestizo en la obra de J. M. Arguedas', *His(US)*, 72, 1995:15–26, is too superficial. P. Elmore, '*Los ríos profundos* de Arguedas: las lecciones de la memoria', *RHM*, 49:76–91, treats it as a *Bildungsroman*. J. A. Jiménez Micó, 'J. M. Arguedas y la modernidad', *RCEH*, 20:241–65, is on modernity in *Todos los sangres*. J. O'Bryan-Knight, *The Story of the Storyteller*, Amsterdam, Rodopi, 1995, iv + 195 pp., covers *La tía Julia, Historia de Mayta* and *El hablador*, applying Bahktin. M. Valdés Moses, *The Novel and the Globalization of Culture*, NY, OUP, 1995, 262 pp., includes an essay on Vargas Llosa's *The War at the End of the World*. J. L. Geddes, 'Community and conversion in Vargas Llosa's *The Storyteller*', *Literature and Theology*, 10:370–77, is on masking and unmasking in author, narrator and reader. F. Reati, 'Erotismo e historia en *Elogio de la madrastra*', *QIA*, 78, 1995:33–43, is on the novel's pessimism. M. Krakusin, *La novelística de Bryce Echenique*, M, Pliegos, 208 pp. R. M. Porras León, 'El humor y su texto en *La vida exagerada de Martín Romaña*', *Imprévue*, no. 1:29–56, is mechanical and humourless. I. P. Márquez, '*Crónica de músicos y diablos* de Gregorio Martínez', *Chasqui*, 23.1, 1994:53–59, introduces this 1991 novel. N. Vilanova, 'Dinámica de la narrativa peruana reciente', *BHS(L)*, 73:289–96, is a useful survey. G. Portocarrero et al., **La aventura de Mariátegui*, Lima, Universidad Católica, 1995, 592 pp.

PUERTO RICO

J. Marzán, **The Poetry of Palés Matos*, Rutherford, Fairley Dickenson U.P., 1995, 199 pp. M. Kerkhoff, 'Entrevista con Ana Lydia Vega', *La Torre*, 36, 1995:573–610, with useful declarations. J. Perivolaris, 'Subjectivity in L. R. Sánchez's *Quintuples* (1985)', *JHR*, 3, 1994–95:397–414, is on its ambiguous Puerto Ricanness. S. S. Hintz, **Rosario Ferré*, NY, Lang, 1995, x + 276 pp. C. S. Rivera, 'The doll on *Papeles de Pandora*', *Chasqui*, 23.2, 1994:95–101, is on female rebellion. L. S. Zee, 'Rosario Ferré's "La muñeca menor" and Caribbean myth', *ib.*, 102–11, is on the use of Taino elements. J. A. Jaffe, 'Ferré's *Maldito amor* and *Sweet Diamond Dust*', *LALR*, 46, 1995:66–82, is on her emendations to the translation. M. J. Bustos Fernández, 'Subversión de la autoridad narrativa en *Maldito amor* de Rosario Ferré', *Chasqui*, 23.2, 1994:22–29, is on its parody of authorial authority. J. Hoeg, 'F. Contreras Castro's *Unica mirando el mar*', *RCEH*, 20:491–504, is on its subversion of reality. C. L. Montañez interviews R. Ramos-Perea, *LATR*, 30.1:97–104, on his work in the theatre and his ideas.

EL SALVADOR

F. Jaeger, '*Historias prohibidas de pulgarcito* de R. Dalton', *CAm*, 203:108–15, is on his innovative technique. D. García, 'De la poesía a la política', *La Torre*, 34, 1995:243–60, is on Dalton's poetic stance.

URUGUAY

F. Lucio, 'Del erotismo a la desolación', *Quimera*, 142, 1995:42–46, is on the centenary of J. de Ibarbourou. J. Girón Alvarado, **Voz poética y máscaras femeninas en Delmira Agustini*, NY, Lang, 1995, 238 pp. Y. López, 'Delmira Agustini, sus lectores iniciales', *La Torre*, 34, 1995:261–77, is on the critical reception of her early work. A. Beaupied, 'Otra lectura de 'El Cisne' de Delmira Agustini', *LF*, 22:131–42, is on its paradoxical feminism. J. Berry-Bravo, 'Poemas de amor de I. Villarino', *La Torre*, 34, 1995:175–89, examines 'No te amaba' and 'Carta I'. A. Bergero, 'Detrás de *Disparates entretenidos*',

NTC, 16–17:191–213, relates them vaguely to Hernández's socio-political outlook. F. Graziano, **Gaze and Sexual Rituals in Felisberto Hernández*, Lewisburg, Bucknell U.P., 280 pp. See too his 'Tocar el piano, tocar la mujer', *RevIb*, 174:129–35, on music and femininity in Hernández. M. L. Fischer, 'F. Hernández o el arte de la memoria', *ETL*, 25:63–70, is on 'la maneabilidad de los recuerdos'. C. Cana-pero, 'The economy of space in the short stories of Quiroga', Hunter, *Short Story*, 71–85, is on the settings in *Los exiliados*. H. J. Verani, 'Onetti: la aventura de la escritura', *NRFH*, 43, 1995:125–44, is too introductory. J. Maloof, 'Male subjectivity and gender relations in *El pozo*', *Chasqui*, 23.1, 1994:44–52, is feminist on Linacero's misogyny. B. L. Lewis, 'Metonomic metafiction in Onetti', *HR*, 64:491–506, comments on four works. J. A. Rosado, '*Para esta noche* of Onetti', *LALR*, 46, 1995:33–47, sees it as an allegorical *novela negra*. E. Fish-burn, '"La inmigrante" de Armonía Somers', *JHR*, 3, 1994–95:367–76, is on its breaking of taboos. G. Pérez-Sánchez, 'Entrevista: Cristina Peri Rossi', *Hispamérica*, 72, 1995:59–72, gets answers to impertinent questions. M. Riera, 'Entrevista: Cristina Peri Rossi', *Quimera*, 151:15–24, has useful declarations. *NTC*, 16–17, has an interview and six articles on Mario Levrero. R. Mandressi, 'Nacionalismo teatral en la historiografía uruguaya del teatro', *LATR*, 29.2:147–64, criticizes it. J. Cordones-Cook, 'El teatro negro uruguayo de A. Castillo', *ib.*, 85–94, is very descriptive. A. Blasi, 'Valery Larbaud y las letras uruguayas', *Symposium*, 49:243–49, a survey. P. D'Allemand, 'Ángel Rama: el discurso de la transculturiza-ción', *NTC*, 16–17:133–51, is uncritical on his criticism.

VENEZUELA

A. Hidalgo, **La novela moderna en Venezuela*, NY, Lang, 192 pp. J. Castro Urioste, 'Poder y resistencia en *Doña Bárbara*', *ETL*, 25:41–49, is on its self-subversion. R. González Echevarría, '*Cañaima* y los libros de la selva', *CAm*, 201, 1995:22–31, is on Gallegos as the great precursor. F. Aínsa,'*La isla de Robinsón* de A. Uslar Pietri', *Hispamérica*, 72, 1995:101–10, is on history and utopia. J. Miranda, 'El cuento breve en Venezuela' *CHA*, 555:85–93, suggests that 'El osario de Dios' by A. Armas (1969) is a turning point.

BRAZILIAN LITERATURE

By Mark Dinneen, *Spanish, Portuguese and Latin American Studies,*
University of Southampton

1. General

R. R. Mautner Wasserman, *Exotic Nations: Literature and Cultural Identity
in the United States and Brazil 1830–1930*, Ithaca, Cornell U.P., 1994,
288 pp., looks at the discourse of the exotic, from its origins in colonial
writing, through to its development in romanticism, with reference to
Alencar, and culminating in its use by Mário de Andrade to redefine
national identity in *Macunaíma*. The work seeks to show how European
views of the exotic in the Americas were reformulated by U.S. and
Brazilian writers in order to create an original expression of national
culture. Sérgio Buarque de Holanda, *O espírito e a letra*, SPo,
Companhia das Letras, 2 vols, 419, 679 pp., is a collection of H.'s
critical studies which were previously published in journals. Volume
1 includes those articles written between 1920 and 1947, with notable
studies on Modernism and, especially, Mário de Andrade, whilst
volume 2 contains essays from 1948 to 1959 on a wide range of
writers, including Vieira and Romero. Id., *Livro dos prefácios*, SPo,
Companhia das Letras, 430 pp., gathers together the prefaces H.
wrote for books by other authors. Literature is covered in the final
section, with essays on Gonçalves de Magalhães, Lima Barreto, and
Manuel Bandeira, among others. Lígia Militz da Costa, *Ficção
brasileira: paródia, história e laberintos*, Santa Maria, Univ. Federal de
Santa Maria, 1995, 118 pp., uses various paradigms to study seven
authors, including Machado de Assis, Mário de Andrade, Roberto
Bittencourt Martins, and Chico Buarque de Holanda. J. Marchetti
Polinesio, *O conto e as classes subalternas*, SPo, Annablume, 1994,
333 pp., suffers from too broad a coverage. It examines a series of
Italian and Brazilian short story writers, including Machado de Assis,
Rubem Fonseca, Mário de Andrade, and Simões Lopes Neto to study
the ways in which the marginalized sectors of society are represented
in their work. H. Barbosa Filho, *Os desenredos da criação*, Paraíba,
UFPB, 228 pp., attempts to assess recent literary activity in the state
of Paraíba through studies on 15 prose writers and 15 poets from the
region. Those covered include Aldo Lopes, Ricardo Soares, and
Sérgio de Castro Pinto. E. J. Palti, 'Imaginación histórica e *identidad
nacional* en Brasil y Argentina: un estudio comparativo', *RevIb*,
62:47–69, reviews the discussion on the question of national identity
in writers such as Alencar, Gonçalves de Magalhães, and Alberto
Torres to highlight similarities and differences with the corresponding

debate in Argentine literature. L. R. Velloso Cairo, 'Do florilégio à antologia da poesia brasileira da invenção: uma reflexão sobre a paradigma da história da literatura brasileira', *Procs* (Brasília), 1285–92, looks at the development of histories of Brazilian literature, highlighting the work of Cândido, Coutinho, and Haroldo de Campos in breaking with the pattern which had prevailed since the 19th century. E. Ribeiro Pires Vieira, '*Nudity versus royal robe*: signs in rotations from (in)culture to (in)translation in Latin America', McGuirk, *Brazil*, 1–15, discusses post-colonial translation theory to examine how new translations of literary works, free from colonial or neo-colonial schemes of thought, can be produced. W. Martíns, 'Brazilian literature in the nineties', *Review: Latin American Literature and Arts*, 53:5–7, is a brief overview of current Brazilian literature that serves as an introduction to a series of extracts from the work of new writers.

2. COLONIAL

J. A. Ruedas de la Serna, *Arcádia: tradição e mudança*, SPo, USP, 1995, 179 pp., attempts a new interpretation of the Brazilian movement by studying it in relation to arcadianism in Portugal. The contradictions of *arcadismo* are emphasized, with particular attention given to T. A. Gonzaga and Correia Garção. L. C. Villalta, 'Gonzaga or the reverse of *fanfarrão*: the power of language and the language of power', McGuirk, *Brazil*, 70–82, attempts a new reading of Gonzaga's *Cartas chilenas* to discuss the relationship between history and fiction, and between language and power. M. R. Amoroso, 'On the portrayal of indians in the colonial epic: *Muhuraida* or *The Triumph of the Faith*', *ib.*, 113–24, examines how literature constructs the history and culture of the Brazilian indian through a study of the poem written by Wilkens in 1785 on the suppression of the Mura Indians. A. J. Saraíva, *O discurso engenhoso: ensaios sobre Vieira*, L, Gradiva, 179 pp., studies the structure, style and use of language in V.'s sermons in a collection of essays previously published individually in French. G. V. de Sousa, *'Theatrics and politics of culture in sixteenth-century Brazil', *Journal of Dramatic Theory and Criticism*, 8.2, 1994:89–102. P. Fonseca, 'Caminha e a *carta* de "achamento" do Brasil: ideário e estratégias narrativas, confrontados em Colombo', *LBR*, 33.1:99–120, compares the underlying ideology of the writing of Caminha and Columbus, identifying similarities in both thematic content and form. M. Silva, 'Gregório de Matos: paródia como transtextualização', *ib.*, 121–30, examines M.'s poetry in the light of Hutcheon's theory of parody, and highlights links between M.'s work and that of Camões. M. T. Pinto Cavalcante, 'Gregório de Matos: a voz do Brasil em busca de autonomia', *Procs* (Brasília), 1363–67, identifies ideological traits in M.'s satirical poetry which differentiate it from the work of major European poets of the period, and mark it out as a distinctly Brazilian literary expression. Presenting a counterview is L. H. S. Costigan, 'Colonial literature and social reality in Brazil and the Viceroyalty of Peru: the satirical poetry of Gregório de Matos and Juan del Valle y Caviedes', pp. 87–100 of *Coded Encounters: Writing, Gender and Ethnicity in Colonial Latin America*, ed. F. J. Cevallos-Candau et al., Amherst, Univ. of Massachusetts Press, 1994, 298 pp., which argues that, though M. broke with the formal literary conventions of colonial Brazil by employing popular oral language in his poetry, his work reveals the conservative ideology of the dominant classes, and that it is therefore misleading to interpret it as pre-nationalist or revolutionary. M. F. Soares and T. B. Baumann, *'A construção do outro através do uso da língua indígena: o teatro de Anchieta', *Revue d'Ethnolinguistique Amerindienne*, 19–20, 1995:301–12.

3. THE NINETEENTH CENTURY

E. P. Bueno, *Resisting Boundaries: The Subject of Naturalism in Brazil*, NY, Garland, 1995, 198 pp., studies novels by Aluísio Azevedo, Júlio Ribeiro, Adolfo Caminha, and Manoel de Oliveira to show how such works reveal the tensions, divisions and conflicts within Brazilian society at the end of the 19th c., when a homogeneous national identity was being ideologically constructed. P. B. de Castro, *De la Peninsular hacia Latinoamérica: el naturalismo social en Emilio Pardo-Bazán, Eugenio Cambaceres y Aluísio de Azevedo*, NY, Lang, 1994, 153 pp. R. Schwartz, 'The historical meaning of cruelty in Machado de Assis', *MLQ*, 7.2: 165–179, is a translation of a chapter from his *Um mestre na periferia do capitalismo: Machado de Assis*, SPo, Duas Cidades, 1990. The article focuses on *Memórias póstumas de Brás Cubas* to examine M.'s treatment of class conflict in 19th-c. Brazilian society. G. Pinheiro Passos, *A poética do legado: presença francesa em 'Memórias póstumas de Brás Cubas'*, SPo, Annablume, 158 pp. R. Krueger, 'The first collection of Brazilian slave texts: its interdisciplinary and international importance', *Procs* (Brasília), 938–43, briefly discusses some of the few published texts written by Brazilian slaves on their experience. R. Villela Cavaliera, 'Influência e intertextualidade em *Lucíola* (José de Alencar)', *ib.*, 976–81, studies the links between *La Dame aux camélias* by Dumas *fils* and A.'s novel of 1862. P. Puntoni, *'A confederação dos Tamoyos* de Gonçalves de Magalhães: a poética da história e a historiografia do Imperio', *NovE*, 45:119–30, argues that though the poem is mediocre in terms of literary quality, it is highly significant for Brazilian historiography.

4. TWENTIETH CENTURY

POETRY

T. Acona Lopez, *Marioandradiando*, SPo, Hucitec, 127 pp., is an important study of the work of Mário de Andrade. The seven essays it contains, covering diverse aspects of his verse, his studies on folklore, and his prose, including *Mucunaíma*, serve to emphasise A.'s versatility. M. Marcondes de Moura, *Murilo Mendes: a poesia como totalidade*, SPo, USP, 1995, 204 pp., is a detailed study of the imagery and techniques of M.'s poetry which seeks to demonstrate how it achieves considerable originality through the fusion of diverse and sometimes contradictory elements. At a broader level, it also attempts to assess the poet's contribution to the development of modern Brazilian poetry. E. de Almeida Pereira, 'Contemporary Brazilian poetry: invention and freedom in the Afro-Brazilian cultural tradition', *JLACS*, 5.2:139–54, examines the ways in which the concerns of the black community are debated within the different currents of modern Afro-Brazilian poetry. S. Santiago, 'The course of literary modernity in Brazil', *ib.*, 175–82, briefly assesses the legacy of the Modernist movement in order to highlight major characteristics of Brazilian literary production in recent decades. W. Lopes, *Bandeira: estrela permanente no céu Pasárgada*, Recife, Comunitarte, 103 pp., is a brief study in homage to the poet, examining how the circumstances of his life, such as ill health, marked his work. J. Batista B. de Brito, *Signo e imagem em Castro Pinto*, Paraíba, UFPB, 1995, 279 pp., analyses in detail the work of the Paraiban poet, using the theories of Michael Riffaterre and Gaston Bachelard. C. Richardson-Durham, **The beat of a different drum: resistance in contemporary poetry by Afro-Brazilian women', *Afro-Hispanic Review*, Columbia, 14.2, 1995:21–26. Margaret R. Parker, *The Story of a Story across Cultures: The Case of the 'Doncella Teodor'*, London, Támesis, 149 pp., includes reference to Brazilian *cordel* versions of *Donzela Teodora* in a study of this widely diffused popular story which attempts to reach an understanding of its lasting popularity within the contexts of different cultures. I. M. Fonseca dos Santos, 'Voz, memória, identidade: cantos tradicionais de mulheres brasileiras', *Procs* (Brasília), 1150–57, discusses the construction of female identity in Brazilian popular literature, and the role of women within that tradition. N. Novaes Coelho, 'A poesia feminina na América latina da primeira metade do século: Cecíla Meireles (Brasil), Gabriela Mistral (Chile), Juana de Ibarbourou (Uruguai)', *ib.*, 1215–21, discusses the concern with spiritual values in the work of the three poets. A. M. Lisboa, 'Uma leitura de *Solombra* de Cecília Meireles', *ib.*, 1238–44, examines M.'s use of imagery, rhythm and metre. M. N. Soares Fonseca, 'Paisagens com árvore e arco-íris', *ib.*, 1311–16, is a comparative study of the poetry of Edimilson Almeida Pereira and that of the Haitian, René Depestre. J. M. Parker, 'João Cabral: 45 ou cai(u) fora?', *ib.*, 1326–31, discusses whether Melo Neto can legitimately be considered a member of the 1945 Generation. M. L. Gonçalves Balestriero, 'Modernidade em Mário Faustino', *ib.*, 1332–37, focuses on the tension between intuition and rationality in F.'s poetry. R. Mata Sandoval, '*Transblanco*: una apropiación creativa de Octavio Paz por Haroldo de Campos', *ib.*, 1380–85, discusses C.'s interest in P.'s work, focusing on his translation into Portuguese of one particular poem, *Blanco*. M. R. Duarte de Oliveira, 'Tarsiwald: diálogos entre telas e textos', *ib.*, 747–51, outlines the development of Oswald de Andrade's *Pau-Brasil* and *Antropofagia* poetry alongside the painting of Tarsila do Amaral. On the same theme, V. Dantas, 'Entre *A negra* e a mata virgem', *NovE*, 45:100–16, seeks to shed light on the development of Modernist ideas by examining the relations between Oswald de Andrade, Mário de Andrade, and Tarsila do Amaral in the early 1920s. H. de Campos, 'Oswald de Andrade: from concealment to exposition', McGuirk, *Brazil*, 198–210, highlights A.'s crucial role in Brazilian Modernism through a brief review of his theories and poetry.

DRAMA

A. Gouveia de Araújo, *Os homens cordiais: apresentação da violência oficial na literatura dramática brasileira pós-64*, Paraíba, UFPB, 170 pp., is a valuable and well-argued study of a difficult period for the Brazilian theatre. It focuses on plays by Dias Gomes, Jorge Andrade, and Millôr Fernandes in order to examine how the dramatists treat the issue of state violation of human rights during the military dictatorship. L. H. Damasceno, *Cultural Space and Theatrical Conventions in the Works of Oduvaldo Vianna Filho*, Detroit, Wayne State U.P, 290 pp., is a translation of his *Espaço cultural e convenções teatrais na obra de Oduvaldo Vianna Filho*, Campinas, UNICAMP, 1994. It offers the most complete study yet produced of the work of V.F., covering in detail the development of his career as a playwright and drama theoretician, but is also valuable for the information provided on the responses of the Brazilian theatre to the social and political turbulence experienced by the country in the 1960s and 70s. R. Anderson, 'The muses and the destruction of *Arena contra Zumbi*', *LATR*, 29.2:15–28, seeks to show how Boal's play of 1965 broke with the broadly realist code which had orientated his work in the theatre until then. G. Ravetti and S. Rojo, 'Maria Adelaide Amaral ou a crise da classe média brasileira', *ib.*, 30.1:43–54, considers five plays by the dramatist, only one of which has been published, focusing on their common theme of middle-class frustration and alienation. D. S. George, '*Encenador* Gerald Thomas's *Flash and Crash Days*: Nelson Rodrigues without words', *ib.*, 75–88, studies the work of G.T. to show how the director-designer has become a major creative force in the contemporary Brazilian theatre. A. J. Lappin, 'Parody and piety in the *Auto da compadecida*', *PortSt*, 12:145–57, highlights the importance within Suassuna's play of the communal values central to traditional backlands catholicism. E. Szoka, **A Semiotic Study of Three Plays by Plínio Marcos*, NY, Lang, 1995, 150 pp.

PROSE

Nelson H. Vieira, *Jewish Voices in Brazilian Literature: a Prophetic Discourse of Alterity*, Gainesville, U.P. of Florida, 256 pp., is a well-researched and informative study of the work of Lispector, Samuel Rawet, and Moacyr Scliar, which is chiefly concerned with the issues of race and cultural difference raised by the writers. It argues that, in different ways, their work obliges the reader to confront Brazil's multicultural and multiracial nature, which has been concealed by continual efforts to create an image of a socially integrated and culturally harmonious society. L. B. Barr, *Isaac Unbound: Patriarchal Tradition in the Latin American Novel*, Tempe, Arizona State U. P., 201 pp., includes Moacyr Scliar in the writers studied in an exploration of the representation of Jewish culture and experience in the Latin American novel. Marta Peixoto, *Passionate Fictions: Gender, Narrative and Violence in Clarice Lispector*, Minneapolis, Minnesota U.P., 1994, 116 pp., offers an original analysis of a range of L.'s work, centring on a critique of Hélène Cixous's earlier interpretations. G. Pontiero, 'Clarice Lispector: dreams of language', pp. 271–89 of *A Dream of Light and Shadow: Portraits of Latin American Women Writers*, ed. M. Agosin, Albuquerque, New Mexico U.P., 1995, 324 pp., presents a survey of L.'s life and literary career, highlighting her experimentation with language as one of her major achievements. S. T. Walden '*Grande Sertão: veredas*: de dragão a Brasilidade', *LBR*, 33.1:131–41, discusses the significance of symbolism in Rosa's novel, within the context of the debate on cultural identity in Brazilian literature. N. Lindstrom, 'Narrative experiment and social statement: Helena Parente Cunha', *ib.*, 141–50, examines P.C.'s creative writing in order to study how the author reconciles her preoccupation with the nature of writing with the presentation of social issues, especially those relating to women. *RCF*, 15.3, 1995, contains a number of short essays on the work of Osman Lins. Mary L. Daniel, 'Ethnic love/hate in the *inéditos* of Lima Barreto', *His(US)*, 79:389–99, looks at the way in which L.B.

confronts racial issues in Brazil at the turn of the century, through reference to his novels and personal diaries. S. A. Reily, '*Macunaíma's* music: national identity and ethnomusicological research in Brazil', pp. 71–96 of *Ethnicity, Identity and Music: The Musical Construction of Place*, ed. M. Stokes, Oxford, Berg, 1994, 212 pp., discusses Mário de Andrade's interest in Brazilian popular music and how *Macunaíma* has provided inspiration for composers seeking to produce a distinctly national musical expression. Z. Nunes, 'Anthropology and race in Brazilian Modernism', pp. 115–25 of *Colonial Discourse/Postcolonial Theory*, ed. F. Barker et al., Manchester,. MUP, 1994, 288 pp., re-examines Modernist thinking on race by studying *Macunaíma* within the context of anthropological writing in Brazil in the 1920s. S. G. T. Vasconcelos, 'The magic of words: João Guimarães Rosa and the backlands', *PortSt*, 12:158–70, considers how R. experiments with language in order to deal with the dichotomy between the formal prose of the erudite writer and the popular language of the backlands. M. Dinneen, *Listening to the People's Voice*, London, Keegan Paul, 296 pp., focuses on the novels of Ariano Suassuna, studied within the context of nationalist and regionalist thought, to examine the ways in which the author assimilates expressions of popular culture, especially *literatura de cordel*, into his writing. A. Prysthon, 'Diogo Mainardi and the postmodern Brazilian narrative', McGuirk, *Brazil*, 163–71, highlights the humour, parody and mannerism in M.'s novels of the late eighties and nineties. E. de Assis Duarte, *Jorge Amado: Romance em tempo de utopia*, RJ, Record, 277 pp., is a perceptive examination of the novels of social criticism which A. published between 1931 and 1954, demonstrating how the author's work developed during the period as a result of the consolidation of his political commitment and changes in his approach towards form. A. Mendonça Sampaio, *Jorge Amado, o romancista*, SPo, Maltese, 103 pp., is a concise survey of A.'s novels, highlighting the main characteristics of each. There is little critical analysis, but it serves as a useful introduction to the author's work. M. C. Coelho and M. T. Azinheira, *Jorge Amado: Capitães de areia*, L, Europa-America, 72 pp., is a basic guide to the novel aimed at undergraduate students. R. M. Levine, 'The cautionary tale of Carolina Maria de Jesús', *LARR*, 29:1,1994: 55–81, is a fascinating account of the life of a black *favelada* whose published diary became a bestseller in the 1960s. L. argues that the disdain shown for her work by the literary establishment reveals the deeply-lying prejudices about race and class that exist in Brazilian society. L. F. Valente, 'Reflexões sobre o novo romance histórico brasileiro', pp. 77–96 of *Proceedings of the Brazilian Studies Association: First Conference*, ed. A. E. Riedringer, Albuquerque, Brazilian Studies Association, 1994, 269 pp., examines the relationship between historiography and the work of Márcio Souza, J. Ubaldo Ribeiro, and M. Scliar. J. M. Wisnik, 'La gaya ciencia: literatura y música popular en Brasil', *RO*, 174, 1995:53–72, discusses the adaptation of literature for popular music, with reference to Guimarães Rosa. S. Frankl Sperber, 'Literaturas populares e tradições: permanência e aproveitamento pelas literaturas eruditas', *Procs* (Brasília), 1140–45, discusses the role of myth in Mário de Andrade's *Macunaíma* and Ramos's *São Bernardo*. M. M. Gonzalez, 'O discurso da neopicaresca brasileira', *ib.*, 1202–06, considers the role of the picaresque in novels by Suassuna, Scliar, Sabino, and Márcio Souza, among others. Elódia Xavier, 'A narrativa de autoria feminina dos anos oitenta: a mulher em crise', *ib.*, 1222–27, refers to Patrícia Bins, Lya Luft, Márcia Denser, and Sonia Coutinho in a discussion of how women writers dealt with issues of female identity in the 1980s. C. Schwantes, 'Escrita feminina no Brasil hoje', *ib.*, 1228–31, considers work by Jamardo Failace, H. Jobim, Luft and Denser within the light of French and Anglo-American feminist literary theory in an attempt to identify key features which characterize contemporary women's writing. M. B. S. Assaf Bacha, 'Brasília: os descaminhos da utopia na obra de Darcy Ribeiro', *ib.*, 1181–85, discusses the ways in which R.'s work, especially *Maíra*, questions concepts of utopia in Brazil. T. R. Costa Serra, 'The mythological structure in *Augusto Matraga's Hour and Turn* by João Guimarães Rosa', *ib.*, 1246–50, discusses the role of myth in R.'s short story, and sees within it the basis for *Grande sertão: veredas*. S. M. Van Dijck Lima, 'O popular e o erudito en uma obra transtextual', *ib.*, 1257–62, examines sources used by Hermilo Borba Filho for his novel *Agá*. M. J. Evangelista, 'Nélida Piñon: a criação dentro da criação. Uma leitura de *A força do destino*', *ib.*, 1263–71, discusses intertextuality within P.'s 1978 novel. E. Pibernat Antonini, 'Identidade e consciência de latino-americanidade', *ib.*, 1293–98, focuses on the novels of Erico Veríssimo, comparing *O continente* with *Incidente em Antares*. Z. Bernd, 'Formas e sentidos do híbrido na literatura brasileira', *ib.*, 1306–10, discusses the fusion of popular oral tradition and erudite literary culture in the work of João Ubaldo Ribeiro. A. Facó, 'Rosa e Borges: da modernidade à pós-moderni-dade', *ib.*, 1338–45, is a comparative study of the aesthetic approaches of Guimarães Rosa and Borges. D. Nascimento, 'Memórias culturais na pós-modernidade de *Macunaíma*', *ib.*, 1346–50, presents basic points for a post-modernist reading of Mário de Andrade's best known work. P. Petrov, 'Aspectos pós-modernistas no discurso ficcional de Rubem Fonseca', *ib.*, 1351–56, considers F.'s novels within the light of post-modernist aesthetics. L. Ruas Pereira, 'Na esteira de Lobato', *ib.*, 1373–79, looks at L.'s legacy for children's literature in Brazil.

IX. ITALIAN STUDIES

LANGUAGE

By MAIR PARRY, *Senior Lecturer in Italian, University of Bristol,*
and RODNEY SAMPSON, *Senior Lecturer in French, University of Bristol*

1. GENERAL

Italiano e dialetti nel tempo. Saggi di grammatica per Giulio C. Lepschy, ed. Paola Benincà et al., Ro, Bulzoni, ix + 409 pp., henceforth *Lepschy Vol.*, addresses a wide range of topics — a well deserved tribute to a major contributor to so many branches of Italian linguistics. Giovan Battista Pellegrini, *Varia Linguistica*, Alessandria, Orso, 1995, x + 426 pp., gathers together 21 articles on etymology, toponymy, and classification that span another eminent and prolific career. The flourishing state of Italian linguistics is reflected in the following volumes of conference proceedings: *Italian Studies in Linguistic Historiography. In ricordo di Antonino Pagliaro. Gli studi italiani di storiografia linguistica, Rome 23–24 January 1992*, Münster, Nodus, 1994, 195 pp.; *Donna e linguaggio. Convegno internazionale di studio, SAPPADA/PLODN (Belluno)*, ed. Gianna Marcato, Padua, CLEUP, 1995, 632 pp., henceforth Marcato, *Donna*; *Italia ed Europa nella linguistica del Rinascimento: confronti e relazioni. Atti del Convegno internazionale, Ferrara, Palazzo Paradiso, 20–24 marzo 1991*, ed. Mirko Tavoni et al., Modena, Parini, 1996, XXX pp., henceforth *Atti* (Ferrara); *Aspects of Romance Linguistics, Selected Papers from the Linguistics Symposium on Romance Languages XXIV, March 10–13, 1994*, ed. C. Parodi et al., xiv + 530 pp., henceforth *Papers* (Los Angeles); *Lingua e dialetto nella tradizione letteraria italiana. Atti del Convegno di Salerno, 5–6 novembre 1993*, Ro, Salerno, xiv + 636 pp., henceforth *Atti* (Salerno). The appearance of new journals and working papers, such as *Rivista Italiana di Onomastica (RIOn)*, *Romanistik in Geschichte und Gegenwart (RomGG)*, *Plurilinguismo. Notiziario del Centro Internazionale sul Plurilinguismo (PNCIP)*, and the *British Quaderni di Ricerca, Centro di Dialettologia e Linguistica Italiana di Manchester (QRCDLIM)*, is a further sign of buoyancy. A. Castellani, 'Sulla formazione del sistema paragrafematico moderno', *SLI*, 21:3–47. M. Palermo, 'I manuali redazionali e la norma dell'italiano scritto contemporaneo', *ib.*, 88–115. Salvatore C. Sgroi, *Bada come parli. Cronachette e storie di parole*, T, SEI, 1995, ix + 411 pp., whose ambiguous title is not to be read in the puristic sense, is a useful compendium of recent newspaper pieces by S. on contemporary, especially lexical, usage.

2. HISTORY OF THE LANGUAGE, EARLY TEXTS, AND DIACHRONIC STUDIES

L. Banfi, 'Una nuova redazione in versi della "Leggenda di Santa Margherita" secondo il manoscritto Trotti 502 della Biblioteca Ambrosiana', *QFLR*, 3.11:7–32. G. Billanovich, 'Come nacque un capolavoro: la *Cronica* del non più anonimo romano', *AAL*, 6, 1995: 195–211, attributes the 14th-c. work plausibly to Bartolomeo Valmontone. Ilio Calabresi, **Glossario giuridico dei testi in volgare di Montepulciano: saggio d'un lessico della lingua giuridica italiana, iv: Testo 23. I tre statuti dei calzolai di Montepulciano: 1326–1731*, 1995, Ro, CNR, xciii + 699–1049 pp. A. Stussi, 'Venezia 1309', *Lepschy Vol.*, 341–49, analyses three vernacular copies from the Venetian chancellery. Id., 'Padova 1388', *ID*, 58:69–83, gives a critical commentary on an early Paduan text. **Cronachetta di Urbino, 1404–1444*, ed. Giovanni Scatena, Urbino, Quattro Venti, 1995, 59 pp. Leon Battista Alberti, *Grammatichetta e altri scritti sul volgare*, ed. Giuseppe Patota, Ro, Salerno, 89 pp. Gualdo Riccardo, **Il lessico medico del De regime pregnantium di Michele Savonarola*, F, Accademia della Crusca, 327 pp. Anna Laura Lepschy, *Varietà linguistiche e pluralità di codici nel Rinascimento*, F, Olschki, 201 pp., contains perceptive analyses of particular cases from the fascinating range of literary usage in the 16th c., highlighting for example the grammatical and lexical variation found in particular regional koines, the relationship between language and characterization, and the use of verb tenses, as in the two (previously unpublished), 'Serve e padrone nella Veniexiana' (53–108) and 'Sui tempi nel primo canto del Boiardo' (127–36). B. Richardson, 'Rustic language in a sixteenth-century Florentine comedy: *La Biagia da Decomano*', *ISt*, 51:96–112, shows through a deft analysis of plurilingualism and dialect usage in what is probably the first Italian rustic play to be printed, how just when 'Trecento Tuscan was becoming widely accepted in Italy as the basis for a standard literary language, recognition was accorded to dialect as an alternative and autonomous literary medium'.

Atti (Ferrara), 1, contains the following study relevant to the *Questione della Lingua*: A. A. A. Paternoster, 'Dalle *Prose della volgar lingua* di P. Bembo alla *Deffence et illustration de la langue française* di J. Du Bellay: lo sviluppo di una retorica unificatrice' (219–32). *Atti* (Ferrara), ii, has M. Lieber, 'Giovan Giorgio Trissino (1478) e Martin Lutero (1483–1546): due autori in cerca della lingua nazionale. La sperimentazione lessicale' (45–56); E. Banfi, 'Alla ricerca di una norma: Italia e Grecia alla vigilia dell'età moderna' (89–98); L. Binotti, 'Liburnio traduttore della Carta di Cortés. L'immagine del nuovo mondo e la *questione della lingua* in Italia' (131–44); Jan De Clerq and P. Swiggers, Le *De italica pronunciatione et orthographia libellus* (1569) de John David

Rhys' (147–61). C. Scavuzzo, 'Girolamo Ruscelli e la norma grammaticale nel Cinquecento', *SLI*, 22:3–31. Girolamo Muzio, *Battaglie per difesa dell'italica lingua*, ed. Carmelo Scavuzzo, Messina, Sicania, 1995, 439 pp. Riccardo Drusi, *La lingua cortigiana romana: note su un aspetto della questione cinquecentesca della lingua*, Venice, Il Cardo, 1995, 236 pp. M. Lieber, 'Sprachkultur im Zeitalter der italienischen Renaissance — Gian Giorgio Trissino und die italienische Sprache', *RomGG*, 2:15–44. Claudio Tolomei, *Il Cesano de la lingua toscana*, ed. Ornella Castellani Pollidori, F, Accademia della Crusca, 115 pp., has been completely revised. Alessandro Tassoni, *Postille al primo vocabolario della Crusca*, ed. Andrea Masini, F, Accademia della Crusca, li + 258 pp. B. Richardson, 'La riforma ortografica dal 1501 al 1533: confronti tra l'Italia e la Francia', *Atti* (Ferrara), 1, 257–66, takes Trissino's new characters as the point of departure for interesting comparisons. C. Bloc-Duraffour and S. Lazard, 'Standardisation de la typographie à Venise au cours des XVIᵉ–XVIIᵉ siècles', *ib.*, 267–85.

M. Maiden, 'Ipotesi sulle origini del condizionale analitico come "futuro del passato" in italiano', *Lepschy Vol.*, 149–73, convincingly attributes the demise of the simple conditional in this function to a desire to stress the deictic, temporal value of the verb using the aspectual marker of completion. S. Bozzola, 'Contributo alla storia dell'ortografia. F. F. Frugoni e il secondo Seicento', *SGI*, 16:75–118. L. Serianni, '*Vonno*, "vogliono": un meridionalismo inavvertito nella lingua letteraria sei–settecentesca', *SLI*, 21:48–53. S. Raffaelli, 'I titoli dei libri nell'Ottocento. Un sondaggio linguistico', *SLI*, 22:32–50, offers orthographic, phonetic, morphological, syntactic, and lexical analyses. H. W. Haller, 'Tra friulano e toscano: la scrittura bilingue di Caterina Percoto', Marcato, *Donna*, 210–10, examines the linguistic choices in P.'s Italian prose on the level of code, lexis, and morphosyntax, and offers a fascinating insight into the problems confronting a female writer from the Italian periphery in the varied but generally pro-Tuscan linguistic climate of Risorgimento Italy. M. G. Dramisino, 'Le correzioni linguistiche al *Marco Visconti* di Tommaso Grossi', *SGI*, 16:119–88, includes a comparison with Manzoni's interventions in *I promessi sposi*. L. Serianni, 'La prosa di Maria Bellonci, ovvero la ricerca dell'acronia', *SLI*, 22:50–64, examines B.'s writings from 1939–85. Maria Catricalà, *Studi per una grammatica dell'invenzione: l'italiano brevettato delle origini (1860–1880)*, F Manent, 112 pp.

3. History of Linguistic Theory

T. Bolelli, 'Linguistica di ieri e di oggi', *AAL*, 6, 1995:847–60, surveys the main currents of linguistics over the past two centuries

S. Albertini, 'Questione linguistica e questione politica nelle opere minori di Dante', *CJIS*, 18, 1995:111–35, explores the links between D.'s views on politics and language in the *Convivio*, *De Vulgari Eloquentia*, and *De Monarchia*. L. Serianni, 'Sul dantismo di Alfonso Varano. Rilievi linguistici', *GSLI*, 561:26–54, is sceptical over the influence of Dante on V.'s language and style. *Atti* (Ferrara), 1, contains several articles relating to Italy: L. Stepanova, 'La terminologia linguistica dantesca e la sua fortuna nel Rinascimento' (211–18), analysing Dante's terms, *illustre*, *cardinale*, *aulicum*, and *curiale*; M. Tavoni, 'Osservazioni sulle prime grammatiche dell'italiano e dello spagnolo' (333–46), identifying crucial differences resulting from the social and cultural environment; S. Vanvolsem, 'La grammatica volgare di M. Alberto de gl'Acharisi ... tournée de tuscan en françois' (347–63); M. Lliteras and E. Ridruejo, 'La gramática racional en las obras de Correas y de Buonmattei' (365–79); G. Skytte, 'Nascita della grammatica ragionata nel '600. Un confronto tra la *Grammatica* di Benedetto Buonmattei e la *Grammaire de Port Royal*' (381–89); M. G. Bianchi, 'Lodovico Castelvetro, la ricerca etimologica e lo studio della lingua letteraria' (549–64); M. Gazzotti, 'Riflessione linguistica e studi comparativi nell'attività di Jacopo Corbinelli' (565–79). Milena Montanile, **Le parole e la norma: studi su lessico e grammatica a Napoli tra Quattro e Cinquecento*, Na, ESI, 163 pp. Maria Catricalà, **L'italiano tra grammaticalità e testualizzazione: il dibattito linguistico-pedagogico del primo sessantennio postunitario*, F, Accademia della Crusca, 1995.

4. Phonology

J. J. Ohala and M. G. Busà, 'Nasal loss before voiceless fricatives: a perceptually-based sound change', *RIL*, 7, 1995:125–44, includes Italian data in a discussion positing that pre-fricative nasal loss is a counterpart to the known phenomenon of spontaneous nasalization in vowels adjacent to voiceless high airflow fricatives. A. Castellani, 'Grafemi e fonemi: il caso di Antonio di ser Girolamo da Orvieto (con una giunta sul monottongamento di "uo" a Orvieto e a Roma)', *SLI*, 21, 1995:145–54. M. Loporcaro, 'On the analysis of geminates in Standard Italian and Italian dialects', pp. 153–87 of *Natural Phonology: The State of the Art*, ed. B. Hurch and R. A. Rhodes, Berlin–New York, Mouton de Gruyter, 348 pp., persuasively argues on the basis of diachronic and dialectal data that geminates are phonologically not single segments but sequences of two identical segments. Further studies in this area are F. Rainer, 'Auslautdopplung im Italienischen', *Italienisch*, 35:44–54, where gemination is examined in items arising through word formation; and on *raddoppiamento sintattico* there are V. Formentin, 'Attestazioni di raddoppiamento sintattico provocato da "-t" e "-nt" finali in un manuscritto del Trecento', *SLI*, 21, 1995:54–87, and M. Absalom, 'Raddoppiamento sintattico or syntactic doubling: a misnomer?', *Working Papers in Linguistics*, 15, 1995:1–14, which looks at previous work on the supposedly syntactic basis of RS and concludes that the phenomenon is not conditioned by syntactic structures. J. Hajek, 'The *gorgia toscana* isn't what it used to be: changing attitudes from one millennium into the next', *CJIS*, 19:61–74, offers a lucid reassessment of the past, present, and possible future of the GT.

5. MORPHOLOGY

U. Seewald, *Morphologie des Italienischen*, Tübingen, Niemeyer, 132 pp., gives a clear and well-illustrated introduction ideal for a student text. A concise opening chapter on basic terms and concepts is followed by a review of inflexional and derivational mophology, the former briefly and the latter more extensively. There is little explicit preoccupation with theoretical issues, an essentially structuralist perspective being adopted along with some input from valency theory in the handling of derivational morphology. An evaluation of the merits of Classical-style WP and 20th-c. IA and IP approaches to inflexional morphology appears in P. Matthews, 'Morfologia all'antica', *Lepschy Vol.*, 191–205, where the Italian verb serves as subject matter.

M. Chini, *Genere grammaticale e acquisizione. Aspetti della morfologia nominale in italiano L2*, Pavia, Francoangeli, 340 pp., explores nominal gender in second language acquisition of Italian, presenting the results of a detailed experimental investigation of speakers of four different L1 backgrounds. Patterns of gender usage are found to be guided by L2 structure as well as more abstract factors of linguistic organization. A. M. Thornton, 'On some phenomena of prosodic morphology in Italian: accorciamenti, hypocoristics and prosodic delimitation', *Probus*, 8:81–112, identifies the minimal word as a disyllabic trochee and views this as a target shape for various phonological and morphological processes. I. Vogel and D. J. Napoli, 'The verbal complement in Italian compounds', pp. 367–81 of *Contemporary Research in Romance Linguistics*, ed. J. Amastae et al., Amsterdam, Benjamins, 1995, argues convincingly for interpreting the first element of items like *lavapiatti* as an uninflected verb stem. S. Scalise, 'Preliminari per lo studio di un affisso: -*tore* o -*ore*?', *Lepschy Vol.*, 291–307, explores formal aspects of the deverbal derivational suffix -*(t)ore* and proposes an allomorphic interpretation: -*ore* appears after past part. stem of learned verbs and -*tore* after present stem of other verbs. A. Bisetto, 'Il suffisso -*tore*', *QPL*, 4, 1995 [1996]: 39–71.

M. Sala Gallina, 'Lo statuto del clitico nella dislocazione a destra: pronome vero o marca flessionale?', *AGI*, 81:76–94, explores the variable status of clitics as grammaticalized or as dislocated cataphoric forms. An attractive account for auxiliary selection using notions of prototypicality and markedness of subject choice appears in G. Centineo, 'A lexical theory of auxiliary selection in Italian', *Probus*, 8:223–71, while P. M. Bertinetto and M. Squartini, 'La distribuzione del Perfetto Semplice e del Perfetto Composto nelle diverse varietà dell'italiano', *RPh*, 49:383–419, explores patterns of past tense usage in 11 localities across Italy using a questionnaire. M. Loporcaro, 'Italienische Dialektologie und allgemeine Sprachwissenschaft', *VR*, 55:16–32, highlights morphological and syntactic phenomena found in Italian dialects of considerable interest to general linguists, namely subject-controlled gender marking in verbs, inflected infinitives, raising of indirect objects to subject position in passives, and variable patterns of past participle agreement with direct objects.

A. Nocentini, 'Tipologia e genesi dell'articolo nelle lingue europee', *AGI*, 81:3–44, offers a typological review of the rise of the article in 12 European languages including Italian. A much bolder proposal on the article appears in M. Alinei, 'L'etimologia di *magnano* "calderaio ambulante" e l'inizio dell'articolo nelle parlate neolatine', *QS*, 17:191–202; the author claims that the word derives from Germanic *alaman(nan)* 'all men' and that the initial element *ala-* was identified with an already existing definite article, thus presupposing the existence of the definite article already in the spoken Italic of the Bronze Age. From detailed consideration of dialectal and philological data M. Loporcaro, 'Un capitolo di morfologia storica italo-romanza: it. ant. *ne* "ci" e forme meridionali congeneri', *ID*, 58, 1995:1–48, concludes that while 'partitive' *ne* derives from INDE, the 1st pl. clitic pronoun *ne* (and dialectally *ni, nni,* etc.) originated from NOS. A comparably wide-ranging database is exploited in M. Maiden, 'On the Romance inflectional endings *-i* and *-e*', *RPh*, 50:147–82, where it is argued that these endings, both in Italian and Romanian, derive overwhelmingly from forms originally containing final *-s*. F. Fanciullo, 'Tra fonologia e morfologia: vicende di un suffisso greco-romanzo nell'Italia meridionale', *AGI*, 81:95–119, suggests the likely Greek antecedents to the rise of the proparoxytonic suffix -' Vllu / -' Vlla found widely in southern dialects. C. Agostinelli, 'Sull'origine degli infinitivi sincopati "corre", "scerre", "sciorre", "sverre", "torre"', *SLI*, 22:65–73.

E. Pizzuto and S. Corazza, 'Noun morphology in Italian Sign Language', *Lingua*, 98:169–96, provides new data on LIS (Italian Sign Language) nominal morphology and its variability in different cities, and also on the interaction between nominal morphology and classifier predicates. M. Chini and G. Crocco Galeas, 'Verbalparadigmen, Prototypizität und natürliche Morphologie: Überlegungen am Beispiel des Erstspracherwebs des Italienischen', *QPL*, 14, 1995 [1996]: 73–110.

6. SYNTAX AND SEMANTICS

Guglielmo Cinque, *Italian Syntax and Universal Grammar*, CUP, 1995, 332 pp., contains important essays (some previously unpublished) within the Principles and Parameters framework that offer valuable insights into a range of syntactic features: NP extraction, relative clauses, quantifiers, *si* constructions, 'Complement Object Deletion', ergative adjectives, pseudo-relative constructions after verbs of perception, leftward movement of *tutto*, and the order òf noun and adjective (the typical Italian surface order is considered to result from the movement of the noun from post-adjectival position). Id., 'Posizione del soggetto nel DP italiano', Lupu, *Studi*, 436–63, modifies an earlier proposal in the light of recent theoretical developments, arguing that genitive subjects are base-generated to the left of the NP, not to the right. Id., 'Genitivo e genitivi pronominali nel DP italiano', *Lepschy Vol.*, 67–85, identifies and accounts for a number of puzzling restrictions on possessive structures. P. Benincà, 'La struttura della frase esclamativa alla luce del dialetto padovano', *Lepschy Vol.*, 23–43, systematically analyses Paduan data, drawing comparisons with Italian, to arrive at the following order of fronted constituents: Hanging Topic/(Left Dislocation)/Wh-exclamative/Left Dislocation/Wh-interrogative. L. Rizzi, 'Residual Verb Second and the Wh-Criterion', Belletti, *Parameters*, 63–90, contains sections of theoretical relevance to the analysis of Italian, especially interrogatives; R. Zanuttini, 'On the relevance of tense for sentential negation', *ib.*, 181–207, draws on Italian and dialect data to argue that negative markers which are functional heads, for example It. *non*, can only occur in conjunction with the functional category Tense, whereas this restriction does not hold for adverbial negatives such as Pied. *nen* or Mil. *minga*. M. M. Parry, 'La negazione italo-romanza: variazione tipologica e variazione strutturale', *Lepschy Vol.*, 225–57. G. Graffi, 'Alcune riflessioni sugli imperativi italiani', *ib.*, 143–48, offers a persuasive account of the idiosyncratic morphology and syntax of Italian imperatives, which in G.'s view comprise just 2nd sg., 1st plur., and 2nd plur. A. Giorgi and F. Pianesi, 'Per una teoria delle rappresentazioni temporali', *LFQDLLC*, 1, 1995:69–95, examines the relationship between the syntax and semantics of verb tenses in Italian and Latin. C. Poletto, 'Three kinds of subject clitics in Basso

Polesano and the theory of *pro*', Belletti, *Parameters,* 269–300, analyses dialect data supporting L. Rizzi's theory in which the formal licensing and the identification of *pro* are kept distinct. In 'Complementizer deletion and verb movement in Italian', *UVWPL,* 5, 1995 [1996]: 49–79, she interprets optional and stylistically marked structures such as *Credo sia già partito* as cases of verb movement to the Complementizer position (or rather 'domain', since the generative model used postulates a split CP). M. R. Manzini, 'Il congiuntivo', *Lepschy Vol.,* 175–90, explains the distribution of the subjunctive in terms of a syntactic dependency whereby the indefinite T(ense) is bound by a phrasal operator (negative, interrogative, or conditional). C. Poletto and A. Tomaselli, 'Verso una definizione di elemento clitico', Dolci, *Studi,* 159–224, offers a stimulating theoretical discussion of cliticization that compares Romance data, exemplified by Italian and the dialects, with German. L. Mereu, 'On the status of subject clitics in languages and the Null Subject Parameter', pp. 315–39 of *Teoria del linguaggio e analisi linguistica. XX Incontro di Grammatica Generativa,* ed. G. Borgato, Padua, Unipress, 1994, refers to Italian dialect data in her typology of subject clitics based on a functional rather than a configurational characterization. Complement cliticization is the subject of C. Robustelli, 'Fenomeni di cliticizzazione in italiano antico', *Lepschy Vol.,* 273–90, which concentrates on a small but significant group of cases of cliticization to the infinitive in causative constructions. A valuable appendix to the Italian translation of an important manual, Liliane Haegeman's *Manuale di Grammatica Generativa. La Teoria della Reggenza e del Legamento,* ed. Adriana Belletti, Mi, Hoepli, is M. T. Guasti, 'Aspetti della sintassi dell'italiano' (589–639), which also analyses pronominal cliticization and causatives, as well as restructuring verbs and verb movement. M. T. Guasti, 'Semantic restrictions in Romance causatives and the incorporation approach', *LI,* 27: 294–313, uses Italian as the language of exemplification. A. Giorgi and F. Pianesi, 'Verb movement in Italian and syncretic categories', *Probus,* 8: 137–60, discusses complementizer deletion and interrogatives. Also within the Minimalist framework V. Egerland, 'Spec head agreement, Case theory and the syntax of participles: absolute participial clauses in Old Italian', *RGG,* 20: 1995 [1996]: 33–68, demonstrates that syntactic differences between usage in 14th.-c. and modern texts are 'perfectly systematic and regular'. A. Belletti and L. Rizzi, 'Su alcuni casi di accordo del participio passato in francese e italiano', *Lepschy Vol.,* 7–22.

Bertinetto, *Temporal Reference,* contains important theoretical contributions, many of which are based entirely or partially on Italian data: for example, J. Pustejovsky and F. Busa, 'Unaccusativity and event composition' (159–77), argues within a framework of Generative

Lexicon theory that unaccusativity is 'the result of a kind of foregrounding of the event structure associated with the predicate, similar in some respects to argument-changing operations such as passivization'. Also included in vol. 1 are: P. M. Bertinetto and M. Squartini, 'An attempt at defining the class of "gradual completion" verbs' (11–26); A. Bonomi, 'Aspect and quantification' (93–110); D. Delfitto and P. M. Bertinetto, 'A case study in the interaction of action and actionality: the Imperfect in Italian' (125–42); A. Sanfilippo, 'Thematic affectedness and aspect compositionality' (179–93); W. Castelnovo, '*Ora* as a perspective adverb' (237–54); W. Castelnovo and R. Vogel, 'Reported speech' (255–72); V. Lo Cascio, 'On the relation between tense and aspect in Romance and other languages' (273–93); V. Bianchi, M. Squartini, and P. M. Bertinetto, 'Perspective point and textual dynamics' (309–24); L. Dini, 'Comparative ellipsis and event reconstruction' (325–40); A. Giorgi and F. Pianesi, 'From semantics to morphosyntax: the case of the Imperfect' (341–63). Vol. 2 includes: A. Giacalone Ramat, 'Tense and aspect in learner Italian' (289–309). Aspect and actionality are also theoretically crucial in P. M. Bertinetto and D. Delfitto, 'L'espressione della "progressività/continuità": un confronto tripolare (italiano, inglese e spagnolo)', *Lepschy Vol.*, 45–66, and in Rosaria Solarino, *I tempi possibili. Le dimensioni temporali del gerundio italiano'*, Padua, Unipress, 131 pp., a much-needed, comprehensive, and systematic analysis of a wealth of data. A. Giacalone Ramat, 'Sulla grammaticalizzazione dei verbi di movimento: *andare* e *venire* + gerundio', *AGI*, 80, 1995:168–203. L. Ciarlo, 'Il sistema della temporalità nell'acquisizione di lingua prima. Studio di un caso', *BALI*, 19, 1995:107–23, offers Italian evidence for the early acquistion of temporal deixis. E. Weiberg, 'Reference to past events in bilingual Italian–Swedish children of school age', *Linguistics*, 34:1087–114. W. Bassano, 'Il ruolo della L1 nello sviluppo della perifrasi progressiva nell'italiano L2', *LFQDLLC*, 1, 1995:97–123. M. Cresci, 'L'acquisizione del clitico *ne* nell'italiano lingua materna', *ib.*, 171–85. G. Bernini, 'Stadi di sviluppo della sintassi e della morfologia della negazione in italiano', *LFQDLLC*, 3:7–33. M. T. Guasti, 'L'acquisizione dell'interpretazione anaforica e deittica dei pronomi', *ib.*, 127–44, includes Italian exemplification.

M. Cennamo, 'Transitivity and VS order in Italian reflexives', *STUF*, 48, 1995:84–105, seeks to identify word-order constraints in the notoriously complex area of *si* constructions, through the skilful analysis of actual usage in written (mainly journalistic) texts. The choice of *si* VN, or N *si* V is governed by syntactic, semantic, and pragmatic factors, involving the type of *si* construction (reflexive middle, impersonal), the discourse status of the noun (± Given), the type of sentence (predicative / presentative), the transitivity of the verb (a scalar notion), with tense and intonation also relevant. G. Centineo, 'A lexical theory of auxiliary selection in Italian', *Probus*, 8:223–71. D. Adger, 'Economy and optionality: interpretations of subjects in Italian', *Probus*, 8:117–35, deals with the apparent optionality of pre- or postverbal position for subjects with unaccusative verbs in Italian and argues that positioning is in fact dependent on well-formedness conditions relating to discourse. M. Berretta, 'Ordini marcati dei costituenti maggiori di frase: una rassegna', *LFQDLLC*, 1, 1995:125–70. L. Mereu, 'Verso una tipologia dell'accordo verbo-soggetto', *RivL*, 7, 1995 [1996]:333–67, is a comparative study that includes Italian dialect data. H. Siller-Runggaldier, 'Kasus, syntaktische Funktionen und semantische Rollen im Italienischen', *RomGG*, 2:189–204. C. Casadio, 'Pronomi partitivi: il contrasto *weak/strong*', *LS*, 30, 1995:551–63, examines Italian data, offering a new perspective for the semantic analysis of indefinite domains. P. Ramat and D. Ricca, 'Prototypical adverbs: on the scalarity/ radicality of the notion of adverb', *RivL*, 6, 1994 [1995]:289–326, include Italian data in an attempt to define this elusive category.

7. PRAGMATICS AND DISCOURSE

Giacalone Ramat, *Pragmatics*, contains many contributions relating to Italian, for example: M. E. Conte, 'Epistemico, deontico, anankastico' (3–9), which uses Italian exemplification to show that regulations can involve anankastic modality (introducing a necessary condition) and not only deontic modality; N. Vincent and D. Bentley, 'Conditional and subjunctive in Italian and Sicilian: a case study in the province of Palermo' (11–33), combining a wide-ranging theoretical discussion of modality and tense in conditional sentences with a sociolinguistic analysis of data that reveal a clear tendency towards harmonizing the markers of tense and modality in both clauses; M. Chini, '"Meno male che non elo un topo, se no mi mangia il gatto, pe finta". Precursori e genesi dei costrutti ipotetici in una bambina italofona' (143–72). E. Cresti, 'L'ontogenesi del predicato nell'acquisizione dell'italiano', *SGI*, 16:346–76. A. Scarano, 'Frasi relative e pseudo-relative in italiano', *ib.*, 377–423, also adopts a semantic and pragmatic approach. A. Kauppinen, 'The Italian *indicativo imperfetto* compared to the Finnish conditional verb form. Evidence from child language', *JP*, 26:109–36. M. Jacquemet, 'Power alliances in court. Turning turncoats into witnesses', *Folia Linguistica*, 30, 1996:189–215, draws on data from two very different sets of trials against the Neapolitan *camorra* (1983–85 and 1986) to examine 'the issues of power, authority and control as expressed in, and constructed through, verbal interaction' between *pentiti* and judges. E. Radtke, 'Segnali di cortesia nell'italiano parlato', *RomGG*, 2:163–88, concludes with a plea for the recognition of the structural importance of such 'segnali' in everyday conversation. L. Dascalu Jinga and L. Vanelli, '"Mi raccomando eh!"' A pragmatic and phonetic analysis of the Italian interjection *eh*', *LS*, 31:393–431.

B. J. Birner and G. Ward, 'A crosslinguistic study of postposing in discourse', *LSp*, 39:113–42, includes a comparison of English existential and presentational *there*-sentences with Italian presentational *ci* constructions and Italian subject inversion: the constraints on the postposition of the logical subject are related to its discourse status — it must be 'discourse-new', though not necessarily 'hearer-new' or morphologically indefinite. G. Skytte, 'Per una grammatica della risposta', *Lepschy Vol.*, 309–21. *L'italiano che parliamo*, Santarcangelo di Rimini, Fara, 1995, 76 pp., contains three articles: F. Casadei, 'Flessibilità lessico-sintattica e produttività semantica delle espressioni idiomatiche: un'indagine sull'italiano parlato' (11–33), arguing that idioms are frequently not used as unanalysable syntactic and semantic units; G. Fiorentino, 'Parlato e complessità sintattica: analisi del parlato argomentato in contesto didattico-espositivo' (35–58), showing how important it is to consider the type of text and level of formality in any discussion of differences between written and spoken Italian; V. Samek-Lodovici, 'Sul focus strutturale' (59–76), adopting a generative framework to postulate a Focus position adjoined to VP. **La costruzione del testo in italiano: sistemi costruttivi e testi costruiti. Atti del seminario internazionale di Barcellona, 24–29 aprile, 1995*, ed. María de las Nieves Muñiz Muñiz and Francisco Amella, F, Cesati — Barcelona, Univ. of Barcelona, 212 pp. M.-E. Conte, 'Dimostrativi nel testo: tra continuità e discontinuità referenziale', *LS*, 31:135–44, analyses the textual functions and restrictions on the use of *questo* and *quello*.

8. LEXIS

An impressive range of dictionaries has appeared. The new edition of the respected dictionary *Lo Zingarelli*, ed. M. Dogliotti and L. Rosiello, Bo, Zanichelli, 2144 pp., brings substantial improvements, notably many new lemmata and additional colour illustrations together with the welcome incorporation into the dictionary text of the *nomenclatura* sections where collocations and hyponyms of lexical items of broad semantism are enumerated. *C-dir: Dizionario italiano ragionato su CD-rom*, ed. A Gianni, F, D'Anna, containing one CD-rom disk for PCs with at least 4Mb RAM, is arranged with broad lemmata sometimes subsuming large numbers of derivationally related items. There is good cross-referencing between lemmata and attractive screen presentation, but when consulting a longer entry it might be helpful to know the total number of screen pages it has and the page at which the user is. G. Devoto and G. C. Oli, *Il dizionario della lingua italiana,* F, Le Monnier, 1995, has also appeared in a CD-rom version. C. Marelli, *Le parole dell'italiano,* Bo, Zanichelli, reviews the Italian lexicon through the analysis of dictionaries and corpora. R. Rosselli and R. Eynard, *Dizionario di base della lingua italiana,* T, SEI — F, Sàndron, xxxvii + 1240 pp., offers a rich array of attractive material intended for school use; entries are accompanied by data on synonyms and antonyms, and there is guidance on grammatical usage and numerous colour plates are provided. A similar audience is targeted by T. De Mauro and G. G. Moroni, *Dizionario di base della lingua italiana,* T, Paravia, 1499 pp., where a slightly smaller lexical range is covered but in a perhaps clearer format. An associated fascicle, T. De Mauro and A. Cattaneo, *Dizionario visuale,* 137 pp., provides colour illustrations of objects in thematic fields together with the associated lexical items. G. Turrini, *Capire l'antifona: dizionario dei modi di dire,* Bo, Zanichelli, 1995, 662 pp., is a dictionary of idiomatic expressions accompanied by an alphabetic index of key words. A substantially enlarged edition of the useful D. Cinti, *Dizionario dei sinonimi e dei contrari,* Novara, De Agostini, 712 pp., has appeared. V. Ceppellini, *Il dizionario pratico di grammatica e linguistica,* Novara, De Agostini, 623 pp., is a user-friendly reference work for basic linguistic terms and concepts.

Lexikalische Analyse romanischer Sprachen, ed. P. Blumenthal, G. Rovere, and C. Schwarze, Tübingen, Niemeyer, 163 pp., contains a variety of insightful articles exploring how lexical items are most appropriately characterized in the light of their semantic and morpho-syntactic properties, using approaches based principally on valency theory and functionalism. Seven of the articles in this well-produced collection operate on Italian and reflect the extensive theoretical work being carried out currently on the lexicon of the language: P. Blumenthal, 'Subjektrollen bei polysemen Verben' (7–21); P. Cordin and M. G. Lo Duca, 'Configurazioni argomentali: analisi dei verbi "reciproci" in italiano' (23–32); Z. Fabián, 'Sulle connessioni tra le reggenze verbali e le unità fraseologiche verbali' (33–40); G. Rovere, 'Verbi comuni in contesti tecnici' (101–12); M.-T. Schepping, 'Zur Valenz abgeleiter italienischer Nomina' (113–23); A. Stein, 'Argumentstruktur italienischer Verben' (135–47); F. Venier, 'I verbi sintagmatici' (149–56). The problem of classifying compound lexemes is attacked by T. De Mauro and M. Voghera, 'Scala mobile. Un punto di vista sui lessemi complessi', *Lepschy Vol.,* 99–131, where seven syntactic-semantic criteria are proposed as a classificatory basis.

T. Hohnerlein-Buchinger, *Per un sublessico vitivinicolo*, Tübingen, Niemeyer, viii + 247 pp., examines the etymology and semantic-morphological characteristics of the names of grape varieties and wines. Fifteen names receive extensive treatment and a brief sketch is given of 147 more. **Indice della lingua legislativa italiana: inventario lessicale dei cento maggiori testi di legge tra il 1723 e il 1973*, ed. M. Biagini, F, Giuntina, I, (A–E), 1993, and II, (F–P), 1995, are parts of a massive compilation in three volumes. Lexical usage in the press is explored in M. Lieber, '"Maratona televisiva", "Mafia-Marathon", "Marathonis" — ein Beispiel gegenwärtiger Deonomastik in der italienischen (und deutschen) Pressesprache', *Italienisch*, 33, 1995:92–95, and an aspect of political discourse in M. Bischofsberger, 'Il caso di *postmoderno* nel discorso politico. In vista di una ricerca di semantica storica', *QS*, 17:297–324. S. Stimolo, **Onorevole parli chiaro*, Mi, Rizzoli, 1994, contains a collection of new political words and expressions. Michele Cortelazzo, *Annali del lessico contemporaneo. Neologismi '95*, Padua, Esedra, 90 pp.

P. D'Achille, 'Prime apparizioni di ideofoni ed esotismi in libretti d'opera', *LN*, 57:1–6, finds early attestations of several 'exotic' and onomatopoeic words. Several interesting lexicographical studies on usage in the field of musicology appear in *Tra le note: studi di lessicologia musicale*, ed. F. Nicolodi and P. Trovati, Fiesole, Cadmo, ix + 226 pp., for example, F. Rossi, 'Qualche problema di lessicografia e di lessicologia musicali' (1–21); L. Aversano, 'Terminologia violinistica tra Sei e Settecento' (23–56); L. Putignano, 'Primi appunti sul *Piccolo lessico del musicista* di Amintore Galli' (105–28); A. Quaranta, '"Decadentismo", "Impressionismo" e altri "Ismi" di fine secolo: il "caso Debussy" e la critica italiana del primo Novecento' (129–62); and S. Raffaelli, 'Termini musicali nei titoli dei film italiani' (181–204). Individual lexical items are discussed in C. Cordié, '*Canguro* (come "avido di riempirsi la borsa")', *LN*, 56, 1995:114–15; A. Fabi, 'Ancora *scala mobile*', *ib.*, 115; S. C. Sgroi, '*Tondo e corsivo*', *ib.*, 115; Id., '*Comporre* in tipografia', *ib.*, 57:25–26; Id., '*Malfidato* (un settentrionalismo): "inaffidabile" o "diffidente"?', *QS*, 17:325–27; D. Trolli, 'El sonnolento mal de subetía', *LN*, 57:7–11; S. C. Trovato, 'Tangeloso', *ib.*, 11–13; F. Rainer, 'Fr. *ducroire*: un italianismo passato inosservato', *ib.*, 14; P. Janni, 'Linguisti e linguaioli in Germania e in Italia', *ib.*, 15–20; M. Cortelazzo, '*Inciucio*', *ib.*, 49. A. Castellani has two studies, '*Scialacquare*', *SLI*, 21, 1995:242–43, and '"Velopattino" (e altro)', *ib.*, 244–47. P. Cherchi, 'L'arte di Michelazzo', *LN*, 57:26, cites an attestation of the idiom *l'arte di Michelazzo, mangiare, bere e andare a sollazzo* already in 1561, and G. Petrolini, 'Il *marangone* e la *marangona*', *ib.*, 33–48, proposes as etymon for these items a form composed of *marra* 'hoe' + RUNCARE 'to hoe'. A lengthy study of the history of a range of words relating to the language of espionage appears in P. Preto, 'Le parole dello spionaggio', *LN*, 56, 1995:97–114, while M. Vena, 'Retrodatazioni e aggiunte lessicali dalle *Rime e sentenze morali* e dal *Theogenius* di Leon Battista Alberti', *Italica*, 72, 1995:488–511, increases our knowledge of the dating and existence of several dozen lexical items. M. Loporcaro, 'Un problema d'etimologia: sul *che fico!* del linguaggio giovanile', *SLI*, 13, 1995:343–64, boldly proposes as etymon Romanesco *ficaccio efficace*.

In the double volume of *TLP*, 33–34, 1995–96, various articles on lexical topics appear: P. de Bernardo Stempel, 'Tratti linguistici comuni ad appellativi e toponimi di origine celta' (109–36); G. Giacomelli, 'Omofonia o sviluppo semantico? Un caso italiano' (137–50), dealing with *bordello* 'brothel' and regionally 'boy' which are shown to be homophones; C. A. Mastrelli, 'Ital. *foglietta* "misura per liquidi"' (267–76), sees this word as a borrowing from Occitan; W. Schweickard, 'Un prezioso contributo alla lessicografia italiana dell'Ottocento: il *Vocabolario patronimico italiano di nazionalità o sia adjettivario italiano* di Francesco Cherubini (1860)' (483–89). Lexicographical history is also addressed by P. Manni, 'Il *Nòvo dizionario universale della lingua italiana* di Policarpo Petrocchi', *SLI*, 21, 1995:195–241, continuing from *SLI*, 18, 1992:3–44, and *SLI*, 19, 1993:3–46. A. L. Lepschy and G. Lepschy, 'Anglicismi e italianismi', pp. 187–96 of *Scritti di linguistica e dialettologia in onore di Giuseppe Francescato*, Trieste, Ricerche, 1995, xlvii + 363 pp., contrasts the openness of English with the puristic hostility of Italian with regard to borrowings and concludes that borrowing is a natural phenomenon in language and that despite the cries of despair the lexical influence of English on Italian has been slight. M. Fanfani, 'Sugli anglicismi nell'italiano contemporaneo', *LN*, 57:72–92, is the last of a series of contributions in *LN*, 52, 53, 54, 55, analysing borrowings beginning with *a-* and deals with *auditorio / auditorium*. Recent gallicisms are examined in some detail by M. Fantuzzi, 'Non di solo inglese. Note sulla penetrazione di elementi francesi nel lessico dell'italiano contemporaneo', *LN*, 57:72–92. F. Casadei, **Metafore ed espressioni idiomatiche. Uno studio semantico sull'italiano*, Ro, Bulzoni, 496 pp., analyses some 3000 idioms using the Lakoffian theory of metaphor.

M. Cortelazzo, 'Perché non si vuole la presidentessa?', Marcato, *Donna*, 49–52, traces the link between contemporary negative connotations of *-essa* and its history in particular words. S. Spina, 'Lessico, donne e mondo del lavoro: i nomi femminili di mestiere nella letteratura italiana', *ib.*, 129–40. E. Burr, 'Agentivi e sessi in un corpus di giornali italiani', *ib.*, 141–57. Alessio Petralli, *Lingue sciolte. Dalle minoranze linguistiche locali alle nuove tecnologie internazionali*, Bo, CLUEB, 186 pp., henceforth Petralli, *Lingue*, gathers together interesting observations on lexical usage, particularly neologisms in the fields of technology, sport and politics, that appeared first in the 'Plurilingua' column of the *Corriere del Ticino*. S. Marx, 'Überlegungen zur Leistung italienischen Wortguts in der Wochenzeitung *Die Zeit*', *PNCIP*, 3:99–133.

A promising new journal *Rivista Italiana di Onomastica* (*RIOn*) started up in 1995 with coverage of anthroponomy, toponomy, and literary onomastics. Vol. 1 includes: M. G. Arcamone, 'Cognomi italiani da nomi di animali' (12–22); G. Meacci, 'L'*allònimo*' (23–30); S. Raffaelli, 'Un suffisso politico? Nomi di città in -*ia*' (32–40); L. Serianni, 'A proposito di odonimia' (41–50); G. D'Acunti, 'Fenomenologia antroponimica del grifone' (89–111); V. R. Jones, 'Alcune note di onomastica manzoniana: il nome di Lucia' (112–17); E. Caffarelli, 'Dalla prosa di Aldo Palazzeschi: spunti di cronografia e sociografia per l'onomastica letteraria' (118–45); L. Sasso, 'Savinio e i nomi di fumo' (146–59); and P. Marzano, 'Due esempi di percorsi onomastici nella narrativa di Piero Chiara' (160–72). B. Porcelli, 'I nomi in venti novelle del *Decameron*', *Italianistica*, 24, 1995:49–72, examines onomastic usage with some interesting results. A. Quarneti, **Toponomastica di Brisighella*, Faenza, Edit Faenza, 1995. J. Kramer, 'Die Italienisierung der Südtiroler Ortsnamen und die Polonisierung der ostdeutschen Toponomastik', *RomGG*, 2:45–62.

9. SOCIOLINGUISTICS

Gabriella Klein, **La città nei discorsi e nell'immaginario giovanile: una ricerca sociolinguistica a Napoli*, Galatina, Congedo, 1995, 235 pp. C. Marcato, '(Fare) Cestìl nel "parlar giovane" di Udine', Lupu, *Studi*, 598–606, discusses an expression of probable German origin, borrowed via the traditional thieves' slang of the Veneto. C. Marcato and F. Fasco, 'L'atteggiamento dei giovani studenti nei confronti del friulano e del linguaggio giovanile in un'inchiesta sociolinguistica a Tolmezzo', *PNCIP*, 3:83–98. D. Bentley, 'Alcune osservazioni sui costrutti condizionali nella provincia di Palermo', *QRCDLIM*, 1:1–20, confirms in a detailed statistical analysis of sociolinguistic data from Palermo that the level of education is the prime variable governing the use of non-standard structures and that the counter-factual use of the Imperfect indicative is now deemed acceptable, unlike its use in irrealis conditionals. A. A. Sobrero, 'Code-switching in dialectal communities in Italy', *RivL*, 6, 1994 [1995]:39–55, contains important theoretical and methodological considerations, while code-switching between language and dialect in Italy also features in A. Giacalone Ramat, 'Condizioni e restrizioni nel contatto tra lingue', *LS*, 30, 1995:227–41.

Marcato, *Donna*, is full of stimulating articles relating to the Italo-Romance area, for example C. Bazzanella and O. Fornara, 'Segnali discorsivi e linguaggio femminile: evidenze da un corpus' (73–98), gives the lie to some common assumptions; A. De Marco, 'L'influenza del sesso nell'uso dei diminutivi in italiano' (87–98); T. von Bonkewitz, 'Lingua, genere e sesso: sessismo nella grammaticografia e in libri scolastici della lingua italiana' (99–110). Cordin, *Femminile e maschile*, contains G. Marcato, 'Il lessico al femminile tra '800 e '900' (65–80), and P. Cordin, 'Linguaggio femminile e scrittura popolare in diari e memorie di donne trentine (1914–1917)' (81–101). Petralli, *Lingue*, also considers the relationship between language and gender, in addition to sections on linguistic minorities and the linguistic situation in the Ticino.

E. Radtke, 'Ancora su ... *sgamare*', *SLI*, 22:101–05, sees in the rapidity with which dialectal elements pertaining to lexis and syntax are passing first into substandard varieties and slang, and then into racy journalistic prose, evidence of a massive restandardization of the language on the scale of the differentiation between Classical and spoken Latin. J. Trumper, 'Riflessioni pragmo-sintattiche su alcuni gruppi meridionali: italiano "popolare"', *Lepschy Vol.*, 351–67, systematically assesses the influence of Calabrian dialects on the morphosyntactic structure of the Italian spoken in the region. C. Marazzini, 'Plurilinguismo giuridico e burocratico prima dell'Unità d'Italia', *PNCIP*, 3:69–82. *Pagine di scuola, di famiglia, di memorie. Per un'indagine sul multilinguismo nel Trentino austriaco*, ed. Emanuele Banfi and Patrizia Cordin, Trento, Archivio della Scrittura Popolare, 269 pp., examines linguistic diversity during the crucial century and a half up to the Great War. M. Dell'Utri, 'Spigolature trentine: indagini linguistiche su tre lettere dell'inizio del '900', *BALI*, 19, 1995:107–23, highlights characteristic features of *italiano popolare* written by Trentino prisoners of war or refugees. P. Cordin, 'Memorie autobiografiche femminili nell'archivio della scrittura popolare di Trento', Marcato, *Donna*, 235–45. J. Kramer, 'Bemerkungen zum Italienischen in Luxemburg', *RomGG*, 2:219–27.

I. Bonomi, 'La narrativa e l'italiano dell'uso medio', *SGI*, 16, 321–38, investigates in eight texts the frequency of ten morphosyntactic features characteristic of informal discourse. *Versi rock: la lingua della canzone italiana negli anni '80 e '90*, ed. Accademia degli Scrausi, Mi, Rizzoli, 1995, 397 pp. *Parole in musica. Lingua e poesia nella canzone d'autore italiana*, ed. Lorenzo Còveri, Novara, Interlinea, 224 pp. *Potere alla parola: antologia del rap italiano*, ed. Pierfrancesco Pacoda, Mi, Feltrinelli, 208 pp. Gian Paolo Caprettini, *La scatola parlante (l'evoluzione del linguaggio televisivo)*, Ro, Ed. Riuniti, xiii + 211 pp.

10. DIALECTOLOGY

The *Atlante Linguistico Italiano* has at last begun to emerge from the Istituto dell'Atlante Linguistico at the University of Turin. Although the delay caused by years of publication difficulties means that unfortunately it is not as sophisticated from the sociolinguistic and syntactic points of view as more recent regional undertakings and the transcription of ethnographic data does not use the IPA, it covers the whole of Italy (a network of 1065 points, including alloglottic areas), representing a major linguistic achievement that will serve as an invaluable reference tool especially for lexical, phonetic, and morphological study. *Atlante Linguistico Italiano*, I: *Il corpo umano*, ed. Lorenzo Massobrio et al., Ro, IPZS, 1995, vii + 513 pp., contains 93 maps; the *Verbali delle inchieste*, and *Punti 1–661*; II, vii + 1083 pp., continues with *Punti 662–1065*. Paolo Giannoni, *L'AIS ieri e oggi. I principi teorici dell'AIS. L'interpretazione e l'integrazione dei dati in funzione dell'analisi diacronica. Indagine in Toscana (Radda in Chianti, punto 543)*, Basel–Tübingen, Francke, 310 pp. Paola Benincà, *Piccola storia ragionata della dialettologia italiana*, Padua, Unipress, 207 pp., offers a revised, amplified version of the eminently readable and informative 1988 publication. T. Stehl, 'Urbanità linguistica: Die Stadt als Kommunikationsraum in der italienischen Sprachwissenschaft', *Italienisch*, 35:56–71, traces the history of urban dialectology in Italy and applauds recent rapprochement with geolinguistics in the regional linguistic atlases, for example *NADIR* (Salento), *ALEPO* (West Piedmont), and *ALS* (Sicily). H. Goebl, 'La convergence entre les fragmentations géo-linguistique et géo-génétique de l'Italie du Nord', *RLiR*, 60:25–49, reveals striking areal correspondences between dialects and genetic distribution.

Two new collections of dialect studies edited by the same distinguished scholar have appeared: *Saggi dialettologici in area italo-romanza. Nuova raccolta*, ed. Giovan Battista Pellegrini, Padua, CSDI, 1995, vii + 261 pp., henceforth Pellegrini, *Nuova raccolta*, and *Terza raccolta di saggi dialettologici in area italo-romanza*, ed. Giovan Battista Pellegrini, Padua, CSDI, 1996, v + 257 pp., henceforth Pellegrini, *Terza raccolta*. L. Renzi, ' "Ma la diga, no xela venezian éla?" '. Per una storia delle forme allocutive nei dialetti italiani', *Lepschy Vol.*, 259–71, offers a stimulating overview that exhorts others to examine this little-studied but important area. H. W. Haller, 'Traduzioni interdialettali: "La scoperta dell'America" da Pascarella ai genovesi', *RID*, 19:81–96, is an absorbing stylistic and linguistic comparison of the numerous dialect poems inspired by Pascarella's highly successful account in Romanesco. Id., 'Sull'uso letterario del dialetto nel romanzo recente', *Atti* (Salerno), 601–10. On a similar theme,

Giuseppe Anceschi, *'La verità sfacciata'. Appunti per una storia dei rapporti fra lingua e dialetti*, F, Olschki, 211 pp., offers thoughtful considerations on the writings of, for example, Giorgio Baffo, Carlo Porta, G. G. Belli, Vittorio Imbriani, Carlo Dossi, Delio Tessa, and Gadda, relating to this often tortuous relationship. Dialect lexis features in R. Bracchi, 'Dallo scorcio aneddotico all'orizzonte culturale. Esempi di fraseologia meteorologica', *QS*, 17:247–70.

NORTHERN DIALECTS. P. Benincà, 'Agglutination and inflection in northern Italian dialects', *Papers* (Los Angeles), 59–72, discusses unusual verb forms (bearing modal or tense formatives *following* person agreement) in the light of the theoretical debate for and against a lexicalist theory of verb morphology, opting for a syntactic origin for these particular data. L. Vanelli, 'Convergenze e divergenze nella storia del pronome e dell'articolo: esiti di ILLU(M) nei dialetti italiani settentrionali', *Lepschy Vol.*, 369–86, is a clear, comprehensive overview of the diachronic developments and syntactic differences that account for the extensive and initially perplexing morphological variation. L. Zörner, 'Osservazioni sul clitico oggetto maschile della 3ª persona *lo* nei dialetti italiani settentrionali', *RID*, 19:165–77, attributes the variation (in the case of one of the categories) to the diverse nature of support vowels reintroduced in particular contexts following apocope, their quality being frequently determined by analogy with other personal pronoun objects. Her 'Neues zur oberitalienischen Personalendung der 4. Person Präsens *-úma*', *VR*, 55:33–37, draws on data from an early Lombard text to construct a very plausible case for deriving this puzzling suffix from a contextually reduced form of auxiliary HABEMUS, but the Canavese data remains problematic. R. Grazioli, 'The particles *s'* and *d'* in northern Italian ballad texts', *RPh*, 49:262–75, argues on the basis of Piedmontese data that these two particles, which are restricted to literary usage, function as evaluative devices that foreground particular information. Id., 'Aspetti della concisione verbale nei testi delle ballate tradizionali piemontesi: l'uso del vocativo', *RID*, 19:97–118, illustrates the many functions so economically performed by vocatives. These range from scene setting, tracking speakers, and scene changes to evoking intervening events. P. Rizzolati, 'Sul friulano "ont" e le denominazioni del burro nell'Italia nord-orientale', Lupu, *Studi*, 649–61, focuses on reflexes of UNCTU(M).

PIEDMONT. *Il Piemonte linguistico*, T, Museo della Montagna 'Duca degli Abruzzi', 1995, 57 pp., is an exhibition volume with separate linguistic maps, comprising essays by Piedmontese specialists: G. Gasca Queirazza, 'Sviluppo dei dialetti del Piemonte' (7–16); A. Rossebastiano, 'I luoghi e i loro nomi' (23–27); A. Genre, 'La toponomastica: che cos'è?' (28–36); L. Massobrio, 'Il Piemonte negli atlanti linguistici e nelle raccolte dialettali' (37–40); T. Telmon, 'L'atlante parlato del Piemonte' (41–56). Lexical studies include A. Rossebastiano, 'Bela 'n piasa: parole e cose della moda femminile in Piemonte nei secoli XVI–XVII', Marcato, *Donna*, 475–88, and T. Telmon, 'I nomi dell'aratro in Piemonte e in valle d'Aosta', pp. 283–95 of *Il seme l'aratro la messe. Le coltivazioni frumentarie in Piemonte dalla Preistoria alla meccanizzazione agricola*, ed. R. Comba and F. Panero, Cuneo, Società per gli Studi Storici della Provincia di Cuneo.

LIGURIA. Fiorenzo Toso, **Storia linguistica della Liguria*, I, *Dalle origini al 1528*, Recco (Genova), Le Mani, 1995, ix + 232 pp. Pierleone Massajoli, **Dizionario della cultura brigasca*, II: *Grammatica*, Alessandria, Orso, xiv + 91 pp. L. Còveri and M. Campagnol, 'Poesia dialettale al femminile. Un'indagine in Liguria', Marcato, *Donna*, 187–200. E. Melli, 'A proposito della data di nascita e di altre questioni concernenti l'Anonimo Genovese', Lupu, *Studi*, 905–17.

LOMBARDY. **I quatter vangeli de Mattee, March, Luca e Gioann: in dialett milanes*, Mi, NED, 1995, xxvi + 518 pp., has facing Italian text. Riccardo Magri, *Dialetto cremonese di città e dei paesi. Ortografia e grammatica*, *Dizionario italiano-dialetto*, and **Dizionario dialetto-italiano*, Cremona, Turris, 105, 204, and 323 pp. respectively, are directed at the general public. Enrico Cirani and Mario Gardini, *Al dialèt di magiurén: dizionario del dialetto di Casalmaggiore*, Cremona, Turris, xii + 116 pp., contains some contextualized exemplification. Karl von Ettmayer, *Lombardisch-ladinisches aus Südtirol: ein Beitrag zum oberitalienischen Vokalismus: die zugrundeliegenden Dialektmaterialien*, ed. Hans Goebl, San Martin de Tor, Istitut cultural ladin 'Micurà de Rü', 1995, iv + 304 pp.

VENETO. John Trumper and Maria Teresa Vigolo, *Il Veneto centrale: problemi di classificazione dialettale e di fitonomia*, Padua, CSDI, 1995, xi + 232 pp., reviewing the classification of Veneto dialects from the standpoint of each linguistic level, lays particular emphasis on the need for a meticulous consideration of lexical data. Such an approach reveals a greater concentration of Celtic terminology in the mid-southern Veneto area than was previously supposed and confirms the spuriousness of Rheto-Romance as a historical unit: so-called 'Ladin' elements being also found in mid-southern Veneto. The ensuing systematic etymological study of the botanical terminology of the area raises crucial methodological and classificatory issues. P. Barbierato, 'La toponomastica del territorio di Conegliano', Pellegrini, *Nuova raccolta*, 3–52; D. Soranzo, 'Attraverso le antiche carte padovane (noterelle toponomastiche)', *ib.*, 69–88, and 'Leggendo le carte medioevali padovane: proposte toponomastiche', Pellegrini, *Terza raccolta*, 167–217; E. Croatto, 'Saggio lessicale del dialetto della Valle di Zoldo', *ib.*, 219–343, and 'Alcune caratteristiche del lessico cadorino', Pellegrini, *Nuova raccolta*, 111–52; G. Tomasi, 'La cultura del castagno nel veneto settentrionale', *ib.*, 153–73; C. Marcato, 'Contributi alla conoscenza del veneto lagunare di Grado e Marano: il lessico ornitonimico', *ib.*, 175–89; N. Breda, 'Tassonomie popolari e osservazioni demologiche su specie vegetali di area trevigiana (Mosnigo di Moriago)', *ib.*, 191–242; M. T. Vigolo, 'Aggiunte alle denominazioni delle malattie di animali in area veneta e ladina', *ib.*, 243–55, and 'Note su alcuni punti oscuri di fitonomia trevigiana', Pellegrini, *Terza raccolta*, 235–46; G. B. Pellegrini, 'Tedeschismi nei dialetti veneti settentrionali', *ib.*, 1–20; S. Schmid, 'La struttura della sillaba nei dialetti veneti', *ib.*, 125–66. L. Meneghello, 'Batarìa', *Lepschy Vol.*, 207–24, is a delightful romp among the lexical (and other) treasures of Vicentino. Dino Coltro, **Parole perdute: il parlar figurato nella tradizione orale veneta*, Verona, Cierre, 1995, 285 pp. Both F. Ursini, 'L'immagine femminile in un misogino veneziano del '500: Andrea Calmo', Marcato, *Donna*, 341–49, and M. Ceretta, 'L'immagine femminile negli articoli in dialetto di un settimanale vicentino (1889–1981)', *ib.*, 351–63, reveal how language reflects but also conditions attitudes and behaviour.

EMILIA-ROMAGNA.   Adelmo Masotti, *Vocabolario romagnolo italiano*, Bo, Zanichelli, xii + 738 pp., is a noteworthy addition to Zanichelli's imposing range of Italian dictionaries. It offers an excellent overview of today's dialect with its loans and neologisms, and the generous exemplification of full sentences and proverbs makes it a rich source of grammatical as well as lexical information. A. Uguzzoni and M. G. Busà, 'Correlati acustici della opposizione di quantità vocalica in area emiliana', *RID*, 19:7–39. L. Repetti, 'Constraints on prosodic structure: a study of the dialect of Coli (PC)', *SILTA*, 24, 1995:279–84, and 'Syllabification and unsyllabified consonants in Emilian and Romagnol dialects', *Papers* (Los Angeles), 373–82, demonstrate how a generative theory of phonology based on constraints can elegantly explain apparently conflicting data and account for minimal variation in closely related dialects. J. Hajek, 'A first acoustic study of the interaction between vowel and consonant duration in Bolognese', *RIA*, 19, 1995:3–10, tackles the problem of the status of traditional geminate consonants in Bolognese to find that they are indeed long (not tense as has been claimed recently) in the urban dialect, although not in all rural varieties. L. Canepari and D. Vitali, 'Pronuncia e grafia del bolognese', *RID*, 19:119–64, combines a detailed phonetic and phonological description of the many varieties of Bolognese arising from sociolinguistic variation with suggestions for orthographic reform and useful facts about the regional Italian. B. Badini, 'Contrasti di lingua e cultura fra testimonianze femminili bolognesi del Sei-Settecento', Marcato, *Donna*, 211–21. M. Loporcaro, 'Un caso di coniugazione per genere del verbo finito in alcuni dialetti della montagna modenese e bolognese', *ZrP*, 112:458–78. Giuseppe Di Genova, **Grammatica e rimario del dialetto modenese*, Vignola, Vaccari, 94 pp.

CENTRAL AND SOUTHERN DIALECTS. Francesco Avolio, **Bommèspre: profilo linguistico dell'Italia centro-meridionale*, San Severo (Foggia), Gerni, 1995, xxi + 176 pp. R. Sornicola, 'Alcune strutture con pronome espletivo nei dialetti italiani meridionali', *Lepschy Vol.*, 323–40, surveys some little-known data of particular relevance to the pro-drop parameter from the viewpoints of generative and functional / pragmatic theory. F. Fanciullo, 'Tra fonologia e morfologia: vicende di un suffisso greco-romanzo nell'Italia meridionale', *AGI*, 81:95–119. V. Formentin, 'Flessione bicasuale del pronome relativo in antichi testi centro-meridionali', *ib.*, 133–76, notes the prolonged survival of a nom./acc. distinction.

TUSCANY. C. Cecioni, **La terra, e' la s'à nni ssangue: indagine su lingua, cultura e vita del contado fiorentino*, F, CET, 301 pp. G. Giacomelli, 'La Mea e la Nena, due eroine quasi sconosciute della poesia dialettale toscana', Marcato, *Donna*, 173–79. M. Barberini, *Vocabolario maremmano*, Pisa, Nistri-Lischi, xx + 491 pp., offers extensive coverage of the lexicon, completed by brief sections on toponomastic terms and proverbs of the region.

ABRUZZO AND MOLISE. R. Hastings, 'The dialects of Abruzzo and Molise', *QRCEDLIM*, 1:21–38; Id., 'Between Tuscan and Abruzzese: regional Italian in Abruzzo', *ib.*, 39–61. M. Minadeo, *Lessico del dialetto di Ripalimosani*, Campobasso, Enne, xxviii + 397 pp., contains a detailed and extensive dictionary and a selection of texts and proverbs. For a close examination of the dialect of Casacalenda we now have: A. Vincelli, *Grammatica descrittiva del dialetto di Casacalenda*, Campobasso, Enne, 1995, 223 pp., containing a clear overview of phonology and morphosyntax, and also a second edition of his *Vocabolario ragionato del dialetto di Casacalenda* accompanied by a brief addendum of lexical material: *Vocabolario ragionato del dialetto di Casacalenda. Integrazione*.

CAMPANIA. A facsimile has appeared of the 1873 ed. of R. D'Ambra, *Vocabolario napolitano-toscano: domestico di arti e mestieri*, Sala Bolognese, Forni, xi + 548 pp. R. E. Radtke, 'Napoletano *schiocca, scucchia* — un caso di contaminazione semantica', *QS*, 17:203–10. Two theoretically stimulating syntactic analyses are: N. Vincent, 'Appunti sulla sintassi dell'infinito coniugato in un testo napoletano del Trecento', *Lepschy Vol.*, 387–406, which combines a clear esposizione of the conditions governing a now defunct use of the conjugated infinitive in Neapolitan with comparative references to related phenomena in other Italo-Romance varieties; and A. Ledgeway, 'La ristrutturazione e i verbi modali in napoletano', *QRCEDLIM*, 1:62–82, which sees restructuring as a consequence of Case Theory. P. del Puente, 'La metafonia napoletana. Un tentativo di analisi sociolinguistica', *ID*, 58, 1995 [1996]:49–67. M. Dell'Aglio, 'Valori non semantici del suffisso diminutivo nella parlata delle donne salernitane', Marcato, *Donna*, 623–32.

BASILICATA. M. T. Greco, 'La denominazione dei giorni a Picerno e a Tito (Potenza)', *BALI*, 19, 1995:75–77, looks at designations for temporal units such as 'today' rather than names of days of the week.

CALABRIA. J. Trumper and A. Lombardi, 'Il ruolo della morfologia verbale nella determinazione di eteroglosse calabresi significative (ed eventuali ipotesi storiche)', *QRCEDLIM*, 1:83–101. John Trumper, *Una lingua nascosta. Sulle orme degli ultimi 'quadrari' calabresi*, Messina, Rubbettino, 192 pp., is a detailed and fascinating study of the language of Calabrian tinkers. F. Spezzano, *Il gergo della malavita in Calabria*, Cosenza, Pellegrini, 166 pp., attractively presents under 20 thematic headings several hundred lexical items from underworld slang in Calabrian, many of them unique to this dialect. J. Trumper, M. Maddalon, and G. Chiodo, 'L'influenza di eventi macrocosmici su alcune discontinuità linguistiche (Calabria)', Pellegrini, *Nuova raccolta*, 89–105, presents a fascinating account of how linguistic patterns were reshaped in 17th-c. Calabria as a result of major earthquakes and subsequent population displacement. M. Loporcaro, 'Reggino *ssiari* "*aizzare*": ideofoni e lessico ordinario', *QDLC*, 5, 1994:89–92, considers a possible case of onomatopoeic word formation. Id., 'Raddoppiamento fonosintattico dopo III persone plurali del verbo nei dialetti di Conflenti (CZ) e di San Giovanni in Fiori (CS)', *AAL*, 6, 1995:543–53, develops L.'s favourite field of study with the identification of a special instance of RF. J. Trumper, 'Vindex verborum: aspetti importanti dell'elemento albanese nei gerghi italiani di mestiere', Pellegrini, *Terza raccolta*, 109–24, considers designations of tradesmen in various dialects, predominantly of the Centre-South; Id., 'Noterelle su alcuni fitonimi sconosciuti ed alcuni altri mal definiti dell'area del Pollino (CS, PZ: area Lausberg)', *ib.*, 247–57.

PUGLIA. V. Valente, 'Locuzioni pugliesi da tecnicismi giuridici', *ib.*, 85–96, examines cases of legal loans in Pugliese dialects. Immacolata Tempesta, *Contatti *linguistici e sociolinguistici fra Puglia e Salento: gli indefiniti*, Alessandria, Orso, 1995, 86 pp. In A. Miglietta, 'I gradi dell'aggettivo al confine settentrionale del Salento', *BALI*, 19, 1995:79–105, the results are given of a survey of six localities using a detailed questionnaire. G. Colasuonno, *Vocabolario *del dialetto di Palo del Colle*, Bari, Levante, 258 pp. D. Bentley, 'Alcune osservazioni sui

costrutti condizionali nella provincia di Palermo', *QRCEDLIM*,
1:1–20. A. Michel, *Vocabolario critico degli ispanismi siciliani*, Palermo,
CSFLS, 542 pp.

11. ITALIAN ABROAD

C. Milani, 'Note sulla lingua di emigrate italiane in ambiente
anglofono', Marcato, *Donna*, 517–29. J. Vizmuller-Zocco, 'Languages
of Italian Canadians', *Italica*, 72, 1995:512–29, emphasizes the
diversity of Canadian Italian and its uncertainty in the future, and
from the same author there is 'I prestiti linguistici dall'inglese in
italiano e in italiano nordamericano', *Il Veltro*, 40:466–73, in which
lexical accommodation in the two coexisting linguistic systems is
examined. A fascinating study of the Italian used in legal texts
emanating from the chancellery of Ottoman Tunisia appears in
J. Cremona, 'L'italiano in Tunisi. La lingua di alcuni testi del tardo
'500 e del '600', *Lepschy Vol.*, 85–97. G. Alfieri and C. Giovanardi,
'Italiano non letterario in Francia nel Novecento', *SGI*, 16: 189–320,
examines the types of conversational Italian proposed as models for
learners. C. Bettoni and A. Rubino, 'Emigrazione al femminile: il
caso italo-australiano', Marcato, *Donna*, 501–16.

12. SARDINIAN

Francesco C. Casula, *La Carta del logu del regno di Arborea: traduzione
libera e commento storico*, Sassari, Delfino, 1995, 298 pp. E. Blasco
Ferrer, 'Testi sulcitani con commento glottologico. Contributo alla
conoscenza d'un campidanese sui generis', *TLP*, 33–34:39–44,
contains three texts with phonetic transcription. M. Virdis, 'Note di
sintassi sarda medievale', *ib.*, 507–26, argues on the basis of numerous
textual examples for the generation of the subject in D-structure as
an adjunct of V or VP, which produces a postverbal surface subject
in unmarked constructions (preverbal subjects are the result of
movement to TOP or SpecC). A. Dettori, 'Una voce femminile del
medioevo sardo', Marcato, *Donna*, 295–313, analyses one of the
Condaghe di Santa Maria di Bonarcado. Renzo De Martino, *Il dizionario
Maddalenino: glossario etimologico comparato*, Cagliari, Torre, 195 pp.
Lucio Artizzu, *Il dizionario di Cagliari: sa memoria e su tempus*, Cagliari,
Torre, 295 pp. E. Büchi, 'La position des noms de familles sardes à
l'intérieur de la patronymie romane', *TLP*, 33–34:45–65. I. Loi
Corvetto, 'Plurilinguismo nei toponimi medievali sardi', *ib.*, 247–57.
M. Maxia, 'Un toponimo medievale sardo di origine prediale', *ib.*,
291–94. G. Paulis, 'Note di onomastica sarda: soprannomi e etimolo-
gia', *ib.*, 365–80. M. Pittau, 'L'iscrizione nuragica in lettere latine nel

nuraghe Áidu 'Entos (Bortigeli, Sardegna)', *ib.*, 381–95. M. Lörinczi, 'Tassonomia popolare e tassonomia scientifica: il caso del fenicottero di Sardegna', *QS*, 17:271–95. M. S. Casula, 'Imprecazioni al femminile in area sarda (Settimo S. P.)', Marcato, *Donna*, 489–98, is a fascinating comparative study. M. E. Soges, 'Tra identità regionale e tendenza verso i modelli di prestigio. Aspetti del lessico delle donne nell'italiano di Macomer (NU)', *ib.*, 607–15.

E. Radtke, 'Appunti sulla storiografia della filologia sarda nella Germania dell'Ottocento', *TLP*, 33–34:397–407, reminding us of the major contribution of German scholars to Sardinian studies, comments on the analytical and classificatory approaches of W. Meyer Lübke and M. L. Wagner's predecessors. Modern scholarship is largely home-based, but Michael A. Jones (*Sardinian Syntax*, London, Routledge, 1993) deserved inclusion among the few foreign scholars mentioned, especially in view of the traditional neglect of syntax. R. Rindler Schjerve, 'Cambiamento di codice come strategia di sopravvivenza ovvero vitalità del sardo al giorno d'oggi', *ib.*, 409–25, concludes on the basis of a detailed quantitative and qualitative analysis of code-switching that 'il sardo si trova in uno stato di italianizzazione progressiva che nello stato attuale delle cose sembra essere il costo della sua conservazione funzionale'. This is encouraging in that it poses no immediate threat for Sardinian's survival, but the generational discontinuity in its acquistion as L1 bodes ill for its future.

DUECENTO AND TRECENTO I (DANTE)
POSTPONED

DUECENTO AND TRECENTO II
(EXCLUDING DANTE)
By JOAN HALL, *Cambridge*

1. GENERAL

Armando Petrucci, *Writers and Readers in Medieval Italy. Studies in the History of Written Culture*, New Haven, Yale U.P., 1995, xiii + 257 pp., surveys manifold aspects of the subject from its beginnings to the introduction of printing; in particular, an interesting chapter deals with 'Reading and writing *volgare* in medieval Italy'. M. Feo, '"Litterae" e "litteratura" nel medioevo e nell'umanesimo', *Acta* (Copenhagen), 221–41, examines these concepts as interpreted in the Latin works of Brunetto Latini, Petrarch, Boccaccio, and others. C. Segre, 'I volgarizzamenti', Cavallo, *Lo Spazio*, III, 271–98, begins with brief notes on translation from Latin into French and Spanish, then concentrates on the much larger corpus of translations into the Italian *volgare*. The selection of works was based on different criteria: medieval Latin authors were translated for practical/moral reasons, while in the case of classical works the motivation was at least partly aesthetic. In the case of historical and poetic texts, a historical survey of 13th- and 14th-c. prose and verse translations reveals an increasing aesthetic interest in style, with maximum freedom in narrative works.

The field of medieval political discourse is enriched by a mine of material in Cammarosano, *Propaganda*, which contains the papers from an international conference held in Trieste in March 1993. The contributions dealing with Italy (the great majority) include: H. Zug Tucci, 'Dalla polemica antimperiale alla polemica antitedesca' (45–64); J.-C. Maire Vigueur, 'Religione e politica nella propaganda pontificia (Italia comunale, prima metà del XIII secolo)' (65–83); J.-P. Boyer, 'La "foi monarchique": royaume de Sicile et Provence (mi-XIIIe–mi-XIVe siècle)' (85–110); A. Barbaro, 'La propaganda di Roberto d'Angiò re di Napoli (1309–1343)' (111–31); E. Artifoni, 'Retorica e organizzazione del linguaggio politico nel Duecento italiano' (157–82); M. Aurell, 'Chanson et propagande politique: les troubadours gibelins (1255–1285)' (183–202); A. Bartoli Langeli, 'Cancellierato e produzione epistolare' (251–61); N. Grove Marchioli, 'L'epigrafia comunale cittadina' (263–86); A. Di Salvo, '"Celebrazioni politiche d'occasione": il caso dei primi Scaligeri' (287–310); G. M. Varanini, 'Propaganda dei regimi signorili: le esperienze venete del Trecento' (311–43); S. Carocci, 'La celebrazione aristocratica nello Stato della Chiesa' (345–67); G. Andenna, 'La simbologia del potere nelle città comunali lombarde: i palazzi pubblici' (369–93); A. Zorzi, 'Rituali di violenza, cerimoniali penali, rappresentazioni della giustizia nelle città italiane centro-settentrionali (secoli XIII-XV)' (395–425); C. Crouzet-Pavan, 'Gênes et Venise: discours historiques et imaginaires de la cité' (427–53); P. Cammarosano, 'Il comune di Siena dalla solidarietà imperiale al guelfismo: celebrazione e propaganda' (455–67); S. Raveggi, 'Appunti sulle forme di propaganda nel conflitto tra magnati e popolani' (470–89); and M. M. Donato, '"Cose morali, e anche appartenenti secondo e' luoghi": per lo studio della pittura politica nel tardo medioevo toscano' (491–517).

Social attitudes and beliefs in the period are reflected in V. Branca, 'Ripiegamenti spirituali di mercanti fra medioevo e rinascimento', Graciotti, *Spiritualità*, 162–77, arguing from recently studied documents that 14th-15th-c. Tuscan merchants were very conscious of religion, perhaps even more so than the literati of the period. F. Cardini, 'Note per una preistoria dell'esotismo nella Firenze medievale', Goodich, *Convergences*, 49–58, gives a stimulating brief survey identifying three main strands of Florentine views on the East: hostile (linked with the crusade movement); romantic (exotic luxury, splendour, colour); and a new more open and critical view in which Muslim cultural values and Saladin's wisdom and virtue were set against criticism of the Christian world.

L. Gatti, 'Il mito di Marte a Firenze e la "pietra scema". Memorie, riti e ascendenze', *Rinascimento*, 35, 1995:201–39, discusses the myth of Mars (and his statue at the head of Ponte Vecchio) both as guardian of Florence and as the origin of the city's sectarianism and discord. The theme is traced in the writings of Brunetto Latini, Dante, Sacchetti, Villani, Boccaccio, Antonio Pucci, and on into the 15th c., as well as in the visual iconography of Florentine history: an evolution that shows 'come nel contesto frammentario, mobile e incerto del cosmo cittadino, i testi, le immagini e i riti fossero eventi complessi che si aprivano alle interpretazioni più varie, dando così luogo ad una ricchezza di significati ...'

Of interest for the development of the *exemplum* tradition is B. G. Kohl, 'Valerius Maximus in the fourteenth century: the commentary of Giovanni Conversini da Ravenna', *Acta* (Copenhagen), 537–46. According to C. Delcorno, 'Le "vitae patrum" nella letteratura religiosa medievale (secc. XIII–XV)', Graciotti, *Spiritualità*, 179–201, the *Vitae Patrum* served not only as *exempla* for sermons, but also (especially in Tuscan *volgarizzamenti*) as material for private reading, nourishing tendencies to mysticism and contemplative devotion in members of the elite, who sought direct access to the Christian message in that period of crisis of ecclesiastical institutions.

M. Bendinelli Predelli, 'La donna guerriera nell'immaginario italiano del tardo Medioevo', *ItC*, 12, 1994:13–31, surveys the antecedents of Bradamante, Marfisa, and Clorinda in ancient and medieval literature, beginning with the legend of the Amazons and passing through the Franco-Italian tradition. The figure of the warrior maiden, and certain features of her career, are traced in works by Andrea da Barberino, Domenico Scolari, Boccaccio, Pucci, Piero da Siena, and Marco Polo. G. Allaire, 'The warrior woman in late medieval prose epics', *ib.*, 33–43, covers some of the same ground, with additional examples and analytical commentary; the two articles together map what may prove a fertile field for further research. C. Kleinhenz, 'The quest motif in medieval Italian literature', *Kelly Vol.*, 235–51, discusses the nature and function of the Arthurian quest motif in Italian lyric and narrative-didactic poetry, prose romances, and the *novella*. The motif is used both incidentally for allusive (comic) effect, and as a principal theme. M. Saksa, 'Sull'iconografia del cavaliere medievale in Italia', *QMed*, 40, 1995:109–20, focuses on the image of the knight in graphic art, linking it with the literary tradition.

Angela Giallongo, *L'avventura dello sguardo. Educazione e comunicazione visiva nel Medioevo*, Bari, Dedalo, 1995, xii + 516 pp., is a wide-ranging historical survey of the development and influence of concepts of vision, culminating in the conscious use of images as iconographic instruments to propagate religious and secular values, the evolution of an educational system centred on them, and the discovery of different strategies of visual behaviour. Also on vision: N. Pasero, 'Sottrazione del colore: per una ricerca sulla lirica del Duecento', *IR*, 3, 1994:169–86, considers the interaction of symbolic and philosophical values of colour, and the question of why colours are rarely mentioned in 13th-c. love poetry.

2. BOCCACCIO

Varieties of discourse in the *Decameron* are studied by Pier Massimo Forni, *Adventures in Speech. Rhetoric and Narration in Boccaccio's 'Decameron'*, Philadelphia, Pennsylvania U.P., xiv + 155 pp. The aim is to map the complexity of interactions between narration and non-narrative discourse, which 'constantly gloss each other'. Topics include the morphology of verbal interactions in the *cornice*, the issue of narrative pleasure, the analysis of explicit and allusive types of narrative response, the beginnings of the *novelle*. The narrative possibilities of speech are explored, with particular reference to the *novella* of Zima (III 5). The Appendix is a postscript on the theme of incest in the *Decameron*, treated earlier in Forni's *Forme complesse nel 'Decameron'* with reference to the Tancredi story.

D. Delcorno Branca, '"Cognominatio prencipe Galeotto". Il sottotitolo illustrato del Parigino It. 482', *StB*, 23, 1995:79–88, draws an interesting conclusion from a study of the drawings at the *incipit* of the Paris MS of the *Decameron*, which are recognized as the work of B. himself or someone very close to him. The drawing of knights and ladies resembles contemporary illustrations of the French *Lancelot*; this, together with the name of Galeotto in the subtitle and the figure, in the initial, of a monk or teacher reading aloud, suggests an intriguing challenge to Dante's negative gloss of Galehaut in the *Inferno*. G. Bertoli, 'Le prime due edizioni della seconda "rassettatura"', *ib.*, 3–17, reconsiders the sequence and relative accuracy of the earliest printed editions of the *Decameron* (1482).

V. A. Milanese, 'Affinità e contraddizioni tra rubriche e novelle nel *Decameron*', *ib.*, 89–111, examines the structure of the rubrics and their relationship (exegetic or parodistic) with the narrative. The analysis takes account of previous studies by D'Andrea and Usher, largely favouring the former. T. Gabriele, 'Aspects of nudity in the Decameron', Benedetti, *Gendered Contexts*, 31–38, contesting 'notions of nudity in the *Decameron* as a purely female or purely erotic element', argues that nudity usually signals a state or threat of 'vulnerability, danger, and shame'. F. Canovas, 'Forme et fonction de l'énoncé onirique dans le texte médiéval: l'exemple du *Decameron*', *Neophilologus*, 80:555–67, aims to demonstrate that literary dream sequences can be read as *mises-en-abyme*, and that such sequences are not modern but belong to a long tradition and large corpus of medieval texts. The argument focuses on *novelle* IV, 5 and 6, V, 8, and IX, 7.

This year has produced a rich crop of works dealing with individual *novelle*. R. Ferreri, 'La quarta novella del *Decameron*', *RStI*, 14.1:25–35, offers a neat structural analysis of the tale of the monk and the abbot. A particularly original and illuminating study is that of D. D. Vacca, 'Converting Alibech: "Nunc Spiritu copuleris"', *JMRS*, 25, 1995:207–27: '... this novella can be read as a pointed, though oblique, commentary on the patristic and scholastic construction of Christian morality and the understanding of sexuality of Sts. Jerome and Augustine'. M. Wenzel, 'Giovanni Boccaccios *Dekameron*. Die erste Novelle del fünften Tages als ein Sujet der darstellenden Kunst? Ein interdisziplinärer Blick', *ItStudien*, 17:174–85, considers Branca's thesis that B., in the *novella* of Cimone, promoted a new topos in Western figurative art: the nude reclining Venus. A. Baldi, 'La retorica dell'"exemplum" nella novella di Nastagio (Decameron, V, 8)', *ItQ*, 123–24, 1995:117–28, shows that while the story is introduced as an *exemplum*, with precedents in earlier exemplary literature, it subverts Christian morality by contaminating it with courtly values. There is an element of parody: while the narrator

assumes a didactic posture and mimics ritual language, in fact the
novella evokes a joyous and unrepentant sensuality. R. Fedi, 'Strutture
decameroniane', *LS*, 31:353–61, finds a turning point in narrative
development of the *Decameron* between Days V and VI, a change in
the the general tone of the work and in the style of the *novelle*. VI, 1 is
seen as a 'new beginning' — a 'golden section' of the *Decameron* as a
whole, with Oretta's journey mirroring the journey of the *brigata* and
the progress of the *Decameron* itself. Another view of this *novella* is given
by C. Clark-Evans, 'Boccaccio's "narratio interrupta": the *Cornice*
and the First Tale of Day VI', *CJIS*, 18, 1995:136–45, noting the
interruption by servants in the introduction to the day, followed by
Oretta's interruption of the knight's story. The discussion covers
various kinds of interruption in the *Decameron* and the different
techniques used to end a story. L. Russo, 'Chichibìo cuoco: della
leggerezza mentale', *Belfagor*, 51:187–92, is a reprint of a 1938 article
on the question of whether Chichibio is a naïve fool or a witty
maverick, including a note on B.'s use of municipal dialect expressions
for comic effect. F. Alfie, 'Poetics enacted: a comparison of the
novellas of Guido Cavalcanti and Cecco Angiulieri in Boccaccio's
Decameron', *StB*, 23, 1995:171–96, stresses intertextual elements and
structural parallels, showing that B.'s treatment of the two poets
reflects many aspects of the preceding lyric tradition, as well as self-
portrayals of Cavalcanti and Cecco and perhaps their contemporary
reputations.

A. Bisanti, 'Lettura della novella di madonna Isabella', *QMed*, 39,
1995:47–61, focuses on a *novella* said to be dismissed by most critics
as meagre and uninteresting. The author, in agreement with Baratto,
finds it one of the most complex and rich in *colpi di scena*, exploiting
the theatrical possibilities offered by the heroine's two lovers. The
novella also works as an *exemplum* whose message is that love does not
necessarily make one stupid. M. Picone, 'Il romanzo di Alatiel', *StB*,
23, 1995:197–217, offers a complex, fascinating reading of the story
as a parody of Greek romance; a key role is attributed to Antigono,
said to represent B. himself. The final denouement is described as
'una riflessione sul potere della parola e un giudizio sulla validità
della letteratura'. N. Moe, 'Not a love story: sexual aggression, law
and order in *Decameron* X, 4', *RR*, 86, 1995:623–38, outlines the
transformation in style, narrative presentation, and social and ethical
vision, from a tale of passion in *Filocolo* into a tale of property in the
Decameron, where the use of legal discourse glosses over and legitimates
an illicit act of passion. F. Ademollo, '*Decameron* X 8.56 ss. e un'antica
controversia filosofica', *Rinascimento*, 35, 1995:173–78, explores
philosophical references in the *novella* of Tito and Gisippo, especially
in relation to Cicero's *De fato*. In the same *novella*, R. Hyatte,

'Reconfiguring ancient "amicitia perfecta" in the *Decameron* 10, 8',
ItQ, 125–26, 1995:27–37, identifies the perfect virtue of friendship
with the oratorical virtue exalted by Cicero, and suggests an analogy
between the final ethical concord in the *novella* and the harmonious
companionship of the *brigata*.

V. R. Giustiniani, 'Griselda e Ser Ciappelletto, o l'uso dell'inatteso
nel *Decameron*', *ItStudien*, 17:20–26, describes the first and last *novelle*
of the *Decameron* as a symmetrical pair, with both protagonists as
totally unrealistic, artificially constructed and diametrically opposite
casi limiti. The emerging genre of the *novella* is defined as a story with
an unexpected turn of events, which in these two tales is the reversal
of the *caso limite* (sinner to saint, wronged to adored wife), though B.
takes care to provide a plausible underpinning for the improbable
events. A more ambitious analysis of the last tale, and the last day, is
that of R. Hollander and C. Cahill, 'Day Ten of the *Decameron*: the
myth of order', *StB*, 23, 1995:113–70. They challenge the common
idea of Day X as an upbeat conclusion celebrating the triumph of
virtue. Instead, the underlying thread is seen as 'an interrogation of
the myth of order', bringing out 'the destructive consequences that
may result from upholding the law, particularly the rigid terms of
contractual agreements'. The authors argue that the *Decameron*
belongs not to the 'matrix of tragedy/comedy' but to the 'tradition of
Roman satire and Roman comedy', and re-read all the *novelle* of Day
X in that key. Their complex and well-grounded analysis makes a
substantial contribution to the literature on this subject. Two more
studies of the last *novella* are T. Greiner, **'Una matta bestialità?* Zur
Deutung von Boccaccios Griselda-Novelle', *ZRP*, 111, 1995:503–22,
and E. Ruhe, **'Griselda und der Falke. Intratextueller Dialog im
Decameron', *ASNS*, 233:52–64.

R. Gigliucci, 'Argumentum, historia: nota su *Avventuroso Siciliano* e
Decameron', *StB*, 23, 1995:245–53, discusses the common features of
the two works, especially an interest in historical plausibility, and
their relationship with existing traditions and sources. Also on the
Decameron: R. van Stipriaan, **Leugens en vermaak. Boccaccio's novellen in de
kluchtkultuur van de Nederlandse Renaissance*, Amsterdam U.P., xiii +
337 pp.; Joachim Theisen, **Arigos Decameron. Übersetzungs-strategie und
poetologische Konzept*, Tübingen–Basel, Bibliotheca Germanica–
Francke, xv + 670 pp.

E. L. Giusti, 'The widow in Giovanni Boccaccio's works: a negative
exemplum or a symbol of positive praxis?', Benedetti, *Gendered
Contexts*, 39–48, analyses B.'s handling of the widow as a literary
character, bringing out the relation between literary topos and
historical reality. In the *Decameron*, *Il Corbaccio*, *De mulieribus claris*, and

other works, the widow emerges in general as a symbol of self-determination. The treatment of this theme by Francesco da Barberino and others is also discussed. M. Veglia, 'Sul nodo culturale del *Corbaccio*', *SPCT*, 52:79–100, focuses on the idea of false love as a 'peste', a seductive but dangerous conception derived from classical literature and the romance tradition. This issue, defined as a basic doctrinal node of medieval culture, is developed by B. in the *Corbaccio* — a treatise on the risk of *imbestiamento* and spiritual death for those who yield to such love — and also by Dante, Cavalcanti, and others, in particular Petrarch (partly in correspondence with B.). G. Chiecchi, 'Per l'interpretazione dell'egloga *Olimpia* di Giovanni Boccaccio', *StB*, 23, 1995:219–44, shows how B. rethinks the tradition of the bucolic genre and gives it a new Christian-Dantean direction.

P. Hardman, 'Chaucer's articulation of the narrative in *Troilus*: the manuscript evidence', *ChRev*, 30, 1995:111–33, argues that Chaucer's practice differed from B.'s less than appears from printed editions. A detailed examination of narrative divisions in the six MSS of *Troilus*, despite differences, shows significant correspondences with B.'s in the *Filostrato*. Another Boccaccio–Chaucer study is that of Laura D. Kellogg, *Boccaccio's and Chaucer's Cressida*, NY, Lang, 1995, xi + 144 pp., which sets out the character's literary history and descent from Dido; this is followed by separate discussions of her treatment by B. (30 pp.) and Chaucer (44 pp.), with a 20-page appendix on B.'s presentation of Dido in several works. C. Vecce, 'Bembo, Boccaccio, e due varianti al testo delle *Prose*', *Aevum*, 68, 1994:521–31, refers to some MS fragments containing Bembo's comments on Boccaccio, later incorporated in *Prose della volgar lingua*, with implications for Bembo's sources and the aims of his textual analysis. A. Petrucci and F. Petrucci Nardelli, 'Un manoscritto pisano con estratti boccacceschi', *FC*, 20, 1995 [1996]:375–85, describes codex 732 (722) in the library of the University of Pisa, containing pages from B.'s *De casibus virorum illustrium* and the *Genealogia deorum gentilium*. Evidently B. had great influence on the development of painting: a survey by E. Callman, 'Subjects from Boccaccio in Italian painting, 1375–1525', *StB*, 23, 1995:19–78, with black-and-white illustrations, updates earlier listings by P. Watson and V. Branca of Boccaccian themes depicted (mainly) on *cassone* and *spalliera* panels and *deschi*.

3. PETRARCH

B. Stock, 'Reading, writing and the self: Petrarch and his forerunners', *NLH*, 26, 1995:717–30, places P. within a tradition, going back to

Augustine, of self-knowledge through reading (plus meditation) and self-definition through writing. This emerges in the *Secretum* and other spiritual writings, and is expressed poetically in the *Canzoniere*. L. Enterline, 'Embodied voices: Petrarch reading (himself reading) Ovid', Finucci, *Desire*, 120–46, deals with the link between language and sexuality in the *Canzoniere*. By analysing how P. read Ovid and how rhetoric informs sexuality through the emblematic figure of Actaeon, the author sees Petrarchan subjectivity as in a continuous process of Ovidian change, with existential moments of anguish, crises, and alienation that shape a new history of the self. N. Gardini, 'Un esempio di imitazione virgiliana nel *Canzoniere* petrarchesco', *MLN*, 110, 1995:132–44, argues that P.'s use of Virgil is not merely a matter of literary 'practice', but implies a superior idea of literature and a redefinition of the role of the poet. For example, P.'s treatment of the Orpheus myth, derived from Virgil and not from Ovid, expresses his view of Virgil as a spiritual and artistic father and a mythic affirmation of man as artist. P.'s evocations of Virgil and Dante are studied by M. Riccucci, 'L'esordio dei *Triumphi*: tra *Eneide* e *Commedia*', *RLettI*, 12, 1994 [1996]:313–49, with particular reference to the first part of the *Triumphus Cupidinis I* and the *Divine Comedy*; the author finds that P. competed with Dante mainly in the technical-professional arena. Ingrid Rossellini, *Nel trapassar del segno. Idoli della mente ed echi della vita nei 'Rerum Vulgarium Fragmenta'*, F, Olschki, 1995, 206 pp., is a wide-ranging and fertile study of the *Canzoniere*, linking P.'s transgressive love of Laura with the 'trapassar del segno' on the part of Ulysses and Adam in the *Divine Comedy*; the essential difference is seen in P.'s humanistic orientation. Another comparison of Dante and Petrarch is that of G. Bárberi-Squarotti, 'La preghiera alla vergine: Dante e Petrarca', *FC*, 20, 1995 [1996]:365–74, who notes that whereas Dante addresses the Virgin through St Bernard, P. pleads for himself in his own voice, and concludes that P.'s poem falls short of the religious sublimity of the prayer in the *Divine Comedy*.

P. Williams, '*Canzoniere* 366: Petrarch's critique of Stoicism', *ISt*, 51:27–41, deals with the problem of whether, and in what sense, the final *canzone* expresses a repudiation of the poet's love for Laura. Unlike the opening sonnet, which rejects passion *per se* in favour of rational choice, *Vergine bella* is seen as reflecting Augustine's view that passions are good when rightly directed; P. accepts the inferiority of earthly love and prays for the Virgin's divine aid in achieving what his will and reason cannot do unaided. A more secular and literary orientation is evoked by J. C. Warner, 'The frying pan and the phoenix: Petrarch's poetics revisited', *RStI*, 14.1:13–24. Taking the Petrarch criticism of J. Freccero and T. Roche as a point of departure, he enquires to what extent the *Canzoniere* is a story of conversion.

During the long love story unfolding between the secure poles at the beginning and end of the collection (both affirming his repentance and reform), the poet creates suspense and is able to 'enjoy transgression without risking damnation'. P. Kuon, 'Metamorphosen Lauras. Zum Verhältnis von Artifizialität in Petrarcas *Canzoniere*', *ItStudien*, 17:36–56, argues that the element of reality in the *Canzoniere* lies not in Laura herself but in the poet's changing vision of her. The Italian summary concludes that 'Il gioco intertestuale delle metamorfosi di Laura ... presuppone — tutt'altro che gioco gratuito, postmoderno — un pegno reale: la salvezza dell'autore'. N. Tonelli, 'Le parole di Laura nei *Rerum Vulgarium Fragmenta*', *RLettI*, 12, 1994 [1996]:293–312, surveys psychological, literary, and intertextual aspects of the poet's encounters with Laura, with emphasis on her direct speech. S. S. Thomas, 'Petrarch, Tournier, photography and fetishism — the veil in the *Rime Sparse*', *RoQ*, 43:131–41, defines Laura as a 'fetish twice removed: a fetish made from a fetish': the poet converts the woman into an idol, which is then fetishized.

  J. Leclercq, 'Temi monastici nell'opera di Petrarca', Graciotti, *Spiritualità*, 149–62, deals with P.'s treatment of the monastic life in *De otio religioso* and *De vita solitaria*, as evidence of reciprocal relations and exchanges between humanism and monasticism. P.'s monastic doctrine is outlined, and then the texts are analysed with particular reference to the meanings of the verb *vacare*. The upshot is that P. considered the monastic life, for those called to it, as a path towards spiritual tranquillity in union with God; for those without a vocation it was a symbol of *libertà nella pace*. K. A. E. Enenkel, *Die humanistische "vita activa/vita contemplativa". Diskussion: Francesco Petrarcas *De vita solitaria*', *Acta* (Copenhagen), 249–57. M. Feo, 'L'epistola come mezzo di propaganda politica in Francesco Petrarca', Cammarosano, *Propaganda*, 203–26, surveys the political content and contexts of P.'s letters (mostly in the *Familiares* and *Seniles*) to Charles IV, Niccolò Acciaiuoli, Francesco da Carrara, Cola di Rienzo, and Jacopo Bussolari. *A Concordance to the 'Familiares' of Francesco Petrarca*, ed. Aldo S. and Reta A. Bernardo, Padua, Antenore, 1994, 2 vols, 2650 pp., offers a massive and definitive resource for scholars. J. Adler, *Die Besteigung des Mont Ventoux — Francesco Petrarca und die Landschaft*', *CP*, 217–18, 1995:54–71. G. Crevatin, 'Il pathos nella scrittura storica del Petrarca', *Rinascimento*, 35, 1995:155–71, focuses on P.'s authorial interventions in *De viris illustribus*, especially the biographies of Scipio and Caesar, bringing out his literary originality in the context of medieval historiography, emphasizing the dignity of history and the rediscovery of artistic values. F. J. Nichols, 'Petrarch's *Liber sine nomine* and the limits of language', *Acta* (Copenhagen), 741–50, reflects on the problem of speaking of the unspeakable — the corruption of the papal court at Avignon — and on P.'s ideas about language and expression.

William J. Kennedy, *Authorizing Petrarch*, Ithaca, Cornell U.P., 1995, xiii + 391 pp., is a study of the 'authorization' of the *Canzoniere* as a canonical lyric text for a broad 15th–16th-c. European readership and for poets in Italy, France, and England. Several Renaissance commentators are surveyed (most extensively Bembo), and a long chapter is devoted to female Petrarchan poets (especially Colonna, Gambara, Pernette du Guillet, and Louise Labé). A. Kablitz, *'Verwandlung und Auflösung der Poetik des fin'amors bei Petrarca und Charles d'Orléans: Transformationen der spätmittelalterlichen Lyrik diskutiert am Beispiel der Rhetorik des Paradox', Stempel, *Musique*, 261–350; Francesca Gregoratti, *Bibliografia delle opere a stampa su Francesco Petrarca nella biblioteca civica 'Attilio Hortis' di Trieste*, F, Olschki, 192 pp.

4. OTHER AUTHORS

AnI, 13, is devoted to women mystic writers. The introduction by D. S. Cervigni (7–17) stresses their literary importance. M. C. Storini, 'Umiliana e il suo biografo: costruzione di un'agiografia femminile fra XIII e XIV secolo' (19–39), focuses on the *Vita* of Umiliana de' Cerchi (1219–46) written soon after her death by Vito da Cortona. In its language, form, and content this biography is an embryonic example of a new hagiographic narrative mode, a new linguistic and metaphoric system. T. Arcangeli, 'Re-reading a mis-known and mis-read mystic: Angela da Foligno' (41–78), gives a thoughtful feminist-oriented perspective on the problem of finding the 'voice' of a female mystic through layers of distortion imposed by male society and, in the case of Angela, a male scribe. M. A. Sagnella, 'Carnal metaphors and mystical discourse in Angela da Foligno's *Liber*' (79–90), maintains that despite Angela's rejection of her 'sinful' female body, her physical being is ultimately restored and sublimated through mystical union with Christ. Five articles deal with Catherine of Siena: K. Scott, 'Candied oranges, vinegar, and dawn: the imagery of conversion in the letters of Caterina of Siena' (91–108), focuses on three letters of spiritual advice written in 1378, in which the paradoxical nature of Catherine's spiritual journey is expressed through the creative use of symbolism and allegory as well as conventional imagery; S. Noffke, 'The physical in the mystical writings of Catherine of Siena' (109–29), deals with the place of physical experience in Catherine's mystical theology, as seen in her treatise, letters and *orazioni*; C. Rattazzi Papka, 'The written woman writes: Caterina da Siena between history and hagiography, body and text' (131–49), maintains that

Catherine's rejection of the body is evident only in her official (male) representation, not in her own writings where physical imagery is a spiritual element which integrates mind and body; M. Zancan, 'Lettere di Caterina da Siena: il testo, la tradizione, l'interpretazione' (151–61), examines the letters, all but two of them dictated and extensively altered through transcription, seeking to discern the 'forte figura di donna intellettuale' within the fixed image of the Saint; J. Chance, 'St. Catherine of Siena in late medieval Britain: feminizing literary reception through gender and class' (163–203), looks at the way Catherine's writings and legend were disseminated in Britain from the 14th to the early 16th c. G. Marrone, 'Ideologia, creatività e iconografia nella Chiara di Liliana Cavani' (387–400), discusses the treatment of Chiara d'Assisi in Cavani's film *Francesco* (1989). The volume concludes with C. Mazzoni, 'Italian women mystics: a bibliographical essay' (401–35).

S. Noffke, 'Caterina da Siena (Catherine of Siena) (1347–1380)', Russell, *Women Writers*, 58–66, is a straightforward basic introduction to Catherine and her works, with a survey of criticism and a good bibliography. T. Luongo, 'Catherine of Siena: rewriting female holy authority', *Procs* (St. Hilda's), 89–103, examines the way in which the Saint 'communicated and negotiated her authority' as revealed by her letter on the conversion and death of Niccolò di Toldo. D. Valentini, 'In search of the subject: Angela of Foligno and her mediator', *RLA*, 6, 1995: 371–75, argues that Angela, through the 'negotiated' mediation of her scribe Arnaldo, represents an 'essential link in the chain of women who appropriated the written word', and thus in their self-affirmation as subjects. Jacques Dalarun, *Francesco: un passaggio. Donna e donne negli scritti e nelle leggende di Francesco d'Assisi*, Ro, Viella, 1994, 200 pp., outlines the hypothesis of a general movement of feminization of Christianity, beginning with Robert of Arbrissel in the 12th c. and passing through St Francis, whose attitude towards Chiara d'Assisi and women in general is analysed through his writings and those of biographers, especially Tommaso da Celano and Bonaventura. J. P. Byrne, 'Reading the medieval woman's voice: reflections on the letters of Margherita Datini, an Italian housewife on the eve of the Renaissance', *West Georgia College Review*, 25:5–13, comments on the letters of Margherita (the wife of Origo's Merchant of Prato) as they reflect her relations with her husband.

E. Vicentini, 'Il *Milione* di Marco Polo come portolano', *Italica*, 71, 1994:145–52, focuses on the *Milione* as a source of commercial information and guide to ports, which was transcribed and distributed to the merchant classes with adaptations to suit their practical as well as literary interests. C. W. Dutschke, ' "Do you imagine that our readers will expect truth?" Or, Marco Polo and Columbia University', *Columbia Library Columns*, 43.2, 1994:33–40, investigates the views of Marco Polo's early readers as to the veracity or otherwise of his reporting, as revealed by two 15th-c. texts, in particular an annotated MS copy. P. Zumthor, 'The medieval travel narrative', *NLH*, 25, 1994:809–24, includes some interesting comments on Marco Polo. M. Pregliasco, 'Linguaggi e figure dello spazio dei viaggi d'oltremare (sec. XIV-XV). Rassegna di testi e studi', *LItal*, 48:625–39, surveys a good number of travel narratives, mostly Italian. X. von Ertzdorff, *'Et transivi per principaliores Mundi provincias: Johannes Marignoli als weitgereister Erzähler der Böhmenchronik', *Colloquium* (Schweinfurt), 142–73.

Il libro di messer Tristano ('Tristano Veneto'), ed. Aulo Doñadello, Venice, Marsilio, 1994, 647 pp., is a welcome edition of the famous but little known *Tristano Veneto*, the only complete medieval Italian *romanzo* — a direct translation of much of the French prose *Tristan* into the Venetian dialect. The text is enriched with about 150 pp. of introduction and critical apparatus. P. Michon, 'L'épisode de la folie de Tristan dans le *Tristano Panciatichiano*', *MA*, 101, 1995:461–73, compares the narrative in the Italian MS with the *Roman de Tristan en prose*, showing how the translator consulted several texts and adapted the story to suit his taste and that of his public. The discussion includes some comparisons with the *Tavola Ritonda*. D. Delcorno Branca, 'I racconti arturiani del *Novellino*', *LItal*, 48:177–205, traces the complex and problematic derivations of Arthurian stories from various sources, and their treatment in the *Novellino*. P. Atzemi, '*Novellino*, XVIII', *Neophilologus*, 80: 269–73, argues that the 'long version' of the *novella* 'Della vendetta che fece Iddio d'uno barone di Carlo Magno' was probably based not on the Latin version of the pseudo-Turpin, but rather on the Old French 'Johannes translation' of it. All three versions are cited and the details compared, showing that the *Novellino* is closer to the Johannes version. *The Novellino*, trans. Roberta L. Payne, introd. Janet L. Smarr, NY, Lang, 1995, 153 pp., is intended for 'undergraduates' (clearly non-Italianists) and includes no linguistic material. It relies on Favati's edition, with no mention of Segre's more widely accepted compilation. The brief introduction gives a schematic survey of the range, content, typologies, and sources of the *novelle*, repeating the long-discredited theory that the narratives were intended merely as outlines for oral use. The translations convey little or nothing of the *Novellino*'s literary interest, and the book's usefulness must be very limited. S. Amadori, 'Una nuova fonte sacchettiana: il *Liber de introductione loquendi* di Filippo da Ferrara O.P.', *LItal*, 48:420–36, gives a brief but interesting résumé of the history of the *exemplum*, emphasizing the increasing importance of *delectatio* or narration for its own sake, especially as evident in Filippo's 14th-c. *Liber*, which is identified as a probable source for some *novelle* of the *Trecentonovelle*. L. Battaglia Ricci, 'Autografi "antichi" e edizioni moderne. Il caso Sacchetti', *FC*, 20, 1995 [1996]: 386–457, is a study of the criteria adopted in producing printed editions from autograph MSS, with reference to the autograph text of Sacchetti's *rime* in the MS Ashburnham 574 at the Biblioteca Laurenziana in Florence. C. Panzera, 'Per l'edizione critica dei *Documenti d'amore* di Francesco da Barberino', *SMV*, 40, 1994: 91–118, is a comparison and discussion of MS texts and previous editions. F. Giambonini, 'Prima revisione per Giovanni dalle Celle e Luigi Marsili', *Rinascimento*, 34, 1994: 145–52, provides a description and textual annotations of MS III.61 in the Biblioteca dell'Abbazia di Vallombrosa (Florence), as an addendum to Giambonini's critical edition of the letters of the two writers.

A. Fratta, *Le fonti provenzali dei poeti della Scuola Siciliana. I postillati del Torraca e altri contributi*, F, Le Lettere, 150 pp., surveys Torraca's annotations in the 1885–88 critical edition by D'Ancona and Comparetti of *Le antiche rime volgari, secondo la lezione del codice 3973*, and in the diplomatic edition of Bartoli and Casini, along with notes by A. Gaspary and others. D. Billy, 'Sextiniana', *MedRom*, 19, 1994: 237–52, offers a survey of recent theoretical articles on the *sestina*. C. Pulsoni, 'Sulla morfologia dei congedi della sestina', *Aevum*, 69, 1995: 505–20, looks for a rule governing the order of rhymed words in the *congedo*, examining 14th-c. *sestine* (Spanish and Provençal as well as Italian) by Dante, Petrarch, Sacchetti, Cino Rinuccini, Giovanni da Prato, Antonio degli Alberti, Alberto degli Albizzi, Bruscaccio da Rovezzano, Niccolò Beccari, Giusto de' Conti, Luigi Groto, and Lionardo Caviani; the last mentioned appears, through his treatment of the *congedo*, to be one of the unexpectedly few 14th-c. poets actually influenced by Petrarch. A critical edition of another of these is Cino Rinuccini, *Rime*, ed. Giovanna Balbi, F, Le Lettere, 1995, 205 pp. Writing at the end of the Trecento, Rinuccini was a devoted follower of Dante and the Stilnovo, and a keen disciple of Petrarch.

C. A. Mangieri, 'Il v. 108 del contrasto *Rosa fresca aulentissima*', *SPCT*, 52: 5–17, deals with a palaeological problem: the decipherment and correct interpretation of line 108 in the MS. M. Picone, 'Giullari d'Italia. Una lettura del Gatto lupesco', *Versants*, 28, 1995: 73–97, considers the position of the *giullari* in Italy as viewed by Guittone, Dante, and Boccaccio, with a detailed analysis of the *Gatto lupesco* as the imaginary journey of a *giullare* in the world of his extraordinary inventions and ordinary difficulties. M. S. Elsheikh, 'Leggenda del transito della Madonna. Testo aquilano del Trecento',

SPCT, 51, 1995:7–42, provides a new critical edition of the 729-line text, aiming to correct the errors of a previous editor and to 'restituire alla *leggenda* la sua dignità di testimone arcaico del dialetto aquilano nella tradizione letteraria abruzzese'.

The Laude in the Middle Ages, ed. and trans. Vincenzo Traversa, NY, Lang, 1994, 432 pp., could serve as an excellent student's introduction to the history, language, and literature of medieval Tuscany. The introduction sketches the religious, social, and literary background of the *laude*; then 22 of these, taken from a codex (whose bibliographical details are strangely omitted) in the Spencer Research Library in Kansas, are presented in three forms: a transcription from the MS, a modern Italian version, and an English one. The ample contextual notes are supplemented by a glossary and word-index linking archaic and modern forms and offering numerous variants quoted from a wide selection of other texts of the period. C. Del Popolo, 'Per il *Laudario di Modena*', *SPCT*, 52:19–47, provides textual notes on the Laudario supplementing the 1984 study by M. S. Elsheikh.

Anonimo genovese, *Rime e ritmi latini*, ed. Jean Nicolas, Bo, Commissione per i Testi di Lingua, 1994, ccxvi + 631 pp., contains an exhaustive study of the early 14th-c. poet and his language, accompanying the meticulously annotated text (478 pp.) of his vernacular verse: 'un documento preziosissimo sulla parlata ligure della stessa epoca e un esemplare della produzione in versi, colta ma poco artistica, dell'Italia settentrionale'. About 70 pages are devoted to the Genoese dialect, and there are 90 pages of indexes and glossaries. The vernacular works include poems on religious and 'moral' themes and 'attualità', giving a vivid glimpse of Genoese life around 1300. R. Drusi, 'Un leone e un cagnolino fra zoologia e poesia: proposta per un verso di Bonagiunta (Son. IX, 14)', *GSLI*, 173:55–77, discusses the significance of the sonnet's last line, 'catel bactuto fa leon temente', linking it with a familiar 'parabola del reggitore che trae partito dalle sventure altrui'. S. Knaller, *'Caval-cantis Poetik der Ambiguität im Kontext der zeitgenössichen Philoso-phie', *RF*, 106, 1994:28–47.

HUMANISM AND THE RENAISSANCE

By E. HAYWOOD, *College Lecturer in Italian, University College, Dublin*
and P. L. ROSSI, *Lecturer in Italian Studies, Lancaster University*

I. GENERAL

Margaret Aston, *The Panorama of the Renaissance*, London, Thames and Hudson, 367 pp., is a useful work for students despite a few infelicitous errors. The introduction surveys the meaning of the word and the spread of the new cultural ideas. The panorama is subdivided into eight chapters with images which are intended to clarify the text. George Holmes, *Renaissance*, London, Weidenfield and Nicolson, 272 pp., uses art as a starting point to explore themes that elucidate many facets of the Renaissance. Perceptive insights suffer from insufficient space in which to develop the various themes, and it is difficult to find one's way round the excellent illustrations. Franco Brioschi and Costanzo di Girolamo, *Manuale di letteratura italiana*, T, Bollati Boringhieri, 1994–96, 4 vols, xv + 1004, 890, 966, 1141 pp., is aimed directly at the undergraduate audience and adopts a thematic approach, with good surveys on autobiography, treatises, and the development of literature as a means of communication. Giampaolo Dossena, *Storia confidenziale della letteratura italiana: Cinquecento e Seicento*, Mi, Rizzoli, 1994, 389 pp., presents an entertaining scatological survey which may well inspire students to further reading. Peter Brand and Lino Pertile, *The Cambridge History of Italian Literature*, CUP, 701 pp., has three essays by L. Panizza on the Quattrocento respectively dealing with humanism; power, patronage, and literary associations; and literature and the vernacular. B. Richardson discusses prose, and there are essays on narrative poetry (P. Marinelli), lyric poetry (A. Oldcorn), and theatre (R. Andrews). *Subject and Object in Renaissance Culture*, ed. Margreta de Grazia, Maureen Quilligan, and Peter Stallybrass, CUP, xvi + 398 pp., is a stimulating collection of 14 essays which attempt to unravel the complex relationship between human beings and the objects (such as books, clothes, furniture) of everyday life. Lisa Jardine, *Worldly Goods: A New History of the Renaissance*, Basingstoke, Macmillan, xxvi + 470 pp., has a provocative sub-title, and emphasizes the entrepreneurial spirit and acquisitiveness. This interpretation needs much modification but will at least engender lively debate. The year's most original contribution is Suzanne B. Butters, *The Triumph of Vulcan: Sculptor's Tools, Porphyry, and the Prince in Ducal Florence*, 2 vols, F, Olschki, 724 pp., which examines poets and literati, artists, and craftsmen. In histories, orations, and epideictic verse men such as Vasari, Varchi, and Bocchi commented on the febrile activities aimed at commemorating the Medici. This is not a narrowly focused study but a wide-ranging feast of scholarship that is both addictive and instructive. Michael Rocke, *Forbidden Friendships: Homosexuality and Male Culture in Renaissance Florence*, OUP, x + 371 pp., is a particularly important study that will allow us to reassess the meaning of the many descriptions of male gatherings, the innuendoes, and references to homosexuality in Renaissance literature. *Italian Academies of the Sixteenth Century*, ed. David S. Chambers and François Quiviger, London, Warburg Institute, 1995, 215 pp., contains 13 essays which look at organization, interests, and membership from the early academies in the 15th c. to Italian academies in Antwerp and which establish the importance of academies as civic as well as cultural institutions. *La scuola dei Carracci: dall'Accademia alla bottega di Ludovico*, ed. Emilio Negro and Massimo Pirondini, Modena, Artioli, 1994, 352 pp., examines the formation and organization of the academy (initially Desiderati, Incamminati), the particular skills of the founders, and the effects of the new fashion for collecting. *Le trame della moda*, ed. Anna Giulia Cavagna and Grazietta Butazzi, Ro, Bulzoni, 1995, 461 pp., contains 18 essays which examine sumptuary laws, the language of style, methodology, and the use of written records and literature for assessing the importance of dress at court and in society. *Città e corte nell'Italia di Piero della Francesca*, ed. Claudia Cieri Via, Venice, Marsilio, 504 pp., gathers 28 essays which explore biography, humanism, patronage, and the relationship between the city and the court with a particularly good essay by C. Hope on Vasari's life of Piero. As a traditional monograph Charles E. Cohen, *The Art of Giovanni Antonio da Pordenone: Between Dialect and Language*, 2 vols, CUP, xx + 502–902 + 741 pls, is a major study that rewards close reading, but it is more than a work on art history as it covers aspects of Renaissance culture which have wider implications. It considers: the nature of education in the social and cultural context of provincial centres; the usefulness of broad concepts; the religious climate that allowed expressive intensity before Trent; the influence of popular art forms in the theatre. and the nature of the creative process. Mauro Lucco, *Giorgione*, Mi, Electa, 1995, 159 pp., has a good historiographical introduction which emphasizes both the importance of musical metaphors in interpreting early 16th-c. art and the fact that the Paragone also involved poetry and music. *The French Descent into Renaissance Italy 1494–95: Antecedents and Effects*, ed. David Abulafia, Aldershot, Variorum, 1995, 496 pp., has 19 essays which, though primarily aimed at evaluating the intricate complexities of Italian diplomacy in the late 15th c., has studies on Machiavelli, *italianità* and the French invasion, and the Ferrarese court. It also gives an index of microfilms on Italian diplomatic history 1454–94 at

Yale University. Émile Picot, *Les Italiens en France au XVIe siècle*, F, Vecchiarelli, 1995, 1 + 381 pp., is a facsimile of the 1918 study, rich with archival references, that traces the careers of writers, philosophers, artists, and businessmen. Peter Burke et al., *History of Italian Art*, 2 vols, Cambridge, Polity, 1994, xiii + 337, xi + 499 pp., makes selections from the Einaudi *Storia dell'arte italiana* (1979) available in English. Janice Shell, *Pittori in bottega*, T, Allemandi, 1995, 314 pp., uses archival material to reconstruct the daily lives of artists in Milan and to reveal the preoccupations to obtain work, to keep up to date, and to run an efficient business. *Lorenzo the Magnificent: Culture and Politics*, ed. Michael Mallett and Nicholas Mann, London, Warburg Institute, x + 324 pp. + 31 pls, contains 20 essays which look at L.'s many activities, with studies of theatre, collecting Greek MSS, philosophy, and the posthumous image of L. in Machiavelli, Guicciardini, and in Europe. *Lorenzo der Prächtige und die Kultur im Florenz des 15. Jahrhunderts*, ed. Horst Heintze, Giuliano Staccioli, and Babette Hesse, Berlin, Duncker & Humblot, 1995, 213 pp., offers a broad overview of the new 'age of Pericles' over which L. presided, with 17 studies on poetry, chivalry, patronage, Poliziano, Pico della Mirandola, Landino, the anti-Medicean aesthetics of Savonarola, and the study of Greek. Giancarlo Renzi, *La Valtibertina, Lorenzo e i Medici*, F, Olschki, 1995, xi + 286 pp., explores the cultural, political, economic, social, and military importance of the area between Florence and Arezzo with reference to the interests of Florence and the Medici. O. Gori, 'Per un contributo al carteggio di Lorenzo il Magnifico: lettere inedite ai Bardi di Vernio', *ASI*, 154 : 253–378. Rita Delcroix, *Giuliano de' Medici*, F, Camunia, 506 pp., is a biography of Giuliano, Duke of Nemours. *L'Église dans l'architecture de la Renaissance*, ed. Jean Guillaume, Paris, Picard, 1995, 271 pp., has 14 essays which include a socio-cultural study that views the Sagrestia Vecchia as a means of emphasizing Medici wealth and power, and a close reading of Michelangelo's letters revealing a strategy for ensuring the completion of large-scale projects over the long term. Verena Von der Heyden-Rynsch, *I salotti d'Europa*, Mi, Garzanti, 284 pp., traces the phenomenon of the literary salons. Much research is now looking at statutes and laws to assess the social and political significance of literary texts. The following offer much valuable source material for these studies: Laura Ikens Stern, *The Criminal Law System of Medieval and Renaissance Florence*, Baltimore, Johns Hopkins U.P., 1994, xxii + 286 pp., investigating the interplay between the judicial and political aspects of the legal system, and showing how this approach can be used to shed light on political activity; and Giovanni Cascio Pratilli and Luigi Zangheri, *La legislazione medicea sull'ambiente*, 3 vols, F, Olschki, 1994–95, 453–955, 282 pp., consisting of two volumes of laws from the period 1485–1737 and an index volume which traces attitudes to town planning, building regulations, protection of the *patrimonio artistico*, and includes an evaluation of natural resources. The following give the Latin texts with facing translations: *Gli statuti criminali della comunità della riviera del Lago di Garda (1386)*, ed. Antonino Fedele, Brescia, Grafo, 1994, 254 pp.; Lorenzo Angelini, *Lo statuto di Barga del 1360*, Accademia Lucchese di Scienze, Lettere ed Arti, 1994, 133 pp.; *Gli statuti della Valle Brembana Superiore del 1468*, ed. Mariarosa Cortesi, Provincia di Bergamo, 1994, 398 pp.; Oreste Belotti and Paolo Oscar, *Statuto di Costa Volpino 1488*, Provincia di Bergamo, 1994, xxxvii + 83 pp. Paolo Marchetti, *Testis contra se*, Mi, Giuffrè, 1994, 303 pp., studies the role and importance of confession in judicial procedure. The much neglected genre of writing on food and drink is now beginning to receive scholarly attention. Paola Cecchini, *La corte squisita del Duca Federico*, Bo, Calderini, 1995, 106 pp., is a wide-ranging study that uses MS sources and works by M. da Como, B. Sacchi (Platina), F. Colle, V. Cervio, and C. Messisburgo to reconstruct the household furnishings and food at the Montefeltro court. Lucio Lume et al., *Archivi per la storia dell'alimentazione*, 3 vols, Ro, IPZS, 1995, 2029 pp., has 95 essays and is a fascinating collection that uses literature, chronicles, legal documents, and notarial archives to investigate the kind of food necessary and available for consumption at court, in institutions of learning, and in churches. It also draws attention to the great number of early literary works on gastronomy in the Biblioteca Marciana, Venice, and the reasons for their printing. Giampiero Nigro et al., *El coquator ponendo*, Prato, Francesco Datini, 400 pp. + 48 pls, has nine essays in two sections: 'Discorsi, regole e norme'; 'Pratiche e ricette'. This is not a recipe book but a scholarly investigation into the place of food in Renaissance culture. It examines the humanist discussion of the table in Platina, the culture of meals, humanist ideas on medicine, the literature of gastronomy, and the ritual of eating at court. It also has a descriptive catalogue of MSS and books on food and drink. B. Laurioux, 'I libri di cucina italiani alla fine del Medioevo: un nuovo bilancio', *ASI*, 154:33–58. The creation and mutation of fame and reputation is the subject of: Lionello Puppi, *Nel mito di Venezia*, Venice, Cardo, 1994, 111 pp., a collection of five essays which explore the myth of Venice, inspired by the events of the war of Cambrai, together with a stimulating essay that assesses the validity of recent critical positions on terminology and semiotics; Martin Rosenberg, *Raphael and France*, University Park, Pennsylvania State U.P., 226 pp., which looks at how the French adapted the mythical Raphael inherited from Vasari and co-opted the authority of this picture of the Renaissance master's life to support their own aesthetic, social, and political values; P. Paolini, 'Mussolini e Machiavelli', *ON*, 19.1, 1995:195–203, which claims that Mussolini's article 'Preludio al "Machiavelli" ' (*Gerarchia*, 3, 1924:205–09) contains an original interpretation of M.'s political thought, of some interest in the history of M.'s *fortuna*; Massimo Mussini, *Correggio tradotto*, Mi, Cassa di Risparmio di Reggio Emilia, 1995, 321 pp., which examines the myth of C. and how the interpretation of his works derived from literary descriptions rather than the visual evidence and how his style was widely diffused by prints; A. Richard Turner, *Inventing Leonardo. The Anatomy of a Legend*, London, Papermac, 268 pp., which charts the changing face of Western cultural values in their reactions to and interpretations of the L. enigma; William E. Wallace, *Michelangelo at San Lorenzo. The Genius as Entrepreneur*, CUP, 1994, xiv + 266 pp., which explores the myth of M. as solitary anti-social genius and traces how, at the centre of a vast collaborative project, his role as hands-on craftsman evolved into that of architect as gentleman; L. Pon, 'Michelangelo's lives: 16th-c. books by Vasari, Condivi and others', *SCJ*, 27:1015–36, which looks at the creation of the M. myth.

PRINTING AND PUBLISHING. David Woodward, *Catalogue of Watermarks in Italian Printed Maps c. 1510–1600*, F, Olschki, 204 pp., uses photographic techniques to present 335 images of watermarks, with a useful graphic index. This will be a major contribution to a future systematic catalogue. Iain Fenlon, *Music, Print and Culture in Early Sixteenth Century Italy*, London, British Library, 1995, 96 pp., contains the texts of the 1994 Panizzi lectures which investigate the impact of the spread of printing on the publication of treatises, textbooks, manuals, and tutors. *Prima edizione a stampa della Divina Commedia. Studi*, 1, ed. Piero Lai and Anna Maria Menichelli, Comune di Foligno, 1994, 120 pp., has studies on the early incunables of Dante, humanism and the printing industry in Foligno, and the spread of paper manufacturing. Albert Kapr, *Johann Gutenberg: the Man and his Invention*, Aldershot, Scolar, 316 pp., is a well-documented biography which also looks at the spread of printing. Nicoletta Grosso, *Le città d'Europa nel Rinascimento*, Novara, Istituto Geografico De Agostini, 1995, 175 pp., presents full colour images of cities from the *Civitates orbis terrarum*, with an introduction that examines the printing history of this technically complex enterprise. Great erudition is brought to bear in Dennis E. Rhodes, *Silent Printers*, London, British Library, 1995, xix + 286 pp., where over 250 anonymous Venetian printers are identified. Marco Carminati, *Codici miniati del maestro B.F.*, Pavia, Cardano, 1995, 194 pp., examines the problem of identifying the MS illuminator working in 16th-c. Milan with the figure of Francesco Biniasco. *Il calamo e la figura, il 'bel mondo' medievale*, ed. Laura Carlino, Biblioteca Statale di Cremona, 1994, 99 pp., is an exhibition catalogue of illuminated MSS with humanist commentaries on classical and religious texts. Andrea Capaccioni, *Lineamenti di storia dell'editoria umbra: il Quattrocento ed il Cinquecento*, Perugia, Voluminia, 112 pp., is a scholarly study which investigates the activities of typographers, booksellers, customers, and writers. D. Parker, 'Women in the book trade in Italy, 1475–1620', *RQ*, 49:509–41, looks at the conditions that allowed women to take part in this profession. *La Bibliofilia*, 98, includes: P. Scapecchi, 'Una lettera di Atramytteno a Manuzio e le prime testimonianze dell'attività di Aldo a Carpi' (23–30); A. Reynolds, 'Francesco Berni's second published work, *Capitolo del gioco della primiera col comento di messer Pietropaulo da San Chirico*, Rome 1526' (31–43); G. Zappella, 'Aggiunte agli annali della tipografia di Campagna (sec. XVI)' (45–54); E. Barbieri, 'Una ignota edizione della Spagna: Venezia, Giorgio Rusconi, 1507' (233–43); C. Fahy, 'La carta nel libro quattrocentesco e nelle edizioni aldine' (55–57); Id., 'Il formato in 24° di Alessandro Paganino' (59–63).

BIBLIOGRAPHY. *Biblia: La biblioteca volgare*, I: *Libri di poesia*, ed. Italo Pantani, Mi, Bibliografica, xxii + 488 pp., inaugurates an important new series which will be of great value. Even though it does not have the full descriptive critical apparatus of the *Censimento Unico* and relies on secondary sources it has useful cross-referencing indexes. The other planned volumes of 15th- and 16th-c. literary genres are: *La biblioteca umanistica*, *La biblioteca religiosa*, and *La biblioteca professionale*. Alfredo Serrai, *Storia della bibliografia*, VI: *La maturità disciplinare. Indice dei volumi I–VI*, ed. Gabriella Miggiano, Ro, Bulzoni, 1995, 431 pp., is the latest volume of this admirable project and is dedicated to the bibliographers of the early modern period. The series as a whole has made a lasting contribution to our understanding of early modern epistemology and will be the basis for more detailed individual studies. Researchers will be grateful for *I fondi speciali delle biblioteche lombarde*, I: *Milano e provincia*, ed. Istituto Lombardo per la Storia della Resistenza e dell'Età Contemporanea, Mi, Bibliografica, 1995, xxvi + 464 pp., which lists all the special collections with descriptions of their contents. Anna Aletta Avanzati et al., *Kissner e Roma: un fondo bibliografico informatizzato del Gabinetto Comunale delle Stampe, secc. XVI–XIX*, Ro, Artemide, 95 pp., has three introductory essays on the illustrations and bindings followed by a catalogue of the works on Rome with full critical apparatus. Anna Bosco and Luca Seravalle, *Le edizioni del XVI secolo nella Biblioteca Chelliana di Grosseto*, Biblioteca Chelliana, 1995, 199 pp., is the second volume in the series and describes 394 items with full critical apparatus. Lorenzo Baldacchini, *Incunaboli e cinquecentine in Romagna: la Biblioteca Piana e la Biblioteca del Seminario di Sarsina*, Ro, Vecchiarelli, 153 pp., treats the two libraries separately and, again, has full critical apparatus. *Le cinquecentine della*

Biblioteca dell'Archivio di Stato di Roma, ed. Giovanna Falcone, Mi, Bibliografica, 114 pp., lists 427 works, also with full critical apparatus. Giulio Busi, *Libri ebraici a Mantova. Le edizioni del XVI secolo nella Biblioteca della Comunità Ebraica*, F, Cadmo, 256 pp., describes an important collection of 334 works which has many cabbalistic and mystical texts, with full critical apparatus and indexes. James E. Walsh, *A Catalogue of Fifteenth Century Printed Books in the Harvard University Library*, IV, MRTS, 330 pp. + 16 pls, continues an admirable series with entries for publishers in France, the Netherlands, Spain, Portugal, England, and Montenegro. There is a separate section on Hebrew incunables and a supplement of works published in Germany, Switzerland, and Italy that should have been in volumes I and II. Anna Gonzo and Walter Manica, *Gli incunaboli della Biblioteca Civica e dell'Academia degli Agiati di Rovereto*, Provincia Autonoma di Trento, 199 pp., is an impressive piece of scholarship with full critical apparatus that lists 72 incunables. *Private Libraries in Renaissance England*, IV: *PLRE 87–112*, ed. R. J. Fehrenbach and E. S. Leedham-Green, MRTS, 1995, xxx + 348 pp., continues the high standards set by the previous volumes with much Italian material. Guido Ratti, *Piemonte e biblioteche. Vicende culturali, politiche e amministrative tra il IV e il XX secolo*, Alessandria, Orso, 1995, 91 pp., has a discussion of the early libraries set up by Emanuele Filiberto, Pius V, and the Jesuits. Maria Luisa Ricciardi, *Biblioteche dipinte*, Ro, Bulzoni, 103 pp. + 63 pls, links the iconography in the decoration of libraries in Urbino, Venice, Parma, and Rome to the world of learning and to the motivation behind setting up the collections.

2. HUMANISM

The broad intellectual and cultural interests of humanists are explored in *The Cambridge Guide to Renaissance Humanism*, ed. Jill Kraye, CUP, 320 pp., which contains 14 authoritative essays on classical scholarship, printing, education, biblical scholarship, philosophy, philology, science, and literary studies. The fascination of the *Hypnerotomachia* has been the subject of numerous studies. Stefano Borsi, *Polifilo architetto*, Ro, Officina, 1995, 277 pp., now considers the significance of the architectural images within the context of 15th-c. humanistic culture where the antiquarian interest in classical ruins and epigraphy is studied along with the literary texts to uncover the polymathic erudition of the humanist author. D. Fattori, 'Per la biografia di Francesco Colonna. Due schede d'archivio', *La Bibliofilia*, 98:281–88. Leonardo Bruni, *Opere letterarie e politiche*, ed. Paolo Viti, UTET, 896 pp., has an excellent introduction which provides the critical, biographical, and bibliographical analysis, followed by the

Latin and Greek texts with facing translations. The collection excludes works on history, poetry, narrative, translations, and letters. A useful appendix lists the authors and works cited. Ann Moss, *Printed Commonplace-Books and the Structuring of Renaissance Thought*, Oxford, Clarendon, ix + 345 pp., is an impressive study which examines the effect on humanist aspirations, and the relevance to the Ciceronian debate, of texts that 'worked as a memory store of quotations which could be activated to verbalize present experience in the language of familiar moral paradigms and with reference to a cultural history shared by writer and reader'. Edith Wyss, *The Myth of Apollo and Marsyas in the Art of the Italian Renaissance*, Cranbury, Delaware U.P., 182 pp., investigates: humanist studies of the myth; the diversity of its meaning, and its Platonic and Pythagorean links; its Counter-Reformation reading as just punishment; and its use as symbol of wisdom and revelation. *The Medieval Military Revolution*, ed. Andrew Ayton and J. L. Price, London, Tauris, 1995, 208 pp., has an essay on Erasmus's humanist views on war and peace. Ilio Calabrese, *Glossario giuridico dei testi in volgare di Montepulciano. Le Fonti*, IV, F, Pacini, 1995, xciii + 699–1049 pp., has a long introduction which focuses on Poliziano's language and its legal connotations. It analyses the letter by his father to Piero de' Medici and offers new research on P.'s humanism. Poggio Bracciolini, *Del piacere di vivere*, ed. Cecilia Benedetti, Mi, Vita Felice, 1995, 59 pp., is a letter written to Niccolò Niccoli in 1416 when B. left the tense atmosphere of the Council of Constance and experienced the peace of Baden. Sigismondo Tizio, *Historiae senenses*, vol. 1, tome 2, pt 1, ed. Grazia Tomasi Stussi, Ro, Istituto Storico Italiano per l'Età Moderna e Contemporanea, 1995, xiii + 278 pp., is the second volume (vol. 1, tome 1, pt 1, ed. Manuela Doni Garfagnini, 1992) of a critical edition of a monumental work in ten volumes in the Fondo Chigi, Biblioteca Vaticana, which traces the history of Siena between 1267 and 1528; it was written between 1506 and the author's death in 1528 and owes a debt to Flavio Biondo. W. G. Craven, 'Coluccio Salutati's defence of poetry', *RenS*, 10:1–30, examines the difficulty, due to inconsistencies, of attributing a precise position. A. Bolland, 'Art and humanism in early Renaissance Padua: Cennini, Vergerio and Petrarch on imitation', *RQ*, 49:469–87. F. Bausi, 'La dedicatoria a Leone X del *De cardinalatu* di Paolo Cortesi', *BHR*, 58:643–50, looks at the letter of Raffaele Mattei. D. Canfora, 'Due fonti del *De curialium miseriis* di Enea Silvio Piccolomini: Bracciolini e Lucrezio', *ASI*, 154:479–94. S. Dall'Oco, 'Bartolomeo Facio e la tecnica dell' "excursus" nella biografia di Alfonso d'Aragona', *ib.*, 207–51. R. Drusi, 'Abbozzo del principio della "lettera intorno a' Manoscritti antichi" del Borghini', *LItal*, 48:253–55. *Rinascimento*, 35, 1995, includes studies by: L. Boschetto,

'Democrito e la fisiologia della follia. La parodia della filosofia e della medicina nel *Momus* di Leon Battista Alberti' (3–29); P. Godman, 'Florentine humanism between Poliziano and Machiavelli' (67–122); G. Fioravanti, 'Il commento di Ugo Benzi agli *Economici* (pseudo) aristotelici' (125–71); S. Dall'Oco, 'La "Laudatio regis" nel *De rebus gestis ab Alphonso primo* di Bartolomeo Facio' (243–51); S. Perfetti, ' "Cultius atque integrius". Teodoro Gaza, traduttore umanistico del *De partibus animalium*' (253–86); A. Daneloni, 'Niccolò Niccoli, Angelo Poliziano ed il Laur. Plut. 49, 7' (327–42). K. Gouwens, 'Life-writing and the theme of cultural decline in Valeriano's *De litteratorum infelicitate*', *SCJ*, 27:87–96. Lucia Nuti, *Ritratti di città*, Venice, Marsilio, 273 pp. + 86 pls, traces the evolution of differing rhetorical solutions for representing the city from the Middle Ages to the 18th c. This is a well documented study that encompasses the printing industry, and the humanist ideals of Alberti, Calco, Castiglione, Fulvio, and J. de Barbari. The shared interest in humanism by Cosimo il Vecchio and Michelozzo is explored in Antonio Natali, *L'umanesimo di Michelozzo*, F, Maschietto and Musolino, 118 pp., where humanist readings of classical texts, especially Cicero, are shown to have inspired Cosimo to patronage on an impressive scale and these interests to have coincided with M.'s personal interpretation of antiquity. Philippe Costamagna, *Pontormo*, Mi, Electa, 1994, xx + 379 pp., examines the artist's roots in the classicism of the High Renaissance and his response to the religious and artistic preferences of Duke Cosimo. The classical revival in Genoa with its echoes of traditional values and interests, which gave rise to a home-grown humanist response to the threat of Milan in the early 15th c., is the subject of Steven A. Epstein, *Genoa and the Genoese*, Chapel Hill, North Carolina U.P., 396 pp. *Pisanello*, ed. Paola Marini, Mi, Electa, 537 pp., is a collection of 23 essays which assess: the humanists' admiration for P.'s artistic activity; pedagogy and literary activity at the school of Guarino Veronese; and the patronage for his particular vision of the past. The volume succeeds in recreating the world where P.'s approach was valued. The humanist veneration of the antique is attested in Alison Luchs, *Tullio Lombardo and Ideal Portrait Sculpture in Renaissance Venice, 1490–1530*, CUP, 1995, xiv + 210 pp. + 209 pls, which considers L.'s dialogue with the lost values of antiquity, where his ideal forms are seen as 'imaginary evocations of ancient, mythic personalities'. Pietro C. Marani, *Leonardo*, Mi, Electa, 1994, 161 pp., examines the classical elements in L.'s technique and style and how these contributed to his development. Alessandro Vezzosi, *Leonardo da Vinci. Arte e scienza dell'universo*, Mi, Electa, 200 pp., is a useful résumé of L.'s ideas. André Chastel, *Leonardo*, T, Einaudi, 1995, xxii + 226 pp., is a collection of 13 essays which establish L.'s links with humanistic, philosophical, and scientific currents, and emphasize L.'s erudition. *Leonardo da Vinci's Sforza Monument Horse: The Art and the Engineering*, ed. Diane Cole Ahl, Bethlehem, Lehigh U.P., 1995, 152 pp., has nine studies which cover: Biringuccio's *Pyrotechnia*; the ideals of equine management and aesthetics in Renaissance poems, letters, and treatises, especially L. B. Alberti's *De equo animante*; what literary sources tell us about the propagandistic and personal associations of the monument. Howard Burns, Christoph Luitpold Frommel, and Lionello Puppi, *Michele Sanmicheli*, Mi, Electa, 1995, 324 pp., has 21 essays which evaluate the humanist approach and the constant, dynamic reinterpretation of the past to provide solutions for contemporary problems. *Die Rezeption der 'Metamorphosen' des Ovid in der Neuzeit: Der antike Mythos in Text und Bild*, ed. Hermann Walter and Hans-Jürgen Horn, Berlin, Mann, 1995, xv + 294 pp. + 64 pls, establishes Ovid's popularity in 15th- and 16th-c. Italy and how his work was reinterpreted and manipulated to fulfil specific artistic needs. It has studies on Dolce's *Trasformazioni* and Ebreo's *Dialoghi d'amore*, the literary texts behind the *maiolica istoriata*, and the vogue for paintings after Ovid in Venice and Rome. The effect which intellectual and cultural currents had on the visual arts is examined in Joachim Poeschke, *Michelangelo and his World*, NY, Abrams, 272 pp. + 256 pls, which places M. and his contemporaries Sansovino, Cellini, Bandinelli, and Ammannati within the context of a dialogue with classical antiquity, and discusses theoretical standpoints and the shift in subject matter and function. Fiamma Domestici, *I Della Robbia a Pistoia*, F, Octavo, 1995, 318 pp., traces the roots of the Della Robbia style to the stoic ethics of the humanist circle of the early 15th c. and sees it as promoting a pure uncontaminated religious message close to the ideas of beauty required by the reformed Franciscan and Dominican orders. *L'uomo e la natura nel Rinascimento*, ed. Luisa Rotondi Secchi Tarugi, Mi, Nuovi Orizzonti, 562 pp., has 29 essays that investigate the understanding of what is nature and natural in response to the new geographical and astronomical discoveries in literature, theology, and philosophy, and the effects these dicoveries had on popular and elite cultures. How humanist scholarship affected all aspects of life can be seen in Girolamo Mercuriale, *De arte gymnastica*, ed. Michele Napolitano, Ro, Elefante, 237 pp., which deals with the curative benefits of exercise. *Cesare Cesariano: volgarizzamento dei libri IX e X di Vitruvio*, ed. Barbara Agosti, Pisa, Accademia della Crusca, 267 pp. + 11 pls, based on the MS in the Real Academia de la Historia, Madrid, is a faithful transcription of the MS with no attempt at linguistic analysis. The introduction traces the fortune of C.'s work. E. Haywood, 'Classical perceptions of Ireland revisited in Renaissance Italy', *International Journal of the*

Classical Tradition, 2:467–86, looks at the negative attitude to Ireland ascribable to the rediscovery of ancient geographers, especially Strabo. Greek influence is the subject of a number of studies. John Monfasani, *Byzantine Scholars in Renaissance Italy: Cardinal Bessarion and other Emigrés*, Aldershot, Variorum, 1995, xii + 351 pp., has 14 essays on: Bessarion; Perotti and the debate between Platonists and Aristotelians; Platonic paganism; university teaching and Byzantine culture; and Byzantine rhetorical traditions and the Renaissance. *I Greci in Occidente*, ed. Gianfranco Fiaccadori and Paolo Eleuteri, Venice, Cardo, lxxv + 92 pp., uses the collection of the Biblioteca Marciana to trace the importance of Greek works. Each author is discussed under a specific theme with a scholarly assessment of the texts in terms of MS tradition, owners, translations, and diffusion. E. Travi, from 'Pietro Bembo traduttore dell'*Elogio di Elena* di Gorgia da Leontini', *SPCT*, 53:93–104.

SOUTHERN HUMANISM. *Territorio e feudalità nel mezzogiorno rinascimentale. Il ruolo degli Acquaviva tra XV e XVI secolo*, 1, ed. Caterina Lavarra, Galatina, Congedo, 1995, x + 240 pp., throws light on different aspects of the Acquaviva d'Aragona, with studies of the heroic status acquired by pro-Aragonese family head Giulio Antonio at the siege of Otranto (R. Jurlaro), the support for Greek learning and the printing press given by the pro-French elder son, Andrea Matteo (F. Tateo, C. Bianca), and the political role and literary defence of his own status and that of his family by the pro-Spanish younger son, Belisario (L. Miele, I. Nuovo, G. Ferraù, E. Haywood, D. Defilippis, M. De Nichilo). Other articles look at the role of the warrior and at Greek communities and urban development in the Regno (F. Cardini, P. Corsi, B. Vetere). L. Miele, 'Tristano Caracciolo ed un progetto pedagogico per la giovane nobiltà meridionale', *CLett*, 23.3–4, 1995:33–47, shows how the nobility gave serious thought to the education and the career of their children. Lucia Miele, *Studi sull'umanesimo meridionale*, Na, Federico e Ardia, 1994, 216 pp., contains previously published articles on Belisario Acquaviva, Antonio de Beatis, Antonio de Ferrariis Galateo, Giuniano Maio, Orso degli Orsini, and Pontano. M. L. Doglio, 'Il "dichiarar per lettera" del Pontano', *CLett*, 23.3–4, 1995:5–32, provides an overview of the style and contents of P.'s (Latin and vernacular) letters (written in his own name and that of his master), with an appendix of letters in print. T. R. Toscano, 'Un'orazione latina inedita di Bernardino Rota "principe" dell'Accademia dei Sereni di Napoli', *ib.*, 81–109, gives the text, with commentary, of the 'presidential address', delivered in 1546. Mario Spedicato, *Il mercato della mitra, episcopato regio e privilegio dell'alternativa nel regno di Napoli in età Spagnola*, Bari, Cacucci, 237 pp. Giacomo Pace, *Il governo dei gentiluomini*, Ro, Cigno Galileo Galilei,

360 pp., adds to our understanding of the social, economic, and political developments which affected the spread of humanism and new ideas in Sicily. Liliana Monti Saba, *Pontano e la storia*, Ro, Bulzoni, 1995, 201 pp., deals with the much neglected *De bello neapolitano*, describing the war fought, 1458–65, by Ferrante D'Aragona against rebellious barons. *Storia e civiltà della Campania: il Rinascimento e l'età Barocca*, ed. Giovanni Pugliese Carratelli, Na, Electa, 1994, 502 pp., contains 13 studies with essays on feudal structures, the impact of the Counter-Reformation, and the study of the natural world. It covers Simone Porzio, Bruno, Campanella, Nifo, and Telesio. Anna Giannetti, *Il giardino napoletano*, Na, Electa, 1994, 141 pp., examines the use of language to describe the idea of the garden by Pontano, de' Crescenzi, and Sannazaro. Fernando Calabrese, *I Colonna nel Regno*, Mi, Nuovi Autori, 1995, 92 pp., throws light on the period by examining the cultural activities of this important family.

PHILOSOPHY AND HISTORY OF IDEAS. Marsilio Ficino, *Sulla Vita*, ed. Alessandra Tarabochia Canavero, Mi, Rusconi, 364 pp., has a scholarly introduction on F.'s thought, and the language and context of the *De Vita*, with a useful glossary of terms dealing with medicine and astrology. Francesco Bausi, *Nec rhetor neque philosophus*, F, Olschki, 213 pp., is an impressive study with full critical apparatus of the sources, language, and style of Giovanni Pico della Mirandola's early Latin works (1484–87). A. Calciolari, 'Pico tra le postille di Ficino a Giuliano l'Apostata. Ricerche sul *Commento al Salmo XVIII* del Mirandolano', *SPCT*, 53:39–73. H. D. Saffrey, 'Florence, 1492: the reappearance of Plotinus', *RQ*, 49:488–508, examines the *Enneads*. Cesare Vasoli et al., *Dall'Accademia neoplatonica fiorentina alla riforma*, F, Olschki, 145 pp., examines the relationship between humanism, the Renaissance, and the Reformation, and how each of these contributed to changes in European culture. There are essays on humanism and conciliarism, echoes of the Accademia fiorentina in Calvin's Geneva, and the influence of G. Pico della Mirandola on Zwingli, Michelangelo, V. Colonna, and Ochino. L. Valcke, 'Facettes et reflets du mythe mirandolien', *RenR*, 20.1:27–47, re-evaluates the *Oratio de hominis dignitate*. Claudio Strinati et al., *Tiziano amor sacro e profano*, Mi, Electa, 1995, 472 pp., is an illuminating collection of essays which examine: eroticism in terms of Speroni's *Dialogo d'amore*, Plato's *Symposium*, Equicola's *Libro di natura di amore*, Leone Ebreo's *Dialoghi d'amore* and Castiglione; the relationship between Bernardo and Pietro Bembo and the new courtly ethos of neoplatonic love; and the real and depicted woman in Venetian society. Palingène, *Le Zodiaque de la vie*, ed. Jacques Chomarat, Geneva, Droz, 527 pp., gives the Latin text with French translation and has an excellent introduction which sets the writings of Pier Angelo Manzolli (Marcello Palingenio

Stellato) in an intellectual and social framework. Edith Balas, *Michelangelo's Medici Chapel*, Philadelphia, American Philosophical Society, 1995, 196 pp., offers a new neoplatonic interpretation which sees the female forms as the material and virginal aspects of the earth goddess and the male figures as the gods of heaven (the Dioscuri). Both sets relate to ideas on immortality, purification, absolution, rebirth, and renewal. *Astrologia, arte e cultura in età rinascimentale*, ed. Daniele Bini, Modena, Il Bulino, 286 pp., has an English/Italian dual text and presents a balanced account, with a specific chapter on the astrological material in the Biblioteca Estense, which examines the influence, operation, and importance of astrology in Renaissance culture. Marco Vannini, *Mistica e filosofia*, Casale Monferrato, Piemme, 204 pp., has a chapter on *De visione Dei* by Cusanus. Isabella Cortese, *I secreti della signora Isabella Cortese*, Mi, Vita Felice, 1995, 222 pp., is a facsimile of the first edition (1584) of a work, by a mysterious figure, which belongs to the Book of Secrets, a genre popular in both popular and elite cultures. Alfio Bangrazi et al., *Atti del convegno internazionale su Paracelso*, Ro, Paracelso, 1994, 195 pp. Luigi Pepe, *Copernico e la questione copernicana in Italia dal XVI al XIX secolo*, F, Olschki, 293 pp., has 11 essays on: natural philosophy in the universities of Padua, Bologna, and Ferrara; G. B. Amico, Fracastoro, and Arab astronomers; the Gregorian calendar; and G. B. Piccoli and scientific training. Enrico Peruzzi, *La nave di Ermete: la cosmologia di Girolamo Fracastoro*, F, Olschki, 1995, viii + 119 pp., reconstructs F.'s cosmology by giving a close reading of the *Homocentricorum sive de stellis liber unus*. F.'s thought emerges as a complex interaction of Aristotelianism, Averroism, Platonism, Neoplatonism, and Hermeticism. S. Pearce, 'Nature and supernature in the dialogues of Girolamo Fracastoro', *SCJ*, 27:111–32, examines the attempt to construct a philosophical anthropology. A. Perifano, 'L'alchimie dans *De la Pirotechnia* de Vannoccio Biringuccio', *REI*, 42:189–202. A. C. Crombie, *Science, Art and Nature in Medieval and Modern Thought*, London, Hambledon, xv + 516 pp., is a collection of 23 articles which investigates the evolution of scientific objectivity with studies of: the Jesuit insistence upon specific rational criteria for acceptable scientific inquiry; the place and importance of rhetoric in Galileo; mathematics and Platonism in 16th-c. Italian universities and Jesuit educational policy; and the connotations of the term *virtù* in Alberti. Edward Grant, *The Foundations of Modern Science in the Middle Ages*, CUP, 1996, xiv + 247 pp., stresses how Greco-Arabic science, which entered Europe in the late middle ages, signified a dramatic break with the past. Paolo De Simonis et al., *Scienziati ed esploratori chiantigiani*, Radda in Chianti, Centro di Studi Chiantigiani, 107 pp., has studies of the MSS of the Dalla Volpaia family, who collaborated with Poliziano,

Leonardo, and Michelangelo, and the writings of Giovanni da Verrazzano. Paul Zumthor, *La misura del mondo*, Bo, Il Mulino, 1995, 440 pp., studies early modern perceptions of space, and takes into account real images, theoretical abstractions, and archetypal/emotional values to re-evaluate the very language used in descriptions of space. Frank Lestringant, *Mapping the Renaissance World*, Oxford, Polity, 1994, 197 pp., charts the crisis in Renaissance cosmography in the light of religious, methodological, and epistemological concerns. Lew Andrews, *Story and Space in Renaissance Art*, CUP, 1995, 188 pp., uses the writings of Alberti, Manetti, Ghiberti, Leonardo, and Castelvetro to offer a new interpretation of visual and narrative theories. Marisa Dalai Emiliani and Valter Curzi, *Piero della Francesca tra arte e scienza*, Venice, Marsilio, 611 pp., is an excellent collection of 38 essays which gives an insight into early modern epistemology. There are studies on optics, proportion, perspective, and mathematics, while Piero's treatises are examined for their linguistic interest and a methodology is set out for the critical edition of his writings. Martin Clayton, *Leonardo da Vinci: a Curious Vision*, London, Merrell Holberton, 168 pp., reveals how L.'s highly inventive manipulation of all available techniques reflects the development of his philosophical system. Before 1513 the drawing represented the end product of reasoning. After this date the drawing came first and was a basis for investigation. Andrea Carlino, *La fabbrica del corpo: libri e dissezione nel Rinascimento*, T, Einaudi, 1994, xxiv + 267 pp. + 38 pls, is a meticulously researched study which examines the complex interactions between two important strands in the evolution of medical knowledge. It evaluates the relationship between the practical and the theological, between social practices, and taboos relating to the treatment of cadavers, and the texts on anatomy sanctified by tradition and rigid academic interests. Francesco Panarelli, *Il corpo e l'anima*, T, SEI, 208 pp., is an excellent study that sheds new light on the preoccupations of the early modern period. *Immagini del corpo in età moderna*, ed. Paolo Giacomoni, Trento U.P., 1994, 282 pp., has eight essays that examine the various ideas about the body implicit in the microcosm-macrocosm world view. Piero Camporesi, *Il governo del corpo*, Mi, Garzanti, 1995, 169 pp. *Cultures of Natural History*, ed. N. Jardine, J. A. Secord, and E. C. Spary, CUP, 501 pp., has 26 essays that trace the continuous effort of reassessment and refocusing as new knowledge of the natural world was gathered and assimilated.

RELIGIOUS THOUGHT AND THE CHURCH. A number of volumes commemorate the quincentenary of Savonarola's death. *L'età di Savonarola: fra Bartolomeo e la Scuola di San Marco*, ed. Serena Padovani, Venice, Marsilio, 345 pp., looks at the sermons of Savonarola and the Dominican spirituality which affected Fra Bartolomeo's whole life and his art. *L'età di Savonarola: fra Paolino e la pittura a Pistoia nel primo '500*, ed. Chiara d'Afflitto, Franca Falletti, and Andrea Muzzi, Venice, Marsilio, 261 pp., traces the lasting influence and echoes of his teaching. Carlo Falciani, *Il Rosso fiorentino*, F, Olschki, 105 pp. + 85 pls, has an excellent introduction that highlights the profound influence of Savonarola on writers, philosophers, and artists, and shows how the new spiritual ideas led to new forms of expression. Tito S. Centi, *La scomunica di Girolamo Savonarola*, Mi, Ares, 134 pp., revisits the clash between S. and Rome and questions the validity of the excommunication. Steven F. Ostrow, *Art and Spirituality in Counter-Reformation Rome*, CUP, 385 pp., uses an interdisciplinary approach that makes use of sermons, iconography, theological and historical texts, and treatises on art theory, to demonstrate how the Sistine and Pauline chapels in Santa Maria Maggiore expressed the personal, theological, and ecclesiastical concerns of their patrons and the Counter-Reformation church, and pointed to the legitimacy of the papacy and its temporal and spiritual supremacy. Craig A. Monson, *Disembodied Voices*, Berkeley, California U.P., 1995, 354 pp., investigates the cultural lives of the nuns in the convent of Santa Cristina della Fondazza, Bologna, and reveals that for women the 'cloister came to represent the best choice, or at least the lesser evil among life's meagre options'. The study points to the strategies adopted to moderate and mediate the formal structure of the authority imposed upon them. Daniel Bornstein and Roberto Rusconi, *Women and Religion in Medieval and Renaissance Italy*, Chicago U.P., 334 pp., considers how women could be active, influential, and creative when established authorities were weak, yet their power became limited when order was re-established. Paolo Prodi, *Disciplina dell'anima, disciplina del corpo e disciplina della società tra medioevo ed età moderna*, Bo, Il Mulino, 1994, 963 pp., looks at how the notion of discipline, which had its roots in religion, became a fundamental factor in the evolution of religion, manners, law, and civic responsibility. O. Visani, 'Un ritrovato codice di prediche di Bernardino da Siena e della sua cerchia', *LItal*, 48:44–62. Saverio Guida, *Religione e letteratura romanze*, Soveria Manelli, Rubbettino, 1995, 220 pp. The contribution of the secular arm of the Church to the language of jurisprudence is attested in Sandro Serangeli, *Diritto romano e Rota Provinciae Marchiae*, I, T, Giappichelli, 1995, 349 pp. Charles M. de la Roncière, *Religion paysanne et religion urbaine en Toscane (c. 1250–c. 1450)*, Aldershot, Variorum, 1994, x + 319 pp., contains nine articles which examine the multiplicity of religious groups and organizations. Ole Peter Grell and Bob Scribner, *Tolerance and Intolerance in the European Reformation*, CUP, 294 pp., contains 15 essays which establish how the areas affected by the Reformation dealt with dissenting voices. The introduction by Grell sets out the various positions with great clarity. Simonetta Adorni-Braccesi, *'Una città infetta': la repubblica di Lucca nella crisi religiosa del Cinquecento*, F, Olschki, 1994, xvi + 414 pp., reconstructs the evolution of religious dissent within the context of Italian and European politics. It links local concerns to the wider issues of church reform and the crisis of religious belief in the 16th c. The following cast light on the impact of the Council of Trent on culture: Danilo Curti and Marco Gozzi, *Musica e liturgia nella riforma tridentina*, Provincia Autonoma di Trento, 1995, 126 pp., which contains six essays tracing the evolution of Trent's judgements on liturgical music and the relationship between music and poetry; and Bernard Aikema, *Jacopo Bassano and his Public*, Princeton U.P., xiv + 257 pp., which investigates the guidelines drawn up at Trent and examines: the interpretation of ideas central to contemporary spiritual movements; the conscious breaking of established rules of decorum in using the *stilus humilis* instead of the *stilus gravis* and the aim to 'hold the attention of his [Bassano's] audience whom he incited to choose between two conflicting paths of life'. Massimo Firpo and Dario Marcatto, *Il processo inquisitoriale del Cardinal Giovanni Morone*, VI, appx II, Ro, Istituto Storico Italiano per l'Età Moderna e Contemporanea, 1995, 459 pp., makes use of the material in the Archivio del Sant'Ufficio Romano and gives the *Summarium processus originalis* pertaining to the charge of heresy brought against V. Colonna, M. Flaminio, A. Priuli, and P. Carnesecchi. *Witchcraft in Early Modern Europe: Studies in Culture and Belief*, ed. Jonathan Barry, Marianne Hester, and Gareth Roberts, CUP, xiv + 368 pp., contains 13 essays which reflect on Keith Thomas's assumptions, on recent witchcraft scholarship, and on approaches for future research. Marcantonio Flaminio, *Apologia del 'Beneficio di Christo' e altri scritti inediti*, ed. Dario Marcatto, F, Olschki, 225 pp., gives the texts of the *Meditationi et orationi* on Paul's epistle to the Romans, of the *Modo che si dee tenere ne l'insegnare et predicare il principio della religione christiana*, and of unpublished letters to Giulia Gonzaga and Pietro Carnesecchi, as well as that of the *Apologia*. The activities of confraternities in the promotion of cultural life are examined in: *Confraternite, arte e devozione in Puglia dal Quattrocento al Settecento*, ed. Clara Gelao, Na, Electa, 1994, 525 pp., an exhibition catalogue with three essays and a vast array of documentation on the institution, organization, and social and artistic function of the confraternities; Marina Romanello, *Le spose del principe*, Mi, Angeli, 1995, 184 pp., concerning the Casa Secolare delle Zitelle, set up by women in Udine at the end of the 16th c., which enabled them to live together without the restrictions of an official religious institution; R. Chavasse, 'Latin lay piety and vernacular lay piety in word and image: Venice, 1471–early 1500s', *RenS*, 10:319–33. The attempt to give a physical manifestation to spiritual ideals is the subject of: Giovanni Careri, *Bernini: Flights of Love, the Art of Devotion*, Chicago U.P., 1995, 118 pp. + 41 pls, which takes as its starting point the analysis of the term *bel composto* to examine the dynamic set up between the beholder and the form; Christopher A. Reynolds, *Papal Patronage and the Music of St. Peter's, 1380–1513*, Berkeley, California U.P., 1995, xvii + 439 pp., which points to the powerful attractive force exerted by papal patronage on foreigners, and uncovers the cultural values and educational backgrounds of the composers, and the contribution made by the language and rhetoric of the Italian Renaissance; *San Pietro che non c' è*, ed. Cristiano Tessari, Mi, Electa, 307 pp., which has ten essays that present documentary evidence to assess the different approaches, problems, and plans that were part of the grandiose project to build a new St Peter's.

INDIVIDUAL CENTRES. *Alla corte degli Estensi. Filosofia, arte e cultura a Ferrara nei secoli XV e XVI*, ed. Marco Bertozzi, Ferrara, Università degli Studi, 1994, 466 pp., provides a fascinating glimpse of Ferrarese 'high life', with 23 articles on: learning, philosophy, science, humanism, literature, religion, art, and the decadence of Ferrarese civilization. Thomas Tuohy, *Herculean Ferrara: Ercole d'Este, 1471–1505, and the Invention of a Ducal Capital*, CUP, xxxii + 534 pp., makes use of diaries, eulogies, and letters to assess the cultural life of Ferrara between 1471 and 1505 and to reconstruct the physical appearance of the court under Ercole d'Este. *Merlozzo da Forlì: la sua città e il suo tempo*, ed. Marina Foschi and Luciana Prati, Mi, Leonardo Arte, 1994, 445 pp., contains essays that cover the whole gamut of cultural activity in Forlì, including the genre of the chronicle. *Quadri rinomatissimi: il collezionismo dei Pio di Savoia*, ed. Jadranka Bentini, Modena, Artioli, 1994, 237 pp., looks at the patronage of the family at Carpi, Rome, and Ferrara. *Lombardia borromaica, Lombardia spagnola, 1554–1659*, ed. Paolo Pissavino and Gianvittorio Signorotto, 2 vols, Ro, Bulzoni, 1995, 946 pp., contains 23 essays, with studies of the complex issues involved in assessing the presence of Spanish literature in Lombardy and the part played by religious congregations in the organization of schooling. Clifford M. Brown and Guy Delmarcel, *Tapestries for the Courts of Federico II, Ercole, and Ferrante Gonzaga, 1522–63*, Seattle, Washington U.P., 239 pp., uses a vast range of archival evidence to assess the cost and mechanisms of production, together with analyses of how the subject matter and iconography relate to the Gonzaga patrons. Isabella Lazzarini, *Fra un principe e altri stati: relazioni di potere e forme di servizio a Mantova nell'età di Ludovico Gonzaga*, Ro, Istituto Storico Italiano per il Medio Evo, xvi + 523 pp., examines the structure of the Gonzaga court and the administration of power; the wealth of data provided will be the starting point for further studies. *I Gonzaga: moneta, arte, storia*, ed. Silvana Balbi de Caro, Mi, Electa, 1995, 549 pp., contains 59 essays which examine the court, patronage, and the iconography and *imprese* of the family, which formed a backdrop to literary works. Leandro Ventura, *Lorenzo Leonbruno: un pittore a corte nella Mantova di primo Cinquecento*, Ro, Bulzoni, 1995, 354 pp. + 188 pls, sheds light on cultural activities at the court of Isabella d'Este and of Francesco II and Federico II Gonzaga. Raffaele Tamalio, *Federico Gonzaga alla corte di Francesco I di Francia nel carteggio privato con Mantova (1515–1517)*, Paris, Champion, 1994, 447 pp., is a rich collection of letters which sheds much light on the state of French–Italian relations and on the events which had a decisive effect on the formation of Federico's character. *Parma: le tradizioni dell'immagine*, I, ed. Arturo Carlo Quintavalle, Parma U.P., 1994, 190 pp., brings together scholars with different methodological approaches to examine cultural and artistic activity in Parma. Gian Luca Podestà, *Dal delitto politico alla politica del delitto*, Mi, Egea, 1995, xvii + 346 pp., examines the Farnese family's appropriation of property in the Duchy of Parma after its acquisition by Paul III in 1545. An overview of the relationship between town and gown is to be found in Dino Dini, *Pisa e la sua università*, Pisa, ETS, 1995, 676 pp. Paola Benigni et al., *Il potere e la memoria*, F, Edifir, 1995, 86 pp. + 78 pls, examines the problem of sources in reconstructing the history of Piombino. It investigates the dispersal of archival sources, and the possibility of using heraldry, cartography, and coins as sources. *Banchi ebraici a Bologna nel XV secolo*, ed. Maria Giuseppina Muzzarelli, Bo, Il Mulino, 1994, 336 pp., is the fruit of a collaborative research project which makes use of private and public archival sources to reconstruct the complex relationship between the Jewish community and the civic authorities. Ariel Toaff, *Love, Work and Death. Jewish Life in Medieval Umbria*, London, Littman, 297 pp., reconstructs the worldview of Italian Jewry by examining how people lived, and the traditions and culture they shared, and does much to balance the prevalent emphasis on antisemitism. Anna Esposito, *Un'altra Roma: minoranze nazionali e comunità ebraiche tra Medioevo e Rinascimento*, Ro, Il Calamo, 1995, 345 pp., focuses on the impact which the expulsion of Spanish Jews had on the social and cultural life of the well-established Jewish community. Francesco Vossilla, *La Loggia della Signoria*, F, Medicea, 1995, 154 pp., uses a wide range of literary and historical sources to study the social, political, and cultural factors that led to the commissioning, selection, and installation of the sculptural decoration in the loggia. Giovanna Benadusi, *A Provincial Elite in Early Modern Tuscany*, Baltimore, Johns Hopkins U.P., 259 pp., looks at the strategies employed by the major families in Poppi to mediate with the politics of a centralized power. Ugo Procacci, *Studio sul catasto fiorentino*, F, Olschki, xi + 189 pp., is a long-awaited study which analyses how the *catasto* worked, what kind of information may be gleaned from it, and how this can be analysed. Lucia Tongiorgi Tomasi and Fabio Garbari, *Il giardiniere del Granduca: storia e immagini del Codice Casabona*, Pisa, ETS, 129 pp., is a beautifully produced volume dedicated to the collaboration between the Flemish herbalist J. De Goethuysen and the German artist Daniel Froeschl. It adds much to our knowledge of the Medici fascination with exploring the natural world and to our understanding of the cultural climate in late 16th-c. Florence. *Carteggi delle magistrature dell'età repubblicana: Otto di pratica. Missive*, ed. Raffaella Maria Zaccaria, 2 vols, F, Olschki, xxiii + 1170 pp., consists of the inventories of more than 20,000 letters sent to the Otto between 1480 and 1527, together with notes and indexes. This is an invaluable research tool for investigating the foundation of the Medici state before the establishment of the principality. Giorgio Cadoni, *Crisi della mediazione politica e conflitti sociali: Niccolò Machiavelli, Francesco Guicciardini e Donato Giannotti di fronte al tramonto della 'Florentina Libertas'*, Ro, Jouvence, 1994, 262 pp., explores the complex evolution of the debate on the possibility of republican liberty. Franco Cesati, *Le strade di Firenze*, Ro, Newton Compton, 1994, 671 pp., recreates the social geography of the city by listing the streets alphabetically and giving the dates and owners of the palaces. *Erasmo, Venezia e la cultura padana nel '500*, ed. Achille Olivieri, Rovigo, Minelliana, 1995, 366 pp., comprises 27 essays divided into three sections: 'Erasmo a Venezia: edizioni e lettere'; 'Gli intellettuali di fronte ad Erasmo'; 'Erasmo e le corti padane'. The essays investigate the impact of scholarship, the development of humanistic techniques, and religious ideas and piety. *Venezia e l'Europa*, ed. Francesco Vecchiato, Verona, Ed. Universitaria, 1994, 541 pp. F. Cardini et al., *Europa 1492 tra centralità e periferia*, Pordenone, Concordia Sette, 1994, 150 pp., has essays on the impact which the discovery of the New World had on the notion of the early modern state and on the European reaction to the exotic. Brian Pullan, *Poverty and Charity: Europe, Italy, Venice 1400–1700*, Aldershot, Variorum, 1994, x + 339 pp., contains 12 essays which evaluate the role of the church and state in tackling economic and social problems and disease. Robert C. Davis, *The War of the Fists: Popular Culture and Public Violence in Late Renaissance Venice*, OUP, 1994, vi + 232 pp., studies the 'guerre dei pugni', pitched battles fought between artisans for control of city bridges, described in a lengthy chronicle of some 400 pages. Margaret L. King, *The Death of the Child Valerio Marcello*, Chicago U.P., 1994, xviii + 484 pp., is a fascinating and rewarding study initially focused on one particular Venetian family's personal tragedy, but expanding to encompass patronage and reflections on death. Guido

Tigler, *Il portale maggiore di San Marco a Venezia*, Venice, IV, 1995, 579 pp., examines the astrological and theological themes in the iconography and relates them to contemporary, social, and religious preoccupations. Venice's close links with the East can be traced in *I 'documenti turchi' dell'Archivio di Stato di Venezia*, ed. Maria Pia Pedani Fabris, Ro, IPZS, 1994, lxxii + 697 pp. Onorato Caetani and Gerolamo Diedo, *La battaglia di Lepanto (1571)*, Palermo, Sellerio, 1995, 224 pp., is a collection of letters sent by Onorato Caetani, captain general of infantry on the papal armada that helped defeat the Turks. These are from the Archivio Caetani in Rome and give a fascinating running commentary on the dramatic events.

3. POETRY

NARRATIVE POETRY

REWRITINGS AND REAPPRAISALS. Most of this year's offerings are about transformations (within texts, from text to text, or from text to metatext), and about our changing perceptions of the genre. A. Franceschetti, 'Turpino e il suo libro nell'*Orlando innamorato*', *EL*, 21. 3:3–20, assesses the role of 'Turpino personaggio' in *OI*, and the many and original ways Boiardo calls upon 'Turpino storico e cronista,' usually to lend weight to his own extravagant inventions, and to introduce a note of irony. A. Casadei, 'Riusi (e rifiuti) del modello dell'*Innamorato* tra il 1520 e il 1530', *Italianistica*, 24, 1995:87–100, sketches the twilight of the 'moda boiardesca' and the emergence of the 'moda ariostesca', focusing on Marco Guazzo's *Belisardo* and Francesco de' Lodovici's *Anteo* and *Trionfi de Carlo*. A. Scaglione, ' "Amori e dolori" in the *Orlando innamorato*', *Italica*, 73:1–10, argues that Boiardo, by presenting love for the first time as an 'optional negative force in a secular way', that is as something to be avoided, lays the groundwork for what will become with *Orlando furioso* a fully-fledged *Bildungsroman*, providing a 'socially relevant model of leadership' which was to enjoy great success in the rest of Europe and still exercised a powerful influence on 'the colonial high administrators of the British Empire in the age of Queen Victoria'. Stefano Jossa, *La fantasia e la memoria. Intertestualità ariostesche*, Na, Liguori, 194 pp., is an impressive study which attempts to define Ariosto's poetics of rewriting: A. decomposes and recomposes the Ancients by means of dittology and adjectivization, using Petrarch as a model of style and Dante of writing, with Poliziano as a guarantor of *contaminatio*; but he opposes homogeneous syntaxis to Poliziano's heterogeneous parataxis, and thus moves towards the acceptance of a norm, while rejecting the rigidity of Bembo's solution. A. also rewrites himself, within *OF* and from the first to the third redaction, in order to establish linguistic 'modernity'. E. Fumagalli, 'Presenze di commenti ai classici nell'*Orlando furioso*', *Aevum*, 68, 1994:551–70, shows how A.'s use of classical authors is mediated and influenced by their late 15th-c. commentators. F. Sberlati, *'Sospensione e intrattenimento. Tracce di una tradizione orale nel Furioso'*, *Studi Raimondi*, 47–66. S. Favalier, 'Le *Roland furieux* de l'Arioste dans les "tramutazioni" vénitiennes à la bergamasque du XVIᵉ siècle', *REI*, 41, 1995:99–109, illustrates the way in which, with greater frequency than any other work, *OF* became the object of homage and parody in late 16th-c. Venice, in a zany ('Zanni') manner of which A. himself would no doubt have approved. C. Longhi ' "Il giuoco del *Furioso*". Grammatica di una citazione teatrale da Ariosto', *LS*, 31:433–62, is a study of how Edoardo Sanguineti recomposed *OF* for stage performances in 1969–70. S. Ritrovato, '*I Romanzi* di Giovan Battista Pigna (1554): interpretazione di un genere moderno', *SPCT*, 52:131–51, argues that Pigna, in his defence of *OF*, anticipates many of the views of modern critics on the novel/romance. And for the latest on what modern critics think of *OF* see: L. Fortini, 'Rassegna ariostesca (1986–1995)', *LItal*, 48:295–314. Stefano Jossa, *Rappresentazione e scrittura. La crisi delle forme poetiche rinascimentali (1540–1560)*, Na, Vivarium, 376 pp., argues that the change from an 'open' to a 'closed' world in the political sphere (Absolutism, Counter-Reformation) is mirrored by a similar change in the cultural sphere ('the end of Humanism'), as evidenced in the debate on the romance between Giraldi and Pigna, and the differing views of that genre they expressed in *Ercole* and *Eroico* (as well as in the debate between Giraldi and Speroni on tragedy, and the differing views of tragedy they put forward in *Orbecche* and *Canace*). G. Allaire, 'Tullia d'Aragona's *Il meschino altramente detto il Guerino* as key to a reappraisal of her work', *QI*, 16, 1995:33–50, deals with a more personal crisis. It seeks to rehabilitate the chivalric epic by means of which Tullia had sought to rehabilitate herself (from courtesan to intellectual), and by dating it more accurately (1543–46) it shows that T. was a good and versatile poet in her own right, and not the literary creature of Benedetto Varchi. Male poets, it would seem, had loftier ambitions: C. Kallendorf, 'From Virgil to Vida: the *poeta theologus* in Italian Renaissance commentary', *JHI*, 56, 1995:41–62, traces the conflict (and its resolution) between pagan and Christian values in Italian Renaissance editions of Virgil's works, and in Vida's *Christias*. Tasso for his part is all about conflict and change. M. Residori, 'Il Mago d'Ascalona e gli spazi del romanzo nella *Liberata*', *Italianistica*, 24, 1995:453–71, is about how T. uses romance means for epic ends. S. Zatti, 'Tasso e il Nuovo Mondo', *ib.*, 501–21, discusses the cultural imperialism inherent in T.'s epic rewriting of the romance topos of the journey of discovery. G. Güntert, 'Dalla *Gerusalemme liberata* alla *Conquistata*: racconto di nobili imprese e allegoria del contemptus mundi', *ib.*, 381–94, presents the change from *GL* to *GC* as a change from oxymoron to antithesis, from polycentrism to Manicheism, and as a *Weltflucht*, the divine poet of the former coming to terms in the latter with the chasm which separates his humanity from God's divinity. P. Di Sacco, 'Da Ascalona alla "Scalogna". Tasso, la magia e altro', *LItal*, 48:602–24, discusses the retreat of magic (diabolical, natural, and divine) before the onslaught of 'brutal' reality, from *GL* to *GC* and beyond. D. Boillet, 'Clorinde, de la *Jérusalem délivrée* à la *Jérusalem conquise*', *REI*, 42:7–53, analyses the figural representations of the three facets of Clorinda's character: 'vierge guerrière', 'dame sans merci', 'âme égarée'. Claudio Gigante, *'Vincer pariemi più se stessa antica'. La 'Gerusalemme conquistata' nel mondo poetico di Torquato Tasso*, Na, Bibliopolis, 170 pp., considers *GC* as a work in its own right, analysing how it is made and how it holds together, with particular reference to Goffredo's dream and the influence of Homeric realism on the description of battles. Id., 'Il sogno di Goffredo', *StT*, 43, 1995:7–30, discusses the antecedents, autobiographical sincerity, structure, intertextuality and meaning of the dream in *GC* xx, which is to be seen as an integral part of the poem, whose most significant characteristics (paraphrase of the Holy Scriptures, influence of Petrarch's *Trionfi*, 'maniera cortigiana') it shares. T. Mattoli, 'Alle origini delle polemiche sulla *Liberata*. Una lettera di Giulio Giordani del 1583', *RPLit*, 17, 1994:195–220, contains a hitherto unpublished letter in defence of *GL* by a gentleman from Pesaro who a few years earlier had acted host to Tasso. B. Basile, 'Fonti classiche per alcuni versi gnomici tassiani. Recuperi dalle glosse alla *Liberata* di Scipio Gentili', *FC*, 20, 1995 [1996]:491–98, shows how the 1590 *Annotationi* of Gentili, who knew T. and shared his *forma mentis*, can help us to understand *GL*. E. Villa, 'La *Comparatione* di Paolo Beni', *Italianistica*, 24, 1995:649–58, is about Beni's appreciation of the modernity of *GL*. B. Basile, 'La più antica biografia del Tasso', *ib.*, 525–39, reproduces Francesco De Pietri's *Compendio della vita di Torquato Tasso scritta da Gio. Battista Manso* first published in 1619. R. Scrivano, 'Ermeneutica tassiana e pittura', *ib.*, 633–48, discusses and illustrates *GL*-inspired paintings from Tintoretto to Tiepolo. L. Carpanè, 'La fortuna editoriale tassiana dal '500 ai giorni nostri', *ib.*, 541–57, seeks to explain why *GL* is read less today than the *Divine Comedy*, and why that need not be so. Also on the *fortuna* of Tasso see: L. Bolzoni, 'Tra parole e immagini: per una tipologia cinquecentesca del lettore creativo', *LItal*, 48:527–58, who discusses *inter alia* Orazio Toscanella's 1574 commentary on *Orlando furioso* and Galileo's *Considerazioni al Tasso*; K. Ley-Mainz, ' "sii grand'uomo e sii infelice". Zur

Umwertung des Tasso-Bildes am Beginn des Ottocento: Vorausset-zungen und Hintergründe in europäischen Rahmen (La Harpe/ Gilbert — Goethe — Foscolo)', *GRM*, 46:131–73; M. Pieri, 'Dalla commedia dell'arte al sillabo: varie sorti di Torquato mattatore', *Italianistica*, 24, 1995:593–614, which deals with the theatrical guises of T. (as created by Goldoni, Goethe, Rosini, Alberto Nota, and De Sanctis); *La ragione e l'arte. Torquato Tasso e la Repubblica Veneta*, ed. Giovanni Da Pozzo, Venice, Il Cardo, 1995, 254 pp., which is a catalogue of an exhibition on T.'s formative years in Venice, containing many articles; R. Bruscagli, 'Gli studi tassiani di Lanfranco Caretti', *StIt*, 15:67–76; Arnaldo Di Benedetto, *Con e intorno a Torquato Tasso*, Na, Liguori, vii + 370 pp., which contains a new reading of *GL* xii, beside a whole series of previously published articles.

WARFARE (AND 'MANLINESS'). Michael Murrin, *History and Warfare in Renaissance Epic*, Chicago U.P., 1994, xvi + 371 pp., calling on the expertise of military historians and literary critics, travelling from Italy (Pulci, Boiardo, Ariosto, Tasso) via the Iberian Peninsula to England, and covering the period 1483–1610, assesses the way writers of romances coped or did not cope in their works with the 'Gunpowder Revolution', how they did or did not incorporate history into their poems, how the genre came to reflect the different modes of fighting prevalent in different parts of the world, and why the genre was ultimately defeated by, and eschewed, war as it gave way to Milton's 'peaceful epic'. P. Di Sacco, 'Femmine guerriere. Amazzoni, cavalli e cavalieri da Camilla a Clorinda', *Intersezioni*, 16:275–89, sketches the history of the *antianeirai* virgin warrior (equal of man and enemy of man) from Antiquity to Tasso, via Boiardo and Ariosto. Laura Benedetti, *La sconfitta di Diana. Un percorso per la 'Gerusalemme liberata'*, Ravenna, Longo, 148 pp., reads *GL* as a dramatization of the conflict between the sexes, in which the (male) victor over the forces of evil is a 'mutilated individual', and the conquest of the ideal city is achieved by a ruthless domination of women and nature, each one of the female (pagan) protagonists having to renounce her (feminine) prerogatives, and Christian, that is, matrimonial love providing but a fleeting and unsatisfactory resolution to the clash between male and female roles. J. M. Kisacky, 'Magic and enchanted armaments: moral considerations in Boiardo and Ariosto', *Fol*, 30:253–73, shows how B. and A., contrary to tradition, allow knights the use of magic weapons, B. simply for the fun of it, A. so as to castigate them in a chivalric context, while accepting them elsewhere. M. Praloran, *'Vedere, patire, agire: il duello di Lipadusa nel *Furioso*', *Omaggio Folena*, 1089–1106. U. Balzaretti, 'L'*Orlando furioso* in filigrana: Ravenna, le armi da fuoco, la corte, l'ascesa negata di Ruggiero', *Aevum*, 70:563–96, takes modern warfare as a starting point to show

how readers must read between the lines of *OF* in order to decipher the *serio ludere* of Ariosto as he walks a tightrope between praising and condemning the rulers of Ferrara in a poem which might not have been any different had he not been dependent on Este patronage. Moderata Fonte, *Tredici canti del Floridoro*, ed. Valeria Finucci, Modena, Mucchi, 1995, xlvi + 227 pp., offers the text of a *romanzo cavalleresco* and raises the question of how a woman tackled the themes of war, love, and dynasty in a predominantly male genre.

THE MARVELLOUS AND FANTASY. Rosaria Patanè Ceccantini, *Il motivo del 'locus amoenus' nell'Orlando furioso e nella Gerusalemme liberata*, Université de Lausanne, Faculté des Lettres, 59 pp., contains a brief literary history of the topos, and an analysis of how Ariosto and Tasso adapt it to the structural and moral demands of their poems. F. Grazziani, 'Le miracle de l'art: le Tasse et la poétique de la *meraviglia*', *REI*, 42 : 117–39, defines *meraviglia*, which is said to find its supreme expression in the epic poem, as the ethical and metaphysical pleasure of the reader, and the *concettismo* of the lofty and divinely inspired poem. M. Casubolo, 'Imprese tassiane: il *Rinaldo*', *Italianistica*, 24, 1995 : 333–53, catalogues the *imprese* in *Rinaldo*, and interprets them in the light of Cinquecento theories on the matter, arguing that most are the fruit of Tasso's 'gusto per la creazione fantastica'. Gustavo Costa, **Il sublime e la magia da Dante a Tasso*, Na, ESI, 1994, 158 pp.

LANGUAGE. M. Praloran, ' "Lingua di ferro e voce di bombarda". La rima nell'*Innamoramento de Orlando*', *ParL*, 51–52, 1995 : 23–53, shows how Boiardo, in whom is evident 'la gioia della produzione fonica', explores and discovers the potential of varying rhyme schemes, and how he learns to adapt them to the demands of his poetics of representation. G. Cavallini, 'Su alcuni usi dell'aggettivo nel Tasso epico', *Italianistica*, 24, 1995 : 355–69, explores the many different effects to which T. uses adjectives in *GL*. A. Soldani, 'Saggio di un'analisi della *Liberata*: l'ordine delle parole', *StT*, 43, 1995 : 31–91, analyses T.'s use of figures of speech which act as counterpoint to the rhyme scheme, and thanks to which T. achieves a dialectic harmony of metre and syntax, which is the linguistic equivalent of his thematic search for harmony in disunity. P. Galetto, 'Procedimenti interagenti nella poesia del Tasso (Gerus. Lib. c. XIV, ottave 57–71)', *LS*, 30, 1995 : 387–414, is a detailed semantic, linguistic, and rhythmic analysis, which illustrates how T. generates meaning in *GL*, transforming Armida from classical enchantress to modern woman. E. Scotti, 'Il problema testuale della *Gerusalemme liberata*', *Italianistica*, 24, 1995 : 483–500, stresses the need for a reassessment of T. philology, and attempts to establish a proper genealogy of the text of *GL*.

OTHER POETRY

BEFORE THE TRIUMPH OF PETRARCHISM. Mario Martelli, *Letteratura fiorentina del Quattrocento. Il filtro degli anni Sessanta*, F, Le Lettere, 341 pp., sets the (mostly vernacular) cultural, and hence political, scene for the decade in which Lorenzo made his literary debut, in an anthologizing and 'stream of literariness' manner, which ranges over poems and 'plays' by (among others) Lucrezia Tornabuoni, Feo Belcari, Naldo Naldi, Ugolino Verino, Antonio di Cola Bonciani, Luca and Luigi Pulci, besides those of Lorenzo himself. T. Zanato, '*n controrestauri al* Canzoniere *laurenziano*', *RLettI*, 11, 1993:453–533, is a learned and measured, point-by-point reply to Martelli's demolition, in *Interpres*, 11, 1991, of Zanato's edition of L.'s *canzoniere*. R. Bessi, 'Le *Stanze* del Poliziano e la lirica del primo Quattrocento', *LItal*, 48:3–24, reveals that late 14th- and early 15th-c. poets included in the *Raccolta aragonese* had very little (lexical or stylistic) influence on the *Stanze*, and that the only poet of that period who did was Giusto de' Conti. D. Delcorno Branca, **'Fra commento e poesia. Schede per la* Stanze', *Omaggio Folena*, 845–60. Id., 'Per il linguaggio dei rispetti del Poliziano', *Rinascimento*, 35, 1995:31–66, shows, by comparison with the traditions of Tuscan and courtly *rispetti*, how P. is in a class of his own, with few peers and no followers. F. Bausi, 'Per il testo delle *Silvae* di Angelo Poliziano. Ricerche sulla tradizione a stampa', *Schede umanistiche*, 1:5–22, is a study of variants in the incunabula of the *Silvae*. L. Merino Jerez, 'Las *Silvae* de Poliziano comentadas por el Brocense', *HL*, 45:406–29, deals with a commentary by the Spanish humanist Francisco Sánchez de las Brocas, published in Spain in 1544.

PETRARCHISM (MORE OR LESS) TRIUMPHANT. M. Boaglio, 'Il proposito dell'imitazione. Liriche d'esordio e canzonieri petrarcheschi nel primo Cinquecento', pp. 85–118 of *Luoghi e forme della lirica*, ed. Giorgio Bárberi Squarotti, T, Tirrenia, examines the varied responses to the Petrarchan model of Pietro Bembo, Gaspara Stampa, Vittoria Colonna, Michelangelo Buonarroti, and Giovanni Della Casa. In the same volume, S. Calzone, 'Metamorfosi dei codici cromatici da Petrarca ai petrarchisti' (69–84), looks at the changing colours of the master and his disciples, while others look at changing waters: D. Chiodo, 'La scena del bagno' (47–68); C. Peirone, 'Approdi e naufragi' (29–46); and G. Baldissone looks at changing and vanishing sights in 'L'occhio lirico' (9–28). E. Travi, ***Come Pietro Bembo leggeva Petrarca', *Testo*, 27, 1994:49–55. R. Zaiser, 'Pietro Bembo: ein orthodoxer Imitator Petrarcas?', *ItStudien*, 17:186–200, shows how, in his *innamoramento* poem, B. sought to out-Petrarch Petrarch. And in real life Bembo went one better: G. Braden, 'Applied Petrarchism: the loves of Pietro Bembo', *MLQ*, 57:397–423, explains how Petrarch's 'solitary male lyricism' could be made to express 'the mutual passion of a man and a woman', thus allowing B. and his beloveds to act out Petrarchism even as they went to bed together. So L. Martines, 'Amour et histoire dans la poésie de la Renaissance italienne', *Annales*, 51:575–603, may be right when he defends the use as historical documents — to throw light on the 'mental structures' of Renaissance (urban) society, its religious sensitivities, its notions of social status and identity, its attitudes to marriage and property — of the love poetry of the years 1370–1530 (whose authors, it would seem, were reactionary male chauvinists to a man). The ravages and Petrarchan repercussions of male chauvinism are illustrated in Adele Cambria, *Isabella. La triste storia di Isabella Morra. Le Rime della poetessa di Valsinni*, ed. Giovanni Caserta, Venosa, Osanna Venosa, 92 pp., which contains ten sonnets and three *canzoni*, with the life story of their 16th-c. author, who was murdered by her brothers and uncles for loving a man she should not have loved. As always in the south of Italy at the time, the social and political realities are never far beneath the surface. T. R. Toscano, 'Due nuovi manoscritti di rime di Luigi Tansillo in Spagna e una notizia sul recupero del codice Casella', *FC*, 20, 1995 [1996]:80–125, evaluates the way in which a mid 16th-c. *canzoniere* was formed within the confines set by the cultural exigencies of Spain, Naples, and Florence. A. Afribo, 'La ripetizione e altro in Luigi Tansillo', *RLettI*, 12, 1994:351–82, draws a map of the stylistic features, especially in so far as they differ from Petrarch's, of T.'s sonnets and madrigals. Ascanio Pignatelli, *Rime*, ed. Maurizio Slawinski, T, RES, lvi + 159 pp., provides an interesting example, in readable form, of experimentation with the Petrarchan canon in late 16th-c. Italy, by a Neapolitan nobleman who was a fellow-student and friend of Tasso's. The restrictions imposed on experimentation by a different sort of canon are highlighted by V. Martignone, 'Un caso di censura editoriale: l'edizione Dolce (1555) delle *Rime* di Bernardo Tasso', *StT*, 43, 1995:93–112, who discusses an editor more sensitive to the demands of politics than to those of poetry. Experiments within the Petrarchan canon by Bernardo's more famous son are documented by S. Berti, 'La "Canzone alla Bruna" e l'*Ars amatoria* di Ovidio', *LItal*, 48:63–78, who shows how Torquato, though he wished to conceal the fact, contaminated Petrarch with Ovid. (For Ovid's influence on Tasso, see NEO-LATIN POETRY, below.) M. Guglielminetti, 'Quando "appare la persona del poeta". Saggio sulle rime autobiografiche del Tasso (1557–1579)', *REI*, 42:55–84, discusses T.'s discovery of an original autobiographical style within the confines of the lyric tradition, and how some of his poems can be read as the 'lyrical autobiography' of a Romantic *avant la lettre*. S. Prandi, *** "Ne le tenebre ancor vivrò beato": variazioni tassiane sul tema della gelosia', *Studi Raimondi*, 67–84. V. Martignone, 'Varianti d'autore tassiane: un sondaggio sulle *Rime amorose*', *Italianistica*, 24, 1995:427–35, argues that T. used a clearly recognizable and poetically inspired system in revising his poems. M. Zaccarello, 'Postille ad una recente edizione delle Rime Chigiane·del Tasso', *RLettI*, 12, 1994:441–56, suggests some ways in which the critical apparatus of T.'s *Rime d'amore* (ed. F. Gavazzeni et al., Modena, Panini, 1993) might have been improved, especially with regard to variants. Torquato Tasso, *Alle Signore Principesse di Ferrara*, Ferrara–Ro, Gabriele Corbo, 1995, 130 pp., is a collection of poems to Lucrezia and Leonora d'Este put together by T. around 1578 with the purpose of getting the two princesses to intercede on his behalf with their brother, Alfonso II. *Rime de gli Academici Eterei*, ed. Ginetta Auzzas and Manlio Pastore Stocchi, introd. Antonio Daniele, Padua, CEDAM, 1995, 214 pp., is a critical edition of a collection of poems by eleven poets (including T. Tasso, Battista Guarini, and Scipione Gonzaga) published in 1567 and dedicated to Marguerite de Valois, daughter of Francis I and wife of Emanuel Philibert of Savoy.

ON THE MARGINS OF PETRARCHISM (BEYOND AND BEFORE TIME). P. Vecchi Galli, 'Sulla poesia pastorale: per un seminario di studi, una edizione e altro', *SPCT*, 53:75–91, points out how much more we really need to know about the (Tuscan) background to Sannazaro's *Arcadia*, and about the genre in general. Angela Caracciolo Aricò, *L'Arcadia del Sannazaro nell'autunno dell'Umanesimo*, Ro, Bulzoni, 1995, 105 pp., sees S. as transforming Arcadia into a place of protest and refuge for a desperately melancholy latter-day Oedipus, and *Arcadia* as a spiritual autobiography composed under the shadow of the death of S.'s mother and the downfall of the Aragonese dynasty. On the transalpine *fortuna* of S., see F. Lavocat, 'Les traductions françaises de l'*Arcadia* de Sannazar', *RLC*, 1995:323–39. E. Garavelli, 'Il "I Idillio" di Teocrito tradotto da Annibal Caro', *Aevum*, 69, 1995:555–91, discusses the popularity of Theocritus in Renaissance Italy, and provides a critical edition of this early 16th-c. Italian translation of his first eclogue. R. Cavalluzzi, 'Il *rogo amoroso*', *Italianistica*, 24, 1995:371–79, discusses this pastoral poem on the death of a friend's beloved in the context of Tasso's *mal de vivre*. The poem on which T. worked until he was relieved of that *mal* is discussed by A. Maggi, 'La creazione prima della creazione: *Il mondo creato* di Torquato Tasso alla luce de *La sepmaine* di Guillaume du Bartas', *RoN*, 37:59–66, who shows how T. rises to the challenge, not faced by his model, of expressing in words that which *is* not yet. P. Luparia, 'Trinitas creatrix. Appunti sulla teologia platonica del Tasso nel *Mondo creato*', *REI*, 42:85–116, provides an exegesis of the opening of the poem

which shows how the triune God is expressed and praised through
the poetry of threefold diversity in harmony. L. Capra, 'Qualche
riconoscimento di nozioni cosmografiche del Tasso', *Italianistica*, 24,
1995:323–32, draws on several of T.'s works, but especially *Il mondo
creato*, to expound T.'s views on the heavens, the sun, the moon, other
planets, and constellations. G. Jori, 'Dal frammento al cosmo. Idoli e
pietas dai *Dialoghi* al *Mondo creato*', *ib.*, 395–410, outlines T.'s passage
from the error of *idolum* to the certainty of *signum*, and from *eros* to
caritas and faith. M. Saccenti, 'La *gran macchina del mondo* e la
congiuntura Tasso-Marchetti', *ib.*, 615–32, discusses the *fortuna*,
baroque-style, of *Il mondo creato*.

ON THE MARGINS OF PETRARCHISM (LESSER AND UNUSUAL
FORMS). M. Castoldi, 'Fra immagine sacra e preghiera profana. Per
la tradizione di un *Sonetto alla Madonna di Loreto*', *SPCT*, 52:49–78,
discusses a tradition which developed in the shadow of Petrarchism.
G. Bellorini, 'Luigi Cassola madrigalista', *Aevum*, 69, 1995:593–615,
studies the features of the 363 madrigals by a late 15th- early 16th-c.
'poeta stucchevole, lezioso, alessandrino' from Piacenza, which were
first published in 1544 and enjoyed great popularity for over half a
century. M. Damian, *'Struttura dei madrigali michelangioleschi',
Omaggio Folena, 905–20. Martha Feldman, *City Culture and the Madrigal
at Venice*, Berkeley, California U.P., 1995, xxi + 473 pp., explains
Venetian theory within the context of Ciceronian rhetoric and traces
the development of a poetics of linguistic purity, emotional restraint,
euphony, and variety. *Contro le puttane. Rime venete del XVI secolo*, ed.
Marisa Milani, Bassano, Ghedina & Tassotti, 1994, 125 pp., is a
collection of mainly anonymous poems in Venetian and Paduan
dialect, which includes verse by A. Calmo and M. Venier, and the full
text of the *Catalogo delle cortigiane*. A. Romano, 'Osservazioni metriche
e stilistiche sulle poesie di Pietro Aretino', *LS*, 31:505–24, provides a
typology, with commentary, of the metrical forms used by Aretino.
N. Ciampaglia, 'Un inedito *Tractato* meridionale su Ippolita d'Aragona di Frate Bernardino de Renda di Patti: identificazione di una
fonte perduta', *FC*, 20, 1995 [1996]:44–79, gives a preview of a late
15th-c. 480-stanza *planctus* in *ottava rima* on the death of Ippolita
Sforza belonging to the Sicilian tradition of *cantari sacri*, but quite
untypical of the Neapolitan vernacular production of the time.
A. Daniele, *'Sul testo del *Chaos del triperuno* di Teofilo Folengo. Primi
appunti', *Omaggio Folena*, 1015–30. F. J. Santa Eugenia, 'Ottave
quattrocentesche sugli uccelli da caccia', *SFI*, 54:221–60, is a critical
edition of a late 15th-c. Lombard versification of part of the *Liber
ruralium commodorum* of the Bolognese jurist Pietro de' Crescenzi
(*c.* 1233–1320). S. Barelli, 'Innovazioni metriche di Giovan Paolo
Lomazzo e degli "Accademici della Valle di Blenio" ', *Italianistica*, 24,

1995:101–17, illustrates and discusses the subversive tendencies evident in the daring strophic and metrical experiments carried out by Lomazzo in the 'bizzarro magma letterario' of his two collections of poems, *Rabisch* and *Grotteschi*. A. Maggi, 'Depicting one's Self: *imprese* and sonnets in *La Virginia overo la dea de' nostri tempi* by Ercole Tasso', *QI*, 16, 1995:51–60, argues that this work, a combination of sonnets, *imprese*, and cabalistic meditations on the name of the poet's beloved, published in 1593 in Bergamo, is an enigmatic and complex self-portrait, in which the poet's body vanishes out of devotion to the Other. Antonio Delfino and Maria Teresa Benezzani, *Marc'Antonio Ingegneri e la musica a Cremona nel secondo Cinquecento*, Lucca, Libreria Musicale Italiana, 1995, xvi + 469 pp., has essays which deal with the circulation of Tasso's poetry before 1581 and the use made of the works of Tansillo, Bembo, Ariosto, and Sannazaro. *Dall' idillio alla visione*, ed. Raffaele Cavalluzzi, Manduria, Lacaita, 1994, 169 pp., has essays on: musical elements in early 15th-c. Neapolitan literature, concentrating on Sannazaro, Bonifacio, and Britonio; the uncertainty of Tasso when confronted with traditional Aristotelian–Ptolomaic cosmology and his position in the debate over science versus faith. Vincenzo Paladino, *L'opera poetica di Tommaso Campanella*, Alessandria, Orso, 1994, 92 pp., examines the social background and gives an assessment of the early works before turning to C.'s poetry and its fortunes.

COMMENTARY. *Schifanoia*, 15–16, 1995 is dedicated to 'Il commento al testo lirico' and contains: D. De Robertis, 'Commentare il Dante lirico' (13–23), discussing C. Landino among others; A. Bettarini Bruni, 'Il commento dello Pseudo-Colonna alla canzone d'amore del Cavalcanti' (24–45); G. Belloni, 'All'origine della critica degli scartafacci (1495/96–1540)' (61–79), discussing Pontano, Aldo Manuzio, Ugolino Martelli, and Bernardino Daniello on Petrarch; C. Montagnani, 'L'eclissi del codice lirico: una canzone di Niccolò Malpigli nel commento di Pier Andrea De' Bassi' (82–90); R. Rossi, 'Filelfo commenta Petrarca' (91–98); R. Cardini, 'Landino e Dante' (99–109); S. Carrai, 'Un commento quattrocentesco "ad usum mulieris": Jacopo de' Boninsegni sopra un sonetto del Cingoli' (110–20); G. Gorni, 'Un commento inedito alle *Rime* del Bembo da attribuire a Sertorio Quattromani' (121–32); V. Martignone, 'Il commento tassiano alle *Rime amorose*' (133–40); C. Molinari, 'La parte del Guarini nel Commento al *Pastor Fido*' (141–50).

NEO-LATIN POETRY. W. K. Percival, 'A working edition of the *Carmina differentialia* by Guarino Veronese', *RPLit*, 17, 1994:153–77, by providing an (almost) critical edition of an essentially medieval lexicon, shows how even the greatest innovators relied on tried and tested methods, which even today make for good and informative reading (for example, 'Hic vehementer *amat, diligit* iste minus. / Dic *Gallos* gentem, gallinas *gallus* habebit. / Atque sacerdotem Cybelis tu dicto *Gallum!*'). M. Madrid Castro, 'Baptiste Mantuani contra poetas impudice loquentes, cum Sebastiani Murrhonis interpraetacione', *HL*, 45:93–133, provides a critical edition of a poem in elegiac distychs by Battista Spagnoli of Mantua (1447–1516), with a commentary by the German humanist Sebastian Mor (1452–94). L. M. Colker, '*Venus*: a humanist's epigrams on love', *HL*, 44, 1995:107–35, gives the text of a 'not entirely lascivious' collection of 67 Latin poems by an anonymous early 16th-c. Italian as contained in a Columbia University Library MS. L. Castagna, 'Il *Politiani tumulus* di Pietro Bembo (*Carminum* XXVI)', *Aevum*, 69, 1995:533–53, subjects a short and mediocre *texte* to a long and learned *explication*. *Aetates Ovidianae. Lettori di Ovidio dall'antichità al Rinascimento*, ed. Italo Gallo and Luciano Nicastri, Na, ESI, 1995, 379 pp., has 18 essays, including a study of Ovidian influences on Pontano's *Urania* (also, a study of how Ovid was treated in 16th-c. treatises on poetry, and on his presence in Tasso). E. O'Connor, 'Hell's pit and heaven's rose: the typology of female sights and smells in Panormita's *Hermaphroditus*', *MH*, 23:25–51, shows how Beccadelli rewrote classical/pagan and medieval/Christian images of good and bad women in order to express praise or blame. Piero Cecchini, *Giannantonio Campano: studi sulla produzione poetica*, Urbino, Quattroventi, 1995, 145 pp., is about a friend and acolyte of Pomponio Leta's. D. Sacré, 'Le poète néo-latin Girolamo Faletti (†1564)', *HL*, 41, 1992:199–220, provides a biographical sketch of a little-known poet from northern Italy, who settled in Ferrara and then became Ferrarese ambassador to Venice.

4. THEATRE

FESTE

Matteo Casini, *I gesti del principe. La festa politica a Firenze e Venezia in età rinascimentale*, Venice, Marsilio, 448 pp., is an in-depth comparative study of the festive rituals by means of which the state imposed itself upon society and celebrated its power from the 15th to the early 17th c. The work focuses on funerals and enthronements of rulers, state processions and holidays, receptions of foreign dignitaries, and the major civic festival of each city (Venice: Annunciation, Florence: St John). Nicole Carew-Reid, *Les fêtes florentines au temps de Lorenzo il Magnifico*, F, Olschki, 1995, 291 pp., traces the evolution of a new cultural politics aimed at sidelining republican motifs in favour of Medici glorification. It covers the festivals for San Giovanni, carnivals, and diplomatic receptions, and argues persuasively that there was a close relationship between festival and theatre, and a clear political agenda. M. Licht, 'Elysium: a prelude to Renaissance theater', *RenS*, 49: 1–29, provides a description and discussion of the Rome 1473 festivities offered in honour of the marriage of Eleonora of Aragon and Ercole d'Este, which produced a speaking likeness of antiquity, while stopping short of staging classical or classically inspired plays. James M. Saslow, *The Medici Wedding of 1598: Florentine Festival as Theatrum Mundi*, New Haven, Yale U.P., x + 323 pp., reconstructs a multimedia event by providing 'a comprehensive chronological narrative, while at the same time ranging synchronically across a wide social and artistic terrain [. . .] to approach the totality of the event from an interdisciplinary standpoint that highlights the interplay between artistic and social analysis'. Amelio Fara, *Bernardo Buontalenti*, Mi, Electa, 1995, 330 pp., is the first monograph on this multi-talented figure, particularly noteworthy for his scenographic *apparati* for festivals, state funerals, and plays.

SACRE RAPPRESENTAZIONI

Antonia Pulci, *Florentine Drama for Convent and Festival. Seven Sacred Plays*, trans. James Wyatt Cook, ed. J. W. Cook and Barbara Collier Cook, Chicago U.P., xxx + 281 pp., is meant for an English-speaking audience, but has much to offer students of Italian for the insights it offers into the sacred genre, the times, the position of women playwrights, and the life of Luigi Pulci's sister-in-law. E. Cesaretti, 'Preoccupazione devozionale nella *Rappresentazione di San Giovanni e Paolo* di Lorenzo de' Medici', *The Italianist*, 15, 1995: 67–82, illustrates the sincerity of Lorenzo's devotion as it emerges from the text of the play, which, it is argued, was not just an *instrumentum regni*. Teofilo Folengo, *Atto della Pinta. Sacra rappresentazione*, ed. Maria Di Venuta, Lucca, Pacini Fazzi, 1994, 133 pp., is an intriguing late example of the genre (1538–39), written in a mixture of Latin and vernacular, and with a plot running from the Creation to the Annunciation.

COMEDY

Origini della commedia nell'Europa del Cinquecento. Atti del XVII Convegno, Centro Studi sul Teatro Medievale e Rinascimentale (Roma, 30.9–3.10.1993), ed. Myriam Chiabò and Federico Doglio, Ro, Torre d'Orfeo, 1994, 619 pp., includes *inter alia*: G. Chittolini, 'Il mondo signorile padano nello scorcio del Quattrocento' (19–36); G. Monaco, 'Precedenti classici nella commedia europea del Cinquecento' (37–44); L. Bottoni, 'Due commedie per la fondazione del genere: *La Cassaria* e i *Suppositi*' (65–88); G. Ulysse, 'Lettura drammaturgica del *Negromante* dell'Ariosto' (107–29); A. Bruschi, 'Scene prospettiche urbane nel

Cinquecento: progettazione, caratteri. La scena per le *Bacchidi* del
1531' (177–92); R. Ceserani, 'Suggestioni figurative, modelli culturali
ed esperienze teatrali in Ludovico Ariosto' (193–208); F. Ruffini,
'Vitruvio e la città ferrarese' (243–57); R. Barone and A. Stäuble,
'Proposte per una tipologia dei personaggi femminili nella commedia
rinascimentale' (313–39); M. Bruni, 'La "Commedia degli strac-
cioni" di Annibal Caro: un esperimento di teatro cinquecentesco'
(341–63). It also includes two very useful (albeit incomplete) *bibliographies raisonnées*, containing editions of and studies of the comedies
of the period, one for Italy, divided by centres (L. Denarosi, 407–526),
and one for 'abroad', divided by countries (L. Zampolli, 527–615).
Lo 'Stichus' e lo 'Pseudolus' di Plauto: volgarizzamenti rinascimentali, ed.
Laura Rossetto, Ravenna, Longo, 342 pp., is a critical edition, with
analysis, of anonymous vernacular renderings of the two comedies
contained in a 16th-c. Venetian MS in the hand of diarist Marin
Sanudo. Alessandro Parronchi, *La prima rappresentazione della Mandragola*, F, Polistampa, 1995, 132 pp., is a handsomely illustrated book
which brings together all the author's writings on the matter so as to
restate unambiguously (and still convincingly) that *Mandragola* was
performed for the first time on 7 September 1518, that we have a
model of the stage-set for that performance, that Machiavelli acted
the part of Siro on that occasion, and that the character of Fra
Timoteo is based on a real-life contemporary of Machiavelli's.
B. Richardson, 'Rustic language in a sixteenth-century Florentine
comedy: *La Biagia da Decomano*', *ISt*, 51:96–112, discusses linguistic
(and other) features of one of the earliest Tuscan rustic comedies,
which is also the first Italian rustic comedy to have been printed
anywhere, and which derives from the *mogliazzo* genre and the
letteratura nenciale tradition. R. Ferguson, 'The influence of Venetian
popular theatre on Ruzante's *Parlamento* and *Bilora*', *ISt*, 51:113–33,
shows how R. adapted elements from three types of popular theatre
(*vilanesca, buffonesca, bulesca*) to unsettle the expectations of his privileged audiences with a chilling picture of the primal behaviour of the
underprivileged. Piermario Vescovo, *Da Ruzante a Calmo. Tra 'signore
comedie' e 'onorandissime stampe'*, Padua, Antenore, 241 pp., aims to
provide an insight into mid-15th-c. Venetian culture, with special
reference to Ruzante, Andrea Calmo, and the *Scuola dei Liquidi* acting
company, from the crossroads between acting and publishing (plays),
playwriting and letter-writing, the written and the spoken word,
monolinguism and plurilinguism. Roberto Trovato, *Anton Francesco
Grazzini: un commediografo fra tradizione e modernità*, Genoa, La Quercia,
156 pp., is a chronological, play-by-play introduction to Lasca's seven
extant comedies and the farce *Arzigogolo*. Students of Lasca may also
be interested in Stefano Termanini, *Antologia del teatro di Anton Francesco*

Grazzini detto il Lasca, Genoa, La Quercia, 1995, 163 pp., which contains excerpts from *Il Frate*, *La Gelosia*, *La Strega*, and *L'Arzigogolo*.

TRAGEDY

Paola Mastrocola, *Nimica fortuna: Edipo e Antigone nella tragedia italiana del Cinquecento*, T, Tirrenia, 168 pp., argues that Italian tragedy, whose seminal importance in the revival of the genre cannot be overstressed, was born of literary precedent and 'tragic times' (which also saw the birth of modern science and Calvinism), and that it was of two types: the tragedy of Power in the first half of the 16th c., based on the Antigone model, and the tragedy of Truth in the second half of the century, based on the Oedipus model. S. Di Maria, 'Towards an Italian theater: Rucellai's *Oreste*', *MLN*, 111:123–48, aims to demonstrate, by comparing R.'s play with the model it imitates (Euripides's *Iphigenia in Tauris*), offering a semiotic decoding of its 'theatrical discourse', and considering a 'virtual performance' of it, that it is not a dull play and that it succeeded in revitalizing an ancient art form. E. Barbieri, 'Un fantasma bibliografico inglese: F. Negri, *Tragedia del libero arbitrio*, Poschiavo 1547', *La Bibliofilia*, 97, 1995:267–90, proves that the Trinity College Cambridge exemplar of this work was not published at Poschiavo, but in Venice by Antonio Brucioli. M. Residori, 'In margine a una nuova edizione del *Re Torrismondo*', *Italianistica*, 25:121–30, is about the many merits and few failings of V. Martignone's edition of the play (Parma, Guanda, 1993). R. Manica, 'Su *Aminta* e *Torrismondo*', *Italianistica*, 24, 1995:411–26, claims that to ask whether or not these two plays are too literary and not theatrical enough is a question posed with hindsight, which does not take into account how Tasso and his times conceived of literature and the theatre. See too above, under NARRATIVE POETRY: REWRITINGS AND REAPPRAISALS, Stefano Jossa, *Rappresentazione e scrittura*.

PASTORAL

A. Di Benedetto, 'L'*Aminta* e la pastorale cinquecentesca', *GSLI*, 173:481–514, analyses the evolution of the genre, from its Quattrocento antecedents to Tasso and Guarini. D. Chiodo, 'Tra l'*Aminta* e il *Pastor fido*', *Italianistica*, 24, 1995:559–75, presents lesser-known imitations of *Aminta* (Marco Montano, *Teonomia*; Diomisso Guazzoni, *Andromeda*; *Alceo*, a piscatorial setting of *Aminta*; Girolamo Vida, *Filliria*; Maddalena Campiglia, *Flori*, 'una vera pastorale al femminile'), and traces the gradual loss of melancholy and sincerity in the genre's protagonists. A. La Penna, *'Note all'*Aminta* del Tasso', *Omaggio Folena*, 1171–82. I. Gallinaro, 'L' "anagramma purissimo" dell'*Aminta*', *Italianistica*, 24, 1995:577–91, discusses the moralization of *Aminta* by the 17th-c. cleric G. B. Di Leone da Santo Fele (*Aminta moralizzato*, Naples 1691).

5. PROSE

Olga Zorzi Pugliese, *Il discorso labirintico del dialogo rinascimentale*, Ro, Bulzoni, 1995, 143 pp., takes as its starting point Speroni's assertion in his *Apologia dei dialoghi* that the dialogue is 'un piacevole labirinto' and investigates the 'elementi principali di ludismo e danza che concretizzano questo concetto in termini spaziali'. Antonio Stäuble, *Le sirene eterne*, Ravenna, Longo, 206 pp., contains nine essays which, concentrating on classical and biblical echoes, examine: Castiglione and the panegyrics of Urbino; the use of rhetoric; imitation and *facezie*; aspects of the *Cortegiano* and the *Poemetto in prosa* in praise of love. *La presenza dimenticata: il femminismo nell'Italia moderna fra storia, letteratura, filosofia*, ed. Graziella Pagliano, Mi, Angeli, 188 pp., has an essay by F. Brezzi on the Florentine mystic Maddalena de' Pazzi which investigates mysticism as a strategy for self-fulfilment in a male-dominated world, while M. Savini explores the topos of praise of great women in courtly literature and Tasso's reflections on the *virtù femminile e donnesca*. F. Furlan, 'Verba non manent, la donna nella cultura toscana fra Tre e Quattrocento', *Intersezioni*, 16:259–74, discusses works by Alessandro Strozzi, San Bernardino, and Alberti. *Italian Women Writers from the Renaissance to the Present*, ed. Maria Ornella Marotti, University Park, Pennsylvania State U.P., 285 pp., has an essay on M. Fonte's *Il merito delle donne* and L. Marinelli's *La nobiltà et l'eccellenza delle donne* (C. Jordan), and a study of letter-writing and how courtesans responded to, and imitated, canonical standards (F. A. Bassanese). Nuccio Ordine, *Teoria della novella e teoria del riso nel Cinquecento*, Na, Liguori, 176 pp., has three essays on how aspects of physiognomy, medicine, philosophy, and rhetoric were integrated into the therapeutic aim of the *novella comica*. Bruno Porcelli, *Struttura e lingua*, Na, Loffredo, 1995, 452 pp., is divided into two parts: the first sets out the innovations in both the linguistic strategies and the diverse structural models adapted and adopted in Malaspini's *Ducento novelle;* the second has essays on Tasso, and Buonarroti il Giovane. Vittorio Branca, '*Con amore volere': narrar di mercatanti fra Boccaccio e Machiavelli*, Venice, Marsilio, xv + 134 pp., is a reworking of five previously published articles which investigate the much neglected writings of merchants. It reveals a vigorous genre preoccupied with personal reflections. A. Romano, 'Paralipomeni aretiniani. Postille su due opere disperse e sul sepolcro di Pietro Aretino', *SPCT*, 52:113–29, investigates the *Regno de la morte* and the *Giardino spirituale*.

S. Ritrovato, 'I romanzi di Giovan Battista Pigna (1554): interpretazione di un genere moderno', *ib.*, 131–51. A. Cameron, 'Doni's satirical Utopia', *RenS*, 10:463–73, points to the originality of the *Mondo savio*. D. Solfaroli Camillocci, 'Scrivere la propria storia. Memoria familiare e servizio del principe nel "libro" di Gasparo Venturini da Massa', *ASI*, 154:123–53.

ARIENTI, G. SABADINO DEGLI. Carolyn James, *Giovanni Sabadino degli Arienti: a Literary Career*, F, Olschki, 160 pp., is a biography of the humanist known as the Bolognese Boccaccio. It traces the effects of patronage on his literary output and shows how other aspects of his expertise were valued more than his skill as a professional writer.

BANDELLO. Carlo Godi, *Bandello: narratori e dedicatori della prima parte delle novelle*, Ro, Bulzoni, 410 pp., reconstructs the symbiotic relationship between the narrator and the dedicatee that contributes as much to our understanding of B.'s social and cultural world as to the *novelle*.

BRUNO. *NRLett*, 1994, no. 2, contains the proceedings of a conference (Cassino, 11–12 Dec. 1992), with articles by: G. Aquilecchia, 'Dialoghi bruniani e dialoghi tassiani: per una comparazione delle fonti' (19–30); N. Badaloni, 'Riflessioni sul tema dell' "individuo" nella concezione metafisica e morale di G. Bruno' (31–46); L. De Bernart, 'Bruno e i "fondamenti" filosofici della teoria copernicana' (46–74); C. Monti, 'Incidenza e significato della tradizione materialistica antica dei poemi latini di Giordano Bruno: la mediazione di Lucrezio' (75–88); R. Sturlese, 'Le fonti del *Sigillus sigillorum* di Bruno, ossia: il confronto con Ficino a Oxford sull'anima umana' (89–168); C. Vasoli, 'Bruno, Ramo e Patrizi' (169–90). Giordano Bruno, *Un'autobiografia*, ed. Michele Ciliberto, Na, Procaccini, 1994, 120 pp., gives the documents pertaining to B.'s various appearances before the religious authorities, which help to reconstruct B.'s perception of himself and his life's journey. Giordano Bruno, *Immagini 1600–1725*, ed. Simonetta Bassi, Na, Procaccini, 155 pp., assembles critical comments on and images of Bruno. Nuccio Ordine, *Giordano Bruno and the Philosophy of the Ass*, New Haven, Yale U.P., 272 pp., is a systematic study of the figure of the ass, which is revealed as a powerful symbol that encompasses many different qualities including *varietas* and *coincidentia oppositorum* and which can help to clarify some fundamental principles of B.'s epistemology. J. J. Heffernan, 'La *Cena delle ceneri*: verso una conoscenza immaginativa', *Intersezioni*, 16:429–51, examines the psychological dimension of B.'s river journey. E. A. Gosselin, 'A Dominican head in layman's garb? A correction to the scientific iconography of G. Bruno', *SCJ*, 17:673–78, gives Bruno back his tonsure. Giordano Bruno, **De causa, principio et uno*, trans. L. Hersant, Paris, Belles Lettres, lxix + 390 pp.

R. Sturlese, 'La nuova edizione del Bruno latino', *Rinascimento*, 35, 1995:373–95. P. Viti, 'Frammenti bruniani', *ib.*, 231–42, examines fragments of texts in the Florentine Archivio di Stato.

CARDANO. Gerolamo Cardano, *Sul sonno e sul sognare*, ed. Maura Mancia and Agnese Grieco, Venice, Marsilio, 1995, 233 pp., has a good introduction that discusses the underlying allegorical structure of the work and the correspondences between the various images.

CECCHI. *Il 'Sommario de' magistrati di Firenze' di ser Giovanni Maria Cecchi*, ed. Arnaldo D'Addario, Ro, IPZS, 117 pp., is a critical edition of a treatise which sets out the political, administrative, and legal organs of the state. C., though a professional notary, is best known for his comedies.

COMMENDONE. Giovanni Francesco Commendone, *Discorso sopra la corte di Roma*, ed. Cesare Mozzarelli, Ro, Bulzoni, 114 pp., presents the bare text of a work which circulated in MS form but was not published until the 18th c. The text is not a description of the court but more a reflection on how to succeed in a complex world where politics and religion are inextricably linked.

CREMA. Antonio da Crema, *Itinerario al San Sepolcro 1486*, ed. Gabriele Noti, Ospedaletto, Pacini, 193 pp., is part of a project to publish critical editions of texts describing pilgrimage journeys. Da Crema, a Mantuan, made his trip as both a penance and a crusade. His description, which has an immediacy due to the blend of wonderment and spiritual musings, betrays an underlying pre-meditated structure.

DELLA CASA. S. Prandi, 'Ragioni di un commento (in margine al *Galateo*)', *LItal*, 48:592–601, answers criticism on the methodology for the critical edition of the *Galateo* (T, Einaudi, 1994).

LEONARDO. Rhetorical nuances in Leonardo's literary and visual imagery, and the interaction between them, are examined in Eugenia Paulicelli, *Parola e immagine: sentieri della scrittura in Leonardo, Marino, Foscolo, Calvino*, Fiesole, Cadmo, 156 pp., which focuses on the *Paragone*.

MACHIAVELLI. Francesco Nitti, *Machiavelli nella vita e nelle dottrine*, vol. 2, ed. Stefano Palmieri, Bo, Il Mulino, 435 pp., is in a way the first edition as it gives a facsimile of pp. 1–240, which were printed but never published, and adds to these material from various MS sources. S. U. Baldassarri, 'Costanti del pensiero machiavelliano nel *Decennale I* e nel *Capitolo della fortuna*', *ItQ*, 33:17–28. Roger D. Masters, *Machiavelli, Leonardo and the Science of Power*, Notre Dame U.P., 366 pp., is a provocative study that reinterprets M. by assuming an acquaintance with L.; the latter's attempt to integrate scientific knowledge, technical innovation, and social utility is seen as good reason to reconsider M. from the perspective of a scientific approach to human nature and politics. Harvey C. Mansfield, *Machiavelli's Virtue*, Chicago U.P., 371 pp., is an enjoyable collection of articles and essays which cover M.'s irony and modernity. Above all it emphasizes his realism, 'when politics is understood as aiming to win with no reference to a standard above politics'. Niccolò Machiavelli, *De principatibus*, ed. Giorgio Inglese, Ro, Istituto Storico Italiano per il Medio Evo, 1994, xv + 326 pp., is an excellent critical edition containing a much needed in-depth analysis of M.'s language. There is a detailed evaluation of the MS tradition, setting out all the variants of the text, and a sensitive introduction analyses the writing, circulation, and printing of the text. *Machiavelli: Figure-Reputation*, ed. Joep Leerssen and Menno Spieiring, Amsterdam, Rodopi, 200 pp., contains ten essays which place Machiavelli at the intersection of culture and politics, as a 'formative influence in constitutional thought and in the history of ideas and of European self-awareness'. M. C. Figorilli, 'La "tristizia" nei *Discorsi* di Machiavelli', *RLI*, 100.1:39–53.

PATRIZI. Francesco Patrizi, *Della retorica dieci dialoghi*, ed. Anna Laura Puliafito Bleuel, Lecce, Conte, 1994, vi + 61 pp., is a facsimile of the 1562 (Venice) edition accompanied by a short but perceptive introduction.

RUCELLAI. Rita Maria Comanducci, *Il carteggio di Bernardo Rucellai: Inventario*, F, Olschki, xlvii + 111 pp., has an impressive introduction that puts the letters into their historical and cultural context, followed by a list of all the correspondence to and by him. The volume has indexes and a dictionary of all R.'s ciphers.

VASARI. Roland Le Mollé, *Giorgio Vasari*, Paris, Grasset, 1995, 475 pp., is a well-structured biography particularly useful in setting out V.'s range of activities in the service of the Medici. Giorgio Vasari, *Lives of the Painters, Sculptors and Architects*, 2 vols, trans. Gaston de Vere, London, Everyman, lxiii + 1000, 1114 pp., a reissue of what is without doubt the most sensitive, clear translation (1912) of the 1568 edition, has the dedicatory and concluding letters, and a particularly perceptive introduction by David Ekserdjian which discusses the genesis and methodology of the work.

SEICENTO

By MAURICE SLAWINSKI, *Lecturer in Italian Studies, University of Lancaster*

1. GENERAL

LITERARY HISTORY, POETICS, GENERAL CRITICISM. Stefano Tomassini, *L' 'Heroico', ad esempio. Tasso: idea del poema nell'opera di Paolo Beni*, T, Genesi, 1994, 250 pp., publishes ample selections from Beni's commentary on the *Gerusalemme* (1616, and then, revised and expanded, 1626), preceded by a lively, perceptive account of Beni's career and his part in the *Gerusalemme* controversy (including some details of his relationship with, and championing of, Galileo which are new to me). The volume also contains a brief postscript, 'Dietro una battaglia', by M. Pieri, and an excerpt from Beni's catalogue of the Italian books in his library, which one hopes to see published *in toto*.

Ezio Raimondi, *Il colore eloquente. Letteratura e arte barocca*, Bo, Il Mulino, 1995, 116 pp., includes essays on the Baroque as the mirror of modern historical consciousness, on literature in Bologna in the first half of the *Seicento* (the best and most substantial in the collection), on Guercino and literary influences, on Bartoli's observations on painters and paintings (there is also, by way of appendix, a piece on 'Gadda "barocco"'). There are no bibliographical references to the numerous texts cited, nor any indication as to whether any (or all) of the essays had appeared previously (one or two certainly ring a bell). Neither omission wholly detracts from the slim volume's interest, but more than a reaction to the manic over-annotation of much recent *Seicento* criticism they are, I fear, the marks of an authorial *sufficenza* bordering on discourtesy. Closely related territory is covered by G. Parini, '*Ut pictura poesis*. L'Accademia dei Gelati e le arti figurative', pp. 113–26 of *Italian Academies of the Sixteenth Century*, London, Warburg Institute, 1995, 216 pp., hereafter *Italian Academies*. On a parallel theme I also note F. Vazzoler, **'Seguendo il cammino del pittore. Suggestioni letterarie fra Genova e Venezia', pp. 337–46 of *Bernardo Strozzi, Genova 1581 / '82–Venezia 1644. Catalogo della mostra di Genova (Palazzo Ducale 6 maggio–6 agosto 1995)*, ed. E. Gavazza, G. Nepi Sciré, G. Rotondi, Mi, Electra, 1995, 380 pp.; J. V. Mirollo, 'The death of Venus: right reading of Baroque verbal and visual texts', pp. 203–19 of *The Image of the Baroque*, ed. Aldo Scaglione and Gianni Eugenio Viola, NY, Lang, 1995, 240 pp., hereafter *The Image*.

L. Borsetto, 'La "poetica d'Horatio tradotta". Contributo allo studio della ricezione oraziana tra Rinascimento e Barocco', *Atti*

(Licenza), 171–220, is an extensive discussion of *Seicento* translations and periphrases of the *Ars poetica*.

Giacomo Jori, *Le forme della creazione. Sulla fortuna del 'Mondo creato' (secoli XVII e XVIII)*, F, Olschki, 1995, 160 pp., deals with the 'heptameron' poem, from the Italian translation of Du Bartas (1592), through Tasso's posthumous work (via Angelo Grillo and Felice Passero), to Murtola, Marino (contaminations of the tradition in *Adone, Dicerie Sacre*, and *Strage degl'Innocenti*), the prose meditations on the subject by Giovanni Rho (*Essamerone*, 1652) and Giovan Battista Caracciolo (*Creazione del mondo*, 1654), and finally Giuseppe Girolamo Semenzi's 'canzoniere sacro' (*Il Mondo creato diviso nelle sette giornate*, 1666), a somewhat bizarre collection of lyrics where the by then canonical division by topics instituted by Marino is used instead — *ad maiorem Dei gloria* — to celebrate the various aspects of creation.

Interpretazione e meraviglia, ed. G. Galli, Pisa, Giardini, 1994, 249 pp., contains a number of essays of *Seicento* interest, which though they mainly focus on Marino, are of wider relevance: G. Giglioni 'Dalla meraviglia dei sensi alla meraviglia dell'intelletto. Note sul concetto di automa nel XVII secolo' (23–52), discussing the construction and representation of automata, their impact on perceptions of biological organisms, and their impact on philosophical reflections concerning the development of animal and human consciousness; B. Rima, 'Novità, stupore e meraviglia nella retorica del Seicento' (79–95), linking wonder with the 17th-c. preoccupation with 'gli aspetti positivi della magia', though the link is not wholly satisfactory, and the category of 'magic' rather vaguely defined; and G. Pedrojetta, 'Marino e la meraviglia' (97–105), returning to the famous supposed declaration of poetic intent, 'è del poeta il fin la meraviglia', reminding us of its context (a critique of Murtola's attempt to produce a poetry that will celebrate the wonders of nature) and correcting traditional misreadings — but Pedrojetta's view that 'le "meraviglie" mariniane [...] sono meraviglie retorico-verbali, prodigi esclusivi dell'arte del dire', seems no less reductivist. Both these views are somewhat corrected in A. Martini 'La pratica mariniana' (107–19), which takes as its starting point Marino's own use of the word to highlight the wonders of his text, linking this to a near constant of *Seicento* literary theory, its hedonism, and the related theme of the *svogliatura del secolo*, to be understood however not as mere escapism, but as a rejection of the boundaries of traditional morality which has its own gnoseological charge, 'un'ambizione conoscitiva tutta moderna' closely akin to that of the New Science (a kinship which however, in the limited space of the essay, is asserted rather than demonstrated).

R. Merolla, 'Dopo Sisto V. La ricerca letteraria a Roma e la transizione al barocco', *EL*, 21.2:27–47, though more a summary of recent research than an original study, says perceptive things about literary culture not just in the *urbs*, but across that large part of the peninsula which had Rome and the Papacy as its chief point of reference, emphasizing the complex and contradictory nature of the debate between classicists and modernists (a broader and in many ways more useful category than *concettisti*).

F. Guardiani, 'Baroque and neobaroque: the great retrievals', *FoI*, 30:129–36, considers recent arguments concerning the 'baroque' nature of many strands of postmodernism, in relation to our changing understanding of the Baroque as a distinct historical period, observing acutely that 'Baroque leads to modernity while neobaroque moves away from it' (though he would appear to be more sanguine about this backward route to the future than I am!).

BIBLIOGRAPHY, MANUSCRIPTS, LIBRARIES AND ARCHIVES. *Biblioteche romane del Sei e Settecento*, ed. Valentino Romani, Manziana, Vecchiarelli, 28 + [122] pp., is a facsimile reproduction of the relevant parts of the *Nota delli Musei, Librerie, Galerie et ornamenti di statue e pitture ne' Palazzi, nelle case e ne' giardini di Roma* (1664) and of Giovan Battista Piazza's *Eusevologio Romano, overo delle Opere pie di Roma* (1689). It is prefaced by a brief introduction devoted chiefly to a register of 150 public and private Roman libraries of the period. A. Barzazi, 'Ordini religiosi e biblioteche a Venezia tra Cinque e Seicento', *AISIGT*, 21, 1995:141–228, draws on inventories made at the behest of the Inquisitors to analyse the holdings of some twenty monastic and conventual libraries, as well as those of individual fathers, some three decades after the Council of Trent: a somewhat surprising mixture of biblical exegesis, the church fathers and canonists; works related to preaching (homilies, rhetorical, and mnemonic treatises); Latin classics, humanist texts, and more recent encyclopaedias (notably Garzoni's very recent *Piazza universale*); orthodox scholastic, Platonist, and anti-Aristotelian philosophers (Ficino, Patrizi); a sizeable quantity of forbidden heretical works (some of them held for study purposes with the licence of the Provincial, but many seemingly for no better reason than that they were there and no one seemed to know they should not have been!).

Giovanna Bosi Maramotti, *Le muse d'Imeneo. Metamorfosi letteraria dei libretti per nozze dal '500 al '900*, Ravenna, 1994, 410 pp., is a catalogue of publications belonging to a marginal literary genre held in Emilia-Romagna libraries (particularly Ravenna and Bologna). The tally of 40 entries from the *Seicento* (given my own frequent chance encounters with such works) seems surprisingly low. M. Lenci, 'Le raccolte delle *Gazzette* a stampa genovesi in Italia e all'Estero. Inventario

1639–1684', *ABI*, 64:2:43–58, locates a number of these leaflets in miscellanies preserved in a somewhat random selection of libraries in Italy, London, Madrid, and Stockholm.

G. L. Bruzzone, 'La biblioteca del magnifico Giulio Dionisio Pavese (1667)', *ABI*, 63:4, 1995:5–34, publishes the library inventory of a wealthy Savonese related by marriage to Chiabrera, consisting of 461 vols., a few of them theological and philosophical (church fathers, Plato, Ficino, Patrizi), many devotional, some on rhetoric and poetics (Aristotle commentaries by Castelvetro and Piccolomini, works by Trissino and Speroni), and a substantial collection of vernacular literature, classical-conservative in its flavour (several Petrarchists, Ciampoli, Barberini).

N. Scianna, 'Due rari di Vincenzo Coronelli nella Biblioteca dell'Archiginnasio', *L'Archiginnasio*, 89, 1994:279–93, describes two products of the small print and engraving shop established by C. in the Convento dei Frari, Venice. A. B. Parenti, 'Leonardo e Pietro Accolti e l'edizione del 1623 del *De bello a Christianis contra barbaros gesto* di Benedetto Accolti', vol. ii, pp. 665–82 of *Studi in onore di Arnaldo d'Addario*, ed. Luigia Borgia et al., Lecce, Conte, 1995, 4 vols, xxviii + 1760 pp., hereafter *Studi D'Addario*, traces the biography of two descendants of Benedetto, who published his work out of a mixture of family pride and religious motives (not least the hope of encouraging the 'Florentine' pope Urban VIII to launch a new crusade), and provides details concerning the background to, and details of, the operation. I also note P. Gios, 'Informazioni, ricerche e acquisizioni librarie di Gregorio Barbarigo (1656–1658): dall'epistolario', *RSSR*, 49:27–43; A. Ambrosio, **L'erudizione storica a Napoli nel Seicento. I manoscritti di interesse medievistico nel Fondo brancacciano della Biblioteca Nazionale di Napoli*, Catanzaro, Carlone, 168 pp.

BIOGRAPHY, AUTOBIOGRAPHY. Giovan Battista Manso, *Vita di Torquato Tasso*, ed. Bruno Basile, Ro, Salerno, 1995, xlii + 334 pp., is not so much a contribution to Tasso studies as an important milestone in that of the *Seicento* profession of letters: not a literary biography in any sense we would understand, but the most thoroughgoing attempt (at least on the conservative, aristocratic side of the debate) to 'construct' a model man of letters (as persuasively argued in Basile's introduction). Giuseppe Massei, *Vita di Paolo Segneri*, ed. Quinto Marini, Ro, Magnanti, 1995, 100 pp., reproduces the text of a *Breve ragguaglio* of 1698 from a manuscript in the Jesuit Archives in Rome, collated against the edition published in 1701 with Segneri's *Opera omnia*. The mode of the narrative is hagiographical, and this may explain its temporary prohibition by the Order (rather than the Master of the Sacred Palace), which at that time disapproved of Segneri's anti-probabilist views. Franco Barcia, *Salvatore Cadana.*

Diplomazia e ragion di stato alla corte dei Savoia, Mi, Angeli, 144 pp., profiles a Franciscan, esteemed in his day as a preacher, political theorist, and councillor of Charles Emanuel II. The volume includes an account of his life, an essay on his political writings, a survey of 'lost' works, a bibliography of those published (27 editions of ten different titles), and the text of the hitherto unpublished *Relazione* of his 1653 embassy to Portugal (where he unsuccessfully negotiated an anti-Spanish alliance). E. Taddeo, 'L'"ingegnosissimo nipote" ovvero Lodovico Malvezzi', *StSec*, 37:3–27, is a lively reconstruction of the career of a talented but troublesome nephew of the better-known Virgilio, author (*a tempo perso* presumably, since he was fairly constantly embroiled in duels, family feuds, judicial proceedings) of lyrics collected in the splendidly named *Deliri della solitudine* (1634), which oscillate between (very) late Petrarchism and *concettismo*, and *Il Diogene* (1635), a slim pamphlet of moral observations built around the pretext of Alexander's visit to the cynic philosopher. U. Motta, 'Tra Paolo V e la Bibbia: la produzione epigrafica di Antonio Querenghi', *IMU*, 37, 1994:137–69, is chiefly useful for additional information concerning the biography of an important transitional figure, a near-contemporary of Tasso, who like him studied with Speroni and Zabarella, but lived to be a respected Roman literary authority and back-room adviser under Paul V and Urban VIII, and came to represent the continuity between Renaissance and Baroque classicism. D. Fioretti, 'Famiglia e coscienza di sé nell'età barocca: le "Memorie" del conte Nicolò Vannucci', *Studia picena*, 60, 1995:223–65, deals with a more traditional kind of personal journal, not so much autobiography as family *res gestae*, aiming to celebrate the collective identity of a provincial dynasty. See also GENDER, below.

COURT SOCIETY. Girolamo Aleandro, Girolamo Rocco, and Marcello Giovannetti, *Esercizi fisiognomici*, ed. L. Rodler, Palermo, Sellerio, 122 pp., might appear from the title to belong elsewhere, but in fact the three brief texts published (alongside the well-known *Del modo che tener devono i saggi e letterati cortigiani per non essere dalla corte (quasi da novella Circe) in sembianza di brutti animali trasformati*, we have Rocco's *Della cognizione di se medesimo*, and Giovannetti's *Dello specchio*, all from the *Saggi accademici* edited in 1630 by Agostino Mascardi), do not concern physiognomy in the conventional sense, but are rather exercises in defining, through exhortation to moral self-knowledge, the character of a model courtier-*letterato*. R. Merolla, 'Dal *cortegiano* al *servidore*. Modelli primo-secenteschi di trattatistica sul comportamento', *EL*, 19.3, 1994:3–36, is a valuable introduction to discussions of prince-literati relations, particularly the highly polemical and little studied views of Giovan Battista Manzini (*Il servizio negato al Savio*,

1626), though somewhat flawed in my view by not attempting to relate these self-consciously abstract discussions (it would not have done, after all, to be too specific, as most literati still depended on princes' favour) to the realities of Counter-Reformation and absolutism, and a tendency therefore to view them simply as rhetorical exercises.

Frederick Hammond, *Music and Spectacle in Baroque Rome*, New Haven, Yale U.P., 1994, xxiv + 370 pp., provides a useful, if somewhat unoriginal, account of the Barberini court circle and its patronage programme, then details its contribution to music and (particularly) opera: a workmanlike book, though some turns of phrase (the first Palazzo Barberini is located in 'downtown Rome'; Cardinal Francesco graduated 'in both laws') ring a somewhat anachronistic note.

EDUCATION. U. Baldini, 'L'influenza del *cursus* gesuitico nella struttura dei corsi superiori del seminario padovano negli anni del Barbarigo. Note preliminari e di metodo', *Ricerche di storia sociale e religiosa*, 49: 15–26, deals with the curriculum established by Cardinal Gregorio Barbarigo at the end of the *Seicento*. S. Negruzzo, 'La formazione teologica e il sistema delle scuole nella Pavia spagnola', *ASL*, 121, 1995: 49–101, discusses the institutional set-up, the role of the religious orders (notably the Somaschi and Barnabites: the Jesuits were concentrated in Milan and only became involved at Pavia, in a modest way, in the second half of the *Seicento*), and the content and organization of courses.

EPISTOLARY RELATIONS. *Correspondence de Peirasc et Aleandro*, ed. J.-F. Lhote and D. Joyal, I, 1616–18; II, 1619–20, Clermont-Ferrand, Adosa, 1995, 260, 288 pp., is a treasure-house of literary, antiquarian, and occasionally political gossip. The only small criticism of an otherwise well-produced, very carefully annotated edition is that for understandable reasons of space it has been decided to produce a single index, to be published with the final volume of the correspondence, which ceased only with Aleandro's death in 1629. C. Carminati, 'Lettere di Federigo Meninni al padre Angelico Aprosio', *StSec*, 37: 183–217, publishes ten letters between important exponents of late *Seicento* culture, five of them from 1661–62, the others dated 1678–81, preserved in Genoa University Library, whence a wealth of *Seicento* manuscript material has recently emerged. The later letters are undoubtedly the more interesting, with some particularly valuable comments concerning the literary *querelles* of the age, and Marino's unhappy relations with the Jesuits as perhaps due to a series of 'Sonetti Bernieschi' he supposedly wrote against Costantino Pulcarelli, a Neapolitan member of the order. M. Sarnelli, '"Maravigliosa chiarezza", "raccomandazioni" e "mal di pietra": il carteggio

Delfino-Pers', *ib.*, 225–312, brings together 79 letters, predominantly from Cardinal Giovanni Delfino (1617–99), Patriarch of Aquileia, chiefly about the literary news of the day and preserved in the civic libraries of Udine and San Daniele del Friuli, with an appendix of two letters to Carlo di Pers, concerning the posthumous publication of his cousin's *Poesie*. G. L. Bruzzone, 'Sei lettere di P. Isidoro Ugurgieri Azzolini a P. Angelico Aprosio', *BSSP*, 101, 1994:273–88.

GENDER.   Angela Groppi, *I conservatori della virtù: donne recluse nella Roma dei papi*, Ro–Bari, Laterza, 1994, 328 pp., examines the social role of the *conservatori*, half-way houses between school and nunnery where girls from lower-class families with clerical or upper-class patrons might safely prepare for marriage (or the veil), to the benefit of public morality and inter-class harmony. V. Cox, 'The single self: feminist thought and the marriage market in Early Modern Venice', *RQ*, 48, 1995:513–79, takes as its starting point the 'feminist' writings of Lucrezia Marinelli and Modesta Pozzo (1600) and goes on to examine the material condition of Venetian women from the late 16th c., when family strategies to preserve wealth resulted in a dramatic increase in the number of noblewomen taking the veil or remaining spinsters, and also in increased wealth and status — perhaps even power — for those who married. Cox argues plausibly that this may have been behind the 'new wave' of women's writing in this period, and a new sense of self, the *single* self existing autonomously outside and beyond male power, needs, and desires. N. L. Canepa, 'The writing behind the wall: Arcangela Tarabotti's *Inferno monacale* and cloistral autobiography in the seventeenth century', *FoI*, 30:1–23, seems to me to miss the very real interest of this text, in pursuit of women's oppression and their heroic resistence: no substitute for actually reading what *one* woman had to say (preferably alongside the companion *Paradiso monacale*); and while Tarabotti's objections are fairly conventional, as are the literary devices to which Canepa draws attention, the real interest may lie elsewhere — in the way in which Tarabotti constructs herself as a woman of letters through the very force of her objections to forced claustration. Also on Tarabotti: F. Medioli, 'Alcune lettere autografe di Arcangela Tarabotti: autocensura e immagine di sé', *RSLR*, 32:133–41, which casts a rapid glance on her *Lettere familari e di complimento* (1650), and F. De Rubeis, 'La scrittura forzata. Le lettere autografe di Arcangela Tarabotti', *ib.*, 142–55, which publishes seven letters, including one alongside the (self-censured) version published in 1650.

The close link between marginality, self-writing, and 'feminist' consciousness seems to me to be confirmed by a number of studies relating to the other side of claustral biography: not rebellion but the self-assertion of mysticism, sanctity, devotional literature. Stefano

Andretta, *La venerabile superbia. Ortodossia e trasgressione nella vita di Suor Francesca Farnese (1593–1651)*, T, Rosenberg & Sellier, 1994, 256 pp., discusses biographies of a *santa mancata*, in the context of contemporary religious politics and debates on sanctity; but here too what emerges is that a distinct, reflexive female identity appears possible only in the context of what might be termed a 'strategy of exceptionality', claiming for oneself a special and unique status as outsider from which to begin to redefine femininity itself as otherness. A. Jacobson Schutte, '*Per speculum in enigmate*: failed saints, artists and self-construction of the female body in Early Modern Italy', Matter, *Creative Women*, 185–200, sketches (from Inquisitorial records) the stories of three low-born would-be saints who in the mid 17th century sought to model themselves as holy women by representing and quite literally shaping their own bodies. The stories are interesting, though neither the comparison with the emergence of successful women painters nor the generalizations drawn from them are terribly convincing. E. A. Matter, 'The commentary on the rule of Clare of Assisi by Maria Domitilla Galluzzi', *ib.*, 201–11, a rather solemn account of a no less solemn work, is too reverential to reveal why it might still be of interest to us. A. Riccardi, 'The mystic humanism of Maria Maddalena de' Pazzi', *ib.*, 212–24, constructs the account of Maria Maddalena's ecstasies as a Christian-humanist narrative, starting from the premise that 'Early modern mysticism distances itself from the conception of the body expressed by medieval mysticism; it makes the body into a focal point, a determinant place for tensions, in which the integralness of humanity (and thus the *unio mystica*) is realized'. E. B. Weaver, 'Suor Maria Clemente Ruoti, playwright and academician', *ib.*, 282–96, examines the literary career of a Florentine nun (*c.* 1610–90), author of two verse plays, *Jacob* and *Il Patriarca*, pub. 1637, as well as the manuscript *Natal di Cristo*, written twenty years later, which to a degree dramatize issues of gender, and argues that despite its restrictions the convent setting was one which favoured the intellectual development of women. Contributions relating to claustral life are also to be found in *AnI*, 13, 1995: A. Maggi, 'The voice and the silences of Maria Maddalena de' Pazzi' (257–81); K.-E. Barzman, 'Cultural production, religious devotion, and subjectivity in Early Modern Italy: the case-study of Maria Maddalena de' Pazzi' (283–305); O. Pelosi, 'Tra *eros* e *caritas*: le "pene d'amore" di Maria Domitilla Galluzzi' (307–32); M. Courbat, 'Veronica Giuliani: scrittura e riscrittura' (333–49); M. Lollini, 'Scrittura obbediente e mistica tridentina in Veronica Giuliani' (351–69). The fact that the same handful of names keep recurring in all these contributions again makes one question the wider significance claimed for such writings.

More general perspectives on the female religious orders and their role in shaping female identity (including authorial identity) are offered in six contributions of *Seicento* interest in *Donne e fede. Santità e vita religiosa in Italia*, ed. G. Zarri and L. Scaraffia, Ro–Bari, Laterza, 1994, 552 pp.: G. Zarri, 'Dalla profezia alla disciplina'; M. Caffiero, 'Dall'esplosione mistica tardo-barocca all'apostolato sociale (1650–1850)'; A. Prosperi, 'Lettere spirituali'; E. Weaver, 'Le muse in convento. La scrittura profana delle monache italiane (1450–1650)'; M. Modica Vasta, 'La scrittura mistica'; S. Matthews Grieco, 'Modelli di santità femminile nell'Italia del Rinascimento e della Controriforma'.

THE JESUITS. *I Gesuiti a Venezia. Momenti e problemi di storia veneziana della Compagnia di Gesù, Atti del convegno di studi, Venezia, 2–5 ottobre 1990*, ed. M. Zanardi, Padua, Giunta Regionale Veneto-Gregoriana, 1994, 891 pp., covers a vast range of topics over a span of 250 years. Of particular *Seicento* interest are M. Zanardi, 'I "domicilia" o centri operativi della Compagnia di Gesù nello stato veneto 1542–1773' (89–179), which details the development of the Order's network of houses, and its penetration in the region; G. Cozzi, 'Fortuna e sfortuna della compagnia di Gesù a Venezia' (59–88), rehearsing the well-known 1603 expulsion of the Order from the Serenissima and its 1657 return. Various further contributions survey other aspects of the Jesuit impact on Venetian culture: B. Ulianich, 'I gesuiti e la Compagnia di Gesù nelle opere e nel pensiero di Paolo Sarpi' (233–62); G. P. Brizzi, 'Scuole e collegi nell'antica Provincia Veneta della Compagnia di Gesù (1542–1773)' (467–511); U. Baldini, 'La tradizione scientifica dell'antica Provincia Veneta della Compagnia di Gesù. Caratteri distintivi e sviluppi' (531–82); and G. Morelli and E. Sala, 'Teatro gesuitico e melodramma: incontri, complicità e convergenze' (597–611). On a not unrelated topic, Aloisio Antinori, *Scipione Borghese e l'architettura*, Ro, Izzi, 1995, xiv + 450 pp., contains an introductory chapter (3–28) which has some extremely interesting remarks concerning the *Interdetto* and its role, early in Paul V's papacy, in strengthening his links with the Jesuits.

LANGUAGE. M. Dell'Aquila, '*Il Cavalcanti* di Paolo Beni', pp. 9–47 of *La scrittura dispersa. Testi e studi su inediti e rari tra Seicento e Novecento*, ed. Michele Dell'Aquila, Pisa, Giardini, 1995, 122 pp., gives a very traditional reading of the polemic between Beni and the *Cruscanti*. S. Bozzola, 'Contributo alla storia dell'ortografia. F. F. Frugoni e il secondo Seicento', *SGI*, 16:75–118, is an extremely valuable contribution to this still relatively undeveloped field of study, closely related to the current debate concerning the editing of Early Modern Italian texts. It is distinguished from earlier studies both by the attention it pays to extant autographs, and by the fact that it goes well beyond description, or comparison to Salviati's norms, linking Frugoni's practice to various Seicento attempts to argue the case for and against traditional spellings (including subtle phonetic distinctions between 'long' and 'short' *s*) which raise important questions concerning the link between orthography and sound — particularly, though not exclusively, in poetry. A. Mura Porcu, 'Note linguistiche sulla prosa del Seicento: *Il Demetrio Moscovita* di M. Bisaccioni e *La Dianea* di G. F. Loredano', pp. 1–42 of *La cultura fra Sei e Settecento. Primi risultati di una indagine*, ed. Elena Sala Di Felice and Laura Sannia Nowé, Modena, Mucchi, 1994, vii + 314 pp., deals with lexicon, syntax, and period structure, and is largely descriptive, only occasionally venturing into stylistic commentary.

LITERATI, ACADEMIES, ORGANIZATION OF CULTURE. *Commercium Litterarum: Forms of Communication in the Republic of Letters*, ed. Hans Bots and Françoise Waquet, Amsterdam, APA–Holland U.P., 1994, xii + 333 pp., contains only one contribution specifically of Italian interest: D. Gallo, 'Rome, mythe et réalité pour le Citoyen de la République des Lettres', though no doubt the many survey essays in the collection also contain a wealth of relevant material. *Roma moderna e contemporanea*, 3, 1995, is a special issue, ' "Il gran Teatro del Mondo". Roma tra Cinque e Seicento: storia, letteratura, teatro', ed. R. Merolla, which contains six contributions chiefly of interest for the organization of Roman cultural life: M. A. Visceglia, 'Burocrazia, mobilità sociale e "patronage" alla corte di Roma tra Cinque e Seicento' (11–55); V. Frajese, 'Tendenze dell'ambiente oratoriano durante il pontificato di Clemente VIII' (57–80); S. Iucci, 'La trattatistica del segretario tra la fine del Cinquecento e il primo ventennio del Seicento' (81–96); L. Alemanno, 'L'Accademia degli Umoristi' (97–120); R. Merolla, 'L'Accademia dei Desiosi' (121–55); M. Saulini, 'Il Teatro dei Gesuiti' (157–62). M. Fumaroli, 'Académie, Arcadie, Parnassus: trois lieux allégoriques de l'éloge du loisir lettré', *Italian Academies*, 15–35, is elegantly vague, and seems rather to gloss over the fact that unlike Arcadia and Parnassus academies were real places with practical functions. B. Basile, 'Temperamento e scrittura. Nota su Daniello Bartoli', *LS*, 30, 1995:275–82, contrasts the 'conservative' physiognomics of Bartoli, who associated intellectual *ingegno* with the melancholy disposition, and the supposedly more modern view of such contemporaries as his fellow Jesuit Sarbiewski, who stressed the learned skill of linguistic manipulation against poetic 'fury' (but, given the way in which the debate has always oscillated between the two, the use of such labels seems slightly gratuitous, and *gratta gratta*, underneath there lurks yet another baroque *capovolgimento*, since Bartoli's views are ultimately scholastic-Aristotelian, while Sarbiewski's assumptions are fundamentally Christian-Platonist).

D. Bertolini Meli, 'The neoterics and political power in Spanish Italy: Giovanni Alfonso Borelli and his circle', *HistS*, 34:57–89, considers Borelli's involvement in the Messina revolution of 1673–77, and argues that the political views of the 'neoterics' (as late-*Seicento* southern enthusiasts for philosophical and medical novelties liked to style themselves), generally assumed to be radical (even republican) and anti-Spanish, were in fact more varied, dependent on local conditions and on their proximity to the seats of power.

PRINTING AND PUBLISHING.   D. Parker, 'Women in the book trade in Italy, 1475–1620', *RQ*, 49:509–41, brings together the little that is known about women's role in the trade, from operating as publishers and printers in their own right (usually as a result of inheriting the business from a husband, father, or brother) to work as bookbinders. R. Radici, 'Quattro inventari di librai bresciani del '600', *CAB*, 1993 [1995]:155–67, is a rapid survey of booksellers' stocks from the mid-*Seicento*. Mention must also be made of a valuable addition to our knowledge of the economics of printing, previously overlooked: Francesco Calzolari, *Printing a Book at Verona in 1622: The Account Book of Francesco Calzolari junior*, ed. Conor Fahy, Paris, Fondation Custodia—Northeast Kingdom, Vermont, Stinehour Press, 1993, 172 pp. (being the accounts for the printing and distribution of the *Musaeum Francisci Calcealarii*).

TRANSLATION, TRANSMISSION, INFLUENCE.   M. Rebaudengo, 'Letture alfieriane per un "mostruoso spettacolo": Tasso, G. B. Andreini, Milton e l' *Abele*', *GSLI*, 173:78–110, suggests that the 'Adamo' in Alfieri's library was the 1613 drama by G. B. Andreini, and that this may have been a source for his *Abele* (though another possibility could be Loredano's 1640 *romanzo* of the same title). A. Bruni, 'Per la fortuna di Shakespeare in Italia: l'*Aristodemo* e una traduzione inedita del Monti', *SFI*, 53, 1995:223–48, argues that Monti's departure from Dottori's homonymous tragedy is determined by the influence of Shakespeare. A. Martino, 'Die italienische Vorlage des *Hauptman Schreck* (1627)', *WBN*, 22, 1995:102–07, identifies as a source Francesco Andreini's *Bravure del Capitan Spavento* (1607). F. Gambin, 'La traduzione come servizio. In margine alla prima edizione italiana del *Criticon*', *QLL*, 20, 1995:135–50, looks at Giovan Pietro Cattaneo's version (Venice, 1685) and its motives: an interesting question, particularly in view of its late date, but somewhat difficult to determine in view of the fact that we know absolutely nothing of the translator. L. Dolfi, 'Tirso e Cicognini: due don Giovanni a confronto', pp. 129–62 of *La festa teatrale ispanica*, ed. G. B. De Cesare, Na, Istituto Universitario Orientale, 1995, 354 pp., compares Tirso da Molina's *Burlador de Sevilla* and Giacinto Andrea Cicognini's *Convitato di pietra* (1650). I also note D. Bernardi, *'El *Don Chisciotte* de

Lorenzo Franciosini (1622): un caso de (auto)censura', pp. 93–104 of *Atti delle Giornate cervantine*, ed. C. Romero Muñoz, D. Pini Moro, and A. Cancellier, Padua, Unipress, 1995, 136 pp.

TRAVELLERS. Carla Sodini, *I Medici e le Indie Orientali. Il diario di viaggio di Placido Ramponi emissario in India per conto di Cosimo III*, F, Olschki, 120 pp., consists of an expansive introduction to Medici involvement in Eastern trade and evangelization (Ramponi's 'baggage' included holy water founts for Theatine churches in Goa!), and of the somewhat briefer text of a hitherto unpublished diary of 1697–1700. L. Monge, 'La Londra secentesca nell' "Anglipotrida" di Orazio Busino', *AnI*, 14:553–74, consists of a brief discussion of Busino's London sojourn (as chaplain to Pietro Contarini's 1618 embassy) and provides some excerpts from his manuscript account of London life, perhaps of more interest to Jacobean scholars (to whom, however, it was already relatively well known) than to Italianists. Id., 'Pietro Contarini a Roma (1623): il diario inedito di un ambasciatore veneziano', *AtV*, 33, 1995:183–207, consists of a brief biographical note, followed by the diary (which actually deals not with the Roman visit, but with the journey there) by the same Orazio Busino. A. N. Mancini, 'Autobiografia e autocoscienza narrativa nel *Viaggio di Francia* di Sebastiano Locatelli', *AnI*, 14:230–45, considers the (very modest) significance of the journal of the French voyage (1664–65) of a Bolognese priest who then spent the rest of his life in his native city, where over many years he meditated (and rewrote) his one notable experience of the wider world. C. Voielle-Guidi, *'Démêlés et pérégrinations d'un Vénitien en marge à travers six lettres inédites de B[artolomeo] Dotti', *CER*, 18, 1994:211–37.

MISCELLANEOUS CONTRIBUTIONS. Of possible interest to *Seicento* students pursuing related lines of research are: Sandra Cavallo, **Charity and Power in Early Modern Italy: Benefactors and their Motives in Turin, 1541–1789*, CUP, 1995, xv + 280 pp.; and D. Rosselli, ' "Tamquam bruta animalia": l'immagine dei vagabondi a Roma tra Cinquecento e Seicento', *QSt*, 31:363–404.

2. POETRY

L. Alemanno, 'Le "Rime degli Accademici Umoristi"', *FMADIUR*, 1995:275–90, rapidly describes a manuscript anthology compiled in 1612 by no less than Giovan Battista Guarini during his *principato* and preserved in the Biblioteca Estense. It includes verse by Pier Francesco Paoli, Agazio Di Somma, Girolamo Preti, Fabio Leonida, Arrigo Falconio, Alessandro Guarini, Alessandro Sertini, Alessandro Zagarini, Ottavio Rinuccini, Scipione Caetano, Scipione Pascali, Antonio Querenghi, Marcello Macedonio, and Guarini himself (much of which was subsequently published in other collections) and transcribes from it *inediti* by Di Somma and both the Guarini.

V. De Maldé, 'Appunti per la storia dell'elegia volgare in Italia tra umanesimo e barocco', *StSec*, 37 : 109–34, is only marginally of *Seicento* interest, given that according to De Maldé, between the 1580s and 1645 'sull'elegia cade un silenzio, a mia notizia, assoluto', only broken thereafter by a handful of texts, to which De Maldé devotes just four paragraphs.

Luoghi e forme della lirica, ed. Giorgio Bárberi Squarotti, T, Tirrenia, 208 pp., contains two contributions to *Motivgeschichte* of *Seicento* interest. D. Chiodo, 'La scena del bagno nella letteratura italiana' (47–68), takes us from Matelda's 'dunking' of Dante to Montale's Esterina, but has right at its centre Preti's *Salmace* and a number of other *Seicento* texts (by Marino, Errico, Fontanella, Maia Materdona): a wonderfully chosen anthology, though Chiodo's acute ear for the sounds and rhythms of these exquisite verses leads him rather to take the 'baths' out of context. Thus he comments on Marino's 'inferior' imitation of the *Salmace* in Adonis's bath, without taking into account that in *Adone* VIII, far from being the climax of Venus and Adonis's sexual encounter, it is a coldy observed, self-consciously voyeuristic prelude (and contrast) to the orgasmic sequence that follows, where typically the gratification of the senses is placed outside the normal narrative time and space of the poem. The second item is F. Pevere, 'La macchina delle parole. Strumenti scientifici e tecnologici nella poesia del Seicento' (119–48), which returns with vigour to this popular theme, extending the search beyond modern anthologies, and reminding us of a number of less well-known images (spinning machines, organs, watermills, arquebuses alongside the better-known clocks, automatons, compasses, and telescopes) and of their collective role — beyond the various more or less trite moralities to be drawn from them — in documenting changing perceptions of 'nature' and 'art'.

F. Fido, 'Dreams and experiences of elsewhere: voyage poems in seventeenth-century Italian literature', *The Image*, 45–60, is more narrowly focused than the title suggests, dealing principally with poems inspired by Colombus's discoveries (at least two of which, however, it fails to mention: Guidubaldo Benamati's *Mondo Nuovo* of 1622 and Agazio Di Somma's *America* of 1625). His hypothesis that in Italian literature the topos of the sea voyage exhausted itself as seafaring declined is not only somewhat facile, but also in my view rather inaccurate.

A. Ceruti Burgio, 'Tre poeti locali alla corte dei Farnese: Francesco Duranti, Antonio Ongaro, Tiberio Torricella', pp. 121–29 of Id., *Parma Rinascimentale e Ducale. Poesia, arte e società a Parma dal tardo '400 alla fine del '700*, Parma, Zara, 174 pp., hereafter *Parma Rinascimentale*, contains very brief notes on three forgotten (and minor) 'mannerists'.

BASILE. A. Sana, 'Eliodoro nel Seicento italiano, 1: Il *Teagene* di Giovan Battista Basile', *StSec*, 37:29–108, dealing with B.'s Italian verse rewriting of the Alexandrine romance *Æthiopicæ* (1637), which caught the attention of many *Seicento* writers of epic and romance, contains a quantity of matter of interest to students of both genres.

CASABURI. Pietro Casaburi Urries, *Le Sirene*, ed. D. Chiodo et al., introd. G. Bárberi Squarotti, T, RES, xxvii + 348 pp., together with earlier editions of Maia Materdona and Battista (*YWMLS*, 51:486, and 53:498) provides ready access to the bulk of the work of (arguably) the three most significant southern *concettisti* of the mid *Seicento*. A rewriting of southern literary history of the period (hitherto largely based on anthologies) may well be in order as a result, since all three challenge the orthodox view of Neapolitan 'Marinism', to the point that a better term may be 'post-Marinism'. What emerges from C.'s lyrics, originally published between 1676 and 1685, is not Marino's careful balance between outward *facilitas* and underlying iconoclastic irony (to which among his Neapolitan followers Maia comes closest) but a strange marriage of icily correct versification with a nervous display of rhetorical novelty and classical erudition. Less concerned than the slightly older Battista (who may nevertheless have been his most direct model) to celebrate the social rituals of his class, C. is at once dignified and ostentatious, his writing a kind of literary equivalent of the code of conduct by which the southern *nobiltà d'armi* (to which C. himself appears to have belonged) made a show of living, and as much a part of the defence of its social pre-eminence: a far cry from the 'middle-class' assertiveness which characterized so much of the first wave of (northern) *concettismo*.

CHIABRERA. Q. Marini, 'Orazio e i *Sermoni* di Gabriello Chiabrera', *Atti* (Licenza), 241–76, analyses C.'s debt in these very late verse epistles, arguing that he 'non subisce passivamente il fascino della poesia satirica oraziana [...] ma si serve di Orazio per conquistare autonomia dai moduli satirici cinquecenteschi'.

LEMENE. Francesco De Lemene, *Raccolta di cantate a voce sola*, ed. E. Canonica, Parma, Fondazione Bembo–Ugo Guanda, lxxii + 147 pp., is a somewhat bizarre enterprise, whose place in the series must be questioned: not that an elegant versifier like L., marking the transition between *concettismo* and Arcadia, does not deserve attention, but to bury 500 lines of slight verse in 200 pages of *apparato* betrays a lack of critical judgement, while the repetitious commentary is chiefly notable as a warning how not to use information technology: only the use of a machine-readable corpus could have thrown up quite so many echoes of earlier (mainly

Petrarchan/Petrarchist) texts, most of them so remote that they tell us only what we knew all the time, that poets store up and recombine the words of other poets.

MARINO. Giovan Battista M., *Il Tempio e la Sferza*, ed. G. Maragoni, Ro, Vignola, 1995, 154 pp., is the first modern edition of two key works of the Parisian period, antithetical instances of 'occasional' writing: the poem written in 1615 to 'woo' Maria de' Medici and Concini, and the 1616 prose against the Huguenots, produced after Concini's murder to curry favour with the assassin de Luynes. The *invettiva* appears linguistically more varied and interesting than the *panegirico*, though the architecture of the latter's carefully patterned description of an imaginary allegorical edifice in honour of the Queen warrants more careful study. The texts, prefaced by a dense introduction concentrating on the prosodic and rhetorical aspects of the text, are reproduced, as the editor himself declares, with a determined refusal to 'ammodernare il desueto e alieno o [...] uniformare il fluttuante e il variabile'.

B. Fogagnolo, 'Quattro lettere inedite di G. B. Marino a Ridolfo Campeggi', *Aevum*, 70:637–56, publishes four letters dating respectively from 1606, 1612, 1614, and 1620, part of a larger body of correspondence between Campeggi and other *letterati* in the Archivio di Stato, Bologna: none of them throws any major new light on M.'s career or his literary relations, though the 1612 letter does provide further evidence of the depth and seriousness of the crisis precipitated by his Turin arrest of 1611. F. Giambonini, 'Bibliografia delle opere a stampa di G. B. Marino: 1700–1940 (II)', *StSec*, 37:317–65, continues a valuable contribution to the history of the reception and circulation of M.'s works.

The 'Sense' of Marino, ed. F. Guardiani, NY, Legas, 1995, 550 pp., brings together some 25 papers whose unifying theme is 'sense' in the two distinct (yet in Marino's case closely related) acceptances of meaning and what one might, for lack of a better term, define as 'sensory realism' (not just Calcaterra's vague *poetica dei sensi*, but a precise sensory empiricism originating in Telesio). It is refreshing to find a volume devoted to M. which is as much concerned with hermeneutics as with stylistics, and while the scope, interest, and quality of the contributions vary considerably, almost all contain some stimulating new critical angle, or fresh historical data to add to our still far from satisfactory understanding of M.'s socio-cultural context. The following seem of particular significance: P. Cherchi, 'Il re Adone' (9–33), reconsidering the question of Adonis's election to the crown of Cyprus as a specifically political statement (an approach which finds me in wholehearted agreement, though I am not wholly convinced by this reading); A. Franceschetti, 'Ancora su Amore e

Psiche: la molteplicità delle fonti' (35–52), which extends the scope of M.'s fabled 'rampino' to Boiardo, N. da Correggio, and Firenzuola, pointing up the extraordinary omnivorousness of his reading and the complexity of his rewriting; G. Niccoli, 'The wild boar as *Satiro*' (139–55), arguing that the 'humanization' of Adonis's quarry turned rapist and killer poses some disturbing questions about man's animal nature; V. De Maldé, 'Nuovi generi e metri del Marino' (179–210), providing a valuable frame of reference to test M.'s claims of innovation; P. A. Frare, 'Antitesi, metafora e argutezza tra Marino e Tesauro' (299–321), attempting a systematic answer to the oft-posed but never adequately resolved question of the relation between M.'s practice and Tesauro's theorization, based on an extensive selection of sonnets and madrigals: his conclusions support the view that *capovolgimento* based on antithesis, rather than metaphor, is the essence of M.'s *arguzie*, but in view of the insistence of a number of critics that the *Terza parte della Lira* is more metaphorically innovative than earlier compositions, it is somewhat surprising that Frare's selection is restricted to the 1602 *Rime* and the *Galeria*); A. Martini, 'Marino e il madrigale attorno al 1602' (361–93), rightly stressing the novelty and importance of M.'s handling of the madrigal form, even in relation to its remarkable prior evolution at the hand of Tasso, though I wonder whether to define it as a 'mignardise' is not to minimize what in M.'s hands is often the vehicle of his most disturbing insights into the poetics of desire and representation; M. Scarci, 'Marino on stage: *La catena d'Adone*' (451–64), notable both for its contribution to the early history of opera and for drawing attention to the fact that the first (and only?) operatic adaptation of *L'Adone* was produced in Rome (under the auspices of his old Aldobrandini patrons) in 1626 just after the poem's official condemnation. (No less interesting is the fact that it should draw on the Falsirena episode, to which most modern critics have paid only cursory attention.) The collection also contains a number of contributions on M. and contemporary musicians (notably Alessandro Piccinini, Monteverdi, D'India) on which I do not feel qualified to comment.

Paolo Cherchi, *Le metamorfosi dell''Adone'*, Ravenna, Longo, 160 pp., takes as its starting point the narratological research which has dominated much recent work on *L'Adone*, but attempts to go beyond it. Structural analysis here is not as an end in itself, but a key to the 'political' meanings of the poem (in the broad sense of description and critique of the 'massimi sistemi' of Baroque society). While falling short of a comprehensive account, both in the way it is organized in discrete essays (some parts of which had already appeared as articles) and because it leaves large sections of the poem untouched and unaccounted for, it is nevertheless the most ambitious and wide-ranging rereading of the last 20 years. Id., 'The metamorphoses of Adonis', *The Image*, 61–72, is a summary of the opening chapter of the foregoing book. In the same volume we also have F. Guardiani, 'Giovan Battista Marino's *L'Adone*: a key to Baroque civilization' (73–91), which summarizes the course of M. studies over the last 30 years, and argues the case (indisputable, though it still needs to be made) for the poet's absolute centrality to 17th-c. sensibility and our understanding of it.

Angelo Colombo, *'Ora l'armi scacciano le Muse'. Ricerche su Giovan Battista Marino (1613–1615)*, Ro, Izzi, viii + 148 pp., comprises two essays, 'L'eredità mancata del Tasso. G. B. Marino fra la *Liberata* e la *Distrutta*' and 'Periegesi mariniane. Un'epopea burlesca da Torino a Parigi', which though not new (see *YWMLS*, 54:501; 55:572) appear here in substantially expanded and corrected guise.

F. Guardiani and A. Martini, 'Il manierismo e Giovan Battista Marino', *ColH*, 20, 1994: 51–70, returns to a question first raised by Giovanni Pozzi, M.'s place in the Mannerism–Baroque continuum, broadly endorsing his position where M.'s 'mannerist' *elocutio* is concerned, but going on to note how particularly in *L'Adone* the *dispositio* is far more complex and self-questioning (or baroque). F. Graziani, 'De l'épopée chevaleresque à l'épopée de paix: conta-minations et renouvellements du genre de l'Arioste à Marino', *RLC*, 70:475–86, discusses *L'Adone* and Jean Chapelain's prefatory *Discours* in relation to Renaissance theories of and claims for epic poetry, but the upshot is a definition of the poem as an 'oeuvre totalisante' with 'la portée d'une épopée de l'Art', which does not really take us beyond Calcaterra's 'enciclopedia del poetabile'. R. Cavalluzzi, 'L'Atteone di Marino. Il teatro, il sogno e la morte in barocco', pp. 99–126 of *Dall'Idillio alla visione. Passaggi della differenza tra Rinasci-mento e Barocco in area napoletana*, ed. R. Cavalluzzi, introd. Francesco Tateo, Manduria, Lacaita, 1994, 170 pp., hereafter *Dall'Idillio*, con-siders the representations of the Acteon myth in *Adone* V and *La Sampogna*, but does not seem to me to go beyond the usual generalizations (and occasional platitudes) concerning the *Seicento* preoccupation with the relationship between desire and death. E. Paulicelli, *'La Galeria* di Giambattista Marino e gli spazi percorsi dalle parole', pp. 57–81 of Id., *Parola e immagine. Sentieri della scrittura in Leonardo, Marino, Foscolo, Calvino*, Fiesole, Cadmo, x + 156 pp., also to be found in shorter form in *The 'Sense' of Marino* above, starts from the promising premise that ways of looking, representation as the only possible 'reality', and the relationship between words and things (rather than the poetic re-presentation of the visual arts) are the true themes of *La Galeria*, but thereafter seems rather to drift into piecemeal commentary on individual compositions. M. G. Accorsi, 'La *Sampogna* di Marino tra narrazione e teatro. Commento a un'edizione', *SPCT*, 52: 153–76, makes some useful if scattered observations concerning the *Idillio* genre, M.'s contribution to it, and Vania De Maldé's recent edition (*YWMLS*, 55:571), though the exact purpose of publishing them in this fragmentary form (despite the title, neither a review of the edition nor an overview of the text) escapes me.

M. Guglielminetti, 'Il Marino del Coppini', *Mélanges Terraux*, 481–91, rehearses Aquilino Coppini's observations on M. and *marinismo*, already referred to by G. Pozzi, giving the key passages of his letters, but rather taking them at face value and forgetting their didactic intent (addressed as they were, and as the plainness of their Latin reminds us, to two former pupils). It would have been good to see the commentary extended to the whole matter of M.'s reception in Milan (culminating in the Bidelli editions of *La Lira*). One interesting new piece of information does, however, emerge: M.'s temporary retreat to the safety of Venice following Murtola's 1609 attempt on his life. N. Cacciaglia, 'Momenti perugini nell'attività poetica di Giambattista Marino', *AUSP*, 20, 1994:155–78, despite the change of title, is no more than a reprint of an already noted article (see *YWMLS*, 56:563).

ORSINI. Paolo Giordano Orsini, *Rime diverse*, ed. A. M. Luisetti, T, RES, xxii + 218 pp., is principally of documentary interest, relocating an aristocratic dilettante, previously thought a full-blooded *marinista*, to the margins of *concettismo*. Despite a preponderance of forms typical of Marino and his imitators, he comes closer in tone and taste to Chiabrera and Testi. The brief introduction is chiefly concerned to place the poems in the context of O.'s biography; the text is based on the first (and only) edition of 1648, collated with a partial autograph manuscript.

PERS. O. Pelosi, 'The Ellipse and the Circle: an analysis of some lyrics by Ciro di Pers between *Anima in Barocco* and neo-Platonism', *The Image*, 93–107, does little to advance understanding of a fascinating and occasionally great poet.

ROSA. Salvator Rosa, *Satire*, ed. D. Romei and J. Manna, Mi, Mursia, 357 pp., relies for its text on the not entirely reliable Cesareo edition of 1892, subjected to a 'trascrizione critica' which does not, by the new editors' own admission, remove 'dubbi e perplessità non lievi'. It is nevertheless valuable for its extensive body of notes, including significant corrections to the chronology of the poems' composition proposed by Limentani, and a lively introduction which stresses R.'s separateness from courtly satirists, arguing that his verse is marked by class antagonism as well as moral revulsion for the court world, and discussing his debt to Juvenal, Persius, and Lucian.

SALOMONI. Giuseppe Salomoni, *Rime*, ed. C. Giovannini, introd. G. Bárberi Squarotti, T, RES, xxi + 212 pp., adds another valuable piece to the jigsaw of *Seicento* poetry after Marino: S. emerges from this first modern edition of his verse as a highly accomplished *concettista*, with a close eye to Marino, but also to Tasso and Guarini, though one who for all his skill does not move beyond his models, or exceed the cultural boundaries of his native Udine. For the text the editor does not clearly explain why she does not use the first complete edition of his verse (1626) or the earlier partial editions of 1616 and 1620. Given this, and her slightly casual note concerning the adoption of 'le norme più consuete di ammodernamento del testo', one can only wonder how reliable the text actually is. She might also have worked a little harder at identifying dedicatees, poetic corres-pondents, and other contemporary figures referred to in the *Rime*, not all of them as obscure as she claims.

SERGARDI. *The Satires of Lodovico Sergardi: an English translation and Introduction*, ed. and trans. Ronald E. Pepin, 1994, NY, Lang, 136 pp.

TINGOLI. P. Tononi, 'Due documenti inediti per la storia di Lodovico Tingoli, poeta riminese del XVII secolo', *SU*, 66, 1993–94 [1995]: 277–82, publishes the will, and another related document, of an interesting provincial nobleman, well connected in both Rome and Vienna, and the first of a long series of Italian poets (and soldiers) at the Imperial Court.

ZAZZERONI. G. Maragoni, 'Tra verzieri ed erbarî. Note sulle rime boscherecce di Paolo Zazzeroni', *Italica*, 73:336–47, notes with his usual perspicacity some essential semantic, phonetic, and rhythmic mechanisms in the *Giardino di Rime* (1641) by another *concettista* from the Veneto, then goes on to suggest that some echoes of them may have found their way into the supposedly antithetical versification of the following century as represented by Filicaia and Metastasio.

3. DRAMA

DRAMATIC LITERATURE. Federico Della Valle, *Opere*, ed. M. G. Stassi, T, UTET, 1995, 640 pp., is the first (almost) complete edition since the now out-of-print 1955 Mondadori edition, on which most of its text is based. It differs, however, in the addition of some of the prose writings (the *orazioni* of the Milanese period) and the exclusion of the handful of extant lyrics, as well as the manuscript versions of the Reina di Scozia. One is grateful to the publishers, who have kept faith with the 'Classici Italiani' where Mondadori, Ricciardi, and Laterza have thrown in the towel, but the present volume is rather disappointing, since it offers neither greater completeness, nor an improved text, and is accompanied by a very routine introduction and commentary. A. Franceschetti, 'Presenze e funzioni della divinità in tre tragedie barocche', *D'Andrea Vol.*, 241–55.

S. Maira, 'Ermetismo e libertinismo in *Amor nello specchio* di G. B. Andreini. Pretesti per una beffa strutturale', *EL*, 19.2, 1994:47–72, considers an unsettling play centred on the themes of narcissism and hermaphroditism (the plot would appear halfway between Ariosto's story of Ricciardetto and Fiordispina, and Marivaux's 'philosophical' experiments) which whatever its dramatic merits certainly warrants attention, though the attempt to link it with postmodernist poetics seems rather arbitrary. A. Ceruti Burgio, 'Alcuni drammi sacri poco noti del primo Seicento di Antonio Maria Prati', *Parma Rinascimentale*, 137–51, gives a rapid résumé of five extant biblical and hagio-graphical dramas (1612–23).

PLAYS AND PLAYERS. Maurizio Rebaudengo, *Giovan Battista Andre-ini tra poetica e drammaturgia*, T, Rosenberg & Sellier, 1994, 222 pp., is a somewhat overlong account of Andreini's attempt to secure his status and that of his famous actor parents Isabella and Francesco by combining his *capocomico* role with that of playwright. The rather unfocused discussion of individual texts is unlikely to contribute to the immortality he sought. J. Tylus, 'Natural women: Isabella Andreini and the first Italian actresses', *ItC*, 13, 1995:75–85, makes much of exceedingly scant evidence to argue (somewhat predictably) the code-breaking versatility of early actresses, made possible by 'the paradoxical figure of a public woman'. L. George Clubb, 'Un repertorio illustrato per compagnie teatrali', *LItal*, 47, 1995:240–42, announces the discovery (in the New York Public Library) of a book of water-colour illustrations, dating from the end of the 17th–begin-ning of 18th century, which 'ingenuously but vigorously communicate the stage effects' a *Commedia* troupe could produce, possibly 'a reference collection for a *capocomico* [...] and a sample book to show to prospective customers'. More seriously unsubstantiated are the claims of C. Burattelli, 'I Comici dell'Arte nelle tavole in piume d'uccello di Dionisio Menaggio', *BTe*, 37–38:197–212, for the documentary value of an unusual series of pictures (bird-feather collages which include some of the *Commedia* characters) now in the Blacker-Wood Library of Ornithology at McGill University. W. Brooke, 'Louis XIV's dismissal of the Italian actors: the episode of *La Fausse Prude*', *MLR*, 91:840–47 reviews the circumstances of the Comédie Italienne's definitive departure from Paris.

SPECTACLE. S. Mamone, 'Tra tela e scena. Vita d'accademia e vita di corte nel primo Seicento fiorentino', *BTe*, 37–38:213–28, surveys some of the semi-private theatrical activities pursued in the orbit of the Medici court (aristocratic households, academies, *confraternite*), arguing that it is here rather than in the increasingly stereotypical performances produced for the court festivals that the most vital theatrical partnerships and experiments take place. L. Gentili, **La città degli Olimpî. Mitologia e architettura effimera in alcune entrate nuziali della Casa d'Austria*', pp. 31–65 of *Intersezioni. Spagna e Italia dal Cinquecento al Settecento*, ed. Mariateresa Cattaneo, Ro, Bulzoni, 1995, 182 pp., hereafter *Spagna e Italia*.

THEATRES. F. Decroisette, 'Iconografia ufficiale, iconografia sommersa: l'esempio della Pergola', *BTe*, 37–38:229–41, discusses the evidence for the 17th-c. layout of the theatre. F. Bussi, '"Ancien Régime" dei teatri musicali piacentini tra Seicento e Settecento', *ASPP*, 47, 1995:161–67, offers brief notes on performances at the Teatro della Cittadella, from 1669, with some comments on earlier theatres in the city.

OPERA. *Le parole della musica*, I: *Studi sulla lingua della letteratura musicale;* II: *Studi sul lessico della letteratura critica del teatro musicale, in onore di Gianfranco Folena*, 2 vols, F, Olschki, 1995, 424, 334 pp., contains a number of contributions relevant to musicology, opera, and theatre history, as well as lexicography: P. Gargiulo, 'Per la terminologia del teatro d'opera secentesco: fonti teoriche e drammatiche' (I, 31–44); E. Torselli, 'Dalla"Musurgia universalis" al "Musico testore": parole e idee per la musica tra miti antichi e prassi moderna' (I, 45–70); G. Staffieri, 'Lo scenario nell'opera in musica del XVII secolo' (II, 3–31), concerning plot summaries sold ahead of performance (not *canovacci* like those of the *Commedia dell'arte*) whose relationship with the performance and publishing history are discussed; M. T. Muraro, 'Teatro, scena e messinscena: lessico degli addetti ai lavori' (II, 47–55).

Roma moderna e contemporanea, 4, has a special section, 'Il melodramma a Roma tra Sei e Settecento', with two contributions of *Seicento* relevance: C. Gianturco, '"Per richiamare e divertire gli spettatori dalla seria applicazione che l'azione richiede": prologhi, intermedi e balli per il Teatro di Tordinona', relating to performances dating from the 1670s (19–36); G. Rostirolla, 'Alcune note sulla professione di cantore e di cantante nella Roma del Sei e Settecento' (37–74). I also note I. Bajini, **Recitato — cantato. Da un dramma di Antonio Sigler de la Huerta a un libretto d'opera di Giulio Rospigliosi*', *Spagna e Italia*, 67–101, comparing Sigler's *No ay bien sin ageno daño* (1652) and *Dal male al bene*. E. Fortman, 'Musical aliens and alien music: perceptions of Italian and French music in seventeenth-century Paris', *SCFS*, 17, 1995:211–21, deals entirely with opera.

4. PROSE

HISTORIOGRAPHY. T. Zanato, 'Sondaggi sul testo dell'*Istoria* di Davila (in margine a una recente edizione)', *SV*, 30, 1995:125–50, points out with rather tiresome thoroughness the failure, in a recent edition (Arrigo Caterino Davila, *Storia delle guerre civili di Francia*, ed. M. D'Addio and L. Gambino, Ro, 1990, whose omission from earlier surveys is to be regretted), to make adequate use of a (possibly) autograph manuscript, in pursuit, it would appear, of some original authorial practice; but despite the claim that the 'problematica [...] filologico-critica' must be the object of no less editorial effort than the elucidation of the text's historiographical significance (a doubtful proposition: linguistically the work does not seem to me to have any great significance) Zanato himself seems to be rather selective in what he reckons to be of 'philological' interest, and says nothing of that all-important guide to sense (and sometimes innuendo), the punctuation.

SATIRE. L. Binotti, 'Il potere della parola. Parodia e satira tra la Spagna e Venezia', pp. 85–98 of *Il letterato tra miti e realtà del nuovo mondo: Venezia, il mondo iberico e l'Italia*, ed. Angela Caracciolo Aricò, Ro, Bulzoni, 1994, 574 pp, discusses an anonymous Spanish *Aviso de Parnaso* (1617) after the manner of Boccalini, criticizing Venice's alliance with Savoy in the War of Monferrato, and the reply (*Castigo de' Calunniatori*) published in 1618 under the pseudonym Fulvio Valerio Savoiano.

THE 'ROMANZO'. A. Coppola, 'Il *Corriero svaligiato* di Ferrante Pallavicino. Un esempio di "pensiero poetante"', *EL*, 21.3:77–81, makes the all too obvious point that Pallavicino combines 'saggistica' (in the rather general sense of analytical discourse on topics of contemporary interest) and 'narrative', in a way which is character-istic of his age, when certain things were best said under cover of fiction (though even that did not save this author from the stake!). G. Berger, 'Der *Corriere svaligiato* Ferrante Pallavicinos — ein libertin-ischer Briefroman?', *ItStudien*, 17:8–19, suggests (wrongly in my view) that the work is a *capostipite* of the epistolary novel, and compares it to the *Lettres persanes*. A. Fariello, 'Tempo e morte in un romanzo barocco', *EL*, 20.3, 1995:63–82, discusses Pona's *Lucerna* in terms of the relationship between frame and episodes, questioning the extent of his libertinism and arguing that the work (really a collection of *novelle*) is only superficially philosophical and chiefly notable for its rather gratuitous fascination with gruesome deaths. G. Mazzocchi, 'La novela morisca y su relación con la novela barroca italiana: Anton Giulio Brignole Sale y la Storia Spagnuola', *Revista del Departamento de Filologia Moderna, Universidad de Castilla–La Mancha*, 5,

1994: 163–81, identifies a possible source for Brignole Sale in A. de Villegas's *El Abencerraje*, possibly via Montemayor's *Diana*.

BASILE. F. Tarzia, 'Il *Cunto* di Giovan Battista Basile e l' ideazione di un nuovo genere letterario', *FMADIUR*, 1995: 177–200, starts off from the promising premise that the *Cunto* needs to be more firmly placed in relation to, and against, late *Cinquecento* theorizations of minor genres (in this case the *novella*), but then drifts into scattered narratological observations. P. Guaragnella, 'Il mondo dal "di dentro". Un intermezzo de *Lo cunto de li cunti* di G. B. Basile: *La coppella*', *Dall'Idillio*, 127–61. H. McCullough, *'Basile's *Pentamerone*: from the marvellous to the fantastic', *QI*, 15, 1994: 183–90.

BOCCALINI. Harald Hendrix, *Traiano Boccalini fra erudizione e polemica. Ricerche sulla fortuna e bibliografia critica*, F, Olschki, 1995, viii + 406 pp., originates in a doctoral thesis and preserves all the heavy-handed thoroughness of this sub-genre of *Literaturwissenschaft* (including graphs illustrating, *inter alia*, the chronological and geographical frequency of the *Ragguagli* and their imitations!). Quite apart from the valuable though not exhaustive bibliographical section, there is a wealth of useful, even interesting, new information here, but there is also a good deal which need not have been repeated, and an essay less than half the length would have made its point better. B. Bosold, 'Concettismo e arte della prosa da Traiano Boccalini a Baltasar Gracián', *LItal*, 48: 205–29, sets out to 'rescue' the *Ragguagli* from Croce's criticism (founded, I suspect, not so much on aesthetic objections, as on a fundamental lack of sympathy with the world Boccalini was describing and what he had to say about it), and to refocus attention on its 'carattere innovativo ed autonomo'; but though Gracián's theorization of this hybrid genre would indeed appear to reflect closely Boccalini's own intentions and their modernist, anti-classical basis, it remains to be seen how this might alter our view of the text. As things stand, Bosold would appear to challenge earlier attempts to place the text within the 'tradizionale teoria dei generi' with another, only slightly less traditional; quite why we need it to enable us to recognize the shrewdness and wit of Boccalini's account of poetry, poetics, and *letterato*-patron relations escapes me.

CROCE. Giulio Cesare Croce, *Le sottilissime astuzie di Bertoldo (Edizione del 1606)*, ed. P. Cigada, Mi, Berlusconi, 1994, xix + 200 pp., is the first modern edition to be based on the recently rediscovered 1606 Milan imprint, accompanied by a record of the variants and revisions of the 1608 edition, which the editor thinks were largely concerned to raise the moralizing tone further and remove some of the more 'colourful' expressions which associated Croce with libertinism. This is the subject of the first of two prefatory essays: V. Branca, 'La dolce vita veneziana e Bertoldo' (also published elsewhere as

'Barocco villanesco tra Bologna e Venezia', for which see *YWMLS*, 57:535), and P. Camporesi, 'Giulio Cesare della Lira, da uomo di villa a uomo di corte', also included, as part of a larger study, in Id., *Il palazzo e il cantimbanco (Giulio Cesare Croce)*, Mi, Garzanti, 1994, 151 pp., which constitutes something of a revision of C.'s earlier reading of Croce, moving away from seeing him as a popular anti-establishment author and placing him closer both to the literary mainstream and to the Bolognese elite (the *palazzo* of the title).

5. THOUGHT

POLITICAL THOUGHT. D. Vagnoni, 'Esempi di trasformazione semantica nella *Dissimulazione onesta* di Torquato Accetto', *EL*, 21.2:67–88, argues that dissimulation is present as much at the micro-textual level (*elocutio*) as at the macro-level (argument) of Accetto's text.

CAMPANELLA. *La Monarchia del Messia*, ed. V. Frajese, Ro, Ediz. di Storia e Letteratura, 1995, 150 pp., publishes for the first time (collated from two Vatican manuscripts) the Italian text of C.'s defence of the pope's secular authority, written at the time of the Venetian Interdict. Frajese's introduction reconstructs the context and history of its composition and points out its uneasy amalgam of messianic astrology, natural law, and papal absolutism. Textual variants, quotations, and allusions are identified in the footnotes. *Bruniana & Campanelliana* is a new journal dedicated to previously unpublished texts and documents as well as critical studies. The first issue (1, 1995) includes: 'Cinque sonetti inediti di Campanella', ed. G. Ernst (11–20), and by the same scholar, 'Note campanelliane, I: L'inedita "Chiriscopia" a Richelieu; II: La perduta "Disputatio contra graphomantum"' (83–102); E. Canone, 'L'editto di proibizione delle opere di Bruno e Campanella' (43–62); M.-P. Lerner, 'La science galiléenne selon Tommaso Campanella' (121–56); M. Mulsow, '"Sociabilitas". Zu einem Kontext der Campanella-Rezeption im 17. Jahrhundert' (205–33).

W. Eamon, 'Natural magic and utopia in the Cinquecento: Campanella, the Della Porta circle and the revolt of Calabria', *Memorie Domenicane*, 26, 1995:369–402, investigates the link between the Neapolitan scientific milieu, the development of Campanella's philosophical views, the Calabrian 'rebellion', and his prison writings. Though Eamon gives us fair summaries of what is known of each, what seems to me to emerge is really the inadequacy of our knowledge and understanding of most aspects of this extraordinary story, from southern Italy's extraordinary late-*Cinquecento* tangle of rationalism, millenarianism, Catholic reform, and political subversion, through the extent of C.'s engagement with it, to the continuing need to cut through the vast logorrhea of his prison writings, distinguishing between the tactical and expedient and the intellectual core (which one cannot help feeling will turn out to be more modest than *campanellisti* claim). M. S. Sapegno, 'Percorsi dell'Utopia: da More a Campanella', *FMADIUR*, 1995:29–50, makes some perceptive observations concerning the differences between their respective Utopias, and the development of Campanella's political thought, though the treatment of the relationship between his early republican-ism and his later 'conversion' to Catholic absolutism, and the not unrelated issue of the extent and chronology of his rewriting of the *Città del Sole*, only alluded to by Sapegno, could usefully have been dealt with systematically. P. Tuscano, 'Utopia e realismo negli *Aforismi politici* di Tommaso Campanella', *EL*, 21.1:3–25, picks up related themes, outlining some of the salient features of this relatively early text (1601), still republican in sentiment, but already indicative of the views which would lead to the espousal of elective absolutism: mistrust of the masses and a firm belief that power should be the prerogative of an intellectual elite, chosen irrespectively of birth. It must be said, however, that despite Tuscano's attempt to stress the 'non pochi alti insegnamenti', the text reveals more the conventionality of Cam-panella's political thought than any novelty or profundity. S. Zoppi, 'Orazio e Campanella', *Atti* (Licenza), 221–40, reaches the not exactly earth-shattering conclusion that Campanella's poetic is markedly critical of Horatian views. T. Cerbu, **Dissimulation on display: the feint of power in Campanella's *Scelta*', pp. 203–09 of *The Play of Self*, ed. Ronald Bogue and Mihai I. Spariosu, Albany, NY State U.P., 1994, xvi + 268 pp., discusses Campanella's self-repres-entation in the *Scelta di poesie filosofiche*.

GALILEO AND THE NEW SCIENCE. Exhaustion sets in as one attempts to keep track of publications on Galileo's trial and condem-nation, few of them fully justified by new facts or fresh interpretations. Alceste Santin, *Il caso Galilei*, T, SEI, 1995, 164 pp., is a clear traditional account, with no particular interpretative axe to grind, intended for the general reader. The same cannot be said of Giorgio Spini, *Galileo, Campanella e il 'divinus poeta'*, Bo, Il Mulino, 90 pp., a (moderately) polemical pamphlet which rightly seeks to 'correct' the 'extreme' readings of Redondi and Biagioli, except that having attacked the narrowness of their perspectives, Spini replaces them with a no less narrow one of his own. His Galileo is an establishment figure whose views were essentially orthodox (even Copernicanism, he argues, was more widely accepted than is generally assumed; the real radicalism lay with the 'libertine' tradition the author has extensively, if not always very deeply, charted) and were only banned because of a *faux pas* in relation to Urban VIII (the 'divine poet' of the title). This seems to me not merely reductivist, but plain wrong in grossly overstating Galileo's social and intellectual 'integration' (even at the peak of his success he remained something of an outsider without the 'proper' academic or aristocratic qualifications), and in emphasizing the Pope's sense of affront at the *Dialogo* (an important factor, no doubt, but only one of many in the 'horribil congiuntura' of a trial which also involved the most urgent issues of epistemology, textual hermeneutics, and Church politics). Similar ground is covered in Id., 'Galileana minima', *Studi D'Addario*, 1299–1315, which consists of two notes, one on the defence of *Sidereus nuncius* by the Scotsman John Wedderburn, the other on the supposed panegyric of his discoveries by the future Urban VIII (*Adulatio perniciosa*, first published in 1620), minimizing its quality, pointing out its real significance, and describing its subsequent publication history (intriguingly, it was never censured, even after the break with Galileo, despite its implicit approval of Galileo's method and discoveries, which Spini attributes simply to Urban's conviction that he was a great poet). Yet another example of a historian of ideas using Galileo as grist to his mill is B. Dooley, 'Processo a Galileo', *Belfagor* 51 : 1–21, which argues that a not insignificant part in his condemnation was played by the changing modes of intellectual communication: Galileo's views were dangerous as much because of the means by which they were expressed and spread as their content, though paradoxically his condemnation only served to accelerate the new lines of communication.

Galileo e la scienza sperimentale, ed. M. Baldo Ceolin, Padua, Dipartimento di Fisica dell'Università, 1995, 132 pp., contains: T. B. Settle, 'Per una lettura sperimentale delle ricerche di Galileo sul moto: la rete degli esperimenti galileiani' (11–62); L. Olivieri, 'Dalle "scientiae mediae" alle "nuove scienze": linee di sviluppo dell'episte-mologia galileiana' (65–86); C. Maccagne, 'Le matematiche nella concezione galileiana della fisica come scienza sperimentale' (87–102); P. Bozzi, 'Percezione ed esperimento: le ragioni di Simplicio, ossia la base percettiva del moto pendolare e della discesa lungo piani inclinati' (105–31). On the same topic, L. Conti, 'La dimensione sperimentale della relatività galileiana', pp. 549–76 of *Alexandre Koyré: l'avventura intellettuale*, ed. Carlo Vinti, Na, ESI, 1994, 734 pp., hereafter *Alexandre Koyré*, concerns attempts to demonstrate the principle according to which it is impossible to determine from within a system (that is, the Earth) whether that system is in motion or stationary. A. van Helden, 'Telescopes and authority from Galileo to Cassini', *Osiris*, 9, 1994:9–29, considers how acceptance of the (often uncertain) observational data of the new astronomy depended on the 'construction' of the authority of the observer.

M. Biagioli, 'Le prince et les savants: la civilité scientifique au 17ᵉ siècle', *Annales*, 50, 1995:1417–53, compares the varying degrees of 'courtliness' obtaining within the Accademia del Cimento, the Royal Society, and the Académie Royale des Sciences, relating them to the form and degree of involvement of the respective sovereigns. A similar approach is taken in Id., 'Scientific revolution and aristocratic ethos: Federico Cesi and the Accademia dei Lincei', *Alexandre Koyré*, 279–95. Exciting as Biagioli's original ideas were, these articles are rather repetitious and predictable. J. Tribby, 'Dante's restaurant: the cultural work of experiment in early modern Tuscany', pp. 319–37 of *The Consumption of Culture, 1600–1800: Image, Object, Text*, ed. A. Bermingham and J. Brewer, London, Routledge, 1995, xiv + 546 pp., considers 'the emergence of Medici interest in natural experiment between the later 1650s and the 1680s as part of the means by which the [Medici] court established the terms of social privilege in the grand duchy'.

M. De Caro, 'Sul platonesimo di Galileo', *RivF*, 87:25–40, rehearses the (by now traditional) Platonist reading and argues against Wallace's rival Aristotelian one (though he is also mildly critical of some 'Platonist' excesses). I also note M. Finocchiaro, *'Methodological judgement and critical reasoning in Galileo's Dialogue', Proceedings of the Biennial Meeting of the Philosophy of Science Association*, 2, 1994:248–57.

Other contributions on *Seicento* natural philosophy include A. Clericuzio and S. de Renzi, 'Medicine, alchemy and natural philosophy in the early Accademia dei Lincei', *Italian Academies*, 175–94, which surveys the research activities of the Lincei, arguing against the commonplace view that their programme only took shape after, and was determined by, Galileo's enrolment; P. Galluzzi, 'La scienza davanti alla Chiesa e al Principe in una polemica universitaria del secondo Seicento', *Studi D'Addario*, 1317–44, which publishes letters of 1670 by Giovanni Maffei, and by Lorenzo Bellini, Donato Rossetti, G. A. Borelli, Alessandro Marchetti, concerning conflicts between traditionalists and 'galileiani' at Pisa University; F. Bonelli and L. Russo, 'The origin of modern astronomical theories of tides: Chrisogono, de Dominis and their sources', *BJHS*, 29:385–401; G. L. Betti, 'Note sull'edizione bolognese degli *Opuscoli filosofici* di Benedetto Castelli (1669)', *Il Carrobbio*, 22:75–83; Anna Cassini, *'Giovan Domenico Cassini. Uno scienziato del Seicento. Testi e documenti*, Perinaldo, Comune di Perinaldo, 1994, 315 pp.

On Jesuit science we have James M. Lattis, *Between Copernicus and Galileo. Christopher Clavius and the Collapse of Ptolemaic Cosmology*, Chicago

U.P., 1994, xviii + 294 pp., a comprehensive reconstruction of Clavius's role in setting the co-ordinates of Jesuit astronomical and mathematical investigation, and his role in promoting the 'Copernican revolution'; *Christoph Clavius e l'attività scientifica dei Gesuiti nell'età di Galileo*, ed. U. Baldini, Ro, Bulzoni, 1995, 316 pp., which contains mainly essays beyond the scope of this survey, but also includes three contributions of possible interest to literary scholars: D. Aricò, '"In doctrinis glorificate Dominum". Alcuni aspetti della ricezione di Clavio nella produzione scientifica di Mario Bettini' (189–207); R. Gatto, 'L'attività scientifica dei Gesuiti a Napoli' (283–94); A. Clementi, 'I collegi gesuitici in Abruzzo' (295–316).

MAGALOTTI. Antonio Turolo, *Tradizione e rinnovamento nella lingua delle 'Lettere scientifiche ed erudite' del Magalotti*, F, Accademia della Crusca, 1994, 180 pp., analyses the lexis and syntax of the *Lettere* (written in the 1660s and 1690s, but only published in 1721) pointing to the sharp change occurring between the two periods of composition: the seven early letters are marked by Tuscan conservatism, while the latter are packed with *barbarismi* and long catalogues full of exotic and unusual terms. The shift supposedly reflects, on the one hand, the decline of Magalotti's interest in experimental science and, on the other, a broader cosmopolitan perspective based on his new experiences as a widely travelled career diplomat.

REDI. L. Guerrini, 'Una lettera inedita del Carcavi al Magliabechi con un parere sul Redi', *GCFI*, 75 : 180–84, presents a letter of 1669 showing R.'s *Generazione degli insetti* being read and appreciated in Paris.

VANINI. F. De Paolo, *'Vanini in Francia: i confini di una presenza', pp. 317–29 of *Il Seicento francese oggi: situazione e prospettive della ricerca*, ed. Giovanni Dotoli, Bari, Adriatica, 1994, 358 pp.

SETTECENTO

By G. W. SLOWEY, *Lecturer in Italian, University of Birmingham*

1. GENERAL

LIBRARIES, PUBLISHING. D. Brunelli, 'Una proto-industria tipo-grafica del Settecento: la stamperia Scolari in Verona', *Miscellanea Marciana*, 7–9, 1992–94 [1996]:207–30, details the operations of a printer who worked mainly in the area of religious publications. M. Callegari, '"Tipografi-umanisti" a Padova nel '700: i fratelli Volpi e la stamperia cominiana', *AVen*, 180, 1995:31–63, examines the links between the Volpi family of publishers and the university, and in particular their connection with figures such as Vallisneri, Zeno, and Maffei, who were also editors of the *Giornale de' letterati d'Italia*, which regularly carried articles about the publications of the Cominiana press; the article also discusses Gaetano Volpi's influence on the press, underlining his conservative and pro-Jesuit approach to publications, and demonstrates the strong links which the press had with publica-tions of the university, especially in the fields of theology and science. G. Baldi, 'La Biblioteca Civica "Girolamo Tartarotti" di Rovereto: contributo per una storia', *AARA*, 244, 1994 [1995]:41–170, although dealing with the whole history of the library up to the present day, has a detailed first part concerning the early years of the library after its foundation in 1764 and explores its links with other cultural institutions in the city. M. De Gregorio, 'Prima di Bandini. Tentativi di biblioteca universitaria a Siena nel Settecento', *Società e Storia*, 19:253–81, looks at the library of Sallustio Bandini, given to Siena's Studio in 1758, and at the efforts of Pompeo Neri to establish a proper university library in the city. Maria Iolanda Palazzolo, *Editoria e istituzioni a Roma tra Settecento e Ottocento*, Ro, Izzi, 1994, x + 134 pp., collects four essays which have appeared elsewhere.

LITERARY HISTORY AND BACKGROUND. *StSet*, 16, is devoted to 'L'enciclopedismo in Italia nel XVIII secolo' and contains: F. Arato, 'Un'enciclopedia perugina del Seicento: Secondo Lancellotti' (25–41); C. Vasoli, 'Giacinto Gimma' (43–60), examining the *Nova encyclopaedia* and pointing out the ambiguity of G.'s interest in the new sciences alongside his belief in Satanic powers, which are 'la testimonianza della persistenza di credenze e di miti destinata a sopravvivere anche nell'*âge de la raison*'; A. Barzazi, 'Enciclopedismo e ordini religiosi tra Sei e Settecento: la *Biblioteca universale* di Vincenzo Coronelli' (61–83), describing the problems this work had with Church censorship and also its less than favourable reception by Zeno and Muratori; P. Casini, '"On étudie et on raisonne en Italie".

Geometria, scienza e lumi in Italia' (85–96), illustrating d'Alembert's comment by reference to thinkers such as Paolo Frisi, Francesco Algarotti, and Ferdinando Galiani, and to centres such as Rome, Naples, and Bologna; C. Farinella, 'Le traduzioni italiane della *Ciclopaedia* di Ephraim Chambers' (97–160), pointing out the comparatively late appearance in Italy of translations of this work, which was published in 1727, though the preface was only published in 1746 by Pasquali in Venice; later volumes appeared in Naples, and then the bulk of the work in 1748–53, again from Pasquali, and the fact that work was put on the Index did not prevent publication of further supplements; M. Infelise, 'Enciclopedie e pubblico a Venezia a metà Settecento: G. F. Pivati e i suoi dizionari' (161–90), discussing Pivati, who began by translating and producing compilations of foreign encyclopaedias and then produced his own *Nuovo dizionario scientifico e curioso sacro-profano*, also projecting a *Dizionario poligrafico* which was never completed; C. Mangio, 'Censura granducale, potere ecclesiastico ed editoria in Toscana: l'edizione livornese dell'*Encyclopédie*' (191–219), dealing with the censorship of new works and pointing out that it seemed less rigid in Livorno, where many works on the Index were published by the Coltellini press and the *Encyclopédie* itself was reprinted in 1770–79 by the Stamperia dell'Enciclopedia; A. Tosi, 'Le *planches* nelle edizioni toscane dell'*Encyclopédie*' (221–48), discussing Giuntini's Lucca edition of 1756 and the Livorno Coltellini edition of 1763; M. Verga, 'Isidoro Bianchi e le *Notizie de' letterati*' (249–65), assessing the influence of this Palermo periodical and the involvement in its publication of Bianchi and Giovanni Evangelista Di Blasi in the period immediately following the expulsion of the Jesuits, and noting its warm reception of the Livorno edition of the *Encyclopédie*; S. Luzzatto, 'La buona compagnia. Alessandro Zorzi e il progetto di una *Nuova Enciclopedia Italiana*' (267–88), looking at Z.'s attempts between 1775 and 1779 to interest leading figures in the cultural world such as Biffi, Paradisi, and Pietro Verri in his project for a new encyclopaedia; P. Del Negro, 'Due progetti enciclopedici nel Veneto del tardo Settecento: dal patrizio Matteo Dandolo all'abate Giovanni Coi' (289–321), concerning itself with Dandolo's *Spirito dell'Enciclopedia* (1771–74) and Coi's involvement in the Padua reprint of Panckoucke's *Encyclopédie méthodique*; G. Alfieri, '"Stile manifatturato" e "stile instruttivo": la lingua nel progetto comunicativo dell'enciclopedismo italiano' (323–71), analysing the discussions on language and examining the choice of particular styles for the communication of information, with an appendix of contributions from figures such as Frisi, Zorzi, and Alessandro Verri; C. Donato, 'Fortunato Bartolomeo De Felice e l'edizione di Yverdon dell'*Encyclopédie*' (373–96), exploring the cultural background to the publication of the *Encyclopédie* by the Italian-born Swiss, who was always keen to shine in the cultural world of his native Italy; G. Abbattista, 'La "folie de la raison par alphabet"'. Le origini settecentesche dell'*Encyclopaedia Britannica* (1768–1801)' (397–434); P. Castagneto, 'Uomo, natura e società nell'edizioni settecentesche dell'*Encyclopaedia Britannica*' (435–76); F. A. Kafker, 'L'influenza dell'*Encyclopédie* sulla tradizione enciclopedica del XVIII secolo' (477–88). R. Abbrugiati, 'La pensée politique du *Caffè* ou l'expression juridique et économique d'un projet de société', *ChrI*, 46:5–29, examines aspects of the debates carried in *Il Caffè* such as ancients vs moderns, utilitarianism, *italianità*, and cosmopolitanism, moving on to consider discussions on law and economics. R. Pasta, 'Per una rilettura de *Il Caffè* (1764–1766)', *RSI*, 107, 1995:840–75, also looks at themes of the periodical such as criticism of aristocracy and pacifism, detailing in particular the contribution of Alessandro Verri, and highlighting Pietro Verri's interest in keeping the journal going through his rejection of articles which he considered too openly critical of religion or government. P. Luciani, 'La nuova edizione del *Caffè*', *RLI*, 100.1:54–59, is another brief look at the recent new edition of the journal. **Un decennio di storiografia italiana sul secolo XVIII*, ed. Alberto Postigliola, Na, Istituto Italiano per gli Studi Filosofici, 1995, 472 pp. V. Giormani, '1793–1795: la breve stagione concorsuale di Giuseppe Olivi tra Padova e Venezia', *SV*, 30, 1995 [1996]:269–318, outlines O.'s work in the area of natural sciences and examines his relationship with Padua's university and academy. B. Marangoni, 'Minoranze religiose nello studio di Pisa. Le lauree degli acattolici 1737–1799', *BSP*, 64, 1995:147–92, discusses the attitude of the authorities towards the participation of non-Catholics in Pisa University, which moved from an initial limited tolerance to greater discrimination, especially against Jews; there is an appendix of graduates in this category, together with documentation of their progress. A. Borelli, 'Medicina e società a Napoli nel secondo Settecento', *ASPN*, 112, 1994 [1995]:123–77, concentrates on the figure of Domenico Cotugno, one of the most celebrated medical and scientific figures in Europe, to demonstrate the development of interest in new ideas in the south of Italy. M. Federici, 'L'elogio del sovrano. Le orazioni di Adeodato Turchi vescovo di Parma', *AP*, 80:176–97, traces T.'s development from a moderate reforming position in relation to the Enlightenment to a return to the values of the old regime, examining his eulogy of Maria Theresa. S. Stoppato, 'La pratica della retorica e la politica del consenso: detti e proverbi del procuratore Zuanne Emo raccolti dal nobile veneziano Giacomo Nani', *SSLS*, 46:227–42, looks at a representative of one of the most important cultural and political groups in Venice, who was convinced of the necessity for a return to the 'virtù repubblicana' of the old sort F. Lui, 'L'allegoria della virtù. Il programma iconografico di una galleria bolognese nelle lettere inedite di Carlo Bianconi a Giambattista Biffi (1770–1779)', *AAC*, 33–34, 1994 [1995]: 157–75, illustrates very clearly aspects of the transition to neoclassicism and Bianconi's interest in cultural and artistic progress, and publishes, in appendix, six of the letters. G. Bertini, 'Belle arti e accademie a Parma e a Torino nelle lettere di P. M. Paciaudi e G. B. Bodoni', *BMBP*, 8, 1994 [1995]: 54–79, uses the letters to demonstrate the important role played by Paciaudi in raising the status of the Accademia delle Belle Arti in Parma and in attempts to establish a public library, and to examine the development of links between Parma and Turin. O. Capoferri, 'Giovanni Maironi da Ponte, pedagogista illuminato nella Bergamo del Settecento', *Bergomum*, 91.1: 145–59, deals with the way in which education was seen as fundamental for the reform of society, involving the laicization of education and the direct involvement of the government; the article analyses Maironi's *Saggio di educazione nazionale proposto in un discorso accademico* (1779), which was directed at the Venetian government, and reflects debates going on elsewhere in Italy, drawing particularly on Milan and the work of Gian Rinaldo Carli. F. Montecuccoli degli Erri, 'Il console Smith. Notizie e documenti', *AtV*, 182, 1995 [1996]: 111–81, examines S.'s activities as editor and bookseller, his connection with Giambattista Pasquali, and other material concerning his villa at Mogliano Veneto; it adds a copy of S.'s will and of the official valuation of his possessions and fortune. E. Greppi, 'Il conte Antonio Greppi (1722–1799), imprenditore, finanziere, diplomatico nella Lombardia austriaca del Settecento', *ASL*, 121, 1995: 399–429, while dealing with G.'s position in the financial and tax systems of Lombardy, also examines his connections with Pietro Verri. G. Liva, 'L'Archivio Greppi e l'attività della filiale di Paolo Greppi a Cadice', *ib.*, 431–87, is concerned with the extensive correspondence in the family archive. I. Sonzogni, 'Il carteggio Alessandro Furietti–Pierantonio Serassi. Momenti dell'erudizione bergamasca a metà Settecento', *Bergomum*, 91.2: 91–188, publishes the 69 letters of the collection, with an introduction discussing the involvement of the two in the collection of inscriptions and in the editing of the Latin works of Basilio Zanchi and Publio Fontana. S. Roda, 'L'epigrafia selvaggia di Giuseppe Francesco Moyranesio', *QSt*, 93: 631–52, tells of M.'s faking of dozens of Latin epigraphs and manuscripts, many of which were based on material ascribed to an equally false Dalmazzo Berardenco, whose *Vita*, another fake, was published in 1780. On a similar topic is M. Angelini, 'L'invenzione epigrafica delle origini familiari', *QSt*, 93: 653–82, which discusses the falsification of an 8th-c. epigraph, seemingly carried out by a certain Carlo Garibaldi in order to boost his family's legal and financial claims. A. Fabrizi, 'Altre notizie su Francesco Zacchiroli', *GSLI*, 173:110–23, examines Z.'s *Lettere* and other bibliographical material to demonstrate his enthusiasm for Enlightenment ideas, looking also at his *Description de la Galerie Royale de Florence* of 1783 and other works including his translation of Gibbon's *Decline and Fall of the Roman Empire*. B. Capaci, ' "Lo stomaco di calce". Bagni termali e patologie mondane nelle lettere di Caterina Dolfin e Gasparo Gozzi', *Intersezioni*, 16:291–307, presents the particular psychopathology of the literary classes, referring to Giuseppe Pujati's *Della preservazione della salute dei letterati* and showing how members of that society were skilled in describing in detail the pathological aspects of their existence; the article draws on D.'s letters to her husband and those from G. to her, noting G.'s capacity for self-mockery.

2. POETRY, PROSE, DRAMA

B. Danna, 'L'ombra di Voltaire in Italia. Fra satira lucianea e poesia sepolcrale tardosettecentesco', *LItal*, 48:79–94, considers the lesser importance of Voltaire's influence on poetry, as opposed to his influence on theatre, philosophy, and history, examining periodicals like the *Giornale enciclopedico di Venezia* and pointing to anti-Voltaire contributions by writers such as G. B. Contri and those in favour by such as Casanova; there is also reference to Alfieri, Pindemonte, and Foscolo. F. Furlan, 'Traductions et adaptations à la veille de la Révolution: *Ecatonfilea*, *Deifira* et leurs lecteurs', *REI*, 41, 1995: 111–31, discusses the periodical *Conservateur* and the appearance in it in 1756 of *Déiphire*, comparing it with Alberti's 1471 original and with the 1574 Lyons translation as well as Mirabeau's 1780 version from his *Recueil des contes*; the article also looks at Champ-Rion's 1785 version of Alberti's *Ecatonfilea*. Giorgio Pullini, *Il teatro in Italia*, III: Settecento e Ottocento, Ro, Studium, 1995, 395 pp., contains: 'Dalla tragedia al melodramma: poetica' (13–32); 'Dalla tragedia al melodramma serio' (33–65); 'Le poetiche intorno alla commedia' (67–84); 'Dalla commedia all'opera buffa' (125–60); 'La poetica e la tragedia di Alfieri' (161–80). E. Baker, 'Italian opera production during Mozart's travels in Italy 1770–1773', *AARA*, 244, 1994 [1995]: 18–40, is concerned with aspects of theatre production in the cities visited by the Mozarts. E. Tamburini, 'Piante inedite del teatro Alibert: progetti di Francesco Galli Bibiena, i disegni di Pietro Paolo Coccetti. Con una riflessione sui teatri romani del Settecento', *BTe*, 37–38:243–60, traces Bibiena's planned reconstruction of the original Alibert theatre in Rome and the involvement of Coccetti, a local architect, adding some ideas on the structure of other Roman theatres. P. A. Ferrara, 'Gregorio Calaprese and the subjugation of the body in Metastasio's *Drammi per musica*', *Italica*, 73:11–23, deals with C. as a primary source of M.'s 'Cartesian aesthetic' and suggests that C.'s theory of corporeal representation can be widely found in M.'s work, claiming that this is what helps distinguish his work from that of Apostolo Zeno or Gian Francesco Busenello.

3. Individual Authors

ALFIERI. Vittorio Alfieri, *Mirra*, ed. Angelo Fabrizi, Modena, Mucchi, 353 pp., has a substantial introduction. Id., *Della tirannide. Del principe e delle lettere. La virtù sconosciuta*, introd. Marco Cerruti, ann. Ezio Falcomer, Mi, Rizzoli, 393 pp. S. Costa, 'Lo stratagemma della posterità. Sull'epistolario di Vittorio Alfieri', *RLI*, 100, 2–3:5–25, sees A.'s early letters as anticipating the 'grandi temi alfieriani', with A. announcing his dedication to poetry; the letters also foreshadow his later description of himself as a 'vate' and his later judgements on the French Revolution, and demonstrate his concern for his 'propria immagine postuma'. M. Rebaudengo, 'Letture alfieriane per "un mostruoso spettacolo": Tasso, G. B. Andreini, Milton e l'*Abele*', *GSLI*, 173:78–110, discusses the influences on A. of Tasso's *Gerusalemme liberata*, as well as of Andreini's *Adamo*, of which A. had a copy in his library, and which is shown to have a close link particularly with Act I of A.'s *Abele*; the article also looks at A.'s use of Milton's *Paradise Lost* for ideas such as the depiction of Lucifer's two offspring, Sin and Death, from Milton Book II, which appear in Act I of *Abele*. J. Lindon, 'L'Inghilterra di Vittorio Alfieri: storia di un mito', *GSLI*, 173:515–32, for which see *YWMLS*, 57:545. Giacomo Debenedetti, *Vocazione di Vittorio Alfieri*, Mi, Garzanti, 1995, ix + 299 pp., is a reprint of an important work with an introductory essay by F. Fido. Walter Binni, *Studi alfieriani, 2 vols, Modena, Mucchi, 412, 312 pp. C. Domenici, *Alfieri e i tragici greci. Postille edite e inedite nei volumi di Montpellier e Firenze', *StIt*, 14, 1995:79–122.

ARNALDI. D. von Wille, 'Il *Saggio sopra la filosofia in genere* di Lodovico Arnaldi: una traduzione settecentesca inedita del *Discursus praeliminaris* di Christian Wolff', *Studi filosofici*, 18, 1995:89–126, considers A.'s interest in Wolff's philosophy and the criteria he adopted in translating Wolff's terminology and adds a transcription of the MS from the Marciana.

BARETTI. P. M. Prosio, 'Ritratto di Giuseppe Baretti', *StP*, 25:405–11, deals with B.'s activities as a critic in the *Frusta letteraria* and as a travel writer in, for example, the *Lettere familiari*.

BECCARIA. G. Santato, 'La questione attributiva del *Dei delitti e delle pene*', *LItal*, 48:360–98, examines the collective involvement of the Accademia dei Pugni and especially the link between B. and P. Verri, who was instrumental in ensuring that the book was published at Livorno in 1764. This led to rumours about the paternity of the work and to arguments between B. and Verri, particularly in the light of V.'s own claims to be the 'ideatore' of the work. The article points to B.'s 'singolare arrendevolezza' to suggested changes in the MS, but concludes that the book 'è certamente opera del Beccaria ma, va altresì precisato, non solo del Beccaria'.

BELLATI. Francesco Bellati, *Poesie milanesi*, ed. Pietro De Marchi, Mi, All'insegna del Pesce d'Oro, 468 pp., contains 26 poems in Milanese dialect, together with an extensive introduction.

BUTTURINI. S. Rocchini, 'Per una lettura dei *Carmina* di Mattia Butturini', *AMAP*, 108.3:153–83, looks at B.'s involvement in poetry, theatre, and book production in Venice and shows how his *Carmina* of 1785, which draw on Horace and Catullus, emphasize his attachment to old values, to faith in divine justice, to a belief in love and friendship.

CESAROTTI. C. Bracchi, 'Le *Osservazioni sopra Orazio* di Melchiorre Cesarotti', *GSLI*, 173:544–65, noting C.'s view that poets should be allowed to be poets and not treated as infallible authorities, explains how he approached Horace with the intention of indicating what was universally valid in his poetry and warning against the adoption of motifs which belonged to a past civilization, a practice which he saw as common in contemporary lyricists. C. himself considered that in Horace's love lyrics 'tutto è freddo', but found some response to the poetry by listening to the sensations it aroused, while remaining critical of Horace's social and political preparation.

DA PONTE. Lorenzo Da Ponte, **Lettere*, ed. Giampaolo Zagonel, Vittorio Veneto, De Bastiani, 573 pp. M. Saulini, 'Lorenzo Da Ponte: la memoria esorcizza l'esperienza teatrale', pp. 111–21 of *Memorie di Goldoni e memoria del teatro*, ed. Franca Angelini, Ro, Bulzoni, 182 pp., speaks of Da P.'s self-construction as a person loath to participate in the personal feuds of his artistic world and his presentation of himself as 'another' in relation to the European theatre world, considered by New Yorkers as the symbol of European decadence.

GALIANI. G. Nicoletti, **'Quarto contributo galianeo: il carteggio con Saverio Manetti (1757–1775)', *StIt*, 15:79–108.

GIANNONE. H. Trevor-Roper, 'Pietro Giannone and Great Britain', *HJ*, 39:657–75, discusses the influence of G.'s writings, in particular his *Istoria del regno di Napoli*, on Jacobites and later on Gibbon.

GOLDONI. Carlo Goldoni, *L'uomo prudente*, ed. Piermario Vescovo, Venice, Marsilio, 1995, 252 pp. Id., *Il padre di famiglia*, ed. Anna Scannapieco, Venice, Marsilio, 704 pp. Id., *Il poeta fanatico*, ed. Marco Amato, Venice, Marsilio, 279 pp. Id., *La sposa persiana. Ircana in Julfa. Ircana in Ispahan*, ed. Marzia Pieri, Venice, Marsilio, 542 pp. Id., *Il campiello*, trans. Marco Liviero and Chris Banfield, Birmingham, University of Birmingham, 1995, 114 pp. G. Gronda, 'L'edizione nazionale delle opere di Goldoni: i primi tre volumi (1993–1994)', *RLettI*, 12, 1994 [1996]:491–502. Franco Fido, *Le inquietudini di Goldoni. Saggi e letture*, Genoa, Costa & Nolan, 1995, 191 pp., gathers together ten essays (most of which have appeared elsewhere) to illustrate aspects of G.'s work which are less commonly studied, such as his use of proverbs, his presentation of war, and his links with Giandomenico Tiepolo and Voltaire; in addition there are: 'Nobili, popolane, borghesi in maschera: (ancora) sul carnevale goldoniano' (99–112); 'L'"école des oncles" e le ambiguità del lieto fine' (113–24); 'I libretti per musica scritti a Parigi' (147–62). Id., *'Tempo della città, tempo del teatro', FC*, 20, 1995 [1996]: 516–26. *Tra libro e scena. C. Goldoni*, ed. Carmelo Alberti and Ginette Herry, Venice, Il Cardo, 259 pp. Michel Olsen, *Goldoni et le drame bourgeois* (Analecta Romana Instituti Danici, suppl. 23), 1995, 247 pp., contains sections on the theatre of Diderot and on theatre in general, as well as on G. and on his relationship with Pietro Chiari. *Problemi di critica goldoniana*, II, ed. Giorgio Padoan, Ravenna, Longo, 1995, 292 pp., contains: M. Donaggio, 'Per il catalogo dei testi stampati da Giovanni Battista Pasquali, 1735–1784' (9–100); L. Rossetto, 'Tra Venezia e l'Europa. Per un profilo dell'edizione goldoniana del Pasquali' (101–32); M. Bordin, 'Fra "negozio" e "villa". Crisi della morale borghese dal *Prodigo* alla trilogia della *Villeggiatura*' (133–82), discussing G.'s critical presentation of the beliefs and moral values of merchant society, with its emphasis on appearances, and his treatment of the theme of 'villa' or 'campagna' in this context; for Pantalone in *Il cameriere brillante* the country reflects a 'libertà' which 'sa tanto di rinuncia', and in the *villeggiatura* plays this sets the pattern for 'la determinazione suicida' of a class which has lost its way; M. Agnelli, 'Il pubblico veneziano di Carlo Goldoni' (183–230), maintaining that G. in his *Mémoires* creates an ideal public which never really existed, and pointing out that there was no consistent reception of G.'s work in Venice, as is shown more accurately in his letters; A. Zaniol, 'I tempi e le stratificazioni testuali del Goldoni francese: le "spie" del *Matrimonio per concorso*' (231–67), looking at a play written in France in 1763 for the San Luca theatre: G. may, it is suggested, have substantially modified the text in the 1788 Zatta edition, and this may have been something he did in other editions of his plays; A. Fabiano, 'Goldoni e la *Comédie italienne*. Alcuni spunti per una possibile nuova valutazione' (269–80), discussing G.'s links with the Comédie in the context of court privileges which could restrict performance of Italian opera buffa and other stage works; A. Scannapieco, 'Ancora a proposito di Giuseppe Bettinelli, editore di Goldoni' (281–92), dealing with the printing by Bettinelli of texts to be sold at performances of G.'s plays. *YIS*, 11, 1995, is devoted to articles on Goldoni in France: G. Gronda, 'Goldoni drammaturgo europeo' (5–21), examines the production of G.'s years in France, drawing not only on the *Mémoires*, but also on contemporary theatre and journal notices and letters; G. Herry, 'Serait-ce le théâtre qui lui aurait donné una patrie?' (23–40), considers how well G. fitted into his life in France; F. Fido, 'La ragione in ombra e le tentazioni della follia nelle commedie francesi di Goldoni' (41–63), points out how G.'s ability to draw on 'il mondo' was severely restricted by the indifference of the French world which he did not know, and talks of a 'progressiva naturalizzazione di comportamenti aberranti'; C. Marelli, 'Due commedie 'canoniche' rivisitate' (67–98), examines *Il servitore di due padroni* and *La bottega del caffè*; A. Momo, 'Servette e massere: erotismo e sessualità' (99–113), talks of the ambiguous nature of the serving-girl 'tra la libertà trasgressiva del Teatro da cui proviene, e la moralità del Mondo ... in cui viene ad agire'; F. Fido, 'A sonnet lost and found' (159–61); P. Vescovo, 'Appunti di filologia goldoniana' (163–81), discusses the various 18th-c. editions of G. with a view to establishing which readings can be considered as agreed by G. himself; P. Stewart, 'Anche i pensieri parlano ... Nota sui monologhi e sugli *a parte* nelle commedie del Goldoni' (183–89); the issue also contains three articles on productions of G. plays. *Memorie di Goldoni e memoria del teatro*, ed. Franca Angelini, Ro, Bulzoni, 182 pp., includes: F. Angelini, 'Memoria e teatro in Carlo Goldoni' (7–21), which introduces the essays; N. Mangini, 'Su due "topoi" dell'autobiografia goldoniana' (25–34), on which see below under N. Mangini; C. Alberti, ' "La mia vita è una commedia". Il racconto della "vocazione" teatrale nell'età di Goldoni' (35–52), examines contemporary views of the theatre and of actors, illustrating the point from Luisa Bergalli as well as from the more obvious Gozzi and Goldoni; S. Ferrone, 'Il personaggio Goldoni' (53–62), describes a 'Goldoni segreto', looking especially at G.'s mental depressions; G. Herry, 'Goldoni in commedia; il padre, la legge, l'avvocato' (63–77), discusses a kind of autobiographical presence of G. in his plays which, according to the author, contributes greatly to their modernity; P. Puppa, 'I *Mémoires*, ovvero ritratto dello scrittore da giovane' (79–97), talks of love and family relationships; M. Olsen, 'Norme e valori: teatro e *Mémoires*' (99–107), claims that the *Mémoires* do not belong to the genre of personal literature, but are intended to highlight G.'s work, particularly his comedies. N. Mangini, 'Per una verifica di due fondamentali *topoi* dell'autobiografia goldoniana', *Italianistica*, 25, 1:83–89, discusses the way G. adapts facts in order to emphasize his reform of the theatre. G. Cecchi, 'Il teatro goldoniano illustrato in tre edizioni ottocentesche', *BTe*, 37–38:275–93, draws on the editions published by the Società Editrice of Florence (1827–31), by Colombo Coen in Trieste (1857–58), and by Sonzogno in Milan (1827–31).

GOZZI, C. *Carlo Gozzi scrittore di teatro*, ed. Carmelo Alberti, Ro, Bulzoni, 319 pp., contains: G. Luciani, 'Carlo Gozzi o la ricerca di un rinnovamento del teatro comico italiano' (13–32), suggesting that G.'s strong defence of the 'teatro d'attore' led him to abandon any attempt at reform of the comic theatre; G. Herry, '1756–1758: Venezia a teatro ossia Carlo Gozzi prima di Carlo Gozzi' (33–82), examining the relationship between Goldoni and G. in the period in question through their formation and theatrical experiences and looking particularly at the period before G.'s *Tartana* of 1758; N. Mangini, 'Carlo Gozzi, un "rustego" alla corte di una comme-diante' (83–101), discussing G.'s relationship with Teodora Ricci Bartoli; A. Beniscelli, 'Gozzi, Goldoni, l'approdo alle memorie' (103–21), looking at links between the theatre and autobiographical presentation in the *Memorie inutili*; G. Pizzamiglio, 'Alle origini delle *Memorie* gozziane' (123–34), arguing that the *Memorie* must, at least in part, go back to the period before G.'s polemic with Gratarol; A. Momo, 'Due maschere apolidi a Venezia' (135–49), dealing with Pantalone and Tartaglia; F. Vazzoler, 'Un napoletano a Venezia: Agostino Fiorilli (Tartaglia) fra Sacchi e Gozzi' (151–69), examining Fiorilli's contribution to Sacchi's company with an analysis of the linguistic aspects of Fiorilli's performances as Tartaglia; P. Vescovo, 'Per una lettura non evasiva delle *Fiabe*. Preliminari' (171–213), illustrating G.'s familiarity with Enlightenment debates on magic and witchcraft, pointing out the difference between *L'amore delle tre melarance* with its comic parody and *Il corvo* with its note 'del sinistro, del notturno, del pauroso', and highlighting his reactionary view of the Revolution as displayed in *La più lunga lettera* of 1801; C. Alberti, 'Il declino delle maschere. Drammi flebili e commedie serio-facete oltre le favole teatrali' (215–71), examining such plays as *Cavaliere amico* (1752) and plays of the post-1767 period, and documenting changes in attitude to comedy on the part of people such as Domenico Caminer; A. Croce, '*Le droghe d'amore*' (273–87), discussing the play as an example of G.'s Spanish comedy, comparing it with Tirso de Molina's original; the volume concludes with two articles on modern productions. G. Muresu, 'Memoria e ripudio del teatro nelle *Memorie inutili* di Carlo Gozzi', pp. 123–42 of *Memorie di goldoni e memora del teatro*, ed. Franca Angelini, Ro, Bulzoni, 182 pp., concludes that G.'s lack of self-critical ability led him to underestimate the theatrical and narrative strength of his work.

GOZZI, G. M. Amato, '"Un libro cominciato e non finito": l'attività giornalistica di Gasparo Gozzi', *StSet*, 15, 1995:163–84, emphasizes G.'s role as an observer of society and the unifying function of his own character throughout his career as a journalist.

MARTELLI. F. Waquet, 'Allégorie, autobiographie et histoire littéraire: le *Comentario* de Pier Jacopo Martelli', *REI*, 41, 1995:23–38, discusses the *Comentario* which is placed as an introduction to M.'s own selection of his poetry, the *Canzoniere* of 1710. M. examines the arguments between Marinists and Petrarchists, recognizing the supremacy of the latter, while at the same time autobiographically describing his own poetic journey.

METASTASIO. Pietro Metastasio, *Oratori sacri*, ed. Sabina Stroppa, Venice, Marsilio, 283 pp. M. Orcel and R. De Letteriis, 'Lecture de *Didone abbandonata*', *ChrI*, 47–48:223–33, describes the final scene as 'un modèle dramatique' which M. never repeated in his later works. R. Mellace, **L'Achille in Sciro di Pietro Metastasio'*, *StIt*, 14, 1995:55–65.

MONTI. A. Colombo, 'Giunte e ritocchi per l'epistolario montiano. La corrispondenza con Francesco Albergati Capacelli', *GSLI*, 172, 1995:550–80, prints ten of M.'s letters, 1779–1796, revising the version given in Alfonso Bertoldi's 19th-c. edition.

RICCOBONI. B. Alfonzetti, 'Memoria e memorie teatrali in Luigi Riccoboni', pp. 143–53 of *Memorie di Goldoni e memoria del teatro*, ed. Franca Angelini, Ro, Bulzoni, 182 pp., examines R.'s *Histoire du Théâtre Italien*.

SALERNO. Niccola Maria Salerno, *Novelle*, ed. Luigi Reina, Salerno, Elea, xxxvii + 311 pp., is the first modern edition of these 60 *novelle* of 1760.

STROCCHI. Dionigi Strocchi, *Poesie greche e latine volgarizzate*, ed. Umberto Colla, T, RES, 1995, 284 pp., includes poetry excluded from S.'s own edition.

TEOTOCHI. A. L. Franchetti, **'Lettere inedite di Vivant Denon a Isabella Teotochi Albrizzi'*, *StIt*, 15:109–14.

UGOLINI. P. Bernardini, 'Note per la ricostruzione della biografia e dell'attività letteraria e storiografica di Biagio Ugolini (1702–1775)', *SV*, 30, 1995 [1996]:211–36, in addition to discussing U.'s *Thesaurus antiquitatum sacrarum*, contains, in an appendix, the text of the *Considerazioni circa lo stato presente dell'Europa*.

VARANO. L. Serianni, 'Sul dantismo di Alfonso Varano', *GSLI*, 173:26–54, examines V.'s *Visioni sacre e morali* (1789) and attempts to identify possible sources for his poetic language, concluding that it is not to Dante that we should look, but to the tragic theatre and to *opera seria.*

VERRI, P. E. Agnesi, 'Un inedito giovanile di Pietro Verri, "La storia del signor Marco Porzio Catone"', *GSLI*, 173: 435–45, looks at the autograph of a work in the Archivio Sormani Verri and at a non-autograph, but fuller, version which, according to the author, shows V.'s transition 'al superamento dei conflitti interiori' after a difficult earlier phase.

VICO. G. Costa, *'Vico, Platone e l'"abisso delle acque"', *FC*, 20, 1995 [1996]: 499–515. A. Battistini, '"Un angoletto morto della storia". Vico e la cultura europea tra Sei e Settecento', *LItal*, 47, 1995: 549–64.

OTTOCENTO

POSTPONED

NOVECENTO

By JOHN M. A. LINDON, *Professor of Italian Studies, University College London*
(This survey covers the years 1995 and 1996)

1. GENERAL

Manuale di letteratura italiana. Storia per generi e problemi, ed. Franco Brioschi and Costanzo Di Girolamo, IV: *Dall'Unità d'Italia alla fine del Novecento*, T, Bollati Boringhieri, xiv + 1141 pp., combines sections on poetry, narrative, theatre, and 'saggistica' with others devoted to the sociology of publishing and literary communication, literary journals, the avant-gardes, language and the literary use of dialect, and such formal 'institutions' of literature as versification. *La cultura italiana del Novecento*, ed. Corrado Stajano, Ro–Bari, Laterza, xviii + 849 pp., contains (371–422) a concise literary survey from the pen of C. Segre. Giuliano Manacorda, *Storia della letteratura italiana contemporanea 1940–1996*, Ro, Ed. Riuniti, 2 vols, 1996, usefully extends to the last three decades a work originally published in 1967. *Il Novecento*, ed. G. Luti, II: *Dagli anni Venti agli anni Ottanta*, Padua, Piccin–Vallardi, 1993, xii + 656–1779. Monica Farnetti, *Reportages. Letteratura di viaggio del Novecento italiano*, Mi, Guerini, 1994, 176 pp., sketches a first genre-historical overview and demonstrates the constitutive function of travel for much 20th-c. Italian literature. R. Schwaderer, 'Italien in deutschsprachigen Kulturzeitschriften. Die Rezeption der italienischen Kultur und die Entwicklung des literarischen Italienbildes im deutschen Sprachraum seit 1945. Eine Skizze am Beispiel der Zeitschrift *Merkur*', *ASNS*, 148:65–81, is part of a projected comprehensive investigation into Italo-German cultural contacts from 1945 to 1990.

INTELLECTUAL MOVEMENTS, CRITICISM, PERIODICALS, PUBLISHING. *Visioni e archetipi. Il mito dell'arte sperimentale e di avanguardia del primo Novecento*, ed. F. Bartoli, R. Dalmonte, and C. Donati, Trento, Università degli Studi, 510 pp. V. Bagnoli, 'Futurism e *Società dello spettacolo*', *Intersezioni*, 15:425–38, analyses the Futurist programme in terms of its aim to manipulate the collective imagination and sensibility. G. Guglielmi, 'L'antiestetica futurista', *LS*, 30, 1995:293–301, concludes that Futurism, in spite of its ideological aspiration to 'realize' art, remains within the bounds of aesthetics: 'Ne è il rovesciamento, non il superamento'. C. Bongie, 'Declining Futurism: *La battaglia di Tripoli* and its place in the *Manifesto tecnico della letteratura futurista*', *QI*, 15, 1994 [1995]:217–25, draws attention to the *Battaglia* and its intertextual connections with the *Manifesto*, in which it is cited more than once. C. Sartini Blum, 'Transformations in the Futurist technological mythopoeia', *PQ*, 74, 1995:77–97. P. Possiedi, 'La cucina futurista', *ItQ*, 125–26, 1995:39–46, examines the volume of that title published in 1932 by Marinetti and Fillìa, two years after publication of the *Manifesto della cucina futurista* and the opening of a Futurist restaurant in Turin, and finds confirmation that their rise to the Fascist establishment 'portò i futuristi a contraddire il loro stile eversivo'. Andrew Hewitt, *Fascist Modernism: Aesthetics, Politics, and the Avant-Garde, Stanford U.P., 1993, 222 pp., is not confined to the Italian avant-garde, but does highlight Marinetti and the links between Futurism and Fascism in Italy. M. Guglielmi, 'La letteratura americana tradotta in Italia nel decennio 1930–1940: Vittorini e l'antologia *Americana*', *FoI*, 29, 1995:301–12. C. Burdett, 'Visions of the United States: a note on the different styles of Emilio Cecchi and the *Americanisti*', *MLN*, 111:164–70, elaborates on the chasm dividing Cecchi in his anti-American 'prosa d'arte' *America amara* from writers like Vittorini and Pavese who looked admiringly across the Atlantic. Renato Barilli, *La neoavanguardia italiana. Dalla nascita del 'Verri' alla fine di 'Quindici'*, Bo, Il Mulino, 1995, 318 pp., a lucid and authoritative account from one who was a pupil of Anceschi and a member of the Gruppo 63, is articulated in four chapters: 'Verso una poesia "novissima"' (13–84), 'Battaglie per un "nuovo romanzo"' (85–92), 'Il dibattito teorico' (193–238), and 'Vita ulteriore e morte del Gruppo 63' (239–312).

On Croce: F. Arato, 'Croce: storia della cultura e storia della letteratura', *GSLI*, 172:213–26; M. Scotti, 'Orazio e Croce', *Atti* (Licenza), 533–54; R. Ricorda, 'Benedetto Croce, Angelo Conti e "altri estetizzanti"', *LItal*, 47, 1995:402–22. For Conti I also note by the same scholar *Dalla parte di Ariele. Angelo Conti nella cultura di fine secolo, Ro, Bulzoni, 1993. *NC*, 113 (41.1), 1994, was given over to *Il saggio nel Novecento italiano*, ed. Stefano Verdino, with contributions on such figures as Serra, Cecchi, Longhi, Praz, Debenedetti, Contini, and Bo. On three of these I note: M. Biondi, 'L'*Esame di coscienza di una letterato* di Renato Serra, fra manoscritto e stampa', *Luti Vol.*, 255–86; V. Bagnoli, 'Tre articoli di Emilio Cecchi (1906)', *LItal*, 48:437–50; and V. Gueglio, "Carlo Bo, il dialogo e l'agonia', *ON*, 19.5, 1995:107–34, which elaborates on B.'s critical view of 'letteratura come vita, cioè come fatto religioso'. *Da Petrarca a Gozzano. Ricordo di Carlo Calcaterra (1884–1952) con un saggio introduttivo di Carlo Dionisotti, una testimonianza di Oreste Macrì, e lettere di Gozzano, Graf, Contini, Pasolini e altri. Atti del Convegno, S. Maria Maggiore 19–20 settembre 1992*, ed. Roberto Cicala e Valerio Rossi, Novara, Interlinea, 1994, 142 pp., covers the main fields of C.'s criticism, with G. Belloni on Petrarch, E. Raimondi on the Baroque, M. Saccenti on Arcadia, and

M. Guglielminetti on Gozzano. The selection of letters to C. also includes specimens from Attilio Bertolucci and Giorgio Bassani. On a lifelong devotee of Pascoli: L. Picchi, 'Ettore Cozzani critico letterario', *ON*, 19.1, 1995:125–45. On the parallel 'resistance' response to World War II of three heterogeneous intellectuals all living near Cortona in 1943–44: I. Nardi, 'Resistenza in Arcadia: Pancrazi, Origo, Debenedetti', *Luti Vol.*, 327–42. Sketching an outline history for the last four decades: M. Biondi, 'La critica letteraria in Italia nel dopoguerra. Appunti per una storia', *ParL*, 536–38, 1994 [1996]:35–87. L. Re, 'Questioni di genere. Teoria e critica femminista tra Stati Uniti e Italia', *Intersezioni*, 16:357–74.

C. Chiummo, 'Il libro di tutti e la grande industria: *La lettura* di Giacosa e di Simoni (1901–1923)', *ItStudien*, 16, 1995:65–79, chronicles and characterizes the *Corriere*'s monthly literary supplement in its early, pre-Fascist years. A similar analysis extending to the first half-century is E. Morandi, '*La Lettura* (1901–1952)', *ON*, 19.6, 1995 [1996]:193–211, and for good measure there is also Elisabetta Camerlo, **La Lettura, 1901–1945. Storia e indici*, Bo, CLUEB. G. Oliva, 'Le riviste in Abruzzo durante la Grande guerra', *CLett*, 90:155–70. D. Della Terza, 'Tra Napoli e Roma: *Aretusa* e *Mercurio*, due riviste dell'Italia del dopo guerra', *FC*, 20, 1995 [1996]:559–76. E. Gurrieri, 'Indici di *Mercurio* (1944–1948)', *StIt*, 12, 1994 [1995]:169–217. For Triestine publishing and the house, founded by Anita Pittoni, that brought out first editions of works by Svevo, Saba, Giotti, and Giani Stuparich: S. Parmegiani, 'Le Edizioni dello Zibaldone (Trieste 1949–1975)', *EL*, 20.3, 1995:99–118.

2. POETRY, NARRATIVE, THEATRE

Manfred Lentzen, **Italienische Lyrik des 20. Jahrhunderts. Von den Avantgarden der ersten Jahrzehnte zu einer 'neuen Innerlichkeit'* (Analecta Romanica, 53), Frankfurt, Klostermann, 1994, 417 pp., articulates a general account of essential lines of development in eight chapters with reference to the work of some 30 poets. *Il canto strozzato. Poesia italiana del Novecento*, ed. Giuseppe Langella, Novara, Interlinea, 1995, 564 pp. (hereafter Langella, *Canto*), combines an anthology from over 50 poets with some 350 pp. of essays, part devoted to individual poets (see below under Betocchi, Caproni, Gozzano, Luzi, Montale, Quasimodo, Rebora, Saba, Sbarbaro, Ungaretti, and Zanzotto) and part to more general topics: P. Zoboli, 'Spunti di metrica novecentesca' (19–34); G. Rogante, 'Dallo "sperso esistere" alla "terra promessa". La poesia del Novecento davanti all'"ultimo orizzonte"' (37–54); E. Elli, 'Itinerari della parola poetica da Pascoli a Ungaretti' (59–71); G. Langella, 'Verso il silenzio. Poesia e non-poesia dai vociani agli ermetici' (73–96); E. S. Nicolaccini, 'Verso la prosa: da Lucini a Sanguineti' (99–112); R. Ramella, 'Sulle orme di Orfeo' (115–28); G. Lupo, 'Tra terra della memoria e Campi Elisi. Il sistema simbolico dell'ermetismo meridionale' (131–42); P. Zoboli, 'I poeti liguri' (145–55); U. Motta, 'Vittorio Sereni e i poeti della "Linea Lombarda"' (157–71); S. Bulletta, 'Ideologia e linguaggio della neoavanguardia' (173–89). Paola Pepe, *Novecento e Utopia*, T, Tirrenia, 1995, 84 pp., develops a highly conceptualized and over-concentrated discourse on 20th-c. poetry with reference to Bertolucci, Campana, Caproni, Luzi, Montale, Saba, Sereni, and Ungaretti. Luigi Scorrano, *Presenza verbale di Dante nella letteratura italiana del Novecento*, Ravenna, Longo, 1994, 197 pp. Francesco De Rosa and Giuseppe Sangirardi, *Introduzione alla metrica italiana*, Mi, Sansoni, 402 pp., is untypical of general manuals in the attention it gives to the 20th c. A substantial section of the work characterizes and classifies the 'verso libero', as well as discussing 20th-c. 'versificazione tradizionale', and analyses specimen texts by poets ranging from Cardarelli to Zanzotto. Paolo Giovannetti, *Metrica del verso libero italiano (1888–1916)*, Mi, Marcos y Marcos, 1994, 314 pp., chooses for analysis Italian texts ranging from the time of Kahn's formulation of the principles of free verse in France to the appearance of Ungaretti's *Porto sepolto* and Cardarelli's *Prologhi*. The author rejects the critical commonplace that free verse represents a technical and cultural impoverishment and is an external sign of avant-garde *rottura* with the past. His insights are put to good use in Alberto Bertoni, *Dai simbolisti al Novecento. Le origini del verso libero italiano*, Bo, Il Mulino, 1995, 391 pp., a major contribution situating the leading figures (Carducci, Lucini, Pascoli, D'Annunzio, Marinetti) in a secure and detailed historical (and theoretical) perspective. F. Penzenstadler, 'Autoreferentialität in der italienische Lyrik zu Beginn der Moderne', *ItStudien*, 17:106–29, finds Gozzano's poetry, with its irony, paradoxically more 'modern' than Marinetti's (not to say D'Annunzio's). M. Alinei, '*La strada*: una svolta nel rapporto fra lingua e poesia', *ASNP*, 24, 1994 [1995]:1013–22, dismissing the antifascist credentials of Hermeticism, characterizes the post-war movement that gave rise to a poetry journal often seen as a literary pendant to neorealist film, but in fact a parallel, and in large part earlier, phenomenon. S. Zoico, 'Per un'analisi contrastiva. Valeri, Caproni, Sereni traduttori di Apollinaire', *StN*, 22, 1995 [1996]:85–108. *Italian Poetry since 1956*, ed. Peter Hainsworth and Emmanuela Tandello (Supplement to *The Italianist*, 15, 1995, hereafter Hainsworth, *Italian Poetry*), includes the following general contributions: N. Lorenzini, 'Le frontiere del senso nella poesia italiana contemporanea' (12–28); E. Tandello, '"Il disegno profondo della poesia": poetry in the 1980s' (29–43) with the appendix 'A bibliography of Italian poetry 1980–1993' (44–51); and D. Zancani, 'Lyricism and experimentalism in recent Italian dialect poetry' (182–97). Stefano Agosti, *Poesia italiana contemporanea*, Mi, Bompiani, 1995, 185 pp., gathers pieces not included in his earlier collections of essays in the field. *Italian Women Poets of the Twentieth Century*, ed. Catherine O'Brien, Blackrock, Irish Academic Press, 311 pp., presents substantial selections from the work of A. Pozzi and of the following living or recently deceased poets: D. Menicanti, M. Guidacci, B. Marniti, M. L. Spaziani, A. Rosselli, A. Merini, J. Insana, B. Frabotta, V. Lamarque, and P. Valduga.

Emerico Giachery, *Letteratura come amicizia*, Ro, Bulzoni, 258 pp., gathers a rich miscellany more particularly relevant to Montale, Orelli, Pizzuto, Baldini, Guerrini, Pomilio, Scanziani, Jenni, Pierro, Romano Romani, Bonaviri, Marniti, Bononi, Claudio, Fiore, Bonchino, and Chiusano.

Sharon Wood, *Italian Women's Writing 1960–1994*, London, Athlone, 1995, xv + 320 pp., traces 'the links between Italian society and politics and women's cultural response' in terms of women's contribution to narrative: within the threefold chronological division 1900–1922, 1922–64, and 1964–94, she gives particular attention to the work of Neera, Serào, Deledda, and Aleramo; to Banti, Ginzburg, Morante, and Ortese; and to Maraini, Durante, Petrignani, and Capriolo. P. Albarella, 'L'inquietudine e le forme', *Italienisch*, 36:42–54, traces a problematic 'return to the novel', against the background of a claustrophobic reality and of the 'prosa d'arte' fashion for the fragment, with particular reference to Tozzi, Borgese, Pirandello, Gadda, and Vittorini. Robert S. Dombroski, **Properties of Writing: Ideological Discourse in Modern Italian Fiction*, Baltimore, Johns Hopkins U.P., 1994, 208 pp., for the 20th c. particularly concerns *maggiori* such as Pirandello, Svevo, Gadda, Lampedusa, and Calvino. S. Costa, 'Epos e favola nella narrativa contemporanea', *Luti Vol.*, 389–403, surveys the ongoing presence of 'il meraviglioso ariostesco' in the 20th c., from Ferrero and Savinio to Landolfi and Calvino. M. Schmitz-Emans, 'Experimente mit der Zeit: Über Geschichtliches in Romanen von Italo Calvino, Leonardo Sciascia, Umberto Eco und Raffaele Nigro', *ASNS*, 148:295–322. In *NC*, 115 (42.1), 1995, devoted to 'Narrativa italiana contemporanea', the authors represented by separate essays include Celati, Manganelli, Tabucchi, Siti, and Del Giudice. E. Testa, 'Lo stile semplice del racconto/dei racconti?' (27–50), defines the contrast between an expressionistic style and the 'stile semplice' based on spoken usage and exemplified via stylistic analysis of Fenoglio's *Una questione privata*, Bilenchi's *Conservatorio di Santa Teresa*, and Ginzburg's *Lessico famigliare*. Unlike the neorealist use of 'oralità' to characterize social, and especially working-class, categories, the 'stile semplice' takes over as 'lingua *tout court* della narrazione', as in Tabucchi or Celati.

Gianfranco Pedullà, *Il teatro italiano nel tempo del fascismo*, Bo, Il Mulino, 1994, 388 pp., an exemplary essay in sociological theatre history, richly quantified and documented from unpublished sources, explores multiple aspects of the subject, in particular shedding light on the extent and effect of Fascist state intervention at institutional and ideological levels, and also paying attention to the impact of cinema as the primary form of mass entertainment: despite a 'copiosa drammaturgia popolare di carattere nettamente fascista', the project of a Fascist *teatro di massa* was a failure except at the level of the local amateur dramatic societies promoted by the regime (which, however, were outnumbered by Catholic *teatrini*); the professional theatre did not and could not produce Fascist drama merely at the behest of the regime, when public demand required a diet of escapist entertainment, notably 'white telephone' comedy and review.

3. INDIVIDUAL AUTHORS

ALERAMO. A. Hartstock, 'Sibilla Aleramo und die "scrittura femminile"', *Italienisch*, 33, 1995:42–57, traces through her journalism the development of her thinking on women and literature. B. Zaczek, 'Plotting letters: narrative dynamics in the correspondence of Giovanni Papini and Sibilla Aleramo and *La trasfigurazione*', *Italica*, 72, 1995:54–69. A. Nozzoli, 'Il frustino di Sibilla', *Luti Vol.*, 305–25, explores A.'s last novel with particular reference to the autobiographical dimension and its links with Boine and Rebora.

ALVARO. R. Mercuri, 'Mito e memoria in Alvaro', *Italianistica*, 22, 1993 [1994]:153–56, focuses on *L'uomo nel labirinto* and *Gente in Aspromonte* to conclude that 'questa problematica della memoria e del mito è una costante del macrotesto alvariano'. Vincenzo Paladino, **Alvariana e altro Novecento*, Mi, Mursia, 270 pp. Ada Ruschioni, **Alvaro critico e altri saggi*, Mi, Vita e Pensiero, 1995, x + 304 pp.

BACCHELLI. M. De Grandi, 'Frugando tra i versi di Riccardo Bacchelli nel decennio della morte', *Cenobio*, 44, 1995:455–74, concludes that B.'s poems 'restano testimonianza insostituibile per precisare... soprattutto il suo cammino intellettuale, dal crocianesimo storicistico alla fede cattolica'.

BÀINO. P. Sarzana, 'Napoli e le città del mondo nella poesia di Mariano Bàino', *StN*, 22, 1995 [1996]:247–54, briefly examines the avant-garde poet's third collection, *Ônne 'e terra*.

BANTI. B. Montagni, 'Quando Anna Banti si firmava Lucia Lopresti. 1919–1929, un decennio di scritti d'arte', *StIt*, 11, 1994

[1995]:95–106, examines the recently recovered 'incunaboli ban-tiani' for answers to the question why the writer turned to narrative only in 1934 with the short story *Cortile*. The early art historical writings are seen to provide the indispensable foundation for B.'s later work as 'lettrice e interprete del passato' in works such as *Artemisia* and *La camicia bruciata*. D. Valentini, 'Anna and her sisters: the idyll of the convent in Anna Banti', *FoI*, 30:332–50, concerns in particular the short stories of *Le monache cantano* (1942). A. M. Torriglia, 'From mother to daughter: the emergence of a female genealogy in Anna Banti's *Artemisia* and Alba de Céspedes's *Dalla parte di lei*', *Italica*, 73:369–87.

BASSANI. E. Kanduth, 'Il luogo della morte nell'opera di Giorgio Bassani', *Italianistica*, 22, 1993 [1994]:273–79, explores the signific-ance of a characteristic *leitmotiv* of B.'s fiction. C. Varese, 'Tempo e spazio nell'*Airone* di Giorgio Bassani', *ib.*, 281–88, concerns the subjectivized presentation of time and space in a work where 'lo stesso procedere narrativo si esprime prevalentemente nella coscienza ossessiva del personaggio [Limentani]'.

BENNI. B. Marx, 'Il Medioevo alla Berlusconi. Zu Stefano Benni: *La Compagnia dei Celestini* (1992)', *Italienisch*, 34, 1995:42–56, considers Benni's use of medieval fantasy in his critique of a media-dominated consumer society.

BERTACCHI. E. Paccagnini, 'Bertacchi e la letteratura di fine Ottocento', *ON*, 19.6, 1995 [1996]:71–91, characterizes the poet's rhetorical style as a critic, and his extra-literary values as seen in his response to Whitman, De Marchi, De Amicis, and Zanella.

BERTOLUCCI. See PASOLINI, below.

BETOCCHI. G. Langella, 'Trionfo della croce. L'itinerario poetico-religioso di Carlo Betocchi', Langella, *Canto*, 299–307.

BIANCIARDI. J. Soldateschi, 'Non si vive di sola zuppa. Sui racconti di Luciano Bianciardi', *Luti Vol.*, 367–88.

BIGONGIARI. M. C. Papini, 'Dall'Arca alla Torre', *RLI*, 99.1–2, 1995:125–30, looks at the collection P. Bigongiari, *Tutte le poesie (1933–1963)*, gathering three decades of verse, unpublished as well as published, which B. himself has likened to a *Bildungsroman*.

BOINE. M. Mola, 'Boine: i *Discorsi* in parentesi', *FC*, 19, 1994 [1996]:427–46, reassessing the *Discorsi militari*, sees the book as more than a passing aberration on the part of B.

BONAVIRI. Carmine Di Biase, **Giuseppe Bonaviri. La dimensione dell'oltre*, Na, Cassitto, 1994, offers a comprehensive thematic reading of the Sicilian's output of verse and fiction.

BONONI. Giuseppe Fontanelli, *Il solo segno. La 'Trilogia' di Loris Jacopo Bononi*, Venice, Marsilio, 391 pp., conducts, in what is only the second monograph devoted to B., a mainly thematic reading of the three verse collections brought together by Il Polifilo in 1987 and by Marsilio in 1994 (*Diario postumo*, 1969; *Miserere dei*, 1970; *Il poeta muore*, 1973).

BONTEMPELLI. **Massimo Bontempelli scrittore e intellettuale*, ed. Corrado Donati, Ro, Ed. Riuniti, 1992, 366 pp. P. Bianchi, 'La letteratura fra realismo e magia: Massimo Bontempelli', *Testo*, 28, 1994:86–107, reassesses B.'s 'reconstructive' avant-garde positions in his aesthetic theory and criticism. S. Micali, 'Bontempelli e la dissoluzione della *femme fatale*', *Italica*, 73:44–65, examines the three works she considers most significant in B.'s 'smantellamento' of the *femme fatale*: *Eva ultima*, *Nostra Dea*, and *Vita e morte di Adria e dei suoi figli*.

BORGESE. Anna Maria Cavalli Pasini, **L'unità della letteratura. Borgese critico scrittore*, Bo, Pàtron, 1994, 334 pp. M. C. Terrile, 'La narrazione dell'inettitudine in *Rubè* di Giuseppe Antonio Borgese', *Italica*, 72, 1995:40–53, finds the problem with *Rubè* to lie in the relationship between narrator and protagonist, but not in the sense meant by E. Cecchi: it is one of extraneousness between 'classical' narrative forms and what they purport to represent, namely the disintegration of 'una coscienza che si perde'. A. Mauriello, 'Simmetrie narrative nel *Rubè* di Giuseppe Antonio Borgese', *CLett*, 91–92:283–305.

BRACCO. A. Castegnaro, 'Un inedito (?) di Roberto Bracco', *Testo*, 29–30, 1995:184–97, publishes from a MS the sonnet in Neapolitan decasyllables 'Tiempe passate' as offered by the writer in 1929 to two young admirers met at Benedetto Croce's dinner-table.

BRANCATI. R. Ricorda, '"Del dormire con un solo occhio"': Vitaliano Brancati e la scrittura diaristica', *CLett*, 91–92:487–515.

BUFALINO. S. Lazzarin, 'Gesualdo Bufalino: questioni editoriali e interpretative', *Italianistica*, 24, 1995:195–206, prompted by the 1992 Bompiani edition of B.'s *Opere 1981–1988*, concludes that B.'s writing 'rimane in bilico tra circuito culturale "alto" e grande diffusione, tra opposizione al processo di *omologazione finale* e pratiche testuali postmodernistiche omologanti'. L. Cattanei, 'Per la poesia di Gesualdo Bufalino', *ON*, 19.2, 1995:215–22.

BUZZATI. Nella Giannetto, *'Il sudario delle caligini'. Significati e fortune dell'opera buzzatiana*, F, Olschki, 265 pp., is a noteworthy collection from the founder of the Centro Studi Buzzati at Feltre, re-elaborating already published work and adding the unpublished chapters 'Il sudario delle caligini' (9–27), exploring B.'s 'universo simbolico', and 'Paure private, paure collettive, paure di classe nell'immaginario di Dino Buzzati' (105–38), which, highlighting its particular importance in B.'s narrative, seeks to classify the theme of fear 'secondo una tipologia ragionata che giovi ad evidenziarne caratteristiche semantiche e valenze metaforiche e simboliche'. S. Martin, 'Exploding the intertextual: Buzzati and his (?) reader of "I sette messaggeri"', *Italica*, 72, 1995:70–82.

CALVINO. M. M. McLaughlin, 'Words and silence: Calvino criticism 1985–1995', *RoS*:78–105, provides an illuminating guide to work published since the author's death. New book-length studies include: Tommasina Gabriele, **Italo Calvino: Eros and Language*, Toronto, Farleigh Dickinson U.P., 1994, 175 pp.; Marco Belpoliti, **L'occhio di Calvino*, T, Einaudi, xii + 286 pp.; Ulla Musarra-Schroeder, *Il labirinto e la rete. Percorsi moderni e postmoderni nell'opera di Italo Calvino*, Ro, Bulzoni, 226 pp., first discussing C.'s critical thinking in terms of three successive phases and then his fiction according to three corresponding narratological categories: 'il labirinto e la rete', metanarrative experimentation, and what might be termed metaphysical contemplation; and Guido Bonsaver, *Il mondo scritto: forme e ideologia nella narrativa di Italo Calvino*, T, Tirrenia, 298 pp., a systematic analysis, literary-historical, technical-formal, and thematic, of C.'s entire narrative *oeuvre*. Id., '*Il menabò* and the "avanguardie": some observations on the literary debate of the sixties', *ItS*, 50, 1995:86–96, reaffirms that, though he never admitted it, C. was indebted to the 'neoavanguardia' for his development as a writer. R. Chilleri, 'La scrittura di Calvino tra natura e ragione', *StIt*, 12, 1994 [1995]:129–43, tries to define the relation between rationality and the irrational, and between moral earnestness and imagination / play, in C.'s work as a whole. F. Ricci, 'De Chirico city: Calvinian ambulations', *MLR*, 91:78–93, anticipates a book-length study 'demonstrating how his [C.'s] writing often strives to overstep its word-bound limitations by assimilating itself to the painterly arts' and refers particularly to the influence of De Chirico's 'metaphysical' paintings. J. Stephens, 'L'egotista di Grenoble: Calvino e Stendhal', *The Italianist*, 15, 1995:175–212, seeks to pin down Stendhal's pervasive, yet elusive, influence. W. Berger, 'Calvino contra Dumas. Zweimal Montecristo: Von der Providenz zum Dialog', *Italienisch*, 36:18–27, invokes Bakhtin to point the contrast between the ideologically uniform 'monologue' of Dumas's text and C.'s 'polyphonic' rewriting. G. P. Raffa, 'Eco and Calvino reading Dante', *Italica*, 73:388–409, suggests that Eco and Calvino 'may be the postmodern transmitters of the cosmic, encyclopedic impulse that once inspired Dante'. Philippe Daros, **Italo Calvino. Le voyageur dans la carte*, Paris, Hachette, 1994, 288 pp., contains *inter alia* an anthology of C. criticism, including many French contributions, and bibliographies.

For *Il sentiero dei nidi di ragno:* A. Dini, 'Calvino al Premio Riccione 1947', *ParL*, 524–26, 1993 [1994]:33–59. The presence in the Trilogy of numerous elements of 'arte combinatoria' is discussed in K. Becker, 'Kombinatorische Verfahren in Italo Calvinos "Antenati"-Romanen', *RF*, 108: 179–93, while W. Graeber, 'Gravità senza peso: Italo Calvinos *Baron auf den Bäumen*', *Italienisch*, 36: 2–16, reads the work in relation to Calvinian *leggerezza*. G. Nava, 'Calvino interprete di Borges', *ParL*, 532–34, 1994 [1995]: 24–32, takes account of C.'s narrative re-elaboration of Borges (*Le cosmicomiche, Ti con zero, Le città invisibili*), as well as the 1984 lecture on him. B. Ferraro, 'Percorsi narrativi e tracciati temporali nelle *Città invisibili* di Italo Calvino', *Italianistica*, 23, 1994 [1995]: 483–90. F. Ricci, 'The quest for sonship in *Le città invisibili* and "La strada di San Giovanni" by Italo Calvino', *FoI*, 29, 1995: 52–75. H. Felten, 'Italo Calvino: *Il castello dei destini incrociati*. Una lettura plurale', *ItStudien*, 16, 1995: 81–92, reviews (or suggests) contrasting interpretations of the work. J. Usher, 'Calvino and the computer as writer/reader', *MLR*, 90, 1995: 41–54, looks at *Se una notte* as C.'s 'most developed fictional response to the challenge of the literature machine' in the context of his meditation on the computer as a theoretical model. Id., 'From "super-albero" to "iper-romanzo": lexical continuity and constraint in Calvino's *Se una notte d'inverno*', *ItS*, 51: 181–203, interprets the results of applying computer analysis to the work, which show that it is 'characterized by an exceptionally consistent reuse of key words and phrases from one section to another'. L. Barile, 'L'infraordinario in Calvino e Perec', *LItal*, 28: 25–43. M. J. Muratore, 'The reader defied: text as adversary in Calvino's *Se una notte d'inverno un viaggiatore*', *QI*, 15, 1994 [1995]: 111–19, sees 'the increasingly adversarial relationship between artists and their consumers' as the feature distinguishing C.'s text from other examples of 'post-modern self-reflexivity'. P. Kottmann, '*Se una notte d'inverno un viaggiatore:* l'apertura della chiusura', *FoI*, 30: 55–64. M. Belpoliti, 'Il foglio e il mondo. Calvino, lo spazio e la scrittura', *NC*, 41, 1994: 215–42, the second part of an article, focuses on *Palomar*. S. Wright, 'Italo Calvino e la ricerca dell'ordine nella moltiplicità', *ItQ*, 129–30: 59–76, seeks a definition of the structural characteristics of C.'s later works, based on the fragment. H. R. Jauss, 'Il *Monsieur Test* di Valéry e il *Palomar* di Calvino', *Intersezioni*, 16: 73–93. G. Bonsaver, 'Cities of the imagination: traces of Italo Calvino in Jeannette Winterson's fiction', *The Italianist*, 15, 1995: 213–30. See also PARISE, below.

CAMPAILLA. S. Martelli, 'Referenti còlti e immaginario fantastico nella narrativa di Sergio Campailla', *FoI*, 30: 80–91.

CAMPANA. G. Segneri, 'Il Belgio di Campana: il non-luogo dello sguardo recluso', *FoI*, 29, 1995: 286–300. S. Pearce, 'Dino Campana: myth, memory, and the dynamics of poetic creation', *ItS*, 50, 1995: 48–71, studies the mythical framework of the *Canti orfici* and interprets them as 'poetry concerned with the dynamics of poetic creation itself'. G. Boccotti, 'La *Chimera* di Campana e la *Vergine delle rocce* di Leonardo', *StN*, 20, 1993 [1995]:55–71. J.-C. Mileschi, 'Dino Campana: les *Canti Orfici* et la "visione di Grazia"', *REI*, 41, 1995:157–67, shows from the text of the *Canti* how 'madness' and silence are the logical outcome of C.'s quest as poet. E. Pellegrini, 'Dino Campana e la sua immagine: "ciascuno assorto in ciò che formava l'unico senso della sua vita: la sua colpa"', *Luti Vol.*, 287–303. G. Simonetti, 'Su alcuni autografi novecenteschi: Campana e Sereni', *Italianistica*, 24, 1995:119–38, concerns notes on the text of 'La Verna', 'Invetriata' and 'Genova', and 'Le varianti di Sereni "tra sistema chiuso" e tentazione prosastica'.

CAMPANILE. P. L. Cerisola, 'L'umorismo "teatrale" di Achille Campanile', *CLett*, 91–92:415–34.

CAMPO. R. Caira Lumetti, 'Cristina Campo: una sola moltitudine', *ib.*, 649–66.

CAPASSO. E. Villa, 'Aldo Capasso: una presenza poetica del Novecento', *Italianistica*, 22, 1993 [1994]:173–202, traces C.'s *iter*, from the 30s to the 60s, writing poetry in which 'la parola si fa fremito esistenziale oltre ogni retoricità'.

CAPRONI. C Annoni, 'Giorgio Caproni. Poesia come allegoria', Langella, *Canto*, 323–43. S. Bozzola, 'Narratività e intertesto nella poesia di Caproni', *StN*, 20, 1993 [1995]:113–51, takes G. Genot's 'Strutture narrative della poesia lirica' (*ParL*, 212, 1967:35–52) as the cue for an analysis concentrating especially on *Versi livornesi* and *Il conte di Kevenhüller*. L. Surdich, '"In musica + idee": tra Montale e Caproni', *RLI*, 99.3, 1995 [1996]:102–35, purports to be 'il primo e del tutto parziale e provvisorio abbozzo di un parallelo che ... meriterà ulteriori e più organici sondaggi'. Ulrich Fusen, **Akustische Dimensionen und musikalische Parallelen in der Lyrik der 'poeti-musicisti' Eugenio Montale und Giorgio Caproni*, Geneva, Droz, 1995, 342 pp. D. Thompson, '"Genova di tutta la vita": urban landscapes of the soul in the poetry of Giorgio Caproni', Hainsworth, *Italian Poetry*, 71–89. **'Queste nostre zone montane'. Atti del Convegno di studi su Giorgio Caproni (Montebruno, 19–20 giugno 1993)*, ed. Francesco Macciò, Genoa, La Quercia, 1995, 108 pp., gathers papers focusing particularly on the poet's last verse collections in relation to the Val Trebbia as their 'scenario metafisico irrinunciabile'.

CARACCIOLO. L. Parisi, 'Gli scritti giovanili di Alberto Caracciolo', *QI*, 1995 [1996]:81–88, looks at works published between 1941 and 1948 in relation to the late *Religione ed eticità* (1971) and finds fundamental consistency.

CARDARELLI. C. Burdett, 'The success and failure of Cardarelli's neo-classical literary project', *The Italianist*, 15, 1995: 128–49, examines C.'s *prosa d'arte* after *La Ronda*, arguing that in its failed attempt to achieve 'decorous refinement' it exposes the contradictions inherent in the literary ideology of *La Ronda*. A. Benevento, 'Intorno ai carteggi di Vincenzo Cardarelli', *ON*, 19.3–4, 1995: 75–107, looks at the many editions of letters by one of Italy's most prolific 20th-c. epistolographers, for whom letter-writing was 'un'attività vicina e alternativa a quella letteraria, un momento di riflessione e di raccoglimento'.

CASSOLA. G. Manno, 'Cassola neorealista, ovvero tra oggettivismo e mimetismo: un'analisi linguistica della *Ragazza di Bube*', *Versants*, 30: 135–59, confirms C.'s 'tormented' and contradictory relationship with neo-realism: 'evitare di fare il verso alla realtà e allo stesso tempo volerla registrare in modo oggettivo'. Through his *filtraggio* the 'people' emerge linguistically idealized but psychologically demoted.

CATTAFI. V. Puccetti, 'Lettura de *L'osso, l'anima* di Bartolo Cattafi', *CLett*, 91–92: 627–48.

CECOVINI. R. Frattarolo, 'Manlio Cecovini tra memoria e invenzione', *EL*, 20.4, 1995: 73–84. Id., 'Nottole ad Atene', *ib.*, 20.2, 1995: 99–100, briefly discusses the Triestine writer's latest volume.

CELATI. M. Boselli, 'Apparenze e caducità', *NC*, 41, 1994: 253–65, characterizes Celati's *Verso la foce* (1992). C. Nocentini, 'A short story about silence: Celati's *Baratto*', Hunter, *Short Story*, 173–85. See also PARISE, below.

CERONETTI. V. Bezzi, 'Il viaggio di Guido Ceronetti. Un nuovo pellegrinaggio nell'Italia della fine del XX secolo', *StN*, 22, 1995 [1996]: 219–46, examines *Un viaggio in Italia*, whose protagonist undergoes a regenerating 'moderna discesa agli inferi alla ricerca di un'immagine dell'Italia perduta in un passato dai contorni mitici'.

CERRI. S. Martelli, 'Giovanni Cerri e la poesia dialettale molisana', *CLett*, 93: 285–303.

CIALENTE. G. Minghelli, 'L'Africa in cortile: la colonia nelle storie levantine di Fausta Cialente', *QI*, 15, 1994 [1995]: 227–35, considers the oriental 'space' of C.'s *Cortile a Cleopatra* and its function in determining the identity of the characters.

CONTE. A. Meda, 'Il mito nei romanzi di Giuseppe Conte', *StN*, 22, 1995 [1996]: 207–18, explores the Jungian significance of myth in C.'s novels with their search for a way out of the crisis of Western civilization.

CORAZZINI. A. I. Villa, 'Scoperte e recuperi corazziniani', *ON*, 19.6, 1995 [1996]: 93–173, is spin-off from a broader study of Roman 'crepuscolarismo', which will be set in the context of early 20th-c.

neo-idealism; it recontructs C.'s relations with exponents of Rome's poetic fraternity belonging to currents such as neo-mysticism and 'Rinascenza latina'.

D'ARRIGO. G. Alfani, 'Per una definizione di "romanzo monolinguistico": *Horcynus Orca* di Stefano D'Arrigo', *FC*, 19, 1994 [1996]: 393–410. E. Giordano, '*Cima delle nobildonne* di S. D'Arrigo: il volto ambiguo della bellezza', *Italianistica*, 25: 111–18, focuses particular attention of the symbolic figure of Queen Hatshepsut, the adolescent widow of Thutmose II, who became the only woman Pharoah.

D'ARZO. R. Scrivano, 'La "grazia" e le "opere". Metamorfosi di un modello: Bernanos, Lisi, D'Arzo, Pomilio', *ib.*, 22, 1993 [1994]: 237–46, shows how the Italian writers—D'Arzo in 'Casa d'altri' (1952)—radically modify the model of Bernanos's *Journal d'un curé de campagne*.

DE CÉSPEDES. See BANTI, above.

DE CRESCENZO. W. Wehle, 'Einfache Gefühle in schwierigen Verhältnissen. Luciano De Crescenzo: *Croce e delizia*', *Italienisch*, 34, 1995: 78–89, highlights the links with Boccaccio and *La Traviata*: 'Als *burla*, als Schwank, verwendet er [De Crescenzo] die Oper *La Traviata*'.

DE DONNO. O. Macrì, 'Dialetto e poesia in Nicola G. De Donno', *EL*, 21.3: 109–16, illustrates D.'s 'individualismo dialettale' in his use of Salentine.

DELEDDA. S. Briziarelli, 'Woman as outlaw: Grazia Deledda and the politics of gender', *MLN*, 110, 1995: 20–31. G. Sanguinetti Katz, 'Immagini e strutture in un racconto della Deledda', *QI*, 15, 1994 [1995]: 205–15, illustrates D.'s presentation of the family via a detailed examination of 'Battesimi', which she considers a particularly significant text. P. Blelloch, 'Grazia Deledda's and Gavino Ledda's writing on Sardinia: two sides of the same reality', *ItQ*, 125–26, 1995: 47–58, draws a rather generic comparison which she sums up thus: 'half a century later, with full political and social awareness, he [Ledda] condemns the same situation that existed in Deledda's time. The folklore and spiritualism of Deledda have become Ledda's historical and social conscience'.

DEL GIUDICE. M. Bresciani Califano, 'Atlante occidentale: l'oggetto e la forma nascosta', *Luti Vol.*, 405–16.

D'ELIA. 'Il presente, la poesia, la critica: conversazione con Gianni D'Elia', Hainsworth, *Italian Poetry*, 104–20, is an interview given to Emmanuela Tandello in May 1994.

DE LIBERO. R. Esposito Di Mambro, 'Tradizione e innovazione nel sistema espressivo di Libero de Libero', *CLett*, 91–92: 473–85.

G. Salvadori, 'La Ciociaria in *Amore e morte* di Libero de Libero', *ib.*, 90:239–47.

DI GIACOMO.   L. Mirone, 'Le *Novelle napolitane* di Salvatore di Giacomo', *ib.*, 22, 1994:773–91.

DURANTI.   S. W. Vinall, 'The portrayal of the Second World War in the early works of Francesca Duranti and Rosetta Loy', *The Italianist*, 15, 1995:231–47, compares and contrasts two woman novelists whose childhood was overshadowed by the war, with particular reference to their blend of personal and historical material in their first novels, *La bambina* (1976) and *La bicicletta* (1974). S. Lucamante, 'La geometria del romanzo: i "grafici narrativi" di Francesca Duranti', *FoI*, 29, 1995:313–23.

ECO.   S. Debenedetti Stow, 'La teoria della (cor)relatività, ovvero la crociata di Sherlock Eco. (Proposte per l'analisi del testo de *Il nome della rosa* e *Il pendolo di Foucault* di Umberto Eco)', *RStI*, 13.1, 1995:118–50, interprets the texts as a 'discorso sui libri' and on 'i lussuriosi della parola'. K. Ackermann, 'Umberto Ecos *Pendolo di Foucault*: Autobiographie als Metafiktion', *Italienisch*, 36: 28–40, likewise develops an (uncontroversial) general interpretation of the novel. D. W. Landrum, 'Casaubon and the key to all mythologies: the limits of interpretation in *Foucault's Pendulum*', *ItQ*, 125–126, 1995:59–65. 'A colloquio con Umberto Eco. A cura di Thomas Stauder', *Italienisch*, 35:2–13, comprises the salient parts of an interview (1995) devoted to *L'isola del giorno prima*. N. Bouchard, 'Umberto Eco's *L'isola del giorno prima*: postmodern theory and fictional praxis', *Italica*, 72, 1995:193–208, attempts an epistemological and stylistic discussion of E.'s third novel. See also CALVINO, above.

ERBA.   N. Bortolotti, 'L'ultimo Erba', *Testo*, 27, 1994:87–98, analyses *Variar del verde* to show how 'la dimensione ironico-dissacrante che caratterizzava le opere precedenti si affievolisce qui, per lasciar posto a quel sottofondo malinconico e chiaroscurale che costituisce il senso e la ragione della scrittura erbiana'. The neo-baroque element in E.'s poetry is also explored and found to be 'crepuscular', not 'hermetic', in derivation.

FABBRI.   P. Di Sacco, 'Diego Fabbri (1911–1980)', *StN*, 22, 1995 [1996]:7–43, offers a chronologically articulated account of F.'s career as a dramatist.

FENOGLIO, B.   E. Saccone, 'War and peace in Beppe Fenoglio's partisan novels', *MLN*, 111:31–37, concludes that war, for F., is always a war of resistance, not a defence of something positive. P. Cooke, 'The red and the blue: the depiction of the Italian partisan Resistance in Fenoglio's *Il partigiano Johnny*', *MLR*, 91:365–81, shows F. reflecting historical reality with regard to the tensions between Communist and 'autonomous' forces in the Resistance movement.

FENOGLIO, M.   Marisa Fenoglio, *Casa Fenoglio*, Palermo, Sellerio, 1995, 172 pp., written at Marburg, centres first on the matriarchal 'madama Milcare' and her relationship with the city and then on the city itself as revisited by the expatriate authoress.

FERRUCCI.   A. Carrera, 'La nascita del creatore. Un'interpretazione dell'opera narrativa di Franco Ferrucci', *StN*, 20, 1993 [1995]:7–52, offers an overall appreciation of the expatriate's work. R. LaValva, 'Il narratore errante di Franco Ferruccio', *FoI*, 30:351–67.

FIORE.   A. L. Giannone, 'Per una storia della poesia meridionale del '900: *Ero nato sui mari del tonno* di Vittorio Fiore', *CLett*, 90:187–97.

FO.   F. Fido, 'Dario Fo e la Commedia dell'Arte', *Italica*, 72, 1995: 298–306, challenges the commonplace analogy between F. and the *commedia*, emphasizing the political dimension of his work. J. Farrell, 'Fo and Feydeau: is farce a laughing matter?', *ib.*, 307–22, looks at F.'s early one-act farces and defines him as 'guffawing at absurdities that were man-made' with a view to their elimination.

GADDA.   S. Zancanella, 'Rassegna di studi gaddiani 1974–1994', *LItal*, 47, 1995:467–84. R. Colombi, 'Uno "sviluppo possibile": il linguaggio dilatato. Lingua e stile in Carlo Emilio Gadda', *CLett*, 91–92:359–76. C. Fresina, 'C. E. Gadda. Le "bavardage" de l'ingénieur', *REI*, 41, 1995:47–66, taking Roscioni's 1969 monograph as starting point, develops his analysis of G.'s 'epistemology' with closer reference to G.'s narrative *oeuvre*. R. De Lucca, 'Revealed truth and acquired knowledge: considerations on Manzoni and Gadda', *MLN*, 111:58–73, exploring the 'specificity' of literature as defined by the two authors, concludes that G.'s 'resolution of the crisis that led Manzoni to abandon art, as crisis of rationality…, is the realization that all human discourses are mixtures of reality and unreality'. Francesco Mattesini, *Manzoni e Gadda*, Mi, Vita e Pensiero, 86 pp., includes 'Gadda, l'"Apologia manzoniana" e Montale' (31–49) and 'Manzoni e Gadda' (51–74). M. Kleinhans, 'Carlo Emilio Gaddas Kampf zwischen San Giorgio und San Luigi Gonzaga. Versuch einer Symbolanalyse', *ItStudien*, 16, 1995:109–38, explores symbolism in *San Giorgio in casa Brocchi*. A. Sbragia, 'Fear of the periphery: colonialism, class, and the South American outback in Carlo Emilio Gadda', *MLN*, 111:36–57, reflects on G.'s preoccupation with the evil 'periphery' in relation to his spell in Argentina, to Fascism and to *La cognizione del dolore*. Ferdinando Amigoni, *La più semplice macchina: lettura freudiana del 'Pasticciaccio'*, Bo, Il Mulino, 1995, 192 pp., maintains that under a veil of irony G. provides clues to the interpretation of a work whose obscurity is 'estremamente funzionale e solo di superficie' and whose tautology and ludic inconclusiveness are only apparent: particular weight is given to 'Psicologia e letteratura' (1948) and to G.'s assertion in his 1977 interview with Arbasino: 'Alla psicanalisi mi sono avvicinato e ne ho largamente attinto idee e moventi conoscitivi con una intenzione e in una consapevolezza nettamente scientifico-positivistica ...' Amigoni concludes, *inter alia*, that Liliana Balducci is a combination of three Freudian components and that the portrait of Countess Menegazzi is based on a passage of Freud's *Psychopathology*. R. Diaconescu-Blumenfeld, 'Regemination in Gadda's *Pasticciaccio*', *QI*, 16, 1995 [1996]: 117–21, sees the work as shot through with duality, from the 'opposition against which every turn twists' to exploration of 'gender polarity at every level of textuality'. L. Alessandri, 'L'autore nel *Pasticciaccio*', *LS*, 31:79–99, addresses G.'s 'baroque language'. A. Cortellessa, 'I capitoli postumi della *Meccanica* di Carlo Emilio Gadda', *StN*, 20, 1993 [1995]:93–111. L. Caretti, 'Le bandelle di Carlo Emilio Gadda', *StIt*, 11, 1994:121–23, concerns two autobiographical book-cover notes dating from 1957 and 1958. S. Casini, 'Lettere di Carlo Emilio Gadda a Onofrio Martinelli e Adriana Pincherle (1946–1962)', *ib.*, 125–41, publishes a rich batch of missives to Florentine friends, all but one written after G.'s move to Rome.

GAETA. B. Rossi, 'Benedetto Croce e Francesco Gaeta: l'amicizia, la morte e il tentativo di una consacrazione poetica attraverso Guido Gozzano', *CLett*, 90:199–219.

GARRONE. C. Cordié, 'Dino Garrone ed il mito di Cristoforo Colombo (L'Adriatico, il Polo Nord, l'avventura)', *ib.*, 91–92:459–71, is an affectionate evocation of the Novarese writer afflicted by recurring 'ulissismo dannunziano'.

GATTO. E. Ajello, 'Alfonso Gatto, architetto', *Italienisch*, 35:14–26, looks at G.'s articles for *Casabella* in terms both of their content and of their unusual *prosa d'arte* style.

GINZBURG, L. *L'itinerario di Leone Ginzburg*, ed. Nicola Tranfaglia, pref. Norberto Bobbio, T, Bollati Boringhieri, xiv + 111 pp., gathers four papers which illustrate G.'s personality and conspiratorial career, his literary criticism, and his activity as a cultural organizer.

GINZBURG, N. R. Kroll, 'Zur Textualisierung des "ich" in "autobiographischen Texten" von Natalia Ginzburg und Elsa Morante', *Italienisch*, 33, 1995:24–40, studies a literary strategy based on conscious rejection of direct 'confession' and resulting in incomplete self-representation, even with regard to femininity. G. Minghelli, 'Ricordando il quotidiano. *Lessico famigliare* o l'arte del cantastorie', *Italica*, 72, 1995:155–73. B. Carle, 'Natalia Ginzburg's narrative *Voci della sera*', *QI*, 14, 1993 [1995]:239–54, applies Genette in a structural analysis of the text. L. Fontanella, 'Natalia Ginzburg tra finzione e memoria. Una lettura di *Voci della sera* e *Lessico famigliare*', *ParL*, 536–38, 1994 [1996]:133–46.

GIUDICI. R. Zucco, 'Fonti metriche della tradizione nella poesia di Giovanni Giudici', *StN*, 20, 1993 [1995]: 171–208. B. Bartolomeo, 'Giudici e Campanella. Lettura di "Ha poco tempo, lo so, Monsignore"', *ib.*, 153–70, extends the discussion to the whole of 'Fortezza' and 'Frate Tommaso' to highlight 'un gioco compositivo in bilico tra letteraria allusività del linguaggio poetico e le sue proprietà risemantizzanti'.

GOZZANO. M. A. Morettini Bura, 'Gozzano post-moderno', Langella, *Canto*, 193–205. R. Carnero, 'L'altrove esotico nelle poesie di Guido Gozzano', *ON*, 19.1, 1995: 177–93, shows how the '*bric-à-brac esotico*' of G.'s poetic imagination survives contact with reality more or less intact: 'sembra che il Gozzano non abbia imparato nulla di più di quanto già sapeva prima di partire. Egli in Oriente cerca delle conferme, rifiuta il reale quando non coincide con l'attesa'. Id., 'L'India di Guido Gozzano e l'India di Hermann Hesse: appunti per un confronto', *RLMC*, 48, 1995: 57–84, finds much to contrast, as well as to compare, between the authors of *Verso la cuna del mondo* and *Aus Indien*. P. Fasano, 'Il bello stile negli esili versi. Colloqui con Dante di Guido Gozzano', *RLI*, 98.3, 1994 [1995]: 5–29, dilates acutely on G.'s parodistic borrowing from Dante, which he owed to the mediation of D'Annunzio and Pascoli, 'depositari' of the early 20th-c. classicizing *koiné*, but from which he returned to the original 'sacred texts' of Italian poetry. Hence, 'il meccanismo della parodia si fa, per così dire, esponenziale...' through a re-use of D'Annunzio's *dantismi* which consciously refers to both authors. M. Sarnelli, 'Una lettera inedita di Guido Gozzano ad Arturo Onofri e addenda sul cinema. (Testimonianze di A. Varaldo, N. Oxilia e A. Guglielminetti)', *ib.*, 99.1–2, 1995: 159–67, edits a letter of 1908 responding to Onofri's *Poemi tragici*; also discusses and documents the contrasting ways in which intellectuals close to him viewed the advent of the cinematograph: all, however, variously reflect an elitist conception of culture and its 'fruitori'. M. Masoero, 'Una "sommossa" studentesca di inizio secolo: Guido Gozzano e compagni', *StP*, 25: 423–31, concerns an episode that occurred at G.'s *liceo* at Savigliano in 1903.

GRAMSCI. C. Di Frede, 'Gramsci e il meccanico gioco d'altri tempi', *ON*, 19.6, 1995 [1996]: 183–92, concerns the imprisoned G.'s purchase (1928) of the most prestigious toy of the day, a Hornby Meccano, for his son Delio, and his subsequent doubts as to its value because of its 'American' and middle-class connotations.

GUERRA. S. Corsi, 'Tonino Guerra, un suo *Avviso* e l'ὑπερα-ποθνήσκειν', *ON*, 19.1, 1995: 227–31, proposes interpreting G.'s 'Piròun' (in the late prose 'Du masnóin da cafè) in terms of the classical conception of ὑπεραποθνήσκειν.

GUIDACCI. C. O'Brien, 'The poetic world of Margherita Guidacci', Hainsworth, *Italian Poetry*, 90–102.

JOVINE. F. D'Episcopo, 'L'effetto Pirandello nella narrativa di Francesco Jovine', *CLett*, 90:171–85.

LA CAVA. A. Piromalli, 'Mario La Cava nella letteratura nazionale', *ib.*, 91–92:559–67.

LANDOLFI. R. Scrimieri, '*La biere du pecheur*: una poetica della *accidia*', *LS*, 31:267–91, shows how the narrator's *accidia* determines distinctive formal aspects of the Landolfi novel, such as its fragmentariness and the use of *innesti*. These transform the text into the vehicle for its own interpretation. D. Patrignani, '"Il Malinconico scialacquatore": il motivo della dissipazione nella narrativa di Tommaso Landolfi', *CLett*, 91–92:517–37. B. Stasi, '"Un che di sposato alla vita": Landolfi e D'Annunzio', *ib.*, 539–57. C. Crepaldi, 'Un caso di ipertestualità in Landolfi', *LS*, 30, 1995:597–604, shows there to be a close semantic and structural parallel between L.'s *Il nuovo mausoleo* and Gogol's *The Overcoat*, which L. had translated.

LEDDA. C. Testa, 'Ledda's *Padre padrone*: from the *Bildungsroman* to the novel of superfluousness', *FoI*, 30:103–26. See also DELEDDA, above.

LEVI, C. D. Sperduto, 'Modificazioni cronologiche nel *Cristo si è fermato a Eboli*', *EL*, 20.2, 1995:89–93, suggests that 'absence of time' in L.'s Lucania and the chronological liberties he takes in his account of *confino* there are interrelated. L. Baldassaro, '*Paura della libertà*: Carlo Levi's unfinished preface', *Italica*, 72, 1995:143–54. C. A. Schweizer, 'Carlo Levis Reise durch "der Linden Doppelnacht"', *ASNS*, 147, 1995:81–103, focuses on the image of Germany presented in *La doppia notte dei tigli* (1959).

LEVI, P. Mirna Cicioni, *Primo Levi: Bridges of Knowledge*, Oxford, Berg, xv + 222 pp., provides an excellent comprehensive introduction to Levi: clear, concise and sensitive to the Jewish context, the literary dimension and the tensions at the heart of his writing. A. Sempoux, 'Une approche de Primo Levi', pp. 95–99 of *La Littérature des camps* (unnumbered special issue of *LR*, 1995). D. M. Sachs, 'The language of judgment: Primo Levi's *Se questo è un uomo*', *MLN*, 110, 1995:755–84, makes shrewd observations on the work's 'shifting voices and temporal multiplicity' and under the heading 'Intellectual resistance'. S. Nezri, 'Primo Levi: un conflitto tra memoria e letteratura', *StP*, 24, 1995:347–53, compares L.'s testimony on Auschwitz with that of Jean Samuel to highlight in Levi the element of literary elaboration which he eventually came to view with pessimism. E. Neppi, 'Sopravvivenza e vergogna in Primo Levi', *StCrit*, 11:419–50, sees the question 'why have I survived?' as the *filo rosso* running all the way through L.'s *œuvre*, which is thus viewed essentially as an apologia. On the same basis, A. Finco, 'Primo Levi: lo spettro di Auschwitz', *RStI*, 12.2, 1994 [1995]:54–60, shows no hesitation in ascribing L.'s death to suicide. G. Farinelli, 'Primo Levi e la difesa dell'uomo umano: quale insegnamento?', *ON*, 19.1, 1995:147–66, reflects on *Se questo* and its message for the present day.

LISI. For his *Diario di un parroco di campagna* (1942), see D'ARZO, above.

LOI. Franco Loi, **Diario breve. Scritti sulla poesia e sulla letteratura*, Forlì, Nuova Compagnia, 1995, 77 pp. 'Poesia e dialetto: conversazione con Franco Loi', Hainsworth, *Italian Poetry*, 122–36, is the text of an interview with Emmanuela Tandello.

LORIA. R. Scrivano, 'L'identità sconosciuta. Note per un ritratto di Arturo Loria', *CLett*, 91–92:443–58. M. Marchi, 'Uno scrittore "disperso e inascoltato": Arturo Loria', in Id., *Palazzeschi e altri sondaggi*, 189–214 (see PALAZZESCHI, below).

LOY. H. H. Wetzel, 'Rosetta Loy: *Sogni d'inverno* (1992)', *Italienisch*, 34, 1995:32–40, on the basis of *Sogni d'inverno*, finds the secret of L.'s success to lie in her shrewd dosage of ingredients such as historical analysis, nostalgia, and 'plasticity' of imagination, plus a measure of *kitsch*. F. Brizio Skov, 'Rosetta Loy e Lalla Romano: ritratto di due scrittrici contemporanee', *RStI*, 14.2:206–11, briefly defines the two writers from a feminist perspective. See also DURANTI, above.

LUZI. G. Rogante, 'La poesia di Mario Luzi: dal canto al frammento', Langella, *Canto*, 309–21. N. Caranica, *Capire Luzi, Ro, Nuova Universale Studium, 1995, 288 pp. S. Pastore, 'Ripetizione e disgiunzione nella poesia di Mario Luzi', *Italianistica*, 23, 1994 [1995]:491–520. G. Singh, 'Tradizione e modernità nella poesia di Luzi', *ib.*, 22, 1993 [1994]: 247–62. B. Carle, 'Mario Luzi's pictorial *poesis*: *Avvento notturno* (1940) and *Viaggio terrestre e celeste di Simone Martini* (1994)', *Italica*, 73:66–82. M. Fabbri, 'Stare a Sinesio come Sinesio sta a Ipazia', *CLett*, 91–92:569–85, addresses L.'s *Libro di Ipazia*. C. O'Brien, 'A reading of Mario Luzi's "Oscillano le fronde" and "Vola alta, parola"', Hainsworth, *Italian Poetry*, 156–65. G. Fontana, 'Parole, silenzi. Su "Nel corpo oscuro della metamorfosi" di Mario Luzi', *StCrit*, 10, 1995:143–71, studies the genesis of the *poemetto* with the help of Pavia MSS, which are edited in an appendix: the creative process is seen as taking on the character of a 'rito di purificazione della parola'. Id., 'Il teorema e il testo. Appunti su Luzi traduttore di Mallarmé', *ib.*, 417–53.

MAGRELLI. V. Zeiler, '"Getto e pollone delle tenebre". I percorsi poetici dell'io nelle poesie di Valerio Magrelli', *ItStudien*, 17:201–30, examines each of M.'s three verse collections in turn before offering an overview of their themes, only to confirm conclusions already commonplace in Italy. P. Hainsworth, 'Three poems by Valerio

Magrelli', Hainsworth, *Italian Poetry*, 166–81, samples each of the three collections *Ora serrata retinae*, *Nature e venature*, and *Esercizi di tiptologia*.

MAGRIS. E. Guagnini, '*Le voci* di Claudio Magris. Ideologia e tecnica di un racconto', *ib.*, 27–34, seeks the antecedents and essential features of this short-story study of telephonic communication.

MALAPARTE. G. Luti, 'Le due "tecniche" di Malaparte', *RLI*, 98.3, 1994 [1995]: 30–37, compares M.'s original *Technique du coup d'état* (Paris 1931) and the 1948 Italian edition, where the work underwent considerable (but little appreciated) restructuring attributable to changed circumstances and to the evolution of M.'s political views. Id., 'Il sangue di Malaparte', *CLett*, 91–92: 399–414, concerns the short-story collection *Il sangue* (1937). W. De Nunzio Schilardi, 'Bambini vittime ed eroi nella *Pelle* di Curzio Malaparte', *ib.*, 93: 271–84.

MALDINI. R. Behrens, 'Konstruierte Heimat, mild ironisch. Sergio Maldinis Roman *La casa a nord-est* und der italienische Mythos von Mitteleuropa', *Italienisch*, 34, 1995: 10–30, analyses the 1991 novel against the background of the Italian 'myth' of Central Europe and in terms of the contrast between 'italianità' and a 'nordic' frontier otherness set in Friuli.

MALERBA. C. E. Trevisan, 'Il segreto de *Il pianeta azzurro* di Luigi Malerba', *QI*, 14, 1993: 57–73, shows how what at first seems merely a *giallo* turns out to be an enigmatic intrigue developing social, moral, and philosophical issues, and finally acquires a metanarrative dimension. Margherita Heyer-Caput, **Per una letteratura della riflessione: elementi filosofico-scientifici nell'opera di Luigi Malerba*, Bern, Haupt, 1995, 324 pp.

MANGANELLI. M. Mari, 'Evoluzione del *Discorso sopra la difficoltà di comunicare coi morti* di Giorgio Manganelli', *StN*, 22, 1995 [1996]: 173–97, compares the four MS drafts of the *Discorso* preserved at Pavia with each other and with the published text.

MARAINI. G. Sumeli Weinberg, 'La forza della negatività: la dialettica del soggetto parlante nella *Lunga vita di Marianna Ucrìa* di Dacia Maraini', *ON*, 19.3–4, 1995: 177–86, shows how in the novel, 'ad ogni fase di approfondimento dell'io femminile, il discorso dell'autrice entra in rapporto dialettico con la storia vista nel suo insieme di fenomeni socio-culturali che hanno condizionato la realtà della donna fino ai giorni nostri'. G. Santagostino, '*La lunga vita di Marianna Ucrìa*: tessere la memoria sotto lo sguardo delle chimere', *Italica*, 73: 410–28. R. Galle, 'Archaisierendes Erinnern. Zu Dacia Marainis *Bagheria*', *Italienisch*, 34, 1995: 58–77, reflects on the nature of the 'remembered self' present in the foreground of the work but only sketched through fragmentary reminiscences. Also on M.'s feminism: Barbara Heinzius, *Feminismus oder Pornographie? Zur Darstellung von Erotik und Sexualität im Werk Dacia Marainis*, St Ingbert, Röhrig, 1995, xix + 430 pp., and A. Forti-Lewis, 'Virginia Woolf, Dacia Maraini e *Una stanza per voi*: l'autocoscienza politica e il testo', *RStI*, 12.2, 1994 [1995]: 29–47. D. Cavallaro, '*I sogni di Clitennestra*: the *Oresteia* according to Dacia Maraini', *Italica*, 72: 340–55, sees M.'s play as exemplifying women writers' attempt to modernize and transform Aeschylus's trilogy.

MATTIONI. G. Baroni, 'La recente narrativa di Stelio Mattioni', *ON*, 19.5, 1995: 183–200, focuses mainly on *Il mondo di Celso* but also situates M. in relation to Triestine predecessors and contemporaries. There is also (193–200) a valuable bibliography compiled by A. Rondini.

MENGHINI. Remo Fasani, *Felice Menghini: poeta, prosatore e uomo di cultura*, Chur, Pro Grigioni Italiano—Locarno, Dadò, 1995, 253 pp., includes a selection of M.'s work as well as Fasani's critical essay.

MICHELSTAEDTER. *Sotto il segno di Michelstaedter. Il valore di una identità*, ed. Toni Iermano, Cosenza, Periferia, 1994, 111 pp. S. Campailla, 'Le immagini della persuasione', *CLett*, 91–92: 329–36.

MONTALE. R. Orlando, 'Il "razionalismo" di Montale fra Bergson e Šestov', *ASNP*, 24, 1994 [1995]: 973–1012, pursuing M.'s fundamental philosophical positions, highlights the importance of Lev Šestov's critique of Bergson and holds that M. 'si sia arroccato su una linea sostanzialmente post-kantiana, razionalistica, se si vuole, di fronte a cui le tentazioni del vitalismo e dell'irrazionalismo bergsoniano non hanno cessato di esercitare i loro ammalianti influssi, ma pur sempre come impossibile evasione'. P. Zoboli, 'Il "recto" e il "verso" del libro poetico di Montale', Langella, *Canto*, 269–87. E. Vineis, 'Variantistica e parole-chiavi: accertamenti montaliani', *LS*, 30, 1995: 283–92, starting from L. Rosiello's 1965 *Analisi statistica* quantifying M.'s 'parole-temi', examines variants in poems from *Ossi*, *Occasioni*, and *Bufera* which tend to confirm Rosiello's findings. V. Pacca, '"La foce del Bisagno": un'immagine montaliana', *RLettI*, 12, 1994 [1996]: 429–40, explores the links between M., Anna degli Uberti, the Bisagno estuary where they would meet (1919–23), and its significance in M.'s poetry as a symbol of life's deathward movement. F. Bausi, 'Una donna di Montale: Esterina', *StIt*, 12, 1994 [1995]: 119–27, concerns links with the poetry of Zanella, Poliziano, and Marradi, as well as the figure of Esterina. L. Blasucci, 'Livelli figurali di "Casa sul mare" (Montale, *Ossi di seppia*)', *Italianistica*, 22, 1993 [1994]: 133–44. E. Bonora, 'Dagli *Ossi di seppia* a *Le occasioni*. Lettere di Montale a Debenedetti', *GSLI*, 173: 348–91, edits 17 letters and postcards (1923–28) with an introductory essay tracing the complex transition from *Ossi* to *Le occasioni*. Eugenio Montale, *Le occasioni*, ed. Dante Isella, T, Einaudi, xvii + 249 pp. E. Giachery, 'Riflessioni interpretative su passi montaliani', *CLett*, 91–92: 377–91, concerns poems in *Le occasioni*. L. Greco, 'Strutture formali ed emergenza storica: ancora su "A Liuba che parte" di Eugenio Montale', *FoI*, 30:320–31. C. Scarpati, 'Due varianti montaliane', *ib.*, 393–97. E. Rovegno, **Per entrar nel buio. Lettura di Finisterre di Eugenio Montale*, Genoa, ECIG, 1994. G. Borghello, 'Il sicomoro di Montale', *Italianistica*, 22, 1993 [1994]:145–52. R. Orlando, 'Tema e *imagery* di *Tempo e tempi* (Montale, *Satura*)', *ASNP*, 24, 1994:439–54. É. Ó Ceallacháin, 'Montale's retreat: the home as privileged poetic space in *Diario del '71 e del '72* and *Quaderno di quattro anni*', Hainsworth, *Italian Poetry*, 52–70. On interrelated poems (April 1971 and February 1972) of the *Diario*: P. Zanotti, 'A proposito del "Re pescatore"', *Italianistica*, 24, 1995:139–52, shows how, in the process of composition, '"Kingfisher" è diventato qualcosa come un "Re pescatore" a prospettiva rovesciata ... ed è per questo motivo che ha assunto un nome allusivo e comprensibile solo alla luce della poesia precedente'. Also for the *Diario*: M. Martelli, 'Biglietto d'auguri', *Luti Vol.*, 37–42. É. Ó Ceallacháin, '"Non qui scuola di canto": Montale's late versions of Yeats', *ItS*, 50, 1995:72–85, re-examines Montale's renderings of 'When you are old', 'Sailing to Byzantium', and 'After long silence'. C. Di Biase, '*Diario postumo. Oltre la soglia. Nel centenario della nascita di Montale* (1896–1996)', *EL*, 21.3:21–32. F. De Rosa, 'Note sulla più recente critica montaliana', *Italianistica*, 24, 1995:171–90, taking its cue from Pietro Cataldo's *Montale* (Palermo 1991), usefully addresses the new tendencies apparent in M. criticism in the early 1990s. *Una dolcezza inquieta. L'universo poetico di Eugenio Montale*, Mi, Electa, 259 pp., is the catalogue of a centenary exhibition held at Genoa and Milan. G. Giudici, 'Oltre Montale', *LItal*, 48:521–26, reflects briefly on the significance of the centenary. L. Pisanello, 'La "collaborazione" Montale-Furst', *StN*, 20, 1993 [1995]:73–91, sheds further light on M.'s relations (discussed by M. Soldati in *Rami secchi*, 1989) with the American whom M. engaged to write for him. R. Bettarini, 'Montale: "carissima signora (non però Signora) ..."', *StIt*, 15:115–38, presents a series of brief missives sent her by M. in 1979–80 while, with G. Contini, she was working on the critical edition of M.'s verse (Turin 1980). See also GADDA, above.

MORANTE. B. Marx, 'Zwischen Pseudographie und Selbstinszenierung: zu Elsa Morante', *Italienisch*, 35:28–43, interprets M.'s narrative strategy as tending toward the creation of a narrative voice beyond the gender divide and the barrier of sexual differentiation. M. A. McDonald Carolan, 'The missing mother: procreation vs creation in Morante's early fiction', *RStI*, 13.1, 1995:100–17, from the short stories of *Il gioco segreto*, argues that M. 'subverts the biological, productive function of the female in order to elevate the creative power of woman'. R. LaValva, 'Sortilegi della menzogna: *Wuthering Heights* e Emily Bronte', *ItQ*, 123–24, 1995:49–59, sees a case of 'memoria letteraria profonda' in the evident affinity between *Menzogna e sortilegio* and *Wuthering Heights*. F. Siddell, 'Jottings and jewels in Elsa Morante's *Alibi*', *FoI*, 29, 1995:91–102. M. Ferrecchia, '*L'isola di Arturo* e *Aracoeli* di E. Morante. Due stili, un linguaggio', *CLett*, 91–92:587–610. *StN*, 21, 1994 [1995], is given over to the 17 conference papers *Vent'anni dopo 'La storia': omaggio a Elsa Morante*, ed. Concetta D'Angeli and Giacomo Magrini. Ranging across M.'s whole output, they include notably: P. V. Mengaldo, 'Spunti per un'analisi linguistica dei romanzi di Elsa Morante' (11–36); G. Magrini, 'Gli specialisti originari' (37–51); G. Nava, 'Il *Gioco segreto* di Elsa Morante: i modi del racconto' (53–78); and C. Garboli, 'Le finte lettere di Anna' (149–74), written also as the introduction to a new Einaudi edition of *Menzogna e sortilegio*. Two contributions extend to Pasolini: M. Fusillo, '"Credo nelle chiacchiere dei barbari". Il tema della barbarie in Elsa Morante e in Pier Paolo Pasolini' (97–129), and W. Siti, 'Elsa Morante nell'opera di Pier Paolo Pasolini' (131–48). See also GINZBURG, N., above.

MORAVIA. Renzo Paris, *Moravia. Una vita controvoglia*, F, Giunti, 378 pp., an anecdotal 'life' from one of M.'s friends, widely incorporates the testimony of other acquaintances and of M.'s sister. Documentation of particular interest are the score of letters to Adriana Pincherle and an unpublished 'taccuino' of Leonetta Cecchi Pieraccini.

MORETTI. Marino Moretti–Giuseppe Prezzolini, **Carteggio 1920–1977*, ed. Michele Ferrario, Ro, Ediz. di Storia e Letteratura–Dipartimento dell'Istruzione e Cultura del Cantone Ticino, 1995, xiv + 202 pp. See also PALAZZESCHI, below.

MORSELLI. R. Rinaldi, 'I romanzi a una dimensione di Guido Morselli', *CLett*, 91–92:667–91.

NEGRI. M. G. Bajoni, 'Due lettere inedite di Ada Negri', *Testo*, 29–30, 1995:198–201, transcribes from the MSS brief missives (1912 and 1913) from N. to her publisher Emilio Treves. Salvatore Gennaro, **Una piccola amicizia di Ada Negri*, Olgiate Olona, Grafica Olona, 1995, 83 pp. A. Gorini Santoli, *Invito alla lettura di Ada Negri*, Mi, Mursia, 1995, 208 pp.

ONOFRI. Massimo Maggiari, 'Palingenesi e sogno nel primo Onofri', *QI*, 15, 1994:197–203, briefly explores theme and image in the 'crepuscular' *Liriche* (1907).

ORENGO. In Stefania Lucamante, 'Intervista con Nico Orengo', *RStI*, 14.2:138–51, the author discusses *inter alia* each of his novels.

OXILIA. Giuseppe Farinelli, 'Nino Oxilia', *CLett*, 91–92:337–58, reappraises the poetry of Gozzano's 'crepuscular' friend.

PALAZZESCHI. A. Dei, 'Moretti e Palazzeschi: una sconosciuta recensione a *Lanterna*', *StIt*, 14, 1995:177–81, presents and reproduces Moretti's brief review (October 1907) which, unlike that of *Cavalli bianchi* which appeared a year earlier, has escaped scholarly attention. It groups P. with other *crepuscolari* under the labels 'poeti esotici' and 'giovanissimi decadenti italiani' three years before G. A. Borgese coined the expression *poesia crepuscolare*. S. Pegoraro, 'La poesia-teatro di Aldo Palazzeschi', *FC*, 19, 1994 [1996]:447–62. Marco Marchi, *Palazzeschi e altri sondaggi*, F, Le Lettere, 333 pp., opens with three pieces on P.: 'La parabola di Perelà' (17–56), for a somewhat longer version of which see 'Palazzeschi. Storia del *Codice di Perelà*', *Luti Vol.*, 223–54; 'Palazzeschi, Teresa e Carolina. Lettura di *Sorelle Materassi*' (57–97), also published as 'Lettura di *Sorelle Materassi*', *RLI*, 100.1:60–85; and 'Il Codice e il Doge. Note al testo a due edizioni' (99–127). C. Papini, 'Un racconto dimenticato: *Madre* di Aldo Palazzeschi', *RLI*, 98.3, 1994 [1995]:126–29, reprints from the magazine where it appeared in 1950 a short story not previously reproduced. See also SABA, below.

PAPINI, G. See ALERAMO, above.

PAPINI, G. A. M. Martelli, 'Le *Vanità* di Gianni A. Papini', *Versants*, 27, 1995:41–65, offers readings of selected poems from *Tutte le vanità* and also of 'Addio sul Lemano', which was separately published in *Cenobio* in 1994.

PARISE. Raffaele Manica, Silvio Perella, and Fabio Pierangeli, *'Né un'astronave né un destino'. Calvino, Parise, Celati*, Ro, Nuova Cultura, 1995, 197 pp., collects contributions all devoted to P. except for F. Pierangeli, 'Italo Calvino tra incipit e finali' (9–60): Id., 'Le tracce madreperlacee della memoria nei *Sillabari*' (61–80); R. Manica, 'Occasioni per Parise' (81–110), also on P.'s relations with Celati; S. Perrella, '*Sillabari*' (111–117); Id., 'L'ultimo Parise' (119–27); and Id., 'L'inutile impresa e la grata sorpresa dei *Sillabari*' (129–34).

PARRONCHI. L. Baldacci, 'Parronchi poeta', *RLI*, 99.1–2, 1995:46–57, offers a sensitive and critically sophisticated overview of P.'s career as a poet. R. Capek Habekovic, 'The horizontal lyricism of Parronchi's *Pietà dell'atmosfera* and *Il rispetto della natura*', *RStI*, 14.2:213–22, compares two collections (1970 and 1990 respectively) that in different ways continue the emphasis on 'the drama of human existence' with which, in the 1950s, P. turned his back on his initial hermeticism.

PASINETTI. C. Della Coletta, 'Historiographic metafiction: P. M. Pasinetti's *Melodramma*', *QI*, 15, 1994:121–36, with L. Hutcheon sees the postmodern historical novel as raising questions about the cognitive status of both fictional and historical knowledge. *Melodramma* (1993) 'initiates a dialogue between fiction and reality ... a non-conclusive, contradictory discussion that ... problematizes our relation to the world and the forms in which we inscribe it'. The same scholar, 'Il teatro della storia e il mondo del romanzo: *Melodramma* di P. M. Pasinetti', *StN*, 20, 1993 [1995]: 237–62, stresses the 'three-act' work's 'fluttuante e corale oralità' and the presence in it of multiple perspectives and temporal dimensions which subvert the 'teleological linearity' of historical discourse.

PASOLINI. M. Nota, 'Charmes frioulans de Pier Paolo Pasolini', *Versants*, 30: 105–34, defines P.'s work in Friulan as 'poésie archaïque-contemporaine, s'inscrivant effectivement dans le cadre italo-euro-péen moderne, par ses contenus, mais se rattachant également à la tradition du *trobar clus* provençal, par le choix de la langue'. A stimulating commentary, in terms of 'sdoppiamento', on selected poems from the 1974 revised edition of the Friulan collection is afforded by Jean-Michel Gardair, *Narciso e il suo doppio. Saggio su 'La nuova gioventù' di Pasolini*, Ro, Bulzoni, 168 pp. G. Magrini, 'Pasolini, Spitzer, Bertolucci: *Recit* senza accento', *ParL*, 536–38, 1994 [1996]: 19–34, reads the Pasolini poem in relation to Spitzer's analysis of the 'récit de Théramène' in *Phèdre* and notes Pasolinian influence in Bertolucci's 'Discendendo il colle'. J. Wöhl, ' "Un amaro scherzo shakespeariano". Anmerkungen zu Pier Paolo Pasolinis Gedicht "In morte del realismo"', *Italienisch*, 33, 1995: 58–73, illustrates a characteristic use of intertextuality with reference to the *Divina Commedia* (in 'Divina Mimesis') as well as to Shakespeare's *Julius Caesar*. R. Gordon, 'Rhetoric and irony in Pasolini's late poetry', Hainsworth, *Italian Poetry*, 138–55. Id., 'Identity in mourning: the role of the intellectual and the death of Pasolini', *ItQ*, 123–24, 1995: 61–74. E. Capodaglio, 'Congetture sugli Appunti di *Petrolio*', *StCrit*, 11: 331–67. Giuseppe Zigaina, *Hostia. Trilogia della morte di Pier Paolo Pasolini*, Venice, Marsilio, 1995, xxxii + 463 pp., completes a 20-year 'analisi "linguistica" della morte di Pasolini', defined as 'morte sacrificale ... a valorizzazione semantica (retroattiva) dell'ope-ra', by bringing together Zigaina's numerous writings on the subject (see also *YWMLS*, 56: 613). Anglo-Saxon, and especially North-American, interest in P. shows no sign of abating. Recent monographs include: Thomas E. Peterson, **The Paraphrase of an Imaginary Dialogue: the Poetics and Poetry of Pier Paolo Pasolini*, NY, Lang, 1994, 356 pp.; Sam Rohdie, **The Passion of Pier Paolo Pasolini*, Bloomington, Indiana U.P.—London, British Film Institute, 1995, 230 pp; and David Ward, *A Poetics of Resistance: Narrative and the Writings of Pier Paolo Pasolini*, Cranbury, N.J., Associated University Presses, 1995, 215 pp., systematically works through P.'s fiction from the Friulan novels to

Petrolio before proceeding to the theoretical writings, the journalism and the verse tragedies. Ward finds in P. an underlying tension between the 'epistemological' (i.e. cognitive) and 'performative' functions of narrative, and stresses P.'s ideologically motivated resistance to conventional narrative codes buttressing bourgeois hegemony. M. Marchi, 'Suggestioni da descrizioni. Il saggismo poetico dell'ultimo Pasolini', in Id., *Palazzeschi e altri sondaggi*, 235–81 (see PALAZZESCHI, above) and in **Antologia Vieusseux*, 1995. See also MORANTE, above.

PATTI. P. Giannantonio, 'Ercole Patti, tra cronaca e invenzione', *Italianistica*, 22, 1993 [1994]:157–72, dwells on the diaristic dimension in the narrative work of this 'ulisside della vita e vagabondo della penna'.

PAVESE. G. Davico, 'Luoghi pavesiani oggi: Brancaleone', *StP*, 24, 1995:83–91, documents P.'s period of *confino* in Calabria. M. Brunetta, 'Pavese lettore nella biblioteca del Collegio Trevisio di Casale Monferrato', *StN*, 22, 1995 [1996]:47–84, highlights the importance of P.'s readings in myth and anthropology, as attested by Father G. Baravalle and by P. himself in *Il mestiere*, for the *Dialoghi con Leucò* and his subsequent development in general. P. M. Prosio, 'Pavese, la guerra, la fede: per una lettura autobiografica della *Casa in collina*', *ON*, 19.3–4, 1995:109–25, while noting the external *dis*similarities between the stories of Pavese and Corrado in the period September 1943–November 1944, seeks to confirm the autobiographical status of Corrado in relation to the two key moments of P.'s life at that time: non-participation in the Resistance and religious involvement at the Collegio Trevisio. The pro-Fascist comments of the 1943–44 *taccuino* published in *La Stampa* in 1990 are therefore (wrongly, in my view) dismissed as 'momenti di umore, sfoghi immediati, estemporanei appunti', so that the guilt-stricken Corrado of the 1948 novel can represent the P. of that earlier period. C. Cortinovis, 'L'architettura dei *Dialoghi con Leucò*', *Testo*, 27, 1994:67–86, explores the internal organization and overall sense of the dialogues with the help of the various indexes devised by P. during their composition. D. De Camilli, 'Cesare Pavese e i nomi dei personaggi', *Italianistica*, 22, 1993 [1994]:211–36, conducts a detailed review of P.'s choice of names for his characters to find that, almost in spite of his allusive intentions, P. 'pescò nella realtà': hence, 'l'esperienza narrativa di P. può servire a testimoniare che l'*interpretatio nominis* ha perso parte della sua applicabilità nella letteratura contemporanea'.

PIERRO. E. Giachery, 'Madre mortale e madre immortale: un memorabile "ritorno" di Albino Pierro', *ib.*, 22, 1993 [1994]:263–71. M. Veglia, 'Poesia di Lucania. Una testimonianza su Albino Pierro',

SPCT, 51, 1995:175–86, elaborates on the paradoxes of P.'s dialect poetry, arguing that the Tursi dialect and memories of Lucania do not alone account for the high quality of the verse: the conversion to dialect was 'l'accertarsi e il radicarsi di quanto le preesisteva' in P.'s Italian verse, and 'saranno le poesie italiane ad offrirci la spiegazione della conversione stessa e del carattere, che ne discese, delle parole di Tursi'. G. Jovine, 'Nascita della poesia dialettale di Albino Pierro', *CLett*, 90:249–69. F. Zambon, 'Albino Pierro "nella gabbia del mondo". Appunti su *Nun c'è pizze di munne*', *StN*, 22, 1995 [1996]:159–72. 'Sei voci su Albino Pierro', ed. Alfredo Stussi, *ASNP*, 24, 1994 [1995]:939–72, are the proceedings of a round table (Pisa 1993) on P.'s poetry, with contributions by L. Blasucci, T. Bolelli, M. Feo, G. Nencioni and A. Roncaglia, and a brief conclusion from Stussi himself.

PIOVENE.   A. M. Mutterle, 'Attenzione, distrazione, stramberia ne *La vedova allegra*', *StN*, 22, 1995 [1996]:143–58, characterizes the 1931 short-story collection.

PIRANDELLO.   P. Di Sacco, 'Rassegna pirandelliana (1988–1993): edizioni e studi', *Testo*, 26, 1993 [1994]:106–27. Id., 'Aggiornamenti pirandelliani: le *Novelle per un anno*, il teatro e i "miti", Marta Abba, la retorica umoristica', *ON*, 19.1, 1995:235–56, selects and discusses recent contributions with a view to identifying some of the main trends in P. studies. V. Paladino, 'L'"altrove" di Pirandello', *ib.*, 19.6, 1995 [1996]:53–69, seeks to demonstrate, with reference to many texts, a lifelong drive on the part of P. to transcend contingency. A. Ciccarelli, 'Appunti su Pirandello e la tradizione', *EL*, 20.1, 1995:51–70, sees the presence of Ariosto in *Così è, se vi pare*, of Leopardi in *Il giuoco delle parti*, and of Dante, Leopardi, and Manzoni in *Il fu Mattia Pascal*. M. L. Patruno, 'Pirandello critico. Il *Discorso* su Giovanni Verga', *CLett*, 90:221–37. Paola Daniela Giovanelli, *Dicendo che hanno un corpo. Saggi pirandelliani*, Modena, Mucchi, 1994, 620 pp., gathers mainly unpublished material to form a highly structured overall interpretation programmatically based on the intention to 'commentare Pirandello con il solo Pirandello' (and in fact co-ordinating an impressive range of internal references within the whole corpus of P.'s writings) but also inspired by Gino Gori's theory of the grotesque.

Independently of this, and invoking Bachelard's comment on man's 'besoin d'animaliser' and the new vogue of the bestiary from the turn of the century, E. Bacchereti, 'L'"animalesca filosofia". Appunti per un "bestiario" pirandelliano', *Luti Vol.*, 161–91, explores P.'s zoomorphic imagery in his short stories. Giancarlo Mazzacurati, *Pirandello nel romanzo europeo*, Bo, Il Mulino, 1995, 376 pp., the second edition of a collection of essays on P.'s novels, expands to include

'L'arte del titolo, da Sterne a Pirandello' (309–49). On *L'esclusa*:
I. Nardi, 'Pirandello, il lettore e Marta Ajala nella selva del
naturalismo', *CLett*, 91–92: 209–21. L. Kroha, 'Il "desiderio" di
Mattia Pascal ovvero *Liolà*: Pirandello maschilista?', *QI*, 15, 1994
[1995]: 75–94, interprets the novel in terms of the *maschilismo* of *Liolà*,
that is to say, attributing to Mattia a subconscious desire to establish
a relationship with Pomino. P. Gibellini, 'Mattia Pirandello fu Pascal',
CLett, 91–92: 189–96. V. Paladino, 'Il caso de *Il fu Mattia Pascal*', *ib.*,
197–208. A. Palermo, 'La "strana" storia de *I vecchi e i giovani*', *FC*,
20, 1995 [1996]: 546–58, moves from the epithet 'strana', a key word
in the text, to the strangeness of the novel itself (which Sciascia
defined 'forse l'opera di Pirandello più pirandelliana') and of the
history of its reception ('vicenda segnata dalla più pirandelliana
paradossalità'). L. Kroha, 'Scrittori, scrittrici e industria culturale:
Suo marito di Pirandello', *ON*, 19.5, 1995: 167–82, returns to the
possible connection between Silvia Roncella and Sibilla Aleramo and
shows how P. reverses three commonplaces: for women the new
'cultural industry' does *not* threaten the autonomy of the artist but, on
the contrary, offers them an unprecedented autonomy; women
writers do *not* pose an economic threat to the 'cultural industry' itself,
but only to the male monopoly; writing does *not* masculinize women,
instead the novel represents male femininization. G. Corsini, 'La
strategia del silenzio in Pirandello', *ib.*, 153–66, draws examples
mainly from *Quaderni di Serafino Gubbio operatore* and *Novelle per un anno*
to show that, in a world (Pirandello's) where language is inherently
false, silences tend to be moments of revelation. R. Scrivano, 'Crisi
dell'identità e crisi della comunicazione nei *Quaderni di Serafino Gubbio
operatore*', *EL*, 20.1, 1995: 33–49. Angelo Pietro Cappello, *Come leggere
'Uno, nessuno e centomila' di Luigi Pirandello*, Mi, Mursia, 1995, 118 pp.
N. De Vecchi Pellati, 'Il regime retorico dell'ironia e del paradosso
nell'esordio de *La patente* di Pirandello', *EL*, 21.4: 15–33, attempts a
close reading of the opening of a *novella* that represents 'la quintessenza
del pirandellismo'. A. Neiger, 'Un norvegese in Sicilia. Una lettura
della novella *Lontano* di Pirandello', *CLett*, 91–92: 223–33. G. Scogna-
miglio, 'Lo sconvolgimento del tempo e la drammatica delle apparenze in *Una giornata* di Luigi Pirandello', *ib.*, 235–45. D. Della Terza,
'Pirandello: dal racconto al teatro: da *La signora Frola e il signor Ponza
suo genero* al *Così è (se vi pare)*', *ib.*, 197–208. S. Zappulla Muscarà, '*La
giara*, dal testo narrativo al testo drammatico', *ib.*, 247–61.

Corrado Donati and Anna T. Ossani, *Pirandello nel linguaggio della
scena. Materiali bibliografici dei quotidiani italiani (1962–1990)*, Ravenna,
Longo, 1993, 222 pp. I. Fried, 'From the roles of the wandering
companies to Pirandello's roles and masks', *The Italianist*, 15,
1995: 116–27, seeks to define the nature of P.'s modernity as a

dramatist. M. A. F. Witt, 'Author(ity) and constructions of actress in the drama of Pirandello and Genet', *CLS*, 32:42–57. On individual plays: G. Bardin, 'Pirandello e il Gatto di Schrödinger', *StIt*, 12, 1994 [1995]:113–18, develops the analogy between the experiment proposed by the Viennese physicist and the plot of *Così è (se vi pare)*; J. Mazzaro, 'Pirandello's *Sei personaggi* and expressive form', *CD*, 30:503–24; G. Genco, '*Sei personaggi in cerca d'autore*: il dramma di "prendere il palcoscenico"', *ON*, 19.6, 1995 [1996]:213–26, considers the play as 'metatheatre' and focuses particularly on the 'characters'; M. Maggi, '*Enrico IV*: la maschera e il nulla', *EL*, 20.2, 1995:71–81; A. Meda, '*Lazzaro* e la riscrittura pirandelliana del mito biblico', *QI*, 14, 1993 [1994]:41–56, relates to the volume noted in *YWMLS*, 56:616; C. Gardenio Granata, 'Una memoria ariostesca nell'ultimo dramma pirandelliano', *EL*, 20.1, 1995:71–80, suggests a link between *I giganti della montagna* and the pages on *Orlando furioso* in the essay on humour. N. D. Nichols and J. O. Bazzoni, *Pirandello and Film*, Lincoln, Nebraska U. P., 1995, 248 pp., concentrates on P.'s efforts to turn *Sei personaggi* into a filmed screenplay. On P.'s influence in film-making: D. Bini, 'Enrico IV tra Pirandello e Bellocchio', *QI*, 14, 1993 [1995]:277–87, and G. Striuli, 'Pirandello's influence on Nino Manfredi's film *Nudo di donna*', *ib.*, 15, 1994 [1995]: 95–109, finds the 1982 film firmly 'anchored in Pirandellian tradition'. G. Pullini, 'Il dramma di Pirandello nell'epistolario con Marta Abba', *LItal*, 48:559–91. Luigi Pirandello, **Lettere a Marta Abba*, ed. Benito Ortolani, Mi, Mondadori, 1995, xliv + 1656 pp. *Pirandello's Love Letters to Marta Abba*, ed. and trans. Benito Ortolani, Princeton U.P., 1994, xlv + 371 pp. *YSPS*, 15–16, 1995–96, comprises several book reviews and the following articles: U. Fanning, 'Adultery: the paternal potential' (7–18), M. Günsberg, '"Goffamente parata": women and age in Pirandello's plays' (19–33); J. Stella, 'Mattia Pascal and the tragedy of being' (34–53); P. Puppa, 'Savinio versus Pirandello' (54–70); G. Jouët-Pastré, 'La femminilità in *Káos*: i fratelli Taviani reinterpretano Pirandello' (71–87), and 'Intervista ai fratelli Taviani' (88–96); M. Casey, 'Dov'è l'uscita' (97–99); O. Ragusa, 'The Pirandello–Abba correspondence' (100–24).

PIROMALLI. V. Paladino, 'La poesia di Antonio Piromalli. Memoria e contestazione ontologica', *ON*, 19.1, 1995:221–25, situates *Sei tu il bolero* in terms of its affiliations.

PIZZUTO. G. Alvino, 'Cinque "pagelle" inedite di Antonio Pizzuto', *StCrit*, 10, 1995:367–83.

POMILIO. For his *L'uccello nella cupola*, see D'ARZO, above. C. Di Biase, '"Una lapide in via del Babuino", racconto postumo di Mario Pomilio', *Italianistica*, 22, 1993 [1994]:317–23. Id., 'Pomilio e Manzoni', *CLett*, 91–92:611–26.

PORTA. K. Z. Moore, '*Melusine* and modernity: Antonio Porta's *Nuova Scienza* as a *Vita Nuova*', *Italica*, 72, 1995: 174–92. John Picchione, **Introduzione a Antonio Porta*, Ro–Bari, Laterza, 1995, 185 pp.

POZZI. G. Strazzeri, 'La conquista di un'identità tecnica nella poesia di Antonia Pozzi', *Acme*, 48.3, 1994 [1996]:67–77, briefly defines Pozzi's verse in terms of its diction and syntax, and of its metre and other formal characteristics. A. Cenni, 'Antonia Pozzi e Vittorio Sereni, in un tempo vero di immagini', *RLI*, 99.3, 1995 [1996]:163–70, anticipates a volume of poetry and letters by the two poets dating from the time of their friendship.

PRATOLINI. G. Benvenuti, 'Ricordo di Vasco Pratolini', *ON*, 19.1, 1995:97–122, is a 'personal overview' of the writer's career prompted by recent editions of his works and other signs of a revival in critical interest. A. Parronchi, 'Due lettere di Pratolini a Pancrazi', *Luti Vol.*, 63–76. G. Manghetti, 'Vasco Pratolini a Mario Puccini (1947–1956). Dalle carte d'archivio', *ib.*, 343–65.

PREZZOLINI. A. Mantovani, 'Prezzolini e le riviste d'avanguardia', *Intersezioni*, 15, 1995:275–310, concerns the period 1900–10. **Giuseppe Prezzolini: The American Years 1929–1962*, ed. Silvia Betocchi, F, Gabinetto Vieusseux, 1994, 115 pp.

PRISCO. A. Benevento, '*Il cuore della vita*. Un libro di viaggi di Michele Prisco', *EL*, 21.3:117–20.

QUASIMODO. Giuseppe Savoca, **Concordanza delle poesie di Salvatore Quasimodo: testo, concordanza, liste di frequenza, indici*, F, Olschki, 1994, xxiv + 320 pp., contains a presentation by Oreste Macrì. N. Cacciaglia, 'La poetica civile di Salvatore Quasimodo', Langella, *Canto*, 289–97. G. Hays, '*Le morte stagioni*: intertextuality in Quasimodo's *Lirici greci*', *FoI*, 29, 1995:26–43. C. F. Goffis, 'Salvatore Quasimodo traduttore di J. Ruskin o di M. Proust?', *CLett*, 91–92:435–41, concerns La '*Bibbia d'Amiens' introdotta da Proust*. Salvatore Quasimodo, **Saggi critici per dodici poeti*, ed. Lina Angioletti, Na, Marotta, 1993, for the 25th anniversary of Q.'s death, brings together his critical essays (1965–68) on contemporary poets such as Giuseppe Zanella, Giuseppe Rea and Angioletti herself.

RABONI. E. Minardi, 'Su *Ogni terzo pensiero* di Raboni', *NC*, 43:73–82, briefly addresses the significance of R.'s 'return to origins' with regard to his 'radical renewal' of poetic form.

REBORA. S. Pautasso, 'Rebora: un discorso aperto', *CLett*, 91–92:307–16. R. Cicala, 'Appunti su Clemente Rebora espressionista e mistico', Langella, *Canto*, 219–28.

RICCHI. A. Panicali, 'La parola e il sogno nella poesia di Renzo Ricchi', *ON*, 19.6, 1995 [1996]:237–49, elaborates on the spiritual 'autobiografismo' of the poetry of *Le radici dello spirito*. F. Tei, 'L'anima in palcoscenico. Il teatro della meditazione di Renzo Ricchi', *ib.*, 19.2, 1995:99–124, surveys a quarter-century's work for the stage, with its emphasis on religious and existential themes, now collected in Renzo Ricchi, **Teatro*, F, Ponte alle Grazie, 1993, and Renzo Ricchi, **La coscienza in scena*, F, Polistampa. A selection of his plays is now available also in English, with a useful, albeit too brief, introduction: Renzo Ricchi, *Five One-Act Plays*, introd. and trans. Renzo D'Agnillo, Dublin, UCD Department of Italian, 111 pp.

RIMANELLI. S. L. Postman, 'A voyage of the mind as "diversivo" through Giose Rimanelli's *Biglietto di terza*', *RStI*, 13.2, 1995 [1996]:29–41, defines R.'s Canadian adventure as 'an autobiography presented in autodiogetic form as a history of a journey' and as the third work in 'the essential Italian trilogy' of America after Soldati's *America primo amore* and Cecchi's *America amara*.

ROCCATAGLIATA CECCARDI. G. Cavallini, 'I settenari di Ceccardo', *CLett*, 91–92:263–81, concerns the Genoese poet Ceccardo Roccatagliata Ceccardi (1871–1919).

ROMANO. *Intorno a Lalla Romano. Saggi critici e testimonianze*, ed. Antonio Ria, Mi, Mondadori, xiii + 473 pp., gathers some 40 contributions to the conference held in Milan in September. S. Wood, '"La mia maniera di essere": an interview with Lalla Romano', *The Italianist*, 15, 1995:373–83. See also LOY, above.

ROSSI. L. Porro Andrioli, 'Le relazioni interpersonali nella poesia di Aldo G. B. Rossi', *ON*, 19.1, 1995:205–19, samples and discusses *Emmaus e Nuove Poesie*, the latest collection of verse from a Catholic priest.

RUFFATO. G. L. Barbieri, 'Il paradigma della complessità poetica: l'opera di Cesare Ruffato', *ON*, 19.6, 1995 [1996]:227–35, while reluctant to view R.'s 'neo-baroque' verse as 'meta-poetry', does argue that 'ciò non toglie che il gioco sul codice sia protagonista assoluto di questi testi'.

SABA. Giuseppe Savoca and Maria Caterina Paino, **Concordanze del 'Canzoniere 1921' di Umberto Saba*, F, Olschki, 505 pp. M. C. Moretti, '"Guardare e ascoltare". Il *Canzoniere* onesto di Saba', Langella, *Canto*, 231–49. A. Girardi, 'Dall'aulico al quotidiano. Noterella sulla lingua di Saba', *StN*, 22, 1995 [1996]:133–41. A. Dei, 'Saba a Palazzeschi. Lettere 1911–1934', *StIt*, 12, 1994:147–67, presents a series of 14 missives (letters and postcards), only one of them already published, and defines the nature of the two poets' friendship. A. Galetto, 'Saba — Carimandrei: "Cronistoria" di una classicità consapevole', *StN*, 22, 1995 [1996]:109–31.

SANGUINETI. A. Pietropaoli, 'Sanguineti Angelus Novissimus', *LS*, 30, 1995:415–44, is devoted to S.'s verse collection *Senzatitolo* (1992).

SANTUCCI.   M. Seita, 'La cultura classica nel romanzo *Il velocifero* di Luigi Santucci', *Paideia*, 49, 1994:205–15.

SANVITALE.   S. Wright, 'In viaggio *Verso Paola* tra identità individuale e storia', *ItQ*, 127–28:61–75, examines the 1991 short novel which, unlike her earlier works, presents the author with the challenge of creating a male protagonist.

SATTA.   R. F. Farini, 'Il romanzo di Nuoro: *Il giorno del giudizio* di Salvatore Satta', *EL*, 20.4, 1995:61–72.

SAVINIO.   *Ariel*, 10.1–2, 1995 [1996], devoted entirely to S., focuses on the theatre, but also includes P. Di Sacco, 'Rassegna di studi saviniani' (259–85). F. Secchieri, 'La *Nuova enciclopedia* di Alberto Savinio', *Italianistica*, 24, 1995:153–67.

SBARBARO.   E. Elli, '*Pianissimo* e altro di Sbarbaro', Langella, *Canto*, 207–17. A. Romanello, 'Il poeta nella grande città: introduzione a *Pianissimo*', *LItal*, 48:230–51. A. Perli, 'Sbarbaro traduttore di Huysmans', *StIt*, 14, 1995:151–70, sees an affinity between the two figures, not only in their careers, but in the themes and situations of their works, and also shows how in S.'s translation of *A rebours* (1944) 'il lavorio stilistico sovverte... lo stesso ordinamento logico-sintattico, ripristinando modi e cadenze tipici dell'espressionismo dei primi *Trucioli*'. These findings are basically confirmed by S. Pavarini, 'Sbarbaro traduttore: *A rebours* di J.-K. Huysmans', *LS*, 31:329–52, whose analysis delves more deeply into the nature of S.'s recreation of the original and into the 'poetics of translation' by which he was guided.

SCIASCIA.   G. Finocchiaro Chimirri, 'Il "pamphlet" prima del "giallo": l'incontro memorabile Sciascia-Courier', *Italianistica*, 22, 1993 [1994]:289–96, fills a lacuna in Sciascia interpretation by investigating the ongoing presence, open or cryptic, of the pamphleteer P.-L. Courier in his works. S. Ben Ahmed, 'Il saggio come concezione metafisica in Leonardo Sciascia', *QI*, 15, 1994 [1995]:237–46, examines the fusion of essay and *giallo* in *Il giorno della civetta*. M. Belpolito, 'Nel chiarchiaro. Sciascia, la luce e la morte', *NC*, 43:119–23. D. Della Terza, '*Candide* in Italia: l'esempio di Leonardo Sciascia (come una premessa ottocentesca)', *RLMC*, 48, 1995 [1996]:263–74, and E. Scarano, 'Sciascia, Candido, Candide', *Italianistica*, 22, 1993 [1994]:297–315, look at S.'s way of reading Voltaire in his own *Candido*. T. O'Neill, 'La scoperta dell'America, ovvero Ipotesi per come componeva Sciascia', *LItal*, 47, 1995:565–97, explores the role of literary models and influences in S.'s 'ricostruzioni documentarie'. Recent book-length contributions include: Joseph Farrell, **Leonardo Sciascia*, Edinburgh U. P., 1995, x + 181 pp.; Matteo Collura, *Il maestro di Regalpietra. Vita di Leonardo Sciascia*, Mi, Longanesi, 390 pp., which is more than a biography (offering as it does, for example, a guide to S.'s writings in the context of his life and of the society whose injustices and barbarities he denounced) and which well deserves the acclaim with which it has been received; and Carlo Spalanca, **Da Regalpietra a Parigi: Leonardo Sciascia tra critica italiana e critica francese*, Caltanissetta–Ro, Sciascia, 1994, 320 pp.

SERENI. G. Mazzoni, 'Le prime raccolte di Sereni', *ASNP*, 25, 1995 [1996]:485–508, rests on an often overlooked distinction between the two groups of poems that constitute *Frontiera*: the earlier one, in its syntax and metre (and subjectivism), is essentially 'hermetic', and not modelled on Montale's *Occasioni*, the novelty of which S. nonetheless appreciated; the later poems move away from the initial 'sintassi scarsa e paratattica' towards 'modelli sintattici mutuati in modo rigido dalla tradizione premoderna e ostentatamente letterari, costruiti . . .' while remaining un-Montalian: 'il libro evolve verso l'autobiografismo lirico che trova la sua forma compiuta nella raccolta successiva [*Diario*]'. G. Einaudi, 'Gli *Strumenti umani* e le lettere di Sereni nell'Archivio Einaudi', *StCrit*, 11:51–54, quotes letters (March 1964–September 1965) documenting the history of the verse collection. See also CAMPANA and POZZI, above.

SERRAO. L. Bonaffini, 'Achille Serrao e la poesia neodialettale napoletana', *RStI*, 14.2:152–66, defines S. in comparison (and contrast) with Neapolitan contemporaries and the Neapolitan tradition: 'Serrao . . . taglia corto coi precedenti illustri della linea Russo–Di Giacomo, per ricollegarsi con i grandi momenti della lirica napoletana, da Basile al Capurro'.

SILONE. E. Straub, 'Ignazio Silone und die Schweiz', *ItStudien*, 17:130–56, presents fresh biographical data on S.'s Swiss exile and looks at his views on Swiss democracy. B. Moloney, 'Nettie Sutro's German translation of Silone's *Fontamara*', *MLR*, 91:878–85, argues that the German version of the novel was based on an Urtext subsequently revised by Silone for publication in Paris and that indeed 'the revision process began even while the German text was in the press'. Id., 'Ignazio Silone and *Il Risveglio*: the 1945 version of Silone's *Fontamara*', *ItS*, 51:134–66, edits the extracts of the novel that appeared in *Il Risveglio*. M. Gambacciani, 'Sul *Viaggio a Parigi* di Silone', *Italianistica*, 24, 1995:191–94, looks briefly at the collection in the light of V. Esposito's 1993 retranslation (see *YWMLS*, 56:623) of Sutro's German translation (*Die Reise nach Paris*, Zurich, 1934). Esposito's inclusion, in Italian, of the latter's essay on Silone, virtually unknown in Italy, is considered particularly useful. L. Fasciati, 'L'"unico libro" di Ignazio Silone', *Cenobio*, 45:355–72, finds running through S.'s fiction 'temi, motivi, caratteri e personaggi che si assomigliano, che si ripetono, che si corrispondono'.

SINISGALLI. M. Maggiari, '*On the Elysian Fields* by Leonardo Sinisgalli', *FoI*, 29, 1995:44–51. P. Jodogne, '"Rue Sainte Walburge" di Leonardo Sinisgalli', *Italianistica*, 22, 1993 [1994]:203–09, concludes that the title, while probably derived from personal experience of Liège, 'non ha ... funzione referenziale, ha solo una funzione poetica'.

SLATAPER. Sandra Arosio, **Scrittori di frontiera: Scipio Slataper, Giani e Carlo Stuparich*, Mi, Guerini Scientifica, 234 pp. F. Angelini, 'Slataper e il teatro: il caso Hebbel (1910–1920)', *Ariel*, 9.3, 1994 [1995]: 89–103.

SPATOLA. B. Zecchi, '*L'Oblò* di Adriano Spatola: il racconto del racconto che non c'è', *ItQ*, 127–28:49–60, analyses S.'s experimental novel, to conclude that it is an example of 'testo autoreferenziale': 'testo senza "significato", scrittura vuota, buco, oblò'.

STUPARICH, G. A. Benevento, '"Lettere a Giani" di Elody Oblath Stuparich', *CLett*, 22, 1994:807–10. See also SLATAPER, above.

SOLDATI. R. Manica, 'Quel che suona Laura. Variazioni su Soldati', *ParL*, 528–30, 1994:26–40, mainly concerns the piano recital in the short story *Il concerto*.

STRATI. G. Polimeni, 'Polifonia e scrittura nel *Selvaggio di Santa Venere* di Saverio Strati', *ON*, 19.2, 1995:199–213, analyses the way in which alternation of narrative voices becomes the 'struttura portante' of the 1977 novel, begun in 1952.

SVEVO. E. Schächter, 'The enigma of Svevo's Jewishness: Trieste and the Jewish cultural tradition', *ItS*, 50, 1995, 24–47, documents S.'s repudiation of his Jewish background, also shedding new light, *inter alia*, on his marital relations. F. Catenazzi, 'Ancora su Svevo e dintorni', *Aevum*, 70:747–50, following up his recent volume *L'italiano di Svevo* (see *YWMLS*, 56:624), argues that various now non-standard features of S.'s Italian were current usage among the novelists of his day and not the personal idiosyncrasies they are widely imagined to be. M. Palumbo, 'Svevo e i suoi autori', *MLN*, 111:1–30, singles out Darwin, Schopenhauer, and Freud as especially important. C. Annoni, '*L'orologio di Flora* e il dottor Sofocle: Svevo lettore dei classici', *Testo*, 26, 1993:48–80. Id., 'Giunta a *L'orologio di Flora*. Caute proposte per l'intertesto di Svevo', *ib.*, 28, 1994:62–85. E. Guagnini, 'Svevo e Joyce', *ItStudien*, 16, 1995:93–108, re-examines the two writers' relations in the light of work by Dario de Tuoni, Stelio Crise, and Giancarlo Mazzacurati. On the novels: A. Brambilla, 'I. Svevo, *Una vita*: testo profano e testo sacro', *Testo*, 26, 1993:102–05; E. Giordano, '"Mamma mia": *Una vita* e lo sguardo materno', *FoI*, 29, 1995:76–90; M. Verdicchio, 'Ironia nel primo Svevo: *Una vita* e *Senilità*', *RStI*, 12.2, 1994 [1995]:14–28, maintaining that the two novels are no less ironic, in their way, than *Coscienza*; T. C. Riviello,

'The role of the protagonists and the women in Italo Svevo's *Una vita* and *La coscienza di Zeno*', *ib.*, 13.1, 1995:88–99, attempting a 'contrastive analysis' of the two novels; L. Curti, 'Zeno guarisce dell'ottimismo. Schopenhauer e Freud nella *Coscienza*', *RLettI*, 12, 1994 [1996]:401–27, maintaining that Zeno is ill only in his optimistic belief that a doctor can cure his unhappiness and arguing that the novel is really the story of his recovery from such optimism; G. Langella, 'La "dolce malattia". Intorno a una pagina di Svevo', *LItal*, 47, 1995:271–89, concerning Zeno's supposed diabetes; M. Farnetti, 'La prefazione del dottor S.', *Luti Vol.*, 193–206; G. Savelli, 'Il dottor S. e la storia virtuale di Zeno', *StCrit*, 11:93–110, interpreting Dr S.'s preface, with its 'contractual ambiguity', as the key to the novel's interpretation; and P. Bartoloni, 'Zeno Cosini, an Italian novelist?', *RStI*, 14.2:198–205, reconsidering the thesis that Zeno is the 'real author' of the novel, put forward in G. Palmieri, *Schmitz, Svevo, Zeno* (see *YWMLS*, 56:624) and in the introduction to: Italo Svevo, *La coscienza di Zeno. Edizione rivista sull'originale a stampa*, ed. Giovanni Palmieri, pref. Maria Corti, F, Giunti, 1994, xi + 460 pp., which also reaffirms the editor's view that Zeno expresses himself in a language which S. 'ha inventato *ad hoc* per il suo personaggio scrivente'. On *Il vegliardo*: G. Langella, 'Il testamento letterario di Svevo', *CLett*, 91–92:5–29. Id., **Il tempo cristallizzato. Introduzione al testamento letterario di Svevo*, Na-Ro, ESI, 1995, 228 pp. G. A. Camerino, 'Nota su un'edizione dei romanzi sveviani', *CLett*, 22, 1994:803–06, concerns the 1993 UTET edition, ed. G. Ioli. C. Verbaro, 'Il lettore burlato: riflessioni in margine a *Una burla riuscita*', *Luti Vol.*, 207–22.

TABUCCHI. E. Schulze-Witzenrath, '"Un giallo molto *sui generis*": Antonio Tabucchis *Il filo dell'orizzonte*', *ItStudien*, 16, 1995:177–92, shows how in the 1985 novel T. 'hat ... das Detektivschema in bemerkenswerter Weise enttrivialisiert'. G. Kurtz, 'Antonio Tabucchi — Entgrenzungen', *RF*, 107, 1995:163–70, seeks to define the characteristics of T.'s fiction, and 'Antonio Tabucchi: *Sostiene Pereira*', *ib.*, 414–19, suggests a number of alternative categorizations of the recent novel. *SpR*, 12, 1996–97, is entirely given over to the substantial *Antonio Tabucchi: A Collection of Essays*, ed. Bruno Ferraro and Nicole Prunster, covering the main areas of interest in T.'s narrative and comprising the following: B. Ferraro, 'Antonio Tabucchi's actors, characters and ghosts' (3–25); G. Bertone, 'Notes for a reconnaissance of Tabucchi's works' (29–43); R. Bodei, 'The geometry of equality: Antonio Tabucchi and the civil dimension' (44–48); I. Lanslots, 'Tabucchi's waiting rooms' (51–60); L. Lepschy, 'The role of memory in Antonio Tabucchi's *Piccoli equivoci senza importanza*' (61–70); N. Trentini, 'Towards a study of dream in Antonio Tabucchi' (71–96); T. Arvigo, 'From *Notturno indiano* to *Il filo dell'orizzonte*:

"landscape of absence" and "landscape of disappearance"' (99–108); R. Ceserani, 'The art of fixing shadows and writing with light: Tabucchi and photography' (109–124); G. Palmieri, 'Antonio Tabucchi's iconic temptations' (125–40); A. Botta, 'Antonio Tabucchi's *Requiem*: mourning modernism' (143–57); L. Surdich, 'The constant search for oneself' (158–72); M. Bertone, 'Paths to testimony in *Sostiene Pereira*' (175–85); F. Brizio-Skov, '*Sostiene Pereira*: the crisis of the intellectual between history and literature' (186–201); M. Jansen, 'What about Pereira? Can he be trusted?: a testimony of "true fiction" in *Sostiene Pereira*' (202–14); A. Sempoux, 'A note on the phrase "sostiene Pereira"' (215–16). There are also useful bibliographies.

TAMARO. L. Rorato, 'Childhood prisons. Denied dreams and denied realities: the ritualization of pain in the novels of Susanna Tamaro', *RoS*, 28:61–78, usefully scrutinizes not just the best-selling *Va' dove di porta il cuore* but the whole corpus of T.'s fiction, which has not yet received much critical attention in Italy.

TESTORI. Carlo Bo, *Testori. L'urlo, la bestemmia, il canto dell'amore umile*, ed. Gilberto Santini, Mi, Longanesi, 1995, 104 pp., gathers upwards of a score of articles.

TOMASI DI LAMPEDUSA. Giuseppe Aromatisi (Giuseppe Tomasi di Lampedusa?), *Scritti ritrovati*, pref. Francesco D'Orsi Meli, introd. Andrea Vitello, Palermo, Flaccovio, 1993, 228 pp., carries a lengthy introduction. R. de Forcade, 'Tomasi di Lampedusa, Giuseppe Maggiore e l'operazione "antigattopardo"', *ON*, 19.2:185–97, shows that *Il Gattopardo* was prompted and influenced by Maggiore's *Sette e mezzo* (Cuneo, 1952) as was claimed when the Palermo bookseller S. F. Flaccovio (who had helped T. get *Il Gattopardo* published) and Giuseppe Ghibaudo, the Cuneo printer, in May 1963, republished Maggiore's novel for it to be presented by the press agencies as the 'authentic' *Gattopardo*. G. M. Tosi, 'Letteratura e solitudine: gli anni '50 e il "Caso Lampedusa"', *FoI*, 30:65–79.

TOZZI. R. Luperini, *Federigo Tozzi. Le immagini, le idee, le opere*, Ro–Bari, Laterza, 1995, xiv + 246 pp. A. E. Galvan, 'Tozzi precursore fra esistenzialismo e *nouveau roman*', *EL*, 21.3:97–108, presents a persuasive, well-documented argument. Marco Marchi, *Palazzeschi e altri sondaggi* (see PALAZZESCHI, above) includes 'Le novelle di Tozzi' (135–59) and 'Tozzi "minore" (Baudelaire, Dante e Leopardi, Viani)' (161–80). F. Secchieri, 'Lettura di *Un'allucinazione* di Federigo Tozzi', *SPCT*, 51, 1995:159–73, observes that the novelty of the work (and of most of T.'s short-story writing) lay in the way it deliberately eluded naturalistic conventions and turned (to apply Jean Ricardou's phrase) the 'récit d'une aventure' into 'l'aventure d'un récit'.

G. Melloni, 'Lo sguardo teatralizzato e la dissimulazione dell'espro-prio nella *Casa venduta* di Federigo Tozzi', *LS*, 31:293–328, highlights the structure of the story, with its 'diegetically framed' theatrical nucleus, and the function of 'teatralizzazione': not just one narrative device among many, but one of the 'nuclei generatori della poetica tozziana', rooted in his vision of existence. Id., 'La scrittura come "vertigine della dissoluzione". Una proposta di lettura di *Con gli occhi chiusi* di Federigo Tozzi', *StCrit*, 11:23–50, starting from the novel's conclusion, considers the phenomenology of vertigo in this work and T.'s *oeuvre* in general. E. Saccone, 'Con gli occhi chiusi', *MLN*, 110, 1995:1–19. Id., 'Allegoria e sospetto. Il caso di *Tre croci*', *FC*, 20, 1995 [1996]:527–45, dwells particularly on the image of the three crosses and the significance of the work's conclusion.

UNGARETTI. E. Giglia, 'Ungaretti: ragioni di una poesia', Lan-gella, *Canto*, 251–67. R. Gennaro, 'Ancora su Bergson nel primo Ungaretti', *StIt*, 15:35–65, after documenting U.'s attendance at Bergson's Collège de France lectures on Spinoza in 1914, shows that in the poetry of the period 1915–19 'la traccia bergsoniana... investe innanzitutto i temi del tempo e della memoria, ma riguarda anche il panismo, il linguaggio, il sentimento dell'assenza e del nulla'. W. Musolino, 'Physics and metaphysics: capture and escape. Two war poems of Wilfred Owen and Giuseppe Ungaretti', *FoI*, 30:311–19, concerns 'Veglia'. D. De Robertis, 'Ungaretti: l'"Inno alla morte"', *Italianistica*, 22, 1993 [1994]:121–31, in memory of G. Varanini, analyses the first poem by U. he came to know: read aloud by his father even before its inclusion in *Sentimento del tempo* (1933). Alessandra Zingone, **Deserto emblema. Studi per Ungaretti*, Caltanissetta–Ro, Sciascia, 328 pp.

VASSALLI. C. Della Coletta, 'L'altra metà del Seicento: da *I promessi sposi* di Manzoni a *La chimera* di Vassalli', *Italica*, 73:348–68, develops an illuminating contrast between the two historical novels.

VITTORINI. P. Diffley and C. Honess, '"Il cuore dell'infanzia, Siciliano e di tutto il mondo": the function of childhood in the novels of Elio Vittorini', *RoS*, 27:31–48. C. Honess, 'Sardinia as an apprenticeship: Vittorini's *Sardegna come un'infanzia* as a prelude to *Conversazione in Sicilia* and *Il Sempione strizza l'occhio al Fréjus*', *The Italianist*, 15, 1995:150–74, finds numerous anticipations of the second and third works in the first. P. Guaragnella, 'Icone di un sogno. Su *Viaggio in Sardegna* di Elio Vittorini', *LS*, 31:49–77, confirms the highly literary style of the work in an analysis pointing to derivation from, among others, Cecchi, Sbarbaro, Quasimodo, and Ungaretti, and discusses the dreamlike character of V.'s vision of Sardinia. M. Seidel, 'Kommunikation als Handlung: Metapoetische Strukturen und Aspekte in Vittorinis *Conversazione in Sicilia*', *ItStudien*,

16, 1995:149–75, defines the 'Erzählerrede' as an integral component of the story, to be understood as 'ein aktuelles Handeln des Erzählers... das den Erzählgegenstand, das Geschehen, wesentlich überhaupt erst im Akt des Schreibens konstituiert'.

VOGHERA. K. Pizzi, 'Guido and Giorgio Voghera: a "secret" anxiety of influence', *ItS*, 50, 1995:112–22, probes psychoanalytically 'into the subtext of *Il segreto*' and finds the father–son confrontation between the two Triestine writers.

VOLPONI. P. G. Conti, '*Le mosche del capitale* di Paolo Volponi: spazio disciplinato e spazio disciplinante', *EL*, 21.3:33–59, shows how in form and descriptive technique the novel reflects the reality of Italy's 'neocapitalism'.

WALSER. A. Coppari, 'La scrittura del pudore. Note su Robert Walser', *NC*, 41, 1994:243–52.

ZANZOTTO. U. Motta, 'La neolingua di Andrea Zanzotto', Langella, *Canto*, 345–60. M. Moroni, 'Andrea Zanzotto: l'"io" come unità minima di testimonianza critica', *Italica*, 73:83–102, maintains that Z., in his poetics, has stuck to this option longer and more coherently than any other member of the Novissimi or the Gruppo 63 in general. N. Gardini, 'Lingua e pensiero nel primo Zanzotto: dagli ermetici a Montale', *ON*, 19.2, 1995, 73–97, seeks to enhance critical appreciation of Z.'s earliest work (*Dietro il paesaggio*, 1951) via detailed analysis of its 'montalismo'. L. Zille Cozzi, 'Metamorfosi della negazione e della morte nella poesia di Andrea Zanzotto', *StN*, 20, 1993 [1995]:209–35. A. Balduino, 'Per una rappresentazione musicale di M. De Stefani su testi tratti dal *Galateo in bosco* di A. Zanzotto', *ib.*, 22, 1995 [1996]:199–206. Velio Abati, **Andrea Zanzotto. Bibliografia 1951–1993*, F, Giunti, 1995, 237 pp.

X. ROMANIAN STUDIES*

LANGUAGE

By MARTIN MAIDEN, *Professor of the Romance Languages, University of Oxford*

GENERAL. Eugen Coseriu, *Prelegeri şi conferinţe (1992–93)*, ed. S. Dumistrăcel, Iaşi, Dosoftei, 1994, 189 pp., is a collection of lectures given by C. on his receiving a doctorate *honoris causa* from Iaşi University, concluding with 'Unitate lingvistică — unitate naţională', (181–89), a trenchant reassertion of the essential unity of Romanian and 'Moldavian'. An insight into the linguistic preoccupations of Sever Pop is offered in M. Popa, 'Sever Pop în corespondenţă cu Romulus Todoran', *LiL*, 40.1, 1995:108–15. Surveys of scholarly work in various branches of Romanian linguistics are: J. Brumme, 'Die rumänistische Linguistik in der DDR', *Balkan-Archiv*, 19–20, 1994–95:237–66; M. Iliescu and O. Winkelmann, 'Neuere Beiträge zur Grammatik der rumänischen Sprache', *ib.*, 267–86; G. Birken-Silvermann, 'Kontaktlinguistische Beiträge zur Rumänistik: Stand und Perspektiven der deutschsprachigen Forschung', *ib.*, 287–316. W. Dahmen, 'Situaţia actuală şi perspectivele românisticii germane', *LiL*, 40.3–4, 1995:87–102, is an overview of the notable contribution of scholars from the German-speaking world to the study of the Romanian language. Paul Schveiger, 'Limba română: între deschidere şi purism', *ib.*, 39.2, 1994:39–42, questions the usefulness of language planning for Romanian.

HISTORY OF THE LANGUAGE. Maria Cvasnîi Cătănescu, *Limba română. Origini şi dezvoltare*, Humanitas, 217 pp., offers a succinct and accessible, albeit derivative, synthesis of Romanian linguistic history, supplemented by a collection of historical texts. A. Lombard, 'Destinul limbii latine în Răsărit', *LiL*, 40.1, 1995:5–14, reviews and reasserts some major issues in the history of Romanian and underlines the special scientific importance of the language for Romance linguists. V. Ţara, 'Despre fixarea şi evoluţia normelor limbii române literare', *ib.*, 39.2, 1994:86–88. G. Brâncuş, 'Argumente lingvistice pentru continuitatea românească la nordul Dunării', *ib.*, 40.2, 1995:5–15, stresses among other things the importance of vocabulary inherited from Latin, particularly in the agricultural sphere, indicative of a sedentary presence since Roman times. T. Ferro, 'Aspecte "balcanice" din limba română; convergenţe pe plan romanic', *ib.*,

---

* The place of publication of books is Bucharest unless otherwise stated.

41.1:17–27, shows on the evidence of other (particularly Italo-) Romance varieties that some of the supposed 'Balkan' features of Romanian, such as the so-called 'neuter' gender, the proliferation of reflexive verbs, and the use of morphological elements based on verbs of volition, such as *-va* in *cineva*, might have purely Romance origins.

The historical phonology of Romanian seems to have been rather neglected in the period under review, with the exception of R. Sampson, 'Romanian vowel nasalization and the palatal nasal /ɲ/', *SEER*, 73, 1995:601–12, who deftly resolves an apparent problem of vowel nasalization by arguing that at the time of nasalization /ɲ/ had not yet been formed; its postulated antecedent /ɲ.j/, however, was one of a set of hormorganic sequences of nasal consonant + oral consonant which regularly triggered nasalization. Extensive reference to Romanian is made in M. Maiden, 'On the Romance inflectional endings -i and -e', *RPh*, 50:147–82, where it is argued that these endings, both in Italo-Romance and Romanian, derive overwhelmingly from proto-Romance forms in final *-s*. Elena Dragoş, *Elemente de sintaxă istorică română*, Ed. Didactică şi Pedagogică, 1995, 173 pp., is marred in places by some factual inaccuracies and misleading or simplistic representations. In particular, the author shows little awareness of the significance of parallel developments in other Romance languages (for example, enclisis of the type *dusu-s-a* is too summarily attributed to Slav influence). G. B. Pellegrini, 'Concordanze balcaniche nell'uso dell'articolo determinativo', Lupu, *Studi*, 201–18, discusses the appearance of the article in proper names, place names, greetings, and exclamations, in Albanian and Greek, as well as Romanian. L. Renzi, 'A proposito della teoria di Graur sulla posposizione dell'articolo rumeno', *ib.*, 227–45, makes a most interesting appeal to Wackernagel's Law in order to account for the suffixing of the Romanian article. V. Iancu, 'Cum vorbesc românii din Ungaria. Calcul lingvistic', *ib.*, 149–61, examines calquing in the standard Romanian used in Hungary. Alexandru Ligor, *Vechi tipărituri în limba română şi unitatea naţională*, Chişinău, Universitas — Cîmpina, Verva, 1994, 115 pp., contains much that is relevant to the study of the unification of Romanian, particularly in its written form.

The period under review has seen some important work on the linguistic situation in Moldova. Romanianists, Romance linguists, and anyone interested in the factors which make a linguistic variety into a 'language' will applaud the appearance of *Studies in Moldovan*, ed. D. Dyer, NY, Columbia U.P., xx + 225 pp., where M. Bruchis, 'Moldavian national history' (3–28), and W. Crowther, 'Nationalism and political transformation in Moldova' (31–51), elucidate the general historical and political background to the modern language problem. D. Deletant, 'Language policy and linguistic trends in the

Republic of Moldavia, 1924–1992' (53–87), offers a particularly clear and wide-ranging historical account, tracing among other things the vicissitudes of the Latin and Cyrillic alphabets in Moldavia and examining the phenomenon of so-called linguistic 'enrichment' of the 'Moldavian language'. D. Dyer, 'The making of the Moldavian language' (89–109) includes a contrastive structural survey of Muntenian and Moldavian, both literary and dialectal. Partly basing himself on Weigand's now antiquated linguistic atlas (significantly, the otherwise more detailed and reliable Romanian linguistic atlases of the past few decades obediently ignored what lay beyond the river Prut), Dyer shows very clearly that literary Moldavian is effectively identical to literary Romanian while lacking the distinctive traits of the dialects spoken within Moldova/Moldavia; the dialects of Moldova, moreover, do not form a discrete linguistic entity either, since their characteristic features are shown to be shared with the dialects of Romanian Moldova. C. King, 'The politics of language in the Moldovan Soviet Socialist Republic' (111–30), deals with developments since the late 80s, showing how the language question has become emblematic of a wider social and political issue. V. Guţu Romalo, 'Componenta latino-românică a limbii române literare', *LiL*, 39.3–4, 1994:5–12, argues that the emergence of literary Romanian as a force for national unity accounts for the attacks upon Romanian in Moldavia during the Soviet period. I. Datcu, 'N. Iorga despre limba românilor dintre Prut şi Nistru', *ib.*, 80–85, forcefully reasserts Iorga's view of the unity of Bessarabian varieties with Romanian proper. L. Fassel, 'Limba română în teritoriile plurilingve: exemplul Basarabiei (1918–1940)', *ib.*, 40.1, 1995:98–107, focuses mainly on the influence of Romanian on German in that region. D. Dyer, *'Moldavian linguistic realities', Non-Slavic Languages of the USSR. Papers from the Fourth Conference*, ed. H. I. Aronson, Columbus, OH, Slavica, 234–53.

TEXTS. *Crestomaţia limbii române vechi*, 1: *(1521–1639)*, ed. E. Buză et al., Editura Academiei Române, 1994, 246 pp., comprises 72 texts, one third of which are of non-literary origin, and a glossary. The volume is prefaced by a very helpful introductory section explaining the background to the texts, the criteria for their selection, and the general editorial strategy. The typeface is gratifyingly clear (still not always the case with books published in Romania). Given the sometimes indeterminate value of the Cyrillic letters (of the letter *jat'*, for example), it is perhaps a pity that the Cyrillic texts have been transcribed into what is, in effect, modern Romanian orthography, although the editors are scrupulous in indicating the transcriptional procedure followed. The completion of this trilogy of texts is to be eagerly awaited. G. Piccillo, 'Il *Katekismu Krestinesku* di Silvestrio

Amelio (1719). Parte seconda: commento', *Balkan-Archiv*, 19–20, 1994–95:9–132, is a detailed philological and linguistic commentary on this text written by an Italian missionary. R. Windisch, 'Biblia din 1688 de la Bucureşti', *ib.*, 539–46, draws a number of linguistic conclusions from this newly accessible text, and questions the supposed original unity of the Romanian written language. M. Gherman, 'Semnificaţia unui text românesc necunoscut', Lupu, *Studi*, 838–41, highlights the role of Hieronymus Megiser in making the Romanian language known in the West during the 17th c.

ORTHOGRAPHY. Petcu Abdulea, *Dicţionar de omografe*, Editura Didactică şi Pedagogică, 1995, 318 pp., gives a complete list of Romanian homographic words. This volume's utility would have been increased if the author had distinguished between homographs which are genuinely likely to cause confusion, and the many others which syntactic or pragmatic context would readily differentiate. The book contains, by the way, a good deal of information for those interested in stress oppositions in Romanian (which are not generally indicated orthographically). L. Fassel, ' "Ţara arde şi baba se piaptănă" oder über die rumänische Orthographie', *Balkan-Archiv*, 19–20, 1994–95:380–84, casts a critical eye on some anomalies of the recent spelling reforms in the light of S. Dumistrăcel's remarks on the subject. Id., 'Discuţii în jurul ortografiei române', *LiL*, 40.2, 1995:29–35, adduces further arguments against the reforms and in favour of a system based on the 1953 model. T. Hristea, 'Ortografia şi ortoepia neologismelor româneşti (cu specială referire la împrumuturile recente)', *ib.*, 40.2, 1995:36–53.

GRAMMAR. Dumitru Bejan, *Gramatica limbii române*, Cluj, Echinox, 1995, 413 pp., is a reliable reference grammar set in firmly traditional mould, but likely to be of use to native speakers rather than to non-natives. In places it is less detailed than it needs to be: to take one point of detail among many, the vexed question of the formation of the second person singular imperative of non-first-conjugation verbs (in -*i* or in -*e*) is not properly addressed, and I could find no mention of the fact that some imperatives normally in -*i* have -*e* when a clitic pronoun follows. The volume would also have benefited from an index, and the list of contents is insufficient for reference purposes. Gheorghe Constantinescu-Dobridor, *Sintaxa limbii române*, Editura Ştiinţifică, 1994, 601 pp., appears to be a thorough, traditionally oriented and well-illustrated account of Romanian syntax, and has a concluding chapter dedicated to 'Tendinţe în sintaxa limbii române contemporane'. But the utility of this book, too, is greatly impaired by the lack of an index or adequate list of contents. Virginia Motapanyane, *Theoretical Implications of Complementation in Romanian*, Padua, Unipress, 1995, 157 pp., is a fine example of the application of sophisticated theoretical tools (M. works within the general framework of Chomsky's Minimalist Program) to the analysis of the syntax of modern Romanian (including some illuminating references to older Romanian usage). M. develops a lucid and theoretically rigorous account of a number of particularly complex issues in Romanian syntax, and even the non-specialist in syntactic theory will, given a little effort, find it a rewarding read. Alexander Grosu, *Three Studies in Locality and Case*, London, Routledge, 1994, xii + 256 pp., dedicates two of his studies to 'Romanian determiners and functional categories' (147–97) and 'Null operators in Romanian' (199–226). L. Schippel, ' "Că", "pentru că", "fiindcă" — probleme de sintaxă contrastivă germano-română', *LiL*, 39.3–4, 1994:13–16. L. Tasmowski-De Ryck, 'Cîteva observaţii privind folosirea articolului definit şi a articolului adjectival', *ib.*, 39.2, 1994:14–19, examines the use of 'cel' in contexts where it is not syntactically obligatory, and concludes that it has contextual or cultural reference assuming a common universe of discourse shared by interlocutors. M. Van Peteghem, 'Altul şi celălalt: despre limita între referinţa hotărîtă şi nehotărîtă', *ib.*, 39.2, 1994:20–28, examines the difference between these forms (contrasting them with French) and argues for a gradient notion of definiteness such that, of the two Romanian forms, both of them morphologically definite, 'celălalt' has greater definiteness than 'altul'. G. Ciompec, 'Aspekte der grammatischen Kategorie der Komparation in der gegenwärtigen rumänischen Sprache', Lupu, *Studi*, 74–85. T. Capotă, 'Sistemul comparaţiei în limba română', *LiL*, 41.2:11–22. A. Voineag Merlan, 'Coordonarea "discontinuă" în limba română vorbită populară', *ib.*, 41.2:4–10. D. Dumitrescu, 'On the syntactic structure and discourse function of multiple constituent repetitive and nonrepetitive questions in Romanian', Lupu, *Studi*, 86–114, deals with questions conjoining more than one Wh-constituent. G. Giusti, 'Lo statuto categoriale del morfema infinitivale *a* in romeno alla luce di un'analisi contrastiva tra lingue romanze e germaniche', *ib.*, 132–48. G. Pană Dindelegan, 'Pronumele "o" cu valoare neutră şi funcţia cliticelor în limba romănă', *LiL*, 39.2, 1994:9–16. Ş. Găitănaru, 'Pronumele nehotărît în limba română, *ib.*, 40.1, 1995:30–33. J. Felix, 'Asimetrie între conţinut şi expresie la articolul românesc', Lupu, *Studi*, 115–21. M. Iliescu, '*Său, sa* ou *lui, ei* en roumain contemporain', *ib.*, 162–72, throws interesting new light on the distinction between these two classes of third-person possessives. G. Gruiţa, 'Flexiunea mixtă şi consecinţele ei în sistemul morfematic românesc', *LiL*, 39.2, 1994:43–47, surveys a number of cases of 'hybridism' of the type *nepoţica–nepoţele* in the suffixal and inflectional morphology of modern nouns and verbs. A. Beyrer,

'Stufen der Entwicklung im rumänischen Präpositionalgefüge', *Balkan-Archiv*, 19–20, 1994–95:317–33, traces the sources of preposition formation in Romanian. M. Vulpe, 'Termes de parenté et noms propres: possibilitiés combinatoires et restrictions distributionnelles', Lupu, *Studi*, 283–90. M. Barindi, 'Una particolarità sintattica della lingua del folclore rumeno', *ib.*, 293–312, is a fascinating and judicious study which extends into the Romanian domain the phenomenon of syntactically 'partitive' subjects of unaccusative verbs, encountered also in the folklore of some northern Italian dialects. A. Cuniţă, 'Verbes datifs d'attribution ou de privation? Remarques sur l'ambiguïté d'une structure syntagmatique', *ib.*, 503–16. T. Cristea, ' "Idée critique", mondes possibles et créativite', *ib.*, 491–502, makes reference to Romanian uses of the subjunctive. A. Costăchescu, 'La relation adversative en Italien et en Roumain', *ib.*, 464–90, deals, for Romanian, with the functions of *dar, ci, însă.* L. Ionescu-Ruxăndoiu, 'Notes sur quelques formes de la deixis dans le daco-roumain parlé', *ib.*, 173–83, deals mainly with the 'social' deixis of address forms.

LEXICON AND ONOMASTICS. Elena Ciobanu et al., *Dicţionar practic al limbii române*, Floarea Darurilor, 1995, 464 pp., includes etymological information. G. Tohăneanu, *Dicţionar de imagini pierdute*, Timişoara, Amarcord, 1995, 271 pp., explains the etymological meaning of many recent borrowings from other languages into Romanian, and exemplifies their use. Id., 'Neologisme — imagini uitate', *LiL*, 40.2, 1995:54–57, challenges the assumption that neologisms are stylistically neutral, and discerns in them a poetic assertion of the fundamental 'Latinity' of Romanian. E. Toma, 'Traduction ou pseudo-traduction (dans le langage scientifique du XIXᵉ siecle)?', Lupu, *Studi*, 259–64. A. Bidu-Vrănceanu, 'Dinamica vocabularului românesc după 1989. Sensuri "deviate" ale termenilor tehnico-ştiinţifici', *LiL*, 40.1, 1995:38–44, studies the contemporary adaptation of originally specialized terminology into general literary usage. D. Craşoveanu, 'Consideraţii asupra limbajului publicitar actual', *ib.*, 45–48, concludes a distinctly disapproving survey by recommending — apparently without irony — that commercial firms should employ a linguistic specialist to advise them on appropriate usage. A. Stoichiţiu Ichim, 'Observaţii privind influenţa engleză în limbajul publicistic actual (I)', *ib.*, 41.2:37–45. S. Goicu, 'Cuvîntul "sînt" ("sfînt") în onomastica românească', *ib.*, 40.3–4, 1995:16–21. L. Ionescu Ruxăndoiu, 'Structuri sociale şi forme de expresie lingvistică', *ib.*, 41.1:11–16. M. Sala, 'Principios metodológicos en la etimología rumana', *TLP*, 33–34, 1995–96:455–58. The third section of Alain Ruzé, *Vestiges celtiques en Roumanie*, Bern, Lang, 1994, 195 pp. + 2 maps, considers some lexical and onomastic questions, including (the very rare) 'Eléments celtiques dans la langue roumaine' (125–31). Eugen Munteanu, *Studi de lexicologie biblică*, Iaşi, Editura Universităţii 'Al. I. Cuza', 1995, 373 pp., examines the influence of the 'classical languages' (Greek, Slavonic, and, to a lesser extent, Latin) on the lexicon of the translation of religious texts into Romanian in the 17th c., arguing that such influences had a much larger role than is generally appreciated in the formation of standard Romanian vocabulary, both in intellectual and popular usage. V. Pamfil, 'Despre terminologia creştină de origine latină în limba română', Lupu, *Studi*, 193–200. S. Reinheimer Râpeanu, 'L'élément slave ancien du romain en perspective romane. (Quelques noms d'animaux)', *ib.*, 219–26. A survey of onomastic studies in Romania is V. Frăţilă, 'Die Namenforschung in Rumänien', *Balkan-Archiv*, 19–20, 1994–95:403–12. Id., 'De nouveau sur les toponymes du Banat: *áscura* et *călcadza*', Lupu, *Studi*, 122–31. L. Groza, 'Parallélismes phraséologiques franco-roumains. Le cas des expressions "demander l'aman" et "faire des salamalecs" ', *RLiR*, 60:403–12. T. Hristea, 'L'étymologie populaire et ses rapports avec l'attraction paronymique', Lupu, *Studi*, 583–97, makes frequent reference to Romanian examples.

DIALECTOLOGY. *Interferenzen in den Sprachen und Dialekten Südosteuropas*, ed. H. Gehl and M. Purdela Sitaru, Tübingen, Institut für donauschwäbische Geschichte und Landeskunde, 1994, 339 pp., is a collection of articles some of which bear on the mutual influence of Romanian and German in the Banat region. N. Mocanu, 'Situaţia actuală a labialelor în subdialectul bănăţean', Lupu, *Studi*, 182–92. S. Semcinski, 'Unele consecinţe ale contactelor lingvistice româno-ucrainene asupra graiurilor moldoveneşti ale limbii române', *LiL*, 39.3–4, 1994:86–88, argues that various lexical features, together with phonological characteristics such as vowel raising, are attributable to the influence of neighbouring Ukrainian dialects. V. Frăţilă, 'Aggiunte romene al REW. Nuove parole di origine latina', *MedRom*, 19, 1995:325–44, drawing particularly on his native dialect (that of the lower Târnave), and other recent dialectological studies, identifies some rare Romanian reflexes of Latin words, among them CARUS, FLAMMA, GESTIRE, and PECUS. G. Carageani, 'Aromeno e la romanità occidentale', Lupu, *Studi*, 35–51, questions, on structural grounds, whether Aromanian is properly classed together with Daco-Romanian as 'eastern' Romance. L. Fassel, 'Der linguistische Status des Aromunischen: eine unnötige Kontroverse', *Balkan-Archiv*, 19–20, 1994–95:385–401. M. Caragiu Marioţeanu, 'Païen, chrétien et orthodoxe en aroumain', Lupu, *Studi*, 52–73, examines religious terminology and vocabulary.

PRAGMATICS AND STYLISTICS. Changes in style of address in postwar Romania and since the Revolution are the subject of A. Roceric, 'Politeness and politics. Romanian *domn* vs *tovarăş*', Lupu, *Studi*, 246–58. L. Groza, 'Despre jocurile de cuvinte în frazeologia limbii române', *LiL*, 41.2, 32–36. C. Florescu ' "Familiar" ca tip de conotaţie', *ib.*, 39.3–4, 1994:17–21, identifies the characteristics of 'familiar' language (as distinct from 'slang' or 'popular' usage) in Romanian. C. Cruceru, 'Dialogul la cronicari', *ib.*, 39.1, 1994:17–21, discerns in the language of Moldavian and Muntenian chroniclers the origins of dialogue as a literary device in Romanian. Id., 'Marin Preda şi fascinaţia cuvîntului zilnic rostit de oameni', *ib.*, 39.3–4, 1994:22–25, discusses M.P.'s integration of structures from everyday speech into his literary style. M. Cvasnîi Cătănescu, 'Retorica românească medievală. Varlaam "Răspunsul împotriva Catihismului calvinescu" ', *ib.*, 40.1, 1995:19–29.

LITERATURE

POSTPONED

XI. RHETO-ROMANCE STUDIES

By Kenneth H. Rogers, *University of Rhode Island*

1. Bibliographical and General

Hans Goebl, *'Che cos'è un geotipo? Il problema dell'unità ladina intesa in chiave ascoliana', pp. 103–32 of *Italia settentrionale: crocevia di idiomi romanzi*, ed. Emanuele Banfi et al., Tübingen, Niemeyer, 1995. Giovan Battista Pellegrini, *'L'ASLEF ed il "retoromanzo" secondo C. Battisti', *BALM*, 29–35:53–97.

2. Friulan

GENERAL. Andrea Cuna and Federico Vicario, 'Testi e frammenti friulani del Trecento e del Quattrocento dall'Archivio di Stato di Udine', *Ce fastu?*, 71:7–34, inventory Cividale texts from the early 14th c. to the mid-15th c., with philological commentary and a call for the creation of genuine tools for Friulan philology: a history of the language, a historical grammar, and a completion of the etymological dictionary of Friulan. Giovanni Frau, *'Un caso friulano di paraetimologia multipla (*stracéis* con forme similari) e una parola rumena di presunta origine slava (*streasina*)', pp. 113–20 of *Scritti di linguistica e dialettologia in onore di Giuseppe Francescato*, ed. Facoltà di Lettere e Filologia, Trieste, Università degli Studi, 1995, hereafter *Francescato Vol.*

PHONOLOGY. Paola Benincà, 'Il pluralepalatale in friulano: saggio di analisi autosegmentale', *Francescato Vol.*, 25–46.

MORPHOSYNTAX. Giorgio Cadorini, 'Quelques hypothèses sur des aspects de la morphologie du frioulan prélittéraire. Contribution à l'étude de la Romania continentale centrale après la fragmentation du protoroman', *RLiR*, 60:463–83, provides evidence for a wide band of Proto-Romance, from the Po valley to Catalonia, in which the two-case system in the noun, long attested in Occitan and Old French, already existed. C.'s analysis is based largely, but not exclusively, on onomastic material; he urges (482–83) a thorough re-examination of early Dolomitic Ladin and Swiss Romansh nominal structures in the light of his theory. Maria Iliescu, *'Le conditionnel frioulan', *Francescato Vol.*, 159–66.

ONOMASTICS. Paola Barbierato, *'La toponomastica del territorio di Conegliano', pp. 3–52 of *Saggi dialettologici in area italo-romanza*, ed. G. B. Pellegrini, Centro Studio per la Dialettologia 'O. Parlangèli', Padua, 1995. Mauro Bugliato, *'I nomi di luogo a Driolazza', *Sot la*

Nape, 77, 1995:57–76; Enos Costantini, *'I nomi degli Avasinesi: cognomi e nomi di famiglie ad Avasinis', *Sot la Nape*, 77, 1995:77–86.

SOCIOLINGUISTICS AND LANGUAGES IN CONTACT. Pera Rizzolatti, *'Friulano e veneto a Pordenone', *Francescato Vol.*, 261–68.

3. LADIN

GENERAL. Walter Belardi, *'Periferia' e 'centro': un'antitesi nella 'questione dell lingua' di alcune storicità linguistiche* (Biblioteca di Ricerche Linguistiche e Filologiche, 37), Ro, Dipartimento di Studi Glottoantropologici, Il Calamo, 1995, 428 pp., contains three chapters relevant to Ladin linguistics. 'Prodromi inavvertiti della questione della lingua in Val Gardena: Arcangelo Lardschneider lessicografico' (133–84) is an appraisal of L.'s dictionary, compiled between 1906 and 1924. While favourably inclined towards the dictionary, B. notes that L. did not always share the widely-held views of his contemporaries on what constituted 'real' Gardenese words, as opposed to unassimilated Germanisms. In 'La questione del "ladin dolomitan"' (185–318) B. uses examples based on H. Schmid's construction of 'Rumantsch grischun' to demonstrate how a common written Ladin might be created from the six major dialect areas. The author warns against too rapid an introduction of such a written standard, pointing out (285) that the Dolomitic Ladin community is already a linguistic community, and that the various regional political parties would become (in fact, have already become) involved. In the third paper, 'Un caso di discrazia sociolinguistica tra generazioni: le vicende del gardenese scritto' (319–99), B. traces the history of written Gardenese in this century. He finds that older writers shun excessive neologisms, whereas younger writers welcome them. B. sees a gap in thinking between the Gardenese 'elite' and the rest of the population; but in spite of differences of opinion as to the standard to follow, writing in Gardenese is spreading.

ONOMASTICS. Guntram A. Plangg, *'Interferenze nella toponomastica fassana', pp. 171–78 of *Italia settentrionale: crocevia di idiomi romanzi*, ed. Emanuele Banfi et al., Tübingen, Niemeyer, 1995.

SOCIOLINGUISTICS AND LANGUAGES IN CONTACT. Lois Craffonara, 'Sellaladinische Sprachkontakte', pp. 285–329 of *Minderheiten in der Romania*, ed. Dieter Kattenbusch, Wilhelmsfeld, Egert, 1995, vi + 396 pp., recounts the history of language conflict in the area, mainly trilingual, from 1418 to the present. C. sees massive borrowings from the international Romance vocabulary, especially in the last decade, and believes that the obligatory use of subject pronouns with the verb may be due to German influence, while such changes as the shift in diphthong stress from *núof* to *nuóf* may be due to Italian. Otto Gsell,

'Zwischen drei Stühlen? Zur Sprachproblematik der Dolomitenlad-
iner', pp. 199–213 of *Mehrsprachigkeit in Europa — Hindernis oder
Chance?*, ed. Uta Helfrich and Claudia Maria Riehl, Wilhelmsfeld,
Egert, 1994, vii + 213 pp., is a somewhat pessimistic appraisal of the
shift from Ladin to German or Italian in the near future, based on
what G. sees as the diminished competence in Ladin of the young.
The author cites outright borrowings into Ladin, such as *airbag*, and
calques such as *cënta de segurëza* (207); and he asks, in conclusion, what
good is a 'roof' (Überdachundsprache) when the walls are down?

4. Swiss Romansh

GENERAL. Arthur Baur, *La retoromanca: historio kaj nuntempo de la kvara
nacia lingvo de Svislando*, Bellinzona, Dubois, 1995. Ines Gartmann,
*'Publicaziuns: tscherna bibliografica', *Annalas da la Societad Retoru-
mantscha*, 108, 1995:275–302.

SOCIOLINGUISTICS AND LANGUAGES IN CONTACT. Rico Cathomas,
*'Il svilup dalla competenza linguistica tier minoritads: ina avischina-
ziun socio-, psico- e pedalinguistica en duas parts', *ib.*, 7–26. Clau
Solèr, *'Sprachwandel und Sprachwechsel bei ausgegleichenem
Bilinguismus,' pp. 263–75 of *Soziolinguistische Variation: Bilinguismus,
Multilinguismus, Sprachkontakt, Sprachvergleich; Dialektgebrauch und Einstel-
lung zu Sprachvarietäten*, ed. Wolfgang Vierek, Stuttgart, Steiner, 1995.

3

CELTIC LANGUAGES

I. WELSH STUDIES

LANGUAGE

By DAVID THORNE, *Reader in Welsh Language and Literature, University of Wales, Lampeter*

1. GENERAL

M. Löffler, 'The Welsh language in Wales: public gain and private grief?', *Journal for the Study of British Cultures*, 2:187–200, is a balanced account of the decline, the present condition and the prospects of survival of the Welsh language. B. F. Roberts, '"A gentle and amiable prince": Louis-Lucien Bonaparte and Welsh studies', *THSC*, 2:79–99, explores Bonaparte's genuine interest in the Welsh language, its dialects, and in Welsh books and journals. G. H. Jenkins, '"Tis a tongue not made for every mouth": the Welsh language in early modern Wales', *The Celtic History Review*, 2:8–10, is a brief discussion of the demeaning attitude of English writers towards the Welsh language. J. G. Jones, 'The national petition on the legal status of the Welsh language', *WHR*, 18:92–124, reviews the weaknesses and modest achievements associated with the 1942 Welsh Court Act which sought to define the legal status of the Welsh language.

2. GRAMMAR

Gareth King, *Intermediate Welsh*, London, Routledge, 156 pp., is a useful reference and practice book for students who have managed the initial stages of learning Welsh. Peter Wynn Thomas, *Gramadeg y Gymraeg*, Cardiff, Univ. of Wales Press, x + 837 pp., is a valuable comprehensive reference grammar of modern Welsh usage based on wholly synchronic principles. Id., 'Safonau Cymraeg ysgrifenedig', *SC*, 29:269–93, examines the results of the survey of the acceptability of variants in contemporary written Welsh. A. Shisha-Halevy, 'Structural sketches in Middle Welsh syntax (1)', *ib.*, 127–224, introduces what will eventually form a series of corpus-based profiles of certain subsystems in Middle Welsh grammar. The discussions in Borsley, *Celtic Syntax*, assume the principles-and-parameters framework; the comparative perspective presented is both internal and external to the Celtic family. R. D. Borsley and I. Roberts in their introduction (1–52), provide a sketch to the basic assumptions about syntactic theory that are common to the contributions collected here and discuss a number of aspects of the syntax of Celtic languages that are of particular interest from a principles-and-parameters perspective. R. Hendrick, 'Some syntactic effects of suppletion in the Celtic copulas' (75–96), addresses the issue of how syntax and morphology interact by referring to examples from Welsh, Breton, and Irish. M. Tallerman, 'Fronting constructions in Welsh' (97–124), presents an alternative analysis of both the cleft (mixed) and abnormal constructions in Welsh. A. Rouveret, '*Bod* in the present tense and in other tenses' (125–70), argues for a unitary characterization of the verb *bod* in Welsh, although *bod* has several forms in the third person of the present indicative. I. Roberts and U. Shlonsky, 'Pronominal enclisis in VSO languages' (171–99), ties together similar aspects of the clitic systems of Welsh and Semitic (Arabic and Hebrew). E. Poppe, 'Negation in Welsh and Jesperson's cycle', *JCLin*, 4:99–107, investigates typological aspects of the development of the negation of a verbal phrase in Welsh in the light of Otto Jesperson's comments on a cyclic behaviour for a historical development of negation. David A. Thorne, *Gramadeg Cymraeg*, Llandysul, Gomer, 480 pp., is a comprehensive description of contemporary Welsh literary usage which includes useful sections on registers and dialect variation. D. Willis, 'Dweud y drefn: myfyrdodau ar hanes trefn geiriau yn y Gymraeg', *Y Traethodydd*, 151:160–72, provides a brief description of word order in the verbal phrase in Welsh. E. Poppe, 'Convergence and divergence: the emergence of a "future" in the British languages', *TPS*, 94:119–60, presents evidence for the uses of the future paradigms in Modern Welsh and Modern Breton from medieval texts. Based on the inherent aspectuality of the verb, an explanation for the present and future readings of the Welsh verbs is advanced; some typological parallels for the developments in Welsh and Breton are discussed. Id., 'Tense and mood in Welsh grammars c. 1400–1621', *NLWJ*, 29:17–38, examines the categories of tense and mood in the work of early Welsh grammarians.

3. Etymology and Lexicography

Gwilym T. Jones and Tomos Roberts, *Enwau Lleoedd Môn: The Place-names of Anglesey*, Anglesey, Univ. of Wales, Bangor, ix + 182 pp., is a bilingual volume discussing the geographical and historical place names of Anglesey. A. Falileyev, *SC*, 29:295–96, has notes on OW *ciluin* and Middle Welsh *cwys*. E. P. Hamp, *ib.*, 297–300, writes on *Andiatis*, *Eden*, *cyfys*, *llesg*, *cyfre*, *trew*, *ystrew*. V. Orel, *ib.*, 301–04, discusses *Corúinom, ailam, lisTaś TiTaś, Pionti arsnas*, from the Botoritta inscription. Parts 45 and 46 of *GPC* (ed. G. A. Bevan) cover PILYN-PRAIN, PRAIN-PUREN respectively. P. Morgan, 'The place-name as surname in Wales', *NLWJ*, 29:63–75, examines the distribution patterns of those Welsh locative surnames which form a small proportion of the surnames of the Welsh people.

4. SOCIOLINGUISTICS

C. M. Jones, 'Motivation and gender: a Welsh case study', *Journal of Celtic Language Learning*, 2:6–19, demonstrates the significance of gender orientated motivational differences among participants attending an immersion course. Marion Löffler, '*Iaith nas Arferir, Iaith Farw Yw*': *Ymgyrchu dros yr Gymraeg rhwng y ddau Ryfel Byd*, Aberystwyth, UWCASWC, 28 pp., assesses the contribution of two important voluntary organizations, established between the two world wars, *Undeb Cenedlaethol y Cymdeithasau Cymraeg* and *Urdd Gobaith Cymru*, to the preservation of the Welsh language by creating opportunities for their members to use their native language through a plethora of recognized social networks. Dot Jones, *The Coming of the Railways and Language Change in North Wales 1850–1900*, Aberystwyth, UWCASWC, 23 pp., focuses on the language ability of railway workers as a force for language change in North Wales and concludes that the railway revolution, together with migration and education, must be considered a primary factor in accounting for language shift in 19th-c. Wales. D. Prys, 'Gender and sex in Welsh nouns', *Planet*, 121:88–91, demonstrates that assumptions about a person's sex based on noun gender cannot be made in the Welsh language and that a set of directives issued and deemed useful in one language cannot be adopted by another.

EARLY AND MEDIEVAL LITERATURE

By NERYS ANN JONES, *Department of Celtic, University of Edinburgh*

Cyfres Beirdd y Tywysogion, the seven-volume series of editions of the work of the 12th- and 13th-c. court poets of the Welsh princes is completed with the publication of Rhian M. Andrews et al., *Gwaith Bleddyn Fardd a Beirdd Eraill Ail Hanner y Drydedd Ganrif ar Ddeg*, Cardiff, Univ. of Wales Press, xxvi + 667 pp., a substantial volume presenting the work of eight late 13th-c. poets. Equally substantial is the *Festschrift* presented to the general editor of the series, R. Geraint Gruffydd, on his retirement as director of the University of Wales Centre for Advanced Studies in Welsh and Celtic. Contributions to *Beirdd a Thywysogion: Barddoniaeth Llys yng Nghymru, Iwerddon a'r Alban*, ed. B. F. Roberts and M. E. Owen, Cardiff, Univ. of Wales Press–Aberystwyth, The National Library of Wales, xxxii + 356 pp., include D. S. Evans, 'Iaith y llys a Beirdd y Tywysogion' (60–74), an introduction to some of the linguistic characteristics of *Gogynfeirdd* verse. P. Lynch, 'Yr awdl a'i mesurau' (258–87), and N. A. Jones, 'Y Gogynfeirdd a'r englyn' (288–301), are two articles on the metrics of the corpus. Y Chwaer Bosco, 'Awen y Cynfeirdd a'r Gogynfeirdd' (14–38), surveys the use of the term *awen* 'inspiration' and M. Haycock, 'Medd a mêl farddoni' (39–59), provides a comprehensive study of the associations of mead and mead-drinking in the work of both the Poets of the Princes and their predecessors. C. McKenna, 'Bygwth a dychan mewn barddoniaeth llys Gymraeg' (108–21), examines the evidence for the use of satire by the *Gogynfeirdd*, whilst M. E. Owen, 'Noddwyr a beirdd' (75–107), draws on the *topoi* and vocabulary they used, as well as on what is known of the patronage they enjoyed and of the way their work was transmitted, in order to piece together as full a picture as possible of their role and status in medieval Welsh society. Aspects of the work of two individual *Gogynfeirdd*, 12th-c. Cynddelw Brydydd Mawr and 13th-c. Bleddyn Fardd, are focused upon in A. Parry Owen, '"A mi, feirdd, i mewn a chwi allan": Cynddelw Brydydd Mawr a'i grefft' (143–65), and R. M. Andrews, '*Triwyr a gollais: Yr awdlau marwnad i dri mab Gruffudd ap Llywelyn gan Fleddyn Fardd*' (166–79). G. A. Williams, 'Owain Cyfeiliog: bardd-dywysog?' (180–201), argues, on the basis of the high number of collocations that are common to their work, that the poems traditionally attributed to prince-poet Owain Cyfeiliog belong to his court-poet, Cynddelw Brydydd Mawr, whilst R. Bromwich, 'Cyfeiriadau traddodiadol a chwedlonol y Gogynfeirdd' (202–18), examines the allusions made by the *Gogynfeirdd* to the native lore of Wales and concludes that

Cynddelw might have played an important role in the creation of 'The Triads of the Island of Britain'. The royal patrons of the *Gogynfeirdd* are the subject of two interdisciplinary studies. *Gruffudd ap Cynan: A Collaborative Biography*, ed. K. L. Maund, Woodbridge, The Boydell Press, xi + 217 pp., includes J. E. Caerwyn Williams, 'Meilyr Brydydd and Gruffudd ap Cynan' (165–86), an edition, translation and discussion of Meilyr Brydydd's elegy to the 11th-c. prince of Gwynedd. The meat of the book, however, is a series of discussions on various aspects of Gruffudd's Life commissioned sometime during the 12th or 13th centuries. D. E. Thornton, 'The genealogy of Gruffudd ap Cynan' (79–108), K. L. Maund, 'Gruffudd, grandson of Iago: *Historia Gruffud vab Kenan* and the construction of legitimacy' (109–16), J. Jesch, 'Norse historical traditions and *Historia Gruffud vab Kenan*: Magnús Berfættr and Haraldr Hárfagri' (117–48), N. A. Jones, '*Historia Gruffud vab Kenan*: the first audience' (149–56). *Yr Arglwydd Rhys*, ed. N. A. Jones and Huw Pryce, Cardiff, Univ. of Wales Press, xxii + 230 pp., contains a wide-ranging study of the role of Rhys ap Gruffudd, 12th-c. prince of Deheubarth, as a patron of the arts by J. E. Caerwyn Williams, 'Yr Arglwydd Rhys ac "Eisteddfod" Aberteifi 1176: y cefndir diwylliannol' (94–128), and also a detailed discussion of the eulogies sung to him by the *Gogynfeirdd* by N. A. Jones, 'Canu mawl Beirdd y Tywysogion i'r Arglwydd Rhys' (129–44). The spirit of life in the court which Rhys and his descendants held at Dinefwr in Carmarthenshire is evoked in Morfydd E. Owen, *Bwrlwm Llys Dinefwr: Brenin, Bardd a Meddyg/The Din of Dinefwr: Prince, Poet and Physician*, Carmarthenshire Antiquarian Society Monograph Series, Llandybïe, 6: 16 + 16 pp., by means of a series of portraits of individuals drawn from the evidence of the native law tracts, court poetry and the medical books of the period. A wide range of sources, including contemporary poetry, is also used by B. F. Roberts in order to present medieval attitudes towards the holy island of Bardsey in 'Enlli'r Oesoedd Canol', Jones, *Enlli*, 21–48.

A useful introduction to the religious literature of medieval Wales for a non-Welsh readership is provided by Oliver Davies, *Celtic Christianity in Early Medieval Wales: The Origins of the Welsh Spiritual Tradition*, Cardiff, Univ. of Wales Press, xii + 193 pp. It contains translations of poems of praise, penance and confession dating from the 10th to the 13th c., and synopses of some early saints' Lives as well as of the 14th-c. visionary work *Ymborth yr Enaid*: the author's study of these texts as a reflection of the spiritual values and needs of the age in which they were composed is more convincing than his quest for traces of pre-Christian 'Celtic' features. There is nothing original in J. Ryan, 'Kyssegrlan Vuched or Ymborth yr Eneit', *New Blackfriars, A Monthly Review edited by the English Dominicans*, October

1996, 452–57, but A. Breeze, 'Master John of St. Davids, Adam and Eve, and the Rose amongst Thorns', *SC*, 29:225–35 breaks new ground with a detailed investigation into the sources of a poem on Adam and Eve beginning 'Ef a wnaeth Panthon', and of a passage on the Virgin Mary as a rose amongst thorns in the didactic poem known as 'Difregwawd Taliesin', both works attributed by Breeze to a 12th-c. poet, Master John of St Davids.

Although the syntax of the language of the Book of Aneirin has often been used as part of the argument for dating the *Gododdin*, until recently no comprehensive study of it has been available. Graham R. Isaac, *The Verb in the Book of Aneirin: Studies in Syntax, Morphology and Etymology*, Tübingen, Niemeyer, 483 pp., makes good that deficiency with a close syntactic analysis of the sentences of the corpus, followed by the collection and classification of all finite verbs except *bot*. Appended to this study is a series of notes on the analysis of certain passages in the *Gododdin* which will be of interest to literary scholars. A further note by Isaac suggesting a new reading of one of the *Gododdin* stanzas is to be found in 'CA ll. 1234 Oed quenuin hic caraitet', *SC*, 29:300–01. C. Cessford challenges the traditional view that the enemies of the *Gododdin* were Anglo-Saxons in 'Where are the Anglo-Saxons in the Gododdin poem?', *Anglo-Saxon Studies in Archaeology and History*, 8:95–98, and in 'Yorkshire and the Gododdin poem', *Yorkshire Archaeological Journal*, 68:241–43, and compares archaeological and literary evidence in 'Pictish Silver and the Gododdin poem', *PASJ*, 9:30–31. D. A. Bray, 'A Woman's Loss and Lamentation: Heledd's song and *The Wife's Lament*', *Neophilologus*, 79:147–54, is a most welcome comparative study in which the situations of the two female protagonists are viewed against the background of two similar heroic cultures, and their expression of grief read within the context of heroic poetry. P. Sims-Williams, 'The death of Urien', *CMCS*, 32:25–56, scrutinizes the accounts of Urien Rheged's slaying in two 9th-c. sources, the *Historia Brittonum* and the *englynion* cycle, 'Canu Urien', concluding that they are both illustrations of the theme of the loss of British sovereignty in the 'Old North'. During the course of this accomplished paper Sims-Williams also tackles the difficult but tantalizing questions of the date of Urien's death, the identity of his killer, the reason for his decapitation and the relationship between 'Canu Urien' and the Llywarch Hen cycle. Daniel Huws, *Five Ancient Books of Wales* (H. M. Chadwick Memorial Lectures, 6), Cambridge, 23 pp., provides a thought-provoking account of the five earliest manuscript collections of Welsh poetry, while P. Russel, 'Scribal (in)competence in thirteenth-century North Wales: the orthography of the Black Book of Chirk (Peniarth MS 29)', *NLWJ*, 29:129–76 explains the orthographic peculiarities of this important literary and legal MS by the fact that the scribes were copying from an exemplar written in OW orthography, and tentatively suggests that BBCh was the product of some form of secular law-school in North Wales. Elissa R. Henken, *National Redeemer: Owain Glyndŵr in Welsh Tradition*, Cardiff, Univ. of Wales Press, xii + 250 pp., although primarily a study of Glyndŵr folklore, contains a survey of the role of the redeemer-hero in medieval Welsh vaticinatory poetry. J. A. Doig, 'The prophecy of the "Six Kings to Follow John" and Owain Glyndŵr', *SC*, 29: 257–67, traces the origins and development of this popular prophecy and examines its possible use by Glyndŵr and his allies as anti-Lancastrian propaganda in the early years of the 15th c. R. Wallis Evans, 'Proffwydoliaeth Dewi Sant', *LlC*, 19: 168–71, publishes three texts of St. David's prophecy. R. G. Gruffydd, 'Why Cors Fochno?', *THSC*, 2: 5–19, is an attempt to discover why Cors Fochno in northern Cardiganshire appears in vaticinatory poetry from the late 11th c. onwards as the site of one of the final victories of the Welsh against the English. In arguing his hypothesis that a battle was actually fought at Cors Fochno in the mid-6th c. between the British, led by Maelgwn Gwynedd, and the Irish, Gruffydd uses place name evidence to demonstrate that the 12th-c. *Life of St. Padarn* may be based on genuine historical information.

Huw M. Edwards, *Dafydd ap Gwilym: Influences and Analogues*, Oxford, Clarendon, xiii + 300 pp., is a thorough study of the cultural and literary influences which contributed to the distinctive poetic voice of Dafydd ap Gwilym. He examines the evidence relating to the popular poets of medieval Wales and the way their submerged tradition reveals itself in bardic verse, before attempting to identify the elements in early *cywydd* poetry which may owe something to both the native popular verse tradition and to the effect of European literary fashion. Dylan Foster Evans, *"Goganwr am gig ynyd": The Poet as Satirist in Medieval Wales*, Aberystwyth, Research Papers of UWCASWC, 41 pp., explores the role and status of satire in 14th-c. Wales, drawing attention to its traditional style and metre, and to the learning and technical accomplishment of its practitioners. Id., 'Y bardd a'i farf: y traddodiad barfol', *Dwned*, 2: 11–29, traces the development of a sub-genre of humorous poetry where the poet berates his own beard. He concludes with the intriguing suggestion that these *cywyddau* were in fact lightly-disguised poems of request for a shave! In the 14th and 15th c., poems requesting all kinds of gifts, by the poets themselves or on behalf of their patrons, were highly popular in Wales, as is shown in B. O. Huws's prolegomena to a study of the genre, 'Golwg ar y canu gofyn', *YB*, 21: 37–50. Id., 'Cerdd unnos', *Dwned*, 2: 119, provides an additional reference to those given in R. I. Daniel's article in *Dwned*, 1 : 55–66, to a poem claimed to be composed in the space of one night, and in 'Datgan cerddi', *Dwned*, 2 : 120–21, he draws attention to a comparison in a poem by Ieuan Llawdden (*fl.* 1450) which might shed some light on the nature of the accompaniment to which the *cywyddau* would be sung. N. Jacobs, 'Adjectival collocations in the poetry of the early *Cywyddwyr*: a preliminary survey', *CMCS*, 31 : 55–70, affords an insight into the poetic techniques of the first generation of *cywydd* poets by analysing the way loose adjectival compounds are constructed in their work, and R. G. Gruffydd in his Sir John Rhŷs Memorial Lecture, 'Wales's second grammarian: Dafydd Ddu of Hiraddug', *PBA*, 90 : 1–28 (the substance of which has been published in Welsh in *LlC*, 18 : 205–20) illuminates both the obscure figure of the reviser of Einion Offeiriad's bardic grammar and 14th-c. poetics in general.

R. G. Gruffydd, 'A glimpse of Welsh medieval court procedure in a poem by Dafydd ap Gwilym', *Fryde Vol.*, 165–78, provides a translation and commentary upon a poem to the Cock-Thrush (*GDG*, 123) in which the poet's relationship with his beloved is expressed in quasi-legal terms, while M. T. Davies, 'Dafydd ap Gwilym and the friars: the poetics of antimendicancy', *SC*, 29 : 237–55, examines Dafydd's so-called antimendicant poems (*GDG*, 136–38) and shows how the poet's attitude towards the transitory nature of life also manifests itself in the imagery and style of his love and nature poetry. D. Huws, 'The transmission of a Welsh classic: Dafydd ap Gwilym', *Fryde Vol.*, 179–202, tackles the puzzle of why no collection of the work of Dafydd ap Gwilym was made during the first hundred years after the poet's death, and in the process presents a comprehensive survey of the manuscript tradition of Dafydd's poetry from *c.* 1450 to 1748. Helen Fulton, *Dafydd ap Gwilym: Apocrypha*, Llandysul, Gomer, xxxix + 267 pp., takes a new approach to the problems of the manuscript transmission of *cywyddwyr* poetry by basing her editions on single master manuscripts belonging to the 16th century. This volume contains a selection from the 177 poems attributed to Dafydd in the manuscript but rejected by Thomas Parry in his definitive edition of the canon. As is usual in the 'Welsh Classics Series', each edited text is accompanied by an English translation and notes.

Ann Parry Owen, *Gwaith Llywelyn Brydydd Hoddnant, Dafydd ap Gwilym, Hillyn ac eraill*, Aberystwyth, UWCASWC, xvii + 217 pp., is an edition of the poems added to the Hendregadredd MS *c.* 1325–50 when it was being used as the court book of Ieuan Llwyd of Glyn Aeron. The collection consists mainly of *awdlau* and *englynion* addressed to Ieuan himself, to members of his family and to other local noble families. Also included in the volume is the work of another contemporary Ceredigion poet, Llywelyn Ddu ab y Pastard,

edited by D. F. Evans. A full discussion of one of the *Hendregadredd*
poems, Dafydd ap Gwilym's lengthy *englynion* series of praise to the
cross at Carmarthen, is provided in Ann Parry Owen, 'Englynion
Dafydd Llwyd ap Gwilym Gam i'r Grog o Gaer', *YB*, 21 : 15–36. M.
P. Bryant-Quinn, ' "Enaid y Gwir Oleuni": y Grog yn Aberhonddu',
Dwned, 2 : 51–93, is a revised edition of one of the most accomplished
poems of this genre, the 15th-c. *cywydd* of praise to the cross at Brecon,
formerly attributed to Huw Cae Llwyd. On the basis of internal
evidence, it is proposed that this magnificent poem might be the work
of Huw's less well-known contemporary, Ieuan Brydydd Hir. R. I.
Daniel, 'Agweddau ar waith Llywelyn ab y Moel', *Dwned*, 2 : 31–50, is
a revision of the canon of the 15th-c. soldier-poet who fought with
Glyndŵr. As well as re-examining the dating and historical context of
Llywelyn's poems, the author provides for the first time in print a
fuller version of the well-known *cywydd* 'I Goed y Graig Lwyd'.
Finally, D. J. Bowen concludes his study of poets and patrons of
15th-c. Wales with a masterly survey of the praise tradition in 'Beirdd
a noddwyr y bymthegfed ganrif (Rhan III)', *LlC*, 18 : 1–28.

Sioned Davies, *Crefft y Cyfarwydd: Astudiaeth ar Dechnegau Naratif yn Y
Mabinogion*, Cardiff, Univ. of Wales Press, x + 261 pp., combines a
close analysis of the stylistic features of the 11 native tales known as *Y
Mabinogion* with a knowledge of recent international research on oral
literature and the development of literacy, to produce a simulating
study of the techniques of the *cyfarwydd*, the oral story-teller of
medieval Wales. C. Lloyd-Morgan, 'The branching tree of medieval
narrative: Welsh *cainc* and French *branche*', *Mills Vol.*, 36–50, is a
detailed examination of the meaning and usage of the two terms in
the literary tradition of Wales and France, leading to the conclusion
that there was probably no direct connection between them. The
conclusion of J. Hemming, '*Ami and Amile*: a partial source for *Pwyll?*',
CMCS, 32 : 57–93, on the other hand, is that the opening section of
the First Branch of the *Mabinogi* may well have been influenced by an
11th-c. French or Latin version of the original French legend.
D. November, 'Y Fenyw a'r Mabinogi', *Y Traethodydd*, 151 : 233–50,
provides a somewhat impressionistic feminist reading of the Four
Branches, while S. Ito-Morino, 'The journey across the wilderness:
structural analysis of the three Welsh Arthurian romances (2)', *StCJ*,
7 : 27–43, attempts to demonstrate that the central theme of the
Arthurian romances is 'a Journey between two worlds'. *The Mabinogi:
A Book of Essays*, ed. C. W. Sullivan III, NY–London, Garland,
xxi + 387 pp., is a useful collection of 16 papers on the Four Branches
previously published in journals during the 1970s and 1980s. G.
Thomas, 'Pedair Cainc y Mabinogi', *Cof Cenedl*, 11 : 3–27, provides
an eminently readable general introduction to the Four Branches

based on sound modern research, while W. J. McCann, 'Tristan: the Celtic and Oriental material re-examined', Grimbert, *Tristan and Isolde*, 3–35, contains a discussion of the material concerning Trystan/ Drystan in Middle Welsh, based mainly on the work of Rachel Bromwich. M. E. Owen, 'The medical books of medieval Wales and the physicians of Myddfai', *The Carmarthenshire Antiquary*, 31 : 34–44, is a lucid introduction to the medical literature preserved in the Welsh vernacular and what it tells us about the practice of medicine in late medieval Wales, consisting of a survey of the manuscripts and their contents and a discussion of the evidence for the importance of Meddygon Myddfai in the transmission of medical learning in the Welsh language.

Two most useful guides to recent work in the field of medieval Welsh literature are Rachel Bromwich, *Medieval Welsh Literature to c. 1400, including Arthurian Studies: A Personal Guide*, Cardiff, Univ. of Wales Press, iv + 50 pp., and J. T. Koch, 'The Celtic Lands' in Lacy, *Arthurian Literature*, 239–322.

LITERATURE SINCE 1500

By KATHRYN JENKINS, *Lecturer in Welsh, University of Wales, Lampeter*

Glanmor Williams, 'Iaith, llên a chrefydd yn yr unfed ganrif ar bymtheg', *LlC*, 19:29–40, analyses the reaction of the Welsh to the Renaissance and Protestant Reformation. J. G. Jones, 'John Penri: Piwritan a Chymro', *ib.*, 41–69, offers a comprehensive survey of Penri's life and career and emphasizes his especial contribution to Welsh history and religious literature. Id., 'Maurice Kyffin a Huw Lewys: dau amddiffynnydd y ffydd Brotestannaidd yng Nghymru ym 1595', *YB*, 21:51–72, studies two key figures and notes the significance of their all-important translations, namely, *Deffynniad Ffydd Eglwys Lloegr*, and *Perl Mewn Adfyd*, published in 1595, for the continuation of the Reformation in Wales. G. Bowen, 'Robert Gwyn o Benyberth, awdur Catholig', *THSC*, 2:33–58, outlines the career of one of the most prolific authors of the Elizabethan era, noting that he wrote 7 works, 2 of which are not extant. Id., *Y Drych Kristnogawl*, Cardiff, Univ. of Wales Press, 1322 pp., is a full edition of Alun Mathias's copy of Cardiff MS 3240, and contains an extensive introduction. C. Lloyd Morgan, 'Ar glawr neu ar lafar: llenyddiaeth a llyfrau merched Cymru o'r bymthegfed ganrif i'r ddeunawfed', *LlC*, 19:70–78, notes that the development of women's literature in Wales is very much in contrast to the similar development in Europe, and that patterns of literacy probably account for this. In a most interesting minor article, R. G. Gruffydd, 'Atgof am ddyddiau ysgol yr Esgob Richard Davies (1506?–1581)', *Y Casglwr*, 56–57:4, refers to a verse by Davies in the introduction to the 1567 New Testament where he describes the method by which he was taught the Ten Commandments.

B. F. Roberts, 'Lloyd-Lhuyd-Llwyd', *Y Traethodydd*, 151:180–83, looks at the various spellings of his surname used by the antiquarian Edward Lhuyd, noting his consistent use of the accustomed spelling after 1688. N. Lloyd, 'Sylwadau ar iaith rhai o gerddi Rhys Prichard', *NLWJ*, 29:257–80, offers a significant and startling analysis. By carefully comparing different manuscript and printed versions of his work she concludes that the printed versions published by Stephen Hughes do not represent the poet's true voice. Id., 'Cerddi Huw Morys i Barbra Miltwn', *YB*, 21:97–119, analyses three poems in their historical context and publishes an edited version of their texts. G. W. Owen and D. Llwyd Morgan, 'Rhai sylwadau ar arddull Morgan Llwyd', and 'Morgan Llwyd a'r Iddewon', *ib.*, 73–80, 81–96, discuss important aspects of Llwyd's work, dwelling particularly on the poetic nature of his prose style in *Llythur ir Cymru Cariadus*, and his eschatological longings.

K. Jenkins, 'Cân y Ffydd', *Cylchgrawn Cymdeithas Hanes y Methodistiaid Calfinaidd*, 20:5–30, discusses the development of the Methodist hymn from the beginning of the Methodist movement in Wales in the middle of the 18th c. to the present day, dwelling particularly on characteristic themes and stylistic traits. B. F. Roberts, 'Emynau Ewrop yn y Gymraeg', *Bwletin Cymdeithas Emynau Cymru*, 3:151–65, is a comprehensive survey of translations of hymns of the European tradition into Welsh with particular emphasis on German influence. E. W. James, 'Merched a'r emyn yn Sir Gâr', *Barn*, 402–03:26–29, looks at the work of four female hymnists in the Dinefwr area of Carmarthenshire, noting the development of the Welsh hymn and the paucity of women hymnwriters. E. Evans, *Pursued by God*, Bridgend, Evangelical Press of Wales, 191 pp., is a translation with introduction of 507 verses of William Williams Pantycelyn's epic poem *Theomemphus*, (the original being roughly three times as long), and emphasizes the faithful depiction of Biblical teaching rendered by the poet. G. Carr, 'Bwrlwm bywyd y Cymry yn Llundain yn y ddeunawfed ganrif', pp. 59–87 of *Cof Cenedl*, 11, ed. G. H. Jenkins, Llandysul, Gomer, 184 pp., studies the activities of various societies and figures dwelling in the English capital, but in close contact with literary and linguistic developments in Wales. R. Ifans, 'Celfyddyd y cantor o'r Nant', *YB*, 21:120–46, dissects the *anterliwtiau* and looks especially at the craft of characterization. An historical novel by R. D. Jones, *Fy Hen Lyfr Cownt*, Llandysul, Gomer, xvii + 85 pp., has been reprinted containing an Introduction by K. Jenkins. The novel is in the form of a diary and is an imaginary account of the last decade of the life of the extraordinary hymnist, Ann Griffiths (1776–1805). The Introduction notes the genius of the hymnist and outlines relevant historical background on plot and characterization.

D. A. Jones, in a number of articles, draws attention to the significance of the literary activities of Thomas Levi (1825–1916). In 'Hen Swynwr y "Sorfa Fach" ', *Cof Cenedl*, 11:89–116, he offers a biographical portrait, based on his monograph, *Thomas Levi*, Caernarfon, Pantycelyn, 60 pp., which states quite categorically that the subject incorporates the values and public duties of 19th-c. Wales, and was a pioneer in the field of magazine publishing for children: he was the first editor of *Trysorfa'r Plant*, which gained cross-denominational support and which reached a monthly readership of 44,000. Id., 'Llond Poced o Ddoethineb', *Y Casglwr*, 58:18, also refers to Levi, and looks at the popularity at this time of the pocket essay. H. T. Edwards, 'The Welsh collier as hero', *Welsh Writing in English*, 2:22–48, analyses the stereotypical portrayal of the collier in Welsh literature, and notes the moralist literature of the 19th c. E. Cass, 'Robert Jones Derfel: a Welsh poet in the *Cotton Factory Times*', *Llafur*, 7:53–67, discusses the context of British working-class literature, referring in particular to a weekly paper of the cotton operatives of Lancashire, which contained poems sent in by readers, listing those contributed by R. J. Derfel between 1891–1905. J. G. Jones, 'Cipdrem ar emynau Ieuan Glan Geirionydd', *Bwletin Cymdeithas Emynau Cymru*, 3:126–40, outlines the life and career of the noted poet and hymnist and emphasizes the literary and theological quality of his work and his natural bent toward stoicism. R. Ifans, 'Carol blygain fwyaf poblogaidd ein Iaith', *Y Traethodydd*, 151:25–39, analyses the scriptural allusions, typological and otherwise, in Eos Iâl's famous carol. D. E. Davies, 'Watkin Hezeciah Williams', *ib.*, 116–20, celebrates the contribution of the poet-preacher, dwelling on his education at Carmarthen College. M. L. Parry-Jones, 'Baledi Levi Gibbon, Thomas Harris, Stephen Jones, ac eraill', *LlC*, 19:85–129, is a study and classification of various forms of popular ballads as illustrated by the afore mentioned poets. B. F. Roberts, ' "My dear little boy": nodyn ar lythyrau Islwyn at Martha Davies', *YB*, 21:147–62, looks at the correspondence of Islwyn and his wife, and notes the complexities of their relationship owing to the premature death, previous to their marriage, of the poet's celebrated sweetheart Anne Bowen. K. Jenkins, ' "Angau Arfog Miniog Mawr": dau fardd. Un braw', *THSC*, 2:167–83, discusses the poetry of Robert ap Gwilym Ddu, though similarities are drawn, and contrasts are made, with the work of T. H. Parry-Williams, noting the overriding obsession of both with the theme of death in their poetry.

R. Poole, 'The politics of place', *Planet*, 119:66–71, studies the antagonism between the Welsh and English literary traditions in 20th-c. Wales. *Moelwyn: Bardd y Ddinas Gadarn*, ed. B. F. Roberts, Caernarfon, Pantycelyn, 100 pp., is a celebration of the life, poetry, theology, and criticism of J. G. M. Hughes, and contains contributions on these aspects by M. Evans (34–66), M. Lloyd Davies (67–84), and K. Jenkins (85–97), as well as that of the editor. *Bro Fy Mebyd a Cherddi Eraill*, Denbigh, Gee, 167 pp., is a selection with preface by D. Jones of the poetry of Wil Ifan, placing particular emphasis on his winning *vers libre pryddest* of 1925: the preface also notes the influence of Ceiriog and John Morris-Jones. Thomas Parry, *Amryw Bethau*, Denbigh, Gee, 324 pp., is a collection of essays on Welsh *literati* by one of this century's foremost scholars, and contains an important biographical foreword by J. E. C. Williams. D. Ifans, 'Annwyl Kate, Annwyl Saunders — Atodiad', *NLWJ*, 29:341–46, brings to light unpublished correspondence between Saunders Lewis and Kate Roberts regarding their conversation on Welsh prose which was subsequently published, *Crefft y Stori Fer*. R. Humphreys, *Lloffion o Ddyddiadur Ambrose Bebb 1920–1926*, Cardiff, Univ. of Wales Press, xii + 338 pp., is a collection of prose from Bebb's most prolific period: the Introduction dwells on French influence, and portrays the subject as a natural born researcher. E. Humphreys, 'O Barch i Ambrose Bebb', pp. 192–203 of *Gwarchod y Gwreiddiau*, ed. R. Llwyd, Llandysul, Gomer, 248 pp., depicts Bebb as a true prose artist who was shackled by his scholarship. J. E. Davies, 'Canmlwyddiant *Y Llenor*', *Y Casglwr*, 56–57:28–29, is an appreciation of the value and content of the notable periodical, together with an analysis of W. J. Gryffudd's role as editor.

W. O. Roberts, 'Gair am eiriau: nofela yn y ganrif nesaf', *Llais Llyfrau*, 4:4,11, suggests that the novel is a literary form which changes and adapts to the needs of each new generation, and that the new millennium could well see the rise of the world novel, *y nofel byd*. In the light of CD-ROM technology, R. G. Jones, 'Dyfodol y llyfr', *Llais Llyfrau*, 3:6–8, considers the endurance of the book, and suggests the survival of only popular literature in the form of the printed word. S. P. Rowlands, 'D'eud y gwir, goblyn!', *Taliesin*, 95:63–68, looks at the concept of truth in fiction. B. M. Matthews, 'O Frynhyfryd i Finafon', *ib.*, 69–76, is a brief discussion of the novels of Eigra Lewis Roberts. J. Rowlands, 'Chwarae â chwedlau: cip ar y nofel Gymraeg ôl-fodernaidd', *Y Traethodydd*, 151:5–24, is a defence of post-modernism, and praises the work of authors such as Robin Llywelyn and Mihangel Morgan. Id., 'Y Corff Mewn Llenyddiaeth', *Taliesin*, 96:11–25, analyses the nuances of pornographic and erotic literature. G. Williams, 'Dadorchuddio coesau'r bwrdd', *ib.*, 26–37, is a collection of quotations dealing with the topic of sex in 20th-c. Welsh literature from *Atgof*, Prosser Rhys, to reviews of the first pornographic novel in Welsh, *Dirmyg Cyfforddus*. K. Crockett, 'Plymio i'r dwfn:rhy-wioldeb rhwystredig *Un Nos Ola Leuad*', *ib.*, 38–52, discusses sexuality as a personal issue in Caradog Prichard's novel, and analyses the complex relationship between religion and sexuality. R. Crowe, 'Llên y Cymry, hoyw, (try)loyw?', *Taliesin*, 93:63–79, considers the unexpected references to gays in some of the most renowned literature of the 20th c.

I. M. Williams, *Dramâu Saunders Lewis: Y Casgliad Cyflawn. Cyfrol I*, Cardiff, Univ. of Wales Press, xii + 696 pp., is an edited collection where each play is prefaced by a critical essay which seeks to understand Lewis's intellectual development and the influences upon him. The editor overtly notes the pinnacles and failures amongst the plays considered. In a review article of the volume, D. G. Jones, 'Golygu dramâu Saunders Lewis', *Taliesin*, 96:102–14, criticizes the editor for interfering with the text, and at times for not making sufficient critical comment. H. Davies, 'Saunders Lewis a Theatr Garthewin', *YB*, 21:169–83, traces the playwright's connections with Robert Wynne and his wife, and recounts the circumstances of the performances of Lewis's plays at Garthewin. J. P. Clancy, 'Gwenlyn Parry a barddoniaeth theatr', *ib.*, 212–21, is an analysis of the language of *Y Tŵr*, and discusses the dramatist's depiction of reality. T. Jones, 'Idwal Jones: dramodydd a digrifwr', *Ceredigion*, 12:59–80, studies the life and career of the poet-dramatist, paying particular attention to the period of the First World War, and his contribution to the limerick in Welsh.

C. M. Jones, 'Tafodiaith a Barddoniaeth', *YB*, 21:222–27, is an introduction to the study of the use of dialect in literature and refers to the notable poem *Pwllderi* by Dewi Emrys. G. T. Hughes, 'Grym a garw: naws ein barddoniaeth Gymraeg', *Llais Llyfrau*, 2:8–9, suggests that the Welsh language remains a living and vibrant medium for poetry writing. E. W. James, ' "Byd gwyn fydd byd a gano": W. S. Gwynn Williams, T. Gwynn Jones, ac *Old Welsh Folk Songs* (1927)', *Canu Gwerin*, 19:75–89, looks at the work of T. Gwynn Jones in editing and translating songs in partnership with W. S. Gwynn Williams. E. W. Jones, 'Rhan o feddyliau'r hil: edrych yn ôl ar T. Gwynn Jones', *Taliesin*, 94:77–100, is an appreciation of the poetry of T. Gwynn Jones, with particular praise for *Madog*. T. E. Pritchard, 'Mae yno flas y cynfyd', *Barddas*, 226:6–8, traces the connections of the poet R. Williams Parry with Eifionnydd. A further contribution to the *Bro a Bywyd* series has appeared: *Waldo Williams*, ed. J. Nicholas, Swansea, Barddas, 103 pp. H. T. Edwards edited another volume in the series presenting the cultural activities of the South Wales Valleys: *Cwm Aman*, Llandysul, Gomer, 382 pp., contains 14 contributions, including an article on the poet-preacher Nantlais, by T. G. Jones (88–105). B. M. Hughes, '*Y Da Cyfoes': Rhai Agweddau ar Farddoniaeth Gymraeg 1945–1952*, Llandybïe, Barddas, 62 pp., studies the poetry of that period and emphasizes the polemics in poetical debate and the quality of the work of Gwenallt, T. H. Parry Williams, and Saunders Lewis, and the significance of *Adfeilion*, T. Glynne Davies. R. G. Gruffydd, 'Nodyn ar soned "Mabon" gan Saunders Lewis', *YB*, 21:163–68, looks at the echelons of meaning in the poem's figurative language and suggests that it is one of this century's most important sonnets. D. S. Jones, 'Nid gwely ond rhodd', *ib.*, 184–203, is an analysis of *Hunllef Arthur*, the epic poem of Bobi Jones. M. S. Roberts, 'Bobi Jones a mawl', *ib.*, 204–11, notes the way in which the poet uses praise to express a positive reality.

II. BRETON AND CORNISH STUDIES

By HUMPHREY LLOYD HUMPHREYS, *School of Modern Languages, University of Wales, Lampeter*

I. BRETON

Hor Yezh continues publication of previously mentioned work: P. Herbert, 'Anvioù laboused Europa', 206:5–22, and G. Kerouanton, 'O pennaouiñ gerioù war harzoù Bro-Leon', 205:110–43 (see *YWMLS*, 55:641 for both). L. Raoul, 'Roll ar c'helaouennoù brezhonek adalek dibenn an eil brezel-bed', *Hor Yezh*, 205:6–7, although only a MS list accompanied by histograms, provides a useful synoptic chronological picture of the 80 Breton-language periodicals which have appeared since 1945. G. Emelyanoff, 'Ar gelaouenn *L'Union agricole et maritime* dindan renerezh Leon ar Berr (1914–28)', *ib.*, 206:35–51, after a short presentation of the periodical, gives a full bibliography of all Breton material it published.

La Bretagne linguistique, 10, is made up of the *Actes du Colloque BADUME – STANDARD – NORME: Le double jeu de la langue*, whose 30 papers explore, over a wide range of languages, the relationship between the norm, the regional standard and the most local forms of speech for which a neologism of Breton origin is used (< /ba dy-m/, a common realization of literary *e-barz du-mañ* 'in my/our district; back home'). The editors, J. Le Dû and Y. Le Berre, in 'Parité et disparité: sphère publique et sphère privée' (7–25), present the theme and, with the support of chiefly Breton examples, propose to remedy some of the inadequacies of the traditional *di*glossic model; H. Ll. Humphreys, 'Réflexions sur les localismes et le supralocalisme en anglais, en gallois et en breton' (81–95), sketches a comparison of the situations in the three languages with succinct reference to their historical conditioning; F. Broudic, 'Langues parlées, langues écrites en Basse-Bretagne 1946–1990' (69–79), compares the situation of Breton on the basis of a survey conducted by seminarists and of his own later and more sophisticated investigations. F. Favereau, 'Normalisation d'un conte breton: à la recherche de l'impossible norme' (121–31), approaches the problems 'from below'. Th. Cottour and J.-P. Nouy, 'L'alphabétisation en Bretagne', *Ar Men*, 72:16–25, gives a good concise introduction to the subject.

F. Kervella, 'Distagadur ar brezhoneg', *Hor Yezh*, 207:7–44, is a presentation of a standard pronunciation of Breton. It is an unfinished updating of previous work which contains a modicum of useful observations but is uneven and sometimes confused. J.-Y. Urien, 'Conflit syntaxique autour de l'attribution: attribution et relation médiate', *Klask*, 3 : 7–33, complements the author's article, *ib.*, 1 : 101–28 (see *YWMLS*, 51 : 559). L. A. Timm, 'Pronominal A-forms in Breton: a discourse-based analysis', *JCL*, 4 : 1–33, contains much useful discussion on the predominantly non-prepositional values of *ahanon* ... etc., although the paradigm is shockingly mis-represented with *anezh-* generalized despite the counter-evidence of the examples! S. Hewitt, 'Kenneth Jackson's notes on Breton morphology and syntax', *JCL*, 4 : 109–13, assesses 500 pp. of MS notes, advocating that this substantial body of material marshalled by a leading specialist should be made available to modern scholars.

R. Mogn, 'Anvadurezh keltiek plant Breizh — Pteridophyta', *Hor Yezh*, 205 : 110–43, begins a classified inventory of plant names. The *Bull. de la Soc. archéologique du Finistère*, 123 (1994), has some short items in its 'Chronique de langue et de littérature bretonnes': J.-F. Simon, 'Du sens du mot *apoteiz*: un bilan provisoire' (468–70); Middle Breton is represented by G. Le Menn, 'L'inscription en moyen breton de la cloche de Plouézoc'h (1545)' (465–68), and id., '*Sell pe ri* ou *Sell petra ri*: au sujet d'une devise en breton' (464–65); E. Vallerie, 'Un texte négligé sur les origines du diocèse de Quimper: la *Vita Menulfi episcopi*' (453–57); B. Tanguy, 'Saint Vellé et Guicquelleau' (447–53), discusses the saint's name and the *Gwi(k)-/Plou-* alternance.

The most substantial item on place name studies is M. Madeg, *Renabl anoiou kêriadennou Bro-Leon hag o distagadur*, Brest, Emgleo Breiz/ Ar Skol vrezoneg, 3 vols, 421, 241, 168 pp. Vol. 1 is a generally sound and practically useful presentation of the problems confronting the compiler of an oral inventory in this field. The polemical tone adopted, in particular in referring to exclusively etymological conceptions of the study of place names, is somewhat disagreeable and probably counterproductive, although basically by no means unjustified; vol. 2 gives an alphabetical list in a moderately narrow transcription of some 18,000 names of inhabited places; vol. 3 is a parish by parish listing giving spellings favoured by the author. This is a very important piece of synchronic place name research. E. Vallerie, *L'Art et la manière de prononcer ces sacrés noms de lieu de Bretagne*, Douarnenez, Le Chasse-Marée-Ar Men, 310 pp., is aimed at a non-specialist readership and presents in 'imitated pronunciations' the names of every commune in the historical province in standard French and in Breton and/or Gallo. There are on the one hand a number of omissions and errors while much other information is given, administrative status at present and under the Ancien Régime fairly systematically, everything else very variably and anecdotally.

Two important books have appeared in the field of oral literature. Y.-F. Kemener, *Carnets de route de Yann-Fañch Kemener: Kanaouennoù Kalon Vreizh — Chants profonds de la Bretagne*, Morlaix, Skol Vreizh,

359 pp., contains 166 songs, which are presented in a dialectalized version of *peurunvan* spelling, accompanied by the melody and a French translation; a selection is contained in the accompanying CD. These are from collections made in the 1970s and 1980s by the most remarkable interpreter of Breton song among the younger generation — perhaps the last to grow up in close contact with traditional singers, albeit in a transformed society. Kemener recalls this period (9–22) and gives summary biographies of 57 singers who taught him their repertoire (63–80); A. Le Meut discusses problems of musical transcription (53–60); J. Rio, against the background of past collections, gives a thematic presentation (23–33); F. Favereau's contribution (34–52) on the language (very similar to that described by Humphreys, see *YWMLS*, 57:612), though, generally sound, is not very carefully constructed — why 30 examples of habitual presents in *-a*, but no mention at all of the provection of sonants? The bibliography is by no means as complete as it could have been and it is a pity to find no discography of Kemener or other singers mentioned. M.-A. Constantine, *Breton Ballads*, Aberystwyth, CMCS Publications, 269 pp., after presenting 19th-c. collectors and their informants and discussing the nature of the tradition, proceeds to detailed commentaries of two pieces from Luzel's *Gwerziou*, sixteen versions of 'Iannik Kokard' (love and leprosy), and two of 'Mari Kelenn' (infanticide and penance) and concludes with a discussion on how writing up or translating the oral versions can distort their original 'message'. Id., 'Prophecy and pastiche in the Breton ballads: Groac'h Ahès and Gwenc'hlan', *CMCS*, 30:87–121, concludes that two pieces from the Penguern collection, both suspected forgeries, contain genuinely popular traditional elements. F. Postic, 'La peste d'Elliant', *Ar Men*, 80:18–30, provides a presentation and commentary of the theme. L. Kergoat, 'Live yezh ar c'hanaouennoù pobl', *Klask*, 3:43–55, discusses, with examples from Plogonnec, the rather random mingling of literary and local forms in the language of traditional singers. F. Favereau, 'Phonologie des rimes et des vers dans la poésie chantée à Poullaouen', *ib.*, 35–41, is a more narrowly focused corpus illustrating many similar points. A. Gleoneg, 'Leurenniñ e vuhez', *ib.*, 75–81, discusses problems raised by the collection and interpretation of autobiographical ethnotexts.

Literary literature is represented by G. Denez, 'Barzhoniezh maread *Gwalarn*: modern pe get', *ib.*, 107–14, who discusses to what extent the poetry of this interwar school could be considered modern. F. Favereau, 'L'évolution du discours bretonnant chez Pierre-Jakez Hélias', pp. 167–77 of M. Lagrée and J. Sainclivier, *L'Ouest et le politique: Mélanges offerts à Michel Denis*, Rennes, PUR, considers aspects of the writer's attitude towards Breton particularism. P. Bourdoulous,

'L'*Ave Maria* breton', *Hor Yezh*, 205:78–81, reprints a 1915 presentation, with brief notes, of eight versions dated 1576–1776. C. Lanchec, 'Ar vuhez pemdeziek el levrioù relijiel', *Klask*, 3:93–105, discussing attitudes to daily life in devotional literature, is illustrated exclusively from Marion's *Magasin spirituel er Beurerion en artisantet er servitourion hac en dud diar er mæzeu* (1790); text references, and the use of the original spelling would have made this more useful to scholars. P. Tabuteau, 'Un damsell ouzh buhez pemdeziek ar soudarded vreton war an talbenn e-pad ar brezel bras', *ib.*, 67–73, presents the observations of three Breton writers on life on the front, 1914–18. D. Carré, 'Loeiz Herrieu er brezel bras: ul lizher a dalbenn ar Champagne', *ib.*, 83–92, publishes an annotated letter from one of these writers.

2. CORNISH

Cornish Studies, 4, pays far more attention to Cornish language and literature than earlier numbers, with five articles of substance occupying about a third of the space. B. Deacon, 'Language revival and language debate: modernity and postmodernity', *ib.*, 88–106, is a carefully documented examination of the Cornish revival scene from a sociological and ideological perspective. N. J. A. Williams, '"Linguistically sound principles": the case against Kernewek Kemmyn', *ib.*, 64–87, generally reiterates for a more general readership points discussed in the author's *Cornish Today* (*YWMLS*, 57:614); attribution of the simplification of an 'original' threefold quantitative distinction for vowels to English influence seems quite unnecessary — after all, such systems are extremely rare and inherently unstable. N. Kennedy, '*Cornish Today*: a Modern Cornish perspective', *ib.*, 171–81, is a review article primarily concerned with defending aspects of Gendall's Modern Cornish particularly criticized by Williams. It is stimulating to see contributions by internationally recognized figures in other fields. Glanville Price, 'Negative particles in Cornish', *ib.*, 147–51, compares the nineteen Middle Cornish examples of discontinuous negatives with the Welsh *(ni)...ddim*, Breton *(ne)...ket* and French *(ne)...pas*, arguing against their being calques of French. B. Murdoch, 'Is *John of Chyanhor* really a Cornish *Ruodlieb*?', *ib.*, 45–63, examines the relationship between the late Cornish tale and the 11th-c. Latin poem from southern Germany, which may also throw light on the *Charter Fragment*. O. J. Padel, 'Notes on the new edition of the Middle Cornish "Charter endorsement"', *CMCS*, 30:123–27, provides corrections or expanded notes to Toorians' edition (see *YWMLS*, 56:650), to which he gives his enthusiastic general approval.

III. IRISH STUDIES

EARLY IRISH

By UÁITÉAR MAC GEARAILT, *Irish Department, St Patrick's College, Dublin City University*

1. LANGUAGE

J. F. Eska, 'On the crossroads of phonology and syntax: remarks on the origin of Vendryes's restriction and related matters', *SC*, 28:39–62, reviews the literature on Vendryes's restriction and provides important new insights on its origins, taking into account, for instance, the evidence of some Uto-Aztecan languages 'which are attested in a transitional stage between that reconstructed for Indo-European and that attested in Gaulish and early Insular Celtic'. D. Shields, 'Old Irish *līn* "Numerus": another Indo-European/Near Eastern connection?', *ZCP*, 48:287–89, offers a new explanation for the semantic shift in Old Irish *līn* (Lat. *plēnus* etc.) 'full' to 'numerus', referring to external rather than internal forces of change. R. Matasović, 'Old Irish dative singular of neuter n-stems', *SCJ*, 8:59–63, argues that the dative sg. ending of Old Irish n-stems, *-imm*, may be derived from the PIE instrumental sg. ending *-mi*, which is attested in Balto-Slavic. E. P. Hamp, '*Fían*', *ib.*, 87–95, returns to the related terms *Féni*, for which he recently suggested the reconstruction **ueid(h)-n-ioi*, and *Fian* <**ueid(h)nā*. Although their surface shapes are considered to be 'phonologically and in stem source morphologically' connected, their background has not been identified. The purpose of this article is to make clear the semantics of *fian*, which have been difficult to perceive and explain.

K. McCone, *Towards a Relative Chronology of Ancient and Medieval Celtic Sound Change*, Maynooth, An Sagart, 195 pp., aims to establish a relative chronology of the principal sound changes that occurred from Proto-Indo-European via Proto- and Insular Celtic to Old and Middle Irish. There are six chapters dealing with the phonology and orthography of the Celtic languages (I); from Proto-Indo-European to Proto-Celtic (II); the voiceless labiovelar, syllabic nasals, lenition and the Celtic family tree (III); primitive Irish (IV); from Early Old Irish to Middle Irish (V); and the great British vowel shift (VI). P. de Bernardo Stempel, 'Tratti linguistici comuni ad appellativi e toponimi di origine celtica in Italia' pp. 109–36 of *Studia ex Hilaritate: Mélanges de Linguistique et d'Onomastique Sardes et Romanes offerts à Monsieur Heinz Jürgen Wolf, publiés par Dieter Kremer et Alf Monjour dans les Travaux de Linguistique et de Philologie XXXIII–XXXIV*, considers lexical material of Celtic origin in Italian in the light of what is now known about Celtic, especially as it developed on the Continent. Borsley, *Celtic Syntax*, contains many references to Early Irish. E. P. Hamp, *Tascio-*, *ŽCP*, 46 : 13, offers a simple explanation of *Tascio-* and Old Irish *tadg*. In *Indogermanica et Caucasistica: Festschrift für Karl Horst Schmidt zum 65. Geburtstag*, ed. R. Bielmeier and R. Stempel, Berlin, de Gruyter, 1994, P. de Bernardo Stempel, 'Das indogermanische *m(V)no*-Verbaladjektiv im Keltischen' (281–305), considers a number of issues of relevance to Early Irish.

K. McCone, 'Zum Ablaut der keltischen *r*-Stämme', pp. 275–84 of *In honorem Holger Pedersen: Kolloquium der Indogermanischen Gesellschaft vom 26. bis 28. März 1993 in Kopenhagen*, ed. J. E. Rasmussen, Wiesbaden, Dr Ludwig Reichert, Verlag, 1994, xvi + 520 pp., examines Celtic and especially Old Irish *r*-stems (*athair, máthair* etc.) to see how far the original ablaut has survived and how the problems associated with this stem (listed on opening page) may be overcome. J. F. Eska, 'On syntax and phonology within the Early Irish verbal complex', *Diachronica*, 13.2 : 225–57, deals with the development of the dual flexional system of the Early Irish verb and the absence of expected phonological mutations after initial preverbs. He attributes the former to syntactic movement within the verbal complex and proposes a system which also has the advantage of explaining why responsives and the imperative do not participate in the normal dual flexional system. In *Evans Vol.*, the following contributions may be noted: A. Harvey, 'Suggestions for improving the notation used for Celtic historical linguistics' (52–57), J. T. Koch, 'Further to Indo-European *g^{wh} in Celtic' (79–95), P. Mac Cana, 'Composition and collocation of synonyms in Irish and Welsh', P. Russell, 'Brittonic words in Irish glossaries' (166–82), K. H. Schmidt, 'Rekonstruktion und Transormation des Protokeltischen' (183–95), P. Sims-Williams, 'Indo-European *g^{wh} in Celtic, 1894–1994' (196–218). P. de Bernardo Stempel, 'Zum Genus Femininum als ableitbarer Kategorie im Keltischen', pp. 427–46, Analecta Indoeuropaea Cracoviensia, Vol. II: *Kuryłowicz Memorial Volume. Part I*, ed. W. Smoczyński, makes interesting observations concerning *ī*- and *ā*-stems, the 'lexikalischer Distinktiv' quasi-prefix *ban-* and gender assignment in Goidelic dialects, the loan suffix *-es* in Old Irish and its likely origin, and the etymology of Old Irish *caille*. She also deals briefly with some Irish kinship terms and syntactical matters.

R. Hofman, 'The linguistic preoccupations of the glossators of the St. Gall Priscian', pp. 111–26 of *History of Linguistic Thought in the Early Middle Ages*, ed. V. Law, Amsterdam–Philadelphia, Benjamins, 1993, considers why the Carolingian Irish glossators of Priscian had so little interest in comparing Irish and Latin, whereas their pre-Carolingian counterparts, for example, the author of *Auraicept na nÉces*, had. Id.,

The Sankt Gall Priscian Commentary. Part I, 2 vols, 1996, Münster, Nodus Publicationen, 754 pp., presents a comprehensive edition of the St Gall commentary on Priscian. This impressive work is part of the series *Studien und Texte zur Keltologie*. Volume I contains an introduction on Priscian and Ireland, a description of the manuscripts, sections on the gloss commentary, the sources, and the editorial approach, as well as the text itself (Books 1–5). Volume II presents a translation and commentary, with indices (*terminorum Latinorum, terminorum Hibernicorum, nominum, verborum et elocutionum Hibernicorum*, and *fontium*) and bibliography. E. Poppe, 'Die mittelalterliche irische Abhandlung *Auraicept na nÉces* und ihr geistesgeschichtlicher Standort', pp. 55–74 of *Theorie und Rekonstruktion*, ed. K. D. Dutz and H.-J. Niederehe, Münster, Nodus Publicationen, 1996, discusses the medieval Irish linguistic tract, *Auraicept na nÉces*, which he describes as '*summa* des sprachwissenschaftlichen Denkens der mittelalterlichen Schulen Irlands', and shows that early Irish scholars were conversant with aristotelian philosophy and logic.

I. Genee, 'Pragmatic aspects of verbal noun complements in Early Irish: *do* + verbal noun in the Würzburg glosses', *JCLin*, 3:41–73, deals with a subclass of verbal noun constructions in the 8th-c. Würzburg glosses. She argues that pragmatic factors play an important role at the early stage of the development of infinitival constructions in Irish. P. McQuillan, 'Towards a theory of modality for the Irish verb: subjunctive and indicative in Early Irish', *ib.*, 4:35–75, shows how the subjunctive and indicative interact in Early Irish and discusses what is meant by the term *modality* and how it is applicable to Irish. N. Müller, '"With"-relations and suffixed pronouns in Early Irish', *ib.*, 89–97, examines 'with'-relations in Early Irish as expressed by the prepositions *co^n* and *la* and suggests a link between the particular participant hierarchy in 'with'- relations expressed by *co^n* and the fact that *co^n* does not have a pronominal paradigm. *Dán do Oide: Essays in Memory of Conn R. Ó Cléirigh 1927–95*, ed. A. Ahlqvist and V. Čapková, Dublin, Institiúid Teangeolaíochta Éireann contains the following contributions relating to Early Irish: L. Breatnach, 'On the flexion of the *ā*-stems in Irish' (49–57), which adds to Thurneysen's paradigms, in *A Grammar of Old Irish*, illustrating the flexion of the *ā*-stems in Old Irish; D. Disterheft, 'Syntactic innovation in Early Irish' (123–33), offers some reflections on syntactic change in Early Irish. P. Kelly, 'Variation in Early Irish linguistic terminology' (243–46), examines how a number of basic Latin linguistic terms are adapted to the model of Irish words and suggests that the existence of variants gives an insight into the process of vernacularization; K. McCone, 'A note on palatalization and the present inflection of weak *i*-verbs' (303–13), contributes some fresh observations on palatalization in the present forms of *i*-verbs; L. Mac Mathúna, 'A lexical trek through some Early Irish "valleys"' (325–36), illustrates the dominance of *glenn*, later *gleann*, in the lexical field VALLEY throughout the history of the Irish language; R. Ó hUiginn, 'Dar le' (545–57), outlines the history and development of the phrase *dar le* in Early and Modern Irish.

D. Wodko, *Sekundäradjektive in den altirischen Glossen. Untersuchungen zur präfixalen und suffixalen Wortbildung*, Innsbruck, Institut für Sprachwissenschaft, 1995, viii + 357 pp., provides an excellent description and analysis of secondary adjectives formed with a range of prefixes and suffixes, for example, *so-*, *do-*, *-dae*. P-Y. Lambert, 'Le complément du comparatif de supériorité en vieil-irlandais', *ÉC*, 31 : 167–77, deals first with comparative constructions in Brittonic and then considers early Irish constructions with (i) prepositionless dative, (ii) prepositions *ol*, *ré*, and *sech*, (iii) *oldáas*, and (iv) *indáas*, *adáas*. He comments on the preposition *ind*, as distinct from *i^n* 'in', noting less frequent use of *oldáas* than *indáas* in the Milan glosses, where however it is preferred to *indáas* after comparative adverbs, especially ones formed with *ind-*. *Ind*-adverbs, like *ind-már* 'grandement', are compared with the later variety with geminating *co* 'as far as, up to' + accusative, for example *co mmór*. *Ind-* + dative may well be the earliest form of the complement of the comparative, having taken over from the independent dative. He compares OW *int*, Old Breton *ent/int*, i.e. the Modern Welsh predicative particle *yn*. The final section of the article concerns adverbial formations, such as *bes síre*. Id., 'Préverbes gaulois suffixés en *-io-*: *ambio-*, *ario-*, *cantio-*', *ib.*, 115–21, follows L. Breatnach's and P. Russell's articles on Old Irish nouns derived from prepositions with a study of Gaulish preverbs with suffix *-io-*, *ambio-*, *cantio-*. Taking the latter to be phonetically parallel to Irish *céite*, he analyses it (i.e. **kntiom*) as a nominal derivative of the preposition **knti-* (Gaul, *canti-*, W. *cant*, Ir *cét(a)-*) 'en association avec, entièrement'. In the final section of the paper he speculates on the origin and meaning of the element *-o-/-io-*. X. Tremblay, 'Études sur le verbe vieil-irlandais', *ib.*, 151–65, deals with (I) R. Thurneysen's class B V verbs in Old Irish, i.e. verbs with present nasal infix, in particular those which 'ignore[nt] la métaphonie *i>e* de la syllabe intonée', e.g. *at-gnin*, *at-baill*, *ara-chrin* (cf. *crenaid* (Sanskrit *krīnāti*) < **qrināt* < **k^{w}ri-n-éh$_2$-t*). Proposing that they are a direct reflex of presents in **n-eh$_1$-* and **n-eh$_3$*, he reconstructs an example of each of these types of present and of an **n-eh$_2$* present (*crenaid*) and suggests that Irish provides 'le premier témoin matériel non ambigu de presents à nasale infixée en -*n-eh$_1$-* et *n-eh$_3$*', which are lacking in Greek but which have parallels in *-nā-/-nī-* presents in Sanskrit. He also discusses (II) the suppletive present perfective and preterite of *-cuirethar* 'throws, puts', *ro-laë*, agreeing with an explanation proposed by McCone and then rejected by him in favour of another. E. P. Hamp, 'Old Irish *arbar* n. "corn"', *ib.*, 89–90, provides clarifications concerning the formation of *arbar* and explains how 'a complex total paradigm may have produced' it. J. T. Koch, 'The conversion and the transition from Primitive to Old Irish *c.* 367–*c.* 637', *Emania*, 13 : 39–50, considers the evidence for 'the most rapid and profound series of linguistic changes of any two- to three-century span in the history of the [Irish] language'. Among the issues he addresses are the problems of dating, the change from Primitive to OIr., the Christian Latin loan words in Irish and their date, Ogam and OIr. orthography, parallel changes in Brittonic and their causes, pre-Celtic substrata in pre-Christian Ireland.

R. Baumgarten, '"*Cr(a)ide hé* ..." and the Early Irish copula sentence', *Ériu*, 45 : 121–26, considers a point of syntax in a Middle Irish epigram which occurs as an example of the metre 'suirge mall' in a metrical tract. P. Mac Cana, 'The historical present and the verb "to be"', *ib.*, 127–50, examines the status and behaviour of the verb 'to be' in the context of the historical present. P. Schrijver, 'The Celtic adverbs for "against" and "with" and the early apocope of *-I*', *ib.*, 151–89, argues that Old Irish *fri* and *la* reflect Proto-Celtic **writ-i* and **(p)let-i*, i.e. Primitive Indo-European datives or locatives of the root nouns **urt* and **pl(e)th$_2$*. F. O. Lindeman, 'Varia I: Old Irish *ithid*', *ib.*, 191–94, discusses the Indo-European origins and development of OIr. *ithid* 'eats'. L. Breatnach, 'Varia II: 1. Irish *geined* and *geinit*, Gaulish *geneta*, Welsh *geneth*', *ib.*, 195–96, presents four examples of Ir. *geined*, which is not given in *DIL*, and explains its meaning and its relationship to *geinit*. L. Breatnach, 'Varia II: 2. Prepositions with added vowel in relative compound verbs', *ib.*, 197–98, discusses relative forms of compound verbs with a vowel added to the preverb, e.g. well-known *imma-* and *ara-*, and presents hitherto unnoticed examples with other preverbs. K. McCone, 'OIr. *senchae*, *senchaid* and preliminaries on agent noun formation in Celtic', *Ériu*, 46 : 1–10, shows that a *t*-stem *senchae* (*-ad*) is a 'chimera reflecting typical Middle Irish modifications of an OIr. *io*-stem', which leaves us with an OIr. *io*-stem *senchae* (cf. *Senchae mac Ailella* in the Ulster tales) and 'an arguably Old Irish *i*-stem *senchaid*'. He concludes however that *senchae* is the oldest and 'hence the only etymologically relevant form'. He takes the first element to be *sen* < **seno-* 'old' and considers *chae* to be derived from the agentive *o*-grade formation with accented thematic suffix **k^{w}ois-ó-s* 'seer, witness', the full form being **seno-k^{w}oisos*. J. Uhlich, 'On the fate of intervocalic **u* in Old Irish, especially between neutral vowels', *ib.*, 11–48, surveys the phonological changes that affected intervocalic **u* and sets out to ascertain how 'original groups consisting of **u* between two neutral vowels developed into

Old Irish'. The article is divided into eighteen sections, the last of which gives the main results of the investigation. S. Schumacher, 'Old Irish **tucaid, tocad* and Middle Welsh *tynghaf tynghet* re-examined', *ib.*, 49–57, shows that the Middle Welsh phrase *tynghaf tynghet* is a *figura etymologica*, with both noun and verb having a firm etymological and morphological base in Celtic and Indo-European. In Middle Welsh *tynghaf* 'I destine' and *tyngaf* 'I swear' were indistinguishable. However, he argues, at the time when the early poems in which they occur were composed the difference between them was quite clear and their etymological relationship was transparent. He also shows that *tynghet* and its Old Irish cognate *toceth/tocad* cannot be derived from the Celtic primary verb 'to swear'. He thus rejects J. Koch's recently published view that *tynghaf tynghet* and Gaulish *toncnaman toncsiiontio* arose from a Common Celtic taboo deformation of an ancient oath formula **tongū (do) Lugue lugiom* 'I swear an oath to Lugus'. F. O. Lindeman, 'Varia I: On a possible Celtic–Greek etymological correspondence', *ib.*, 165–66, remarks on the future of Greek φέρω 'bears' and one of its forms οἴσω, which he takes to represent the (full-grade) *s*-aorist subjunctive stem *$*H_3ey$-s-e/o-*, the original 3 sg. active being reconstructable as *$*/H_3$ēy-s-t/* 'bore'. If Celtic also inherited the latter, he suggests, one could expect Common Celtic *$*āy$-s-t*, which would ultimately become OIr. **aí* (conjunct). He gives a number of examples of this form from early Irish, with the preverb **to-* and meaning 'bore, gave birth to'. He also deals with *toud* 'to bring forth (offspring)'. Id., 'Varia II: On some Celtic compound verb forms', *ib.*, 167–70, offers an explanation for the peculiarity whereby in loose composition a preverb originally ending in a vowel does not cause lenition of the initial of the verb in Old Irish, for instance in *do beir, fo cain* etc.; cf. the contribution by J. Eska referred to earlier. K. McCone, 'Old Irish *con-dieig* "asks, seeks", verbal noun *cuin(d)gid*: a problem of syncope and verbal composition', *Éigse*, 28, 156–59, discusses a problematical feature of the verb *con-dieig*.

A. Breeze, '*Slab* "mud", an Old Irish ghostword: English *slob* "untidy person"', *ZCP*, 47:87–88, suggests that OIr. *slab* in the line *berid buarslaib resliabh* in the poem *Cétamain, cain cucht* is a ghostword. Id., 'Irish *brat* "cloak, cloth": English *brat* "child"', *ib.*, 89–92, considers the derivation of English *brat* 'child' from Irish *brat* 'rugged garment' and supplies evidence of the transition of sense which has hitherto been lacking. Id., 'Old English *gop* "servant" in riddle 49: Old Irish *gop* "snout"', *Neophilologus*, 79:671–73, explains the Old English hapax legomenon *gop* in riddle 49 of the Exeter Book as a loan from OIr., i.e. *gop*, which as well as 'beak, snout' can also mean something like 'beak- or snout-faced menial'. Id., '*Deorc* "bloody" in *The Dream of the Rood*: Old Irish *derg* "red, bloody"', *Éigse*, 28:165–68, suggests Irish origins for the word *deorc* in an early English text. Id., 'Irish *Beltaine* "May Day" and *Beltancu*, a cattle-rent in pre-Norman Lancashire', *Éigse*, 29:59–63, explains the associations of the term *Beltancu* with Ir. *Beltaine*. Id., 'Middle English *daisser* and Irish *deisréad* "sprinkler"', *ib.*, 150–52, suggests the Middle English word *daissers* 'sprinklers' is a borrowing from Irish *deisréad*, the term for a sprinkler of holy water, which is found in the 12th-c. *Acallam na Senórach*.

2. LITERARY CRITICISM AND TEXTS

J. Carey, 'The rhetoric of *Echtrae Chonlaí*', *CMCS*, 30:41–65, undertakes a detailed analysis of the early OIr. tale *Echtrae Chonlai*, which represents 'some of the earliest Irish storytelling to have survived'. Carey brings to light some of the subtleties of the tale and succeeds in his aim of elucidating some of its underlying ideology. G. R. Isaac, 'The end of the world in Welsh and Irish: a common disaster', *SC*, 28:173–74, draws attention to parallels between the *Oianau* of Myrddin and the Mórrígan's prophecy of the end of the world at the close of *Cath Maige Tuired*, the most remarkable being *Gwraget heb gvilet. gwir heb gurhid: mná can féli, fir gan gail* 'Women without modesty, men without valour'. C. Sterckx, 'Images monétaires et mythes celtes', *ZCP*, 47:1–17, suggests that while many of the images and figures on Gaulish coins cannot be explained satisfactorily, many others can be of service to students of mythology, if used with prudence and objectivity. He cites examples of parallels in Gaulish which are sufficiently well supported by medieval mythological sources to be recognized as reflexes of analogical myths, Sucellos and the Dagda Eochaid Ollathair of Irish tradition, Epona and Rhiannon of Welsh and Breton tradition. He disputes some of the claims made by Sjoestedt, Duval and others concerning images on Gaulish coins and proposes four criteria for recognizing parallels between such representations and myths in later Celtic traditions. L. D. Myrick, 'The steleographic transmission of prediluvian scéla: an apocryphal reference in the Irish *Lebor Gabála*', *ib.*, 18–31, examines an account in a late interpolation in §97 of *Lebor Gabála* of the transmission of prediluvian knowledge to posterity after the flood. According to this, Cham fashioned three four-sided pillars, one each of lime, clay and wax, and inscribed prediluvian *scéla* upon them. The wax pillar miraculously survived the flood and historical knowledge back to the time of creation was preserved. She examines some Jewish and Greek variants, which assign the invention and preservation of technology to giants or monsters. She also considers the most likely medieval sources of the apocryphal material as it stands in the LG interpolation and in three early medieval Irish variants on the same theme. P. L. Henry, '*Táin roscada*: discussion and edition', *ib.*, 32–75, edits a number of *roscada* which represent 'an archaic stratum of obscure if not at times unintelligible rhythmical verse or prose' in the OIr. version of *Táin Bó Cúailnge*. Each text is accompanied by a translation and notes. Isabel Kobus, '*Imtheachta Aeniasa*: *Aeneis*-Rezeption im irischen Mittelalter', *ib.*, 76–86, considers the Mid.Ir. version of Virgil's *Aeneid*, dealing with the manuscript tradition, date, sources, structure, omissions, and characterization. A. J. Hughes, *ZCP*, 48:17–28, 'Some aspects of the salmon in Gaelic tradition past and present', deals (in part I) with the metaphorical use of the salmon in medieval Gaelic bardic poetry and (in part II) with the belief that salmon could be identified by their physical appearance, a belief which, he suggests, is implied in a passage concerning the river Drowes in the *Vita Tripartita*. S. N. Tranter, 'Systems of classification in the first middle Irish metrical tract and their implications', *SCJ*, 8:97–115, compares versification practices in medieval Ireland and Iceland. *(Re)Oralisierung*, ed. H. L. C. Tristram, Tübingen, Narr, 501 pp., has a number of contributions concerning early Irish: U. Mac Gearailt, 'Change and innovation in eleventh-century prose narrative in Irish' (443–96), considers the development of a Mid.Ir. prose, particularly in the 11th c. He refers primarily to Recensions I and II of the *Táin*, *Cath Ruis na Ríg*, and the two Mid.Ir. versions of *Togail Troí*; A. Bruford, 'The hermit disturbed and undisturbed' (177–206), returns to the Early Modern Irish story of *Murchadh mac Briain and the Hermit* to describe and compare all the fourteen texts which have survived 'in the detail they deserve'; R. Ó hUiginn, 'Cú Chulainn and Connla' (223–46), deals with the background and development of the story of how Cú Chulainn killed his only son, which appears in YBL as *Aided Óenfir Aífe*; S. Mac Mathúna, 'Motif and episodic clustering in early Irish voyage literature' (247–62), sets out to clarify the relationships of a number of texts belonging to early Irish voyage literature, for example the Irish language *immrama* 'voyages', *Navigatio Sancti Brendani Abbatis*, and the voyage sections of the Irish and Latin versions of the Life of St. Brendan. He also examines the relationship of motifs and anecdotes in this literature to those recorded from oral tradition; E. M. Slotkin, 'What allows fixed texts to enter Gaelic oral tradition?' (55–65), explains the conditions under which literary works, which can have early Irish origins, might enter into oral tradition.

Progress in Medieval Irish Studies, ed. K. McCone and K. Simms, Maynooth, An Sagart, 275 pp., contains 11 chapters on research in the field of early Irish language and literature. They are as follows: K. McCone, 'Prehistoric, Old and Middle Irish' (7—53); T. Ó Cathasaigh, 'Early Irish narrative literature' (55–64); L. Breatnach, 'Poets and poetry' (65–77); M. Herbert, 'Hagiography' (79–90); T. O'Loughlin, 'The Latin sources of medieval Irish culture: a partial *status quaestionis*' (91–105), L. Breatnach, 'Law' (107–21); C. Etchingham, 'Early medieval Irish history' (123–53); M. Ryan, 'Early medieval Ireland: some archaeological issues' (157–63); D. McManus, 'Classical modern Irish' (165–87), C. Breatnach, 'Early Modern Irish prose' (189–206); K. Simms, 'Literary sources for the history of Gaelic Ireland in the post-Norman period' (207–15). This exhaustive progress-report also contains a bibliography and author index. C. Etchingham, *Viking Raids on Irish Church Settlements in the Ninth Century: A Reconsideration of the Annals*, Maynooth, An Sagart, vi + 79 pp., presents a detailed account of annalistic evidence for the chronology and geographical distribution of Viking raids on churches. The book contains six sections: 1. Introduction: Aims and Historiographical Context, 2. Chronology of Raids, 3. Geographical Distribution of Raids, 4. Purpose of Raids, 5. Raids in a Wider Context (pp. 48–57, which are missing from at least one copy), 6. Conclusion. P. Ó Riain, *The Making of a Saint: Finbarr of Cork 600–1200*, London, Irish Texts Society, Subsidiary Series 5, traces the development of the cult of St Finbarr from its beginnings in the 7th c. down to the 12th c.

J. Carey, 'An edition of the pseudo-historical prologue to the *Senchas Már*', *Ériu*, 45 : 1–32, presents an edition of the so-called 'pseudo-historical prologue' to the *Senchas Már*, with translation, textual notes, two appendixes, and an introduction describing manuscripts and suggesting dates of composition. T. O'Loughlin, 'The library of Iona in the late seventh century: the evidence from Adomnán's *De Locis Sanctis*', *ib.*, 33–52, discusses the evidence in *De Locis Sanctis* regarding the books which were available in Iona during Adomnán's abbacy in the last decades of the 7th c. C. Swift, 'Tírechán's motives in compiling the *Collectanea*: an alternative interpretation', *ib.*, 53–82, reconsiders the motives of Tírechán in writing the *collectanea* found in the 9th-c. Book of Armagh and questions the consensus which argues that he was writing with the specific intention of promoting Armagh. J. Borsje, 'The *bruch* in the Irish version of the Sunday Letter', *ib.*, 83–98, discusses one of the monsters in the Old Irish Sunday Letter in order to illustrate the difference between the 'native Irish', 'imported', and 'integrated' monsters which she postulates. F. J. Byrne and P. Francis, 'Two lives of Saint Patrick: *Vita Secunda* and *Vita Quarta*', *JRSAI*, 124:5–117, provide translations of two Lives of

Patrick, with introduction and detailed commentary on linguistic and other matters. These lives help to elucidate the development of the Patrick legend as represented in the Old Irish Tripartite Life. The authors suggest that they may have been written by Colmán na mBretan, abbot of Slane, who died in 751. T. O'Keeffe, 'Lismore and Cashel: reflections on the beginnings of Romanesque architecture in Munster', *ib.*, 118–52, describes Romanesque material from the monastery of Lismore and considers Cormac Mac Carthaig's patronage of churches at Lismore in the 1120s. D. McCarthy, 'The origin of the *latercus* paschal cycle of the insular Celtic churches', *CMCS*, 28:25–49, returns to the theme of the *latercus*, having identified in an earlier article, co-written with D. Ó Cróinín, its technical characteristics and established its dependence on the *Liber Anatolii*. He shows that it is not, as hitherto believed, a forgery by insular computists and offers some suggestions concerning its origin and date. K. Olsen, 'The cuckold's revenge: reconstructing six Irish *roscada* in *Táin Bó Cúailnge*', *ib.*, 51–69, takes on the daunting difficulties, linguistic and otherwise, associated with the *roscada* in the Recension I *Táin* and presents 'one possible reading' of the six *roscada* which make up the conversation between Ailill, Medb, and Fergus after the latter's sword is taken by Ailill's charioteer. M. T. Flanagan, '*Historia Gruffud vab Kenan* and the origins of Balrothery, Co. Dublin', *ib.*, 71–94, queries O'Donovan's suggestion that *Baile an Ridire* is the Irish original of *Balrothery*, north Co. Dublin, and suggests an alternative derivation involving a Welsh personal name, such as those occurring in documents of the late 12th or early 13th c. The implications for the Irish dimension and content of the biography of Gruffudd ap Cynan (*ob.* 1137) are considered.

A. S. Mac Shamhráin, *Church and Polity in Pre-Norman Ireland: The Case of Glendalough* (Maynooth Monographs, 7), Maynooth, An Sagart, 1996, xxv + 274 pp., continues the task of reassessing church and polity in early medieval Ireland by means of a case study focusing on the well-documented centre of Glendalough. T. O. Clancy and G. Márkus, *Iona: The Earliest Poetry of a Celtic Monastery*, Edinburgh U.P., 1995, present the Gaelic and Latin poetry of those who lived and studied on the island of Iona after the time of Colm Cille. An introductory section provides a historical context. Then follows part II with the original versions of the poems and translations *en face*. Part III presents a translation of the early prose text *Apgitir Chrábaid*, whose author studied on Iona. Part IV contains a description of the books known to have been in use in 7th-c. Iona, notes, abbreviations, bibliography, and index. D. Ó. Cróinín, *Early Medieval Ireland: 400–1200*, London, 416 pp., gives an account of Irish society and culture from the early Christian period to the time of the Normans. B. T. Hudson, *Prophecy of Berchan: Irish and Scottish High-Kings of the Early Middle Ages*, London, Greenwood, 288 pp., presents the text of an Early Irish history of the kings of Ireland and Scotland from the 9th to the 11th c., with translation and commentary. He examines the prophecy of Berchán as a historical record concerning the kings of Ireland and Scotland. He also supplies biographies of individual kings, listing important events in their careers, giving the length of their reign, and the circumstances of their death. *A Military History of Ireland*, ed. T. Bartlett and K. Jeffery, CUP, 1995, 565 pp., contains a number of relevant contributions, for instance that by M. T. Flanagan, 'Irish and Anglo-Norman warfare in twelfth-century Ireland' (52–75), who considers Irish and Norman warfare in the light of contemporary sources such as the annals. There are also contributions by T. Charles-Edwards, on the earlier period, and K. Simms, on the later period.

P. Mac Cana, 'Y Canu Mawl yn Iwerddon cyn y Normaniaid', pp. 122–42 of *Beirdd a Thywysogion: Barddoniaeth Llys yng Nghymru, Iwerddon a'r Alban*, ed. B. F. Roberts and M. E. Owen, Cardiff, Univ. of Wales Press, outlines the evidence for the existence before the 12th c. of a tradition of panegyric poetry similar to that of the post-Norman period. D. Gabriel, 'The power of the woman over the man in mediaeval Irish prose tales', *SCJ*, 7:61–86, sets out to determine the sources and nature of women's power over men as it is described in early Irish tales, to show how that power affects both men and women, and to point out its limits. D. N. Dumville, 'The world of the *síd* and the attitude of the narrator in *Táin Bó Fraích*', *ib.*, 21–25, draws attention to the episode of Fráech's cure and shows how the author distances himself from the Otherworld-interpretation of the cure, 'presumably out of a sense ... that a cleric should not be encouraging open recognition of beneficient Otherworldly powers'.

B. Maier, *Lexikon der keltischen Religion und Kultur*, Stuttgart, Kröner, 1994, xv + 392 pp., presents clear, brief explanatory notes on all important figures, places, institutions etc. associated with Celtic religion, with accurate representation of pronunciation and all relevant bibliographical references. Erzählkunst, Münster, Lit, 96 pp., 1996, provides a brief but clear account of the development of early Irish tales, narrative techniques, and tale-types. This is volume 1 of the new series *Forum Celticum: Studien zu keltischen Sprachen und Kulturen*, ed. J. Corthals and E. Ternes. J. Carey, *The Irish National Origin-Legend. Synthetic Pseudohistory. With a Memoir of Edmund Crosby Quiggin by D. N. Dumville*. (Quiggin Pamphlets on the Sources of Mediaeval Gaelic History), 1, Cambridge, Department of Anglo-Saxon, Norse and

Celtic, 1994, xvi + 27 pp., gives a concise, stimulating account of the origins and development of Irish pseudohistory up to the time of the first version of *Lebor Gabála*, i.e. the 11th c. D. N. Dumville et al., *Saint Patrick, 493–1993*, Woodbridge, Boydell, 1993, ix + 334 pp., deal in six essays and brief discussions with various aspects of Patrick's life and the Patrician problem. *The Epic in History*, ed. L. Sharon Davidson and S. N. Mukherjee, Sydney, 1994, 205 pp., contains a contribution by B. Martin on verbal exchanges called 'flytings' which are found in the *Táin*. D. A. Bray, *A List of the Motifs in the Lives of the Early Irish Saints*, Helsinki, Academia Scientiarum Fennica, 1992, 138 pp., lists the motifs found in many of the medieval Irish saints' Lives.

G. Márkus, 'What were Patrick's alphabets?', *CMCS*, 31 : 1–15, discusses the meaning and purpose of the 'alphabets' mentioned in medieval Irish texts concerning Patrick, for example by Tírechán (7th c.). J. Corthals, 'Early Irish *retoirics* and their late antique background', *ib.*, 17–36, argues that early Irish *roscada* emerged in the 6th c. in imitation of Latin poetry and rhetorical style and were included in the curriculum of the schools concerned with learning in the vernacular. Id. 'Zur Entstehung der archaischen irischen Metrik und Syntax', in *Gedenkschrift für Jochem Schindler*, ed. H. Eichner and H. C. Luschützky, deals in greater detail with the same subject and the syntax and morphology of such poetry. K. Hollo, 'Conchobar's "sceptre": the growth of a literary topos', *CMCS*, 29 : 11–25, discusses the development of the literary topos involving the royal sceptre of Conchobor mac Nessa in early Irish tales. M. Thomas Davies, 'Protocols of reading in early Irish literature: notes on some notes to *Orgain Denna Ríg* and *Amra Coluim Cille*', *ib.*, 32 : 1–23, compares a typical modern textual note, by D. Greene in his edition of *Orgain Denna Ríg*, and glosses from the commentary on *Amra Coluim Cille* (ACC) and considers what this suggests about how modern readers/ scholars might approach the interpretation of early Irish texts. After discussing some glosses from ACC he suggests that the commentary to which they belong is neither 'worthless' nor 'silly' but represents 'a positive, sophisticated, and consistent hermeneutic' which 'evinces little anxiety about arriving at the singular, correct, intended meaning of the text' and 'seems committed to unearthing as many potential meanings as possible'. C. D. Wright, *The Irish Tradition in Old English Literature*, CUP, 1993, xiii + 321 pp., reveals the Irish elements in Old English texts such as the homily Vercelli IX. E. Bhreatnach, *Tara. A Select Bibliography*, Dublin, Royal Irish Academy, 1995, ix + 173 pp., surveys the historical, literary, and archaeological studies which treat of the ancient royal site of Tara (Temair), Co. Meath. O. Szerwiniack, 'D'Orose au *Lebor Gabála Érenn*: les gloses du manuscrit Reg. Lat.

1650', *ÉC*, 31 : 205–17, refers to M. Scowcroft's recent *Ériu* articles on the development of *Lebor Gabála* and in particular the view that '*Historia Brittonum* [*ca.* 829–30 A.D.] comprises the earliest extant version of the *Lebor Gabála* tradition'. He agrees with J. Carey that 'le *Lebor Gabála* est né au XIᵉ siècle' and suggests that 'avant cette date, il est abusif d'employer ce titre'. As an example of the 'anciens éléments épars' which were later to become part of that 'ensemble cohérent' he presents glosses on two books of Orosius by an Irish glossator working on the continent. These are contained in the 9th-c. Vatican manuscript Reginensis latinus 1650 and they may have played a role 'dans l'élaboration progressive de l'archétype du *Lebor Gabála*'. P. Russell, 'Notes on words in early Irish glossaries', *ib.*, 195–204, gives detailed consideration to entries in early Irish glossaries, particularly that of Cormac and that entitled *Dúil Dromma Cetta*, under the headings *Íarus*, *Imbas for-osnai*, and *Lúathrinde*. P. L. Henry, '*Amra Con Roi* (*ACR*): discussion, edition, translation', *ib.*, 79–94, provides a useful edition of the 8th-c. poem *Amra Con Roí*, with translation, discussion, and notes. An interesting feature of the poem is the long list of gifts, in section II, for which the poet, Ferchertne, gives thanks to Cú Roí. C. Vielle, 'Matériaux mythiques gaulois et annalistique romaine: éléments antiques d'un cycle héroïque celtique', *ib.*, 123–49, examines material reflecting Celtic influence in Latin texts, for example by the annalist Claudius Quadrigarius, compares similar features in Irish and other Celtic traditions, and concludes that they represent a Gaulish heroic cycle. The two types of mythic hero which are represented in these Latin sources involve two separate cycles and 'correspondent aux deux héros irlandais-types' [*sic*], the hero 'of' and the hero 'outside' the tribe, 'le chien-guerrier' and 'le loup-chasseur'; i.e. Cú Chulainn and Finn in Irish tradition. B. Sergent, 'Celto-hellenica III: Achille et Cúchullain', *Ollodagus*, 4 : 195–205, compares the Greek hero Achilles and Cú Chulainn. *The Celtic Connection*, ed. G. Price, Gerrards Cross, Colin Smythe, 1992, xii + 361 pp., contains three essays devoted to Irish by M. Ó Murchú, P. Ó Riain, S. Mac Mathúna. P. M. Freeman, 'Greek and Roman views of Ireland: a checklist', *Emania*, 13 : 11–13, provides a very useful reference list of works by Greek and Roman authors who refer to Ireland, with dates, references to standard editions, and a brief résumé of content.

R. B. Warner, 'Tuathal Techtmar: a myth, or ancient literary evidence for a Roman invasion?', *ib.*, 23–32, attempts to find evidence for an incursion into Ireland from the Roman world in early Irish pseudo-histories and myths, focusing particularly on the career of Tuathal Techtmar. He suggests that 'a steady Romanization of Irish culture' took place in the later part of the Iron Age, over the first to the fourth centuries AD. K. Muir, 'The east Ulster perspective on the Ulster Cycle tales', *Emania*, 14:51–63, deals with east Ulster place names in Ulster tales such as the *Táin, Cath Ruis na Ríg*, and *Mesca Ulad*. W. Sayers, 'Homeric echoes in *Táin Bó Cúailnge*', *ib.*, 65–73, reviews some 'Homeric echoes' in the *Táin*. He also takes into account the Irish version of Pseudo-Darys' *De Excidio Troiae Historia, Togail Troí*. C. Sterckx, 'A Celtic Apollo at Navan?', *ib.*, 75–76, points out, apropos of an article by R. B. Warner in *Emania*, 12, close structural parallelism between Macha's fate in the Ulster Cycle and the drama of Leto, daughter of a Titan, who is seduced by Zeus in Greek tradition. He sees significance in similarities between the birth of the Greek Apollo after nine days and the nine-day debility suffered by the Ulstermen, which was punishment for their treatment of the pregnant Macha and with which the 'Apollonian' Fíor was connected. He refers also to the Decamnoctiaca of the Gaulish Apollo Grannos. R. Warner, 'Navan and Apollo', *ib.*, 77–81, suggests that there was a god whose influence was widespread over Europe. He was the life-giving god Apollo whom the Celts of Gaul and Britain associated with local Celtic gods with similar attributes. Warner suggests that he was the god to whom the Navan enclosure was dedicated and to whom the 40-metre 'temple' was erected and burned. Conmáel mac Ébir (Cunomaglus) was an early Irish 'doublet' and Cú Chulainn was his later embodiment. C. Lynn, 'That mound again: the Navan excavation revisited', *Emania*, 15:5–10, returns to the subject of an earlier article, the interpretation of the mound at Navan (Old Irish *Emain Macha*), this time discussing possible associations with hostels such as that described in *Togail Bruidne da Derga*. A. Condon, 'Telach Óc and Emain Macha c. 1100', *ib.*, 39–46, refers to an article by R. Warner in *Emania* 12 and clarifies some points relating to the first poem in *Lebor na Cert*. He goes on to suggest that it is a reflex of the great circuit of Ireland made by Muirchertach Ua Briain in 1101. F. Ó Béarra, 'Táin Bó Cuailnge: Recension III', *ib.*, 47–65, offers a fine translation of the Recension III *Táin*, with an introduction on the manuscript tradition and other aspects of the tale. N. B. Aitchison, 'Votive deposition in Iron Age Ireland: an early medieval account', *ib.*, 67–75, considers a passage by Tírechán concerning a well which Patrick is claimed to have believed was a place of pagan worship and of votive deposition. Id., *Armagh and the Royal Centres in Early Medieval Ireland: Monuments, Cosmology, and the Past*, Suffolk, 1994, considers a broad range of issues relating to Armagh and royal centres in early medieval Ireland. W. Sayers, 'Charting conceptual space: Dumézil's tripartition and the fatal hostel in early Irish literature', *The Mankind Quarterly*, 34:27–64, discusses the literary portrayal of the hostel in early Irish literature. M. Herbert, 'Goddess and king: the sacred marriage in early Ireland', pp. 264–75 of *Women and Sovereignty*, ed. L. O. Fradenburg, Edinburgh UP, 1992, vi + 334 pp., discusses the sovereignty goddess and kingship in early medieval Irish tradition.

D. McManus, '*Úaim do rinn*: linking alliteration or a lost *dúnad?*', *Ériu*, 46:59–63, offers some clarifications concerning the meaning of the third of the *.ui. hernailí dēg na filideachta* with which a *fili* must be familiar, i.e. *Úaim do rinn. i. co rob do rinn na cethramthan do rāith araile.* J. Carey, 'On the interrelationships of some *Cín Dromma Snechtai* texts', *ib.*, 72–92, discusses the corpus which R. Thurneysen held to be derived from the lost *Lebor* or *Cín Dromma Snechtai*. He considers the possible affiliation of several of the texts in question and attempts to identify significant relationships within the group. The sections of the article are as follows: (I) the Mongán tales, (II) *Tucait Baile Mongáin* and *Baile Chuinn Chétchathaig*, (III) the *immacallam* texts, *Immram Brain*, and the Mongán tales (IV) *Echtrai Chonlai* and *Immram Brain*, (V) the so-called 'Midland group', (VI) *Tochmarc Étaíne*. B. Murdoch, '*Saltair na Rann* XXV–XXXIV: from Abraham to Joseph', *ib.*, 93–119, continues his valuable commentary on the text of the 10th-c. verse composition *Saltair na Rann*, which he began with his work on the Adam and Eve Story in 1976. R. M. Scowcroft, 'Abstract narrative in Ireland', *ib.*, 121–58, attempts to 'set forth a theory and examples of the abstract modality in medieval Irish narrative composition'. The following sections explore 'four major aspects of this phenomenon as well as a variety of sources and techniques in the literature itself': 1. etymological narrative, 2. the drink of sovereignty, 3. history and mythology, 4. le borgne et le manchot, 5. narrative inversion. J. T. Koch, in collaboration with J. Carey, *The Celtic Heroic Age: Literary Sources for Ancient Celtic Europe and Early Ireland and Wales*, Malden, 1995, 400 pp., provides a detailed survey of primary literary materials of the early Celtic-speaking peoples.

D. N. Dumville, 'Cath Fedo Euin', *Sc. Gael. Stud.*, 17:114–27, examines an annalistic notice concerning a battle between the Cruithin and Dál Riata at Fid Euin in AD 629 to see whether there is sufficient evidence to sustain what scholars have deduced from derived versions of it. These mention four more victims of that battle, three of whom are said to be *nepotes* of Aedán mac Gabráin, king of Dál Riata: Rigullan, Faílbe, and Oisiric mac Alfrith. J. W. Gleasure, 'The Rawlinson B512 version of *Scéla Mucce Meic Dathó*, *ib.*, 143–45, offers a list of corrections of minor points of detail in Meyer's and Thurneysen's text of *Scéla Mucce* from Rawlinson B 512. P. Mac Cana, 'A literary footnote: the Nun of Beare', *ib.*, 205–12, wonders, in relation to the early Irish poem of the Caillech Bérri ('the Old

Woman of Beare'), 'how fully and how accurately can we hope to gauge the range and complexity of the poet's imagery'. He refers in particular to § 20 of D. Ó hAodha's recent edition and discusses the views of other scholars, including those of B. K. Martin from an interesting article written in 1969 (*Medium Aevum* 38). Enlarging on an earlier suggestion that the poem is a sophisticated comment on social and ideological tensions in 9th-c. Ireland, he goes on to cite an analogue in the Therigatha, the Pali songs of Buddhist nuns, in particular that ascribed to Ambapali. P. A. Breatnach, 'The new edition of the hagiography of St Finbarr', *CMCS*, 32:111–18, offers a detailed review of P. Ó Riain's edition of the Life of Finbarr, *Beatha Bharra. Saint Finbarr of Cork. The Complete Life.*

C. G. Buttimer, 'Longes mac nUislenn reconsidered', *Éigse*, 28:1–41, expresses the view that *Longes mac nUislenn* is biographical and includes within its compass the life-cycle of Derdriu. Considering the story to consist of five different phases (*Birth, Espousal, Exile, Return, Death*), he investigates the features which give each segment its 'distinctive texture'. M. Ní Dhonnchadha, '*Caillech* and other terms for veiled women in medieval Irish texts', *ib.*, 71–96, discusses examples of the word *caillech* meaning 'married woman', 'bride of Christ'/'virgin nun', and 'penitent spouse'/'holy widow' in turn and identifies synonyms in Latin and Irish in support of the various definitions proposed. J. Harris, 'The Middle Irish adaptation of Lucan's *Bellum Civile*: an exercise in creative conventionality', *ib.*, 103–28, presents a fresh and stimulating reappraisal of the Irish adaptation *In Cath Catharda*. J. Carey, 'Eithne in Gubai', *ib.*, 160–64, discusses the name *Eithne in Gubai*. T. Ó Broin, 'Doomed kings?', *Éigse*, 29:64, discusses the interpretation of a passage from *Baile in Scáil*. T. Ó Concheanainn, 'Textual and historical associations of Leabhar na hUidhre', *ib.*, 65–120, discusses the origins, make-up, and history of the early 12th-c. manuscript Leabhar na hUidhre, and also the sources of its texts, the lost manuscript *Cín Dromma Snechtai* and the entry of its texts into the Connacht tradition, the contents of *Cín Dromma Snechtai*, the *Táin* and *Tochmarc Emire*, and much more. J. Carey, 'A posthumous quatrain', *ib.*, 172–74, reveals some interesting features in a quatrain which appears in the margin of a page in Leabhar Breac, including the use of Mag Mell 'Delightful Plain' to designate the Christian heaven. J. Stevenson, 'Literacy and orality in early medieval Ireland', pp. 11–22 of *Cultural Identity and Cultural Integration: Ireland and Europe in the Early Middle Ages*, Dublin, 1995.

R. M. Keogh, 'Does the Armorican forest hold the key to Saint Patrick's escape?', *SH*, 28:145–57, re-examines the information in Patrick's *Confessio* on his escape from Ireland and suggests the year

409 gains support as the date of that event. C. Etchingham, 'Bishops in the early Irish church: a reassessment', *ib.*, 35–62, shows that the importance of the bishop in the early Irish church has been underestimated. He gives the views of previous scholars, discusses the evidence of the primary sources concerning the functions and standing of bishops, considers the sphere within which the bishop exercised power, and examines the evidence for superior episcopal jurisdiction. R. Chapman Stacey, *The Road to Judgement: From Custom to Court in Medieval Ireland and Wales*, Philadelphia, Pennsylvania U.P., 1994, xvi + 342 pp., makes a consierable contribution to the study of Irish and Welsh institutions. The book is devoted largely to the theme of suretyship. The first five chapters deal primarily with Irish law: 1. Law and law book in medieval Ireland, 2. Contractual suretyship in Irish law, 3. The social context of personal suretyship, 4. Hostage-sureties in Irish law, 5. The road to judgement. L. M. Bitel, *Isle of the Saints: Monastic Settlement and Christian Community in Early Ireland*, Ithaca, Cornell U.P., 1990, xvi + 269 pp., gives a very fine description of religious life in Ireland between AD 800 and 1200. P. Brown, *The Rise of Western Christendom: Triumph and Diversity, A.D. 200–1000*, Oxford, Blackwell, xiii + 353 pp., makes many interesting references to early Irish religious life, culture, and literature.

J. Corthals, 'Affiliation of children: Immathchor nAilella 7 Airt', *Peritia*, 9:92–124, offers an edition of a short Old Irish (*c.* 700) legal text concerning a lawsuit on the assignment of twins after their mother, Sadb, has been repudiated by their father, Ailill Aulomm. D. Mac Lean, 'The status of the sculptor in Old-Irish law and the evidence of the crosses', *ib.*, 125–55, examines 8th-c. legal tracts such as *Uraicecht Becc* which set out the legal and social status of the craftsman and the relationship between a master craftsman and his dependents and apprentices. N. McLeod, 'Irish law: significant numbers and the law of status', *ib.*, 156–66, suggests a method for generating the numerical series upon which early Irish law texts appear frequently to draw. D. Bracken, 'Immortality and capital punishment: patristic concepts in Irish law', *ib.*, 167–86, suggests that an early legal poem on capital punishment, found in the pseudo-historical prologue to the *Senchas Már*, should be interpreted in the context of Hiberno-Latin and patristic literature. 'It is,' he argues, 'the product of the same ecclesiastical milieux that produced Hiberno-Latin literature itself.' E. Johnston, 'Transforming women in Irish hagiography', *ib.*, 197–220, deals with three aspects of the transformation of women in early Irish literature. She first explores the image of the sovereignty goddess and then discusses the notion of a woman possessing a masculine soul. She also discusses the evidence for the transvestite saint and suggests that these represent aspects of the Irish church's ideology. B. Jaski, 'The Vikings and the kingship of Tara', *ib.*, 310–53, provides a detailed study of the influence of the Vikings on political developments in Ireland from *c.* 850 to 980. M. Ní Mhaonaigh, '*Cogad Gáedel re Gallaib*: some dating considerations', *ib.*, 354–77, shows that rather than dating from the time of Brian Bórama (*ob.* 1014), the work of political propaganda entitled *Cogad Gáedel re Gallaib* probably dates from the time of Muirchertach Ua Briain (*ob.* 1119), most likely from the period 1103–13. S. Duffy, 'Ostmen, Irish and Welsh in the eleventh century', *ib.*, 378–96, argues against the view, expressed for instance by K. Maund, that contacts between Ireland and Wales in that century rarely amounted to more than raids by Irish-based Vikings. He argues that relations between the two countries were more complex, that both Ostmen and Irish kings had close political links with Wales, and that *Historia Gruffud vab Kenan* is a useful primary source on the subject.

3. ONOMASTICS

K. H. Schmidt, 'Keltische Namen', pp. 762–74 of *Namenforschung: Ein internationales Handbuch zur Onomastik*, ed. G. Hilty and H. Löffler, Bd. 1, Berlin, Walter de Gruyter, provides much information on Celtic names under six headings: 1. Quellen, 2. Stand der Forschung, 3. Typische Namenbildungen, 4. Bedeutungen und Schichten, 5. Repräsentative Darstellungen und Referenz-Arbeiten, 6. Literatur (in Auswahl). N. Ó Muraíle, 'The Irish genealogies as an onomastic source', *Nomina*, 16:23–47, discusses important sources of early Irish names. J. Uhlich, *Die Morphologie der komponierten Personennamen des Altirischen*, Bonn, M. Wehle, 1993, xxxv + 309 pp., presents a comprehensive and thorough study of compound personal names in OIr. F. J. Byrne, '*Dercu*: the feminine of *mocu*', *Éigse*, 28:42–70, uncovers and discusses the correlative feminine form of the Ogham gentilic formula *mucoi*, i.e. *dercu*, of which at least six instances occur 'disguised' in the published genealogies. D. Ó Murchadha, 'Cenn Ebrat, Sliab Caín, Belach Ebrat, Belach Legtha/Lechta', *Éigse*, 29:153–71, discusses the location of the places named in the title. Id., 'Nationality names in the Irish annals', *Nomina*, 16:49–70, considers names such as *Ériu*, *Féni*, *Goídil*, *Cruthin*, *Picti* in the medieval annals (Annals of Ulster, Annals of Four Masters etc.). W. Sayers, 'Vífill — captive Gael, freeman settler, Icelandic forbear', *Ainm*, 6:46–55, investigates 'the rather curious' name of Vífill which was borne by three individuals associated with Icelandic settlement history. Sayers concentrates on one of these, an aristocrat captured in war who was freed from slavery by one Auðr daughter of Ketill and given land by her in Iceland. He suggests that *vífill*, a term for the beetle or chafer whose root is well represented in Germanic, is a calque on an Irish name containing *dóel* (*Dubthach Dóel Ulad, Dubthach Dóeltenga*), or *cíar* (*Ciarán*).

MODERN IRISH

POSTPONED

IV. SCOTTISH GAELIC STUDIES

By RICHARD A. V. COX, *Lecturer in Celtic, University of Aberdeen*

Volume 17 of *SGS*, ed. D. MacAulay, J. Gleasure and C. Ó Baoill, University of Aberdeen, iv + 402 pp., was presented as a *festschrift* to Professor Derick S. Thomson on 28 February 1997; the bibliography covers the period 1943–92. Lexical studies include S. Grannd, 'The lexical geography of the Western Isles' (146–49), which plots the distribution of *flùr*, *dìthean* and *sìthean*. The resulting pattern raises the intriguing question why, seemingly dwarfing any unfinished etymological business. C. Ó Dochartaigh, 'Two loans in Scottish Gaelic' (305–13), looks at the distributionally contrastive pairs, *nàbaidh-coimhearsnach* and *roth-cuibheall*, in order to illustrate the limitations involved in applying data from the *Linguistic Survey of Scottish Gaelic* to the study of lexical geography. R. L. Thomson's 'Edward Lhuyd's Geiriau Manaweg III' (369–75), continues Thomson's analysis of Lhuyd's Manx material from the early 1700s and compares about 800 lexical items with the equivalent responses from Lhuyd's Scottish Gaelic material, which illustrates the rather complex relationship between the Gaelic dialects of Argyllshire, Inverness-shire, and Man at that time. In the field of onomastics, George Broderick, *Placenames of the Isle of Man*, 1. *Sheading of Glenfaba*, 2. *Sheading of Michael*, Tübingen, Niemeyer, 1994, xliv + 377, 1995, xlii + 301 pp., are the first volumes to emerge from his survey of the island. He provides a detailed documentary history and etymology for the names which are listed by parish. There are many cross-references to Scottish Gaelic and to Irish, although there are some oversights in the representations. While there is no index of elements, words cited in the commentary are indexed. Angus Watson, *The Ochils: Placenames, History, Tradition*, Perth, Perth and Kinross District Libraries, 1995, 159 pp., gives the first detailed account of the place nomenclature of this area. It provides a useful witness to the intensive nature of Gaelic settlement there, and Watson gives a sound exposition, as far as it goes, of name structure and the historical background, as well as a quick survey of the significance of groups of elements (in which *sìthean* 'fairy mound' falls into the belief and culture category, whereas it may have easily applied to a topographical feature). The absence of pronunciations for less accessible name forms and the absence of an index of elements is a drawback. Other lexical corpora are provided in G. Stockman, 'Lexical correspondences in Scotland and Antrim', *SGS*, 17:361–68, which gives an interesting list of items found in both locations — and most of which are common in their Scottish Gaelic form. The entry *i mbeultaobh* is an apparent blow for the dative plural school regarding *beulaibh* and *cùlaibh*. G. W. MacLennan, 'More Gaelic dialectology', *ib.*, 255–62, looks at some lexically or morphologically unusual words and phrases from Donegal. The explanation for the origin of *acha dtaobh dó* with the sense 'about' is not convincing. One cannot help thinking that there is a connection with Scottish Gaelic {*acha a^N*} with the sense of 'to, till' (for example, *trobhad ach a(m) faic thu seo* 'come till you see this'), so that *acha dtaobh dó* might have had an earlier sense 'whichever way, either way (of it)'. J. L. Campbell, 'The Rev. Dr Kenneth MacLeod's collection of Gaelic asseverations, exclamations, and imprecations', *ib.*, 71–81, is an interesting and unusual lexical corpus. Calum MacFhearghuis, *Hiort: Far na Laigh a' Ghrian*, Stornoway, Acair, 172 pp., gives an account, glossed with anecdote and song, of the history and lore of St Kilda and its people. While not fully sourced, there is much detail. Many of the words of songs composed by St Kildans have been lost (and the author fills some of the gaps with his own), but there are some points of linguistic interest in the surviving material, for example, *bhiolach* for *bhiorach*, *cha do dh'fhaod thu riamh èirigh* and *nach do dh'fhaod thu thighinn*; *na do theach* for *na do thaigh*; *cha dèan leighean dlan mi*. *Gaelic Words and Phrases from Wester Ross*, compiled by Roy Wentworth, Gairloch, R. G. Wentworth, xii + 315 pp., is a much enlarged version of that prepared (under the same title) in 1993, with its main English–Gaelic section followed by a Gaelic–English glossary. The foreword describes it as 'a dialect supplement … to the dictionaries presently available'. Its strength lies more in its presentation of usage (for example, under *hurry* forms of *greas*, *cabhag* and *deithearach* are used to provide equivalent for '*hurry up!, we'll have to hurry, she hurried me, you were hurried*') than as a dialectal corpus (for example, *adhbart* for *adhbrann*). R. Black, 'James Macintyre's Calendar', *SGS*, 17:36–60, reproduces Macintyre's text of proverbs and sayings relating to the calendar, compiled in the early 19th c., with detailed notes along with a description of the manuscript. S. Walker, 'Gàidhlig an Cinntir', *Gairm*, 175:209–11, is an erratic and more anecdotal than scientific account of some place names in Kintyre. H. Pálsson's 'Towards a glossary of Norse place names in Lewis and Harris', *SGS*, 17:314–24, is a discursive treatment of a number of classified Old Norse elements with some interesting parallels and contrasts drawn between usage in Norway, Scotland and Iceland; its Achilles heel is that it fails to take due account of the phonological development of Old Norse to Scottish Gaelic. *Scotland o Gael an Lawlander*, ed. Derrick McClure, Glasgow, Gairm Publications, viii + 119 pp., is a bilingual anthology of Gaelic poems (by D. Thomson, D. MacAulay, A. MacNeacail, and Myles Campbell) translated into Scots. It also has a vocabulary list with Scots words from the translations, along with the Gaelic words from the original poems, given an English gloss. The periodical *Gairm*, continues in the vanguard of register development with G. MacAoidh, 'Reul-eòlas air son luchd-tòiseachaidh', *Gairm* 174: 140–45 and 175: 217–21, though not without the attendant difficulties of currency: *mul* 'pole' rather than *pòla*; familiarity with sense: *meanbh-dhomhan* 'baby universe'; sense range: *neònachas* 'phenomenon' (otherwise 'curiosity'); and familiarity with form and wieldiness: *nàdur-fheallsanach beachdail* 'theoretical physicist'. N. C. Dorian, 'Personal-pattern variation in East Sutherland Gaelic', *SGS*, 17: 103–13, discusses variation in linguistic form beyond that determined merely by geographical, age, and register-based factors, as in /(x)a rɔ/ and/or /(x)a t rɔ/ *cha robh* 'was not' (the latter by analogy with the use of the preterite particle in other instances of verbs in /r/-). Variation also occurs in lenited vs unlenited *fios*; *ris, leis*, and *gus* vs *ri, le*, and *gu* with plural nouns; *gus an* vs *ach an* 'until', etc. There is plenty of scope for the comparative research that Dorian hopes will be undertaken in the future. D. G. Howells, 'The irregular verb', *ib.*, 179–80, illustrates the suppletive nature of the irregular verb in Scottish Gaelic, and argues that this development is normal in an Indo-European context. S. Watson, 'Hiatus-filling /h/ in Irish and Scottish Gaelic', *ib.*, 376–82, discusses the origin of the use of a glottal fricative (instead of glottal action or stop, or intonation) to mark hiatus in certain Gaelic dialects, suggesting the cause of the development lies in the 'weakening' of intervocalic *-th-* and the expected subsequent variation between zero (or glottal stop) and inherited /h/, with the consequence of analogous formations with /h/ in positions which formerly constituted hiatus (original or not). (On p. 377 in phonetic transcriptions, for non-word-initial [e] read [ə], for [c] read [ɔ].) K. E. Nilsen, 'Some notes on the Gaelic of eastern Nova Scotia', *ib.*, 292–94, discusses the use of *w*, for non-palatal lenited and unlenited *l*, and of *m* for unlenited non-initial non-palatal *n* in Scotland and Nova Scotia, with an emphasis on distribution rather than phonological development. The unusual plural allomorph, for example in /aməwən/ for *amannan*, is seen as related to the latter change, although it is not explained how, and cited as a possible Nova Scotian innovation. W. F. H. Nicolaisen, 'Gaelic *-ach* > Scots *-o* in Scottish place names', *ib.*, 278–91, analyses the written records of place names showing this development (for example, Ardo < Ardoch < Ardach). A phonological development *-ach* [αχ] > *-och* [ɔχ] > [o:χ] > *-o* [o:] is postulated, with the earlier development of Old English *-hōh* > *-o* (for example, Kelso, Minto) cited in supporting evidence. The range of reflexes deriving from Gaelic *-ach* is seen in *Dornoch*, *Durno*, and *Dornock*, and Nicolaisen wonders whether there may not also be a local pronunciation **Dornach* (misprinted **Dornoch*). W. Gillies, 'Some thoughts on the *toschederach*', *ib.*, 128–42, researches the etymology of the name of this (uncertain) administrative official, arguing that an original compound from *tóiseach + dóer-rath* 'base clientship' with later interference from *deóradh* 'stranger' etc. provides a solution to the range of variant forms found, including Manx *toshiagh joarey*.

D. MacAulay, 'Some thoughts on time, tense and mode, and on aspect in Scottish Gaelic', *ib.*, 193–204, tries to highlight some of the more interesting features of Gaelic temporal and modal systems, indicating that traditional categories used to describe them are not very well suited to doing so and suggesting an alternative approach. R. A. V. Cox, 'Tense and aspect in the Scottish Gaelic verbal system: a working paper on definitions and presentation', *ib.*, 82–86, similarly tackles its subject from a synchronic point of view and argues for a more Gaelic-oriented approach. D. Adger, 'Aspect, agreement and measure phrases in Scottish Gaelic', Borsley, *Celtic Syntax*, argues in defence of 'a generalised version of Visibility' as seen in an analysis of measure phrases in Scottish Gaelic (200–22). Issue may be taken with some of the examples used: *'s e am ministear a tha mi a' ceilidh* [*sic*] *a-nochd* (207); *'s e a' cheist sin a fhreagairt a tha doirbh* (208) (?rather *'s e tha doirbh, a' cheist sin a fhreagairt*); also *'s ann falbh a tha doirbh*, with rejection of *'s e falbh a tha doirbh* (?rather the latter, as distinct from *'s ann a' falbh a tha sinn* or similar — an appended footnote explains the apparent anomaly here, but confusion on the part of informants in interview seems likely). There is confusion between the use of nouns as temporal adverbs (for example, *seachdain*, ?elliptical for *fad seachdain*) and expressions of other measures, for example, *tri mile not*; thus *feumaidh a' cho-labhairt tri mile not* [*sic*] *a chosg* (not a good example) is seen as impossible due to the impossibility of **feumaidh a' cho-labhairt seachdain a mhairsinn*. No allowance is made for a distinction between *tha Daibhidh* [*sic*] *air falbh* and *tha Daibhidh air a bhith a' falbh*. Roibeard Ó Maolalaigh, *Scottish Gaelic in Three Months*, Henley-on-Thames, Hugo's Language Books, 224 pp., explains the main principles of grammar for the most part in a clear and accessible style and format. Treatment is generally traditional, although he uses the useful, more recent terms 'independent', 'dependent' and 'relative' with regard to verbal forms, and (to no advantage) the terms 'nominative' and 'prepositional' for the radical ('subject/object') and dative cases; and some sections (for example, §67a on the conjunction 'because' and §90 on the comparative and superlative) would benefit from revision. Innovatively (and rightly) the IPA is used to show pronunciation. *Mo Chiad Fhaclair*, compiled by Moray Watson, Stornoway, PRG and Acair, 96 pp., is intended as an elementary children's dictionary for use in schools and employs pictures along with simple definitions and explanations of headwords. Some lexical categories (parts of the body, clothes, etc.) are dealt with as an appendix in the format of a word-picture dictionary. It follows the Gaelic orthographic conventions of 1981 (for example, *aosta* rather than *aosda*) though the tendency to write 'io' (for example, *lion, mios, sios*) as opposed to 'io' for normal /iə/, if attempting to avoid a homograph with 'io' for /i:/ (for example, *pìob, Bìoball*), is misguided. Excepting the latter English loans, /iə/ is historically /i:/ here (so Arran /mǐ:s/), and 'io' avoids a homograph with /i/ (for example, *fios, lios, mion*).

D. Dumville, '*Cath Fedo Euin*', *SGS*, 17 : 114–27, examines the value of the annal entry for this battle, fought between Cruithin and Dál Riata in AD 629, as historical evidence, in the light of previous deductions from it; and urges that careful analysis should be made before similar material derived from the 'Clonmacnoise Chronicle' is used. J. Bannerman, 'The residence of the king's poet', *ib.*, 24–35, details evidence showing that the *ollam ríg*'s residence during the 13th c. may have lain at Balvaird, 10 miles to the south of Scone, and suggests that the king's poet had a continuing functional role up to the time of Robert Bruce's accession in 1306. B. Ó Cuiv, 'Further comments on the Ó Gnímh family of Co. Antrim', *ib.*, 298–304, continues his research into the origin of this family and its relationship with the Agnews of Galloway.

Donald E. Meek, *The Scottish Highlands: The Churches and Gaelic Culture* (Gospel and Cultures Pamphlet 11), Geneva, WCC Publications, viii + 69 pp., gives an overview of the communication of the Christian faith in the Highlands in the context of Gaelic language and culture. In reflecting on whether the latter was strengthened or weakened during this process, Meek gives a very useful account of the influence of the churches in the development of the literary language, including the 'transformation' of the Bible to Scottish Gaelic, ultimately from earlier Classical Gaelic texts. The predominance of negative images with regard to the churches' support for the development of a modern Gaelic culture is acknowledged, although it is argued that the level of blame should be restricted because support was not always lacking and because other factors detrimental to Gaelic language and culture existed also. The Highland Churches are urged to take some responsibility for the future development of Gaelic culture on historical grounds. N. Grant, 'Gaelic and education in Scotland', *SGS*, 17 : 150–58, provides an overview of the influence of the educational system on the question of the maintenance and survival of the Gaelic language. K. MacKinnon, 'Social class and Gaelic language abilities in the 1981 census', *ib.*, 239–54, describes how analysis of the returns shows that the general migration of Gaelic speakers away from Gaelic areas has been 'strongly structured in occupational and social class terms'. I. MacAonghais, 'Sgeulachd', *ib.*, 181–92, transcribes the recording of four episodes of Fenian tales from Domhnall Chaluim Bàin in Tiree in 1960. J. E. Rekdal, 'A controversy over copyright — The episode of Colum Cille's copying of St Finnian's Psalter in Mánus Ó Domhnaill's *Betha Colaim Chille*', *ib.*, 325–35, examines several episodes from this 16th-c. Life to reveal elements of pre-Christian and Christian tradition, arguing that the specialized discourse, of which these traditions had become a part in later Lives, suggests that the dichotomy between them had been turned into a convention within the genre of saints' Lives. A. Bruford, 'Workers, weepers, and witches: the status of the female singer in Gaelic society', *ib.*, 61–70, speculates on an unbroken tradition, but changing status, of the female Gaelic poet from pre-Christian times to the present century. T. P. McCaughey, '*Cumha le Iain Dhùn Ollaidh*', *ib.*, 213–20, addresses the question of how the *cumha* '*Och ón mo thuras o'n dé!*', connected with traditions about a Spanish princess whose body was washed ashore, came to be ascribed to Iain Ciar Dhùn Ollaidh. C. Ó Baoill, '*Caismeachd Ailean nan Sop*', *ib.*, 295–97, transcribes the primary text of this poem by Eachann mac Iain, *c.* 1537, found in Hector Maclean's 18th-c. manuscript. D. Meek, 'Images of the natural world in the hymnology of Dugald Buchanan and Peter Grant', *ib.*, 263–77, explores the differing aims of these poets from the 18th and 19th c., respectively, and the extent to which each uses the imagery of nature in his work. While its frequent use by Buchanan (reflecting the influence of his English models, though it is framed in a Highland context) is to reflect God the Creator, its sparsity in Grant's hymns should be understood set against their dominant natural image of the world as a place to be endured rather than enjoyed. J. Shaw, 'Brief beginnings: Nova Scotia and Old World bards compared', *ib.*, 342–55, follows the unbroken threads of tradition from the 18th c., along with some innovation in theme, that have continued in Nova Scotian verse into this century; it is set against the weight of romantic nostalgia and associated technical forms that burdened much of 19th-c. verse from Scotland. C. Whyte, 'A note on Dàin do Eimhir XIII', *ib.*, 383–92, examines the significance of the inclusion of a reference to *an Audiart a bhuair De Born* (as an unhappy pair of lovers) in this poem, suggesting that Sorley MacLean was likely to have been familiar with Pound's work inspired by the Provençal troubadour poet, Bertran de Born. I. C. Smith, 'A sensuous perception: one aspect of Derick Thomson's poetry', *ib.*, 356–60, notes that Thomson has always been aware of the contrast in himself between book learning and 'simple sensuousness'. Smith draws out this sensuousness, arguing that 'its pure delightfulness is one of Thomson's finest gifts' and that he need not have worried about the danger of book learning.

Finally, fittingly, *Alasdair Mac Mhaighstir Alasdair: Selected Poems*, ed. Derick S. Thomson, Edinburgh, Scottish Academic Press, vi + 223 pp., is the first in the Scottish Gaelic Texts Society's new 'minor series' and benefits greatly from the editor's research into the life and work of this poet. The 14 poems selected, each with an explanatory preface and copious notes, are representative of the poet's core work. The introduction contains biographical details, comment on the language and metrics of the selection, as well as an overview of Mac Mhaighstir Alasdair's poetry.

4

GERMANIC LANGUAGES

I. GERMAN STUDIES

LANGUAGE

By Charles V. J. Russ, *Reader in the Department of Language and Linguistic Science, University of York*

1. General

SURVEYS, COLLECTIONS, BIBLIOGRAPHIES

A wide range of the different faces of the typological characteristics of German feature in *Deutsch — typologisch*, ed. E. Lang and G. Zifonun (Jb. des Instituts für Deutsche Sprache, 1995), Berlin, de Gruyter, vii + 700 pp., which contains the following: E. Lang, 'Das Deutsche im typologischen Spektrum. Einführung in den Band' (7–15); B. Comrie, 'Sprache und Sprachen: Universalien und Typologie' (16–30); E. König, 'Kontrastive Grammatik und Typologie' (31–54); B. Primus, 'Dependenz und Serialisierung: das Deutsche im Sprachvergleich' (57–91); C. Platzak, 'Germanic verb second languages' (92–120); B. Haftka, '"Deutsch ist eine V/2-Sprache mit Verbendstellung und freier Wortfolge"' (121–41); C. Wilder, 'V-2 Effekte: Wortstellungen und Ellipsen' (142–80); B. Lenz, 'Negationsverstärkung und Jespersens Zyklus im Deutschen und in anderen europäischen Sprachen' (183–200); K. Donhauser, 'Negationssyntax in der deutschen Sprachgeschichte. Grammatikalisierung oder Degrammatikalisierung?' (201–17); E. Hentschel, 'Negation in Interrogation und Exklamation' (218–26); V. Ehrich, 'Verbbedeutung und Verbgrammatik: Transportverben im Deutschen' (229–60); S. Olsen, 'Partikelverben im deutsch-englischen Vergleich' (261–88); J. Grabowski and P. Weiss, 'Das Präpositioneninventar als Determinante des Verstehens von Raumpräpositionen: *vor* und *hinter* in fünf Sprachen' (289–311); E. Lang, 'Lexikalisierung und Wortfeldstruktur — typologisch betrachtet. Räumliche Dimensionsausdrücke als Fallstudie' (312–55); Ö. Dahl, 'Das Tempussystem des Deutschen im typologischen Vergleich' (359–68); J. O. Askedal, 'Überlegungen zum Deutschen als sprachtypologischem "Mischtyp"' (369–83); U. Engel and E. Geller, 'Das Verb in seinem Umfeld. Die deutsche Standardsprache im Licht des Schwäbischen, des Jiddischen und des Polnischen' (384–401); M. Starke, 'Germanische und romanische

Pronomina: stark — schwach — klitisch' (405–27); W. Abraham, 'Personalpronomina, Klitiktypologie und die Struktur des "Mittelfeldes"' (428–69); K.-M. Köpcke and D. Zubin, 'Prinzipien für die Genuszuweisung im Deutschen' (473–91); W. U. Wurzel, 'Morphologischer Strukturwandel: Typologische Entwicklungen im Deutschen' (492–524); N. Fuhrhop, 'Fugenelemente' (525–50); T. A. Hall, 'Silben- und Morphemstruktur in der Phonologie des Deutschen' (553–68); U. Kleinhenz, 'Zur Typologie phonologischer Domänen' (569–84); K. Alter, 'Der Zusammenhang von Akzentuierung und Phrasierung im Sprachvergleich' (585–614); and P. Eisenberg, 'Zur Typologie der Alphabetschriften: Das Deutsche und die Reform seiner Orthographie' (615–31). National varieties of German are treated by U. Ammon, 'Typologie der nationalen Varianten des Deutschen zum Zweck systematischer und erklärungsbezogener Beschreibungnationaler Varietäten', *ZDL*, 63 : 157–75, and Id., 'Die nationalen Varietäten des Deutschen im Spannungsfeld von Dialekt und gesamtsprachlichem Standard', *Muttersprache*, 106 : 243–49. Austrian German is examined in detail by *Österreichisches Deutsch. Linguistische, sozialpsychologische und sprachpolitische Aspekte einer nationalen Variante des Deutschen*, ed. R. Muhr et al. (Materialien und Handbücher zum österreichischen Deutsch als Fremdsprache, 2), Vienna, Hölder-Pichler-Tempsky, 1995, 402 pp., which contains a large number of contributions. Also noted: P. Hessmann, 'Österreichisches Deutsch oder Standardsprache Österreichisch?', *GM*, 41, 1995 : 19–23.

An outstanding work on German and Lëtzebuergesch is *Luxembourg and Lëtzebuergesch. Language and Communication at the Crossroads of Europe*, ed. G. Newton, Oxford, Clarendon, xviii + 286 pp. N. has assembled an excellent team who deal with a wide range of issues: G. Newton, 'Luxembourg: the nation' (5–37); Id., 'German, French, Lëtzebuergesch' (39–65); C. V. J. Russ, 'Lëtzebuergesch: a linguistic description' (67–96); J.-P. Hoffmann, 'Lëtzebuergesch and its competitors: language contact in Luxembourg today' (97–108); F. Hoffmann, 'Lëtzebuergesch, spoken and written, developments and desirabilities' (109–22); Id., 'The domains of Lëtzebuergesch' (123–41); Id., 'Linguistic variation and varieties in the Grand Duchy of Luxembourg' (143–56): J.-P. Hoffmann, 'Beyond the boundaries: Lëtzebuergesch outside the Grand Duchy' (157–79); G. Newton, 'Lëtzebuergesch and the establishment of national identity' (181–215); and F. Hoffmann, 'Textual varieties of Lëtzebuergesch' (217–50). The central message is that Lëtzebuergesch is a language in its own right and faces choices as to how it should develop. This is a well produced volume with maps and illustrations.

Handbuch der mitteleuropäischen Sprachminderheiten, ed. R. Hinderling and L. M. Eichinger, Tübingen, Narr, xvi + 510 pp., is a major work on Central European linguistic minorities. It includes the following contributions on varieties related to German or within the Germanic-speaking area: A. G. H. Walker, 'Nordfriesland, die Nordfriesen und das Nordfriesische' (1–30); K. M. Pedersen, 'Die deutsche Minderheit in Dänemark und die dänische Minderheit in Nordschleswig' (31–61); M. Norberg, 'Die Sorben — Slawisches Volk im Osten Deutschlands' (61–77); R. Jodlbauer, 'Die Burgenländer Kroaten' (77–119); Id., 'Die Kärntner Slowenen' (119–67); M. Krizman, 'Die slowenische Minderheit in der österreichischen Steiermark' (185–99); L. M. Eichinger, 'Südtirol' (199–263); A. R. Rowley, 'Die Sprachinseln der Fersentaler und Zimbern' (263–87); P. Zürrer, 'Deutsche Sprachinseln im Aostatal' (287–311); D. Kattenbusch, 'Ladinien' (311–35); E. Diekmann, 'Das Rätoromanische in der Schweiz' (335–85); G. Kolde and A. Näf, 'Die Westschweiz' (385–413); R. Harnisch, 'Das Elsass' (413–59); H. Fröhlich, 'Luxemburg' (459–79); M. Hinderdael and P. Nelde, 'Deutschbelgien' (479–97); and D. Stellmacher, 'Niederdeutsch' (497–507). Also noted: R. Harnisch, 'Zur sprachlichen Situation im Elsaß', *DSp*, 23, 1995:289–315; P. Wiesinger, 'Zur Sprachsituation und Sprachpolitik in den Minderheitengebieten Österreichs', *Sprachenpolitik in Grenzregionen*, ed. R. Maru (Veröffentlichungen der Kommission für Saarländische Landesgeschichte und Volksforschung, 29), Saarbrücken, Kommissionsverlag, pp. 337–60; F. Grucza, 'Zur Geschichte und Bedeutung der deutschen Sprache in Mitteleuropa', *Fest. Helbig*, 717–27; C. Baechler, 'Le Reich allemand et les minorités nationales 1871–1918', *Revue d'Allemagne*, 28:31–48; A. Ziegler, *Deutsche Sprache in Brasilien: Untersuchungen zum Sprachwandel und zum Sprachgebrauch der deutschstämmigen Brasilianer in Rio Grande do Sul* (Kultur der Deutschen im Ausland, 2), Essen, Die Blaue Eule, 258 pp. German in Europe is the subject of M. Schlossmacher, 'Der Gebrauch von Deutsch in den Organen der europäischen Union', *DSp*, 23, 1995:219–39, and J. Born and W. Schütte, *Eurotexte: Textarbeit in einer Institution der EG* (SDSp, 1), 1995, 456 pp. The use of German in primarily non-German communities is treated in T. Biegel, *Sprachwahlverhalten bei deutsch-französischer Mehrsprachigkeit. Soziolinguistische Untersuchungen mündlicher Kommunikation in der lothringischen Gemeinde Walscheid* (Studien zur Allgemeinen und Romanischen Sprachwissenschaft, 4), Frankfurt, Lang, xii + 252 pp., and M. Waas, *Language Attrition Downunder. German Speakers in Australia* (Studien zur Allgemeinen und Romanischen Sprachwissenschaft, 3), Frankfurt, Lang, 212 pp. An item on standardization is G. Schnegelsberg, 'Gegenstände der Normung und Normierungsalternativen. Wissenschaftstheoretische Implikationen für ein Gesamtkonzept', *Muttersprache*, 106:147–61. A general work is R. Schrodt, *Warum geht die deutsche Sprache immer wieder unter? Die*

Problematik der Werthaltungen im Deutschen (Passagen Diskursforschung), Vienna, Passagen Vlg, 1995, 344 pp. The legacy of East and West German surfaces in the following: M. Kreisel, **Leistungsermittlung und Leistungsbewertung im Muttersprachunterricht der DDR. Klassen 5 bis 10 — Determinanten und Tendenzen* (Beiträge zur Geschichte des Deutschunterrichts, 32), Frankfurt, Lang, 258 pp.; C. Bergmann, 'Über das "Herausbrechen" und "Zersetzen" von Menschen. Semantische Verschiebungen im Sprachgebrauch des Ministeriums für Staatssicherheit der ehemaligen DDR', *Muttersprache*, 106:289–301; N. Nail, 'Handeln und Sprachhandeln an der Berliner Mauer. Zur frühen Dekonstruktion einer Staatsgrenze', *ib.*, 302–07; and H. D. Schlosser, 'Ost und West im Talkshowtest. Kommunikatives Verhalten von alten und neuen Bundesländern', *ib.*, 308–18.

INTERDISCIPLINES

First language acquisition appears in N. Müller and Z. Penner, 'Early subordination: the acquisition of free morphology in French, German and Swiss German', *Linguistics*, 34:135–65, and D. Ingram and W. Thompson, 'Early syntactic acquisition in German: Evidence for the modal hypothesis', *Language*, 72:97–120. Bilingual education and language acquisition are featured in the following: S. Mahlstedt, **Zweisprachigkeitserziehung in gemischtsprachigen Familien. Eine Analyse der erfolgsbedingenden Merkmale*, Frankfurt, Lang, 233 pp.; H. Kuntz, **Sprachbarrieren und Lernblockaden beim emanzipatorischen Deutschunterricht in einem Entwicklungsstand: Fallstudie anhand der scheduled castes and tribes in Indien*, Munich, Iudicium, lxxxii + 324 pp., and D. M. Weiss, **Beeinflussung der Wahrnehmung durch Zweisprachigkeit: eine Studie zur Farbwahrnehmung bei Zweisprachigen* (EH, XXII, 167), 230 pp. German as a foreign language is dealt with in **Deutsch als Zweit- und Fremdsprache. Methoden und Perspektiven einer akademischen Disziplin*, ed. N. Dittmar and M. Rost-Roth (Werkstattreihe Deutsch als Fremdsprache, 52), Frankfurt, Lang, 316 pp.; J. Iluk, 'Verstehen und Gebrauch deutscher unterrichtsbezogener Redemittel', *DaF*, 33:18–22; L. Götze and P. Suchsland, 'Deutsch als Fremdsprache. Thesen zur Struktur des Faches', *ib.*, 67–72; G. Heinrici, 'Deutsch als Fremdsprache ist *doch* ein fremdsprachenwissenschaftliches Fach!', *ib.*, 131–35; L. Götze, 'Grammatikmodelle und ihre Didaktisierung in Deutsch als Fremdsprache', *ib.*, 136–43; F. G. Königs, 'Deutsch als Fremdsprache — ein Fach auf der Suche nach seinen Konturen', *ib.*, 195–200; and G. Neuner, 'Deutsch als zweite Fremdsprache nach Englisch. Überlegungen zur Didaktik und Methodik und zur Lehrmaterialentwicklung für die "Drittsprache Deutsch"', *ib.*, 211–17.

More technical, IT approaches, are T. Portele, *Ein phonetisch-akustisch motiviertes Inventar zur Sprachsynthese deutscher Äußerungen* (SI, 32), vi + 170 pp.; A. Lehr, *Kollokationen und maschinenlesbare Korpora. Ein operationales Analysemodell zum Aufbau lexikalischer Netze* (RGL, 168), vii + 383 pp.; *Lexikon und Text. Wiederverwendbare Methoden und Ressourcen zur linguistischen Erschließung des Deutschen*, ed. H. Feldweg and W. Hinrichs (Lexicographica Series Maior, 73), Tübingen, Niemeyer, xii + 266 pp.; A. Lehrndorfer, *Kontrolliertes Deutsch: linguistische und sprachpsychologische Leitlinien für eine (maschinell) kontrollierte Sprache in der Technischen Dokumentation* (TBL, 415), 248 pp.; and C. Traber, *SVOX: the Implementation of a Text-to-Speech System for German* (TIK-Schriftenreihe, 7), Zurich, Hochschulverlag, 234 pp. Also noted: F. Krier, 'Zur Steuerung von Kommunikationsvorgängen in einem Ideolekt', *DSp*, 23, 1995:269–87. Language and gender are treated in S. Oelkers, '"Der Sprintstar und ihre Freundinnen." Ein empirischer Beitrag zur Diskussion um das generische Maskulinum', *Muttersprache*, 106:1–15, and D. Cherubim, 'Mannomann!', *ib.*, 117–34.

GENERAL LINGUISTICS, PRAGMATICS AND TEXT LINGUISTICS

General linguistic themes are treated in B. Bartschat, *Methoden der Sprachwissenschaft. Von Hermann Paul bis Noam Chomsky*, Berlin, Schmidt, 190 pp., and O. Reichmann, 'Der rationalistische Sprachbegriff und Sprache, wo sie am sprachlichsten ist', *Akten* (Vancouver), 1, 16–31. Style and text analysis feature in *Stil in Fachsprachen*, ed. B. Spillner (Studien zur Allgemeinen und Romanischen Sprachwissenschaft, 2), Frankfurt, Lang, 181 pp.; G. Lerchner, 'Stilistische Solidaritäten. Stilgeschichte zwischen Literatur- und Sprachhistoriographie', *ZGer*, 6:337–48; *Beiträge zur Text- und Stilanalyse*, ed. A. Feine and H.-J. Siebert (SST, 19), 194 pp.; *Ebenen der Textstruktur. Sprachliche und kommunikative Prinzipien*, ed. W. Motsch (RGL, 164), xii + 332 pp.; E. Stock, 'Text und Intonation', *Sprachwissenschaft*, 21:211–40; N. R. Wolf, 'Wortbildung und Text', *ib.*, 241–61; F. Jürgens, 'Textsorten- und Textmustervariationen am Beispiel der Todesanzeige', *Muttersprache*, 106:226–42; C. Fraas,*Gebrauchswandel und Bedeutungsvarianz in Textnetzen: die Konzepte* IDENTITÄT *und* DEUTSCHE *im Diskurs zur deutschen Einheit* (SDSp, 3), 175 pp.; A. Endlich, 'Anmerkungen zur Sprache der Programmzeitschriften', *ib.*, 135–46.; M. Toman-Banke, *Die Wahlslogans der Bundestagswahlen 1949–1994*, Wiesbaden, Deutscher Universitätsverlag, 417 pp.; A. Schmitz-Forte, *Die journalistische Reisebeschreibung nach 1945 am Beispiel des Kölner Stadt-Anzeigers und der Süddeutschen Zeitung* (EH, 1, 1460), 1995, 457 pp.;

R. Charpiot, 'Textanalyse. Rundfunk- und Fernsehansprache des Bundespräsidenten Gustav Heinemann zum 100. Jahrgang der Gründung des Deutschen Reiches, 17. Januar 1971', *NCA*, 14:209–19; H. Girnth, 'Texte im politischen Diskurs. Ein Vorschlag zur diskursorientierten Beschreibung von Textsorten', *Muttersprache*, 106:66–80; S. Schlickau, *Moderation im Rundfunk: diskursanalytische Untersuchungen zu kommunikativen Strategien deutscher und britischer Moderatoren* (Arbeiten zur Sprachanalyse, 25), Frankfurt, Lang, 246 pp.; W. Franke, 'Ratgebende Aufklärungstexte. Überlegungen zur linguistischen Beschreibung ratgebender Beiträge der Massenmedien', *ZGL*, 24:249–72; B. C. Gilliar, *The Rhetoric of (Re)unification. Constructing Identity through East and West German Newspapers* (Berkeley Insights in Linguistics and Semiotics, 20), Frankfurt, Lang, 122 pp.; S. Stein, *Formelhafte Sprache: Untersuchungen zu ihren pragmatischen und kognitiven Funktionen im gegenwärtigen Deutsch* (Sprache in der Gesellschaft, 22), Frankfurt, Lang, 1995, 380 pp.; F. Januschek, 'Sich verstricken oder sich raushalten? Einflußnahme auf rechte Diskurse in Politik und Medien — ein Erfahrungsbericht', *OBS*, 53:133–47; U. Störiko, *'Wir legen Word auf gutes Deutsch': Formen und Funktionen fremdsprachiger Elemente in der deutschen Anzeigen-, Hörfunk- und Fernsehwerbung*, Viernheim, Cubus, 1995, xiii + 553 pp.; and Y.-I. Bak, *Das Frage-Antwort-Sequenzmuster in Unterrichtsgesprächen (Deutsch-Koreanisch)* (Beiträge zur Dialogforschung, 12), Tübingen, Niemeyer, ix + 207 pp. Specialist languages feature in the following: L. Hoffmann, 'Intraserielle und interserielle Vergleiche von Fachtexten. Ein Beitrag zur Unterscheidung von Textsorten', *Fest. Helbig*, 563–74; S.-L. Chen, *Pragmatik des Passivs in chemischer Fachfunktion. Empirische Analyse von Labordiskursen, Versuchsanleitungen, Vorlesungen und Lehrwerken* (Arbeiten zur Sprachanalyse, 23), Frankfurt, Lang, 1995, ix + 292 pp.; S. Göpferich, *Textsorten in Naturwissenschaften und Technik. Pragmatische Typologie — Kontrastierung — Translation* (Forum für Fachsprachenforschung, 27), Tübingen, Narr, 1995, xiii + 521 pp.; M. Hundt, *Modellbildung in der Wirtschaftssprache. Zur Geschichte der Institutionen- und Theoriefachsprachen der Wirtschaft* (RGL, 150), 1995, ix + 316 pp.; B. Kissig, *Fachsprachliche Wortgruppen in englischen und deutschen Texten der Mikroprozessortechnik* (Leipziger Fachsprachen-Studien, 8), Frankfurt, Lang, xiv + 267 pp.; R. Tatje, *Die Fachsprache der Mineralogie. Eine Analyse französischer und deutscher Fachzeitschriftenartikel* (Studien zur allgemeinen und romanischen Sprachwissenschaft, 1), Frankfurt, Lang, 1995, 335 pp.; E. Kasparek, 'Erfahrungen mit Sprache in einer Rechtsanwaltspraxis', *OBS*, 51:61–74; S. Walther, 'Zur Bedeutung von Sprache in der Krankenpflege. Ein Bericht aus Theorie und Praxis', *ib.*, 53:27–47; and *Wissenschaftliche Technolekte*, ed. C. Lauren and M. Nordmann (Nordeuropäische Beiträge aus den

Human- und Gesellschaftswissenschaften, 10), Frankfurt, Lang, 229 pp. Conversational analysis in its widest sense finds treatment in H. Bassler, *Wissenstransfer in intrafachlichen Vermittlungsgesprächen. Eine empirische Untersuchung von Unterweisungen in Lehrwerkstätten für Automobil- mechaniker* (RGL, 162), xi + 488 pp.; M. Beck, *Klären und streiten: Gesprächserziehung in Schule und außerschulischer Bildung* (Sprechen und Verstehen, 10), St. Ingbert, Röhrig, 265 pp.; C. Spiegel, *Streit: eine linguistische Untersuchung verbaler Interaktionen in alltäglichen Zusammen- hängen* (FIDS, 75), 1995, 289 pp.; K. Ehler, *Konversation: höfische Gesprächskultur als Model für den Fremdsprachenunterricht* (Studien Deutsch, 21), Munich, Iudicium, 288 pp.; R. Patzelt, 'Gesprächsanalyse als Verfahren der Unterrichtsreflexion für Lehrerinnen und Lehrer', *OBS*, 53:75–97; S. Streck, '"Was issn' des eigentlich — Supervision?" Zur Präferenz für Höflichkeit bei der konversationellen Aushandlung eines psychologischen Begriffs in klinischen Interviews', *ib.*, 52:169–95; J. Schwitalla, 'Telefonprobleme. (Leidvolle) Erfahrungen mit einem neuen Medium', *ZGL*, 24:153–74; and *Schlichtung. 1. Streit schlichten: gesprächsanalytische Untersuchungen zu institutionellen Formen konsensueller Konfliktregelung*, ed. W. Notdurft (SIDS, 5), viii + 431 pp. The language of young people is dealt with in P. Schlobinski and K. A. Schmid, 'Alles ist eine Frage des Stils. Zur sprachlichen Kommu- nikation in Jugendcliquen und -szenen', *Muttersprache*, 106:211–25.

2. HISTORY OF THE LANGUAGE

The fundamental relationship between writing and pronunciation is treated in P. Wiesinger, *Schreibung und Aussprache im älteren Frühneuhoch- deutschen. Zum Verhältnis von Graphem — Phonem — Phon am bairisch- österreichischen Beispiel von Andreas Kurzmann um 1400* (SLG, 42), x + 265 pp. The contributions to *Fest. Wellmann* show how multi- faceted the historical study of German can be. They include: W. Fleischer, 'Phraseologismen in einem Familienblatt des 19. Jahrhunderts' (13–28); E. Glaser, 'Das Beizbüchlein in der Abschrift der Clara Hätzerlin. Ein Zeugnis Augsburger Schreibsprache im 15. Jahrhundert (Tonvokalismus)' (29–46); H. Graser, 'Zum Mittelhoch- deutschen der Augsburger Tertiarenregel' (47–58); H. Hahn, 'Trainer Wörgötter: "Habe mich für den Offensivverteidiger Wellmann entschieden." Der Wandel der Spielsysteme und seine Auswirkungen auf die Bezeichnungen für Fußballspieler' (59–91); G. Kettmann, 'Zur Konstanz der frühneuhochdeutschen Orthogra- phie in stadt- und landesherrlichen Kanzleien' (131–38); E. Koller, 'FNHDaF: Vier Briefe Eleonores von Portugal' (161–73); W. König,

'Zur Sprache der Juden in Ichenhausen. Ein Beitrag zur Rekonstruktion des Jiddischen in Ichenhausen sowie seiner ehemaligen Funktion in der deutschen dialektalen Alltagssprache' (175–90); H. Moser, 'Das erste Mirakelbuch von Maria Waldrast. Portrait eines Sammeltexts aus dem 15. Jahrhundert' (191–205); H. Ortner, 'Das sprachgeschichtliche Schicksal der pathetischen Sprech- und Schreibweise. Darf man, wenn man nicht Hölderlin heißt, "'s Maul nicht aufmachen"?' (213–45); L. Ortner, 'Die Textsorte Briefinserat (im Jahr 1900 und heute). Oder: *Herzchen! Ob Erhaltenem viel Freude*' (247–88); M. Pümpel-Mader, 'Anredeformen und Beziehungsgestaltung in den Briefen von Sigmund Freud und C. G. Jung' (289–312); M. Siller, 'Die Entwicklung der Suffixe -*lîch* und -*rîch* im Frühneuhochdeutschen. Am Beispiel der tirolischen Urkunden- und Kanzleisprache' (313–59); A. Simeckova, 'Zur Zweisprachigkeit im Böhmen des 17. Jahrhunderts. Heinrich Hiesserles von Chodaw Reisebuch und Lebenserinnerungen' (361–69); M. Walch, 'Zur Sprache des Berliner Weltgerichtsspiels. Die Flexion des Verbs' (371–406); G. Winkler, 'Endlichkeit und Unendlichkeit — der Aspekt des Zeitraums in der deutschen Adjektivbildung' (407–27); and N. R. Wolf, 'Deutsch im frühneuzeitlichen Vatikan' (429–39). The contributions reflect the concern of H. Wellmann for word formation and linguistic change. They represent solid scholarly research on these subjects. Also noted: S. Grosse, 'Wann beginnt die deutsche Gegenwartssprache?', *Fest. Mollay*, 99–111; T. Roelecke, **Periodisierung der deutschen Sprachgeschichte. Analysen und Tabellen* (SLG, 40), xi + 494 pp.; F. Simmler, 'Entwicklungsetappen bei der Entstehung der nhd. Schriftsprache. Die Bezeichnungen für Kleidung, Schuhwerk und Bettzeug in der deutschsprachigen Regula Benedicti-Tradition', *Sprachwissenschaft*, 21 : 141–210; C. M. Stephens, 'On the grammaticalization of German *können, dürfen, sollen, mögen, müssen*, und *wollen*', *AJGLL*, 7, 1995 : 179–206; and E. Pastor, '"Seit wann siezen wir uns eigentlich?" Zur Geschichte der pronominalen Anredeformen im Deutschen. Ein Streifzug durch Literatur- und Sprachgeschichte', *GM*, 42, 1995 : 3–17.

The earliest stages of German are represented by: J. Koivulehto and T. Vennemann, 'Der finnische Stufenwechsel und das Vernersche Gesetz', *BGDSL*, 118 : 163–82; A. Bammesberger, 'The preterite of Germanic strong verbs in classes four and five', *NOWELE*, 27 : 33–43; D. Boutkan, **The Germanic 'Auslautgesetze'* (Leiden Studies in Indo-European, 4), Amsterdam, Rodopi, 1995, 476 pp.; W. Griepentrog, **Die Wurzelnomina des Germanischen und ihre Vorgeschichte* (IBS, 82), 1995, 510 pp. Gothic is treated in R. Coleman, 'Exponents of futurity in Gothic', *TPS*, 94 : 1–29.

The following illustrate aspects of Old High German: G. W. Davis and G. K. Iverson, 'Segment organization in the High German consonant shift', *AJGLL*, 7, 1995:111–27; F. Kortland, 'The High German consonant shift', *ABÄG*, 46:53–57; T. F. Shannon, 'Towards a cognitive explanation of perfect auxiliary variation: Some modal and aspectual effects in the history of Germanic', *AJGLL*, 7, 1995:129–63; and N. F. Onesti, 'Sintassi e stile nel *Ludwigslied*', *StG*, 1995:7–28. The OHG dictionary, *Althochdeutsches Wörterbuch*, proceeds at its leisurely pace: vol. 4, fasc. 14, Berlin, Akademie, cols 998–1075.

Items on Middle High German include H. Weddige, **Mittelhochdeutsch. Eine Einführung*. Munich, Beck, xii + 210 pp., and J. Singer, **Grundzüge einer rezeptiven Grammatik des Mittelhochdeutschen*, Paderborn, Schöningh, xvi + 293 pp. The *Mittelniederdeutsches Wörterbuch* continues with vol. 2, fasc. 26, *päschen-nacht — pippouw*, Neumünster, Wacholtz, 1995, cols 1409–1535.

Late MHG is represented by P. Ernst, 'Probleme der Rekonstruktion oberschichtiger Sprachformen am Beispiel Wiens im Spätmittelalter', *ZDL*, 63:1–29; H. J. Simon, 'Zur Problematik einer Geschichte der deutschen Abtönungspartikeln anhand eines Sprachlehrbuchs von 1424', *Sprachwissenschaft*, 21:262–300; and O. Sauerbeck, 'Der Schwund von *-ere*(-), *-ene*(-) bei Adjektiv und Pronomen im ausgebildeten Neuhochdeutschen', *ZDP*, 115:84–98.

Die Sprache der ersten deutschen Wochenzeitungen im 17. Jahrhundert, ed. G. Fritz and E. Strassner (Medien in Forschung + Unterricht, A, 41), Tübingen, Niemeyer, x + 357 pp., is the fruit of a research project in this very important area. It contains contributions on the nature and structure of the earliest newspapers, their syntax and vocabulary. The illustration of the whole volume is exemplary with its copious graphs. The contributors examined five papers, two from 1609 and three from 1667. Newspapers were a new text type and important early diffusers of innovative words and forms. The main areas that they treated were political events, military matters, court events, and business. They contain many foreign words and in some cases provide the first record of a particular word. The syntax investigation dealt with complex sentences and the structure of the noun phrase. Quite a few passive forms are used and most sentences show a subordinate clause after the main clause. An important book on a subject which, up to now, has been somewhat neglected. A must for all history of German buffs!

A very welcome volume is the very detailed *Kleines frühneuhochdeutsches Wörterbuch*, ed. C. Baufeld, Tübingen, Niemeyer, xxii + 264 pp. It contains words from the main Early NHG readers and also from a corpus of 100 texts in the period 1350–1600. One very useful help is the marking of earlier and later meanings with (a) and (b) respectively. This is a great help to historical semantic studies. The specialist area or geographical provenance of a word is also marked. The latter, however, does not seem to occur very often. A much needed lexical help at a price that students could afford. A major help for the study of Martin Luther's language is *Luthers Deutsch. Sprachliche Leistung und Wirkung*, ed. H. Wolf, Frankfurt, Lang, 387 pp., which contains past and present articles on Luther's language. Other items on L.: G. S. Koby, 'Revising biblical translation: Luther's lexical choices in Matthew between 1522 (*Septembertestament*) and 1545', *AJGLL*, 7, 1995:207–46; H. Wolf, 'Luthers sprachliche Selbstbeurteilungen', *ZDP*, 115:349–70; U. Schröter, 'Luthers Sprachauffassung und deren Bedeutung für die deutsche Sprache im Zusammenhang mit der Bibelübersetzung (1522–1545/46) und der Problematik ihrer Revision', *LB*, 85:99–129, and C. Funk, **Fortbewegungsverben in Luthers Übersetzung des Neuen Testaments* (EH, 1, 517), xiv + 331 pp. Items on the history of German in eastern Europe include I. T. Piirainen, 'Der Sachsenspiegel aus Schweidnitz/ Swidnica. Ein Beitrag zum Frühneuhochdeutschen in Schlesien', *NMi*, 96, 1995:309–14, and Id., 'Das Stadtprotokoll von Kesmark/ Kežmarok aus den Jahren 1554–1614. Ein Beitrag zum Frühneuhochdeutschen in der Slowakei', *Fest. Mollay*, 267–73. Also noted: J. Schiewe, **Sprachenwechsel — Funktionswandel — Austausch der Denkstile. Die Universität zwischen Latein und Deutsch* (RGL, 167), ix + 372 pp.; Z. Gerner, 'Flugschriften des deutschen Bauernkrieges. Ergebnisse einer syntaktisch-semantischen und formalen Analyse unter kommunikativem Aspekt', *Studien zur Germanistik*, 3, 1995:143–62; and H. Nitta, 'Zur Wortstellung im Frühneuhochdeutschen unter besonderer Berücksichtigung der Satzklammer', *ZDP*, 115:371–81.

The 18th c. furnishes a number of studies. M. Konopka, *Strittige Erscheinungen der deutschen Syntax im 18. Jahrhundert* (RGL, 173), xi + 253 pp., is an innovative work that seeks to examine the statements of 12 grammarians from all parts of the German-speaking area to see where some controversial usage is to be found. Then a further corpus is used to examine actual usage. The result is not an either/or description of usage but the recognition that the difference between sources is one of frequency. The constructions dealt with include bracketing, *zu* + infinitive, subordinate clauses, and clauses with verb omitted. A book to be studied carefully. Also noted: P. Wiesinger, 'Die Einführung der allgemeinen deutschen Schriftsprache in Österreich in der zweiten Hälfte des 18. Jahrhunderts', *Fest. Mollay*, 393–410; B. van Benthem, **Die laienmedizinische Fachsprache im Spiegel therapeutischer Hausbücher des 18. Jahrhunderts* (GAG, 612), 482 pp.; W. W. Menzel, **Vernakuläre Wissenschaft. Christian Wolffs*

Bedeutung für die Herausbildung und Durchsetzung des deutschen als Wissen-schaftssprache (RGL, 166), vii + 279 pp.; **Studentensprache und Studenten-lied in Halle vor hundert Jahren. Neudruck des 'Idiotikon der Burschensprache' von 1793 und der 'Studentenlieder' von 1781. Eine Jubiläumsausgabe für die Universität Halle-Wittenberg dargebracht vom Deutschen Abend in Halle,* Halle, Fliegenkopf, 1990, xxxix + 127 pp.; and A. Linke, 'Höflichkeit und soziale Selbstdarstellung in Anstandsbüchern des 18. Und 19. Jahrhunderts', *OBS*, 52 : 70–104.

3. ORTHOGRAPHY

A momentous event this year has been the publication of two main works reflecting the new reformed German spelling system. *Duden. Die deutsche Rechtschreibung*, 21st edn, Mannheim, Dudenverlag, 928 pp., and *Die neue deutsche Rechtschreibung*, ed. U. Hermann et al., Gütersloh, Bertelsmann, 1040 pp. Also noted on this subject: **Die neue Rechtschreibung. Wörter und Regeln leicht gelernt*, ed. H. Beuschel-Menze and F. Menze, Reinbek, Rowohlt, 190 pp.; K. Heller, 'Rechtschreibreform', *DaF*, 33 : 238–40; R. Looser, **Gescheiterte Rechtschreibreformen in der Schweiz: die Geschichte der Bemühungen um eine Reform der deutschen Rechtschreibung in der Schweiz 1945 bis 1966* (TVS, 22), 1995, 511 pp.; and G. Gréciano, 'Zur Orthographie der Phraseologie', *Fest. Helbig*, 451–62. An historical study is K. P. Wegera, 'Zur Geschichte des Adjektivgroßschreibung im Deutschen. Entwicklung und Motive', *ZDP*, 115 : 382–92.

4. PHONOLOGY

To be warmly welcomed is R. Wiese, *The Phonology of German*, Oxford, Clarendon, x + 351 pp. Much of modern phonology has moved so quickly that it has been almost impossible to catch up. W. offers us a detailed overview of German phonology from a modern post-generative perspective. The volume includes the phoneme system of German, the prosodic structure of German, showing how syllables are built up, prosodic morphology, lexical morphology, underspeci-fication, phonological rules and alternations, which includes umlaut and devoicing, and stress in words, compounds, and phrases. There is a useful index of all words treated. This is a clearly produced, highly informative volume. G. Muthmann, *Phonologisches Wörterbuch der deutschen Sprache* (RGL, 163), vi + 498 pp., takes up an older tradition which did not find imitators of producing a dictionary based on the alphabetic listing of words in their phonemic or phonetic form. There is a detailed introduction tackling the difficult, but not insuperable, problem of order. By its nature this dictionary has to take a standard, uniform description of German, but variation is allowed, particularly in foreign words. This is an extremely useful book which is necessary for any serious study of German phonology. U. Willi, *Die segmentale Dauer als phonetischer Parameter von 'fortis' und 'lenis' bei Plosiven im Zürichdeutschen* (ZDL, Beiheft 92), Stuttgart, Steiner, x + 250 pp. One of the last contributions by the late H. Penzl is on the nature of evidence for umlaut, 'Zum Beweismaterial für den *i*-Umlaut im Nordisch-Westgermanischen', *AJGLL*, 8:93–104. Also on umlaut: R. Wiese, 'Phonological vs. morphological rules: on German umlaut and ablaut', *JL*, 32:113–35, and G. K. Iverson and J. C. Salmons, 'The primacy of primary umlaut', *BGDSL*, 118:69–86. Also noted: H. Takahashi, **Die richtige Aussprache des Deutschen in Deutschland, Österreich und der Schweiz nach Maßgabe der kodifizierten Normen* (Duisburger Arbeiten zur Sprach- und Kulturwissenschaft, 27), Frankfurt, Lang, 277 pp.; C. Hall et al., *Deutsche Aussprachelehre. Ein Hand- und Übungsbuch für Sprecher des Finnischen*, Helsinki, Finn Lectura, 1995, 260 pp., which has been extended and changed in various ways, and W. H. Vieregge, *Patho-Symbolphonetik. Auditive Deskription pathologischer Sprache* (ZDL, Beiheft 100), xi + 239 pp. *Untersuchungen zu Stimme und Sprache/ Papers on Speech and Voice*, ed. A. Braun (ZDL, Beiheft 96), v + 166 pp., contains a range of papers, the following treating German data: H. Grassegger, 'Koartikulatorische Einflüsse auf die Produktion von Anlautplosiven bei österreichischen (steirischen) Sprechern' (12–18); A. Braun, 'Zur regionalen Distribution von VOT im Deutschen' (19–32); H. Helfrich, 'Zur Wahrnehmung des Stimmhaft-stimmlos-Kontrastes — Eine signalentdeckungstheoretische Analyse' (33–53); P. Martens and H. Scheeren-Martens, 'Lese-Regeln zur Aussprache deutscher Vokale' (75–124); R. Pfeiffer-Rupp, 'Das Internationale Phonetische Alphabet nach der Reform von 1989/1993 (Terminologie, Tabellierung, semiotische Motivation, Typemik und subtypemische Taktik)' (134–66). Also noted: **Beiträge zur deutschen Standardaussprache. Bericht von der 16. Sprechwissenschaftlichen Tagung am 15. und 16. Oktober 1994. Zum Gedenken an H, Krech*, ed. E. M. Krech and E. Stock (Hallesche Schriften zur Sprechwissenschaft und Phonetik, 1), Hanau, Dausien, 252 pp.; J. A. Wipf, 'Vorschläge zur Bewertung von Ausspracheleistungen', *DaF*, 33:34–38; and M. T. Müller, 'Aussprachübungen mit Phantasie und Bewegung. Anregungen aus dem Schauspieltraining', *ib.*, 39–40.

5. MORPHOLOGY

The following items deal with inflectional morphology: A. Bittner, *Starke 'schwache' Verben, schwache 'starke' Verben. Deutsche Verbflexion und Natürlichkeit* (SDG, 51), xiii + 224 pp.; M. Neef, *Wortdesign. Eine deklarative Analyse der deutschen Verbflexion* (SDG, 52), 308 pp.; M. Kefer, 'Superlativbildung auf *st* oder *est?*', *ZGL*, 24:287–98; R. Joeres, 'Der Friede oder der Frieden. Ein Nominalproblem der Substantivflexion', *Sprachwissenschaft*, 21:301–36; and K. Pittner, 'Zur morphologischen Defektivität des Pronomens *wer*', *DaF*, 33:73–77.

Derivational morphology is treated in J. Meibauer, 'Wortbildung und Kognition. Überlegungen zum deutschen -*er*- Suffix', *DSp*, 23, 1995:97–123; A. Greule, 'Reduktion als Wortbildungsprozeß der deutschen Sprache', *Muttersprache*, 106:193–203; J. Erben, 'Vorstöße oder Verstöße. Versuch einer Einschätzung von A. Kerrs Neologismen (Theaterkritiken 1905–1933)', *Fest. Wellmann*, 1–15; N. Hortzitz, 'Die Wortbildung im Dienst der Meinungssprache. Am Beispiel von Substantivkomposita mit *Jude* in antijüdischen Texten', *ib.*, 107–30; A. and M. Kienpointner, '"Sind nun Frauen die besseren Autofahrer?" Veränderungen der geschlechtsspezifischen Sprachgebrauchs im Gegenwartsdeutschen', *ib.*, 139–60; W. Motsch, 'Affixoide. Sammelbezeichnung für Wortbildungsphänomene oder linguistische Kategorie?', *DaF*, 33:160–68; J. Erben, 'Wortbildung und Textbildung', *Fest. Helbig*, 545–52; W. Motsch, 'Semantische und pragmatische Aspekte der Wortbildung', *ib.*, 513–31; B. Symann, *Stiefkind Grammatik. Untersuchungen zur kindlichen Wortbildung* (Item linguistische Studien, 1), Essen, Item, 1995, 290 pp.; B. Lenz, *unAffigierung. Unrealisierbare Argumente, unausweichliche Fragen, nicht plausible Antworten* (SDG, 50), 1995, ix + 242 pp.; A. Klosa, *Negierende Lehnpräfixe des Gegenwartsdeutschen* (Germanische Bibliothek, n. F., 3. Reihe: Untersuchungen, 22), Heidelberg, Winter, xii + 494 pp.; B. Lawrenz, 'Der Zwischen-den-Mahlzeiten-Imbiß und der Herren-der-Welt-Größenwahn: Aspekte der Struktur und der Bildungsweise von Phrasenkomposita im Deutschen', *ZGL*, 24:1–15; R. K. Bloomer, 'Die pleonastischen Zusammensetzungen der deutschen Gegenwartssprache', *AJGLL*, 8:69–90; E. Donalies, '*Da keuchgrinste sie süßsäuerlich*. Über kopulative Verb- und Adjektivkomposita', *ZGL*, 24:273–86; W. Fleischer, 'Zur Wortbildungsaktivität reflexiver Verben', *Fest. Helbig*, 533–44; R. Schmidt, 'Die "Entübelung" von Wortstrukturproblemen. Zum Head-Status von Präfixen im Deutschen und Schwedischen', *DaF*, 33:86–91; and F. Eppert, 'Wie brauchbar ist -*nis* als Genus- und Artikelindikator', *ib.*, 15–18.

Historical studies are R. Joeres, *Wortbildungen mit -macher im Althochdeutschen, Mittelhochdeutschen und Neuhochdeutschen* (Germanische Bibliothek, n. F., 3. Reihe: Untersuchungen, 24), Heidelberg, Winter, 357 pp., and G. Winkler, *Die Wortbildung mit -lich im Alt-, Mittel- und Frühneuhochdeutschen* (Sprache — Literatur und Geschichte, 11), Heidelberg, Winter, 1995, 465 pp.

6. SYNTAX

Another crack at presenting the grammar of German is provided by B. Dodd et al., *Modern German Grammar. A Practical Guide*, London, Routledge, 492 pp., accompanied by a 105-pp. *Workbook*. This volume covers both the structural and functional approaches to grammar. The text is set out in a typologically clear and eye-catching way. There is also an introduction showing how to use the book. Usefully there is an account of the 'proposed' spelling reform which has, of course, been overtaken by events. The workbook is also divided into structures and functions and has a key. Only time and experience will tell if this is the book that is suitable for a particular course on German language. It is certainly worth a try.

Other items on different aspects of grammar include: W. Hackel, **Verfahrensgrammatik. Eine alternative Grammatikbeschreibung für den Sprachunterricht*, Frankfurt, Lang, 95 pp.; B. M. Farenkia, 'Aspekte einer kommunikativ-funktionalen Grammatik aus der Fremdperspektive', *DaF*, 33:156–59; U. Hirschfeld, 'Grammatik und Phonetik', *Fest. Helbig*, 11–22; K.-E. Sommerfeldt, 'Wortfelder mit mehreren Wortarten — Probleme einer Inhaltsgrammatik', *Muttersprache*, 106:55–65; N. Fries, 'Grammatik und Emotionen', *LiLi*, 26:37–69; J. Buscha, 'Zur Theorieneutralität von Referenzgrammatiken', *Fest. Helbig*, 3–9; and G. Neuner,'Progressionsverfahren bei der Lehrwerkentwicklung. Beispiel: Grammatik', *ib.*, 685–706.

Features of the noun phrase are treated in G. Kolde, **Nominaldetermination. Eine systematische und kommentierte Bibliographie unter besonderer Berücksichtigung des Deutschen, Englischen und Französischen*, Tübingen, Niemeyer, viii + 618 pp.; V. Agel, 'Finites Substantiv', *ZGL*, 24:16–57; P. Petkov, 'System- und normbedingter Kasusgebrauch' *ZGL*, 24:58–63; G. Lipold, 'Das Satz "subjekt" als Serialisierungsproblem im Gegenwartsdeutschen', *Fest. Mollay*, 233–41; W. Abraham, 'Von semantisch zu syntaktisch begründeter Kasusrektion im Deutschen', *Fest. Helbig*, 351–65; P. Pavel, 'Die Kasustranspositionen im Deutschen', *ib.*, 367–76; V. Agel, 'Dem Jubilar seine Festschrift: ein typologisches Kuckucksei in der deutschen Substantivgruppe', *Fest. Mollay*, 1–18; H. J. Heringer, 'Prinzipien der Genuszuweisung', *Fest. Helbig*, 203–16; C. Fortmann, **Konstituentenbewegung in der DP-Struktur: zur funktionalen Analyse der Nominalphrase im Deutschen* (LA, 347), vi + 173 pp.; G. Zifonun, 'Minimalia grammaticalia: das nichtphorische *es* als Prüfstein grammatischer Theoriebildung', *DSp*, 23, 1995:39–60; D. Bresson, 'Dictionnaire syntaxique électronique des noms prédicatifs de l'allemand', *Lingvisticae Investigationes*, 19, 1995:387–400; and K. Willems, '*Derer* als Demonstrativpronomen und als Relativpronomen. Zum Problem des Sprachwandels', *Muttersprache*, 106:36–54.

Items on other parts of speech include E.-M. Heinle, 'Zur Frequenz der Wortart Adverb', *Fest. Wellmann*, 93–106; W. Abraham, 'Wieso stehen nicht alle Modalpartikel in allen Satzformen? Die Nullhypothese', *DSp*, 24:16–57; D. Homberger, '*indem*. Anmerkungen zu einer schwierigen Konjunktion', *Muttersprache*, 106:22–35; H. Glinz, 'Formalstrukturen und Bedeutungsstrukturen: Propositionen — verbale Semanteme — dominante und inhaltliche Teile', *Fest. Helbig*, 41–52; and G. Starke, 'Das Adjektiv als Verbergänzung im Deutschen', *ib.*, 339–50.

Sentence structure appears in I. Behr and H. Quintin, *Verblose Sätze im Deutschen* (Eurogermanistik, 4), Tübingen, Stauffenberg, xii + 264 pp.; G. Gréciano, 'Zur Aktualität des "Prädikatskomplexes"', *SN*, 68:83–90; A. Näf, 'Die w-Exklamativsätze im Deutschen — zugleich ein Pladoyer für eine Rehabilitierung der Empirie in der Sprachwissenschaft', *ZGL*, 24:135–52; O. Leirbukt, 'Über Setzung und Nichtsetzung des Korrelats bei Relativsätzen mit *wer*', *Fest. Helbig*, 151–63; R. Grosse, 'Konzessivsätze unter soziologischen und historischen Aspekten', *ib.*, 139–45; F. Freund and B. Sundqvist, '"Konzessiv" oder "kontradiktorisch"?', *ib.*, 147–50; J. Geilfuss-Wolfgang, **Über gewisse Fälle von Assoziation mit Fokus* (LA, 358), viii + 358 pp.; W.-T. Jung, **Syntaktische Relationen im Rahmen der Dependenzgrammatik* (BGS, 9), 184 pp.; **On Extraction and Extraposition in German*, ed. U. Lutz and J. Pafel (Linguistik aktuell, 11), Amsterdam, Benjamins, xii + 315 pp.; U. Schneider, 'Die Thema-Rhema-Gliederung im Deutschen und ihre Bedeutung für den Unterricht des Deutschen als Fremdsprache', *DaF*, 33:78–85; H.-W. Eroms, 'Die Thema-Rhema-Gliederung aus grammatischer Perspektive', *Fest. Helbig*, 53–67; W. Heinemann, 'Negation und Textkonstituition', *ib.*, 553–62; Christoph and Czeslawa Schatte, 'Negationszeichen in Entscheidungsfragesätzen', *ib.*, 129–37; O. Leys, 'Das Ziel als Distanzbeziehung', *LB*, 85:55–67; and M. Schecker, 'Klammer-Konstruktionen', *Fest. Mollay*, 61–72.

Verbal construction features in J. Lunze, 'Plain middles and *lassen* middles in German: reflexive constructions and sentence perspective', *Linguistics*, 34:645–95; S. Krogh, 'Neuhochdeutsch *lassen* mit Objekt und Infinitiv. Einige Bemerkungen zu Gunnar Bech, "Studien über das deutsche verbum infinitum"', *ZGL*, 24:64–79; E. Hentschel and H. Weydt, 'Das leidige *bekommen*-Passiv', *Fest. Helbig*, 165–83; H. Vater, 'Zum Reflexiv-Passiv im Deutschen', *ib.*, 185–92; C. Maienborn, *Situation und Lokation. Die Bedeutung lokaler Adjunkte von Verbalprojektionen* (SDG, 53), ix + 292 pp.; B. and G. Wojtak, 'Werben für

Verben? Betrachtungen im Grenzfeld zwischen Lexikon und Grammatik', *Fest. Helbig*, 235–85; J. Mbassi, 'Polysémie et univocité: le cas de l'impératif allemand', *NCA*, 14:191–94; M. Lefèvre, 'Temps et phase en allemand', *ib.*, 14:87–98; J. Amrhein, 'Die Semantik von *werden*. Grammatische Polysemie und die Verbalkategorien Diathese, Aspekt und Modus (Fokus, 14), Trier, Wissenschaftlicher Vlg, 134 pp.; N. R. Wolf, '*würde*. Zur Verwendung einer Hilfsverbsform', *Fest. Helbig*, 193–202; G. Starke, 'Partizipialkonstruktionen und freie Fügungen am Satzanfang mit und ohne Subjektbezug', *DaF*, 33:10–14; and J. Sternkopf, 'Die Verba dicendi in stabilen Wortkomplexen', *Muttersprache*, 106:338–43.

Contrastive studies include K. Solfjeld, 'Sententiality and translation strategies German-Norwegian', *Linguistics*, 34:567–90; M. Doherty, 'Passive perspectives, different preferences in English and German — a result of parameterized processing', *ib.*, 591–643; S. Masi, **Deutsche Modalpartikeln und ihre Entsprechungen im Italienischen. Äquivalente für doch, ja, denn, schon und wohl* (Bonner Romanistische Arbeiten, 59), Frankfurt, Lang, 287 pp.; Y.-B. Kim, **Die deutschen Relativsätze und ihre Entsprechungen im Koreanischen. Kontrastive Syntax und Übersetzungsproblematik* (EH, 1, 1543), 242 pp.; J. Bermann and A. Frank, **Deutsche und französische Syntax im Formalismus der LFG* (LA, 168), vii + 383 pp.; H. Czepluch, **Kasus im Deutschen und Englischen. Ein Beitrag zur Theorie des abstrakten Kasus* (LA, 349), xii + 376 pp.; M. Nekula, **System der Partikeln im Deutschen und Tschechischen unter besonderer Berücksichtigung der Abtönungspartikeln* (LA, 355), xiv + 219 pp.; and G. Buchgeher-Coda, **Die deutschen Wechselpräpositionen und ihre italienischen Entsprechungen in lokativer und direktionaler Funktion*, Turin, Tirrenia, 1995, 447 pp.

7. SEMANTICS

K. B. Beaton, *A Practical Dictionary of German Usage*, Oxford, Clarendon, xvii + 921 pp., reflects a tradition of dealing with German vocabulary which is extremely useful for the English-speaking learner. The usage in the title is that of words and does not include grammatical constructions. The presupposition for this volume is the clear understanding of the differentiated meaning of English words and then one can proceed to their German equivalents. This is certainly essential when dealing with English-German translation. How relevant that may be when today this takes rather a back-seat is a moot point. The English words are listed alphabetically. The presentation of the English and German is very clear. There are then two appendices, one listing English words and one German words so that one can find anything in the dictionary easily. The examples of usage strive to be modern but do not give their exact sources. The vocabulary dealt with is largely traditional and English loans are not frequent. This is a book which deserves to be widely used. Let us hope that linguists of vision will think so.

H. Olschansky, *Volksetymologie* (RGL, 175), 713 pp., is a long overdue volume on this fascinating subject. O. traces the research into this topic which goes back to A. Schmeller, although he is not usually given proper recognition. It is also something which occurs in other neighbouring disciplines, notably *Volkskunde*. Despite attempts at trying to find another designation for the phenomenon the word *Volksetymologie* remains unassailed and is, reluctantly, used in this work. The phenomenon affects isolated words chiefly on the synchronic level and, despite its name, is used by people from all social backgrounds. After two theoretical and illustrative chapters there are four separate bibliographies whose entries are commented on and quotations cited. There is also an index of popular etymologies from German. This book fills a hole in this aspect of the historical development of German vocabulary. Also noted: A. Burkhardt, 'Zwischen Poesie und Ökonomie. Die Metonymie als semantisches Prinzip', *ZGL*, 24:175–94; F. Wang, *Die konzessive Beziehung in der deutschen Gegenwartssprache. Untersuchung zu ihrer Syntax, Semantik und Pragmatik* (EH, XXI, 158), 174 pp.; B. Stiebels, *Lexikalische Argumente und Adjunkte. Zum semantischen Beitrag von verbalen Präfixen und Partikeln* (Studia Grammatica, 39), 322 pp.; P. A. Mumm, 'Generische Bezeichnung. Onomasiologische Aufgaben und ihre Lösungen durch das neuhochdeutsche Artikelsystem', *Sprachwissenschaft*, 20, 1995:420–67; and A. Steube, 'Compositionally constructed epistemic meaning and reference in German', *Fest. Helbig*, 117–27.

The semantics of individual words and groups of words feature in: A. von Stechow, 'The different readings of *wieder* "again": a structural account', *Journal of Semantics*, 12:87–138; M. Dalmas, 'Tanz auf dem doppelten Boden der Tatsachen. Zu den diskursiven Funktionen von *eigentlich*', *Fest. Helbig*, 217–37; J. Schröder, 'Zu Verben der visuellen Wahrnehmung (Kerngruppe)', *ib.*, 317–25; S. Jahr, 'Semantische Valenz substantivischer Fachwörter auf textueller Ebene', *ib.*, 377–87; O. Kovtun, 'Zum fachsprachlichen und allgemeinsprachlichen Gebrauch von *Manager, Management* und *managen*', *Muttersprache*, 106:344–49; D. Kaiser, 'Sprache der Nähe — Sprache der Distanz: eine relevante Kategorie für den DaF-Unterricht?' *DaF*, 33:3–9; R. S. Bauer and C. Chlosta, 'Sprichwörter: ein Problem für Fremdsprachenlehrer wie -lerner?!' *ib.*, 91–102; and G. Zifonun, 'Ungewöhnliche Verwendungen von *mit* (I)', *ib.*, 218–22.

Lexicographical studies are headed by *Wörterbuch der Valenz etymologisch verwandter Wörter. Verben, Adjektive, Substantive*, ed. K.-E. Sommerfeldt and H. Schreiber, Tübingen, Niemeyer, vi + 298 pp. This volume represents an extension for valency theory to include communicative and pragmatic aspects, to describing vocabulary in terms of lexical fields, and to include the word classes of verbs, adjectives and nouns in etymologically connected groups. After a theoretical introduction the fields are presented. They represent both concrete and abstract words, including movement, transport, cleaning, emotions, feelings. For each field there is first an overview of its members. Then for each etymological sub-group there are examples, semantic and syntactic features, and special notes. By comparing the semantic features one can see how the different sub-groups differ in meaning. The decoding of the abbreviations for the semantic and syntactic features is not always straightforward and requires practice. Indeed one *n* in *Sn* is missing (by deduction it means nominative). There is a complete alphabetical list of all words at the end of the volume. This book is primarily intended for the learner of German, but he will need to have a good background in valency before consulting it with profit, and should persevere as it is worth the effort. Also noted: M. Kammerer, *Bildschirmorientiertes Abfassen von Wörterbuchartikeln: dargestellt am Beispiel des Frühneuhochdeutschen Wörterbuches* (Lexicographica. Series Maior, 68), Tübingen, Niemeyer, 1995, vii + 210 pp.; *Wörterbücher in der Diskussion. II. Vorträge aus dem Heidelberger Lexiokographischen Kolloquium*, ed. H. E. Wiegand (Lexicographica. Series Maior, 70), Tübingen, Niemeyer, xv + 364 pp.; *Lexikographie zwischen Theorie und Praxis. Das deutsch-ungarische Wörterbuchprojekt*, ed. R. Hessky (Lexicographica. Series Maior, 71), Tübingen, Niemeyer, vi + 102 pp.; *Das Lernerwörterbuch Deutsch als Fremdsprache (=LWB) in der Diskussion*, ed. I. Barz and M. Schröder (Sprache — Literatur und Geschichte, 12), Heidelberg, Winter, xii + 266 pp.; J. Kornelius, 'Vom Printwörterbuch zum elektronischen Kollokationswörterbuch. Theoretische, methodische und praktische Überlegungen zur Erstellung eines Kollokationswörterbuchs', *Lexicographica*, 11, 1995:153–71; L. Elekfi, 'Wortartbezeichnungen in deutsch-ungarischen Wörterbüchern', *Fest. Mollay*, 73–84; H.-P. Kromann, 'Deutsche Wörterbücher aus der Perspektive eines fremdsprachigen Benutzers', *Fest. Helbig*, 501–12; S. J. Schierholz, 'Grammatik im Wörterbuch. Zur Wörterbuchbenutzung aus fremdsprachiger Perspektive', *DaF*, 33:223–32; and I. Fischer, '*Klassische* Germanen versus *moderne* German? Die Gegensatzrelation bei Adjektiven im Langenscheidt Großwörterbuch Deutsch als Fremdsprache', *DaF*, 33:233–37. The *Deutsches Wörterbuch*, Stuttgart–Leipzig, Hirzel, continues with vol. 2, fasc. 6, *ander—angen*, cols

801–960, fasc. 7, *angen—Ankunft*, cols 961–1120, and vol. 8, double fasc. 3–4, *Erbgut—erlauben*, cols 1601–1920. This is a mammoth, largely unsung, enterprise which is proceeding competently. The number of compound forms exceeds any other German dictionary and the entries are clearly set out, although crammed with information. Fascicles 6 and 7 are full of *an*-compounds. However, there are some other interesting words: *Anfechtung* (without a quotation from Luther!); *angeben* 'to boast' goes back to the 17th c.; the first record of *Anglizismus* is in 1744; *anhand*, there seems a large unexplained gap between *an der Hand* from the 18th c. to *anhand* in the 20th; *Animation* for '(film) animation' is first recorded in 1976; *ankommen* is listed with many idiomatic phrases. *A* seems a very long letter! Vol. 8 has a plethora of compounds with *er-*, also *Erdapfel*, the regional synonym for 'potato'; *erfahren*, already lexicalized as an adjective in its own right in MHG. This is a fundamental work for German lexicography and one hopes that financial and other support will long be made available for it.

Borrowing is always a popular area. This year sees the publication of A. W. Stanforth, *Deutsche Einflüsse auf den englischen Wortschatz in Geschichte und Gegenwart* (RGL, 165), xiii + 200 pp., which has been a long time in the making. After a review of the literature and the setting up of a theoretical framework there follows a chronological account of German borrowings in English. This is followed by a discussion of their pronunciation and spelling, their grammatical treatment, their semantic integration and functional and stylistic aspects. Finally there is an evaluation of their role. In an appendix J. Eichhoff examines German loans in American English. An index of words might have been good, but the typographical layout of the work is such that they are immediately recognizable. The numbers are not easily exactly quantifiable but are relatively slight, 0.5% of the English vocabulary. Over 75% are simple loan words and almost 95% are nouns. This is a very clearly written, excellent study. A fascinating volume is *Eurolatein. Das griechische und lateinische Erbe in den europäischen Sprachen*, ed. H. H. Munske and A. Kirkness (RGL, 169), vi + 341 pp., which contains the following contributions: N. Holzberg, Neugriechisch und Eurolatein' (1–11); M. Habermann, 'Latinismen in deutschen Fachtexten der frühen Neuzeit' (12–46); J. Schiewe, 'Kontinuität und Wandel des akademischen und wissenschaftlichen Wortschatzes im Übergang der Universitäten vom Lateinischen zum Deutschen' (47–64); H. Schmidt, 'Lehnpräpositionen aus dem Lateinischen in der deutschen Gegenwartssprache' (65–81); H. H. Munske, 'Eurolatein im Deutschen: Überlegungen und Beobachtungen' (82–105); H. Keipert, 'Das Lateinische in der Geschichte der russischen Sprache' (106–28); H.-P. Stoffel, 'Zur

Wortbildung, Semantik und Etymologie von russischen Lexemen auf *de(z)-...-(iz)acij* + *a* im eurolateinisch-internationalen Kontext' (129–51); M. Scheler, 'Zur Rolle des griechischen und lateinischen Elements im englischen Wortschatz' (152–70); C. Schmidt, 'Zur Europäisierung der französischen Nomina agentis: die Internationalismen *-(o)graphe* und *-(o)logue/-(o)logiste*' (171–93); M. Höfler, 'Zur Datierung von Eurolatinismen in der französischen Lexikographie' (194–205); W. Rettig, 'Die Latinität des französischen und des italienischen Wortschatzes' (204–18); J. Volmert, 'Die Rolle griechischer und lateinischer Morpheme bei der Entstehung von Internationalismen' (219–35); A. Kirkness, 'Zur lexikographischen Dokumentation eurolateinischer Wortbildungseinheiten: Vergleichende Beobachtungen am Beispiel *aero-*' (236–74); H. Henne, 'Das Eigene im Fremden. Vom semantischen Stellenwert der Wörter' (275–83); F. J. Meissner, 'Eurolexis und Fremdsprachendidadtik' (284–305); and M. Habermann and A. Kirkness, 'Auswahlbibliographie' (306–36). This is an extremely wide-ranging volume. This whole question of national versus European language structures is the coming topic in the 21st c. Also noted: A. Effertz and U. Vieth, *Das Verständnis wirtschaftsspezifischer Anglizismen in der deutschen Sprache bei Unternehmern, Führungskräften und Mitarbeitern der neuen und alten Bundesländer* (Freiberger Beiträge zum Einfluß der angloamerikanischen Sprache und Kultur auf Europa, 1), Frankfurt, Lang, 191 pp.; E. Szwejkowska-Olsson, '*Virulent, vehement,* und *versiert* — oder über die *Viren* der deutschen Sprache. Zum Fremdwortgebrauch in vornehmlich wissenschaftlichen Texten', *MS*, 90:38–44; A. Dresch, '*Adventure Look* und *Sport-Appeal.* Das Phänomen "modischer" Anglizismen in Men-Lifestyle-Zeitschriften', *DSp*, 23, 1995:240–68; H.-J. Kann, 'Neue Germanismen in *Time*', *Sprachdienst*, 40:102–05; and B. Carstensen and U. Busse, *Anglizismenwörterbuch*. III. *P—Z*, Berlin, de Gruyter, 1022–1752.

Contrastive semantic studies include: H. Schumacher, 'Kontrastive Valenzlexikographie', *Fest. Helbig*, 387–415; B. Gutermann, *Die Raumdarstellung in deutschen und französischen technischen Texten. Sprachvergleichende Untersuchungen zur Frequenz der Darstellung räumlicher Relationen, zu ihrer sprachlichen Form und zu Inhalt-Form-Beziehungen* (EH, XXI, 160), 306 pp.; and Y. Wenliang, 'Interkulturelle Interferenzen Chinesisch — Deutsch. Am Beispiel des universitären Lebens', *Muttersprache*, 106:263–71.

Items dealing with the historical development of words and phrases include: N. Oettinger, 'Die Wortbildung von deutsch *Heim*', *Fest. Wellmann*, 207–12; R. Beekes, 'The etymology of German *Funke* "spark"', *ABÄG*, 46:1–8; R. Schmidt-Wiegand, 'Er redet wie ihm der Schnabel gewachsen ist. Eine Redensart und ihre Herkunft aus dem Sprichwort', *NdW*, 35, 1995:227–35; R. Hochholzer, **Himmel und Hölle: onomasiologische und semasiologische Studien zu den Jenseitsbezeichnungen im Althochdeutschen* (RBDSL, B, 60), 240 pp.; D. Benkartek, **Ein interpretierendes Wörterbuch der Nominalabstrakta im Narrenschiff Sebastian Brants von Abenteuer bis Zwietracht*, Frankfurt, Lang, 449 pp.; J. Knobloch, 'Vom Bildungswert etymologischer Wortforschung', *Sprachwissenschaft*, 20, 1995:468–74; Id., 'Etymologische Beobachtungen zum deutschen Wortschatz. Teil 2', *Muttersprache*, 106:16–21; and A. Sons, 'Das Chinabild in der deutschen Sprache. Ein historisch-linguistischer Überblick', *ib.*, 97–116. Also noted: G. Müller and A. Steinhauer, 'Wörter des Jahres 1995', *Sprachdienst*, 40:1–17.

8. Dialects

An important and ambitious work is *Mittelrheinischer Sprachatlas*, ed. G. Bellmann. 1. *Vorkarten, Vokalismus*, 1, 1994. 11. *Vokalismus*, 2, 1995, 2 vols, Tübingen, Niemeyer, ix + 88 maps, maps 89–176. Intensive preparatory work was carried out in order to select the phonological and morphological items to be solicited. Eight field workers were used, who transcribed the answers of informants in IPA script during highly structured interviews. Informants were predominantly male, had manual jobs, and had lived in their own locality all their lives. They were separated into two groups on the basis of age, +/−75 and +/−35 and mobility. The new thing about this atlas is that for many maps answers from the two series of informants were mapped on to one map, called *Kontrastblatt*. This enables us to see what forms are changing. On one page there is a *Basisblatt* which maps the forms of the word according to the group of older inhabitants. On the opposite page there are two maps with a smaller number of localities, one repeating the *Basisblatt* with a reduced number of entries while the other shows changes by using red symbols. This gives the atlas a dynamic which dialectologists will want to pursue in detail. The introductory volume gives a detailed account of the methods and contains several appendices, bibliography, index of names and topics, the questionnaires, alphabetical list of key words, and sociolinguistic information on each informant. An excellently produced atlas. Lexical material appears in another atlas, *Bayerischer Sprachatlas*. *Sprachatlas von Bayerisch-Schwaben*. 1. *Wortgeographie*, 1, ed. W. König and C. Feik, Heidelberg, Winter, xxiv + 619 pp. + 158 maps. The material was gathered for this in a period of five years. The informants were between 55 and 70 and had lived in their locality most of their lives. In most localities more than one informant was used. Several field workers took part in the interviews, using a questionnaire of over 2,000 questions. They realize that they are not presenting the typical dialect of the locality but of the informants. The material is presented in the form of commentaries and lists of all the responses. Then in the second half of the atlas there are traditional maps. This has the advantage of giving the researcher more raw data than normal. The symbols for the maps are very clear, showing the different areas immediately. A careful study will show how far Swabian and Bavarian are lexically different. Also noted: *Wolgadeutscher Sprachatlas*, ed. N. Berend, Tübingen, Francke, 320 pp.; K. Siewert, 'Karte der Rotwelsch-Dialekte in Deutschland', *ZDL*, 43:282–88; **Stand und Aufgabe der deutschen Dialektgeographie*. ii. *Brüder-Grimm-Symposion zur Historischen Wortforschung. Beiträge zu der Marburger Tagung vom Oktober 1992*, ed. E. Bremer and R. Hildebrandt (Historische Wortforschung, 4), Berlin, de Gruyter, viii + 293 pp.; and A. N. Rauch, **Krankheitsnamen im Deutschen. Eine dialektologische und etymologische Untersuchung der Bezeichnungen für Diphtherie, Febris Scarlatina, Morbilli, Parotitis Epidemica und Varicellae* (*ZDL*, Beiheft 84), 1995, xvii + 208 pp.

'. . . *im Gefüge der Sprachen.' Studien zu System und Soziologie der Dialekte. Festschrift für Robert Hinderling zum 60. Geburtstag*, ed. R. Harnisch et al. (*ZDL*, Beiheft 90), 1995, xii + 301 pp., contains the following contributions: A. R. Bachmann and F. X. Scheuerer, 'Zur Verbalflexion im Bairischen. Der mehrformige Plural am Beispiel der südlichen Oberpfalz' (1–12); L. M. Eichinger, 'Ist Regionalität eine sinnvolle Kategorie in der Sprachwissenschaftsgeschichte?' (31–50); H.-W. Eroms, 'Passivkonstruktionen im Bairischen' (51–68); R. Harnisch, 'Fortis und Lenis im Bairischen — naturaliter' (69–93); R. Jodlbauer, 'Überlegungen zu einem Vergleich der Situation sprachlicher Minderheiten' (95–113); W. König, 'Das Jenische der Wasenmeister. Zum Funktionswandel einer Sondersprache' (115–29); A. R. Rowley, 'Bibliographie zur Lexikographie der bairischen Dialekte in Deutschland' (131–59); M. Schnabel, 'Konkrete Phonologie—abstrakte Morphologie. Ein Beitrag zum Problem der Konkret- und Abstraktheit bei phonologischen und morphologischen Beschreibungen, dargestellt am Dialekt von Weingarts (Oberfranken)' (161–76); E. Seidelmann, '"Z Büslinge I de Hörgass." Beobachtungen über Sprachvariation, Sprachspott und Sprachbewußtsein im Alemannischen' (177–87); D. Wagner, 'Orschärische Orwese' (189–204); E. Wagner, 'Zum Vorhaben eines "Ostfränkischen Handwörterbuchs" (Kleinen Ostfränkischen Wörterbuchs)' (205–18); C. J. Wickham, 'postmodern mundart. Zum Schnubiglbaierisch des Felix Hoerburger' (219–36); W. Winkler, 'Gesellschaft und Dialekt bei Johann Andreas Schmeller. Beweggründe eines Betroffenen' (237–49); L. Zehetner, 'Ein Wörterbuch der deutschen Sprache in Altbayern. Warum und wie es entsteht' (251–68); R. Zimmer, 'Dialekt und Texttyp' (269–301).

Low German studies include *Von Dünkirchen bis Königsberg. Ansätze und Versuche einer niederdeutschen Einheitssprache*, ed. F. Debus (Berichte aus den Sitzungen der Joachim Jungius-Gesellschaft, 14, 2), Göttingen, Vandenhoeck & Ruprecht, 45 pp.; *Notwehr ist erlaubt. Niederdeutsch im Urteil von Verehrern und Verächtern. Texte aus Mecklenburg und Pommern vom 16. bis zum 20. Jahrhundert*, ed. R. Herrmann-Winter, Rostock, Reich, 1995, 319 pp.; M. Schröder, *Humor und Dialekt. Untersuchungen zur Genese sprachlicher Konnotationen am Beispiel der niederdeutschen Folklore* (Name und Wort, 14), Neumünster, Wachholtz, 1995, 459 pp.; D. Hansen-Jaax, *Transfer bei Diglossie: synchrone Sprachkontaktphänomene im Niederdeutschen*, Hamburg, Kovac, 1995, v + 192 pp.; J. Ruge, *Der landwirtschaftliche Fachwortschatz in der Wilstermarsch: generationsspezifische Untersuchungen zu seiner Entwicklung*, Hamburg, Verlag Dr. Kovac, 1995, 532 pp.; and G. Rohdenburg, '"Drei Körbe reifes Obst." Kongruenzbeziehungen zwischen pseudopartitiver Konstruktionen im Nordniederdeutschen', *ZDL*, 43:289–94. Berlin is represented by P. Schlobinski, 'Zur *r*-Vokalisierung im Berlinischen', *ZDL*, 43:195–204, and G. Zimmermann, 'Das Berlinische. Gebrauch und Einschätzungen der Berliner Stadtvarietät (Historischer Rückblick)', *Muttersprache*, 106:319–37.

Central German features in C. Chapman, 'Anomalies in the strong verb paradigms of two West Central German dialects', *ZDL*, 43:49–57.

Alemannic is represented by H. Bickel, *Traditionelle Schiffahrt auf den Gewässern der deutschen Schweiz: Wort und Sache nach den Materialien des Sprachatlasses der deutschen Schweiz* (Sprachlandschaft, 17), Aarau, Sauerländer, 1995, 480 pp.; G. Schiltz, *Der Dialektometrische Atlas von Südwest-Baden (DASB): Konzepte eines dialektometrischen Informationssystems*. I. *Textband*. II. *Kartenband*, 1. III. *Kartenband*, 2. IV. *Kartenband*, 3 (Studien zur Dialektologie in Südwestdeutschland, 5), 4 vols, Marburg, Elwert, v + 220, v + 188, v + 191, v + 204 pp.; H. Ruef, *Sprichwort und Sprache. Am Beispiel des Sprichworts im Schweizerdeutschen* (SLG, 36), 1995, ix + 303 pp.; B. Rüegger et al., *Mundart und Standardsprache im reformierten Gottesdienst. Eine Zürcher Untersuchung* (Sprachlandschaft, 18), Aarau, Sauerländer, 318 pp.; and S. Dal Negro, 'Fenomeni di grammaticalizzazione e decadenza linguistica nel *titsch* di Formazza', *Linguistica e filologia*, 2:123–34.

Bavarian studies include V. Martin, 'Modelle der Umgangssprache. Überlegungen zum theoretischen Status eines linguistischen Begriffs am Beispiel des Wiener Deutsch', *ZDL*, 43:129–56, H. Baumgartner, *Dialekt im Wasserburger Land. Ein schulisches Projekt*, Wasserburg, Wasserburger Vlg, xlvii + 110 pp., and U. Götz, 'Zum analogen Umlaut im Bairischen', *Sprachwissenschaft*, 21:18–36. Noted on East Franconian: S. Krämer, *Die Steigerwaldschranke. Zum Aufbau einer ostfränkischen Dialektgrenze* (WBDP, 14), 1995, 175 pp.

The following dialect dictionaries are proceeding: *Hamburgisches Wörterbuch*, fasc. 13, *Hans—Hillige*, Neumünster, Wacholtz, 1995, cols 513–640; *Hesse-Nassauisches Volkswörterbuch*, vol. 4, fasc. 39, *wanstig-wegwerfen*, Marburg, Elwert, 1995, cols 513–76; vol. 4, fasc. 40, *Wegwurf-Wespel*, 1995, cols 577–640; *Pfälzisches Wörterbuch*, vol. 6, fasc. 46, *Stumpen-wasser—Urban-aufseher*, Stuttgart, Steiner, 1995, cols 769–960; fasc. 47, *Urbansberg—Weib*, 961–1152; *Brandenburg-Berlinisches Wörterbuch*, vol. 4, fasc. 1–2, *Schwabbel—Stein*, Berlin, Akademie, 1995, cols 1–256; *Preußisches Wörterbuch*, vol. 5, fasc. 4, *schuppen—Schutzmann*, Neumünster, Wachholtz, 1995, cols 385–512; and *Nordsiebenbürgisch-Sächsisches Wörterbuch*, vol. 4, *N—Sch*, ed. G. Richter et al., Cologne, Böhlau, 1995, xxxii + 1046 cols.

9. Onomastics

Personal names are represented by A. Muschg, 'Beginnen wir mit Emma', *ColH*, 23:9–18; W. Seibicke and J. Lutz, 'Die beliebtesten Vornamen des Jahres 1995', *Sprachdienst*, 40:41–47; T. Finkenstaedt, 'Vornamen in Wildsteig/Obb. 1637–1980', *Blätter für oberdeutsche Namenforschung*, 30–31, 1993–94:45–73; and H. Hornbruch, *Deonomastika. Adjektivbildungen auf der Basis von Eigennamen in der älteren Überlieferung des Deutschen* (SA, 31), 396 pp.

Place names are exemplified by *Flur und Name. Ausgewählte Deutungen*, ed. T. Banzer et al., Triesen, Vlg Liechtensteiner Namen-buch, 119 pp.; W. Kleiber and W.-D. Zernecke, *Der Klauer. Ein rheinhessischer Flurname. Dokumentation und Deutung* (Akad. der Wiss. und der Lit., Mainz: Abh. der Geistes- und sozialwiss. Kl., 7), Stuttgart, Steiner, 88 pp.; L. Kiss, 'Deutsche Ortsnamen in Rußland', *Fest. Mollay*, 191–202; R. Bauer and W.-A. Reitzenstein, 'Bibliographie zur Namenforschung für Bayern 1991–1993 und Nachträge', *Blätter für oberdeutsche Namenforschung*, 30–31, 1993–94:74–81; G. Burgermeister, *Die Flurnamen der Gemeinde Bettingen*, Basel, Helbing & Lichtenhahn, 1995, vi + 103 pp.; A. Burri, *Die Siedlungs- und Flurnamen der Gemeinde Worb. Ein Beitrag zur Namengrammatik* (SD, 42), 1995, 543 pp.; E. Kühebacher, *Die Ortsnamen Südtirols und ihre Geschichte. II. Die geschichtlich gewachsenen Namen der Täler, Flüsse, Bäche und Seen* (Veröffentlichungen des Südtiroler Landesarchivs, 2), Bozen, Athesia, 387 pp.; H. Ramge, 'Vom Färbelies und der alten Weschnitz. Zur historischen Topographie des Bensheimer Raumes um 800', *Archiv für hessische Geschichte und Altertumskunde*, 53, 1995:1–33; *Altdeutsches Namenbuch. Die Überlieferung der Ortsnamen in Österreich und Südtirol von den Anfängen bis 1200*, ed. I. Hausner and E. Schuster

(Institut für Österreichische Dialekt- und Namenlexika), fasc. 7, *Gleißenfeld, Ober-, Unter-Häslein, Deutsch-*, Vienna, Vlg der Österr. Akad. der Wissenschaften, 1995, pp. 419–98; and S. Bingenheimer, **Die Flurnamen der Gemeinden um den Wissberg in Rheinhessen* (Mainzer Studien zur Sprach- und Volksforschung, 20), Stuttgart, Steiner, 508 pp.

MEDIEVAL LITERATURE

By DAVID A. WELLS, *Professor of German at Birkbeck College, University of London*

1. GENERAL

Lexikon des Mittelalters, x, Munich, LexMA, 1995, viii + 2222 cols, continues this admirable reference work under a new publisher. This volume shares with its predecessors a dominant concern with personalities, among them 17 Rogers, 26 Rudolphs, 35 Richards and over 70 Roberts. Among the numerous articles of significant background interest for medieval literary studies the following deserve special mention: the treatment of Classical authors in the period (Pliny, Plutarch, Seneca), *Pommern, Prämonstratenser, Prag, Preußen, Regensburg, Regnum Teutonicorum, Reichsstädte, Renaissance, Renovatio, Sankt Gallen, Sachsen, Salzburg, Schachspiel, Schrift* and *Schule* and their compounds, *Schwaben, Sexualität, Speculum humanae salvationis, Speyer.* There is a particularly full account of *Ritter* and its compounds (J. Fleckenstein). Of immediate importance for German studies are a wealth of individual studies, generally compact but embracing all essential factual and bibliographical information, and prepared by a number of well-known specialists in the field. Among the authors N. H. Ott has the lion's share numerically, with either the complete contribution or the German sub-section on *Psalmen, Psalter, Raber, Vigil, Reinfried von Braunschweig, Reisen, Reisebeschreibung, Roland, Salomo, Schlaraffenland, Schwank, Seyfried der Hürne, Sieben weise Meister, Spielmannsdichtung,* and *Sprichwort.* Similarly prolific is U. Müller who contributes *Politische Dichtung, Refrain, Satire, Schmähdichtung,* and *Seifried Helbling.* No less informative are the entries on the Germanic aspects of *Polytheistische Religionen* (R. Simek), *Prachteinband* (O. Mazal), *Predigt* (H.-J. Schiewer), *Rabenschlacht* (J. Haustein), *Rätsel* (V. Schupp), *Reimchronik* (U. Liebertz-Grün), *Reimgebet* (U. Schulze), *Reinbot von Durne* (K. Kunze), *Reinmar* (R. Bauschke, P. Sappler, V. Schupp), *Renart* (F. P. Knapp), *Rezeptliteratur* (G. Keil), *Roman* (V. Mertens), *Rosengarten* (J. Heinzle), *Rosenplüt, Hans* (H. Brunner), *Runen* (R. Simek), *Sankt Georgener Predigten* (K. O. Seidel), *Sachsenspiegel* (R. Lieberwirth), *Sächsische Weltchronik* (E. Schubert), *Sage* (K. Graf), *Schwarzwälder Predigten* (H.-J. Schiewer), *Seuse, Heinrich* (H. Backes), *Siegfried* and *Sigenot* (J. Heinzle), *Spervogel* (U. Schulze), *Spiegelliteratur* (G. Roth), *Spruchdichtung* (U. Schulze), and *Stabreim(-dichtung)* (S. Sonderegger). Many of these entries form part of a broader, European-wide treatment of the subject in question, and are thus justified as a contextualization of the often more detailed information found in the *Verfasserlexikon.* The interdisciplinarity of the work makes for some inevitable unevenness, so that, for example, the thin treatment of *Poetik* contrasts with the relatively detailed survey of *Rhetorik* (J. Knape on the German dimension), while the concluding article on *Stadt*, with numerous sub-sections, is notable for transcending the bounds of the volume. W. Röcke, *MDG*, 43.1:70–74, and R. Brandt, *ib.*, 43.3:71–76, debate the place and structure of medieval German studies in the curriculum. In Schiewer, *Forschungsberichte*, there are substantial surveys of recent research on the linguistic basis of medieval German studies (R. Peilicke, 153–89), and on anthropological approaches to the literature of the period (C. Kiening, 11–129). F. P. Knapp, Kugler, *Interregionalität*, 11–21, considers the basis of regional literary history, especially in the case of Austria, and U. Wyss, *ib.*, 45–63, examines the work of R. Borchardt and J. Nadler. H. Beckers, *Queeste*, 2, 1995:146–62, documents literature of the period from the Lower Rhineland. Gernot U. Gabel, *Verzeichnis französischer Dissertationen (1885–1990) zur deutschsprachigen Literatur vom Mittelalter bis zum 20 Jahrhundert*, Hürth, Gemini, 144 pp., is a useful bibliographical resource containing 868 numbered titles, classified by literary periods. The Middle Ages are well represented with 63 items, most of them naturally from recent decades, including some largely unknown studies. P. Dinzelbacher, *Mediaevistik*, 6, 1993[1995]:45–84, supplies a substantial critical bibliography of work on visionary and eschatological literature published since about 1980.

German Poetry from the Beginnings to 1750, ed. Ingrid Walsøe-Engel, pref. George C. Schoolfield (The German Library, 9), NY, Continuum, 1992, xxxviii + 338 pp., is a useful addition to this attempt to present German literature in 100 volumes of translations, here accompanied, as befits the subject-matter, by the original texts on facing pages. After *Muspilli* and a few examples of the charms and other early anonymous lyric the major poets of *Minnesangs Frühling* are all reasonably well represented, followed by 11 items from Walther and much scantier treatment of the later Middle Ages (Neidhart, Steinmar, Oswald von Wolkenstein only). A. Krass, *WS XIV*, 87–108, makes adaptations of the *Stabat mater* the basis of a consideration of medieval approaches to translation, and H. Wenzel, Williams, *Knowledge*, 93–116, considers the function of metaphor in the context of the polarity of orality and written text. S. Goldmann, *Euphorion*, 90:134–49, traces the origins of Curtius's conception of the topos. Brian Murdoch, *The Germanic Hero. Politics and Pragmatism in Early Medieval Poetry*, London–Rio Grande, Ohio, Hambledon, x + 188 pp., gives a vivid presentation of the subject on the basis of a very full range of texts, including, besides the expected works from all the Germanic languages, the Roland epic, *Herzog Ernst*, and Konrad

von Würzburg's *Heinrich von Kempten*. The exclusion of the MHG
Dietrich epic does not detract from M.'s overarching view that the
hero is an essentially positive figure preoccupied with the maintenance
of social order; the omission of the Icelandic prose sagas renders it
less obviously unambiguous. U. Schwab, *ABÄG*, 46:189–215, supplies a critical report on recent Italian work on the Germanic hero. A
series of handbooks in Italian is introduced with Claudia Händl, *Dalle
origini all'età precortese*, 1995, and Michael Dallapiazza, *L'epica cortese*
(La letteratura tedesca medievale, 1, 2), 2 vols, Pisa, ETS, 203,
150 pp. *The Cultural Patronage of Medieval Women*, ed. June Hall
McCash, Athens, Georgia U.P., xxi + 402 pp., includes a survey of
female patronage by the editor and interesting background studies of
the application of the subject to early Byzantium (A. L. McClanan),
the medieval West to the 12th c. (J. M. Ferrante), and religious houses
(M. H. Caviness). The subsequent chapters focus helpfully on specific
examples from the high and late Middle Ages, but with an emphasis
almost exclusively on France and England the limitations of the
collection as a comprehensive treatment of the topic are obvious.

Franz Xaver Scheuerer, *Zum philologischen Werk J. A. Schmellers und
seiner wissenschaftlichen Rezeption. Eine Studie zur Wissenschaftsgeschichte der
Germanistik* (SLG, 37), 1995, xii + 255 pp., is a detailed study of
Schmeller's editorial and other philological activity. Wolfgang Beutin,
Zur Literaturgeschichte des Mittelalters, der Renaissance und des Barocks (Vom
Mittelalter zur Moderne, 10), Hamburg, von Bockel, 1994, 174 pp.,
contains reprinted essays. *Mittelalter-Rezeption V. Gesammelte Vorträge des
V. Salzburger Symposions (Burg Kaprun, 1990)*, ed. Ulrich Müller and
Kathleen Verduin (GAG, 630), xi + 510 pp., is a fifth volume in this
sub-series with numerous studies on reception and revival of medieval
themes.

The *Katalog der deutschsprachigen illustrierten Handschriften des Mittelalters*, vol. II, fascs 4, 5, ed. Norbert H. Ott and Ulrike Bodemann,
Munich, Beck, pp. 241–320 + 22 illus., vi + pp. 321–463 + 57 illus.,
continues this admirably detailed work of reference with the conclusion of the second volume. These fascicles conclude the article on
Bibelerzählung (see *YWMLS*, 55:703) and otherwise contain the very
substantial treatment of *Biblia pauperum* together with other articles
much more modest in scope but interesting through their variety: the
works of Hans Vintler and Heinrich Schlüsselfelder of the *Blumen der
Tugend* type, Ulrich Füetrer's *Buch der Abenteuer*, and Anton von Pforr's
Buch der Beispiele der alten Weisen. The supporting material continues to
include a good representative array of illustrations and, no less
valuable, admirably detailed indexes. It is easy to imagine that the
next edition of this fine work will be produced in electronic format.

A. Mentzel-Reuters, *DAEM*, 51, 1995:169–94, reports on recently published manuscript catalogues. The *Gesamtindex mittelalterlicher Handschriftenkataloge. Kumulation der seit 1945 in der Bundesrepublik Deutschland erschienenen Handschriftenkataloge*, ed. Bernd Michael, Wiesbaden, Harrassowitz, 1995, appears in a 24-microfiche edition. Of especial importance is Karin Schneider, *Die mittelalterlichen Handschriften aus Cgm 4001–5247* (Die deutschen Handschriften der Bayerischen Staatsbibliothek München, 7), 2nd edn, Wiesbaden, Harrassowitz, 735 pp. Karin Schneider, *Die Fragmente mittelalterlicher deutscher Versdichtung der Bayerischen Staatsbibliothek München (Cgm 5249/ 1–79) (ZDA*, supp. 1), Stuttgart, Steiner, 121 pp., inaugurates what promises to become a most welcome new series, following typography and layout of the *ZDA* and evidently designed for monographs exceeding the usual article length. S.'s introduction explains the background to the fragments from some 400 vernacular manuscripts chiefly from the 13th and 14th cs, and the body of the study consists of full codicological descriptions according to the modern Munich system. With its full indexes this is a catalogue of lasting value. Other recent codicological work includes Peter Jörg Becker and Tilo Brandis, *Altdeutsche Handschriften* (Patrimonia, 87), Berlin, Kulturstiftung der Länder–Staatsbibliothek zu Berlin-Preußischer Kulturbesitz, 1995, 40 pp.; P. J. Becker, 'Ankauf einer Sammlung von vierzig altdeutschen Handschriften', *Mitteilungen. Staatsbibliothek zu Berlin-Preußischer Kulturbesitz*, n. F., 3, Berlin 1994:123–30; U. D. Oppitz, 'Die "Deutschen Manuskripte des Mittelalters" (Zb-Signatur) der ehemaligen Stolberg-Wernigerodischen Handschriftensammlung', pp. 187–205 of *Geographia spiritualis. Festschrift für Hanno Beck*, ed. Detlef Haberland, Frankfurt, Lang, 1993, 351 pp.; and *Incunabula Gottingensia. Inkunabelkatalog der Niedersächsischen Staats- und Universitätsbibliothek Göttingen*. 1. *Adagia-Biblia*, ed. Helmut Kind, Wiesbaden, Harrassowitz, 1995, x + 322 pp. U. Winter, *MJ*, 28.2, 1993:103–12, informs on Magdeburg Domgymnasium manuscripts in Berlin, and F. Heinzer, *Scriptorium*, 49, 1995:312–19, on the relocation of the Donaueschingen manuscripts to Karlsruhe and Stuttgart.

OTHER WORKS

Horst Fuhrmann, *Überall ist Mittelalter. Von der Gegenwart einer vergangenen Zeit*, Munich, Beck, 328 pp., is in spite of the title an excellent sequel to F.'s *Einladung ins Mittelalter* (see *YWMLS*, 49:619) and a model of how medieval studies can be presented to a wider public without compromising scholarly standards. There are well-documented and readable chapters on a fascinating array of topics which still have a contemporary resonance: welcome and departure rituals, economy, pious forgery, attitudes to the Germans and figures such as Barbarossa, Quedlinburg, money-lending and the Jews, celibacy, orders of knighthood and the award of honours, death, and the work of U. Eco, W. Kammeier, and E. H. Kantorowicz. Hans-Henning Kortüm, *Menschen und Mentalitäten. Einführung in Vorstellungswelten des Mittelalters*, Berlin, Akademie, 373 pp., is conceived as an introduction which seeks to familiarize Germanists with the chief insights derived from French scholarship founded on the concept of *mentalité* and its later modification by that of the *imaginaire*. The book is structured into two main parts: chapters on the nobility, knightly class, the Church, towns, marginal groups, peasants, and intellectuals; and diachronic studies of conceptions of the natural world, space, and time; sickness, age, and death; love and sexuality; and religion. Excellent bibliographies accompany each chapter and the work succeeds both as a basis for information on approaches to the individual topics and as a guide to the underlying philosophical approach as a whole. Werner Faulstich, *Medien und Öffentlichkeiten im Mittelalter 800–1400* (Die Geschichte der Medien, 2), Göttingen, Vandenhoeck & Ruprecht, 298 pp., like the work of Haiko Wandhoff (see p. 725 below) identifies media and communication as a significant lacuna in recent accounts of the period, but sees his task as the more general one of illustrating how the different social groupings of the Middle Ages were linked by various communicative modes. Besides a survey of general changes from early to later Middle Ages there are a range of detailed studies showing how the term 'medium' can be applied to any number of persons or objects: historiographer, knight, fool, minstrel, diploma, carnival, lecture, disputation, mendicant preacher, priest, glass window, drama, itinerant, letter. A substantial chapter is devoted, not surprisingly, to 'das Schreibmedium Buch'. The degree of genuinely new insight this approach affords is variable, but it can focus on neglected topics, e.g. the rural storyteller. The illustrations, though poorly reproduced, make their intended points. Malte Hossenfelder, *Antike Glückslehren. Quellen in deutscher Übersetzung* (KTA, 424), xxxiv + 390 pp., is a lucid German translation of a body of Hellenistic philosophical texts designed to show the emergence of the subjective view of happiness. The introduction lucidly traces the development of late-Classical thought in this area. H. argues forcefully that the cynics, stoics, Epicureans, and sceptics are not merely epigonal thinkers in the wake of Plato and Aristotle, but of fundamental importance as currents in later European thought. Hence the significance of this book as background to the medieval conception of Fortuna. *'Scientia' und 'ars' im Hoch- und Spätmittelalter*, ed. Ingrid Craemer-Ruegenberg and Andreas Speer (Miscellanea Mediaevalia, 22), 2 vols, Berlin, de Gruyter, 1994, xxx + 1–513, xii + 518–1065 pp., includes contributions on Latin scientific, educational, and historiographical terminology in the 11th–15th cs. *Europäische Technik im Mittelalter 800–1200 [1400]. Tradition und Innovation. Ein Handbuch*, ed. Uta Lindgren, Berlin, Gebr. Mann, 642 pp., is a comprehensive treatment of medieval technology, magnificently produced and including copious illustrations. Over 60 contributions by a team of specialists deal, in almost exclusively non-technical language, with all major aspects of building, agrarian technology, the metal trades, energy sources, mining, military, nautical, astronomical, and geographical technology, and book production. The whole of this material is placed in a coherent historical context with introductory and concluding sections on the Classical background and the transition to the Renaissance. The wider cultural implications are brought into sharp prominence with the section on the dissemination of technical knowledge, which includes chapters on the *artes mechanicae*, the important role of women in technology, patronage, references to technology in literature, the literary aspects of craft and city emblems, the medieval conception of the machine, and the introduction of patents. The documentation of the volume is impressive: besides a 46-page bibliography of the subject individual bibliographies accompany each contribution. Gudrun Theresia Stecher, *Magnetismus im Mittelalter. Von den Fähigkeiten und der Verwendung des Magneten in Dichtung, Alltag und Wissenschaft* (GAG, 622), 1995, 162 pp. Gernot Böhme and Hartmut Böhme, *Feuer, Wasser, Erde, Luft. Eine Kulturgeschichte der Elemente*, Munich, Beck, 344 pp., is a readable and scholarly treatment which has much of interest for literature and the wider cultural background. Beginning with the role of the elements in myths of the creation of the universe and of man, and in myths of destruction by water and fire, the authors proceed by way of philosophical and cosmological conceptions to neo-Platonism and specific instances of the elements as components of man. A full chapter is devoted to medieval and early modern scientific and alchemical ideas. Finally, there are sections on the literary and artistic representation of the elemental forces and their taming and recurrence. P. Zumthor, *Acta* (Seeon), 317–27, discusses the performative function of medieval cartography, and K. Bertau, Kugler, *Interregionalität*, 81–105, considers the geographical movement underlying the major cultural changes in European history.

R. N. Swanson, *Religion and Devotion in Europe, c. 1215-c. 1515*, CUP, 1995, xv + 377 pp., is intended as a general outline survey but in fact succeeds in presenting a very wide range of detailed information on the period and in reflecting recent scholarly debate with cautious and balanced personal judgement. S. structures the material into an account of medieval Catholicism and its requirements; access to the faith, including a section on the Bible, books, and literacy which, although the chief emphasis of the study is non-literary, gives due weight to the rise of vernacular literature and the drama in particular; forms of religious life and devotion; life as pilgrimage, charity, and commemoration; the priest; attitudes to non-Catholics and their beliefs; and the practical reality of religion. A particular feature is the careful rejection of the over-emphasis on a distinction between popular and 'élite' religion. Bernhard Schimmelpfennig, *Das Papsttum. Von der Antike bis zur Renaissance*, 4th impr., WBG, ix + 392 pp., is essentially a reissue of a work originally published in slightly different format (see *YWMLS*, 46:666–67). While revision of the text is relatively minor, a very substantial supplementary bibliography (pp. 336–58) has been added. Winfried Becker, Günter Christ, Andreas Gestrich, and Lothar Kolmer, *Die Kirchen in der deutschen Geschichte. Von der Christianisierung der Germanen bis zur Gegenwart*, ed. Peter Dinzelbacher (KTA, 439), xv + 692 pp., is designed as an outline history of the Church in Germany by four historians rather than theologians. The Middle Ages receive their fair share of the limited space (L. Kolmer, pp. 1–196), with separate chapters on the chief early medieval periods, the Investiture Contest, the laity in the 12th and 13th cs, the decline of the papacy, the Great Schism, and late-medieval piety with its rehabilitation of the laity. The basic bibliography and glossary help to make this a good first reference source. Adriaan H. Bredero, *Bernhard von Clairvaux (1091–1153). Zwischen Kult und Historie. Über seine Vita und ihre historische Auswertung*, trans. Ad Pistorius, introd. Ulrich Köpf, Stuttgart, Steiner, 270 pp., is a welcome German edition of what proves to be a seminal study. B. takes a new look at St Bernard's life, works, canonization and hagiographical treatment, and argues that his representation in succeeding ages has often been distorted in the light of the evidence. Gabriel Audisio, *Die Waldenser. Die Geschichte einer religiösen Bewegung*, trans. Elisabeth Hirschberger, Munich, Beck, 281 pp., traces the history of the heresy from its 12th-c. origins to the present day, the greater part of the study focusing on the Middle Ages since A. argues that Protestant assimilation at the Reformation effectively saw the end of the movement as an independent force. There is a chapter on the literary activity of the Waldensians in the light of their emphasis on the Bible and preaching, A. contesting the older view that they constituted an independent oral culture. M. Bose, *MAe*, 65:187–210, studies the medieval interpretation of Solomon. R. Fulton, *Viator*, 27:85–116, reviews the Marian exegesis of the Song of Songs. Meinolf Schumacher, *Sündenschmutz und Herzensreinheit. Studie zur Metaphorik der Sünde in lateinischer und deutscher Literatur des Mittelalters* (MMS, 73), v + 737 pp., is a most valuable thesis by a pupil of

Friedrich Ohly which fills a significant lacuna in the coverage of theological conceptions in terms of *Bedeutungsforschung*. There is an excellent introductory survey of recent work on the theory of metaphor in general, of particular studies of medieval metaphorical usage, and of work on the metaphor of sin to date. A survey of the Latin and German terminology of the pollution of sin is followed by treatments of the application of the concept of impurity to sexual and other sins; the concepts used of the inner man; different persons, and the parts of the body, in relation to the metaphorical usage; reference to specific objects, places, animals, and kinds of dirt; and the most substantial chapter on metaphorical usage relating to the purification from sin. A wide range of literature is cited: the tradition of the medieval commentaries on Job emerges as of particular importance in the background to the earlier vernacular works, where beside the obvious OHG penitential texts the early sermon collections receive relatively more prominence than the corpus of Early MHG poetry. The text reads lucidly and avoids the obvious pitfalls of an unending series of examples. Access to this wealth of material is facilitated by detailed indexes of biblical citations, authors and works, and themes and concepts. Norbert Schnitzler, *Ikonoklasmus — Bildersturm. Theologischer Bilderstreit und ikonoklastisches Handeln während des 15. und 16. Jahrhunderts*, Munich, Fink, 355 pp., reflects a new approach to the subject of iconoclasm which rejects the older emphasis on merely its radical exemplification in the Reformation period in favour of a much subtler approach, focusing on the wider symbolic and spiritual significance of the attitude to visual images in general and on the late-medieval debate about the theological place of images in Christian worship. For the latter it emerges that there is no coherent body of edited sources, and S.'s work goes far to remedy this. The texts are handled with sensitivity, with careful diffferentiation between the rhetoric of the debate and establishment of typical attitudes as *topoi* on the one hand and the actual working-out in theological doctrine and historical event on the other. An important chapter addresses the anti-Semitic aspect of the subject. The response to the recurring fundamental question of whether art was indeed the 'book of the illiterate' has implications for studies of the 'text and image' type. The question of the veneration of images is also discussed by L. E. Saurma-Jeltsch, *Acta* (Seeon), 406–28. Peter Dinzelbacher, *Angst im Mittelalter. Teufels-, Todes- und Gotteserfahrung: Mentalitätsgeschichte und Ikonographie*, Paderborn, Schöningh, 295 pp., is another monograph from this exciting and accessible writer on medieval religious topics. Starting from a Kierkegaardian definition of *Angst* as a fear unrelated to an object, D. has little difficulty in showing its medieval relevance by way of a quotation from Hartmann's *Erec* on different types of fear, but the main emphasis emerges through a chronological treatment. Illustrations of the early medieval saint in battle against the demonic are followed by chapters on the presence of the devil in the high Middle Ages and the subsequent increase in fear of the diabolic and its different expression, and on the early modern fear of death and the plague and their interaction with the divine. D. is at home in all forms of medieval literature and art and the study is at once vivid and scholarly.

Clemens Ottmers, *Rhetorik* (SM, 283), vii + 255 pp., contains an introduction on the definition and historical development of rhetoric, in which a rebirth of interest is perceived, followed by chapters on the theories of rhetorical form, divisions of a speech, argument, style, and performance. Unlike some other treatments O. takes Aristotle rather than Cicero and Quintilian as the base from which later developments are traced. There is a single, classified, bibliography at the end of the work. W. Blank, *Fest. Steger*, 3–16, comments on the rhetoric of allegory. *Theorie der Metapher*, ed. Anselm Haverkamp, 2nd rev. edn, WBG, vi + 512 pp., is the revision of a work which first appeared in the Wege der Forschung series in 1983 (see *YWMLS*, 45:625). The 18 contributions and bibliography have been augmented by a select bibliography of the latest literature and a brief *Nachwort* in which H. places the subject in its contemporary context. W. Harms, *Acta* (Seeon), 575–95, studies medieval and later examples of the symbolic and representational use of letter shapes.

C. Kiening, Brall, *Personenbeziehungen*, 347–87, takes a broad look at the role of personification in the expression of relationships. G. Althoff, *FmSt*, 30:60–79, studies the understanding of the role of the emotions in the medieval period, and O. Langer, Brall, *Personenbeziehungen*, 163–88, the conceptions of friendship and love in Aelred of Rievaulx and elsewhere, while G. Althoff, *ib.*, 457–76, records ritualized forms of non-verbal communication, and also, *Acta* (Seeon), 239–52, considers the communicative role of a king's ritualized tears. C. Meier, *FmSt*, 30:315–42, considers the interpretation of work in 12th-c. Latin texts. *Der Wald in Mittelalter und Renaissance*, ed. Josef Semmler (Studia Humaniora, 17), Düsseldorf, Droste, 1991, 239 pp., has a number of contributions of background interest. Müller, *Herrscher*, is the first of seven ambitious volumes seeking to present medieval 'myths' of a total of 21 different categories. The introduction, in admitting the lack of clarity of definition of myth, points to the strength as well as the weakness of the approach, which allows each contributor considerable flexibility in the discussion of each figure. Besides more obviously literary figures detailed below, there are studies of the literary and mythological associations of Harun ar-Rashid (A. Khattab), Genghis Khan (U. Müller), Marco Polo

(A. Classen), Columbus (A. Köchl and R. Bachinger), and a number of saints including Michael (W. Wunderlich), James (R. Averkorn), Nicholas (W. Mezger), Brigitte (D. A. Bray), Gall (M. Jochimsen), Winifred (N. Bruce-Comissar), Wolfgang (P. Streng), Francis (J. Le-Goff), Elizabeth of Thuringia (H. Beutin), and Roch (G. F. Strasser). H. Kugler, Kugler, *Interregionalität*, 175–93, surveys the myths of origins of the Franks, Saxons, and Bavarians.

The New Cambridge Medieval History. II. *C. 700–C. 900*, ed. Rosamond McKitterick, CUP, 1995, xxxi + 1082 pp., bears only limited resemblance to its predecessor and is a tribute to the wealth of detailed historical scholarship of the past generation, here lucidly summarized by 27 eminent contributors in 30 chapters, only 13 of which (pp. 18–380) are concerned with political history in the narrow sense and these are far from being mere factual narratives. The remainder of the book displays all the virtues of a discursive approach disciplined by restricted space; topics include kingship, aristocracy, and forms of government; social, military, and economic organization; the papacy, Church organization and liturgy, monasticism, and lay religion; the Carolingian Renaissance, education, theology, book production, art and architecture. While R. McKitterick's introductory survey of the sources and their interpretation notes the significance of creative literature as a link between orality and literacy, her affirmation of the primacy of Latin is reflected in D. Ganz's account of book production, so that the relative neglect of vernacular literature is disappointing, given the welcome presence of cultural history in the concluding chapters. The dominance of the Franks and Carolingians which gives the volume its coherence leads naturally to the problem of linguistic usage in Continental Western Europe, but the focus on the nature of the shift from Latin to Romance in Francia (M. Banniard), however much reflecting contemporary scholarly interest, necessarily creates an impression of imbalance. On the other hand literary scholars would do well to heed the significance of the conclusion substantiated from several historical quarters that literacy even in this period was much more widespread than has usually been supposed. With its copious bibliographies, genealogical tables, and indexes, this supremely informative volume deserves immediate recognition as the chief English-language reference work on the period for scholar and layman alike. Otto Krabs, *Wir, von Gottes Gnaden. Glanz und Elend der höfischen Welt*, Munich, Beck, 266 pp., traces the theme of sacral kingship and divine right from the early Middle Ages to the end of absolutism. Barbarossa and Frederick II are seen as exemplifying the high medieval ideal, while Percy E. Schramm and Ernst H. Kantorowicz provide reliable sources for a treatment which proves too anecdotal and discursive to be satisfying.

Egon Boshoff, *Ludwig der Fromme*, Darmstadt, Primus, ix + 305 pp., is a lucid biography which does justice to the relative rehabilitation of Charlemagne's son in recent times. Appropriate detail is devoted to the preparatory part of L.'s career as ruler of Aquitaine, and there is much on the dynastic and social background. The concluding summary chapter considers the cultural and educational achievements of the reign against the background of their relative neglect in favour of those of Charlemagne and Charles the Bald. Gerd Althoff, *Otto III.* (Gestalten des Mittelalters und der Renaissance), WBG, x + 245 pp., follows the pattern set by other titles in this recent new series (see *TWMLS*, 52:605). There is an introductory review of the interpretation of the youthful monarch's reign by 19th-c. and 20th-c. historians, followed by an account of his life and reign in six concise and highly readable chapters. The last restates A.'s view that the concept of biography must for the period in question be subordinated to an awareness of the particular cultural pressures facing a ruler at the turn of the 11th c. and the representative and ritualistic function of the sources by which he must be judged. This shows a welcome sensitivity to the literary and subjective aspects of the topic. Odilo Engels, *Stauferstudien. Beiträge zur Geschichte der Staufer im 12. Jahrhundert*, ed. Erich Meuthen and Stefan Weinfurter, Sigmaringen, Thorbecke, ix + 350 pp., is an enlarged version of a collection of collected essays originally published as a *Festschrift* in 1988. The 12 substantial contributions presented here date originally from between 1971 and 1995 and are classified into four sections: general studies of the Hohenstaufen and Welf dynasties in the period; Rhineland history, including comments on the geographical distribution of creative literature; historiography; and recent work on Barbarossa, Godfrey of Viterbo and the myth of Trojan origins, and Henry the Lion. *Quellenkunde zur deutschen Geschichte im Spätmittelalter (1350–1500)*, ed. Winfried Dotzauer, WBG, xv + 589 pp., is a remarkable classified bibliography of 1,781 numbered titles (besides appendices on Burgundy and the Teutonic Order). The content goes far beyond purely political history, with sections on economy, the town, the Church and its organization in the widest sense, the sciences, and social history including the classes, minorities, trades, travel and transport, and the universities. While creative literature in the narrow sense is excluded, theological works including sermons and mysticism do find a place, as do Latin and vernacular chronicles of all categories. Each subsection is accompanied by helpful narrative text whch explains the genre of work documented and its historical and cultural background. This work is a source-book for the period in the widest sense.

C. Stephen Jaeger, *The Envy of Angels. Cathedral Schools and Social Ideals in Medieval Europe, 950–1250*, Philadelphia, Pennsylvania U.P.,

1994, xvi + 515 pp., focuses on the relative obscurity of 11th-c. learning in the cathedral schools, perhaps, in the light of recent research, overstating our ignorance of figures such as Honorius Augustodunensis. J.'s careful surveys and close readings of the texts enhance their status as the basis of the development of the code of courtesy, with a humanistic ideal of harmony of physical presence and ethical and cultural values, and point to the essential similarity of schools in France and Germany. The decline of the schools and their ideal under the pressure of forces such as social ambition and intellectual independence is then traced with a range of examples, leading to the transformation of the old learning into 'widely shared social ideals and literary models'. This of course dovetails with J.'s well-known earlier research on courtly culture. In the present study reference to MHG literature is, perhaps surprisingly, relatively limited, with the important and expected exception of Gottfried's *Tristan*. There are many details of interest in the argument, for example the question of gesture, where the emphasis on comportment takes a different approach to studies more related to the work of F. Ohly and *Bedeutungsforschung*, while the sensitive interpretation of the Wise and Foolish Virgins of Strasbourg Cathedral points to wide implications of the thesis for our understanding of the visual arts. *Strukturen der Gesellschaft im Mittelalter. Interdisziplinäre Mediävistik in Würzburg*, ed. Dieter Rödel and Joachim Schneider, Wiesbaden, Reichert, xix + 384 pp., is a collection of 21 essays with a welcome interdisciplinary slant, with much of interest for historiography and the social background to literature. D. Huschenbett (35–49) examines the literary significance of the treatment of a story of domestic love and murder in Thuringia in successive chronicles, while R. Weigand, H. Möhring-Müller, and D. Ruhe study aspects of marriage and of women's material and educational status. K. Wittstadt considers clerical reform in late-medieval Würzburg, while aspects of conflict and its peaceful resolution are the subject of work by J. Schneider, J. Morsel, C. Proksch, and D. Willoweit, H. Brunner (101–14) commenting on the explicitly literary presentation of warfare. Würzburg forms the focus of contributions on the late-medieval economy. N. R. Wolf (337–48) traces the origins of the concept of *gesellschaft*, and the chronicles are again the major sources in treatments by J. Petersohn of the transportation of corpses over long distances and by K. Arnold and H.-P. Baum of the anti-Jewish pogroms in Würzburg. Jörg Rogge, *Für den Gemeinen Nutzen. Politisches Handeln und Politikverständnis von Rat und Bürgerschaft in Augsburg im Spätmittelalter* (Studia Augustana, 6), Tübingen, Niemeyer, ix + 332 pp., falls primarily into the field of social and political history, but is fruitful for background knowledge of the late-medieval town and the conditions in which literature was produced. R. focuses on the relationship of the council to the guilds and on the political attitudes of their members, and shifts the emphasis from the usual 16th-c. focus of interest back into the later Middle Ages. While a significant part of the evidence derives from chroniclers such as Burkard Zink, Hektor Mülich, Wilhelm Rem, Matthias Langenmantel, and Georg Preu, important inferences for literary history might be drawn from R.'s radical distinction between their politics and those of the great majority of guildsmen who were illiterate. *Träger und Instrumentarien des Friedens im hohen und späten Mittelalter*, ed. Johannes Fried (Vorträge und Forschungen, 43), Sigmaringen, Thorbecke, 633 pp., is an impressive collection of 16 essays, with introduction and conclusion, on many aspects of the theme of peace, founded on the fundamental insight that war was the usual state of affairs in the period and that the maintenance of peace implied a variety of public and private responsibilities. Besides K. Grubmüller's essay on the explicitly literary evidence (see p. 727 below), K. Schreiner (37–86) reviews at length the use of religious and symbolic expressions of peacemaking; J. L. Nelson (87–114) studies the Carolingian situation in 840–43; O. G. Oexle (115–50) the role of *conjuratio* in peacemaking; J. Fleckenstein (151–68) the role of the knightly class in the tension between war and peace; T. Reuter (169–201) the actual conditions of insecurity and violence on the roads; G. Dilcher (203–27) the legal aspects of the peace; R. Härtel (525–59) failed attempts at peacemaking and the breaking and abuse of peace; and K. Arnold (561–86) artistic images of war and peace. Other contributions consider the role of the papacy and specific instances and conceptions of peace in different European countries. Heinz Schreckenberg, *Die christlichen Adversus-Judaeos Texte und ihr literarisches und historisches Umfeld (1.-11. Jh.)*, 3rd rev. edn (EH, XXIII, 172), 1995, 783 pp., is a substantial reworking and updating of what has become a standard source work for medieval texts relating to the Jews. The chronological arrangement of the vast body of material, which includes Old and New Testament background texts, besides the classified bibliographies and detailed indexes, facilitates the reader's task. The vernacular dimension of the subject-matter is not neglected: the OHG translation of Isidore of Seville, the *Physiologus*, and Williram von Ebersberg are all covered in appropriate detail. David M. Olster, *Roman Defeat, Christian Response, and the Literary Construction of the Jew*, Philadelphia, Pennsylvania U.P., 1994, xi + 209 pp., is concerned with 7th-c. history and the manner in which Christian apologists, perceiving their religion to be under threat, 'constructed' a literary Jewish opponent as a recognizable and defeatable evil. The thesis is highly important for later dialogue literature and for the history of anti-Jewish attitudes in general.

2. GERMANIC AND OLD HIGH GERMAN

W. Goffart, *Traditio*, 50, 1995:9–30, interestingly considers the ideological implications of recent and current views of Germanic antiquity. Lotte Motz, *The King, the Champion and the Sorcerer. A Study in Germanic Myth* (Studia Medievalia Septentrionalia, 1), Vienna, Fassbaender, 148 pp., takes a new look at the functions of the chief gods of the Germanic pantheon in the light of the findings of modern comparative religion. Allan A. Lund, *Germanenideologie im Nationalsozialismus. Zur Rezeption der 'Germania' des Tacitus im 'Dritten Reich'*, Heidelberg, Winter, 1995, 182 pp. + 16 pls, is a fascinating account of the treatment and interpretation of Tacitus in the scholarship, literature, and propaganda of the Third Reich, based, as the copious bibliography (pp. 107–65) shows, on an impressive range of sources. L. quotes extensively to show the remarkable extent to which the ideology was ultimately related to the *Germania*, but is also careful to place the study in the context of the understanding of the conception of *Germanen* in general. P. Lendinara, *AION(FG)*, n.s., 2, 1992:25–49, considers the comments of Venantius Fortunatus on the writings of the Germanic barbarians, and W. Haubrichs, *Colloquium* (Bristol), 35–58, cites a range of early medieval historical texts with a view to defining the nature of honour in the period.

H. Schmeja, *Akten* (Sterzing), 13–24, surveys the pre-literary inscriptions from the Tyrol. Robert Nedoma, *Die Inschrift auf dem Helm B von Negau. Möglichkeiten und Grenzen der Deutung norditalischer epigraphischer Denkmäler* (Philologica Germanica, 17), Vienna, Fassbaender, 1995, 108 pp. + 27 pls, shows that the earlier literature on this subject, apparently treated in exhaustive detail, has failed to take both extralinguistic factors and non-Germanic epigraphic tradition into account. The evidence, most of it inevitably of a highly technical nature, points to a more precise identification of this earliest Germanic onomastic source of pre-Roman North Italic provenance as a Venetic local alphabet, while the condition of the helmet and the circumstances of its discovery suggest that the two portions of text represent two names of one and the same owner. A. V. A. J. Bosman and T. Looijenga, *ABÄG*, 46:9–16, present and interpret a runic inscription on a recently discovered scabbard mount, and L. Peeters, *ib.*, 17–52, incorporates a wide range of biblical and Germanic reference in an essentially Christian interpretation of the Franks casket, while H. Penzl, *BGDSL*, 117, 1995:369–80, considers the runic system as a language, and K. Düwel, *AION(FG)*, n.s., 2,

1992:7–23, considers the runes as magic symbols. *ABÄG*, 45, is devoted to 'Frisian Runes and Neighbouring Traditions'. The 17 contributions range widely over cultural, archaeological, and numismatic topics, with several concerned with the relationship to evidence from England and Denmark. A checklist of inscriptions by T. Looijenga is of fundamental value, while the cautious scepticism of R. I. Page and new work on the origin of the runes as a whole by H. Williams reveal how little is really known. R. Coleman, *TPS*, 94:1–29, studies the expression of the future in Gothic, and R. Del Pezzo, *AION(FG)*, n.s., 2, 1992:51–60, comments on the Gothic inscriptions in Naples.

R. McKitterick's views on Carolingian multilingualism and their applicability to German are scrutinized by E. Hellgardt, *BGDSL*, 118:1–48, and V. Santoro, *Linguistica e filologia*, Bergamo, 2:229–47, comments on the place of the vernacular in Carolingian culture. *'The Gentle Voices of Teachers.' Aspects of Learning in the Carolingian Age*, ed. Richard E. Sullivan, Columbus, Ohio State U.P., 1995, xiv + 361 pp., is a collection of essays on facets of Carolingian cultural history linked by the insight formulated in R. E. Sullivan's introduction (1–50) that a comprehensive synthesis of the period is lacking. Sullivan (51–105) also reviews the forces and classes forming the background to the period. J. J. Contreni (106–41) surveys the educational system in practice; R. L. Crocker (142–70) explains, with examples, the Frankish reception of Roman liturgical chant; B. M. Kaczynski (171–85) comments on the Franks' understanding of Jerome's philology; L. Nees (186–226) notes the political context of some works of Carolingian art; T. F. X. Noble (227–60) studies the *Libri Carolini*; and D. Ganz (261–83) traces the historiographical background to the ideology which has informed Carolingian studies.

Elvira Glaser, *Frühe Griffelglossierung aus Freising. Ein Beitrag zu den Anfängen althochdeutscher Schriftlichkeit* (SA, 30), 661 pp., studies the neglected early scratch glosses from five manuscripts indisputably from Freising, especially MS Clm 6300 which with some 448 numbered items (including those not identifiable) is revealed as one of the most prolific sources of OHG glosses generally, and the analysis of which occupies pp. 80–482 of this Bamberg *Habilitationsschrift*. The layout of the material generally follows the well-established format of the series, with a separate chapter on the cultural-historical background to Freising and the particular significance of, and problems associated with, scratch glosses, which are understood to serve a variety of functions. The documentation is exhaustively detailed, lending conviction to the discriminating conclusions which indicate both similarities and differences among the usage of the manuscripts studied, but a general tendency to single-word glossing as distinct from interlinear versions or glossaries, and an emphasis on the elucidation of patristic rather than biblical texts from which an association with the particular interests of Bishop Arbeo (764–84) is inferred. E. Glaser, *AION(FG)*, n. s., 2, 1992:119–36, points to the role of scratch glosses in the early tradition, and E. Langbroek, *ABÄG*, 46:59–90, comments in detail on H. Mayer's work on the Salzburg scratch glosses (see *YWMLS*, 56:733). N. Henkel, *WS XIV*, 46–72, considers the linguistic and literary status of the OHG interlinear texts, and C. März, *ib.*, 73–86, focuses on more fundamental questions about the function and ultimate purpose of the glosses and related translations. M. Gebhardt, *Akten* (Sterzing), 25–37, surveys nine Tyrolean manuscripts containing OHG glosses, H. Tiefenbach, *Sprachwissenschaft*, 21:127–40, comments on the OS Lamspringe Juvencus glosses, and M. J. Schubert, *Poetica*, 28:48–65, includes the Kassel Glosses and other early texts in a study of 'German for foreigners', while in Molinari, *Teoria*, E. Fazzini (159–79) writes on the glosses of the *Lex Baiuvariorum*, and E. Glaser (181–205) on early glossing in Freising. M. G. Saibene, Molinari, *Teoria*, 207–40, studies the style of the Isidore translation, and M. G. Cammarota, *Linguistica e filologia*, Bergamo, 2:161–91, the *Monsee-Wiener Fragmente*.

Jörg Riecke, *Die schwachen jan-Verben des Althochdeutschen. Ein Glie-derungsversuch* (SA, 32), 702 pp., is a Regensburg dissertation which is well suited to this series, but is significantly more restricted to narrowly linguistic subject-matter than many earlier volumes. R. establishes a rigid demarcation of the dialectal and temporal boundaries of the class of weak verbs in question, to which surprisingly little earlier scholarship has been devoted. The material is set out in the form of lemmata followed by detailed references and commentary as appropriate on the basis of classification by derivation. The conclusions indicate a corpus of 1,054 verbs in total. Use of the index thus provides the reader with a helpful and informative lexicographical aid. Heike Hornbruch, *Deonomastika. Adjektivbildungen auf der Basis von Eigennamen in der älteren Überlieferung des Deutschen* (SA, 31), 396 pp., a Münster dissertation from the school of R. Schützeichel, defines its subject-matter as appellative terms derived from proper names, with the important qualification that the emphasis falls on adjectives rather than nouns, although the chapter on the latter which follows the theoretical prolegomena includes interesting groups of examples such as the suffixes in personal names, names of plants, and ethnic names. The greater part of the study is given over to a series of articles on adjectives from proper names, 305 OHG and OS examples being identified, with subsequent documentation of the MHG development of a representative corpus; with 243 MHG examples in the -*isch* suffix alone, usage is shown to be historically stable. There is a good summary of the chief findings and admirable indexes of the words studied and of their sources. A. Masser, *Sprachwissenschaft*, 21 : 1–11, studies the OHG and OS renderings of John 2. 4, and A. Wagner, *ZDA*, 125:297–321, the early baptismal vows and the cultural implications of their translation.

Steffen Krogh, *Die Stellung des Altsächsischen im Rahmen der germanischen Sprachen* (SA, 29), 413 pp., seeks a fundamental definition of Old Saxon in its relationship to neighbouring West Germanic languages, covering much traditional historical ground but with a clarity rarely achieved in older studies. After an introductory survey of the essentials of the historical position of the continental Saxons 26 monuments, including glosses, are passed in review. The two most substantial chapters analyse the sounds and endings with a view to comparison with the other languages, syntactic features being regarded, perhaps regrettably, as unreliable indicators of independent development. The conclusions point to a weakening of many of the arguments favouring the status of OS as a mixed language and a reassertion of it and the other individual West Germanic languages as the primary linguistic entities of the region. Consideration of the wider historical and cultural factors is a welcome feature of the work. *Heliand und Genesis*, ed. Otto Behagel and Burkhard Taeger, 10th rev. edn (ATB, 4), xliv + 294 pp., appears twelve years after the previous edition (see *YWMLS*, 46:670). The preface, expanded introduction, and textual changes take account of more recent publications, notably A. N. Doane's edition of the *Genesis* and D. Hoffmann's metrical study (see *YWMLS*, 53:628–29), and U. Schwab's criticisms of Behagel's conception of the text, which are rejected. T. Hofstra, *NOWELE*, 28–29:387–98, suggests that Joachim Camerarius (1500–74) may have composed the *Heliand* Preface B, and J. E. Cathey, *LJb*, 37:31–46, highlights the theme of wisdom and eloquence in the *Heliand*. V. Santoro, *Romanobarbarica*, 12, Rome, 1993:223–49, studies the Old Saxon Bedan homily. J. Semmler, pp. 33–57 of *Das Buch in Mittelalter und Renaissance*, ed. Rudolf Hiestand (Studia Humaniora, 19), Düsseldorf, Droste, 1994, 220 pp., investigates a Carolingian missal in the context of Old Saxon and Old Low German activity in Essen in the 9th and 10th cs.

W. Haubrichs, *WS XIV*, 13–45, gives examples of Otfrid's translation technique, and Cornelia Epping-Jäger, *Die Inszenierung der Schrift. Der Literalisierungsprozeß und die Entstehungsgeschichte des Dramas*, Stuttgart, M & P, 558 pp. (see pp. 759, 775 below), includes interpretations of the OHG baptismal vows and of Otfrid's preface *Ad Liutbertum* in the light of communication theory.

Notker der Deutsche von St. Gallen, *De interpretatione. Boethius' Bearbeitung von Aristoteles' Schrift 'peri hermeneias'. Konkordanzen, Wortlisten und Abdruck des Textes nach dem Codex Sangallensis 818*, ed. Evelyn Scherabon Firchow, Berlin, de Gruyter, 1995, xx + 664 pp.; and Notker der Deutsche von St. Gallen, *Categoriae. Boethius' Bearbeitung von Aristoteles' Schrift 'kategoriai'. Konkordanzen, Wortlisten und Abdruck des Textes nach den Codices Sangallensis 818 und 825*, ed. Evelyn Scherabon Firchow and Richard Hotchkiss, 2 vols, Berlin, de Gruyter, xxvi + 1243 pp., are new editions which transcribe the manuscripts closely and exploit computer technology. Notker der Deutsche, *Die kleineren Schriften*, ed. James C. King and Petrus W. Tax (Die Werke Notkers des Deutschen, 7; ATB, 109), cxxxii + 349 pp., is a fourteenth volume which finally completes the edition begun in 1972. The basic layout of the texts of course follows the pattern established at the outset, but the general appearance cannot now be regarded as impressive in view of the changes in typography and printing technology of the past two decades. The texts appear in the sequence of the Seven Liberal Arts envisaged by N., and are concluded with the letter to Bishop Hugo von Sitten. In addition to the expected works we find, controversially, the *Distributio, De dialectica*, and the *St Gall Tractate*. Studies justifying their inclusion are promised. In general each of the two editors assumes responsibility for a text and the related introductory matter, allowing for a welcome flexibility of approach given the variable nature of the problems attending each work. *The St. Gall Tractate: A Medieval Guide to Rhetorical Syntax*, ed. Anna A. Grotans and David W. Porter, Columbia, SC, Camden House, 1995, ix + 149 pp., is a most useful diplomatic edition with translation on facing pages of the seminal text sometimes ascribed to Notker which forms a helpful complement to the ATB edition. The introduction (by Grotans) is substantial, with detailed palaeographical information as well as analysis of the content and evident function of the text. A. A. Grotans, *OGS*, 25:46–89, describes and studies a Berlin manuscript of Notker's *Nova rhetorica* from 15th-c. Bavaria, and V. Santoro, Molinari, *Teoria*, 241–54, comments on Notker as translator. Cornelia Staeves, *Notkers Hermeneutik-Übersetzung. Möglichkeiten der zweisprachigen Textbearbeitung* (EH, 1, 1582), 213 pp.

E. Hellgardt, *Colloquium* (Bristol), 301–19, assesses the place of conflict in gnomic literature, and M. Eikelmann, *ib.*, 320–22, summarizes a dissertation on conflict in the proverb. K.-P. Wegera, *GerLux*, 8:73–86, surveys the late-medieval reception of the *Physiologus*, and D. Peil, *MJ*, 30.1, 1995:61–80, shows that the medieval *Physiologus* tradition had relatively little influence on later emblembooks.

3. MIDDLE HIGH GERMAN

GENERAL

Hilkert Weddige, *Mittelhochdeutsch. Eine Einführung*, Munich, Beck, xii + 210 pp., is designed as a linguistic complement to W.'s *Einführung in die germanistische Mediävistik* (see *YWMLS*, 49:614). W. acknowledges his debt to the standard *Mittelhochdeutsche Grammatik*, pointing out that it was founded by Hermann Paul as a simple student guide. Proceeding from the premiss that in practice linguistic study is today based in literature, W. supplies a very brief survey of the early development of German followed by chapters on phonology and morphology well illustrated with diagrams and maps. Sections on syntax and semantics then lead into a vivid alphabetical dictionary of key courtly terms (pp. 92–137) with literary examples, and a final section of well-annotated texts for translation practice. Johannes Singer, *Grundzüge einer rezeptiven Grammatik des Mittelhochdeutschen*, Paderborn, Schöningh, xvi + 293 pp., is conceived as an 'analytical' and 'receptive' grammar designed for the modern reader of MHG texts, and using the terminology primarily appropriate to modern German. That there is a need for grammars which emphasize the differences between modern and medieval German is beyond question. Whether the reader of the MHG text — presumably including the student novice — is really assisted in his task by a grammar aligned to the principles of cognitive linguistics, its 'structures' and 'processes' emphasized at every turn, is more questionable. The choice of Hartmann von Aue's language as representative is unexceptionable. But the very fact that much fundamental information on, for example, dialects, textual tranmission, basic sound changes, lists of strong and irregular verbs, etc., has to be provided in an appendix and often in a form taken straight from established reference works, surely casts doubt on the ultimate value of this work. Christa Baufeld, *Kleines frühneuhochdeutsches Wörterbuch. Lexik aus Dichtung und Fachliteratur des Frühneuhochdeutschen*, Tübingen, Niemeyer, xxxii + 264 pp., is introduced as a modest aid to study in the continuing absence of full-scale dictionaries of the literature of the period. In fact it is a handy and accessible guide to the vocabulary of 107 identified and numbered texts of the period 1350–1600. That these are drawn from the standard readers necessarily makes for an emphasis on scientific and specialized, at the expense of creative, literature, but the dictionary is no less welcome all the same. F. Urbanek, *MJ*, 30.2, 1995:1–27, includes MHG examples in a study of the rhetorical *genera dicendi*. H. Zutt, *Fest. Steger*, 17–32, surveys the semantic and cultural dimension of MHG *bieten*.

R. Brandt, pp. 31–56 of *Vergessen. Entdecken. Erhellen. Literaturwissenschaftliche Aufsätze*, ed. Jörg Drews (Bielefelder Schriften zu Linguistik und Literaturwissenschaft, 2), Bielefeld, Aisthesis, 1993, 206 pp., comments on the orality-writing debate. Haiko Wandhoff, *Der epische Blick. Eine mediengeschichtliche Studie zur höfischen Literatur* (PSQ, 141), 416 pp., is a Berlin dissertation by a pupil of Horst Wenzel which builds on the recent interest among medievalists in oral and written tradition, but also on the wider developments in communication theory accompanying the rise of electronic media. Much attention is paid to depicting, in arguably over-simplified terms, the early medieval cultural situation of essential illiteracy in order to contrast the transition marked by the rise of vernacular court epic. Reference is made to a good range of works of the 12th and 13th cs, and W. identifies hitherto neglected textual passages relevant to the general theme. However, the value of the thesis perhaps lies less in any new contribution to knowledge than in showing how the insights of communication theory of the past generation can provide a new, but certainly not exclusive, context for viewing MHG epic. W. Haug, *Acta* (Seeon), 190–204, applies the oral-written polarity to the question of performance. U. Müller, Ingold, *Autor*, 33–53, sees in the Neidhart tradition an exemplification of the problem of the conception of a medieval author, and R. Krohn, pp. 43–59 of *Fragen nach dem Autor. Positionen und Perspektiven*, ed. Felix Philipp Ingold and Werner Wunderlich, Konstanz U.P., 1992, 313 pp., comments on the relationship of medieval poets and performers to their subject-matter, while J.-D. Müller, Ingold, *Autor*, 17–31, traces the medieval Latin background to the concepts of author and authority.

I. Ten Venne, *Mélanges Spiewok*, 407–22, considers the Thuringian regional dimension, and *Beiträge zur Geschichte der Literatur in Thüringen*, ed. Detlef Ignasiak (Palmbaum-Studien, 1), Rudolstadt, Hain, 1995, 255 pp., includes reference to the Thuringian court, while H. Tervooren, pp. 39–47 of *Die Stadt im Mittelalter* (see p. 756 below), also *Fest. Hoffmann*, 231–40, comments on the character of literature from the Lower Rhine area.

U. Storp, Brall, *Personenbeziehungen*, 137–62, studies the role of the father in the definition of lineage and identity, and I. Bennewitz, *Colloquium* (Bristol), 157–72, notes father-daughter incest in a range of MHG texts, while T. Nolte, *Poetica*, 27, 1995:225–53, examines the uncle-nephew relationship in MHG literature, and L. Miklautsch, Brall, *Personenbeziehungen*, 89–107, comments on mother-daughter relationships in Veldeke, Gottfried, and Neidhart. Karin Rinn, *Liebhaberin, Königin, Zauberfrau. Studien zur Subjektstellung der Frau in der deutschen Literatur um 1200* (GAG, 628), 349 pp. I. Bennewitz, *Acta* (Seeon), 222–38, considers the construction of femininity in MHG literature. James A. Schultz, *The Knowledge of Childhood in the German Middle Ages, 1100–1350*, Philadelphia, Pennsylvania U.P., 1995, xx + 318 pp., is a thoughtful and wide-ranging study which succeeds in combining reference to a very large number of MHG texts with a coherent analysis and sensibly restrained use of contemporary insights derived from non-medieval disciplines such as cultural anthropology and psychoanalysis. After a very clear review of the semantic evidence S. classifies his material in chapters on the status and nature of childhood; nurture, nursing, and education; the ties and relationships of childhood, including separations and unusual situations; adolescence and rites of passage; different types of narrative; and the historical development. The conclusions point to a pattern more complex than either the idea of an absence of a medieval conception of childhood (P. Ariès) or the assumption that it is a historical constant (I. Zingerle). While S.'s dependence on creative literature is convincingly justified, there are occasions when one feels more concession might have been made to the usage of literary convention.

Maren Clausen-Stolzenburg, *Märchen und mittelalterliche Literaturtradition*, Heidelberg, Winter, 1995, x + 438 pp., takes a fundamentally new and clear-headed look at a problem still coloured by the influence of the Grimm brothers. The conclusions of the Kiel dissertation are as important for medieval literature — chiefly of the 15th c., but also texts as early as Eilhart's *Tristan* — as for the Grimms' *Märchen* themselves. Through an acute analysis of a wide range of biblical passages and the salient figures and themes of works dealing with subjects traditionally viewed as *märchenhaft* — fairies, witches, foundlings, prophecy and fulfilment, unfulfilled murder contracts, envy of the good deed, deliverance tests, and many others — C.-S. shows beyond doubt that allegedly 'folk-tale' motifs in Grimm, but also in a host of MHG verse and prose romances, are in fact integral parts of the common literary heritage and firmly rooted in written narrative tradition. Besides the numerous references to the literary sources the evidence of popular reading from the early printed book to the early 19th c. corroborates the thesis in detail. A. Classen, *Neohelicon*, 22.2, 1995:9–51, uses a range of MHG courtly and other literature to support N. Elias's thesis of the relative tolerance of explicit sexual reference in the period. *Gepeinigt, begehrt vergessen. Symbolik und Sozialbezug des Körpers im späten Mittelalter und in der frühen Neuzeit*, ed. Klaus Schreiner and Norbert Schnitzler, Munich, Fink, 1992, 415 pp., includes, with MHG literary references, K. Schreiner (41–84) on the fall of man and N. H. Ott (223–41) on changes in legal gesture. *Höflichkeit*, ed. Harald Haferland and Ingwer Paul (OBS, 52), 224 pp., includes a contribution by the two editors (pp. 7–69) on the theory of politeness, referring to major MHG works and their use of polite gesture, including stirrup service. In Brall, *Personenbeziehungen*, H. Wenzel (191–218) links the representation of bodily gesture to the themes of seeing and hearing, and U. Küsters (271–320) distinguishes *ersehen* and *merken*, first and 'second' sight, in the visual encounters of courtly love-relationships, while U. Zellmann (389–425) studies partings in several works. G. S. Williams, Fietz, *Semiotik*, 82–96, comments on the narrative function of laughter in medieval narrative, and H. Kugler, Brall, *Personenbeziehungen*, 251–67, looks at spatial movement in the Arthurian romance and the fabliau, while H. Wenzel, *ZGer*, 6:9–20, considers the multidimensional perspective of time for different medieval social classes. A. Classen, pp. 109–20 of *Shifts and Transpositions in Medieval Narrative. A Festschrift for Dr Elspeth Kennedy*, ed. Karen Pratt, Woodbridge, Brewer, 1994, xxi + 206 pp., studies the transposition of dream to reality in MHG narrative, and E. Feistner, *GRM*, n. F., 46:257–69, discusses the function of disguise in a range of MHG texts, while J. W. Thomas, *GN*, 27:110–11, records the motif of invisibility in MHG narratives, T. Cramer, Williams, *Knowledge*, 151–92, considers criteria for identifying monstrous beings, and G. Roth, *Colloquium* (Bristol), 285–97, documents perjury in a range of literature.

K. Grubmüller, *Träger und Instrumentarien* (see p. 718 above), pp. 17–35, reviews the semantic background to *vride* in MHG, showing that, so far from being the equivalent of Latin *pax*, it means merely a passive state of absence of the conflict assumed to be the norm. In *Burg und Schloß als Lebensorte in Mittelalter und Renaissance*, ed. Wilhelm G. Busse (Studia Humaniora, 26), Düsseldorf, Droste, 1995, vi + 262 pp., B. Haupt (129–45) reviews the role of the *kemenate* in various MHG texts, and G. Binding (83–107) surveys the living quarters in Hohenstaufen castles, while H. Jeske, *Sprachwissenschaft*, 21:12–17, studies the MHG usage of the architectural term *berfrit*.

Various MHG and some earlier works are cited in Müller, *Herrscher*, in contributions dealing with the mythical roles of Charlemagne (K.-E. Geith), Barbarossa (R. Krohn), Henry the Lion (D. Brosius), Richard Lionheart (R. Krohn), Saladin (M. Maher), Frederick II (U. Müller), St Martin (F. V. Spechtler), St Anne (V. Nixon), St Vitus (G. F. Strasser), St Barbara (M. van Dijk), and St George (J. L. Flood). V. Mertens, *BGDSL*, 118:358–78, considers the narration of the *Nibelungenlied*, *Klage*, and Wolfram's *Titurel*, and J.-M. Pastré, *Reinardus*, 9:109–19, detects in Ulrich von Zatzikhoven's *Lanzelet* and in the *Nibelungenlied* analogues to Celtic motifs identified by V. J. Propp. V. DiMarco, *LJb*, 37:47–66, mentions the MHG Alexander poems in a treatment of the hero's encounter with the Amazon Queen, and B. Haupt, *ZDP*, 115:321–37, identifies the Munda Sion episode as a link between the *Strassburger Alexander*, Hartmann's *Erec*, and the St Brendan legend.

Frühmittelhochdeutsche Literatur. Mittelhochdeutsch/Neuhochdeutsch, ed., trans., and comm. Gisela Vollmann-Profe (UB, 9438), 295 pp., includes Frau Ava's *Jüngstes Gericht, Ältere Judith, Vorauer Marienlob, Melker Marienlied, Vom Rechte*, and excerpts from *Wiener Genesis, Millstätter Sündenklage, Kaiserchronik, St. Trudperter Hohelied*, and *Vorauer Alexander*. More familiar works which already appear in Reclam editions have been consciously omitted. The prose translations on facing pages provide a straightforward guide to meaning. Basic bibliography accompanies references to the relevant articles in the *Verfasserlexikon*, and one could only wish for more of the admirably informative notes (pp. 231–87). J. Barlow, *FmSt*, 29, 1995:86–95, adds to knowledge of the myth of the Franks' Trojan origins. From Italy we note *Il 'Merigarto'*, ed. and comm. Paola Spazzali, Milan, Minute, 1995, 206 pp., and P. Spazzali, 'Il *Merigarto* e Prüll', *Acme*, 49.3, 1994:35–41. N. Staubach, *FmSt*, 29, 1995:167–206, compares the opening of the *Kaiserchronik* with Freculphus of Lisieux's treatment of Augustinian history in his world chronicle.

J. G. Sang, pp. 363–72 of *Dimensions. A. Leslie Willson and Contemporary German Arts and Letters*, ed. Peter Pabisch and Ingo R. Stoehr, Krefeld, van Acken, 1993, 408 pp., writes on the mythical aspects of *Herzog Ernst*, and T. A.-P. Klein, *SM*, 36, 1995[1996]:1053–57, supplies textual annotation to a forthcoming edition of Odo of Magdeburg's *Ernestus*. A. Cipolla, Molinari, *Teoria*, 255–99, studies the problem of translation in the *Alexanderlied*, and Müller, *Herrscher*, has chapters on the myths of Alexander the Great (R. Bräuer) and Roland (U. Müller), with literary documentation. B. Gutfleisch-Ziche, *ZDA*, 125:142–86, studies the transmission of the *Rolandslied*, and D. P. Sudermann, *MP*, 92, 1994–95:413–37, interprets its opening, while B. Janz, *Mediaevistik*, 7, 1994[1996]:119–42, studies the legal and temporal associations of Genelun's capture and betrayal, and J. Ashcroft, *Papers* (Amherst), 301–08, comments on Pfaffe Konrad's association with the court of Henry the Lion. D. Gottschall, *AION(FG)*, n.s., 4, 1994:53–74, continues the debate on the language and place of origin of the *Lucidarius*.

Otto Betz, *Hildegard von Bingen. Gestalt und Werk*, Munich, Kösel, 247 pp., seeks to characterize H.'s work and thought in a vivid and immediate way while remaining true to the sources. With substantial excerpts from the work in translation B. ranges over her life and background, mysticism, symbolism, praise of the senses, conceptions of sickness and health and of music and wisdom, ethical polarities, and angelology. F. Betz contributes a chapter on H.'s contemporary relevance. *Tiefe des Gotteswissens — Schönheit der Sprachgestalt bei Hildegard von Bingen. Internationales Symposium in der Katholischen Akademie Rabanus Maurus Wiesbaden-Naurod vom 9. bis 12. September 1994*, ed. Margot Schmidt (MGG, 1, 10), 1995, ix + 239 pp., is the fruitful proceedings of a conference dedicated to H. but in fact of significance for the period in general. I. Müller (1–17) addresses the authorship of the medical and scientific texts; A. Derolez (19–28) comments on the new edition of the *Liber divinorum operum*; A. Carlevaris (29–48) analyses H.'s understanding of Scripture, and C. Meier (49–83) her conception of work; H. J. Pretsch (85–98) illuminates the background to her Swabian correspondence; E. Gössmann (99–116) explores her use of maternal imagery; M. Schmidt (117–42) focuses on her understanding of the physical and spiritual senses; P. Escot (143–53) explains the mathematical associations of her thought; R. Cogan (155–65) studies the music of 'O quam mirabilis'; R. Blumenfeld-Kosinski (167–79) compares her conception of man and woman with that of Christine de Pizan; R. Pernoud (181–92) writes on her sermons; B. W. Hozeski (193–207) adopts a literary approach to the *Liber vitae meritorum*; and S. Flanagan (209–22) compares her treatment of the Ursula legend with that of Elisabeth of Schönau. M. W. Adamson, *Sudhoffs Archiv*, 79, 1995:173–92, edits a herbal, medical, and dietetic vernacular appendix to Hildegard of Bingen's *Liber simplicis medicinae*.

MIDDLE HIGH GERMAN HEROIC LITERATURE

Reiner Tetzner, *Germanische Heldensagen. Nach den Quellen neu erzählt* (UB, 8751), 356 pp., is a companion volume to T.'s *Germanische Göttersagen* (see *YWMLS*, 54:661). The sources are essentially the *Nibelungenlied*, which receives a substantial *Nacherzählung*, and the Dietrich epic from the *Deutsches Heldenbuch*. The glossary of names is again a useful appendix. Walter Kofler, *Der Held im Heidenkrieg und Exil. Zwei Beiträge zur deutschen Spielmanns- und Heldendichtung* (GAG, 625), ii + 362 pp. Müller, *Herrscher*, has chapters on the mythical links of various figures including Attila (I. Nemeskürty and M. Springeth), Brünhild (P. Steger), Siegfried (O. Ehrismann), Volker (W. Lenschen), and Dietrich (J. L. Flood).

On the *Nibelungenlied* we note Ragnhild Boklund-Schlagbauer, *Vergleichende Studien zu Erzählstrukturen im 'Nibelungenlied' und in nordischen Fassungen des Nibelungenstoffes* (GAG, 626), ix + 239 pp., and Neil Thomas, *Reading the 'Nibelungenlied'* (Durham Modern Languages

Series; German, 5), Durham U.P., 1995, 119 pp., while I. Praël, *ASNS*, 233:241–59, compares the *Nl.* with the Old Indian *Mahabharata*. H.-W. Goetz, *LiB*, 43:54–62, pursues the debate on Augustinian conceptions in the *Nl.*, C. Jost, *ib.*, 63–69, considers its reception as an operatic source from the 18th c. on, and J. Fourquet, *ib.*, 44:5–9, comments on the names *Nibelungen* and *Burgonden*. W. Hoffmann, *Mediaevistik*, 6, 1993[1995]:121–51, supplies a critical review of literature on Siegfried published 1978–92. A. Guillaume, *Mélanges Spiewok*, 195–207, considers the religious ethos of the *Nl.*, while V. Mertens, Haferland, *Erzählungen*, 59–69, links Hagen's narration of the young Siegfried's adventures to his fundamental opposition to the hero, and I. R. Campbell, *ABÄG*, 46:131–41, seeks to cast light on the opaque detail of *âventiure* 14; Id., *GR*, 71:23–34, analyses Hagen's motives in requesting Rüdiger's shield (av. 37). A. Classen, *JEGP*, 95:359–81, reviews the early printed transmission of the *Jüngeres Hildebrandslied*. Reception studies include John Evert Härd, *Das Nibelungenepos. Wertung und Wirkung von der Romantik bis zur Gegenwart*, trans. Christine Palm, Tübingen, Francke, 219 pp., and N. Thomas, pp. 121–31 of *Celtic and Germanic Themes in European Literature*, ed. Neil Thomas, Lewiston, NY, Mellen, 1994, xi + 135 pp., a discussion of the *Nl.* in the Third Reich. Monika Deck, *Die Nibelungenklage in der Forschung. Bericht und Kritik* (EH, I, 1564), 254 pp. J. Bumke, Haferland, *Erzählungen*, 71–83, differentiates the accounts of the fall of the Burgundians in the different versions of the *Klage*, and J.-D. Müller, *ib.*, 85–98, links Swämmel's reports to the genesis of the heroic retelling of history.

M. Smith, *AUMLA*, 86:33–47, investigates Kudrun's motives, and W. McConnell, *FCS*, 17, 1990: 229–43, writes on death in *Kudrun*, while E. Cziep, *Imagination*, 11.1:7–11, characterizes the text and illustration of the work in the *Ambraser Heldenbuch*. Sabine Lenschow, *Die Funktion und Verwendung der Propria in der mittelhochdeutschen Dietrich-Epik*, introd. Friedhelm Debus (DOLMA, B, 1), x + 313 pp., is a Kiel dissertation which introduces a new series of onomastic studies. The introductory chapters include a general review of the application of onomastics to literary studies and the surveys of the history and genre of the Dietrich epic are equally useful. The discussions of the texts include lexical summaries of the chief aspects of the proper names, structural surveys which point to their fundamental formal role, and statistical data. J. Fourquet, pp. 9–14 of *Westjiddisch = Le yiddish occidental. Mündlichkeit und Schriftlichkeit. Actes du colloque de Mulhouse*, ed. Astrid Starck (Reihe Sprachlandschaft, 11), Aarau, Sauerländer, 1994, 184 pp., comments on *Dukus Horant*.

THE COURTLY ROMANCE

J. Bumke, *Acta* (Seeon), 118–29, comments in general terms on approaches to criticism of text and transmission in the court epic, and M. Curschmann, *ib.*, 149–69, sees Lambert of Ardres's chronicle as a text of relevance for understanding courtly culture in Germany. N. J. Lacy, Müller, *Herrscher*, contributes a chapter on the myth of Arthur, and I. Kasten, Kugler, *Interregionalität*, 161–74, looks at the suprarégional dimension of the conception of *amour courtois*. Hubert Speckner, *Dichtung und Wahrheit im Mittelalter. Das Leben der höfischen Gesellschaft im Spiegel der höfischen Literatur*, Vienna, Praesens, 1995, 222 pp., seeks to detect the evidence of 'everyday life in the Middle Ages' in Veldeke's *Eneas*, Hartmann, Gottfried, and Wolfram. Aware that the only positive basis for such a task rests on the insight that the idealizing works include some elements of reality, the book scarcely resolves the acknowledged problem of subjectivity in their identification. Nevertheless, against the background of recent work on *Realienkunde*, there are useful reviews of what the literature has to tell us about clothing, horses and weapons, castles and tents, food and drink, money, women, knighthood (the most substantial and also perhaps the most controversial section), the relations between the sexes, festivals, education, and the feudal system. P. Giloy-Hirtz, Brall, *Personenbeziehungen*, 61–87, notes relationships between women in the courtly romance. Natascha Wieshofer, *Fee und Zauberin. Analysen zur Figurensymbolik der mittelhochdeutschen Artusepik bis 1210*, Vienna, Praesens, 1995, 206 pp., focuses on the female fairies and sorceresses in six works which, with the addition of Gottfried's *Tristan*, are identical to those studied in G. Ehrismann's seminal work of 1905 on the *Märchen* and courtly romance: Hartmann's *Erec* and *Iwein*, Wolfram's *Parzival*, Ulrich's *Lanzelet*, and Wirnt's *Wigalois*. There are careful surveys of earlier research and definitions of the figures identified as magical, the internal evidence of the works being seen as crucial. Analysis of the texts points to the realms of healing, prophecy, education and wisdom, protection, fortune, and love, in association with specific objects and spheres of influence, as crucial to women with magical powers. The further conclusion that female magic is exclusively positive in contrast to the malign and demonic associations of its masculine counterpart is all the more convincing for not being presented within a feminist framework. Stephan Maksymiuk, *The Court Magician in Medieval German Romance* (Mikrokosmos, 44), Frankfurt, Lang, ix + 185 pp., is an admirably clear and concise treatment of a fascinating subject. Adopting a 'history of mentalities' approach, M. traces the importance of political sorcery in Classical, Celtic, and Germanic society and sees the medieval context of magical belief in the gulf between the Christianity of the educated clerics and popular culture. Since the belief in sacral kingship and the fluid boundary between magic and miracle both invited tolerance of magical advisers, the role of court magicians in Ulrich von Zatzikhoven's *Lanzelet*, Wolfram's *Parzival*, Wirnt von Gravenberg's *Wigalois*, Heinrich von dem Türlin's *Crône*, and Johann von Würzburg's *Wilhelm von Österreich* can all be shown to reflect historical reality. L. Petzoldt, *Fest. Schenda*, 549–68, studies the figure of Virgil as a magician. R. Wetzel, Schiewer, *Forschungsberichte*, 190–254, provides a selective survey of research on the Tristan legend in German literature for the period 1969–94, and D. Buschinger, *Mélanges Spiewok*, 69–78, compares the death of the lovers in different versions of *Tristan*. C. Huber, *Colloquium* (Bristol), 59–73, addresses the problem of slaying or sparing the defeated opponent, as exemplified in Hartmann's and Chrétien's *Erec* romances and in the *Prosa Lancelot*.

H. Fromm, Haferland, *Erzählungen*, 27–39, studies the rhetorical *ordo narrandi* in Veldeke's *Eneas* in the light of his sources, while P. Kern, *WS XIV*, 109–33, argues that the reception of Ovid played a significant role in the adaptation of Virgil's *Aeneid* by Veldeke and in the *Roman d'Eneas*, and S. Westphal, *Exemplaria*, 8:231–58, considers Veldeke's Camilla and other martial women. H. A. Burmeister, *ZDA*, 125:322–29, prints fragments of the Upper German *Servatius* from Prague, asserting an early dating. V. Mertens, *Mélanges Spiewok*, 280–95, considers Eilhart's *Tristan* in the Berlin Meusebach manuscript, and R. J. Cormier, *FCS*, 17, 1990:57–66, studies Eilhart's tower of pleasure. H. Boková and K. Gärtner, *BGDSL*, 118:333–57, print newly-discovered fragments of Herbort von Fritzlar's *Liet von Troye*, and R. Hahn, *Colloquium* (Bristol), 102–12, treats the portrayal of warfare in the work, while M. Mecklenburg, Haferland, *Erzählungen*, 41–57, interprets Herbort's treatment of Ulysses's narrative.

HARTMANN VON AUE

H. Brunner, *Colloquium* (Bristol), 113–22, compares the view of war in H. and Chrétien de Troyes. Werner Schröder, *Irrungen und Wirrungen um den Text von Hartmanns 'Erec'* (Akad. der Wiss. und der Lit., Mainz. Abh. der geistes- und sozialwiss. Kl., Jg 1996, no. 11), Stuttgart, Steiner, 24 pp., addresses the implications of the Wolfenbüttel fragments for the text of *Erec*, and in particular polemicizes against the conception of a second romance as argued in different forms by K. Gärtner and E. Nellmann. S. sees the W text as a variant like any other, reflecting East Central and Low German reception of Hartmann. Brigitte Edrich-Porzberg, *Studien zur Überlieferung und Rezeption von Hartmanns Erec* (GAG, 557), 1994, 316 pp. E. C. Lutz,

DVLG, 70:3–47, argues that the *Erec* romances reconcile the epic tradition of rhetorical description with the cosmological diagram of the *mappa mundi* type, I. R. Campbell, *MDU*, 88:4–16, interprets the Cadoc episode as an important stage in Erec's restoration of his relationship with Enite, and R. W. Fisher, *ABÄG*, 46:119–30, interprets the role of shame in *Erec*, while M. H. Jones, *Colloquium* (Bristol), 74–90, evaluates the outcome of the battles, J. Fuhrmann, *Mélanges Spiewok*, 177–84, writes on law in *Erec*, H. Wandhoff, *Acta* (Seeon), 170–89, emphasizes the work's aural and visual features, and R. Pérennec, Kugler, *Interregionalität*, 107–26, points to the uniqueness of its conversational narrative style. U. Ernst, *Euphorion*, 90:1–40, draws the manuscript transmission of *Gregorius* and its source into the argument about its genre, arguing it is a saint's life rather than a courtly romance, its theological content in no way lessened. While the evidence is interesting, it is for consideration whether U.'s assumption of a secular-spiritual dichotomy is more imagined than real. A. Classen, *Seminar*, 32:221–39, places Gregorius's tablet at the centre of a discussion of medieval reading, and E. Wenzel and H. Wenzel, Haferland, *Erzählungen*, 99–114, interpret the tablet as a symbol of a second life the hero must incorporate into his own life. Hartmann von Aue, *Der arme Heinrich*, ed. Hermann Paul and Kurt Gärtner (ATB, 3), 16th rev. edn, xxxvi + 63 pp., is the first new edition since 1984 (see *YWMLS*, 46:676–77). The changes are substantial. G. takes the approach of the previous editor, Gesa Bonath, further by incorporating all the MS B variants in a new apparatus, while another important innovation is the proper assimilation of the Benediktbeuern E fragments in which modern scientific techniques have revealed further textual evidence. The introduction has been wholly recast and updated. David Duckworth, *The Leper and the Maiden in Hartmann's Der arme Heinrich* (GAG, 627), vi + 153 pp., interprets the work substantially against the background of the accounts of leprosy in the gospels and in Bernard of Clairvaux. C. Lorey, *Fest. Marahrens*, 19–48, comments on guilt in *Iwein*, and H. Kugler, *OGS*, 25:90–118, interprets *Iwein* against the background of the theory of good and bad government, while H. Kugler, Haferland, *Erzählungen*, 115–24, uses the term 'window' to characterize the narrative of Ginover's abduction, and R. Kalkofen, *Daphnis*, 24, 1995:571–601, includes *Iwein* in a comparative study of the 'self-conscious narrator'. Volker Schupp and Hans Szklenar, *Ywain auf Schloß Rodenegg. Eine Bildergeschichte nach dem 'Iwein' Hartmanns von Aue*, Sigmaringen, Thorbecke, 120 pp., is an attractive account of material on which both authors have published extensively, intended to summarize scholarship on the Rodenegg murals and their background some 20 years after their discovery. Szklenar supplies a detailed history of the lords of Rodank from the late 11th c. until their 13th-c. decline, with a survey of the later fate of the castle, and a comprehensive account of the murals and their position and condition, accompanied by excellent colour plates. Schupp provides interpretative studies of the scenes and their relationship to Hartmann. His final chapter, a survey of research on the dating, comes to the conclusion that hitherto no satisfactory evidence for a precise dating has been identified.

WOLFRAM VON ESCHENBACH

Hartmut Beck, *Raum und Bewegung. Untersuchungen zu Richtungskonstruktion und vorgestellter Bewegung in der Sprache Wolframs von Eschenbach* (ES, 103), 1994, 289 pp., from the school of K. Bertau, is a useful theoretical and semantic study which provides a context for the many literary explorations of the themes of journey, quest, space and landscape. B. provides a detailed classification of the use of appropriate adverbs and particles in relation to different types of distance and the related motion. A careful distinction is drawn between shorter and longer distance and the functions associated with it — social, antagonistic, directed to an aim, active and passive, change of venue, past and present time. The key role of W.'s characters in the depiction of motion emerges from the concluding summary. Paul Kunitzsch, *Reflexe des Orients im Namengut mittelalterlicher europäischer Literatur. Gesammelte Aufsätze* (DOLMA, B, 2), x + 213 pp., consists of reprints of 15 essays by this Orientalist scholar first published between 1969 and 1989. The introduction draws the threads together and justifiably points to the vital role of onomastics in determining the Oriental influence upon W. above all. Together this research is a significant milestone in asserting the essentially learned character of W.'s work. H. Beckers, *WS XIV*, 391–404, publishes newly-discovered fragments of *Parzival* from Westphalia, and E. Nellmann, *ib.*, 134–48, shows how W. creatively misunderstands Chrétien, while F. P. Knapp, *DVLG*, 70:351–68, considers W.'s departure from the bipartite structure of the romance in *P.* in the context of its system of beliefs and presentation of events as *historia*. Arthur Groos, *Romancing the Grail. Genre, Science, and Quest in Wolfram's 'Parzival'*, Ithaca–London, Cornell U. P., 1995, xvii + 270 pp., links and elaborates a series of earlier studies to form a new interpretation of *P.* which at every turn emphasizes, within a broadly Bakhtinian framework, the 'multiplicity of discourses' — romance, hagiography, chronicle, scientific and medical treatise — used in the work at the expense of the single authorial voice usual in its period. While G. adopts Bakhtinian concepts selectively and critically, the real achievement of the study perhaps lies less in the application of currently popular theory than in the fusion of erudition and urbanity with which G. shows the interpretative relevance of W.'s remarkable familiarity with contemporary medical and astronomical knowledge. Hence the theoretical approach has certainly stimulated, but is not essential to, the understanding of 'inconclusive speech acts' in the final chapter, Trevrizent's retraction being notable among them, as evidence of pluralistic and self-contradictory narrative discourse. Holger Noltze, *Gahmurets Orientfahrt. Kommentar zum ersten Buch von Wolframs 'Parzival'* *(4,27–58,26)* (Würzburger Beiträge zur deutschen Philologie, 13), Würzburg, Königshausen & Neumann, 1995, vii + 304 pp., is a Bochum dissertation by a pupil of Eberhard Nellmann and a welcome addition to the recent detailed commentaries on *P.* Appropriately for such a coherent section of the text, the introductory chapter consists largely of a detailed survey of previous interpretations of Book I. There is little on the historical and theoretical background to the commentary form, but N. proceeds pragmatically, often starting with Ernst Martin's data, incorporating recent research as comprehensively as possible and (rightly) not refraining from giving his own view as necessary. Topics dealt with at greater length in the excursuses include primogeniture and disinheritance, specifically Oriental details, and sources. K. Smits, *ZDP*, 115:26–41, interprets *P.* 2,1–4 in terms of urination, and T. Bein, *ib.*, 433–36, the persona of the *ich* of *P.* 108,17, while W. Haubrichs, *Haferland, Erzählungen*, 125–54, links the report of Gahmuret's death and burial to contemporary funerary and memorial practice, and E. Schmid, *WS XIV*, 377–90, considers Herzeloyde's words at the end of Book II. F. P. Knapp, *BGDSL*, 118:49–68, discusses the grail in the context of theories differentiating the magic, miraculous, and mysterious, and R. Breyer, *ZGer*, 6:61–75, traces a change in the function of Cundrie in her role of messenger, while W. Delabar, *Brall, Personenbeziehungen*, 321–46, points to the role of personal interaction in the episode of the blood drops in the snow, M. Eikelmann, *ZDA*, 125:245–63, interprets the Schanpfanzun episode of Book VIII, and J. Fourquet, *Mélanges Spiewok*, 165–75, understands Book IX as 'adaptation'. Isolde Neugart, *Wolfram, Chrétien und das Märchen: Erzählstrukturen und Erzählweisen in der Gawan-Handlung* (EH, I, 1571), 200 pp. E. Brüggen, *Acta* (Seeon), 205–21, interprets the Joflanze episode.

In *WS XIV*, E. Horváth (409–22) studies the fate of the Hamburg *Willehalm* manuscript and others now returned from Moscow, and J. Heinzle (423–29) records readings relevant for his edition, while K. Gärtner and K. Klein (430–43) print a Magdeburg fragment newly discovered in Berlin, and C. Bertelsmeier-Kierst (444–51) points to the scribal tradition of fragment F 84 shared by the oldest

Lohengrin fragments. B. Wachinger, *Akten* (Vancouver), 1, 49–59, takes a broad look at the ethical layers in *Whm*, and E. Schmid, Kugler, *Interregionalität*, 127–42, studies W.'s treatment of its 'French' aspects. Christoph A. Kleppel, *'vremder bluomen underscheit.' Erzählen von Fremdem in Wolframs 'Willehalm'* (Mikrokosmos, 45), Frankfurt, Lang, 271 pp., is a Munich dissertation by a pupil of W. Harms which makes a substantial contribution to understanding a nexus of problems often identified singly but rarely explored in such coherent depth. Close textual analysis against the background of theoretical works emphasizing the dependence of alterity on the individual or collective perception of the beholder leads to careful differentiation of the signals by which alterity is conveyed, many of them, naturally, in the military sphere. Equally good is the chapter on the relationship between the known and the foreign as exemplified by three figures who cross the boundary: Gyburc and Rennewart, as expected, but also Willehalm whose adventures are fruitfully linked to the subject of the thesis with reference to work on the distinction between real and figurative disguise. U. Liebertz-Grün, *GRM*, n. F., 46:383–405, shows how conflicting authorial voices in *Whm* give an ambivalent view of the value of the martial and crusading ethos, and E. Ukena-Best, pp. 5–40 of *Zwischen Schrift und Bild. Entwürfe des Weiblichen in literarischer Verfahrensweise*, ed. Christine Krause (Heidelberger Frauenstudien, 1), Heidelberg, Mattes, 1994, viii + 260 pp., notes the cleverness of the women in *Whm*, while C. J. Young, *Colloquium* (Bristol), 348–58, studies the treatment of conflict in the *Whm* manuscript illustrations. There is an Italian edition of W.v.E., *Titurel*, ed. Michael Dallapiazza, trans. Lucia Antonini (Biblioteca medievale, 35), Parma, Pratiche, 1994, 118 pp., and H. Brackert, Haferland, *Erzählungen*, 155–75, interprets the inscription on the dog's lead.

GOTTFRIED VON STRASSBURG

Gottfried von Straßburg, *Tristan. Nach dem Text von Friedrich Ranke neu herausgegeben, ins Neuhochdeutsche übersetzt, mit einem Stellenkommentar und einem Nachwort*, ed. Rüdiger Krohn. 3. *Kommentar, Nachwort und Register*, 4th rev. edn (UB, 4473), 1995, 390 pp., though set in larger fount, is over 100 pages longer than the first edition of 1980 (see *YWMLS*, 42:726–27). The commentary proper has been fully reworked and brought up to date in the light of the latest research, as has the bibliography, a task facilitated by the appearance of H.-H. Steinhoff's second bibliographical volume (see *YWMLS*, 48:693). In the introduction K. answers his critics and justifies his sensible decision not to seek to incorporate the commentary of L. Okken (see below) which in view of its different orientation is a complementary rather than a rival work. Lambertus Okken, *Kommentar zum Tristan-Roman Gottfrieds von Strassburg*, 2nd rev. edn (APSL, 57, 58), 2 vols, x + 1–694, 695–1107 pp., is a completely revised version of O.'s earlier work (see *YWMLS*, 47:663) into which both the subsequent supplementary volume of 1988 (see *YWMLS*, 51:651) and more recent literature up to early 1996 have been incorporated. The revision is welcome not least because of the greatly improved visual appearance and layout of the material which benefits from the latest printing technology. As reviews of the first edition indicated, an 'objective' commentary which disregards the particular expertise and interests of the compiler is impossible (and probably undesirable), and O. explicitly emphasizes his views on the significance for *T.* of Classical Latin and Oriental parallels. The appendices on music and medicine have also been updated. There is more on the implications for G. of the newly-discovered Carlisle fragments of the *Tristan* of Thomas from R. A. Wisbey, *Times Literary Supplement*, 12 March 1996:13, and W. Haug, Haferland, *Erzählungen*, 177–87, discusses their implications for the understanding of G.'s conception of love. M. S. Batts, pp. 647–54 of *Übersetzen, verstehen, Brücken bauen. Geisteswissenschaftliches und literarisches Übersetzen im internationalen Kulturaustausch*, ed. Armin Paul Frank (Göttinger Beiträge zur internationalen Übersetzungsforschung, 8), 2 vols, Berlin, Schmidt, 1993, 897 pp., comments on recent *T.* translations. B. Schirok, *Fest. Steger*, 33–51, discusses the narrative levels of text and excursus in *T.*, A. Classen, *Mélanges Spiewok*, 79–98, considers Gottfried's communicative strategies, and C. B. Palmer, *MDU*, 88:17–30, adopts a Freudian approach to Tristan's allegedly homoerotic relationships with Marke and Morold, while E. D. Blodgett, *Fest. Marahrens*, 1–18, comments on music and subjectivity in *T.*, and U. Draesner, Schilling, *Wechselspiele*, 77–101, interprets the role of songs and their performance in the Isolde Weisshand episode. M. Javor Briški, *ANeo*, 29:13–25, traces the epic and symbolic function of education in the work. Hans Bayer, *Gottfried von Straßburg und der 'Archipoeta'. Die literarischen Masken eines Ehr- und Namenlosen* (Spolia Berolinensia, 8), Hildesheim, Weidmann, vii + 260 pp., pursues his theories on the heretical associations of the classical courtly poets to draw G. into the web. A complex range of evidence from a variety of sources argues that G., a canon regular and leading member of Frederick I's chancery, was banished for heresy and forgery after the 1184 Synod of Verona and thereafter adopted various literary 'masks' to conceal his advancement of subversive political and religious views. These include not only the mysterious Gunther of Pairis (as the reader might naturally have expected) but also authorship of the Abelard-Heloise correspondence, some of the Archpoet's works, and the *Tegernsee Antichrist Play*. Parodied as Brun the bear in *Reinhart Fuchs* and confronted by the polemic of no less a literary opponent than Walther von der Vogelweide, it is no wonder that G.'s views made little headway and it has been left to Bayer to unmask him. S. C. Van D'Elden, *Papers* (Amherst), 343–51, comments on the interpretation of Tristan illustrations.

OTHER ROMANCES

In *Colloquium* (Bristol), K. Ridder (173–88) surveys the role of amorous and political intrigue in the later romance, and D. Huschen-bett (189–203) illustrates the complicated place of marriage in the historical development of the the genre. I. Hahn, Brall, *Personenbezie-hungen*, 37–60, points to the complexity of the fundamental themes of Wirnt von Gravenberg's *Wigalois*, and J. Eming, *Colloquium* (Bristol), 91–101, considers the problem of conflict resolution in the work, while G. Borgnet, *Mélanges Spiewok*, 33–44, studies its political dimension, and W.-O. Dreessen, *Westjiddisch* (see p. 730 above), pp. 84–98, the Yiddish version. Annegret Wagner-Harken, *Märchen-elemente und ihre Funktion in der Crône Heinrichs von dem Türlin. Ein Beitrag zur Unterscheidung zwischen 'klassischer' und 'nachklassischer' Artusepik* (DLA, 21), 1995, 457 pp. Werner Schröder, *Herstellungsversuche an dem Text der 'Crône' Heinrichs von dem Türlin mit neuhochdeutscher Übersetzung und Kommentar. II. Herstellungsversuche an dem Text der 'Crône' Heinrichs von dem Türlin. Zweiter Teil: Die Becherprobe* (Akad. der Wiss. und der Lit., Mainz. Abh. der geistes- und sozialwiss. Kl., Jg 1996, nos. 2, 4), 2 vols, Stuttgart, Steiner, 202, 138 pp., points to the absence of a critical text to replace the inadequate edition of G. H. F. Scholl and seeks to demonstrate the possibilities in the first volume on the basis of an analysis of four sections, including prologue, epilogue, and the glove test episode. The second volume adopts the same approach to the goblet test (lines 918–2631), dividing it into three and omitting the catalogues of names. S. includes diplomatic prints and translations together with detailed commentary in support of his readings, and the reader is left wondering whether still more can be expected along the lines of S.'s other recent editorial activity. The same editorial principles are applied in a somewhat more satisfying manner in *Das Ambraser 'Mantel'-Fragment*, ed. Werner Schröder (Sitzungsberichte der Wiss. Gesellschaft an der Johann Wolfgang Goethe-Univ. Frankfurt am Main, 33, no. 5), Stuttgart, Steiner, 1995, 57 pp., which presents a complete and welcome new edition of the 994 lines juxtaposed with Hartmann's *Erec* in the Ambras MS. S. follows B. Kratz's scepticism about the earlier editor O. Warnatsch's belief that Heinrich von dem Türlin was the author (see *YWMLS*, 39:648), and argues much more convincingly that the textual resemblances to the *Crône* reflect its familiarity to the anonymous author of *Der Mantel*. Cornelia Reil, *Liebe und Herrschaft. Studien zum altfranzösischen und mittelhochdeutschen Prosa-Lancelot* (Hermaea, n. F., 78), Tübingen, Niemeyer, viii + 268 pp., is a wide-ranging and ambitious reappraisal of the nature and function of love in the prose romances, which avoids the term 'courtly' and is heavily coloured by the approach and language of Walter Haug. While full account is taken of the earlier romance tradition, the emphasis falls on a detailed study of selected episodes of the text. R. argues consistently that the love-affair of Lancelot and Ginover is primarily represented in its political context, the whole cycle being conceived as a kind of history of Arthurian government. The comparison with Tristan's love is particularly illuminating. It is however questionable whether such a reading, as R. suggests, necessarily relegates to a secondary role the spiritual or allegorical dimension often associated with the works. M. Unzeitig-Herzog, *WS XIV*, 149–70, demonstrates differences in the translation practice of versions of the *Prosa-Lancelot*, and M. Meyer, *Colloquium* (Bristol), 204–14, considers the role of Galahot, while K. S. Sneeringer, *Neophilologus*, 80:425–33, finds a 'typological' significance in the skin-colour of the hero. V. Honemann, Haferland, *Erzählungen*, 221–32, seeks to classify the many monologues, reports, and narratives in Stricker's *Daniel*, and I. Kasten, *ib*., 189–98, traces the link between the illustration of the goblet in Konrad Fleck's *Flore und Blanscheflur* and the story-line of the romance. H. Alex, *WS XIV*, 405–08, prints a *Jüngerer Titurel* fragment from Trento. Wolfgang Wegner, *Albrecht, ein poeta doctus rerum naturae? Zu Umfang und Funktionalisierung naturkundlicher Realien im 'Jüngeren Titurel'* (EH, 1, 1562), 308 pp. Holger Höcke, *'Willehalm'-Rezeption in der 'Arabel' Ulrichs von dem Türlin* (EH, 1, 1586), 333 pp.

Konrad von Würzburg is represented by Susanne Rikl, *Erzählen im Kontext von Affekt und Ratio. Studien zu Konrads von Würzburg 'Partonopier und Meliur'* (Mikrokosmos, 46), Frankfurt, Lang, 256 pp., while T. R. Jackson, Brall, *Personenbeziehungen*, 219–49, interprets the Achilles-Deidamia episode in his *Trojanerkrieg*, and F. J. Worstbrock, Haferland, *Erzählungen*, 273–84, shows how the narration of the death of Hercules provides an insight into Konrad's understanding of the substance of his material. Elisabeth Lienert, *Geschichte und Erzählen. Studien zu Konrads von Würzburg 'Trojanerkrieg'* (WM, 22), xiii + 438 pp., is an ambitious and wide-ranging Würzburg *Habilitationsschrift* which seeks to provide a comprehensive interpretation of the work. The introduction points to the problems posed by the essentially 'historical' romances, and focuses on the programmatic function of the prologue. By far the largest section of the body of the study addresses K.'s treatment of his sources, with much on the earlier medieval Trojan legend as a whole and also subsidiary chapters on his reception of the classical MHG romance tradition. The role of the narrator, the composition and structure of the work and its guiding themes and perspectives are the subject of the second main section. Finally, L. considers the reception and continuation of the work, and its influence on texts such as the *Göttweiger Trojanerkrieg*. Further evidence of the intense current interest in the Trojan romances is shown by another work from the Würzburg school on another important successor text to Konrad's, *Das Elsässische Trojabuch ('Buch von Troja I')*. *Kritische Ausgabe*, ed. Christoph Witzel (WM, 21), 1995, cxix + 173 pp. One of the most popular but anonymous Trojan prose texts has been renamed on the basis of fairly certain evidence of its provenance. From the 15 extant manuscripts and fragments W. selects a *Leithand-schrift* (B1) and presents a very clear edition with critical apparatus. The codicological introduction includes details of the contents of each manuscript, and the index of proper names is another valuable aid to the study of the tradition of the Trojan tradition as a whole. H. Wandhoff, *Poetica*, 28:66–96, studies the incorporation by the Arthurian romance of pictorial scenes of the Trojan legend. Manfred Kern, *Agamemnon weint oder arthurische Metamorphose und trojanische Destruktion im 'Göttweiger Trojanerkrieg'* (ES, 104), 1995, iii + 251 pp., is a Vienna dissertation from the school of Helmut Birkhan which seeks to re-evaluate the *G.T.* on the basis of the fundamental insight that the poet forces the Trojan subject-matter into an Arthurian frame-work. The theoretical background is developed from a discussion of the postclassical aesthetic and an adapted framework of intertex-tuality. The subtle interplay of the Trojan and Arthurian worlds leads K. to adopt the term 'Hintergrundstrahlung' as a characteristic of the text. Both thematic and structural aspects of the dichotomy are addressed, while the most useful parts of the thesis are probably those which point to the reception of earlier Arthurian tradition.

C. Bertelsmeier-Kierst and J. Heinzle, *ZDP*, 115:42–54, reaffirm, against H. Thomas, their dating of the *Lohengrin* fragments. C. Bertelsmeier-Kierst and D. Heinig, *ZDA*, 124, 1995:436–56, cast new light on the fragmentary evidence of Ulrich von Etzenbach's *Alexander*, and W. Wunderlich, Haferland, *Erzählungen*, 259–71, studies Ulrich's treatment of the narration of Apelles's grave paint-ings, while M. Bärmann, *Die Ortenau*, 73, 1993:515–42, comments on Berthold von Herbolzheim and his *Alexander*, and T. Ehlert, *ZDA*, 125:87–92, studies the sources of the Waldeck *Alexander* fragment. W. Röcke, Haferland, *Erzählungen*, 285–301, distinguishes the manner in which knowledge of marvels of nature and of the East is presented in *Reinfried von Braunschweig*, and J. T. Schaefer, *Mélanges Spiewok*, 351–63, supplies a comparative study of *Tristan als Mönch*.

V. Mertens, Brall, *Personenbeziehungen*, 109–34, studies the conception of love in the late prose romances, and R. Schlusemann, *ABÄG*, 46:171–87, includes the German translation of the *Roman van Heinrich en Margriete van Limborch* in a comparative manuscript study, while S. B. Pafenberg, *ColGer*, 28, 1995:265–84, points to the place of evil and predestination in Thüring von Ringoltingen's *Melusine*. Ulrich Füetrer, *Lannzilet: aus dem 'Buch der Abenteuer' Str. 1123–6009*, ed. Rudolf Voss (SME, 3), v + 485 pp., is conceived as the completion of the edition of the first 1,122 lines by K.-E. Lenk (see *YWMLS*, 51:655–56), although an independent piece of work which generally proceeds more conservatively than Lenk. There is a codicological introduction and lists of emended passages. The text is presented in a clear layout with two columns to the page. A substantial apparatus is printed together at the end, followed by a substantial commentary on both linguistic and literary details and a short list of the passages which refer to six historical contemporaries of F., besides himself. This is a most useful edition of an unusually late verse romance, the presentation and resolution of the conflicts of which are discussed by H.-J. Ziegeler, *Colloquium* (Bristol), 323–39. Ruth Harvey, *Marquard vom Stein: Der Ritter vom Turn. Kommentar*, ed. Peter Ganz, Nigel Palmer, Lothar Schmitt, and Christopher Wells (TSM, 37), 204 pp., complements the posthumously published edition of Harvey (see *YWMLS*, 50:719–20), whose *Nachlaß* included a meticulous textual commentary comparing Marquard's version with the French original and the English text. The editors provide a concise but detailed introduction surveying all recent scholarship on the text and bring knowledge of the transmission up to date. They make no attempt to supply what Harvey failed to complete — notably an account of Marquard's life and an interpretation of the woodcuts — but what appears here is rich in textual and thematic detail. The different narrative levels in the same work are the subject of U. Gaebel, Haferland, *Erzählungen*, 393–409.

LYRIC POETRY

The *Repertorium der Sangsprüche und Meisterlieder des 12. bis 18. Jahrhunderts*, Tübingen, Niemeyer, continues with index vols 14–16. R. Berens, *GerLux*, 8:1–72, makes a new study of the Manesse MS, of which there is a revised diplomatic edition, *Die große Heidelberger Liederhandschrift. (Codex manesse). Mit einem Verzeichnis der Strophenanfänge. In getreuem Textabdruck*, ed. Fridrich Pfaff and Hellmut Salowsky, Heidelberg, Winter, 1995, xii + 1601 cols. K. Klein and H. Lomnitzer, *BGDSL*, 117, 1995:381–403, report the rediscovery of a folio of the Jena Song Manuscript. Peter Dronke, *The Medieval Lyric*, 3rd edn, Woodbridge, D. S. Brewer, xxi + 288 pp., is a welcome reissue of this study, as much a standard work as it has remained controversial. There is a substantial new preface in which D. points to the significance for his general approach of Bernhard Bischoff's Provençal strophes discovered in 1984 and surveys the most important recent bibliographical additions in each of the major language areas. Gale Sigal, *Erotic Dawn-Songs of the Middle Ages. Voicing the Lyric Lady*, Gainesville, Florida U.P., xii + 241 pp., is a wide-ranging critical study based on a range of texts in Provençal, French, English, and German, accompanied by a not unbearably heavy load of feminist baggage. All the works are present in A. T. Hatto's *Eos*. The overall thrust of the book is an emphasis on the active, participatory role of the woman portrayed in the *alba* genre, who is contrasted with 'the silent, worshipped lady created in the canso', allegedly the only female lyric figure identified in previous criticism. If this appears astonishing to medieval Germanists, its explanation may lie in a bibliography which excludes all literature in German and most in any language other than English, or in evident ignorance of poets such as Der von Kürenberg and recent critical approaches to Reinmar. Wernfried Hofmeister, *Sprichwortartige Mikrotexte als literarische Medien, dargestellt an der hochdeutschen politischen Lyrik des Mittelalters* (Studien zur Phraseologie und Parömiologie, 5), Bochum, Brockmeyer, 1995, ix + 574 pp., seeks to develop a new approach to the analysis of the presence and function of proverbial and sententious elements (broadly conceived) in medieval poetry. The methodology worked out by H. in the first half of the study owes much to modern structuralist and semiotic approaches and to communication theory, and on his own admission the recourse to the appropriate jargon is so considerable that he obligingly aids the reader with a 'terminologischer Wegweiser'. The texts included range from the political lyrics of Walther by way of the most important postclassical poets to Oswald von Wolkenstein, Michel Beheim, and Hans Rosenplüt. There are minutely detailed analyses of the chief literary and linguistic features identified. H. weighs up the possible implications of his approach, which almost inevitably suffers from a certain neglect of the more conventional scholarly literature on the texts treated. Dedicated to the relationship between performance and text, *Acta* (Seeon) has a section on the lyric, with contributions by P. Strohschneider (the role of the performer, 7–30); H. Meier and G. Lauer (evidence of performance in the Codex Buranus, 31–47); H. Tervooren (the place of 'performance' in interpretation, 48–66); and T. Bein (singing about singing, and the dialogue with the audience, 67–92). A. Classen, *SM*, 36, 1995[1996]:211–39, pursues the theme of love in the Minnesang as a game. In Schilling, *Wechselspiele*, M. Eikelmann

(19–42) considers the role of narrative and epic elements in the love-lyric as narrowly conceived with its conventional assignment to the lyric genre, while G. Wolf (153–77) reviews the texts defined as *Gegensang* and considers their role in performance, seeing their treatment as mere parody as too narrow. In *Colloquium* (Chiemsee), C. Edwards (1–25) surveys the evidence for the early pastourelle in Germany, with an appendix of texts; I. Kasten (27–41) looks at the degree of accommodation of the form to the genre system of the courtly lyric; J. Ashcroft (57–65) studies instances of a woman's monlogue exemplifying a dilemma; J. Margetts (101–14) considers the relatively uncommon treatment of deprivation in the lyric; T. Tomasek (115–28) documents songs referring to the preparation of flax; H.-J. Behr (195–202) reviews the largely stagnant history of the dawn song after Wolfram; and A. Robertshaw (245–56) comments on the late-medieval political lyric. Susanne Fritsch-Staar, *Unglückliche Ehefrauen. Zum deutschsprachigen 'malmariée'-Lied* (PSQ, 134), 1995, 496 pp., is a dissertation by a pupil of H. Tervooren which treats the subject exhaustively for the medieval and early modern periods, and includes a copious appendix of texts.

D.-R. Moser, *Fest. Schenda*, 513–31, considers the poets of the *Carmina Burana*, and F. P. Knapp, *Akten* (Sterzing), 129–40, addresses their linguistic and cultural pluralism. W. Fritsch-Rössler, *ZDP*, 115:18–25, interprets Meinloh von Sevelingen, MF 13, 1, and C. Edwards, pp. 13–30 of *Celtic and Germanic Themes* (see p. 730 above), studies the fairy mistress in Morungen, while W. E. Jackson, *FCS*, 17, 1990:157–68, compares Morungen, MF 141, 37, with Oswald von Wolkenstein, Kl. 65, and J. Ashcroft, Schilling, *Wechselspiele*, 123–52, tries to make sense of Rugge/Reinmar MF 108, 22, on the basis of knowledge of Walther and Hartmann. C. Ortmann, *Colloquium* (Chiemsee), 81–99, sets up a typology of Hartmann's crusading lyric.

Walther von der Vogelweide, *Leich, Lieder, Sangsprüche. Mit Beiträgen von Thomas Bein und Horst Brunner*, 14th rev. edn, ed. Christoph Cormeau, Berlin, de Gruyter, lxv + 344 pp., is a complete reworking of Lachmann's edition which, while naturally orientated towards an emphasis on transmission and reception, follows a modified principle of the *Leithandschrift* and often supports Lachmann's readings. Horst Brunner, Gerhard Hahn, Ulrich Müller, and Franz Viktor Spechtler, *Walther von der Vogelweide. Epoche — Werk — Wirkung*, Munich, Beck, 273 pp., is a thoroughly welcome addition to this series, starting from the premise in Hahn's introduction that most W. research of recent decades has (rightly) been concerned with problems of detail. Müller writes lucidly on the transmission and editing and contributes, with S. Neureiter-Lackner, on the reception of W. with much information on modern approaches to performance. The works as a whole are

covered in three chapters on the love-lyric (Hahn), *Spruchdichtung*
(Müller), and the *Leich*, 'Alterslieder', and songs on the Holy Land
and crusading theme: these are a collective *tour de force*, supplying
admirable coverage of recent critical literature in the briefest possible
space. The book is not only the excellent student introduction it
purports to be, but a work of reference providing an up-to-date
starting-point for further research. *Walther von der Vogelweide. Actes du
Colloque du Centre d'Études Médiévales de l'Université de Picardie Jules Verne
15 et 16 Janvier 1995*, ed. Danielle Buschinger and Wolfgang Spiewok
(Greifswalder Beiträge zum Mittelalter, 39; Wodan, 52), Greifswald,
Reineke, 1995, v + 177 pp., contains nine essays, chiefly on Walther,
who is also the chief example in a study of the problems of defining
medieval 'literary geography' by A. Ebenbauer, Kugler, *Interregionalität*, 23–43. V. Mertens, *JFinL*, 27, 1995:178–92, discusses
problems relating to the performance of Walther's love-songs, and
C. Edwards, *Colloquium* (Bristol), 250–63, emphasizes the learned
elements in his use of imagery and dialectic, while E. Lienert, *GRM*,
n. F., 46:369–82, comments on his attitude to past and present time,
and C. März, *Colloquium* (Chiemsee), 43–56, considers the implications of the relationship of his *Leich* and *Carmina Burana*, 60/60a.
S. Ranawake, *ib.*, 67–79, points to Provençal influence on the
crusading motifs in his songs, and J. Haustein, *ib.*, 217–26, studies his
reception in MS k.

　　H. Kästner, Schilling, *Wechselspiele*, 209–43, considers the consequences for 13th-c. didactic verse of the competition between
mendicant preachers and itinerant poets for the attention of the lay
audience. J.-D. Müller, Schilling, *Wechselspiele*, 43–76, places Neidhart and Hadloub at the centre of a study of the tendency of the later
lyric to ritualize, narrate, and fictionalize the performer's role, and
E. Lienert, *ZDA*, 125:264–74, interprets Gottfried von Neifen's
Wiegenlied as a parody of the dawn-song, while U. Kühne, *ib.*,
125:275–96, comments on the *œuvre* of Der Marner in the light of J.
Haustein's work (see *YWMLS*, 57:688). Michael Bärmann, *Herr Göli.
Neidhart-Rezeption in Basel* (QFLK, 4), 1995, x + 343 pp. Claudia
Breitfeld et al., *Otto von Botenlauben. Minnesänger — Kreuzfahrer —
Klostergründer* (Bad Kissinger Archiv-Schriften, 1), Würzburg, Schö-
ningh, 1994, 505 pp., includes contributions on all aspects of O.'s life,
family, work, and background by T. Heiler, W. Störmer, C. Breitfeld,
E. Bünz, B. U. Hucker, D. Huschenbett, R. Kahsnitz, P. Rückert,
J. Wabra, H. Wagner, and P. Weidisch. In *Colloquium* (Chiemsee),
E. Bremer (129–45) studies the lyric of Ulrich von Winterstetten, and
S. Schmolinsky (147–56) the allegorical usage of Der Wilde Alex-
ander, whose song VI is the subject of F. J. Worstbrock, *BGDSL*,
118:183–204. D. Peil, Schilling, *Wechselspiele*, 179–207, interprets the

roles and relationships of the sexes in Reinmar von Zweter, and M. Schilling, Schilling, *Wechselspiele*, 103–21, addresses the role and function of the songs in Ulrich von Liechtenstein's *Frauendienst*, while D. Hempen, *GN*, 27:19–22, writes on the lepers in the same work. B. Wachinger, *ZDA*, 125:125–41, traces the origin of the Tannhäuser ballad, and E. Wenzel, Kugler, *Interregionalität*, 143–60, discusses Süsskind von Trimberg, while K. Stackmann, *BGDSL*, 118:379–92, responds to critics of the dictionary to the Göttingen Frauenlob edition, and J. Rettelbach, *Colloquium* (Chiemsee), 177–93, interprets Frauenlob's alleged 'Selbstrühmung' as a polemical persiflage by another hand.

Ursel Fischer, *Meister Johans Hadloub. Autorbild und Werkkonzeption der Manessischen Liederhandschrift*, Stuttgart, M & P, 263 pp., accompanies the recent studies of G. Lübben and G. Paule from the Constance school of C. Ortmann (see *YWMLS*, 56:753–54), explicitly described as one of a triad of works and sharing with its companions an identical programmatic introduction (pp. 11–44). Against the background of the thesis that the rise of the written manuscript tradition of the lyric in the late 13th c. with the collection of earlier works marks an enhancement, indeed canonization of the genre, F. gives an account of the Hadloub transmission and takes as her starting-point his 'Manesse strophes'. The reference to the collecting of songs then forms the basis of an interpretation of his work as a whole, which is repeatedly seen to accommodate to the new literary situation. E. Hages, *Colloquium* (Chiemsee), 157–76, discusses Wizlaw von Rügen's exploitation of 13th-c. lyric tradition. M. Huber, *Acta* (Seeon), 93–106, studies evidence of fabricated performance in the transmission of the Monk of Salzburg, and D. Hirschberg, *Colloquium* (Chiemsee), 203–16, analyses his *di trumpet* (MR 15). K. Stackmann, *Literatur, Musik und Kunst* (see p. 761 below), pp. 132–61, supplies a fundamental introduction to the Meistergesang, exploring its intellectual background, content, and function. Ulrike-Marianne Schulz, *Liebe, Ehe und Sexualität im vorreformatorischen Meistersang: Texte und Untersuchungen* (GAG, 624), 1995, 316 pp. H. Vögel, Schilling, *Wechselspiele*, 245–73 + 7 pls, considers the love-lyric of Hugo von Montfort in performance and manuscript production. M. Nix, Schiewer, *Forschungsberichte*, 130–52, supplies a bibliographical review of discussion of the problems relating to the so-called 'historical song', and G. Roth, *Colloquium* (Chiemsee), 257–80, compares two historical songs from Silesia by Leonhard Assenheimer and Heinz Dompnig, while M. Baldzuhn, *ib.*, 227–43, interprets Hanz Folz's songs 89–94. E. Glaser, *Fest. Wellmann*, 29–46, analyses Clara Hätzlerin's graphemic system.

DIDACTIC, DEVOTIONAL AND RELIGIOUS LITERATURE

H. Wenzel, Kugler, *Interregionalität*, 65–79, cites a number of didactic poets on changes in communicative media and their consequences. T. B. McGuire, *FCS*, 16, 1990:189–97, points to the psychomachia in Herrad of Landsberg, and G. Pichler and H. Reichert, *ZDA*, 125:202–10, print new fragments of Priester Wernher's *Maria*. H.-J. Schiewer, Haferland, *Erzählungen*, 199–219, considers a corpus of 48 narrative exempla included in early German sermons. In *Symposium* (Roscrea), N. Henkel (1–21) links Priester Wernher, Konrad von Fussesbrunnen, and Konrad von Heimesfurt with the production of courtly literature *c.* 1200, and P. Kurmann and E. C. Lutz (23–54) study the literary and iconographical portrayal of the crowning of Mary, while H.-J. Ziegeler (55–77) analyses the Marian poems of MS Heidelberg Cpg 341, and B. Gutfleisch-Ziche (79–96) renews interest in the structure and function of the Millstatt manuscript. M. Stolz (97–117) discusses Wilhelm Müncher's *Psalterium glossatum*, and K. Gärtner (119–51) edits and discusses the exegesis of the Creation in the *Christherre-Chronik*, while M. Sherwood-Smith (153–65) points to the significance of Peter Comestor's *Historia Scholastica* as a source for vernacular authors, and F. Shaw (167–81) surveys chronometric traditions in the world chronicles. W. Röll (183–95) reviews Bible translation into Yiddish in the 14th and 15th cs, and J. L. Flood (197–213) studies the association of various saints with the new diseases recorded from the end of the period, while N. Miedema (215–35) considers the link between the late-medieval veneration of relics and pilgrimage to Rome. W. Frey, *Colloquium* (Bristol), 125–41, considers the role of the Jews in events of the Christmas cycle in a range of religious poetry and drama.

K. Liman, Brall, *Personenbeziehungen*, 429–55, analyses the communicative technique of a number of chronicles. Danielle Jaurant, *Rudolfs 'Weltchronik' als offene Form. Überlieferungsstruktur und Wirkungsgeschichte* (BG, 34), 1995, x + 407 pp., is a detailed study based on analysis of the manuscript contents. Konrad von Halberstadt O. P., *Chronographia Interminata 1277–1355/59*, ed. Rainer Leng (WM, 23), x + 286 pp., brings to light a largely unknown source for the years in question with an edition of the second part of a world chronicle which begins with the Creation and also includes much non-historical material. The text and its presentation follow the format of the MGH series, and accordingly include a wealth of source-reference and other annotation. The introduction (pp. 1–117) is also richly informative, with much on the structure of the work, its relationship to its genre, and its encyclopaedic and Joachimite content besides its compilatory technique and author's life and background. M. Vittor, *Mélanges Spiewok*,

423–38, compares the Genesis of Heinrich von München's *Weltchronik* with a French 13th-c. version, and G. Wolf, pp. 61–71 of *Fragen nach dem Autor* (see p. 725 above), considers the role of the author in family chronicles of the 15th and 16th cs, while J. Wolf, *ZDA*, 125:51–86, considers Konrad Bollstatter's contribution to historiography in late 15th-c. Augsburg. K. F. Werner, *ZDA*, 124, 1995:375–435, traces the Burgundian origins of the beast epic, and E. Brüggen, *Colloquium* (Bristol), 235–49, reviews the literature on courtesy and table-manners. E. Feistner, *ZDP*, 115:1–17, considers the literary reflection of the popular theory of confession and penance, and R. F. M. Byrn, *Colloquium* (Chiemsee), 281–94, shows that in a range of MHG religious lyric the semantic connotations of *rein* are largely metaphorical and spiritual. A. Vizkelety, *Fest. Mollay*, 385–92, publishes a Marian poem ascribed to St Augustine. C. Ortmann and H. Ragotzky, *Symposium* (Roscrea), 237–53, study the authorial role in Der Stricker's religious *exempla*. Hans-Jochen Schiewer, *'Die Schwarzwälder Predigten.' Entstehungs- und Überlieferungsgeschichte der Sonntags- und Heiligenpredigten. Mit einer Musteredition* (MTU, 105), x + 456 pp., is a landmark in the study of this mysterious author, shifting the emphasis decisively to the transmission of the text, the importance of the previously neglected 'vulgate' version of the *de tempore* sermons being shown by their survival in 30 manuscripts even though S. maintains the received view that Grieshaber's older edition represents the autograph, a unique instance for a 13th-c. German literary text. The meticulous analysis of the documents is of great interest for knowledge of the transmission of the early sermons in general, the literary tradition of which these works are seen to continue, S. also favouring a Franciscan environment. A much shorter chapter deals with the much less interesting *sanctorale* sermons, mainly direct translations of the *Legenda aurea*. An appendix presents five sermons in a sample edition. *Predigten und Stücke aus dem Kreise Bertholds von Regensburg (Teilsammlung Y[III])*, ed. Frank G. Banta (GAG, 621), 1995, xlvi + 206 pp. H. Meyer, *BGDSL*, 117, 1995:404–31, rejects A. E. Schönbach's thesis that Berthold was a pupil of Bartholomaeus Anglicus. *Das Bremer Evangelistar*, introd. and ed. Jochen Splett, Marion Bockelmann, and Andreas Kerstan (QFSK, 234), lxxxv + 387 pp., presents a text related to the *Leben Jesu*. P. Göhler, Haferland, *Erzählungen*, 233–41, sees the third dialogue between father and son in Wernher der Gartenaere's *Helmbrecht* as crucial for indicating the views of the poet, while T. Terada, *Festschrift für Kenji Aoyagi*, Sapporo, 1993, pp. 311–22, views the *Helmbrecht* poet as a cleric, and R. Sprandel, *Otto von Botenlauben* (see p. 744 above), pp. 296–308, considers Hugo von Trimberg's view of the 13th-c. nobility.

Deutsche Mystik, ed., trans., and introd. Louise Gnädinger (dtv, 24064), Zurich, DTV–Manesse, 518 pp., is an attractive anthology of translated excerpts from Hildegard of Bingen (with Latin originals), Mechthild of Magdeburg, Eckhart, Tauler, Rulman Merswin, Heinrich von Nördlingen, Margaretha Ebner, Seuse, and Christine Ebner, together with lyrics. The introductions on each author are more substantial than is usual with such selections. There is a brief bibliography. Kurt Ruh, *Geschichte der abendländischen Mystik*. III. *Die Mystik des deutschen Predigerordens und ihre Grundlegung durch die Hochscholastik*, Munich, Beck, 534 pp., appears just six years after the commencement of this admirably lucid and comprehensive treatment of the mystics (see *YWMLS*, 52:628; 55:728). The apogee of the subject is naturally reached in this volume, but R. devotes 200 pages to its scholastic roots, with concisely informative sections on the Neoplatonic sources; the reception of Dionysius by Thomas Gallus, Robert Grosseteste, and Hugh of Balma; and the relevant aspects of Albert the Great, Aquinas, the 13th-c. Carthusians, and Dietrich von Freiberg. This prepares the ground, already anticipated in earlier volumes, for the substantial chapters on Eckhart, the texts reflecting his influence, contemporary Dominicans, Seuse, and Tauler. In the chapter on Eckhart R.'s earlier book (*YWMLS*, 47:671) is sometimes followed verbatim but more often reformulated, and always modified as necessary to take account of the most recent scholarship. This, together with the detailed bibliographical support underpinning every section of the volume, maintains the impression made by its predecessors that R. has delivered the authoritative standard work of reference on the mystics for the next generation. Alois M. Haas, *Mystik als Aussage. Erfahrungs-, Denk- und Redeformen christlicher Mystik* (STW, 1196), 529 pp., is an impressive collection of 17 essays of both analytical and historical content, the majority of which were published in rapid succession between 1988 and 1992. This gives the work a coherence often lacking in such reprints. There are new studies on mysticism as a means of discovering sense, the theology of mysticism, and Jakob Böhme. H. Unger, pp. 13–33 of *Können, Mut und Phantasie. Portraits schöpferischer Frauen aus Mitteldeutschland*, ed. Annemarie Haase and Harro Kieser (Aus Deutschlands Mitte, 26), Weimar, Böhlau, 1993, 203 pp., characterizes some of the female mystics, and P. Dinzelbacher, Brall, *Personenbeziehungen*, 3–36, surveys texts documenting mystical pregnancy. Mechthild von Magdeburg, *Das fließende Licht der Gottheit. Zweite, neubearbeitete Übersetzung*, introd. and comm. Margot Schmidt (MGG, 1, 11), 1995, xlviii + 460 pp., is a fundamental reworking of a translation which first appeared in 1955. The whole work, including the substantial annotations, is now accommodated to Hans Neumann's edition of 1990–93 (see *YWMLS*,

53:652; 55:729). A textual apparatus has accordingly been abandoned, the notes and select bibliography reflect the current state of research, and access to the text is facilitated by the inclusion of indexes of biblical citations, names, writers, and subjects. S.'s dedication radiates through this fine volume and matches that of Neumann to whose edition it forms a worthy companion. E. Hellgardt, *Symposium* (Roscrea), 319–37, considers aspects of Mechthild von Magdeburg's stylistic technique, and E. A. Andersen, *Colloquium* (Bristol), 264–72, emphasizes her relationship with the Dominicans. Margarete Hubrath, *Schreiben und erinnern. Zur 'memoria' im Liber Specialis Gratiae Mechthilds von Hakeborn*, Paderborn, Schöningh, 149 pp., is a Bonn dissertation which, on the theoretical basis of the insights of H. R. Jauss and G. Kaiser, seeks to demonstrate that *memoria* — broadly conceived as both preservation and actualization of the past — underlies the origin, content, and function of a relatively neglected collective work of *c.* 1290–1310. The monastic conditions of production of the work receive constant mention in the illustration of the thesis, which focuses on the visionary imagery and the representation of the Passion, while the treatment of biblical text is also drawn into the argument through the application of the concept of intertextuality. Christine Ruhrberg, *Der literarische Körper der Heiligen. Leben und Viten der Christina von Stommeln (1242–1312)* (BG, 35), 1995, ix + 487 pp., is a large-scale study of the life, background, and work. Meister Eckhart, *Das Buch der göttlichen Tröstung. Von dem edlen Menschen*, ed., trans., and comm. Günter Stachel, Munich, Kösel, 192 pp., is conceived as a sequel to S.'s earlier treatment of sermons and the *Rede der underscheidunge* (see *YWMLS*, 54:689). Here the very brief biographical introduction focuses on the bare essentials, and is accompanied by pointers to the basis of E.'s thought. The translations of the texts are broken into sections each followed by explanatory commentary, besides introductory matter and notes. U. Kern, '*Scientia' und 'ars'* (see pp. 710–11 above), pp. 569–85, studies Eckhart's theory of the intellect. Volker Frederking, *Durchbruch vom Haben zum Sein. Erich Fromm und die Mystik Meister Eckharts*, Paderborn, Schöningh, 1994, 513 pp. J. Kreuzer, '*Scientia' und 'ars'* (see pp. 710–11 above), pp. 633–49, studies Tauler's thought and mysticism. Peter Ulrich, *Imitatio et configuratio. Die philosophia spiritualis Heinrich Seuses als Theologie der Nachfolge des Christus passus* (Eichstätter Studien, n. F., 36), Regensburg, Pustet, 1995, 200 pp. H.-J. Schiewer, *Symposium* (Roscrea), 289–317, edits and studies an early 15th-c. text from the milieu of beguine mysticism in Basle.

E. Feistner, *WS XIV*, 171–84, proposes a methodological basis for analysing the history of the translation of saints' lives. Madeleine Boxler, '*ich bin ein predigerin und appostlorin.' Die deutschen Maria*

Magdalena-Legenden des Mittelalters (1300–1550). Untersuchungen und Texte (DLA, 22), 619 pp., is useful chiefly as a survey of the substantial body of late-medieval German texts on St Mary Magdalene and as a compendium of texts. A survey of the New Testament data and major patristic and medieval references is followed by a catalogue and typological analysis of 38 texts. A substantial chapter is devoted to the theoretical and practical problems attending an edition of the *Nürnberger Maria Magdalena-Legende III* in the light of current approaches to text and transmission; the interpretation focuses on the reception of the work. Diplomatic transcripts of other texts fill much of the rest of the book (pp. 213–576). Ruth Wolff, *Der heilige Franziskus in Schriften und Bildern des 13. Jahrhunderts*, Berlin, Gebr. Mann, 333 pp. + lxii pp. pls, is a Munich dissertation which confronts the major representations of the life of St Francis in the visual arts with the most significant texts following his rapid canonization: Thomas of Celano's life for the Bardi cycle in Florence and Bonaventure's legends for the Assisi frescoes, besides earlier documents. W. has much to say on the apparent dichotomy between the relative realism of portrayal of a near contemporary and the traditional role of the saint in *Heilsgeschichte* to which the representation is accommodated. The interpretation of the anonymous *Sacrum commercium* tract as a personification allegory is largely convincing even if only older material on the literary side is cited, while close analysis of the works of Thomas of Celano against the background of hagiographical tradition points to development in the underlying conception of hagiography. K. A. Zaenker, *FCS*, 17, 1990: 515–26, traces the cult of St Brendan *c.* 1500, and there is a facsimile edition, with commentary volume, of *Von Sant Branden eyn hübsch lieblich lesen, was wunderß er uff dem môr erfaren hat*, ed. Lutz Unbehaun, 2 cols, 1994, fac. 53 pp., comm. 127 pp.

Konrad von Mure, *Der Liber ordinarius. Die Gottesdienstordnung am Großmünster in Zürich*, ed. Heidi Leuppi (Spicilegium Friburgense, 37), Fribourg U. P., 1995, 616 pp., is a substantial edition and study of the liturgical work. *Brother Hermann's Life of the Countess Yolanda of Vianden*, trans. Richard H. Lawson (SGLLC), 1995, xviii + 72 pp., is a lucid English prose translation of a little-known work, based on John Meier's 1889 edition of the unique 17th-c. transcript of the poem. L. includes line-references to the original at ten-line intervals. The introduction is brief, but points to the essential humanity of the work which emerges above all through the vivid and sensitive characterization. The textual situation is further discussed by G. Newton, *Fest. Hoffmann*, 151–81. M. Schnyder, *Euphorion*, 90:41–61, studies Konrad von Würzburg's Mariological prologue to his *Goldene Schmiede*, and

H. Graser, *Fest. Wellmann*, 47–58, discusses the language and provenance of a Franciscan Rule from Augsburg, while H. Beckers, *ZDP*,
115:338–48, prints a fragment of an early 14th-c. *Minnerede*. Dietrich
von Freiberg, *Abhandlungen über die Akzidentien. Lateinisch — Deutsch. Auf
der Grundlage des Textes der kritischen Ausgabe von Maria Rita Pagnoni-
Sturlese*, trans. Burkhard Mojsisch, introd. Karl-Hermann Kandler
(PBib, 472), 1994, xlviii + 144 pp. B. Murdoch, *SM*, 36, 1995[1996]:
777–96, compares the *Erlösung* with Cornish and Italian gospel
poems, and X. von Ertzdorff and H. Meinhardt, *WS XIV*, 208–30,
study the MHG translation of Thomas Aquinas's *Summa Theologiae*,
while E. Wenzel, *ZGer*, 6:47–60, argues that the purpose of Heinrich
von Hesler's *Apokalypse* is the transmission of orthodox exegesis to the
laity in the face of heretical Joachimite texts, and T. Gervasi, *AION*,
n.s., 4, 1994:75–95, studies names and translations in the *Elsässische
Legenda aurea. Der Heiligen Leben. 1. Der Sommerteil*, ed. Margit Brand,
Kristina Freienhagen-Baumgardt, Ruth Meyer, and Werner Willi-
ams-Krapp (TTG, 44), liii + 584 pp., displays all the benefits of a
team effort in producing a reliable edition of the fundamentally
important late-medieval legendary. The editors emphasize the demonstrably southern and Dominican character of the items included,
besides the use of vernacular sources from the classical courtly period
on, while the role of the work as a source-book in its own right almost
goes without saying. The rich transmission in manuscripts and
printed versions is fully documented and, in view of its extremely
conservative nature, it is no surprise to find the same editorial
approach — a *Leithandschrift* accompanied by readings from the main
branches of the stemma — as was successfully used for a no less
monumental work edited by the same school, the *Elsässische Legenda
Aurea* (see *YWMLS*, 42:740). The layout of the text is a model of
clarity and with the simple but effective indexes the book is a pleasure
to use — truly an edition for many generations to come. Manuela
Niesner, *Das Speculum humanae salvationis der Stiftsbibliothek Kremsmünster.
Edition der mittelhochdeutschen Versübersetzung und Studien zum Verhältnis von
Bild und Text* (Pictura et poesis, 8), Cologne, Böhlau, 1995,
xiii + 397 pp. + 45 pls, commences with a useful survey of research
on the dating, origin, authorship, and function of the *S.H.S.* besides
an account of its particular assimilation of allegory and typology.
There follows an edition of the text of the German verse translation
of the sumptuously illustrated Codex Cremifanensis 243 with an
index of proper names, linguistic analysis and account of the
relationship to the Latin text. The second part of the study seeks to
confront the rather disparate literary and iconographical research
with a 'Text und Bild' approach. By asking the right questions against
the background of an excellent knowledge of the literature to date N.

supplies an illuminating commentary on this important and unusual work. Ulla Williams, *Die 'Alemannischen Vitaspatrum'. Untersuchungen und Edition* (TTG, 45), x + 145* + 438 pp., is another major hagiographical edition from the Würzburg school, following its now well-established principles of focusing on the transmission and reception of such texts as their chief features of interest for the later Middle Ages. The introductory material gives full information on the complicated history and content of the *Vitaspatrum* texts dating back to the 4th-5th cs, their particular spirituality provoking a revival of interest among the Dominicans in particular. Following the late-13th-c. poetic *Väterbuch* W. identifies six prose translations of the 14th and 15th cs, the two earliest of which, complementing each other in content, are the subject of the edition. There is full documentation of the monumental transmission and W. easily demonstrates, on the basis of comparison of translations of an identical Latin source-text, that different translators were responsible for the two sections, the saints' lives and the exempla respectively. The latter number, with appendices, no less than 513. As with the other editions in this series the approach produces a thoroughly readable text which, used in conjunction with the lucid documentation, fully achieves its aim of presenting the subject-matter in the wider context of the tradition it represents. W. Dittmann, Haferland, *Erzählungen*, 303–26, studies the account of the discovery of chess and its significance in Konrad von Ammenhausen's *Schachzabelbuch*, and J. Clerc, *Mélanges Spiewok*, 99–114, examines poverty in Heinrich der Teichner. A. Angenendt, T. Braucks, R. Busch, T. Lentes, and H. Lutterbach, *FmSt*, 29, 1995:1–71, cite a number of late-medieval religious texts in a monograph on devotional practices associated with numbers and counting, and W. C. McDonald, *FCS*, 19, 1992:101–45, surveys late-medieval texts referring to the charnel house, while F. Pensel, *ZDA*, 124, 1995:457–62, edits a Weimar fragment of Marquard von Lindau's *De Nabuchodonosor*.

Christian Bauer, *Geistliche Prosa im Kloster Tegernsee. Untersuchungen zu Gebrauch und Überlieferung deutschsprachiger Literatur im 15. Jahrhundert* (MTU, 107), viii + 305 pp., is a highly appropriate study for this series, focusing on the transmission and function of the vernacular literature in its relation to Latin of a single late-medieval monastery. Tegernsee is exemplary to the extent that its connection with the Melk Benedictine reform points to explicit encouragement of the use of German from the mid-century on and later evidence allows a reconstruction of the library holdings. B. identifies the readership in the restored lay brotherhood, convincingly established before the main part of the study expounds the basis of the organization of the library, the German contents of which are documented in detail. The subsequent analysis casts much light on the purpose and readership of the various types of literature represented, and uses the contemporary Augustinian library of Rebdorf for purposes of comparison. Peter Wiesinger, *Schreibung und Aussprache im älteren Frühneuhochdeutschen. Zum Verhältnis von Graphem — Phonem — Phon am bairisch-österreichischen Beispiel von Andreas Kurzmann um 1400* (SLG, 42), x + 265 pp., includes an appendix of texts. N. H. Kaylor, *FCS*, 18, 1991 : 133–42, writes on Peter von Kastl and his lost 1401 translation of Boethius, and A. Klein, *ZDP*, 115:439–42, demonstrates that Johannes von Indersdorf studied at Vienna, while E. De Felip-Jaud, *Akten* (Sterzing), 269–79, analyses the proverbs in Hans Vintler's *Pluemen der tugent* and its Italian original, and F.-J. Schweitzer, *ib.*, 281–92, considers his approach to superstition.

Karl Tax, *Das Janota-Officium. Geschichte und Sprache eines ripuarischen Stundenbuches* (APSL, 124), viii + 506 pp., studies a 15th-c. book of hours with strong links to the breviary first published by Eugeniusz Janota in 1855, part of the unknown manuscript source reappearing only in 1989. The account of the background to the work and the reconstruction of the original make for an interesting first chapter. The relationship to works of Geert Grote and the Devotio Moderna, and the particular significance of the Psalms and the regional tradition of the translation in which they stand form the focus of two further substantial studies. Finally, a detailed linguistic analysis seems to confirm the inetrmediate position of the work between the Dutch Devotio Moderna and the Lower Rhine tradition. L. Horstkötter, *APr*, 72:255–59, prints a 15th-c. Low German document relating to the Premonstratensian reform movement, and H. Moser, *Fest. Wellmann*, 191–205, introduces a 15th-c. miracle book from Maria Waldrast (Tyrol), while R. Meyer, *Colloquium* (Chiemsee), 295–307, surveys the neglected 15th-c. collection of religious songs from St. Katharinental. W. Schouwink, *FCS*, 20, 1993:291–307, studies the allegorization of dicing and clothing in a 15th-c. sermon, and M. Populer, *MA*, 102:479–527, introduces the devotional notebook of a Frankfurt citizen of the 1470s. *Der Geras-Pernegger deutsche Psalter aus dem 15. Jahrhundert. Text, Untersuchung und kulturgeschichtliche Beurteilung*, ed. Ralph Andraschek-Holzer (Studien und Forschungen aus dem Niederösterreichischen Institut für Landeskunde, 19), Vienna, NÖ Institut für Landeskunde, 1994, viii + 242 pp. W. Milde, *Das Buch in Mittelalter* (p. 722 above), pp. 79–93, studies a Hussite manuscript owned by Heinrich Toke and Flacius Illyricus. B. Eichler, pp. 29–42 of *Sprache und Stil in Texten für junge Leser. Festschrift für Hans-Joachim Siebert zum 65. Geburtstag*, ed. Angelika Feine and Karl-Ernst Sommerfeldt (SST, 17), 1995, 226 pp., considers the development of the late-medieval form of educational literature. W. Röcke, *ZGer*,

6:21–34, notes the Utopian aspects of Johann Hartlieb's *Alexander*, and H.-J. Bachorski, Haferland, *Erzählungen*, 371–91, considers the work's narrative perspectives. D. F. Tinsley, *FCS*, 14, 1988:179–89, points to the tradition of self-portrayal in Hermann von Sachsenheim's *Die Mörin*.

DRAMA. E. E. DuBruck, *FCS*, 21, 1994:17–53, reviews recent work on the medieval drama. In *Akten* (Sterzing), P. Wiesinger (67–93) studies the language and provenance of the oldest Tyrolean plays, M. Siller (193–230) reviews their recent new editions, M. Fink (231–37) records plays in Hall (Tyrol) in the 15th and 16th cs, U. Hennig (239–43) comments on the laments of Mary in the Tyrolean plays, B. Thoran (245–61) discusses the relationship of the *Wächterlied* and the *Canticum hebraicum* in the Sterzing Easter plays, and A. Traub (263–67) notes the transmission of their melodies. G. Wolf, *Acta* (Seeon), 381–405, examines the implications for ritual performance of the stage directions in the *Donaueschingen Passion Play* and in late-medieval chronicles, and P. Macardle, *Symposium* (Roscrea), 255–70, studies the songs in the *St. Galler Mittelrheinisches Passionsspiel*, while G. Wolf, *ib.*, 271–88, looks at the Harrowing of Hell in the Passion and Easter plays. *Das Osterspiel von Muri. Urtext, Spielfassung, Materialien*, ed. Christian Haller, Baden, Baden-Vlg, 1994, 173 pp. C. Dauven-van Knippenberg, *FCS*, 18, 1991:143–58, surveys the dramatic reception of the Longinus legend, and D. F. Duclow, *FCS*, 21, 1994:55–86, studies the Dormition of the Virgin in drama and art, while D. A. Wells, *ABÄG*, 46:159–70, places the work of H. Linke (see *YWMLS*, 57:698) on the procession of apostles in the Last Judgement plays in the historical context of the theme, M. Walch, *Fest. Wellmann*, 371–406, analyses the language of the *Berlin Last Judgement Play*, U. Schulze, *BGDSL*, 118:205–33, studies further aspects of the development of the tradition of the Last Judgement plays, and also, in Haferland, *Erzählungen*, 351–69, identifies the epic components of the *Lucerne Last Judgement Play I*. I. Henderson, *FCS*, 14, 1988:95–103, surveyed the state of 1980s research on this group of plays.

Deutsche Spiele und Dramen des 15. und 16. Jahrhunderts, ed. Hellmut Thomke (Bibliothek der Frühen Neuzeit, 2), DKV, 1186 pp., contains two *Fastnachtspiele* of Hans Rosenplüt and two of Hans Folz, one play each by Balthasar Spross, Pamphilius Gengenbach, Niklaus Manuel, Sixt Birck, Paul Rebhun, Jakob Ayrer, Johannes Stricker, and Ferdinand II of Tyrol, and three pieces of Hans Sachs. The selection aims at a representative portrayal of the early Nuremberg *Fastnachtspiel* and the succeeding works in the genre of higher quality. The editions are wholly new and in general T. succeeds in his aim of presenting near-diplomatic texts with notes to facilitate both scholar and general reader. The introductions and commentaries on each work are as methodically detailed as one has come to expect of this series. S. Jefferis, *FCS*, 15, 1989:165–81; *ib.*, 17, 1990:169–83, compares the play *Aristoteles und die Königin* with its fabliau source, and with wider analogues. Work of the past few years on the *Fastnachtspiel* includes E. E. DuBruck, *FCS*, 14, 1988:39–53 (the role of the peasant); E. Kimminich, *ib.*, 15, 1989:183–208 (the battle of Carnival and Lent); M. W. Walsh, *ib.*, 305–21 (comic abuse of Arthur and the Round Table); J. Koopmans, *ib.*, 16, 1990:131–42 (generic problems); E. Kimminich, *ib.*, 17, 1990:209–27 (the devouring of souls and of fools); E. E. DuBruck, *ib.*, 18, 1991:33–48 (the treatment of the vices); J.-M. Pastré, *ib.*, 19, 1992:165–76 (seduction); D. Price, *ib.*, 209–28 (Hans Folz's anti-Judaism); and M. Przybilski, *ASNS*, 233:323–26 (the background to Hans Folz's use of pseudo-Hebrew in his plays).

SCIENTIFIC AND SPECIALIZED LITERATURE

Graphische Symbole in mittelalterlichen Urkunden. Beiträge zur diplomatischen Semiotik, ed. Peter Rück (Historische Hilfswissenschaften, 3), Sigmaringen, Thorbecke, 834 pp., is with 49 separate contributions from a variety of disciplines and a total of 1,665 illustrations a remarkable testimony to the richness of graphic symbolism. R.'s extensive introductory chapter establishes the necessary parameters of the subject and reviews the contents as a whole. The first section of four essays on the function of graphic symbols opens wider linguistic and literary perspectives than the immediate subject suggests, with work on the theoretical understanding of sign and symbol on an interdisciplinary basis (H. Jung), the legal function of symbolism in documents, including reference to the *Sachsenspiegel* (R. Schmidt-Wiegand), the graphic function (A. Hofmann), and linguistic aspects of the subject (H. Glück). The majority of the contributions are classified according to types of symbolic signature and seal; monograms, including numismatic usage; Frankish, papal, Iberian, North-West European, and East European usage; and notarial usage. Some remarkable general differences are revealed: the almost complete absence of graphic symbols in England and Scandinavia, and in Germany after the 12th c., contrasts with the wealth of evidence from Iberia and an independent tradition in Eastern Europe. The work must surely rehabilitate the study of the visual and representational aspects of documents and charters in a period which has tended to undervalue these functions in the concentration on their textual and legal content. C. Baufeld, *Colloquium* (Bristol), 273–84, characterizes Konrad von Megenberg's critical stance in the *Buch der Natur*, and

C. Fasbender, *BGDSL*, 117, 1995:432–36, interprets his use of *vêch*, while S. Kleine, *Sudhoffs Archiv*, 79, 1995:101–14, explains the source and function of the *Mainauer Naturlehre*. R. Schmidt-Wiegand, *FmSt*, 30:1–18, explains the early medieval basis of technical legal language, while *Die Stadt im Mittelalter. Kalkar und der Niederrhein*, ed. Gerhard Kaldewei (Schriften der Heresbach-Stiftung Kalkar, 1), Bielefeld, Vlg für Regionalgeschichte, 1994, 284 pp., includes work by R. Schmidt-Wiegand (185–216) on the civic aspects of the *Sachsenspiegel*, and W. Peters (217–21) on the Kalkar *Sachsenspiegel*. Information on various fragments of legal texts is published by U.-D. Oppitz in *Zeitschrift der Savigny-Stiftung für Rechtsgeschichte*, 113:345–61; *Memminger Geschichtsblätter*, 1991–92[1993]:67–75; *Tijdschrift voor rechtsgeschiedenis*, 64:191–99; *Braunschweigisches Jb.*, 73, 1992:127–34; *Hildesheimer Jb.*, 65, 1994:233–36, and 67, 1995:325–28; *Jb. für brandenburgische Landesgeschichte*, 46, 1995:70–75. M. Prosser, *JV*, 19:184–95, interprets late-medieval rural legal texts on, among other things, the rights of free-range chickens.

Die Geschichte des medizinischen Denkens. Antike und Mittelalter, ed. Mirko D. Grmek, Munich, Beck, 520 pp., is a well-documented survey of the history of medical thought in the West, including Arabic influence, and welcome against the background of the numerous piecemeal studies published in recent years. G. supplies an introduction and an account of the conception and definition of sickness. Ten further chapters by diferent specialists consider the growth of medical science, Hellenistic, Roman, and Byzantine and Arabic medicine, the treatment of the sick in medieval Christian society, the scholastic discipline, medical therapeutics and the search for a panacea, surgery, works of the *regimen sanitatis* type, and the characteristic diseases of medieval Europe. O. Riha, *Mediaevistik*, 7, 1994[1996]:203–21, argues that medical texts indicate the fundamentally different way of viewing the world in the Middle Ages, and in *Sudhoffs Archiv*, 80:129–49, cites some vernacular authors in a study of the medieval conception of sickness. Britta-Juliane Kruse, *Verborgene Heilkünste. Geschichte der Frauenmedizin im Spätmittelalter* (QFLK, 5), xi + 498 pp., includes, besides the studies, a substantial number of texts on obstetrics and gynaecology, and M. Weiss-Amer, *FCS*, 19, 1992:301–18, records texts on the dietetics of pregnancy. B.-Schnell, *WS XIV*, 185–207, studies the technique of translation in the *Älterer deutscher Macer*.

K. Kranich-Hofbauer, *Editio*, 10:49–67, places the Starkenberg *Rotulus* at the centre of a discussion of the problems facing the editor of late-medieval documents. Karin Zimmermann, *Der Heidelberger Rotulus aus dem Jahre 1401 (UAH XII, 2 Nr. 33). Studien zu den Personennamen (BNF*, n. F., Beiheft 48), Heidelberg, Winter, 417 pp., is an exhaustive study of a document of special interest to social historians but hitherto neither edited nor analysed in full. The roll, listing members of the University supplicating for ecclesiastical benefices, is described as one of six known similar documents from Heidelberg. Z. provides a full introduction to the background, a legible transcription of the preface and 405 numbered entries, and detailed classification and analysis of the personal names and of the family names by origin. There are full indexes besides a linguistic analysis. G. Kettmann, *Fest. Wellmann*, 131–38, considers the relative stability evidenced by the language of late-medieval civic documents. In *Akten* (Sterzing), P. Ernst (39–66) documents the earliest vernacular transmission of civic records from Vienna and Brixen, B. Döring (95–107) contributes linguistic comments on Tyrolean specialized prose literature, K. Brandstätter (359–406) records vernacular material from Trentino, K. Kranich-Hofbauer (407–18) studies the conversational and dialogic aspects of Tyrolean documents, and B. Spreitzer (419–31) examines the role of women and evil in demonological literature from Innsbruck. I. T. Piirainen, *NMi*, 97:231–37, studies the oldest civic record from Pressburg/Bratislava, and T. Hildbrand, *FmSt*, 29, 1995:349–89, makes Swiss documents of *c.* 1300 the basis of a theoretical treatment of the description of written sources, while B. Kasten, *Burg und Schloß* (p. 727 above), pp. 35–82, prints vernacular documents relating to the domestic management of Duke Wilhelm IV of Jülich-Berg, and U. Bodemann, *OGS*, 25:119–34, characterizes the work of Kaspar Engelsüss of Strassburg.

OTHER LATER MEDIEVAL LITERATURE

Brenner, *Literaturgeschichte*, 1–23, deals with the early modern period, but space permits treatment of only the most outstanding 15th-c. works. U. Goebel, *FCS*, 15, 1989:133–45, favours classifying Early NHG literature in terms of text type rather then genre, and A. Classen, *ib.*, 20, 1993:35–64, looks at the treatment of courtly love-motifs in late-medieval narratives. *Novellistik des Mittelalters: Märendichtung*, ed., trans., and comm. Klaus Grubmüller (Bibliothek des Mittelalters, 23), DKV, 1387 pp., contains 38 texts of short narrative works accompanied on facing pages by the rather rigid and certainly unpolished line-by-line translations characteristic of the series to date. G.'s introduction to the genre — and the problem of its boundaries — is based on a classification of the texts into the foundation of the fabliau (Der Stricker, *Das Schneekind*), variants on the theme such as Herrand von Wildonie's *Die treue Gattin*, morality and deception in love (e.g. Konrad von Würzburg's *Herzmäre*,

Aristoteles und Phyllis), sexual comedy, Heinrich Kaufringer's consciously literary exploitation of the genre, and the 15th-c. emphasis on evil and the grotesque (Hans Rosenplüt). The notes focus on matters of linguistic comprehension but are also informative on questions of source and transmission. Werner Schröder, *Variable Verschriftlichung eines Märe. Ein history von eim edelman vnd sinem knechte Heinrich* (Sitzungsberichte der Wiss. Gesellschaft an der Johann Wolfgang Goethe-Univ. Frankfurt am Main, 34, no. 3), Stuttgart, Steiner, 104 pp., returns to earlier work on the fabliaux and addresses the interesting textual problems of what was long known as 'Der Junker (Jungherr) und der treue Heinrich'. S. argues that the shorter version H is closer to the first lost transcript and provides a critical edition with variants from the alternative version D. The latter, however, he sees as an equally valid transmission of what was from the outset an 'open' text. J. Margetts, *Colloquium* (Bristol), 215–32, interprets the place of marital strife in short narrative texts, and K. Grubmüller, *ib.*, 340–47, considers aspects of their downright violence. Id., Haferland, *Erzählungen*, 243–57, classifies types of deceptive narratives used in fabliaux, while W. C. McDonald, *FCS*, 21, 1994:167–91, considers the role of moral instruction in a range of late-medieval narratives of love-affairs, and N. R. Wolf, *Colloquium* (Bristol), 359–70, comments on the linguistic presentation of conflict before and after the invention of printing. K. Skow-Obenaus, *FCS*, 21, 1994:303–22, studies deception in *Die sieben weisen Meister*, and U. Friedrich, *IASL*, 21.1:1–30, sees Heinrich Kaufringer's interpretative sophistication anchored in his playing with metaphors.

W. Schröder, *Euphorion*, 90:348–61, comments negatively on K. Bertau's new edition of the *Ackermann aus Böhmen*, while C. Kiening, *BGDSL*, 118:234–56, offers a more moderate assessment. L. Szalai, *Fest. Mollay*, 341–54, writes on Wittenwiler's *Ring*, and H. Tervooren, *ZDP*, 115:437–38, points to its possible reception in the Rhine-Maas region. E. J. Morrall, *The Library*, 18:216–29, studies the early editions of Aeneas Silvius Piccolomini's *Historia de duobus amantibus*, and F. Fürbeth, *BGDSL*, 117, 1995:437–88, edits translations of his *De origine heraldorum*.

In *Akten* (Sterzing), A. Robertshaw (141–50) comments on Werner Marold's commentary on Oswald von Wolkenstein (see *YWMLS*, 57:701–02), and U. M. Schwob (151–62) considers the place of emotion in his work, while R. Gstrein (163–72) studies his use of melody and rhythm, and A. Traub (173–80) draws compositional comparisons with Guillaume de Machaut. A. Classen, *FCS*, 14, 1988:23–38, introduces O.'s grandson Veit, and *ib.*, 15, 1989:93–105, points to O.'s French and Italian sources. French influence is also the subject of A. H. Touber, *FCS*, 18, 1991:279–84. A. Schnyder, *GRM*,

n. F., 46:1–15, proposes a new reading for O., Kl. 3, and A. Robertshaw, *Tiroler Heimat*, 58, 1994:31–41, studies the local associations of O., Kl. 102, while R. Haub, *ZBL*, 59:177–83, edits a document in O.'s name from Beuerberg. P. Bassola, *Fest. Mollay*, 33–45, writes on the names in Helene Kottannerin, and A. Classen, *FCS*, 17, 1990:33–56, identifies Michel Beheim's autobiographical voice.

A. Fujii, *ZDP*, 115:393–432, proposes a new method for identifying different compositors of early printed works, and A. E. Wright, *FCS*, 19, 1992:319–49, reviews the impact of the Nuremberg printers. Ursula Rautenberg, *Überlieferung und Druck. Heiligenlegenden aus frühen Kölner Offizinen* (FN, 30), xi + 383 pp., adopts the tested method of a detailed study of the products of a limited number of printing-houses in a particular locality, and shows just how fruitful this can be for knowledge of the transition from manuscript to print, the relationship of Latin and vernacular, patrons, the readers, and the market, besides more immediate questions of textual transmission. The chosen body of texts — legends of saints venerated in Cologne — is subjected to meticulous bibliographical description in the appendix (pp. 249–331). Besides the obvious Ursuline legends the chief texts emerge as the *Passienbüchlein von den vier Hauptjungfrauen*, Johannes von Hildesheim's *Historia trium regum*, and legends from the Cologne humanist circle. The particular local interest, which has implications for other cities, is found in the pilgrimage associations of printed texts, while the legend of the Magi whose relics the city possessed is shown to have implications for local politics and exemplification of the encomiastic *laudes urbium* tradition. Cornelia Epping-Jäger, *Die Inszenierung der Schrift. Der Literalisierungsprozeß und die Entstehungsge-schichte des Dramas*, Stuttgart, M & P, 558 pp. (see below, p. 775), includes a communicative approach to the *Belial*, Heinrich Steinhöwel, Niklas von Wyle, and other literature from the end of the period. Albrecht Classen, *The German Volksbuch. A Critical History of a Late-Medieval Genre* (SGLL, 15), 1995, ix + 302 pp., is a useful account of the present state of knowledge of the somewhat fluid form. The first part of the study consists of a large number of concise but informative and well-documented statements about numerous aspects of the definition, popularity, readers, printers, themes, style, structure, 19th-c. rediscovery, and the like, concluding with a list of desiderata. The second chapter is a survey of scholarly research from A. W. Schlegel to the present day, the outlines of which are of interest for many other forms of literature. Finally, C. discusses in more detail Thüring von Ringoltingen's *Melusine*, *Fortunatus*, *Till Eulenspiegel*, and the *Historia von D. Johann Fausten* as individual representatives of the genre. Id., *WW*, 46:1–20, surveys the instructive history of the controversial term *Volksbuch*. G. Nocker, *Akten* (Sterzing), 181–92, studies humanist poetry at the Innsbruck court, and A. Karnein, *MH*, 22, 1995:141–70, characterizes Mechthild von der Pfalz as a patroness, while J. Theisen, *WS XIV*, 294–322, takes a broad-brush approach to the translation activity of the early humanists, and C. Bertelsmeier-Kierst, *ib.*, 323–43, focuses specifically on *Griseldis*. W. Schneider-Lastin, *ZDA*, 125:187–201, presents the codicological evidence of a 15th-c. German translation of Christine de Pizan from Berne, and U. von Bloh, *WS XIV*, 265–93, discusses the 15th-c. Heidelberg translation of *Reinolt von Montalban* and other Dutch works. E. Timm, *Akten* (Vancouver), 1, 60–75, records Yiddish literature in the Italian Renaissance from 1474 on. A facsimile edition of Heinrich Steinhöwel, *Der Ulmer Aesop von 1476/77. Aesops Leben und Fabeln sowie Fabeln und Schwänke anderer Herkunft*, Ludwigsburg, Libri Illustri, 1995, is accompanied by a commentary by Peter Amelung. B. Derendorf, *NdW*, 36:167–82, outlines the tradition of the Low German *Historien-bibel VIII*.

Nine Robijntje Miedema, *Die 'Mirabilia Romae'. Untersuchungen zu ihrer Überlieferung mit Edition der deutschen und niederländischen Texte* (MTU, 108), x + 589 pp., is a major contribution on the neglected text consisting of a description of Classical buildings in Rome, a collection of legends of both pagan and Christian orientation, and a guide to the chief sights of the city. The problems associated with the main theories of dating are reviewed, M. cautiously favouring nothing more than a date before the mid-12th-c. *terminus ante quem*. After briefly differentiating three related works designed as pilgrimage guides, M. supplies a monumentally detailed survey of the Latin, German, and Dutch manuscript tradition, accompanied by a briefer account of the transmission in versions in other languages. The edition seeks to reflect both the diversity of the vernacular transmission and its relationship to the Latin. Both long and short versions of the work are presented in a legible text which is accompanied by a substantial body of detailed commentary and studies of the problem of the genre of the work, and of its reception. This is a thoroughly worthy addition to a prestigious series. K. Ridder, *WS XIV*, 231–64, studies aspects of the translation of Sir John Mandeville's travels. *Reisen in reale und mythische Ferne. Reiseliteratur in Mittelalter und Renaissance*, ed. Peter Wunderli (Studia Humaniora, 22), Düsseldorf, Droste, 1993, vi + 270 pp., includes essays by A.-D. von den Brincken (the fourth continent, 16–34), R. Hiestand (the Sinai in travelogues, 76–102), and J. Semmler (the *Navigatio Brendani*, 103–23), besides other work on the wider European context of voyages of discovery, cartography, monstrous beings, etc. A. Simon, *Colloquium* (Bristol), 142–54, surveys the presentation of Eastern peoples in pilgrimage literature, and H. Neumann, *ZGer*, 6:35–46, writes on the theme of the Terrible Valley in late-medieval travel literature, while D. C. Klepper, *FCS*, 15, 1989:209–31, studies the pilgrimage narrative of Count Palatine Ludwig III by John of Frankfurt, and in *GJ*, 71, N. Miedema (99–125) and F. Schanze (126–40) examine the early maps and itineraries of Erhard Etzlaub. Michael Herkenhoff, *Die Darstellung außereuropäischer Welten in Drucken deutscher Offizinen des 15. Jahrhunderts*, Berlin, Akademie, 350 pp., is a Bamberg dissertation which forms an informative compendium of German incunabula including 'geographical' subject-matter. Early printed editions of the standard medieval encyclopaedic works are differentiated both from later travel and pilgrimage literature and from versions of Greek and Latin classics. This clears the ground for studies of large-scale geographical and cosmographical works and those dealing respectively with the Holy Land and Egypt, the Turkish Empire, and the New World. The statistics point to the dominance of Augsburg and Nuremberg and the generally successful classification of the somewhat disparate material places the different types of text in a mutually illuminating perspective.

Literatur, Musik und Kunst im Übergang vom Mittelalter zur Neuzeit. Bericht über Kolloquien der Kommission zur Erforschung der Kultur des Spätmittelalters 1989 bis 1992, ed. Hartmut Boockmann, Ludger Grenzmann, Bernd Moeller, and Martin Staehelin (AAWG, 208), 1995, 470 pp., contains 16 contributions on a range of topics which fit the title of the volume but often have wider interdisciplinary implications. Apart from K. Stackmann on the Meistergesang (see p. 745 above) of greatest literary interest are the studies of F. J. Worstbrock (9–35), who characterizes Konrad Celtis as a humanist whose work marked a total break with, and probably ignorance of, high medieval German literary culture; B. Guthmüller (109–31), who studies the reception of Classical myth and Ovid in particular *c.* 1500 in terms significant for European literature as a whole; and H. Boockmann (301–20), who considers the political and social background to artistic production in Nuremberg in the same period. V. Schupp, *Fest. Steger*, 52–67, comments on Hartmann Schedel's *Weltchronik*, which U. Jochum, *LiLi*, 103:20–34, includes in a discussion of the literary history of the printed book. Horst-Joachim Frank, *Literatur in Schleswig-Holstein*. 1. *Von den Anfängen bis 1700*, Neumünster, Wachholtz, 1995, 624 pp., includes chapters on the Dance of Death and early printing in Lübeck, while G. H. M. Claassens and B. Sternberg, *ZDP*, 115:55–83, edit newly discovered fragments of a Dance of Death from the Kleve area. J. Van Cleve, *Eulenspiegel-Jb.*, 35, 1995:89–106, draws attention to the technological transformation which accompanied the publication of Brant's *Narrenschiff*, the title-page of which is interpreted by J. Theisen, *Euphorion*, 90:62–75, and chapter 13 by W. C. McDonald, *FCS*, 17, 1990: 245–68, while S. Heimann-Seelbach, *Seminar*, 32:95–103, relates it to the trivium. J. Knape, *Colloquium* (Chiemsee), 309–33, documents Brant's activity as a lyric poet, and prints an appendix of texts, while H. Plard, pp. 223–38 of *La satire humaniste. Actes du colloque international des 31 mars, 1er et 2 avril 1993*, ed. Rudolf de Smet, Louvain, Peeters, 1994, 266 pp., notes his criticism of voyages of discovery, and D. Wuttke, *HL*, 43, 1994:106–31, his understanding of Siamese twins. Dietmar Benkartek, *Ein interpretierendes Wörterbuch der Nominalabstrakta im 'Narrenschiff' Sebastian Brants von Abenteuer bis Zwietracht*, Frankfurt, Lang, 449 pp. J. L. Flood, *AGB*, 45, 1995:283–334, makes a substantial contribution to the translation and reception of *Reynke de Vos*.

THE SIXTEENTH CENTURY

By PETER MACARDLE, *University of Durham*

1. GENERAL

BIBLIOGRAPHY

Michael A. Pegg, *A Catalogue of German Reformation Pamphlets (1516–1550) in Swedish Libraries* (Bibliotheca Bibliographica Aureliana, 150), Baden-Baden, Koerner, 1995, xii + 182 pp. Louis Schlaefli, *Catalogue des livres du seizième siècle (1531–1599) de la bibliothèque du Grand Séminaire de Strasbourg* (Bibliotheca Bibliographica Aureliana, 149), Baden-Baden, Koerner, 1995, 676 pp., reveals the richness of this collection. *Bibliotheca Dissidentium. Répertoire des non-conformistes religieux des seizième et dix-septième siècles.* XVII. Frank Muller, *Jacob Kautz.* Stephen Boyd, *Pilgram Marpeck, Hans Schlaffer, Leonhard Schiemer* (Bibliotheca Bibliographica Aureliana, 146), Baden-Baden, Koerner, 1995, 124 pp., is a concise bibliographical treatment of these four significant radicals, variously influenced by Anabaptist thought. The lists of MSS and printed works, and of secondary literature, are supplemented by facsimiles, summaries and selective translations, and helpful suggestions for future research. Disappointingly, Kautz's MS writings are cited in modern editions, without their original library and archive locations. Sachiko Kusukawa, *A Wittenberg University Library Catalogue of 1536* (Libri Pertinentes, 3), Cambridge, LP Publications, 1995, xli + 258 pp., prints the 'volume' and author catalogues of that library of 1536; in the former list (1–167) she identifies many items from the collection now in Jena. An introduction includes information on the formation of the Wittenberg collection (xi–xix). In *BSRS*, 13, 1995:10–14, K. writes on the same library. V. Honemann, *Pirckheimer Jb.*, 11:15–34, examines the subjects and functions of single-sheet prints; S. Griese, *ib.*, 43–69, investigates contemporary collectors and copiers of such prints. H. Vögel, *Daphnis*, 24, 1995:455–59, infers the existence of a lost edition of *Kaiser Octavian*. M. Bärmann, *ib.*, 25:645–66, identifies recently-discovered fragments of 16th-c. German texts.

2. HUMANISM AND THE REFORMATION

Erika Rummel, *The Humanist-Scholastic Debate in the Renaissance and Reformation*, Harvard U. P., 1995, 249 pp., criticizes recent scholarship for playing down the degree of hostility between these two intellectual movements. R. interestingly suggests that individual 'humanists' and 'scholastics' are best defined in terms of their respective 'cultural affiliations', their attitudes to a set of key questions such as the value of the Classics for Christian education and for theology, and the role of philology in biblical exegesis (p. 14). Though the two factions did indeed coexist reasonably happily in Italy in the earlier Renaissance, R. argues, in the Northern Europe of the 16th c. they were very much in conflict, largely over the place of humanism in university curricula; this developed into the hostilities of the Reformation. R. investigates in particular detail the crucial disagreement between the factions over whether Aristotelian logic was the only appropriate mode of academic argumentation, or whether less formal, rhetorically based modes of argumentation could be adapted to the task, as many humanists such as R. Agricola and Melanchthon attempted to do. This is an important book whose argument is backed up by a wealth of quotations from a wide variety of humanist and scholastic sources, many refreshingly unfamiliar. Armin Sieber, *Deutsche Rhetorikterminologie in Mittelalter und früher Neuzeit* (Saecvla Spiritalia, 32), Baden-Baden, Koerner, 351 pp. Beginning with Notker Labeo and ending with W. Ratke (1619), this study of the development of vernacular rhetorical terminology includes two 16th-c. works, F. Riederer's *Spiegel der wahren Rhetorik* and O. Fuchsperger's *Kunst der wahren Dialectica*. In the historical part of the study (43–203) the treatises are singly analysed; the systematic part (205–85) generalizes the results, on the level of lexis, syntax, and communication. Overall, a lack of continuity in the development of vernacular rhetorical terms is shown. The formation of new words, especially abstract nouns, is, as might be expected, frequent; composite words, however, are relatively few, as are loan translations, except in the discussion of *figurae*. The increase in nominal forms contributes to the development of a communicatively more effective syntax. By contrast with other areas of vocabulary, though, German rhetorical terminology has not, even by the 17th c., succeeded in freeing itself completely from Latin, and Latin marginalia continue to play an important part in German texts. J. Theibault, *CGP*, 23, 1995:65–78, compares peasant rhetoric in the *Bauernkrieg* and the Thirty Years' War. The compendious *850 Jahre Prämonstratenserabtei Weißenau 1145–1995*, ed. Helmut Binder, Sigmaringen, Thorbecke, 1995, 579 pp., contains several essays of 16th-c. interest. G. Wieland's prosopographical sketch of the monastery from foundation to secularization (119–77), which deals in detail with the 15th and 16th cs (140–47), shows that the Reformation induced not a few of the monks to leave the abbey. F.-J. Merk (179–93) examines the work of Johannes Mayer of Ummendorf, abbot 1495–1523; several aspects of his activity suggest the influence of humanism. The career of Mayer's successor, the historian and patron of the arts Jacob Murer, is assessed by P. Eitel (195–218), who concentrates on M.'s reaction to the *Bauernkrieg*. T. Brüggemann (481–88) examines a copy of the Catholic controversialist Jakob Feucht's *Kinder Postill* (1579) which formerly belonged to the monastery library, while H. Binder (489–505) follows what traces can be found of the fate of the library's holdings, particularly its printed books, after their dispersal in 1802.

3. GENRES

DRAMA AND DIALOGUE

Deutsche Spiele und Dramen des 15. und 16. Jahrhunderts, ed. Hellmut Thomke (Bibliothek der Frühen Neuzeit, 2), DKV, 1186 pp. Most of the 15 plays come from the 16th c., from Gengenbach to Ferdinand II von Tirol; a selection reflecting the volume's aims of including plays of quality, representing the various German 'literarische Landschaften' and *Schriftsprachen* and illustrating the development of the genre. The edition is most satisfactory, with minimal editorial interference; original illustrations are reproduced. The commentary (899–1150) discusses textual problems where necessary (e.g. on Manuel, 996–1002). There are sections on each playwright, reflecting up-to-date research, and a concise *Stellenkommentar*. The bibliography judiciously mixes the best of the old (sometimes very old) and the most recent studies. This is an eminently usable collection, beautifully produced, which preserves scholarly exactitude whilst presenting material in an accessible form. J. A. Parente, Jr, *ColGer*, 29:1–11, writes on later Strasbourg school drama.

PROSE AND VERSE

Bernd Moeller and Karl Stackmann, *Städtische Predigt in der Frühzeit der Reformation. Eine Untersuchung deutscher Flugschriften der Jahre 1522 bis 1529* (AAWG, 220), 383 pp., examines 35 representative printed sermons, reproduced (23–196) using a combinination of paraphrase and selective direct quotation. The second part (197–360) submits the texts to analysis of various kinds. The authors' biographical details are examined (197–221). Generic questions regarding *Flugschriften*, particularly sermons, are treated, as well as questions of literary form (222–53). Punctuation, syntax and other features affecting the legibility of the texts are considered in detail (254–83), as is the use of biblical quotation (283–99). The eschatologically-charged theology of the sermons is clearly characterized (300–50). The results (summarized 351–60) largely corroborate what has already been learnt about the period rather than bringing new insights, but such corroboration is valuable. The centrality of preaching to the spread of the

Reformation, the fact that the impetus came from mature members of the Catholic 'establishment': such insights emerge very clearly from the texts. The uniformity of the religious message preached in this early period is undeniable; this fact controverts the thesis of an early Reformation doctrinal heterogeneity championed by some scholars. Bärbel Schwitzgebel, *Noch nicht genug der Vorrede. Zur Vorrede volkssprachiger Sammlungen von Exempeln, Fabeln, Sprichwörtern und Schwänken des 16. Jahrhunderts* (FN, 28), xii + 239 pp., studies the forewords of Protestant 'Kompilationsliteratur': exempla (11–56), fables (57–97), proverbs (98–117), *Schwänke* (118–41), and *Schwankromane* (142–73), setting them not only in the context of the works they introduce but in that of other forewords. The foreword is seen to be a semi-independent text, often concerned less with the actual work it introduces than with legitimizing the *Textsorte* to which the text belongs, as with collections of fables (p. 92). Frequently it is so fixated on situating the work in question in a familiar generic tradition that it ignores individual or innovative aspects of the work itself. Forewords contain much informative reflection on the nature and function of literature — for instance, in the case of the *Schwankroman*, on the dietetically beneficial effects of humorous writing (p. 172). In the case of fables, the forewords actually constitute the 16th-c. theory of the genre (p. 193). They frequently emphasize the didactic effect of works to the extent of ignoring their entertaining elements. An appendix (pp. 197–227) prints a collection of 11 forewords from representative texts. Martin Ehrenfeuchter, *Aspekte des zeitgenössischen Zauberglaubens in Dichtungen des 16. Jahrhunderts* (EH, 1, 1581), 264 pp., considers the ways in which 16th-c. thought on witchcraft and magic found expression in literature, particularly the work of J. Pauli (*Schimpf und Ernst*), H. Sachs, and H. W. Kirchhof (*Wendunmuth*), representing the entire chronological spread of the century. Especially interesting is E.'s distinction between the attitudes of the three authors (pp. 179–225). In contrast to Kirchhof, who believed in witches and advocated their execution, Sachs regarded the whole business as 'traum und fantasey' (189); in this rational attitude he seems to have reflected the judicial moderation of Nuremberg magistrates and the theology of A. Osiander. Elisabeth Tiller, *Frau im Spiegel: Die Selben und die Anderen zwischen Welt und Text. Von Herren, Fremden und Frauen, ein 16. Jahrhundert*, 2 vols, Frankfurt, Lang, 668, vi + 669–973 pp., begins with a conspectus of Renaissance developments in art, science, society, and culture (pp. 9–234); then considers the many discourses on women current in 16th-c. Europe (pp. 235–668). These (male) discourses spoke of women as Other — but an Other numerically equal to men and necessary for human existence; this relativized the dominance of men, and opened up spaces for women to originate their own discourses (p. 666). The third major section (pp. 669–841) discusses various forms of female authorship in Italy, France, and Germany. Bloated though the work is, it offers only the briefest survey of 15 German female authors (pp. 814–32), which contains little that is new; and in general T. does not push far enough beyond summarizing extant scholarship. E. Timm, *Akten* (Vancouver), 1, 60–75, compares the Yiddish *Bovobuch* and *Paris und Wiene* to their Italian originals. P. C. M. Dieckow, *Euphorion*, 90: 76–133, summarizes research on later 16th-c. *Prosaerzählsammlungen*. H. Wiegand, *Chloe*, 22, 1995: 119–47, contrasts German and Latin descriptions of a Heidelberg *Schützenfest* of 1554. A. Lötscher, *Daphnis*, 24, 1995: 17–53, identifies syntactic 'Prestigesignale' in 16th-c. German prose. H. Puff, *ib.*, 55–78, studies the 'Sprachkontakt' of Latin and German in grammar books. F. Simler, *ib.*, 185–239, studies 'Doppelformen' in translations of the Rule of St Benedict. G. Hahn, *Acta* (Seeon), 107–17, contrasts the predominantly oral nature of Lutheran hymns with their fixing and dissemination in written form. J. L. Flood, *Colloquium* (Bristol), 335–50, considers the role of songs in the output of German printers. A. Simon, *GLL*, 49: 387–404, discusses 16th-c. publishers' prefaces.

4. OTHER WORK

Jan Harasimowicz, *Kunst als Glaubensbekenntnis. Beiträge zur Kunst- und Kulturgeschichte der Reformationszeit*, Baden-Baden, Koerner, 212 pp., 125 illus. One essay in this collection is published for the first time: an illuminating study of the radical iconographical difference between early Lutheran funerary art and that of the late medieval period (127–43). A second, on 'Protestantische Bild-Wort-Sprache des 16. und 17. Jahrhunderts' (41–81), has been considerably expanded since its first appearance. Another two are printed for the first time in German. Of particular interest is '"Das große Sterben der Kunst" in den Ländern der siegreichen Reformation' (1–24), previously available only in Polish; it explores ways in which the Reformation altered the conditions for the production of religious art, and hence the quantity and kind produced. The intrinsic interest of the essays is increased by the many unfamiliar pictures and sculptures, largely from Silesia, which illustrate them. Andres Betschart, *Zwischen zwei Welten. Illustrationen in Berichten westeuropäischer Jerusalemreisender des 15. und 16. Jahrhunderts*, Würzburg, Königshausen & Neumann, vi + 379 pp., traces the changes which illustrations of journeys to Jerusalem underwent in the period in question. While the earlier images are pictorial symbols of what is perceptible only to the 'inner eye' (p. 221), the later examples reliably depict visible phenomena (p.

152). This relates to changes in the reasons for visiting the city, as pilgrimage gave way to travel for the sake of knowledge; it also reflects the rise of the scientific world-view, and its increasing prominence in travel-writing. With a change of role comes a change of importance: by the 16th c., illustrations have become an essential part of the texts. B. analyses illustrations using a method comparable to Panofsky's 'iconology' (pp. 31–41), and many of his detailed investigations are original and illuminating. The study catalogues 56 illustrated accounts of journeys to the Holy Land, 30 of them German (pp. 245–376). Albert Fischer, *Daniel Specklin aus Straßburg 1536–1589. Festungsbaumeister, Ingenieur und Kartograph*, Sigmaringen, Thorbecke, 227 pp., traces the career of this remarkable Alsatian polymath, city architect of Strasbourg, and fortifications engineer on numerous projects for the Habsburgs. After a sketch of Alsace in the 16th c., and a biography of S. (pp. 17–46), there follow the three main sections on his work in fortification (pp. 56–162), civil engineering (pp. 163–74), and cartography (pp. 175–200), key areas of Renaissance technology to which he made pioneering practical and theoretical contributions (his work on fortification influenced the 17th-c. French school of Vauban). Not the least significant part of the study are the 100 fine reproductions of S.'s plans and drawings, technically interesting and intrinsically beautiful, many previously unpublished. M. Wiesner-Hanks, *JMRS*, 25, 1995:89–106, discusses the gendering of work in German cities. A. Jordan Gschwend, *BSRS*, 13, 1995:1–9, studies Catherine of Austria's *Kunstkammer*. E. Kühebacher, *Akten* (Sterzing), 109–27, investigates dialect and liturgical language in an Innichen sacristan's book.

5. INDIVIDUAL AUTHORS AND TEXTS

AGRIPPA VON NETTESHEIM, HEINRICH CORNELIUS. M. van der Poel, pp. 199–220 of *Le paradoxe en linguistique et en littérature*, ed. Ronald Landheer and Paul J. Smith (HICL, 350), 244 pp., sees the term 'paradoxon' as too imprecise to describe A.'s *De vanitate scientiarum*.

AMERBACH, FAMILY. *Die Amerbachkorrespondenz im Auftrag für die öffentliche Bibliothek der Universitat Basel*, ed. Alfred Hartmann. 10. *Die Briefe aus den Jahren 1556–1558*, ed. Beat Rudolf Jenny. 11, 1. *Juli 1557-Ende 1558*, Basel, Vlg der Universitätsbibliothek, 1995, cxv–cxxxviii + 393–1011 pp., contains the letters for that period, plus addenda to vols 4–10/11, appendices and indexes.

BOTE, HERMANN. Richard Tenberg, *Die deutsche Till Eulenspiegel-Rezeption bis zum Ende des 16. Jahrhunderts*, Würzburg, Königshausen & Neumann, 1995, 234 pp., lists all the editions and adaptations of *T.E.*, and all documents in which it, or the figure of Till, are mentioned, up to the end of the 16th c. The assembled evidence is in many respects highly suggestive: that Till is first alluded to in German humanist correspondence of 1411 implies that B. may have been the compilator rather than the author of the book (pp. 30–37); there are indications of a strong association of humanists with the text, so that a humanist (T. Conradi?) may have been a co-compilator (pp. 59–65); the social and geographical spread of knowledge of Till seems not to depend solely on print but to involve oral tradition (p. 207). T. attempts to sift truth from fiction in his documentary sources. His compendium shows how reactions to Till varied between approval and outright condemnation. It also charts the increasing use of Till in confessional polemic, and even the beginnings of the commercialization of the Till 'heritage' by the end of the 16th c. (pp. 202–03). J. Schulz-Grobert, 'Setzer und Übersetzer. Zum Status potentieller Bearbeiter des "Eulenspiegelbuchs" in Straβburg', *WS XIV*, 344–58.

COCHLAEUS, JOANNES. Joannes Cochlaeus, *Philippicae I-VII*, ed. Ralph Keen, 2 vols (Bibliotheca Humanistica et Reformatorica, 54/1–2), Nieuwkoop, De Graaf, xxiii + 375, vii + 297 pp., is an excellent edition of these controversial anti-Melanchthon Latin poems of the 1530s and 1540s, which together make up C.'s longest polemical work. Vol. 1 contains all the texts, vol. 2 biographical material on C. (pp. 1–10), introductions to the *Philippicae* (pp. 11–66), an exhaustive commentary (pp. 67–188), and appendices of related texts (pp. 205–67). There are copious biblical and general indexes (pp. 269–97). A translation of the poems would have been a helpful addition. A. Laube, *AR*, 87:119–35, writes on C.'s anti-Lutheran polemical partnership with J. Dietenberger.

ECK, JOHANN. M. Schulze, *Lutherjahrbuch*, 63:39–68, considers E. as a serious theologian, rather than as a mere virtuoso debater.

FEICHTER, VEIT. A. Hofmeister, *Akten* (Sterzing), 339–58, proposes a 'dynamic edition' of F.'s MS *Dommesnerbuch* for Brixen Cathedral; W. Hofmeister, *ib.*, 433–41, examines early modern written legal records in F.'s *Urbar*.

FISCHART, JOHANN. U. Seelbach, *Chloe*, 22, 1995:173–84, argues that F.'s *Eulenspiegel reimensweis* (1572) is not simply a 'Grobianized' version of *Till Eulenspiegel*. H. Oelke, *AR*, 87:149–200, studies F.'s polemical exchange with J. Nas (1568–71).

FRANCK, SEBASTIAN. S. Wollgast, 'Zu Sebastian Francks philosophischen Auffassungen', *Daphnis*, 25:221–305. S. Waldhoff, *Zeitschrift für Kirchengeschichte*, 107:327–54, comments on F.'s critique of Bucer's views on authority.

FRISCHLIN, NICODEMUS. N. Kaminski, *Daphnis*, 24, 1995:79–133, investigates the complex uses of *imitatio* in two plays.

GESSNER, CONRAD. Udo Friedrich, *Naturgeschichte zwischen artes liberales und frühneuzeitlicher Wissenschaft. Conrad Gessners 'Historia animalium' und ihre volkssprachliche Rezeption* (FN, 21), 1995, ix + 276 pp., is a detailed analysis of this important encyclopaedic work. The first major section (pp. 25–132) analyses the *Historia* in the context of early modern encyclopaedic discourse, showing how G. shifts about methodologically, selecting different approaches and different kinds of truth for discussion as the occasion demands. His method, situated ambivalently between *philosophia naturalis* and *philosophia moralis*, is fundamentally literary rather than 'scientific'. The second main section (pp. 143–246) considers contemporary German translations of the *Historia*; these are market-driven attempts to reach an undifferentiated mass readership. The Schwenckfeldian Johann Heiden transforms the original into an explicitly Christian 'Exempelbuch' (p. 251), replete with allegorical and emblematical material. The range and density of this study cannot be adequately summarized. It is a most informative contribution to scholarship on early modern scientific writing.

GÖDING, HEINRICH. H.-J. Behr, *Daphnis*, 25:667–80, discusses G.'s poem celebrating the wedding of Duke Heinrich Julius of Brunswick.

GRUMBACH, ARGULA VON. P. Matheson, 'Breaking the silence: women, censorship and the Reformation', *SCJ*, 27:97–109.

HERGOT, HANS. C. Brinker-von der Heyde, *MDU*, 88:298–309, discusses H.'s *Newe Wandlung eines christlichen Lebens*.

HUTTEN, ULRICH VON. V. Honemann, 'Latein und Deutsch bei Ulrich von Hutten', *WS XIV*, 359–76.

LALEBUCH. J. J. Berns, *Chloe*, 22, 1995:149–72, argues that the learned, literary dimension of the work must be given due attention. R. Kalkofen, *Daphnis*, 24, 1995:571–601, examines the 'self-conscious narrator' in the text.

LAMM, MARCUS ZUM. H. Meise, *Acta* (Seeon), 287–306, comments on the critical manipulation of pictorial representations in L.'s *Thesaurus picturarum* (1544–1606).

LEMNIUS, SIMON. Simon Lemnius, *Bucolica. Fünf Eklogen*, ed. and trans. Lothar Mundt (FN, 29), viii + 224 pp. The text of the poems, and the excellent facing German translation, occupy the bulk of this, the first modern edition of a complete collection of Neo-Latin Eclogues. L.'s poems are often panegyrics on princes, patrons, and cities; they have an autobiographical element; and they constantly allude to personalities and events of their time, occasionally in opaque allegorical mode. This dense texture of reference is carefully identified and explained in the commentary (pp. 164–205). Mundt also identifies other interesting features: for instance, the third Eclogue is the only known hodoeporicon in bucolic form. The edition proper is prefaced by material on L.'s biography and the genesis of the *Bucolica* (pp. 1–9), and a particularly informative section on the Neo-Latin Eclogue tradition (pp. 9–54), which, with its *Forschungsbericht* and its summary of the work of 30 German poets, makes a splendid attempt at charting this poorly documented field.

LIPSIUS, JUSTUS. Jacqueline Lagrée, *Juste Lipse. La restauration du stoïcisme. Etude et traduction de divers traités stoïciens*, Paris, Vrin, 1994, lvii + 76 pp. P. Nelles, 'Juste Lipse et Alexandrie: les origines antiquaires de l'histoire des bibliothèques', pp. 224–42 of *Le pouvoir des bibliothèques. La mémoire des livres en Occident*, ed. Marc Baratin and Christian Jacob, Paris, Albin Michel, 338 pp. J. Papy, 'Giusto Lipsio e la superstizione', pp. 445–56 of *L'uomo e la natura nel rinascimento*, ed. Luisa Rotondi Secchi Tarugi, Milan, Nuovi Orizzonti, 562 pp. D. Sacré, *Lias*, 22, 1995:163–73, discusses an unpublished letter to L. from B. Moretus. E. Ulčinaitė, *Acta* (Louvain), 405–22, considers L.'s influence in early modern Lithuania.

LOCHER, JAKOB. W. Ludwig, *Philologus*, 140:163–82, edits letters of L. to W. Reichart praising the humanist ambience of Ingolstadt University.

LUTHER, MARTIN. Hans Jochen Genthe, *Martin Luther. Sein Leben und Denken*, Göttingen, Vandenhoeck & Ruprecht, 343 pp., written for the 1996 *Lutherjahr*, in some respects connects with the reverential tradition of L. biography of an earlier century, but clearly reflects the historical and theological insights of modern ecumenical scholarship. The L. presented here is not one retrospectively canonized by Lutheran triumphalism, but a man of his age, an age largely 'zwischen den Zeiten' (p. 6) and still open to developments foreclosed by subsequent confessionalization. G. gently debunks the vestiges of pious legend which still stubbornly overlie the facts in the popular consciousness. Especially convincing are the detailed and evocative descriptions and analyses of the specifics of 16th-c. life and thought (such as life in the Augustinian order, pp. 46–70), which neither trivialize, demonize nor otherwise distort the medieval Catholicism from which L. sprang. Artur Göser, *Der Hymnus 'Veni redemptor gentium' bei Müntzer und Luther. Exemplarischer Versuch einer ideologiekritischen Textanalyse*, Würzburg, Königshausen & Neumann, 1995, 256 pp., argues that the function of L.'s hymns is misrepresented by traditional hymnology, which has assumed they are designed to fit, indeed to constitute, the reformed liturgy. G. insists that they are also (and more importantly) expressions of L.'s ecclesiological ideology, which is essentially a continuation of the medieval model of the Church as an institution mediating divine truth and grace and demanding human obedience to the divine Word. With this he contrasts M.'s anarchic model: an 'ecclesia futura' of individuals sanctified by the Spirit. A comparative analysis of L.'s 'Nu kom der heyden heyland' and M.'s 'O herr, erloeser alles volcks', both translations of the Ambrosian hymn 'Veni, redemptor gentium' (pp. 107–79) illustrates G.'s contention that the two versions, even in details of lexis and grammar, reflect these conflicting ideologies. *Luthers Deutsch. Sprachliche Leistung und Wirkung*, ed. Herbert Wolf, Frankfurt, Lang, 388 pp., collects 28 carefully selected, significant essays by various hands, covering many aspects of this complex topic. These include the very first contribution on the subject by a Germanist, Paul Pietsch, in 1883 (pp. 31–41), and range into works of the 1990s, so that the book is at once a collection of intrinsically informative essays on L.'s role in the creation of a NHG standard language and a historical documentation of the progress of this area of scholarship. W.'s historical overview (pp. 9–29) contextualizes the individual essays very clearly, and the work is rounded off by a bibliography of over 700 items (pp. 341–87). *Lutherjb.*, 62, 1995, publishes papers on L.'s contribution to thought on liberation and freedom by K.-H. zur Mühlen (48–66), S. Kjeldgaard-Pedersen (67–80), P. Blickle (83–103), M. U. Edwards (104–20), and M. Brecht (121–51). H. Feld, *Lutherjb.*, 63:11–18, concludes that L. was burnt in effigy at Rome in 1521; G. G. Kraus, *ib.*, 69–101, reviews the assertion that L. was an Antinomian; J. E. Vercruysse, *ib.*, 103–28, surveys the modern Catholic image of L., while E. W. Gritsch, *ib.*, 19–38, and B. Stolt, *CGP*, 23, 1995:53–63, examine aspects of L.'s humour. Z. Zlatar, *Parergon*, 14:57–84, argues that the Leipzig Disputation cannot be seen as the definitive moment of L.'s break with Rome. G. L. Dipple, 'L., Emser and the development of Reformation anticlericalism', *AR*, 87:9–37; L. C. Green, *ib.*, 38–56, examines L.'s understanding of 1 Timothy 2. 4. J. L. Flood, *Colloquium* (Bristol), 3–32, situates the theological controversy between L. and Henry VIII in the process of the discovery of England by Germany and vice versa. R. Sammel, 'The *Passio Lutheri*: parody as hagiography', *JEGP*, 95:157–74.

MELANCHTHON, PHILIPP. Olaf Berwald, *Philipp Melanchthons Sicht der Rhetorik* (Gratia, 25), Wiesbaden, Harrassowitz, vii + 172 pp., is an admirably clear and compact summary of M.'s views on the importance of rhetoric, views expressed in M.'s rhetorical manuals and also in a wide variety of other texts. Anthropologically, M. sees communication as constitutive of community; politically, rhetoric is the foundation of a legal system which is the only protection against tyrannical rule. Political conflict often results from rhetorical incompetence. B. carefully documents M.'s ideas on desiderata for the 16th-c. *vir bonus* (pp. 31–49), on the *affectus* (pp. 50–56), on the importance of *exercitatio* (pp. 87–95), and on *imitatio* (pp. 57–86), where he is seen to value Greek authors especially highly beside the supreme model, Cicero. A useful bibliography of M.'s many writings which touch on rhetoric (pp. 100–42) is included. B. Bauer, *Rhetorica*, 14:37–71, shows how M.'s rhetorical idealism was sadly abused in the *Realpolitik* of interconfessional discussion. C. J. Classen, pp. 297–321 of *The Passionate Intellect. Essays on the Transformation of Classical Traditions Presented to Professor I. G. Kidd*, ed. Lewis Ayres, New Brunswick–London, Transaction Publishers, 1995, xvi + 376 pp., evaluates M.'s use of rhetorical categories in biblical exegesis. C. Methuen, 'The role of the heavens in the thought of Philip Melanchthon', *JHI*, 57:385–403. J. Helm, *Medizinhistorisches Jb.*, 31:298–321, examines M.'s reception of Galen.

MURNER, THOMAS. H. Langer, *Chloe*, 22, 1995:103–18, relates the complex interplay of preaching and satire in M.'s work to his 'heikle Persönlichkeitsstruktur'.

NEMIUS, IOANNES. Martin M. Winkler, *Der lateinische Eulenspiegel des Ioannes Nemius. Text und Übersetzung, Kommentar und Untersuchung* (FN, 24), 1995, vi + 346 pp. The *Triumphus humanae stultitiae*, the first Latin verse translation of *Till Eulenspiegel*, was written in 1558 by N., an Erasmian priest and schoolmaster. As W. points out, N.'s version adapted Till to the more exalted expectations of a Latinate readership, and made him palatable to humanist tastes. This is a carefully produced edition, with a fluent German translation, and a full commentary on factual, linguistic and stylistic points (pp. 178–240) as well as material on N.'s life and work (pp. 5–53). There are thorough sections on the text's major *topoi* of divine wisdom versus human folly, the *mundus inversus*, and *memento mori* (pp. 241–76); and on the way in which N. adapted the ambivalent original in a moralizing and allegorical spirit, producing a simpler and more coherent moral statement (pp. 276–86). A documentation of parallels to Till in Antiquity (pp. 286–325) completes a very useful addition to the corpus of edited Neo-Latin writing.

PARACELSUS. *Analecta Paracelsica. Studien zum Nachleben Theophrast von Hohenheims im deutschen Kulturgebiet der frühen Neuzeit*, ed. Joachim Telle, Stuttgart, Steiner, 1994, xv + 591 pp., contributes richly to the study of the influence of P.'s thought. Several essays discuss little-known Paracelsians, usually with primary bibliographies and calendars or editions of letters or other works. Such figures are Gerhard Dorn (D. Kahn, 59–126); Franz Krell (T. Lederer, 149–66), Georg Baldinus (W.-D. Müller, 213–304), Johannes Scerbecius (P. Voswinckel, 305–34), and Christoph Weickhart (H. Pfefferl, 407–28). J. Paulus (335–406) details 70 others. S. Limbeck (1–58) edits Peter Payngk's *Rhapsodia vitae Theophrasti Paracelsi*, J. Telle (167–212) the 16th-c. alchemical poem 'Vom Stein der Weisen'.

C. D. Gunnoe (127–48) writes on T. Erastus's anti-Paracelsian circle; C. Gilly (425–88) considers the extent to which Paracelsianism became a fully-fledged religion; R. G. Bogner (489–530) details Paracelsian passages placed on the Index; K. Pfister (531–40) writes on P. in several early modern astrological treatises; and W. Kühlmann (541–56) discusses J. C. Adelung's biography of P. For all its diversity this is a well balanced and focused volume, uniformly high in quality and constituting an important addition to our knowledge of German Paracelsianism. H. Rudolph, *CGP*, 22, 1994:106–20, considers the influence of 1 Corinthians 15 on P.'s thought. I. Kästner, *Sudhoffs Archiv*, 79, 1995:115–19, writes on K. Sudhoff's collection of books relating to P. Also noted: *Paracelsus. Das Werk — Die Rezeption, ed. Volker Zimmermann, Stuttgart, Steiner, 1995, 227 pp., containing 13 contributions.

REICHART, WOLFGANG. W. Ludwig, *Daphnis*, 24, 1995:263–99, illustrates the suppression by Lutheran authorities of humanist expression in R.'s epitaphs.

REUCHLIN, JOHANNES. Johannes Reuchlin, *Sämtliche Werke*. 1, 1. *De verbo mirifico. Das wundertätige Wort*, ed. Widu-Wolfgang Ehlers et al., Stuttgart-Bad Cannstatt, Frommann-Holzboog, xv + 447 pp., inaugurates this important 11-volume project, the first-ever complete scholarly R. edition. It is being produced by an interdisciplinary team, in recognition both of R.'s seminal position in several fields and of the improbability of any single discipline taking on such a project. The text of this treatise on the significance of the name of God (IHVH) is based on the editions printed in R.'s lifetime (pp. 413–25), with minimal editorial intervention (pp. ix–x). The facing German translation has been kept as close to the original as possible, even in syntax and word order, the better to give a flavour of the Latin and to indicate its structures (p. 425); nonetheless, it is reasonably fluent and readable. Both aesthetically and in terms of workmanship the edition is superb. The major disadvantage is that the second part of the volume, containing the detailed commentary which will contextualize and explicate this demanding work, is yet to appear and will, it is hinted (pp. xi, xiv), take some time to do so. Johannes Reuchlin, *L'arte cabbalistica (De arte cabalistica)*, trans. and ed. Giulio Busi and Saverio Campanini (Eurasiatica, 38), Florence, Opus Libri, 1995, lxx + 292 pp. Hans Peterse, *Jacobus Hoogstraeten gegen Johannes Reuchlin. Ein Beitrag zur Geschichte des Antijudaismus im 16. Jahrhundert* (Veröffentlichungen des Instituts für europäische Geschichte Mainz, Abteilung abendländische Religionsgeschichte, 165), Mainz, von Zabern, 1995, viii + 194 pp., is a detailed and lucid reconsideration of the R. Affair, views of which are still too strongly conditioned by the *Epistolae obscurorum virorum*. P. carefully reviews the whole sweep of events, paying particular attention to Hoogstraeten, whose views and motivations he examines precisely and dispassionately. H. emerges not as a bigot but as free from personal animus and genuinely concerned that the legitimation of the Talmud or Kabbalah as theological sources would compromise established hermeneutical method. P. also argues convincingly that humanist-scholastic conflict, played down in recent historical views, was significant, as for instance the dissemination of G. Benigno's *Defensio* of R. by Hermann von Neuenahr's humanist circle suggests.

RHENANUS, BEATUS. F. Fuchs, pp. 27–30 of *Lebendige Antike. Rezeptionen der Antike in Politik, Kunst und Wissenschaft der Neuzeit. Kolloquium für Wolfgang Schiering*, ed. Reinhard Stupperich, Mannheim, Palatium, 1995, 223 pp., considers R. as a collector of inscriptions. R. Walter, *Annuaire des amis de la bibliothèque humaniste de Sélestat*, 46 : 67–72, studies R.'s role in the 16th-c. rediscovery of Tacitus. M. Reeve, 'Beatus Rhenanus and the lost Vormaciensis of Livy', *RHTe*, 25, 1995 : 217–54.

SACHS, HANS. Hans Sachs, *Werke in der Reihenfolge ihrer Entstehung*, ed. Wolfgang A. Michael and Roger A. Crockett, 3 vols, Berne, Lang, 321, 375, 256 pp., frees S.'s works from the labyrinthine arrangement in the Keller-Goetze edition, in order to trace the chronological development of S.'s views and literary skill. For this selective edition the editors have chosen material which will be 'ansprechend und sinnvoll' for modern readers (1, 8), a debatable criterion; nonetheless, a wide range of genres is presented. The text follows S.'s own *Folioausgabe*, with minimal editorial intervention. Each text is followed by a brief historical and stylistic commentary. Unfortunately, footnotes are not always entirely satisfactory, especially in the case of Latin material, and the German of some commentaries is marred by major errors in grammar and idiom. Cornelia Epping-Jäger, *Die Inszenierung der Schrift. Der Literalisierungsprozeß und die Entstehungsgeschichte des Dramas*, Stuttgart, M & P, 558 pp., situates S.'s drama in the transition from medieval oral culture to the literacy of modern times. It argues that S. belongs to the intermediate stage of 'Hypoliteralität', when a not fully literate public was developing a demand for kinds of knowledge enshrined in books. Hence many of the habitual criticisms of S.'s drama (unoriginality, weak psychology, formal defects) miss the point that the plays are primarily 'frühneuhochdeutsche Übersetzungsliteratur' (p. 405): the playwright is still tied to the (written) original he is trying to communicate; the audience, eager for the content of written culture, is still limited by the structures of orality, incapable of approaching the written original on its own terms. An extended analysis of the ways in which S.'s *Comedia von der Griselda* mediates between Boccaccio's original tale and the expectations of the 'hypoliteral' German public (pp. 454–516) convincingly illustrates the central thesis. *Hans Sachs and Folk Theatre in the Late Middle Ages. Studies in the History of Popular Culture*, ed. Robert Aylett and Peter Skrine, Lewiston–Queenston–Lampeter, Mellen, xiv + 224 pp., carries on the venerable tradition of British S. scholarship. F. Shaw (1–18) considers S. as a character in Wagner's *Meistersinger*; M. Rogers (19–42) analyses the comedy of the *Fastnachtspiele* as a complex 'game with expectations'; P. Broadhead (43–62) examines the contribution of the dialogues to public debate on the Reformation; B. Murdoch (63–81) comments on S.'s dramatizations of early chapters of Genesis; P. Skrine (83–103) offers a positive re-evaluation of four plays on classical subjects; D. Blamires (105–37) analyses the recurring pattern of the 'victime heroine' in the dramas; J. L. Flood (139–65) discusses some aspects of S.'s adaptations of Boccaccio; J. West (169–86) concludes that the use of compound words may be a significant stylistic feature of S.'s dramatic writing; J. E. Tailby (187–95) relates the *Fastnachtspiele* to the 15th-c. Nuremberg tradition; and R. Aylett (197–224) examines S.'s dramatizations of episodes from *Till Eulenspiegel*. *Pirckheimer Jb.*, 10, 1995, is given over to essays on Sachs. N. Holzberg (9–29) comments on the 'tragedi' of the Horatii and Curiatii; E. Bernstein (31–45) considers S. as 'teutscher tichter'; J. Knape (47–81) analyses the *Meisterlied* adaptation of a story from the *Decameron*; U. Feuerstein and P. Schwarz (83–107) examine the *Meisterlieder* of the year 1546; A. Wingen-Trennhaus (109–49) studies S.'s literary sources in Nuremberg; A. Dortmund (151–55) writes on S.'s adaptation of Terence's *Eunuchus*; A. Schmidt (157–87) gives an informative account of 19th-c. and 20th-c. S. monuments and S. commemoration in Nuremberg. D. Katritzky, *GLL*, 49:32–41, deals with the 18th-c. reception of Sachs. W. A. Coupe, *CGP*, 22, 1994:46–53, analyses the text-image relationship in three broadsheets with texts by S.

SAPIDUS, JOHANNES. P. Schäffer, *Annuaire des amis de la bibliothèque humaniste de Sélestat*, 46:81–98, translates and comments on S.'s *Paraclesis* (1543).

SCHWENCKFELD, CASPAR. R. Emmet McLaughlin, *The Freedom of Spirit, Social Privilege, and Religious Dissent. Caspar Schwenckfeld and the Schwenkfelders* (Bibliotheca Dissidentium, Scripta et Studia, 6), Baden-Baden, Koerner, 271 pp., collects nine already published essays: the last (233–54), detailing the long 'standoff' between Schwenkfelders and official Reformers in Strasbourg, appeared in 1994. In a newly-written introduction (9–35), McL. draws the various studies together into a narrative tracing the development of S.'s theology. He emphasizes its roots in late-medieval Catholicism, which he argues was in many respects Spiritualist in orientation (p. 17). The particular importance of V. Crautwald as an influence on S. is explored (pp. 19–24); and ways in which S. has affected the course of subsequent radical and liberal Protestantism are discussed.

SLEIDAN, JOHANN. L. Druez, 'L'humaniste Jean Sleidan: de la diplomatie à l'histoire', *Cahiers de Clio*, 123, 1995 : 15–32.

STURM, JOHANN. Lewis W. Spitz and Barbara Sher Tinsley, *Johann Sturm on Education: the Reformation and Humanist Learning*, St Louis, Concordia, 1995, 429 pp., supplements English translations of eight of S.'s key educational treatises (pp. 61–339) with a biography and analysis of S.'s pedagogical method (pp. 19–60), a review of the reception of S.'s thinking by his contemporaries (pp. 341–63), and copious notes (pp. 365–415). R. Walter, *Annuaire des amis de la bibliothèque humaniste de Sélestat*, 46 : 73–80, writes on S.'s biography of B. Rhenanus.

TREITZSAUERWEIN, MARCUS. E. Koller, *Akten* (Sterzing), 293–321, demonstrates how T. adapts a report of the wooing of the Portuguese Princess Leonor for the *Weißkunig*.

TRITHEMIUS, JOHANNES. T. Ernst, *Daphnis*, 25 : 1–205, deciphers T.'s cryptological work, the *Steganographia*.

ULSENIUS, THEODERICUS. C. G. Santing, *Sudhoffs Archiv*, 79, 1995 : 138–49, studies U.'s work on syphilis.

VADIAN, JOACHIM. S. Füssel, *Pirckheimer Jb.*, 11 : 7–14, edits *In artis impressoriae laudem* (1511).

WALDIS, BURKARD. Ludger Lieb, *Erzählen an den Grenzen der Fabel. Studien zum 'Esopus' des Burkard Waldis* (Mikrokosmos, 47), Frankfurt, Lang, 1995, 325 pp., reassesses W.'s tendency to narrative digression from the basic stories of the fables he adapts from Aesop. L. argues that W., like La Fontaine, plays with the genre of the fable: the huge variety of ways in which he renarrates the Aesopic material does not reflect any single approach or intention, but rather a fascination with forms and possibilities of narration showing a sophistication unusual in early modern writing. W.'s use of different kinds of fiction occasionally reaches amazing levels of intricacy which push the form of the fable to its limits. This complex study addresses a neglected author, and pushes W. studies well beyond the positivism in which they were stranded in the 19th and early 20th cs.

WICKRAM, GEORG. Elisabeth Wåghäll, *Dargestellte Welt — Reale Welt. Freundschaft, Liebe und Familie in den Prosawerken Georg Wickrams*, Berne, Lang, 286 pp., measures the world depicted in W.'s narratives against the real world of his time, concluding that the treatment of love, friendship, marriage and family life is initially rooted in the late-medieval courtly ethos, but later increasingly reflects the urban burgher world of the 16th c. Particularly the late *Von guten und bösen Nachbarn* depicts a bourgeoisie whose dominant values are security and rectitude. The novels do not imitate reality, but represent a world which should be imitated. Most interesting, perhaps, is the section where W.'s religious ideals are shown to reflect Erasmian and Bucerian thought (pp. 55–79). The compact study deals with some complex topics very briskly indeed (e.g. love in medieval literature, pp. 157–61). But the detailed analysis of individual works is valuable. S. Pastenaci, *WRM*, 19, 1995:49–58, compares *Gabriotto und Reinhard* and *Der Goldfaden*. A. Masser, 'Georg Wickram und der Beginn des bürgerlichen Romans', Thurnher, *Vorträge*, 63–73.

ZELL, KATHARINA. M. H. Jung, *Zeitschrift für Theologie und Kirche*, 107:145–78, considers Z. as 'Laientheologin'.

ZIMMERN, FROBEN CHRISTOPH VON. G. Wolf, *Acta* (Seeon), 381–405, studies 'inszenierte Wirklichkeit und literarische Aufführung' in the *Zimmerische Chronik*.

THE SEVENTEENTH CENTURY

By JILL BEPLER, *Herzog August Bibliothek, Wolfenbüttel*

1. GENERAL

The reference work *German Baroque Writers, 1580–1660 and German Baroque Writers, 1661–1730*, ed. James Hardin (Dictionary of Literary Biography, 164, 168), 2 vols, Gale Research, Detroit–Washington–London, 389, 421 pp., contains bio-bibliographical essays on the standard major literary figures of the period, including a few figures not necessarily usually noted for their literary prowess, such as Leibniz. The volumes provide an excellent introductory survey aimed at an audience not necessarily conversant with the German language. Brenner, *Literaturgeschichte*, 25–48, gives a brief summary of developments in German literature during the period, seeing the courts as new centres of literary activity and the era as characterized by the tension between a need for codification of rules both in politics and in literature and the chaos of the atrocities of the Thirty Years' War. B. identifies Opitz, Gryphius, and Grimmelshausen as the main protagonists. Mara Wade, *Triumphus Nuptialis Danicus. German Court Culture and Denmark. The 'Great Wedding' of 1634* (WAB, 27), 443 pp., 150 illus., examines the festival and literary production associated with the Danish-Saxon marriage alliance of 1634, the most splendid festival held in Europe during the Thirty Years' War. W.'s study illustrates how deeply connected Danish and German culture were during the 17th c., both due to the political ties which meant that the Danish King was a prince of the Empire and to a long tradition of Danish intermarriage with German dynasties. Copenhagen had both a Danish and a German Chancellery throughout the period and Latin, German, and Danish were the languages of its cultural manifestations. W. places the 1634 festivities in the context of Danish court culture from the latter part of the 16th c., showing the influences and developments which led to the ballets, comedies, fireworks and pageants celebrating the wedding. In particular W. highlights the roles played by Martin Opitz, Johann Lauremberg, and Heinrich Schütz. This wide-ranging investigation brings a much-needed realization of the North-European fabric of German culture in the period and further corrects the misconception of German festival culture as solely dependent on models from France and Italy. A. Carrdus, '*Thränen-Tüchlein für christliche Eltern*: consolation books for bereaved parents in 16th and 17th century Germany', *GLL*, 49:1–17, looks at the much-neglected devotional works published in such enormous quantities during the 17th c. She uses these manuals of consolation to reveal the erroneous perception of the era as lacking emotional parental bonding and, concentrating on a work by Sigismund Scherertz, shows how personal experience is generalized to provide exemplary models for dealing with private grief. J. R. Paas, 'Inseparable muses. German Baroque poets as graphic artists', *ColGer*, 29:13–38, uncovers the tip of an iceberg in looking at the artistic activities of certain German writers of the 17th c., recalling that both Castiglione and Henry Peacham considered drawing skill essential to the education of a gentleman. P. concentrates mainly on Nuremberg and the work of Anton Ulrich of Braunschweig-Lüneburg, Sigmund von Birken, and Karl Gustav von Hille, and gives a listing of extant engravings based on sketches by authors. P. stresses the central role of mimetic representation in poetry and in painting in the 17th c., reflected in the story of the competition between Zeuxis and Parrhasios, Greek artists of Classical antiquity, to produce *trompe l'oeil* paintings. A. Herz, 'Der Hase des Zeuxis: von Sandrart über Birken zu Harsdörffer. Harsdörffers unbekannter *Discurs Von der edlen Mahlerey*', *Daphnis*, 25:387–422, alludes to the same story and unfolds a fascinating series of deductions which have led to the identification of Harsdörffer as the author of a hitherto unnoticed treatise on painting, in which the inextricable links between poetry and the visual arts are expounded. *Ob die Weiber Menschen seyn, oder nicht?*, ed. Elisabeth Gössmann (Archiv für philosophische und theologiege-schichtliche Frauenforschung, 4), Munich, Iudicium, 398 pp., is a very useful compendium of texts associated with the question of the intellectual standing attributed to women in the early modern period. Each text is introduced by a commentary and annotated. Williams, *Knowledge*, contains the proceedings of a conference investigating the interaction of discourses of knowledge in the early modern period. G. F. Strasser, 'Science and pseudoscience: Athanasius Kircher's *Mundus Subterraneus* and his *Scrutinum … Pestis*', *ib.*, 219–40, investigates the specific parameters of Jesuit writing on science. J. A. Parente, Jr., 'Carnal knowledge: writing about sex in early modern Germany', *ib.*, 243–61, looks mainly at the factors which have hitherto led modern Germanists to ignore the sexual implications of Baroque texts, seeing the Humanist predilection for erotic poetry as part of the discourse on desire and its control in the period. Garber, *Sozietätsbewegung*, contains the proceedings of a mammoth conference on European academies which took place in Paris in 1989. The years which have elapsed since the conference inevitably mean that a few contributions have been superseded, which in no way lessens the value of the volumes as an impressive compendium to a central aspect of early modern intellectual history.

S. Wollgast, 'Zu Joachim Jungius' *Societas ereunetica.* Quellen — Statuten — Mitglieder — Wirkungen', *ib.*, 1179–1229, sketches the character of the early scientific academy founded by J. and its connections with Italian academies, the Rosicrucian circle of Johann Valentin Andreae, with Hartlib and Durie in England, and those German Protestant princes engaged in the formation of the Fruchtbringende Gesellschaft. Correcting recent concentration on the idea of the latter as purely academy-based, G. Hoppe, 'Traditions- und Spannungsfelder um die Fruchtbringende Gesellschaft im Spiegel ihres Alltags (1617–1629)', *ib.*, 1230–60, sees the knightly oders of earlier centuries as one of the traditions from which the Fruchtbringende Gesellschaft originated, thus explaining the relatively high number of noble *illiterati* in its ranks, members for whom there is no record of cultural activity or even interest. Via Prince Ludwig's correspondence with Christian of Anhalt H. traces the society's links to Italian academies and explores the social and religious framework of its early membership. M. Bircher, 'Die späte Fruchtbringende Gesellschaft und ihre Ständeordnung. Zu einem unbekannten Schulactus, Breslau 1670', *ib.*, 1261–85, looks at the civic context of the work of the later members of the society as reflected in Wende's Silesian school drama, since edited by Bircher in 1991. E. Pietrzak, 'Schlesier in den deutschen Sprachgesellschaften des 17. Jahrhunderts', *ib.*, 1286–1319, explores the role of Silesian writers in the three main German language societies, most of whom came from very modest backgrounds. P. sees Silesia's special political and patriotic literary tradition as one reason why prominent poets from the region did not see the necessity of vying for membership. R. Jürgensen, 'Johann Michael Dilherr und der Pegnesische Blumenorden', *ib.*, 1320–60, examines D.'s role as a patron of the Pegnischer Blumenorden. In keeping with his status as the most senior clergyman in Nuremberg and his noble family ties, D. did not publicly link himself with this basically bourgeois society. As J. shows, he was, however, a focal point for its most important members over several decades. Both Harsdörffer and Birken were literary advisors to D. They contributed poetry and emblems and made stylistic improvements to his innumerable devotional works, and he in turn wrote dedicatory poetry for many works linked to the society. It was, however, in Birken's *Himmel-klingendes Schäferspiel* contained in the memorial volume published on D.'s death in 1675 that his function as the society's *éminence grise* was made clear. U. Seelbach, 'Die Altdorfer Ceres-Gesellschaft (1668–1669)', *ib.*, 1361–80, presents the scant traces of the activities of an Altdorf student poetic society dedicated to the praise of drinking, obviously typical of innumerable such student groups, and known only due to the chance survival of a manuscript with poetry by some of its members. Edith Grether, *Die Poesie der Throne. Die Juristen in der Fruchtbringenden Gesellschaft* (Rechtshistorische Reihe, 127), Berne, Lang, 1995, 236 pp., is a dissertation in the history of law which takes a fascinating subject for investigation, but unfortunately fails to come to grips with either the specific problems of early modern text traditions and their broader contexts or the social history of authorship. D. Ignasiak, 'Die Gründung der Fruchtbringenden Gesellschaft in Weimar und die europäische Rolle der Thüringer Fruchtbringer', *Beiträge zur Geschichte der Literatur in Thüringen*, Rudolstadt, Hain, 1995, pp. 116–37, explores the close links between the early Fruchtbringende Gesellschaft and the Utopian writers Campanella and Andreae and the pedagogical reformers Ratke and Comenius. I.'s main interest, however, is to highlight the central importance of the Thuringian region for the society's history.

2. POETRY

INDIVIDUAL AUTHORS

COLERUS. David Halsted, *Poetry and Politics in the Silesian Baroque. Neo-Stoicism in the Work of Christophorus Colerus and his Circle*, Wiesbaden, Harrassowitz, 272 pp., is a very illuminating study of Breslau as a centre of neo-Stoic thought adapted to the peculiar constraints of its precarious political situation. H. shows how neo-Stoicism was the prime influence on the education policies of the city fathers and its most prominent schoolman, Christophorus Colerus. H. points out the inapplicability of a concept of power based on centralized rule in an interpretation of the role of occasional poetry in Silesia, which he sees 'at the interstices of patterns of power' with 'meaning-giving power' as that of the individual patron and thus subject to constant change. H.'s study explores how C. himself was deeply influenced by his teacher in Strasbourg, Matthias Bernegger, who by juxtaposing exempla from history with contemporary experience, enacted in his teaching the political theories of Justus Lipsius. H. examines both C.'s school dramas and places his long-neglected poetry, both Latin and vernacular, in the context of the 'commerce of literature' which characterized the interchange between the élite classes of such cities. H. looks at the significance of Opitzian precepts and neo-Stoic thought for the poetry of several of C.'s friends and pupils, Tscherning, Titz, Czepko, Johannes Scheffler, and Hofmannswaldau, showing interesting links between neo-Stoicism and mysticism in the cases of Czepko and Scheffler.

CZEPKO. Daniel Czepko, *Sämtliche Werke*. II, 1, ed. Lothar Mundt and Ulrich Seelbach, Berlin, de Gruyter, 821 pp., contains C.'s Latin poetry, both from printed and manuscript sources, in a parallel text edition with German prose translations of all poems by the editors. This superb continuation of the Czepko edition further augments our picture of the poet and the edition as a whole allows easy access both to C.'s Latin and German poetry.

HOFMANNSWALDAU. A. Schubert, 'Auf der Suche nach der menschlichen Natur. Zur erotischen Lyrik Hofmannswaldaus', *Daphnis*, 25:423–65, examines the deeper theological aspects of H.'s erotic poetry in the light of his attitudes to the strictures of society as an expression of the corrupt state of man and physical love as an expression of a non-prelapsarian natural state. S. claims that H. seeks to combine Christian and Classical explanations of the nature of man, seeing his dilemma in resolving the two as an indication of his philosophical position between the Baroque and early Enlightenment.

NEUMARK. R. Althaus, '*Musicalische Neu-erbauete Schäfferey* — Eine von Georg Neumark bearbeitete und 1645 in Königsberg erschienene Ausgabe der *Jüngsterbaweten Schäfferey* von 1632', *Daphnis*, 25:369–85, is a purely music-history based discussion of N.'s brief role as an early link in the reception of Heinrich Albert's solo compositions.

OPITZ. Anna Carrdus, *Classical Rhetoric and the German Poet 1620 to the Present. A Study of Opitz, Bürger and Eichendorff*, Oxford, Legenda, xii + 263 pp., includes (pp. 1–86) an examination of the signifance of rhetoric in the sense of craft for the production of poetry. She deals extensively with O.'s 'Trostgedichte in Widerwärtigkeit des Krieges' as consolation poetry, placing the poem in its rhetorical tradition, especially looking at 10 Scaliger's precepts for the composition of such works. C.'s close reading of the poem throws new light both on the structure of 'Trostgedichte' and on its role as an exemplar for nascent vernacular poetry in Germany.

RIEMER. K. Heldt, '"Das Preißliche Uhr-Werck/ Auf der Neuen Augustus-Burg an der Saalen zu Weißenfels." Politische Casualalle-gorese auf Herzog August von Sachsen-Weißenfels', Sent, *Oper*, 63–93, places R.'s panegyric of the Halle Duke, reproduced in an appendix to the article, in the context of the occasional poetry produced in celebration of August and his family. She shows how the particular dynastic constellation within Electoral Saxony furthered the patronage of such poetry, which was centred on the Duke himself. The central allegory of the clock in R.'s poem is used to praise the regulation of all aspects of society by the just ruler and thus to legitimize his absolute power within the framework of the Christian values to which he remains subject.

3. PROSE

INDIVIDUAL AUTHORS

GREIFFENBERG. C. M. Pumplun, 'Andachtsbuch und Roman. Zur Struktur der *Geburtsbetrachtungen* Catharina Regina von Greiffenbergs (1633–94)', Schmidt-Glintzer, *Fördern*, 215–29, examines G.'s four-volume prose meditations, contrasting their structure with the mainstream of Lutheran devotional prose works. G.'s lengthy meditations do not lend themselves for use as private devotions in the normal sense of *Hausandachten*, which are structured in such a way that short sections containing hymns, prose and prayer may be extracted, usually with the help of indexes, to suit individual needs. P. sees the continuity of G.'s text as closer to the novels of Buchholtz and Anton Ulrich, in which the poet herself, a critic of the pastoral novel, praised the integration of Christian edification and entertainment.

GRIMMELSHAUSEN. P. Brenner, 'Hans Jacob Christoffel von Grimmelshausen: *Der abentheurliche Simplicissimus Teutsch*', *Romane* (Interpretationen), 7–46, summarizes current research positions on the novel and points to the pivotal importance of the print medium and book culture for the novel's concept of experience. B. finds fault with those heuristic models which seek to explain the cosmos of the novel in terms of one system, astrology for example, unable to accept the polyvalence of styles and structures within the text. He sees G.'s techniques as closer to those of Fischart and Rabelais than to those of the picaresque novel. M. Zywietz, 'Grimmelshausens "lyrische Perle" und das Fortwirken mittelalterlichen Musikverständnisses im *Simplicissimus*', *Daphnis*, 25 : 681–94, examines the role of music in G.'s main novel as an indicator of a harmonious sphere to which various elements of disorder or contemplation directly or indirectly refer. *Simpliciana*, 18, contains the proceedings of a conference entitled 'Grimmelshausen und die epische Tradition am Oberrhein' held in Karlsruhe in 1995. Most contributions are concerned with the satirical and Catholic literary traditions of the region which can be traced in G.'s work. G. Weydt, 'Größe und Rätsel des Meisters. Paralipomena zum gesellschaftlichen Status Grimmelshausens', *ib.*, 13–27, sketches the breadth of G.'s reading, both of Classical and medieval texts, in order to raise once more the question of the author's social standing and his intellectual horizons. S. Streller, 'Narrenschiff und Schalksnarr. Oberrheinische Spuren in Grimmelshausens Narrenbild', *ib.*, 45-51, briefly links G.'s adaptation of the 16th-c. tradition of the carnivalesque fool. S. Trappen, 'Konfessionalität, Erbauung und konfessionell gebundene Traditionen bei Grimmelshausen', *ib.*, 53–73, discusses the significance of G.'s Catholicism, the unobtrusiveness of which in his novels is normally interpreted as a sign of his eirenicism. T. convincingly shows that the author's perception of his works as devotional literature means that confessional controversy takes second place to the didactic goal of moral improvement. T. differentiates between the traditions of Catholic and Protestant devotional works, with their dogmatically motivated distinctive motifs and themes, showing how G.'s novels are integrated into an unequivocally Catholic context. This is made clear by looking at the importance of the asceticism of the hermit/saint motif and the tradition of Catholic picaresque novels dominated by notions of pilgrimage, confession, and repentance. T. takes his argument a stage further in his examination of *Proximus und Lympida*, a novel based on the legend of an exemplary devout man, which he links to the tradition of the south German Jesuit novel. R. G. Bogner, 'Erzählte Leichenpredigt, Konfessionspolemik und Satire. Zur katholisch-calvinistischen Kurzprosasammlung in Grimmelshausens erstem *Vogel-Nest*', *ib.*, 123–38, begins by examining a tale-telling competition between Catholics and Calvinists in an alehouse from G.'s *Vogel-Nest*, which G. himself situates in the tradition of earlier satirical novellas by referring to Johannes Pauli's *Schimpff und Ernst*, thus evoking a literary context to which confessional polemics were central. I. M. Battafarano, 'Mit Spee gegen Remigius: Grimmelshausens antidämonopathische Simpliciana im Strom nieder-oberrheinischer Vernunft', *ib.*, 139–64, proceeds from a close comparison of G. and one of his sources, the prosecutor and demonologist Nicolas Remy, from whom G. took a historical account of a witches' sabbath, to a series of deductions which aim to show that G. was also acquainted with Spee's *Cautio criminalis* and that the references to witchcraft and demonology in his literary works are in fact in indirect support of Spee's call for tolerance. R. Zeller, 'Die Schweiz ein "irdisch Paradis" oder eine närrische Welt? Schweiz und Schweizer im *Simplicissimus* und in den *Simplicianischen Schriften*', *ib.*, 165–80, concludes that in his description of Simplicissimus's two contrasting journeys to Switzerland, G. is not interested in a realistic depiction but in presenting aspects of the varying central themes of the novel.

REUTER. G. E. Grimm, 'Christian Reuter: *Schelmuffskys warhafftige curiöse und sehr gefährliche Reisebeschreibung zu Wasser und Lande*. Kapriolen eines Taugenichts. Zur Funktion des Pikarischen', *Romane* (Interpretationen), 47–77, is the reworked version of an essay published in 1987 under the same title, seeing R.'s main character as a parody both of the contemporary political ideal of the cavalier and of the picaresque hero.

SPANGENBERG. W. E. Schäfer, 'Wolfhart Spangenbergs *Ganskönig* (1607)', *Simpliciana*, 18: 29–43, calls attention to the Strasbourg writer S.'s highly popular work, reprinted three times and translated into

Swedish during the author's lifetime. Despite his popularity S. has received very little critical attention beyond that accorded to his *Eselkönig*. Schäfer's study looks at S.'s links with his satirical predecessor Fischart, showing that S. continues the tradition established by F. not just in translating Lucian and in the use of fable motifs, but also in his position as F.'s successor as lector in a Strasbourg printing house where F.'s own works were still being reprinted. S. points to the importance of Strasbourg as a centre of German satirical writing throughout the 16th and well into the 17th c. and explores how S.'s *Ganskönig* skilfully uses a parody of several genres for political and confessional satire.

OTHER WORK

Given the blurred distictions between factual and fictional prose in the early modern period and the fact that many novelists of the period were polymaths also involved in early forms of journalism such as the newspaper, the periodical, and the almanac, an investigation of aspects of the early newspaper is very welcome. *Die Sprache der ersten deutschen Wochenzeitungen im 17. Jahrhundert*, ed. Gerd Fritz and Erich Strassner (Medien in Forschung und Unterricht, A, 41), Tübingen, Niemeyer, 357 pp., is above all a linguistic study, but the work contains very illuminating sections on the development of the newspaper, parallel text types, especially the manuscript newsletter, and the 17th-c. moral and political debate on curiosity and the value of the newspaper. M. Fauser, 'Klatschrelationen im 17. Jahrhundert', Schmidt-Glintzer, *Fördern*, 255–63, examines a type of literature which illustrates well the fringe activity between journalism and fiction, anecdotal collections of conversation material. These were published in great numbers and obviously enjoyed great popularity with the reading public.

4. DRAMA

INDIVIDUAL AUTHORS

LOHENSTEIN. J. O. Newman, 'Sons and mothers: Agrippina, Semiramis, and the philological construction of gender roles in early modern Germany (Lohenstein's *Agrippina*, 1665)', *RQ*, 49:77–113, uses the incest scene between Nero and Agrippina in L.'s school drama in order to examine its underlying discourse of power and morality. N. takes the didactic aim of the play seriously and scrutinizes L.'s footnotes and their Humanist sources, revealing the moral relativism at the heart of this scene, which she interprets as a struggle between custom and political expediency. This explains how within the terms of the play Agrippina could be perceived as a positive figure in the *femme forte* tradition of female rulers, appealing to the specific political situation of Duchess Luise of Liegnitz-Brieg, ruling during the minority of her son, to whom the play is dedicated.

OTHER WORK

B. Rudin, 'Das Fürstlich Eggenbergische Hoftheater in Böhmisch Krumau (1676–1691). Zur ästhetischen Allianz zwischen Wanderbühne und Hofkultur', *Daphnis*, 25:467–88, uses the example of a court theatre in Bohemia to demonstrate the interaction between court and commercial spheres in the employment of groups of strolling players who moved easily between both worlds. R. traces the career of actor-manager Johann Georg Göttner, for whose company the ducal theatre in Böhmisch Krumau was designed. The continuity of documentation for the repertoire of the Bohemian troupe shows the gradual transition from dramatic texts to opera librettos as the latter became the main focus of court performance. This idea is expanded further by B. Jahn, 'Das Libretto als literarische Leitgattung am Ende des 17. Jahrhunderts? Zu Zi(e)glers Roman *Die Asiatische Banise* und seine Opernfassungen', Sent, *Oper*, 143-69, who takes a very instructive look at the cross-currents between opera and the novel. Z.'s novel lends itself to such a study as it contains operatic elements, including an opera libretto, and was itself adapted for the stage in three different opera versions. J. shows how prominently the theatre features in the courtly novel of the late 17th-c. and how both the novel and the libretto are recommended by the etiquette literature of the day as reading for those seeking to perfect their gallantry. This point is undermined by the fact that some librettos were obviously not written for stage performance, but to be read, much like the drama of the Romantic period. U. Deppe, 'Die Festlichkeiten am Dresdner Hof anläßlich der "Durchlauchtigsten Zusammenkunft" 1678. Theater und theatralische Spielformen im Dienste fürstlicher Repräsentation. Die Festkultur am Hofe Johann Georg II.', *ib.*, 95–116, takes up a subject dealt with by Helen Watanabe-O'Kelly in an article in 1990, stressing the political and dynastic background to the 1678 Dresden festivities, in this case concentrating on the allegory of the planets and the role of the stage designer Johann Oswald Harms. M. Wade, 'Die Bedeutung Dänemarks für die Entwicklung der frühdeutschen Oper in Halle und Weißenfels', *ib.*, 191–207, investigates the influence of Duke August's attendance at the Great Wedding of 1634 in Copenhagen on his later commissioning of opera performances in the German language for festivities in his own

residences in the 1660s. M. Bircher, '"ein jeder lebt allda vergnüg-
lich." Herzog August, der Wohlgerathene, Begründer der Hofkultur
von Halle-Weißenfels', *ib.*, 33–62, focuses on Duke August's opera
culture and on the role of Johann Beer at his court, in some respects
a shorter version of the same author's comprehensive study, '"Teutsche Gemühter zu Tugenden und Künsten anfrischen." Die deutsche
Oper in Halle: eine Frucht des Palmenordens unter Herzog August
von Sachsen', pp. 105–68 of '*in Teutschland noch gantz ohnbekandt.'
Monteverdi-Rezeption und frühes Musiktheater im deutschsprachigen Raum*, ed.
Markus Engelhardt (Perspektiven der Opernforschung, 3), Frankfurt,
Lang, xiv + 354 pp. G. Busch, 'Wolfenbüttel, Halle, Weißenfels und
wieder Wolfenbüttel. Glanz und Abglanz höfischen Musiktheaters
zwischen Oker und Saale (1635–1695)', Sent, *Oper*, 209–46, gives an
excellent summary of the development of operatic theatre at the
courts of central Germany in the 17th c., stressing the importance of
the verse song, used both in religious and secular contexts, and
tracing the changes in performances at court from closed activities in
which the court participated both as performers and audience, to a
phase in which performances were directed towards a broader public
as demonstrations of cultural power to their being purely 'presentation' in the sense of entertainment. R. Jacobsen, 'Die Weißenfelser
Libretti und Spielszenarien in Gotha', *ib.*, 247–75, shows the close
cultural links between the Saxon courts by examining two volumes of
opera librettos bound together and found in the library holdings at
Gotha documenting performances given in Weissenfels and obviously
collected by Duke Friedrich of Sachsen-Gotha as inspirations for his
own musical events in Gotha. S. Smart, 'Die Oper in Weißenfels
(1696 und 1708): zur Aufgabe und zum Inhalt der Weißenfelser
Libretti', *ib.*, 277–303, investigates three types of opera libretto
central to the Weissenfels opera and important to the development of
the German-language opera at the end of the 17th c., the mythological, the pastoral, and the historical libretto. T. Fuchs, 'Die
Weißenfelser Hofoper — Beziehungen zu anderen deutschen
Opernbühnen', *ib.*, 305–16, gives a survey of the various links
between the opera centres discussed in the volume, both in terms of
dynastic connections and artistic personnel.

THE CLASSICAL ERA

By DAVID HILL, *Senior Lecturer in German, University of Birmingham*

It is symptomatic of the changing status of the print medium that this year's entry must take note of the new CD-ROM series *Reclam Klassiker auf CD-ROM*, Stuttgart, Reclam, which includes for our period: Goethe, *Faust. Der Tragödie erster Teil*, 1995, *Die Leiden des jungen Werthers*, 1995, and *Iphigenie auf Tauris*; Lessing, *Nathan der Weise*; Schiller, *Wilhelm Tell* and *Kabale und Liebe*. With the correct equipment the user is not only able to access and copy the text and a range of hyperlinked material relating to it, including context-specific notes and an interpretative essay, but can also hear the text (without stage-directions) spoken by a single actor — except in the case of *Faust*, where only selections from the dialogues between Faust and Mephistopheles are available. Each of these CD-ROMs links material hitherto dispersed over a number of books, but the technology makes this a new resource, and of particular value is the ability to search for occurrences of words, although limited here by the use of modernized orthography. A considerable amount of original material, on the other hand, is offered by the same publisher in a three-CD set *Geschichte der deutschen Lyrik in Beispielen*, ed. Dietmar Jaegle, of which the second disk, 'Von der Aufklärung bis zur Romantik', contains the text and recording of 13 poems from our period together with commentaries and substantial interpretative essays. What J. has added to the standard format is a glossary of technical terms relating to the analysis of verse together with hyperlinked information on the period and the life of the author concerned. This adds up to a package that can be used in a number of different ways depending on whether the user starts from the text (printed or spoken), the author's biography, the literary period or the formal rhetoric of poetry.

1. GENERAL

BIBLIOGRAPHY, REFERENCE. Joachim Dyck and Jutta Sandstede, *Quellenbibliographie zur Rhetorik, Homiletik und Epistolographie des 18. Jahrhunderts im deutschsprachigen Raum*, 3 vols, Stuttgart-Bad Cannstatt, Frommann-Holzboog, lxxiii + 614, 615–1310, 1311–1478 pp., offers a bibliography listing chronologically over 4000 publications dealing with rhetoric, homiletics, and letter-writing, including multiple editions and printings. Each entry contains not only the details of the title page and format but also the location of the example cited and additional information when relevant. Vol. 3 contains indexes which allow the user to search for authors or, in the case of anonymous texts, titles. Problems of definition, for example affecting the border-line to aesthetic theory, which is not covered, mean of course that the completeness for which the editors strive is unattainable, but this scarcely detracts from a monumental piece of work· which will undoubtedly inspire and inform much further research.

GENERAL STUDIES AND ESSAY COLLECTIONS. *18. Jahrhundert. Text und Zeugnisse*, ed. Walther Killy and Christoph Perels, Munich, Beck, 1254 pp., is a new edition of this classic anthology. Although the last quarter of the 18th c. is rather under-represented, one is continually impressed by the wealth of material that the editors have collected, often from quite remote sources, and the way that they have used it to build up a complex picture of the age. Within this documentation of 18th-c. German culture there is a certain emphasis on aesthetic and on socio-political matters. Brenner, *Literaturgeschichte*, contains chapters on 'Frühaufklärung' (49–68), 'Aufklärung' (69–94), 'Klassik und Romantik' (95–131). The brevity of this survey means that B. is often reduced to making individual observations on texts which, although clear in their formulation, remain apodictic. Of greatest interest is perhaps the rather controversial periodization, which allows Leibniz, Gottsched, and Gellert to coexist in a world shattered by the Lisbon earthquake and brings together under the term 'Aufklärung' such divergent tendencies as those linked with Klop-stock, Lessing and the *Sturm und Drang*. *Von Dichterfürsten und anderen Poeten. Kleine niedersächsische Literaturgeschichte*. 1. *32 Portraits*, ed. Jürgen Peters and Wilhelm Heinrich Pott, Hanover, Revonnah, 1993, 250 pp., contains a series of short essays presenting writers associated with Lower Saxony from the medieval period up to the early 19th c. but predominantly concerned with our period and including portraits of several that deserve to be better known, including Campe, Zimmermann, and Grosse. This is a popularizing book and does not lay claim to new information, but the regional accent often suggests a fresh approach and is appropriate to a period when it was the region that provided the limits to most people's everyday experience.

PERIODS: AUFKLÄRUNG. Harro Zimmerman conducts a debate on current views of the Enlightenment with Robert Darnton, Jean Mondot, and Werner Schneiders in *Das achtzehnte Jahrhundert*, 20:137–49. Peter-André Alt, *Aufklärung. Lehrbuch Germanistik*, Stuttgart, Metzler, ix + 348 pp., offers a thorough introduction to central themes of the period. Sections on the underlying ideas and on aesthetic theory are followed by sections on each of the genres, verse, drama and narrative. This structure reflects a concern with aesthetic continuities and rather less emphasis on the social context than is common today. The fact that it separates different areas of work by one author is less a problem for the German Enlightenment than the fact that A. draws the period to a rather abrupt conclusion in the early 1770s. The argument is conducted with clarity and precision, and brief surveys of the insights gained by recent research help to emphasize that our understanding of the period is something that is itself historical. *Der Mensch der Aufklärung*, ed. Michel Vouvelle, Campus, Frankfurt–Maison des Sciences de l'Homme, Paris, 381 pp., is an attempt to define the society and ideology of the Enlightenment by separate treatments of a sequence of social types, 'Der Adlige', 'Der Geschäftsmann', 'Der Gelehrte', etc. Given the clear formal division of roles in the 18th c., this is a helpful way of proceeding and allows for the development of informative and interesting perspectives. But if the term *Mensch* is thus successfully analysed in terms of its components, the same is not consistently the case with the other term, *Aufklärung*, for the occasional references to local variants and to historical developments during the century do not entirely prevent the book from creating the impression of an abstract and therefore in the end unhistorical ideal of Enlightenment.

PERIODS: EMPFINDSAMKEIT, STURM UND DRANG. R. Krebs, 'Herder, Goethe und die ästhetische Diskussion um 1770. Zu den Begriffen "énergie" und "Kraft" in der französischen und deutschen Poetik', *GJb*, 112, 1995 [1996]:83–96. C. Zelle, 'Zwischen Rhetorik und Spätaufklärung. Zum historischen Ort der Sturm-und-Drang-Ästhetik mit Blick auf Johann Georg Schlossers "Versuch über das Erhabene" von 1781 (mit einem unveröffentlichten Brief Schlossers im Anhang)', *Lenz-Jb.*, 6:160–81.

PERIODS: CLASSICISM. The debate about the politics of Weimar Classicism continues with: D. Kemper, 'Ideologie und Ideologiekritik: W. Daniel Wilsons Vorwurf der Spitzelei gegenüber Goethe', *GJb*, 112, 1995 [1996]:383–97, and H. Tümmler, 'Replik auf Professor W. Daniel Wilsons "Zeit"-Artikel', *ib.*, 399–402, while W. himself will no doubt provoke further controversy with 'Tabuzonen um Goethe und seinen Herzog. Heutige Folgen nationalsozialistischer Absolutismuskonzeptionen', *DVLG*, 70:394–442, in which he argues that an adequate understanding of the politics of Weimar Classicism is impeded by Nazi interpretations of the role of the critical intellectuals of the time. At a different level, *Das Goethe- und Schiller-Archiv 1896–1996. Beiträge aus dem ältesten deutschen Literaturarchiv*, ed. Jochen Golz, Weimar, Böhlau, 488 pp., celebrates the anniversary of the Weimar archive with a well illustrated collection of essays dealing with textual matters, of which many relate to Classicism: J. Golz, 'Das Goethe- und Schiller-Archiv in Geschichte und Gegenwart' (13–70); V. Wahl, 'Die Überwindung des Labyrinths. Der Beginn der Reorganisation des Goethe- und Schiller-Archivs unter Willy

Flach und die Vorgeschichte seines Direktorats (1954–1958)' (71–103); G. Schmid, 'Vergangenheit und Zukunft der professionellen Archivarbeit im Goethe- und Schiller-Archiv' (105–17); B. Mende, 'Das Gebäude des Goethe- und Schiller-Archivs' (119–60); D. Kuhn, 'Aus dem Goethe- und Schiller-Archiv. Mit der Veröffentlichung von Goethes Schemata zur "Succession der drey Herzoginnen"' (161–74); S. Henke, '"Ich habe mich zu einem Versuch verführen lassen, meinen Götz von Berlichingen aufführbar zu machen." Zur Überlieferung der Bühnenbearbeitungen von Goethes "Götz von Berlichingen" im Goethe- und Schiller-Archiv' (175–93); S. Schäfer, 'Die Briefe von Katharina Elisabeth Goethe an ihre Familie in Weimar. Ein Beitrag zu der noch ausstehenden "Geschichte der Goetheschen Briefregistratur"' (195–213); U. Bischof, '"Mit der innigsten Verehrung …"'. Briefe von Frauen an Goethe' (215–27); M. Koltes, '"… ohne Volks Versammlung noch die Bestimmung als Volksredner zu erfüllen." Goethes strategischer Briefwechsel mit Sulpiz Boisserée' (229–50); J. Sänger, '"Von einem der wundersamsten Stammbücher das man vielleicht gesehen." Das Stammbuch des Barons von Burkana wiederentdeckt' (251–65); H. Nahler, '"Er verfolgte die Wahrheit mit unbesorgter Gründlichkeit." Schillers ästhetische Vorlesungen in der Niederschrift von Christian Friedrich Michaelis' (267–80); G. Arnold, 'Herders Nachdichtung "Aufschriften auf den Königsgräbern bei Persepolis"' (281–91); R. Otto and C. Rudnik, 'Karl Ludwig von Knebel — Goethes "alter Weimarischer Urfreund". Seine Persönlichkeit und sein literarischer Nachlaß' (293–320); R. Wollkopf, 'Die "Wiedervereinigung" von Archivalien und Teilnachlässen im Goethe- und Schiller-Archiv' (463–74); and the volume ends with an invaluable 'Verzeichnis der Bestände im Goethe- und Schiller-Archiv' (475–81). Ursula Salentin, *Anna Amalia. Wegbereiterin der Weimarer Klassik*, Cologne, Böhlau, 201 pp. + 32 pls, offers a sober and balanced biography of Anna Amalia. S. avoids the temptation anachronistically to sentimentalize a private life about which we can only speculate, and shows well the place within a full life of A.'s contribution to the evolution of the 'Weimarer Musenhof'. What also emerges is the fact that her force of personality was decisive in its emergence and that she remained part of its development at least until the last decade of her life. Six months before the death of A. in 1807, Johanna Schopenhauer took up residence in Weimar, and Astrid Köhler, *Salonkultur im klassischen Weimar. Geselligkeit als Lebensform und literarisches Konzept*, Stuttgart, Metzler & Poeschel, 268 pp., offers a fascinating account of the social and cultural dynamics of the salon over which S. presided until she left Weimar in 1829. This level of analysis tells us more about the immediate context of literary production than either individual biographies or studies of society as a whole, and is used here specifically to shed light on two novels whose genesis is closely linked to the salon, Goethe's *Die Wahlverwandt-schaften* and S.'s *Gabriele*. Both of them, K. argues, represent a kind of experimentation with the possibilities and limitations of sociability in Weimar, but Gabriele is more than an imitation of Ottilie, and S. is more concerned than Goethe with discussing the idea of social integration. Further perspectives are offered by H. Schmiedt, 'Die Wiederkehr der Weimarer Klassik in den Kommentaren ihrer Kritiker', *WW*, 46:20–31; M. Böhler, 'Geteilte Autorschaft: Goethe und Schiller. Visionen des Dichters, Realitäten des Schreibens', *GJb*, 112, 1995 [1996]:167–81; B. Kauffmann, 'Weimars deutsches Gesicht. Die Stadt der Klassiker und der Schatten von Buchenwald untrennbar wie Faust und Mephisto', *ib.*, 333–38. J. Golz, 'Dokumente "einsichtiger Freundschaft" im Goethe- und Schiller-Archiv', *ib.*, 360–64, records the acquisition of material belonging to Voigt.

GENRES. There are a number of contributions to our understanding of 18th-c. theatrical practice: D. C. John, 'Heinrich Gottfried Koch: research lost and found', *GN*, 27:101–04, records the discovery of what may be the repertoire lists of this major troupe principal; R. B. Emde, 'Manuskripte und Memoiren von Schauspielerinnen des 18. Jahrhunderts. Ein Leben mit Texten, durch Texte, für Texte, in Texten', *Das achtzehnte Jahrhundert*, 20:181–96; K. Schwind, '"Man lache nicht!" Goethes theatralische Spielverbote. Über die schauspielerischen Unkosten des autonomen Kunstbegriffs', *IASL*, 21:66–112, discusses the way that the writer's increasing control could act as a restriction for the actor. Günter Sasse, *Die Ordnung der Gefühle. Das Drama der Liebesheirat im 18. Jahrhundert*, WBG, 326 pp., discusses the literary reflection of the shift in the 18th c. away from ascribed social roles towards a world of individual choices,in particular the shift from a conception of marriage as a dynastic arrangement to the ideal of personal self-realization in love. In a series of analyses of dramas by Luise Adelgunde Gottsched, Gellert, Lessing, Lenz, Wagner, Goethe, Leisewitz, and Schiller, Sasse examines the tensions between desires and institutions, and does so with such lucidity and intelligence that this is likely to become a classic study of this important motif and in general of the drama, even if it rather underemphasizes the problems of the idealization of love in marriage which feminist criticism has identified. Critical insights of this kind are offered by E. McInnes, ' "Verlorene Töchter": Reticence and ambiguity in German domestic drama in the late eighteenth century,' Jackson, *Taboos*, 27–42, and A. Mathäs, 'Between self-assertion and self-denial: gender and ideology in eighteenth-century domestic tragedy', *LY*, 27, 1995:39–61.

Erich Meuthen, *Selbst-Überredung. Rhetorik und Roman im 18. Jahrhundert* (Litterae, 23), Freiburg, Rombach, 1994, 283 pp., traces the emergence and crisis of individualism through the error inherent in Agathon's 'Schwärmerey', the commanding emotionalism of Saint Preux and Werther to the therapeutic distance of Moritz's *Anton Reiser*. The twist that Meuthen gives to this familiar thesis is to relate it to the decline of rhetoric, or rather, as he persuasively argues, to the transformation of an older, more formal rhetoric into a new rhetoric of immediacy, naturalness, and originality. He thus integrates interpretations of 18th-c. narrative fiction into more modern discussions of the nature of aesthetics and the nature of language, and thereby adds considerably to our understanding of the way that the history of literature in the 18th c. is also a history of the relationship between literature, or text, and reality. F. Jannidis, ' "Individuum est ineffabile." Zur Veränderung der Individualitätssemantik im 18. Jahrhundert und ihrer Auswirkung auf die Figurenkonzeption im Roman', *Aufklärung*, 9.2 : 77–110, discusses the meanings of individuality in the novels of Schnabel, Gellert, and Moritz. Holger Dainat, *Abaellino, Rinaldini und Konsorten. Zur Geschichte der Räuberromane in Deutschland* (STSL, 55), 317 pp., examines the social connotations of the *Räuberroman*, taking an unusually wide set of examples as his basis. What is original and valuable about this study is not so much the analysis of writers, readers and distribution systems as the way that it shows how the robber hero is both excluded from society and integrated into its system of values. Criminality, that is, deviation from a social order legitimated by Reason, Nature, and God, was seen increasingly in the second half of the 18th c. in terms of the individual constellation of circumstances which had condemned the individual to the loss of a secure role within society. The *Räuberroman*, D. argues, was thus able to reflect — albeit in a simplified way — the problem of the individual in a modern society. H. Esselborn, 'Erschriebene Individualität und Karriere in der Autobiographie des 18. Jahrhunderts', *WW*, 46 : 193–210, discusses autobiographical writing by Jung-Stilling, Moritz, and Bräker. A. Montandon, 'Sur les fables allemandes au XVIIIᵉ siècle', *RLC*, 70 : 119–31.

THEMES. Alfred Behrmann, *Das Tramontane oder die Reise nach dem gelobten Lande. Deutsche Schriftsteller in Italien 1755–1808* (BNL, 145), 214 pp., consists of a series of essays, some of which have been published elsewhere, in which he discusses the German experience of Italy and and focuses on specific authors: Winckelmann, Goethe, Moritz, Humboldt, and Seume. These essays preserve the spirit of informality and delight of the lectures they were based on and which, B. argues, is essential to the experience of Italy. There is therefore quite extensive quotation, but in these essays B. succeeds where so many have failed, namely in genuinely combining lightness of touch with informed scholarship, while details are banished to the end-notes. Laroche, *Bildnis*, sets out to analyse the literary function of the portrait in texts which, despite the title of the volume, are largely taken from the late 18th c. Introductory sections review contemporary attitudes to the portrait, in particular the miniature, and its relevance to physiognomics, and indicate the intensity of its use as a motif in the literature of the period. The main body of the book consists of analyses of usages by Gellert, Wieland, Lessing, Jacobi, Heinse, Lenz, Goethe, Brentano, and Hoffmann in which L. shows interestingly how these authors deploy the tension between the portrait and the figure who is being portrayed, but the study seems overwhelmed by the richness of its material. It goes back to a 1977 dissertation and maybe a more thorough use of later theoretical insights would have allowed L. to find further depths of meaning in this productive topic. Janina Knab, *Ästhetik der Anmut. Studien zur 'Schönheit der Bewegung' im 18. Jahrhundert* (EH, 1, 1569), 334 pp., pursues the process by which in the 18th c. the understanding of *Anmut* breaks free from the regulated norms of rhetoric and etiquette and becomes a central component in the evolution of aesthetic and anthropological thought. A provisional end-point of this debate was reached by Schiller's essay *Über Anmut und Würde*, and K. examines the importance of his concept of 'Schönheit der Bewegung' as a link between the intentional and the spontaneous, a transcendent ideal and a unique act of expression. Much of the contemporary debate was dominated by the plastic arts, and a number of well-chosen illustrations help to concretize a volume whose main theses are inevitably rather abstract. An opening chapter also makes for clarity by, paradoxically, beginning with a convincing attempt to show how Kleist destabilized the conceptual system S. had struggled to erect. H. C. Finsen, 'Evidenz und Wirkung im ästhetischen Werk Baumgartens. Texttheorie zwischen Philosophie und Rhetorik', *DVLG*, 70:198–212. The contemporary reception of Homer is discussed by J. Wohlleben, 'Friedrich August Wolfs *Prolegomena ad Homerum* in der literarischen Szene der Zeit', *Poetica*, 28:154–70, and T. Krischer, 'Friedrich August Wolfs *Prolegomena Ad Homerum* und die neuere Homerforschung', *ib.*, 171–80. Further aspects of reception are dealt with by D. Katritzky, 'Hans Sachs im 18. Jahrhundert: Strategien der Rezeption', *GLL*, 49:32–41, and Ernst Hinrichs, Roland Krebs, and Ute van Runset, *'Pardon, mon cher Voltaire ...' Drei Essays zu Voltaire in Deutschland* (Kleine Schriften zur Aufklärung, 5), Wolfenbüttel, Lessing-Akademie–Göttingen, Wallstein, 126 pp., which contains three important essays that significantly extend the work of H. A. Korff: E. Hinrichs, 'Aus der Distanz der Philosophen — Zum Briefwechsel zwischen Voltaire und

Friedrich II' (9–47); U. van Runset, 'Voltaires Deutschlandbild' (49–85); R. Krebs, '"Schmähschrift wider die weiseste Vorsehung" oder "Lieblingsbuch aller Leute von Verstand"? — Zur Rezeption des "Candide" in Deutschland' (87–124). There are errors in the labelling of the illustrations but the three essays are both well informed and cogently argued. J. Hermand, 'Rousseau, Goethe, Humboldt. Ihr Einfluβ auf die späteren Befürworter des Naturgartens', *GRM*, n. F., 46:270–86, investigates the reception of these authors in early-20th-c. garden theory in Germany.

Susanne Kord, *Sich einen Namen machen. Anonymität und weibliche Autorschaft 1700–1900* (EFF, 41), 240 pp., consists of a number of interlocking essays dealing with women's writing during our period and the 19th c., revolving round the thesis that the gradual acceptance of formal arguments for the equality of women towards the end of the 18th c. was accompanied by the ascription to women of 'feminine' roles which in practice excluded them from the canon of 'high' literature. A symptomatic consequence was their increasing use of pseudonyms which concealed their gender. This is a lively and ground-breaking study which draws attention to an enormous body of neglected literature but also suggests appropriate ways of interpreting it. It concludes with a table of pseudonyms, and this is indeed a book that will be a resource as well as an inspiration. Kuzniar, *Goethe*, contains a collection of at times provocative but stimulating and well informed essays on the presentation of gender in the literature of our period. These generally take the form of analyses of individual texts or authors, and are listed separately below, but K.'s introduction (1–32) and a concluding essay by S. Kord, 'Eternal love or sentimental discourse? Gender dissonance and women's passionate "friendships"' (228–49), offer further-reaching general discussions, as does J. Purver, '"Zufrieden mit stillerem Ruhme"? Reflections on the place of women writers in the literary spectrum of the late eighteenth and early nineteenth centuries', *PEGS(NS)*, 64, 1993–95:72–93. French, *Women*, argues that anthologies of letters have tended to ignore areas of experience important to women, and proceeds to analyse the correspondence of — from our period — Meta Klopstock, Louise Gottsched, and Anna Louise Karsch. This is a wide-ranging and lively study, which focuses particularly on the acceptance or otherwise of the role ascribed to the authors as women. S. Richter, 'The ins and outs of intimacy: gender, epistolary culture, and the public sphere', *GQ*, 69:111–24, analyses the cult of friendship in the circle around Gleim. Gail K. Hart, *Tragedy in Paradise. Family and Gender Politics in German Bourgeois Tragedy 1750–1850*, Columbia, Camden House, xiii + 136 pp., examines the role of women in the tradition of the *bürgerliches Trauerspiel*, which, often quite consciously, built on *Miß Sara Sampson*. As this tradition allowed men to move into the realm of the sentimental, she argues, so it excluded women and turned the private sphere into one dominated by male negotiations. Having demonstrated this thesis in a detailed discussion of Lillo, Lessing and Klinger (*Sturm und Drang*), she reveals its force in subtle analyses of plays by Goethe (*Stella, Die natürliche Tochter*) and Wagner. This stimulating study concludes with an examination of the connotations of gender in Kleist's aesthetics and in the three plays with which Hebbel showed that the tradition of the *bürgerliches Trauerspiel* had come to its end. Stefanie Ohnesorg, *Mit Kompaß, Kutsche und Kamel. (Rück-)Einbindung der Frau in die Geschichte des Reisens und der Reiseliteratur* (Sofie, 2), St. Ingbert, Röhrig, 332 pp., offers a history of travel, giving special attention to women as observed by travellers and particularly as travellers themselves, but includes some reflections on fictional travel. O.'s starting-point is the Middle Ages, and there is a concluding section on women and the Orient which takes us into the 19th c., but the greater part of the book is devoted to the 18th c. The problems of the book are, firstly, that it tends to rehearse the history of male travelling and then add on examples of women travelling, and, secondly, that an activity which is so dependent on material conditions is treated in a way that is geographically imprecise: the focus is on German writers, but the conditions of the territories within which they were travelling vary considerably, and examples from France and England are introduced without sufficient reflection on the differences. This book is clearly written and is useful as an introductory survey, showing the limitations of many gender-blind studies of travel, but at the same time it draws attention to the need for a more thorough treatment of the topic. T. Strack, 'Alexander von Humboldts amerikanisches Reisewerk: Ethnographie und Kulturkritik um 1800', *GQ*, 69:233–46.

There have been several studies of the social environment of literature in the 18th c. *Germany. A New Social and Economic History.* II. *1630–1800*, ed. Sheilagh Ogilvie, London, Arnold, xvi + 426 pp., contains a wide range of essays, mainly by German scholars, focusing on a number of aspects of the socio-economic development which provide both the context of literature and its subject-matter. The contributions are clearly structured and, despite the notorious complexity of 18th-c. Germany, offer a convincing presentation of the main patterns. If the emphases are sometimes different from those often found in social histories of literature, then it is probably because the latter are insufficiently aware of the distance between the two realms and the work that is done by literature in reaching out for social issues: this volume is probably the most reliable remedy available for such an imbalance. A case in point is studied by

H. Macher, 'Friedrich Justin Bertuchs Armenschrift von 1782. Bürgerliches Reformdenken im Spannungsfeld von sozialer Praxis, aufgeklärter Humanität und ökonomischem Rationalismus', *IASL*, 20.2, 1995 : 1–55, while a special number of *Aufklärung*, 9.1, is devoted to a comparative study of what is commonly called enlightened absolutism, for which the editor prefers the term 'Reformabsolutismus', and contains: E. Hellmut, 'Der Staat des 18. Jahrhunderts. England und Preußen im Vergleich' (5–24); C. Zimmermann, 'Grenzen des Veränderbaren im Absolutismus. Staat und Dorfgemeinde in der Markgrafschaft Baden' (25–45); C. Ernst and N. Franz, 'Waldreform im 18. Jahrhundert. Die Anfänge der nachhaltigen Forstwirtschaft im "Baumbusch" und im "Kondelwald" im überregionalen Vergleich' (47–73); T. Würtenberger, 'Verfassungsentwicklungen in Frankreich und in Deutschland in der zweiten Hälfte des 18. Jahrhunderts' (75–99); G. Birtsch, 'Absolutismus oder Reformabsolutismus?' (101–09). *Gesinde im 18. Jahrhundert*, ed. Gotthardt Frühsorge, Rainer Gruenter, and Beatrix Freifrau Wolff Metternich (Studien zum achtzehnten Jahrhundert, 12), Hamburg, Meiner, 1995, xi + 466 pp., contains a series of essays dealing with one set of social relations that is particularly evident in the literature of the period: H. Günther, 'Herr und Knecht' (1–12); R. Schröder, 'Gesinderecht im 18. Jahrhundert' (13–39); F. Eder, 'Gesindedienst und geschlechterspezifische Arbeitsorganisation in Salzburger Haushalten des 17. und 18. Jahrhunderts' (41–68); J. Enklaar, 'Rechte und Pflichten des Gesindes auf einem niederländischen Landsitz im 18. Jahrhundert' (69–81); P. Münch, 'Tiere, Teufel oder Menschen? Zur gesellschaftlichen Einschätzung der "dienenden Klassen" während der Frühen Neuzeit' (83–107); G. Frühsorge, 'Einübung zum christlichen Gehorsam: Gesinde im "ganzen Hause"' (109–20); L. Hüttl, 'Das Erscheinungsbild der Dienstboten in der katholischen Frömmigkeitsgeschichte des 18. Jahrhunderts' (121–60); M. Maurer, 'Dienstmädchen in adligen und bürgerlichen Haushalten' (161–87); G. Mühlpfordt, 'Ein Plan zum Wohl des Gesindes (1786)' (189–214); U. Ricken, 'Das Gesinde in der Sprache des 18. Jahrhunderts' (215–24); D. Roche, 'Le précepteur dans la noblesse française: instituteur privilégié ou domestique?' (225–43); R. Mortier, 'Les domestiques dans l'*Encyclopédie* et chez Rousseau' (245–52); W. Frese, 'Die Erinnerungen des böhmischen Lakaien Hansel Commenda' (253–64); Weygo Comte Rudt de Collenberg, 'Haus- und Hofmohren des 18. Jahrhunderts in Europa' (265–80); K.-T. Winkler, ' "My people": Sklaven als Gesinde' (281–307); P. Raabe, 'Der Bibliotheksdiener im 18. Jahrhundert' (309–18); W. Martens, 'Das Gesinde in den Moralischen Wochenschriften' (319–28); R. Sühnel, 'Der unzerbrochene Krug. Richardsons puritanische Kammerzofe

Pamela' (329–37); T. Koebner, 'Die Kammerzofe auf dem Theater
von Molière bis Da Ponte' (339–55); U. Sadji, 'Mohrendiener im
deutschen Drama des 18. Jahrhunderts' (357–67); H. Bauer,
'Dienstmägde, die verlorene Unschuld und das Bild von der menschlichen Seele' (369–82); Beatrix Freifrau Wolff Metternich, 'Über die
Bildwürdigkeit von Gesinde' (383–97); R. Stratmann-Döhler, 'Gesinde im Spiegelbild der Architektur' (399–405); H. Weber, 'Der
Serva-padrona-Topos in der Oper oder Komik als Spiel mit musika-
lischen und sozialen Normen' (407–29); E. Sagarra, 'Quellenbibliographie zur Rechts-, Sozial- und Literaturgeschichte der Dienstboten
(des Gesindes) ca. 1700–1918' (431–57). N. C. Wolf, 'Blumauer
gegen Nicolai, Wien gegen Berlin: Die polemischen Strategien in der
Kontroverse um Nicolais *Reisebeschreibung* als Funktion unterschied-
licher Öffentlichkeitstypen', *IASL*, 21.2:27–65. Herrmann, *Volk*,
contains the papers given at an interdisciplinary conference in
Tübingen in — appropriately enough — November 1990, dealing
with the idea of German nationhood at the end of the 18th c. The
papers revolve around the intersection of literary history, the history
of ideas, and political history, and those most directly relevant in the
present context include: H., 'Volk — Nation — Vaterland: ein
Grundproblem deutscher Geschichte' (11–18); U. A. J. Becher,
'Nation und Lebenswelt. Zu einigen Grundlagen der Politisierung'
(19–34); M. Gilli, '"Volk" bei Georg Forster und den deutschen
Jakobinern' (46–54); J. Rathmann, 'Die "Volks"-Konzeption bei
Herder' (55–61); H. Bosse, 'Patriotismus und Öffentlichkeit' (67–88);
M. Maurer, 'Nationalcharakter und Nationalbewußtsein. England
und Deutschland im Vergleich' (89–100); U. Im Hof, '"Volk —
Nation — Vaterland" und ihre Symbolik in der Schweiz' (131–40);
H. Steinmetz, 'Idee und Wirklichkeit des Nationaltheaters.
Enttäuschte Hoffnungen und falsche Erwartungen' (141–50); G.-L.
Fink, 'Das Wechselspiel zwischen patriotischen und kosmopolitisch-
universalen Bestrebungen in Frankreich und Deutschland
(1750–1789)' (151–84). Wolfgang Martens, *Der patriotische Minister.
Fürstendiener in der Literatur der Aufklärungszeit* (Kontext, 1), Weimar,
Böhlau, xvii + 388 pp., counters the emphasis of current socio-
cultural studies on middle-class secession by constructing the history
of men who have devoted themselves to service to the monarch or the
state. M. examines a large number of literary texts, many of them
novels, and gives a convincing account of the shifts in views of the
state and of the relationship of the middle classes to it which took
place during the 18th c. He brings together a great deal of material,
much of it forgotten, and even if critics come in due course to the
conclusion that his study does not exhaust the possibilities of
interpreting the socio-political meanings of these texts, they will owe

him a debt for having brought together such a wealth of material which directly confronts what all too often tend to be rather generalized claims about the reflection of bourgeois values in the literature of the Enlightenment. J. Vogl, 'Die zwei Körper des Staates', *Acta* (Seeon), 562–74, examines the emergence of the representational and the functional aspects of the modern state, relating this to the portrayal of the theatre in *Wilhelm Meisters Lehrjahre*. An important essay by J. A. McCarthy, ' "Ein Verbrechen, wozu man gezwungen wird, ist kein Verbrechen mehr." Zur Spannung zwischen Rechtspflege und Aufklärungsmoral im 18. Jahrhundert', *Das achtzehnte Jahrhundert*, 20:22–44, examines the role of literary figures in the conflict between the demands of what was felt, especially after 1780, to be a conservative legal system and psychological understanding. A case in point is discussed by M. Luserke, 'Kulturelle Deutungsmuster und Diskursformationen am Beispiel des Themas Kindsmord zwischen 1750 und 1800', *Lenz-Jb.*, 6:198–229. The origins of modern individualism in 18th-c. culture are outlined by A. Hahn and H. Willems, 'Wurzeln moderner Subjektivität und Individualität', *Aufklärung*, 9.2:7–37, and by C. Berthold and J. Greis, 'Prometheus' Erben — über Arbeit, Individualität, Gefühl und Verstand', *ib.*, 111–38. F. Kittler, 'From the recreation of scholars to the labor of the concept', Leventhal, *Reading*, 65–73, discusses the history of the activity of interpretation and links it with the decline of rhetoric at the end of the 18th c. R. T. Gray, 'Buying into signs: money and semiosis in eighteenth-century German language theory', *GQ*, 69:1–14, is a fascinating investigation into the 18th-c. acceptance of semiotic arbitrariness by drawing on the analogy of the productivity available through the money economy. More concretely, Fania Oz-Salzberger, *Translating the Enlightenment. Scottish Civic Discourse in Eighteenth-Century Germany*, Oxford, Clarendon, 1995, ix + 356 pp., offers a subtle and informative study of the reception of Adam Ferguson by Iselin, Garve, Lessing, Schiller, and others. It shows how the appropriation of ideas reveals both the similarities and the differences between the two cultures, and how the writings of the Scottish Enlightenment expose tensions within the German Enlightenment. F.'s common-sense epistemology appealed to the Late Enlightenment in Germany but there was little response to his idea of civic virtue, and his view of history was alien to the basically teleological approach of the Enlightenment. What is of particular interest is the way that O. traces these differences into the very process of translation and the availability or otherwise of terms and connotations in the two languages. Martin L. Davies, *Identity or History? Marcus Herz and the End of the Enlightenment*, Detroit, Wayne

State U.P., 1995, xiv + 344 pp., takes a thoughtful and unconventional view of the Late Enlightenment by examining an individual who has largely disappeared from historical narratives, not so much to rehabilitate him as because he can be used as a lens through which to observe the cultural environment in which he is situated. Marcus Herz, who was at one time the star pupil of Kant but was unable to follow his teacher into his critical phase, was also a doctor who was unable to keep step with medical research and a man who, with his younger wife Henriette, played an important part in the salon life of Berlin in the 1790s and was at the same time an important link in the German Jewish tradition. D. has provided the first full-scale study of H., but of even greater value is the portrait of late-18th-c. cultural life which H. is used to illuminate. Id., 'Reason and revulsion: Marcus Herz and the Enlightenment', *GLL*, 49:136–46. An edited reprint of Johann Samuel Traugott Gehler, *Physikalisches Wörterbuch*, ed. Wolfgang Bonsiepen, Stuttgart-Bad Cannstatt, Frommann-Holzboog, begins with vols 2 and 3 (Natur und Philosophie, 7–8), 1995, 918, 958 pp., which will be an invaluable resource for the study of 18th-c. culture. The first edition of G.'s encyclopaedic dictionary, which was first published 1787–96, is a painstaking summary of the current state of knowledge in the realm of physics, including astronomy, but the whole is infused by the spirit of the Enlightenment, seen perhaps most clearly in topics that touch, or touched, the borderline of science, such as entries under 'Magie' or 'Magnetismus' and in the frequent use of the term 'Aberglaube' to designate popular errors. These magnificent volumes are an important document of the popularization of science and their reprint an invaluable resource for the modern critic.

2. GOETHE

EDITIONS. J. Schillemeit, 'Gs Tagebücher, historisch-kritisch und kommentiert. Zu einem Editionsvorhaben der Stiftung Weimarer Klassik', *Editio*, 10:68–80.

GENERAL STUDIES AND ESSAY COLLECTIONS. Stuart Atkins, *Essays on Goethe*, ed. Jane K. Brown and Thomas P. Saine, Columbia, Camden House, 1995, v + 333 pp., gathers together 17 essays, which have appeared in various places since the late 1940s, a brief prefatory appreciation, and a bibliography of A.'s work. A. has made an enormous contribution to G. scholarship, and these shorter pieces impress by their learning, their thoughtful sophistication and their common sense, and by the number of insights which have subsequently become part of accepted knowledge about Goethe. Hans Richtscheid, *Goethe zum Dank*, ed. Herbert Kappes, Sankt Augustin,

Academia, 1995, xiv + 213 pp., contains over 60 brief essays or fragments published after R.'s death, with a preface, titles and references provided by the editor. They are in three groups according to the three manuscripts in which they were found, the first dealing with particular motifs in G.'s writing, while the second contains more general considerations of G., and the third is devoted to *Faust*. R.'s interest is in the philosophical connotations of individual aspects of G.'s life and work, and his observations, while often illuminating, contain echoes of a tradition of ecstatic *Geistesgeschichte* that present-day literary critics may feel make them rather unspecific and uncritical.

POETRY. David E. Wellbery, *The Specular Moment. Goethe's Early Lyric and the Beginnings of Romanticism*, Stanford U. P., 467 pp., is a dazzling study of G.'s early poetry which takes as its starting-point the I-centeredness of lyric poetry and, within that, the role of the 'du' in G.'s evocations of Love and Nature in his *Sturm und Drang* poetry. W. adopts a contrastive approach, and this problem of the constitution of the subject takes him beyond lyric poetry and beyond G. to authors such as Wieland, Novalis, and Hoffmann and thus to a reconsideration of the literary sensitivities of the *Goethezeit* as a whole. W.'s argument is carefully formulated in dialogue with modern critical theory, and this produces a book of some density, but it is marked by the close and sensitive reading of individual texts, and the demands it makes are the demands of the literary texts he is investigating. This book is important reading for anyone interested in G. and his age, anyone interested in literature. More narrowly focused studies include: W. Riedel, 'Eros und Ethos. Gs *Römische Elegien* und *Das Tagebuch*', *JDSG*, 40:147–80; G. Schulz, '"Liebesüberfluß." Zu Gs Ballade "Die Braut von Corinth"', *ib.*, 38–69; M. Mayer, 'Mit Liebe beziffert. Gs "St. Nepomucks Vorabend"', *JFDH*:70–83; I. Schmitt, '"Ein für allemal tot"? Ein weiterer Deutungsversuch zu Gs Divan-Gedicht "Selige Sehnsucht"', *ZDP*, 115:176–92, discusses death in terms of metamorphosis; A. Meier, 'Carl Friedrich Zelters Lied *Aus der Ferne*: Ein produktives Mißverständnis zum *West-Östlichen Divan*', *Euphorion*, 90:264–73; J. Adler, 'Schellings Philosophie und Gs weltanschauliche Lyrik', *GJb*, 112, 1995 [1996]:149–65. Katharina Mommsen, *Goethe und Diez. Quellenuntersuchungen zu Gedichten der Divan-Epoche* (GSA, 67), 1995, xx + 401 pp., is a new edition of the highly praised 1961 volume (see *YWMLS*, 23:351), to which has been added a new introduction, a selection of reviews of the original book, and a bibliography of M.'s publications.

DRAMA. E. Powers, 'From "Empfindungsleben" to "Erfahrungsbereich": the creation of experience in G.'s *Die Laune des Verliebten*',

GY, 8:1–27; E. H. Denton, '"A kiss is but a kiss:" the pastoral stage in G.'s *Die Laune des Verliebten*', *GR*, 71:101–13; M. Willems, 'Stella. Ein Schauspiel für Liebende. Über den Zusammenhang von Liebe, Individualität und Kunstautonomie', *Aufklärung*, 9.2:39–76. K. Ley, '"sii grand'uomo e sii infelice." Zur Umwertung des Tasso-Bildes am Beginn des Ottocento: Voraussetzungen und Hintergründe im europäischen Rahmen (LaHarpe/Gilbert — Goethe — Foscolo)', *GRM*, n. F., 46:131–73; A. Aurnhammer, 'Tasso-Wallfahrten deutscher Italienreisender', *JFDH*:146–70. D. Barry, '"Ist uns nichts übrig?":' the residue of resistance in G.'s *Iphigenie auf Tauris*', *GLL*, 49:283–96; E. Meuthen, '*Sprich deutlicher daß ich nicht länger sinne*. Über den "Doppelsinn" in Gs *Iphigenie*', *Euphorion*, 90:416–31.

FAUST. Criticism of the textual basis of Schöne's edition (see *YWMLS*, 56:818) continues with R. Kassel, 'Philologische Bemerkungen zu einer neuen *Faust*-Ausgabe', *ib.*, 375–81; G. Kaiser, 'Noch einmal: "Das Unzulängliche / Hier wird's Ereignis" (*Faust* 12106f.)', *ZDP*, 115:279–83; H. R. Vaget, 'Albrecht Schönes *Faust*: Philologie, Exegese, Historie', *GY*, 8:271–87. Individual passages are interpreted by: D. Bremer, '"Wenn starke Geisteskraft [...]". Traditionsvermittlungen in der Schlußszene von Gs *Faust*', *GJb*, 112, 1995 [1996]:287–307; H. Rölleke, '*Vor mir den Tag und hinter mir die Nacht* — Anmerkungen zu einem *Faust*-Vers', *Euphorion*, 90:344–47; P. Michelsen, 'Der Rat der Narren. Die Staatsratsszene in Gs *Faust II*', *JDFH*:84–129; C. A. Grair, 'G., Faust and Sardanapalus: the end of an age', *GY*, 8:238–51; P. A. Bloom and H. R. Vaget, '"Sardanapal!" — The French connection: unraveling *Faust II*, 10176', *ib.*, 252–70. N. Vazsonyi, 'Searching for "the order of things": does G.'s *Faust II* suffer from the "fatal conceit"?', *MDU*, 88:83–94, argues that the search for order in *Faust II* represents a failure to recognize the historical limitations of the concept of order.

NARRATIVE. Stefan Blessin, *Goethes Romane. Aufbruch der Moderne*, Paderborn, Schöningh, 406 pp., returns to the subject of his *Habilitationsschrift* (see *YWMLS*, 41:788–89), and again this is a detailed study of the four individual novels against a historical framework. On this occasion B. places less emphasis on the socio-economic context of the novels and focuses in short introductory chapters on the evolution of modernity. Within this framework he traces how the emergence both of distinct spheres of existence and of the modern sciences is reflected in the novels. B. also argues that the unique quality of G.'s writing lies in the fact that he managed to incorporate into his conception of development those factors which are opposed to development such as are represented by Mignon, and it is this kind of awareness of the richness of the novels which allows B.'s reading the numerous insights which make this book a worthwhile addition to an already extensive literature. Studies of *Werther* include: J. Nelles, 'Werthers Herausgeber oder die Rekonstruktion der "Geschichte des armen Werthers"', *JFDH*:1–37; L. A. Rickels, 'Psy Fi explorations of outer space: on Werther's special effects', Kuzniar, *Goethe*, 147–73; D. Purdy, 'The veil of masculinity: clothing and identity via G.'s *Die Leiden des jungen Werthers*', *LY*, 27, 1995:103–29; J. Black, 'Writing after murder (and before suicide): the confessions of Werther and Rivière', Leventhal, *Reading*, 233–59; B. Leistner, 'Gs "Werther" und seine zeitgenössischen Kritiker', *GJb*, 112, 1995 [1996]:71–82; K. Edmunds, '"der Gesang soll deinen Namen erhalten:" Ossian, Werther and texts of/ for mourning', *GY*, 8:45–65; K. Robertson, 'Poetry or the truth of the tears', *GN*, 27:94–96. Rüdiger Südhoff, *Die intertextuelle Sinnkonstitution im Bildungsroman der Weimarer Klassik. Poetologische Paradigmen der Aufklärungsliteratur in Goethes 'Lehrjahren'*, Stuttgart, Metzler & Poeschel, 1994, 219 pp., examines the way in which *Wilhelm Meisters Lehrjahre* adopts, uses, and transforms two contemporary sets of literary motifs, firstly those surrounding the idea of the visionary artist, and secondly a series of gestures that can be found in Lessing, specifically features shared by the *bürgliches Trauerspiel* and the *rührendes Lustspiel*. Intertextuality is such a pervasive phenomenon that most studies of it can easily be accused of incompleteness, and S. does not, for example, investigate G.'s use of the *Räuberroman* or the *Geheimbundroman*, but his decision to limit himself to particular areas of meaning, those connected with art and the theatre, means that this clearly and intelligently written study has a focus which allows it to shed new light on particular well-known aspects of the novel. By contrast Brandl, *Emanzipation*, is a highly theorized and systematized study of the anthropology inherent in selected texts of the *Goethezeit* which, before going on to compare the *Nachtwachen von Bonaventura*, *Peter Schlemihl*, and *Prinzessin Brambilla*, contains 'Gs "Wilhelm Meisters Lehrjahre": Unbefriedigende Aktualisierung des problembehafteten Systems' (45–176). The framework of the study is provided by the tension between an ideal of emancipatory enlightenment and 'Anthropomorphismus', by which B. means the belief in a transcendental will that controls and contains individual aspirations. This thus leads to discussions of the portrayal of religion, society and subjectivity, which offer an impressive interpretation of many passages of the *Lehrjahre* useful even for those who retain some scepticism about the scheme within which B. places them. The tensions between the ideal of self-realization and the social pressures to conform is also at the heart of a slighter but arguably more balanced study by Walter Beller, *Goethes Wihelm Meister Romane. Bildung für eine Moderne* (Schriftstücke, 2), Hanover, Revonnah, 1995, 283 pp., which takes the two *Wilhelm Meister* novels together and examines the development of the idea of education. What is valuable about this study is the way that it recognizes the openness of the concept of *Bildung* in Wilhelm's development and shows that there is a kind of progress, but one that involves loss, not only in those victims he leaves behind but also in himself. However, the compromises Wilhelm reaches, B. argues, have the merit of allowing him to take an active part in managing the potentialities he has not been able to give free rein to. This B. reads in terms of a discussion of the possibities of responding to the emergence of modernity. K. R. Edmunds, '"Ich bin gebildet genug ... um zu lieben und zu trauern:" Wilhelm Meister's apprenticeship in mourning', *GR*, 71:83–100; M. Redfield, 'The dissection of the state: *Wilhelm Meisters Wanderjahre* and the politics of aesthetics', *GQ*, 69:15–31; E. Dye, 'G.'s *Die Wahlverwandtschaften*: Romantic metafiction', *GY*, 8:66–92; H. Rowland, 'Chaos and art in G.'s *Novelle*', *ib.*, 93–119. Matías Martínez, *Doppelte Welten. Struktur und Sinn zweideutigen Erzählens* (Palaestra, 298), Göttingen, Vandenhoeck & Ruprecht, 227 pp., contains a chapter on *Die Wahlverwandtschaften* in which he examines the tensions between the realism of the novel, which presents actions as the interreactions of real individuals, and myths of atonement; in the end M. seems to privilege the latter and thereby weaken his thesis by not allowing sufficiently clearly that myth is also ideology. More sophisticated is the argument of Elisabeth von Thadden, *Erzählen als Naturverhältnis — 'Die Wahlverwandtschaften'. Zum Problem der Darstellbarkeit von Natur und Gesellschaft seit Goethes Plan eines 'Roman über das Weltall'*, Munich, Fink, 1993, 243 pp., who examines the relationship between science and literature as ways of perceiving and talking about the world. She shows how these issues became acute around the period 1806–09 as G. came to understand that, although science makes claims to universality, both science and the world it is describing are fundamentally subject to change. About half the book deals specifically with the way that *Die Wahlverwandtschaften* reflects this as a narrative structure which thematizes the attempts of individuals to structure their environment, firstly through science and secondly through their organization of the estate. Their limitations are reflected in their failure to organize past and present into a productive synthesis and in the way that, instead, governed by a notion of 'progress', they quarantine the past in archival form. The concept of 'Verzeitlichung', denoting a new relationship to time and therefore to individuality, is central to T.'s argument and also to Fotis Jannidis, *Das Individuum und sein Jahrhundert. Eine Komponenten- und Funktionsanalyse des Begriffs 'Bildung' am Beispiel von Goethes 'Dichtung und Wahrheit'* (STSL, 56), 230 pp., who offers a study of the idea of human development in a text which was planned at the same time as *Die*

Wahlverwandtschaften, namely *Dichtung und Wahrheit*. J. is, as is appropriate to this series, more concerned with the sociological context of ideas, and about half of the book deals with the general conditions of the evolution of the concepts of individuality, development and teleology. These are worthwhile but rather generalized, whereas the study of *Dichtung und Wahrheit* which he then goes on to has the subtlety that is possible with the detailed analysis of linguistic and literary patterns, specifically the way in which G. presents the idea of change, where he examines in particular the portrayal of the development of religious beliefs. Bettina Hey'l, *Der Briefwechsel zwischen Goethe und Zelter. Lebenskunst und literarisches Projekt* (UDL, 81), 167 pp., argues that G.'s correspondence with Zelter, now restored by the *Münchener Ausgabe*, is a text whose organic wholeness, its literariness, has hitherto been neglected. It became clear to both correspondents that they were writing a collection of letters destined for publication and that it would be a kind of sequel and counterpart to the correspondence between G. and Schiller, and this awareness is reflected in the internal organization of the work. H. shows how the structure of the correspondence depends on the roles of the two correspondents — G. emphasizing symbolism, Z. humour — and how individual letters gain depth of meaning within the network of themes and motifs set up by the whole collection. More fundamentally she shows how centrally these letters revolve around the experience of death and transience, beginning with the death of Schiller, and how remorselessly they follow the ageing of both G. and Z. and the losses they endured. In defiance of such forces of disorder G. and Z. use autobiographical techniques in order to make sense of their lives, and thus they come to reflect on the anthropological function of letterwriting as a model of linguistic communication and interpretation. Id., 'Gs und Zelters Reflexionen über die menschliche Stimme', *JDSG*, 40:181–209.

THEMES.   Maike Arz, *Literatur und Lebenskraft. Vitalistische Naturforschung und bürgerliche Literatur um 1800*, Stuttgart, Metzler & Poeschel, 264 pp., offers a comparative study of the vitalism in G.'s thought, arguing for the connections between his approach to scientific matters, namely his rejection both of a telelology of nature and of reductionist and potentially materialist atomism, and his view of human creativity. After an examination of the *Prometheus* fragment, *Werther*, 'Metamorphose der Pflanzen' and 'Metamorphose der Tiere', A. goes on to examine texts by two further writers with anthropological concerns, Chamisso's *Peter Schlemihl* and Büchner's *Lenz*. Vitalism also features in a study by Matthew Bell, *Goethe's Naturalistic Anthropology. Man and other Plants*, Oxford, Clarendon, 1994, 346 pp., which is considerably more thorough and convincing in its location of G.'s writing within the context of 18th-c. anthropology. In a wide-ranging introduction B. shows how the concerns of the Enlightenment led to tensions and slippages between a naturalistic anthropology of human nature and an optimistic ethics. He then follows the development of G.'s reflections on human nature, particularly in response to the development of Herder's thinking, and analyses in some detail the literary realization of these ideas in a range of texts from *Werther*, through the revision of *Wilhelm Meisters Theatralische Sendung* to *Die Wahlverwandtschaften*. B. is thereby able to integrate the subtle analysis of individual texts in a broader account of the development of G.'s thought and locate this, in the end, within the Western tradition of thinking about the relationship between mind and body. Ulrike Landfester, *Der Dichtung Schleier. Zur poetischen Funktion von Kleidung in Goethes Frühwerk* (Litterae, 30), Freiburg, Rombach, 1995, 338 pp., consists of a number of essays reflecting on the meanings attributed to clothing in writings of G. up to 1785, and therefore including the prose *Iphigenie* and *Wilhelm Meisters Theatralische Sendung*, with a prefatory section on the history of the semantics of clothing. Drawing our attention to a surprising range of usages, she shows how clothes and ornaments can be used to stand for people, that is, either to represent them or to represent their absence, to allow human contact or prevent it, and how they can be used to articulate the role that a character plays or to articulate the problem of naturalness. Remo Bodei, *Dekompositionen. Formen des modernen Individuums*, trans. Sabine Schneider (Spekulation und Erfahrung, 11, 36), Stuttgart-Bad Cannstatt, Frommann-Holzboog, 400 pp., is an extended study of the thought of G., Hegel, and the Romantics. One section (pp. 228–88) examines with a typical combination of diffuseness and insight aspects of G.'s reflections on ideas of change, using Bruno and Spinoza as paradigms and including particularly interesting reflections on the female characters who are threatened by the activity of the men.

There have been several studies of the presentation of sexuality in G.'s writing. Helmut Fuhrmann, *Der androgyne Mensch. 'Bild' und 'Gestalt' der Frau und des Mannes im Werk Goethes*, Würzburg, Königshausen & Neumann, 1995, 192 pp., argues that there is a tension in G.'s writing between his more formal, theoretical statements, in which he posits a fundamental, natural difference between men and women, and his literary imagination, which continually drives him to construct male figures which tend towards what would have been felt to be feminine and female figures who adopt male roles. He thus argues that G.'s literary writing is drawn towards a vision of human beings as essentially androgynous. F. proceeds by examining the gender connotations of particular values and thereby avoids the reduction of literary interpretation either to biography or to the explicit portrayal of gender. This approach is a productive one, and the style lively although it is somewhat essayistic and therefore not always able to engage in sufficient detail either with existing interpretations of G. or with modern theories of gender. More specific studies, although they lack the sweep of F.'s argument, are often more successful: S. E. Gustafson, 'Male desire in G.'s *Götz von Berlichingen*', Kuzniar, *Goethe*, 111–24; W. D. Wilson, 'Amazon, agitator, allegory: political and gender cross(-dress)ing in G.'s *Egmont*', *ib.*, 125–46; Rigby, *Transgressions*, contains a chapter on *Iphigenie auf Tauris* (128–49) within a broader discussion of the history from Racine to Hebbel of the connections between tragedy and Enlightenment and its consequences for the portrayal of women; R. D. Tobin, 'In and against nature: Goethe on homosexuality and heterotextuality', Kuzniar, *Goethe*, 94–110; H. Schlaffer, 'G. als Muse. Der Autor und die Schriftstellerinnen seiner Zeit', *GJb*, 112, 1995 [1996]: 183–95.

There have been several further studies of particular motifs in G.'s writing: R. Hahn, '"Dies Werk ist nicht, ein für allemal beurtheilt zu werden [...]." Über Gs Auseinandersetzung mit dem *Nibelungenlied*', *GJb*, 112, 1995 [1996]: 275–86; M. Bell, 'G.'s two types of Classicism', *PEGS(NS)*, 65, 1993–95: 98–115; R. Görner, 'G.'s Ulysses: on the meaning of a project', *PEGS(NS)*, 64, 1993–95: 21–37; I. Honnef-Becker, 'Ist G. eigentlich ironisch? Zum Ironie-Begriff in der Literaturwissenschaft', *ZDP*, 115: 161–75. More general political and philosophical issues are addressed by: N. Rennie, 'Ut pictura historia: G.'s historical imagination and the *Augenblick*', *GY*, 8: 120–41; G. Schmidt, 'G.: politisches Denken und regional orientierte Praxis im Alten Reich', *GJb*, 112, 1995 [1996]: 197–212; K. Mommsen, 'Die Türken im Spiegel von Gs Werk', *ib.*, 243–57; G. Sauder, 'Der junge G. und das religiöse Denken des 18. Jarhhunderts', *ib.*, 97–110; A. Costazza, 'Ein Aufsatz aus der Zeit von Moritz' Weimarer Aufenthalt. Eine Revision der Datierung und Zuschreibung von Gs Spinoza-Studie', *ib.*, 259–74; T. Ziolkowski, 'Friedrich Schlegel und seine drei Tendenzen: krank oder gesund?', *ib.*, 121–34, discusses shifts in G.'s attitudes towards Romanticism around 1805.

Frederick Amrine, *Goethe in the History of Science*, begins with vol. 1, *Bibliography, 1776–1949*, and vol. 2, *Bibliography, 1950–1990* (SMGL, 29–30), xiii + 465, ix + 464 pp., which will provide an indispensable basis for studying the reception of G.'s scientific work. The main body of these two volumes consists of a listing by year of all the scientific publications by G. and of all the responses to them. The definition of the latter category is particularly difficult and particularly important, and, although some decisions will no doubt prove to be contentious, A. has wisely chosen to include not only discussions and reviews but also original scientific work that shows indebtedness to G., but excludes discussions within larger studies of G. or in histories of literature. Of particular value is the fact that entries include not only basic bibliographical information but also an indication of the area of scientific work to which they refer. Vol. 2 concludes with nine indexes which will turn this impressive labour of love into an invaluable practical tool for research both into the history of science and into Goethe. A more analytical approach is adopted by Theda Rehbock, *Goethe und die 'Rettung der Phänomene'. Philosophische Kritik des naturwissenschaftlichen Weltbilds am Beispiel der Farbenlehre*, Konstanz, Vlg am Hockgraben, 1995, xiv + 434 pp., who discusses the position of G.'s optics within the history of science. The debate, she argues, has polarized round, on the one hand, the argument that G. was an unscientific amateur who failed to understand Newton, and, on the other, the view of G. as heralding an alternative kind of science. An adequate understanding of G., and indeed of science, requires an acceptance of the historical evolution of science, and R. therefore reconstructs the 18th-c. context of the reception of Newton, and in particular the criticisms of Berkeley, in order to elaborate a world in which G.'s rejection of Newton was a valid philosophical enterprise, one which, she argues, is best interpreted as a forerunner of the phenomenology of Husserl and Wittgenstein. I. Müller, 'G. und die Medizin seiner Zeit', *GJb*, 112, 1995 [1996]: 55–70, shows how G. combined an affinity to the Hippocratic belief in the balance of natural forces with a general scepticism about the cognitive force of medicine; C. Paulitsch, 'Rekonstruktion eines Farbvariators und seine Entwicklung', *ib.*, 403–05.

INFLUENCE. RECEPTION. Annette Rehrl, *Illustrierte Ausgaben von Goethes Lyrik 1800–1933*, Stuttgart, Metzler & Poeschel, 262 pp., traces the reception of G.'s poetry through the illustrations to collected editions. Introductory sections deal with the history of the illustration before going on to discuss their function in three of the most commonly illustrated poems, 'Heidenröslein', 'Der Fischer', and 'Der Totentanz'. Although R. is aware that other factors are involved, her focus is on the connections between text and illustration, and she shows in a final section how the pattern of historical development reflects not only the evolution of art history but also the history of the understanding of G., with a relative lack of popularity round the middle of the 19th c. followed by the restoration of — and then later the challenge to — a conservative view of his poetry. H. S. Madland, 'Poetic transformations and nineteenth-century scholarship: the "Friederikenliteratur"', *GY*, 8: 28–44. Irmgard Wagner, *Critical Approaches to Goethe's Classical Dramas. Iphigenie, Torquato Tasso, and Die natürliche Tochter*, Columbia, Camden House, 1995, 233 pp., deals with each of these three plays in turn, each one within three chronological sections dealing with the periods up to 1918, between 1918 and 1945, and since 1945 respectively. A brief conclusion compares the critical fates of the three plays, and it is indeed worth noting that the fundamental differences between these plays are reflected in their changing fortunes, but the structure of the book, which consists basically of three separate narratives, points up the reluctance of W. (as indeed of the series itself) to deal with the broader historical context of the academic debate about these plays. This debate must appear as a self-contained dialogue of academics reacting to each other as long as there is no discussion of the wider reception of the texts in schools or in the theatre, let alone of the ideological contexts within which the arguments about texts are deployed and values in them are identified and criticized. Further questions of reception are discussed by: L. Zagari, 'G. und die europäische Romantik in ihrer Wirkung und Gegenwirkung', *ib.*, 213–26; E. Osterkamp, 'Die Geburt der Romantik aus dem Geiste des Klassizismus. G. als Mentor der Maler seiner Zeit', *ib.*, 135–48; E. Bahr, 'Die Widersacher des späten G.: die Jungdeutschen, die Nationalen und die Orthodoxen', *ib.*, 227–41; R. J. Baerlocher, '"Le nom insiffable du Grand G.". Anmerkungen zum Goethe-Bild von George Sand', *ib.*, 309–20; M. Jaeger, 'G. oder Nietzsche. Karl Löwiths philosophische Goethe-Rezeption', *ib.*, 321–31; M. Lemmel, 'Die Bedeutung Gs für Robert Walser. Ein Überblick über Textbefund und Forschungslage', *ib.*, 339–42; G. Martin, 'Von der weltanschaulichen Differenz. Heidegger und G.', *DVLG*, 70:475–500; E. Waniek, 'Apotheosis and death of the author: G. in Itálica', *Neophilologus*, 80:75–90, discusses the image of G. in the novel *Joc de miralls* (1989) by Carme Riera.

BIOGRAPHY. Wilhelm Bode, *Goethes Liebesleben. Dichtung und Wahrheit*, Leipzig, Edition Leipzig, 352 pp, is an illustrated and modernized edition of the 1913 volume in which B. presented what he called 'die erste erotische Biographie des Dichters' (p. 5). Although it has become a classic point of reference for the biographical approach to G.'s writing in terms of his personal experience of love, B. attempts consistently to separate life from literature. As the subtitle indicates, his intention is to contrast G.'s retrospective stylizations with contemporary evidence, and although the modern reader misses the awareness of unconscious motives that would really undermine the sentimentality of earlier biographies, this is perhaps the first sustained attempt to interpret G.'s life 'against' his more public autobiographical writings. M. Jaeger, 'Der glückliche Heide. G. über Winckelmann', *WW*, 46:210–24. K. F. Gille, 'G. an Bucholtz, 14 Februar 1814. Aspekte der Stellung Gs zur Nationalbewegung', *WB*,

42 : 165–87. K. Gerhardt, 'G. und "Das Römische Carneval". Eine Betrachtung zu Text und Bild', *ib.*, 289–96. E.-M. Clauss, 'Im Schatten Werthers. Die Briefe Gs an Frau von Stein', *ib.*, 296–304. Gisela Maul and Margarete Oppel, *Goethes Wohnhaus*, Hanser, Munich, 159 pp., is a detailed description of G.'s house in Weimar. After introductory essays on the history of the house (Gisela Maul) and on G.'s practice of collecting (Erich Trunz), the book contains a description, a photograph and a plan of each room and, what is perhaps more important, a description of each of the art objects in the room, together with notes on G.'s acquisition of them. C. Lichtenstern, 'Jupiter — Dionysos — Eros/Thanatos: Gs symbolische Bildprogramme im Haus am Frauenplan', *GJb*, 112, 1995 [1996]: 343–60; T. Richter, 'Ein Brief Doris Zelters über den Besuch mit ihrem Vater bei G. im Juli 1826', *ib.*, 365–73; A. Ohage, 'Die Goethesche "Familien Tafel" wiederentdeckt', *JDFH*: 130–45.

3. SCHILLER

EDITIONS. *Schillers Werke, Nationalausgabe*, continues with vol. 15, part 2, *Übersetzungen aus dem Französischen*, ed. Willi Hirdt, Weimar, Böhlau, 712 pp., containing translations of three comedies by Picard, the first scene of *Britannicus*, and S.'s masterpiece, *Phèdre*. H. produces a text that is both easily readable and also of great scholarly value, having the French original printed in parallel and consigning to end-notes the considerable complexities of the textual history. He also contributes an informative essay on S.'s relationship to French culture and includes documentation on the reception of these translations. A worthy addition to an edition that is marked by care for the variety of needs that readers can bring to texts. *Der Geisterseher*, ed. Mathias Mayer (UB, 7435), 243 pp., uses a sensible synthesis of different editions of the text, including the *Philosophisches Gespräch*, followed by notes, a bibliography, and an essay in which M. outlines the complex genesis of this fragmentary novel and discusses its relationship to contemporary debates about the supernatural. *Die Räuber. Ein Schauspiel*, ed. F. J. Lamport, London, Bristol Classical Press, 1993, vii + 189 pp., goes back to the 1781 text, with cautious modernization of spelling and punctuation. The introduction provides the reader with the necessary background information and suggests how S.'s break with the conventions of traditional tragedy made him confront the problem of poetic coherence, which he resolved particularly by the use of parallel and contrasting dramatic situations. This useful edition concludes with extensive notes which deal efficiently with linguistic and interpretative difficulties and with the many historical allusions, and with a vocabulary of less common words. *Don Carlos and*

Mary Stuart, trans. Hilary Collier Sy-Quia and Peter Oswald, introd. Lesley Sharpe, OUP, xl + 359 pp., contains new verse versions which generally manage even to reproduce the word-plays of the original and are accompanied by an explanatory note and authoritative introduction in which Sharpe places the two plays in their historical context and discusses problems of their interpretation.

LITERARY WORKS. *Gedichte von Friedrich Schiller. Interpretationen*, ed. Norbert Oellers (UB, 9473), 324 pp., contains: G.-M. Schulz, '"Die Kindsmörderin"' (11–27); G. Kurscheidt, '"Die schlimmen Monarchen"' (28–48); W. Riedel, '"Resignation"' (48–63); H. Koopmann, '"Die Götter Griechenlands"' (64–83); H.-J. Malles, '"Die Künstler"' (84–111); J. Golz, '"Der Tanz"' (112–22); W. Hinderer, '"Das Reich der Schatten"' (123–48); K. Jeziorkowski, '"Der Spaziergang"' (149–78); G. Theile, '"Klage der Ceres"' (179–95); G. Kaiser, '"Der Taucher"' (196–216); K. Pestalozzi, '"Die Kraniche des Ibycus"' (217–36); N. Oellers, '"Das Glück"' (237–54); K. L. Berghahn, '"Das Lied von der Glocke"' (255–82); E. Osterkamp, '"Nänie"' (282–97); H.-G. Werner, '"Kassandra"' (298–311). Joachim Bernauer, *'Schöne Welt, wo bist du?' Über das Verhältnis von Lyrik und Poetik bei Schiller* (PSQ, 138), 1995, 270 pp., is an examination of S.'s aesthetics that moves away from such well researched fields as the dramatic theory and the more philosophical essays, and traces the development of S.'s reflections on poetry as found primarily in his reviews but also in his letters and his own poetry. The focus of this study is on the way that S.'s view of the means of human self-realization changes during the 1780s from an idealization of friendship to a vision of the Utopian nature of art. There is a brief final section on the last decade of S.'s life, which, B. argues, shows no further major changes. His overall conclusions may be unsurprising, but this study proceeds by close textual analysis and its value lies in the clarity with which it defines the steps taken to reach them and in the matter-of-fact way in which it handles S.'s terminology. Michael Hofmann, *Friedrich Schiller. Die Räuber* (OIU, 79), 128 pp., offers an introduction to the play that is particularly successful in its combination of clarity and complexity. H.'s discussions of psychological, philosophical, and aesthetic issues are not only informative but also stimulate the reader to independent reflection and study. R. Harrison, '"Wer die Wahl hat, hat die Qual." Philosophy and poetry in S.'s *Wallenstein*', PEGS(NS), 65, 1993–95:136–61. D. E. von Mücke, 'The spectacle of Maria Stuart's imprisonment', Leventhal, *Reading*, 93–116. Gordon Sebastian Gamlin, *Synergetische Sinnkonstitution und das Bild des 'Macbeth' in Friedrich von Schillers Einrichtung der gleichnamigen Tragödie von William Shakespeare am Weimarer Hoftheater am 14. Mai 1800 unter der Leitung von Johann Wolfgang von Goethe*, Konstanz, Hartung-Gorre, 1995, iv + 104 pp., examines the performance of S.'s translation of *Macbeth* in terms of the interplay of many interventions, including those of Goethe, the actors, and even the audience. There are sections on the position of this performance within a history of the reception of Shakespeare and within a debate about translation, but the most effective parts of this study are those where Gamlin discusses the practicalities of the theatre and shows how S.'s knowledge of them and of the audience's expectations made it necessary for him to recast the Shakespearian original. The concluding analysis of five symptomatic scenes discusses S.'s handling of the supernatural and the comic, where his tendency to clarify and harmonize has the effect not of weakening but of focusing the horror of Shakespeare's play. L. M. Brooks, 'Autobiographical hyperbole: S.'s *Naive and Sentimental Poetry*', Leventhal, *Reading*, 193–209.

THEMES. *Schiller heute*, ed. Hans-Jörg Knobloch and Helmut Koopmann (Stauffenburg Colloquium, 40), Tübingen, Stauffenburg, 225 pp., contains the papers given at a conference in Johannesburg: H. Koopmann, 'S. und das Ende der aufgeklärten Geschichtsphilosophie' (11–25); M. Misch, 'S. und die Religion' (27–43); H.-J. Marquardt, 'Ästhetik der Emanzipation — Emanzipation der Ästhetik? Zu Ss Konzept des literarischen Publikums' (45–58); P. Horn, 'Die "Tochter der Freiheit" und die "Tendenz". Zur Autonomie der Kunst in Ss *Über die ästhetische Erziehung des Menschen* und Schopenhauers *Die Welt als Wille und Vorstellung*' (59–73); B. Kytzler, 'Der unterdrückte Bogen B in den *Räubern*' (75–82); T. Elm, '"Ein Ganzes der Kunst und der Wahrheit." Zum Verhältnis von Poesie und Historie in Ss *Wallenstein*' (83–97); K. Köhnke, 'Ss *Maria Stuart* — philosophische Theorie und dramatische Praxis' (99–113); K. S. Guthke, '*Die Jungfrau von Orleans*. Sendung und Witwenmachen' (115–30); M. Ritzer, 'Not und Schuld. Zur Funktion des "antiken" Schicksalsbegriffs in Ss *Braut von Messina*' (131–50); H.-J. Knobloch, '*Wilhelm Tell*. Historisches Festspiel oder politisches Zeitstück?' (151–65); R. Nethersole, '". . . die Triebe zu leben, zu schaffen, zu spielen": Ss Spieltriebkonzeption aus gegenwärtiger Sicht' (167–88); R.-P. Janz, 'Schiller-Parodien' (189–201); and K. von Delft, 'Deutsche Klassik in afrikaanser Übersetzung. Am Beispiel des *Don Carlos*' (203–23). Norbert Oellers, *Friedrich Schiller. Zur Modernität eines Klassikers*, ed. Michael Hofmann, Frankfurt, Insel, 383 pp., contains 18 essays by this distinguished scholar, with an appreciation in celebration of his 6oth birthday. Many of these are already classic studies, but five of them are new and underline the range of O.'s approaches, whether analysis of a particular text, biographical study or thematic survey. Steven D. Martinson, *Harmonious Tensions. The Writings of*

Friedrich Schiller, Newark, Delaware U.P.–London, AUP, 448 pp., investigates the precarious unity of opposing principles in S.'s work by taking as central image the motif of a stringed instrument in which it is the tension, the strain which might break the instrument, that produces the music. Introductory chapters examine S.'s medical writing and his early poetry but then, after a section on *Der Verbrecher aus verlorener Ehre*, there is only a brief discussion of the early plays before M. comes to the main focus of his study, *Wallenstein, Maria Stuart, Wilhelm Tell*, and the theoretical essays of S.'s maturity. This analysis of the dialectical in S.'s thinking suggests a greater distance than is sometimes assumed between S. and the tradition of Romantic idealism. It is also full of interpretative insights and even the reader who cannot concur with every one of them will benefit from the ideas with which this book is teeming. Whereas M.'s approach is largely interpretative, a more critical perspective is offered by Constantin Behler, *Nostalgic Teleology: Friedrich Schiller and the Schemata of Aesthetic Humanism* (SGS, 26), 1995, vii + 259 pp., which is a fascinating study of the problems inherent in S.'s notion of aesthetic education. S.'s triadic myth, the 'nostalgic teleology' of B.'s title, promises the restoration of harmony and freedom by means of art, but this idealism, B. argues, can equally be read as a strategy for the internalization of normative discipline. In particular B. points to S.'s theoretical underpinning of an ideal of femininity which, he argues, uses the rhetoric of liberation while enforcing the internalization of norms of gendered behaviour. This discussion of the post-structuralist critique of S., and thereby of the German idealist tradition, is presented with admirable clarity and coherence. Markus Ohlenroth, *Bilderschrift. Schillers Arbeit am Bild* (EH, 1, 1524), 1995, 286 pp., examines S.'s imagery in different areas of his writing, its sources and its functions. In the early poetry O. finds imagery that is primarily scientific in its origins, while that in the shorter aesthetic essays from 1791–93 is more moderate and more likely to win the response of the educated general reader. The final main section uses S.'s Matthisson review in order to show how S. employs images drawn from nature in some of his mature poems and *Wilhelm Tell*. N. Werber, 'Technologien der Macht. System- und medientheoretische Überlegungen zu Ss Dramatik', *JDSG*, 40:210–43. L. E. Kurth-Voigt, 'Preexistence and the plurality of lives in the writings of the young S.', *GY*, 8:172–91. Taylor, *Perspectives*, contains 'S.'s Spinozan theory of God and its relation to the person' (5–37), which discusses parallels between Spinoza and the *Ästhetische Briefe*. Hans-Jürgen Schings, *Die Brüder des Marquis Posa. Schiller und der Geheimbund der Illuminaten*, Tübingen, Niemeyer, 247 pp., takes the problematic relationship between the judgements on Posa in the *Briefe über Don Karlos* and his portrayal in the play itself and argues that this can be explained in terms of S.'s attitude to the *illuminati*, many of whose values are represented in Posa. Schings then retraces the complex but largely forgotten history of S.'s dealings with the *illuminati*, and argues that this is the underlying theme of the various stages in the long drawn-out genesis of the play. Schings not only deepens our understanding of *Don Karlos* but provides a coherent interpretation of many documents from S.'s life by filling out a picture of the network of *illuminati* in late-18th-c. Germany. The study ends with an examination of the later development of these Utopian ideas in S.'s *Ästhetische Briefe*. C. M. Craig, 'S. and the issue of armed conflict', *GN*, 27 : 89–94. Hansjoachim Kiene, *Schillers Lotte. Porträt einer Frau in ihrer Welt*, Frankfurt, Fischer, 326 pp., is a biography of Charlotte that in reality revolves around the 'eigentliche Hauptperson', Friedrich Schiller, and uses the figure of Charlotte in order to focus on the private life of her husband. K. creates a fluent narrative out of the known facts, but the picture of Charlotte that emerges is not sharply defined and is all too indebted to the cliché of the woman who fulfils herself through wifely devotion. P. Mattson, ' "Bloβ zufällige Versäumniβ"? Zwei unbekannte Briefe Wilhelm von Humboldts an S.', *JDSG*, 40 : 14–29.

INFLUENCE, RECEPTION. Lesley Sharpe, *Schiller's Aesthetic Essays: Two Centuries of Criticism*, Columbia, Camden House, 1995, xiii + 137 pp., presents a survey of the academic history of S.'s aesthetic essays and is the most successful of this series of reception studies because the academic discussion of such theoretical texts, unlike that of the dramas, is relatively independent of other realms of cultural life such as theatre and school. What becomes clear is the way that in more recent times the political interest in S. has shifted from the plays to these essays. The value of the book, however, is not only that it reconstructs a section of the history of the discipline but perhaps even more that, by illuminating them from so many different angles, it contributes considerably to our understanding of the essays themselves. F. M. Birrell, ' "abenteuerlich miβverstanden?": Habermas' reception and interpretation of S.', *GLL*, 49 : 297–309. H. Rowland, 'Confluence and crosscurrents: S.'s "Das Lied von der Glocke" and Hans Christian Andersen's "Die alte Kirchenglocke" ', *MDU*, 88 : 142–56.

4. INDIVIDUAL AUTHORS
(EXCLUDING GOETHE AND SCHILLER)

ALBRECHT. I. Roebling, 'Sturm und Drang — weiblich. Eine Untersuchung zu Sophie Albrechts Schauspiel *Theresgen*', *DUS*, 48.1 : 63–77.

BRUN. B. Keith-Smith, 'The ballads of Friederike Brun: celebrations of beauty, magic and panic', *CGP*, 24 : 37–55.

BÜRGER. Helmut Scherer, *Lange schon in manchem Sturm und Drange. Gottfried August Bürger. Der Dichter des Münchhausen. Eine Biographie*, Berlin, Scherer, 333 pp., combines fluency with the results of new research by reserving the scholarly apparatus for a planned supplementary volume. S. sweeps aside the sentimentality of the traditional image of B. as victim and shows the extent of the cultural and financial privileges which he enjoyed and which he squandered largely by extravagance and disorganization. Illustrations and the unflinching honesty of B.'s own letters are both effectively used to create a strong feeling of immediacy, at the expense, perhaps, of reflection on the historical significance of B.'s ideas and values, for example in relation to social justice or sexual propriety. There is also little consideration of the nature of B.'s literary achievement, but S. presents the complex circumstances of B.'s private and public life in a thorough and convincing way and makes possible more realistic assessments of the relationship between the man and his writing. *G. A. Bürger und J. W. L. Gleim*, ed. Hans-Joachim Kertscher (Hallesche Beiträge zur europäischen Aufklärung, 3), Tübingen, Niemeyer, xxvi + 264 pp. + 1 table, contains an introductory review by K. of current research (xi–xxvi) followed by: Id., ' "Unser *Bürger* ist ein Halberstädter." Johann Wilhelm Ludwig Gleim und Gottfried August Bürger' (1–13); E. Rohmer, 'Der "Personalcharakter" in der Lyrik Wilhelm Ludwig Gleims. Untersuchungen zum Dichtungsverständnis an einem Beispiel aus den *Liedern für das Volk*' (14–28); S. Mödersheim, 'Igel oder Amor? Zum Briefwechsel zwischen Anna Louisa Karsch und Johann Wilhelm Ludwig Gleim' (29–39); U. Pott, 'Die Freundschaft und die Musen. Gleim in seinen Briefen an die Dichterin Anna Louisa Karsch und ihre Tocher Caroline Luise von Klencke' (40–57); G. Busch, 'Von den Gleimschen Romanzen zur ersten deutschen "romantisch-comischen" Oper' (58–67); G. Mühlpfordt, 'Halle-Leipziger Aufklärer als Lehrer und Anreger Gottfried August Bürgers — sein Werden und Wirken in der Geisteswelt der Mitteldeutschen Aufklärung' (68–96); H. Scherer, 'Die soziale Herkunft des Dichters Gottfried August Bürger' (97–136); H. Ritter, 'Liebe und Ehe bei Gottfried August Bürger — Wirklichkeit und Poesie' (137–48); T. Höhle, 'Über die von Gottfried August Bürger dem *Münchhausen*-Buch hinzugefügten Geschichten' (149–58); B. Wiebel, 'Münchhausens Kugelritt ins 20. Jahrhundert — ein Aufklärungsflug' (159–83); G. Häntzschel, ' Demokratisch, patriotisch, kosmopolitisch. Aspekte der Popularität bei Gottfried August Bürger' (184–94); H. Feger, 'Gottfried August Bürgers

Hauptmomente der kritischen Philosophie. Zur Methode der Popularisierung der Kantischen Philosophie an der Göttinger Universität' (195–208); H.-J. Kertscher, 'Nachahmung — Ideal — Moral. Zu einigen Aspekten in Bürgers ästhetischen Vorlesungen' (209–23); M. Rüppel, '"Was sagen Sie von Mme Bürger?" Elise Bürger (1769–1833) als Schauspielerin und das Theater zur Zeit der "Weimarer Klassik"' (224–38); H.-J. Ketzer, 'Zum Tod eines Dichters:Gottfried August Bürger, gestorben am 8. Juni 1794' (239–46); and H. Scherer, 'Dokumente zur sozialen Herkunft von Gottfried August Bürger — Anhang' (247–52, table). Anna Carrdus, *Classical Rhetoric and the German Poet 1620 to the Present. A Study of Opitz, Bürger and Eichendorff*, Oxford, Legenda, xii + 263 pp., includes 'G. A. B.: Rhetoric and "Volkspoesie"', pp. 87–156, showing how active the classical tradition of rhetoric remained, even amongst writers of the Sturm und Drang who so emphasized naturalness, feeling, and imagination. Examining 'Leonore' and 'Das Lied vom Braven Manne' against the background of B.'s theoretical writing, C. demonstrates the importance of the principle of *enargeia*, modified by B. in the light of his concept of *Popularität*. This perceptive analysis of the connections between theory and practice is a valuable contribution to our understanding of B. in particular and 18th-c. poetry in general.

CAMPE. C. Federle, '"Die Erhaltung des Gleichgewichts": defining and prescribing a technology of self', Leventhal, *Reading*, 153–67, discusses C.'s conception of the relationship between sentiment and reason.

CLAUDIUS. *Matthias Claudius 1740–1815. Leben. Zeit. Werk*, ed. Jörg-Ulrich Fechner (WSA, 21), xxviii + 344 pp., contains the papers of a 1990 symposium: F. G. Friemel, 'Christliche Simplicität' (3–18); C. Degn, 'Claudius und die Obrigkeit' (19–28); W. Freund, 'Claudius' theologiegeschichtliche Stellung aus heutiger evangelischer Sicht' (29–41); W. Martens, 'Claudius und die Französische Revolution' (43–65); B. Becker-Cantarino, 'Rebecca Claudius. Zur sozialgeschichtlichen Realität des "Bauermädchen"' (69–90); A. Lüchow, 'Claudius und Klopstock' (91–109); K. Bohnen, 'Lessing und Claudius. Vom "Doppelgesicht" der Aufklärung' (111–33); J.-U. Fechner, 'Claudius und Herder. Eine Skizze' (135–49); K. Hammacher, 'Jacobi und Claudius' (151–64); H. Weigelt, 'Lavater und Claudius' (165–78); A. Kranefuss, '"Es gibt was Bessers in der Welt." Zum poetischen "Unterricht von göttlichen Dingen" bei Matthias Claudius' (181–207); A. Kadelbach, 'Matthias Claudius und die Gesangbücher im Dänischen Gesamtstaat' (209–38); L. L. Albertsen, 'Claudius als Verfasser von Kirchenliedern' (239–50); H. Rowland, 'Satirische Formen in den Feuilletons und Rezensionen von Matthias Claudius' (251–63); D. Andresen, 'Matthias Claudius' Schrift "An den Naber mit Rat" sprach- und theologiegeschichtlich' (265–75); A. Fink-Langlois, 'Matthias Claudius als Übersetzer von Fénélons religiösen Schriften' (277–310); and W. Kehn, 'Garten und Landschaft bei Claudius' (311–31). H.-Diether Grohmann, *Matthias Claudius als Übersetzer französischsprachiger Schriftsteller. Eine translationskritische Analyse der vom Wandsbecker Boten ins Deutsche übertragenen religionsphilosophischen Werke und utopischen Reiseromane unter Anwendung eines Rahmenmodells der wissenschaftlichten Übersetzungskritik* (Kieler Beiträge zur deutschen Sprachgeschichte, 17), Neumünster, Wachholtz, 1995, 326 pp., has substantial introductory sections reviewing the range of C.'s translation work in the *Wandsbecker Bote* and discussing the most suitable categories for evaluating translations. He then offers a detailed analysis of three sections of C.'s *Die Reisen des Cyrus*, a translation of a novel in French by Andrew Michael Ramsay. Normative judgements are fraught with difficulties, but G. shows that C.'s knowledge of French and his skill at reproducing its structures are considerably greater than had previously been thought. Briefer analyses of further translations confirm this judgement, but make an exception in the case of the later Fénelon translation, which is much freer.

ENGEL. H. Kallweit, 'Ausdruck: Homogenisierung des Textes ans "lebendige Princip" in Seele und Körper', *Acta* (Seeon), 633–53, discuss E.'s views on the physical expression of states of mind.

FORSTER. H. Peitsch, 'Round-trips from the inside to the outside: the changing place of Georg Forster's travelogues in the German literary canon from 1797 to 1989', *CGP*, 24: 17–35.

GELLERT. Claudia Kaiser, *'Geschmack' als Basis der Verständigung. Chr. F. Gellerts Brieftheorie* (EH, 1, 1563), 181 pp., discusses the use of the category 'good taste' in the 18th c. and how G. applies it in his injunctions on letter-writing, in particular his ideal of 'geschmackvolle Natürlichkeit'. In the second half of this study K. reflects on the social basis for G.'s idea of tastefulness and relates it to a revision of the roles of author and reader and the empowerment of social groups hitherto often excluded from writing. This universalism is, she argues, a means by which G. is able to articulate a middle-class social morality based on an idealization of personal experience. B. Witte, 'Christian Fürchtegott Gellert: *Leben der schwedischen Gräfinn von G***. Die Frau, die Schrift, der Tod', *Romane* (Interpretationen), 112–49, discusses the use of social types in G.'s novel.

GLEIM. Substantial contributions are listed under BÜRGER and KARSCH.

GOTTSCHED. P. M. Mitchell, *Johann Christoph Gottsched (1700–1766). Harbinger of German Classicism*, Columbia, Camden House, 1995, x + 131 pp., is a sober and well-informed survey of the career and achievement of G., not only as a literary critic and theoretician but also as a linguist and popular philosopher. The chapters are organized by chronology and genre, and M. offers a sympathetic account of the logic behind G.'s intervention in a wide range of debates. This approach leads him to play down not only G.'s private life, his character and personal motives, but also intellectual episodes in which he played a more passive role, at the hands, for example, of Bodmer and Breitinger or Lessing. A fuller discussion would have allowed M. to evaluate G.'s significance within a shifting constellation of ideas and social forces, but this volume provides a useful basis for an understanding of G.'s project.

HAMANN. *Johann Georg Hamann. Autor und Autorschaft. Acta des sechsten Internationalen Hamann-Kolloquiums im Herder-Institut zu Marburg-Lahn 1992*, ed. Bernhard Gajek (RBDSL, B, 61), 371 pp., contains: M. Wetzel, '"Geschmack an Zeichen"; Johann Georg Hamann als der letzte Denker des Buches und der erste Denker der Schrift' (13–24); B. Weissenborn, 'Auswahl und Verwendung der Bibelstellen in Johann Georg Hamanns Frühschriften' (41–64); M. Rössler, 'Die Verwendung von Kirchenliedern in Hamanns Frühschriften' (41–64); R. Wild, 'Polemik, "innere Figur" und Schuld. Zur Kreativität Johann Georg Hamanns am Beispiel des "Fliegenden Briefes"' (65–78); M. Beetz, 'Dialogische Rhetorik und Intertextualität in Hamanns "Aesthetica in nuce"' (79–106); K. Hizing, 'Von Gesichtszügen und Kreuzzügen. Hamanns Physiognomik des Stils' (107–22); A. Bohnenkamp-Renken, 'Offenbarung im Zitat. Zur Intertextualität Hamannscher Schreibverfahren anhand von "Wolken. Ein Nachspiel Sokratischer Denkwürdigkeiten"' (123–42); T. Studer, 'Rekonkretisierung als Schreibmotiv bei Hamann' (143–57); H. Weiss, 'Hamann zu Hume und Kant. Johann Georg Hamanns Erkenntnis-, Sprach- und Stiltheorie' (161–76); U. Gaier, 'Hamanns und Herders hieroglyphische Stile' (177–96); E. Büchsel, 'Die parodierten Philosophen. Hamann zwischen Voltaire, Herder und Jean Paul' (197–211); J. Ringleben, 'Gott als Schriftsteller. Zur Geschichte eines Topos' (215–76); H. Graubner, 'Hamanns Buffon-Kommentar und seine sprachtheologische Deutung des Stils' (277–304); J. von Lüpke, 'Zur theologischen Dramaturgie in Hamanns Autorschaft' (305–29); J. Kohnen, 'Ostpreußisch-russische Wechselbeziehungen in Königsberg zur Zeit Johann Georg Hamanns' (333–52); A. Michailov, 'Vladimir Koževnikov und sein Hamann-Buch aus dem Jahre 1897. Eine Episode aus der russischen Hamann-Rezeption' (353–68); and V. Bryuschinkin, 'Zur Logik der Kultur. Kant, Hamann und russische Slawophile über Aufklärung' (369–71). I. Hacking, 'How, why, when, and where did language go public?', Leventhal, *Reading*, 31–50.

HEBEL. J. A. Steiger, 'Die Kalendergeschichte als biblisch-narrative Predigt. Johann Peter Hebels *Franziska* im Vergleich mit deren Quelle (G. K. Pfeffel)', *Euphorion*, 90:277–99.

HEINSE. Rosemarie Elliott, *Wilhelm Heinse in Relation to Wieland, Winckelmann, and Goethe. Heinse's Sturm und Drang Aesthetic and New Literary Language* (FLK, 51), 204 pp., offers an analysis of H.'s style which proceeds by a series of comparisons, his *Stanzen* set against Wieland's *Idris und Zenide*, his *Gemäldebriefe* against Winckelmann's aesthetic writings, and *Ardinghello* against *Werther*. E. uses these comparisons in order to elaborate what is specific to H.'s writing and argues that they show him to be a central figure of the *Sturm und Drang*. Style is, of course, not everything, but E. shows how much it can tell us about a writer when the critic too is able to find an appropriate style for dealing with it. And, as Max Baeumer points out in a Preface (9–12), E.'s study of H. adds an important new element to our understanding of the evolution of the literary use of the German language. B. also contributes his own 'Wilhelm Heinse: *Ardinghello und die glückseligen Inseln*', *Romane* (Interpretationen), 240–58.

HERDER. The edition of Johann Gottfried Herder, *Briefe. Gesamtausgabe. 1763–1803*, concludes with vol. 10, *Register*, ed. Günter Arnold, Weimar, Böhlau, x + 865 pp., containing indexes which allow the preceding nine volumes to be searched for H.'s own works (both alphabetically and, within twelve categories, chronologically), for the names of people and their writings, and for the names of periodicals and for biblical, mythological and geographical names. In view of the diversity of his interests this volume promises to be an important tool in the research not only of H. himself but of the whole cultural world of late-18th-c. Germany. *Johann Gottfried Herder. Acaedmic Disciplines and the Pursuit of Knowledge*, ed. Wulf Koepke, Camden House, Columbia, xii + 276 pp., contains a valuable collection of studies going back to a 1990 symposium, focusing on epistemological questions: E. Knodt, 'Hermeneutics and the end of science: H.'s role in the formation of *Natur-* and *Geisteswissenschaften*' (1–12); P. H. Reill, 'H.'s historical practice and the discourse of Late Enlightenment science' (13–21); R. E. Norton, 'H.'s concept of "Kraft" and the psychology of semiotic functions' (22–31); J. Gessinger, '"Das Gefühl liegt dem Gehör so nahe:" the physiological foundations of H.'s theory of cognition' (32–52); H. J. Schneider, 'The cold eye: H.'s critique of Enlightenment visualism' (53–60); P. J. Burgard, 'Literary history and historical truth: Herder — "Shakespeare" — Goethe' (61–77); H. D. Irmscher, 'Der Vergleich im Denken Hs' (78–97); G. Arnold, 'H.'s interdisciplinary conjectures on the origin of human history' (98–105); K. Arens, 'History as knowledge: H., Kant, and the human sciences' (106–19); M. Maurer,

'Geschichte zwischen Theodizee und Anthropologie. Zur Wissenschaftlichkeit der historischen Schriften Hs' (120–36); M. Heinz, 'Grundzüge von Hs Psychologie: *Uebers Erkennen und Empfinden der Menschlichen Seele* (1774)' (137–51); T. Markworth, 'Das "Ich" und die Geschichte: Zum Zusammenhang von Selbstthematisierung und Geschichtsphilosophie' (152–67); M. Bollacher, 'Geschichte und Geschichtsschreibung in Hs *Ideen zur Philosophie der Geschichte der Menschheit*' (168–76); W. Koepke, '*Kulturnation* and its authorization through H.' (177–98); R. Otto, 'H.'s academy conception — theory and practice' (199–211); E. A. Menze, 'H. and world history; philosophical, historiographical, and pedagogical dimensions' (212–19); H. Müller-Michaels, '"For his own self-formation" — on the educative effect of autobiography about 1800' (220–31); M. Bunge, 'H.'s historical view of religion and the study of religion in the nineteenth century and today' (232–44); and S. B. Knoll, 'H. and Kurt Breysig' (245–65). *Sein ist im Werden. Essays zur Wirklichkeitkultur bei Johann Gottfried Herder anläßlich seines 250. Geburtstages*, ed. Wilhelm-Ludwig Federlin (Theion, 6), Frankfurt, Lang, 1995, 228 pp., contains a selection of essays which focus on theological and philosophical aspects: M. Bunge, 'J. G. H.'s view of religion' (9–20); K. Dienst, 'Vom geistlichen Nutzen des konsistorialen Amtes. Zum Umkreis eines Bückeburger (1775) und Weimarer (1790) Circulars von J. G. H.' (21–47); W. Düsing, 'Anthropozentrische Elemente in Hs Naturbegriff' (49–58); W.-L. Federlin, '"Die Homiletik erfodert eine ganz andre Beredsamkeit." Kritik und Bedeutung der Rhetorik in Lessings und Hs Homiletik' (59–82); H.-G. Geyer and D. Stoodt, 'H. im Pantheismusstreit' (83–102); H. von Hintzenstern, 'H. in der Weimarer Kirchenleitung' (103–21); R. Junghans, 'Hs Auslegung von Luthers Kleinem Katechismus' (123–52); T. Namowicz, 'Zur religiösen Komponente in Hs Auffassung von Volk und Nation' (153–69); J. Rathmann, 'Hs Volksbegriff und seine Pfarrertätigkeit' (171–78); J. W. Rogerson, 'Hs Entwurf der Anwendung dreier Akademischer Jahre für einen jungen Theologen' (179–85); B. Schnetzler and R. Aguirre, 'Johannes Müller von Schaffhausen als Herausgeber von Hs Dichtung *Der Cid*' (187–99); and E. Weber, 'H. und die Kultur der Brahmanen' (201–23). Schiewer, *Cognitio*, argues that the conventional periodization of literature has obscured a line of continuity, formed both by personal contact and study, which connects the epistemological approaches of H., Jean Paul and Novalis. By means of a detailed analysis of H.'s *Metakritik der Kritik der reinen Vernunft*, which takes up the largest part of this book, S. shows how this tradition rests on a rejection of the abstractness of Kant's theory of knowledge and how Lambert's approach offered a model for the integration of the form and content of knowledge by reflecting on the role of language in cognition. This study reinstates a relatively unresearched work of H.'s and thereby extends our picture of his philosophy of language and, derived from that, his understanding of human reason, but it also brings alive the contribution of Kant by taking seriously the arguments mounted against him by contemporaries. A similar but broader project is undertaken by Andreas Herz, *Dunkler Spiegel — helles Dasein. Natur, Geschichte, Kunst im Werk Johann Gottfried Herders* (BNL, 146), 551 pp., who in an important contribution to our understanding of H.'s epistemology shows how H. countered the rationalism of the Enlightenment and what he feared would be its revival through Kant with an awareness of the limitations of human knowledge. H. was not on the other hand, he argues, a sceptic but believed that knowledge was available to humans — at least partially — in other forms, through history, nature, art, and love. Although Herz's reluctance to analyse individual texts can mean a certain loss of focus, it is justified, especially in the case of a digressive writer like H., because it makes it possible for him to disentangle lines of argument and locate H. — and his style — within a history of ideas that stretches from the Enlightenment to Nietzsche and the present. R. S. Leventhal, 'Reciprocal influence', Leventhal, *Reading*, 75–90, examines the historical significance of the rhetorical figure of 'gegenseitiger Einfluß' in H.'s essay *Vom Einfluß der Regierung auf die Wissenschaft und der Wissenschaft auf die Regierung*. K. Menges, 'Integration oder Assimilation: Hs Äußerungen über die Juden im Kontext der klassischen Emanzipationsdebatte', *Euphorion*, 90:394–415. Enrique Banús, *Untersuchungen zur Rezeption Johann Gottfried Herders in der Komparatistik. Ein Beitrag zur Fachgeschichte* (EH, XVIII, 82), 449 pp., examines the ways in which the history of comparative studies has been written up and the role that the figure of H. plays within these histories. It is therefore a study of the reception of H., or of the idea of H., and shows how he is made to figure in a number of discourses. In particular B. shows how the ambivalence of H.'s position allowed him to be used both within nationalist and anti-nationalist, rationalist and irrationalist histories. These arguments are then refined and strengthened by a comparison of H.'s role with that of other comparable authors (Goethe, Mme de Staël, the Schlegel brothers) or literary periods (Enlightenment, *Sturm und Drang*). S. Mark Lewis, *Modes of Historical Discourse in J. G. Herder and N. M. Karamzin* (STML, 12), ix + 125 pp., places his emphasis on K., and attempts to make good our lack of knowledge about a man who had an important role as a disseminator of German culture in Russia. L. argues that both in his position within the literary landscape and in some of his ideas, K. shows similarities with H., several of which are directly due to K.'s reading of H. Unfortunately this study does not entirely resolve the problems of causality that studies of influence raise, and this is exacerbated by an imprecision in the English that also prevents the emergence of a thesis that is entirely convincing.

HIPPEL. A. Lindemann-Stark, 'Die Biographie des Theodor Gottlieb von Hippel (1741–1796). Eine Quellensuche', *Euphorion*, 90:237–63. Id. and J. Kohnen, 'Zwischen Vergessen und Wiederentdecken. Bibliographie zu Theodor Gottlieb von Hippel (1741–1796)', *Das achtzehnte Jahrhundert*, 20:197–220. H. H. H. Beck, 'Neither Goshen nor Botany Bay: Hippel and the debate on improving the civic status of the Jews', *LY*, 27, 1995:63–101.

HÖLTY. W. Hettche, '"Wir sind also Freunde." Zwei unbekannte Hölty-Briefe', *JDSG*, 40:5–13.

JUNG-STILLING. S. K. Schindler, 'Homosocial necrophilia: the making of man in Jung-Stilling's idyllic patriarchy', Kuzniar, *Goethe*, 61–76.

KARSCH. *'Mein Bruder in Apoll.' Briefwechsel zwischen Anna Louisa Karsch und Johann Wilhelm Ludwig Gleim*, ed. Regina Nörtemann and Ute Pott, 2 vols, Göttingen, Wallstein, 540, 656 pp., contains 427 of the 1,265 surviving letters between K. and Gleim, edited with painstaking attention to detail and a wealth of supporting information. This correspondence, which lasted from 1761 to 1791, gives fascinating insights into the culture and values of the age and reflects the shifting personal and literary expectations that the two correspondents had of each other and of themselves. It promises in particular to shed light on the relatively neglected writing of K., whose observation of the social world around her is extremely acute, and on the use of the letter as a sophisticated medium of communication in the 18th c.

KLINGER. Michael Müller, *Philosophie und Anthropologie der Spätaufklärung. Der Romanzyklus Friedrich Maximilian Klingers* (Passauer Schriften zu Sprache und Literatur, 4), Passau, Rothe, 1992, 357 pp., is probably the most useful introduction to K.'s late cycle of novels that we now have, disentangling the network of motifs and ideas and exposing the structure of philosophical and political ideas in this sequence of narratives. Unlike many critics, M. makes the sensible decision to examine the cycle as a whole, and even though there is a certain loss of a sense of the relative integrity of the individual novel, this allows him to reveal the complexity of K.'s vision. The number of diagrams with which this study is embellished reveals an eagerness to communicate and to categorize, and this produces a study that is clear and is already a classic. And although it does also show a certain tendency to label concepts and use them as counters in a scheme, it is not entirely unfair to accuse K. of this as well. R. Baasner, 'Dichtung,

Bildung und Beruf. Zum Literaturbegriff des alten Klinger', *ZDP*, 115:193–203, discusses the concept of the 'Dichter' in *Der Weltmann und der Dichter*.

KLOPSTOCK. *Klopstock an der Grenze der Epochen*, ed. Kevin Hilliard and Katrin Kohl, Berlin, de Gruyter, 1995, x + 424 pp., is really two books in one. The first part consists of a series of papers which reconsider the conventional assumption that K. stands between two ages, one dominated by religion, the other by Goethe: K. Kohl, '"Sey mir gegrüßet!" Sprechakte in der Lyrik Klopstocks und seiner deutschen Zeitgenossen' (7–32); K. Weimar, 'Das Wandeln des Wortlosen in der Sprache des Gedichts' (33–45); I. Strohschneider-Kohrs, 'Bilderlogik und Sprachintensität in Klopstocks paraenetischen Elegien der Spätzeit' (46–67); L. L. Albertsen, 'Poetische Form bei Klopstock' (68–79); H. Benning, '*Ut Pictura Poesis — Ut Musica Poesis*. Paradigmenwechsel im poetologischen Denken Klopstocks' (80–96); D. Martin, 'Klopstocks *Messias* und die Verinnerlichung der deutschen Epik im 18. Jahrhundert' (97–116); M. Lee, 'Eingeleiert in Klopstocks Rhythmik: *Der Messias* und Goethes Fragment "Der ewige Jude"' (117–31); J.-U. Fechner, '"ser fịl fọrtrefl."? Zeitgenössische Übersetzungen von Werken Klopstocks und die Frage nach der Epochenschwelle' (132–51); A. Lüchow, '"Die heilige Cohorte." Klopstock und der Göttinger Hainbund' (152–220); and K. Hilliard, 'Klopstocks Tempel des Ruhms' (221–40). The second half of the volume (247–424) consists of an invaluable update by H. Riege of the Klopstock bibliography taking us from 1972 to 1992.

KNIGGE. The bicentenary of K.'s death in 1796 is marked by several publications, including a modern edition of his *Über Eigennutz und Undank. Ein Gegenstück zu dem Buche: Über den Umgang mit Menschen*, ed. Gert Ueding (Promenade, 6), Tübingen, Klöpfer & Meyer, 151 pp., which is an extended essay on the principles of ethical behaviour and their connection with human nature. K. criticizes Kant for obscurantist system-building and appeals to the Enlightenment tradition of Mendelssohn and Garve, but in doing so the unnamed main opponent is probably the materialism of writers like LaMettrie and Helvétius. Of particular interest are the passages where K. moves into social criticism and discusses self-interestedness in various classes and professions: here the typical condemnation of court life rubs shoulders with crude anti-Semitism and perceptive comments on the interests operating in different trades and in the French Revolution. Ernst August Freiherr Knigge, *Knigges Werke. Eine Bibliographie der gedruckten Schriften, Kompositionen und Briefe Adolphs, Freyherrn Knigge und seiner Tochter Philippine von Reden, geb. Freiin Knigge*, Göttingen, Wallstein, viii + 632 pp., is an attractively, if somewhat eccentrically, presented companion to K. studies, offering a full bibliographical guide to both primary and secondary literature, including K.'s musical compositions and the writings of his daughter Philippine. Title-pages are frequently reproduced, even of translations, and the detail of the information available in this volume makes it a valuable resource. *Adolph Freiherr Knigge* (TK, 130), 107 pp., contains, together with the usual biographical sketch and bibliography and the text of a letter to Nicolai (14–20): H. Dittberner, 'Der gute Herr aus Bredenbeck' (3–13); W. Fenner, 'Knigges Brief an Friedrich Nicolai' (21–22); H. Brandes, 'Für eine aufgeklärte Lesewelt. Knigges *Journal aus Urfstädt*' (23–29): K.-H. Göttert, '*Über den Umgang mit Menschen*' (30–34); W. D. Wilson, 'Vom internalisierten "Despotismus" zur Mündigkeit. Knigge und die Selbstorganisation der aufgeklärten Intelligenz' (35–46); J. Dirksen, 'Den Markt umgehen. Knigge als praktizierender Literaturtheoretiker' (47–53); M. Rector, 'Über die Grenzen des Umgangs mit Menschen. Zu Adolph Freiherr Knigges Romanen' (54–66); M. Rüppel, 'Knigge und das Theater' (67–73); A. Fischer, ' "Cantories amant humores." Adoph Freiherr Knigge und die Tonkunst' (74–83); W. Fenner, ' "Bürgerfreund, Aufklärer, Völkerlehrer." Knigge in Deutschland von 1796 bis 1996' (84–90); and C. Stephan, 'Knigges Aktualität' (91–94). Ruth Klüger, *Knigges 'Umgang mit Menschen. Eine Vorlesung'*, Göttingen, Wallstein, 30 pp., contains a selection of extracts from K. and a brief interpretative survey arguing the ambivalence of the socio-political gestures in K.'s work, which on the one hand embodies an anti-aristocratic liberalism and on the other is anxious about the spread of Enlightenment to women and the lower classes.

KRÜGER. Katja Schneider, *Vielleicht, daß wir also die Menschen fühlen lehren. Johann Christian Krügers Dramen und die Konzeption des Individuums um die Mitte des 18. Jahrhunderts* (EH, 1, 1577), 226 pp., examines the contribution of K. (1723–50) to the theatre of the 1740s. The core of this efficiently written study is the analyses of his five comedies, in which S. focuses on the tensions in K.'s presentation of typically Enlightenment values such as 'Vernunft' and 'Tugend'. By setting them in the context of the valorization of the idea of feeling at the time, S. is able to argue that these plays, in their variety, are piecemeal attempts to approach problems which were later to receive sustained treatment in the plays of Lessing and the *Sturm und Drang*. Behind this study there lies a rather old-fashioned idea of Enlightenment and there is room for further examination of K.'s audiences and, more generally, the social basis and connotations of the ideas he uses, but S. deserves credit for her careful analysis of a sequence of comedies whose importance has received insufficient consideration.

LA ROCHE. V. Ottenbacher and H. Zeilinger, 'Wieland-Bibliographie 1993–95', *Wieland-Studien*, 3:299–353, contains a listing of recent publications on L. (341–46). Gudrun Loster-Schneider, *Sophie La Roche. Paradoxien weiblichen Schreibens im 18. Jahrhundert* (Mannheimer Beiträge zur Sprach- und Literaturwissenschaft, 26), Tübingen, Narr, 502 pp., is an investigation of the aesthetic categories inherent in the comments on La Roche's writing made particularly by Wieland but also by La Roche herself and others. Loster-Schneider finds here attempts to define an aesthetic that is appropriate to women and one that therefore offers a positive evaluation of typically feminine forms of experience but at the same time contains an element of special pleading that implicitly subordinates women's to men's writing. She then considers the way that La Roche embodied aspects of this debate in her own writing, and concludes this carefully argued book with an analysis of the attitudes towards writing embedded in the autobiographical text *Mein Schreibtisch* of 1799. Renate Feyl, *Die profanen Stunden des Glücks*, Cologne, Kiepenhauer & Witsch, 272 pp., is described as a novel, but avoids the self-conscious fragmentation of modern fiction and is basically a biography of L. which fills out the known facts with imagined personal reflections and with details which situate L. in the everyday life of the period. The account begins in the early 1770s and uses L.'s contacts with a wide range of contemporary authors to paint a picture of the contemporary cultural scene, but the central focus of the book is inevitably on L.'s struggle to balance the conflicting demands on her as wife, as mother, and as celebrated author. Gesa Dane, 'Sophie von La Roche: *Geschichte des Fräuleins von Sternheim*', *Romane* (Interpretationen), 171–95.

LENZ. '*Ich aber werde dunkel sein.*' *Ein Buch zur Ausstellung Jakob Michael Reinhold Lenz*, ed. Ulrich Kaufmann, Wolfgang Albrecht, and Helmut Stadeler, Jena, Bussert, 147 + 64 pp., contains a rather variable collection of essays designed to accompany an exhibition in Jena, which is reflected in the generous selection of pictures: T. Schnaak, 'Zum Bildungsgang des jungen Lenz' (11–14); Id., 'Das theologische Profil des Vaters in einigen Grundzügen' (15–23); W. Albrecht, 'Lenz und Sophie von La Roche. Empfindsamer Tugendidealismus als Konsensstifter für Sturm und Drang und (Spät-) Aufklärung' (24–31); S. M. Pautler, '"Wehe dem neuen Projektenmacher" — Überlegungen zur sozialreformerischen Programmatik im Werk von J. M. R. Lenz' (32–45); A. Velez, 'Wie "unverschämt" sind Lenz' "Philosophische Vorlesungen"? Diskursive und persönliche Einflüsse auf Lenz' erste moralphilosophische Abhandlung' (46–57); M. Rector, 'Ästhetische Liebesverzichtserklärung. Jakob Lenz' Dramenfragmente *Catharina von Siena*' (58–65); E. Menz, 'Arentins Passion' (66–77); W. Albrecht and U. Kaufmann,

'Lenzens "expositio ad hominem" in historisch-kritischer Edition (mit Faksimile)' (78–91); I. Daum, '"Lettre adressée à quelques officiers de la commission hydraulique de la communication d'eau." An einige Offiziere des Hydraulikausschusses der Wasserverbindung adressierter Brief. Eine französische Schrift aus der letzten Lebenszeit Lenz' (92–108); K. A. Wurst, '"Der gekreuzigte Prometheus." J. M. R. Lenz: Wirkungsgeschichte in Literaturwissenschaft und -kritik' (109–16); B. Dedner, 'Jakob Lenz und Georg Büchner' (117–26); E. Nahke, 'Brief über das Umfeld der "Hofmeister"-Ausstellung von 1950' (127–31); U. Kaufmann, '"Rede, daß ich dich sehe!" Johannes Bobrowskis Lenz-Gedicht und seine Folgen' (132–40); Id., '"Steinreich an Worten . . . bettelarm an Geld." Ein Gespräch mit Henning Boëtius' (141–43); and Id., 'Dichters Wort sucht sich den Ort. Eine Lenz-Trilogie in Goethes Park' (144–47). Takeshi Imamura, *Jakob Michael Reinhold Lenz. Seine dramatische Technik und ihre Entwicklung* (SBL, 52), 476 pp., repeats a great deal of unnecessary information, firstly summarizing the textual state of each of L.'s plays and then providing a routine commentary of a few pages on each of his writings. The second half of the book discusses the question of a development in L.'s dramatic and aesthetic writing up to 1776, but here too I. does not really succeed in developing an independent argument. Symptomatically, the most useful part of this book is the enormous bibliography, which takes up a third of the volume. Uwe Hayer, *Das Genie und die Transzendenz. Untersuchungen zur konzeptionellen Einheit theologischer und ästhetischer Reflexion bei J. M. R. Lenz* (Frankfurter Hochschulschriften zur Sprachtheorie und Literaturästhetik, 9), Frankfurt, Lang, 1995, 209 pp., represents, on the other hand, a serious attempt to rethink the position of L. within a history of theology. H. focuses on the competition between the claims of reason and revelation in the Enlightenment and shows how L., standing at the intersection of various intellectual currents, was able to find an individual resolution of them. There is some discussion of the anthropological and aesthetic implications of these ideas, but H. limits himself to a study of L.'s theological and moral writing (essays and letters) from the early Strasbourg years. Despite this limitation, and despite the fact that he has not been able to take account of the wave of bicentenary publications in 1994, this a significant attempt to situate L.'s intellectual origins within a theological discourse that literary historians neglect at their peril. Essays on individual texts or aspects of L.'s life include: W. Wittkowski, '*Der Hofmeister*: Der Kampf um das Vaterbild zwischen Lenz und der neuen Germanistik', *LitL*:75–92; M. Maurach, 'J. M. R. Lenzens "Guter Wilder". Zur Verwandlung eines Topos und zur Kulturdiskussion in den Dialogen des *Neuen Menoza*', *JDSG*, 40:123–46; J. Landwehr, 'Das suspendierte

Formurteil. Versuch der Grundlegung einer Gattungslogik anläßlich von Lenz' sogenannten Tragikomödien *Der Hofmeister* und *Die Soldaten*', *Lenz-Jb.*, 6:7–61; E. Menz, 'Die Mutter, die Kurtisane. Anmerkungen zu Lenz', *ib.*, 75–92; R. Graf, 'The homosexual, the prostitute, and the castrato: closet performances by J. M. R. Lenz', Kuzniar, *Goethe*, 77–93; A. Martin, 'Pfeffels Brief über Lenz im Steintal', *Lenz-Jb.*, 6:93–99; H. Wender, 'Was geschah Anfang Februar 1778 im Steintal? Kolportage, Legende, Dichtung und Wahnsinn', *ib.*, 100–26; and V. Gündel, 'Jakob Michael Reinhold Lenz' Mitgliedschaft in der Moskauer Fremaurerloge "Zu den drei Fahnen"', *ib.*, 62–74.

LESSING. Wolfgang Albrecht, *Gotthold Ephraim Lessing* (SM, 297), ix + 178 pp., tackles bravely the problems of presenting in a single small volume the life and works of L., with special emphasis on a critical review of the secondary literature. This series offers an invaluable bibliographical resource, but there are clearly difficulties in dealing with a major writer who has received so much critical attention. This is an informative and readable book presented with great lucidity, but the tendency to narrative tends to mean that it misses some of the complexity of L.'s writing, and there is little emphasis on its philosophical implications. A. Schmiesing, 'Remembering and forgetting in *Miß Sara Sampson*', *LY*, 27, 1995:19–37. L. Grevel, '"Beim Wort genommen": Minna von Barnhelms Gesprächsstrategie im Spiegel aufklärerischer Vernunftkonzeption', *ZDP*, 115:481–500, considers the use of the rhetorical repertoire of the Enlightenment in the dialogue of the play. G. E. Grimm, '*Riccaut de la Marlinière, Glücksritter und Franzos* — Die Rezeption einer Lustspielfigur zwischen Gallophilie und Gallophobie', *Euphorion*, 90:383–93. I. Morris, 'The symbol of the rose. A baroque echo in *Emilia Galotti*', *PEGS(NS)*, 64, 1993–95:53–71. A. Schilson, 'Dichtung und (religiöse) Wahrheit: Überlegungen zu Art und Aussage von Lessings Drama *Nathan der Weise*', *LY*, 27, 1995:1–18. Evelyn K. Moore, *The Passions of Rhetoric: Lessing's Theory of Argument and the German Enlightenment* (Library of Rhetorics, 3), Dordrecht, Kluwer, 1993, xix + 122 pp., analyses the *Rettung des H. Cardanus* and L.'s dispute with Goeze in order to join a number of recent critics in arguing that for L. the rhetoric of argumentation is essential to understanding, particularly because it allows for emotion. In both cases M. shows that L. was not only engaging in argument but also discussing the epistemological implications of different kinds of argument. What is of particular value in this brief study is that M. places these deliberations within the history of the 18th-c. reception of Classical rhetoric and of Classical debates about the value — and danger — of rhetoric.

LICHTENBERG. C. Brauers, 'Lichtenberg am Fenster. Der gesunde Menschenverstand und die Krankheit der Beobachtung', *GRM*, n. F., 46 : 16–33, discusses the epistemological problems of empiricism.

MERCK. M.-T. Federhofer, 'Fossilien-Liebhaberei. Johann Heinrich Merck und der naturwissenschaftliche Dilettantismus des 18. Jahrhunderts. Mit drei ungedruckten Briefen Mercks an Sir Joseph Banks', *Lenz-Jb.*, 6 : 127–59.

MENDELSSOHN. W. Goetschel, 'Moses Mendelssohn und das Projekt der Aufklärung', *GR*, 71 : 163–75.

MORITZ. *Anton Reiser. A Psychological Novel*, trans. John R. Russell, Columbia, Camden House, xiv + 286 pp., successfully reproduces the poise of M.'s prose writing, while losing nothing of the realism. An introd. relates the realism of the novel to M.'s treatment of his own experience in it. *Karl Philipp Moritz und das 18. Jahrhundert. Bestandsaufnahmen — Korrekturen — Neuansätze*, ed. Martin Fontius and Anneliese Klingenberg, Tübingen, Niemeyer, 1995, x + 280 pp., contains the papers given at a conference marking the bicentenary of M.'s death: A. Meier, 'Quantité négligeable? Überlegungen zur Moritz-Forschung' (3–11); H. Hollmer and K. Erwentraut, 'Ein Klassiker ohne Text. Kritische Überlegungen zu einer Karl-Philipp-Moritz-Ausgabe' (13–30); A. Klingenberg, 'Editionsprobleme des Moritzschen Gesamtwerks: Grammatiken, Übersetzungen, Journalistisches, Amtliches' (31–46); D. Böck, 'Karl Philipp Moritz — Klassiker ohne Text. Wie ediert man "Gränz = Genies" und "Zwischengeister"?' (47–55); Id., 'Karl Philipp Moritz an Jean Paul. Ein wiederentdeckter Brief' (57–58); H. Schmidt, 'Karl Philipp Moritz über Sprache, Hochdeutsch, Berliner Umgangssprache und märkischen Dialekt' (61–73); F. R. Varwig, 'Sprachpsychologie und Sprechausdruck im Moritzschen Werk' (75–88); J. Jahnke, 'Ähnliche Sprachformen in verschiedenen Moritzschen Textarten' (89–98); W. Martens, 'Zur Einschätzung von Romanen und Theater in Moritz' "Anton Reiser"' (101–09); U. Goldenbaum 'Ästhetische Konsequenzen des Moritzschen "Spinozismus"' (111–22); E. M. Batley, 'Die produktive Rezeption des Freimaurertums bei Karl Philipp Moritz' (123–33); R. Bezold, 'Einige Bemerkungen zu den Beiträgen von Wolfgang Martens, Ursula Goldenbaum und Edward M. Batley' (135–43); A. Costazza, 'Karl Philipp Moritz und die tragische Kunst' (145–76); J. Fohrmann, '"Bildende Nachahmung." Über die Bedeutung von "Bildung" und "Ordnung" als Prinzipien der Moritzschen Ästhetik' (177–86); E. J. Engel, '"Bildende Nachahmung" als "Gründungsmanifest"?' (187–89); T. R. Cadete, 'Die edierte Seele zwischen Scham und Schuld: Überlegungen zum "Magazin zur Erfahrungsseelenkunde"' (193–200); J. Osinski, 'Psychologie und Ästhetik bei Karl Philipp Moritz' (201–14); M. L.

Davies, 'Moritz und die aufklärerische Berliner Medizin' (215–26);
G. Dürbeck, 'Aporien der Erfahrungsseelenkunde' (227–35);
J. Becker, '"Trösterin Hoffnung": Zu Moritz' Götterlehre' (237–47);
H. Scholtz, 'Moritz' Wendung von der Aukklärung zum Kult des
Schönen' (249–53); J. Jahnke, 'Moritz' Antike-Rezeption und G. C.
Maternus de Cilano' (255–59); and S. Badstübner-Gröger, 'Karl
Philipp Moritz in Berlin — Bemerkungen zu seinen Wohnungen und
zu seinen Äußerungen über die Stadt' (260–76). Anne-Marie Bara-
nowski, *Conquête du mouvement et recherche de soi. L'imaginaire de Karl Philipp
Moritz* (Collection Contacts, III, 35), Berne, Lang, 416 pp., is an
analysis of the themes and motifs recurring in *Anton Reiser* and the
Hartknopf novels. The central problem, she argues, is the threat of
isolation of the individual, which is equivalent to death. Both Anton
Reiser and Andreas Hartknopf, like M. himself in his theoretical
work, are striving to regain an organic totality. This is a useful
starting-point, and the close analysis of individual formulations is
often instructive, though B.'s tendency to relate them to fragments of
universal myths is problematic, at least as long as she does not reflect
on their history and context. By contrast Alessandro Costazza,
*Schönheit und Nützlichkeit. Karl Philipp Moritz und die Ästhetik des 18.
Jahrhunderts* (IRIS, 10), Berne, Lang, 221 pp., attempts to relocate M.
within the debates of the Late Enlightenment, and makes a strong
case for the argument that M.'s aesthetic theories have been treated
too much as the solutions for various personal or philosophical
problems which lie outside the realm of aesthetics, and that they must
also be situated within the particular context of 18th-c. aesthetic
theory. He therefore rehearses the emergence of the ideals of beauty
and usefulness in the writings of Gottsched, Sulzer and others, and
shows how M. transcends this approach with his idea of an organic
totality, which allowed him to argue — before Goethe — for the
autonomy of art. In a final chapter C. goes on to show the
consequences of this position for M.'s discussion of the idea of
Enlightenment in the *Berliner Monatsschrift*. Where he discusses M. and
is not just presenting background information, C. is thoughtful and
instructive, and it is to be hoped that he will go on and examine the
consequences of his argument for other areas of M.'s work, particularly his novels. Studies of *Anton Reiser* include: L. Müller, 'Karl
Philipp Moritz: *Anton Reiser*', *Romane* (Interpretationen), 259–301; Id.,
'Die Erziehung der Gefühle im 18. Jahrhundert. Kanzel, Buch und
Bühne in Karl Philipp Moritz' *Anton Reiser* (1785–1790)', *DUS*,
48.2:5–20; W. Vosskamp, 'Poetik der Beobachtung. Karl Philipp
Moritz' *Anton Reiser* zwischen Autobiographie und Bildungsroman',
EG, 51:471–80; H. Gaskill, 'The "joy of grief": Moritz and Ossian',
ColGer, 28, 1995:101–25. Y. Pauly, '"Äußerst wenig Hülfsmittel"?

Quellenkritische Beobachtungen zu Karl Philipp Moritz' *Anthusa*', *GRM*, n. F., 46:406–23. R. Wintermeyer, 'Mystique et méthode dans l'œuvre de Karl Philipp Moritz', *EG*, 51:453–70.

MÖSER. Karl H. L. Welker, **Rechtsgeschichte als Rechtspolitik. Justus Möser als Jurist und Staatsmann* (Osnabrücker Geschichtsquellen und Forschungen, 38), Osnabrück, Verein für Geschichte und Landeskunde von Osnabrück, 1280 pp.

MÜLLER. *Maler Müller Almanach*, ed. Rolf Paulus, Pfaffen-Schwabenheim, Fiedler, 1995, 124 pp., reprints several short extracts from M.'s writing together with a variety of mainly biographical essays: U. Leuschner, '"Der Freundschaft geweihete Scenen." Lessings Bedeutung für Maler Müllers "Metrischen Faust"' (13–25); C. Wingertszahn, 'Maler Müllers "schnackisch" Gedicht an den "lieben Claudius in Wandsbeck" (mit Abbildungen)' (31–44); H. G. Dehe, 'Warum kehrte Friedrich Müller nicht in seine Heimat zurück? Widersprüche im Lebensgang des Maler-Dichters' (45–52); I. Sattel Bernardini, 'Maler Müllers Testament und weitere Quellen zur Nachlaßgeschichte (mit Abbildungen)' (53–76); G. Sauder and R. Paulus, 'Fortschritte der Maler-Müller-Edition' (105–07); and R. Paulus, 'Neue Veröffentlichungen zu Maler Müller seit 1987' (117–21). G. Sauder, 'Maler Müllers dramatische Welt', *Lenz-Jb.*, 6:182–97. U. Leuschner, 'Maler Müllers metrischer Faust. Prolegomena zur Edition, mit einigen grundsätzlichen Überlegungen zu Problemen der Edition aus dem Nachlaß eines "poeta minor"', *Editio*, 10:81–98.

NICOLAI. *Der Briefwechsel zwischen Friedrich Nicolai und Carl Augustus Böttiger*, ed. Bernd Maurach et al., Berne, Lang, 138 pp., continues M.'s work on the letters of B. held in Dresden by presenting here his correspondence with N. and thus the meeting of two generations of Enlightenment publicists. Dating almost entirely from the first decade of the 19th c., these letters document the wide-ranging interests and experience of the two correspondents, their shared involvement in freemasonry and their rejection of Romanticism, but also matters of more personal as well as more academic interest, and allow the modern reader insights into the everyday world of the Late Enlightenment and shed an interesting sidelight on both Classical and Romantic literary circles.

POPOWITSCH. Kurt Faninger, *Johann Siegmund Valentin Popowitsch. Ein österreichischer Grammatiker des 18. Jahrhunderts* (Schriften zur deutschen Sprache in Österreich, 18), Frankfurt, Lang, 257 pp., offers a survey of the now largely forgotten linguist who was the first professor of the German language at the University of Vienna and was considered a major opponent of Gottsched. After an introductory biographical sketch of P. (1705–74), F. outlines his position within the theoretical debates of his day on issues such as the use of *Fremdwörter* and the evaluation of South German dialects, which he regarded as valuable but as no rivals to the unified German language he sought. F. then discusses in some detail his description of German grammar, which he compares favourably with those of P.'s contemporaries, Gottsched, Antesperg, and Aichinger, and shows how his orthographical proposals reveal unusual insights, although he admits that P. was of little direct influence.

SCHNABEL. B. Recker, 'Johann Gottfried Schnabel: *Die Insel Felsenburg (Wunderliche Fata einiger See-Fahrer)*', *Romane* (Interpretationen), 78–111.

SCHIKANEDER. J. K. Brown, 'The Queen of the Night and the crisis of allegory in *The Magic Flute*', *GY*, 8:142–56, takes the ambiguity of the title 'Königin der Nacht', which also means latrine cleaner, as the starting-point of a discussion of allegory at the end of the Enlightenment.

SPIESS. Ulrich Hartje, *Trivialliteratur in der Zeit der Spätaufklärung. Untersuchungen zum Romanwerk des deutschen Schriftstellers Christian Heinrich Spieß (1755–1799)* (EH, I, 1535), 202 pp., examines four novels, *Das Petermännchen, Der Mäusefallen- und Hechelkrämer, Die Löwenritter*, and *Hans Heiling*, and shows how they adopt a broadly similar tripartite narrative structure involving dislocation and disorientation followed by recovery. He discusses the psychological effect of a pattern which allows the reader to identify with impotent characters who are led passively to goals that elude those who strive more consciously for them. H. then traces the tensions between this reliance on a benevolent destiny and S.'s criticisms of social rigidity, which are closer to the principles of the Enlightenment. The argument thus far is not fundamentally new, although it is presented with admirable clarity. However, instead of interpreting these tensions as symptoms of S.'s personal insecurity, H. argues that they represent the contradictory aspirations of his readers, who were flattered by the valorization of the individual but relieved of the obligation to assert themselves. A final comparison with *The Castle of Otranto* shows the dependence of S. on the tradition of the Gothic novel.

VULPIUS. E. T. Larkin, 'Christian August Vulpius: Popular literature as moral orientation', *CGP*, 24:73–91.

VOSS. Johann Heinrich Voss, *Ausgewählte Werke*, ed. Adrian Hummel, Göttingen, Wallstein, 558 pp., is the first modern edition to give a balanced selection of V.'s work, offering a representative range of samples from his poetry, his translation work, his essays on education, and his contributions to literary-political debates. It also contains documentation on the contemporary reception of V. and extensive annotations. Although H. does not offer us the complete V. he offers enough for most readers to gain a good understanding of this many-sided and contentious author, and the texts have been reliably edited to the highest modern standards. This is set to be the standard edition of V. for everyday use.

WEZEL. Johann Karl Wezel, *Pädagogische Schriften*, ed. Phillip S. McKnight (RBDSL, A, 10), 246 pp., contains an extensive introduction (pp. 5–86), followed by 16 short essays by W. which are today difficult to access, including three whose ascription to W. is uncertain. These texts show W. engaging in debates with Basedow, Campe and others who were trying to respond to Rousseau's revolutionary ideas in education, and they show the significance of this under-researched area for an understanding of anthropological ideas in the 1770s and 1780s. They are texts that contain ideas which are important for the interpretation of W.'s novels but they are also significant because they will help to develop a more balanced view of W. himself, as well as of the later stages of the Enlightenment. *Johan Carl Wezel. Akten des Symposiums der Gesamthochschule / Universität Kassel vom 15. bis 18. Oktober 1992*, ed. Michael Glasmeier and Rolf Lobeck, Kassel, Jenior & Pressler, 1994–95, 253 pp., contains the texts of *Die Komödianten* (113–43) and of letters relating to W., ed. A. Klingenberg (13–17), as well as several imaginative, 'creative' responses to W. and the following more academic contributions: A. Klingenberg, 'Johann Karl Wezels Literaturtheorie — Herausforderung für die Literaturwissenschaft?' (18–43); H. Bärnighausen, 'Wezel-Forschung in Sondershausen 1986–91' (44–64); G. Steiner, 'Das feudale Umfeld Wezels' (65–96); M. Glasmeier, 'Künstlertum und Physiognomie' (97–112); H. H. F. Henning, 'Wezels dramatisches Werk und die groteske Satire *Die Komödianten*' (149–66); P. Bexte, 'Tumulte: Die Liebe unter den Bedingungen der Post in Wezels Roman *Herrmann und Ulrike*' (167–80); and D. Weiland, 'Wezel als Autor der *Nachtwachen von Bonaventura* — ein Denkspiel' (187–217). G. Sauder, 'Johann Karl Wezel, *Belphegor oder die wahrscheinlichste Geschichte unter der Sonne*', *Romane* (Interpretationen), 196–239. F. Futterknecht, 'Johann Carl Wezel's *Herrmann und Ulrike* (1790) or The Origin of the Good', Leventhal, *Reading*, 51–63, examines the novel in the context of the evolving nuclear family and its relationship to the state.

WIELAND. Christoph Martin Wieland, *Der neue Amadis*, ed. Jan Philipp Reemtsma and Hans and Johanna Radspieler, Zurich, Hafmanns, 1995, 280 pp., is valuable because it is the first modern edition not to follow the revised version of the *Sämmtliche Werke* but rather to go back to the first edition of 1771, which is freer in metre and therefore shows more clearly W.'s literary achievement. Its greater use of allusion also implies a more sophisticated readership, or perhaps even audience. The text is here presented in unmodernized form with notes on the differences between the three versions of the 1771 edition. Klaus Schaefer, *Christoph Martin Wieland* (SM, 295), viii + 186 pp., is an invaluable guide to the study of W., though it is inevitably selective. A survey of his intellectual and personal development is followed by an examination of particular areas of his work, for example his contribution to the *Bildungsroman*, his translation of Shakespeare, his humorous novels, his verse epics, his response to political issues, his shorter narratives, and the late novels. Although this approach leaves gaps, it allows for the focus and the precision of formulation that makes this series so worth while. H. Schelle, 'Nachträge und Ergänzungen zur Wieland-Bibliographie 12', *LY*, 27, 1995:163–67. Id., 'Wielands *Aristipp* und seine Neuausgaben', *ib.*, 169–90. Thomas C. Starnes, *Der Teutsche Merkur. Ein Repertorium*, Sigmaringen, Thorbecke, 1994, 694 pp., offers a set of indexes that will prove invaluable to the study of this periodical and indeed to any study of the cultural life of late-18th-c. Germany. It contains a summary of the contents of each number of *Der Teutsche Merkur*, listed chronologically, followed by alphabetical lists of contributions, organized by genre: prose articles, verse, notices, reviews, and engravings. There follow a list of contributors and indexes of people mentioned (both real and fictional), place-names, and themes and motifs. If in this final *Sachregister* S. has perhaps been over-generous with incidental detail, that does not detract from the value of this book as a tool for accessing what is probably the most important periodical of its time. *Wieland-Studien*, 3, contains: G. Willems, 'Von der ewigen Wahrheit zum ewigen Frieden. "Aufklärung" in der Literatur des 18. Jahrhunderts, insbesondere in Lessings *Nathan* und Wielands *Musarion*' (10–46); D. Kimmich, 'Christoph Martin Wielands Epikureismus. *Ars vivendi* und der Widerstand gegen eine Dialektik der Aufklärung' (47–74); K. Oebel, '"C'est le Voltaire des Allemands." Zur Kritik Christoph Martin Wielands im vorrevolutionären Frankreich. Eine Untersuchung anhand der Übersetzungen seiner Werke' (75–106); L. Auteri, 'Die Chance der Zweisamkeit. Zur Erfahrung der Liebe bei Wieland' (107–22); T. Lautwein, 'Zur Funktion der Intertextualität in C. M. Wielands Verserzählung "Komababus oder was ist Tugend"' (123–49); U. Handke, 'Christoph Martin Wieland als politischer Journalist. Die Amerikanische Revolution im Spiegel des "Teutschen Merkur"' (150–60); B. Auerochs, 'Platon um 1800. Zu seinem Bild bei Stolberg, Wieland, Schlegel und Schleiermacher' (161–93); D. Martin, 'Der "große Kenner der Deutschen Ottave Rime". Wielands Autorität bei Tasso-Übersetzern um 1800' (194–215); M. H. Schmidt, '"Er war der erste deutsche Gelehrte für mich, der etwas Dichterisches auch in seinem

Aeussern hatte." Die Wieland-Büsten Johann Gottfried Schadows' (216–33); J. Kiefer, 'Christoph Martin Wieland als Mitglied des Lehrkörpers der Erfurter Universität und sein Lehrprogramm' (234–43); R. Moering, 'Achim von Arnims Weimar-Stanzen. Mit einem Gedicht auf Christoph Martin Wieland' (244–72); J. Jacobs, 'Fehlrezeption und Neuinterpretation von Wielands *Agathon*. Anmerkungen zu einem neuen Deutungsvorschlag' (273–81), discussing the argument of Walter Erhart; A. Schneider, 'Zur Datierung eines Briefs aus der Korrespondenz Wielands' (282–83); and V. Ottenbacher and H. Zeilinger, 'Wieland-Bibliographie 1993–95' (299–353). Thomas Lautwein, *Erotik und Empfindsamkeit. C. M. Wielands 'Comische Erzählungen' und die Gattungsgeschichte der europäischen Verserzählung im 17. und 18. Jahrhundert* (Studien zur Neueren Literatur, 3), Frankfurt, Lang, 245 pp., contains analyses of W.'s four 'Comische Erzählungen' of 1765, together with chapters on the history of the genre in the 18th c. and on the development represented by these four compared with the 'Erzählungen' of 1752. L. offers sensitive and illuminating readings of the texts, and it is perhaps not surprising that, although he introduces comparisons where relevant, the value of the book lies more in incidental observations than in its conclusions. The absence of a theoretical framework and the use of extensive quotation make this a rather slight volume, but the directness of L.'s responses to the texts make it neverthless worth reading. K. Manger, 'Christoph Martin Wieland: *Geschichte des Agathon*', *Romane* (Interpretationen), 150–70. J. P. Reemtsma, 'Christoph Martin Wieland: *Aristipp und einige seiner Zeitgenossen*', *ib.*, 302–22. S. Richter, 'Wieland and the homoerotics of reading', Kuzniar, *Goethe*, 47–60. U. Hentschel, 'Seraph und/oder Sittenverderber? Erotik, Sexualität und Moral im Selbstverständnis Christoph Martin Wielands', *LY*, 27, 1995:131–61.

WINCKELMANN. Jeffrey Morrison, *Winckelmann and the Notion of Aesthetic Education*, Oxford, Clarendon, 274 pp., is based on an examination of W.'s influence on understandings of art in the 18th c. An introductory chapter gives an outline of the meanings associated with Rome as a destination in the Grand Tour and as a focus for current debates on art, before going on to analyse W.'s views on aesthetic experience with reference to Ingarden. The following sections compare these with those of W.'s pupils, Johann Hermann von Riedesel and Johann Jacob Volkmann, and then argue in a final, particularly illuminating chapter that it was Goethe who, although not in the same sense a pupil and although — or perhaps because — he was aware of the relativity of some of W.'s dicta, came closest to appreciating W.'s vision of the meaning of aesthetic experience, and especially of its educational importance. This important contribution to our understanding of 18th-c. aesthetics successfully integrates a broad range of information by means of a clearly structured argument and its development through the interpretation of particular texts. S. Richter, 'Sculpture, music, text: Winckelmann, Herder and Gluck's *Iphigénie en Tauride*', *GY*, 8:157–71; Id., 'Winckelmann's progeny: homosocial networking in the eighteenth century', Kuzniar, *Goethe*, 33–46; C. MacLeod, 'The "third sex" in an age of difference: androgyny and homosexuality in Winckelmann, Friedrich Schlegel, and Kleist', *ib.*, 194–214.

THE ROMANTIC ERA

By SHEILA DICKSON, *Lecturer in German, University of Strathclyde*

1. GENERAL STUDIES

Romantik-Brevier, ed. Hartwig Schultz, Stuttgart, Reclam, 283 pp., compiles an appealing selection of material for the browser. Brenner, *Literaturgeschichte*, 95–131, offers only a very superficial overview of the Romantic period.

THEMES. Subjectivity and individualism are a main focus this year. Andrew J. Webber, *The Doppelgänger. Double Visions in German Literature*, Oxford, Clarendon, xii + 379 pp., is a study of major importance which goes beyond a discussion of theory and practice of the motif to a searching analysis of subjective identity. There is an introductory chapter, and chapters on Jean Paul, E. T. A. Hoffmann, and Kleist, and W.'s subtle investigation of individual texts persuasively elucidates his theoretical working model of the *Doppelgänger* revealing epistemological, aesthetic and psychosexual patterns and structures. Rüdiger Görner, *Grenzgänger. Dichter und Denker im Dazwischen*, Tübingen, Klöpfer & Meyer, 168 pp., has short chapters on Georg Forster, Hölderlin, Chamisso and others, in which G. can only convey a brief impression of individualism, and does so in an appropriately idiosyncratic way. On the individualism of German Idealism, Remo Bodei, *Dekompositionen. Formen des modernen Individuums*, Stuttgart-Bad Cannstatt, Frommann-Holzboog, 400 pp., pays brief visits to Novalis and Hölderlin and 'das unbekannte Ich'. Iris Denneler, *Die Kehrseite der Vernunft. Zur Widersetzlichkeit der Literatur in Spätaufklärung und Romantik*, Munich, Fink, 361 pp., examines the contradictory interest in the non-rational and deviant in the former period and its reflection in works by Schiller, Kleist, Tieck, and E. T. A. Hoffmann. D. examines a broad range of rules and conventions that are undermined and broken. Romanticism is thus interpreted almost exclusively as a reaction against the *Aufklärung*. This is not so much an argument as a framework of interpretation, extending from social criticism to the role of the sexes to moral and aesthetic education. Edmund Brandl, *Emanzipation gegen Anthropomorphismus: Der literarisch bedingte Wandel der goethzeitlichen Bildungsgeschichte* (EH, 1, 1520), 1995, 886 pp., is a tremendously detailed examination of a progressive emancipation of the subject in a variety of aspects of life. The reader is swamped with details and diagrams, but the conclusions that emancipatory terms increase while anthropomorphic ones decrease, that *Wilhelm Meister*, *Nachtwachen*, *Peter Schlemihl*, and *Prinzessin Brambilla* present the same conflicts in progressively radical terms, and that there is no question of a Classical/Romantic opposition here, are very flat. Also on the Romantic subject, Dirk von Petersdorff, *Mysterienrede. Zum Selbstverständnis romantischer Intellektueller* (SDL, 139), x + 447 pp., examines antique and 18th-c. influences on early-Romantic self-interpretation and the cult of genius. Romantic mythology and religion are discussed in detail, and in the context of a variety of early-Romantic writers. The result is a solid, well-researched study, which contributes new ideas to the discussion in this area. On the Romantic individual Kuzniar, *Goethe*, has three essays, by M. B. Helfer on *Lucinde*, C. MacLeod on Winckelmann, Schlegel, and Kleist, and J. Pfeiffer on Kleist's letters. The first is an interesting textual interpretation, the second does not clearly distinguish between homosexual and androgynous, while the third goes no further than establishing the broad ambiguity of masculine feelings in this era. The cult of the individual is discussed further in Yvonne-Patricia Alefeld, *Göttliche Kinder. Die Kindheitsideologie in der Romantik*, Paderborn, Schöningh, 414 pp., which has a large amount of material on Novalis and a chapter on E. T. A. Hoffmann. Bernd Laroche, *'Dies Bildnis ist bezaubernd schön' Untersuchungen zur Struktur und Entwicklung der Bildnisbegegnung in der deutschen Literatur des 16.-19. Jahrhunderts* (EH, 1, 1522), 1995, 371 pp., carefully reconstructs the role and significance of the portrait in Romantic literature with particular reference to *Godwi* and *Die Elixiere des Teufels*. The picture becomes removed from its relationship to reality and becomes a trigger for the observer's inner eye. The subjectivity and perspectivism of Romantic vision are illustrated by detailed textual reference, and therein lies the merit of the study. H. Eichner, 'Die deutsche Romantik — Zeit des Umbruchs?', *Akten* (Vancouver), 1, 1–13, is more general, and considers Romanticism as a time of change in a descriptive summary of certain main ideas.

On Romantic mythology, Walburga Lösch, *Der werdende Gott. Mythopoetische Theogonien in der romantischen Mythologie* (BBNDL, 21), 274 pp., provides more background information than analysis of the specifics of the chosen subject. As a result it is a very general survey. Viktor Žirmunskij, *Deutsche Romantik und moderne Mystik*, St. Ingbert, Röhrig, 212 pp., is a reprint and a translation of a work which appeared in 1913, as a tribute to the author. Of related interest is P. Mayer, 'Reinventing the sacred: The Romantic myth of Jacob Böhme', *GQ*, 69:247–59.

There are three essays on German literature in *Romantic Geographies. Proceedings of the Glasgow Conference, September 1994*, ed. Colin Smethurst, Glasgow, Univ. of Glasgow French and German Publications, xiv + 305 pp., by H.-W. Schmidt, 'Transcending geography: Jean Paul's imaginary landscapes' (27–40), who traces a victory of the imagination over geography, S. Dickson, 'Hapless but hopeful: the travellers' tales of Hoffmann' (99–112), emphasizing the importance of the imagination in Hoffmann's journeys, and E. Décultot, 'Peindre le paysage: Franz Sternbald et le problème de la *Landschaftsmalerei*' (83–98), a discussion of Tieck's new concept of landscape painting which no longer needs to 'signify'. Herrmann, *Volk*, has essays on early 19th-c. nationalism including Forster and Fichte.

Paul Ridder, *Gesund mit Goethe. Die Geburt der Medizin aus dem Geist der Poesie*, Münster, Lit, 386 pp., is disappointingly one-sided as the extremely technical medical discussion makes merely side-references to poets and poetry.

GENRES. Winfried Freund, *Deutsche Märchen. Eine Einführung* (UTB, 1902), Munich, Fink, 198 pp., begins with a plea for a return to reading *Märchen* as 'poetische Botschaften der Hoffnung in dürftiger Zeit' instead of academic or psychoanalytical treatises (p. 14) but the individual readings do not offer convincing reasons. Pages 81–96 were missing from my copy. *An Anthology of German Novellas*, ed. Siegfried Weing, Columbia, SC, Camden House, xxii + 277 pp., includes several Romantic Novellen, and the text is annotated in English for undergraduate use. Detlev Kremer, *Prosa der Romantik* (SM, 298), vi + 221 pp., reviews major themes that motivate, and are reflected in, Romantic prose, such as imagination, love, the artist, and new mythology. The material and the argumentation can become very involved, and the study loses accessibility through its attempt at comprehensiveness.

French, *Women*, has general chapters on gender, history, and genre, and a chapter on Caroline Schlegel-Schelling and Rahel Varnhagen, followed by a chapter on Bettine von Arnim's *Goethes Briefwechsel mit einem Kinde* and *Die Günderode*. The former emphasizes the aesthetic form; letter-writing as an act of narration, the latter the highly personal form, affording Bettine the scope for ironic self-reflexivity. The role of Goethe's mother in the former work is examined and her importance emphasized.

2. INDIVIDUAL AUTHORS

ARNIM, BETTINE VON. B. v. A., *'Ist Dir bange vor meiner Liebe?' Briefwechsel mit Philipp Hössli*, ed. Kurt Wanner, Frankfurt–Leipzig, Insel, 244 pp., which includes letters and Hössli's diary, is a most interesting new source of material on B. and also more generally as a socio-historical document. There is a useful introduction to set the scene. *Internationales Jahrbuch der B. v. A.-Gesellschaft*, 6–7, 1994–95, has essays by W. Schmitz, 'B. in Weimar' (109–42), which comments on

cultural history and in particular Thomas Mann's sceptical commentary in *Lotte in Weimar* on B.'s project of the 'gebildeter Kulturstaat'.
I. Leitner and S. von Steinsdorff, 'Die vollkommenste Grammatik
der Liebe, die jemals komponiert wurde' (143–57), discuss *Goethe's
Briefwechsel mit einem Kinde* as a grammar, philosophy and theology of
love, as poetic theory, and as the *Bildungsroman* of the female artist,
with B. eventually usurping Goethe as the personification of enthusiasm. The volume also contains an essay by I. Scheitler, 'Griechenlyrik
(1821–1828). Literatur zwischen Ideal und Realität' (188–234), and
publishes manuscripts by Helmina von Chézy, Gisela von Arnim,
and Louise Otto-Peters. B. v. A., *Lieder und Duette für Singstimme und
Klavier. Handschriften, Drucke, Bearbeitungen*, ed. Renate Moering, Kassel, Furore, 88 pp., is an interesting new source of information for
Germanists as well as musicians. In addition to the texts, Moering
documents B.'s place in Romantic music and in Romantic art in
general in a well-informed commentary. Also noted: B. Greiner,
'Echo-Rede und "Lesen" Ruths. Die Begründung von Autorschaft in
B. v. As Roman *Goethes Briefwechsel mit einem Kinde*', *DVLG*, 70:48–66.
C. Hilmes, '"Lieber Widerhall." *Bettine von Arnim: Die Günderode* —
eine dialogische Autobiographie', *GRM*, 46:424–38.

ARNIM, L. A. VON.   Michael Andermatt, *Verkümmertes Leben, Glück
und Apotheose. Die Ordnung der Motive in A. v. As Erzählwerk*, Berne, Lang,
629 pp., examines semantic and narrative structures in a range of
A.'s texts, arguing that each one, as a variation in theme, motif, and
content, can only be understood in the context of the whole. He
establishes an intertextuality of constants and variables in the areas of
the erotic (love) and family, and professional, state-political and
natural-cosmic orders. All levels either succeed, fail, or remain in an
ambiguous state of suspension. Andermatt then discusses the characteristics of A.'s narrative, which make interpretation difficult for the
reader, links this fundamental ambivalence to Schlegel's concept of
irony, then further contextualizes A.'s body of motifs into the
Romantic discourse of analogy and polarity. This is a very ambitious
project and is carried out carefully. The main value of the study is in
its detail, as none of the conclusions are particularly new or surprising.
Internationales Jb. der B. v. A.-Gesellschaft, 6–7, 1994–95, has two essays
on Arnim, by R. Simon, 'Text und Bild. zu A. v. As *Isabella von
Aegypten*' (168–87), who examines allegorical levels of meaning and
their 'fortschreitendes Verknüpfen', and S. Nienhaus, 'A. v. As
Aufhebung der Naturwissenschaften in der Poesie' (158–67), who
examines A.'s final rejection of science in favour of art due to the
latter's freedom of reference. R. Burwick, 'Physiology of perception:
A. v. A.'s practical and historical aesthetics', Burwick, *Imagination*,
156–76, also emphasizes the importance of A.'s scientific studies and

the polarity of science and art. This is supported by means of analogies between poetic reception and electric stimulation, between body and soul and the activity of electromagnetic forces.

BRENTANO, CLEMENS. C. B., *Sämtliche Werke und Briefe*, ed. Jürgen Behrens et al., vol. 32, *Briefe*. IV. *1808–1812*, ed. Sabine Oehring, Stuttgart, Kohlhammer, 524 pp., continues this excellent edition, and covers an important period of correspondence in B.'s life. The texts are sensitively edited and hence accessible to the widest range of Romantic scholars. *Requiem für eine romantische Frau. Die Geschichte von Auguste Bußmann und C. B.*, ed. Hans Magnus Enzensberger (IT, 1778), 289 pp., is a new amended version of a 1988 publication, which now includes a *capriccio*, previously published in 1992. Susanne Scharnowski, *'Ein wildes, gestaltloses Lied.' C. Bs Roman 'Godwi oder Das Steinere Bild der Mutter'*, Würzburg, Königshausen & Neumann, 209 pp., is a most stimulating and convincing analysis of B.'s novel in the context of the letter novel, early Romantic thought, and, consequently, as a presentation of the themes of identity and communication as both epistemological and aesthetic questions. S.'s argument is firmly based on a convincing, and appealing, detailed analysis of the various components and levels of B.'s narrative. N. Saul, 'Clemens and the women. Gender, genre and madness in B.', *PEGS*, 64–65:161–81, examines B.'s games with gender identity which might suggest a progressive understanding of gender, but which are proved to be a reductive colonization of the female. Also noted: K. Klopschinski, 'Über eine "wunderliche Begebenheit mit einem Kopf"'. Eine unbekannte Quelle zu C. Bs *Geschichte vom braven Kasperl und dem schönen Annerl'*, *DVLG*, 70:600–09; G. Birrell, 'Paternal order and disorder in B.'s *Geschichte vom braven Kasperl und dem schönen Annerl'*, *MDU*, 88:60–82; and C. Testa, 'Utopia and its double: B.'s *Die Chronika eines fahrenden Schülers'*, *GR*, 71:134–46.

CHAMISSO. G. Weiss, 'Südseeträume: Schlemihls Suche nach dem Glück', *Aurora*, 56:111–26, interprets the importance of the South Pacific as a symbol of transcendence and a Utopian world, which even Schlemihl cannot reach in this life, neither through society with its master/slave hierarchy, nor through nature, which for Schlemihl is an object of observation, not a Rousseauian paradise.

EICHENDORFF, JOSEPH VON. *Sämtliche Werke des Freiherrn J. v. E. Historisch-Kritische Ausgabe*, ed. Wilhelm Kosch, August Sauer, Hermann Kunisch, and Helmut Koopmann, vol. VI, 1, *Historische Dramen und Dramenfragmente. Text und Varianten*, ed. Harry Fröhlich, Tübingen, Niemeyer, xiv + 642 pp., contains two published dramas and also E.'s sketches and fragmentary outlines of scenes. The editor leaves open the question of poetic quality and emphasizes the ideological and historical interest of these texts which document E.'s political views in the turbulent period 1804–54. The editorial policy of including earlier completed stages, but not immediate corrections or partial reworkings, in the main text, followed by the final version, is intended to retain the impression of 'work in progress' without making the reading of the text impossible. This work has been meticulously carried out to provide invaluable new sources for study of the author and the period. J. v. E., *In freudenreichem Schalle. Eine Sammlung oberschlesischer Märchen*, ed. Eckhard Grunewald, Würzburg, Bergstadt, 79 pp., is a new edition of these texts with critical commentary, helpful to the general reader, which puts the *Märchen* in context and details sources and motifs. *Aurora*, 56, has essays by A. Riemen on E.'s journey in the Harz in comparison with the travels of Goethe and Heine (1–16), W. Hentschel on general travelling experiences in the late 18th and early 19th c. (95–109), and A. Davidson, who uncovers traces of E. in Thomas Mann's *Der Zauberberg* (17–46). F. Heiduk provides information on the brothers E. as students in Breslau (127–32) and documents relating to the 'Jubelfeyer' of 1803 (133–48). I. Holtmeier continues her E. bibliography (149–54). Sabine Karl, *Unendliche Frühlingssehnsucht. Die Jahreszeiten in Es Werk*, Paderborn, Schöningh, 323 pp., examines the symbolism of each season individually, then links them with E.'s concepts of poetry, life and salvation. The textual analysis is persuasive, and the wider implications valuable. Johannes Kersten, *E. und Stifter. Vom offenen zum geschlossenen Raum*, Paderborn, Schöningh, 228 pp., compares the two authors' exploitation of spacial symbolism, with sections on such motifs as the forest, the mountains, and the garden. This is a descriptive study with careful attention to detail. Thomas Winkler, **Werkgenetische Untersuchung zu J. v. Es 'Die Zauberei im Herbste'. Versuch einer Ordnung der überlieferten Texte*, Hamburg, Kovac, 270 pp.

FICHTE. J. G. F., *Gesamtausgabe der Bayerischen Akademie der Wissenschaften*, ed. Reinhard Lauth and Hans Gliwitzky, Reihe I, *Werke*. 9. *Werke 1806–1807*, ed. Reinhard Lauth, Hans Giwitzky et al., Stuttgart-Bad Cannstatt, Frommann-Holzboog, 1995, x + 327 pp., has 'Die Anweisung zum seeligen Leben' and 'Ueber Machiavelli', presented as illustrations of F.'s reorientation from abstract theory to concrete involvement in history in the crucial year 1806. This volume continues the excellent editing and documenting of F.'s work.

FOUQUÉ. *F. de la Motte Fs Biographie seines Lehrers Sachse aus dem Jahre 1830*, ed. Horst Häker, Frankfurt (Oder), Kleist-Gedenk- und Forschungsstätte, 30 pp., contains text and commentary.

GRIMM, JACOB AND WILHELM. *Gs Märchen International. Zehn der bekanntesten Grimmschen Märchen und ihre europäischen und außereuropäischen Verwandten. 1. Texte. 2. Kommentar*, ed. Ingrid Tomkowiak and Ulrich

Marzolph, 2 vols, Paderborn, Schöningh, 212, 66 pp., aims to promote intercultural understanding by comparing the Grimms' texts with variations from other countries, reproduced in volume 1 with source references. The commentary volume consists of general information on the *Märchen* form and more detailed commentaries on each text. This is informative and helpful as groundwork. *Brüder G. Kinder- und Hausmärchen. Ausgabe letzter Hand*, ed. Heinz Rölleke, Stuttgart, Reclam, 1002 pp., is based on the Grimms' final edition, but includes all texts from earlier editions not reproduced in this. There is also a bibliography and an afterword. The volume is aimed at a non-scholarly audience.

HAUFF, WILHELM. M. Thum, 'Re-visioning historical romance. Carnivalesque discourse in W. H.'s *Jud Süß*', Cramer, *Neues*, 25–42, argues a persuasive case for this work as a carnivalesque deconstruction of the anti-Semitic stance it is accused of propagating.

HOFFMANN, E. T. A. E. T. A. H., *Fantasy Pieces in Callot's Manner*, trans. Joseph M. Hayse, NY, Union College Press, xx + 327 pp., makes this collection in its entirety available to an English-speaking audience. It has useful explanatory notes on the text for non-Germanists. This year's *E. T. A. H.-Jb.* has articles by C. Diedrichs (7–19) on H.'s *Die Räuber* and the games Hoffmann plays with his reader's expections and imagination, B. Reifenscheid (20–32) on H. as illustrator and the importance of the sketch and caricature as a stimulus for his literary work, and R. Heinritz and S. Mergenthal, 'Abgründe des Schauerromans' (33–40), who compare motifs and techniques in H. and James Hogg, with Matthew Lewis as mutual source. The two former writers are shown to have transferred the religious to the psychological. R. Schmidt, 'Ein doppelter Kater?' (41–53), compares H.'s *Kater Murr* with Christa Wolf's *Neue Lebensansichten* with reference to Bakhtin and Kristeva. (An English translation of this essay is published in *Contemporary German Writers, their Aesthetics and their Language*, ed. Arthur Williams, Berne, Lang, pp. 9–34.) Also in this volume of the *Jahrbuch*, H.-G. von Arburg, 'Der Physiognomiker als Detektiv und Schauspieldirektor: Johann Ludwig Christian Hakens *Blicke aus meines Onkels Dachfenster in's Menschenherz* (1802)' (54–68), and A. Obrich, 'Bibliographie der Sekundärliteratur über E. T. A. H. 1981–1993, Teil 1, 1981–87'. Claudia Librand, *Aporie des Kunstmythos. Die Texte E. T. A. Hs* (Litterae, 42), Freiburg, Rombach, 315 pp., traces a development from a negative aesthetic in *Die Elixiere des Teufels* and *Der Sandmann* to a positive aesthetic of mediation in *Prinzessin Brambilla* in which the two main characters can transcend the dualism of art and life. More minor works such as *Meister Martin der Küfner* and *Der Artushof* are shown to trivialize or ignore the dualism, thus merely faking a synthesis. L.'s systematic approach offers an interesting avenue of interpretation. Johannes Wiele, *Vergangenheit als innere Welt. Historisches Erzählen bei E. T. A. H.* (EH, 1, 1554), 478 pp., establishes H.'s experience of history and politics and argues that historical narration enabled him to grapple with contemporary political issues, for example in *Das Fräulein von Scuderi*, and that H. thematized the problem of subjective mediation of the past by demonstrating it to be 'erzählendes Neu-Interpretieren'. *Doge und Dogaresse* is discussed in particular detail, and the interpretation does yield interesting detail. Wulf Segebrecht, *Heterogenität und Integration. Studien zu Leben, Werk und Wirkung E. T. A. Hs* (Helicon, 20), Frankfurt, Lang, 231 pp., is a collection of S.'s publications over a period of almost 30 years. The material is not, therefore, new, and the less familiar essays were usually written for a quite specific context, such as an afterword in an edition or for a themed conference. Others offer biographical information on H. in Bamberg. Also on H. and Bamberg, two companion volumes by Rainer Lewandowski, director of the E. T. A. H. Theatre in Bamberg, make poetic and critical use of the theme in *Sie sind auch kein Bamberger, wie ich höre*, Bamberg, Fränkischer Vlg, 1995, 137 pp., which is the text of a play, consisting in the main of H.'s writings and other contemporary sources, and *Fiktion und Realität. E. T. A. H. und Bamberg*, Bamberg, Fränkischer Vlg, 1995, 251 pp., which is a lively, informative biographical investigation, devolving in part from research for the play. There is much anecdotal information of interest on H.'s time in Bamberg, but L. also goes beyond this by considering his later works in the light of these experiences. Matias Martinez, *Doppelte Welten. Struktur und Sinn zweideutigen Erzählens*, Göttingen, Vandenhoeck & Ruprecht, 227 pp., has a chapter on *Der Zusammenhang der Dinge* in relation to purpose and chance in human action. He examines the role of vision and the relationship of life and art, two central themes in H.'s works, and presents an intelligent analysis of them. Also noted, S. Dickson, 'E. T. A. H.: Mind, mythology and meaning', *FMLS*, 32 : 251–63. A. Bresnick, 'Prosopoetic compulsion: Reading the uncanny in Freud and H.', *GR*, 71 : 114–33.

HÖLDERLIN. *Internationale H.-Bibliographie (IHB) auf der Grundlage der Neuerwerbungen des H.-Archivs des Württembergischen Landesbibliothek 1993–1994. Quellen und Sekundärliteratur, Rezeption und Rezensionen. II. Materialband*, ed. H.-Archiv, Werner Paul Sohnle, and Marianne Schutz, Stuttgart-Bad Cannstatt, Frommann-Holzboog, viii + 516 pp., is, like its predecessors, an invaluable source of information for H. scholars. *F. H.*, ed. Heinz Ludwig Arnold and Andreas Döhler (TK, 7), 295 pp., has essays on H. as poet, writer, and thinker. H. Dittberner, 'Hs Stolz' (7–23) is a discursive introductory essay, while H.-J. Molles, 'Weltverzicht als Männerwerk' (24–32), discusses

H.'s earliest poetry as a statement on his struggles between theological duty and poetic desire. Also on poetry, R. Colombat analyses 'Abendphantasie' and 'Des Morgens' (79–90) as complementary perspectives on the possiblities of integrating the subject and the divine. W. Groddeck, ' "Stutgard" oder "Die Herbstfeier" ' (135–44), attempts to establish the authenticity of the edited versions of the text; M. Knaupp, ' "... eine / Last von Scheitern ..." ' (182–92), takes the same approach with 'Mnemosyne'. B. Böschenstein, 'Das Gut des Gesangs' (213–20), is another attempt at textual criticism, this time of 'Wie Meeresküsten', to illustrate the paradox of a fragmentation which encompasses totality. M. Franz argues for 'Hs Gedicht "Andenken" ' (195–212) to be understood as a monument to Susette Gontard after her death. On H.'s late poetry, C. Wingertszahn, ' "Die Aussicht scheint Ermunterung." Hs spätes Gedicht "Das fröhliche Leben" ' (223–36), demonstrates the highly sophisticated and artistic qualities of 'Das fröhliche Leben' to prove the quality of this work, which is often only considered in the context of H.'s illness. The theme of this poem is shown to be a central motif in his last poems. H. Heissenbüttel, 'H. oder die Schwierigkeit, Poesie zu vertonen' (237–50), examines the relationship between language and music in general, and the lack of relationship between H.'s poetry and contemporary music in particular. On H.'s thought, J. Schmidt writes on 'Hs dichterische Rezeption der stoischen Ethik und Naturphilosophie' (33–50), followed by U. Gaier on 'H. und die Theorie der Organisation' (51–61), which examines the traditions (Herder in particular) on which H. drew. R. Görner, 'Wanderungen zwischen den Extremen. Hs Sinngebung des Exzentrischen' (62–74), discusses the motif of the wanderer as an illustration of eccentric development. On history, K. Grätz, 'Der Übergang vom Alten zum Neuen' (99–117), elucidates its increasing and changing importance in *Der Tod des Empedokles*. H. brings together two models of history, the Christian-eschatological and antique-cyclical, and demonstrates that the two can be compatible from the perspective of a single cycle. H. Bothe, 'Vom Versuch, ein deutscher Tyrtäus zu sein. Notizen zum Verhältnis von Dichtung, politischer Tat und Nationalbewuβtsein bei H.' (118–31), emphasizes the significance of reason in H.'s nationalism and the links between poetry and politics. C. Anders (91–98) characterizes *Hyperion* as 'engagierte Literatur' and argues that the contemporary reader feels equally challenged. The volume also contains a 'Vita F. H.' (251–67) by H.-J. Malles and a selected bibliography by H.-J. Malles and Sarah Schmidt (268–92). Theresia Birkenhauer, *Legende und Dichtung. Der Tod des Philosophen und Hs Empedokles*, Berlin, Vorwerk, 607 pp., analyses the development of H.'s ideas on the Empedokles theme from his original project of *Der*

Tod des Socrates. She argues persuasively that this parallels a development in H.'s theory of tragedy which questions the autonomy of character by presenting extreme changes in states of consciousness in a character in conflict, thus dismantling the classical projection of Greek tragedy. Gisela Dischner, '... *bald sind wir aber Gesang.' Zur H.-Linie der Moderne*, Bielefeld, Aisthesis, 250 pp., and Gert Hofmann, *Dionysos Archemythos. Hs transzendentale Poiesis*, Tübingen-Basle, Francke, xii + 264 pp., both review H.'s understanding of Dionysian concepts. The latter argues for Dionysos as representative of the aesthetic-creative state and a transcendental reflection of poetic activity, the former focuses on the creative process of the word in a world alienated from the gods and Dionysos as 'kommender Gott'. Both emphasize the importance of H.'s dialogue with his contemporaries, and D. uses this as a base to trace H.'s line of interpretation via Nietzsche (the first to understand it) to Rilke, George, Trakl, Benn, and Celan. *Gedichte von F. H. Interpretationen*, ed. Gerhard Kurz, Stuttgart, Reclam, 224 pp., presents interpretations of selected H. poems in some detail. The pitch is too high for the foreign learner, but there is reference material of interest for the Germanist. Also noted: R. Berbig, 'Ein Fest in den Hütten der gastlichen Freundschaft: Zum Verhältnis von Freundschaft und Heimat bei F. H.', *MDU*, 88 : 157–75.

KLEIST. Two volumes by Helmut Sembdner have been revised and reprinted, namely *H. v. Ks Lebensspuren. Dokumente und Berichte der Zeitgenossen*, Munich, Hanser, 542 pp., with new sources illuminating previously peripheral material, and *H. v. Ks Nachruhm. Eine Wirkungsgeschichte in Dokumenten*, Munich, Hanser, 660 pp., with new material particularly on K.'s suicide. *KlJb* has the proceedings of a conference on 'Zeitgenossenschaften', with contributions on K.'s teacher Christian Ernst Wünsch by C. Meiner (1–32), which questions his influence on K.'s early works, and on Johann Daniel Falk by R. Wartusch (188–200), who rejects Helmut Sembdner's theory of mutual poetic influence. Another teacher, Heinrich August Kerndörffer, and the influence of contemporary theory of declamation, is investigated by M. Kohlhäufl (142–68). H.-J. Becker (35–49) presents Wilhelm Traugott Krug as a contrast to K. by means of their relationship with Wilhelmine von Zenge, and reviews Georg Christian Wedekind's career and political views as K.'s doctor in the intriguing period 1803–04. K. is put in a wider literary context by J. Knape (91–105), who compares early letters to their sisters by Goethe, Mozart, Brentano and K. as particularly intimate modes of communication, and by U. Japp, who writes on the contemporary comic theatre (108–20) to establish that K. was influenced by the widest possible range of sources, including contemporary theatre, and that evidence of the latter is present with respect to specific works rather than in general trends. K.'s own work is scrutinized by P. Michelsen (123–39), who considers the tragedy of Alkmene's recognition of the truth in *Amphytrion*, R. Charbon (77–88), who analyses K.'s stance on race and racism in *Die Verlobung*, concluding that K.'s perspective is that of a white European, though not a racist, who undermines the whole concept of superiority of race, and S. Doering (171–86), who places K.'s Oriental references in the contemporary fashion for the Orient, but argues convincingly that K. was fundamentally interested in the mysteries of the human mind, which remain the same whatever the geography. The similarities and differences that characterize K.'s relationship to Romanticism are further emphasized by F. Strack (201–18), illustrated by K.'s critical exploitation of specific Romantic themes and motifs. A similar focus is evident in *BKF* which contains the proceedings of a conference 'K. and Brandenburg', as in this volume too contemporaries and predecessors figure far more strongly than K. himself. Gernot Müller, *Man müßte auf dem Gemälde selbst stehen. K. und die bildende Kunst*, Tübingen, Francke, 1995, viii + 336 pp., is a valuable investigation of K.'s dialogue with visual art in his ideas and works, which is placed in the context of his scepticism towards language and knowledge. M. identifies four phases and five forms of expression articulating the relationship between literature and visual art and examines each quite systematically. The final section on references to visual art in the Novellen is equally carefully written. Seán Allan, *The Plays of H. v. K. Ideals and Illusions*, CUP, xx + 315 pp., is an indispensable work of reference: it could make K.'s work more accessible to the English speaker by virtue of being written in English and providing translation of quotations and references to published English translations, and it will be a useful source for the general and specialist reader, documenting current research and controversies surrounding K. As an investigative study of ideals of perfection and transcendental metaphysics it contributes significantly to the Kleist debate. Bianca Theisen, *Bogen-Schluss. Ks Formalisierung des Lesens*, Freiburg, Rombach, 233 pp., examines the paradoxes of K.'s judgements and conclusions in their implications for the reader, without radically changing our awareness of textual ambiguity. Johannes Endres, *Das 'depotenzierte' Subjekt. Zu Geschichte und Funktion des Komischen bei H. v. K.*, Würzburg, Königshausen & Neumann, viii + 222 pp., establishes a general context, from Lessing to Hegel, and projects forwards from Heine to Freud, before turning attention to K.'s comic strategy, by means of a careful reinterpretation of his reception of Schiller. The focus is thus wider than the title suggests, and E.'s survey shows evidence of careful research. Beatrice Martina Guenther, *The Poetics of Death. The Short Prose of K. and Balzac*, Albany,

State Univ. of New York Press, x + 216 pp., locates the historical context of the authors' representations of death in their responses to Napoleon, but the chapters on K. analyse the stories in far more general terms as expressions of the awareness of the mortality of truth and knowledge which leads to a refusal to impose any single belief system, a subversion of the concept of 'Bildung' and a move from mimesis to self-referential narrative. In fact this study is very general and does not develop the investigation of the motif of death satisfactorily. Sabine Doering, *H. v. K.* (Literaturwissen für Schule und Studium), Stuttgart, Reclam, 124 pp., is a useful and reliable introduction for undergraduate use. H.-J. Knobloch, 'Ein Traum in Preußischblau', *Aurora*, 56:47–56, argues that *Prinz Friedrich von Homburg* encourages the regeneration of a new Prussian State, not that of the past, with an ideal, which is recognized as a Utopia, of community and humanity, but which justifies any aggression to defend it. Also noted: K. Zeyringer, '"Wo kömmt der Witz mir her?" Eine "Lustspielfigur par excellence" — zu Ks *Amphitryon*', *DVLG*, 70:552–68; B. Greiner, '"Das ganze Schrecken der Tonkunst." *Die heilige Cäcilie oder die Gewalt der Musik*: Ks erzählender Entwurf des Erhabenen', *ZDP*, 115:501–20; J. Wilson, '"Taking by storm": The discourse of spontaneity in K.'s *Die Marquise von O...*', *Seminar*, 32:283–92; and M. Chaouli, 'Devouring metaphor: Disgust and taste in K.'s *Penthesilea*', *GQ*, 69:125–43.

MEREAU, SOPHIE. *S. M.-Brentano. Liebe und allenthalben Liebe. Werke und autobiographische Schriften*, ed. Katharina von Hammerstein, 3 vols, DTV, 315, 305, 325 pp., collects the novels *Das Blütenalter der Empfindung* and *Amanda und Eduard*, poems and stories, such as *Marie* and *Elise*, and diaries and other prose. This is a useful body of material, and it is accompanied by helpful commentary and glosses.

NACHTWACHEN VON BONAVENTURA. Thomas Böning, *Widersprüche. Zu den 'Nachtwachen von Bonaventura' und zur Theoriedebatte*, Freiburg, Rombach, 598 pp., takes Nietzsche and deconstruction as interpretative points of orientation to interpret the *Nachtwachen* as a modern if not postmodern text. The scope of the survey is extensive, and the reader is asked to cope with a large amount of material within a very loose framework. This detracts from the accessibility of the study, which offers, however, a significant new contribution to our understanding of the text. Also noted: Daniela Weiland, 'Wezel als Autor der *N. v. B.* — ein Denkspiel', pp. 187–217 of *Johann Carl Wezel. Akten des Symposiums der Gesamthochschule/Universität Kassel vom 15. bis 18. Oktober 1992*, ed. Michael Glasmeier and Rolf Lobeck, Kassel, Jenior & Pressler, 1994–95, 253 pp. (see p. 833 above).

NOVALIS. Berbeli Wanning, *N. zur Einführung*, Hamburg, Junius, 219 pp., has too much material for the non-specialist and too little new research for the specialist. There are interesting ideas and pertinent comments, but this is offset by a naive acceptance of such clichés as Sophie as 'überirdisches Wesen' for N. (p. 52). N. features prominently in G. L. Schiewer, *Cognitio symbolica* (see p. 850 below). G. Rommel, 'Imagination in the transcendental poetics of N.', Burwick, *Imagination*, 95–122, stresses the need for an integrated approach to N.'s theoretical and poetic works. Knowledge is gained through a combination of poetry, reason and language. H. Uerlings, 'N. in Freiberg. Die Romantisierung des Bergbaus', *Aurora*, 56:57–77, takes an opposite position to T. Ziolkowski on Romantic institutions to argue for a split between professional and poetic activity, and the mine as symbol for an inward path with a necessary return to the surface. Neither is convincingly argued, and U. merely reiterates the importance of Freiberg and contemporary research for the development of this motif. Also noted: H. Hartmann, 'Die Poesie als Creator Spiritus: Klingsohrs Weinlied im Kontext des *Heinrich von Ofterdingen*', *MDU*, 88:43–59.

RICHTER, JEAN PAUL. *J. Ps Sämtliche Werke*, ser. 2, *Nachlaß*, vol. 6, *Dichtungen, Merkblätter, Studienhefte, Schriften zur Biographie, Libri legendi*. 1, *Text*. 11. *Apparat*, ed. Götz Müller, Janina Knab, and Winfried Feifel, 2 vols, Weimar, Böhlau, xii + 936, x + 388 pp., is an invaluable source of material, in various stages of refinement, on J.P.'s thoughts, ideas, and personal experiences as building blocks for his literary production. The editorial apparatus is impressively comprehensive and systematic, without being overwhelming. Andreas Erb, *Schreib-Arbeit. J. Ps Erzählen als Inszenierung 'freier' Autorschaft*, Wiesbaden, Deutsche Universität, 266 pp., examines J.P.'s position as creative writer faced with the social and economic constraints of bourgeois society around 1800. His texts are shown to address the question of how genius can be achieved through a process of education. Heike Döll, *Rollenspiel und Selbstinszenierung. Zur Modellfunktion des Theaters in J. Ps 'Titan' und 'Komet'* (BSDL, 46), 255 pp., approaches the subject via chapters on Käte Hamburger, Lessing, and 18th-c. theory and practice, followed by J.P.'s theory of the novel and humorous theatre, and concludes that theatre is not just a model, but a *sine qua non*. The main focus of argument confirms the demand for and limits of individual autonomy in J.P.'s work. Stephen Fennell, *Gleich und Gleich. Die Messianik bei J. P.*, Würzburg, Königshausen & Neumann, x + 237 pp., examines Messianic thought and its influence on J.P.'s narrative technique. A theoretical chapter is followed by chapters on individual works to ascertain relationships of identity in figurative language between author, hero, and God. The argument is interesting and F.'s line of approach is revealing. Elvira Steppacher, *Körpersprache in J. Ps 'unsichtbarer Loge'*, Würzburg, Königshausen & Neumann,

129 pp., examines the role of metaphor as mediator of body in language in expressing man's double nature as sensuous and spiritual being, then compares the narrator's 'suffering' with the Passion of Christ. This volume is in fact part of a longer dissertation, which may explain the disjointed and incomplete feel of the work. Rolf Vollmann, *Das Tolle neben dem Schönen*, Frankfurt, Eichborn, 263 pp., assures the reader that 'keine Wissenschaft, sondern eher Scherz und Unterhaltung' will be found in this volume. Thus disarmed, the reader is likely to enjoy, and may learn much from this lively biography. Gesine Lenore Schiewer, *Cognitio symbolica. Lamberts semiotische Wissenschaft und ihre Diskussion bei Herder, J. P. und Novalis* (FN, 22), x + 283 pp., examines the influence of Johann Heinrich Lambert on Herder, and argues that both these thinkers influenced the theories of language and knowledge in J.P.'s poetic conception and Novalis's philosophical work. The case is stronger with reference to J.P. and the study provides useful background material.

SCHLEGEL, DOROTHEA. M. B. Helfer, 'Dorothea Veit-Schlegel's *Florentin*: Constructing a feminist Romantic aesthetic', *GQ*, 69:144–60.

SCHLEGEL, FRIEDRICH. Claudia Brauers, *Perspektiven des Unendlichen. F. Ss ästhetische Vermittlungstheorie*, Berlin, Schmidt, 368 pp., reinterprets the development of S.'s thought as a continuing process of restriction with his final position of Catholic Restoration as conclusion, rather than volte-face. This is an extremely careful, detailed study of S.'s writings between 1795 and 1818. Also noted: Albert Meier, '"Gute Dramen müssen drastisch sein": Zur ästhetischen Rettung von F. Ss *Alcaros*', *GY*, 8:210–37; J.S. Librett, 'Figuralizing the oriental, literalizing the Jew: On the attempted assimilation of letter to spirit in F. S.'s *Über die Sprache und Weisheit der Inder*', *GQ*, 69:260–76.

STEFFENS, HEINRICH. This year sees the completion of the reprint of H. S., *Was ich erlebte. Aus der Erinnerung niedergeschrieben*, vols 2–5 (Natur und Philosophie, Texte und Untersuchungen, 2–5), Stuttgart-Bad Cannstatt, Frommann-Holzboog, II, 1995, vi + 440 pp.; III, 1995, xii + 341 pp.; IV, xiv + 451 pp.; V, xiv + 494 + lxxiii pp. The final four volumes follow hard on the publication of vol. I (see *YWMLS*, 57:803). Vol. V has useful appendices for reference. This is a high quality reproduction of an important source of information on the Romantic period.

TIECK, LUDWIG. William Crisman, *The Crises of 'Language and Dead Signs' in L. T.'s Prose Fiction*, Columbia, SC, Camden House, x + 202 pp., offers close readings of key prose texts across the range of T.'s career, with the aim of identifying and examining each as a continuing and changing exploration of communication and expression of dread of the inability to communicate. The study builds on a solid appreciation of previous T. scholarship to develop an original and well-founded analysis of speech-acts, which suggest that T.'s enquiries prefigure 20th-c. language philosophy. Mara Nottelmann-Feil, *L. Ts Rezeption der Antike*, Frankfurt, Lang, 270 pp., is a very useful survey of T.'s sources, and his changing attitude towards them. Wolfgang Rath, *L. T.: Das vergessene Genie. Studien zu seinem Erzählwerk*, Paderborn, Schöningh, 548 pp., is an extremely solid piece of scholarship, illuminating T.'s life and life philosophy and their interaction with his work. The background material on Romanticism is valuable too. R. G. Päsler, '*Nachrichten von altdeutschen Gedichten*. Anmerkungen zu L. Ts Handschriftenstudien in der Bibliotheca Vaticana', *E. T. A. Hoffmann-Jb.*, 4:69–90, reconstructs T.'s work in the library and his textual editing of his sources. G. Opie, 'An indescribable terror: narrative strategies in Tieck's *Der blonde Eckbert*', Hunter, *Short Story*, 39–53, is a very basic exposé of this text.

WACKENRODER. L. R. Furst, 'In other voices: W.'s *Herzensergießungen* and the creation of a Romantic mythology', Burwick, *Imagination*, 269–85, perceives this work as a fiction rather than a scholarly tract, and as an attempt to create an aesthetic religion based on the visionary rather than the visual. F. sees in this the Romantic idealization of the past and yearning for a Golden Age in the future.

LITERATURE, 1830–1880

By BOYD MULLAN, *Lecturer in German in the University of St Andrews*

1. GENERAL

REFERENCE WORKS AND GENERAL STUDIES. A major new biblio-graphical resource has become available in the form of *Inhaltsanaly-tische Bibliographien deutscher Kulturzeitschriften des 19. Jahrhunderts*, ed. Alfred Estermann, 10 vols (in 15), Munich, Saur, which began publication in 1995 and has been completed this year with the appearance of vols 9 and 10. It provides a comprehensive index of names and contents for 20 leading journals of the period 1815–80, among them such organs as the *Telegraph für Deutschland*, the *Hallische Jahrbücher*, *Die Gartenlaube*, and *Westermanns Monatshefte*. It will certainly be highly valued by Germanists lucky enough to work in institutions that can afford to purchase it.

Brenner, *Literaturgeschichte*, makes a good fist of the daunting, and currently somewhat unfashionable, task of outlining the historical development of German literature over the past six centuries. It is divided into 12 chapters of between 25 and 30 pages, each of which deals with a significant epoch (for example, *Barock*, *Aufklärung*, *Realismus*) and presents its representative authors and literary move-ments within the social, political, and cultural context of the time. Anyone tempted to yawn dismissively at this point should pause for a moment and be aware that despite the modest space at his disposal Brenner has packed into the book an enormous amount of exactly the sort of useful fact that is needed by students — and indeed by professional Germanists wishing to familiarize themselves more closely with fields outside their own immediate specialisms. Despite the claim in the publisher's prospectus that the book is not intended as a reference work it does in fact read rather like a series of articles in a literary encyclopaedia, except that it provides a continuous guiding thread from one article to another. Two of the chapters fall into our period and are concerned with *Biedermeierzeit* and *Realismus*; depending on their importance authors and movements merit anything from half a page to three pages of discussion. Tribute should be paid to Brenner's style which is lucid and fluent throughout. *Der große Romanführer: 500 Hauptwerke der Weltliteratur. Inhalte, Themen, Personen*, ed. B. Gräf, Stuttgart, Hiersemann, xvi + 760 pp., summar-izes the contents of what the editor considers the most important and influential novels of world literature from ancient times to the present. The difficulties of defining what is meant by a novel are not ignored: Gräf's not unreasonable solution to the problem is to adopt a wide and flexible definition which allows him to accommodate many works of non-European fiction (including even one from ancient Egypt!). Two firm rules that help limit the potentially unmanageable number of entries are that novels not originally written in German must have been translated into German, and that each author is represented by only one novel. This second rule works well enough for certain authors like Hölderlin, but has the frustrating effect of cutting out nearly all the work of authors such as Fontane or Thomas Mann. Of the 500 novels summarized 57 are by German-speaking authors, eight of whom fall into our period (Fontane, Freytag, Heyse, Immermann, Keller, Meyer, Mörike, and Stifter). Sometimes the basis of selection is puzzling. Why, for example, does Chamisso's *Schlemihl* merit inclusion when Novalis's *Ofterdingen* does not? And why do La Roche and Dürrenmatt appear when Gutzkow, Gotthelf, Ludwig, and Raabe are left out? Some of the summaries are recycled from *Reclams Romanführer* which was first published in 1962, though this fact is nowhere acknowledged. The summaries are however informative and reliable and the book is handsomely printed and bound. Viera Glosíková, *Handbuch der deutschsprachigen Schriftsteller aus dem Gebiet der Slowakei (17.-20. Jahrhundert)* (Veröffentlichungen der Kommission für Literaturwissenschaft, 15), Vienna, Vlg der Österr. Akad. der Wiss., 1995, 172 pp.

THEMES. Among the themes that have attracted significant interest this year are: the relationship between literature and politics, German political exiles, intercultural studies, the treatment of taboo subjects, Don Juan and the *femme fatale*, women's writing, Jewish affairs, and the ever-popular Kaspar Hauser. *Literatur und Nation: Die Gründung des Deutschen Reiches 1871 in der deutschsprachigen Literatur*, ed. Klaus Amann et al. (LGGL, 36), 507 pp., is one of the major scholarly achievements of the year. Its aim is to trace the reaction of German-speaking writers and intellectuals to the 'kleindeutsch' solution which Bismarck brusquely applied to the problem of German unification following the Prussian victories of 1866 and 1870. The work is divided into three main sections which approach the topic from a German, an Austrian, and a Swiss perspective, though within this broad framework space is found to discuss the position of ethnic minorities such as the Jews in the Habsburg lands. The decision to produce a collective volume rather than a monograph reflects the editors' awareness of the fact that the *Reichsgründung* evoked drastically differing reactions among different groups of people in the German-speaking world. The individual contributors thus deliberately illuminate the topic from a wide — and always interesting — variety of perspectives, and there is no doubt that this diversity greatly enhances the intellectual richness of the volume. The book is handsomely produced and illustrated, and an index of names ensures that it is user-friendly. The individual articles are: M. Derndarsky, 'Perspektiven der Reichsgründung: Die deutsche Frage und ihre Lösung durch Bismarck' (13–29); A. Schumann, 'Glorifizierung und Enttäuschung: Die Reichsgründung in der Bewertung der Literaturgeschichtsschreibung' (31–43); U. Köster, 'Die ideale Deutung der Reichsgründung und ihr Funktionswandel im Kaiserreich' (49–62); M. Marquardt, 'Das deutsche Reich als ideengeschichtliche Konstruktion im Werk Wilhelm Diltheys' (63–77); M. Thormann, 'Für die "nationale Hälfte des Bewußtseins": Der Beitrag der *Grenzboten* zur kleindeutschen Nationalstaatsgründung 1871' (79–92); R. Hartmann, 'Von "Bruderkrieg", "Erbfeind" und Reichsgründung in der Lyrik der *Gartenlaube* zwischen 1867 und 1871' (93–105); R. Parr, 'Real-Idealismus: Zur Diskursposition des deutschen Nationalstereotyps um 1870 am Beispiel von Ernst Wiechert und Theodor Fontane' (107–26); H. O. Horch, 'Enthusiasmus und Resignation: Berthold Auerbach und die Reichsgründung 1871' (127–52); P. Sprengel, 'Der Liberalismus auf dem Weg ins "neue Reich": Gustav Freytag und die Seinen 1866–1871' (153–81); E. Meyer-Krentler, '"Gibt es nicht Völker, in denen vergessen zu werden eine Ehre ist?" Wilhelm Raabe und die deutsche Einigung' (183–203); M. Haider, 'Deutsche Reichsgründung und österreichisches Selbstverständnis in politischer Sprache' (207–31); W. Michler, 'An den Siegeswagen gefesselt: Wissenschaft und Nation bei Wilhelm Scherer' (233–66); J. Sonnleitner, 'Bismarck in der österreichischen Literatur' (267–303); W. Wiesmüller, '"... dann wächst Deutschthum dem Preußenthume über das Haupt": Adalbert Stifter und die deutsche Frage' (305–16); R. Langer, 'Grillparzer und die deutsche Reichsgründung' (317–41); C. Stiller, 'Die Reichsgründung 1871 und die "Antisemitenfrage". Jüdische Perspektiven auf das Zweite Deutsche Reich: Josef Popper-Lynkeus, Karl Emil Franzos, Berthold Auerbach' (343–68); W. Klimbacher, 'Ferdinand Kürnberger und Adolf Fischhof: Zwei ehemalige "Märzkämpfer" in deutschnationaler Euphorie: Literarisch-politische Reaktionen auf Krieg und Reichsgründung 1870–71' (369–96); M. Nöllke, 'Der "verfluchte Civilist" und die "deutsche Heldenarmee": Daniel Spitzers Reaktion auf die Reichsgründung 1870–71' (397–408); C. Seefranz, 'Die schöne Nation: Robert Hamerlings ästhetische Reichsgründung' (409–38); A. Opela, '"Vom Strande der Adria": Aspekte der deutschösterreichischen Kultur in Triest 1866–1871' (439–58); R. Zeller, 'Schweizer Autoren und die Reichsgründung: Gottfried Keller und C. F. Meyer' (461–77). Jonathan F. Wagner, *Germany's 19th Century Cassandra: The Liberal Federalist Georg Gottfried Gervinus* (AUS, IX, 175), 1995, xvi + 222 pp., is primarily concerned with Gervinus's politics, emphasizing his commitment to liberal causes (the *Göttinger Sieben*, the 1848 Revolution) and his opposition to Bismarck's unification of Germany. Richard T. Gray, *Stations of the Divided Self: Contestation and Ideological Legitimation in German Bourgeois Literature, 1770–1914*, Stanford U.P., 1995, xviii + 390 pp., examines the tension between art and politics in German *Bürger* literature from the Enlightenment to the First World War. Gray's main contention is that middle-class German literati were divided against themselves, and struggled more against the sociopolitical and economic principles of their own social group than against any 'class' oppressor from without. The book relies heavily on modern literary theory (Foucault, Habermas, Adorno) and, although learned, is not always easy to read. Six canonical texts are selected from periods of major sociopolitical and literary upheaval and subjected to intensive analysis. The two 19th-c. ones are Heine's *Ideen. Das Buch Le Grand* and Büchner's *Woyzeck*. Gössmann, *Poetisierung*, includes: J. Scholz, 'Deutschland in der Lyrik des Vormärz' (161–97); W. Hinck, '"Land der Rätsel und Schmerzen": Heinrich Heines Deutschlandbild' (199–216); Manfred Windfuhr, '"Unsere großen Meister": Heines intellektuelles Deutschlandbild' (217–39); and H. Ehlert, '"Deutschland, das sind wir selbst": H. Hs Deutschland' (337–41). Gordon A. Craig, *The Politics of the Unpolitical: German Writers and the Problem of Power, 1770–1871*, OUP, 1995, 204 pp., considers the extent to which ten major German literary figures, one of whom is Heine, show political engagement in their works.

Alter, *Exilanten*, includes: H. Chambers, 'Johanna Kinkel's novel *Hans Ibeles in London*: A German view of England' (159–73); P. Howe, '"This world of diamonds and mud: Women travellers in mid-nineteenth century London' (174–97); U. Schmidt-Brümmer, 'Zwischen Gouvernantentum und Schriftstellerei: Amalie Bölte in England' (198–224); and S. Neuhaus, '"Poesie der Sünde" — "Triumph — der Moral": Großbritannien in den Reiseberichten und Romanen des frühen Rodenberg' (254–69). Other essays in the book are listed below under FONTANE. *Romanticism and Beyond: a 'Festschrift' for John F. Fetzer*, ed. C. A. Bernd et al. (California Studies in German and European Romanticism and in the Age of Goethe, 2), NY, Lang, viii + 280 pp., has contributions on 'Heine als Exilant in Paris' and 'On trying to bury Wagner'.

Nationale Grenzen und internationaler Austausch: Studien zum Kultur- und Wissenschaftstransfer in Europa, ed. L. Jordan et al. (Communicatio, 10), Tübingen, Niemeyer, 1995, ix + 360 pp., assembles papers given at a 1992 conference organized by the Heinrich-Heine-Institut in Düsseldorf. It has five contributions relating to Heine: B. Kortländer, 'Begrenzung — Entgrenzung: Kultur und Wissenschaftstransfer in

Europa' (1–19); J. A. Kruse, ' "'...alle edeln Herzen des europäischen Vaterlandes": Heine und Europa' (53–72); K. Sauerland, 'Heines Wirkung: Ein deutscher Skandal und ein europäisches Ereignis?' (73–83); J. Archipov, 'Heine und die russische Lyrik: Beispiele von Lermontov bis Blok' (84–93); and S. Zantop, 'Zwischen Aneignung und Enteignung: Heine in Südeuropa' (94–108). There is also an article by H. Steinecke on the influence of Sir Walter Scott on the German novel, 'Der "reichste, gewandteste, berühmteste Erzähler seines Jahrhunderts": Walter Scott und der Roman in Deutschland'. G. Rémi, 'Entre fascination et répulsion. La France dans la poésie politique du *Vormärz* (1840–1848): Hoffmann von Fallersleben, Herwegh, Freiligrath', *ChrA*, 5: 189–221. M. Thormann, ' "Cultur-volk" und "Raubthier": Das Frankreichbild der liberalen Kultur-zeitschrift *Die Grenzboten* (1848–1871)', *GLL*, 46: 44–56.

Jackson, *Taboos*, has a short introduction by the editor followed by ten contributed chapters which review the treatment of taboo subjects — mostly sexual or political — from the 18th c. to the present day. The general standard of the contributions is high and it was certainly a good idea to draw them together into one thematic volume because this enhances still further the impact that they each make individually. The two chapters that fall directly into our period are those of M. Swales, who offers comment on Stifter (*Das alte Siegel, Kalkstein, Der Nachsommer*) and Fontane (*Effi Briest*), and of D. Jackson who examines a wide range of taboos in the writings of the Poetic Realists, both sexual (homosexuality, prostitution, syphilis) and political (no overt criticism of Bismarck or Prussia, strict reticence in the portrayal of social deprivation in the lower classes). Jackson's chapter also brings out well the role of editorial censorship and of self-censorship in excluding taboo topics from Realist writing.

Don Juan und Femme fatale, ed. Helmut Kreutzer (Literatur und andere Künste), Munich, Fink, 1994, 198 pp., has 12 articles on the history of the theme of Don Juan and his mythic female counterparts such as Cleopatra, Heine's sphinx, Salome, and Kundry, who share with him an extreme and destructive eroticism. The contributors are drawn from a range of specialisms and are concerned not only with literature but also with the plastic arts, film and opera, and with material originating in several European countries and even North America. The main focus of interest is the second half of the 19th c. and the early part of the 20th c. The articles of most direct interest to Germanists are those of G. Helmes on the progressive *Verbürgerlichung* of the Don Juan theme in German literature from Lenau to Frisch with interesting comment on Heyse, Julius Hart, Sternheim, Broch, Zweig, and Horváth; C. Hilmes on Heyse's *Kleopatra*; and J. M. Fischer on Wagner's *Parsifal*.

Autobiographien von Frauen: Beiträge zu ihrer Geschichte, ed. M. Heuser (UDL, 85), vii + 434 pp., publishes 20 conference papers concerned with the theory and history of autobiography as a genre. It has three contributions that fall into our period: O. Niethammer, '"Wir sind von der Natur und durch die bürgerliche Gesellschaft bestimmt, uns mit dem Kleinlichen zu beschäftigen..."': Formen und Inhalte der Autobiographien bürgerlicher Frauen in der Mitte des 19. Jahrhunderts'; K. von Hammerstein, 'Selbst — Geschichte(n) — Schreiben: Dokumente persönlicher Lebensführung und politischen Engagements einer Vormärzlerin: Louise Aston'; E. D. Becker, 'Marie von Ebner-Eschenbach: Meine Kinderjahre. 1906'. Also noted: Christine Otto, *Variationen des 'poetischen Tendenzromans': Das Erzählwerk von Louise Otto-Peters* (Frauen in der Literaturgeschichte, 1), Pfaffenweiler, Centaurus, 1995, 318 pp.

Gabriele von Glasenapp, *Aus der Judengasse: Zur Entstehung und Ausprägung deutschsprachiger Ghettoliteratur im 19. Jahrhundert* (CJ, 11), vi + 320 pp. GLL, 49, has a special German-Jewish number containing among other articles: Hans O. Horch, '"Was heißt und zu welchem Ende studiert man deutsch-jüdische Literaturgeschichte?" Prolegomena zu einem Forschungsprojekt' (124–35); Florian Krobb, '"Durch heutige Sprache und Kunstform wieder beleben ...." Expressions of Jewish identity in German literature around 1848: Salomon Kohn, Hermann Schiff, Leopold Kompert' (159–70).

*Der imaginierte Findling: Studien zur Kaspar-Hauser-Rezeption, ed. Ulrich Struve (BNL, 143), 1995, 237 pp., is marginally relevant to our period, as is P. A. Mackenzie, 'Kaspar Hauser in America: The innocent abroad', *GLL*, 49:438–58.

Ludwig Fertig, '... und abends auf den Helikon!' Dichter und ihre Berufe von Lessing bis Kafka, WBG, vi + 359 pp., explores the means by which a large number of writers — for the most part unhappily — earned their living. Some, like Grillparzer the archivist and Fontane the pharmacist, are generally familiar, but Raimund the confectioner and Nestroy the operatic bass singer will be less so. Most of the text consists of extracts from letters and diaries in which the writers give vent to their feelings. The book can be quite amusing but it is not academically ambitious. Wolfgang Hegele, *Literaturunterricht und literarisches Leben in Deutschland (1850–1990): Historische Darstellung — Systematische Erklärung*, Würzburg, Königshausen & Neumann, 272 pp. K. Riha, 'Großstadt-Wahrnehmung: fünf Autoren, fünf Städte — als Beispiel', *Stadtkultur — Kulturstadt: Eine Bestandsaufnahme aus Anlaß des 'Europäischen Kulturmonats' Graz, Mai 1993*, ed. G. Melzer, Graz, Leykam, 1994, pp. 159–82, has some discussion of Heine and Stifter. *Bibel und Literatur — Bibel als Literatur, ed. Jürgen Ebach et al., Munich, Fink, 304 pp., has a chapter by G. Hartung on 'H. H. und die Bibel'. F. E. Foster, 'Images of the press in German literature in and after 1848', *GLL*, 49:422–37, considers the portrayal of journalists and journalism in works of Freiligrath, Spielhagen, Freytag, and Raabe. E. Bahr, 'Die Widersacher des späten Goethe: Die Jungdeutschen, die Nationalen und die Orthodoxen', *GJb*, 112, 1995:227–41, discusses Goethe reception in the post-Romantic period, with consideration of the attitudes of Heine, Wienbarg, and Börne. *Kleine Lauben, Arcadien und Schnabelewopski: Festschrift für Klaus Jeziorkowski*, ed. Ingo Wintermayer, Würzburg, Königshausen & Neumann, 1995, 240 pp., includes: S. Konrad, 'Fontanes *'L'Adultera*: Eine kritische *Wahlverwandtschaften*-Lektüre'; M. Blum, '"Das ist eben das, was man sich verheiraten nennt": Zu zwei Frauenbildern bei Theodor Fontane'; A. Knapp, 'Die Vergartenlaubisierungen des Wilhelm Busch'.

MOVEMENTS AND PERIODS. *Forum Vormärz Forschung*, 1, 1995 [1996], is a new journal which devotes most of its first volume to the relationship between literature and the press in the Germany of the 1830s and 1840s under the title *Journalliteratur im Vormärz*, ed. R. Rosenberg et al., Bielefeld, Aisthesis, 308 pp. The contributions concerned with this theme are: G. Frank, 'Romane als Journale: System- und Umweltreferenzen als Voraussetzung der Entdifferenzierung und Ausdifferenzierung von "Literatur" im Vormärz' (15–47); H. Brandes, 'Journalkritik und neuere Genres in den Zeitschriften des Jungen Deutschland' (49–58); M. Lauster, 'Moden und Modi des Modernen: Der frühe Gutzkow als Essayist' (59–95); M. Vogt, 'Georg Weerths *Schnapphahnski*: Zur Form des ersten Feuilletonromans in Deutschland' (97–106); J. Requate, 'Die Entstehung eines journalistischen Arbeitsmarktes im Vormärz: Deutschland im Vergleich zu Frankreich' (107–30); W. Rasch, 'Zur Geschichte des *Telegraph für Deutschland* 1838–1843' (131–60); W. Büttner, 'Adalbert von Bornstedt und die Brüsseler Kommunisten' (161–75). The remaining articles in the volume are: B. Kortländer, 'Übersetzen — "würdigstes Geschäft" oder "widerliches Unwesen": Zur Geschichte des Übersetzens aus dem Französischen ins Deutsche im Vormärz' (179–203); L.-P. Linke, 'Return of the vanishing "Greatest American Author": Charles Sealsfield (Karl Postl) auf dem Weg der (Re-)Kanonisierung' (205–12); B. Füllner, '"Es ist ein gutes Stück: ich glaube, daß es Euch Freude machen wird — lustig ist es wenigstens": Zur Entstehung und Überlieferung von Georg Weerths *Humoristischen Skizzen aus dem deutschen Handelsleben*' (213–35); U. Zemke, 'Gefährliche Reisen: Tropenreisen und Tropenmedizin im Vormärz' (237–49). All the contributions to this first volume are of an impressive standard and get the journal off to a promising start. *Vormärzliteratur in europäischer Perspektive. 1. Öffentlichkeit und nationale*

Identität, ed. Helmut Koopmann et al., Bielefeld, Aisthesis, 323 pp., is the first of three projected volumes which will explore European literature in the period leading up to the revolutions of 1848 from an interdisciplinary and comparative perspective. In this first volume the focus of interest is the literature of the German *Vormärz,* with the term *Vormärz* being interpreted in the broader sense to mean all German literature of the years 1830–48, and not merely of the shorter period 1840–48. It was an excellent idea of the editors to include a comprehensive index of names and keywords to the book. Although the general quality of the contributions is high, the chapters likely to be of special interest to Germanists are: P. Stein, 'Zum Verhältnis von Literatur und Öffentlichkeit bis zum deutschen Vormärz. Oder: Wie schlüssig ist Jürgen Habermas' *Strukturwandel der Öffentlichkeit* für die Literaturgeschichte?' (55–85); H. Koopman, 'Chamisso, Börne, Heine: Exil in Deutschland, Exil in Frankreich' (91–110); H. Brandes, 'Die unruhige Nation: Frankreich im Blickpunkt der jungdeutschen Journale' (111–22); H. Lengauer, '"Von eurer Freiheit habt ihr nichts behalten, Als das ungewaschene Maul": Grillparzer und England' (123–45); E. Bourke, 'Daniel O'Connell: Ein Riese unter Zwergen oder ein rechter Lump? Der irische Agitator in deutscher Vormärzperspektive' (159–74); R. Jones, 'Gutzkow and the Catholic issue' (175–88); J. Purver, 'Steps beyond the private sphere: Women writers of the Vormärz and the challenge to exclusion' (247–63); and E. Sagarra, 'Selbstbestimmung durch Fremdbestimmung: On the history of *Der deutsche Michel* as a cartoon image in the Vormärz' (281–92).

Nachmärz: Zum Ursprung der ästhetischen Moderne in einer nachrevolutionären Konstellation, ed. T. Koebner et al., Wiesbaden, Westdeutscher Vlg, 395 pp., is an important publication that fills a surprising gap in the historiography of German literature. Although a great deal has been written in recent years about the *Vormärz,* the editors rightly point out that its correlative, the *Nachmärz,* remains a shadowy concept which urgently needs serious study. The general thrust of the book's 23 articles is that reaction to the failed revolution of 1848 was an important stimulus to the development of the modernist movement in German literature, art and music; the *Nachmärz* is seen as the 'laboratory' of modernism. The articles which are primarily concerned with German literature of our period — and which are of generally excellent quality — are: K. Briegleb, '"Das bessere Lied" — Nachmärz im Vormärz: Zu Heinrich Heines Weg der Kunst Dezember 1841 — Januar 1844' (20–42); G. Sautermeister, 'Heine und Baudelaire: Eine vergleichende Lektüre' (43–78); G. Mattenklott, 'Der Streit als symbolische Form: Lessing, Heine,

Nietzsche' (80–87); T. Koebner, '"Hinschwinden aus der Gegenwart." Richard Wagner nach der Revolution: Ein essayistischer
Exkurs' (144–53); G. Martens, '"Was wüßte deutsches Hornvieh mit
den délicatesses einer solchen Natur anzufangen!" Nietzsche über
Heinrich Heine' (246–55); S. Gilman, 'Freud liest Heine liest Freud'
(273–89); M. Böhler, '"Fettaugen über der Wassersuppe" — frühe
Moderne-Kritik beim späten Gottfried Keller: Die Diagnose einer
Verselbständigung der Zeichen und der Ausdifferenzierung auto-
nomer Kreisläufe' (292–305); H. Ohde, 'Der Shawl des Theodor
Storm. Oder: Das Schreiben und der Markt. Ein literaturhistorisches
Divertimento' (306–11); and A. Glück, 'Stifter — Naturreservate und
künstliche Paradiese nach 1848' (312–45). P. Boden, 'Im Käfig des
Paradigmas: Biedermeierforschung 1928–1945 und in der Nach-
kriegszeit', *Euphorion*, 70:423–44, gives a succinct critical overview of
the changing fortunes of *Biedermeier* as a critical term.

DRAMA. W. E. Yates, *Theatre in Vienna: A Critical History,
1776–1995*, CUP, xx + 328 pp., is one of the outstanding publications of the year. Not only is it the first general survey in English of
the large and important topic of Viennese theatre history, but it is in
fact also the best book on the subject in any language. Yates begins
his survey with the reforms of Joseph II in the late 18th c., which
paved the way for both the transformation of the old court theatre
into the *Burgtheater* and the foundation of the popular theatres in the
city suburbs. He then traces the development of the Viennese
theatrical scene through the 19th c. to the present day, always
attempting to combine theatre history in the narrower sense (buildings, directors, dramatists, actors, repertoire) with an account of the
theatre's changing relationship to society and the state. Here he notes
such matters as changes in the composition of the audience or the
growth of anti-Semitism, and the role of state censorship. An entire
chapter of the book is in fact given over to the topic of censorship,
before and after the watershed year of 1848. Almost inevitably, it is
the 19th c. that has pride of place in the work; five of its nine chapters
are devoted to this golden age. Attention is paid to the fortunes of
both the prestigious *Burgtheater* and the lively strongholds of the
popular theatre that flourished in the suburbs. There is also a chapter
on the history of opera and operetta in the city. The publisher has
risen splendidly to the occasion, for the book is exceptionally
handsomely produced. It contains numerous interesting, and sometimes rare, photographs and illustrations, and a useful map of the
city. A 23-page bibliography and full indexes of names and titles
round off a volume that is in every way exemplary. *Naturalism and
Symbolism in European Theatre 1850–1918*, ed. C. Schumacher (Theatre
in Europe: A Documentary History), CUP, xxvi + 532 pp., has four

chapters running to 80 pages on post-1850 German theatre, but apart from brief treatment of the Meiningen Court Theatre and Wagner's *Festspielhaus* in Bayreuth, has disappointingly little to say about developments before 1890. Austrian theatre is scarcely mentioned in the book at all. These are serious gaps which are only partly redeemed by the comparatively good accounts of theatrical developments after 1890, notably Naturalism, Neo-Romanticism, and the work of Max Reinhardt in Berlin. Harro Müller, *Giftpfeile: Zu Theorie und Literatur der Moderne*, Bielefeld, Aisthesis, 1994, 248 pp., is a collection of 16 essays by the author on a wide range of topics and authors from the 17th c. to the 20th c. Most of them have been published before, including the two on Grabbe. There is however a new one on Büchner, 'Theater als Geschichte — Geschichte als Theater: Büchners *Dantons Tod*', pp. 169–83. The book is introduced by a lively essay on the theory and problems of literary historiography — on the question how it can make sense of literature — and this is the preoccupation that links the various essays in the book together. In the Büchner essay Müller identifies two radically differing views of history. One is that of Robespierre and St Just — for whom history is 'erhabenes Drama' and a tragedy; the other is that of Danton — for whom it is a grotesque 'drame' in Victor Hugo's sense. *Aspekte des politischen Theaters und Dramas von Calderón bis Georg Seidel: Deutsch-französische Perspektiven*, ed. H. Turk et al. (*JIG*, A, 40), 452 pp., has 18 contributions including: G. Scheilin, 'Grabbes drei letzte Stücke: *Napoleon oder die hundert Tage*, *Hannibal* und *Die Hermannsschlacht*, als Modelle zur Umformung des politischen Theaters im 19. Jahrhundert'; P. Langmeyer, 'Geschichte als Natur: Die Mythisierung historischer Zeit und ihre Relativierung in Grabbes Drama *Napoleon oder die hundert Tage*'; M. Scheffel, 'Drama und Theater im Erzählwerk Theodor Fontanes'. Gail H. Hart, *Tragedy in Paradise: Family and Gender Politics in German Bourgeois Tragedy 1750–1850*, Columbia, SC, Camden House, xiv + 136 pp., is interested not so much in the portrayal as in the *removal* of women from the scene in the *bürgerliches Trauerspiel* of the 18th and 19th cs. She interprets their systematic removal as a means of eliminating the 'feminine' threat that they supposedly represented to the male-dominated, middle-class society of the age and at the same time of relieving the anxieties of the predominantly male middle-class audience for which the plays were written. The texts discussed in the seven chapters of the book nearly all belong to the 18th c., with only Hebbel's *Maria Magdalena* (here erroneously spelt *Maria Magdalene*) falling into our period. Predictably, the chapter on Hebbel's play takes the form of a thorough-going — and success-ful(!) — character-assassination of the male figures in the piece. *Thalia's Daughters: German Women Dramatists from the 18th Century to the*

Present , ed. Susan L. Cocalis et al., Tübingen, Francke, vi + 329 pp., has essays on the dramatic works of Droste-Hülshoff, Birch-Pfeiffer, and Ebner-Eschenbach. Susanne Fröhlich, *Strichfassungen und Regie-bücher: Kulturpolitik 1888–1938 und Klassikerinszenierungen am Wiener Burg- und Volkstheater* (Beiträge zur Neueren Geschichte Österreichs, 4), Frankfurt, Lang, 119 pp., has comment on Grillparzer, Raimund, and Nestroy. H. Arntzen, 'Anpassung und Widerstand: Die deutsche Komödie zwischen 1820 und 1848', *Grabbe-Jb.*, 13, 1994:50–66, briefly discusses comedies by Grabbe, Büchner, Raimund, Nestroy, Bauernfeld, and Hebbel. A. Fink-Langlois, 'Masaniello en Alle-magne: le droit de résistance de C. Weise au Vormärz', *RG*, 26:41–74, discusses Wilhelm Zimmermann's *Masaniello, der Mann des Volkes* of 1833 and Alexander Fischer's *Mas'Aniello* of 1839. H. Scheible, '"Ich kann schreiben nach jeder Richtung": Journalistenkomödien vor Schnitzler', *Sprachkunst*, 26, 1995:213–54, has comment on Freytag's *Die Journalisten*, Bauernfeld's *Der literarische Salon*, and Nestroy's *Freiheit in Krähwinkel*.

NARRATIVE PROSE.   *Erzählkunst der Vormoderne*, ed. R. Tarot et al. (Narratio, 11), Berne, Lang, 470 pp., is a collection of essays, some of them by students of Tarot, which aims to trace 'pre-modernist' changes in the narrative perspective favoured by writers of prose fiction in 19th-c. Germany. A dozen of the 20 texts studied fall into our period. The main thesis of the volume is that there was a slow but gradual shift away from what Tarot (borrowing his terminology from Plato) calls 'diegetisch-fiktionales Erzählen' (p. 34) towards a 'mime-tisch-fiktionale Erzählweise' (p. 39). Putting it very simply, what this amounts to is that the mediating voice of the 18th-c. narrator (*diegesis*) is progressively displaced by more direct means of portrayal (*mimesis*). The contributions of Tarot himself and his co-editor G. Scherer on Gutzkow's *Wally die Zweiflerin*, Büchner's *Lenz*, and Sealsfield's *Die Farbigen* are worth reading, but most of the others are thin, and the majority of readers are likely to find that the volume's preoccupation with methodology becomes wearisome. K. Habitzel and G. Mühlberger, 'Gewinner und Verlierer: Der historische Roman und sein Beitrag zum Literatursystem der Restaurationszeit (1815–1848/49)', *IASL*, 21.1:91–123, investigates the remarkable success of the historical novel in *Restaurationszeit* Germany and considers the role played in this success by publishers, lending libraries, periodicals, and censorship. M. Thormann, 'Realismus als Intermezzo: Bemerkungen zum Ende eines Literatur- und Kunstpro-gramms', *WB*, 42:561–87, considers some aspects of the development of Realist theory with particular reference to *Die Grenzboten*. S. Weing, 'Verisimilitude and the nineteenth-century German novella',

Cramer, *Neues*, 1–24. A. Graf, 'Literarisierung und Kolportagero-
man: Überlegungen zu Publikum und Kommunikationsstrategie
eines Massenmediums im 19.Jahrhundert', *Fest. Schenda*, 277–91.

REGIONAL LITERATURE. *Literaturgeschichte Österreichs: Von den
Anfängen im Mittelalter bis zur Gegenwart*, ed. H. Zeman et al., ADEVA,
viii + 604 pp., tries hard to do justice to the whole of Austrian
literature from the Middle Ages to the present. The book is a
collaborative effort with chapters from nine contributors, though
more than a third of it is by Zeman himself. Rather unexpectedly, the
usual anguishing over the question of what constitutes Austrian
literature and what distinguishes it from other German-language
literature is absent. It is simply announced in the foreword that
Austria is here taken to include all the territories of the Babenbergs
and the Habsburgs, though the main emphasis is certainly placed on
Austria proper. An attempt is made to view the writers in a wide
social and cultural context, and to take account of connections with
other art forms (music, opera, painting). It is however disappointing
to have to report that the book probably tries to do too much. Despite
its considerable length of 600 closely printed pages it can find not
quite 100 pages for the 19th c. A very large number of 19th-c. writers
are listed, but the treatment is thin; even the most important authors
get no more than a handful of pages. This may be enough for the
student and the general reader at whom the book is primarily aimed,
but it is of limited value to the specialist.

Konflikte — Skandale — Dichterfehden in der österreichischen Literatur, ed.
W. Schmidt-Dengler et al. (PSQ, 137), 1995, 291 pp., has:
B. Doppler, 'Die Ludlamshöhle und ihr Verbot' (80–91); J. Sonnleitner, 'Bauernfeld — Saphir — Nestroy: Literarische Streitfälle im
österreichischen Vormärz' (92–117); H. Schmidt-Bergmann, '"An
die Ultraliberalen in Deutschland": Nikolaus Lenau und das Junge
Deutschland' (118–28); C. Seefranz, 'Schrille Dissonanzen: Zur
kontroversiellen Rezeption Richard Wagners in der liberalen Ära'
(129–50). *Von Franzos zu Canetti: Jüdische Autoren aus Österreich. Neue
Studien*, ed. M. Gelber et al. (CJ, 14), ix + 428 pp., has: J. L.
Sammons, 'Betrachtungen zu den Heine-Studien von K. E. Franzos
und G. Karpeles'; I. Schedletzky, 'Ost und West in der deutsch-
jüdischen Literatur von H. Heine bis J. Roth'; and G. Stieg, 'Canetti
und Nietzsche'. Viera Glosíková, *Handbuch der deutschsprachigen Schriftsteller aus dem Gebiet der Slowakei (17.-20. Jahrhundert)* (Veröffentlichungen der Kommission für Literaturwissenschaft, 15),
Vienna, Vlg der Österr. Akad. der Wiss., 1995, 169 pp., lists many
minor writers, now nearly all forgotten. K. Zeyringer, 'Text und
Kontext: Österreichische Literatur. Ein Konzept', *JDSG*, 40:438–48,
traces the history of the long-running debate about the question of

whether there is such a thing as specifically Austrian literature from the 18th c. through the 19th c. (Gervinus, Scherer, Minor) to the present day.

LITERARY LIFE, SOCIETIES AND JOURNALS. *Literarische Gesellschaften in Deutschland: Ein Handbuch*, ed. Christiane Kussin, Berlin, Aufbau, 1995, 390 pp., is a second, revised edition of the original publication of 1991. It provides information about a large number of societies which aim to further research on major authors. Fifteen of the societies, ranging from the Georg-Büchner-Gesellschaft to the Theodor-Fontane-Gesellschaft, fall into our period. A. Spies, 'Towards a prosopography of Young Hegelians', *GSR*, 19:321–39, provides an interesting statistical analysis of the contributors to the *Hallische Jahrbücher*.

2. INDIVIDUAL AUTHORS

ANZENGRUBER. *Peter Rosegger — Ludwig Anzengruber: Briefwechsel 1871–1889*, ed. K. Fliedl et al. (LGGL, 33), 1995, 237 pp.

BÖRNE. I. Rippmann, ' "Allen stümpernden Liebhabern der National-Ehre": Spuren des Wartburgfestes bei Ludwig B.', *Das Wartburgfest und die oppositionelle Bewegung in Hessen*, ed. B. Dedner (MSL, 7), 1994, pp. 255–87. W. Labuhn, 'Presse und Öffentlichkeit 1819–1991: Eine Doppelbetrachtung', *ZDP*, 115, *Sonderheft*, 179–87, discusses the impact of press censorship with brief comment on some 19th-c. authors, including B. and Heine.

BÜCHNER. Terence M. Holmes, *The Rehearsal of Revolution: Georg Büchner's Politics and his Drama 'Dantons Tod'* (British and Irish Studies in German Language and Literature, 12), Berne, Lang, 1995, 214 pp., addresses the apparent contradiction that a man personally engaged in revolutionary activity could write a drama which in the view of most critics (notably Viëtor) takes a pessimistic view of the French Revolution. Holmes's thesis is that, far from illustrating the futility of revolution, the play is an attempt at political diagnosis. B. 'rehearses' the events of the Revolution (hence the title of the book) in order to see what went wrong and to show how the revolution for which he was working in the 1830s could succeed. As a committed Communist B. advocates 'permanent revolution', which means the complete annihilation of the *ancien régime* and the avoidance of the 'half-way house' of liberal compromise that Danton represents. In the play the Revolution is seen to be endangered by both the liberals, led by Danton who wants to end it, and the *outré* Robespierre. Robespierre fails because his ambition and vanity lead him to believe that revolution can be achieved only through the seizure of absolute power and the exclusion of the *Volk*. This is the mistake that leads to his downfall at the hands of the Thermidor conspirators. The play can thus be read as an arraignment of both 'counter-revolutionary tendencies' (p. 91). B.'s message is that revolution can succeed only through the class struggle. Holmes's case is daring and likely to be controversial, but the book is lucidly written and closely argued. Ikumi Waragai, *_Analogien zur Bibel im Werk Büchners: Religiöse Sprache als sozialkritisches Instrument_ (EH, I, 1533), 140 pp. Matthias Morgenroth, *_Formen und Funktionen des Komischen in Büchners 'Leonce und Lena'_ (SAG, 314), 1995, 156 pp.

W. Wende, '"Ein _Huhn_ im Topf jedes Bauern macht den gallischen _Hahn_ verenden"': Zur politischen Unmündigkeit des Volkes in G. Bs _Dantons Tod'_, Csobádi, _Volk_, 485–99, brings out well the sharp ideological differences between the social revolutionary B. and the liberal reformers of the German _Bürger_ class, and considers the implications of these differences for the political struggle in the play. H. Hiebler, 'G. Bs literarische Praxis in _Leonce und Lena_: Individuum und Kollektiv im Getriebe des materialistischen Idealismus', _ib._, 501–19, argues that, far from being a frivolous Romantic _Literaturkomödie_, B.'s play attacks the social and political system of the age. T. Rothschild, 'Das Volk wehrt sich: Revolutionäre Gewalt im Drama', _ib._, 545–54. Rüdiger Görner, _Die Kunst des Absurden: Über ein literarisches Phänomen_, WBG, xii + 177 pp., has 'Drei Deutungsmuster des Absurden: Goethe — Kierkegaard — Nietzsche' (12–24), and 'Das Absurde als Form der Zeitkritik bei Georg Büchner' (25–34). R. Selbmann, '"Auf den Menschen reimt sich die ganze Natur"': Über das Verhältnis von Chemie und Literatur im 19. Jahrhundert', _Euphorion_, 70:153–65, has brief comment on _Woyzeck_. Klaus Müller-Salget, 'Der Tag, an dem Woyzeck den Mord beging: Zu einem Textproblem in Bs Dramenfragment', _ZDP_, 115:288–93, brings impressive ingenuity to a stubborn textual problem concerning the time of year when the murder takes place, and proposes a convincing solution. C. Doazan-Jost, 'Hugo von Hofmannsthal et la première représentation au théâtre du _Woyzeck_ de G. B.', _RG_, 26:75–91, discusses the version of the text prepared by Hofmannsthal for the performance of the play in the _Residenztheater_ in Munich in 1813 to mark the centenary of B.'s birth. B. Dedner, '"Wartburg-Spuren" bei G. B.', _Das Wartburgfest und die oppositionelle Bewegung in Hessen_, ed. B. Dedner (MSL, 7), 1994, pp. 231–53. A. Mádl, 'Büchner-Übersetzungen und -Rezeption in Ungarn', _Fest. Mollay_, 243–50. Kathryn R. Edmunds, '_Lenz_ and _Werther_: B.'s strategic response to Goethe', _MDU_, 88:176–96. J. Reddick, '"Man muß nur Aug und Ohren dafür haben"': _Lenz_ and the problems of perception', _OGS_, 24, 1995:112–44.

DROSTE-HÜLSHOFF. A.v.D.-H., *Historisch-kritische Ausgabe. Werke, Briefwechsel*, ed. Winfried Woesler, Tübingen, Niemeyer, has added vol. x, 2: *Droste-Briefe 1843–1848. Kommentar*, ed. W. Woesler, x + 1514 pp.; and vol. xi, 2: *Briefe an die Droste 1809–1840. Kommentar*, ed. B. Plachta, xiv + 958 pp. The excellent two-volume edition of A.v.D.-H., *Sämtliche Werke*. i. *Gedichte*. ii. *Prosa, Versepen, Dramatische Versuche, Übersetzungen*, ed. B. Plachta and W. Woesler, 2 vols, DKV, 1006, 1005 pp., noted in these pages two years ago, has now been issued in paperback by the same publishers at an attractive price. A.v.D.-H., *Sämtliche Briefe*, ed. W. Woesler, 3 vols in one (DTV, 2416), reprints the contents of volumes viii, 1, ix, 1, and x, 1, of the HKA published by Niemeyer. What this new book offers is therefore the text of all the letters written by Droste in a reliable edition, but not the extensive commentaries of Gödden and Woesler, for these were published in the HKA as separate volumes. A useful attempt has however been made to compensate for the missing commentary by the inclusion of specially prepared biographical notes on the recipients of the letters and a 40-page index of all the names mentioned in them. At its affordable price the book represents very good value for money.

Walter Gödden, *Tag für Tag im Leben der Annette von Droste-Hülshoff: Daten Texte, Dokumente*, Paderborn–Munich, Schöningh, 343 pp., is an attractive and informative little volume. It inevitably covers much of the same ground as the author's *Dichterchronik* of Droste's life reviewed in these pages two years ago. On this occasion however the academic footnotes are abandoned in favour of numerous photographs, illustrations, and facsimiles. An astonishing amount of material is included in the book's modest compass, and it is all presented with model clarity. Also by Walter Gödden, *Sehnsucht in die Ferne: Annette von Droste-Hülshoffs Reisen durch die Biedermeierzeit*, Düsseldorf, Droste, 309 pp., does not claim to be a demanding work of scholarship, but does raise the intriguing question why Droste travelled so much. It appears that in all some nine years of her life were spent on the move, even though she never travelled as far afield as some of her friends and contemporaries such as Adele Schopenhauer or Louise von Gall, and wrote no travel literature of the kind popular in the 19th c. Gödden argues that travel was a liberating experience for her, taking her out of the intellectual narrowness of her home surroundings and stimulating her literary creativity (she always travelled with a case full of manuscripts of work in hand). The book quotes extensively from her letters, many of which are concerned with her travels, and considers her contribution to L. Schücking's *Das malerische und romantische Westfalen*. Doris Maurer, *Annette von Droste-Hülshoff: Biographie*, Meersburg, Turm Vlg, 264 pp., cannot hold the candle to either of Gödden's biographies. It is aimed at a popular readership and gives no source references of any kind for its numerous quotations. Bodo Plachta, '*1000 Schritte von meinem Canapee': Der Aufbruch Annette von Droste-Hülshoffs in die Literatur*, Bielefeld, Aisthesis, 1995, 194 pp., is a collection of essays all written by Plachta, some of which have been published before. Herbert Kraft, *Annette von Droste-Hülshoff* (RoM, 517), 1994, 154 pp.

'*Spiel nur war das — wir sind Dichter!' Joseph von Eichendorff. Seine literarische und kulturelle Bedeutung*, ed. W. Gössmann et al., Paderborn, Schöningh, 1995, 371 pp., has a chapter by Gössmann, 'Naturverständnis als Kunstverständnis: Goethe — Eichendorff — Droste'. D. Gallon, 'Second sight in the poetry of A.v.D.-H.', *Celtic and Germanic Themes in European Literature*, ed. N. Thomas, Lewiston–NY, Mellen, 1994, pp. 31–45. M. Meyer, 'Die "Dichtergedichte" der A.v.D.-H.: Probleme einer Identitätsbildung', *Mélanges Spiewok*, 297–319. A. Rösler, '"O Germanien, mein Vaterland": Das Deutschlandbild der Droste', Gössmann, *Poetisierung*, 349–55. G. B. Pickar, 'The "Bauernhochzeit" in Droste's *Die Judenbuche*: A contemporary reading', *Weltbürger — Textwelten: Helmut Kreutzer zum Dank*, ed. L. Bodi et al., Frankfurt, Lang, 1995, pp. 68–93. Frauke E. Lenckos, '"Allein mit meinem Zauberwort": A.v.D.-H.'s late poetry, *Letzte Gaben* (1862)', *GR*, 71:280–95. C. Liebrand, 'Verkehrter Mythos: "Umschriften" in A.v.D.-Hs Romanfragment *Ledwina*', *Aurora*, 56:79–93.

EBNER-ESCHENBACH. The fifth of six planned volumes of E.-E.'s diaries has appeared, *Tagebücher V (1898–1905)*, ed. K. K. Polheim et al., Tübingen, Niemeyer, viii + 628 pp. Ferrel Rose, *The Guises of Modesty: Marie von Ebner-Eschenbach's Female Artists*, Columbia, SC, Camden House, 1994, viii + 213 pp., is based on a Yale dissertation of 1991. Writing from a feminist perspective, Rose argues that E.-E.'s portrayal of female artist figures was deeply influenced by her awareness of her own inferior position as a woman writer. To gain acceptance with the literary establishment she censored certain themes and plots out of her work, adopted a strategy of self-irony in *Aus Franzensbad*, or disguised the female dramatist as Schiller in *Doctor Ritter*. After an introductory chapter which gives a general survey of E.-E.'s life and work, three texts that are representative of different stages in her career — *Aus Franzensbad, Lotti, die Uhrmacherin, Meine Kinderjahre* — are selected for detailed analysis. D. Klostermaier, 'Anton Bettelheim: Creator of the E.-E. myth', *MAL*, 29:15–43, considers the shortcomings of Bettelheim's two biographies of E.-E. written in 1900 and 1920. L. K. Worley, 'Telling stories/telling histories: Marie von Ebner-Eschenbach's "Er laβt die Hand küβen"', Cramer, *Neues*, 34–56. R. Thum, 'Oppressed by generosity; Dismantling the gilded marital cage in Marie von Ebner-Eschenbach's "Erste Trennung"', *ib.*, 57–66.

FONTANE. T. F., *Grete Minde*, ed. H. Nürnberger (DTV, 2377), 156 pp., reprints the text of the Munich edition published by Hanser, but with a revised and extended commentary and a specially written 'Nachwort'. Stefan Neuhaus, *Freiheit, Ungleichheit, Selbstsucht? Fontane und Großbritannien* (Helicon, 19), Frankfurt, Lang, 444 pp., is a 1995 Bamberg dissertation. It is divided into three main parts, the first of which deals with the extent and the nature of F.'s knowledge of Britain. His initial uncritical enthusiasm on the occasion of his first visit in 1844 was to give way to an increasingly critical view during his later visits as his distaste grew for the materialism that he found in British society. The second part is concerned with his admiration for Scott and the enormous influence that Scott's work, especially the novels, had on him. His admiration for Scott largely accounts for his love of 'romantic' Scotland. The third part of the book then examines the presence of British influences in four of F.'s own novels, *Cécile, Unwiederbringlich, Frau Jenny Treibel*, and *Der Stechlin*. Neuhaus is highly knowledgeable about both F. and the 19th-c. Britain that he encountered, and he is not afraid to challenge orthodox or lazy critical opinions. Some of his discussions would however benefit from being shorter; this is especially true of the first part of the book which runs to over 150 pp. and could almost stand as a dissertation in itself. Reine Chevanne, *Fontane et l'Histoire: Présences et Survivances* (EH, 1, 1528), 2 vols, 1995, ii + 834 pp. Regine Dieterle, **Vater und Tochter: Erkundung einer erotisierten Beziehung in Leben und Werk Theodor Fontanes* (ZGS, 47), 304 pp. *'Ich bin nicht für halbe Portionen': Essen und Trinken mit Theodor Fontane*, ed. L. Berg-Ehlers et al., Berlin, Aufbau, 1995, 139 pp., is a collection of passages from various writings of F. about food and drink.

Fontane-Blätter, 61, has: G. Erler, ' "Nervenpleite", der Harz und das "Unsterblichkeits-Packet": Fs Briefe an seine Frau vom August 1877' (6–26); P. Goldammer, 'F.-Autographe aus dem Archiv des Verlages F. A. Brockhaus' (27–39); D. Sangmeister and B. Zand, ' "Warum wir unseren T. F. so lieb hatten": F. und Franz Servaes. Unbekannte Briefe und Rezensionen aus den Jahren 1890 bis 1905' (40–54); W. A. Niemirowski, 'Henryk Sienkiewicz über Bismarck. Mit einem Brief Fs an Theophil Zolling vom 3. April 1895' (55–65); C. Jolles, *'Unwiederbringlich* — der Irrweg des Grafen Holk' (66–83); P. Rieck, 'Polnische Thematik im Werk T. Fs' (84–115); Irmela von der Lühe, ' "Wer liebt, hat recht": Fs Berliner Gesellschaftsroman *L'Adultera*' (116–33); W. Henkel, 'Das F.-Haus in Schiffmühle' (180–82); H. Kinzelmann, 'T. F.: *Denkmal Albrecht Thaer's zu Berlin* — eine Ergänzung' (188–92); L. Otting, 'Zur Geschichte eines F.-Porträts' (193–95); M. Horlitz and P. Schaefer, 'Auswahlbibliographie: Neuerscheinungen und -erwerbungen des F.-Archivs bis

Dezember 1995' (202–17). *Fontane-Blätter*, 62, has: R. Berbig, 'T. F. und das "Rütli" als Beiträger des *Literarischen Centralblattes für Deutschland*: Mit einem unveröffentlichten Brief an Friedrich Zarncke und bislang unbekannten Rezensionen Fs aus dem Jahr 1853' (5–26); I. Nitsche '"Die novellistischen Interessen waren stärker im mir als die historischen": Ein bisher unbekannter Brief T. Fs an Johann David Erdmann Preuss' (27–30); R. Böschenstein, 'Caecilia Hexel und Adam Krippenstapel: Beobachtungen zu Fs Namengebung' (31–57); P. Kunze, 'T. F. und die Sorben' (58–75); C. Grawe, '"Einen frischen Trunk Schiller zu tun": T. Fs Schillerkritiken 1870–1889. (1. Teil)' (76–87); B. Plachta, 'T. F. und Ferdinand Freiligrath' (88–111); J. Osinski, 'Aspekte der F.-Rezeption bei Günter Grass' (112–26); D. Glass and P. Schaefer, 'F. weltweit: Bibliographie der Übersetzungen' (127–53).

Alter, *Exilanten*, includes: L. Berg-Ehlers, 'Der verhinderte Sprachlehrer T. F. und was ihm an Lehrbüchern zur Verfügung gestanden hätte' (101–19); R. Berbig, '"Der Typus eines Geschichtenmachers": Gustav Friedrich Waagen und T. F. in England' (120–41); R. Muhs, 'Max Schlesinger und Jakob Kaufmann: Gegenspieler und Freunde Fs' (292–326); and J. Thunecke, '"Von dem, was er sozialpolitisch war, habe ich keinen Schimmer": Londoner "Kulturbilder" in den Schriften T.Fs und Julius Fauchers' (340–69). Walther Killy, *Von Berlin bis Wandsbeck: Zwölf Kapitel deutscher Bürgerkultur um 1800*, Munich, Beck, 250 pp., attempts to convey an impression of everyday *Bürger* life in the Germany of the early 19th c., using private sources such as autobiographies, diaries, and letters. One chapter entitled 'Fs Swinemünde (1827)' concerns F.'s reminiscences of the Baltic coastal resort as it was in his early childhood. Lilo Weber, *'Fliegen und Zittern': Hysterie in Texten von Theodor Fontane, Hedwig Dohm, Gabriele Reuter und Minna Kautsky*, Bielefeld, Aisthesis, 293 pp., contains discussions of *Cécile, Schach von Wuthenow, Irrungen, Wirrungen* and *L'Adultera*. L. Grevel, *Beim Wort genommen: Interpretationsbeispiele dialogischer Schlüsselszenen in literarischen Texten* (Università di Pisa, Istituto di Lingua e Letteratura Tedesca: Quaderni, 8), Pisa, Nistri Lischi, 1995, 138 pp., has a chapter on *Frau Jenny Treibel*. Michael Scheffel, 'T. F. und *Der Deutsche Krieg von 1866*: Ein Beitrag aus germanistischer Sicht', *Hannovers Übergang vom Königreich zur preußischen Provinz 1866: Beiträge zu einer Tagung am 2. Nov. 1991 in Göttingen*, ed. R. Sabelleck (Schriftenreihe des Landschaftsverbandes Südniedersachsen, 1), Hanover, Hahn, 1995, pp. 245–63. H. Ester, 'Effi, Rollo und die Ordnung', *Zäsur: Zum Abschied von Gregor Pompen am 1. September 1993*, ed. I. Laisina, Nijmegen U.P., 1994, pp. 115–21.

J. Osborne, 'Vision, supervision, and resistance: Power relationships in T. F.'s *L'Adultera*', *DVLG*, 70:67–79, considers the function of

Tintoretto's painting *L'Adultera* (from which F.'s novel takes its title) in highlighting symbolically the theme of marital conflict, the determination of van der Straaten to exercise control over Melanie and her equal determination to resist. S. Hotho-Jackson, '"Dazu muß man selber intakt sein": Innstetten and the portrayal of a male mind in F.'s *Effi Briest*', *FMLS*, 32:264–76, approaches the text from a Freudian perspective. Detlef Kremer and Niklaus Wegmann, 'Wiederholungslektüre(n): Fs *Effi Briest* — Realismus des wirklichen Lebens oder realistischer Text?', *DUS*, 47.6, 1995:56–75, is mainly concerned with the pedagogics of introducing F.'s novel in the schoolroom. Also noted: R. Böschenstein, 'Namen als Schlüssel bei Hoffmann und bei F.', *ColH*, 23:67–91; B. Plett, '"... kein Schriftsteller für den Familientisch mit eben eingesegneten Töchtern": Vorschläge zur Betrachtung des Frauenbildes und des "Unmoralischen" in Fs Romanen', *DD*, 1995:256–63; H. Müller-Michaels, 'T. Fs Wanderjahre: Episoden aus den *Wanderungen durch die Mark Brandenburg*', *ib.*, 277–87; I. Tippkötter, 'T. F.: Kriegsgefangen. Über die Wahrnehmung des Fremden', *ib.*, 264–76; L. Köhn, 'Die Schrecken des Modernen; Fs Begründung realistischer Erzählprosa: *Aus den Tagen der Okkupation* (1871)', *DVLG*, 70:610–43; J. Osborne, '"Ja, vierundsechzig, Kinder, da fing es an": Zu T. Fs *Der Schleswig-Holsteinische Krieg im Jahre 1864*', *GRM*, 46:439–49; H. Kügler, '"In Deutschland ist keine Bleibe mehr." Fonty und die deutsche Einheit: Zur Zeitkritik und zur Fontanerezeption in G. Grass' neuem Roman *Ein weites Feld* — ein Lektürevorschlag', *DD*, 1995:301–04; J. Wertheimer, 'Effis Zittern: Ein Affektsignal und seine Bedeutung', *LiLi*, 26:134–40; H. Tanzer, 'T. Fs *Irrungen, Wirrungen*: Zur Gefühlsstruktur der Liebenden zwischen Authentizität und Sentimentalität', *DUS*, 48. 2:40–49; B. Plachta, 'Geschichte und Gegenwart: T. Fs *Schach von Wuthenow* in Uwe Johnsons *Jahrestagen*', *Euphorion*, 70: 206–18; A. Amberg, 'Poetik des Wassers: T. Fs *Stechlin*: Zur protagonistischen Funktion des See-Symbols', *ZDP*, 115:541–59; B. Dotzler, '"... diese ganze Geistertummelage": Thomas Mann, der alte F. und die jungen Medien', *Thomas-Mann-Jb.*, 9:189–205; M. Stern, 'Autobiographik als Akt der Selbstheilung bei T. F.', *Raabe-Jb.*, 37:119–33; Young Zu Kim, 'Fs Idee der Synthese', *Procs* (Brasília), 967–75. See also S. Konrad and M. Blum, p. 858 above.

FREILIGRATH. *Grabbe-Jb.*, 14, 1995, is devoted entirely to the work of Freiligrath (see under GRABBE). It includes: L. Körner and S. von Wiedekind, 'H. F. Freiligrath: Vita und Itinerar' (27–33); K. Hutzelmann, 'Der Dichter als Schriftsteller und Herausgeber: Die Prosaarbeiten F. Fs. Ein Bericht' (34–63); K. Roessler, 'F. F. über die Schulter geschaut: Neues aus Briefen und Manuskripten 1839–1844'

(64–114); E. Neuss, 'Der Name F. und die Siedlungsnamen auf -rath' (115–28); F. U. Krause, 'Der Name F. als Lautkontinuum und die Frage der Aussprachenormierung' (129–46); F. W. Bratvogel, ' "Ganz der Poet, den wir fordern": F. und seine Leser' (147–57); G. Vonhoff, 'Moving westwards: Zur Bedeutung der Amerikabilder in Fs Übersetzungen amerikanischer Gedichte' (158–74): E. Fleischhack, 'Gedichte an und über F.: Ein Teilaspekt der Rezeption' (175–94); W. Büttner, 'F. F. im Revolutionsjahr 1848' (195–208); J. Ruland, 'F. F. und die deutsche Denkmalpflege' (209–25); P. Hasubek, 'Eine Geste des Dankes und der Verehrung: Zum Verhältnis von F. und Immermann' (226–35); J. Grywatsch, 'Zwischen Bewunderung und Skepsis: Die Droste und F. im gegenseitigen Urteil' (237–57); H. P. Ganser, 'Johann Gaudenz von Salis-Seewis und F. F.' (258–65); A. Schücking-Homeyer, 'Eine Schriftstellerin aus dem Freundeskreis der Freiligraths: Louise von Gall' (266–79); I. Hufnagel and K. Roessler, 'Das F.-Zimmer in der Krone Assmannshausen und seine Manuskripte' (280–98); Berthold Auerbach, 'Rede auf F. F., gehalten am 7. September 1867 zu Darmstadt' (299–317). K. Nellner completes the volume with bibliographies of new publications on Grabbe, Freiligrath, and Weerth. E. Sagarra, ' "Pad mit seinem Irish Bull": German Exiles and the "Irish Question" ', Alter, *Exilanten*, 225–40, has comment on F.'s poem 'Irland'. H. Rösch, 'Die Londoner Schiller-Feier 1859', *ZDP*, 115, *Sonderheft*, 94–111, examines the part played in the London celebrations by various German exiles, including Freiligrath and Gottfried Kinkel. M. Manczyk, 'Die Rübezahlsage in der deutschen und polnischen Literatur', *GeW*, 107, 1995:49–58, has brief comment on F.'s poem 'Aus dem schlesischen Gebirge'.

FREYTAG. *Gustav Freytag: Briefe an die Verlegerfamilie Hirzel.* II. *1865–1877*, ed. M. Galler and J. Matoni (Schriften der Stiftung Haus Oberschlesien, Literaturwissenschaftliche Reihe, 4, 2), Berlin, Gebr. Mann, 1995, 379 pp., presents the second and final part of F.'s correspondence with his Leipzig publisher. M. Galler, 'Demaskierung der Macht', *Orbis Linguarum*, 2, 1995:99–104. R. Theel, 'Kommunikationsstörungen: Gustav Freytags Kritik an Parteipresse und Politikgeschäft in seinem Lustspiel *Die Journalisten* (1852)', *Euphorion*, 70:185–205.

GOTTHELF. Gerhard Gey, *Die Armenfrage im Werk Jeremias Gotthelfs: Zu einer Frühform christlichen sozialpolitischen und sozialpädagogischen Denkens und Handelns*, Münster, Lit, 1994, iii + 211 pp., is a 1994 Trier dissertation.

GRABBE. Ladislaus Löb, *Christian Dietrich Grabbe* (SM, 294), x + 170 pp. *Christian Dietrich Grabbe: Ein Dramatiker der Moderne*, ed. Detlev Kopp, Bielefeld, Aisthesis, 199 pp., has an introductory chapter by the editor, followed by ten other contributions. Five of these — all of them valuable — offer scholarly investigations of G.'s dramas and his biography, and for professional Germanists these articles are likely to be the most interesting part of the book: C. Wiemer, 'Palimpsest des Posthistoire: Gs Seismographie der neuen Medien in *Napoleon oder die hundert Tage* und *Scherz, Satire, Ironie und tiefere Bedeutung*' (21–46); A. Stammberger, 'Der Vers im Monolog als Mittel innerer und äußerer Bewegung: Aspekte der Dynamik von Sprache und Geschehen in Goethes *Iphigenie auf Tauris* und Gs *Don Juan und Faust*' (47–93); G. Nickel and E. Schreiter, ' Zwei Lektüren von C. D. Gs *Don Juan und Faust*' (95–117); M. Vogt, '"... wo die Steine sprechen": Objekte als Akteure im Drama der Moderne' (119–28); E. Fleischhack, 'Georg Fein bei G. in Detmold: Eine noch unbekannte Begegnung im Herbst 1828' (129–36). Other contributions in the book are concerned with recent (and controversial) productions of G.'s plays. The volume is rounded off by D. Kopp, 'Bibliographie C. D. G.' (183–99). Olaf Kutzmutz, **Grabbe: Klassiker ex negativo*, Bielefeld, Aisthesis, 1995, 223 pp., is a 1995 Münster dissertation.

The *Grabbe-Jb.* has broadened its scope and will in future concern itself with the three 19th-c. Detmold writers, Grabbe, Freiligrath and Weerth. Vol. 13, 1994, includes W. Broer, 'Louise Christiane Clostermeier — ein Frauenleben des 19. Jahrhunderts' (98–118). This article assesses the life and personality of G.'s much-enduring wife. K. Nellner contributes short bibliographies of new publications on G., Freiligrath, and Weerth. Also noted: Raleigh G. Whitinger and John L. Plews, 'The anti-heroical consistency of C. D. G.'s historical dramas: poetological discourse and intertextuality in *Gothland, Hohenstaufen,* and *Napoleon*', *ColGer*, 29:39–60. See also the articles listed in *Aspekte des politischen Theaters*, p. 861 above.

GREGOROVIUS. *Eine Reise nach Palästina im Jahre 1882*, ed. H.-W. Kruft, Munich, Beck, 1995, 103 pp.

GRILLPARZER. William C. Reeve, *The Federfuchser/Penpusher from Lessing to Grillparzer: A Study Focused on Grillparzer's 'Ein Bruderzwist in Habsburg'*, McGill-Queen's U.P., 1995, 168 pp. A. K. Kuhn, 'Myth, matriarchy, *Männerphantasie*: Rereading G.'s *Libussa*', *Playing for Stakes: German-Language Drama in Social Context. Essays in Honour of Herbert Lederer*, ed. A. K. Kuhn et al., Oxford–Providence, Berg, 1994, pp. 139–60. M. Dorninger, 'Der Küchenjunge Leon: Eine Gestalt F. Gs in ihrem figuralen Umfeld', *Die lustige Person auf der Bühne: Gesammelte Vorträge des Salzburger Symposions 1993*, II, ed. P. Csobádi et al. (Wort und Musik: Salzburger Akademische Beiträge, 23), Anif/Salzburg, Müller-Speiser, 1994, pp. 623–38. J. Salaquarda, '"Er ist *fast* immer einer der *Unserigen*": Nietzsche und G.', Borsche, *Nietzsche,*

234–56, considers G.'s reception by Nietzsche. F. Lönker, 'Das Spiel der Bilder in Gs *Jüdin von Toledo*', *JDSG*, 40:262–76. Manfred Koch, 'Gottes Finger und die Handzeichen der Liebe: Zum Motivkomplex Hand — Sprache — Speise in Gs Erzählung *Der arme Spielmann*', *Euphorion*, 70:166–84.

Grillparzer-Jb., 19, is largely devoted to the theme of G. and music and includes: G. Stradner, 'Das Grillparzer-Violoncello' (9–20); E. W. Partsch, '*Träumen und Wachen* (WAB 87): Anton Bruckner vertont G.' (21–26); E. Tunner, '*Der arme Spielmann* und *Die Macht der Gewohnheit*: Musikbezüge bei F. G. und Thomas Bernhard' (27–33); L. M. Kantner, 'Giacomo Meyerbeer in der Beurteilung Gs' (35–39); T. Antonicek, '"Da nimmt die werthe Cither/Er wieder von der Wand ..."': Christian Freiherr von Zedlitz und die Musik' (55–63); H. Kretschmer, 'Die Verlassenschaftsabhandlungen der Schwestern Fröhlich' (65–92); E. Hilscher, 'G. und die Musik: Eine Bibliographie (bis Ende 1994)' (93–108); R. Geissler, 'G. und die Zukunft' (109–23); D. C. G. Lorenz, 'Die schöne Jüdin in Stifters *Abdias* und Gs *Die Jüdin von Toledo*' (125–39); W. Woesler, 'Eine Abschrift von Gs *Entzauberung* im Nachlaβ A. v. Droste-Hülshoffs und ihre Folgen' (141–45); S. P. Schleichl, 'Konnte G. Deutsch? Gedanken zu einer Geschichte der deutschen Literatursprache in Österreich seit 1800' (147–69); P. Leisching, 'Das Innsbrucker Ehrendoktorat für F. G.' (171–76).

GROTH. J. Hartig, 'Sag- und Sprichwörter im Prosawerk K. Gs', *NdW*, 35, 1995:85–103. F. Debus, 'Aspekte zur "Aldietschen Beweging" im Spiegel des Briefwechsels zwischen Johan Winkler und K. G.', *Goossens Vol.*, II, 1185–97. The *Jahresgabe der Klaus-Groth-Ges.*, 36, is almost all devoted to the journey that G. made to Capri in the winter of 1895–96, and reproduces the extensive correspondence associated with the visit.

GUTZKOW. K. G., *Berlin: Panorama einer Residenzstadt*, ed. W. Rasch, Berlin, Morgenbuch, 1995, 258 pp., is a selection of journalistic articles written by G. at various stages in his long career between 1831 and 1873 on the theme of life in G.'s home city of Berlin. The choice of the articles and the title of the book are both the work of the editor. Most of the material has not been republished since its first appearance in such organs as the *Telegraph für Deutschland* and the *Augsburger Allgemeine Zeitung*. The book is arranged in four sections which deal with everyday life in Berlin, the politics of Prussia, the Berlin theatre (Raupach, Tieck, Birch-Pfeiffer), and literary life in the city (Alexis, Mühlbach, Lewald). The volume is attractively produced and illustrated. Erich Fritscher, **Karl Gutzkow und das klassizistische Historiendrama des 19. Jahrhunderts: Studien zum Trauerspiel 'Philip und Perez'* (MBSL, 30), 386 pp., is a 1994 Heidelberg dissertation.

HEBBEL. Herlinde N. Ayers, **Selbstverwirklichung/Selbstverneinung: Rollenkonflikte im Werk von Hebbel, Ibsen und Strindberg* (STML, 15), 1995, 184 pp. T. Kawahara, 'Versuch über Hs *Maria Magdalena*: Der Ehrgeiz in der bürgerlichen Gesellschaft und natürliche Bedürfnisse der Menschen', *DB*, 96:86–95 (Japanese with German summary). Volker Nölle, 'Die unterdrückte "Auferstehung": Hs *Agnes Bernauer* im Lichte von Bachofens *Mutterrecht*', *ZDP*, 115:204–25. H. Fröschle, 'Hs Verhältnis zu Uhland: Zur Problematik der Wirkung in der Literatur', *Suevica; Beiträge zur schwäbischen Literatur- und Geistesgeschichte*, 7, 1993[1994]:49–80.

H.Jb., 51, has: M. Ritzer, 'Tragödie und Realismus: Zur Aktualität der Gattung in der Jahrhundertmitte' (7–32); H. Kaiser, '*Schnock* und anderes aus Hs epischem Labor: Über den Ursprung seines Dramas aus Erzählexperimenten' (33–48); H. Aust, 'Hebbel aus realistischer Sicht (am Beispiel von Theodor Fontanes Kritik über *Herodes und Mariamne*)' (49–63); H. Bachmaier, 'Spekulation oder Wahrnehmung: Zur Hebbel-Stifter-Kontroverse' (65–75); H. R. Brittnacher, 'Sündenbock und Opferlamm: Soziologischer Realismus in Hs *Agnes Bernauer*' (77–99); A. Rudolph, 'Geschichtliche Verantwortungsgemeinschaft im Karfunkel: Shakespearerezeption und Zeitbezug in F. Hs Lustspiel *Der Diamant*' (101–28); L. Stockinger, 'Anmerkungen zu Hs Position im Religionsdiskurs der Moderne' (129–49); W. Häusler, '"Die Czechen und Polacken schütteln/Ihr strupp'ges Karyatidenhaupt": F. H. und die "Bedientenvölker" der Habsburgermonarchie' (151–212); and H. Thomsen, 'Theaterbericht' (213–30). See also G. H. Hart, p. 861 above.

HEINE. The *Säkularausgabe* of H.'s *Werke, Briefwechsel, Lebenszeugnisse*, has added vol. 16–17K, Teilband 1, *De L'Allemagne. Kommentar*, ed. C. Pichois et al., Berlin, Akademie, 1995, 285 pp., and vol. 4K, *Tragödien, Frühe Prosa 1820–1831. Kommentar*, ed. E. Richter, Berlin, Akademie, 543 pp. Beate Wirth-Ortmann, *Heinrich Heines Christusbild: Grundzüge seines religiösen Selbstverständnisses*, Paderborn, Schöningh, 1995, 244 pp., is a 1994 Düsseldorf dissertation. This fact no doubt explains the author's deference to the secondary literature on H. and her tendency to quote from it at sometimes unnecessary length. It appears from her foreword that she was a philosopher before she was a Germanist, and in the book she sticks fairly resolutely to her last, for the book is concerned more with H.'s religious beliefs than with his creative writings. The poems and *Reisebilder* are frequently mentioned, but there are no extended discussions of any of them as literature. For Germanists the most interesting chapter in the book will be the last one. This deals with H.'s conversion in 1848 to faith in a personal God, not the God of the Judaism into which he was born or the Protestantism into which he was baptized. Sabine Bierwirth, *Heines*

Dichterbilder: Stationen seines ästhetischen Selbstverständnisses, Stuttgart, Metzler, 1995, xii + 485 pp., is a Düsseldorf dissertation. Edith Lutz, *Der 'Verein für Cultur und Wissenschaft der Juden' und sein Mitglied H. Heine* (Heine-Studien), Stuttgart, Metzler, 290 pp., has some comment on *Der Rabbi von Bacherach*. Sabine Schneider, *Die Ironie der späten Lyrik Heines* (Ep, 148), 1995, 245 pp., is a 1993 Tübingen dissertation. M. M. Dobrinac, **Die Heinrich-Heine-Rezeption im kroatischen, serbischen und slowenischen Sprachgebiet des ehemaligen Jugoslawien von 1945 bis zur Mitte der 70er Jahre mit Bezug auf die sozialistisch-revolutionäre Wirklichkeit des Landes* (EH, 1, 1498), 276 pp., is a 1994 Essen dissertation. Jocelyne Kolb, *The Ambiguity of Taste: Freedom and Food in European Romanticism*, Ann Arbor, Michigan U. P., 1995, xiii + 346 pp., has a chapter on 'H. and the aesthetics of the tea table', pp. 115–223. Also noted: Ralf Schnell, *Heinrich Heine zur Einführung* (Zur Einführung, 130), Hamburg, Junius, 1996, 249 pp.; *Dichtung ist ein Akt der Revolte: Literaturpsychologische Essays über Heine, Ibsen, Shaw, Brecht und Camus*, ed. Gerhard Danzer, Würzburg, Königshausen & Neumann, 280 pp.

Karlheinz Fingerhut, '"Auf den Flügeln der Reflexion in der Mitte schweben" — Desillusionierung und Dekonstruktion: Hs ironische Brechung der klassisch-romantischen Erlebnislyrik und eine postmoderne "doppelte" Lektüre', *DUS*, 47.6, 1995:40–55, offers a postmodernist reading of H.'s 'Donna Clara'. W. Hinck, '"Land der Rätsel und der Schmerzen": H. Hs Deutschlandbild', Gössmann, *Poetisierung*, 199–216. M. Windfuhr, '"Unsere großen Meister": Materalien zu Hs intellektuellem Deutschlandbild', *ib.*, 217–39. H. Ehlert, '"Deutschland, das sind wir selber": H. Hs Deutschlandbilder', *ib.*, 337–41. I. Stipa, 'Translating H.'s lyrics: A passe-partout masquerade of the self ?', *Fest. Exner*, 191–98. M. Winkler, 'Mythology in H.'s writings on religion and philosophy in Germany', *Fest. Jurgensen*, 285–95. R. Robertson, '"Herr Peregrinus": Persona, race and gender in H. H.'s *Die Harzreise*', *Brücken über dem Abgrund/Bridging the Abyss. Auseinandersetzung mit jüdischer Lebenserfahrung, Antisemitismus und Exil. Festschrift für H. Zohn*, ed. A. Colin et al., Munich, Fink, 1994, pp. 145–57. S. S. Prawer, 'Moses Mendelssohn zwischen H. und Marx', *Moses Mendelssohn und die Kreise seiner Wirksamkeit*, ed. M. Albrecht (WSA, 19), 1994, pp. 411–30. K. Fingerhut, 'Comique, satire et déconstruction', *ChrA*, 5:41–62. L. Calvié, 'Histoire politique et parodie littéraire: France-Allemagne, du comte de Thorenc au tambour Legrand', *ib.*, 29–39. U. Hofstaetter, '"Wolfgang Apollo": Das Goethe-Bild des jungen H. in dem Reisebild *Die Nordsee. Dritte Abteilung*', *Journal of Human and Cultural Sciences*, Tokyo, 26, 1995:1–35. J. L. Sammons, 'H.'s last year', *YR*, 84:144–51. C. Perels, 'Zum Sprachverständnis H. Hs', *JFDH*:232–45. B. A. Kruse, 'Die Liebe als Umgestaltung der modernen Subjektivität: Zur frühen Lyrik Hs',

DUS, 48. 2:21–38. A. Riemen, 'Harzreisen: Eichendorff zwischen Goethe und H.' *Aurora*, 56:1–16. See also the articles listed under Gössmann, *Poetisierung*, p. 855 above, Jordan, pp. 855–56 above, and Koebner, pp. 859–60 above.

HEYSE. B. Mullan, 'Death in Venice: The tragedy of a man and a city in P. H.'s *Andrea Delfin*', *ColGer*, 29: 97–114.

IMMERMANN. F. U. Krause, 'Karl Immermann als Geschichts-schreiber der literarischen Stimmungen seiner Generation', *Grabbe-Jb.*, 13, 1994:119–43.

JHERING, RUDOLF VON. M. Fuhrmann, 'R. v. J. als Satiriker: Die *Vertraulichen Briefe über die heutige Jurisprudenz* literarisch betrachtet', *DVLG*, 70:80–97, gives a detailed analysis of the six satirical letters, which were first published in the *Preußische Gerichtszeitung* in the 1860s and attacked various aspects of the contemporary legal system, and sees in them the influence of both ancient satire (Horace) and of the more modern tradition of the *Epistolae obscurorum virorum*, Pascal's *Lettres à un provincial*, and Montesquieu's *Lettres persanes*.

KELLER. G. K., *Sämtliche Werke*, ed. T. Böning et al., has been completed by the addition of vol. 3, *Der grüne Heinrich: Zweite Fassung*, ed. Peter Villwock (Bibliothek deutscher Klassiker, 133), DKV, 1251 pp., and vol. 7, *Aufsätze, Dramen, Tagebücher*, ed. D. Müller (Bibliothek deutscher Klassiker, 137), DKV, 1160 pp. Both volumes maintain the excellent standards of scholarship and book production that one has come to associate with this publisher and this edition of K.'s works, except that one must ask why the seventh volume does not include an index of names to the entire edition. Given the length and density of the critical apparatus in each of the seven volumes, a comprehensive index is surely an absolute necessity. Nevertheless, these two volumes complete a K. edition that is in every other respect outstanding and will be the standard one for the foreseeable future. An interesting feature of the seventh volume is that K.'s essays and newspaper articles are arranged chronologically, rather than by theme as in earlier editions, so that the development of his interests and opinions can be more easily traced. Some of the material in this volume, the early 'Studienbücher' and the diary that he kept in the 1840s, is published in much fuller and more reliable form than ever before. G. K., *Romeo und Julia auf dem Dorfe*, ed. E. and M. Swales, London, Bristol Classical Press, xxx + 78 pp., follows the usual pattern of this useful series. The editors provide a 24-page introduc-tion which is clear and stimulating and does not talk down to its intended readership.

U. Kienzle, 'Hochstapler auf der Opernbühne I. Alexander Zemlinsky: *Kleider machen Leute*', *Die lustige Person auf der Bühne: Gesammelte Vorträge des Salzburger Symposions 1993*, II, ed P. Csobádi et

al. (Wort und Musik: Salzburger Akademische Beiträge, 23), Anif/
Salzburg, Müller-Speiser, 1994, pp. 701–09, examines the use made
of K.'s Novelle by Zemlinsky and his librettist Leo Feld in the comic
opera which was first performed in 1910. P. Goldammer, '"Ich bin
wider meinen Willen abermals in großen Rückstand gerathen": G.
Ks unveröffentlichte Briefe an den Verlag F. A. Brockhaus aus den
Jahren 1847–1854', *JDSG*, 40:30–58, reproduces the text of 23
letters from K. to Heinrich Brockhaus with explanatory comment
and footnotes. Also noted: Heinrich Lauinger, *Formen und Funktionen
des Schmollens in den Seldwyla-Novellen von Gottfried Keller*, Berlin, Frieling,
1994, 176 pp.; G. Sautermeister, 'Erinnerungsarbeit in Ks Bildungsroman *Der grüne Heinrich*', *CEtGer*, 29, 1995:75–82; V. Dürr, '"Nun
sag, wie hast du's mit der Religion?" G. K.'s critique of Reformed
Protestantism in *Meretlein* and later narratives', *ColGer*, 29:115–40.

KÜGELCHEN, WILHELM VON. W.v.K., *Erinnerungen aus dem Leben des
Alten Mannes: Tagebücher und Reiseberichte*, ed. H. Schöner et al., Munich,
Koehler & Amelang, 1994, 304 pp. W.v.K., *Das eigene Leben ist der beste
Stoff: Briefe an die Schwester Adelheid, an Wilhelm Volkmann und Ludwig
Richter*, ed. A. Knittel et al., Munich, Koehler & Amelang, 1995,
212 pp. These two volumes make available previously unpublished
material by K. which supplements his autobiography, the *Jugenderin-
nerungen eines alten Mannes* of 1870. A. P. Knittel, 'Bilder-Bücher der
Erinnerung: W. v. Ks *Jugenderinnerungen eines alten Mannes* im Kontext
ihrer Zeit', *WB*, 42:545–60.

LAUBE. A. Todorow, '"Stürmisches Bravo von der Galerie":
Redner und Publikum in der Mitte des 19. Jahrhunderts. Ein Bericht
aus dem *Ersten deutschen Parlament* von Heinrich Laube (1849)', *Rhetorik*,
14, 1995:1–13.

LENAU. É. Tokei, 'Exotismus und Kosmopolitismus im 19. Jh.:
Zigeunerdarstellungen bei N. L. und Franz Liszt', *Fest. Mollay*,
379–83.

LEWALD. F. L., *Jenny* (DTV, 2387), 384 pp., is a reprint of the
original text of 1843.

MARLITT. W. A. Coupe, 'Eugenie Marlitt: In defence of a writer
of Kitsch', *GLL*, 49:42–58, combines scholarship with wit in this
reappraisal of his remarkable subject.

MEYER. P. Sprengel, 'Der andere Tizian: Kunst und Wirklichkeit,
Lyrik und Novellistik bei C. F. M. (Zu *Angela Borgia* und *Die Versuchung
des Pescara*)', *ColGer*, 26:141–55. Id., 'Zugänge zur Unterwelt: Todes-
Lust und Mythologie im Spätwerk C. F. Ms', *WW*, 46:363–79, has
perceptive comment on *Die Hochzeit des Mönchs* and *Die Richterin*.

MÖLLHAUSEN, BALDUIN. *Geschichten aus dem Wilden Westen*, ed.
A. Graf (DTV, 2634), 1995, 311 pp. A. Graf, '"Wenn eine Arbeit
fertig ist, wird sie eben zur Waare": Der Briefwechsel zwischen

Joseph Kürschner und Balduin Möllhausen (1884–1898)', *AGB*, 41, 1994:215–54.

MÖRIKE. Isabel Horstmann, **Eduard Mörikes 'Maler Nolten'. Biedermeier: Idylle und Abgrund* (MGS, 17), 307 pp. Irene Schüpfer, **'Es war, als könnte man gar nicht reden.' Die Kommunikation als Spiegel von Zeit- und Kulturgeschichte in Eduard Mörikes 'Maler Nolten'* (SDLNZ, 32), 253 pp. H. Arbogast, '"... in meinem nahen Versteck'': Über Eduard Mörikes Gedichte', *JDSG*, 40:525–40. R. Breymayer, 'Buch und Schmetterling: Ein Porträt von Hölderlins Nürtinger Dekan Jakob Friedrich Klemm (1733–1793). Mit einem Hinweis auf die Motivparallele in Ms Gedicht "Im Weinberg"', *Suevica: Beiträge zur schwäbischen Literatur- und Geistesgeschichte*, 7, 1993 [1994]:83–113.

NESTROY. The HKA of N.'s *Sämtliche Werke*, ed. Jürgen Hein et al., Vienna, Deuticke (formerly Jugend & Volk), has added *Stücke*, 15, *Gegen Thorheit giebt es kein Mittel. Die verhängnißvolle Faschings-Nacht*, ed. L. A. Huish, 1995, xv + 478 pp.; *Stücke*, 8, 1, *Die Familie Zirn. Knieriem und Leim. Die Fahrt mit dem Dampfwagen*, ed. F. Walla, xvi + 414 pp.; *Stücke*, 10, *Der Treulose*, ed. J. Hüttner, xvi + 575 pp; *Stücke*, 22, *Die beiden Herrn Söhne. Das Gewürzkrämer-Kleeblatt*, ed. W. E. Yates, xx + 554 pp.; and *Stücke*, 38, *Frühere Verhältnisse. Hauptling Abendwind*, ed. P. J. Branscombe, xiv + 288 pp. J. Hein, 'Wiener Volkstheater und "Wiener Volksstücke"', *DUS*, 47, Heft 5, 1995:17–29, gives a brief general survey of the Viennese *Volksstück* with special mention of Raimund's *Der Verschwender* and Nestroy's *Der Talisman*. F. Jary-Janecka, 'Das verführte, betrogene Volk ...: Nestroys Zweifel daran, wenn's ein wienerisches ist', Csobádi, *Volk*, 521–34. F. Walla, '"Da werden doch die deutschen Affen nicht lange zurückbleiben": Neue französische Quellen zu Stücken J. Nestroys', *EG*, 51:283–305. H. Mojem, 'Unedle Zivilisierte: Zur Zielrichtung der Satire in Nestroys *Häuptling Abendwind*', *JDSG*, 40:276–96.

NIETZSCHE. F. N., *Werke: Kritische Gesamtausgabe*, ed. Giorgio Colli and Mazzino Montinari, Wolfgang Müller-Lauter, and Karl Pestalozzi, Berlin, de Gruyter, has produced vol. I, 1, *Nachgelassene Aufzeichnungen Anfang 1852-Sommer 1858*, xiv + 397 pp. F. N., *Die nachgelassenen Fragmente: Eine Auswahl*, ed. G. Wohlfart (UB, 7118), 314 pp. F. N., *On the Genealogy of Morals*, trans. Douglas Smith, OUP, xxxviii + 170 pp., contains a good 30-page introduction, 24 pages of notes to the text and a helpful index of names, themes and important terms.

Alan D. Schrift, *Nietzsche's French Legacy: A Genealogy of Poststructuralism*, NY–London, Routledge, 1995, xviii + 198 pp., gives an authoritative and well-written analysis of the use made of N.'s thought by modern French theorists, including Derrida, Foucault, Deleuze, and Cixous. Schrift's rare ability to deal with this difficult material in clear

English sets an example that deserves to be followed by all who aspire to publish on poststructuralism. Nicholas Martin, *Nietzsche and Schiller: Untimely Aesthetics*, OUP, xii + 219 pp., argues that, contrary to what is widely believed, N.'s aesthetic thought does not in all respects represent a radical break with the tradition of Schiller and the 18th c., and that there are significant points of contact between *Die Geburt der Tragödie* and Schiller's *Ästhetische Briefe*. Both texts were written at a time of major cultural (and political) upheaval and both demonstrate a belief in the power of art to reform human nature. Both writers, it is claimed, are ultimately concerned with art 'not for art's' but for life's sake' (p. 190). Successive chapters deal with N.'s knowledge of and changing attitude to Schiller; the two authors' philosophy of history; their view of the ancient Greeks and the role alloted them in the two texts; and the nature and function of aesthetic creation and experience. Although the book is primarily concerned with two particular texts, it also guides us very competently through much of the aesthetic thought of the 18th and 19th cs (Winckelmann, Kant, Schopenhauer) as it influenced N. and/or Schiller. The book is well and clearly written and shows a refreshing independence of mind.

Borsche, *Nietzsche*, contains a number of articles relevant to mainstream *Germanistik*: H. Cancik, '"Philologie als Beruf"': Zu Formengeschichte, Thema und Tradition der unvollendeten vierten Unzeitgemäßen F. Ns' (81–96); E. Behler, 'Die Sprachtheorie des frühen N.' (99–111); T. Borsche, 'Natur-Sprache: Herder — Humboldt — N.' (112–30); D. Behler, 'Synästhesie in Ns *Die Geburt der Tragödie*' (131–43); L. Crescenzi, 'Philologie und deutsche Klassik: N. als Leser von Paul Graf Yorck von Wartenburg' (208–16); H. G. Hödl, 'Verklärt-reine Herbstlichkeit: Einige Anmerkungen zu Ns erster Bekanntschaft mit Goethe' (257–67); V. Vivarelli, 'N., Goethe und der historische Sinn' (276–91); F. Gerratana, '"Jetzt zieht mich das Allgemein-Menschliche an": Ein Streifzug durch Ns Aufzeichnungen zu einer "Geschichte der literarischen Gattungen"' (326–50); M. Kohlenbach, 'Die "immer neuen Geburten": Beobachtungen am Text und zur Genese von Ns Erstlingswerk *Die Geburt der Tragödie aus dem Geiste der Musik*' (351–82); and M. Brusotti, 'Verkehrte Welt und Redlichkeit gegen sich: Rückblicke Ns auf seine frühere Wagneranhängerschaft in den Aufzeichnungen 1880–1881' (435–60).

Carsten Zelle, **Die doppelte Ästhetik der Moderne: Revisionen des Schönen von Boileau bis Nietzsche*, Stuttgart, Metzler, 1995, 416 pp. Norbert Reichel, *Der Traum vom höheren Leben: Nietzsches Übermensch und die Conditio humana europäischer Intellektueller von 1890–1945*, WBG, 1994, 187 pp. Werner Stegmaier, **Nietzsches 'Genealogie der Moral'*, WBG, 1994, xiii + 267 pp. Anne Tebartz-van Elst, **Ästhetik der Metapher: Zum Streit zwischen Philosophie und Rhetorik bei Friedrich Nietzsche*, Freiburg,

Alber, 1994, 237 pp., is an Aachen dissertation. **Nietzsche and the Feminine*, ed. P. J. Burgard, Virginia U.P., 1994, xiii + 349 pp., is a collection of essays which view N. from the perspective of modern feminism. Daniel Müller, **Wider die 'Vernunft in der Sprache': Zum Verhältnis von Sprachkritik und Sprachpraxis im Schreiben Nietzsches*, Tübingen, Narr, 1995, 253 pp.

J. Salaquarda, *Nietzsche*, WBG, viii + 397, is a second, revised edition of an important collection of essays first published in 1980. Silvio Vietta, 'Zweideutigkeit der Moderne: Ns Kulturkritik, Expressionismus und literarische Moderne', *Die Modernität des Expressionismus*, ed. T. Anz et al., Stuttgart, Metzler, 1994, pp. 9–20. G. Finke-Lecaudeym, 'Die Rhetorik des Doppelpunktes in Ns *Morgenröthe*', *CEtGer*, 27, 1994:81–92. L. Call, 'Woman as will and representation: N.'s contribution to postmodern feminism', *WGY*, 11, 1995:113–29. M. Leis, 'Ns dionyische Metamorphosen oder: Eine literarische Himmelfahrt', *Diagonal*, 1995:63–71. A. Gellhaus, '"Ästhetische Erziehung des Menschengeschlechts": Lessing und Schiller bei N.', *ZDP*, 115, *Sonderheft*, 112–21. J. Salaquarda, 'Noch einmal *Ariadne*: Die Rolle Cosima Wagners in Ns literarischem Rollenspiel', *Nietzsche-Studien*, 25:99–125. P. Pütz, 'Götzendämmerung und Morgenröte bei Nietzsche und Thomas Mann', *Thomas-Mann-Jb.*, 9:207–21.

PÜCKLER-MUSKAU. G. Krebs, '*Der Lebendigste aller Verstorbenen*: Zum wiedererwachten Interesse an Fürst v. P.-M.', *JFinL*, 27, 1995:193–202.

RAABE. *R.-Jb.*, 37, has: H. Birus, 'Rs Erzählanfänge — aus komparatistischer Sicht' (1–27); U.-W. Ketelsen, 'Wilhelm Jensen — oder der Typus des Berufsschriftstellers in der zweiten Hälfte des 19. Jahrhunderts' (28–42); D. Arendt, '"Die Wissenschaft vom Tode, um zum Leben zu gelangen": Die Rolle des Arztes im Werk W. Rs' (43–68); R. G. Czapla, 'Mythen im Wandel: Zur nordischen Mythologie in W. Rs *Else von der Tanne* und Arno Schmidts *Die Wasserstraße*' (69–91); M. Haslé, 'Der Verdauungspastor: Magen-Sprache und peristaltische Schreibweise in Rs *Stopfkuchen*' (92–113); R. Schillemeit, 'Ideologie statt Philologie' (114–18); and W. Dittrich, 'Raabe-Bibliographie 1996' (215–21). Also noted: J. Bertschik, '"...das soll mir jetzt das rechte Fressen sein in der verhungerten, lustigen Zeit!" Kriegskannibalismus im Erzählwerk W. Rs', *Orbis Linguarum*, 2, 1995:59–70; J. Pfeiffer, 'Wahnsinn, Typhus, Tod: Ausschließungssysteme in W. Rs Roman *Unruhige Gäste*', *DVLG*, 70:213–26.

RAUPACH. H. J. Koning, 'Ernst Raupach (1784–1852): Ein schlesischer Erfolgsdramatiker des 19. Jahrhunderts', *JSFWUB*, 35, 1994:175–90.

REUTER. Wolfgang Beutin, *Der Demokrat Fritz Reuter*, Hamburg, von Bokkel, 1995, 145 pp.

RÜCKERT. Claudia Wiener, *Friedrich Rückerts 'De idea philologiae' als dichtungstheoretische Schrift und Lebensprogramm* (Veröffentlichungen des Stadtarchivs Schweinfurt, 10), Schweinfurt, Stadtarchiv, 1994, 309 pp., is a 1994 Würzburg dissertation. *Die zeitlose Gültigkeit der Weisheit des deutschen Brahmanen: Festvortrag des elften Preisträgers des Friedrich-Rückert-Preises der Stadt Schweinfurt, Johannes Mehlig*, ed. W. Fischer (Rückert zu Ehren, 6), Würzburg, Ergon, 1995, 43 pp.

SAAR. The HKA of F. v. S., *Kritische Texte und Deutungen*, ed. K. K. Polheim et al., Tübingen, Niemeyer (formerly Bouvier, Bonn), has added vol. 6, *Ginevra*, ed. S. Schröder, 268 pp., and vol. 7, *Leutnant Burda*, ed. V. Kribs, x + 239 pp. Both volumes follow the by now well-established pattern of the edition. Each contains Saar's text; a critical apparatus with all the variant readings; an enormously detailed account of the story's genesis, publication history, and reception; a lengthy interpretation; and a full bibliography. The risk with any editorial enterprise of this kind is of course that some of the material — especially the interpretation — will date. Nevertheless, the editors have done their job well and the interpretations on offer here are as shrewd and well-balanced as they are thorough. The books have a pleasing format, and are attractively printed and bound. Also noted: R. Hillenbrand, 'Unendliche Schatten an der Wand: Das *punctum saliens* in F. v. Ss *Braut von Habrovan*', *Sprachkunst*, 26, 1995:255–61.

SACHER-MASOCH. H. J. Werlen, 'From *Geschlechtscharakter* to *Geschlecht und Charakter*: The "nature" of "woman" debate in S.-M.'s *Venus in Furs*', *Neophilologus*, 80:1–10. G. K. Hart, 'Das Ewig-Weibliche nasführet dich: Feminine leadership in Goethe's *Faust* and Sacher-Masoch's *Venus*', *Interpreting Goethe's 'Faust' Today*, ed. J. K. Brown et al. (SGLLC), 1994, pp. 112–22.

SCHEFFEL. J. H. Voigt, 'Der Trifels auf dem Fünften Kontinent: J. v. Ss dichterische Spuren in Australien', *Fest. Jurgensen*, 265–73. W. Wunderlich, '*Wer war der Greis, den Worms solch Lied gelehrt?*: Der erfundene Dichter. J. v. Ss Version vom Autor des *Nibelungenliedes*', *Euphorion*, 89, 1995, 239–70.

STIFTER. The HKA of S.'s *Werke und Briefe*, ed. A. Doppler et al., Stuttgart, Kohlhammer, has added vol. 2, 3–4, *Bunte Steine, Apparat. Kommentar*, ed. W. Hettche, 2 vols, 1995, 430, 330 pp. Christian Begemann, *Die Welt der Zeichen: Stifter-Lektüren*, Stuttgart–Weimar, Metzler, 1995, viii + 427 pp., takes as his starting point the fact that S. has long been held to be a 'difficult' and elusive author, in that under the simple-seeming surface of his writing critics have often registered disturbing contradictions, an ambivalent attitude to the world of reality, and a sense of disorientation within it. It is Begemann's intention in the book to investigate these 'aporias' and the special 'logic' that underlies them using the methods of poststructuralist criticism. What emerges is that S. is a deconstructive author in the best modern way and considerably ahead of his time in the 19th c. In the first of his nine chapters Begemann examines S.'s 'semiotic' view of the world as evidenced by his essay *Wien und die Wiener* and at the same time sets out the theoretical groundwork for the rest of the book. Subsequent chapters are then devoted to detailed analyses of a number of S.'s representative stories and novels and to S.'s conception of art. Readers who are not well versed in deconstructionist theory are likely to find some of the book hard going, though in fairness to the author it should be said that his German style is clear (or at any rate as clear as his critical method allows) and that his discussions of individual texts contain much good comment. Christian-Paul Berger, '... *welch ein wundervoller Sternenhimmel in meinem Herzen ...': Adalbert Stifters Bild vom Kosmos* (Schriftenreihe des Adalbert-Stifter-Instituts des Landes Oberösterreich, ser. 41), Vienna–Cologne, Böhlau, 252 pp., is a 1995 Innsbruck dissertation. Berger's thesis is that there is a firm link between, on the one hand, the belief of S. the scientist in the divinely established order of the cosmos and, on the other, the literary and educational ideals instilled in him in the course of his own Josephinian education at Kremsmünster. Much of the book is concerned with the solar eclipse that S. observed in Vienna in 1842 and the impression that it made on him. To this reviewer however the book was virtually unreadable. Despite its claim to be an interdisciplinary work of interest to Germanists it belongs almost wholly to the history of philosophy or science and is not really a work of *Germanistik* at all. Furthermore, it contains a great deal of pointless name-dropping and clumsy jargon ('Phänotext' and 'Genotext' are but two examples), and there is excessive and irritating use of both bold and italic print which serves absolutely no purpose. Few, if any, Germanists will wish to struggle with it for long. Joseph C. Jeter, *Adalbert Stifter's 'Bunte Steine': An Analysis of Theme, Style and Structure in Three Novellas* (Austrian Culture, 18), NY–Berne, Lang, 197 pp., begins with a rather rambling survey of existing secondary literature on *Bunte Steine* and argues that what links the six stories of the collection is a complex of three themes that runs through all of them. These are the ego of the individual, the society with which he interacts, and the initiatives and actions which link the two together. This far from startling thesis is then supported by detailed textual analyses of *Granit*, *Kalkstein*, and *Katzensilber*. In each text Jeter demonstrates 'the thematic interplay of ego, initiative, and socialization'. It is difficult to disagree with anything that he says, but predictably it adds nothing of substance to our understanding of Stifter. Wolfgang Matz, *Adalbert Stifter oder diese fürchterliche Wendung der Dinge: Biographie,* Munich, Hanser, 1995, 405 pp. Franziska Schössler, **Das unaufhörliche Verschwinden des Eros: Sinnlichkeit und Ordnung im Werk Adalbert Stifters* (Ep, 168), 1995, 260 pp., is a 1994 Freiburg dissertation. Johannes Kersten, *Eichendorff und Stifter: Vom offenen zum geschlossenen Raum,* Paderborn, Schöningh, 1996, 228 pp., is a Düsseldorf dissertation concerned with the differing treatment of space in the work of the two authors.

Adalbert Stifter: Dichter und Maler, Denkmalpfleger und Schulmann. Neue Zugänge zu seinem Werk, ed. H. Laufhütte et al., Tübingen, Niemeyer, xvi + 583 pp., is an important volume which publishes the proceedings of a conference held in 1994 at Passau. The approach taken is a most fruitful interdisciplinary one, with no less than 26 expert contributions from the fields of literature, aesthetics, and the visual arts. To the present reviewer the best essays were those dealing with S.'s interest in the visual arts — a fascinating aspect of the man which has so far received relatively little attention. The quality of the research on offer throughout the book is exceptionally high, and Niemeyer have with good reason done the editors proud by turning out an extremely handsome volume. It will certainly hold its value for many years to come as a major contribution to S. studies. The individual articles are: C. Begemann, ' "Realismus" oder "Idealismus"? Über einige Schwierigkeiten bei der Rekonstruktion von Ss Kunstbegriff' (3–17); K. Möseneder, 'Stimmung und Erdbeben; A. Ss Ikonologie der Landschaftsmalerei' (18–57); F. von Ingen, 'Band und Kette: Zu einer Denkfigur bei S.' (58–74); S. Appuhn-Radtke, ' "Priester des Schönen": A. Ss Künstlerbild zwischen theoretischem Anspruch, literarischer Darstellung und gesellschaftlicher Realität' (75–95); J. Lachinger, 'A. S. — Natur-Anschauungen: Zwischen Faszination und Reflexion' (96–104); L. Schneider, 'Das Komma im Frack: A. S., von Hebbels Kritik aus betrachtet' (105–18); J. Kastner, 'Die Liebe im Werk A. Ss' (119–34); J. Storck, 'Eros bei S.' (135–56); W. Seifert, 'Literaturidee und Literaturdidaktik bei A. S.' (157–84); W. Lipp, 'A. S. als "Conservator" (1853–1865): Realität und Literatur' (185–203); A. Doppler, 'S. im Kontext der Biedermeiernovelle' (207–19); M. Lindner, 'Abgründe der Schuld: Transformationen des goethezeitlichen Bildungskonzepts in Ss *Studien*' (220–45); L. M. Eichinger, 'Beispiele einer Syntax der Langsamkeit: Aus A. Ss Erzählungen' (246–60); S. Schmitt, 'A. S. als Zeichner' (261–308); M. Wünsch, 'Normenkonflikt zwischen "Natur" und "Kultur": Zur Interpretation von Ss Erzählung *Der Hochwald*' (311–34); M. Titzmann, 'Text und Kryptotext: Zur Interpretation

von Ss Erzählung *Die Narrenburg'* (335–73); W. Lukas, 'Geschlechter-
rolle und Erzählerrolle: Der Entwurf einer neuen Anthropologie in
A. Ss Erzählung *Die Mappe meines Urgroßvaters'* (374–94);
W. Kühlmann, 'Von Diderot bis S.: Das Experiment aufklärerischer
Anthropologie in Ss Novelle *Abdias'* (395–409); Ć. von Zimmermann,
'*Brigitta* — seelenkundlich gelesen: Zur Verwendung "kalobiotischer"
Lebensmaximen Feuchterslebens in Ss Erzählung' (410–34); H.-W.
Eroms, 'Ansätze zu einer sprachlichen Analyse von Ss Erzählweise in
den *Studien* am Beispiel der Erzählung *Zwei Schwestern'* (435–54);
B. Ehlbeck, 'Zur poetologischen Funktionalisierung des Empirismus
am Beispiel von Ss *Kalkstein* und *Witiko'* (455–75); H. Barak, '"Gute
Freundin" und "glänzender Künstler": Die dichterisch gestaltete
Wirklichkeit in Ss Erzählung *Turmalin'* (476–85); H. Laufhütte, 'Der
Nachsommer als Vorklang der literarischen Moderne' (486–507); H.-P.
Ecker, '"Darum muß dieses Bild vernichtet werden": Über wissen-
schaftliche Sinnspiele und poetisch gestaltete Medienkonkurrenz am
Beispiel von Ss *Nachkommenschaften'* (508–23); V. Maidl, 'Ss Rezeption
in den böhmischen Ländern' (527–37); E. Schmid, 'Viele Wege
führen in die Ewigkeit: A. Ss Einzug in die Walhalla' (538–65).

Also noted: M. Beckmann, 'Stifters "Sanftes Gesetz": Selbstwie-
derholung in der Wirklichkeit', *Neophilologus*, 80:435–59; T. Wirtz,
'Schrift und Familie in A. Ss *Mappe meines Urgroßvaters'*, *ZDP*,
115:521–40; L. N. Polubojarinowa, 'A. Ss *Bunte Steine*: Zum Problem
der zyklischen Aufbauform', *JASI*, 2, 1995:17–41; W. Fritsch-
Rössler, 'Ss *Nachsommer* und Goethes *Wahlverwandschaften'*, *ib.*, 42–73;
A. Hapkemeyer, 'A. Ss *Haidedorf*: Zur ästhetischen Wahrnehmung der
Horizontale', *ib.*, 74–83.

STORM. T. S., *Werke in einem Band*, ed. P. Goldammer (DTV),
1995, 959 pp., is an attractive and inexpensive volume. Thomas
Mann, *Theodor Storm Essay*, ed. K. E. Laage, Heide, Boyens, 120 pp.,
prints the text of Mann's famous essay of 1930 and all the poems of S.
mentioned in it. Laage adds useful explanatory footnotes to the essay
and gives a detailed and illuminating account of its genesis and the
use that Mann made of the sources (mainly editions of S.'s works and
his correspondence with Kuh, Heyse and Keller) that he consulted
when writing it. The book tells us a good deal about both S. and
Mann and is attractively printed and presented. Gunter H. Hertling,
*Theodor Storms 'Meisterschuß' 'Aquis submersus': Der Künstler zwischen
Determiniertheit und Selbstvollendung*, Würzburg, Königshausen & Neumann, 1995, 103 pp., starts from the surprising — and surely false —
premise that critical opinion has underestimated a Novelle that
Turgenev considered S.'s very best (the word 'Meisterschuß' is his).
Hertling's re-evaluation takes the form of a detailed textual analysis
in three main chapters, one devoted to the framework and one to

each of the two parts of Johannes's chronicle. The analysis is readable and competent and H.'s judgements are generally sound, though he passes too lightly over the notoriously difficult problem of tragic guilt in the tale. He is probably at his best when discussing the painterly aspects of the story and S.'s extensive use of visual imagery. He does not attempt to break new ground in matters of interpretation beyond arguing that Storm shares C. F. Meyer's belief in the power of art to overcome transience and death (p. 14). Although the paintings of Johannes fail to withstand the destructive passage of time, he nevertheless succeeds in defeating it through his art as a *writer*. Interestingly, Hertling thus reaches a conclusion very close to that of A. Nuber (noted in this survey in vol. 56) that Storm subscribes to a general 19th-c. belief in the aesthetic primacy of literature over painting. The book can be recommended as a useful aid for undergraduate students. *Storm-Portraits: Bildnisse von Theodor Storm und seiner Familie. Mit 70 zeitgenössischen Bildern, Zeichnungen, Drucken und Photographien*, ed. Gerd Eversberg, Heide, Boyens, 1995, 80 pp. *Theodor Storm: Anekdoten, Sagen, Sprichwörter und Reime aus Schleswig-Holstein*, ed. Gerd Eversberg (Editionen aus dem Storm-Haus, 6), Heide, Boyens, 1994, 192 pp., attempts to identify and reprint all the popular anecdotes and legends that S. contributed in the 1840s to Biernatzki's *Volksbuch* and Müllenhoff's *Sagen, Märchen und Lieder der Herzogtümer Schleswig, Holstein und Lauenburg* (1845). The editor has added just over 100 pages of commentary and notes. *Storms erste große Liebe: Theodor Storm und Bertha von Buchan in Gedichten und Dokumenten*, ed. Gerd Eversberg (Editionen aus dem Storm-Haus, 8), Heide, Boyens, 1995, 193 pp., reproduces all S.'s poems and diary entries associated with this strange and painful affair, together with the surviving correspondence between him and Bertha and her foster-mother. In a 23-page introductory essay Eversberg brings out well the profound importance of the relationship for S.'s emotional and poetic development, though it is disappointing to see that he subscribes to the currently fashionable, but speculative, assumption that S.'s world view and his attitude to love were significantly influenced by Feuerbach. Barbara Burns, *Theory and Patterns of Tragedy in the Later Novellen of Theodor Storm* (SAG, 325), 273 pp., places S. in the literary and cultural context of the 19th c. and gives close analyses of *Renate, Ein Doppelgänger, John Riew', Der Herr Etatsrat, Ein Bekenntnis*, and *Zur Chronik von Grieshuus*. Wiebke Strehl, **Vererbung und Umwelt: Das Kindermotiv im Erzählwerk Theodor Storms* (SAG, 332), 162 pp. P. Goldammer, ' "Ich bin und bleibe Ihre getreueste Verehrerin": Marie Jensen und Theodor Storm', *Raabe-Jb.*, 37 : 134–47.

Schriften der T.-S.-Ges., 45, has: D. Artiss, 'T. Ss symbolische Tierwelt — dargestellt an seinen Vorstellungen von Wolf, Hund und

Pferd' (7–22); P. Goldammer, '"Mein, den Jahren nach, ältester Freund": Zu Ss Briefwechsel mit Heinrich Schleiden' (23–26); M. Stein, 'Tod und Weiblichkeit in T. Ss Novelle "Auf der Universität": Eine Textanalyse aus intertextueller Perspektive' (27–45); G. Eversberg, 'Der Briefwechsel zwischen T. S. und Heinrich Seidel' (47–96); K. Dohnke, 'Kongruenzen und Divergenzen, Sprache und Stoff: Aspekterealistischen Erzählens bei T. S. und Johann Hinrich Fehrs' (97–116); R. Selbmann, 'Vergoldeter Herbst: Ss "Oktoberlied", Emanuel Geibel und der Realismus in der Lyrik' (117–26); P. Goldammer, '"Mich verdrießt dieser Artikel...": T. S. und das Brockhaussche Konversationslexikon. Mit zwei bisher unveröffentlichten Storm-Briefen' (127–33); G. Ciemnyjewski, '"Natürliche" versus "künstliche" Gesellschaftsordnung: Zum Gesellschaftskritischen in Ss "Posthuma"' (135–38); W. Hettche, 'Zwei Rätsel und ihre Lösung: Zu Gerd Eversbergs Beitrag "Rätsel und Wortspiele von T. S."' (139); E. Jacobsen, 'Storm-Bibliographie' (141–53); G. Eversberg, 'Storm-Forschung und Storm-Gesellschaft' (155–62).

WAGNER. R.W., *Späte Schriften zur Dramaturgie der Oper*, ed. E. Voss (UB, 5662), 250 pp. Lutz Köpenick, *Nothungs Modernität: Wagners 'Ring' und Die Poesie der Macht im 19. Jahrhundert*, Munich, Fink, 1994, 270 pp., examines the *Ring* in the light of Walter Benjamin's ideas on the aestheticizing of politics as expressed in his essay *Das Kunstwerk im Zeitalter seiner technischen Reproduzierbarkeit* and the *Passagenwerk*. The action of the *Ring* is interpreted as an allegory of the political struggles of the 19th c. Particular attention is paid throughout to Siegfried's magic sword Nothung. Thus, for example, in chapter 2 the forging of the sword is seen as an allegory of W.'s conviction of the need for the *Bürger* class of the 19th c. to arm itself for the revolutionary struggle for freedom, in which he had himself participated on the barricades of Dresden in 1849. The foreword leads one to fear the donning of yet another methodological straitjacket, but this anxiety is quickly dispelled when one reads further. Far from being obsessed with methodology, the book is lively and well written, and K. deploys his impressive knowledge of W. and the culture of 19th-c. Germany to make much valuable comment on the political resonance of the tetralogy. Peter Wapnewski, *Weißt du, wie das wird . . .? Richard Wagner, 'Der Ring des Nibelungen'. Erzählt, erläutert und kommentiert*, Munich, Piper, 1995, 330 pp. Id., Haferland, *Erzählungen*, 445–54, interprets Siegfried's last song in *Die Götterdämmerung*. Andrea Schneider, *Die parodierten Musikdramen Richard Wagners: Geschichte und Dokumentation Wagnerscher Opernparodien im deutschsprachigen Raum von der Mitte des 19. Jahrhunderts bis zum Ende des Ersten Weltkrieges* (Wort und Musik, 27), Anif/Salzburg, Müller-Speiser, vi + 522 pp., does a monumental job in tracing and documenting the history of W. parodies. Considerations of space force her to limit her attention to parodies of the librettos only (the music is ignored), and to confine herself to German-language parodies written between the middle of the 19th c. and the end of the First World War. The work is divided into two main parts: the 'Textteil' (19–272) contains Schneider's historical account of the subject and her critical comment on the parodies of each of the main music dramas from *Der fliegende Holländer* to *Parsifal*, while the 'Dokumentationsteil' (273–443) gives the location of the manuscripts and printed texts consulted, plot summaries of the parodies, details of performances and reviews, and any relevant secondary literature. There is also an exquisitely entertaining 'Abbildungsteil' (481–522) containing such items as newspaper caricatures and mock playbills. The book lays the foundations for much future research. It complements, but does not replace, Dieter Borchmeyer's *Wagner-Parodien* of 1983, because Schneider lacks the space to reproduce the actual text of the parodies *in extenso*. *Gesamtkunstwerk: Zwischen Synästhesie und Mythos*, ed. Hans Günther (Bielefelder Schriften zu Linguistik und Literaturwissenschaft, 3), Bielefeld, Aisthesis, 1994, 296 pp., discusses various views and aspects of the *Gesamtkunstwerk* and includes a chapter on Wagner's conception of it. Wolf-Daniel Hartwich, 'Religion und Kunst beim späten Wagner: Zum Verhältnis von Ästhetik, Theologie und Anthropologie in den "Regenerationsschriften"', *JDSG*, 40:297–323, examines the complex of ideas expressed in W.'s 'Religion und Kunst', 'Heldentum und Christentum', and 'Erkenne dich selbst'. Particularly interesting is Hartwich's account of the influence of Gobineau on W.'s thinking. Karl S. Guthke, 'Schopenhauer, Richard Wagner lesend', *JFDH*:246–63, revisits Schopenhauer's marginal notes on the *Ring* and argues that — contrary to what is widely believed — he had no great opinion of W.'s poetic powers. Also noted: Michael Tanner, **Wagner*, Princeton U.P., 256 pp.; F. Salvan-Renucci, '"Wißt ihr, wie das ward?": Einsicht durch Erinnerung im *Ring des Nibelungen*', *CEtGer*, 29, 1995:153–65; G. Campioni, 'Wagner als Histrio: Von der Philosophie der Illusion zur Physiologie der décadence', Borsche, *Nietzsche*, 461–88; Rebecca Saunders, 'Shaking down the pillars: Lamentation, purity and Mallarmé's "Hommage" to Wagner', *PMLA*, 111:1106–20; P.-H. Wilberg, 'Von der "Unfreiheit" eines Künstlermenschen: Über Ws ästhetische Schriftstellerei', *SuF*, 48:706–21.

WEBER, FRIEDRICH WILHELM. *Friedrich Wilhelm Weber: Arzt — Politiker — Dichter*, ed. 'Vereinigung der Freunde des Dichters F. W. Weber e. V.', Paderborn, Bonifatius, 1994, 232 pp., contains 11 essays to mark the centenary of the death of this minor lyricist who died in 1894 and who is best remembered for his verse epic *Dreizehnlinden*.

WEERTH. *'Nur unsereiner wandert mager durch sein Jahrhundert': Ein Georg-Weerth-Lesebuch*, ed. M. Vogt, Bielefeld, Aisthesis, 206 pp., reprints a representative selection of W.'s poems, journalistic prose, and letters in the hope of raising the profile of this relatively little-known writer whom Engels famously described as 'den ersten Dichter des deutschen Proletariats'. Of particular interest are the excerpts from *Humoristische Skizzen aus dem deutschen Handelsleben* and *Leben und Taten des Ritters Schnapphahnski*, for they convey a clear impression of W.'s radical political zeal and the satirical wit which was his main weapon. The editor has provided some 20 pages of explanatory notes and a useful 'Weerth-Chronik'. Even with the benefit of an objective re-evaluation after the *Wende*, W. is not likely to become a canonical author, but he is certainly a revealing cultural indicator for *Vormärz* Germany. *Literatur in Westfalen: Beiträge zur Forschung*, 3, ed. W. Gödden, Paderborn, Schöningh, 1995, 292 pp., has a chapter by B. Füller and M. Vogt on 'Überlegungen zu einer neuen Edition sämtlicher Werke von G. W.'.

LITERATURE, 1880–1945

POSTPONED

LITERATURE FROM 1945
TO THE PRESENT DAY

By DAVID BASKER, *Lecturer in German, University of Wales Swansea*

1. GENERAL

T. Anz, 'Literaturkritik und Literaturwissenschaft. Aufgaben und Möglichkeiten heutiger Literaturkritik', Ingold, *Autor*, 199–209. E. Aurenche, *La Mémoire Coupable. Les Écrivains de langue allemande des années 70–80 et le passé nazi, Berne, Lang, 1994, x + 281 pp. S. Baackmann, *Erklär mir Liebe. Weibliche Schreibweisen von Liebe in der deutschsprachigen Gegenwartsliteratur, Hamburg, Argument, 1995, 223 pp. M. R. Becher, 'Der verspätete Gast an der Tafel der Erkenntnis. Notizen zu Literatur und Wissenschaft', Ingold, *Autor*, 133–39. U. Bernard, 'L'unification allemande dans la caricature internationale', *ChrA*, 5:169–86. 'Gegenwart', Brenner, *Literaturgeschichte*, 298–328. 'Nachkriegszeit', *ib.*, 269–97. M. Derbacher, *Fiktion, Konsens und Wirklichkeit. Dokumentarliteratur der Arbeitswelt in der BRD und der DDR, Frankfurt, Lang, 1995, 204 pp. T. S. Eberle, 'Auf den Spuren des verschwundenen Autors. Eine soziologische Rasterfahndung', Ingold, *Autor*, 73–100. E. Emter, *Literatur und Quantentheorie. Die Rezeption der modernen Physik in Schriften zur Literatur und Philosophie deutschsprachiger Autoren (1925–70), Berlin, de Gruyter, 1995, x + 358 pp. W. M. Fues, *Text als Intertext. Zur Moderne in der deutschen Literatur des 20. Jahrhunderts, Heidelberg, Winter, 1995, v + 268 pp. K. Fujii, 'Landschaften des Verfalls', *DB*, 95, 1995:12–21. S. L. Gilman, *Jews in Today's German Culture, Bloomington, Indiana U.P. , 1995, 132 pp. K. Hosaka, 'Der Rücktritt der Nachkriegsliteraturdiskurse', *DB*, 95, 1995:1–11. *Brauchen wir eine neue Gruppe 47? 55 Fragebögen zur deutschen Literatur, ed. J. Kaiser and G. Guntermann, Bonn, Nenzel, 1995, 155 pp. *1945–1995. Fünfzig Jahre deutschsprachiger Literatur in Aspekten, ed. Gerhard P. Knapp and Gerd Labroisse (ABNG, 38–39), 1995, 702 pp. U. Krechel, 'Die gefälschte Bestürzung', Ingold, *Autor*, 183–92. M. Luchsinger, *Mythos Italien. Denkbilder des Fremden in der deutschsprachigen Gegenwartsliteratur, Cologne, Böhlau, viii + 251 pp. K. T. Mai, *Das Bild der 'Dritten Welt' in Werken der deutschen Gegenwartsliteratur vom Ausgang der vierziger bis in die achtziger Jahre (EH, 1, 1519), 1995, 257 pp. S. Mews, 'The role of language and culture in the German quest for national identity', *Procs* (Brasília), II, 638–43. R. Möbius, *Autoren in den neuen Bundesländern. Schriftstellerporträts, Leipzig, Thom, 1995, 261 pp. S. Petersen, *Korrespondenzen zwischen Literatur und bildender Kunst im 20. Jahrhundert. Studien am Beispiel von S. Lenz — E. Nolde, A. Andersch — E. Barlach — P. Klee, H. Janssen — E. Jünger und G.

Becker (EH, XXVIII, 227), 1995, 314 pp. J. Rosenkranz-Kaiser, **Feminismus und Mythos. Tendenzen in Literatur und Theorie der achtziger Jahre*, Münster, Waxmann, 1995, 184 pp. J. L. Sammons, 'Zu den Grundlagen des Antiamerikanismus in der deutschen Literatur', *Akten* (Vancouver), I, 33–47. W. Schivelbusch, **Vor dem Vorhang. Das geistige Berlin 1945–1948*, Munich, Hanser, 1995, 342 pp. Klaus M. Schmidt and Ingrid Schmidt, **Lexikon Literaturverfilmungen. Deutschsprachige Filme 1945–1990*, Stuttgart, Metzler, 1995, x + 473 pp. E. Schumacher, 'Nach der Party: Techno — Literatur — Theorie', *MDG*, 42.3, 1995:42–50. **Deutsche Dichter des 20. Jahrhunderts*, ed. H. Steinecke, Berlin, Schmidt, 1994, 912 pp. A. M. Stokes, **A Chink in the Wall. German Writers and Literature in the INF-Debate of the Eighties* (NYUOS, 47), 1995, 217 pp. V. Wehdeking, *Die deutsche Einheit und die Schriftsteller. Literarische Verarbeitung der Wende seit 1989*, Stuttgart, Kohlhammer, 1995, 192 pp., sets itself the ambitious task of contributing to better mutual understanding between the citizens of old and new *Bundesländer* beyond the literary sphere. W. is much more convincing where he leaves behind the noble sentiment and focuses on analysis of specific texts: M. Walser's *Die Verteidigung der Kindheit*, M. Maron's *Stille Zeile sechs*, and W. Hilbig's *ich* are the principal subjects of a study which restricts itself primarily to narrative prose works which have as their theme issues surrounding the process of unification. Id., 'Zwei Ansichten vom Fall der Mauer. Deutsche Literatur im Umgang mit der neuen Einheit', *LiB*, 45:66–71. R. Wittman, **Auf geflickten Straßen. Literarischer Neubeginn in München 1945 bis 1949*, Munich, A1, 1995, 109 pp.

WEST GERMANY, AUSTRIA, SWITZERLAND. *Austria 1945–55. Studies in Political and Cultural Re-emergence*, ed. A. Bushell, Univ. of Wales Press, ix + 160 pp., focuses on political, historiographical, and literary developments in the ten years between the end of Nazi occupation of Austrian territory and the signing of the *Staatsvertrag* which brought an end to Allied occupation in 1955. A. B.'s opening essay sets out clearly some of the difficulties in assessing a period of political and cultural history in which the very existence of an Austrian nation-state, let alone its relationship to the National Socialist past, was open to question. B. goes on to measure official attempts to create a positive Austrian national identity against both developments in the Federal Republic and the attitudes of some young Austrian writers to the new state. R. Knight then surveys postwar Austrian historiography, providing a concise analysis of the main assumptions which historians have brought to their accounts of the period, assumptions which he is able to distil down to four distinct narratives. Subsequent chapters concentrate on prominent literary figures in the ten years in question: A. Barker on Doderer, M. Mitchell on Franz Theodor Csokor and the Austrian PEN Club, A. Hammel on Hilde Spiel, S. Low on George Saiko, and J. Thunecke on Albert Paris Gütersloh. Overall the study offers interesting new perspectives on a period of Austrian literary history which is frequently overshadowed by the history of the two Germanies. *Österreichische Tagebuchschriftsteller*, ed. D. G. Daviau, Vienna, Atelier, 1994, viii + 433 pp. C. Ehetreiber, 'Die Grazer Gruppe', *ZGB*, 4, 1995:51–69. *Provinz, sozusagen. Österreichische Literaturgeschichten*, ed. E. Grohotolsky, Graz, Droschl, 1995, 278 pp. A.-M. Heintz-Gresser, 'Mythe et pouvoir dans la société suisse: l'exemple de "l'ensauvagement"', *CEtGer*, 30:163–69. C. Karolak, 'Unbewältigte Zukunft. Kriegs- und Fortschrittsvisionen in der westdeutschen Sciencefiction-Literatur der 50er Jahre', *DK*, 46:233–42. S. H. Kaszyński, *Österreich und Mitteleuropa. Kritische Seitenblicke auf die neuere österreichische Literatur* (UAM, 41), 1995, 199 pp. D. C. G. Lorenz, 'Austrian authors and the dilemma of national and regional identity at the end of the twentieth century', *MAL*, 29.3–4:13–29. *Österreichische Autorinnen und Autoren. Debuts der letzten zwanzig Jahre*, ed. H. Lunzer, Vienna, Böhlau, 1995, 210 pp. G. E. Moser, 'Subjekt und Sprache. Theorien der Postmoderne und österreichische Gegenwartsliteratur', *WB*, 42:379–98. *Literatur über Literatur. Eine österreichische Anthologie*, ed. P. Nachbaur and S. P. Scheichl, Innsbruck, Haymon, 1995, 320 pp. F. Pilipp, 'Tabus und Utopie: Aspekte zur sprachphilosophischen Identität österreichischer Autoren', *MAL*, 29.3–4:57–74. C. Rigler, *Generationen. Literatur im Forum Stadtpark 1960–95*, Graz, Droschl, 1995, 315 pp. W. Schmidt-Dengler, *Bruchlinien. Vorlesungen zur österreichischen Literatur 1945 bis 1990*, Salzburg, Residenz, 1995, 559 pp. S. Schuster and A. Wallner, *Österreichische Literatur 1995. Ein Pressespiegel*, Vienna, Dokumentationsstelle für neuere österreichische Literatur, 128 pp. *Austria, 1938–88. Anschluss and Fifty Years*, ed. W. E. Wright, Riverside, Ariadne, 1995, 323 pp.

GDR. D. Bathrick, *The Powers of Speech. The Politics of Culture in the GDR*, Lincoln, Nebraska U.P., 1995, 303 pp. M. Bettin, 'Die DDR-Zensur und die Selbstzensur in den Augen der Autoren des Prenzlauer Bergs', *SGP*, 22, 1995:191–203. H. Fuhrmann, 'Vorausgeworfene Schatten. Lyrik in der DDR — DDR in der Lyrik', *WW*, 46:454–81. C. B. Grant, *Literary Communication from Consensus to Rupture. Practice and Theory in Honecker's GDR* (APSL, 116), 1995, 244 pp. J.-R. Groth, *Widersprüche. Literatur und Politik in der DDR 1949–1989. Zusammenhänge, Werke, Dokumente*, Frankfurt, Lang, 1994, 312 pp. U. Heukenkamp, 'Ortsgebundenheit. Die DDR-Literatur als Variante des Regionalismus in der deutschen Nachkriegsliteratur', *WB*, 42:30–53. A. Jäger, *Schriftsteller aus der DDR. Ausbürgerungen und Übersiedlungen von 1961 bis 1989. Studie*, Frankfurt, Lang, 1995, viii + 202 pp. C. Meyer, **Vertauschte Geschlechter — verrückte Utopien. Geschlechtertausch-Phantasien in der DDR-Literatur der siebziger Jahre*, Pfaffenweiler, Centaurus, 1995, 257 pp. H.-C. von Nayhauss, 'Zur Entwicklung der DDR-Literatur von den Anfängen bis 1990', *Orbis Linguarum*, 2, 1995 : 3–14. P. O'Doherty, 'German-Jewish writers and themes in GDR fiction', *GLL*, 49 : 271–81. *Berliner Geschichten. 'Operativer Schwerpunkt Selbstverlag.' Eine Autoren-Anthologie: wie sie entstand und von der Stasi verhindert wurde*, ed. U. Plenzdorf, K. Schlesinger, and M. Stade (ST, 2256), 1995, 316 pp., offers fascinating insight into the conflicts between leading GDR writers and the state censors. The anthology of Berlin stories, which includes contributions from 18 different authors (notably from Plenzdorf, G. de Bruyn, S. Heym, and G. Kunert), was originally conceived in the 1970s; its publication in the GDR was prevented by the intervention of the *Stasi*. Now that those restrictions no longer obtain, the editors have included in their edition an introduction, charting the difficulties with which the project met at the hands of the censors, and documentary evidence relating to the *Stasi*'s successful attempts to prevent the appearance of the volume in the GDR. This first edition thus clearly sets the stories in the context of cultural politics in the East Germany of the 1970s and contributes to the ongoing reassessment of GDR literary history which has been taking place since unification. M. Schenkel, **Fortschritts- und Modernitätskritik in der DDR-Literatur. Prosatexte der achtziger Jahre*, Tübingen, Stauffenburg, 1995, 334 pp. C. Schmidt, *Rückzüge und Aufbrüche. Zur DDR-Literatur in der Gorbatschow-Ära* (BSDL, 44), 1995, 291 pp. S. Vollprecht, **Science-fiction für Kinder in der DDR* (SAG, 285), 1994, 135 pp.

MINORITY LITERATURE.   D. Bechtel, '"Sur une terre étrangère": la littérature juive féminine de langue allemande depuis 1970', *Germanica*, 17, 1995 : 79–100. R. Kegelmann, **An den Grenzen des Nichts, dieser Sprache ...' Zur Situation rumäniendeutscher Literatur der achtziger Jahre in der Bundesrepublik Deutschland*, Bielefeld, Aisthesis, 1995, 231 pp. I. Söhrman, 'La culture allemande en Roumanie', *Germanica*, 17, 1995 : 13–24.

2.   LYRIC POETRY

A. Berger, '"Das alte Haus der Sprache." Traditionssprache und Sprachinnovation in der österreichischen Lyrik seit 1945', *ZGB*, Beiheft 3 : 5–18. C. Gürtler, 'Von der Natur und dem Naturunschönen, von der Liebe, vom Speisen und vom Turnen. Aktuelle Tendenzen der Lyrik in Österreich', *ib.*, 139–52. S. Klettenhammer, 'Wider die "verwelkte Metapher zwischen den verrosteten ethnischen Gitterstäben". Themen und Tendenzen der Lyrik aus Südtirol seit den siebziger Jahren', *ib.*, 105–37. W. Wiesmüller, 'Naturlyrische Traditionen in Österreich seit 1945', *ib.*, 165–96. H. Denkler, 'Im Schatten des "Dritten Reiches"': Erblast und Wirkungschance moderner geistlicher Lyrik in Deutschland', *Orbis Linguarum*, 2, 1995:15–22. **Nachkrieg und Unfrieden. Gedichte als Index 1945–95*, ed. H. Domin and C. Greve (FT, 12526), 1995, 302 pp. K. S. Guthke, 'Urlaubsreise mit oder ohne Weltuntergang. Intertextualität und moderne Lyrik', *WW*, 46:55–76. C. Klein, '*Sagen was die / Sager ändert.* La poésie concrète: écriture comique / écriture politique', *ChrA*, 5:157–68. E. Kratschmer, **Dichter, Diener, Dissidenten. Sündenfall der DDR-Lyrik. Ein Abriß. Beispiele und Kommentare*, Jena, Universität, 1995, 348 pp.

3. DRAMA

F. W. Sinhuber, **Drama und Zeitgeist in Österreich von 1980 bis 1990*, Vienna, WUV-Universität, 1995, 176 pp. P. Weber, **Das Deutschschweizer Hörspiel. Geschichte — Dramaturgie — Typologie* (ZGS, 46), 1995, 568 pp.

4. PROSE

A. Corkhill, '1945 and onwards. Female gender and participation in the German short story', *MLR*, 91:414–26. N. Klages, **Look Back in Anger. Mother-Daughter and Father-Daughter Relationships in Women's Autobiographical Writings of the 1970s and 1980s* (SMGL, 71), 165 pp. C. Mauelshagen, **Der Schatten des Vaters. Deutschsprachige Väterliteratur der siebziger und achtziger Jahre* (MGS, 16), 1995, 324 pp. F. M. Schicketanz, **Liebe nach dem Krieg. The Theme of Love in Post-War German Fiction*, Würzburg, Königshausen & Neumann, 1995, 163 pp. *Contemporary German Fiction*, ed. A. Leslie Willson, NY, Continuum, xi + 244 pp., is a collection of translations into English of short stories by 22 modern German writers. The editor offers a very brief survey of the genre in German writing since 1945 and the biographies which conclude the volume give basic details of the authors' lives. The selection of stories for translation is an imaginative one; M. Hamburger's translation of P. Bichsel and I. R. Stöhr's of S. Nadolny are among the best. This is a useful introduction to this area of modern German literature, although, of course, it has the non-specialist in mind.

5. INDIVIDUAL AUTHORS

ACHTERNBUSCH, HERBERT. R. Hüser, 'Fremdwort Bier', *ZDP*, 114, 1995:129–57.

AICHINGER, ILSE. A. Reiter, 'Die Erfahrung des Holocausts und ihre sprachliche Bewältigung: zu I. As *Die grössere Hoffnung*', *GLL*, 49:236–42.

ANDERSCH, ALFRED. I. Battafarano, 'Zwischen Kitsch und Selbstzucht — und auch noch Spuren von Antisemitismus? Marginalia zu A.: eine Forschungskontroverse Sebald, Heidelberger-Leonard und Weigel betreffend', *Morgen-Glantz*, 4, 1994:241–57. D. Baumeister, *A. A. Erzählform und Grenzen der Fiktion im Roman 'Winterspelt'* (EH, 1, 1536), 1995, 137 pp. I. Heidelberger-Leonard, 'A. revisited', *ZDP*, 114, 1995, Sonderheft:36–49. K. R. Scherpe, 'Moral im Ästhetischen. A. Weiss, Enzensberger. Ein Vortrag', *WB*, 42:109–27. See also p. 889 above.

ANDRES, STEFAN. M. Braun, '"Ein kläglicher Prophet in seinem Fisch." S. A. und die Probleme der inneren Emigration', *ZDP*, 115:262–78. J. Klapper, *S. A. The Christian Humanist as a Critic of his Times*, Berne, Lang, 1995, 188 pp.

AUSLÄNDER, ROSE. C. Helfrich, *'Es ist ein Aschensommer in der Welt.' R. A. Biographie*, Weinheim, Beltz Quadriga, 1995, 365 pp., offers a considerable amount of new material concerning the life of A., information which provides interesting new perspectives on the method of composition and content of her lyric poetry. Most revealing are the chapters covering A.'s personal relationships and the influence of the philosopher C. Brunner on her work. Perhaps less successful are H.'s accounts of the poems themselves, but as a source for a biographical interpretation of A.'s work, this volume is of undoubted value. H. Vogel and M. Gans, *R. A. Hilde Domin. Gedichtinterpretationen*, Batmannsweiler, Schneider, 280 pp.

BACHMANN, INGEBORG. K. R. Achberger, '"Das alltägliche Unerhörte." I. B.'s modernist novellas', Cramer, *Neues*, 207–34. K. Antonowicz, 'Malina oder das Auseinandergeraten — die Symbolik des Namens Malina und die Erzählproblematik des *Malina*-Romans', *ColH*, 23:93–124. P. Beers, 'I. B. "Ook ik heb in Arcadië gewoond"', *DK*, 45, 1995:243–52. C. Decker, '"wenn je etwas gut und ganz werden soll": B.'s "Unter Mördern und Irren" and the political culture of the *Stammtisch*', *MAL*, 29.3–4:43–56. R. Duffaut, 'I. B.'s alternative "states": re-thinking nationhood in *Malina*', *ib.*, 30–42. I. Dusar, *Choreographien der Differenz. I. Bs Prosaband 'Simultan'*, Cologne, Böhlau, 1994, 317 pp. I. Egger, 'Mehrsprachigkeit. Zu einem Motiv der österreichischen Literatur am Beispiel von I. B.', *DVLG*, 70:692–706. H. Gehle, *NS-Zeit und literarische Gegenwart bei I. B.*, Wiesbaden, DUV, 1995, 284 pp. I. C. Gil, '"Tot sein und atmen …" O complexo de Antígona no romance *Malina* de I. B.', *Runa*, 23–24, 1995:309–25. P. Grell, *I. Bs Libretti* (EH, 1, 1513), 321 pp. S. Grimm-Hamen, 'La condition poétique selon I. B.', *NCA*,

14:351–71. B. Helbling, *Vernetzte Texte. Ein literarisches Verfahren von Weltenbau. Mit den Fallbeispielen I. B., Uwe Johnson und einer Digression zum Comic Strip 'Doonesbury'* (Ep, 138), 1995, 181 pp. A. Holschuh, 'Relevanz, Philologie und Baackmanns Arbeit über Bs "Undine geht"', *GQ*, 68, 1995:430–35. H. Kundnani, 'The story of an illness. I. B.'s *Malina*', *GLL*, 49:59–71. P. H. Neumann, 'I. Bs Fragment "Das Gedicht an den Leser" — eine Antwort auf die "Sprachgitter"-Gedichte Paul Celans', *CJb*, 6, 1995:173–79. F. Rétif, 'Aux frontières du possible et de l'impossible. L'autre révolte', *Austriaca*, 21:167–74. I. Runtic, 'Der Ort des Schreckens und die Art der Zerstörung in I. Bs früher Lyrik', *ZGB*, Beiheft 3:31–40. F. Strzelczyk, 'Im Labyrinth: zum Verhältnis von Macht und Raum bei B. und Dürrenmatt', *Seminar*, 32:15–29. B. Stuber, *Zu I. B. 'Der Fall Franza' und 'Malina'*, Rheinfelden, Schäuble, 1994, 262 pp. S. Weigel, '"Kein philosophisches Staunen" — "Schreiben im Staunen." Zum Verhältnis von Philosophie und Literatur nach 1945: Benjamin, Adorno, B.', *DVLG*, 70:120–37. Id., 'La polyphonie de l'autre. Traumatisme et désir dans l'autobiographie imaginaire de B.', trans. D. Lassaigne, *RGI*, 5:165–82. E. Zeller, 'I. B: *Der Fall Franza*', *Runa*, 23–24, 1995:327–37. See also CELAN, PAUL; JELINEK, ELFRIEDE.

BAUM, VICKI. L. King, 'V. B. and the "making" of popular success: "mass" culture or "popular" culture?', *WGY*, 11, 1995:151–69. K. von Ankum, 'Motherhood and the "new woman": V. B.'s *stud. chem. Helene Willfüer* and Irmgard Keun's *Gilgi — eine von uns*', *ib.*, 171–88.

BECHER, JOHANNES R. J.-F. Dwars, 'Ein ungeliebter Ehrenbürger. J. R. B. in Jena. Mit Dokumenten seiner Klinikaufenthalte', *JDSG*, 39, 1995:87–110.

BENN, GOTTFRIED. I. Arends, *Die späte Prosa G. Bs. Wirklichkeitserfahrung und Textkonstitution* (BSDL, 43), 1995, 214 pp.

BERNHARD, THOMAS. *Kontinent B. Zur T.-B.-Rezeption in Europa*, ed. W. Bayer, Vienna, Böhlau, 1995, 511 pp. J. Benay, 'La femme, objet de la dramaturgie bernhardienne', *Austriaca*, 21:187–207. T. Bianca, 'Comitragedies: T. B.'s marionette theater', *MLN*, 111:533–39. J. P. Caetano, 'A poesia de T. B. e Peter Handke', *Runa*, 23–24, 1995:359–75. Hyun-Chon Cho, *Wege zu einer Widerstandskunst im autobiographischen Werk von T. B.*, Frankfurt, Lang, 1995, 228 pp. F. Eyckeler, *Reflexionspoesie. Sprachskepsis, Rhetorik und Poetik in der Prosa T. Bs*, Berlin, Schmidt, 1995, 293 pp. J. Federico, 'Heimat, death, and the other in T. B.'s *Frost* and *Verstörung*', *MAL*, 29.3–4:223–42. G. Fuchs, 'Weltverdammung als Selbstrettung. Zum Spätwerk T. Bs', *Austriaca*, 20, 1995:117–34. R. Han, *Der komische Aspekt in Bs Romanen* (SAG, 275), 1995, 214 pp. T. Heyl, *Zeichen und Dinge, Kunst und Natur. Intertextuelle Bezugnahmen in der Prosa T. Bs*

(MSLKD, 22), 1995, 265 pp. H. Hughes, '"daβ jetzt ein Exempel statuieren werde": on T. B.'s *Exempel*', *GLL*, 49:373–86. W. Huntemann, 'Wandlungen des Makabren bei T. B., dargestellt anhand seiner Kurzprosa', *Filologia germańska*, 20, 1995:3–11. A. Kaiser, '"Ein Meister": T. Bs Autobiographie und die Tradition des Bildungsromans', *MAL*, 29.1:67–91. B. Mariacher, 'Schreibend die Existenz verlängern. Anmerkungen zu T. Bs Erzählung *Ja* (1978)', *Studien zur Germanistik*, 3, 1995:93–101. C. W. Martin, *The Nihilism of T. B. The Portrayal of Existential and Social Problems in his Prose Works* (APSL, 121), 1995, 277 pp. M. Mittermayer, *T. B.* (SM, 291), 1995, ix + 220 pp. S. Schlichtmann, *Das Erzählprinzip 'Auslöschung'. Zum Umgang mit Geschichte in T. Bs Roman 'Auslöschung. Ein Zerfall'* (TSL, 27), 149 pp. S. Vidulic, 'Zur Lyrik T. Bs. Forschungsstand. Die Lyrik als Vorgeschichte', *ZGB*, Beiheft 3:19–29. H. Waitzbauer, *T. B. in Salzburg. Alltagsgeschichte einer Provinzstadt 1943–55*, Vienna, Böhlau, 1995, 148 pp.

BICHSEL, PETER. *P.B.*, ed. Rolf Jucker, Cardiff, Univ. of Wales Press, ix + 131 pp., is the third in the series of volumes connected with visits to the Centre for Contemporary German Literature at University of Wales Swansea. The volume opens with three previously unpublished prose pieces by B., one of which was written during his stay in Swansea. Following a biographical sketch by the editor, an informative interview with the author is divided into two sections: 'Der literarische B.' and 'Der politische B.'. The critical essays begin with C. Tresch's analysis of B.'s work as a 'Kolumnenschreiber'. M. Pender offers a reading of the volume of stories *Zur Stadt Paris*; R. C. Spiers examines the conflict between romanticism and realism in the mind of the narrator of *Die Jahreszeiten*; and H. Hoven looks at B.'s attitude towards, and treatment at the hands of, Germanists. The study concludes with a select, but very detailed bibliography. The combination of primary texts, biographical detail, interview, and critical analyses makes this first study in English devoted exclusively to B.'s work both stimulating and informative. See also p. 893 above.

BIENEK, HORST. H. O. Horch, 'Gleiwitz, Lubowitz, Auschwitz. Die Dimension der Schoah in den Gleiwitz-Romanen H. Bs', *ZDP*, 114, 1995, Sonderheft:85–112.

BIERMANN, WOLF. W. Król, 'Zur Rezeption W. Bs in den beiden deutschen Staaten', *SGP*, 22, 1995:165–77. P. Werres, 'W. B. and Brechts Dialektik', *Brecht Yearbook*, 21:245–58.

BOBROWSKI, JOHANNES. E. Haufe, *B.-Chronik. Daten zu Leben und Werk*, Würzburg, Königshausen & Neumann, 1994, 121 pp. J. Joachimsthaler, 'Abschied von der "Innerlichkeit". Zu J. Bs Lyrik während des Krieges', *Convivium*, 1995:49–64. E. Schmitt, 'La nature, mémoire de l'homme dans les petits textes en prose de B.: tentative de recréation d'une union brisée', *TI*, 10, 1995: 183–200.

BÖLL, HEINRICH.   **H. B. und Köln. Mit einer Wanderung durch H. Bs Köln von Martin Stankowski*, ed. V. Böll, Cologne, Kiepenheuer & Witsch, 1994, 314 pp. F. Finlay, **On the Rationality of Poetry: H. B.'s Aesthetic Thinking* (APSL, 122), 284 pp. **H. B. Bilder eines Lebens*, ed. H. Scheurer, Cologne, Kiepenheuer & Witsch, 1995, 128 pp. M. Serrer, 'Parallelisierung und Grenzverwischung. Zur Darstellung von Juden im Werk H. Bs', *ZDP*, 114, 1995, Sonderheft: 50–64.

BORN, NICOLAS.   J.-W. Kremp, **Inmitten gehen wir nebenher. N. B.: Biographie, Bibliographie, Interpretationen*, Stuttgart, M & P, 1994, 459 pp.

BRANDSTETTER, ALOIS.   E. S. Firchow and P. E. Firchow, 'Interview mit A. B.', *MAL*, 29.1: 23–38.

BRAUN, VOLKER.   W. Grauert, **Ästhetische Modernisierung bei V. B. Studien zu Texten aus den achtziger Jahren* (Ep, Reihe Literaturwissenschaft, 137), 1995, 235 pp. D. Haffad, 'Zu V. Bs Drama *T*. Erinnern an Geschichte als Versuch von Bewältigung gegenwärtiger Erfahrung', *CEtGer*, 29, 1995: 215–28. A. Visser, ' "Ost-itis"? Zu V. Bs "Wende" — Texten in "Rot ist Marlboro" ', *WB*, 42: 68–88. R. H. Watt, 'Sex and socialism in V. B.'s *Hinze-Kunze-Roman*', *MLR*, 91: 124–37.

BRINKMANN, ROLF DIETER.   S. K. Schindler, ' "Der Film in Worten": R. D. Bs postmoderne Poetik', *Seminar*, 32: 44–61. D. Stolz, ' "Zuviele Wörter./Zuwenig Leben." oder "He, he, wo ist die Gegenwart?" Lyrik und Fotografie am Beispiel von R. D. B.', *StZ*, 33, 1995: 98–117.

DE BRUYN, GÜNTER.   A. Kreutzer, **Untersuchungen zur Poetik G. d. Bs* (BLL, 12), 1995, 240 pp. See also p. 892 above.

CANETTI, ELIAS.   H. Knoll, 'Der Massenmensch oder: die Kontinuität des Denkens. Zur anthropologischen Struktur des Werks von E.C.', *WB*, 41, 1995: 605–12. P. Rybałtowski, 'Individualität zu Tode gehetzt? Zu E. Cs Roman *Die Blendung*', *Orbis Linguarum*, 2, 1995: 285–88. L. Schieth, 'Ein Bekenntnis zum Leben in kultureller Vielfalt. E. Cs europäische Autobiographie', *DK*, 46: 169–80.

CELAN, PAUL.   C. Bohrer, 'P. C.: eine Auswahlbibliographie der Primär- und Sekundärliteratur 1993–94', *CJb*, 6, 1995: 207–15. A. Gellhaus, 'Die Polarisierung von *Poesie* und *Kunst* bei P. C.', *ib.*, 51–91. C. Ivanovic, 'Trauer — nicht Traurigkeit. C. als Leser Benjamins. Beobachtungen am Nachlaß', *ib.*, 119–59. K. Manger, ' "... machs Wort aus." Cs poetischer Imperativ', *ib.*, 7–23. S. Moses, ' "Verwaist im Gewittertrog" ', *ib.*, 93–106. P. H. Neumann, 'Fragezeichen "Flimmerbaum". Zu einem Gedicht aus "Die Niemandsrose" ', *ib.*, 227–32. C. Parry, 'Meridian und Flaschenpost. Intertextualität als Provokation des Lesers bei P. C.', *ib.*, 25–50.

G.-M. Schulz, 'Vergessene Anführungszeichen oder eine Begegnung der besonderen Art zwischen zwei Texten', *ib.*, 233–40. B. Wiedemann, 'Warum rauscht der Brunnen? Überlegungen zur Selbstreferenz in einem Gedicht von P. C.', *ib.*, 107–18. W. Wögerbauer, 'Zur strukturbildenden Funktion der Liebesbeziehung in der Dichtung P. Cs', *ib.*, 161–72. S. Brömsel, 'Scheitern eines Dialoges', *WB*, 42:252–66. W. Emmerich, 'Begegnung und Verfehlung. P. C. — Ingeborg Bachmann', *SuF*, 48:278–94. B. Fassbind, **Poetik des Dialogs. Voraussetzungen dialogischer Poesie bei P. C. und Konzepte von Intersubjektivität bei Martin Buber, Martin Heidegger und Emmanuel Levinas*, Munich, Fink, 1995, 276 pp. **Word Traces. Readings of P. C.*, ed. A. Fioretos, Baltimore, Johns Hopkins U.P. , 1994, xxv + 404 pp. A. Gellhaus, 'Das Datum des Gedichts. Textgeschichte und Geschichtlchkeit des Textes bei C.', *Text*, 2:79–96. E. Günzel, **Das wandernde Zitat. P. C. im jüdischen Kontext* (Ep, Reihe Literaturwissenschaft, 151), 386 pp. B. Heber-Schärer, **P. C.: Gespräch im Gebirg. Eine Untersuchung zum Problem von Wahrnehmung und Identität in diesem Text Cs* (SAG, 298), 1994, 126 pp. C. Ivanovic, **'Kyrillisches, Freunde, auch das . . .' Die russische Bibliothek P. Cs im Deutschen Literaturarchiv Marbach. Aufgezeichnet, beschrieben und kommentiert*, Marbach, Deutsche Schillergesellschaft, 164 pp. S. Könnecker, **'Sichtbares, Hörbares'. Die Beziehung zwischen Sprachkunst und bildender Kunst am Beispiel P. Cs*, Bielefeld, Aisthesis, 1995, 176 pp. T. Naaijkens, 'Abtrünnig erst bin ich treu. Funktionalität beim Übersetzen von Cs *Mohn und Gedächtnis* ins Niederländische', *DK*, 45, 1995:253–71. R. Zschachlitz, 'Le langage de la domination et les mythes modernes. La critique du langage chez P. C. et l'École de Francfort', *CEtGer*, 30:131–44. See also BACHMANN, INGEBORG; WEISS, PETER.

DODERER, HEIMITO VON. I. Henkel, **Lebens-Bilder. Beobachtungen zur Wahrnehmung in H. v. Ds Romanwerk* (MBSL, 28), 1995, 222 pp. K. Luehrs, '"Fassaden-Architektur." Zur Struktur der Wiener Romane H. v. Ds', *ZDP*, 114, 1995:560–79. M. Mosebahc, 'Stumme Musik der Geometrie — zur Epik H. v. Ds', *SuF*, 48:789–90. See also p. 890 above.

DRACH, ALBERT. A. Fuchs, '"... da Hitler zu Ermordungszwecken nach und nach alle Juden dringend braucht": Labyrinth und Abjektion in A.Ds *Unsentimentale Reise*', *GLL*, 49:243–55.

DÜRRENMATT, FRIEDRICH. J. Daiber, 'Fiktive autobiographie und autobiographische Fiktion. F. Ds Stoffe', *WW*, 46:446–54. T. Roelcke, **Dramatische Kommunikation. Modell und Reflexion bei D.*, *Handke, Weiss*, Berlin, de Gruyter, 1994, xii + 312 pp. See also BACHMANN, INGEBORG.

EICH, GÜNTER. M. Djordevic, 'G. E. zwischen Literatur und Rundfunk. *Die schönsten Geschichten aus 1001 Nacht* als Funkerzählungen', *JDSG*, 39, 1995:350–57. P. Maas, 'Der Schrei des Prometheus. Zugänge zum Spätwerk G. Es', *GerLux*, 7, 1995:11–26. S. Martin, **Die Auren des Wort-Bildes. G. Es Maulwurf-Poetik und die Theorie des versehenden Lesens*, St. Ingbert, Röhrig, 1995, 424 pp.

ENZENSBERGER, HANS MAGNUS. *Debating E. Great Migration and Civil War*, ed. G. Fischer, Tübingen, Stauffenburg, xvi + 226 pp., brings together three groups of articles concentrating on E.'s essays *Die große Wanderung* (1992) and *Aussichten auf den Bürgerkrieg* (1993). Following an introduction by D. Roberts, the first group sets these two recent essays in the context of E.'s 'intellectual journey' since the 1960s and of the position of the intellectual in the Federal Republic. Five essays then focus specifically on his analysis of the civil war in the former Yugoslavia, although here, too, changes in E.'s critical position and his status as a representative figure amongst German intellectuals are familiar points of reference. The final section comprises six chapters on different aspects of *Die große Wanderung* and the controversy which the essay fuelled concerning the questions of immigration and citizenship. Sixteen separate articles on two relatively short essays might, on first sight, seem excessive, but the volume succeeds in addressing a range of fascinating issues surrounding not only E.'s own career as a literary figure and social analyst, but also the political situation of the Federal Republic as a whole in late 20th-c. Europe. U. Nam, **Normalismus und Postmoderne. Diskursanalyse der Gesellschafts- und Geschichtsauffassung in den Gedichten H.M.Es* (EH, 1, 1514), 1995, 282 pp. See also ANDERSCH, ALFRED.

FASSBINDER, RAINER WERNER. **Das ganz normale Chaos. Gespräche über R.W.F.*, ed. J. Lorenz, Berlin, Henschel, 1995, 446 pp.

FICHTE, HUBERT. H. Kuroda, 'Homosexuelle Ästhetik. Anmerkungen zu H. F.', *DB*, 96:117–26.

FRISCH, MAX. K. Hayanagi, 'Kann das *Ich* durch Dichtung ausgedrückt werden? M. Fs "Dichtung der Permutation"', *DB*, 96:96–105. D. Jacobsen, 'Tod im Tessin. M. Fs Erzählung *Der Mensch erscheint im Holozän*', *WB*, 42:399–417. B. Rowińska-Januszewska, 'M. F. — ein unruhiger Europäer', *DK*, 46:161–67.

FRISCHMUTH, BARBARA. L. A. Ingalsbe, 'Ein Gespräch mit B. F.', *MAL*, 29.1:39–51.

FÜHMANN, FRANZ. D. Tate, **F.F.: Innovation and Authenticity. A Study of his Prose-Writing* (APSL, 117), 1995, 263 pp. E. Sauermann, 'Fs Trakl-Essay — zensuriert?', *MBA*, 14, 1995:111–15.

GRASS, GÜNTER. T. Angenendt, **'Wenn Wörter Schatten werfen.' Untersuchungen zum Prosastil von G. G.* (KSL, 6), 1995, 240 pp. H. Aust, 'Diskussion zu G. G., *Ein weites Feld*', *Fontane-Blätter*, 61:171–79.

A. Flügel, *'Mit Wörtern das Ende aufschieben.' Konzeptualisierung von Erfahrung in der 'Rättin' von G. G.* (BBL, 15), 1995, 276 pp. J. Goheen, 'Intertext — Stil — Kanon: zur Geschichtlichkeit des Epischen in G. Gs *Hundejahre*', *CGP*, 24:155–66. C. Ivanovic, 'Fonty trifft Johnson. Zur Fiktionalisierung Uwe Johnsons als Paradigma der Erzählstrategie in G. Gs *Ein weites Feld*', *Johnson-Jb.*, 3:173–99. N. Kim, **Allegorie oder Authentizität. Zwei ästhetische Modelle der Aufarbeitung der Vergangenheit: G. Gs 'Die Blechtrommel' und Christa Wolfs 'Kindheitsmuster'* (EH, 1, 1534), 1995, 259 pp. U. Müller, 'Das neue Buch von G. G. ist tatsächlich, zumindest bisher, *der* Roman der Wende', *LiB*, 43:2–5. **Zerreißprobe. Der neue Roman von G. G. 'Ein weites Feld' und die Literaturkritik. Eine Dokumentation*, ed. G. Oberhammer and G. Ostermann, Innsbruck, Innsbrucker Zeitungsarchiv, 1995, 335 pp. F. F. Plagwitz, 'Die Crux des Heldentums: zur Deutung des Ritterkreuzes in G. Gs *Katz und Maus*', *Seminar*, 32:1–14. R. Scherf, **Katz und Maus' von G. G. Literarische Ironie nach Auschwitz und der unausgesprochene Appell zu politischem Engagement*, Marburg, Tectum, 1995, 357 pp. R. Yorioka, 'Den Verlust erzählen. Über G.G. nach der Vereinigung Deutschlands', *DB*, 95, 1995:45–54.

HANDKE, PETER. U. Dronske, 'Dichten und dauern. P. H. als Lyriker', *ZGB*, Beiheft 3:85–95. W. Frietsch, **Die Symbolik der Epiphanien in P. Hs Texten. Strukturmomente eines neuen Zusammenhanges*, Sinzheim, Pro universitate, 1995, 167 pp. Y. Hirako, 'P. H. und Botho Strauss', *DB*, 95, 1995, 55–65. C. Marschall, **Zum Problem der Wirklichkeit im Werk P. Hs. Untersuchungen mit Blick auf Rainer Maria Rilke* (SD, 43), 1995, 211 pp. L. Scheidl, '*Wunschloses Unglück* de P. H. História paradigmática para as gerações nascidas entre as duas guerras. O contexto político e social da Austria', *Runa*, 23–24, 1995:339–58. U. C. Steiner, 'Das Glück der Schrift. Das graphisch-graphematische Gedächtnis in P. Hs Texten: Goethe, Keller, Kleist (*Langsame Heimkehr, Versuch über die Jukebox, Versuch über den geglückten Tag*)', *DVLG*, 70:256–89. See also BERNHARD, THOMAS; DÜRRENMATT, FRIEDRICH; WENDERS, WIM.

HÄRTLING, PETER. N. Hess, **'Die Fremde ist das Normale.' Fremde und Heimat in P. Hs 'Der Wanderer'* (EH, 1, 1492), 1995, 133 pp.

HEIN, CHRISTOPH. G. Bauer Pickar, 'C. H.'s *Drachenblut*. An internalized novella', Cramer, *Neues*, 251–78. M. Hatsumi, 'Normativität von Chronik. Über C. H.', *DB*, 95, 1995:22–32. C. Kiewitz, **Der stumme Schrei. Krise und Kritik der sozialistischen Intelligenz im Werk C. Hs*, Tübingen, Stauffenburg, 1995, 308 pp. P. McKnight, **Understanding C. H.*, Columbia, South Carolina U.P., 1995, xvi + 199 pp.

HERMLIN, STEPHAN. J. Ross, 'Remembering the revolt: S. H.'s "Die Zeit der Gemeinsamkeit" (1949)', *GLL*, 49:256–70.

HILBIG, WOLFGANG. C. Forderer, 'Doppelgängerfiguren und Abwesenheitssyndrom. Zur "ontologischen Schwäche" von W. Hs Protagonisten', *WB*, 42:54–67. R. Michaelis, 'Laudatio auf W. H. Bremer Literaturpreis 1994', *StZ*, 32, 1994:9–13. R. Paar and A. Disselnkötter, '"Das Wesen aber läßt man besser aus dem Spiel." Metamorphosen in W. Hs Roman *Ich*', *Diagonal*, 1995, 2:99–111. **W.H. Materialien zu Leben und Werk*, ed. U. Wittstock (FT, 12253), 1994, 247 pp. See also p. 890 above.

HUCHEL, PETER. M. Gansel, 'Quelques réflexions sur "mythe et pouvoir" à travers quelques poèmes de P. H.', *CEtGer*, 30:153–61. H. Nijssen, **Der heimliche König. Leben und Werk von P. H.*, Nijmegen U.P., 1995, 593 pp. **P. H. Leben und Werk in Texten und Bildern*, ed. P. Walther (IT, 185), 335 pp.

JANDL, ERNST. *E. J.*, ed. H. L. Arnold (TK, 129), 113 pp., opens with four poems by the author himself. The volume also contains some twelve separate articles on J.'s work. Not surprisingly, a number of these focus on his lyric poetry: J.'s poetics, his early work, a sense of place in his poetry, his work in the 1960s, the cycle of poems entitled 'tagenglas', and the poems he wrote between 1982 and 1992 are all subjects of individual analysis. Other contributions move away from the field in which J. is best known: H. Heissenbüttel looks at the radio plays of J. and F. Mayröcker; K. Wagner examines his writing for the theatre; H. Haider comments on J.'s contributions to cultural politics; and R. Innerhofer assesses the importance of the 'Grazer Autorenversammlung' founded by J. in 1973. K. Pfoser-Schewig's select bibliography concludes a volume which not only offers insight into J.'s lyric poetry but also reveals his part in changing the cultural establishment in Austria. D. Horvat, 'Zur Lyrik E. Js', *ZGB*, Beiheft 3:65–72.

JELINEK, ELFRIEDE. Y. Hoffmann, '"Sujet imposible" suivi de "Ich will seicht sein" et d'un entretien avec E. J.', *Germanica*, 18:153–75. **E. J.: Framed by Language*, ed. J. B. Johns and K. Arens, Riverside, Ariadne, 1994, 309 pp. G. Laudin, 'De la violence sociale à la violence mythique. Le lamentable parcours des héroïnes du théâtre d'E. J.', *Austriaca*, 21:175–86. G. Pailer, '"... an meinen Mörder geglaubt, wie an meinen Vater." Zur Bachmann-Rezeption bei Christa Wolf und E. J.', *WB*, 42:89–108. A. S. Ribeiro, '"Vorgänge im Insektenvolk": signos da violência em *Die Ausgesperrten*, de E. J.', *Runa*, 23–24, 1995:401–24. M. Szczepaniak, 'Böse Mütterlichkeit. Dekonstruktion des Mutter-Mythos im Prosawerk E. Js', *Convivium*, 1995:79–91.

JOHNSON, UWE. R. Berbig, '"Having learned my lesson." Margret Boveris Autobiographie *Verzweigungen* und ihre Herausgeber Elisabeth und U. J.', *DVGL*, 70:138–70. G. Bond, '"weil es ein Haus ist, das fährt." Rauminszenierungen in U. Js Werk', *Johnson-Jb.*, 3:72–96. H. Helbig, 'Last and final. Über das Ende der *Jahrestage*', *ib.*, 97–122. H.-J. Klug, 'Mutmaßungen über einen Spitznamen', *ib.*, 207–10. N. Mecklenburg, '"Trostloser Ehrgeiz der Faktentreue" oder "trostlose Prämisse der fiktion"? U. Js dokumentarischer Realismus', *ib.*, 50–71. B. Neumann, 'Wann starb eigentlich U. J.? Eine Gegendarstellung', *ib.*, 211–13. U. Neumann, '"Behandeln Sie den Anfang so unnachsichtig wie möglich." Vorläufiges zu Romananfängen bei U. J.', *ib.*, 19–49. Id., 'Kleines Wörterbuch der Gemeinplätze zu U. J.', *ib.*, 201–06. J. Siemon, 'Liebe Marie, dear Mary, dorogaja Marija. Das Kind als Hoffnungsträger in U. Js *Jahrestagen*', *ib.*, 123–45. P.-M. Stahlberg and U. Schmitz, 'Begegnung mit U. J.', *ib.*, 9–13. *U. J. zwischen Vormoderne und Postmoderne. Internationales U. J. Symposium 22.-24.9.1994*, ed. C. Gansel and N. Riedel, Berlin, de Gruyter, 1995, xiv + 345 pp. S. Hanuschek, *U. J.*, Berlin, Morgenbuch, 1994, 89 pp. H. Helbig, *Beschreibung einer Beschreibung. Untersuchungen zu U. Js Roman 'Das dritte Buch über Achim'*, Göttingen, Vandenhoeck & Ruprecht, 256 pp., deals with the narrative strategies of 'der (erzähltechnisch) problematischste Roman U. Js' (10). Separate sections of the study deal with the opening of *Das dritte Buch über Achim*, its structure, the narrative situation in the novel, and, most revealingly, with the relationship between the aesthetic theory of Georg Lukács and J.'s text. At each stage H. deals carefully with the views of earlier critics on the novel and sets out his own position clearly and convincingly. His conclusion that the novel is 'ein Versuch, den Veränderungen der Welt erzählend zu entsprechen' (247) is a convincing one. The study makes an important contribution to the analysis of J.'s literary technique through the interpretation of a novel which, in comparison with *Mutmaßungen über Jakob* and *Jahrestage*, has received relatively little attention in its own right. M. Hofmann, 'Dr. med. Vet. Arthur Semig: ein Jude in Jerichow. Zur Erinnerung an die Opfer des Nationalsozialismus in U. Js *Jahrestagen*', *ZDP*, 114, 1995, Sonderheft:65–84. A. Kaiser, *Für die Geschichte. Medien in U. Js Romanen*, St Ingbert, Röhrig, 1995, 247 pp. S.-M. Ku, *'Sie sind kein guter Verlierer'. Die Disproportionalität zwischen dem Bewußtsein des Individuums und der herrschenden Gesellschaftsideologie in U. Js 'Mutmaßungen über Jakob'*, Wuppertal, Deimling, 1995, 191 pp. B. Plachta, 'Geschichte und Gegenwart. Theodor Fontanes *Schach von Wuthenow* in U. Js *Jahrestagen*', *Euphorion*, 90:206–18. I. Rabenstein-Michel, 'Zu Begriff und Funktion des Gedächtnisrasters bei U. J.: *Jahrestage* und *Eine Reise nach Klagenfurt*', *CEtGer*, 29, 1995:49–61. B. Schulz, *Lektüren von Jahrestagen. Studien zu einer Poetik der 'Jahrestagen' von U. J.* (UDL, 77), 1995, vii + 227 pp. J. Zetzsche, *Die Erfindung photographischer Bilder im zeitgenössischen Erzählen. Zum Werk von U. J. und Jürgen Becker* (FBG, 27),

1994, 352 pp. See also BACHMANN, INGEBORG; GRASS, GÜNTER; WEISS, PETER.

KANT, HERMANN. *Die Akte Kant. IM 'Martin', die Stasi und die Literatur in Ost und West*, ed. K. Corino, Reinbek, Rowohlt, 1995, 509 pp.

KASACK, HERMANN. G. O. Stimpson, **Zwischen Mystik und Naturwissenschaften. H. Ks 'Die Stadt hinter dem Strom' im Lichte des neuen Paradigmas* (EH, I, 1503), 1995, 353 pp.

KEUN, IRMGARD. R. Tamaru, 'Die Möglichkeiten, ein *Mädchen* zu sein. Weibliche Angestellte als *Mädchen* bei I. K.', *DB*, 95, 1995: 108–15. See also BAUM, VICKI.

KIRCHHOFF, BODO. U. Struve, 'Gespräch mit B. K.', *DeutB*, 26: 1–16.

KLUGE, ALEXANDER. C. Brauers, 'An sich ein Lernprozeβ ohne tödlichen Ausgang. A. Ks Ästhetik der Lücke', *ZDP*, 115, Sonderheft: 169–78.

KLÜGER, RUTH. I. Heidelberger-Leonard, 'Auschwitz, Weiss und Walser. Anmerkungen zu den "Zeitschaften" in R. Ks *weiter leben'*, *Peter Weiss Jb.*, 4, 1995: 78–89. H. Müller, '"Sag, daβ du fünfzehn bist" — *Weiter leben*. R. K.', *Runa*, 23–24, 1995: 385–400.

KOEPPEN, WOLFGANG. J. R. Bedenk, '"Ich bin sehr beschäftigt." Nachruf auf W. K. (23.6.1906 bis 15.3.1996)', *LiB*, 44: 56–57. J. Hessing, '"Da wurde es meine Geschichte" — zu einem spät entdeckten Text von W. K.', *ZDP*, 114, 1995, Sonderheft: 23–35. **Nach der Heimat gefragt . . .' Texte von und über W. K. Begleitheft zur W.-K.-Ausstellung: 'Mein Ziel war die Ziellosigkeit'*, ed. G. Müller-Waldeck, Berlin, Schelzky & Jeep, 1995, 95 pp. H. Schauer, 'W. K. — ein verspäteter Modernist. Die Darstellung des Wertzerfalls nach 1945 im Roman *Tauben im Gras'*, *Studien zur Germanistik*, 3, 1995: 83–91.

KOLBE, UWE. Y. Usami, 'Die Lyrik des Prenzlauer Bergs — am Beispiel von U. K. und Bert Papenfuβ-Gorek', *DB*, 95, 1995: 33–44.

KÖPF, GERHARD. M. M. G. Delille, 'Portugal als Europametapher bei G. K.', *DK*, 46: 225–32.

KRACAUER, SIEGFRIED. G. Koch, **K. zur Einführung*, Hamburg, Junius, 179 pp.

KRONAUER, BRIGITTE. D. Thormählen, 'Schattenspiele. Das Wirkliche als das Andere bei B. K.', *StZ*, 32, 1994: 379–90.

KUNERT, GÜNTER. K. Dunne, **Der Sündenfall. A Parabolic Key to the Image of Human Existence in the Work of G. K. 1960–90* (EH, I, 1494), 1995, 345 pp. E. Kasper, **Zwischen Utopie und Apokalypse. Das lyrische Werk G. Ks von 1950 bis 1987* (UDL, 80), 1995, v + 193 pp. See also p. 892 above.

KUNZE, REINER. *Sprachvertrauen und Erinnerung. Reden zur Ehrenpromotion von R. K. am 15. Dezember 1993 an der Technischen Universität Dresden*, ed. W. Schmitz, Hauzenberg, Pongratz, 1994, 60 pp.

LENZ, SIEGFRIED. D. Merchiers, 'L'évocation du passé dans *Deutschstunde* et *Heimatmuseum* de S. L.', *CEtGer*, 29, 1995:179–90. Id., 'Réalité politique et dimension mythique: *Heimatmuseum* de S. L.', *CEtGer*, 30:171–81. F. Müller, *S. L. 'Deutschstunde'* (OIU, 80), 128 pp., follows the familiar pattern of the series in introducing a text for use in teaching. M. provides a survey of secondary literature, a biography of L., and information on art and education under National Socialism as a background to his interpretation of the text. This interpretation begins with an analysis of the structure of *Deutschstunde*, followed by some general observations on the genre of the *Rahmenerzählung*. M. then takes the protagonists in turn, offering comments on characterization and motivation. The study concludes with some observations on narrative technique and the use of irony. The *Materialien* contained in the collection of teaching aids are illuminating in particular as far as the Nazi conception of *entartete Kunst* is concerned. This study provides a clear introduction to a text which in itself is not especially complex and it is ideally suited for presenting L.'s work to the uninitiated. E. Schmitt, 'Les Russes dans la Prusse orientale de S. L. et de Arno Surminski: une nouvelle étape dans la "liquidation" du passé', *ChrA*, 5:239–52. See also p. 889 above.

LOEST, ERICH. F. Dieckmann, 'Der Realist als Frontkämpfer. Über E. L.', *SuF*, 48:316–21.

MARON, MONIKA. J. Bekasiński, 'Das Böse und das Häßliche in M. Ms Roman *Die Überläuferin* und K. Strucks Erzählung *Trennung*', *Filologia germańska*, 20, 1995:63–70. See also p. 890 above.

MAYRÖCKER, FRIEDERIKE. D. Riess-Beger, **Lebensstudien. Poetische Verfahrensweisen in F. Ms Prosa* (Ep, Reihe Literaturwissenschaft, 147), 1995, 269 pp. See also JANDL, ERNST.

MENASSE, ROBERT. W. Neuber, 'Gespräch mit R. M.', *DeutB*, 25, 1995:241–54. R. S. Posthofen, '"Es sind poetische Wälder — Gefallen findet, wer sir gefällt": R. Ms Roman *Schubumkehr*', *MAL*, 29.3–4:131–56.

MITTERER, FELIX. G. Sanford, 'Zum Heimatbegriff in einigen Stücken F. Ms', *MAL*, 29.3–4:117–30. A. Strasser, 'Subjekt oder Objekt? Der Idiot in der Dorfgemeinschaft am Beispiel von F. Ms *Kein Platz für Idioten*', *Germanica*, 18:137–51.

MONÍKOVÁ, LIBUŠE. B. Haines, '"New places from which to write histories of peoples": power and the personal in the novels of L. M.', *GLL*, 49:501–12.

MORGNER, IRMTRAUD. S. Hanel, **Literarischer Widerstand zwischen Phantastischem und Alltäglichem. Das Romanwerk I. Ms*, Pfaffenweiler,

Centaurus, 1995, 76 pp. A. Lewis, *Subverting Patriarchy. Feminism and Fantasy in the Works of I. M.*, Oxford, Berg, 1995, vi + 315 pp. A. Riemann, 'Meinem einzigen Verlangen. Die phantastische Rebellion der I. M.', *FemSt*, 12.1, 1994:56–69.

MÜLLER, HEINER. M. Braun, *Drama um eine Komödie. Das Ensemble von SED und Staatssicherheit, FDJ und Ministerium für Kultur gegen H. Ms 'Umsiedlerin oder das Leben auf dem Lande' im Oktober 1961*, Berlin, Links, 1995, 165 pp. *H. M. — Rückblicke, Perspektiven. Vorträge des Pariser Kolloquiums 1993*, ed. T. Buck and J.-M. Valentin (LU, 25), 1995, 180 pp. *H. M. 'Contexts' and 'History'. A Collection of Essays from the Sydney German Studies Symposium 1994 'H. M./Theatre — History — Performance'*, ed. G. Fischer, Tübingen, Stauffenburg, 1995, viii + 273 pp. C. Klein, 'Matériau M(édée/üller)', *Germanica*, 18:115–35. M. Mieth, *Die Masken des Erinnerns. Zur Ästhetisierung von Geschichte und Vorgeschichte der DDR bei H. M.* (EH, 1, 1476), 1994, 283 pp. G. Pickerodt, 'Zwischen Erinnern und Verdrängen. H. Ms Autobiographie *Krieg ohne Schlacht. Leben in zwei Diktaturen*', *CEtGer*, 29, 1995:63–71. J. Schlich, *A propos Weltuntergang. Zu H. M. u. ä.*, Heidelberg, Manutius, 144 pp. E. Schumacher, 'Theater nach Brecht. Gespräch mit H. M. 1984', *SuF*, 48:827–38. E. Wizisla, 'Über Brecht. Gespräch mit H. M.', *ib.*, 223–37. R. Tschapke, *H. M.*, Berlin, Morgenbuch, 97 pp.

MÜLLER, HERTA. K. Bauer, 'Zur Objektwerdung der Frau in H. Ms *Der Mensch ist ein großer Fasan auf der Welt*', *Seminar*, 32:143–54. W. Hinck, 'Das mitgebrachte Land. Rede zur Verleihung des Kleist-Preises 1994 an H.M.', *KlJb*, 1995:6–13. H. Koopmann, 'Rede zur Verleihung des Kleist-Preises 1994', *ib.*, 3–5. T. R. Kuhnle, 'La résistance des monades: *Herztier* de H. M.', *Germanica*, 17, 1995:25–38.

MUSCHG, ADOLF. A. Classen, 'Seinskonstruktion im Leseakt: A. Ms *Der rote Ritter* als Antwort auf eine mittelalterliche These', *EG*, 51:307–27.

ÖZDAMAR, EMINE SEVGI. A. Seyhan, 'Lost in translation: remembering the mother tongue in E. S. O.'s *Das Leben ist eine Karawanserei*', *GQ*, 69:414–26.

REICHART, ELISABETH. L. Demeritt and P. Ensberg, '"Für mich ist die Sprache eigentlich ein Schatz": interview mit E. R.', *MAL*, 29.1:1–22. J. Wigmore, 'E. R.'s "La Valse" and the text of abuse', *GLL*, 49:488–500.

RICHTER, HANS WERNER. A. Nickel, *H. W. R. — Ziehvater der Gruppe 47. Eine Analyse im Spiegel ausgewählter Zeitungs- und Zeitschriftenartikel* (SAG, 290), 1994, 413 pp.

ROSEI, PETER. *P. R.*, ed. G. Fuchs and G. A. Höfler, Graz, Droschl, 1994, 433 pp. K. Thorpe, 'Poe in Venice or the narration of a literary hallucination: *Wer war Edgar Allan?* by P. R.', *CGP*, 24:185–96.

ROTH, GERHARD. S. Ryan, **G. R.: eine Bibliographie. Werke und Rezeption 1966–94*, Dunedin, Otago U. P., 1995, xi + 132 pp. W. Tietze, **Das mikroskopische Gedankenglas. Mythen und Techniken der Autorschaft — in Kommentar zum Werk G. Rs*, Munich, Fink, 1995, 352 pp.

SCHLÖNDORFF, VOLKER. D. Berghahn, 'Fiction into film and the fidelity of discourse: a case study of V. S.'s re-interpretation of *Homo faber*', *GLL*, 49:72–87.

SCHMIDT, ARNO. P. Ahrendt, **Der Büchermensch. Wesen, Werk und Wirkung A. Ss. Eine umfassende Einführung*, Paderborn, Igel, 1995, 417 pp. S. Fischer, 'Datierung literarischer Texte als Inszenierung der Schriftstellerbiographie A. Ss "Pharos"', *Text*, 2:97–104. L. Gümbel, **Ich. Synthetischer Realismus und ödipale Struktur im Frühwerk A. Ss. Eine typologische Untersuchung* (Ep, Reihe Literaturwissenschaft, 139), iii + 356 pp. J. Klein, **A. S. als politischer Schriftsteller*, Tübingen, Francke, 1995, 212 pp. M. Sagorny, **Harte Attacken & warme Gefühle. Wie A. S. Karl May verarztet*, Paderborn, Igel, 1994, 116 pp.

SEGHERS, ANNA. H. A. Doane, 'Die Unzulänglichkeit der neuen Zeit. Zu A. Ss Novelle *Der gerechte Richter*', Cramer, *Neues*, 165–84. W. Wende, 'Fragmentarische Systemkritik einer überzeugten Sozialistin. A. S., *Der gerechte Richter*', *LiLi*, 26:148–59.

STRAUSS, BOTHO. K. Bauer, 'Gegenwartskritik und nostalgische Rückgriffe: die Abdankung der Frau als Objekt männlichen Begehrens und die Erotisierung der Kindfrau in B. S' *Paare Passanten*', *GQ*, 69:181–95. J. Daiber, **Poetisierte Naturwissenschaft. Zur Rezeption naturwissenschaftlicher Theorien im Werk von B. S.* (TSL, 26), 202 pp. S. Lämmermann, **'Für unser Werk, mein Liebster!' Die Thematisierung von Produktion im Erzählwerk von B. S.* (EH, 1, 1558), 450 pp. H. Uchimura, 'Die Phantasie des Verlustes. Zu B. S' Essay "Anschwellender Bocksgesang"', *DB*, 96:106–16. See also HANDKE, PETER.

STRITTMATTER, ERWIN. R. G. Gataullin, 'Zur stilistischen Funktion der Anthroponyme im Roman *Der Wundertäter* von E. S.', *SGP*, 21, 1995:49–54. G. Hansen, **Christliches Erbe in der DDR-Literatur. Bibelrezeption und Verwendung religiöser Sprache im Werk E. Ws und in ausgewählten Texten Christa Wolfs* (BLL, 14), 1995, 281 pp.

SÜSKIND, PATRICK. J. Rozen, 'Fréquence et importance de *und* dans *Das Parfum* de P. S.', *NCA*, 14:79–86.

SYBERBERG, HANS JÜRGEN. S. Brockmann, 'S.'s Germany', *GQ*, 69:48–62.

TIMM, UWE. K. Bullivant, 'Reisen, Entdeckungen, Utopien: Zum Werk U. Ts', *DeutB*, 25, 1995:255–62.

TROTTA, MARGARETHE VON. R. W. McCormick, 'Cinematic form, history, and gender in M. v. T.'s *Rosa Luxemburg*', *Seminar*, 32:30–43. J. Mouton, 'M. v. T.'s sisters: "Brides under a different law"', *WGT*, 11, 1995:35–47. J. K. Ward, 'Enacting the different voice: *Christa Klages* and feminist history', *ib.*, 49–65.

TURRINI, PETER. M. Bobinac, 'Schrecken der Kindheit und ewige Beziehungskisten. Zur Lyrik P. Ts', *ZGB*, Beiheft 3:153–63. G. K. Schneider, '"Und dennoch sagt der viel, der *Heimat* sagt": Ts Ansichten über Österreich und die österreichische Seele', *MAL*, 29.3–4:169–86.

WALSER, MARTIN. **Leseerfahrungen mit M. W. Neue Beiträge zu seinen Texten*, ed. H. Doane and G. Bauer Pickar, Munich, Fink, 1995, x + 269 pp. **New Critical Perspectives on M. W.*, ed. F. Pilipp, Columbia, Camden House, 1994, xii + 196 pp. S. Taberner, 'M. W.'s *Die Gallistl'sche Krankheit*: self-reflectivity as illness', *GLL*, 49:358–72. See also p. 890 above; KLÜGER, RUTH.

WEISS, PETER. A. Bernhard, **Kultur, Ästhetik und Subjektentwicklung. Edukative Grundlagen und Bildungsprozesse in P. W.' 'Ästhetik des Widerstands'*, Frankfurt, Dipa, 1994, 340 pp. *Peter Weiss Jb.*, 3, 1994, includes: I. Breuer, 'Die *Marat/Sade*-Oper von P. W. Eine Nachbemerkung zu den Fassungen des Stücks' (7–41); M. Hofmann, 'Antifaschismus und poetische Erinnerung der Shoah. Überlegungen zu P. W.' *Ästhetik des Widerstands*' (122–34); C. Kammler, 'Selbstanalyse — politisches Journal — Lebensphilosophie. Der widersprüchliche Verlauf von P. W.' *Rekonvaleszenz*' (105–21); R. Koch and M. Rector, 'Arbeitshypothese Optimismus. Gespräch mit Manfred Haiduk über P. W.' (42–75); M. Neumann, 'Mißlungener Restaurationsversuch. Ein Plädoyer für die Erstfassung des *Hölderlin* von P. W.' (76–104); H. Wender, 'Entwicklungsstufen und Fassungen in der Textgeschichte des *Marat/Sade*. Anmerkungen zum Beitrag von Beise und Breuer PWJ 1 (1992)' (153–65). *Peter Weiss Jb.*, 4, 1995, includes: B. Feusthuber, 'Gespaltener Kopf. Durchbohrtes Herz. Anmerkungen zu P. W.' *Die Ästhetik des Widerstands* und Anne Dudens *Das Judasschaf*' (90–101); M. Hofmann, 'Das Gedächtnis des NS-Faschismus in P. W.' *Ästhetik des Widerstands* und Uwe Johnsons *Jahrestagen*' (54–77); H. Mayer, 'Kann sich die Bühne eine Auschwitz-Dokumentation leisten? P. W. im Gespräch (Oktober 1965). Kommentar von Christoph Weiss' (8–30); M. Neumann, 'Stellungnahme zum "Offenen Brief" von Manfred Haiduk und Gunilla Palmstierna-Weiss' (150–52); G. Palmstierna-Weiss and M. Haiduk, 'Offener Brief an die Redaktion des *Peter-Weiss-Jahrbuchs*' (140–50); J. Vogt, 'Treffpunkt im Unendlichen? Über P. W. und Paul Celan' (102–21); C. Weiss, 'Happy-End mit guten Deutschen. Anmerkungen zur Rezeption von Steven Spielbergs *Schindlers Liste* und P. W.' *Ermittlung*'

(34–53). K. H. Götze, *Poetik des Abgrunds und Kunst des Widerstands. Grundmuster der Bildwelt von P. W.*, Opladen, Westdeutscher Vlg, 1995, 235 pp. Id., 'Recherche d'identité et théâtre politique. Le choix du genre chez P. W. dans les années soixante et soixante-dix', *Germanica*, 18:97–114. Id., 'Soudaineté et construction. Modes du souvenir chez P. W. et Walter Benjamin', *CEtGer*, 29, 1995:109–19. *Die Bilderwelt des P. W.*, ed. A. Honold and U. Schreiber, Hamburg, Argument, 1995, 239 pp. J. Kuhn, *'Wir setzten unser Exil fort.' Facetten des Exils im literarischen Werk von P. W.*, St. Ingbert, Röhrig, 1995, 333 pp. S. Packalén, 'P. W. und das dialogische Prinzip', *SN*, 67, 1995:209–27. M. Rector, 'Der zensierte Sympathisant. Zur selektiven Rezeption von P. W. in der DDR', *SGP*, 22, 1995:139–63. F. Trommler, 'Das gelebte und das nicht gelebte Exil des P. W. Zur Botschaft seiner frühen Bilder', *Exilforschung*, 13, 1995:82–95. See also ANDERSCH, ALFRED; DÜRRENMATT, FRIEDRICH; KLÜGER, RUTH.

WELLERSHOFF, DIETER. B. Happekotte, *D. W. — rezipiert und isoliert: Studien zur Wirkungsgeschichte* (EH, I, 1496), 1995, 329 pp. G. K. Schneider, 'D. W.'s novella *Die Sirene*. Calling hours from anywhere, at anytime, for anyone', Cramer, *Neues*, 235–50.

WENDERS, WIM. L. P. Koepnick, 'Negotiating popular culture: W., Handke and the topographies of cultural studies', *GQ*, 69: 381–400. A. Oksiloff, 'Eden is burning: W. W.'s techniques of synaesthesia', *ib.*, 32–47.

WOHMANN, GABRIELE. R. Atkins, 'Chernobyl and beyond: Green issues in the recent works of G. W.', *CGP*, 24:197–214.

WOLF, CHRISTA. J. Bekasiński, 'DDR Schriftsteller zwischen der kommunistischen Ideologie und dem realen Sozialismus. (Am Beispiel C. Ws)', *Filologia germańska*, 20, 1995:13–25. H. M. Brown, 'Authentizität und Fiktion: C. Ws Kleistbild', *KlJb*, 1995:167–82. H. Lehnert, 'Novellentradition und neueste deutsche Geschichte. C. Ws *Was bleibt* als "Gegennovelle" zu ihrer *Moskauer Novelle*', Cramer, *Neues*, 185–206. C. Paver, '"What we must invent for the sake of the truth": expiating the past through narrative invention in C. W.'s *Nachdenken über Christa T.*', Hunter, *Short Story*, 103–29. See also GRASS, GÜNTER; JELINEK, ELFRIEDE; STRITTMATTER, ERWIN.

WÜHR, PAUL. M. Titzmann, 'Gespräch mit P. W.', *DeutB*, 26:81–99.

. II. DUTCH STUDIES

LANGUAGE

By ROEL VISMANS, *Department of Dutch Studies, University of Hull*

I. GENERAL

A regrouping of Dutch Studies journals has taken place in the Netherlands, reflecting the changes in emphasis that have occurred in the field over the past decade. The three journals *Nieuwe Taalgids*, *Spektator*, and *Forum der Letteren*, which used to have a general coverage, have disappeared. Instead two new journals have emerged: *Nederlandse Letterkunde* and *Nederlandse Taalkunde*, reflecting the importance and relative independence of language and literary studies. Both are published by Martinus Nijhoff, Groningen, who also publish an existing third journal, *Taalbeheersing* (in its 18th year) which focuses on language acquisition and language learning issues.

Jaarboek van de KANTL, 1994, 195 pp., and 1995, 143 pp.; *VMKA*, 1994, no. 1, 152 pp., and nos. 2–3, 126 pp.; *VMKA*, 1995, no. 1, 142 pp., and nos. 2–3, 142 pp.; and *VMKA*, 1996, no. 1, 136 pp., survey KANTL's activities and contain many contributions by its members. Most noteworthy is *VMKA*, 1995, nos. 2–3, which is entirely dedicated to Jan-Frans Willems, the 19th-c. Flemish literary and cultural leader. *Nederlands in culturele context*, ed. Th. A. J. M. Janssen, P. G. M. de Kleijn, and A. M. Musschoot, Woubrugge, IVN–Münster, Nodus, 1995, 402 pp., contains the proceedings of the twelfth Colloquium Neerlandicum of Dutch academics abroad, with five sections: on history in literature, the reception of Dutch literature abroad, early printing in Antwerp, politeness in Dutch, and Dutch drama. *Studies in Netherlandic Culture and Literature*, ed. M. A. Bakker and B. H. Morrison, Lanham, UPA, 1994, 253 pp., and *Contemporary Explorations in the Culture of the Low Countries*, ed. W. Z. Shetter and I. Van der Cruysse, 320 pp., contain the proceedings of the Sixth and Seventh Interdisciplinary Conference on Netherlandic Studies, held in 1992 and 1994 at Calvin College and Indiana University respectively. Like the conferences of the International Association for Dutch Studies, those of the American sister association present the increasingly wider spectrum of Dutch Studies as it is practised worldwide, with contributions on not only linguistics and literature, but also history, art history, and other disciplines from the humanities and social sciences. This is also reflected in H. van der Horst, *The Low Sky. Understanding the Dutch*, The Hague, Nuffic, 299 pp., which presents a popular contemporary critique of the Netherlands, but always with an historical angle in mind. A more traditional definition of Dutch Studies is implicit in the 75th anniversary collection of Dutch at the Free University, Amsterdam, *Het is kermis hier*, ed. T. van Dijk and R. Zemel, Amsterdam, Stichting Neerlandistiek VU–Münster, Nodus, 1994, 166 pp., and in *Voortgang. Jaarboek voor de Neerlandistiek*, 15, 1995, *ib.*, 275 pp. The former contains 15 contributions by the University's Dutch Studies staff, including the inaugural lecture of J. D. F. van Halsema. The latter consists of nine literary and three linguistic contributions, mainly with an historical slant and emphasis on the 17th c. L. Beheydt, *Kenterende culturele identiteit*, The Hague, Algemeen Nederlands Verbond (ANV), 32 pp., is B.'s inaugural lecture as extraordinary professor in the culture of the Low Countries. Sponsored by the ANV which promotes the Dutch language and culture, B. reviews the need for a broad language and culture policy in the light of the discussion about cultural identity and the (future of) the Dutch language. *Nederlands-Buitenlands*, Amsterdam, LVVN, 1994, 110 pp., contains the texts of papers given during the annual conference of the Landelijke Vereniging voor Neerlandici (National Society for Dutch Studies) on translation into and out of Dutch, with contributions from, amongst others, K. M. van Leuven-Zwart, F. Ligtvoet, E. van Altena, and P. C. Paardekooper.

Linguistics in the Netherlands 1995, ed. M. den Dikken and K. Hengeveld, Amsterdam, Benjamins, x + 238 pp., contains a large number of articles about Dutch or with interesting Dutch data, covering scrambling (S. Barbiers), the *wat voor* construction (H. Bennis), time auxiliaries (H. Broekhuis and K. van Dijk), the passive (L. Cornelis and A. Verhagen), discourse (J. van Dam van Isselt), Dutch-Indonesian language mixture (H. Giesbers), the effect of grammatical exercises on learners of Dutch as a second language (J. Lalleman and K. Prosa), control relations (M. Petter), 'zero semantics' (G. Postma), the adverb *moeilijk* (T. van der Wouden), verb clusters in Stellingwerfs dialect (C. Zwart), and directional prepositions (J. Zwarts). Likewise, *Linguistics in the Netherlands 1996*, ed. C. Cremers and M. den Dikken, Amsterdam, Benjamins, ix + 268 pp., has work on inalienable possession (S. Baauw and H. Broekhuis, L. Cornips and M. de Wind), the so-called 'reflexive adjunct middle' construction (L. Cornips), negative polarity items (M. Honcoop), intonation and particles (R. S. Kirsner and V. J. van Heuven), metrical complexity (J. G. Kooij), lexical stress and word recognition (K. van Leyden and V. J. van Heuven), orthography (A. Nunn and A. Neijt), quantification and the exclamative (G. Postma), free indirect discourse in newspaper reports (G. Redeker), cohesion and information flow (J. Renkema), and object drop in imperatives (J. Visser). *The Berkeley Conference on Dutch Linguistics 1993*, ed. T. F. Shannon and J. P. Snapper, Lanham, UPA,

1995, xix + 266 pp., contains articles by N. Van Deusen-Scholl (language policy), G. Extra (ethnic minority languages), L. Beheydt (the development of Dutch linguistics), A. Foolen (modal particles), Th. Janssen (the semantics of *maar*), T. F. Shannon (extraposition), H. Broekman (verb clusters), M. Haverkort and W. de Geest (clitics), W. Abraham (typology), and A. Buccini (New Netherlands Dutch). *Jaarboek van de Stichting Instituut voor Nederlandse Lexicologie. Overzicht van het jaar 1994*, Leiden, Stichting Instituut voor Nederlandse Lexicologie, 1995, 98 pp., and *Jaarboek van de Stichting Instituut voor Nederlandse Lexicologie. Overzicht van het jaar 1995*, *ib.*, 91 pp., are the annual reports of the Dutch Institute for Lexicology for 1994 and 1995. Apart from factual reports, the former contains obituaries of J. van Oostrom and A. C. Crena de Iongh, and an article on family names (by T. H. Schoonheim and W. J. J. Pijnenburg), the latter two articles on the new Dutch spelling (M. C. van den Toorn) and the morphology of feminine names and job titles (A. J. van Santen). S. De Vriendt, *Van geen kleintje vervaard. Essays over Nederlandse taalwetenschap*, Brussels, Vubress, 1995, 228 pp., is a collection of 14 of De Vriendt's essays published on the occasion of his retirement from the Free University, Brussels, spanning the period 1970–94. I. van Eijk, *Het Totale Taalboek*, Amsterdam, Balans, 1995, 254 pp., is a reference book aimed at the popular market, but well written and accessible.

2. LINGUISTICS

G. Booij, *The Phonology of Dutch*, Oxford, Clarendon, 1995, xi + 205 pp., claims to be the first comprehensive study of the Dutch sound system. It discusses not only the individual sounds of Dutch, but also prosody of words and connected speech, and spelling. The theoretical framework is that of non-linear generative phonology. E. Blaauw, *On the Perceptual Classification of Spontaneous and Read Speech*, diss., Utrecht, Utrecht, LEd, 1995, ix + 224 pp., studies the prosodic differences between spontaneous and read speech (in Dutch) by means of a number of experiments. Speech with average prosodic features is often classified as read, whereas deviant prosody is often interpreted as being spontaneous. The differences are dependent on situation, especially in spontaneous but also in read speech (e.g. fairy-tales as opposed to the news). A. van Wieringen, *Perceiving Dynamic Speechlike Sounds. Psycho-Acoustics and Speech Perception*, diss., Amsterdam, 1995, 256 pp., studies the dynamic transitions between plosives and vowels, and their perception by the human auditory and perceptive system. H. van den Heuvel, *Speaker Variability in Acoustic Properties of Dutch Phoneme Realisations*, diss., Nijmegen, vii + 176 pp., studies the variations that can occur in the realization of phonemes both by different speakers and by one speaker. The study concentrates on length and spectral composition of phonemes, concentrating on /a/, /i/, /u/. One of the conclusions is that variability is a function of the frequency of a sound in the relevant sound system.

K. Cook, *Dubbel Dutch. A Practical Guide for Foreign Students of Dutch*, Groningen, BoekWerk, 1995, 256 pp., is a glorified vocabulary book, arranged alphabetically, with indexes in Dutch and English and an elementary bibliography. It has all the expected hiatuses (e.g. hardly anything on modal particles or tense), but does try to provide explanations. W. I. M. van Calcar, *Een toegepaste grammatica. Grondslag voor het vak Nederlands*, Apeldoorn, Garant, 1994, 165 pp., wants to fill a gap by making traditional grammar approachable for modern linguists (who 'have lost faith in it') and applied linguists/language teachers (who 'think that they can do without'). It is divided into two parts. Part 1 lays the theoretical foundation, whilst part 2 illustrates how applied grammar works in education.

P. Ackema, *Syntax below Zero*, diss., Utrecht, Utrecht, LEd, 1995, ix + 354 pp., starts from the premiss that morphological processes take place in a separate domain from syntactic ones (the domain 'below zero'), but that both kinds of processes are subject to the same rules and principles. This is tested against the empty category principle, noun incorporation, and passive and perfect constructions in Germanic languages with examples from Dutch and English. G. Booij and A. van Santen, *Morfologie. De woordstructuur van het Nederlands*, Amsterdam, AUP, 1995, ix + 211 pp., is a non-theory-specific introduction to morphology in general and the morphology of Dutch in particular. It also discusses the interaction of morphology with other linguistic levels (phonology and syntax) and with psycholinguistics. E.-P. Kester, *The Nature of Adjectival Inflection*, diss., Utrecht, Utrecht, LEd, xviii + 327 pp., is a comparative study of adjectival inflection in Germanic and Romance languages. Based on Chomsky's Minimalist Programme, it also contains a detailed analysis of the partitive genitive construction in Dutch (e.g. *iets moois*, 'something beautiful').

P. Hendriks, *Comparatives and Categorial Grammar*, diss., Groningen, 1995, 265 pp., is a study of comparatives in Dutch and English within a computational-linguistic theoretical framework. It argues that in most cases, including subdeletion (e.g. 'she bought more books than he bought cds'), the comparative conjunction is a coordinator rather than a subordinator, except in comparative deletion (e.g. 'she bought more books than he sold'). J. Nuyts and W. Vonk, *Discourse Factors in the Use of Epistemic Expressions in Dutch: an Experimental Investigation* (Antwerp Papers in Linguistics, 88), Univ. Antwerpen, 66 pp., looks at the way in which information structure affects the expression of epistemic modality. In particular it looks at the extent to which and the way in which epistemic elements are focalized. The study shows that such focalization rarely occurs, but if it does, the use of a predicative modal adjective is preferred (e.g. *het is waarschijnlijk dat . . .*, 'it is probable that . . .').

S. Kouwenberg, *A Grammar of Berbice Dutch Creole*, Berlin, Mouton de Gruyter, 1994, xviii + 693 pp., is a detailed study of 'the only uncontroversial Dutch-lexicon creole still spoken today' along the Berbice river in (British) Guyana. Part I covers syntax extensively, and has chapters on morphology and phonology. Part II discusses specific constructions such as relatives clauses, focus and predicate cleft constructions, and passive. Part III contains a number of texts and a discussion of the vocabulary of the language, whilst Part IV is the vocabulary list itself.

3. HISTORY OF THE LANGUAGE

The Department of Dutch at the Free University, Amsterdam, specializes in, amongst other things, the history of Dutch linguistics and has published a number of books on the issue. *Linguistics in the Low Countries in the Eighteenth Century*, ed. R. de Bonth and J. Noordegraaf, Amsterdam, Stichting Neerlandistiek VU–Münster, Nodus, 193 pp., and J. Noordegraaf, *The Dutch Pendulum. Linguistics in the Netherlands 1740–1900*, ib., xvi + 189 pp., survey two centuries of linguistic description. The former is a collection of conference papers with contributions on the so-called Schola Hemsterhusiana (A. Feitsma and J. Noordegraaf), Balthazar Huydecoper (R. de Bonth and G. H. Jongeneelen), gender (G. R. W. Dibbets), the republication of C. Kiliaan's *Etymologicum* (T. Extra), the Belgian *Journal Encyclopédique* (J. De Clerq), and the influence of British rhetoric (E. Sjoer). The latter is a collection of previously published papers by N. covering a wide spectrum of linguists from the 18th and 19th cs. In a similar vein, N. has collected a number of his previously published essays about Dutch linguists' views on the origins of language, artificial languages and linguistic idealism in *Oorsprong en ideaal. Opstellen over taalzoekers*, ib., 1995, 144 pp.

J. Huizinga, *Inleiding en Opzet voor Studie over Licht en Geluid*, ib., 96 pp., is a critical edition, introduced by J. Noordegraaf and E. Tros, of H.'s unpublished doctoral dissertation on a comparative study of words which express impressions of light and sound, which H. wrote in 1896. These days H. is not known as a linguist, of course, but as an extremely important historian. This edition is intended to add to our view of this complex figure. *Voor rede vatbaar. Tien voorredes uit het grammaticale werk van Van Hoogstraten, Nyloë, Moonen, Sewel, Ten Kate, Huydecoper (1700–1730)*, ed. R. J. G. de Bonth and G. R. W. Dibbets, *ib.*, 1995, xiv + 192 pp., is a critical edition of ten prefaces of linguistic works from the early 18th c. G. R. W. Dibbets, *De woordsoorten in de Nederlandse triviumgrammatica, ib.*, 1995, iv + 349 pp., is a detailed study of the treatment of parts of speech in the Dutch trivium tradition between *c.* 1530 and *c.* 1660. A. Verwer published his sketch of the Dutch language in 1707 in Latin. It was republished in 1783 and J. Knol translated it into modern Dutch before his death in 1991. The result of this is a facsimile edition and translation: A. Verwer, *Schets van de Nederlandse taal. Grammatica, poëtica, retorica. Naar de editie van E. van Driel vertaald door J. Knol*, ed. Th. A. J. M. Janssen and J. Noordegraaf, *ib.*, 361 pp.

G. van Berkel and K. Samplonium, *Nederlandse plaatsnamen. De herkomst en betekenis van onze plaatsnamen*, Utrecht, Het Spectrum, 1995, xiv + 279 pp., provides the etymology of and further comments on *c.* 6,000 place names. It only covers the Netherlands, not Flanders. W. van Osta, *Toponymie van Brasschaat*, 2 vols, Ghent, KANTL, 1995, xiv + 1157 pp. + 10 maps, is an extremely detailed toponymical study of the town of Brasschaat, north of Antwerp. It contains a thorough methodological justification, a geographical and historical sketch of the town, a description of the local dialect, and a history of the town's name itself. L. van Durme, *Galloromaniae Neerlandicae Submersae Fragmenta, ib.*, 650 pp. + 36 maps, is a detailed toponymical study of Gallo-Roman elements in place names along the Dutch-French linguistic boundary in Belgium, concentrating on the region of western Brabant and eastern East Flanders.

P. Schrijver, 'De etymologie van de naam van de Cannenefaten', *ABÄG*, 41, 1995: 13–22, sketches the etymology of the name of a tribe living between the mouths of the rivers Rhine and Meuse in Roman times. The conclusion is that it is a combination of a Celtic word for 'leek' and a Germanic word for 'masters'. This is explained by the magical, and by implication heroic, qualities ascribed to plants of the genus allium. A. Quak, 'Über die Dehnung in offener Silbe im älteren Niederländischen', *ABÄG*, 42, 1995: 149–57, discusses the lengthening in open syllables in early Middle Dutch. T. Birkmann, 'Zur Worttrennung am Zeilenende in den altfriesischen Handschriften des Brokmerbriefes', *ib.*, 3–12, discusses the breaking-off of words at the ends of lines in an Old Frisian manuscript and what it tells us about the sound and syllable structure of Old Frisian. T. Riad, 'The quantity shift in Germanic: a typology', *ib.*, 159–84, provides a typology of the Germanic languages in terms of the different outcomes of the 'quantity shift', which changed their prosodic structures.

Two contributions to *Procs* (Odense) concern Afrikaans: P. van Reenen and A. Coetzee, 'Afrikaans, a daughter of Dutch' (71–101), discusses the importance of early variants of Afrikaans, Cape Dutch, and Creole Dutch, in terms of the retention of Dutch dialect properties. J. van Marle, 'On the interplay of inherited and non-inherited features in Afrikaans derivational morphology' (103–15), concerns the extent to which the morphology of Afrikaans is directly copied from standard Dutch.

4. SOCIOLINGUISTICS AND DIALECTOLOGY

J. Treffers-Daller, *Mixing Two Languages. French-Dutch Contact in a Comparative Persepctive*, Berlin, Mouton de Gruyter, 1994, xi + 300 pp., is a study of 'language mixture in the speech of bilingual Brusselers'. It looks at the various categories of mixture, such as borrowing of individual words, code-mixes of larger units, and code-switching between sentences. One of the main conclusions is that such a categorization is largely unsustainable, because the various categories share many characteristics. Comparisons are drawn with other bilingual cities, such as Strasbourg. Code-switching is also the topic of A. Backus, *Two in One. Bilingual Speech of Turkish Immigrants in The Netherlands*, diss., Tilburg, Tilburg U.P., 420 pp. Here code-switching is seen as a continuum of phenomena ranging between the extremes 'insertion' (borrowing of individual words from the other language) and 'alternation' (changing from one language to the other at clause boundaries). The study is based on data collected from spontaneous conversations between Turkish teenagers and shows a shift between first- and second-generation immigrants from insertion to alternation. In the second generation insertion is two-way, whereas in the first generation it is one-way, from Turkish to Dutch. The author warns that the conclusion must not be interpreted as loss of Turkish in the second generation: it is merely a shift in choice. He also predicts that code-switching may lead to language change in the sense that a Turkish variant of Dutch can be expected to emerge, whose structural deviations from standard Dutch are rooted in structural character-istics of Turkish.

R. Vousten, *Dialect als tweede taal. Linguïstische en extra-linguïstische aspecten van de verwerving van een Noordlimburgs dialect door standaardtalige jongeren*, Amsterdam, Thesis, 1995, ix + 152 pp., studies the acquisi-tion of dialect by teenagers who are native speakers of standard Dutch. Their success in doing so is dependent on three main linguistic factors: the 'degree of systematicity in the language input', the 'degree of complexity in the second language', and the 'degree of markedness of elements in the second language'. Environmental factors also play a role. H. Van de Velde, *Variatie en verandering in het gesproken Standaard-Nederlands (1935–1993)*, diss., Nijmegen, ix + 268 pp., is a study of changes in the pronunciation of standard Dutch between the mid-1930s and the early 1990s. It contrasts the developments in the northern standard with those in the southern (Flemish) one by comparing the realization of a number of key phonemes: voiced fricatives, postvocalic /r/, word-final /n/, the long vowels /e/ and /o/ and the diphthong /ei/. Data are drawn from radio recordings, which motivates the start date, because the first reliable and usable recordings date from the mid-1930s. The main conclusion is that the northern standard has changed considerably (e.g. almost universal devoicing of voiced fricatives, diphthongization of /e/ and /o/), whereas it has not in the south. The main reason for this is that the southern 'standard Dutch is still an abstract standard'. *Dialect in Beweging. 100 jaar na de enquêtes van Willems en Aardrijkskundig Genootschap*, Groesbeek, Stichting Nederlandse Dialecten, 1995, 279 pp., reports on the results of a large-scale survey in which regional newspapers in the Netherlands and Flanders co-operated in the distribution of dialect questionnaires. The (over 10,000) returns were compared with two similar questionnaires conducted a century earlier. The results are discussed under twelve regional headings. T. Boves and M. Gerritsen, *Inleiding in de sociolinguïstiek*, Utrecht, Spectrum, 1995, 352 pp., is a new introductory textbook in sociolinguistics. The justification for a new textbook is that much has changed since the first such book in Dutch. A great deal of research as been done on the sociolinguistics of Dutch, which means that many examples and illustrations are taken from Dutch. A. A. Weijnen, *Etymologisch dialectwoordenboek*, Assen, Van Gorcum, xxvii + 269 pp., provides the etymology of dialect words, listing in each entry geographical area, etymology, comment, and bibliographical reference. M. van Oostendorp, *Tongval. Hoe klinken Nederlanders?*, Amsterdam, Prometheus, 242 pp., is a popular introduction into a number of aspects of Dutch and (Dutch) linguistics. *Pidgins and Creoles. An Introduction*, ed. J. Arends, P. Muysken, and N. Smith, Amsterdam, Benjamins, 1995, xvi + 412 pp., contains (apart from a good general introduction, articles on genesis and specific features, and a comprehensive list of languages) a number of contributions on creoles relevant to Dutch: Papiamento (S. Kouwenberg and P. Muysken) and Sranan (L. Adamson and N. Smith) spoken in (former) Dutch colonies, and Berbice Dutch (S. Kouwenberg) which is Dutch-based.

G. H. Cocks, *Woordenboek van de Drentse Dialecten*, Assen, Van Gorcum, lxix + 703 pp., is the first volume (A–L) of a dialect dictionary of the north-eastern province Drenthe. Volume 2 is to appear in 1997. It is a professionally compiled dictionary, with a comprehensive introduction on the methodology applied in its compilation. Each entry is arranged dialect-standard with grammatical information, indications of geographical area, and example sentences accompanied by its provenance. C. Hoppenbrouwers, *De taal van Kempenland. Van ààwbätte tot zwiemele*, Eindhoven, Kempen Uitgevers, 384 pp., is a dialect dictionary of the Kempen region in the Netherlands. It has a good introduction, and entries consist of grammatical information and a commentary about etymology and usage, as well as the occasional reference. There are a number of maps and further illustrations. P. Bloemhoff-de Bruijn, *Het dialekt van Wijhe. Klank- en vormverschijnselen*, Kampen, IJsselakademie, 1994, 64 pp., and J. J. Spa, *Het dialekt van de stad Vollenhove. Klank- en vormleer*, *ib.*, 96 pp., are the first two in a series of projected descriptions of dialects on the border of the provinces Gelderland and Overijssel. They are mainly concerned with phonology and morphology, although the latter also contains a section on 'syntactic peculiarities'. J. Pannekeet, *Het Westfries. Inventarisatie van dialectkenmerken*, Wormerveer, Stichting Uitgeverij Noord-Holland, 1995, 443 pp., is a description of the dialects of West Friesland, a region in the northeast of the province North Holland. Twenty chapters discuss phonology, morphological and syntactic characteristics, and usage. The book is accompanied by a cassette with readings of two stories by the author. The set-up is largely contrastive with standard Dutch, but is hampered by the absence of an index.

5. ORTHOGRAPHY

YWMLS, 56:960–61, discussed the proposals for spelling reform and foreshadowed a new official spelling guide. *Woordenlijst Nederlandse taal*, The Hague, Sdu–Antwerp, Standaard, 1995, 1055 pp., marks the introduction of the new spelling (officially since 1 September 1996; also available on computer diskette and CD-ROM). The introduction of the new spelling was accompanied by a number of publications explaining the new rules. The official one from the Dutch Language Union (Nederlandse Taalunie) is *Spelling. Hoe anders? De wijzigingen in een notendop*, The Hague, Nederlandse Taalunie, 8 pp. Other titles include W. Daniëls, *Roze(n)geur en mane(n)schijn. De nieuwe spelling toegelicht*, The Hague, Sdu, 1995, 70 pp., and F. van de Laar, *De nieuwe spelling van het Nederlands. Van aalbes tot zuurstofcylinder*, Utrecht, Kosmos, 1995, 103 pp. More polemical and critical reactions to the debate about the new spelling and the way it was introduced are V. De Donder and G. C. Molewijk, *De sitroen van de ginekoloog / De citroen van de gynaecoloog*, Amsterdam, Meulenhoff–Antwerp, Icarus, 1994, 94 pp., and W. Daniëls and F. van de Laar, *Spellingchaos. Een buitenparlementair onderzoek naar de nieuwe spelling*, Utrecht, Scheffers, 96 pp. The former brings together a defender and an opponent of spelling change. For once the opponent is content with the result of the latest changes because they are intended to be definitive. The defender argues that spelling change is a result of language change and therefore inevitable and even natural. The latter publication is a critique not only of the individual spelling changes, but also of the procedures followed by the authorities in the establishment and implementation thereof.

6. APPLIED LINGUISTICS

T. van der Geest, *Over letterenonderzoek: de methodologie van het Neerlandistische onderzoek in het bijzonder de methodologie van de taalbeheersing*, Assen, Van Gorcum, 1995, ix + 241 pp., provides a critical discussion of the research methodologies prevalent in arts areas, with research into linguistic competence as a case study. In particular, it contrasts quantitative with qualitative research methods. J.-A. Mondria, *Vocabulaireverwerving in het vreemde-talenonderwijs. De effecten van context en raden op de retentie*, diss., Groningen, xiv + 363 pp., examines 'the effects of context and guessing on retention' in the acquisition of foreign language vocabulary. By means of three experiments the study establishes that retention is better if new words are offered in a (preferably textual) context, and that the effect of guessing on retention is not significantly greater than that of 'the meaning-given method'. It is more time-consuming and hence less efficient.

L. Verhoeven, *Ontluikende geletterdheid. Een overzicht van de vroege ontwikkeling van lezen en schrijven*, Lisse, Swets & Zeitlinger, 1994, 239 pp., is a study of the early stages of literacy, i.e. pre-school literacy. It starts from the position that literacy begins to develop well before formal instruction and that its development depends on environmental factors. The book takes in literacy in a bilingual context (especially that of immigrants in the Netherlands).

The Cross-Linguistic Study of Bilingual Development, ed. G. Extra and L. Verhoeven, Amsterdam, North-Holland, 1994, 288 pp., contains the proceedings of a conference held under the auspices of the Royal Netherlands Academy of Arts and Sciences. Contributions specific to Dutch cover the separate development hypothesis based on a case study of a Dutch-English bilingual child (A. de Houwer), early bilingual development in Turkish children in the Netherlands (H. van der Heijden and L. Verhoeven), the acquisition of syntax in first and second language by Turkish and Moroccan children in the Netherlands (J. Aarssen, P. Bos, and L. Verhoeven), first-language text cohesion in a Turkish-Dutch bilingual setting (A. Schaufeli), and the influence of Turkish and Moroccan Arabic on the development of the Dutch of adult learners (P. Broeder, G. Extra, and R. van Hout). J. Aarssen, *Relating Events in Two Languages. Acquisition of Cohesive Devices by Turkish-Dutch Bilingual Children at School Age*, diss., Tilburg, Tilburg U.P., ix + 203 pp., deals with the acquisition of sentence-internal anaphors, relativization, topic continuity, and temporality, and concludes that having to acquire these devices in two languages at the same time has no detrimental effects on the overall linguistic development of bilingual children. H. A. K. Klatter-Folmer, *Turkse kinderen en hun schoolsucces. Een dieptestudie naar de rol van de sociaal-structurele oriëntatie, taalvaardigheid en onderwijskenmerken*, diss., Tilburg, *ib.*, 323 pp., tries to explain the poor educational standing of Turkish children in the Dutch education system by relating the personal characteristics of a group of Turkish children and the characteristics of their schools to their educational achievements. It follows a group of 29 children closely in the last year of primary and the first year of secondary education, and tracks their educational achievements in the subsequent two years. The conclusion is that socio-cultural background and language proficiency in both Dutch and Turkish are significant factors in educational achievement. M. Verhallen-van Ling, *Lexicale vaardigheid van Turkse en Nederlandse kinderen. Een vergelijkend onderzoek naar betekenistoekenning*, diss., Amsterdam, Amsterdam, IFOTT, 1994, xii + 206 pp., is a comparative study of the vocabulary of Dutch and Turkish children. The study concentrates on the quality of the vocabulary rather than the quantity (quantitative differences were already known to exist), measured by experiments on meaning assignment and formal definition. Qualitative differences turn out to be 'more profound than first appears through superficial observation'. H. B. Kook, *Leren lezen en schrijven in een tweetalige context. Antilliaanse en Arubaanse kinderen in Nederland*, diss., Amsterdam, IFOTT, 1994, x + 186 pp., tries to identify the most influential factors in the acquisition of literacy for bilingual children. The study is carried out with children in the Netherlands whose mother tongue is Papiamentu. The main conclusion is that language-independent factors are important in the initial stages of literacy and that a high proficiency in both Papiamentu and Dutch will stimulate it. A good Dutch vocabulary is important in the later stages for reading proficiency. The object of D. de Haan, *Deep Dutch. Towards an Operationalization of School Language Skills*, diss., Amsterdam, IFOTT, 1994, 383 pp., is the linguistic aspects of school language. This is called 'deep Dutch'. Verbal contextualization and metalinguistic skills are thought to be significant in this. Experiments in which groups of pupils of differing achievement levels are tested indicate that this is true for contextualization, but not for metalinguistic skills. There is no correlation between this and ethnic background (and hence linguistic ability in Dutch). T. Ammerlaan, *'You get a bit wobbly ...' Exploring Bilingual Lexical Retrieval Processes in the Context of First Language Attrition*, diss., Nijmegen, vi + 360 pp., looks at factors involved in language attrition among a group of Dutch emigrants in Australia. It concentrates on the word level and tries to estimate the extent of English interference in the retrieval of Dutch words. The study is based on two picture-naming experiments. The informants spoke little Dutch in their everyday lives, but women were more likely to 'practise' their Dutch than men. On the whole attrition was less severe than estimated by the informants themselves. A significant factor for retention turned out to be the length of time spent in the Netherlands prior to emigration. Similarities between English and Dutch were significant.

7. LEXICOLOGY

D. J. Eppink, *De stille kracht van taal. Over de wederzijdse beïnvloeding van het Nederlands en het Indonesisch*, Amsterdam, Contact, 1995, 133 pp., explores the mutual influence that Dutch and Bahasa Indonesia have had on each other over 350 years of colonial history. F. Jansen and H. Roza, *Nieuwlands. De jongste taalaanwinsten*, Amsterdam, Arbeiderspers, 1995, 136 pp., is an inventory of neologisms collected over a two-year period between 1993 and 1995. A. J. Kowalska-Szubert, *De kool en de geit. Nederlandse vaste verbindingen met een dier- of plantelement*, diss., Utrecht, Utrecht, LEd, 179 pp., is a study of expressions with the name of an animal or plant (or both, as in the title). It is divided into four chapters: grammatical characteristics, semantics, etymology, and expressions containing a derivational element.

8. FRISIAN

The wealth of publication on Frisian warrants a seprate section. T. Hoekema, *Beknopte Friese vormleer*, Leeuwarden, Afûk, 83 pp., is a brief survey of the Frisian parts of speech and their morphology. P. H. Breuker, D. Gorter, and J. F. Hoekstra, *Orientation in Frisian Studies*, Leeuwarden, Fryske Akademy, 61 pp., is a brief survey of the academic field. *Wat oars as mei in echte taal. Fryske Stúdzjes ta gelegenheid fan it ôfskie fan prof. dr. A. Feitsma as hechleraar Fryske Taal en Letterkunde*, ed. P. H. Breuker, J. Noordegraaf, and H. D. Meijering, *ib.*, 1994, 246 pp., is a *Festschrift* on the occasion of Feitsma's retirement as Professor of Frisian at the Free University, Amsterdam. H. S. Buwalda, S. H. Buwalda, and A. C. B. van der Burg, *Woordeboek fan 't*

Bildts en list fan toponimen, ib., 784 pp., is a dictionary of the dialect of Het Bildt, an area in the north-west of Friesland. The dialect is the product of centuries of language contact between Frisian and Dutch. *Friezen. In bondel stúdzjes oer persoansnammen,* ed. R. A. Ebeling, K. F. Gildemacher, and J. A. Mol, *ib.*, 192 pp., is a collection of studies on Frisian names. K. F. Gildemacher, *Waternamen in Friesland,* diss., Amsterdam, *ib.*, 1993, 610 pp., is a hydronymical study of Frisian. D. Gorter, *Het Fries als kleine Europese taal, ib.*, 28 pp., and P. H. Breuker, *Obe Postma als auteur van het sublieme, ib.*, 59 pp., are the texts of two inaugural lectures (given on the same day) as professors of Frisian studies in Amsterdam, G. as Professor of Frisian Linguistics, B. of Frisian Literature. D. Gorter and R. J. Jonkman, *Taal yn Fryslân op 'e nij besjoen, ib.*, 1995, 90 pp., marks the third publication of the results of a sociolinguistic questionnaire (the first appeared in 1968, the second in 1984), resulting in a comprehensive survey of the Frisian sociolinguistic situation. S. Jong and A. M. J. Riemersma, *Taalpeiling yn Fryslân. Onderzoek naar de beheersing van het Fries en het Nederlands aan het einde van de basisschool,* diss., Tilburg, *ib.*, 1994, 265 pp., and J. Ytsma, *Frisian as a First and Second Language. Sociolinguistic and Socio-Psychological Aspects of the Acquisition of Frisian among Frisian and Dutch Primary School Children,* diss., Tilburg, *ib.*, 1995, 208 pp., are studies on the fluency of pupils in both Frisian and Dutch at the end of primary education.

LITERATURE

By SABINE VANACKER, *Lecturer in Dutch Studies, University of Hull*

1. GENERAL

*Een beeld van belezenheid. Over culturele geletterdheid: lezingen van de Algemene Conferentie van de Nederlandse Taal en Letteren 1993 en van de Conferentie van de Universiteit Gent in 1994 over culturele geletterdheid, ed. Ronald Soetaert and Luc Top, Den Haag, Sdu Uitgevers–Stichting Bibliographia Neerlandica, combines the papers of two conferences under the auspices of the Dutch Language Union concerning cultural literacy. *Oosthoek lexicon Nederlandse & Vlaamse literatuur*, ed. Christine Brackmann and Marijke Friesendorp, Utrecht, Kosmos–Z & K, 390 pp., is a biographical lexicon of over 1,600 authors, genres, movements, and key concepts within Dutch and Flemish literature from the Middle Ages up to 1996, followed by a list of the main Dutch and Flemish literary prizes and a short bibliography. Literature entries in the encyclopaedia, *Grote Oosthoek Encyclopedie*, have been revised, updated and expanded with very recent items to make a useful reference work for the general lover of literature. Sadly, children's literature and adolescent literature have been excluded from the reference work, as have many regional novels. The lexicon, however, has taken into account authors writing in other languages who have a strong Dutch link, like Belle van Zuylen who wrote in French, the humanist Erasmus, and some modern South African writers. The entries on separate authors include a very brief biography, and focus on their literary *œuvre* and its reception history, while there is cross-referencing to the wider literary and cultural context such as movements, and genres. Paul van Aken, *Niemand te hoog. Humanisme, Vrijzinnigheid en Vlaamse literatuur*, Brussels, VUB Press, 1995, 287 pp., offers an introduction to humanist and free-thinking elements within Flemish literature. The title stems from the dedication to the fascinating *Zedekunst dat is Wellevenskunste*, by the 16th-c. Dutch humanist Coornhert, who considered the values and relative importance of being a human being in this world, written during a chaotic period of religious and political struggle, which also resulted in a rupture with Flanders and a temporary end to the 'rich and often critical literature of Flanders'. Within the similarly chaotic ideological and religious period of the 20th c., humanism and free thought are considered in the Flemish context, involving a very diverse selection containing novels, essays, diaries, and perhaps highlighting less well-known authors. *Van pen tot laser: 31 opstellen over boek en schrift aangeboden aan Ernst Braches bij zijn afscheid als hoogleraar aan de Universiteit van Amsterdam*

in oktober van het jaar 1995, ed. Ton Croiset van Uchelen and Hannie van Goinga, Amsterdam, De Buitenkant, 343 pp., is a collection of 31 essays on books and literacy dedicated to Ernst Braches. A similar work is Samuel IJsseling, *Boeken-wijsheid. Filosofische notities over boeken, lezers en schrijvers*, Kampen, Kok Agora, 1995, 45 pp., a brief collection of philosophical 'notes' on writing, writers and readers. Rudi van der Paardt, **Een vertrouwd gevoel van onbekendheid. Opstellen over antieke intertekstualiteit* (Leidse opstellen, 26), Leiden, Dimensie, discusses intertextuality in classical literature, while Marcel F. Fresco and Rudi van der Paardt, **Naar hoger honing. Plato en platonisme in de Nederlandse literatuur*, Groningen, Historische Uitgeverij, considers the effect of Plato and Platonic philosophy within Dutch literature. Hugo Bousset, **Geritsel van papier. Essays*, Amsterdam, Meulenhoff–Antwerp, Kritak, is the latest collection of essays by the Flemish academic and critic. Rutger Kopland (R. H. van den Hoofdakker), *Het mechaniek van de ontroering*, Amsterdam, Van Oorschot, 1995, 220 pp., collects his essays on poetry and art for the last 25 years, investigating the relationship between poetry and science, especially the connection with his field of interest, psychiatry. The title refers to the mechanics of feeling moved by an aesthetic experience, and questions what causes this aesthetic effect. Rudolf Geel, *Volmaakte schrijvers schrijven niet. Over het scheppingsproces van literaire en andere teksten*, Amsterdam U.P., 1995, 116 pp., considers the mystery surrounding writing and literacy. Discussing not only novels but also letters and speeches, the collection points to the high status awarded to writing. A number of aspects concerning writing are looked at from a theoretical perspective, such as the notion of 'enforced' voluntary writing. Writing is compared to chess, combining intuition with systematic thought, but an activity in which the writer's opponent is himself. Ernst van Alphen et al., *Op poëtische wijze. Een handleiding voor het lezen van poëzie*, Bussum, Coutinho–Heerlen, Open Universiteit, 190 pp., offers a systematic introduction, for university students, to the analysis of poetry. For poetry, no consistent critical theory has been developed, and as a result this book combines theories by Veronica Forrest-Thomson, Jonathan Culler and Michael Riffaterre, focusing on poetry as the location of communication, rendering the reading attitude of the reader and the speaking attitude of the poet of overall importance. In the case of poetry, however, specific additional rules of communication are seen to pertain, with reader and writer accepting the creation of an extra meaning. This book is a very useful survey of a practical approach to poetry analysis and practical criticism.

Reizen door de Europese literatuur. Modellen voor het literatuuronderwijs, ed. Martine De Clercq and Siem Bakker, Leuven–Amersfoort, Acco,

1995, 115 pp., seeks, via the genre of the travel story and its historical evolution in European literature, to highlight the common European tradition. The collection offers a varied selection of subjects around this theme, starting with Martine de Clercq's discussion of whether a history of travel literature can be written. Until recently, the travel story has been the neglected 'box room' of literature and literary criticism. The travel motif has transformed itself for verse narratives, has appeared in science fiction and in prose accounts of expeditions and explorations. From a philosophical perspective, the travel motif can be regarded as a metaphor for a new, distanced perspective on reality, and a fascination with the Other. Berry Dongelmans, Peter van Zonneveld, and Frits van Oostrom, with the co-operation of Marco de Niet, *Dierbaar Magazijn. De bibliotheek van de Maatschappij der Nederlandse Letterkunde*, Amsterdam U.P., discusses the library of the society for Dutch literature. *Een theatergeschiedenis der Nederlanden. Tien eeuwen drama en theater in Nederland en Vlaanderen*, ed. R. L. Erenstein, Amsterdam U.P., presents a major theatre history of the Low Countries from its medieval origins to the present. Maaike Meijer, *In tekst gevat. Inleiding tot een kritiek van representatie*, Amsterdam U.P., 193 pp., is an introduction to feminist text analysis and a feminist perspective on culture studies. The author aims to introduce students to the literary theories predominant in a feminist interpretation, such as structuralist methods of analysis, narratology, deconstruction, intertextuality, discourse analysis, and film theory. Each chapter considers a few texts from one of these theoretical perspectives or focuses on a specific theoretical issue central to the consideration of gender in representation. Meijer stresses the importance of introducing feminist criticism into the study of Dutch literature, but also advocates a move to wider culture studies involving not only poetry and prose, but also posters, songs, children's books, and non-fiction in her analysis of the two 'grammars of difference' in culture, gender, and colour. Also inspired by feminism is Hendrika Alberta Paasman, *Levens in letters. Autobiografieën van Nederlandse schrijfsters*, Amsterdam U.P., 300 pp. So far literary criticism has failed to develop a model for female autobiography, until the arrival of feminist literary criticism attempted to rectify this situation. This book regards autobiographies as works of fiction, involved in the creation of an autobiographical persona rather than the correct recording of biographical truth. The 13 autobiographies by 11 women writers show a surprisingly large and a comparable output; five are analysed to test the existing theories on literary autobiography.

A number of authors consider prose genres, like the historical novel, the moon travel story, or science fiction. Serge Heirbrant, *Componenten en compositie van de historische roman* (Literatuur in veelvoud,

7), Leuven–Apeldoorn, Garant, 1995, a Ghent doctoral thesis, considers the components and the composition of the historical novel. J. J. A. Mooij, *De andere aarde. Maanreisverhalen door de eeuwen heen*, Kampen, Kok Agora–Kapellen, Pelckmans, 162 pp., discusses the quirky, eccentric genre of moon travel stories from the classical period to the present day, focusing mainly on Western European and American stories. A genre dominated by French, English, and American authors, it is at present being continued in science fiction with authors like Arthur C. Clarke, but a number of Dutch authors are considered. There is a rare discussion of detective fiction in Dutch by Jacobus Willem van der Weide, *Detective en anti-detective. Narratologie, psychoanalyse, postmodernisme*, Nijmegen, Uitgeverij Vantilt. Wilma van der Pennen, *Lezen over Science Fiction*, Den Haag, NBLC Uitgeverij, 1995, 42 pp., is a brief introduction of bibliographical research into science fiction.

Finally, an increasing number of works deal with literature from the perspective of the Dutch and Belgian colonial past. The most ambitious overview of Dutch colonial literature is undoubtedly E. M. Beekman, *Troubled Pleasures. Dutch Colonial Literature from the East Indies 1600–1950*, Oxford, Clarendon, 654 pp. Especially strong in its analysis of the early period of the Dutch presence in present-day Indonesia, the book deals with writings by European colonists about the new country and people, starting with mariners' journals around 1600 and ending around World War II. Dutch colonial literature is characterized as having produced exceptional writing, more innovative than previously assumed, and of huge influence on the rest of Dutch literature, both as regards the modern, speech-like Dutch prose style and regarding the content. More recent colonial writing is nearly always Romantic in its outlook, while typically modern colonial themes include doubt, alienation, memory and time, and love of nature. The colonial experience can indeed be termed 'troubled pleasures', since despite the delight at the new freedom, the classlessness and the exotic nature of the colony, the writers never acquire 'certainty and confirmation'. Beekman does not really address the issues of defining 'Dutch colonial literature' and indicating its relationship with 'Dutch literature' or analysing it in terms of recent (post)colonial literary theory, refusing to use the texts as 'exhibits for an ideological debate'. He occasionally takes his bearing from semiotics and uses Bakhtin's concept of the polyphonic novel with interesting results in the cases of Multatuli and Couperus, but on the whole this is a traditional, but highly interesting survey of the canon of Dutch colonial literature. An interesting comparison with Beekman's book is provided by *Weer-werk. Schrijven en terugschrijven in koloniale en postkoloniale literaturen*, ed. Theo D'haen (Semaian, 15),

Leiden, Vakgroep Talen en Culturen van Zuidoost-Azië en Oceanië, Rijksuniversiteit te Leiden, 163 pp., which considers the relationships between Dutch and other European literature and that pertaining to the colonial experience. In his introduction, D'haen highlights how much contemporary societies have been affected by imperialism and colonialism: both English and Dutch literature have contributed to this ideology. Wim Rutgers, *Beneden en boven de wind. Literatuur van de Nederlandse Antillen en Aruba*, Amsterdam, De Bezige Bij, 468 pp., is an important first detailed history of the oral and scripted literature in the Dutch Antilles and Aruba, from the first European contacts in the 17th c. Besides a historical survey the book introduces the little-known and relatively young literature of Dutch Antilles and Aruba, but views this literature in the context of the oral tradition, the strong story telling tradition as well as the background of writing serving to a large extent as the support for speeches and plays.

2. THE MIDDLE AGES

*Niet alleen kijken: over het gebruik van handschriften en handschriftencollecties. Vijf lezingen bij het afscheid van prof. dr. P. F. J. Obbema als conservator westerse handschriften van de Universiteitsbibliotheek Leiden, ed. A. Th. Bouwman, Leiden, Bibliotheek der Rijksuniversiteit te Leiden, 108 pp., contain five lectures on the topic of manuscripts and manuscript collections, held at the retirement of P. F. J. Obbema as curator of Western manuscripts at Leiden University Library. Pieter Obbema, *De middeleeuwen in handen. Over de boekcultuur in de late middeleeuwen*, Hilversum, Verloren, 203 pp., is a nicely presented survey of the book culture in the late Middle Ages with which the departing curator intends to awaken the love of medieval manuscripts. The three main sections deal with the science of manuscripts, failed preservation, and a detailed study of a number of individual manuscripts. The introduction emphasizes the importance for researchers of using the actual manuscripts, since the confrontation with manuscripts provides an important historical experience. Intended for a non-academic audience, the book restricts its use of jargon. *Middeleeuwse Verzamelhandschriften uit de Nederlanden, Congres Nijmegen 14 oktober 1994*, ed. Gerard Sonnemans (Middeleeuwse studies en bronnen, 1), Hilversum, Verloren, 160 pp., has three main sections and complements Verloren's editions of medieval manuscript collections. Manuscript collections present the researcher with the paradox of the collector's intended unity combined with a certain amount of chaos. The Congress on medieval manuscript collections at Nijmegen was organized on the occasion of the presentation of the Geraardbergse manuscript, and aimed to focus research on a neglected

subject, i.e. the actual manuscript collections themselves, rather than their constituent texts. The introduction considers the critical reaction to the series' first two editions of manuscript collections: the main criticism concerned the choice of a diplomatic edition of the texts, without philological comment, which the editors felt would involve a very ephemeral interpretation of the texts. A first section on the structure and cohesion of the collection is followed by a second section on types of collections based on formal aspects. The next manuscript to be published in this series is *Het Tübingse Sint-Geertruihandschrift, Hs. Tübingen, Universitätsbibliothek Me.IV.3*, ed. Hans Kienhorst and Gerard Sonnemans (Middeleeuwse Verzamelhandschriften uit de Nederlanden), Hilversum, Verloren, 149 pp., a diplomatic edition published in collaboration with the Constantijn Huygens Instituut. This manuscript collection contains seven Middle Dutch poems and a Middle Dutch prose passage from the *Moralia in Job*, the latter copied at the Sint-Geertrui convent in Amsterdam. The volume ends with a summary in English, a bibliography, and an appendix on other Middle Dutch manuscripts in the same convent. Paul Wackers et al., *Verraders en bruggenbouwers. Verkenningen naar de relatie tussen Latinitas en Middelnederlandse letterkunde* (Nederlandse literatuur en cultuur in de middeleeuwen, 15), Amsterdam, Prometheus, 361 pp., discusses the bilingual writing culture of the Middle Ages. Translation from high-status Latin into the vernacular languages was presented as a negative process, but nevertheless an important mutual influence occurred. In fact, northern medieval Europe combined two cultures, a Germanic, vernacular, and oral culture and the written Latin culture of the Judaeo-Christian and Classical tradition, which had the monopoly of religious and scientific texts. Although medieval interpretations frequently saw translation from Latin as a betrayal, it in fact built bridges between these cultures.

Jan van Ruusbroec: mystiek licht uit de Middeleeuwen, ed. Paul Verdeyen (Keurreeks; 150), Leuven, Davidsfonds, 167 pp., is the completely revised second edition of this book, combining an outline of the life of Ruusbroec, with a selected anthology of his work. Whereas the original edition had been written for a specific, spiritually-minded audience, the Ruusbroec text has now been organized in ten chapters highlighting the most important aspects of his teachings. This new edition takes into account recent research into his life and writings but still many uncertainties remain. *Het leven van Lutgard: Bloemlezing uit het Kopenhaagse handschrift*, ed. Yolande Spaans and Ludo Jongen, (Middelnederlandse tekstedities, 3), Hilversum, Verloren, 336 pp., offers a selection from the Copenhagen manuscript. The biography of the 13th-c. Lutgard was written by Thomas van Cantimpré, but as a conventional saint's life the *Vita Lutgardis* is not a historically reliable document. An introduction surveys the historical and cultural context of her life. The Middle Dutch translation, two parts of which are presented here, is dated between 1263 and 1274 and represents a more detailed, colourful, and extensive version than the Latin original. There are full indexes and a bibliography.

3. THE RENAISSANCE

O. S. Lankhorst and P. G. Hoftijzer, *Drukkers, boekverkopers en lezers in Nederland tijdens de Republiek. Een historiografische en bibliografische handleiding* (Nederlandse cultuur in Europese context; 1. IJkpunt 1650), Den Haag, SDU Uitgevers, 1995, 227 pp., is an important historiographical and bibliographical introduction to the literary life of the Republic, reviewing printers, booksellers, and readers. *Door eenen engen hals: Nederlandse beschouwingen over vertalen 1550–1670*, ed. Theo Hermans (Verhaalhistorie, 2), 's Gravenhage, Stichting Bibliographia Neerlandica, 159 pp., focuses on another aspect of literary life, the process of translation. In his introduction, Hermans characterizes the Renaissance as a period of intensive and innovatory translation practice and theory. The innovations in certain sciences like mathematics or philosophy were fundamentally connected with the need to translate certain new concepts into Dutch. Not only was there an enormous rise in the number of translations during this period, but also the centre of translation practice moved from Antwerp, before 1570, northwards to Amsterdam. The book offers an interesting introduction to the practice and theory of translation and includes name index and bibliography. *Van sint Jans onthoofdinghe. Zestiende-eeuws Amsterdams rederijkersstuk van Jan Thönisz*, ed. Paul Laport, Frédérique de Muij, and Marijke Spies (Uitgaven/Stichting Neerlandistiek VU, 20), Amsterdam, Stichting Neerlandistiek V–Münster, Nodus, 114 pp., is a 16th-c. play about John the Baptist by the unknown rhetorician poet Jan Thönisz, previously only available in manuscript. The text is presented with a parallel translation into modern Dutch, opening it up to non-specialists. The introduction outlines the history of Amsterdam at the beginning of the 16th c. and the literary context of the work. With the play running to 722 lines, five sections, six rondels, and a refrain, the author reveals a strong rhyming talent, and much humour. There is a selective bibliography. *Jan van Hout. Verzen voor de Leidse loterij en de rederijkerswedstrijd van 1596*, ed. Johan Koppenol, Leiden, Internationaal Forum voor Afrikaanse en Nederlandse Taal en Letteren, concerns lyrics by another rhetorician poet. Machteld van Royen and Fred Wolthuis, *Heinric en*

Margriete van Limborch. Chronologische bibliografie, Groningen, Universiteitsdrukkerij, Rijksuniversiteit Groningen, is a chronological bibliography relating to this text. *Visie in veelvoud: Opstellen van prof. dr. E. K. Grootes over zeventiende-eeuwse letterkunde*, ed. M. Spies and J. Jansen, Amsterdam U.P., collects a number of essays by Grootes on 17th-c. literature, while R. Lindeman, Y. Scherf, and R. M. Dekker, *Reisverslagen van Noord-Nederlanders van 16e· tot begin 19e eeuw. Een chronologische lijst*, Leiden, Internationaal Forum voor Afrikaanse en Nederlandse Taal en Letteren, is a chronological list of travel narratives by travellers from the Northern Netherlands from the 16th to the beginning of the 19th c.

A number of books reinterpret the Dutch national anthem. There is a critical revision of the questions of authorship, dating, and ideological tendency by Abraham Maljaars, *Het Wilhelmus: Auteurschap, datering en strekking. Een kritische toetsing en nieuwe interpretatie*, Kampen, Kok. E. Hofman, *Nieuw licht op het Wilhelmus en zijn dichters*, Zoetermeer, Boekencentrum, 123 pp., also tries to tackle the many unsolved mysteries concerning the text, inspired by the recent discovery of a second collection of popular songs containing an older version of the 'Wilhelmus'. This, the book claims, results in important revisions. Also considered is the place of the text in the tradition of the 'schriftuurlijke lied', lyrics with a close relationship to the Bible. These are the sources of Dutch Protestant literature, and tell of the lives of the faithful during the religious wars read as parallels with biblical situations. Although there is indeed a close connection with these biblical songs, Hofman concludes that the 'Wilhelmus' does not justify a theological thesis, and is not intended to improve biblical knowledge. Despite the many remaining mysteries, its status as an apology or propaganda song is maintained.

A Selection of the Poetry of Sir Constantijn Huygens (1596–1687), ed. Peter Davidson and Adriaan van der Wiel, Amsterdam U.P., 228 pp., presents a number of the poems with parallel translations into English. The selection includes sections from 'Batava Tempe', 'Hofwijk', and 'Werk van Dagen', and shows H.'s stylistic range. The translations have had to abandon rhyme and occasionally vary the metre. The Dutch source text is based on J. A. Worp's edition of the poems, since no complete modern edition exists. The appendices list a selection of poems written or translated into French, Latin, and Italian, a brief selection of H.'s writings in English, and a short essay on his relationship with English literature. *De Hollandse jaren van Hugo de Groot (1583–1621). Lezingen van het colloquium ter gelegenheid van de 350-ste sterfdag van Hugo de Groot ('s-Gravenhage, 31 augustus-1 september 1995)*, ed. H. J. M. Nellen and J. Trapman, Hilversum, Verloren, is an anniversary collection of lectures. Jacob Cats, *Sinne- en Minnebeelden*, ed. Hans Luijten, Assen, Van Gorcum, presents the poetry of 'Father Cats' in three parts. *Minne- en zinnebeelden. Een bloemlezing uit de Nederlandse emblematiek*, ed. Hans Luijten and Marijke Blankman, Amsterdam U. P., presents an anthology of Dutch emblematics. R. van Stipriaan, *Leugens en vermaak. Boccaccio's novellen in de kluchtcultuur van de Nederlandse renaissance*, Amsterdam U.P., 357 pp., discusses 17th-c. Dutch interest in Boccaccio's *Decamerone*, using narratives as dramatic plots, primarily among writers of the farce. Strangely, the earliest Dutch translation of Boccaccio occurred only in 1564 and the earliest stage adaptation in 1602. The status of the farce in the literature of the Dutch Republic is investigated, besides themes of deceit, judgement, illusion, ambiguity, and fiction. These, however, combine with a general feature of the Dutch Renaissance culture, a 'ludic culture of concealment' stemming from Erasmus. The interesting thesis is followed by an extensive bibliography and a list of motifs from the *Decamerone* in Dutch literature. Els Stronks, *Stichten of schitteren: de poëzie van zeventiende-eeuwse gereformeerde predikanten*, Houten, Den Hertog, 345 pp., discusses the opposite pole of the 17th-c. Dutch literary spectrum, the poetry of Dutch Calvinist ministers. The book focuses on three song writers belonging to the Nadere Reformatie and their audiences: Ridderus, who mainly wrote for mothers, children, and servants, Sluiter, who addressed even the most uneducated of his congregation, and Lodenstein, who wrote for private gatherings. A final chapter considers their attitude to Classical mythology, which proved the secular poet's erudition but the pagan aspects of which presented a problem for Calvinist poets, so that increasingly they felt the need to avoid this material. *Journael ofte Gedenckwaerdige beschrijvinghe vande Oost-Indische Reyse van Willem Ysbrantsz. Bontekoe van Hóorn. Descriptieve bibliografie 1646–1996*, ed. Garrelt Verhoeven and Piet Verkruijsse (Bijdragen tot de geschiedenis van de Nederlandse boekhandel. Nieuwe reeks, 1), Zutphen, Walburg, is a descriptive bibliography concerning the famous 17th-c. narrative of the disastrous sea voyage to the Dutch East Indies.

4. THE EIGHTEENTH CENTURY

Willem van den Hull, *Autobiografie (1778–1854)*, ed. Raymonde Padmos (Egodocumenten, 10), Hilversum, Verloren, 736 pp., includes bibliography, genealogy, and name index. The interesting autobiography of an introspective outsider is an important stage in the development of the genre in the Netherlands. Also noted: Q. M. R. Ver Huell, *Levensherinneringen 1787–1812*, ed. L. Turksma, Westervoort, Van Gruting. Gerrit Paape, *Mijne vrolijke wijsbegeerte in mijn ballingschap*, ed. Peter Altena (Egodocumenten, 11), Hilversum,

Verloren, 159 pp., offers an equally enlightening insight into the same period via the writer Gerrit Paape (1752–1803), a one-man book factory, an unofficial publisher and bookseller, as well as a commercial writer who produced a great volume of work. P. had an exceptional talent, and his autobiography/philosophy is interesting work because of his openness and his 'cunning innocence'.

An evocative portrait of the 18th c. is presented in Hella S. Haasse, *Uitgesproken, opgeschreven. Essays over achttiende-eeuwse vrouwen, een bosgezicht, verlichte geesten, vorstenlot, satire, de pers en Vestdijks avondrood*, Amsterdam, Querido, 187 pp. The novelist here explores 18th-c. beliefs on friendship, the new image of women, the origins of the press, the notions of satire, and insights which lead to an understanding of the inspiration behind H.'s work. An evocation of Boswell's life in Utrecht, and the turning point in his life, leads to a discussion of the cultural situation in the 18th-c. Netherlands, as well as a comparison with the level of book reading in the 20th c. Friendship between women, with its emotional excessiveness, formed a welcome release for women who could not express themselves to men and were often caught in loveless marriages and in situations of enforced passivity. Numerous examples receive detailed treatment in this book which presents a wide-ranging collection of essays, combining historical research with a creative imagining of the cultural periods discussed. *Verlichte geesten: een portrettengalerij voor Piet Buijnsters*, ed. Kees Fens, Amsterdam, Querido, 223 pp., is a collection in honour of P. J. Buijnsters, focusing on his specialism of 18th-c. Dutch literature. Authors include Hans Bots, J. J. Kloek, R. Vermij, J. van den Berg, W. van den Berg, Pierre H. and Simone Dubois, R. Schenkeveld-van der Dussen, and F. Grijzenhout in a wide-ranging collection aimed at both specialists and the general public. *De vormingsjaren van A. C. W. Staring. Brieven en documenten betreffende zijn studietijd in Harderwijk en Göttingen, 1784–1789*, ed. M. Evers, Hilversum, Verloren, 319 pp., covers the important period in S.'s life, studying agriculture studies and psychology in Germany, a period forming his identity as a modern landowner, estate manager, and Gelderland poet. The text includes his travel notes, a journal of an autumn journey through Germany in 1787, and the diary of the return journey, besides many personalia. S. added a new aesthetic perspective on his environment, and with his enlightened ideals was in many respects typical of his period.

5. THE NINETEENTH CENTURY

Hieronymus van Alphen, **Literair-theoretische geschriften*, ed. Jacqueline de Man, Assen, Van Gorcum, presents two volumes of his literary-theoretical writings, while the collected work by Nescio is published in Nescio, *Verzameld werk*, ed. Lieneke Frerichs, Amsterdam, Nijgh en Van Ditmar–Van Oorschot. Jo Tollebeek, Frank Ankersmit, and Wessel Krul, *Romantiek en historische cultuur*, Groningen, Historische Uitgeverij, discusses Romanticism and a historical culture. F. A. Hartsen, *Nederlandsche toestanden: Uit het leven van een lijder*, Hilversum, Verloren, 221 pp., is introduced by Nop Maas and belongs to Verloren's biographical series. A long introduction presents H.'s writings, so diverse that they are called the 'Sjaalman's bundle', in a reference to H.'s relationship with Multatuli and his very similar outlook. H.'s friend, Eduard Douwes Dekker, is discussed in Jacob Hoogteijling, *Door de achterdeur naar binnen. Over de wording van Multatuli's 'Max Havelaar'*, Amsterdam, Thesis Publishers, 297 pp. This book on the evolution of his major novel, *Max Havelaar*, focuses on Multatuli's claim in a letter of having written the book in 17 days. In a number of separate chapters, the book considers different topics concerning the genesis of the text with different approaches. The author opts for Stuiveling's 1949 edition of the manuscript, complemented by annotations and some 'paratext' collected from the correspondence. The book ends with a consideration of previous *Max Havelaar* research and an English summary.

6. 1880 TO 1945

Three books discuss the life and writings of Frederik van Eeden. Marianne Mooijweer, *De Amerikaanse droom van Frederik van Eeden*, Amsterdam, De Bataafsche Leeuw, is on his American dream, while R. Th. R. Wentges, *De neus van Frederik van Eeden. Een beschouwing over de betekenis van reuk en geur in zijn werk*, Amsterdam, Candide, discusses the meaning of the sense of smell in his work. Jan Fontijn, *Trots verbrijzeld. Het leven van Frederik van Eeden vanaf 1901*, Amsterdam, Querido, 667 pp. brings the second part of his acclaimed biography of the author, psychiatrist, philosopher and social reformer. Van Eeden's later life is described as increasingly torn between his idealism and the clash with reality. A fellow 1880s poet, Herman Gorter, is portrayed in Herman de Liagre Böhl, *Met al mijn bloed heb ik voor U geleefd. Herman Gorter 1864–1927*, Amsterdam, Balans, while two books discuss Louis Couperus: H. T. M. van Vliet, *Eenheid in verscheidenheid. Over de werkwijze van Louis Couperus*, Amsterdam, Veen, and Bas Heijne, *Het gezicht van Louis Couperus*, Amsterdam, Veen. Hans Goedkoop, *Geluk. Het leven van Herman Heijermans* (Open Domein, 31), Amsterdam, De Arbeiderspers, discusses the life of the naturalist dramatist. Elsbeth Etty, *Liefde is heel het leven niet. 1869–1952*, Amsterdam, Balans, supplies an account of the life and work of the poet Henriëtte Roland Holst. Ferdinand Victor Toussaint van Boelaere, *Prosper van Langendonck. Essay*, ed. Raymond Vervliet, Leiden, Internationaal Forum voor Afrikaanse en Nederlandse Taal en Letteren, 92 pp., presents an edition of this essay about Prosper van Langendonck, with an introduction and annotations by Raymond Vervliet. The essay offers only a partial view of a complex personality, whose poetry indicates an ambivalent love for earthly existence, combined with a yearning for the Absolute. His disillusion, his opposition of ideal and truth, make him a typical *fin-de-siècle* poet, connected with Baudelaire, Poe, and de Musset, while still appreciative of the preceding poetic tradition.

Alice Nahon 1896–1933. Kan ons lied geen hooglied wezen, ed. Ria van den Brandt, Antwerp, Houtekiet–Baarn, Bosch & Keuning, 303 pp., rejects the image of Nahon as the simple, passive, religious girl writing poetry, the 'good Flemish sacrificial virgin from days gone by'. Nahon is still well-known, although her popularity declined after World War II. She was a paradoxical publishing phenomenon, highly popular with readers but also little known. This collection seeks to include new perspectives on her work, including women's studies. This new Nahon is discovered to be more humoristic than previously assumed. Numerous aspects of her life and work are studied by, among others, Ria van den Brandt, Staf Aertzen, Manu van der Aa, Céline Beijer, Caroline Vander Stichele, An de Vos, Jonneke Bekkenkamp, Veronica Vasterling, Ria van den Brandt, Dirk de Geest, Magda Michielsens, Patrick Vanleene, Marysa Demoor, Victor Striker, and Daan van Speybroeck. These short essays are followed by a number of unpublished poems edited by Hilde Van den Hooff. Marc Reynebeau, *Dichter in Berlijn. De ballingschap van Paul van Ostaijen (1918–1921)*, Groot-Bijgaarden, Globe–Baarn, De Prom, focuses on a specific period in the poet's life, his stay in Berlin from October 1918 to May 1921. Paul Van Ostaijen's belief in the autonomy of art means the biographer has to tread carefully in relating the work to the author. Reynebeau consequently stresses that his book investigates the development of the persona Van Ostaijen. Despite Van Ostaijen's early acceptance into the canon, the period of his political exile is surprisingly little documented, perhaps because of the suggestions of drug use and possible homosexuality associated with this period. Other books commemorating the poet in his anniversary year are Wim Meewis, **Paul van Ostaijen*, Leiden, Internationaal Forum voor Afrikaanse en Nederlandse Taal en Letteren, Buelens and E. Spinoy, **De stem der Loreley. Over Paul van Ostaijen*, Amsterdam, Bert Bakker/ Standaard Uitgeverij, Henri-Floris Jespers and Guido Lauwaert, **Paul van Ostaijen. Allen zijn mij vreemdelingen*, Houtekiet/De Prom. Two catalogues of exhibitions: *Paul van Ostaijen*, and *Paul van Ostaijen en de gebroeders Jespers*, are both published by Pandora. José Boyens, **De* *genesis van 'Bezette Stad'. Ik spreek met de mannen en regel alles wel. Brieven van Oscar Jespers aan Paul van Ostaijen 1920–1921 over het ontstaan van 'Bezette Stad' en de Antwerpse groepering Sienjaal*, Antwerp, Pandora, outlines the genesis of his poetry collection *Bezette Stad*, as well as the Antwerp avant-garde group Sienjaal, by means of letters from his painter-friend Oscar Jespers. Jean F Buyck, **Paul van Ostaijen en de kunstkritiek*, Antwerp, Pandora, focuses on his relationship to art criticism, while a yearly publication about the book world in the Low Countries also contains two articles about the poet, *Mekka. Jaarboek voor lezers 1996*, Dedalus.

Three other inter-war authors are also the subject of a monograph. Michel van Nieuwstadt, **De verschrikkingen van het denken. Over Menno ter Braak*, Groningen, Historische Uitgeverij, concerns the editor of the combative literary journal *Forum*, while H. Brandt Corstius and Maarten 't Hart, **Het gebergte. De tweeënvijftig romans van S. Vestdijk*, Amsterdam, Nijgh & Van Ditmar–De Bezige Bij, present the 52 novels of another *Forum* colleague, Simon Vestdijk. Hans Anten, **Het behoorlijk vernis van de rede. Over poëtica en proza van F. Bordewijk*, Groningen, Historische Uitgeverij, presents the poetics and the prose work of the author of the novels in the 'Neue Sachlichkeit' style. Jan van der Vegt, *Hendrik de Vries (1896–1989). Een biografische schets* (De Prom bibliofiel, 34), Baarn, De Prom, 113 pp., is a biographical sketch of the poet Hendrik de Vries. A 'unique figure in Dutch poetry', he was especially influenced by his childhood experiences and his love for Spain, while his poetry combines a conventional form with the important themes of passion, fantasy, and the dream. This short biographical sketch uses interviews, among others with the late Hendrik de Vries himself, as well as letter collections, emphasizing the importance of his drawings and paintings. This brief biography, published for the 100th anniversary of his birth, is to precede a more extensive biography, and includes a selected bibliography of his poems and poem translations, as well as publications about him. The postwar generation of poets, the 'vijftigers', considered De Vries old-fashioned, but by 1970s his status with the new generation of poets had improved again. He received positive attention from the journal *Maatstaf*, and in 1976 was presented with the P.C. Hooftprijs.

Paul Buurman, *Duitse literatuur in de Nederlandse dagbladpers 1930–1955. Een historisch-documentair receptie-onderzoek*, Amsterdam U.P., 385 pp., opens on common modern-Dutch clichés concerning Germany, to investigate the effects of the Occupation on the reception of German literature in the Netherlands. First, a general societal framework is outlined, discussing the concept of 'pillarization' in the Dutch media, the debate concerning the literary canon in the Netherlands, and the available research on the reception of German literature in this period. 'Pillarization' as a structuring principle in Dutch public life is described in its personal effect, with every religious and ideological segment of Dutch society forming a separated 'cultural group'. Hence the canonic choice of certain texts must be related to certain groups of readers with a specific social, professional, religious or ideological profile. The book concludes that Dutch papers did not restrict their review activity solely to the writing of exiles, but also evaluated those who chose to work within the Nazi society. *Een tweede eeuw? Jaarboek 1 van het Stijn Streuvelsgenootschap 1995*, ed. Piet Thomas, Tielt, Lannoo, 278 pp., is the first yearbook of the Stijn Streuvels Society, which was founded in 1995 in order to break through the academic silence around the author. The book aims to present the current status of research, since the publication of Hedwig Speliers's important recent biography, and hopes to continue the Streuvels revival. There is much new biographical, literary, and critical research here from a variety of perspectives, by, among others, Bert Vanheste, Dirk de Geest, Jozef Boets, Hedwig Speliers, Karel van Deuren, Daniël Vanacker, Romain Vanlandschoot, Marcel de Smedt, Jooris van Hulle, Rudolf van de Perre, Roger Rennenberg, and Piet Thomas. This first volume of a new periodical closes with a bibliography and a survey of archival material in Flanders, including addresses and contacts.

7. 1945 TO THE PRESENT DAY

Frank Berndsen, *Moderne literatuur. De benadering van een theoreticus*, Groningen, Passage, offers a theoretical approach to modern literature. *De Gerrit Achterberg-collectie van de Stads- of Athenaeumbibliotheek te Deventer*, ed. F. E. van Wijk (Polyptychon, 1), Amsterdam, Schiphouwer & Brinkman, 153 pp., contains a survey of the collection owned by the City Library of Deventer, followed by a contribution on the publication history of Achterberg's work by P. G. de Bruijn. F. E. van Wijk sketches the Achterberg collection. P. G. de Bruijn's publication history highlights Achterberg's dominant need to be printed and his basic distrust of publishers, resulting in a great many collections on the one hand and frequent quarrels with publishers on the other. The catalogue itself is divided into collected works, anthologies, separate collections and separately published poems, poems published in journals and other collections, translations, letters, and secondary literature. Another bibliographic overview is G. Harinck, *Bibliografie van dr. G. Puchinger 1937–199*, with an introduction by J. de Bruijn, Amsterdam, VU Uitgeverij, 137 pp., while Jos Joosten, *Feit en tussenkomst. Geschiedenis en opvattingen van 'Tijd en Mens' (1949–1955)*, Nijmegen, Vantilt, is a doctoral thesis outlining the history and the ethical-humanist principles of the experimental literary journal *Tijd en Mens*. Frans Ruiter and Wilbert Smulders, *Literatuur en moderniteit in Nederland 1840–1990*, Amsterdam, De Arbeiderspers, investigate modernity in the literature of the last 150 years.

Ton Anbeek, *Het donkere hart. Romantische obsessies in de moderne Nederlandstalige literatuur*, Amsterdam U.P., 214 pp., considers romantic influences in modern Dutch, and Flemish, literature. His engaging discussion starts with the tricky issue of dating Romanticism, surveying major authors like Keats, Shelley, Byron, Coleridge, Wordsworth, Hugo, Lamartine, George Sand, and the young Goethe. Two case studies from modern Dutch and Flemish literature investigate the continuous travel of Slauerhoff and Jeroen Brouwers, their misogyny, existential alienation, wish for destruction, attitude to writing, love of innocence, and their exploration of the darker sadistic side. The next chapters focus on a number of sub-aspects of the Romantic spirit, with discussion of works by Rheinvis Feith, Multatuli, Adriaan van Dis, Gerard Walschap, Herman Teirlinck, Gerard Reve, Top Naeff, and others. Mirjam Meijer, *Mijn broer Ischa. Het verhaal van een joods gezin* (Kans katernen, 8), Amsterdam, De Kan, remembers the late Ischa Meijer and his childhood in the story of a Jewish family. Denise de Costa, *Anne Frank en Etty Hillesum. Spiritualiteit, schrijverschap, seksualiteit*, Universiteit Utrecht, Balans, 360 pp., is a doctoral dissertation offering a feminist reading of these two young Jewish writers, who both died in concentration camps. De Costa focuses on their spirituality, sexuality, and their status as writers. The author aims to change the nature of their interpretation and 'canonization' taking into account gender and ethnic identity, by way of a detailed analysis of their work. De Costa emphasizes the importance of a new look at both these authors, beyond their iconization, and favours a consideration of the specificity of their positions, regarding them as writers rather than only victims of the Shoah. Another work dealing with the Second World War is *De lage schaduw van vijftig jaar. Voorstellingen van de Tweede Wereldoorlog in literatuur en geschiedenis*, ed. Elrud Ibsch, Anja de Feijter, and Dick Schram (Literatuur in veelvoud, 9), Leuven–Apeldoorn, Garant, which focuses on representations of the war in literature and history. Writing by women features in the series *Schrijfsters over schrijfsters*, Amsterdam, Meulenhoff–Antwerp, Manteau, 1996-, an ongoing project by the Anna Bijns Foundation.

Hugo Claus's major multi-interpretational novel is analysed by Dina and Jean Weisgerber, *Claus' geheimschrift. Een handleiding bij het lezen van 'Het verdriet van België'*, Brussels, VUB Press, 1995, 132 pp. They offer only suggestions for reading this novel, stressing the reader, in the end, has to decide on an interpretation. Claus's novel is a complex book full of 'riddles', ambiguous allusions, polysemic language and references, as Claus's aim was to create a 'Babylonic confusion' in his description of Belgium. A symphonic, polyphonic novel which contains both experimentation and the literary tradition, *Het verdriet van België* is both a postmodern 'open' text, and a modernist text which offers a basic message attacking the lie and evil. René Marres, **Over de interpretatie van 'De donkere kamer van Damokles' van W. F. Hermans*, Leiden, Internationaal Forum voor Afrikaanse en Nederlandse Taal en Letteren, interprets Willem Frederik Hermans's war novel, while Jeroen Brouwers, **Het aardigste volk ter wereld. Willem Frederik Hermans in Brussel. Bijdrage aan zijn biografie*, Amsterdam, Atlas, is a partial biography, picturing the author's exile in Brussels. Koopman & Van Ommen, *Een ontmoeting met de Tovenaar. Over Willem Frederik Hermans in foto's en teksten* (De Prom bibliofiel, 33), Baarn, De Prom, 126 pp., is based on two public and private interviews with the author shortly before his death in 1995, combined with photographs of the occasion. The two authors print the correspondence preceding the interview, the impressions of the evening, interspersed with anecdotes from Hermans's life. Peter Henk Steenhuis, *Alles is altijd uit de bijbel. Schriftuurlijke verwijzingen in 'De ontdekking van de hemel'*, Amsterdam, De Bezige Bij, 1995, 91 pp., hunts for biblical references in Harry Mulisch's recent major novel. Written in an informal, chatty way, the book also deals with the formal composition of the text, where chapters are structures in relation to the structure of the Bible, including references to Genesis, Malachi, Matthew, and the Apocalypse. Mulisch repeats the mirror function of the Old and New Testament in his novel, to suggest that the human development of technology means the death of God, the end of language, emotionality and, with Auschwitz, Hiroshima and the discovery of DNA, the end of heaven. Similarly, Vincent de Haas, *De opgebroken straat. Een intertekstuele analyse van 'De komst van Joachim Stiller' in het licht van Lukas 24*, Zoetermeer, Boekencentrum, 264 pp., also a thesis from the theological faculty of the University of Tilburg, undertakes an intertextual analysis, looking for traces of Luke 24 in Hubert Lampo's novel. The first part of the book looks at both texts separately, using narratology. In the novel, the existence of two basic strands is noted, the apocalyptic strand and the epiphany, according to which all characters, as well as space and time, can be organized. Stiller is regarded as part of the tradition of literature on Jesus, using Ziolkowski's *Fictional Transfigurations of Jesus*, and the author calls for expanding the intertextual reading between the Bible and literature. Frans Berkelmans, *Aan het water. Over Het veerhuis, de tweede bundel van Ida Gerhardt* (Acanthus, 2), Egmond-Binnen, Abdij van Egmond,

133 pp., belongs to a series about the connection between art and spirituality. As the author of traditional nature poetry, Ida Gerhardt's poetry lacks a real study. The collection analysed here, her second, was always published together with the first, but in fact took her poetical evolution a step further. The overall structure highlights nature versus culture, a love for the Dutch landscape, and individual happiness, with the war poem as a cautioning counterpoint. Petra Veeger, *Manoeuvres. Proza uit de jaren vijftig en zestig: over Hella Haasse, Nel Noordzij, Aya Zikken, Andreas Burnier*, Delft, Eburon, 239 pp., analyses four female texts from the 1950s and 1960s, illustrating the second feminist wave in the Netherlands. In 1978, Sybren Polet identified a category of novels as 'counter prose', or 'experimental prose', but he mainly recognized male practitioners. Andreas Burnier, however, combines her experimentalism with thematic and stylistic innovation: her novel attacks social conventions, rejects the reader as consumer of literature, and adds female focalization. Since all these novels belong to the same period as the literary journal *Merlyn* (1962–66), close reading is used. But this technique is used more to gauge the effect of the novels on the reader, who is wrongfooted, manipulated into another perspective on the female text, into an eye-opener on the ideology. Thus, the reader is forced to come face to face with her or his method of reading. Hence this very interesting and useful analysis further opens up the literary history to the presence of female authors. *Groepsportret. Wie is wie in De tandeloze tijd van A. F. Th. van der Heijden*, ed. Jan Brands and Anthony Mertens, Amsterdam, Querido, 88 pp., catalogues the hundreds of characters in Van der Heijden's cycle of novels, *De tandeloze tijd*. The famous cartoonist Peter van Straaten contributed their imaginary portraits. The authors indicate how Van der Heijden has written all his novels according to a master plan, since detailed information appears in *De slag om de Blauwburg* which only finds its true meaning in later stories of *Onder het plaveisel*. Over 3,000 pages of text in fact maintain a thematic coherence, although each part of the novel can be read as a separate unit. The characters are alphabetically organized, with short descriptions of their function and the page references involved. The three main locations, Geldrop, Nijmegen and Amsterdam are presented with maps. The main character of the cycle is Albert Egberts and his life story, intensified in the novels, is here represented in all chronological detail. The whole book proves the enthusiasm of the authors for Van der Heijden's work which they compare to Proust's. Paul Sars, *Adriaan van Dis. De zandkastelen van je jeugd* (De school van de literatuur), Nijmegen, Sun–Leuven, Kritak, 149 pp., is intended for a wide audience, introducing both established and young authors. The volume devoted to the writer and broadcaster Adriaan van Dis traces

the 'sometimes difficult development towards writing'. Van Dis's youth is of major importance, as can be seen in his first short story *Nathan Sid* (1983), and his novel *Indische duinen* (1994). For the author, 'Adriaan van Dis *is* Nathan Sid', and his novels interlink reality and fiction. There is a full biography of Van Dis, who is seen as typical of his period, in his openness to other cultures, and his affinity with other societal writers like Ellen Ombre, Anil Ramdas, and Stephan Sanders. Finally, *Monika van Paemel, Armand van Assche, Janine de Rop, Gery Helderenberg, Omer de Dier* (Oostvlaamse literaire monografieën, 11), Ghent, Cultureel Jaarboek Provincie Oost-Vlaanderen, 224 pp., is part of a series highlighting the literary contributions from this province of East Flanders. The life and work of each author in turn is characterized by, respectively, Paul van Aken, Hugo Brems, Filip Rogiers, Rudolf van de Perre, and Frans van Campenhout.

III. DANISH STUDIES*

LANGUAGE

By Tom Lundskær-Nielsen, *Lecturer in Danish,*
Department of Scandinavian Studies, University College London

1. General

Retskrivningsordbogen, 2nd edn, Dansk Sprognævn–Aschehoug, 669 pp., is the first update of the influential 1986 edition. It includes information not only on the changes in spelling since then but also on the 'new comma'. Two other important publications by the same body are *Grammatisk talt. Anbefalede sproglige betegnelser,* ed. Henrik Galberg Jacobsen (Dansk Sprognævns skrifter, 24), Dansklærerforeningen, 60 pp., which contains an alphabetical list of recommended linguistic terms in Danish, and Henrik Galberg Jacobsen, *Sæt nyt komma. Regler, grammatik, genveje og øvelser* (Dansk Sprognævns skrifter, 25), Dansklærerforeningen, 79 pp., which is a complete guide (with exercises) to the use of the new comma. Henrik Galberg Jacobsen and Peder Skyum-Nielsen, *Dansk sprog. En grundbog,* Schønberg, 255 pp., is a valuable general introduction to Danish language with references at the end of each chapter, while Henrik Galberg Jacobsen and Peter Stray Jørgensen, *Politikens Basisbog om Dansk Sprogbrug,* Politiken, 135 pp., is a more elementary reference guide offering practical information on spelling, grammar, and the use of written Danish. Frans Gregersen et al., *Dansk sproglære,* Dansklærerforeningen, 376 pp., is a textbook covering a wide variety of topics in Danish language and with a glossary of linguistic terms. Søren Brandt, *Pas på sproget. En håndbog,* Amanda, 123 pp., offers detailed advice on a long list of problematic words and ends with a short survey section and some useful references. *Content, Expression and Structure. Studies in Danish Functional Grammar,* ed. Elisabeth Engberg-Pedersen et al., Amsterdam–Philadelphia, Benjamins, 510 pp., contains a number of studies of Danish from a functional perspective, as well as a few articles of a more general theoretical nature. Among the studies of, or involving, Danish are: P. Durst-Andersen and M. Herslund, 'The syntax of Danish verbs: Lexical and syntactic transitivity' (65–102); L. Schack Rasmussen and L. Falster Jakobsen, 'From lexical potential to syntactic realization: A Danish verb valency model' (103–57); P. Harder, L. Heltoft, and O. Nedergaard Thomsen, 'Danish directional

---

* The place of publication of books is Copenhagen unless otherwise indicated.

adverbs: Content syntax and complex predicates — a case for host and co-predicates' (159–98); L. Heltoft and L. Falster Jakobsen, 'Danish passives and subject positions as a mood system: A content analysis' (199–234); I. Baron, 'Information structure and the anatomy of the noun phrase: The expression of subject and object in Danish noun phrases' (235–59); E. Kristiansen, 'Topic continuity and prosody: An experimental study in Danish' (261–81); N. Davidsen-Nielsen, 'Discourse particles in Danish' (283–314); E. Spang-Hanssen and H. Rue, 'The functions of locative prepositions' (361–83); and K. Lund, 'Communicative function and language-specific structure in second language acquisition: A discussion of natural sequences of acquisition'. *RASK. Internationalt tidsskrift for sprog og kommunikation*, 4, Odense U.P., 130 pp., includes J. M. Dienhart, 'C-Models and negation in English, Danish and German' (65–91). *Form and Function in Language*, ed. Sharon Millar and Jacob Mey (RASK Supplement, 2), Odense U.P., 1995, 247 pp. *Hermes. Tidsskrift for Sprogforskning*, 16, 17, ed. Henning Bergenholtz et al., Det Erhvervssproglige Fakultet, Handelshøjskolen i Århus, 278, 292 pp. **NyS*, 21. *Nydanske studier & almen kommunikationsteori*, ed. Anne Holmen et al., Dansklærerforeningen, 115 pp., has among its articles E. Møller, 'Dialogiske genrer i den mundtlige diskurs', and U. Røyneland, 'Sproghandlingen som analyseenhed i samtaleforskningen'. **Tidsskrift for Sprogpsykologi*, 3.1–2, ed. Lars Henriksen and Marie Louise Quist, 100, 86 pp., focuses mainly on studies of reading strategies among different groups of people. *Glæden ved sproget*, Modersmål-Selskabet, C. A. Reitzel, 115 pp., includes J. Hoffmeyer, 'Max erobrer virkeligheden — i sproget'; P. Jespersen, 'Samtalens nødvendighed'; E. A. Nielsen, 'Hvad Gud har sammenføjet . . .', and K. Rifbjerg, 'Det rige sprog'.

2. HISTORY OF THE LANGUAGE, PHONOLOGY, MORPHOLOGY, LEXIS, SYNTAX, AND SEMANTICS

Allan Karker, *Politikens sproghistorie: udviklingslinjer før nudansk*, Politiken, 92 pp., is a separate, revised and extended version of the author's concise survey of Danish language history that appeared in previous editions of *Politikens Nudansk Ordbog*. N. Grønnum, 'Danish vowels — scratching the recent surface in a phonological experiment', *ALHa*, 28:5–63. E. Bojsen and E. Hansen, 'Tus og tusse', *Nyt fra Sprognævnet*, no.2:10–11. L. Brink, 'En af de eneste', *Mål & mæle*, 19.1:26–30. P. Jarvad, 'Kerneord og oplevelseskultur', *Nyt fra Sprognævnet*, no.1:1–9. H. Galberg Jacobsen, 'Hvor ofte er jævnligt?', *ib.*, no.2:11–12. I. L. Pedersen, 'Ærkekøbenhavnsk eller ravjysk? Pæredansk er det i hvert fald', *ib.*, 1–5. E. Hansen, 'Homeshopping', *ib.*, 6–8, and 'Dansk grammatik i skrift og tale', *Mål & mæle*, 19.1:11–15.

A. Karker, 'Tiørens fald', *Nyt fra Sprognævnet*, no. 1 : 13–15. Id., 'Akkusativ med infinitiv–tyve år efter', *ib.*, no. 3:1–8. *Sentence Analysis, Valency and the Concept of Adject*, ed. Niels Davidsen-Nielsen (Copenhagen Studies in Language, 19), Samfundslitteratur, 157 pp., includes L. Schøsler, 'Cheese and/or dessert' (15–49); O. Nedergaard Thomsen, 'Adjects and hierarchical semantic structure in Danish' (51–110); L. Heltoft, 'On the alleged universality of the adject' (111–26); and O. Togeby, 'The locative argument' (127–42). Lene Schøsler and Karen Van Durme, *The Odense Valency Dictionary: An Introduction* (Odense Working Papers in Language and Communication, 13), Odense Univ., 53 pp., is an introduction to an ongoing research programme that aims to provide a comprehensive valency analysis of verbs, nouns, and adjectives in Danish. As part of the same programme, two relevant articles appear in *Adjektivernes valens*, ed. Karen Van Durme (Odense Working Papers in Language and Communication, 12), Odense Univ., 85 pp.: L. Schøsler (assisted by J. Daugaard and K. Van Durme), 'Prædikativanalysen i dansk' (3–19), and P. S. Kjærsgaard, 'Danske participialer og valens' (49–84). L. Heltoft, 'Det danske nominals udtryks- og indholdssyntaks — et dependensanalytisk forsøg', *Ny forskning i grammatik*, ed. Michael Herslund (Fællespublikation, 3), Odense U.P., and by the same author, 'Grammatikalisering af semantiske roller i dansk', *Semantiske roller*, ed. Lone Schack Rasmussen (Odense Working Papers in Language and Communication, 10), Odense Univ., pp. 43–64. This volume also contains P. Widell, *Aspektuelle verbalklasser og semantiske roller — Den dobbelte aspektkalkule* (135–68). M. Paludan-Müller, 'Der faldt en dame', *IDUN*, Osaka, 12 : 149–58. O. Nedergaard Thomsen, 'Pronouns, word order, and prosody', *ALHa*, 28 : 131–38. S. Hedegård Nielsen, 'Komma — en hjælp eller plage?', *Mål & mæle*, 19.1 : 23–30. V. Sandersen, 'Om bløde pakker, bløde mænd og andet blødt', *Nyt fra Sprognævnet*, 4 : 10–15. The syntax and semantics of a whole word-class is found in Jette Lamberth Nielsen, *En syntaktisk og semantisk undersøgelse af præpositionen* (Odense Working Papers in Language and Communication, 9), Odense Univ., 1995, 90 pp.

3. DIALECTOLOGY, CONTRASTIVE LINGUISTICS, AND BILINGUALISM

Danske Folkemål, 38, C. A. Reitzel, 119 pp., contains several dialect studies: M. Bjerrum, '*nymæres, for-des-ene* og *på det jævnslette*. Tre sønderjyske udtryk', and 'Om sproget i Gerners Hesiodi Dage'; I. Ejskjær, 'Dialekternes alder', also K. M. Pedersen, 'Verbalsubstantiver på *-ende* i de danske dialekter' and 'Substantiver på *-fuld*'. Bent Jul Nielsen and Inge Lise Pedersen, **Studier i talesprogsvariation og* *sprogkontakt. Til Inger Ejskjær på halvfjerdsårsdagen den 20. maj 1996* (Institut for Dansk Dialektforskning, Universitets-Jubilæets danske Samfunds skrifter, 537), C. A. Reitzel, 351 pp., includes the following articles: F. Gregersen, 'The individual, the concept of *langue*, and the regiolect'; A. Gudiksen, 'Om rødblissede heste og sortstjernede køer. En studie i orddannelse'; T. Kristiansen, 'De talendes eget skøn: sproglige selvvurderinger blandt børn, unge og voksne på Næstved-egnen'; I. L. Pedersen, ' "Der kan jo være nogen der kan itte tåle det." Om hovedsætningsordstilling i bisætninger'; and J. Scheuer, 'Jobsam-tale mellem én jyde og adskillige københavnere'. T. Lundskær-Nielsen, 'Form and use of the Passive in Danish and English', *Proceedings of the Tenth Biennial Conference of the British Association of Scandinavian Studies*, University of Surrey, pp. 43–53. M. Stølen, 'The Folkehøjskolesang as site for contact between Danish and American languages and cultures', *The Origin and Development of Emigrant Languages*, ed. Hans Frede Nielsen and Lene Schøsler, pp. 157–67.

4. LEXICOGRAPHY, GRAMMARS, AND RHETORIC

Politiken has published several dictionaries on Danish language. *Politikens retskrivnings- og betydningsordbog*, ed. Marianne Højmark, 2nd edn, Politiken, 711 pp., has been substantially revised to take account of the latest changes in spelling. *Politikens Store Nye Nudansk Ordbog*, 2 vols, Politiken, 1394 pp., is a thorough revision of *Politikens Nudansk Ordbog*, without the section on language history (published separately, see p. 941 above) and without proper nouns and etymologies, concentrating instead on word meanings, synonyms, idioms, constructions, and spelling. *Politikens Store Fremmedordbog*, Politiken, 929 pp., is a comprehensive dictionary of foreign words in Danish, with a reversed index (one looks up the Danish word to find the foreign term). The entries offer brief semantic explanations and state the original language, but provide no etymology of the items. *Politikens Dansk Visuel Ordbog*, Politiken, 672 pp., has a number of headings, each with colour pictures and illustrations and matching words, plus an index. Two specialist dictionaries are Linda B. Smith, *Engelsk-dansk idiomordbog*, Paludan, 1995, 158 pp., and Helle Pals Frandsen, *Juridisk ordbog dansk-engelsk*, Gad, 207 pp. (the English-Danish version already exists). Explanatory articles are E. Hansen, 'Den nye retskrivningsordbog', *Nyt fra Sprognævnet*, no. 4: 1–5, and H. Galberg Jacobsen, 'Og andre ordbøger', *ib.*, 6–9. A Danish grammar aimed at foreign learners is provided by Barbara Fischer-Hansen and Ann Kledal, *Grammatikken: håndbog i dansk grammatik for udlændinge*, Special-pædagogisk forlag, Herning, 1994, 335 pp. Keld Gall Jørgensen, *Stilistik. Håndbog i tekstanalyse*, Gyldendal, 206 pp., is an introduction to linguistic and stylistic textual analysis and includes a list of common grammatical and stylistic terms. *Det nye korstog. Sproganalytiske vinkler på en sagprosatekst,* ed. Keld Gall Jørgensen and Uwe Geist, Roskilde U.P., is an anthology containing a number of linguistic and literary analyses of the same text from different perspectives. Finn Frandsen, *Medierne og sproget,* Aalborg U.P., 181 pp., contains a selection of articles on the relationship between language and the media. O. Togeby, 'Stiltræk', *SPRÅU. Sprogvidenskabelige arbejdspapirer fra Aarhus Universitet,* 3, Aarhus U.P.

LITERATURE

POSTPONED

IV. NORWEGIAN STUDIES*

LANGUAGE

By ARNE KRUSE, *Lecturer in Norwegian, Department of Scandinavian Studies,
University of Edinburgh*

1. GENERAL

A useful bibliographical work for Scandinavian linguists with an interest in German or for German scholars in the field of Scandinavian linguistics is Kurt Braunmüller, *Deutsch- Skandinavisch im Vergleich. Eine bibliographische Übersicht über linguistische und lexiographische Arbeiten (1945–1995)* (Studia Nordica, 4), Novus, 239 pp. Rolv Mikkel Blakar, *Språk er makt*, Pax Forlag, 238 pp., is a reprint of the now classic work from 1973, including some major additions. In a long introduction B. reflects on which parts of the text have become dated and which are still relevant. A new chapter sets the topic of 'language is power' into a more explicit framework of communication theory. In a separate chapter, H. E. Nafstad deals with how children from different sociocultural backgrounds will experience the school differently. A book on illiterate bilinguals in the classroom is A. Hvenekilde, V. Alver, E. Bergander, V. Lahaug, and K. Midttun, *Alfa og omega. Om alfabetiseringsundervisning for voksne fra språklige minoriteter*, Novus, 334 pp., based on a research project on illiterates from linguistic minorities in today's Norway. The authors discuss methods of teaching literacy to this group and point to possible ways forward. J. Svennevik, M. Sandvik, and W. Vagle, *Tilnærminger til tekst. Ny forskning fra pragmatikk, semiotikk og stilistikk*, Cappelen/LNU, 1995, 357 pp., covers analyses of style, conversation, text and argument, and is meant for students of Scandinavian and media at university level. F.-E. Vinje, *Ordet*, 4, 1995:22–27, writes critically and negatively about the state of the language used by journalists in the newspapers *Dagbladet* and *Aftenposten*. V. finds the language full of inconsistencies and uncertainties, lacking a sense of appropriate registers, and marred by fashionable expressions.

PERIODICALS AND JOURNALS. *Språk i Norden 1996*, ed. Ståle Løland, Jørgen Schack, Eivor Sommardahl, Kristján Árnason, Åsta Norheim, and Birgitta Lindgren, 240 pp., is the yearly issue published by the Nordic Language Secretariat and the Nordic language boards. The main topic of this volume is how fiction contributes to the

---

* The place of publication of books is Oslo unless otherwise indicated.

development of the language. There are contributions on this aspect of Norwegian by D. Gundersen (5–17) and K. Venås (59–72), D. F. Simonsen reflects upon the consequences for the Nordic languages now that Denmark, Finland and Sweden are members of the EU (126–36), and G. Wiggen discusses majority and minority languages in a Nordic perspective (137–74). *Nordlyd*, 23, 1995, ed. I. Broch, T. Bull, and T. Swan, Tromsø Univ. Working Papers on Language and Linguistics, prints the Proceedings of the 2nd Nordic Conference on Language and Gender, held in Tromsø 3–5 November 1994. Several articles are in English, otherwise there are summaries in English. An introductory article by the editors (51–61) sums up and comments on language and gender research in the Nordic countries, and informs us that 'both in Sweden and Denmark pragmatic research, discourse and conversation analysis have been more prominent than in Norway'. J. H. Junttila (113–34) discusses the relationship between gender, social networks and language choice in Finnish and American immigrant groups in Scandinavia, A. Krogstad (147–61) analyses how Norwegian politicians communicate in TV debates and finds that — in contrast to most studies — Norwegian female politicians have actually dominated such debates, T. L. Hoel (162–73) focuses on gender-related patterns of interaction in the high-school classroom and suggests that structured and rule-regulated interaction may contribute to changing the traditional male domination in the classroom, and T. Swan, 'Gender and language change: the case of Norwegian' (298–315), says that both men and women are on the way to becoming invisible in modern Norwegian, as gender markers in the language are becoming obsolete. In *MM*, no. 1, F. Hertzberg (95–102) discusses the possible pedagogical and psychological effects of the fact that many text books in Norwegian higher education are now in English.

2. HISTORY OF THE LANGUAGE AND TEXTUAL STUDIES

On the centenary of the death of Ivar Aasen we saw, in 1996, the 'Ivar Aasen year' with official support and many activities related to the work of Norway's possibly greatest and certainly most influential linguist. Naturally, there have been an exceptional number of publications on Aa. this year, including two most thorough biographies. Stephen Walton, *Ivar Aasens kropp*, Det Norske Samlaget, 864 pp., is an unorthodox biography in many ways as it is structured around Aa.'s body parts and presents unusual angles to Aa., e. g. placing Aa. in a European context and analysing his relationship to the cultural élite in Norway. W. is faithful to Aa.'s life and work, but critical of the myth of Aa. in its more nationalistic forms. Another big, but more conventional biography is Kjell Venås, *Då tida var fullkomen. Ivar Aasen*, Novus, 688 pp. Here we are told in a traditional, chronological manner about Aa.'s background and intellectual growth. Kjell Venås, *Livssoga åt Ivar Aasen*, Ivar-Aasen-året, 28 pp., is a brief biography of Aa.'s life and work with a useful list of important publications by and about him. Jostein Krokvik, **Ivar Aasen*, Norsk Bokreidingslag, Bergen, is a richly illustrated biography with the emphasis on Aa. as the social liberator and creator of a national language. In the series publishing the lesser-known works by Aa., the most recent volume is Jarle Bondevik, Oddvar Nes, and Terje Aarset, *Målsamlingar frå Bergens Stift av Ivar Aasen* (ser. A. Tekster, 2), Bergen, Norsk Bokreidingslag, 1995, 288 pp. *Språknytt*, 1, is an extended number wholly dedicated to Aa., and so is *Syn og Segn*, no. 1. Among the articles in the latter periodical are K. Venås (11–21) on how Aa., with a most radical cultural programme, as an individual was a true conservative; A. Apelseth (33–47) on the mistaken view of Aa. as part of the reactionary National Romantic movement, since his roots and work are much more influenced by the ideals of the Enlightenment; O. Monsson (22–32) follows this view and writes on how important 18th-c. linguistics was for Aa., more so than the early historic-comparative linguistic school which emerged in the early 19th c.; G. Øyehaug (48–54) represents the opposing, more traditional view and writes that Aa. was 'the first to practice comparative dialectology influenced by the comparative method that Rasmus Rask and others were using'. Two articles on Aa. in English are S. Walton, 'A feature of the post-modern politics of identity', *Norwegian Literature 1996* (*The Norseman*, Special Issue nos. 4–5:4–9), and A. Kruse, 'Ivar Aasen and Knud Knudsen — the centenary and the legacy', *Northern Studies*, 31:57–68. The fiction author Edvard Hoem writes about his relationship to Nynorsk in *Mitt tapre språk*, Samlaget, 95 pp., making the point that Nynorsk to him is not only a tool or medium but a key to the unconscious and to history. Jostein Krokvik, *Norskrøtt skriftmåls store fall*, Norsk Bokreidingslag, Bergen, 1995, 104 pp., points to reasons for the drop in support for the Nynorsk standard since World War II. K. blames eagerness to approach the Bokmål standard in official language planning, resulting in structural inconsistencies in the current Nynorsk standard.

A language issue much highlighted in the media has been the recommendation from the Norwegian Language Board (Norsk Språkråd) to Norwegianize the spelling of a number of foreign, mostly English, loan-words. Two long newspaper articles, arguing for two different points of view, are D. Gundersen in *Aftenposten*, 30 January, and A. Sandved, *ib.*, 31 January; G., a member of the Language Board, describes and defends the reform, and S., representing the linguistically conservative section, shows irritation at the Board's not leaving these matters to the so-called free development of the language. On the same topic are two articles in *Språklig samling*, 1, by E. Papazian, 'Æ — en stygg bokstav?' (5–7), and A. Torp, 'Hvorfor stinker æ-en?' (8–10), both questioning why, in this and former spelling reforms, the letter *æ* is hardly ever chosen to represent the corresponding English sound, mostly written *a*. J. Bjones, 'Språk-normering i den siste tiårsperioden', *Syn og Segn*, 1995, no. 1 : 43–50, examines decisions regarding the Nynorsk written standard made by the Norwegian Language Board within the last ten years and points to important questions the Board has omitted, like how to deal with the prefixes *an-* and *be-* and the suffixes *-heit* and *-else*. Lars Vikør and Helge Omdal, *Språknormer i Norge. Normeringsproblematikk i bokmål og nynorsk*, Landslaget for norskundervisning, 187 pp., is an attempt both to inform about what is allowed within the written standards of Nynorsk and Bokmål and to raise questions about the justifications for the wide variety of spelling alternatives in Norwegian. An introductory chapter presents the different principles behind language planning, two chapters each deal with Nynorsk and Bokmål, and a final chapter argues that the language-user should be brought more into consideration in future discussions about a 'wide' or a 'narrow' norm.

Studies in the Development of Linguistics in Denmark, Finland, Iceland, Norway and Sweden, ed. Carol Henriksen et al., Novus, 378 pp., is the result of a conference on Nordic linguistics in Oslo in 1994, where the aim was to fill gaps in our knowledge of the history of linguistics in the Nordic countries. Some of the articles are in English. Among the contributions we find E. H. Jahr, 'Nynorsk språkforskning: en historisk oversikt' (84–101); A. R. Linn: 'The creation of Norwegian and the creation of its creator. Stylistic features in works by and about Ivar Aasen' (150–74); and B. Mæhlum, 'Norsk og nordisk sosiolingvistikk: en historisk oversikt' (175–224). In *Language Contact across the North Atlantic*, ed. P. Sture Ureland and I. Clarkson (LA, 359), 552 pp., B. Mæhlum (313–32) gives theoretical perspectives on the dialect strategies of children on Spitsbergen, A. Kruse (255–68) classifies Scandinavian-American place-names, P. Hallaråker (269–83) discusses the position of Nynorsk in the Norwegian-American press, and A. Hjelde has two articles, the first on phonological changes in a Norwegian dialect in America (283–96) and the second on genders given to English nouns used in Norwegian–American (297–312). All articles are in English. H. Fix, *ABÄG*, 42, 1995 : 13–29, discusses word and syllable division in the *Gamalnorsk Homiliebok*. J. Haugan, 'Kva er norrønt språk', *Norsklæreren*, no. 4:43–47, is an attempt to define what is meant by 'norrøn' and 'Old Norse'. M. Schulte, *Akten* (Greifswald),

416–30, discusses the time-span of the development of the i-umlaut. In *ABÄG*, 46, W. Heitzmann (91–104) discusses the term *þrunginnþistill* in *Skírnismál*, and L. Motz (105–17) investigates the frame setting and the type of direct speech we find in certain Eddic poems and suggests that they arose within a performance of magical or religious significance. In *MM*, no. 1, O. Sandaaker (31–56) investigates the textual genesis of *Ágrip* and *Morkinskinna*, H. Fix (57–65) traces the use of the verbs *ríta, rita* and *skapa, skepja* in the Old Norse *Elucidarius* tradition, and C. Tolley (67–79) shows that Snorri's depiction of Óðinn in *Ynglinga Saga* is likely to have been influenced by the description of Lappish or Sami shamanism found in *Historia Norvegiae*.

3. RUNOLOGY

Ottar Grønvik, *Fra Vimose til Ødemotland. Nye studier over runeinnskrifter fra førkristen tid i Norden*, Norwegian U. P., 301 pp., deals with 20 runic inscriptions from Scandinavia and one from England (the Undley bracteate) from the period AD *c.* 200–600. Several 6th-c. inscriptions that have withstood previous attempts at interpretation are analysed by G. against the background of being written in a language in an earlier stage than previously thought. G. also shows that there are no inscriptions with randomly mixed language at various stages of development, but that they all respectively belong to one particular stage of language development. Sceptical about the theory that certain inscriptions prove that runes are used for magical purposes, G. sets out to show that many inscriptions are religious documents, giving us glimpses of pagan rites and burial cults. In *Samtiden*, 1995, no. 1, O. Grønvik (84–88) summarizes the debate that followed the controversial book by K. Aartun, *Runer i kulturhistorisk sammenheng* (see *YWMLS*, 57:940). G. proceeds to apply Aa.'s theory to two concrete examples of early runic stones, but finds no justification for it. In *MM*, no. 1, there is a detailed and negative review of Aa.'s book by K. F. Seim (107–18). J. Meijer, *ABÄG*, 41, 1995:29–36, writes about metathesis in Viking Age Runic inscriptions. T. Spurkland, 'Runer og skriftlighet i middelalderen', *Norskläreren*, no. 4:35–42, is an introduction to runes showing the parallel usage of runes and Latin letters for different purposes during the Middle Ages. Several Norwegian runic inscriptions are commented upon by Thomas Birkmann, 'Von Ågedal bis Malt: die skandinavischen Runeninschriften vom Ende des 5. bis Ende des 9. Jahrhunderts', *Reallexikon der germanischen Altertumskunde. Ergänzungsbände,*12, Berlin–NY, de Gruyter, 1995, 428 pp. H. Dyvik, *MM*, no. 1:3–21, opposes T. Spurkland's doctoral thesis on a phonographematical analysis of the runic material from Bryggen in Bergen, with a reply from S. (21–29).

Several Norwegian runic inscriptions are commented upon in Enver A. Makaev, *The Language of the Oldest Runic Inscriptions. A Linguistic and Historical-Phonological Analysis* (Filologisk-filosofiska serien, 21), Stockholm, Kungliga Vitterhets och Antikvitets Akademien, Stockholm, 137 pp.

4. DIALECTOLOGY

Einar Lundeby, *Østfoldmål*, Østfold mållag, 1995, 104 pp., is a popular introduction to the dialect of the county of Østfold. An introductory chapter discusses the common view that this dialect is 'ugly', there is a presentation of the phonology and the morphology, and finally L. gives several transcribed samples of the dialect. In an exceptionally detailed review, J. Øverby, *Talatrosten*, Univ. of Oslo, Målførearkivet, 1995, pp. 36–93, points to a number of errors and weak points in the book, while R. V. Fjeld, *ib.*, 9–22, presents the dialect of Aremark in Østfold, and A. Dalen, *ib.*, 33–36, points to French loan-words in the dialect of Trøndelag. Njål Vere, *Listamålet.* III. *Grammatikk, ordbok, stadnamn og folkeminne*, own publication, 1995, 528 pp. (Vol. I came out in 1992, and vol. II in 1994.) The massive monograph on the dialect of Lista, the southernmost tip of Norway, is completed with this volume, including not only a grammar and a dictionary, but also thousands of place-names as well as folklore from the area. Egil Pettersen, *Ka e' tiss?*, Alma Mater, is a popular history of the dialect of Bergen, from the earliest writers who used it up the present day. *Nordnorske dialektar*, ed. Ernst Håkon Jahr and Olav Skare, Novus, 260 pp., attempts to make available the most important information written about dialects in the north of Norway. In the first part of the book, J. and S. give an overview of the dialects in question including maps and commented dialect samples. The second half of the book is a collection of previously published material on dialectology in Northern Norway, both articles outlining common features and differences as well as works focusing on more specialized topics. A special edition of *Nordica Bergensia*, 6, deals with syntactic variation within Scandinavian dialects. A theoretical contribution by K. K. Christensen (15–23) shows how Chomskyan grammar can be applied in dialect syntax studies; an empirical investigation into the wide variation in the Scandinavian languages when it comes to the syntax of the nominal phrase is done by L.-O. Delsing (24–74); H. Sandøy (90–102) shows that there is a semantic difference in the use of the indefinite pronoun *somme* between East and West Norwegian; L. Hellan (103–12) discusses the position of the reduced forms of personal pronouns (clitics) in the Trønder dialect; E. Mørck (113–38) shows how dialectal practice sometimes breaks away from the standard position of the attributes *til* and *nok* within hypotagma; T. Fiva (139–55) and H. Nilsen (156–65) both deal with interrogative sentences in North Norwegian dialects; and Ø. A. Vangsnes (166–88) presents a feature located to the county of Rogaland where it is usual to start a question with *om*. In *Svenska landsmål och svenskt folkliv 1995*, ed. Maj Reinhammar, Uppsala Univ., Institute of Dialect and Folklore Research, 472 pp., M. Barnes (29–36) gives a critical survey (in English) of previous attempts to identify the language of the 15 Scandinavian-language documents from Orkney and Shetland, with presentation and discussion of each document, A. Bjørkum (45–52) samples the vocabulary from the Hardanger area in the poetry of Olav H. Hauge, and A. Dalen (53–59) discusses the word *kru* or *kruvi* in the dialect of Nord-Trøndelag, which D. identifies as the Old Irish *cró* 'enclosure for livestock', otherwise found in Iceland and the Faroes.

5. ONOMASTICS

T. Ness, *Navn i fjorden. Oslo, Asker, Bærum*, Orion, 143 pp., takes the reader on a journey along the inner part of the Oslo Fjord and explains the background to the names of the locations as he meets them. The book includes a reprint of the relevant three chapters of G. Indrebø, *Stadnamn fraa Oslofjorden* (1929), still the standard work on place-names from the area. Peter Hallaråker, *Stadnamn i Møre og Romsdal. Innsamling, teori, metode og praksis* (Forskingsrapport, 8), Høgskulen i Volda/Møreforsking Volda, 1995, 424 pp., is a final report on the ten-year project to collect all place-names possible in the county of Møre and Romsdal. The book will be valuable not only to those interested in the specific project, but to those with an affinity to place-name studies in general. In the ten chapters we are first given a summary of the background and the financial and practical aspects of the project itself, then more general discussions about the need for place-names, a theoretical analysis of names and appellatives and, finally, guidelines on how to normalize place-names in writing. O. Stemshaug writes the Norwegian contribution, 'Name studies in Norway' (32–37), in the important handbook *Namenforschung. Ein internationales Handbuch zur Onomastik*, ed. E. Eichler et al., Berlin–NY, de Gruyter, 1995, pp. 32–39, and informs about the history of onomastics in Norway, archives, publications, and the legislation concerning names. To mark the 75th anniversary of the Norwegian Name Archive, there is an extended annual report from the Sector for Name Research, Univ. of Oslo, *Norsk stadnamnarkiv 75 år, 1921–1996, Avdeling for namnegransking. Årsmelding 1995*, ed. Tom Schmidt, Dept. of Scandinavian and Literary Studies, Univ. of Oslo,

235 pp. Among the contributors are T. Andersson (19–25) on the lake-name *Losna*, with the meaning 'the light one'; E. J. Ellingsve (53–60) on the treatment of place-names as a category in Norwegian linguistics; Å. K. Hansen (61–70) on how national feelings have influenced the debate on whether the Scandinavian names in Normandy are of Danish or Norwegian origin; M. Harson (71–84) on an unprinted manuscript after Oluf Rygh; A.-K. Pedersen (95–112) on the names and languages in multilingual areas in Finnmark; A. Svanevik (143–50) on the river-name *Glåma*; G. Nedrelid (151–63) on surnames in Norway and in Scandinavia; T. Schmidt (163–81) on foreign female names in Aslak Bolt's cadastre; and finally a detailed and interesting account by B. Helleland on the activities of the 75-year-old Norsk stadnamnakiv.

In *Namn og nemne*, 12, 1995, H. Pálsson (7–22) traces several of the possible place-names in *Vǫluspá* back to northern Norway and claims that the seer herself might be of Sami decent; M. L. Aljoksjina (23–34) examines to what degree place-names have grammatical genders; E. Ellingsve (35–50) spotlights Oluf Rygh's hypothesis that the specific element in farm-names with the generic *-stad* is likely to be a personal name and shows that many of his arguments are circular; A. Landøy (51–69) examines trends in personal names in the 19th c.; O. Stemshaug (71–79) shows that the personal name *Vinjar* is not connected with the same family name; and A. Karbø and K. Kruken (89–112) give a preliminary report on horse names from a project on Norwegian domestic animals. In *Namn og nemne*, 13, 1996, V. Haslum (7–34) sets out to define the term place-name; P. Hallaråker (35–51) discusses definite versus indefinite forms of place-names; B. Helleland (53–66) interprets the mountain names *Onen* and *Vassfjøro*; J. Sandnes (67–71) and E. Ellingsve (71–74) continue the debate on Oluf Rygh's treatment of the *stad-* names; and A. Karbø and K. Kruken (75–95) present names of sheep, pigs, dogs, and foxes. B. Helleland, *Akten* (Greifswald), 137–51, writes on place-names as evidence of social and religious life in pre-Christian Norway. H. Stangnes, *Ottar*, Tromsø Museum, 4, 1995: 28–37, laments how place-names disappear. M. Harsson, *Apollon*, Univ. of Oslo, 3:16–19, writes on the relationship between farm names and family names. T. Schmidt, *Historisk tidsskrift*, 74, 1995:218–39, is critical of what he finds is the somewhat careless way some historians and archaeologists use place-names to draw conclusions, and J. Sandnes, *ib.*, 465–67, discusses the palaeography and the localization of the Old Norse name *Langaskip-reiða*. N. Nystu, *MM*, no. 1:103–05, suggests that the names *Skjellåa*, *Skjellbreia*, and *Skjøla* refer to old boundaries. T. Larsen, *Språklig samling*, 3, 1995 (repr. *Nytt om namn*, 23:29–37), summarizes how the act on place-names has functioned in practice since it was passed by

Parliament in 1991. The first ever compilation of articles on Sami names has appeared, *Sámi báikenamat virggálas geavahusas Ruota, Suoma ja Norgga bealde*, Sami College–Nordic Sami Institute–Centre for Sami Studies at the Univ. of Tromsø, 1995 ('Official use of Sami place-names in Sweden, Finland and Norway'), with summaries in English and Russian. Also noted is a compilation of articles by British scholars mostly on Norse names, *Scandinavian Settlement in Northern Britain*, ed. Barbara E. Crawford, London–NY, Leicester U.P., 1995, 248 pp. H. Pálsson, 'Aspects of Norse place names in the Western Isles', *Northern Studies*, Edinburgh, 31:7–24, warns about onomastic pitfalls and sketches a possible methodological approach to Gaelic place-names of Norse origin.

An important event in the field of personal names is the publication of the new edition of *Norsk personnamnleksikon*, ed. Kristoffer Kruken, Det Norske Samlaget, 1995, 388 pp. Compared to the first edition (1981) this has twice the number of name entries, *c.* 6,500. There are also more and updated name statistics from the medieval period to the present and a useful index. A report of a symposium on family names is *Slektsnamn i Norden. Rapport frå NORNAs tjueførste symposium i Oslo 17.-20. september 1992*, ed. Kristoffer Kruken (NORNA-rapporter, 58), Uppsala, 1995, 233 pp., where G. Nedrelid (167–83) uses the census of 1801 to confirm the general suspicion that the few family names that existed in Norway at this early stage were mostly of Danish or German origin, but also to find that the practice of using Norwegian farm names as family names may go back to the first half of the 18th c.; A. Weel (185–99) writes about family names in Fredrikstad in the 19th c. and shows how the use of family names belonged to the upper classes while the use of patronymics was the norm in the lower social groups; A. Svanevik (213–20) discusses the Danish-German-influenced family names based on Norwegian farm names of the type *Wold* from the farm *Voll*. In a theoretical contribution, K. Bakken (37–51) points to features characteristic of all patronymics; T. Schoonheim (23–35) compares personal last names in the Netherlands and in Norway in the 13th c.; and P. Furuberg (129–39) discusses Finnish personal names from the Norwegian Finnskog. *Gudlabadne*, Odda, Jondal, Odda and Ullensvang mållag, 133 pp., is an attempt to register and encourage the use of local personal names from the Hardanger area. B. Maylath, *Names*, 44:41–58, outlines problems and possible solutions to the use of personal names in translations of the works of Ibsen. M. finds that while some names may be translated directly, e.g. *Straamand* > *Strawman*, and other names may be given a metaphorical translation, e.g. *Dr. Rank* > *Dr Goodman*, some names ought not to be translated, e.g. *Brand* and *Eyolf*.

6. SEMANTICS, MORPHOLOGY, SYNTAX

J. T. Faarlund, S. Lie, and K. I. Vannebo, *Norsk referansegrammatikk*, Norwegian U.P., is the most extensive grammar ever published on the Norwegian language. Covering both Bokmål and Nynorsk it is meant to be a handbook as well as a comprehensive description of the language. This is likely to be a standard grammar for Norwegian for years to come. J. T. Faarlund, *Norsk morfologi. Bøyingssystemet i nynorsk og bokmål*, Det Norske Samlaget, 1995, 134 pp., is the second edition of the book that first appeared in 1988. Some major changes have been made following the method used in the previously mentioned work. As a result, the former separate chapter on adverbs has now disappeared. *Lingvistisk analyse av avvikende språk* (Working Papers in Applied Linguistics, 1), Dept of Linguistics, Univ. of Oslo, 1995, 73 pp., is a compilation of six articles all written by speech therapists on various forms of linguistic deviation, most of them phonological deviation in children. Anne Cathrine Wollebæk, *Oversettelse av similer — akseptabel transkodering?* (Working Papers in Applied Linguistics, 2), Dept of Linguistics, Univ. of Oslo, 178 pp., is in two parts, the first on the theory and methodology of translation studies where W. concludes that the discipline is still in a pre-scientific stage, and the second a practical analysis of the translation of similies in an English novel translated into Norwegian. The topic on translating so-called false friends between Norwegian and German is studied by G. Lietz, *Akten* (Greifswald), 356–67. *Papers from the XVth Scandinavian Conference of Linguistics*, ed. I. Moen, H. G. Simonsen, and H. Lødrup, Dept of Linguistics, Univ. of Oslo, 1995, 543 pp., have the following contributions related to Norwegian: B. B. Brynildsen, 'Event structure as a factor in interpreting and translating free ING-adjuncts' (67–78); R. T. Endresen, 'The *og/å* polysemi in spoken Norwegian' (113–22); R. T. Enerstvedt and A. M. Vonen, 'Bilingualism and literacy in Norwegian deaf children' (123–28); H.-O. Enger (129–35) on questions starting with *om* — a syntactic innovation in the dialect of Stavanger; T. Fretheim, 'Pragmatic implications of "not until" in Norwegian' (169–80); L. Joosten, 'Variation in the syntactic status of infinitive markers' (231–42); A. Livanova, 'Semantic classification of morphological gradators with adjectives in Norwegian' (316–25); T. Midtgård, 'Yes/no interrogatives as wh-questions: the syntax and intonation of a Norwegian grammatical construction' (316–25); and T. A. Åfarli, 'A unified analysis of relative clause formation in Old Norse' (533–43). K. E. Kristoffersen, *ANF*, 110, 1995:85–130, summarizes 19th-c. research on Old Norse syntax. H. O. Enger, *Norsklæraren*, 5:36–43, asks the seemingly banal question 'How many genders are there in Norwegian?', and gives some unexpected answers, e.g. that most forms of modern Norwegian lack gender distinctions in the plural. E.'s point is that the number of genders is dependent upon the criteria we use to define gender. R. Veland, *MM*, no. 1:81–94, discusses the use of adjectives for nationality, especially the use of *norvégien* in French.

7. Lexicography

J. H. Rosbach, *Ord i flukt*, Pax Forlag, 161 pp., is another collection from R. of small articles on words following certain topics. On each word R. outlines old and new use, etymology, proverbs, etc. S. Evensberget and D. Gundersen, *Bevingede ord*, Kunnskapsforlaget, 1995, 1013 pp., lists *c.* 13,000 literary quotations, proverbs, etc. A new type of dictionary is Gero Lietz, *Norsk-tysk ordbok over lumske likheter*, Norwegian U.P., 196 pp., where the focus is on the many 'false friends' between Norwegian and German. K. Hofstad, S. Løland, and P. Scott, **Norsk dataordbok*, Norwegian U.P., lists 4,400 computer terms in Norwegian and English. The (lack of) standardization of computer terminology between the Scandinavian languages is the topic of P. Weiss, *Akten* (Greiswald), 447–57. Note should be taken of the launch in the year under review of a new journal, *Nordic Yearbook of Library, Information and Documentation Research*, Novus.

LITERATURE SINCE THE REFORMATION

By ØYSTEIN ROTTEM, *Copenhagen*

1. GENERAL

As a field of academic research children's literature has aroused a growing interest during the last ten years. In *Norsk barnelitteratur — lek på alvor. Glimt gjennom hundre år*, LNU/Cappelen, 202 pp., one of the leading experts, Harald Bache-Wiig, presents a sample of his studies. A chosen number of classical texts is closely read with the stress laid on their historical context. Amongst the writers presented are Rasmus Løland, Zinken Hopp, and Tormod Haugen. Rolf Romøren, 'Barnelitteratur, modernitet, modernisme. Perspektiv og forskningsoversikt', *NLÅ*, 1995:211–30. The cultural radicalism of the inter-war years was one of the main interests of the recently departed Leif Longum, *Å krysse sine spor. Artikler, essays, innlegg 1957–1995*, Bergen, Nordisk institutt, Universitetet i Bergen, 1995, 222 pp., was published in connection with his retirement as a university teacher in 1995. The collection includes articles on Johan Borgen, Jens Bjørneboe, and Paal Brekke. The publication of *Virkelighetens forvaltere. Norsk Sakprosa. Første bok*, ed. E. B. Johnsen, Universitetsforlaget, 1995, 262 pp., and *Forbildets forbilder. Norsk Sakprosa. Andre bok, ib.*, 266 pp., is part of a comprehensive research programme whose aim is to present the history of Norwegian faction. The two volumes at hand include well-written articles on a wide range of matters, such as biographies, medical journals, textbooks, encyclopaedias, and cookery books. Nils J. Ringdal and Terje H. Larsen, *Kardinaler og kremmere. Norske forleggere gjennom hundre år*, Den norske Forleggerforening, 1995, 367 pp. *Holdepunkter. En litteraturhistorisk kildesamling*, ed. L. Longum and S. Aa. Aarnes, LNU/Cappelen, 340 pp. *Samtale med et svin. En antologi om litteraturkritikk*, ed. S. Lie and L. Nysted, Cappelen, 1995, 205 pp. *Det glatte lag. Tanker om litteraturkritikk*, Aschehoug, 223 pp. Geir Hjorthol, *Populærlitteratur. Ideologi og forteljing*, Samlaget, 1995, 286 pp., is a most useful introductory book to the study of popular literature, with models, methods, and theories illustrated in analyses of works by Gunnar Staalesen, Jon Michelet, and others. *Under lupen. Essays om kriminallitteratur*, ed. A. Elgúren and A. Engelstad, LNU/Cappelen, 1995, 316 pp. Bjørn Hemmer, *Sørlandet og litteraturen*, Kristiansand, Høyskoleforlaget, 1995, 371 pp., is a fine piece of popular scholarship with careful presentations of writers from the southern part of Norway, such as Vilhelm Krag, Engvald Bakkan, and Øystein Lønn. Øystein Rottem, *Lyst-Lesninger. Åtte essays om kjønn og identitet i norsk litteratur*, LNU/Cappelen, 347 pp., is mainly devoted to the study of the historical changes of men's gender roles, illustrated through studies of writers such as H. Ibsen, K. Hamsun, S. Hoel, A. Mykle, F. Alnæs, E. Gjelsvik, and K. Faldbakken.

2. THE SIXTEENTH TO NINETEENTH CENTURIES

GENERAL

Jørgen Sejersted, 'Barokken og norsk kanon', *Nordica Bergensia*, 1995, no. 6:108–45. Jostein Fet, *Lesande bønder. Litterær kultur i norske allmuges-amfunn før 1840*, Universitetsforlaget, 1995, 442 pp.

INDIVIDUAL AUTHORS

DASS, P. Asle K. Brovoll, *Fra Helgelands skjær til Namdalens læhn. Petter Dass og Nærøy*, Alstadhaug, Bruvoll, 1995, 38 pp. ENGELBRETSDATTER, D. Inger Vederhus, ' "Saa foor han Melancholisk frem." Sentrale biletkrinsar i salmar av Dorothe Engelbretsdatter', *Kirke og Kultur*, 1995:45–56. Vigdis B. Øystese, ' "Sidste ære-Mindis smertelig Dict." Dorothe Engelbretsdatters minnedikt over ektemannen', *Nordica Bergensia*, no. 10:47–71. HOLBERG, L. Peter Christensen, *Lys og mørke. Ludvig Holberg — en moderne klassiker*, Århus U. P., 1995, 221 pp. Ingeborg Mjør, 'Heltar i tid og rom. Narrativ struktur i to romanar frå 1700-talet', *Nordica Bergensia*, 1995, no. 6:210–33. *Ludvig Holberg. A Study in Influence and Reception*, ed. S. H. Rossel, Amsterdam, Rodopi, 1994, 238 pp. WESSEL, J. H. Alvhild Dvergsdal, 'Nedrighet og øvrighet i *Kierlighed uden Strømper*. Wessels diktning i karnevalistisk belysning', *Edda*:3–18.

3. THE NINETEENTH CENTURY

GENERAL

Kare Glette, *Høvesdikting (leilighetsdikting) i Tønsberg 1840–1890. Ein studie i regional litteratur*, Novus, 1995, 151 pp. Henning Howlid Wærp, 'Romantikkens ruiner — og begrepet det pittoreske. Med eksempler fra J. S. Welhaven, Bernhard Herre, Mauritz Hansen', *Edda*, 1995:176–81. Sivert Ødegaard, 'Naturalismens estetikk i norsk litteraturhistoriografi', *NLÅ*:83–100.

INDIVIDUAL AUTHORS

BJØRNSON, B. Jan Olav Gatland, 'Enn om vi kledde fjellet — Bjørnson og mannleg vennskap', *Edda*, 1995:24–39. Asbjørn Aarnes, 'Bjørnstjerne Bjørnson og Victor Hugo', *Edda*:212–19.

COLLETT, C. Mainly based on private letters and diary notes, Torill Steinfeld's picture of the young C. in *Et kvinnehjertes historie. Den unge Camilla Collett*, Gyldendal, 458 pp., is both vivid, well-documented, and brilliantly presented. At the same time it is a profound study of the social situation of the intellectual woman at that time. T. Steinfeld, 'Camilla Collett og Henrik Jæger: et bidrag til norsk kanonhistorie', *Edda*:133–50.

GARBORG, A. Åsfrid Svensen, '"Alt dult i myrkre vankar." Haugtussa som fantastisk litteratur', *NLÅ*, 1995:76–87. Anne-Lisa Amadou, 'Arme Jørgen: Arne Garborg som oversetter av Molière', *Edda*:220–22.

HAMSUN, K. Several aspects of H.'s writing are treated in *Hamsun i Paris. 8 foredrag fra Hamsun-dagene i Paris 1994*, ed. R. Boyer and N. M. Knutsen, Hamarøy, Hamsun-Selskapet, 1995, 145 pp. Of special interest are T. Kunnas's article on the similarities between H. and Nietzsche, O. Gouchet's comparative study of the interrelationship between H.'s *Børn av Tiden* and Thomas Mann's *Buddenbrooks*, and H. V. Holm's examination of H. as a 'polyphone' writer. Included are also articles on H. and Paris (by A. Kittang), H.'s poetry (by R. Boyer), and fantastic elements in H.'s writing (by B. O. Henriod). The great diversity of topics treated at the first international Hamsun conference at the University of Tromsø in 1995 reflects the actual state of Hamsun scholarship as a broad and lively one. Thus, the contributions in *Hamsun i Tromsø. 11 foredrag fra Hamsunkonferansen i Tromsø 1995*, ed. N. M. Knutsen, Hamarøy, Hamsun-Selskapet, 218 pp., includes reports on the position of H. in Germany (H. Uecker), France (R. Boyer), Russia (E. Pankratova), and Romania (S. T. Baciu). H. F. Dahl, 'Hamsun, Quisling og det norske rettsoppgjøret', and L. F. Larsen, '*Lars Oftedal* (1889) — en politisk pamflett?', deal with the 'old' theme of Hamsun and politics in a new and stimulating way. Gender roles and the picture of women in H.'s writing are examined by J. Lorentzen, 'Den mannlige hysteriker. Nagel og Knut Hamsuns Mysterier', and K. Riishede, 'Drømmen om kjærligheden — kvindebilledet hos Knut Hamsun'. A. Kittang and E. Arntzen designate respectively the modernity and the mythical aspects of H.'s aesthetics. The influence of Schopenhauer is traced by Ø. Rottem, and P. Aaslestad and S. Gimnes analyse H.'s short stories and *På gjengrodde stier*. Tore Stuberg, *Hamsun, Hitler og pressen. Knut Hamsun i norsk offentlighet 1945–1955*, Leseselskapet, 1995, 139 pp. Bo Eldbrønd-Bek, 'Hamsun i Amerika. En samtale med Harald S. Næss', *NLÅ*, 1995:49–75. Ø. Rottem, '"Humbug det også, bare humbug …"' — Nietzsche, Hamsun og Den Store Illusjon', *Bogens Verden*, 1995:126–29. Thomas Seiler, 'Knut Hamsuns *Pan* als patriarchaler Schöpfer-Mythos', *Edda*, 1995:267–77. Hans Peter Thøgersen,

'Knut Hamsun og Johannes V. Jensen — det nye menneske — ', *Dansk udsyn*, 1995, 74:141–62. Included in Sven Willner, *Vandring i labyrinter och andre essäer*, Helsingfors, Söderström, 1995, 233 pp., is a chapter on Hamsun and Finland. Akos Doma, **Die andere Moderne*. *Knut Hamsun, D. H. Lawrence und die lebensphilosophische Strömung des literarischen Modernismus* (AKML, 396), 1995, 284 pp. The two new volumes of H.'s letters, *Knut Hamsuns brev*. II. *1896–1907*, 1995. III. *1908–1914*, ed. Harald S. Næss, Gyldendal, 375, 563 pp., are as admirably edited as the first. Planned as a work in six volumes it will, when finished, be of inestimable significance for further studies in H.'s life and work. Ø. Rottem, *Hamsuns liv i bilder*, Gyldendal, 255 pp. Arne Tuvmyr, *Knut Hamsun og hans kors*, Kristiansand, Norgesforlaget, 532 pp. Dolores Buttry, 'Mellomakt: Knut Hamsuns "På Bankerne" mellom *Sult* og *Mysterier*', *NLÅ*:29–38. Erik Bjerck Hagen, 'Truth and ethics in Hamsun's *Mysteries*', *Edda*:307–16.

IBSEN, H. Mogens Pahuus, *Selvutfoldelse og selvhengivelse. Livssynet hos Henrik Ibsen og Henrik Pontoppidan*, Ålborg U. P., 1995. *Ibsen Research Papers/Yibusheng yan jiu lun wen ji*, ed. Meng Shengde and A. Sæther, Beijing, Chinese Literature Press, 1995, 456 pp., contains papers presented at 'The first Ibsen Works Seminar held in Beijing on May 8–9, 1995'. Among the contributors are K. Bang-Hansen, E. Eide, Gao Zhongfu, B. Hemmer, Wang Ning, Wang Zhonxiang, and A. Aarseth. Thomas F. Van Laan, 'Ibsen and Shakespeare', *ScSt*, 67, 1995:287–305. Kirsti Boger, 'Morgenstjernen og menneskets herskermakt. En analyse av Lucifer-/Vensusmotivet i Henrik Ibsens *Catalina*', *Edda*, 1995:111–26. Ole John Askedal, 'Ludwig Tiecks *Franz Sternbalds Wanderungen*, *Bonaventuras Nachtwachen* og Henrik Ibsens *Peer Gynt*', *Ergo*, 1995:28–56. Ørnulf Hodne, 'Henrik Ibsens bruk av folketradisjon i *Peer Gynt*', *Norskrift*, 86, 1995:35–60. Thore Roksvold, 'Spenning i *En Folkefiende*', *ib.*, 85, 1995:47–63. Egil A. Wyller, '*Når vi døde vågner*. Ibsens kerubiske epilog', *Nytt norsk tidsskrift*, 1995:146–61. Sara Jan, 'William Archer's translations of Ibsen, 1889–1908', *Scandinavica*, 34, 1995:5–36. Hans Aaraas, *Peer Gynt. En drøm om en drømmer og hans drøm*, Gyldendal, 1995, 160 pp. Erik M. Christensen, 'Henrik Ibsen som Profet 1871', *Edda*:27–32. Erik Østerud, 'Tableau and Thanatos in Henrik Ibsen's *Gengangere*', *ScSt*, 68:473–89. Anne-Marie V. Stanton-Ife, 'A woman's place/female space in Ibsen's *Fruen fra havet*', *Scandinavica*, 35:221–36. Robert Ferguson, *Henrik Ibsen. Mellom evne og higen*, Gyldendal, 476 pp., is a biography which gives a subjective and rather negative portrait of I. as a man and artist. Well-written as it is, it is worthwhile reading as a personal and popular introduction. The articles in Vigdis Ystad, '-*livets endeløse gåde.' Ibsens dikt og drama*, Aschehoug, deal with many sides of I.'s work in a stimulating but rather traditional way.

KIELLAND, A. Tor Obrestad, *Sannhetens pris. Alexander Kielland. En beretning*, Cappelen, 477 pp., is the most comprehensive K. biography ever written, presents much new information about the personal life of the writer, and thus gives the reader new insights into his work. Hans H. Skei, 'Kiellands novelletter og noveller i dag', *Edda*:297–306.

OBSTFELDER, S. Martin Nag, *Sigbjørn Obstfelder. Uro og skaperkraft*, Solum, 328 pp. Margreta Tveisme, 'Ord og eld. Ei lesing av Sigbjørn Obstfelders "Ene"', *Nordica Bergensia*, no. 10:72–93.

SKRAM, A. Sivert Ødegaard, 'Amalie Skram naturalist eller romantiker? En punktanalyse av hennes debutroman *Constance Ring*', *Edda*, 1995:55–67. S. Ødegaard, 'Livsbehov og destruksjon som litterære tema. Et bidrag til forståelse av Amalie Skrams roman *Forraadt*', *Edda*:151–61. Åsfrid Hegdal, 'Mellom frihet og determinisme? Amalie Skrams Oline som naturalistisk karaktertype — en analyse av skikkelsens betydning i *Hellemyrsfolket*', *ib.*, 223–36. I. Engelstad, L. Køltzow, and G. Staalesen, *Amalie Skrams verden*, Gyldendal, 253 pp., is a richly illustrated and popular introduction to the writer.

WERGELAND, H. Alvhild Dvergsdal, '*Sujetter for Versemagere* (1841) av Henrik Wergeland. Utviklingstrekk i Wergelands seine lyrikk', *Syn og Segn*, 1995:258–73, 351–64. Jostein Greibrokk, '"Den hedeste Flamme i Nordmandens Indre ..." Forskyvning eller forvandling i Henrik Wergelands tankeunivers?', *Edda*:201–11. Georg Johannesen, *Den første Sommerfugl. Bidrag til Henrik Wergelands resepsjonshistorie. Til 151-årsdagen for hans død 12. juli 1845–1966*, LNU/Cappelen, 118 pp.

AASEN, I. Stepen J. Walton, 'Nokre drag ved Ivar Aasens ungdomsdikting', *NLÅ*:179–98. Magne Myhren, 'Ivar Aasen og ordtøket — fra granskingsemne til nydikta verseline', *ib.*, 199–229.

4. THE TWENTIETH CENTURY

GENERAL

A new edition of Cappelen's 1975 *Norges litteraturhistorie*, ed. E. Beyer, is planned to include three newly-written volumes by Ø. Rottem, covering the post-war years. The first volume, *Fra Brekke til Mehren*, Cappelen, 1995, 553 pp., brings the presentation up to 1965. *Nordisk kvindelitteraturhistorie*. III. *Vide verden 1900–1960*, ed. E. Møller Jensen, Rosinante, 608 pp. *Nazismen og norsk litteratur*, ed. B. Birkeland, A. Kittang, S. U. Larsen, and L. Longum, Universitetsforlaget, 1995, 468 pp., is a revised and enlarged edition of a most useful book from 1975. Hans H. Skei, *På litterære lekeplasser. Studier i moderne metafiksjonsdikning*, Universitetsforlaget, 1995, 192 pp. Øivind Danielsen,

Staten og den litterære republikk, Norges forskningsråd, 1995, 191 pp. Jahn Thon, *Tidsskriftets forståelsesformer — Profil og profilister 1959–89*, LNU/Cappelen, 252 pp., is a presentation of the history of the famous literary magazine *Profil*, written by one of its former editors. Among the Norwegian writers treated in *Modernismens kjønn*, ed. I. Iversen and A. B. Rønning, Pax, 292 pp., are H. Garborg (A. B. Rønning), Hamsun (J. Lorentzen), C. Sandel (J. Øverland), G. Hofmo (U. Langås), and K. Moe (D. von der Fehr). Norwegian writers treated in Gitte Mose, *Den endeløse historie — en undersøgelse af det fantastiske i udvalgte danske-svenske-norske romaner efter 1978*, Odense U.P., 208 pp., include J. Kjærstad, T. Å. Bringsværd, K. Fløgstad, and M. Osmundsen. Alf van der Hagen, *Dialoger. II. Åtte forfattersamtaler*, Oktober, 292 pp. Leif Longum, 'Frigjøringsprogram og ideologisk våpen. Psykoanalysen i 1930-årenes norske/nordiske offentlighet og litteratur', *Motskrift*, no. 1:57–68. Idar Stegane, 'Norsk lyrikk 1980–1995. Skisse til eit oversyn', *Nordica Bergensia*, no. 11:6–17. Sigurd Aa. Aarnes, 'Den norske litterære kanon i dag', *Nordica Bergensia*, 1995, no. 6:63–81. Asbjørn Aarseth, 'Litterær kanonisering i mediepluralismens århundre', *ib.*, 82–107.

INDIVIDUAL AUTHORS

ALNÆS, F.   Truls Gjefsen, *Finn Alnæs. Titan og sisyfos*, Aschehoug, 1995, 307 pp., is an excellent biography in which the relations between A.'s life and work are illuminated in an ideal way.

ANKER, N. R.   Bente G. Arentz-Hansen, 'To forteljarar og ein kjønnsideologi. Ei samanlikning av dei to romanane *Benedicte Stendal* (1909) og *Vi skriver en roman* (1930), med særleg vekt på egforteljarstrategiane og kjønnsideologien til Nini Roll Anker', *Norskrift*, 86, 1995:96–112.

BULL, O.   Andreas G. Lombnæs, 'Natur/Subjekt/Språk. Lesninger i Olaf Bulls forfatterskap. Doktordisputas, Universitetet i Oslo 10. desember 1994. 1. opponent Erik A. Nielsen. 2. opponent Otto Hageberg. Svar fra doktoranden', *Edda*:69–88. Fredrik Wandrup, *En uro som aldri dør. Olaf Bull og hans samtid*, Gyldendal, 1995, 456 pp., is a biography which thoroughly investigates all sides of the life and work of a poet who ranks among the most brilliant in Norway. At the same time W. gives a lively and penetrating presentation of the time and the milieu.

CHRISTIE, E.   Sissel Furuseth, 'Stillstand og bevegelse i den lyriske teksten — Erling Christies *Jailhouse Rock*', *Motskrift*, no. 1:101–18.

DUUN, O.   Heming Gujord, 'Den kanoniserte Olav Duun', *Nordica Bergensia*, 1995, no. 6:160–76. Otto Hageberg, 'Litteraturforsking som motstand. Refleksjonar med utgangspunkt i Rolv Thesens bok om

Olav Duun', *NLÅ*, 1995:151–62. O. Hageberg, *Olav Duun. Biografiske og litteraturhistoriske streiflys*, Samlaget, 1995, 122 pp. O. Hageberg, *Forboden kjærleik. Spenningsmønster i Olav Duuns dikting*, Samlaget, 256 pp., is a penetrating study of the structure of a chosen number of the early works. Based on Freud and psychoanalytic theory H. manages to revise the view of D. as an 'ethical realist'.

EINAN, E.   Heming Gujord, ' "Sovetreet med selvets krone duver." En tankegang i Ellen Einans tekstlandskap', *Nordica Bergensia*, no. 11:171–87.

FALKEID, K.   'Trekkfuglhjertet. En side ved Kolbein Falkeids lyrikk', *Nordica Bergensia*, no. 10:136–54.

FANGEN, R.   *Frihet — ansvar — tjeneste. Ronald Fangens liv og visjon*, ed. Reidar Huseby, Verbum, 1995, 216 pp.

FLØGSTAD, K.   Jan Inge Sørbø, 'Det vi diktar opp skal bli sannare enn røynsle. Om Kjartan Fløgstads lyrikk', *NLÅ*, 1995:163–74. Dag Østerberg, 'Kjartan Fløgstads forfatterskap', *Syn og Segn*, 1995:56–67.

FOSSE, J.   Leif Johan Larsen, 'Smerte, sorg og dristighet. Om Jon Fosses forfatterskap', *Norsklæraren*, 1995, no. 4:46–54. Espen Stueland, *Å erstatte lykka med eit komma. Essay om cesur og rituell forseintkomming i produksjonen til Jon Fosse*, Samlaget, 235 pp.

HAGEN, I. R.   *Ingeborg Refling Hagen — uklar myte eller bevisst pedagog. Artikler om pedagogiske ringvirkninger*, ed. S. Lappegard, Vallset, Opplandske bokforlag, 1995, 139 pp. Ingrid Elise Wergeland, *Slik som kjærlighet vekker deg. En bok om Ingeborg Refling Hagen*, Aschehoug, 1995, 326 pp.

HANSEN, I. E.   Unni Langås, 'Lyrikeren Inger Elisabeth Hansen', *Nordica Bergensia*, no. 12:69–86.

HAUGE, A.   Per Thomas Andersen, 'Heterotopia i Ryfylke. Fornyelse og tradisjon i Alfred Hauges romantrilogi Århundre', *NLÅ*:101–20.

HAUGE, O. H.   Ole Karlsen, 'Olav H. Hauges På ørnetuva (1961) — ei samling mellom ulike poesitradisjoner?', *Motskrift*, no. 1:133–72. Hadle Oftedal Andersen, 'Olav H. Hauge som folkedikter', *Nordica Bergensia*, 1995, no. 6:177–84. H. O. Andersen, 'Modernisme midt i tradisjon. Om sonetten "Gullhanen" av Olav H. Hauge', *Nordica Bergensia*, no. 10:116–35.

HAUGEN, P. H.   Dealing with the aesthetics, the poetic language and the main themes in the works of H. and Lunden, the large number of articles included makes *Store oskeflak av sol. Om Paal-Helge Haugens og Eldrid Lundens forfatterskap*, ed. O. Karlsen, LNU/Cappelen, 1995, 260 pp., the hitherto most comprehensive presentation of the two poets in question. The angles of view differ from readings inspired by Lacan to biographical methods. Among the contributors are A. Linneberg, S. Weibel, U. Langås, L. P. Wærp, G. Hjorthol, and B. Rekdal.

Literature since the Reformation 963

HAUGEN, T. *Tormod Haugen — en artikkelsamling*, ed. O. Losløkk and B. Øygarden, Gyldendal, 1995, 234 pp.
HELSETH, S. *Den blyge torden*. *Personlige essays om Sigurd Helseths forfatterskap*, Cappelen, 1995, 181 pp.
HERBJØRNSRUD, H. Asbjørn Holm, 'Vannbærerens utydelige ansikt — om en novelle av Hans Herbjørnsrud', *Edda*, 1995:226–36.
HOEL, S. Håvard Skar, 'Trollringens strukturelle psykologi. Sigurd Hoels siste roman lest opp mot Peter Brooks' sammenstilling av strukturalisme og psykoanalyse', *NLÅ*:54–65. Sune Auken, 'Den uudholdelige indsigt — Om fortælleren i Sigurd Hoels *Møte ved milepelen*', *Nordica*, 13:197–216.
HOFMO, G. Ivar Havnevik, 'Etterkrigsdebutanten Gunvor Hofmo', *NLÅ*:39–53.
HOLM, P. R. Helge Ridderstrøm, 'Sjelens plutselige stormer: Sansning og det sublime i Peter R. Holms lyrikk', *Edda*, 1995:127–45.
HOVLAND, R. Sønnøv Sundsaasen, 'Intertekstualitet og sluttspill i *Ein motorsykkel i natta*. En ungdomsroman av Ragnar Hovland', *NLÅ*:164–78.
JACOBSEN, R. Erling Aadland, *'Forundring. Trofasthet.' Poetisk tenkning i Rolf Jacobsens lyrikk*, Gyldendal, 353 pp.
JOHANNESEN, G. *Johannesens bok. Om og til Georg Johannesen*, Cappelen, 399 pp.
KINCK, H. E. Even Arntzen, *Vraal og hans litterære søsken. Intertekstualitet i Hans E. Kincks Driftekaren og Paa Rindalslægret*, Tromsø, Institutt for språk og litteratur, Universitetet i Tromsø, 1995, 309 pp. Gudleiv Bø, 'Hans E. Kinck — nasjonalromantikar for 1905-generasjonen', *NLÅ*, 1995:108–33. *Perspektiver på Hans E. Kincks forfatterskap*, ed. G. Bustø, LNU/Cappelen, 194 pp. *Renessanser. Åtte studier i Hans E. Kincks forfatterskap*, ed. H. E. Aarseth, Universitetsforlaget, 1995, 278 pp.
KJÆRSTAD, J. Vera Ableitinger, 'Das Labyrinth der Schrift. Metafiktive und postmoderne Elemente in Jan Kjærstads *Homo Falsus* und Svend Åge Madsens *Lad tiden gå*', *Skandinavistik*, 25, 1995:111–34. Gitte Mose, 'Don Jonas møder Don Juan og Don Johannes. Forførere og forførelse i Jan Kjærstads *Forføreren* og Søren Kierkegaards *Enten-Eller*', *NLÅ*:121–32. Irene Handland, 'Det fiksjonelle rommet — sonebygging i Jan Kjærstads *Det store eventyret*', *Norskrift*, 92:29–46. I. Handland, 'Frå Don Juan til Jonas Wergeland', *ib.*, 47–68.
LØVEID, C. Vibeke S. Andreassen, 'Å plukke fjøra av unge høner. Ei lesing av *Måkespisere* av Cecilie Løveid', *Nordica Bergensia*, no. 11:80–102.
MAHRT, H. B. Terje Borgersen, 'Å tegne tidens ansikt. Et essay om Haakon Bugge Mahrts *Modernisme*', *Motskrift*, no. 1:7–37. Petter Aaslestad, '"Vi maa alle stræbe efter aa bli mere polyfoniske" —

Modernisme-affinitet i Haakon Bugge Mahrt: "Kjære Europa"', *ib.*, 39–55.

OMRE, A. Olav Solberg, 'Språk, psykologi og tema i Arthur Omres romaner *Smuglere* og *Flukten*', *Norskrift*, 86, 1995:1–34.

PRØYSEN, A. *Alf Prøysen — idylliker eller opprører? Artikler om Alf Prøysens forfatterskap*, ed. K. Imerslund, Vallset, Oplandske bokforlag, 1995, 122 pp.

SANDEL, C. Ruth Essex, *Cora Sandel: Seeker of Truth* (Writing about Women, 10), NY, Lang, 1995, 248 pp. Ellen Rebekka Rees, 'Cora Sandels *Kjøp ikke Dondi*: "... som de snakker de menneskene"', *Scandinavica*, 34, 1995:221–36. Janneken Øverland, *Cora Sandel. En biografi*, Gyldendal, 1995, 399 pp.

SCHJERVEN, T. Anne Beate Storm-Larsen, 'Metaperspektiv og sentrallyrikk i Torgeir Schjerven: *Tanker og andre personlige bedrifter (kjærlighet og død)*', *Nordica Bergensia*, no. 11:139–57.

SCOTT, G. Svein Slettan, 'Naturen som læremester. Natur og oppdragelse i Gabriel Scotts barnebøker', *Norskrift*, 88:29–52.

SANDEMOSE, A. Dagmar Brendt, 'Ein tekstlingvistisk analyse av Aksel Sandemoses *Vi pynter oss med horn*', *Nordica Bergensia*, 1995, no. 5:121–39.

SOLSTAD, D. Andreas Lombnæs, 'Genrens nullpunkt. Dag Solstads kortprosa mellom realisme og realisme', *NLÅ*, 1995:175–86. Arvid Nærø, 'Ingen vei tilbake? Teknikk og anskuelse i Dag Solstads roman *Genanse og verdighet* — en kommentar', *Agora*, 13, 1995:147–55.

STENERSEN, R. Bjørn Olsen, 'Rolf Stenersen og surrealismen', *Motskrift*, no. 1:89–100. Espen Søbye, *Rolf Stenersen. En biografi*, Oktober, 1995, 420 pp.

STAALESEN, G. Odd Magnar Syversen, *Gunnar Staalesen — en bibliografi*, Løten, Bokmakeriet, 1995, 11 pp.

UNDSET, S. Tordis Ørjasæter, *Sigrid Undset og Roma*, Aschehoug, 160 pp.

VESAAS, H. M. *Klarøygd, med rolege drag. Om Halldis Moren Vesaas' forfatterskap*, ed. O. Karlsen, LNU/Cappelen, 156 pp.

VESAAS, T. Olav Vesaas, *Løynde land. Ei bok om Tarjei Vesaas*, Cappelen, 1995, 464 pp. Steinar Gimnes, 'Modernisme og resepsjon. Innleiing til ei nylesing av Tarjei Vesaas' roman *Sandeltreet* (1933)', *Motskrift*, no. 1:69–88. Even Arntzen, 'Den poetiske genesis. Om Tarjei Vesaas' *Kjeldene*', *Edda*:55–67.

VIK, B. Thomas Seiler, '"Det er litt av den samme tåken i blikket hennes." Weiblichkeit als Differenz in Bjørg Viks Erzählung *Snart er det høst*', *Skandinavistik*, 26:20–31.

ØKLAND, E. Svein Sletta, 'På frifot. Grunndrag i Einar Øklands barnelyrikk', *NLÅ*:133–63.

V. SWEDISH STUDIES*

LANGUAGE

POSTPONED

LITERATURE

By BIRGITTA THOMPSON, *Lecturer in Swedish at University of Wales Lampeter*

1. GENERAL

The fourth edition has appeared of Bernt Olsson and Ingemar Algulin, *Litteraturens historia i Sverige*, Norstedts, 1995, 619 pp., including updatings of the most recent literature and an extended bibliography with works published up to the mid-1990s. Göran Hägg, *Den svenska litteraturhistorien*, Wahlström & Widstrand, 692 pp., explains in an 11-page postscript the reasons for and strategy behind this impressive one-man project, one of the advantages being a uniform perspective. The emphasis is on narrative and linguistic techniques, and there is no shortage of subjective and provocative evaluations, such as the reappraisal of Emilie Flygare-Carlén as a truly great novelist, while on the other hand he disparages Strindberg's novels, heaps praise on Söderberg, and gives short shrift to some of the most modern poetry. It is entertaining reading and good for revision and outline purposes. *A History of Swedish Literature*, ed. Lars G. Warme (A History of Scandinavian Literatures, 3), Nebraska U.P., xvi + 585 pp., is a comprehensive reference work for the international market by nine scholars from Europe and America. It traces Swedish literature from its beginnings in the Middle Ages to the present day in its historical and social context, and is a worthy updated successor to Alrik Gustafson's 1961 standard work. Although women writers are treated throughout the book, there are special chapters both on women's and also on children's literature. Mats Malm, *Minervas äpple. Om diktsyn, tolkning och bildspråk inom nordisk göticism*, Stockholm-Stehag, Brutus Östlings Bokförlag Symposion, 299 pp., is a doctoral dissertation on Swedish and Danish 'Gothicism', and focuses on literary production from Olof Rudbeck to about 1820, i.e. from 17th-c. classicism to early-19th-c. romanticism, the overarching objective being 'to achieve theoretical understanding of the shifts which took place in the conception of poetry and aesthetics as well as in the techniques of imagery and translation'. *Svenska*

---

* The place of publication of books is Stockholm unless otherwise indicated.

Akademiens Handlingar, 22, 1995 [1996], Svenska Akademien–
Norstedts, contains documents from the annual commemoration day
on 20 December 1995, among them a tribute to Albert Engström,
37 pp.; from the Swedish Academy Archive, 'Henrik Schücks anteck-
ningar till Svenska Akademiens historia 1883–1912. III. Svenska
Akademien och litteraturen 1883–1900', ed. Bo Svensén, 146 pp.;
and B. Svensén, 'Det första akademitrycket. Om ett hittills obeaktat
dokument rörande Svenska Akademiens instiftelse', 24 pp. Cecilia
Sjöholm, *Föreställningar om det omedvetna. Stagnelius, Ekelöf och Norén*,
Stockholm-Stehag, Brutus Östlings Bokförlag Symposion, 334 pp., is
a thought-provoking doctoral dissertation which investigates the
unconscious as a cultural, variable, and in many ways literary
construction; theories by Freud, Kristeva, and Lacan form part of the
methodological basis. The role of femininity as a key to the
unconscious is stressed, and the choice of case-studies is well
motivated: the belief in an unknown source of poetical imagination is
created in the romantic poetry of Erik Johan Stagnelius (47–115),
questioned in Gunnar Ekelöf's poetry from the early 1930s (117–201),
and opposed in the postmodern texts of Lars Norén from the 1960s
(203–80). Dag Nordmark, *Tiljorna vid vägen. Studier i den svenska
landsortsteaterns historia till ca 1850*, Gideå, Vildros, 1995, 303 pp., also
deals with repertoire and authors. Karin Naumann, *Utopien von
Freiheit. Die Schweiz im Spiegel schwedischer Literatur* (BNP, 23), 1994,
220 pp. + 16 illus., investigates the cultural contacts between
Switzerland and Sweden from the 15th c. onwards, the emphasis
being on the 'emigrants at the turn of the century', and the 20th c.,
from Edith Södergran and Eyvind Johnson to writers of the 1990s.
Parnass, nos. 4–5, is devoted to the literary society Romantiska
Förbundet. M. Malm, 'Trogen översättning?', *TidLit*, 25.1:69–86.
Boel Westin, *Children's Literature in Sweden*, Swedish Institute, 72 pp., is
the second, revised and extended edition of the 1991 booklet.

2. FROM THE RENAISSANCE TO THE GUSTAVIAN AGE

Valborg Lindgärde, *Jesu Christi Pijnos Historia Rijmvijs Betrachtad. Svenska
passionsdikter under 1600- och 1700-talet* (Litteratur Teater Film, Nya
serien, 12), Lund U.P., i + 429 pp., a doctoral dissertation, discusses
14 works of poetry, the earliest from 1641, and the latest from 1787
by a friend of Bellman's. The German influence is strong, and five of
the poems are renderings of identifiable German originals. It is
demonstrated how this rather uniform poetry makes full use of the
resources of rhetoric and dialectic to allow the reader to share an
intellectual and emotional experience. M.-C. Hess, 'Schweden und
Sparta', *Akten* (Greifswald), 514–24, discusses Rousseau reception.

Literature 967

BELLMAN, CARL MICHAEL. Marianne Nyström, *Lovisa Bellman född Grönlund. En bok om Carl Michael Bellmans hustru* (Stockholmsmonografier, 107), Stockholmia förlag, 1995, iv + 318 pp. Following Nyström's 1994 book on B., this informative study of Mrs B.'s family and bourgeois life in the period gives a somewhat depressing picture of B.'s marriage because of his constant shortage of money and the couple's lack of shared interests. B. van Boer, 'The collaboration of Joseph Martin Kraus and Carl Michael Bellman', *ScSt*, 68:461–72.

BUDDE, JÖNS. M. Lamberg, 'Jöns Budde. En misogyn munk i Nådendal?', *FT*: 199–208.

DALIN, OLOF VON. A. Swanson, 'Argus on the stage. Dalin the playwright', *ScSt*, 68:401–14. J. Massengale, 'The songs of Olof von Dalin', *ib.*, 415–60.

HOLMSTRÖM, ISRAEL. B. Olsson, 'Israel Holmström. En författarskapsinventering', *Samlaren*, 116, 1995[1996]:5–41, is an investigative report on existing manuscripts, mainly transcripts of poems attributed to H. in various archives, concluding that much remains to be done, primarily further text-critical work. Nevertheless, this research, which began in the 1960s, has revealed the existence of a comprehensive and versatile *œuvre* by comparing holdings in various archives hitherto not properly investigated.

KELLGREN, JOHAN HENRIC. T. Hanson, 'Attributionen av ett inlägg i striden Pro sensu communi 1787', *Samlaren*, 116, 1995 [1996]:148–52.

LENNGREN, ANNA MARIA. B. Audén, 'Förebilden för Anna Maria Lenngrens Betti-dikt', *Samlaren*, 116, 1995[1996]:152–61. *Parnass*, no. 3, is devoted to L.

LINNÆUS, CARL. P. Graves, 'Introduction', pp. 7–25 of Carl Linnæus, *The Lapland Journey. Iter Lapponicum 1732*, ed. and trans. Peter Graves, Edinburgh, Lockharton Press, 1995, 207 pp., provides useful background information on L., his provincial journeys in Sweden, and publication details of his travel books together with notes and stylistic considerations.

SWEDENBORG, EMANUEL. Lars Bergquist, *Biblioteket i lusthuset. Tio uppsatser om Swedenborg*, Natur och Kultur, 286 pp.; as a preliminary to a forthcoming biography on S., these ten essays analyse S.'s theosophical works as well as his importance for Erik Gustaf Geijer (168–84), Carl Jonas Love Almqvist (185–201), and August Strindberg (202–22). Olof Lagercrantz, *Dikten om livet på den andra sidan. En bok om Emanuel Swedenborg*, Wahlström & Widstrand, 205 pp., interprets S.'s enormous *œuvre* from his second period, i.e. almost 30 of his last years, as fiction about life after death, and transforms him from a mystic into a writer who wrote about Utopia after death in the spirit of enlightenment, embracing ideals similar to Lagercrantz's own on living with dignity. *Parnass*, 1994, no. 4, is devoted to S.

3. ROMANTICISM AND LIBERALISM

Lars Lönnroth, *Skaldemjödet i berget. Essayer om fornisländsk ordkonst och dess återanvändning i nutiden*, Atlantis, 225 pp., concentrates on the Icelandic sagas, but makes reference to influences on later literature, e.g. P. D. A. Atterbom's 1811 poem 'Skaldar-mal' with commentary in *Phosporus*, characterizing it as a bold venture for modern poets on the basis of Nordic mythology (114–45), and two *Völuspa* paraphrases in two later poems (169–207), namely Viktor Rydberg's 'Vårdträdet' (1888) and Gunnar Ekelöf's 'Höstsejd' (1934). Ami Lönnroth and Per Eric Mattsson, *Tidningskungen Lars Johan Hierta — den förste moderne svensken*, Wahlström & Widstrand, 320 pp., is not only an impressive biography of Hierta and his dramatic and successful life, best known as the founder of the liberal newspaper *Aftonbladet*, but also a comprehensive description of Stockholm society and Hierta's associations with writers at the time, not least as a publisher of Fredrika Bremer and Almqvist's scandalous novel *Det går an*, as well as controversies with Tegnér.

ALMQVIST, CARL JONAS LOVE. N. Vosbein, 'Fra C. J. L. Almqvists skriveværksted', *Samlaren*, 116, 1995[1996]: 42–51, discusses a manuscript of a plan for a large-scale project that was never completed; it provides insight into A.'s early efforts to become a writer and create a new kind of poetry. L. Krumlinde, 'En spännande affär', *ib.*, 162–65, discusses Hierta's sale of *Aftonbladet* and A.'s involvement in the affair. J. Almer, ' "Jag tror jag vet Poesiens framtid bättre än min egen." C. J. L. Almqvist om föreningen mellan himmelskt och jordiskt i diktkonsten', pp. 9–23 [preface] of C. J. L. Almqvist, *Avhandling om huvuddragen i den poesi som kan väntas av framtiden*, ed. and trans. Anna Forssberg (MLIGU, 20), 101 pp. M. Florin, 'Almqvist och kartans behag. En geografi över hela världen', *BLM*, 65.3:40–41. J. Svedjedal, 'Om två slags lässätt. Om receptionen av C. J. L. Almqvist', *ib.*, 65.6:21–25. P. Wålarö, 'Amorinas förvandling. Förändringen av den metafysiska uppbyggnaden i Almqvists båda versioner', *Fenix*, 12.3–4:82–147.

ATTERBOM, PER DANIEL AMADEUS. P. Söderlund, 'Den olycksaliga ön. Atterboms *Lycksalighetens ö* i ett litteratursociologiskt perspektiv', *TidLit*, 25.3–4:21–29.

BREMER, FREDRIKA. L. A. Lofswold, 'Blaming the messenger. Mary Howitt's translation of Fredrika Bremer's *Hemmen i den Nya Verlden*', *Scandinavica*, 35:213–31. Å. Arping, 'Att mäta kvinnligheten.

Fredrika Bremer och den sexualiserade litteraturhistorieskrivningen',
TidLit, 25.3–4:89–107. *Parnass*, 1995, nos. 3–4, is devoted to B.
RUNEBERG, JOHAN LUDVIG. M. Ekman, 'Nödvändigheternas kon-
flikt i Runebergs *Nadeschda*', *HLS*, 71:53–70 (SSLF, 604).
RYDBERG, VIKTOR. *Parnass*, 1995, no. 5, is devoted to R.
STAGNELIUS, ERIK JOHAN. Horace Engdahl, *Stagnelius Kärleken*,
Nora, Nya Doxa, 85 pp., is a helpful commentary on S.'s longest
poem, 'Kärleken. En metafysisk lärodikt', published in *Liljor i Saron*,
1821, as a kind of explanatory introduction to the work itself, and
helpfully unravels the mysteries of Greek mythology to make the
modern reader see the many different levels S. is operating on.
TEGNÉR, ESAIAS. *Under det höga valvet. En Tegnérbok sammanställd av
Smålands akademi*, ed. Marian Ullén, Norstedts, 261 pp., is a reminder
of various aspects of T., and includes Vilhelm Ekelund's assessment
of T., 'Mjältsjukan', T.'s relation to nature, his achievements as a
bishop and his educational ideals, and T. and America. *Möten med
Tegnér*, ed. Ulla Törnqvist, Lund, Tegnérsamfundet, 177 pp., commemorates the 50th anniversary of the T. Society with excellent
contributions by L. Vinge on T. as priest and poet (7–32), Å. K. G.
Lundquist on reviews of *Frithiofs saga* (33–73), N. Palmborg on the
homage to Oehlenschläger in Lund 1829 (74–112), C. Svensson on
the poem 'Ragnarok' (113–35), and C. Fehrman on T.'s mental
illness (136–76). Other T. Society publications include Gunnar
Fredriksson, *Om eviga idéers aktualitet*, Lund, 30 pp.; Svante Nordin,
Tegnértraditionen och andra traditioner, Lund, 1995, 25 pp.; Sigrid Com-
büchen, *Att läsa Bibeln för andra gången*, Lund, 1994, 36 pp.

4. THE LATER NINETEENTH CENTURY

Maria Nikolajeva, *När Sverige erövrade Ryssland. En studie i kulturernas
samspel*, Stockholm-Stehag, Brutus Östlings Bokförlag Symposion,
376 pp., is a reception study of Swedish literature in Russia about the
turn of the century, investigating the interaction of cultures, mainly
on the basis of Iurii Lotman's theories of cultural semiotics. Anna
Lyngfelt, *Den avväpnade förtroligheten. Enaktare i Sverige 1870–90* (SLIGU,
29), ii + 202 pp., is a doctoral dissertation analysing one-act plays of
the period and their origins (notably by Benedictsson, J. Grönstedt,
A. C. Leffler, and Strindberg), thus modifying the claim by Strindberg
at the end of the 1880s that it was he who introduced a new short
dramatic form based on French models. Jørgen Knudsen, *Georg
Brandes. Symbolet og manden 1883–1895*, 2 vols, Copenhagen, Gyldendal, 1994, 325, vi + 327–668 pp., is the third part of the comprehensive biography of this leading Scandinavian critic, showing
interchanges, influences, and relations between him and Swedish

writers of whom several are singled out and treated in detail, as well as referred to *passim*. Sigvard Lindqvist, *Symbolism i det svenska 1890-talets litteratur*, Jönköping, Wettern-förlaget, 1995, 150 pp., investigates symbolism, both as a predominant subject for discussion in journals and as a literary influence. Å. Åberg, '"Det moderna genombrottet" i svensk landsort. Bokköp och tidningspress i Västerås 1870–1895', *Samlaren*, 116, 1995[1996]: 52–74, focuses on the literary tastes of the general public.

BENEDICTSSON, VICTORIA. Charlotte Jørgensen, *Ernst og Victoria. Et dobbeltportræt af Victoria Benedictsson*, Copenhagen, Munksgaard-Rosinante, 170 pp., is a welcome piece of research, especially after the publication of Jørgen Knudsen's third part of his Brandes biography which accuses B. of being a liar in her diary comments on the affair with Brandes. This penetrating psychological study stresses that B. was two persons, the woman Victoria and the author Ernst; that the male, artistic spirit within her was incompatible with her sensitive, female body, which was ruthlessly used as a source of inspiration. In Jungian terms, B.'s life is a failed individuation process. On the other hand, Bodil Wamberg, *Lykken er en talisman. En kærlighedshistorie fra 1880'ernes København*, Copenhagen, G. E. C. Gad, 1995, 103 pp., claims to be objective, but reproduces yet again the familiar story of a poor, loving woman and an evil, sadistic seducer, each of whom recognizes the other as a catalyst of both suicide and Don Juan tendencies. Unfortunately, both works treat B.'s writings merely as biographical reference material. Corinna Vonhoegen, '*Das Weiß öffnen, um das Schwarz hervorkommen zu lassen.*' *Zur Schrift in der Dramatik Victoria Benedictssons und Cecilie Løveids* (TUGS, 37), 235 pp., is a doctoral dissertation that analyses female drama writing with reference to texts by B. and the Norwegian writer Cecilie Løveid a century later in the light of theories by Derrida, F. A. Kittler, and Kristeva.

ENGSTRÖM, ALBERT. *Parnass*, 1995, no. 1, is devoted to E. and Strindberg.

HEIDENSTAM, VERNER VON. Magnus von Platen, *Verner von Heidenstam och Emilia Uggla. Ett äktenskap*, Fischer & Co., 1994, 213 pp., relating to H.'s first marriage, is based on archive material made public 50 years after H.'s death.

LAGERLÖF, SELMA. *Bron mellan Nås och Jerusalem. Om Nåsböndernas utvandring till Jerusalem i verklighet och dikt. Lagerlöfstudier 1996*, ed. Vivi Edström et al., Ingmarsspelen, Nås, and Selma Lagerlöf-sällskapet, 135 pp., investigates the 1896 reality behind the novel in authentic documents and also the novel itself. Hanna Greta Näslund, *Studier i Selma Lagerlöfs symboliska diktning i slutet av 1890-talet och företrädesvis En herrgårdssägen*, Carlssons, 190 pp., is of little scholarly significance.

Reijo Rüster and Lars Westman, *Selma på Mårbacka*, Bonniers, 184 pp., is a lavishly illustrated work depicting in photographs and text life on L.'s estate, with its many practical and not least financial problems; the pictures are of more interest than the text. K. Hvidt, 'En brevveksling mellem Georg Brandes og Selma Lagerlöf. Endnu en kvinde i Brandes liv', *NT*, 72 : 199–218, publishes for the first time letters that became available in 1990 when the Lagerlöf archive at the Swedish National Library was made public. *Parnass*, 1994, no. 5, is devoted to L.

STRINDBERG, AUGUST. Ulf Olsson, *Levande död. Studier i Strindbergs prosa*, Stockholm-Stehag, Brutus Östlings Bokförlag Symposion, 512 pp., investigates the allegorization of S.'s prose fiction from *Röda rummet* to *Inferno*, with Walter Benjamin's theory of modern allegory as its basis, and claims to provide new insight through close reading directed by three categories, namely commodity form, modernity, and allegory. Unfortunately, the theoretical framework manages to obscure both the author's conclusions and S.'s texts. *August Strindbergs brev 20*, ed. Björn Meidal, Bonniers, 360 pp., covers June 1911–May 1912. *Strindbergiana*, 11, ed. Boel Westin, Atlantis, 160 pp., concentrates on S.'s drama (*Den starkare, Advent, Till Damaskus I* and *Ett drömspel*) in papers by respectively A. Lyngfelt (82–97), J. E. Olsson (98–117), O. Holmgren (118–33), and G. Rossholm (134–57); it also includes contributions by N. Solomin, on S.'s anti-Semitism (9–30); M. Karlsson, on S.'s relevance for the Japanese writer Akutagawas (31–50); K. Wennberg, in conversation with S.'s daughter Anne-Marie Hagelin (51–56); A. Ollfors, on bibliographical notes relevant to *Gamla Stockholm* (57–60); E. Höök, on music in colour (61–70); and S. Grimal on a reassessment of S.'s French in *Inferno* (72–81). Catherine C. Fraser, *Ensam och Allén*, Ordfronts förlag, 1994, 124 pp., analyses the relationship between works by S. the artist and S. the writer. *Parnass*, 1995, no. 1, is devoted to S. and Albert Engström. Björn Meidal, *Samlaren*, 116, 1995[1996]: 143–48, discusses alleged source material in Carl Öhman's book published in 1961, *Strindberg and the Origin of Scenic Expressionism*. E. Törnqvist, 'The Strindbergian one-act play', *ScSt*, 68 : 356–69. A.-C. Snickars, 'Ynk eller brasa', *FT*: 516–21.

5. THE TWENTIETH CENTURY

A welcome publication is *Nordisk kvinnolitteraturhistoria. III. Vida världen 1900–1960*, ed. Elisabeth Møller Jensen, Höganäs, Bra Böcker, 608 pp. (see *YWMLS*, 55 : 1036), which continues in the same vein as the previous two. In the climate of rapid social and political change this century, female writers come into their own with self-confident novels and bold experimental poetry. The chapter-headings signal the new conditions: 'Jaget', 'Begäret', 'Kön och krig'. Many names, such as Selma Lagerlöf and Edith Södergran, do not lend themselves to unambiguous labelling, but together they open up new horizons for 20th-c. literature. *Från Sörgården till Lopnor. Klassiska läseböcker i ny belysning*, ed. Bo Ollén (SSBI, 57), Carlssons, v + 262 pp., discusses the importance of the new project in the early years of this century designed to produce new, high-class reading material for schools. The co-operation of a number of leading writers resulted in the publication of Selma Lagerlöf's *Nils Holgerssons underbara resa genom Sverige* (43–73), Verner von Heidenstam's *Svenskarna och deras hövdingar* (74–106), Sven Hedin's *Från pol till pol* (107–60), an anthology of poetry (161–87), and Anna Maria Roos's *Sörgården* and *I Önnemo* (188–239); most have appeared in new revised editions half a century later. Birgitta Svensson, *Den omplanterade svenskheten. Kulturell självhävdelse och etnisk medvetenhet i den svensk-amerikanska kalendern Prärieblomman 1900–1913* (SLIGU, 27), 1994, 218 pp., discusses how national identity manifested itself among Swedish immigrants, who felt they were both ethnic Swedes and loyal Americans, and helped to mould a very special form of literature, based on Swedish patriotism with traces of the classical and Old Norse tradition of the previous century. Kristin Järvstad, *Att utvecklas till kvinna. Studier i den kvinnliga utvecklingsromanen i 1900-talets Sverige*, Stockholm-Stehag, Brutus Östlings Bokförlag Symposion, 300 pp., is a doctoral dissertation and a thematic study on the female novel of development. It focuses on three trilogies, very different in time and setting, namely Agnes von Krusenstjerna's Tony trilogy from the 1920s, Irja Browallius's Birgit trilogy from 1957–61, and Ingrid Sjöstrand's Törnrosa trilogy, 1985–90. In spite of their differences, the analysis reveals common features which differ from the male counterpart in the *Bildungsroman*, and concludes that free development is still a chimera for the heroines in this type of novel. Peter Hansen, *Romanen och verklighetsproblemet. Studier i några svenska sextiotalsromaner*, Stockholm-Stehag, Brutus Östlings Bokförlag Symposion, 352 pp., a doctoral dissertation, investigates the problem of reality and realism in 1960s novels by Torsten Ekbom, Per Olov Enquist, and Per Olof Sundman by focusing on current literary historical trends and their consequences for narrative techniques. In so doing he tries to unravel what the text appears to say as well as what it appears to intend. Per Ringby, *Avantgardeteater och modernitet. Pistolteatern och det svenska teaterlivet från 1950-tal till 60-tal*, Gideå, Vildros, 1995, 416 pp., is a doctoral dissertation and presents an analysis of the debate on committed art and literature in 1965. Lars Forssell, *Loggbok. Essäer och artiklar om litteratur och kultur 1944–91*, Hägglunds, 244 pp., is a collection of articles published in journals and newspapers, such as *BLM, Dagens Nyheter,* and *Expressen.* As well as highly readable essays on individual writers, there are discussions about poetry, the writer and democracy, books and advertising, and the scope of the cultural section in a daily paper. Articles on writers deal with Sigfrid Siwertz, Bo Bergman, Verner von Heidenstam, Elin Wägner, Viktor Rydberg, Jan Fridegård, Lars Ahlin, Evert Taube, Strindberg, and the unfortunate influence of Fredrik Böök. Johan Svedjedal, *Gurun och grottmannen och andra litteratursociologiska studier. Om Birger Sjöberg, Vilhelm Moberg, Bruno K. Öijer, Sven Delblanc, Bob Dylan och Stig Larsson,* Gedins, 227 pp., investigates the relationship between commercial conditions in the book-publishing world and attitudes and themes in a sample of modern writers, also the assumption that commercial success is not compatible with artistic quality. The study considers Sjöberg's 1920s best-seller *Kvartetten som sprängdes,* Moberg's 1930s novels, Öijer and Delblanc in the title essay, and the novels by Stig Larsson. *Stilstudier. Språkvetare skriver litterär stilistik,* ed. Olle Josephson (Ord och stil, Språkvårdssamfundets skrifter, 27), Uppsala, Hallgrens och Fallgrens Studieförlag AB, 188 pp., discusses in eight essays the present status of linguistic analysis of literary language, evaluating its value and place as a tool for interpretation. This interesting and thought-provoking work covers a wide range of examples: P. Cassirer on Hjalmar Söderberg's short story 'Pälsen' (85–124); G.Widmark on Sara Lidman's and Torgny Lindgren's use of regional varieties of language (46–65); and B. Söderberg on a comparison of the introductory paragraphs in Eyvind Johnson's *Hans nådes tid* and Strindberg's *Hemsöborna* (66–84). In addition, there are analyses of brief samples by Elmer Diktonius, Ernst Brunner, Solveig von Schoultz and Jan Guillou, as well as a comparative study of the way a number of Swedish and English novels (in translation) present dialogue. A welcome reprint of the 1958 edition together with the 1960 *Appendix* and a newly-written preface to this second edition is Göran Printz-Påhlson, *Solen i spegeln. Essäer om lyrisk modernism,* Bonniers, xii + 352 pp., considered to be one of the most influential aesthetic works of the post-war era. Staffan Söderblom, *Diktens tal. En poetik,* Bonniers, 135 pp., investigates the 'silence' of poetry as its very essence. He discusses works by several modern poets, the most significant being Tomas Tranströmer and Anna Rydstedt. Per Wästberg, *Lovtal,* Wahlström & Widstrand, 353 pp., is an anthology of the twelve tributes made to the writers who have so far won the prestigious 'Pilotpris', from Birgitta Trotzig to Lars Gustafsson, giving personal insight into and individual characterizations of works by the other ten authors, namely Sven Delblanc, Lars Gyllensten, Tomas Tranströmer, Olof Lagercrantz, Willy Kyrklund, Verner Aspenström,

Lars Forssell, Karl Vennberg, Lars Norén, and Kerstin Ekman. In addition, there are portraits of a further five writers: Verner von Heidenstam, Gösta Gustaf-Janson, Artur Lundkvist, Bengt Söderbergh, and Carl Fredrik Reuterswärd. Carl-Erik af Geijerstam, *Röster i drömmen och andra essäer*, Bonnier Alba, 197 pp., contains not only personal reminiscences of several Finland-Swedish writers, such as Gunnar Björling and Rabbe Enckell, but also essays on Vilhelm Ekelund, Jan Fridegård, and Walter Ljungquist. Torsten Ekbom, *Bildstorm*, Bonniers, 1995, 410 pp., presents in a wide-ranging and impressive volume various aspects of international modernism in art, music, architecture, and literature. Essays deal with the avant-garde poets Öyvind Fahlström, Åke Hodell, and Carl Fredrik Reuterswärd, as well as the Finland-Swedish modernism of the 1920s and later. *Fem par. Finlandssvenska författare konfronteras*, ed. Roger Holmström (SSLF, 592), Helsinki, 1995, 149 pp., comprises studies in Finland-Swedish literature with essays on Arvid Mörne, Ralf Nordgren, Edith Södergran, Eva-Stina Byggmästar, Håkan Mörne, Pirkko Lindberg, Sally Salminen, Ulla-Lena Lundberg, Anders Cleve, and Kjell Westö. *Från kulturväktare till nightdrivers. Studier i finlandssvensk 1900-talslitteratur*, II, ed. Roger Holmström (SSLF, 599), Helsinki, 203 pp., deals with the period after 1945 and is a welcome and authoritative follow-up to the 1986 anthology *Från dagdrivare till feminister*, edited by Sven Linnér, both intended partly to remedy the lack of a comprehensive and scholarly description of Finland-Swedish literature in the 20th c. Without dealing specifically with individual writers, the six essays analyse trends and themes in post-war literature, such as the cultural climate at the end of the 1940s, nature poetry, children's literature, detective novels, and the writer and society. *Rudan, vanten och gangstern. Essäer om samtida finlandssvensk litteratur*, ed. Michel Ekman and Peter Mickwitz, Helsinki, Söderströms, 1995, 233 pp., is an attempt by younger critics and writers to focus interest on new writers and today's literary climate in general. *Konsten att berätta för barn*, ed. Gunnar Berefelt (SCB, 26), 278 pp., contains 15 informative essays which examine aesthetic aspects of literature for children and young people, mainly works from the 1940s and 1950s. V. Edström, 'Att erkänna barnanaturen. Sagans röst i barnlitteraturen från sekelskiftet till Astrid Lindgren', pp. 213–29 of *Ur barndomens historia*, ed. Gunnar Berefelt (SCB, 25), 229 pp., charts the development of the fairy-tale in the period. *Horisont*, 43.6, is a special issue on Swedish and Finland-Swedish children's literature. B. Westin, 'Drömmens texter. Äventyret som rêverie i barnlitteraturen', *TidLit*, 25.2:3–20. L. Kåreland, 'Musiken, postmodernismen och ungdomsromanen. Exemplet Bernt Danielssons *Steff*', *ib.*, 43–55. L. Wendelius, 'Modernitet och traditionalism. Den amerikanska imperialismen i svensk debatt och dikt

1898–1910', *Samlaren*, 116, 1995[1996]: 75–94, surveys the issue with emphasis on the public opinion makers Harald Hjärne and Rudolf Kjellén, and the writers K. G. Ossiannilsson and Gustaf Janson. M. Jansson, 'Torsten Fogelquist och modernismen: en litteraturkritisk skärningspunkt', *Edda*: 45–53. L. Keustermans, 'Manlighet och mannens kärlekspoesi i Norden', *ib.*, 357–64. S. Bergsten, 'Den sönderplockade rosen. Ett tema i modern svensk lyrik', *TidLit*, 25.2: 56–68. M. Wasilewska-Chmura, 'Musik som lösning av den modernistiska diktens formproblem. Några aspekter på den estetiska debatten i Sverige under 1940-talet', *Akten* (Greifswald), 313–20. K. Hoff, 'Versuch einer Poetik der neuen Dokumentarliteratur,' *ib.*, 254–64, surveys the issue on the basis of novels by Lars Jakobson and Ola Larsmo. E. Zillén, 'Den svenska konkretismens manifest: tillämpad vs. proklamerad poetik', *ib.*, 321–27. R. Yrlid, 'Den undflyende dokumentarismen. En granskning av hur den svenska sextiotalsdokumentarismen skildras i några litteraturhistoriska översikter och ett förslag till en definition', *TidLit*, 25.1: 87–98. B. Holm, 'The village in the world. The sense of place in modern Swedish literature', *Procs* (Brasilia), 604–11, deals with Sara Lidman, Per Olov Enquist, and Torgny Lindgren. *NT*, 72: 313–20, 351–60, is part of a special issue on Scandinavian literature in 1995. M. Lundström, 'Om några av vårens debutanter. En duktig skara', *BLM*, 65.3: 50–51. *BLM*, 65.5, is devoted to translating. B. Gunnarsson, 'Om tre svenska samtidsromaner. Nittiotalet som schablon och ödesdrama', *BLM*, 65.5: 48–50, deals with Claes Holmström, Robert Kangas, and Kjell Espmark. P. A. Tjäder, 'Om svenskt sekelslut. Berättelser om 1900-talets infernaliska dynamit', *BLM*, 65.6: 49–51. *TidLit*, nos. 3–4, is devoted to sociological aspects of literature, and includes: J. Svedjedal (3–20), L. Furuland (129–38), and M. Björkman (139–47) on current research, trends and perspectives; E. Pernell on *Camera obscura* and modern poetry in 1946–47 (44–58); S. Jonsson on Stellan Arvidson (59–75); A. Nordenstam on female literary scholars (76–88); J. Ingvarsson on the avant-garde publication *Gorilla* in 1966–67 (108–28). H. Svahn, 'Författarens ansvar. Etiska och moraliska ställningstaganden av några finlandssvenska författare under åren 1939–1947', *HLS*, 71: 133–57 (SSLF, 604). R. Andtbacka, 'Om litterära grannrelationer och poetisk radikalism', *Horisont*, 42.5–6, 1995: 2–4, considers recent Finland-Swedish poetry. M. Mazzarella, 'Det undflyende jaget. Masken i finlandssvensk memoarlitteratur', *ib.*, 43.2–3: 131–35, uses her own work from 1993, *Att skriva sin värld*, as the starting-point, but focuses on Bertel Gripenberg, Henrik Tikkanen, Christer Kihlman, and Göran Schildt among others. *FT*, nos. 2–3, surveys Finland-Swedish novels and poetry in 1995. Within the field of popular literature, three 48-page Jury books (1–3),

Bromma, Jury, by Ulla Trenter and Karl G. and Lilian Fredriksson, discuss detective novels by respectively Stig Trenter and Henning Mankell, while Ulf Örnkloo lists the best books in the genre 1971–96. Johan Wopenka, *På smekmånad med Gröna Skräcken. Kioskhäften i Sverige — en förteckning*, Gothenburg, BJW-förlaget, 1995, 220 pp., is the first-ever comprehensive bibliography and survey of pulp magazines in Swedish launched 1930–60.

AHLIN, LARS.   Christer Ekholm, *Om Om. En 'obduktion' av Lars Ahlins roman Om* (MLIGU, 18), 59 pp., discusses this elusive novel, and, according to its author, is probably just as elusive but infinitely poorer than its object. B. Agrell et al., 'Den anstötliga jämlikheten. Om sönderklippta kvitton, Valdus Larsson, två ordningar och Lars Ahlins romaner', *OB*, nos. 3–4: 14–22.

ANDERSSON, DAN.   Jörgen Dicander, *'Du ska inte behöva lida så länge till.' Tendenser och tillflöden i Dan Anderssons religiösa författarskap*, Malung, Dalaförlaget, 206 pp., investigates A.'s works as religious writings with early influences from the revivalist movement, and later also from Schopenhauer, Plato, Eckhart, Böhme, Spinoza, Kant, and the Indian mysticism of Bhagavad-Gita.

ARA, AGNETA.   M. Sandin, 'Det som skiljer oss åt skall vara en dörr: Agneta Aras verklighetsmagi', *Horisont*, 43.1 : 38–45. M. Slotte, 'Tassavtryck och stjärnor: samtal med Agneta Ara', *ib.*, 46–49.

BENGTSSON, FRANS G.   *Frans G. Bengtsson-lyrik med kommentarer*, ed. Lennart Ploman (Frans G. Bengtsson-sällskapet, 4), Lund, 1994, 100 pp., includes essays on B.'s poetry by nine of the B. Society members, among them Bertil Romberg and Svante Nordin. The collection of love poetry, *Inför kvinnan ställd*, and eight individual poems are analysed. *Frans G. Bengtsson-studier*, 1, ed. Lennart Ploman (Frans G. Bengtsson-sällskapet, 5), Lund, 1995, 36 pp., comprises five lectures given in April 1995, as well as supplementary comments on the poem 'En ballad om franske kungens spelmän'. *Parnass*, no. 6, is devoted to B.

BERGLUND, ANNE-MARIE.   K. Davidsson, 'Flykten frånvanligheten', *Horisont*, 42.5–6, 1995 : 22–27.

BERGMAN, HJALMAR.   *'Mitt hjärtas stad.' Hjalmar Bergmans Florens. Symposium i Florens 1994*, ed. Berit Wilson (Hjalmar Bergman Samfundet, 10), 173 pp., includes papers on B.'s connections with Florence since he was there in 1901 as an 18-year-old art student: M. Wirmark on B.'s first impressions of the city and on Florentine art (9–21, 22–72); M. C. Lombardi on the short story 'Den underbara modellen' (73–78); papers by S. R. Ek, Y. Haglund-Croce, K. Dahlbäck and Ö. Lindberger, on various aspects of the novel *Savonarola*, ranging from the authentic and historical facts behind it to narrative techniques; E. Lindberger on B.'s aesthetic declaration of artistic creativity in 1929 (136–60); and K. Petherick on B. and religion (161–73). *Parnass*, 1995, nos.3–4, is devoted to B. and film. BERGMAN, INGMAR. *Ingmar Bergman. Film och teater i växelverkan*, ed. Margareta Wirmark, Carlssons, 248 pp., provides background to B. the writer, although it deals with the interaction of film and theatre in papers at a 1995 Lund symposium with contributions by Egil Törnqvist, Birgitta Steene, and Henrik Sjögren, among others. M. J. Blackwell, 'The Silence. Disruption and disavowal in the movement beyond gender', *Scandinavica*, 35 : 233–68.

BJÖRLING, GUNNAR. L. Bäckström, 'Och att Björling', *Horisont*, 42. 5–6, 1995 : 36–39.

BOUCHT, BIRGITTA. B. Wallén, 'Döden som språk och skeende. Ett tematiskt raster i Birgitta Bouchts författarskap', *FT*:187–98.

BOYE, KARIN. *Karin Boyes liv och diktning*, VIII, Karin Boye Sällskapet, 93 pp., contains extracts from her brother Ulf's diary in connection with B.'s disappearance in 1941 and the correspondence between B. and Bonniers in 1922–41. Erik Lindholm, *På vandringsstig med diktarinnan Karin Boye*, Eget förlag, 64 pp., is an attractive and unpretentious volume by the founder of the B. Society, and provides a personal and affectionate presentation of B. through her poems, some previously unpublished, and an account of a meeting with B.'s old mother in 1956.

CARPELAN, BO. A. Johnsson, 'Ljus och något mera', *BLM*, 65.1 : 56–57.

DELBLANC, SVEN. Lars Ahlbom, *Sven Delblanc* (Litterära profiler), Natur och Kultur, 303 pp., is the first comprehensive monograph on D. and an excellent introduction in its admirably concentrated and lucid treatment of D.'s novels. *Kära Alice! Sven Delblancs brev till sin syster i Canada kommenterade av henne själv*, ed. Lars Helander, Sveriges Radios förlag, 1995, 103 pp., provides further insight into the family background, with their dominating, bullying father featured in these letters to his much younger half-sister Alice Boychuk.

DIKTONIUS, ELMER. *Elmer Diktonius brev*, ed. Jörn Donner and Marit Lindqvist (SSLF, 595), Helsinki, 1995, 456 pp., includes D.'s colourful letters in Swedish to a number of colleagues, among them Eyvind Johnson, Gunnar Ekelöf, and Erik Lindegren; a separate publication contains his letters in Finnish, *Kirjeitä ja katkelmia*, Helsinki, 1995.

EKELUND, VILHELM. Anders Olsson, *Ekelunds hunger*, Bonnier Alba, 121 pp., is an excellent introduction to E.'s works and attempts to explain the poet's shift to writing aphorisms.

EKELÖF, GUNNAR. J. Trinkwitz, 'Gunnar Ekelöfs *Ett fotografi*', *Akten* (Greifswald), 294–301. M. Jacobsson, '"Du är modern som är jungfru." En läsning av två dikter fran Gunnar Ekelöfs Diwandiktning utifrån hypogrammet Jungfrun-Modern', *TidLit*, 25.1:27–52. C. Franzén, 'Med blicken på Eurydike. Om det negativas makt hos Mallarmé och Ekelöf', *Edda*: 256–69. A. Melberg, 'Om svårigheten att läsa Mölna-Elegin', *ib.*, 270–75. B. Landgren, 'Polyederns gåta. Gunnar Ekelöfs dikt Melancholia i *Färjesång*', *ib.*, 328–43.

EKMAN, KERSTIN. A. Johnsson, 'Det som bestämmer en som människa', *BLM*, 65.5:39–41.

ENQUIST, PER OLOV. Eva Ekselius, *Andas fram mitt ansikte. Om den mytiska och djuppsykologiska strukturen hos Per Olov Enquist*, Stockholm-Stehag, Brutus Östlings Bokförlag Symposion, 415 pp., is a doctoral dissertation that manages to show how E.'s allegedly documentary and socially orientated works are in fact part of a lyrical tradition, opening up mythical and metaphysical dimensions. The recurrent theme of Hans Christian Andersen's fairy-tale about the Snow Queen and the boy with the ice puzzle becomes a metaphor for E.'s narrative technique.

ERIKSSON, HELENA. A. Mortensen, 'En egensinnig och aktuell avantgardism', *BLM*, 65.6:56–57.

ERIKSSON, ING-MARIE. T. von Vegesack, 'Skandalen Märit. Ing-Mari Eriksson — en litterär brottsling', *BLM*, 65.4:22–29; see also *ib.*, 65.5:51–52.

ERIKSSON, ULF. J. Arnald, 'Konsten att skapa i den döda vinkeln mellan resignation och envishet', *BLM*, 65.1:54–55.

FIORETOS, ARIS. 'Av alla färgerna de grå', discussion between F. and Durs Grünbein, *BLM*, 65.1:4–12. T. Götselius, 'Femton gastar på död mans kista', *ib.*, 65.2:55–57.

FORSSTRÖM, TUA. B. Pettersson, 'Så tuktas en snöleopard. Om Tua Forsströms poesi på engelska', *FT*:115–20.

GRAVE, ELSA. E. Lilja and I. Vilhelmsen, 'Social verklighet och text samt något om Elsa Graves metaforspråk', *TidLit*, 25.3–4:30–43.

GRIPE, MARIA. Carina Lidström, *Sökande, spegling, metamorfos. Tre vägar genom Maria Gripes skuggserie*, Stockholm-Stehag, Brutus Östlings Bokförlag Symposion, 1994, 189 pp., is a doctoral dissertation that will undoubtedly stimulate further research into G.'s works. It investigates G.'s *Skuggan* books as a process of development from a thematic point of view, comprising literary devices and themes also found in G.'s earliér works.

GUSTAFSSON, LARS. Ingemar Friberg, *'Jag är alltid annorlunda.' En studie i identitetsproblematiken i Lars Gustafssons tidiga författarskap mellan åren 1959 och 1967* (AUUUSH, 132), 619 pp., is a doctoral dissertation covering G.'s œuvre, both poetry and prose, from *Poeten Brumbergs sista dagar och död* to *Den egentliga berättelsen om herr Arenander*, and focusing on the novels in 'Främlingstrilogin'. The study discusses the relationship between the writer and the philosopher in the speculative and metaphysical orientation of the early novels, and thereby provides insight into 'the core of G.'s *œuvre*'. *Under den synliga skriften. Nedslag i Lars Gustafssons författarskap*, ed. Thomas Nydahl, Natur och Kultur (also *Ariel*, nos. 3–4, special issue), 96 pp., is a collection of essays. P. Berf, 'Reflexionen zu Möglichkeiten und Grenzen von Sprache und Literatur in Lars Gustafssons theoretischen Schriften', *Akten* (Greifswald), 240–53. H. Järv, 'En filosofs förvillelser', *Fenix*, 11.1, 1994–95:3–18.

HERMANSON, MARIE. P. Nilsson, 'En saga i verkligheten. Intervju med Marie Hermanson', *BLM*, 65.6:16–20.

HULDÉN, EVERT. S. Storå, 'Evert Huldén — reception och position', *FT*:121–32.

HULDÉN, LARS. 'Lars Huldén om sitt begynnande liv', ed. I.-B. Wik, *HLS*, 71:19–52 (SSLF, 604).

ISAKSSON, ULLA. Inger Littberger, *Ulla Isakssons romankonst*, Bonniers, 342 pp., is a doctoral dissertation, the first comprehensive academic study of this popular writer who merits only a brief mention in *Nordisk kvinnolitteraturhistoria*. It analyses closely five of her novels from a thematic and narratological perspective, stressing multifaceted and existential aspects. In her choice and treatment of themes, 'God, love and woman', I.'s ideals clearly belong to an older generation of feminist writers.

JANSSON, TOVE. Erik Kruskopf, *Skämttecknaren Tove Jansson*, Esbo, Schildts, 159 pp., deals with J. as a cartoonist, not least in the development of the Moomins. Lena Kåreland and Barbro Werkmäster, *Livsvandring i tre akter. En analys av Tove Janssons bilderböcker Hur gick det sen?*, *Vem ska trösta knyttet?*, *Den farliga resan* (SSBI, 54), Uppsala, Hjelm Förlag, 1994, 160 pp., presents three picture-books on the same theme — the inner journey of the mind leads to a discussion of existential problems and different phases in the development towards personal independence.

JOHNSON, EYVIND. Erland Lagerroth, 'Den klarnade erfarenhetens förvärv i *Hans nådes tid*', pp. 123–49 of Id., *Den klarnade erfarenhetens förvärv. Brott och straff, Processen, Stäppvargen, Varulven och Hans Nådes tid lästa av Erland Lagerroth*, Gothenburg, Korpen, 166 pp. The purpose of the studies of these five novels is existential, or, in the words of J., 'the gaining of clarified experience'. The analysis focuses on survival under any regime of political oppression, but also on J.'s own experiences of Swedish politics in the Second World War. L. Dahlberg, '"Om verkligheten i en roman." Eyvind Johnson och den självbiografiska romanen', *Edda*: 276–89. *Parnass*, no. 2, is devoted to J.

KIHLGÅRD, PETER. M. van Reis, 'Koncipieringen av en far', *BLM*, 65. 6:52–53.

KLINKMANN, SVEN-ERIK.   C. Braw, ' "Undret i det lilla." ' Om perspektiv och symboler i Sven-Erik Klinkmanns författarskap', *Horisont*, 43.4:45–58.

LIDMAN, SARA.   N. Björk, 'Ett långsamt lyssnande, ett ständigt vidgande av ord', *BLM*, 65.5:36–38.

LIDMAN, SVEN.   Knut Ahnlund, *Sven Lidman. Ett livsdrama*, Atlantis, 560 pp., deals with the dramatic turns of L.'s life, calling it the story of a destiny. It traces his shockingly sensual early life and poetry, followed by novels written in nationalistic vein, and culminating in his existential crisis and religious conversion. L. became the great preacher of the Pentecostal movement, until a bitter schism made him sever all his former ties and turn his relentless energy into writing his confessional memoirs in four volumes. The fragment of an unpublished fifth volume recently came to light, prompting Ahnlund's outstanding book.

LINDÉN, GURLI.   E.-S. Byggmästar, 'Samtal i ett öppet landskap med Gurli Lindén', *Horisont*, 42.5–6, 1995:40–43.

LINDGREN, ASTRID.   Arne Reberg, *Uppväxt med Astrid Lindgren*, Utbildningsförlaget Brevskolan, 201 pp., is a personal appreciation of L. and the extraordinary importance of her works, not only for generations of children but also for adults. It focuses initially on the child reader's experience but manages to give a rounded summary of her *œuvre* as a whole. *Astrid Lindgren och folkdikten*, ed. Per Gustavsson, Carlssons, 144 pp., is a collection of lectures on folklore and popular and provincial traditions in L., the importance of her childhood and her captivating oral technique. V. Edström maintains that the collection of stories and fairy tales *Sunnanäng* is one of the most important works of fiction in the 1950s. *Röster om Astrid Lindgren*, ed. Göran Eriksson (ABF-seminarium oktober 1995), ABF, 86 pp., stresses the varied nature of L.'s *œuvre*, and includes contributions by V. Edström, by M. Strömstedt on the essence of love and male and female characteristics, and by I. Ström on life after death and religion.

LINDORM, ERIK.   Evald Palmlund, *Eric Lindorm. Ett författarliv*, Carlssons, 492 pp., is the first detailed study of the life and writings of L., and stresses that he was essentially bourgeois, in spite of being labelled a representative of an early generation of working-class and even proletarian authors, because of links in his youth with the young socialist movement.

LJUNGQUIST, WALTER.   B. Georgii-Hemming, 'Sanningen att säga eller Utan tvekan kan jag inte säga någonting. Tankar kring Walter Ljungquists *Azalea*', *Horisont*, 43.4:9–16.

LUGN, KRISTINA.   Maria Österlund, ' "Det måste finnas en reserv- utgång." ' Om rumsligheten i Kristina Lugns lyrik', pp. 101–77 of Pia

Ingström et al., *Hemmet, rummet och revolten. Studier i litterärt gränsöverskridande* (LIÅA), 284 pp., is one of three essays by the latest generation of feminist literary scholarship.

LUNDKVIST, ARTUR. Jan Arnald, *Genrernas tyranni. Den genreöverskridande linjen i Artur Lundkvists författarskap*, Aiolos, 1995, 310 pp., is a doctoral dissertation of considerable importance as the first comprehensive work on L.'s extensive *œuvre*. It follows the development of L.'s early ambition to 'make prose into poetry', which eventually became a desire to do away with the dividing lines between the various literary forms. The analysis focuses on three samples from different periods: *Eldtema* (1939), *Malinga* (1952), and four later works, comprising the 'Tetralogy' (1978–84) where, according to Arnald, L. has achieved his ambition. H. Koch, 'Artur Lundkvist', *SBR*, no. 2: 2–3.

MARTINSON, HARRY. Johan Stenström, **Aniara. Från versepos till opera*, Malmö, Corona, 1994, 457 pp., is a doctoral dissertation on the development of the libretto and the resulting stage production. *Parnass*, 1994, no. 3, is devoted to Martinson. Eva Hannus, 'Verklighet till döds. Harry Martinsons kamp mot den onda civilisationen', *HLS*, 71:159–84 (SSLF, 604).

MELINESCU, GABRIELA. G. Lundin, 'Satir hos Gabriela Melinescu: ett utkast', *Horisont*, 43.1:36–37.

MOBERG, VILHELM. Two collections of articles by M., *I det ofria ordets tid*, ed. Anna-Karin Carlstoft (Vilhelm Moberg-sällskapet, 7), Carlssons, 125 pp., and *Att upptäcka Amerika 1948–1949*, ed. Gunnar Eidevall (Vilhelm Moberg-sällskapet, 6), Carlssons, 1995, 109 pp., give insight into the background and contemporary setting of *Rid i natt!* and *Utvandrarna* respectively. *Parnass*, no. 1, is devoted to M.

NILSSON PIRATEN, FRITIOF. *Parnass*, 1995, no. 6, is devoted to Nilsson. Bo Magnusson, 'Några reflexioner kring Fritiof Nilsson Piratens novell *Vänner emellan*', *Horisont*, 42.5–6, 1995:90–94.

NORÉN, LARS. B. Gustavsson and H. Jansson, '2 x Lars Norén och hans döda pjäser', *Horisont*, 43.1:60–63.

NYMAN, VALDEMAR. C. Nynäs, 'Undret kommer då du slutar att vilja eller Allt beror på vad vi gör medan vi väntar. Två romaner av Valdemar Nyman', *FT*:446–64.

OSWALD, GÖSTA. **Breven till Ranveig*, ed. Torsten Ekbom, Atlantis, 1995, 328 pp., provides insight into both O. and literature of the 1940s in general.

OTERDAHL, JEANNA. Ying Toijer-Nilsson, *Jeanna Oterdahl. Liv och verk* (SSBI, 58), Rabén & Sjögren, 256 pp., is a thoroughly researched biography of O. as an eminent critic, educationalist and writer, stressing her importance for children's and young people's literature.

PARLAND, HENRY. R. Åsbacka, 'Att skriva sig fri. Om Henry Parland och Marcel Proust', *FT*:133–45.

PERCIVAL [BACKLUND, PERCY]. Z. Alagic, 'En solrevolutionärs syn på världen och sitt skapande: en intervju med Percival', *Horisont*, 43.1:50–59.

RUIN, HANS. N.-E. Forsgård, 'Poesiens samlande nu. Hans Ruin och tidens anlete', *HLS*, 71:185–206 (SSLF, 604).

SAND, ARNE. P. A. Tjäder, 'Sand för vinden. En doldis i den svenska litteraturen', *BLM*, 65.4:30–35.

SANDMAN LILIUS, IRMELIN. Susanne Ahlroth-Särkelä, *Upptäcktsresor i en värld som ständigt är ny*. *Irmelin Sandman Lilius barnbokskritik i Dagens Nyheter och Hufvudstadsbladet 1973–93* (MLIÅA, 23), 135 pp., introduces a writer of children's books as a literary critic of the same genre, and attempts to evaluate her impact.

SEM-SANDBERG, STEVE. A. Ehnmark, 'Gripen av berättelsen men irriterad på berättaren', *BLM*, 65.2:50–51.

SILFVERSTOLPE, GUNNAR MASCOLL. L. Gustafsson, 'Samtal med en stengäst: om Silfverstolpes statydikt', *BLM*, 65.1:44–50.

SJÖGREN, PEDER. Anders Tyrberg, *Skuldkänslans broderskap. En bok om Peder Sjögrens romaner*, Carlssons, 361 pp., is a doctoral dissertation, and deals with S.'s seven novels. Tyrberg shows that S. was not really an outsider as far as the 1940s generation was concerned, and indicates influence from Sartre and similarities with Lars Ahlin and Stig Dagerman. By concentrating on S.'s advanced narrative techniques, he exposes a common preoccupation with the theme of guilt, and parallels with E. Lévinas's moral philosophy.

SONNEVI, GÖRAN. A. Johnsson, 'Trösten i att inte vara skild från oändligheten', *BLM*, 65.6:44–45.

STENIUS, YRSA. A.-S. Lindholm, 'Jag har berättat denna historia därför att den angår mig. En undersökning av Yrsa Stenius essäsamling *Makten och kvinnligheten*', *HLS*, 71:207–41 (SSLF, 604).

STIERNSTEDT, MARIKA. U. Wittrock, 'Kvinnor på den offentliga scenen — Ellen Key och Marika Stiernstedt', *Samlaren*, 116, 1995[1996]:95–106, considers the influence of Ellen Key on S.

STRÖMBERG, RAGNAR. A. Johansson, 'Det sublima i Ragnar Strömbergs poesi', *TidLit*, 25.1:3–26. L. Elleström, 'Ett intensivt förhållande till tomheten', *BLM*, 65.6:54–55.

SVENBRO, JESPER. T. Götselius, 'Och nu stå alla minnen upp', *BLM*, 65.1:51–53.

SÖDERBERG, HJALMAR. R. Jarvi, 'Hjalmar Söderberg on August Strindberg. The perspective of a theater critic and the influence of a dramatist', *ScSt*, 68:343–55. *Parnass*, 1994, no. 1, is devoted to S.

SÖDERGRAN, EDITH. Edith Södergran, *Brev*, ed. Agneta Rahikainen (SSLF, 563, 2), Helsinki, 312 pp., is the second volume of the critical edition of S.'s collected works in three volumes. It contains all known preserved letters from 1907 to S.'s death in 1923. *Åttio år Edith Södergran. Verk och reception 1916–1995. En bibliografi*, ed. Carita Backman and Siv Storå (SSLF, 606), Helsinki, 224 pp., is a comprehensive bibliography which covers works by S., also in translation, as well as literature on her. *Parnass*, 1995, no. 2, is devoted to S.

SÖDERHJELM, ALMA. Marja Engman, *Det främmande ögat. Alma Söderhjelm i vetenskapen och offentligheten* (SSLF, 602), Helsinki, 480 pp., a doctoral dissertation by a historian, is the biography of a remarkable 'cultural personality' and the first woman professor in Finland, and deals at length with S.'s many and varied activities: as an academic, as a Swedish-speaking individual in Finland and a Finlander in Sweden, as a theatre and film critic, and as an author of poetry and novels.

TRANSTRÖMER, TOMAS. A. Johnsson, 'En tunn bok med hög specifik vikt', *BLM*, 65.2:52–54, deals with *Sorgegondolen. Allt om böcker*, no. 4–5, is a special issue on T.

TROTZIG, BIRGITTA. K. Bak, 'Polyfont och monofont. Om Birgitta Trotzigs intertextuella poetik', *Akten* (Greifswald), 233–39. E. Ström, 'Texter som bildar ett förklaringsberg', *BLM*, 65.6:38–39.

TUNSTRÖM, GÖRAN. *Röster om Göran Tunström*, ed. Kurt Stern (ABF-seminarium mars 1994), ABF, 88 pp., includes contributions by B. Munkhammar, M. Bergh, A. Rahikainen and T. himself. A. Johnsson, 'Hur länge lyser vi?', *BLM*, 65.4:50–52.

TUOMINEN, MIRJAM. I.-B. Wik, '"Kassandras klarsynta skälvning."' Tal och tystnad i Mirjam Tuominens produktion', *Horisont*, 43.5:26–37. T. Korsström, 'Häxan, barnet, bödeln, slätten. Mirjam Tuominen i Nykarleby', *ib.*, 38–45.

VREESWIJK, CORNELIS. Ulf Carlsson, *Cornelis Vreeswijk: artist, vispoet, lyriker*, Malmö, Corona, 332 pp., is a doctoral dissertation on V., regarded by some as the successor of Carl Michael Bellman and Evert Taube. It analyses the relationship between V.'s songs and poetry, and his various roles in life.

WÄGNER, ELIN. L. Ekelund, 'Elin Wägner på torpet Björkelund vid Vättern: en impressionistisk skiss', *Horisont*, 43.1:64–66. *Parnass*, 1994, no. 2, is devoted to W.

WEISS, PETER. M. Bergh, '"My secret life": Peter Weiss franska förbindelser', *BLM*, 65.1:29–38.

ÖSTERGREN, KLAS. D. Landmark, 'Supandets allegorier. Om Klas Östergrens sydsvenska romansvit', *Horisont*, 43.5:56–59.

5

SLAVONIC LANGUAGES*

I. CZECH STUDIES

LANGUAGE

By Marie Nováková and Jana Papcunová,
Ústav pro jazyk český Akademie věd České republiky, Prague

1. General and Bibliographies

Basic problems of present-day Czech are summed up in the proceedings *Spisovnost a nespisovnost dnes (Sborník příspěvků z mezinárodní konference 'Spisovnost a nespisovnost v současné jazykové a literární komunikaci')*, Brno, Masaryk Univ., 261 pp. F. Čermák (14–18) deals with the relationship of common and standard Czech in spoken communication today; F. Daneš (19–27) discusses the theory of standard language based on works of the Prague Linguistic Circle; Z. Hlavsa (28–32) and M. Jelínek (36–42) refer to criteria for the codification and systematic character of standard Czech; J. Chloupek (33–35) characterizes standard Czech as a formal variant of the national language; J. Kořenský (43–47) draws attention to the relationship of the standard language and communication success; J. Kraus (48–52) gives reasons for care for language culture and correctness; P. Sgall (53–58) looks for origins of overcorrectness in Czech; and O. Uličný (59–63) submits a recapitulative view of present-day Czech. A number of further contributions examine the concept of the standard language and use of the standard form of Czech from various points of view (D. Davidová, I. Nebeská, S. Romportl, Z. Rusínová, I. Svobodová, M. Šipkova, J. Bartošek). M. Dokulil (98–102) focuses on Czech orthography, while M. Krčmová (103–05), and Z. Palková (106–09) discuss orthoepy. Studies by O. Martincová, V. Schmiedtová, F. Uher, and M. Žemlička relate to Czech vocabulary. J. Bachmannová, M. Janečková, and S. Kloferová refer to the correlation between dialects and the standard language. Other papers focus on proper names, on the relationship between standard/

---

* For languages using the Cyrillic alphabet names are transliterated according to the Library of Congress system, omitting diacritics and ligatures.

substandard language in literary communication, literature, translation, mass media, and in school practice. Furthermore, the proceedings *Jazyk a jeho užívání. Sborník k životnímu jubileu profesora Oldřicha Uličného*, ed. Iva Nebeská and Alena Macurová, Prague, Charles Univ., 314 pp., comprise a great number of linguistic topics, therefore, the most important papers are mentioned in appropriate sections. Another comprehensive work exploring Czech from various points of view is a book of essays by Světla Čmejrková, František Daneš, Jiří Kraus, and Ivana Svobodová, entitled *Čeština, jak ji znáte i neznáte*, Prague, Academia, 259 pp. (first broadcast in a radio serial in 1993–96). The authors elucidate various language phenomena from morphology, stylistics, structure of text and language communication in cultural and historical context and often in comparison to foreign languages. Iva Nebeská, *Jazyk, norma, spisovnost*, Prague, Karolinum, 159 pp., presents in her monograph a survey of development up to now and the present state of the Czech language standard. J. Hronek and P. Sgall, *JazA*, 33:36–39, deal with some topical questions of language culture. Two articles concern the question as to whether the national language is endangered. J. Kraus, *NŘ*, 79:1–9, and V. Šaur, *ib.*, 10–14, refer to the paper by A. Stich regarding the same question and bring further experience in this matter.

BIBLIOGRAPHIES: M. Nováková has prepared a contribution to the Czech Slavonic bibliography for *Bibliografia językoznawstwa slawisticznego za rok 1993*, ed. Zofia Rudnik-Karwatowa, vol. 1, Wa, Slawistyczny Ośrodek Wydawniczy, 373–418 (314 items). Z. Tyl and M. Tylová, **Bibliographie linguistique de l'année 1993*, ed. M. Janse and S. Tol, Dordrecht–Boston–London, Kluwer, 797–812, compile a selective bibliography of Czech linguistics (303 entries). *SPFFBU — řada jazykovědná*, A44, includes two personal bibliographies: of Adolf Erhart (for the period 1987–95), 143–44, and of Jan Balhar (for the years 1957–96), 145–50. The bibliography of Oldřich Uličný, *Jazyk a jeho užívání*, Prague, 299–315, includes his works from linguistics, informatics and translations (1960–96).

2. HISTORY OF THE LANGUAGE

The study by G. Thomas, 'Towards a history of Modern Czech purism: the problem of covert germanisms', *SEER*, 74:401–20, covers the development of Czech purism since the National Revival until the present day and the impact of the journal *Naše řeč* upon the cultivation of the language; he also analyses loans from German. P. Kosek, *SPFFBU — řada jazykovědná*, A44, 115–21, concentrates on the conjunction *jak* based on a homily by Damascén Marek, *Trojí chléb nebeský*, Prague, 1728. J. Pleskalová, *NŘ*, 79:204–06, examines the role of the so-called hypocoristics in Old Czech (based on material from Kosmas's chronicle and other Old Czech documents). P. J. Šafařík is introduced as a predecessor and not as a founder of Czech historical grammar in a paper by D. Šlosar, *Slavia*, 65:123–27. Several studies are devoted to the language and its level of development in the works of authors of the past: J. Skutil, *České období Jana Amose Komenského*, Brno, Moravské zemské muzeum, 221 pp., on the language of the Czech works of Comenius; M. David, *Výběr*, 33:30–35, analyses the Czech homily by Mikuláš Krupěhorský from the 16th c.; M. Červenka, *ČL*, 44:171–80, follows the beginnings of the Czech dactyl in a ballad by Šebestián Hněvkovský, *Vnislav a Běla*; J. Traxler, *Český lid*, 83:139–53, analyses the language of a newly discovered work by Jan Jeník z Bratřic, *Písně krátké lidu obecného českého* (1832). Finally, Jana Jančáková and Karel Kučera publish *Starší české texty s přehledem morfologie staré češtiny a cvičeními*, Prague, Charles Univ., 109 pp.

3. MORPHOLOGY AND WORD FORMATION

K. Osolsobě, *SPFFBU — řada jazykovědná*, A44, 59–70, summarizes the results of a comprehensive automatic morphological analysis of Czech; K. Trost, *ib.*, 75–89, focuses on the specific feature of Slavonic languages — aspect; he examines the correlation between perfectivity/imperfectivity and iterative verbs. S. Kloferová, *NŘ*, 79:187–91, comments on gender doublets both in standard Czech and dialects. Jaroslav Hubáček, *Tvoření slov v češtině*, Ostrava, Ostravská Univ., 42 pp., briefly sketches word formation in Czech. D. Šlosar has written two studies devoted to Czech compound words: *NŘ*, 79:192–95, discusses the productivity of V–(K)–S compounds (e.g. *lamželezo, trativod, kazimír*), moreover, he, *Jazyk a jeho užívání*, 103–11, gives a survey of compounds since Proto-Slavonic, Old Church Slavonic, Old Czech until present-day Czech. P. Piťha, *PBML*, 65–66:53–65, describes pronominal expressions of possessivity in Czech.

4. SYNTAX AND TEXT

P. Karlík, *NŘ*, 79:66–72, deals with the position and function of verbs in the sentence; he investigates the relationship between the verb as a word class/the predicator as an expression, which meaning more or less reflects respective aspects of extralinguistic factors/the predicate as a central component of syntactic structures and utterances. Furthermore, Id., in a study on the basic functions of deagentization in Czech communication, *SPFFBU — řada jazykovědná*,

A44, 97–104, analyses motives leading the speaker to remove the agent from the position of subject. L. Nebeský and P. Novák, *SaS*, 57: 249–63, investigate the character of Czech word order. F. Štícha, *NŘ*, 79: 26–31, points out a remarkable and in grammars often neglected phenomenon in Czech, which is the intercrossing of sentences. The predicate of the subordinate clause is formally incorporated into the preceding subordinating clause and thus formally, but not as far as the contents is concerned, coordinated with its predicate (structures of the type *Kam že to pojedeš?*). S. Romportl, *SPFFBU — řada jazykovědná*, A44, 71–74, describes Czech deverbative words, gerunds and constructions with them. A. M. Perissutti, *ib.*, 105–14, discusses indefinite determiners *O, nějaký* and *jakýsi*. Another study by P. Karlík, *Jazyk a jeho užívání*, 74–80, is on the use of the Czech past conditional.

5. ORTHOGRAPHY

The aim of the monograph by Radoslava Brabcová, *Novinky z pravopisu a tvarosloví*, Dobřichovice, Kava-Pech, 80 pp., is to sum up new orthographic phenomena with special respect to the cases, in which most mistakes occur.

6. LEXICOLOGY AND PHRASEOLOGY

Many authors have applied their attention to this topic. Only the most significant contributions have been chosen. First, *Studia lexicologica* by Josef Filipec, ed. E. Eichler, Munich, Sagner, 171 pp., should be mentioned. It is an anthology of the author's studies from 1957–95 referring to Czech lexicology and lexicography. Furthermore, *Slovník českých synonym*, by Karel Pala, Jan Všianský and František Čermák, Prague, Nakl. Lidové noviny, 439 pp., has been published this year. Then, there is a great number of papers concerning various subjects. E. Mleziva, *SaS*, 57: 283–96, on the impact of new social changes after 1989 on Czech vocabulary; F. Čermák, *ib.*, 30–46, on the system, functions, forms and semantics of Czech prepositions; Id., *ib.*, 81–90, on phraseology in newspaper editorials, analysing 131 idioms from the newspaper *Lidové noviny* in 1995. An interesting topic is chosen by M. Nekula, *Jazyk a jeho užívání*, 87–92, who examines lexicalized units and idioms denoting ethnic groups; L. Stepanova, *ib.*, 81–86, focuses on set phrases with the meaning 'to get nothing' in Czech. V. Šaur, *JazA*, 33: 15–20, sketches perspectives of Czech etymology; M. Ireinová, *NŘ*, 79: 167–68, focuses on some neologisms in Czech and on their suitability (*osušovna, vloženka, signálka*). I. Němec, *ib.*, 57–60; explains the prefix *pro-* in the word *prostředek*;

M. Homolková, *ib.*, 21–25, discusses the verb *protiřečit* in Old and modern Czech; F. Štícha, *ib.*, 135–40, is on the expression *jen tak* in Czech; and V. Malinovský, *ib.*, 246–51, draws attention to inappropriate use of the expression *ovšem*. J. Hajič, *PBML*, 65–66:29–51, presents an interesting paper entitled 'Semi-automatic classification of Czech nouns', related to computational lexicography. TERMINOLOGY. P. Flegl, *NŘ*, 79:85–98, and A. Černá, *ib.*, 124–28, are on Czech psychologic terminology, the former on the development of Czech characterologic terminology, the latter on the beginning of psychologic terminology prior to the 15th c.; D. Cypriánová, *ib.*, 103–05, on linguistic terminology in two volumes of the journal *Naše řeč*; A. Měšťan, *Slavia*, 65, 139–40, on the contribution of P. J. Šafařík to Czech and Slovak legal terminology. Last but not least, Milan Pohunek, *Rybářský slovník*, Plzeň, Fraus, 126 pp., compiles fishing terminology.

7. SEMANTICS AND PRAGMATICS

Two fundamental semantic studies have been written by J. Hoffmannnová, 'The structure of the semantic context of TIME in various text types', *Prague Linguistic Circle Papers 2*, Amsterdam, Benjamins, 319–30, and M. Ueda, 'On the semantics and discourse functions of Czech hybrid conditionals', *Jazyk a jeho užívání*, 36–45. J. Panevová, *ib.*, 14–23, expounds the meaning of cases, specifically of the instrumental in Czech. Irena Vaňková, *Mlčení a řeč v komunikaci, jazyce a kultuře*, Prague, Institut sociálních vztahů, 280 pp., studies the semantic role of silence in Czech communication.

Z. Rusínová, *SPFFBU — řada jazykovědná*, A44, 91–95, explores the use of diminutives in Czech from the pragmatic point of view; she follows the speaker's attitude to diminutives and the intensification of quantity in discourse. Onomatopoeic words and pragmatics are topics of an essay by R. Blatná, *Jazyk a jeho užívání*, 93–102. These words, according to the author, have notional and pragmatic meaning, which defines their functions in discourse.

Finally, V. Pfeffer, *Normy normalizace*, Opava, Slezská Univ., 118–22, concentrates on the language of normalization, i.e. on the character and development of Czech in the period of normalization in the 1970s.

8. SOCIOLINGUISTICS AND DIALECTOLOGY

Konstanty a proměny mluvených útvarů českého národního jazyka. Sborník prací Filozofické fakulty Ostravské univerzity, řada Linguistica 2, Ostrava, 151 pp., comprises contributions by E. Jandová, M. Horsáková, D. Davidová,

I. Bogoczová, M. Grygerková, E. Demlová, N. Bayerová, and J. Hubáček. Most of these contributions deal with North-Moravian dialects.

DIALECTS. E. Šipková, *NŘ*, 79:212–14, explains the use of the suffix *-va/-vá* in the formation of prepositions (*kroměvá*) in the dialect of the Moravian region Haná; K. Fic, *ib.*, 196–203, describes the formation of agricultural naming units in Czech dialects; J. Jančáková, *Jazyk a jeho užívání*, 129–38, examines the dialect of reemigrants from Malá Zubovština in Ukraine, that shows evident features of North-East Bohemian dialects from the surroundings of Hradec Králové; M. Krčmová, *ib.*, 119–28, describes routine speech in East Moravia. L. Hašová, *ČMF*, 78:88–96, investigates the language situation in the city of Nejdek near Carlsbad and analyses the utterances of respondents who are not native Czechs. A. Jaklová, *NŘ*, 79:15–20, deals with fishing slang.

9. STYLISTICS

The major work in this field is *Od tvaru k smyslu textu. Stylistické reflexe a interpretace* by Karel Hausenblas, Prague, Charles Univ., 226 pp., referring to the development of the discipline in Czech.

M. Jelínek, *Jazyk a jeho užívání*, 240–50, describes Czech administrative-legal style; S. Čmejrková, *ib.*, 265–74, relates to the language and style of magazines for girls; Z. K. Slabý, *Zlatý máj*, 40:55–56, follows the style and language of Czech fairy tales, the question of archaisms in them and changes of their style (e.g. adaptations for film or television); N. Kvítková, *NŘ*, 79:61–65, analyses the language of contemporary religious discourses; D. Svobodová, *ib.*, 99–102, comments on English expressions in Czech journalistic style (based on material of newspapers and magazines in 1994).

ASPECTS OF THE LANGUAGE OF INDIVIDUAL WRITERS. An interesting monograph by Alexandr Stich, *Od Karla Havlíčka k Františku Halasovi (lingvoliterární studie)*, Prague, Torst, 331 pp., comprises 13 essays on the language and works of Karel Havlíček Borovský, Jan Neruda, Alois Jirásek, Václav Holan, František Halas and others. Jiřina Hůrková, *Poézie, jak jsi krásná. (O tvorbě Josefa Kainara)*, Prostějov, IPOS ARTAMA, 39 pp., analyses the poetic work of Josef Kainar. M. Jankovič, *ČL*, 44:115–45, discusses the style of Bohumil Hrabal; J. Bartůňková and J. Zeman, *Jazyk a jeho užívání*, 222–29, follow language humour, contrasts on the level of language codes and the use of proper names in the theatre of the absurd (so-called Jára Cimrman's plays) by Ladislav Smoljak and Zdeněk Svěrák; P. Mareš, *ib.*, 212–21, explores the question of multilinguism in prose works for children by Václav Čtvrtek and Vladimír Henzl; and finally, F. Štícha,

NŘ, 79:78–84, deals with the language and style of memoirs by the actor Vlastimil Brodský.

10. ONOMASTICS

One of the fundamental studies is the article by E. Michálek, *NŘ*, 79:53–54, regarding the Church Slavonic features in Old Czech personal and place names. L. Havlíková, *Slavia*, 65:89–98, also refers to historical place names and expounds the name Velká Morava (Magna Moravia) and other old Moravian toponyms. L. Olivová-Nezbedová, *NŘ*, 79:54–55, explains the use of the suffix *-čice* in Czech field names; L. Švestková, *ib.*, 165–67, examines the denoting of wayside crosses in South Bohemia; R. Vermouzek and J. Vodička, *Vlastivědný věstník moravský*, 48:51–54, cover names of ponds and mills in the river basin of the Moravian stream Ponávka. M. Čechová, *NŘ*, 79:129–34, deals with the names of Czech travel agencies. E. Uhrová and F. Uher, 'Die Onymie in künstlerischen Autobiographien vom Standpunkt des tschechisch-deutschen Sprachgebiets', *BBGN — řada germanistická*, R1, 21–29, relates to literary onomastics, based on Bohumil Hrabal's trilogy, *Svatby v domě*, and on its German translation.

11. LANGUAGES IN CONTACT AND COMPARATIVE STUDIES

Comparative studies, comparing Czech with other languages, are a famous topic of present-day linguistic production. The authors often compare Czech with several languages, or, on the other hand, only with one language. It is necessary to mention a monograph *Slovanská věta*, by Helena Běličová and Ludmila Uhlířová, Prague, Euroslavica, 277 pp. The authors expound the structure of the simple sentence in Czech and in the modern Slavonic languages. Further, Charles E. Townsend and Laura A. Janda submit a comprehensive monograph, *Common and Comparative Slavic: Phonology and Inflection with Special Attention to Russian, Polish, Czech, Serbo-Croatian, Bulgarian*, Columbus, Ohio, Slavica, 310 pp. The authors concentrate on the development of the Slavonic languages, on their phonology and morphology (also from the comparative point of view) and give surveys of Slavonic languages, Czech on pp. 269–77. A noteworthy study 'On implicitness in language and discourse. A contrastive view' by, F. Štícha, *Prague Linguistic Circle Papers 2*, Amsterdam, Benjamins, 331–46, compares various ways of explicit and implicit expression in Czech, English, French, and German. J. Šabršula, *ib.*, 177–89, compares single morphemes, words and sentences in Czech, French, and Latin.

Most attention is attracted by the comparing of Czech and English: B. Mosey and J. Chamonikolasová, 'Nucleus position and tone unit length in English and Czech', *SPFFBU — řada anglicistická*, S2, 15–21, deal with sentence stress in discourse; S. Čmejrková, 'Academic writing in Czech and English', *Academic Writing*, Amsterdam, Benjamins, 137–52, discusses the language of science, special style and standard of writing; J. Hladký, *ČMF*, 78:79–87, follows gemination as a word-formative element in both languages; Id., *The Czech and the English Names of Mushrooms*, Brno, Masaryk Univ., 320 pp., also compiles English names of mushrooms and adds their Czech equivalent in a glossary. Aleš Klégr, *The Noun in Translation. A Czech–English Contrastive Study*, Prague, Karolinum, 241 pp., expounds shift in the meaning in translation of nouns from Czech into English.

Czech–Russian confrontation is represented by a study by P. Dachtlerová, *ČMF*, 78:4–13, on computer terms from the lexical point of view; Czech–Polish confrontation is the subject of a monograph by a Polish Bohemicist Janusz Siatkowski, *Czesko-polskie kontakty językowe*, Wa, Energeia, 272 pp., on Czech–Polish language contacts. Finally, Amr Ahmed Shaturny, *ČJL*, 47:32–34, mentions some agreements in standard and substandard Czech and Arabic.

12.   CZECH ABROAD

Recently, Czech linguistics has taken considerable interest in the language of Czech emigrants and in the state of their language awareness and knowledge. Most authors are interested in American Czech: I. Dubovický, *Český lid*, 83:229–47, discusses questions concerning their identity and functions of their national language (Czech) in this situation; K. Kučera, *Jazyk a jeho užívání*, 112–18, on splitting in the development of American Czech; A. Vašek, *SPFFBU — řada anglicistická*, S2, 71–87, on language acculturation in American Czech. M. Toncrová, *Národopisná revue*, 6:23–25, reports on the language of the Czech minority in Vienna.

13.   BILINGUAL DICTIONARIES

The most important work is *Anglicko-český slovník s nejnovějšími výrazy*, comp. Josef Fronek, Prague, Leda, 1204 pp., which concentrates on the colloquial language. R. Mirchi, *První česko–perský slovník*, Prague, Pardis, 558 pp., fills up a gap in the branch by publishing the first Czech–Persian dictionary. Teresa Zofia Orłoś and Joanna Hornik are the compilers of *Czesko-polski słownik skrzydlatych słów*, Kw, Universitas, 374 pp.; they expound Czech familiar quotations and give their Polish and English equivalents.

LITERATURE

II. SLOVAK STUDIES

LANGUAGE

POSTPONED

LITERATURE

POSTPONED

III. POLISH STUDIES

LANGUAGE

By JOHN BATES, *University of Glasgow*

1. PHONOLOGY, MORPHOLOGY, AND WORD FORMATION

B. Kreja, 'Nadtypy i typy słowotwórcze — ich struktura i dynamika', *JPol*, 76: 11–16; M. Łaziński, 'Bezokolicznik czasownika dokonanego jako człon wymagany w zdaniu', *PJ*, no. 1 (530):21–29, which discusses the aspect of verbs accompanying the semantically related '*zdążyć/zdążać, zdołać, potrafić, udać się*', is an attempt to treat an issue that has been traditionally somewhat neglected in dictionaries and grammar books; G. Sawicka, 'Morfologia bez granic', *PJ*, no. 4 (353):43–57.

GENDER AND INFLECTION. M. Kucała, 'Odpowiedź redakcji: 682. Odmiana nazwiska *Werth*', *JPol*, 76: 233–34; H. S., 'Znów o kłopotach z odmianą czasowników na *-ywać*', *PJ*, nos 5–6 (354–55): 107–08.

PREFIXES. B. Kreja, 'Drobiazgi słowotwórcze: 44. O formacjach z przedrostkiem *niedo-* typu *niedorozwój, niedolisek*', *JPol*, 76: 160–63; R. S., '*Anty-*', *PJ*, no. 3 (352):72–76; Id., '*Neo-* i *post-*', *PJ*, no. 4 (353):74–78.

SUFFIXES. B. Kreja, 'O formacjach na *-ostwo* w języku polskim. (Stan dzisiejszy i historia)', *JPol*, 76:88–96; M. Kucała, '*Franciszek* i inne imiona na *-ek*', *ib.*, 248–53; A. Skudrzykowa, 'Nazwiska żeńskie z przyrostkiem *-owa* we współczesnej polszczyźnie ogólnej', *ib.*, 17–23.

WORD ORDER. M. Demojedowa, 'Czy polszczyzna ma szyk swobodny?', *PJ*, nos 5–6 (354–55): 7–14; F. Sławski, 'Kilka uwag o miejscu enklityki w języku polskim', *JPol*, 76:242–47.

HISTORICAL. K. Maćkowiak, 'Archaizmy w refleksji leksykalno-stylistycznej polskiego Oświecenia', *PL(W)*, 87:159–69; W. R. Rzepka and W. B. Twardzik, 'Archaizmy fleksyjne w *Rozmyślaniu przemyskim*', *JPol*, 76:97–102; Id., 'Archaizmy fleksyjne w *Rozmyślaniu przemyskim* (2)', *ib.*, 321–27.

2. SYNTAX

E. Łuczyński, 'Przecinek w wypowiedzeniu złożonym. Wybrane problemy normatywne', *PJ*, no. 4 (353):23–33; Id., 'Zróżnicowanie stylistyczne interpunkcji polskiej', *JPol*, 76:29–39; Id., 'Po co nam ortografia i interpunkcja?', *ib.*, 184–90; M. Ruszowski, 'Odchylenia

od norm składniowych w prozie dwudziestolecia międzywojennego',
ib., 141–46.

3. LEXICOLOGY AND PHRASEOLOGY

Praktyczny słownik poprawnej polszczyzny. Nie tylko dla młodzieży, ed.
Andrzej Markowski, Wa, Wyd. Naukowe PWN, 480 pp. Maciej
Grochowski, *Słownik polskich przekleństw i wulgaryzmów*, Wa, Wyd.
Naukowe PWN, 185 pp., has an appendix containing synonyms.
M. Zaśko-Zielińska and I. Borkowski, '*Słownik polszczyzny potocznej*
J. Anusiewicza i J. Skawińskiego na tle polskiego dorobku leksyko-
graficznego', *PJ*, no. 3 (352):35–49; M. Borejszo, 'W kręgu słown-
ictwa bożonarodzeniowego', *PJ*, no. 1 (530):1–11; Id., 'W kręgu
słownictwa bożonarodzeniowego (c.d.)', *PJ*, no. 2 (531):1–11; E.
Breza, '*Pszenżyto* i *świdzik*', *JPol*, 76:227–28; A. Czamara, '*Made in
Europe* — Leksykalne zapożyczenia z języka angielskiego w polskim
polu wyrazowym handlu i usług', *PJ*, nos 5–6 (354–55):23–30; Z.
Saloni, 'Homonimia a hasła w słownikach polskich', *JPol*, 76:303–14;
J. Wiktorowicz, 'Einige kritische Bemerkungen zur Deutsch-Pol-
nischen Lexikographie', *KN*, 43:3–9; R. Wołosz, 'Errata do *Indeksu a
tergo do Słownika języka polskiego pod redakcją Witolda Doroszewskiego*', *PJ*,
no. 3 (352):64–67.

INDIVIDUAL WORDS. L. Bednarczuk, '*Wajdelota*', *JPol*, 76:264–73;
H. Duda, '*Yamaże* czy *yamasze?*', *ib.*, 168–73; A. A. Kalashnikov,
'Славянские этимологии. Польск. oszczarki', *Slavianovedenie*
no. 1:15–17; J. Lasoń, '*Okręt podwodny* czy *łódź podwodna?*', *JPol*,
183–84; W. Mańczak, 'W sprawie *absolutnie* "absolutnie nie"', *ib.*,
217–18; T. Piotrowski, 'Kto pisze *rekwiem*, ręka do góry . . . O
normach ortograficznych', *ib.*, 218–21; K. Pisarkowa, '*Dobna* na
Kiriwinie', *ib.*, 258–63; R.S., '*Land* i *-land*', *PJ*, no. 1 (530):75–79;
S. Urbańczyk, 'O *rekwiem* i *requiem*', *JPol*, 76:221–23; B. Walczak,
'Jeszcze o *polocie* i *lotniku*', *ib.*, 103–07.

PHRASES. S. Bąba, '*Być między młotem a kowadłem*', *JPol*,
76:398–400; Id., '*Być (znajdować się) w oku cyklonu*', *ib.*, 76–78; Id.,
'*Mysz się nie przemknie*', *ib.*, 230–33; Id., '*Skoczyć sobie do gardła*', *ib.*,
78–79; Id., '*Wisieć u czyjejś klamki*', *ib.*, 397–98; Id., '*Wpędzić kogoś do
grobu*', *ib.*, 228–30, and M. Kucała, 'Dopisek', *ib.*, 230; J. Miodek,
'*Przekładać się* — "znajdować odbicie, odpowiadać, przylegać" ', *PJ*,
no. 1 (530):80–81.

4. SEMANTICS AND PRAGMATICS

The volume *Dziennikarstwo i świat mediów*, ed. Zbigniew Bauer and
Edward Chudziński, Kw, Oficyna Cracovia, 303 pp., includes:

W. Pisarek, 'Podstawy retoryki dziennikarskiej' (133–48); G. Majkowska, 'O języku mediów' (149–61), registers the neologisms, loan words, and particles such as *euro-* and *eko-* which are becoming ever more prevalent in Polish media language. Jerzy Bralczyk, *Język na sprzedaż*, Wa, Biblioteka 'Rzeczypospolitej', Business Press Ltd, n.d., 198 pp., is written with customary gusto and analyses the grammar, syntax, and varieties of language used in Polish advertising. *Literatura i władza*, ed. Bożena Wojnowska, Wa, IBL, 271 pp., includes: M. Głowiński, 'Władza ludowa przemawia do pisarzy' (115–29), an interesting analysis of three key speeches delivered to writers by Bierut, Berman, and Gomułka, especially the implications of the phrase 'nie nadążać'. K. Bakuła, 'O zmarłych należy mówić tylko dobrze. Wartościowanie w nekrologu, kondolencjach i mowie pogrzebowej', *Polonistyka*, 49:225–28; I. Burkacka, 'Konstrukcje z imiesłowem przysłówkowym w ocenie użytkowników języka', *PJ*, no. 2 (531):12–31; A. Chojecki, 'Gdy mówi mowa', *TD*, nos 2–3 (38–39):233–40; A. Dutka, 'L'opacification du dire en polonais: les glosses métaénonciatives dans une approche non-communicationelle', *KN*, 43:23–34; M. Fleischer, 'Zeit- und Raumbezeichnungen als Weltbildkomponenten. Systemtheoretische und konstruktivistische Perspektive (an polnischen Material)', *WSl*, 41:232–60; E. Gajewska, 'Zabieranie głosu w rozmowie — między teorią językoznawczą a jej wykorzystaniem w dydaktyce języków obcych', *JPol*, 76:174–81; A. Grybosiowa, 'Zmiany w świadomości językowej współczesnych Polaków', *PJ*, no. 1 (350):65–71, analyses deviations from theoretical norms in respect of declension, pronunciation and syntax; I. Kanińska-Szmaj, 'Slogan reklamowy', *PJ*, no. 4 (353):13–22; Z. Leszczyński, 'Przysłowiowe nowotwory rymowe', *JPol*, 76:328–37; J. Lizak, 'Funkcyjna i semantyczna wartość związków frazeologicznych w czasopismach dla dzieci', *PJ*, no. 4 (353):58–64; J. Maćkiewicz, ' "Kiedy słowo jest bronią", czyli erystyka w ujęciu potocznym', *JPol*, 76:108–13; K. Mosiołek-Kłosińska, 'Językowa prezentacja preciwników politycznych w wypowiedziach kandydatów w kampanii 1995 r.', *PJ*, no. 1 (530):12–20; by the same author, 'Slogany wyborcze jako wypowiedzi podsumowujące treści głoszone przez polityków (na materiale tekstów z kampanii prezydenckiej 1995 r.)', *PrzH*, no. 4 (337):105–18; J. Ożdżyński, 'Formy pierwszej osoby w wypowiedzi wykładowej (na przykładzie wykładu z geografii)', *PJ*, no. 1 (530):50–64; R.S., 'Nowomowa', *PJ*, no. 2 (531):58–64; M. Sobocińska, 'Jak uczyć i jak oceniać uczniów? O koncepcji nauczania języka ojczystego w szkołach Wielkiej Brytanii', *Polonistyka*, 49:93–96; D. Świerczyńska, 'Wolność dupce w swej chałupce. (Językowe gry przysłowiowe)', *TD*, nos 2–3 (38–39):240–49; E. Walusiak, 'Struktura semantyczna wypowiedzeń ze spójnikiem *byle*', *PJ*, no. 2 (531): 32–39; D. Wesołowska, '*Nowomowa* koniecznie potrzebna', *JPol*, 76: 349–55; A. Wieczorkiewicz, 'O funkcji i retoryce wypowiedzi muzealnej', *Konteksty*, 50: 37–53; B. Wiemer, 'Obserwacje nad dyskursem polskich uczniów w Niemczech. I. Składnia zdania i użycie zaimków osobowych', *PJ*, no. 4 (353): 34–42; Id., 'Obserwacje nad dyskursem polskich uczniów w Niemczech. II. Leksyka', *PJ*, nos 5–6 (354–55): 15–22; M. Wojtak, 'O "polityce w słowiech". Formy adresatywne w XVIII wieku', *JPol*, 76: 81–87. K. Wojtczuk, 'Właściwości stylu ogłoszeń prasowych jako gatunku tekstów', *PJ*, nos 5–6 (534–35): 31–40; R. Zimny, 'Niektóre cechy składni współczesnego sloganu reklamowego', *JPol*, 76: 147–54.

M. Bugajski and A. Wojciechowska, 'Teoria językowego obrazu świata w badaniu idiolektu pisarza', *PJ*, no. 3 (532): 17–25; M. Gawełko, 'O częstym stosowaniu podmiotu zaimkowego *to*', *PJ*, nos 5–6 (354–55): 1–5; B. Klebanowska, 'Jak pisać *pół godziny?*', *PJ*, no. 2 (531): 65–70; A. Kominek, 'O znaczeniu konotacyjnym nazwy *Kościół*', *PJ*, no. 3 (532): 26–34; A. Pajdzińska and R. Tokarski, 'Językowy obraz świata — konwencja i kreacja', *PL(W)*, 87: 143–58. H. Grochola-Szczepanek, 'O niektórych formach grzecznościowych mieszkańców wsi Rzepiska na Spiszu', *JPol*, 76: 40–44; W. Mańczak, 'Staropolskie *puł* "pół" ', *ib.*, 285–88; L. Moszyński, '*Słonecznik* "obiekt pogańskiego kultu" — archaizm, neosemantyzm czy neologizm Szymona Budnego?', *ib.*, 274–80; A. Sieradzka-Mruk, 'Nawiązanie do perykop biblijnych w kazaniach i homiliach', *ib.*, 135–40.

5. DIALECTOLOGY

Z. Gałecki, 'Podlaskie *ciorzyć* "bić, chłostać" i "mocno padać" (o deszczu)" ', *JPol*, 76: 164–67; R. Lisztwan, 'Teksty gwariowe. 85. Z Zaolzia w powiecie Frýdek-Místek', *ib.*, 45–49; H. Popowska-Taborska, 'Z dziejów kaszubskiej leksykografii (najwcześniejsze dociekania etymologiczne)', *ib.*, 254–57; J. Siatkowski, 'Etymologia dial. *burszówki, burtówki* "snopki w pierwszej warstwie poszycia dachu" ', *ib.*, 281–84.

6. INDIVIDUALS AND INDIVIDUAL WORKS

K. BRANDYS. R. Dźwigoł, 'Dialogiczność w powieści epistolarnej Kazimierza Brandysa *Wariacje pocztowe*', *JPol*, 76: 130–34.
RYSIŃSKI. A. Bochnakowa, 'Przypowieści polskie Salomona Rysińskiego. Wersja rękopiśmienna i XVII-wieczne wydania drukiem', *JPol*, 76: 114–20.

RZEWUSKI. B. Bartnicka, 'Dziewiętnastowieczne nazwy osób w powieściach Henryka Rzewuskiego', *PJ*, no. 3 (532):1–16; by the same author 'Dziewiętnastowieczne nazwy osób w powieściach Henryka Rzewuskiego (c.D.)', *PJ*, no. 4 (353):1–12. SCHULZ. B. Sieradzka, 'Listy Brunona Schulza — części początkowe i końcowe', *JPol*, 76:121–29. SIENKIEWICZ. Z. Przybyła, ' "Żyłka filologiczna" Sienkiewicza-publicysty', *JPol*, 76:356–68.

7. POLISH AND OTHER LANGUAGES

A. Bajda and E. Kołodziejek, 'O nazwach niektórych części ciała w polskich i angielskich frazeologizmach', *PJ*, no. 3 (352):50–56; B. Cooper, 'The Slavonic f-word and cognates', *NZSJ*:149–65, includes the Polish verb *(wy)jebać*; A. Czechowska-Błachiewicz, 'Über den Gebrauch deutscher Entlehnungen im heutigen Polnisch der Einwohner von Łódź', *KN*, 43:319–23; P. Drzymała, 'Szczególne przypadki użycia zaimków osobowych w celowniku w językach polskim, włoskim i francuskim', *SRoP*, 21:3–16, concludes that Polish has more similarities with Italian than French; J. Florczak, 'Économie sémasiologique et onomasiologique. Tentative d'une analyse contrastive d'expressions verbales en français et en polonais', *ib.*, 27–58; W. Heinemann and J. Wiktorowicz, 'Temporale Partikeln und Erwartungshaltungen in Deutschen und Polnischen', *KN*, 43:239–58; F. L. Ionilă, 'Citera observați i asupra unitaților frazeologice din limbile romana si polona, referitoare la denumiri ale corpului omenesc', *SRoP*, 21:59–64, compares idioms 'containing terms standing for parts of the human (and/or animal) body' in Romanian and Polish; L. A. Janda, 'Figure, ground, and animacy in Slavic declension', *SEEJ*, 40:325–55, considers Polish nominative plural virile and masculine genitive singular endings in conjunction with elements of Czech and Russian morphology; H. Mieczkowska, 'Iteratiwa w języku polskim i słowackim', *JPol*, 76:315–20; T. N. Moloshnaia, 'Грамматическая категория глагольной репрезентации в современных славянских языках', *Slavianovedenie*, no. 4:35–44; J. Nalepa, 'Ze studiów nad hydronomią Polski i Połabia: Poprad', *ib.*, 289–98; T. Z. Orłoś, 'Polskie *pomnik*, czeskie *pomník*, *památnik*', *ib.*, 299–302; J. Perlin, 'O sylabiczności spółgłosek w świetle faktów polskich', *PJ*, no. 1(530):43–49, contains a comparative analysis of vowel elision in various languages; A. M. Ramer, 'A letter from an incompletely neutral phonologist', *JPh*, 24:478–89, contains *inter alia* reflections on the devoicing of final consonants in Polish and other languages with potentially enormous ramifications for work in phonetics; J. Sypnicki and G. Vetulani, 'Sur l'aspect en français et en polonais', *SRoP*, 21 : 115-22; J. Winarska, 'Polski modulant *więc* i jego angielskie odpowiedniki', *JPol*, 76 : 155-59; L. Zaręba, 'Frazeologia antroponimiczna związana z kulturą narodową. Polsko-francuskie i francusko-polskie studium porównawcze', *PJ*, no. 1 (530) : 30-42; Id., 'Frazeologia antroponimiczna związana z kulturą narodową. Polsko-francuskie i francusko-polskie studium porównawcze', *PJ*, no. 2 (531) : 40-49.

8. ONOMASTICS

J. Kobylińska, 'Językowy obraz wsi beskidzkiej w XVII wieku na przykładzie nazw ziemi i jej mieszkańców w Księgach gromadzkich wsi Kasina Wielka', *JPol*, 76 : 337-48; B. Kreja, 'Skąd się biorą potrzebne ludziom nazwy? (Krótko o słowotwórstwie)', *ib.*, 369-77; K. Zierhoffer and Z. Zierhofferowa, 'Historia polskich nazw stolicy Bawarii *Monachium*', *ib.*, 51-52; K. Zierhoffer, 'Rzeki <*Nero* abo *Czarna>* i *Vabus*', *ib.*, 53; A. Żukowski, 'Polskie nazwy w Afryce Południowej (na tle nazewnictwa pochodzenia europejskiego)', *PJ*, no. 3 (352) : 57-63.

LITERATURE

POSTPONED

IV. RUSSIAN STUDIES

LANGUAGE
POSTPONED

LITERATURE FROM THE BEGINNING TO 1700
POSTPONED

LITERATURE, 1700–1820
POSTPONED

LITERATURE, 1820–1880
POSTPONED

LITERATURE, 1880–1917
POSTPONED

LITERATURE FROM 1917 TO THE PRESENT DAY
POSTPONED

V. UKRAINIAN STUDIES
POSTPONED

VI. BELARUSIAN STUDIES
POSTPONED

VII. SERBO-CROAT STUDIES
POSTPONED

VIII. BULGARIAN STUDIES*

By ADELINA ANGUSHEVA, *University of Sofia*, and
GALIN TIHANOV, *Merton College, Oxford*
(This survey covers the years 1992–96)

LANGUAGE

1. BIBLIOGRAPHIES

Bibliographies on the study of Bulgarian language published between 1989 and 1995 are edited by M. Karpacheva, 'Библиография на българската езиковедска литература, 1990 (второ полугодие)', *BulEz*, 41, 1991:282–305, 'Библиография на българската езиковедска литература, 1991 (първо полугодие)', *ib.*, 619–30, 'Библиография на българската езиковедска литература, 1992 (второ полугодие)', *ib.*, 43–44, 1994:229–50, 'Библиография на българската езиковедска литература, 1993 (първо полугодие)', *ib.*, 251–65, 'Библиография на българската езиковедска литература, 1993 (второ полугодие)', *ib.*, 266–87, 'Библиография на българската езиковедска литература, 1994 (първо полугодие)', *ib.*, 557–75, 'Библиография на българската езиковедска литература, 1995 (първо полугодие)', *ib.*, 45, 1995:529–44, and by M. Tsonkova, 'Българистиката в хуждата езиковедска периодика през 1990 (с доПалнение за 1989)', *ib.*, 41, 1991:635–36, 'Българистиката в хуждата езиковедска периодика през 1992, 1993 (с доПалнение за 1990, 1991)', *ib.*, 43–44, 1994:576–77.

2. HISTORY OF THE LANGUAGE

The investigations of A.-M. Totomanova and H. Miklas are dedicated to the problems of grapho-phonetics: H. Miklas, 'От Преславския събор до Преславската школа. Въпроси на графемиката', *Pal*, 17.3, 1993:3–12; A.-M. Totomanova, 'Един особен знак в приписките на поп Иван Кръвоноси в Асеманиевото евангелие', *ib.*, 18.2, 1994:72–75. K. Kostova, 'За някои особености в правописа и езика на Октоих N544 от НБКМ', *ib.*, 20.2:129–34, discusses the relationship between orthography and the language of Ochtoechos's text. Linguistic features of particular medieval Slavic texts are explored by M. Iovcheva and L. Taseva, 'Езикови особености на Слово за силата на Йосиф', *ib.*, 19.4, 1995:64–74,

---

* The place of publication of books is Sofia unless otherwise stated.

and by T. Popova, 'Графика и правопис на Книгата на пророк Исай по ръкопис F.I.461 от XIV век от Руската национална библиотека', *ib.*, 20.2:57–63.

T. Mostrova, 'Сложни съществителни имена със суфикс -*тел* в паметници от XIV век', *BulEz*, 43–44, 1994:402–10, looks at the peculiarities of compound nouns in 14th-c. monuments. Concerning the general history of the verb in the Slavic languages G. Rikov, 'Следи от индоевропейските перфектни формации в славянските езици', *ib.*, 1–9, examines the traces of Indo-European perfect tense forms. The problems of the aorist are explored by D. J. Birnbaum, 'Aorist taxonomies in Old Church Slavonic', *Pal*, 20.1:14–25. The use and distribution of syntactic constructions in medieval Slavic texts are discussed by I. Ivanova, 'За един тип модални конструкции в Учителното евангелие на Константин Преславски', *ib.*, 18.2, 1994:66–71; while J. Stashevski, 'Функциите на конструкцията *dativus absolutus* в Житието на св. Симеон Неман', *ib.*, 17.2, 1993:109–15, interprets this construction. T. Ilieva, 'Предаването на гръцкото минъло несвършено време в старобългарския превод на 13-те слова на св. Григорий Богослов по ръкопис от XI век', *ib.*, 17.1, 1993:54–66, explores the translation of the Greek imperfect in an Old Bulgarian text.

K. Vachkova, 'Опит за хронологическа характеристика на българския книжовен език', *BulEz*, 43–44, 1994:418–25, offers a new classification of the development of the Bulgarian literary language. V. Stankov and M. Ivanova, *ib.*, 426–36, analyse the role of tradition in its formation in comparison with that of Serbian. A. Daskalova, 'За българския книжовен език през XVI век (по данни от Житието на Никола Софийски)', *ib.*, 389–401, is dedicated to more detailed questions of the historical development of the literary language in the 16th c. E. Mircheva, 'Проблеми на установяването на книжовноезиковата норма в новобългарските дамаскини от XVII век', *Pal*, 20.3:96–113, discusses the norms of Modern Bulgarian in its earlier stages. The features of translation of the book of Damascene Stouditos are explored by V. Vasilev, 'Общи писменоезикови черти в преписите на архаичните дамаскини', *ib.*, 17.2, 1993:99–108, and Id., 'Правописна, морфологична и лексикална преправка на словата в Троянския дамаскин', *ib.*, 17.4, 1993:72–88. S. Zherev, 'Ю. Венелин и развитието на филологическите възгледи в България през втората четвърт на XIX век', *BulEz*, 43–44, 1994:98–105, studies the impact of Iuri Venelin on the linguistic knowledge of 19th-c. Bulgaria.

3. EPIGRAPHICS

Several publications elucidate the meaning, linguistic features, and historic significance of particular medieval inscriptions: S. Mikhailov, 'По разчитането на един оловен печат на цар Симеон', *Pal*, 14.1, 1990: 111–12; N. Ovcharov, 'Едно уточнение по шуменския Шишманов надпис на Срацо, внук на великия епикернии Срацимир', *ib.*, 18.4, 1994: 115–18, Id., 'Ново тълкуване на Ямболския надпис от 1356–1357 година', *ib.*, 19.2, 1995: 102–06, Id. 'Надписите от XIV век в Марков манастир до Скопие и политическият възход на кралете Вълкашин и Марко', *ib.*, 19.3, 1995: 32–46; S. Smiadovski, 'Ктиторският надпис на деспот Деян (?) от Земенския манастир и датирането на стенописите', *BulEz*, 41, 1991: 110–17, Id., 'Към Боянските стенописни надписи (2)', *ib.*, 43–44, 1994: 18–22, Id., 'Надписите към изображенията на Вселенските събори в Елешнишкия манастир (XVI в.) — извори и проблеми', *Pal*, 17.3, 1993: 77–83, 'Надписите към стенописите от църквата "Св. Никола" краи село Станичене, Нишко (1331–1332)', *ib.*, 18.3, 1994: 17–43; and E. Bakalova and S. Smiadovski, 'Ивановските стенописни надписн — текст и функция', *ib.*, 19.1, 1995: 22–65. New information and a new interpretation of pre-Christian runic inscriptions is given by R. Sefterski, 'Рунически надписи от село Чукурово, Софийско', *ib.*, 17.3, 1993: 81–99, and by S. Mikhailov, 'Към тълкуването на бронзовата седмолачна розета от Плиска', *ib.*, 19.2, 1995: 94–101, who discusses the meaning of the signs on Pliska's bronze amulet. T. Rozhdestvenskaia, 'Древнеболгарская эпиграфическая традиция и новгородская эпиграфика XI–XV вв.', *ib.*, 14.2, 1990: 51–58, is a comparative survey of Old Russian and Old Bulgarian epigraphic traditions.

4. PHONETICS AND PHONOLOGY

Particular problems of historical phonology are discussed by A.-M. Totomanova, 'Съществувала ли е палатална съгласна *с* в старобългарски?', *Pal*, 20.3: 114–19, who questions the existence of palatal consonant /s/ in medieval Bulgarian; by T. Laleva, 'Някои последци от среднобългарското смесване на носовките', *ib.*, 19.3, 1995: 70–72, who analyses the results of nasals' mixing in the Bulgarian language after the 12th c., and by L. Stefova, 'Един ранен пример за прехода *у>й* в български', *ib.*, 19.3, 1995: 73–77. L. Nikolova, 'Ново доказателства относно съдържанието на понятието говорен звук', *BulEz*, 43–44, 1994: 127–31, discusses the use of some phonological terms. D. Rainova, 'Статистическо определяне на мястото на българското словно ударение в системата на езика', *ib.*, 45, 1995:458–63, presents the results of a statistical analysis of the place of the accent in the Bulgarian language.

5. Morphology and Word Formation

P. Dzhambazov, 'За основите подходи в словообразувателните проучвания', *BulEz*, 42, 1992:173–80, is a comprehensive survey of the different methods applied to investigations into word-building. I. Atanosova, 'Някои количествени параметри при употребата на местоимения в съвременния български език', *ib.*, 96–104, gives a quantitative analysis of the distribution of Bulgarian pronouns. NOUN. On the history of morphology A.-M. Totomanova, 'Представите за сричката у Константин Костенечки', *Pal*, 19.2, 1995:57–62, assesses notions of the syllable in a 15th-c. treatise. S. Kolkovska, 'Словообразуване на имена за действия от именни глаголи (с оглед на терминологията)', *BulEz*, 43–44, 1994:478–80, and 'Типология на термините-названия на процеси', *ib.*, 135–41, addresses word-building processes. E. Pernishka, 'Някои типологични характеристики на имената за лица в книжовния български и словашки език', *ib.*, 437–40, compares noun types in Bulgarian and Slovak. VERB. R. Radeva, *Словообразувателна и семантична структура на деноминалните глаголи в съвременния български език*, КО, 1993, gives a comprehensive survey of the relationship between the word-building and semantics of a given type of verb; J. Penchev, 'Време и модалност', *BulEz*, 43–44, 1994:81–86, outlines the relationship between the two categories. I. Kharalampiev, 'За бъдъщето на футурните глаголни форми в българския език', *ib.*, 42, 1992:1–11, and 104–13, discusses the development of the future tenses. Kh. Panteleeva, 'Наблюдения над функционирането на простото (синтетично) условно наклонение през Възръждането', *ib.*, 43–44, 1994:183–90, studies the function of the conditional mood in the language of the Bulgarian Revival. M. Deianova, 'Към установяването на едино страдателно причастие в съвременния български', *ib.*, 42, 1992:166–73.

6. Syntax and Text

The general differences between the methods of classical and transformational syntax are outlined by I. Trifonova, 'Главни различия между класическия и трансформационно-пораждащи синтактичен подход', *BulEz*, 43–44, 1994:484–92. S. Papazova, 'За мястото на допълненията в изречението в български език', *ib.*, 42, 1992:21–29, discusses the structure of the sentence in Modern Bulgarian and the position of objects. P. Doshkov, 'Анализ по параметър свързаност и прагматика на изречения с удвоено допълнение', *ib.*, 43–44, 1994:121–27, studies sentences with a double object. M. Lakova, 'Въпросителни адвербиални словосъчетания къто формант на въпросителните изречения в българския език', *ib.*, 474–83 and 45, 1995:42–49, analyses some characteristics of Bulgarian interrogative sentences. R. Vlakhova, 'Особености на *verba dicendi* във въвеждащия израз на конструкциите с чужда реч', *ib.*, 163–68, outlines the peculiarities of *verba dicendi* in constructions involving indirect speech. I. Nedev, 'Към характеристиката на безсъюзните сложни изречения, чиито втори компонент изразява аргументация', *EzLit.*, 38.5–6, 1993:39–48, studies the features of given types of compound sentence.

7. ORTHOGRAPHY

M. Grigorova, 'Правописни и правоговорни въпроси свързани с някои наречия', *BulEz*, 43–44, 1994:491–92, 'За някои акцентни грешки при числителните имена', *ib.*, 543, and 'Някои правоговорни тенденции при употребата на думи с числително значение', *ib.*, 66–67, studies various orthographic and orthoepic questions associated with adverbs and numerals. R. Rusinov, 'Правопис на един тип сложни имена', *ib.*, 65–66, addresses the orthography of compound nouns.

8. LEXICOLOGY AND PHRASEOLOGY

The general principles of the formation and standardization of dictionaries of Modern Bulgarian are discussed by E. Pernishka, 'Българският език и българският речник', *BulEz*, 42, 1992:380–85, and by R. Stancheva, 'Критерии за оценка на лексикалната правилност', *ib.*, 91–96. I. Kovchev, 'Словообразователен тип и словообразователен модел', *ib.*, 365–71, is theoretical.

Several investigations outline lexicological problems of Old Bulgarian: C. Voss, 'Zum lexikalischen Bestand des Textes der altbulgarischen Paränesis von Ephraim dem Syrer', *Pal*, 18.2, 1994:50–65; M. Tsibranska, 'Глосарят в Синтагмата на Матей Властар', *ib.*, 18.3, 1994:52–62; K. Kostova, 'Наименованието îêðêàîêÿ (ирканиа) в Светославовия изборник от 1073 година', *ib.*, 19.4, 1995:71–74. R. Marti, 'Проблеми на значението на славянската лексика от кирило-методиевско време', *ib.*, 18.4:23–39, explores

the meaning of some lexemes in early medieval texts on the life of
Saint Cyril. Some particular lexical problems of the late 9th- and
10th-c. Bulgarian translations of the Preslav school are elucidated by
M. Iovcheva and L. Taseva, 'Преславската лексика в превода на
Псевдо-Методиевото Откровение', *ib.*, 18.3, 1994:44–51, and
by E. Blakhova and Zh. Ikonomova, 'Лексические совпадения
бесед Григория Двоеслова и Второго Жития Вячеслава с
лексика Иоана Екзарха', *ib.*, 17.3, 1993:13–26. L. Domuschieva,
'Старинни лексеми — компоненти на старобългарски и диа-
лектни композита', *BulEz*, 43–44, 1994:466–70, finds Old Bulgarian lexemes still preserved in Bulgarian dialects. D. Ivanova-
Mircheva, 'Субстантивацията в старобългарската лексикална
система', *ib.*, 9–18, gives a comprehensive survey of the process of
substantivization in Old Bulgarian. N. Dedialkova and L. Iordanova,
Неологизми в съвременната българска поезия, 1993, and 'Нео-
логични речници — основни принципи, сходства и различия',
BulEz, 42, 1992:479–89, discuss theoretical and practical problems
in the study of neologisms in Modern Bulgarian. K. Cholakova,
'Фразеологизми, оформени с начален компонент *като*', *ib.*,
43–44, 1994:29–35, explores the construction and meaning of the
class of idioms beginning with 'as'. T. Panova, 'Българската военна
терминология от позициите на терминологичната норма', *ib.*,
42, 1992:29–36, discusses the typology and formation of military
terminology.

DICTIONARIES.   F. Angelieva and S. Petrova, *Кратък гръцко-
български фразеологичен речник*, KO, 1993, 240 pp. M. Nikolova,
Кратък руско-български и българско-руски бизнес речник, 1993,
30 pp. L. Manolova, *Кратък речник на българската езиковедска
терминология*, BAN, 107 pp.

9. ETYMOLOGY

The etymology of several Bulgarian words with the meaning of
'morning', 'steep' or expressing New Year folk rituals is outlined by
T. A. Todorov, *BulEz*, 43–44, 1994:202–04, 443–47, and 493–96.
I. Duridanov, *ib.*, 45, 1995:225–28, examines the etymology of words
with the meaning 'to blaze', 'to flare'. A comprehensive survey of the
etymological problems of different Bulgarian words is given in his
book *Етимологични етюди. Произход на българските думи*, BAN,
1994, 331 pp.

10. SEMANTICS AND PRAGMATICS

M. Parzulova, 'Семантични омоними, подучени вследствие
термигологизацията на общоупотребими думи', *BulEz*, 43–44,

1994:174–83, and 'За семантичната омонимия', *ib.*, 45, 1995:42–49, discusses the appearance of homonyms as a result of the process of terminologization. E. Pernishka, 'Семантични отношения в речника и тяхното лексикографско отражение', *ib.*, 43–44, 1994:167–74, investigates the expression of the semantic relations between words in dictionaries, and also, 'Семантични изменения и разговорност', *BEzLit*, 35.5, 1992:11–15, semantic changes in the spoken language. K. Ilieva, 'Семантични признаци на частите на речта в съвременния български език', *BulEz*, 43–44, 1994:93–98, examines the semantic characteristics of speech components.

A. Gradinarova, 'Семантичното развитие на отглаголните съществителни на -*не* в съвременния български език', *ib.*, 42, 1992:61–69, summarizes the changes and development of deverbal nouns. S. Kolkovska, 'Категориална семантика и граматическо значение на имената за действие на -*не*', *ib.*, 45, 1995:18–30, discusses the correlation between the grammatical and semantic features of nouns expressing acts. L. Antonova-Vasileva, 'Лексико-семантичен анализ на някои глаголи, означаващи емоционални прояви на човека в българските говори', *ib.*, 100–07, explores the semantic features of verbs expressing emotional reactions in Bulgarian dialects. A. Armianova, 'Семантичните отношения между обобщителното местоимение *всичкият* и прилагателното име *целият*', *ib.*, 42, 1992:58–61, analyses the semantic differences between these particular pronouns. M. Valchanova, 'Някои наблюдения върху семантиката на рефлексийната частица *си*', *ib.*, 45, 1995:414–26, explores the semantics of the particle си. S. Kaldieva-Zakharieva, 'Някои семантични паралели в областта на българската и руманската фразеология', *ib.*, 43–44, 1994:441–46, outlines the semantic similarity of idioms in Romanian and Bulgarian. V. Stankov, 'За една семантична особеност на категорията определеност/неопределеност на имената в български език', *ib.*, 45, 1995:151–58, studies the semantic features of definite and indefinite nouns. P. Kostadinova, 'Субкатегоризацията на рода — формални семантични и формално-семантични категории', *ib.*, 43–44, 1994:465–74, studies the semantic characteristics of gender. E. Kocheva, 'За някои семантични особености на лексиката в дамаскини от XVIII век', *ib.*, 42, 1992:283–89, investigates the semantic features of post-medieval Bulgarian texts. M. Lakova, 'Семантика, прикрепена към синтактичните единици и към синтактичните отношения в изречението', *ib.*, 449–54, studies the semantics of sentence components. D. Genova, 'За значението на изречението и семантичното и прагматичното съдържание на изказа', *EzLit*,

38.2, 1993:95–106, explores the semiotic and pragmatic aspects of the sentence.

11. SOCIOLINGUISTICS AND DIALECTOLOGY

Questions of the phonetic characteristics of Bulgarian dialects are investigated by: Kh. Marinska, 'За вторичната диалектна полифтонгизация', *BulEz*, 42, 1992:36–40; V. Zhobov, 'Предна, затворена, закръглена гласна /ü/ в българските диалекти', *EzLit*, 38.1, 1993:21–24; I. Kochev, 'Ятовата изоглосна област', *BulEz*, 43–44, 1994:22–29; and B. Shaura, 'Старинна българска ятова изоглоса', *ib.*, 458–65.

Morphological characteristics of Bulgarian dialects are addressed by L. Domuschieva, 'Сложни *nomina agentis* с наставка -ица в българските говори', *ib.*, 42, 1992:294–99, and by M. Tetovska-Troeva, *Десубстантивни деятелни имена в българските говори*, BAN, 1992, 174 pp. L. Antonova-Vasileva, 'Морфологични редувания в парадигмата за сегашно време на глаголите в българските диалекти', *BulEz*, 43–44, 1994:470–74, looks at the changes in verb stems of the present tense in Bulgarian dialects. T. Boiadzhiev, 'Зоонимите в българските диалекти', *EzLit*, 38.5–6:15–25, studies the specificity of animal names in various Bulgarian dialects.

From the perspective of historical dialectology B. Velcheva and E. Scatton, 'One for all and all four one: yers and nasals in Rodopi dialects', *Pal*, 19.2, 1995:3–8, deal with the development of the vowel system in the dialects of the Rodopi mountains, and R. Aleksander, 'Ударението на имената от среден род в родопските говори, историко-географски подход', *BulEz*, 42, 1992:393–95, explores the accent in Rodopi dialects. G. Kolev, 'Наблюдения над функ-ционално-семантичната характеристика на родопската опре-делителна система', *EzLit*, 38.1, 1993:24–30, outlines the semantic features of the system of articles in Rodopi dialects. A general survey of the Rodopi dialects is presented in S. Keremidchieva, *Говорът на Ропката (Родопска граматика)*, 1993. N. Nedelchev, *Диалектът на българските католици (Северен павликянски говор)*, Veliko Tarnovo, 1994, 323 pp., discusses the dialect of Bulgarian Catholics.

G. Armianov, *Българският жаргон. Лексико-семантичен и лексикографски аспект*, KO, 1995, is an authoritative exploration of Bulgarian jargon. M. Videnov, 'Наблюдението на проф. Стойко Стойков за зигзагообразното приближаване на диа-лекта до книжовния език', *BulEz.*, 42, 1992:361–65, elaborates on Stoikov's ideas on the connection between the literary language and dialects. The same author, 'Цитиране в разговорната реч', *ib.*, 43–44, 1994:131–34, explores the sociolinguistic problems of the use of quotations in colloquial speech, as well as reduplication in colloquial speech, 'Една неописана особеност на българската разговорна реч', *EzLit*, 38.3–4, 1993:34–54.

12. ONOMASTICS

I. Duridanov, 'Заселването на славяни в Тракия по данните на топонимията', *BulEz*, 43–44, 1994:405–17, examines the toponymy of South-Eastern Bulgaria as a source for the study of the invasion by the Slavic tribes of the Balkan peninsula. E. Georgieva, 'Модели и принцнпи на именуване във вътрешноградските части на Тетевен, Тявна и Елена', *BEzLit*, 35.1, 1992:1–8, investigates the patterns in the process of naming the different parts of the town in the Central Bulgarian region.

13. LANGUAGE CONTACT AND COMPARATIVE STUDIES

A. Dobreva, 'Les iranismes dans la langue bulgare', *LingBal*, 35.3–4, 1992:145–53, discusses some of the earliest layers of the Bulgarian language. Lexical, morphological, and phonetic aspects of language contact between both modern and medieval Greek and Bulgarian are discussed by: M. Dimitrova, 'The Greek loan-words in the gospel manuscript from Turlis village', *ib.*, 127–36; E. Chausheva, 'Перфектът в български и новогръцки език', *BulEz*, 45, 1995:151–58; and by B. Velcheva, 'Language interference and universal constraints (nasalization and denasalization in Bulgarian and Greek)', *LingBal*, 35.3–4, 1992:115–18. A comprehensive survey of the typological similarities of compound nouns in Hungarian, Finnish, and Bulgarian is given by V. Delcheva, 'За някои типологически особености на сложните съществителни имена в унгарски, фински и български', *BulEz*, 45, 1995:49–56. V. Kolesnik, 'Das Funktionieren der Anthropoformen in der Sprache der bulgarischer Ansiedler im Süden der Ukraine', *LingBal*, 35.1–2, 1992:77–80, looks at features of the language of Bulgarian settlers in the Ukraine. The problems of similarities and contacts between Bulgarian and Russian are discussed by S. Peicheva, 'Функции русского языка в современном болгарском обществе', *BR*, 1992, no. 1:4–11, and by Kh. Parvev, 'Пак за руско-българските езикови вразки, но не само за тях', *BEzLit*, 38.1–2, 1995:1–15. Questions of phonetics and intonation are discussed from a comparative point of view by T. Aleksieva, 'Структура фонетического слова в русском и болгарском языке', *BR*, 1993, no. 1:48–55.

I. Chongarova, 'Формально сходная лексика русского и болгарского языков как объект лексикографирования', *BR*, 1992, no. 1:35–43, outlines the problems of false similarity between several Bulgarian and Russian lexemes. V. Zaitseva, 'О добавлениях нулевой и повторной информации в синхронном переводе', *BR*, 1993, no. 4:38–46, investigates the features of simultaneous translation from Bulgarian into Russian and vice versa.

14. STUDIES OF THE BALKAN LANGUAGES

The linguistic features of the union of Balkan languages are discussed by: S. Schich-Bronsert, 'Zum balkanspezifischen Charakter einiger "dass"-sätze im Balkanslawischen und Balkanoromanischen', *Ling-Bal.*, 32.3–4, 1989:103–10; H. Schaller, 'Die Schriftsysteme der Balkansprechen: Entwicklung und System', *ib.*, 32.1–2, 1989:27–41; I. Schich, 'Osmanisch-türkische Reflexionen im Balkanslawischen unter besonderer Berücksichtigung der Phraseologie und Lexikologie', *ib.*, 35.1–2, 1992:59–66; E. Hamp, 'Albanais *shkrap*, aroumain *skrac*', *ib.*, 67; and K. Viktorova, 'Une correction nécessaire à l'étude comparative de T. Vl. Tzavian "Syntaxe structurale de l'union linguistique balkanique" ', *ib.*, 35.3–4, 1992:181–84. Discussing the relationship between language and mentality, P. Asenova, 'La mentalité balkanique: vues de l' "homo balkanicus" sur certaines qualités humaines', *ib.*, 97–113, outlines the common characteristics of the Balkan population.

15. STYLISTICS

Stylistic features of modern Bulgarian prose are discussed by M. Kitanova, 'Някои особености, свързани със стилистичната функция в съвременната българска художествена проза', *BulEz*, 45, 1995:470–72. K. Ankova-Nikova, 'Наблюдения върху публицистичния стил на съвременния български книжовен език. (Стини особености)', *ib.*, 465–67, writes on modern Bulgarian journalistic style.

LITERATURE

1. GENERAL

Explorations of particular genres or genre theory mirror different features of modern theoretical debates. G. Tihanov, 'Литературният жанр: възможности за теоретизирането му', *LitMis*, 39–40.1:14–38, gives a comprehensive survey of the theoretical problems of literary genres. L. Lipcheva-Prandzheva,

'Историческият роман — жанрова същност и граници', *ib.*, 36.1–2, 1992:58–80, discusses the characteristics of the genre of the novel. V. Stefanov, 'Четене — историческо моделиране', *ib.*, 38.2, 1994:114–26, outlines the problems of reading and reshaping the image of history in Bulgarian literature. A. Licheva, 'За "вечните майки" и техните български литературни синове', *ib.*, 37.3, 1993:26–38, addresses the problems of gender and generation in Bulgarian literature as well as the image of the mythical mother in the works of Bulgarian writers. B. Zlatanov, 'Дискурсивни аспекти на българските литературни истории', *ib.*, 39–40.1:3–14, discusses the different interpretations of Bulgarian literature in the discourse on literary history. S. Stoicheva and S. Petkov, 'Обетовата книга', *ib.*, 77–96, deal with the problems of canon and anthologization of Bulgarian literature. R. Kuncheva, 'Перспективата на ранния структурализъм в изследванията на интонацията. Понятието фонетична линия на Й. Мукарживски', *ib.*, 37.1, 1993:35–48, studies the structuralists' heritage in the exploration of the intonation of poetry. D. Mancheva, 'Структурни принципи в театъра на абсурда', *ib.*, 38.3, 1994:130–42, explores the structural principles of drama of the absurd.

2. Reception of Foreign Literatures in Bulgaria

A. Shurbanov, 'Европа и българската литература', *LitMis*, 37.2, 1993:79–98, provides a general overview of the impact of European culture on Bulgarian literature. The impact of the cultural milieu on the translation of literary texts is discussed by E. Mateva, 'Критика как фактор в переводческом процесе', *BR*, 1992, nos 3–4:13–16, and by M. Zlatanova, 'За някои тенденции в издаването на преводна литература', *ib.*, 25–28. N. Danova, 'Още за гръцкия канал на общуване на българите с европейската културе. Случаят К. Фотинов', *LitMis*, 37.2, 1993:50–59, analyses the role of Konstantin Fotinov in the transmission of European ideas through the mediation of Greek culture. V. Trendafilov, 'Между бунтовника и администратора. Бележки върху рецепцията на викторианската литература в България', *ib.*, 36.1–2, 1992:138–52, studies the reception of Victorian literature in Bulgaria. A. Bakracheva, ' "Таи се точнуват романите . . ." Особености на реалистичното повествование в английския просвещенски роман и българската следосвобожденска белетристика', *ib.*, 37.1, 1993:48–79, compares the realistic novels of the English Enlightenment and the Bulgarian post-Revival period. The genre of dialogue in the German Reformation and Bulgarian Revival is studied by N. Andreeva-Popova, 'Диалогът в литературата на немската реформация и българското Възраждане', *ib.*, 38.4, 1994:15–48. N. Aretov, 'Привлекателният образ на великия скептик: българската рецепция на Волтер', *ib.*, 38.2, 1994:89–114, examines the reception of Voltaire in Bulgarian culture.

The problems of the reception of particular Russian authors such as Griboedov and Fet in Bulgaria are interpreted by S. Vlakhov, 'Афористика А. С. Грибоедова в болгарском переводе', *BR*, 1992, nos 3–4:2–13, and by I. Petrova, 'Личностное и творческое присутствие Афанасия Фета в культурном сознании болгар', *BR*, 1991, no. 3:3–10. G. Germanov, 'Интерпретации на български проблеми в творчеството на Ф. М. Достоевски', *BR*, 1992, no. 1:11–17, discusses the representation of Bulgarian history in Dostoevskii's works. The history of the reception of the Russian novel among the Bulgarian intelligentsia is outlined from a cultural and sociological point of view by A. Anchev, 'Интерес болгарской интеллигенции к русскому роману первой половины XIX века', *BR*, 1991, no. 1:37–53. The sociology of literary reception and the cultural significance of Russian immigrants in Bulgaria are interpreted by Kh. Manolakiev, 'Руската емиграция в България и проблемите на литературната рецепция или "Случаят Пушкин 1937 г." ', *LitMis*, 37.2, 1993:114–31. A. Lipatov, 'Взаимодействие латинского Запада и византийского Востока: кирилло-мефодиевская традиция, истоки польской литературы и проблемы славянской взаимности', *Pal*, 17.1, 1993:67–80, discusses the interaction of West and East within a broad comparative framework of medieval Slavic traditions.

3. FROM THE MIDDLE AGES TO THE END OF THE EIGHTEENTH CENTURY

Two authoritative and important encyclopedias have been edited in the last four years: an encyclopedia of Old Bulgarian literature, *Старобългарска литература. Енциклопедичен речник*, ed. D. Petkanova, KO, 1992, 520 pp., which covers the authors, copyists, works, important manuscripts, and general features of various topics connected with medieval Bulgarian literature, its development, book production, centres, and scriptoria; and *Кирилометодиевска енциклопедия*, vol. 2, KO, 1995, dedicated to all topics related to the Cyrillo-Methodian traditions in medieval Slavic culture.

General problems of text structure, genre, and mode in medieval Slavic literature are discussed by N. Ingam, 'Повествователен модус и литературен жанр в средновековните православни литератури: тезиси', *Pal*, 17.3, 1993:36–47; V. Izmirlieva, 'Stories and names: modes of Eastern rhetoric of sainthood', *ib.*, 18.3, 1994:11–16; and by M. Mladenova, 'Макроструктура и микроструктура на текста', *ib.*, 18.4, 1994:75–85 (on the material of apocryphal gospels). The differences and similarities of literary and verbal representation of sacred images are discussed by E. Bakalova, 'Живописна интерпретация на сакрализирания образ в средновековното изкуство', *ib.*, 18.1, 1994:96–107. Specific topics of medieval sensitivity and religiousness (such as the lament, Christian love, saints' face and route, wisdom) are outlined by D. Petkanova, 'Плачът и сълзите в средновековната литература', *ib.*, 18.2, 1994:82–93; by L. Denkova, 'Философски аспекти на християнска любов в средновековата традиция', *ib.*, 17.1, 1993:81–97, 'Пътят в модела на светтоста', *ib.*, 19.1, 1995:66–77, 'Средновековното талкуване на лицето: примерът на старобългарската литература', *ib.*, 20.1:86–98, and 'Софя — изборът на светостта (наблюдения върху епизода в Пространното житие на Константин-Кирил)', *LitMis*, 38.4, 1994:3–15; and by S. Babalievska, 'Темата за християнска любов в ранната старобългарска литература', *Pal*, 18.2, 1994:36–45.

An authoritative comparative study of Old Bulgarian and Byzantine apocryphal texts is presented by A. Miltenova and V. Tapkova-Zaimova, *Историко-апокалиптичната книжнина във Византия и в средновековна България*, KO. The textological problems of early Glagolitic texts are investigated by G. Minchev, 'Мястото на новооткритите листове от Синайския евхологои сред другите текстове от ръкописа. Филологически и литургически анализ на молитвите от денонощния богослужебен цикъл', *Pal*, 17.1, 1993:21–36, and by S. Parenti, 'Глаголический список римско-византийской литургии св. Петра', *ib.*, 18.4, 1994:3–14. The reforms of Patriarch Euthymius and his followers are discussed by; M. Hebert, 'The linguistic and literary reforms of Patriarch Euthymius. A return to the sources', *ib.*, 17.3, 1993:52–62; K. Kabakchiev, 'Превеждал ли е Евтимий Търнововски литургически книги според сведенията на Григорий Цамблак', *BulEz*, 42, 1992:304–09; and by P. Lukin, ' "Сказание о письменах" Константина Костенечкого и "исправление церковных книг" в Сербии при Стефане Лазаревиче', *Pal*, 14.2, 1990:69–80.

Textological problems and the problems of content and the compilation of particular manuscripts are discussed by: F. Thomson, 'The Symeonic Florilegium: problems of its origin, content, textology and edition. Together with an English translation of the eulogy of Tzar Symeon', *ib.*, 17.1, 1993:37–53; R. Pavlova, 'Пролог Ps 705 от Народната Библиотека на Сърбия в Белград', *ib.*, 20.2:110–28; M. Tsibranka, 'Дяк Димитър Кратовскн и

неговият Номоканон от 1466 година', *ib.*, 19.1, 1995:91–98;
A. Turilov, 'Сборник отрывков пергаменных рукописей из
Уваровского собрания ГИМ', *ib.*, 18.4, 1994:15–22; Ts. Raleva,
'Зографский список Сборника царя Симеона', *ib.*, 17.4,
1993:22–58; Kh. Toncheva, 'За някои палеографски особености
на Лобковския (Хлудовия) паримейник — среднобългарски
паметник от края на XIII—началото на XIV век', *ib.*, 19.2,
1995:45–56; and R. Charamella, 'Нови данни за Берлинския
дамаскин', *ib.*, 20.2:120–29.
Recently discovered copies of medieval Bulgarian texts are presented by: V. Velinova, 'Нови преписи на произведения на
Климент Охридски в руски книгохранилища', *Pal*, 19.3,
1995:55–69; B. Mircheva, 'За още един препис на Службата на
Константин-Кирил Философ', *ib.*, 17.2, 1993:22–35; K. Ivanova
and P. Matejic, 'An unknown work of St Romil of Vidin (Ravanica)',
ib., 17.4, 1993:3–15; and by A. Miltenova, ' "Слово за
Антихриста" — един малко познат български апокриф', *ib.*,
17.4, 1993:59–71.
The reception and distribution of the works of various Byzantine
authors in medieval Slavic literature are discussed by: C. Voss, 'Die
Handschift Nr. 137 (69) der Nationalbibliothek Bukarest: eine bisher
kaum bemerkte Neuübersetzung der Paranesis Ephraims des Syrers',
ib., 18.2, 1994:27–44; A. Mincheva, 'Постническите слова на
Исаак Сирин в Киевския Фрагмент от XIII–XIV век', *ib.*, 14.4,
1990:19–38; V. Tapkova-Zaimova and A. Miltenova, 'Видения на
пророк Даниил във Византия и в средновековна България',
ib., 39–46; L. Taseva and M. Iovcheva, 'Апокрифният апока-
липсис на Иоан Богослов (по препис N639 от московската
синодална библиотека)', *ib.*, 19.3, 1995:47–54; and by T. Slavova,
'Архивният хронограф и Тълковната Палея', *ib.*, 18.4,
1994:48–63.
E. Rogachevska, 'Цикл молитв Кирилла Туровского в южно-
славянских рукописях, хранящихся в Болгарии', *ib.*,
20.3:76–84, studies the diffusion of the works of Kiril of Turov in
South Slavic literatures. S. Nikolova, 'Повестта "Стефанит и
Ихнилат" в българската средновековна литература и
книжнина', *ib.*, 14.3, 1990:20–42, looks at the reception of the
Eastern novel in Bulgarian literature.
Several investigations focus on textological problems of the genre
of hymnography: V. Zhelizkova, 'Тропарите в състава на
Простия пролог', *ib.*, 19.1, 1995:78–90; M. Iovcheva, 'Цикълът
молебни стихири за пророците, мъчениците и светителите в
Охтоиха', *ib.*, 20.2:43–56, approaches the textological and linguistic
problems of hymns dedicated to the prophets and saints in the

Ochtoechos; G. Popov, 'Из гимнографското наследство на Константин Преславски', *ib.*, 19.3, 1995:3–31, discusses the original hymnographic works of Konstantin of Preslav; B. Nikolova, 'Чин за ръкополагане на епископ, митрополит, патриарх', *ib.*, 19.1, 1995, examines the texts of specific Christian rituals.

Astrological knowledge and the notions of the human body, nature and the universe in medieval Bulgarian literature are investigated by: M. Georgiev, 'Анатомо-физиологични понятия и представи в старобългарската книжнина (I. Конфигурация на човешкото тяло)', *ib.*, 14.2, 1990:23–38, and 'Анатомо-физиологични понятия и представи в старобългарската книжнина (II. Мисление, реч, активност, движение)', *ib.*, 14.3, 1990:65–79; A. Angusheva, 'Структурни особености на гадателните книги в старобългарската литература', *LitMis*, 17.6, 1993:78–101; K. Miteva, 'Някои наблюдения върху естественонаучните представи в Шестоднев и Небеса на Иоан Екзарх', *Pal*, 18.3, 1994:63–76; and by T. Slavova, 'За планетите и техните подредби в старобългарската книжнина', *ib.*, 18.1, 1994:68–73.

The reflection of a pagan outlook in medieval Byzantine and Slavic literature is discussed by J. Moroz, 'За един субстратен пласт в разказа за свети Никола', *ib.*, 19.3, 1995:98–108, and 'Метаморфоза языческих представлений в Слове Григория Богослова "За честния краст и двамата разбойници"', *ib.*, 14.3, 1990:85–95; and by T. Slavova, 'Славянски митологически компилации', *ib.*, 17.3, 1993:63–76.

The written culture of Proto-Bulgarians and their religious outlook are investigated by: K. Kostova, 'Към въпроса за религиозните представи и произхода на прабългарите', *ib.*, 17.1, 1993:12–20, and 'Ритмични структури в прабългарските надписи на гръцки език', *BulEz*, 42, 1992:272–75; and by F. Filipov, 'По въпроса за религията на прабългарите и българската държава през езическия период (681–864)', *Pal*, 17.1, 1993:3–11.

Palaeographical and codicological questions concerning medieval Slavic books are discussed by E. Mussakova, 'Кодикологични бележки върху Врачанското евангелие (НБКМ 19)', *ib.*, 20.2:64–82, and 'Der kyrillische Palimpsest in Cod. Vat. Gr. 2502 und sein Schmuck', *ib.*, 18.1, 1994:37–57. V. Putsko, 'Портретные изображения авторов и донаторов в древнеболгарской книге', *ib.*, 14.4, 1990:68–83, discusses the sociology of manuscript decoration. R. Zaumova, 'Паисеви предходници', *LitMis*, 37.2, 1993:132–37, looks at the predecessors of the first writer of the Bulgarian Revival.

THE BIBLE AND OLD BULGARIAN LITERATURE

T. Slavova, 'Следи от Методиев период на библейската книга Битие', *Pal*, 19.4, 1995:53–70, proves Methodios's participation in the translation of Genesis. Several investigators look into the translations of particular biblical books into Old Bulgarian (= Old Church Slavonic): T. Mostrova, 'Старобългарският превод на книгата на пророк Йеремия по преписи от XIV–XVI век', *ib.*, 19.2, 1995:9–26; L. Taseva and M. Iovcheva, 'Преводчески особености в книгата на пророк Йезекиил по ръкопис F.I.461 от Руската национална библиотека', *ib.*, 19.4, 1995:40–52.

The question of the number of biblical books included in Slavic indices of canonical texts is examined by I. Gritsevskaia, 'Канон славянской Библии в индексах истинных книг', *ib.*, 14.3, 1990:39–48. E. Dogramadzhieva, 'Състав на славянските ръкописни четвероевангелие', *ib.*, 17.2, 1993:3–21, discusses the content of Slavic gospels. B. Khristova, 'Тълкуванията на старозаветни и новозаветни книги в средновековната култура', *ib.*, 18.2, 1994:76–81, writes on the function of interpretations of biblical texts.

The textological, lexicological, and, especially, phonetic characteristics of particular manuscripts containing biblical texts are investigated by: M. Bakker, 'Discovered on Mount Athos: the Karakalski Apostol', *ib.*, 14.2, 1990:61–67; I. Khristova, 'Наблюдения над ръкопис 508 от сбирката на Народната библиотека "Св.св. Кирил и Методий" ', *ib.*, 17.2, 1993:90–98; M. Matejic, 'A Slavic gospel in Los Angeles', *ib.*, 62–89; T. Laleva, 'Атинското четвероевангелие', *ib.*, 20.1:41–51; and by A.-M. Totomanova, 'Среднобългарските фрагменти в барберинския палимпсест', *ib.*, 26–40. Texts related to biblical readings are analysed by T. Popova, 'Неделя на Хананеиката — едно интересно четиво от богослужебния апарат на четириевангелията', *ib.*, 18.4, 1994:103–08, and by E. Dogramadzhieva, 'Самостоятелни тълковни творби включени в помощния апарат на славянските ръкописни четвероевангелия', *BulEz*, 42, 1992:299–304. Textological questions of the Slavic psalter are studied by M. MacRobert, 'The Greek textological basis of the early redactions of the Church Slavonic Psalter', *Pal*, 14.2, 1990:7–15; A. Todorov, 'Псалми новой части Бычковской псалтыри', *ib.*, 14.1, 1990:49–71; and I. Karachorova, 'Особености в текста на Радомирския псалтир', *ib.*, 14.4, 1990:47–60. Problems of the impact of the first translations of biblical texts into Old Bulgarian (= Old Church Slavonic) on the translation of the Bible into Modern Bulgarian are discussed by D. Ivanova, 'Първият новобългарски превод на Евангелието и старата писмена традиция', *BulEz*, 43–44, 1994:411–18, and 'Приемственост и традиция в новобългарските преводи на Евангелието', *Pal*, 17.4, 1993:89–106. Computer applications to the process of investigating Slavic biblical texts are presented by M. Bakker and J. van der Tag, 'Collating Greek and Slavic Apostolos manuscripts', *ib.*, 18.2, 1994:94–112, and M. Camuglia, 'The Psalter, its tradition and the computer: a new method of textual analysis', *ib.*, 20.1:3–13.

HAGIOGRAPHY

Several investigations are dedicated to the cult and hagiographical representation of SS Cyril and Methodios: M. Spasova, 'Към въпроса за първоначалния текст и авторството на Похвално слово за Кирил и Методий', *Pal*, 20.3:55–75; S. Babalievska, 'Бележки върху проложното житие на Кирил и Методий', *ib.*, 18.3, 1994:77–82; E. Vereshchagin, 'Последование под 30-м января и Миней 98 (f.381) РГАДА (Москва) — предполагаемый гимн первоучителя славян Кирилла', *ib.*, 18.1, 1994:3–21; B. Mircheva, 'Някои структурни особености на преписите на ранната Служба за Константин-Кирил Философ', *ib.*, 22–36; S. Panova, 'Ehrung der Heiligen Kyrill und Metodii im XVIII Jh.', *ib.*, 19.2, 1995:62–93; V. Todoranova and D. Kenanov, 'Към историята на Кирило-Методиева култ през XVII век', *ib.*, 14.2, 1990:92–95; and K. Petkov, 'Традиции в спомена за Кирил и Методий в България през XIII–XIV век — опит за нова интерпретация', *ib.*, 17.2, 1993:46–61.

S. Babalievska, 'Модели и типове моделиране на житийното повествование', *LitMis*, 37.6:69–78, meditates on general questions of the literary problems of the saints' lives. The cultural context and source representation of the cult of archangel Michael in medieval Bulgaria are examined by D. Cheshmedzhiev, 'Към въпроса за култа на Архангел Михаил в средновековна България', *Pal*, 20.1:52–61. D. Kenanov, 'История на уводната част на Метафрастовото житие за св. Николай Мирликийски', *ib.*, 18.3, 1994:83–90, investigates the sources of a Byzantine *vita* in Slavic translation. E. Uzunova, 'Историят на един новонамерен ръкопис (Хилендарският препис на житието на Йоаким Осоговски-Сарандапорски от 1789 г).', *ib.*, 20.2:3–43, presents the newly discovered *vita* of the hermit saint Ioakim Osogovski. B. Velcheva, 'Ранният славянски превод на Житието на св. Мария Египетска в един ръкопис от XV век', *ib.*, 20.3:30–54, proves that the Life of St Mary of Egypt was translated into Old Bulgarian during the times of the Preslav school. Byzantine and

Slavic texts dedicated to two other women saints are examined by E. Mineva, 'Непубликувани византийски стихири за св. Петка Търновска от XV век', *ib.*, 85–95, and M. Petrova, 'Към въпроса за южнославянските преводи на житието на мъченица Параскева-Петка Римлянка', *ib.*, 20.2:83–109. The saints' calendars of particular manuscripts are explored by T. Popova, 'За една особеност в синаксара на Лондонското евангелие', *BulEz*, 41, 1991:445–49, and S. Vakareliiska, 'Съвпадения и разлики в месецослова на два близки евангелски ръкописа: Курсоновото (Видинско) и Банишкото евангелие', *Pal*, 18.1, 1994:58–67.

HISTORIOGRAPHY

Features of the translation of Byzantine chronicles in the Slavic milieu are discussed by Kh. Trendafilov, 'Наблюдения върху славянския превод на Хрониката на Георги Синкел', *Pal*, 14.4, 1990:100–10, and by R. Stankov, 'Славянский перевод Хроники Георгия Амартола в издании В. М. Истрина', *ib.*, 18.1, 1994:74–88. The image of history in aprocryphal texts is treated by A. Turilov, 'Кичевский сборник с "Болгарской апокрифической летописью" ', *ib.*, 19.4, 1995:2–39, and by V. Tapkova-Zaimova, 'Мирът и войната във византийската и българската историко-апокалиптична книжнина', *LitMis*, 37.6, 1993:128–34.

4. THE PERIOD OF NATIONAL REVIVAL

During the last few years fruitful scholarly debates have focused on the literature of this period. Features of post-medieval literature in the context of European culture are discussed by E. Mircheva, 'Проблеми на българската литература XVII–XVIII век в светлината на общи балкански и европейски процеси', *LitMis*, 37.6, 1993:134–44, and S. Strashimirova, 'Ранновъзрожденската литература: аксиологичен ракурс и компаративен дискурс', *ib.*, 37.2, 1993:25–36. The dynamics of the penetration of European ideas into Bulgarian literature and their complex and contradictory reception in it are investigated by: R. Damianova, 'Чуждото — страх и влечение. Българското възраждане и Европа', *ib.*, 37.3, 1993:112–16; L. Mikhova, 'За метаморфозите на своето и чуждото в културите и художествени представи през Възраждането', *ib.*, 117–27; and V. Trendafilov, 'Свое и чуждо във възрожденската литература', *ib.*, 37.2, 1993:36–50. D. Lekov, 'Българската литературна интелигенция през Възраждането и проблемът Русия-Западна Европа', *ib.*, 37.3, 1993:103–11, discusses the dilemmas and cultural dominants of

Bulgarian writers of the Revival period. N. Aretov, 'Възрожденски представи за мястото на България в световната цивилизация', *ib.*, 37.2, 1993:16–25, discusses the ideas of the writers of the period on the place of Bulgaria in European culture. S. Sivriev, 'За "високата" и "низката" литература през Възраждането', *ib.*, 108–14, outlines the main characteristics of different literary layers during the Bulgarian Revival.

INDIVIDUAL AUTHORS

BOTEV, KH. On B.'s poetry: L. Bumbalov, 'Генеалогично пространство и време на жатварката в "Хаджи Димитър" от Ботев', *BEzLit*, 38.1–2, 1995:29–33, and I. Ilinova, 'Глупците и свободата в Ботевия дискурс', *ib.*, 33–40.
SLAVEIKO, P. R. D. Chavdarova, ' "Изворът на белоногата" — още един прочит', *EzLit*, 38.1–2, 1993:106–12, discusses the literary techniques of S.'s poem.

5. LITERATURE FROM 1877 TO THE SECOND WORLD WAR

The notions of genres spread in the literary circle 'Мисъл' are interpreted by G. Tihanov, 'Жанровото съзнание на кръга "Мисъл" — експлицитен модел и имплицитни алтернативи', *LitMis*, 36.1–2, 1992:80–99. The symbolism of colours, their meaning and function in the literary works of Bulgarian symbolists are studied by M. Dachev, 'Семиотика на цвета. Цвят и смисъл в поезията на българските символисти', *ib.*, 37.3–4, 1993:178–97. I. Peleva, 'Плебеи и аристократи. История на името', *ib.*, 37.2, 1993:98–107, addresses the semiotics of names and the process of naming literary heroes from I. Vazov to G. Milev.

INDIVIDUAL AUTHORS

DEBELIANOV, D. S. Khadzhikosev, 'Фаустовски мотив в лириката на Д. Дебелянов', *EzLit*, 38.2, 1993:38–44, discusses the philosophical problems of D.'s poetry.
IAVOROV, P. I. Peleva, 'Македония и краят на историята (Яворовите "Хайдушки копнения" срещу език на националната кауза)', *LitMis*, 38.2, 1994:126–50, interprets the discourse of history and national problems in Ia.'s literary works. S. Tsanov, 'Небиблейският Йов в поезията на А. К. Яворов (Наблюдения върху палинодията "Бежанци" — "Покаяние")', *ib.*, 150–64, examines the reinterpretation of biblical motifs in two of Ia.'s poems.
IOVKOV, IO. The philosophical message and artistic traits of Iovkov's work are interpreted by V. Galonzka, 'Йордан Йовков —

"Жетварят" изображено пространство и метафизична цялост',
LitMis, 37.1, 1993:79–103.

KONSTANTINOV, A. K.'s masterpiece 'Баи Ганьо' is discussed
from the standpoint of different methodological approaches by:
R. Shivachev, ' "Бай Ганьо — културно-исторически проблем',
LitMis, 38.1, 1994:146–69; M. Kirova, ' "Бай Ганьо" поглъщият
човек', *ib.*, 170–92; and R. Lebedova, 'Праезикът на бай Ганьо',
BEzLit, 38.5, 1995:7–13.

MILEV, G. Ts. Atanasova, 'Естетика на антиреализма. (Г.
Милев и списание "Везни")', *LitMis*, 38.4, 1994:65–81, defines the
poetry of M. as belonging to the aesthetics of antirealism. A. Des-
potova-Tsander, ' "Главата ми кървав фенер" (Към темата за
Iвата световна война в творчеството на Г. Милев)', *ib.*, 81–89,
examines the representation of the war in M.'s works.

MINKOV, S. Ts. Petrova, 'Светослав Минков: "Голем"-
изацията към сатиричен похват', *LitMis*, 39–40:140–47,
explores the techniques of satire in M.'s prose.

SLAVEIKOV, P. P. P. Antov, 'Митът за Прометей и П. Славей-
ков', *LitMis*, 36.1–2, 1992:118–38, explores mythic images in the
poetry of S.

STOIANOV, Z. S. Tsanov, 'Митологизацията на личността на
В. Левски и националната история в "В. Левски. Дяконът.
Чърти от живота му" от З. Стоянов', *LitMis*, 37.2, 1993:159–65,
outlines the methods of the representation of the historical figure
Vasil Levski in the biography written by S.

STRASHIMIROV, A. E. Mutafov, 'Повествователният спев у А.
Страшимиров', *LitMis*, 39–40.1:97–118, examines narrative technique in the works of S., while R. Lebedova, 'За художествената
структура на повестта "Змеи" от А. Страшимиров', *EzLit*,
38.5–6, 1993:79–89, explores the structure of one of his works.

TODOROV, P. The reception of the mythical and imaginary in the
works of T. is discussed by D. Iugova, 'Фолклорно-митологична
знаковост в идилиите на П. Тодоров', *LitMis*, 38.1, 1994:118–31.

VAZOV, I. P. Antov, 'Равнища на карнавалност в "Под
игото" ', *LitMis*, 37.2, 1993:138–46, reads V.'s masterpiece through
Bakhtin's ideas. P. Parashkevov, *EzLit*, 38.3, 1993:19–33, discusses
the features of V.'s story *Една българска*.

6. LITERATURE FROM THE SECOND WORLD WAR TO THE PRESENT

INDIVIDUAL AUTHORS

BAGRIANA, E. M. Tsaneva, 'Между "Вечната" и "Святата" (за
нравстено-психологическите измерения на женствеността в

поезията на Багряна)', *LitMis*, 37.3, 1993:3–14, analyses the feminine writing and psychological depth of B.'s poetry. B. Nonev, 'Е. Багряна, Вл. Василев и другите', *EzLit*, 38.2, 1993:20–38, discusses the impact of the literary milieu on B.'s works.

GABE, D. The philosophical aspects of G.'s poetry are explored by M. Nikolchina, 'Отвикване от езика. "Глъбини" на Дора Габе', *LitMis*, 38.3, 1994:15–25.

MARANGOZOV, TS. R. Dimcheva, 'Скептицизмът на Цветан Марангозов: основни идеи и творчески изяви', *LitMis*, 38.3, 1994:10–21.

MUTAFCHIEVA, V. M. Karabelova, 'Недовършен разговор. Анкета с В. Мустафчиева', *LitMis*, 38.4, 1994:153–72, questions the writer of historical novels on her literary works and views.

STANEV, E. N. Ilchevska, 'История и съвременост в "Легенда за Сибин, преславсля княз" на Е. Станев', *EzLit*. 38.5–6, 1993:90–98, investigates the philosophical messages and actuality of S.'s historical novel.

STRATIEV, S. R. Dimcheva, 'Из живота и творчеството на Ст. Стратиев. Анкета', *LitMis*, 39–40.1:147–73, is an interview with the dramatist.

ABBREVIATIONS

I. ACTA, FESTSCHRIFTEN AND OTHER COLLECTIVE AND GENERAL WORKS

Acta (Copenhagen): *Acta Conventus Neo-Latin Hafniensis. Proceedings of the Eighth International Congress of Neo-Latin Studies, Copenhagen, 12 August to 17 August 1991*, ed. Rhoda Schnur et al. (Medieval and Renaissance Texts and Studies), Binghamton, 1994, xix + 1015 pp.

Acta (Los Angeles): *Historical Linguistics 1993. Selected Papers from the 11th International Conference on Historical Linguistics, Los Angeles, 16–20 August 1993*, ed. Henning Andersen (Current Issues in Linguistic Theory, 124), Amsterdam, Benjamins, 1995, x + 460 pp.

Acta (Seeon): '*Aufführung' und 'Schrift' in Mittelalter und früher Neuzeit*, ed. Jan-Dirk Müller (Germanistische Symposien Berichtsbände, 17), Stuttgart, Metzler, xviii + 675 pp.

Actas (Alcalá): *La literatura en la época de Sancho IV. (Actas del Congreso Internacional 'La literatura en la época de Sancho IV', Alcalá de Henares, 21–24 de febrero de 1994)*, ed. Carlos Alvar and José Manuel Lucia Megías, Alcalá U.P., 573 pp.

Actas (Granada): *Medioevo y Literatura. Actas del V Congreso de la Asociación Hispánica de Literatura Medieval. Granada, 1993*, 4 vols, ed. Juan Paredes, Granada U.P., 1995, 545, 560, 551, 560 pp.

Actas (Irvine): *Asociación Internacional de Hispanistas. Actas Irvine-92. III. Encuentros y desencuentros de culturas. Desde la edad media al siglo XVIII*, ed. Juan Villegas, Irvine, CA, University of California, Irvine, Department of Spanish and Portuguese, 1994.

Actas (León): *Humanismo y Císter. Actas de I Congreso Nacional de Humanistas Españoles*, ed. O. C. S. O. Pascual and R. de Francisco, León U.P., 733 pp.

Actas (Mexico): *Caballeros, monjas y maestros en la Edad Media. Actas de las 'V Jornadas Medievales'*, ed. Lillian von der Walde, Concepción Company, and Aurelio González (Publicaciones Medievalia, 13), Mexico, UNAM, ix + 557 pp.

Actas (Salamanca): *Actas del III Congreso de la Asociación Hispánica de Literatura Medieval. Salamanca, 1989*, 2 vols, ed. Maria Isabel Toro Pascua, Salamanca, Departamento de Literatura Española e Hispanoamericana, 1994, 1181 pp.

Actas (Santiago de Compostela), VI: *Actas do XIX Congreso Internacional de Lingüística e Filoloxía Románicas, Universidade de Santiago de Compostela, 1989*. VI. *Sección VI. Galego. Sección VII. Romania Nova*, ed. Ramón Lorenzo, Corunna, Fundación 'Pedro Barrié de la Maza, Conde de Fenosa', 1994, 884 pp.

Actas (Santiago de Compostela), VII: *Actas do XIX Congreso Internacional de Lingüística e Filoloxía Románicas, Universidade de Santiago de Compostela, 1989*. VII. *Sección IX. Filoloxía medieval e renacentista. A: Crítica textual e edición de textos. B: Historia e crítica literarias*, ed. Ramón Lorenzo, Corunna, Fundación 'Pedro Barrié de la Maza, Conde de Fenosa', 1995, 974 pp.

Actas (Santiago de Compostela), VIII: *Actas do XIX Congreso Internacional de Lingüística e Filoloxía Románicas, Universidade de Santiago de Compostela, 1989*. VIII. *Sección X. Historia da lingüística e da filoloxía románicas. Sección XI. Traballos en curso e programas de investigación nacionais e internacionais*, ed. Ramón Lorenzo, Corunna, Fundación 'Pedro Barrié de la Maza, Conde de Fenosa', 866 pp.

Actas (Santiago-Corunna): *Actas do Simposio de Lexicografía Actual: Elaboración de Diccionarios, Santiago de Compostela/A Coruña, 9–11 de outubro de 1995*, ed. C. García, I. González Fernández, and M. González González (*Cadernos da Lingua*, anexo 3), Corunna, Real Academia Galega, 196 pp.

Actas (Valencia): *Max Aub y el laberinto español: Actas del congreso internacional celebrado en Valencia y Segorbe del 13 al 17 de diciembro de 1993*, ed. Cecilio Alonso, 2 vols, Valencia, Ayuntamiento de Valencia, 976 pp.

Actes (Andorra): *Tradició clàssica. Actes de l'XI Simposi de la Secció Catalana de la SEEC (1993)*, ed. Mercè Puig Rodríguez-Escalona, Andorra, Conselleria d'Educació, Joventut i Esports, 697 pp.

Actes (Berkeley): *Actes del Setè Col·loqui d'Estudis Catalans a Nord-Amèrica, 1993*, ed. August Bover, Joan Martí-Olivella, and Mary Ann Newmann, Barcelona, Publicacions de l'Abadia de Montserrat, 301 pp.

Actes (Frankfurt), I–III: *Actes del Desè Col·loqui Internacional de Llengua i Literatura Catalanes. Frankfurt, 1994*, ed. Axel Schönberger and Tilbert Dídac Stegmann, 3 vols, Barcelona, Publicacions de l'Abadia de Montserrat, 423, 446, 473 pp.

Actes (Groningen): *Aspects de l'épopée romane. Mentalités — Idéologies — Intertextualités*, ed. Hans van Dijk and Willem Noomen, Groningen, Egbert Forsten, 1995, ix + 526 pp.

Akten (Greifswald): *Arbeiten zur Skandinavistik. XII. Arbeitstagung der deutschsprachigen Skandinavistik 16.–23. September 1995 in Greifswald*, ed. Walter Baumgartner and Hans Fix (Studia Medievalia Septentrionalia, 2), Vienna, Fassbaender, 598 pp.

Akten (Sterzing): *Literatur und Sprache in Tirol. Von dem Anfängen bis zum 16. Jahrhundert. Akten des 3. Symposiums der Sterzinger Osterspiele (10.–12. April 1995)*, ed. Michael Gebhardt and Max Siller (Schlern-Schriften, 301), Innsbruck, Wagner, 454 pp.

Akten (Vancouver), I–III: *Alte Welten — neue Welten. Akten des IX. Kongresses der Internationalen Vereinigung für Germanische Sprach- und Literaturwissenschaft (IVG). 1. Ansprachen. Plenarvorträge.* II. *Abstracts.* III. *Abstracts*, ed. Michael S. Batts, 3 vols, Tübingen, Niemeyer, vii + 94, xxvi + 282, xxvi + 290 pp.

Alter, *Exilanten: Exilanten und andere Deutsche in Fontanes London*, ed. Peter Alter and Rudolf Muhs (Stuttgarter Arbeiten zur Germanistik, 331), Stuttgart, Heinz, x + 491 pp.

Atti (Ferrara), I–II: *Italia ed Europa nella linguistica del Rinascimento: confronti e relazioni: Atti del Convegno internazionale, Ferrara, Palazzo Paradiso, 20–24 marzo 1991*, ed. Mirko Tavoni et al., Modena, Parini, 1230 pp.

Atti (Licenza): *Orazio e la letteratura italiana. Contributi alla Storia della fortuna del poeta latino. Atti del Convegno svoltosi a Licenza dal 19 al 23 aprile 1993 nell'ambito delle celebrazioni del bimillenario della morte di Quinto Orazio Flacco*, Rome, Istituto Poligrafico e Zecca dello Stato, 1994, 624 pp.

Aviva, *Heritage: The Heritage of the Jews of Spain*, ed. Doron Aviva, Israel, Levinsky College of Education, 1994, 430 pp.

Banquets: Banquets et manières de table au moyen âge (Senefiance, 38), Aix-en-Provence, CUER MA, 564 pp.

Belletti, *Parameters: Parameters and Functional Heads. Essays in Comparative Syntax*, ed. Adriana Belletti and Luigi Rizzi, OUP.

Benedetti, *Gendered Contexts: Gendered Contexts: New Perspectives in Italian Cultural Studies*, ed. Laura Benedetti, Julia L. Hairston, and Silvia M. Ross, New York, Lang, 221 pp.

Berriot, *Mythe: Le Mythe de Jérusalem: Du Moyen Age à la Renaissance*, ed. and pref. Salvadore Evelyne Berriot, Saint-Étienne U.P., 1995, 270 pp.

Bertinetto, *Temporal Reference: Temporal Reference, Aspect and Actionality.* I. *Semantic and Syntactic Perspectives.* II. *Typological Perspectives*, ed. Pier Marco Bertinetto, Valentina Bianchi, James Higginbotham, and Mario Squartini, 2 vols, Turin, Rosenberg and Sellier, 1995, 412, 310 pp.

Borsche, *Nietzsche: 'Centauren-Geburten'. Wissenschaft, Kunst und Philosophie beim jungen Nietzsche*, ed. Tilman Borsche, Federico Gerratana, and Aldo Venturelli (Monographien und Texte zur Nietzsche-Forschung, 27), Berlin, de Gruyter, 1994, xiii + 545 pp.

Borsley, *Celtic Syntax: The Syntax of the Celtic Languages. A Comparative Perspective*, ed. Robert D. Borsley and Ian Roberts, CUP, 368 pp.

Brall, *Personenbeziehungen: Personenbeziehungen in der mittelalterlichen Literatur*, ed. Helmut Brall, Barbara Haupt, and Urban Küsters (Studia Humaniora, 25), Düsseldorf, Droste, 1994, xxvi + 476 pp.

Brandl, *Emanzipation: Edmund Brandl, Emanzipation gegen Anthropomorphismus: Der literarisch bedingte Wandeler goethzeitlichen Bildungsgeschichte* (Europäische Hochschulschriften, I, 1520), Berne–Frankfurt, Lang, 1995, 886 pp.

Brenner, *Literaturgeschichte: Peter J. Brenner, Neue deutsche Literaturgeschichte. Vom 'Ackermann' zu Günter Grass*, Tübingen, Niemeyer, viii + 379 pp.

Brownlee, *Cultural Authority: Cultural Authority in Golden Age Spain*, ed. Marina S. Brownlee and Hans Ulrich Gumbrecht, Baltimore–London, Johns Hopkins U.P., 1995, xvii + 321 pp.

Burwick, *Imagination: The Romantic Imagination: Literature and Art in England and Germany*, ed. Frederick Burwick and Jürgen Klein (Studies in Comparative Literature, 6), Amsterdam–Atlanta, GA, Rodopi, xvi + 456 pp. + 94 pp. + illus.

Cameron, *Champ: Le Champ littéraire 1860–1900: Études offertes à Michael Pakenham*, ed. Keith Cameron and James Cairns, Amsterdam, Rodopi, 345 pp.

Cammarosano, *Propaganda: Le forme della propaganda politica nel Due e nel Trecento*, ed. Paolo Cammarosano, Rome, École Française de Rome, 1994, 528 pp.

Cavallo, *Lo spazio: Lo spazio letterario del Medioevo*, ed. Guglielmo Cavallo, Claudio Leonardi, and Enrico Menestò, 3 vols, Rome, Salerno Editrice, 1995, 665, 717, 701 pp.

Chance, *Gender: Gender and Text in the Later Middle Ages*, ed. Jane Chance, Gainesville–Tallahassee–Tampa–Boca Raton–Pensacola–Orlando–Miami–Jacksonville, Florida U.P., xv + 342 pp.

Colloque (Aix-en-Provence): *Le Clerc au Moyen Age. Colloque du CUER MA, Aix-en-Provence, mars 1995* (Senefiance, 37), Aix-en-Provence, CUER MA Université de Provence (Centre d'Aix), 1995, 664 pp.

Colloque (Orléans): *L'Eau au Moyen Age. Symboles et usages. Actes du colloque d'Orléans — mai 1994*, ed. Bernard Ribémont, Orléans, Paradigme, 174 pp.

Colloquium (Bristol): *Spannungen und Konflikte menschlichen Zusammenlebens in der deutschen Literatur des Mittelalters. Bristoler Colloquium 1993*, ed. Kurt Gärtner, Ingrid Kasten, and Frank Shaw, Tübingen, Niemeyer, xii + 383 pp.

Colloquium (Chiemsee): *Lied im deutschen Mittelalter. Überlieferung, Typen, Gebrauch. Chiemsee-Colloquium 1991*, ed. Cyril Edwards, Ernst Hellgardt, and Norbert H. Ott, Tübingen, Niemeyer, viii + 350 pp.

Colloquium (Schweinfurt): *Literatur im Umkreis des Prager Hofs der Luxemburger: Schweinfurter Kolloquium 1992*, ed. Joachim Heinzle, L. Peter Johnson, and Gisela Vollmann, Berlin, Schmidt, 1994, 321 pp.

Corbin, *Mother Mirror:* Laurie Corbin, *The Mother Mirror. Self-Representation and the Mother-Daughter Relationship in Colette, Simone de Beauvoir, and Marguerite Dumas* (Currents in Comparative Romance Languages and Literatures, 32), New York–Washington, DC–Baltimore–Bern–Frankfurt am Main–Berlin–Vienna–Paris, Lang, 169 pp.

Cordin, *Femminile e maschile: Femminile e maschile tra pensiero e discorso*, ed. Patrizia Cordin, Trento, Università degli Studi, 1995, 167 pp.

Cramer, *Neues: Neues zu Altem. Novellen der Vergangenheit und der Gegenwart*, ed. Sabine Cramer (Houston German Studies, 10), Munich, Fink, ix + 281 pp.

Csobádi, *Volk: 'Weine, weine, du armes Volk!' Das verführte und betrogene Volk auf der Bühne. Gesammelte Vorträge des Salzburger Symposions 1994*, ed. Peter Csobádi, Gernot Gruber, Jürgen Kühnel, Ulrich Müller, Oswald Panagl, and Franz Viktor Spechtler, 2 vols, Anif-Salzburg, Speiser, 1995, 840 pp.

Cunha *Vol.: Miscelânea de estudos lingüísticos, filológicos e literários In Memoriam Celso Cunha*, ed. Cilene da Cunha Pereira and Paulo Roberto Dias Pereira, Rio, Nova Fronteira, 1995, lxviii + 998 pp.

D'Andrea *Vol.: Da una riva all'altra. Studi in onore di Antonio D'Andrea*, ed. Dante Della Terza, Florence, Cadmo, 1995.

Deyermond, *Iberia: Historical Literature in Medieval Iberia*, ed. Alan Deyermond (PMHRS, 2), London, Department of Hispanic Studies, Queen Mary and Westfield College, 132 pp.

Dolci, *Studi: Studi di grammatica tedesca e comparativa*, ed. Roberto Dolci and Giuliana Giusti, Venice, Università degli Studi 'Cà Foscari', 1995.

Dulac, *de Pizan: Une Femme de Lettres au Moyen Age. Études autour de Christine de Pizan*, ed. L. Dulac and B. Ribémont, Paradigme, Orléans, 1995, 528 pp.

Dutton *Vol.: Nunca fue pena mayor (Estudios de Literatura Española en homenaje a Brian Dutton)*, ed. Ana Menéndez Collera and Victoriano Roncero López, Cuenca, Universidad de Castilla-La Mancha, 693 pp.

Evans Vol.: Hispano-Gallo-Brittanica. Essays in Honour of Professor D. Ellis Evans on the Occasion of his Sixty-fifth Birthday, ed. Joseph F. Eska, R. Geraint Gruffydd, and Nicolas Jacobs, Cardiff, University of Wales Press, 1995, xxxv + 335 pp.

Fest. Exner: Poetry Poetics Translation. Festschrift in Honor of Richard Exner, ed. Ursula Mahlendorf and Laurence Rickels, Würzburg, Königshausen & Neumann, 1994, 352 pp.

Fest. Faucher: Rand und Band: Abgrenzung und Verknüpfung als Grundtendenzen des Deutschen. Festschrift für Eugène Faucher zum 60. Geburtstag, ed. René Métrich and Marcel Vuillaume (Eurogermanistik, 7), Tübingen, Narr, 1995, x + 338 pp.

Fest. Helbig: Deutsch als Fremdsprache. An den Quellen eines Faches. Festschrift für Gerhard Helbig zum 65. Geburtstag, ed. Heidrun Popp, Munich, Iudicium, 1995, lii + 833 pp.

Fest. Hinderling: '. . . im Gefüge der Sprachen.' Studien zu System und Soziologie der Dialekte. Festschrift für Robert Hunderling zum 60. Geburtstag, ed. Rüdiger Harnisch, Ludwig M. Eichinger, and Anthony Rowley (ZDL, Beihefte, 90), Stuttgart, Steiner, 1995, xi + 301 pp.

Fest. Hoffmann: Brücken schlagen . . . 'Weit draußen auf eigenen Füßen?' Festschrift für Fernand Hoffmann, ed. Joseph Kohnen, Hans-Joachim Solms, and Klaus-Peter Wegera, Frankfurt, Lang, 1994, 409 pp.

Fest. Jurgensen: Lesen und Schreiben: Literatur, Kritik, Germanistik. Festschrift für Manfred Jurgensen zum 55. Geburtstag, ed. Volker Wolf, Tübingen, Francke, 1995, xx + 338 pp.

Fest. Marahrens: Analogon rationis. Festschrift für Gerwin Marahrens zum 65. Geburtstag, ed. Marianne Henn and Christoph Lorey, Edmonton, Alberta U.P., 1994, xiii + 518 pp.

Fest. Mollay: Im Zeichen der ungeteilten Philologie. Festschrift für Professor Dr.sc. Karl Mollay zum 80. Geburtstag, ed. Péter Bassola (Budapester Beiträge zur Germanistik, 24), Budapest, Universität, Germanistisches Institut, 1993, vii + 436 pp.

Fest. Schenda: Hören. Sagen. Lesen, Lernen. Bausteine zu einer Geschichte der kommunikativen Kultur. Festschrift für Rudolf Schenda zum 65. Geburtstag, ed. Ursula Brunold-Bigler and Hermann Bausinger, Bern, Lang, 1995, 822 pp.

Fest. Steger: Texttyp, Sprechergruppe, Kommunikationsbereich. Studien zur deutschen Sprache in Geschichte und Gegenwart. Festschrift für Hugo Steger zum 65. Geburtstag, ed. Heinrich Löffler, Karlheinz Jakob, and Bernhard Kelle, Berlin–New York, de Gruyter, 1994, xviii + 539 pp.

Fest. Stern: 'Verbergendes Enthüllen': zu Theorie und Kunst dichterischen Verkleidens. Festschrift für Martin Stern, ed. Wolfram Malte Fues and Wolfram Mauser, Würzburg, Königshausen & Neumann, 1995, 452 pp.

Fest. Wellmann: Sprachgeschichtliche Untersuchungen zum älteren und neueren Deutsch. Festschrift für Hans Wellmann zum 60. Geburtstag, ed. Werner König and Lorelies Ortner (Germanische Bibliothek, 3rd ser., 23), Heidelberg, Winter, x + 445 pp.

Fietz, *Semiotik: Semiotik, Rhetorik und Soziologie des Lachens. Vergleichende Studien zum Funktionswandel des Lachens vom Mittelalter zur Gegenwart*, ed. Lothar Fietz, Tübingen, Niemeyer, viii + 377 pp.

Finucci, *Desire: Desire in the Renaissance: Psychoanalysis and Literature*, ed. Valeria Finucci and Regina Schwartz, Princeton U.P., 1994, viii + 273 pp.

French, *Women: Lorely French, German Women as Letter Writers: 1750–1850*, Madison, Fairleigh Dickinson U.P., 324 pp.

Fryde Vol.: Recognitions: Essays Presented to Edmund Fryde, ed. Colin Richmond and Isobel Harvey, Aberystwyth, The National Library of Wales, 546 pp.

Garber, *Sozietätsbewegung: Europäische Sozietätsbewegung und demokratische Tradition. Die europäischen Akademien der Frühen Neuzeit zwischen Frührenaissance und Spätaufklärung*, ed. Klaus Garber, Heinz Wismann, and Winfried Siebers (Frühe Neuzeit, 26–27), 2 vols, Tübingen, Niemeyer, xxx + 1840 pp.

García de la Concha, *Fray Luis: Fray Luis de León. Historia, Humanismo y Letras*, ed. Victor García de la Concha and Lera San José, Salamanca, Ediciones Universidad de Salamanca-Junta de Castilla y León — Ediciones Universidad de Castilla-La Mancha, 707 pp.

Giacalone Ramat, *Pragmatics: From Pragmatics to Syntax. Modality in Second Language Learning*, ed. Anna Giacalone Ramat and Grazia Crocco Galèas, Tübingen, Narr, 1995, 440 pp.

Glaudes, *Terreur: Terreur et représentation*, ed. Pierre Glaudes, Grenoble, ELLUG, Université Stendhal, 354 pp.

Goodich, *Convergences: Cross-Cultural Convergences in the Crusade Period*, ed. Michael Goodich, Sophia Menache and Sylvia Schein, New York, Lang, 1995, xxvii + 334 pp.

Goossens *Vol.: Lingua Theodisca. Beiträge zur Sprach- und Literaturwissenschaft. Jan Goossens zum 65. Geburtstag*, ed. José Cajot, Ludger Kremer, and Hermann Niebaum (Niederlande-Studien, 16), 2 vols, Münster–Hamburg, Lit, 1995, 1–676, 677–1259 pp.

Gössmann, *Poetisierung: Poetisierung — Politisierung. Deutschlandbilder in der Literatur bis 1848*, ed. Wilhelm Gössmann and Klaus-Hinrich Roth, Paderborn, Schöningh, 1994, 387 pp.

Graciotti, *Spiritualità: Spiritualità e lettere nella cultura italiana e ungherese del basso medioevo*, ed. Sante Graciotti and Cesare Vasoli, Florence, Olschki, 1995, xiv + 414 pp.

Grimbert, *Tristan and Isolde: Tristan and Isolde: A Casebook*, ed. Joan Tasker Grimbert, New York–London, Garland, 1995.

Gruffydd *Vol.: Beirdd a Thwysogion: Barddoniaeth Llys yng Nghymru, Iwerddon a'r Alban, Cyfwynedig i R. Geraint Gruffydd, BA, DPhil, FBA*, ed. Morfydd E. Owen and Brynley F. Roberts, Aberystwyth, University of Wales Press, Cardiff and National Library of Wales, xxxii + 356 pp.

Haferland, *Erzählungen: Erzählungen in Erzählungen. Phänomene der Narration in Mittelalter und Früher Neuzeit*, ed. Harald Haferland and Michael Mecklenburg (Forschungen zur Geschichte der älteren deutschen Literatur, 19), Munich, Fink, 454 pp.

Harris, *Culture: Changing Times in Hispanic Culture*, ed. Derek Harris, Aberdeen, Centre for the Study of the Hispanic Avant-garde.

Herrmann, *Volk: Volk — Nation — Vaterland*, ed. Ulrich Herrmann (Studien zum achtzehnten Jahrhundert, 18), Hamburg, Meiner, 407 pp.

Holmes, *Women's Writing: Diana Holmes, French Women's Writing 1848–1994*, London, Athlone, xviii + 320 pp.

Holtus, *Lexikon, II/2: Lexikon der Romanistischen Linguistik (LRL). II.2. Die einzelnen romanischen Sprachen und Sprachgebiete vom Mittelalter bis zur Renaissance*, ed. Günter Holtus, Michael Metzeltin, and Christian Schmitt, Tübingen, Niemeyer, 1995, xlii + 753 pp.

Homenaje Ouimette: La cultura española de entre siglos (XIX–XX). Homenaje a Victor Ouimette, ed. and introd. David A. Boruschoff, Jesús Pérez-Magallón, and Kay Sibbald (*RCEH*, 21.1, Special no.), Edmonton, 250 pp.

Hughes, *Erotic: French Erotic Fiction. Woman's Desiring Writing, 1880–1900*, ed. Alex Hughes and Kate Ince, Oxford–Washington, DC, Berg, viii + 191 pp.

Hunter, *Short Story: The Short Story: Structure and Statement*, ed. William Fiddes Hunter, Exeter, Elm Bank, ix + 198 pp.

Ingold, *Autor: Der Autor im Dialog. Beiträge zu Autorität und Autorschaft*, ed. Felix Philipp Ingold and Werner Wunderlich, St Gall, UVK, 1995, 210 pp.

Jackson, *Taboos: Taboos in German Literature*, ed. David Jackson, Providence, Berghahn, 216 pp.

Jones, *Enlli: Enlli*, ed. R. Gerallt Jones and Christopher J. Arnold, Cardiff, University of Wales Press, ix + 246 pp.

Kelly *Vol.: Conjonctures: Medieval Studies in Honor of Douglas Kelly*, ed. Keith Busby and Norris J. Lacy (Faux titre, 83), Amsterdam–Atlanta, GA, Rodopi, 1994, xxii + 596 pp.

Knight, *Women: Women and Representation*, ed. Diana Knight and Judith Still (Women Teaching French Occasional Papers, 3), Nottingham, WIF Publications, University of Nottingham, 1995, 143 pp.

Kugler, *Interregionalität: Interregionalität der deutschen Literatur im europäischen Mittelalter*, ed. Hartmut Kugler, Berlin, de Gruyter, 1995, vi + 204 pp.

Kuzniar, *Goethe: Outing Goethe and his Age*, ed. Alice A. Kuzniar, Stanford U.P., xiii + 297 pp.

Lacy, *Arthurian Literature: Medieval Arthurian Literature. A Guide to Recent Research*, ed. Norris J. Lacy, New York–London, Garland, xii + 471 pp.

Laroche, *Bildnis:* Bernd Laroche, *'Dies Bildnis ist bezaubernd schön.' Untersuchungen zur Struktur und Entwicklung der Bildnisbegegnung in der deutschen Literatur des 16.–19. Jahrhunderts* (Europäische Hochschulschriften, I, 1522), Berne–Frankfurt, Lang, 1995, 371 pp.

Leventhal, *Reading:* Robert S. Leventhal, *Reading after Foucault. Institutions, Disciplines, and Technologies of the Self in Germany, 1750–1830*, Detroit, Wayne State U.P., 1994, ix + 269 pp.

Lomax *Vol.: New Frontiers in Hispanic and Luso-Brazilian Scholarship: como se fue el maestro, for Derek W. Lomax in Memoriam*, ed. Trevor J. Dadson, R. J. Oakley, and P. A. Odber de Baubeta, Lewiston–Queenston–Lampeter, Mellen, 1994, 573 pp.

Lupu, *Studi: Studi rumeni e romanzi. Omaggio a Florica Dimitrescu e Alexandru Niculescu*, ed. Coman Lupu and Lorenzo Renzi, 3 vols, Padua, Unipress, iii + 410, 411–745, 747–1086 pp.

Luti *Vol.: I segni e la storia. Studi e testimonianze in onore di Giorgio Luti*, Florence, Le Lettere, viii + 518 pp.

Matter, *Creative Women: Creative Women in Medieval and Early Modern Italy*, ed. E.-Ann Matter and John Coakley, Philadelphia, Pennsylvania University Press, 1994, xiv + 356 pp.

McGuirk, *Brazil: Brazil and the Discourse of America: Narrative, History and Fiction, 1492–1992*, ed. B. McGuirk and S. R. de Oliveira, New York, Mellen, 214 pp.

Mélanges Spiewok: Europäischer Literaturen im Mittelalter. Mélanges en l'honneur de Wolfgang Spiewok à l'occasion de son 65ème anniversaire, ed. Danielle Buschinger (Wodan, 30; Greifswalder Beiträge zum Mittelalter, 15), Greifswald, Reineke, 1994, xxxix + 448 pp.

Mélanges Terraux: Mélanges de poétique et d'histoire littéraire offerts à Louis Terraux, ed. Jean Balsamo, Paris, Champion, 1994.

Millington, *Hispanisms: New Hispanisms: Literature, Culture, Theory*, ed. Mark I. Millington and Paul Julian Smith (Ottawa Hispanic Studies, 15), Ottawa, Dovehouse, 1994, 229 pp.

Mills Vol.: Romance Reading on the Book. Essays on Medieval Narrative presented to Maldwyn Mills, ed. Jennifer Fellows, Rosalind Field, Gillian Rogers, and Judith Weiss, Cardiff University of Wales Press, xii + 307 pp.

Molinari, *Teoria: Teoria e pratica della traduzione nel medioevo germanico*, ed. Maria Vittoria Molinari, Padua, Unipress, 1994, 388 pp.

Müller, *Herrscher: Herrscher, Helden, Heilige*, ed. Ulrich Müller and Werner Wunderlich (Mittelalter Mythen, 1), St Gall, UVK, xiv + 781 pp.

Olin *Vol.: Religious Orders of the Catholic Reformation: Essays in Honor of John C. Olin on his Seventy-fifth Birthday*, ed. Richard L. de Molen, New York, Fordham U.P., 1994.

Omaggio Folena: Omaggio a Gianfranco Folena, ed. Pier Vincenzo Mengaldo et al., Padua, Editoriale Programma, 3 vols, 1993, xlvii + 904, vi + 905–1888, v + 1889–2525 pp.

Papers (Amherst): *Literary Aspects of Courtly Culture. Selected Papers from the Seventh Triennial Congress of the International Courtly Literature Society, University of Massachusetts, Amherst, USA, 27 July–1 August 1992*, ed. Donald Maddox and Sara Sturm-Maddox, Cambridge, Brewer, 1994, 360 pp.

Papers (El Paso): *Contemporary Research in Romance Linguistics. Papers from the 22nd Linguistic Symposium on Romance Languages, El Paso / Cd. Juárez, February 1992*, ed. Jon Amastae et al. (Amsterdam Studies in the Theory and History of Linguistic Science, IV. Current Issues in Linguistic Theory, 123), Amsterdam–Philadelphia, Benjamins, 1995, vii + 381 pp.

Papers (Los Angeles): *Aspects of Romance Linguistics: Selected Papers from the Linguistic Symposium on Romance Languages XXIV, March 10–13, 1994*, ed. Claudia Parodi, Carlos Quicoli, Maria Saltarelli, and María Luisa Zubizarreta, Washington, DC, Georgetown U.P., xiv + 530 pp.

Papers (Seattle): *Grammatical Theory and Romance Languages: Selected Papers from the 25th Linguistic Symposium on Romance Languages (LSRL XXV), Seattle, 2–4 March 1995*, ed. Karen Zagona (Current Issues in Linguistic Theory, 133), Amsterdam, Benjamins, vi + 330 pp.

Pratt, *Roland and Charlemagne: Roland and Charlemagne in Europe: Essays on the Reception and Transformation of a Legend*, ed. Karen Pratt (King's College London Medieval Studies), London, King's College London Centre for Late Antique and Medieval Studies, 218 pp. + pls

Procs (Brasília): *Language and Literature Today. Proceedings of the XIXth Triennial Congress of the International Federation for Modern Languages and Literatures./Actes du XIXe Congrès de la Fédération Internationale des Langues et Littératures Modernes. Brasília 22–30 August 1993*, ed. Neide de Faria. I. *Modernity and Postmodernity. Technologies and Translation in the 'Global Village'. The Canon and Canonicity: Global Perspectives.* II. *Languages and Literatures in the 'Global Village'. Interdisciplinary Approaches to Language and Literature.* III. *The Literatures of Latin America*, 3 vols, Universidade de Brasília, xxxvi + 1–502, xviii + 503–1014, xviii + 1015–1391 pp.

Procs (Odense): *The Origins and Development of Emigrant Languages. Proceedings from the Second Rasmus Rask Colloquium, Odense University, November, 1994*, ed. Hans F. Nielsen and Lene Schøsler (*RASK*, supp. 6; *NOWELE*, supp. 17), Odense U.P., xi + 318 pp.

Procs (Oporto): *Das grosse Abenteuer der Entdeckung der Welt im Mittelalter. La grande aventure de la découverte du monde au moyen âge. VI. Jahrestagung der Reineke-Gesellschaft (Porto in Portugal, 30.05–04.06.1995)*, ed. Danielle Buschinger and Walter Spiewok (Greifswalder Beiträge zum Mittelalter, 56), Greifswald, Reineke, 1995[1996], vii + 166 pp.

Procs (St Hilda's): *Women, the Book and the Worldly. Selected Proceedings of the St Hilda's Conference, 1993*, ed. Lesley Smith and Jane H. M. Taylor, Woodbridge, Brewer, 1995, 193 pp.

Rigby, *Transgressions: Catherine E. Rigby, Transgressions of the Feminine. Tragedy, Enlightenment and the Figure of Woman in Classical German Drama* (Reihe Siegen, 130), Heidelberg, Winter, vi + 270 pp.

Robinson, *Writers: Modern Women Writers*, comp. and ed. Lillian S. Robinson, 4 vols, New York, Continuum, xxxiii + 838, ix + 819, ix + 830, viii + 904 pp.

Romane (Interpretationen): *Interpretationen. Romane des 17. und 18. Jahrhunderts* (Universal-Bibliothek, 9474), Stuttgart, Reclam, 328 pp.

Russell, *Women Writers: Italian Women Writers: A Bio-Bibliographical Sourcebook*, ed. Rinaldina Russell, Westport, CT, Greenwood, 1994, 476 pp.

Scarlett, *Body: Elizabeth A. Scarlett, Under Construction: The Body in Spanish Novels*, Charlottesville–London, University Press of Virginia, x + 232 pp.

Schiewer, *Cognitio: Gesine Lenore Schiewer, Cognitio Symbolica. Lamberts semiotische Wissenschaft und ihre Diskussion bei Herder, Jean-Paul und Novalis* (Frühe Neuzeit, 22), Tübingen, Niemeyer, x + 283 pp.

Schiewer, *Forschungsberichte: Forschungsberichte zur germanistischen Mediävistik, 5/1*, ed. Hans-Jochen Schiewer (*Jahrbuch für Internationale Germanistik*, Reihe C, 5/1), Bern, Lang, 267 pp.

Schilling, *Wechselspiele: Wechselspiele. Kommunikationsformen und Gattungsinterferenzen mittelhochdeutscher Lyrik*, ed. Michael Schilling and Peter Stroschneider (*Germanisch-Romanische Monatsschrift*, Beiheft 13), Heidelberg, Winter, 279 pp.

Schmidt-Glintzer, *Fördern: Fördern und Bewahren. Studien zur europäischen Kulturgeschichte der frühen Neuzeit. Festschrift anläßlich des zehnjährigen Bestehens der Dr. Günther Findel-Stiftung zur Förderung der Wissenschaften*, ed. Helwig Schmidt-Glintzer (Wolfenbüteler Forschungen, 70), Wiesbaden, Harrassowitz, 304 pp.

Sent, *Oper: Die Oper am Weißenfelser Hof*, ed. Eleonore Sent (Weißenfelser Kulturtradition, 1), Rudolstadt, Hain, 319 pp.

Siganos, *Solitudes: Solitudes, Écriture et représentation*, ed. André Siganos, Grenoble, ELLUG, Université Stendhal, 1995, 242 pp.

Smith, *Essays: Essays in Memory of Michael Parkinson and Janine Dakyns*, ed. Christopher Smith (Norwich Papers, 4), Norwich, University of East Anglia, xiii + 390 pp.

Solà-Solé Vol.: Essays in Honor of Josep M. Solà-Solé. Linguistic and Literary Relations of Catalan and Castilian, ed. Suzanne S. Hintz, NY–Bern–Frankfurt, Lang, 334 pp.

Šrámek, *Spisovnost: Spisovnost a nespisovnost dnes. Sborník příspěvků z mezinárodní konference*, ed. Rudolf Šrámek, Brno, Masarykova univerzita, 261 pp.

Stempel, *Musique: Musique naturelle: Interpretationen zur französischen Lyrik des Spätmittelalters*, ed. Wolf Dieter Stempel, Munich, Fink, 1995, 512 pp.

Studi Raimondi: Mappe e letture. Studi in onore di Ezio Raimondi, ed. Andrea Battistini, Bologna, Il Mulino, 1994, 484 pp.

Sturrock, *Guide: The Oxford Guide to Contemporary Writing*, ed. John Sturrock, OUP.

Symposium (Roscrea): *Die Vermittlung geistlicher Inhalte im deutschen Mittelalter. Internationales Symposium, Roscrea 1994*, ed. Timothy R. Jackson, Nigel F. Palmer, and Almut Suerbaum, Tübingen, Niemeyer, viii + 337 pp.

Taylor, *Perspectives: Rodney Taylor, Perspectives on Spinoza in Works by Schiller, Büchner, and C. F. Meyer. Five Essays* (North American Studies in Nineteenth-Century Literature, 18), Berne, Lang, 1995, 159 pp.

Thieroff, *Tense*, 11: *Tense Systems in European Languages*, 11, ed. Rolf Thieroff (Linguistische Arbeiten, 338), Tübingen, Niemeyer, 1995, ix + 343 pp.

Vázquez Vol.: Homenaxe á profesora Pilar Vázquez Cuesta, ed. R. Lorenzo and R. Alvarez, Santiago de Compostela U.P., 829 pp.

Williams, *Knowledge: Knowledge, Science, and Literature in Early Modern Germany*, ed. Gerhild Scholz Williams and Stephan K. Schindler, Chapel Hill–London, North Carolina U.P., 310 pp.

Willis Vol.: Portuguese, Brazilian and African Studies. Studies Presented to Clive Willis on his Retirement, ed. T. F. Earle and Nigel Griffin, Warminster, Aris & Phillips, 1995, xii + 440 pp.

Wing, *Belief: Belief and Unbelief in Hispanic Literature. Papers from a Conference at the University of Hull, 12–13 December 1994*, ed. Helen Wing and John Jones, Warminster, Aris & Phillips, 1995, vi + 185 pp.

WS XIV: Wolfram-Studien XIV. Übersetzen im Mittelalter. Cambridger Kolloquium 1994, ed. Joachim Heinzle, L. Peter Johnson, and Gisela Vollmann-Profe, Berlin, Schmidt, 483 pp. + 18 pls.

II. GENERAL

abbrev.	abbreviation, abbreviated to
Acad., Akad.	Academy, Academia, etc.
acc.	accusative
ann.	annotated (by)
anon.	anonymous
appx	appendix
Arg.	Argentinian (and foreign equivalents)
Assoc.	Association (and foreign equivalents)
Bel.	Belarusian
BL	British Library
BM	British Museum
BN	Bibliothèque Nationale, Biblioteka Narodowa, etc.
bull.	bulletin
c.	century
c.	circa
ch.	chapter
col.	column
comm.	commentary (by)
comp.	compiler, compiled (by)
Cz.	Czech
diss.	dissertation
ed.	edited (by), editor (and foreign equivalents)
edn	edition
fac.	facsimile
fasc.	fascicle
Fest.	Festschrift, Festskrift
Fin.	Finnish
Fr.	France, French, Français
Ger.	German(y)
Gk	Greek
Gmc	Germanic
IE	Indo-European
illus.	illustrated, illustration(s)
impr.	impression
incl.	including, include(s)
Inst.	Institute (and foreign equivalents)
introd.	introduction, introduced by, introductory
It.	Italian
izd.	издание
izd-vo	издательство
Jb.	Jahrbuch
Jg	Jahrgang
Jh.	Jahrhundert
Lat.	Latin
lit.	literature
med.	medieval
MHG	Middle High German
Mid. Ir.	Middle Irish
Mil.	Milanese
MS	manuscript
n.d.	no date
n.F.	neue Folge

no.	number (and foreign equivalents)
nom.	nominative
n.s.	new series
OE	Old English
OF	Old French
OHG	Old High German
O Ir.	Old Irish
OS	Old Saxon
OW	Old Welsh
part.	participle
ped.	педагогический, etc.
PIE	Proto-Indo-European
Pied.	Piedmontese
PGmc	Primitive Germanic
pl.	plate
plur.	plural
Pol.	Polish
pref.	preface (by)
Procs	Proceedings
publ.	publication, published (by)
Ren.	Renaissance
repr.	reprint(ed)
Rev.	Review, Revista, Revue
rev.	revised (by)
Russ.	Russian
s.	siècle
ser.	series
sg.	singular
Slg	Sammlung
Soc.	Society (and foreign equivalents)
Sp.	Spanish
supp.	supplement
Sw.	Swedish
Trans.	Transactions
trans.	translated (by), translation
Ukr.	Ukrainian
Univ.	University (and foreign equivalents)
unpubl.	unpublished
U.P.	University Press (and foreign equivalents)
Vlg	Verlag
vol.	volume
vs	versus
W.	Welsh
wyd.	wydawnictwo

* before a publication signifies that it has not been seen by the contributor.

III. PLACE NAMES

B	Barcelona	Na	Naples
BA	Buenos Aires	NY	New York
Be	Belgrade	O	Oporto
Bo	Bologna	Pń	Poznań
C	Coimbra	R	Rio de Janeiro
F	Florence	Ro	Rome
Gd	Gdańsk	SPo	São Paulo
Kw	Kraków, Cracow	StP	St Petersburg
L	Lisbon	T	Turin
Ld	Leningrad	V	Valencia
M	Madrid	Wa	Warsaw
Mi	Milan	Ww	Wrocław
Mw	Moscow	Z	Zagreb

IV. PERIODICALS, INSTITUTIONS, PUBLISHERS

AA, Antike und Abendland
AAA, Ardis Publishers, Ann Arbor, Michigan
AAA, Archivio per l'Alto Adige
AAASS, American Association for the Advancement of Slavic Studies
AAC, Atti dell'Accademia Clementina
AAL, Atti dell'Accademia dei Lincei
AALP, L'Arvista dl'Academia dla Lenga Piemontèisa
AAM, Association des Amis de Maynard
AAPN, Atti dell'Accademia Pontaniana di Napoli
AAPP, Atti Accademia Peloritana dei Pericolanti. Classe di Lettere Filosofia e Belle Arti
AARA, Atti della Accademia Roveretana degli Agiati
AASB, Atti dell'Accademia delle Scienze dell'Istituto di Bologna
AASF, Annales Academiae Scientiarum Fennicae
AASLAP, Atti dell'Accademia di Scienze, Lettere ed Arti di Palermo
AASLAU, Atti dell'Accademia di Scienze, Lettere e Arti di Udine
AASN, Atti dell'Accademia di Scienze Morali e Politiche di Napoli

AAST, Atti dell'Accademia delle Scienze di Torino
AAVM, Atti e Memorie dell'Accademia Virgiliana di Mantova
AAWG, Abhandlungen der Akademie der Wissenschaften in Göttingen, phil.-hist. Kl., 3rd ser., Göttingen, Vandenhoeck & Ruprecht
AB, Analecta Bollandiana
ABa, L'Année Balzacienne
ABÄG, Amsterdamer Beiträge zur älteren Germanistik
ABB, Archives et Bibliothèques de Belgique — Archief– en Bibliotheekswezen in België
ABDB, Aus dem Antiquariat. Beiträge zum Börsenblatt für den deutschen Buchhandel
ABDO, Association Bourguignonne de Dialectologie et d'Onomastique, Fontaine lès Dijon
ABHL, Annual Bulletin of Historical Literature
ABI, Accademie e Biblioteche d'Italia
ABN, Anais da Biblioteca Nacional, Rio de Janeiro
ABNG, Amsterdamer Beiträge zur neueren Germanistik, Amsterdam, Rodopi

ABor, Acta Borussica
ABP, Arquivo de Bibliografia
   Portuguesa
ABR, American Benedictine Review
ABr, Annales de Bretagne et des
   Pays de l'Ouest
ABS, Acta Baltico-Slavica
AC, Analecta Cisterciensa, Rome
ACCT, Agence de Coopération
   Culturelle et Technique
ACer, Anales Cervantinos, Madrid
ACo, Acta Comeniana, Prague
AColl, Actes et Colloques
Acme, Annali della Facoltà di
   Filosofia e Lettere dell'Università
   Statale di Milano
ACP, L'Amitié Charles Péguy
ACUA, Anales del Colegio
   Universitario de Almería
AD, Analysen und Dokumente.
   Beiträge zur Neueren Literatur,
   Berne, Lang
ADEVA, Akademische Druck- und
   Verlagsanstalt, Graz
AE, Artemis Einführungen,
   Munich, Artemis
AE, L'Autre Europe
AEA, Anuario de Estudios
   Atlánticos, Las Palmas
AECI, Agencia Española de
   Cooperación Internacional
AEd, Arbeiten zur
   Editionswissenschaft, Frankfurt,
   Lang
AEF, Anuario de Estudios
   Filológicos, Cáceres
AEL, Anuario de la Escuela de
   Letras, Mérida, Venezuela
AELG, Anuario de Literarios
   Galegos
AEM, Anuario de Estudios
   Medievales
AF, Anuario de Filología, Barcelona
AFA, Archivo de Filología
   Aragonesa
AfAf, African Affairs
AfC, Afrique Contemporaine
AFe, L'Armana di Felibre
AFF, Anali Filološkog fakulteta,
   Belgrade
AFH, Archivum Franciscanum
   Historicum
AFHis, Anales de Filología
   Hispánica

AfL, L'Afrique Littéraire
AFLE, Annali della Fondazione
   Luigi Einaudi
AFLFUB, Annali della Facoltà di
   Lettere e Filosofia dell'Università
   di Bari
AFLFUC, Annali della Facoltà di
   Lettere e Filosofia dell'Università
   di Cagliari
AFLFUG, Annali della Facoltà di
   Lettere e Filosofia dell'Università
   degli Studi di Genova
AFLFUM, Annali della Facoltà di
   Lettere e Filosofia dell'Università
   di Macerata
AFLFUN, Annali della Facoltà di
   Lettere e Filosofia dell'Università
   di Napoli
AFLFUP(SF), Annali dellà Facoltà di
   Lettere e Filosofia dell'Università
   di Perugia 1. Studi Filosofici
AFLFUP(SLL), Annali della Facoltà
   di Lettere e Filosofia
   dell'Università di Perugia. 3.
   Studi Linguistici-Letterari
AFLFUS, Annali della Facoltà di
   Lettere e Filosofia dell'Università
   di Siena
AFLLS, Annali della Facoltà di
   Lingua e Letterature Straniere di
   Ca' Foscari, Venice
AFLN, Annales de la Faculté des
   Lettres et Sciences Humaines de
   Nice
AFP, Archivum Fratrum
   Praedicatorum
AFrP, Athlone French Poets,
   London, The Athlone Press
AG, Anales Galdosianos
AGB, Archiv für Geschichte des
   Buchwesens
AGI, Archivio Glottologico Italiano
AGJSG, Acta Germanica. Jahrbuch
   des Südafrikanischen
   Germanistenverbandes
AGP, Archiv für Geschichte der
   Philosophie
AH, Archivo Hispalense
AHAW, Abhandlungen der
   Heidelberger Akademie der
   Wissenschaften, phil.-hist. Kl
AHCP, Arquivos de História de
   Cultura Portuguesa

AHDLMA, Archives d'Histoire Doctrinale et Littéraire du Moyen Âge

AHF, Archiwum Historii Filozofii i Myśli Społecznej

AHP, Archivum Historiae Pontificae

AHPr, Annales de Haute-Provence, Digne-les-Bains

AHR, American Historical Review

AHRF, Annales Historiques de la Révolution Française

AHRou, Archives historiques du Rouergue

AHSJ, Archivum Historicum Societatis Jesu

AHSS, Annales: Histoire — Science Sociales

AI, Almanacco Italiano

AIB, Annali dell'Istituto Banfi

AIBL, Académie des Inscriptions et Belles-Lettres, Comptes Rendus

AIEM, Anales del Instituto de Estudios Madrileños

AIEO, Association Internationale d'Études Occitanes

AIFMUR, Annali dell'Istituto di Filologia Moderna dell'Università di Roma

AIFUF, Annali dell'Istituto di Filosofia dell'Università di Firenze

AIHI, Archives Internationales d'Histoire des Idées, The Hague, Nijhoff

AIHS, Archives Internationales d'Histoire des Sciences

AIL, Associação Internacional de Lusitanistas

AILLC, Associació Internacional de Llengua i Literatura Catalanes

AISIGT, Annali dell'Istituto Storico Italo-Germanico di Trento

AION(FG), Annali dell'Istituto Universitario Orientale, Naples: Sezione Germanica. Filologia Germanica

AION(SF), Annali dell'Istituto Universitario Orientale, Naples: Studi Filosofici

AION(SL), Annali dell'Istituto Universitario Orientale, Naples: Sezione Linguistica

AION(SR), Annali dell'Istituto Universitario Orientale, Naples: Sezione Romanza

AION(SS), Annali dell'Istituto Universitario Orientale, Naples: Sezione Slava

AION(ST), Annali dell'Istituto Universitario Orientale, Naples: Sezione Germanica. Studi Tedeschi

AIPHS, Annuaire de l'Institut de Philologie et de l'Histoire Orientales et Slaves

AIPS, Annales Instituti Philologiae Slavica Universitatis Debreceniensis de Ludovico Kossuth Nominatae — Slavica

AIV, Atti dell'Istituto Veneto

AJ, Alemannisches Jahrbuch

AJCAI, Actas de las Jornadas de Cultura Arabe e Islámica

AJFS, Australian Journal of French Studies

AJGLL, American Journal of Germanic Linguistics and Literatures

AJL, Australian Journal of Linguistics

AJP, American Journal of Philology

AKG, Archiv für Kulturgeschichte

AKML, Abhandlungen zur Kunst-, Musik- und Literaturwissenschaft, Bonn, Bouvier

AL, Anuario de Letras, Mexico

AlAm, Alba de América

ALB, Annales de la Faculté des Lettres de Besançon

ALC, African Languages and Cultures

ALE, Anales de Literatura Española, Alicante

ALEC, Anales de Literatura Española Contemporánea

ALet, Armas y Letras, Universidad de Nuevo León

ALEUA, Anales de Literatura Española de la Universidad de Alicante

ALFL, Actes de Langue Française et de Linguistique

ALH, Acta Linguistica Hungaricae

ALHA, Anales de la Literatura Hispanoamericana

ALHa, Acta Linguistica Hafniensia
ALHisp, Anuario de Lingüística Hispánica
ALHist, Annales: Littérature et Histoire
ALit, Acta Literaria, Chile
ALitH, Acta Litteraria Hungarica
ALLI, Atlante Linguistico dei Laghi Italiani
ALM, Archives des Lettres Modernes
ALMA, Archivum Latinitatis Medii Aevi (Bulletin du Cange)
ALo, Armanac de Louzero
AlS, Almanac Setòri
ALT, African Literature Today
ALUB, Annales Littéraires de l'Université de Besançon
AM, Analecta Musicologica
AMAA, Atti e Memorie dell'Accademia d'Arcadia
AMAASLV, Atti e Memorie dell'Accademia di Agricultura, Scienze e Lettere di Verona
AMal, Analecta Malacitana
AMAP, Atti e Memorie dell'Accademia Patavina di Scienze, Lettere ed Arti
AMAPet, Atti e Memorie dell'Accademia Petrarca di Lettere, Arti e Scienze, Arezzo
AMAT, Atti e Memorie dell'Accademia Toscana di Scienze e Lettere, La Colombaria
AMDLS, Arbeiten zur Mittleren Deutschen Literatur und Sprache, Berne, Lang
AMDSPAPM, Atti e Memorie della Deputazione di Storia Patria per le Antiche Province Modenesi
AMGG, Abhandlungen der Marburger Gelehrten Gesellschaft, Munich, Fink
AmH, American Hispanist
AMid, Annales du Midi
AML, Main Monographien Literaturwissenschaft, Frankfurt, Main
AmIn, América Indígena, Mexico
AMSSSP, Atti e Memorie della Società Savonese di Storia Patria
АН, Академия наук
AN, Americana Norvegica

ANABA, Asociación Nacional de Bibliotecarios, Arquiveros y Arqueólogos
AnAlf, Annali Alfieriani
AnEA, Anaquel de Estudios Arabes
ANeo, Acta Neophilologica, Ljubljana
ANF, Arkiv för nordisk filologi
AnI, Annali d'Italianistica
AnL, Anthropological Linguistics
AnM, Anuario Medieval
AnN, Annales de Normandie
AnnM, Annuale Medievale
ANQ, American Notes and Queries
ANTS, Anglo-Norman Text Society
AnVi, Antologia Vieusseux
ANZSGLL, Australian and New Zealand Studies in German Language and Literature, Berne, Lang
AO, Almanac occitan, Foix
AÖAW, Anzeiger der Österreichischen Akademie der Wissenschaften
AP, Aurea Parma
APIFN, Актуальные проблемы истории философии народов СССР.
APK, Aufsätze zur portugiesischen Kulturgeschichte, Görres-Gesellschaft, Münster
ApL, Applied Linguistics
APL, Associação Portuguesa de Linguística, Lisbon
APPP, Abhandlungen zur Philosophie, Psychologie und Pädagogik, Bonn, Bouvier
APr, Analecta Praemonstratensia
AProu, Armana Prouvençau, Marseilles
APS, Acta Philologica Scandinavica
APSL, Amsterdamer Publikationen zur Sprache und Literatur, Amsterdam, Rodopi
APUCF, Association des Publications de la Faculté des Lettres et Sciences Humaines de l'Université de Clermont-Ferrand II, Nouvelle Série
AQ, Arizona Quarterly
AqAq, Aquò d'aquí, Gap
AR, Archiv für Reformationsgeschichte

ARAJ, American Romanian
Academy Journal
ARAL, Australian Review of
Applied Linguistics
ARCA, ARCA: Papers of the
Liverpool Latin Seminar
ArCCP, Arquivos do Centro
Cultural Português, Paris
ArFil, Archivio di Filosofia
ArI, Arthurian Interpretations
ARI, Архив русской истории
ARL, Athlone Renaissance Library
ArL, Archivum Linguisticum
ArLit, Arthurian Literature
ArP, Археографски прилози
ArSP, Archivio Storico Pugliese
ArSPr, Archivio Storico Pratese
ArSt, Archivi per la Storia
ART, Atelier Reproduction des
Thèses, Univ. de Lille III, Paris,
Champion
AS, The American Scholar
ASAvS, Annuaire de la Société des
Amis du vieux-Strasbourg
ASB, Archivio Storico Bergamasco
ASCALF, Association for the Study
of Caribbean and African
Literature in French
ASE, Annali di Storia dell'Esegesi
ASEES, Australian Slavonic and
East European Studies
ASELGC, 1616. Anuario de la
Sociedad Española de Literatura
General y Comparada
ASGM, Atti del Sodalizio
Glottologico Milanese
ASI, Archivio Storico Italiano
ASJ, Acta Slavonica Japonica
ASL, Archivio Storico Lombardo
ASNP, Annali della Scuola Normale
Superiore di Pisa, Bologna
ASNS, Archiv für das Studium der
Neueren Sprachen und
Literaturen
ASocRous, Annales de la Société J.-J.
Rousseau
ASolP, A Sol Post, Editorial Marfil,
Alcoi
ASP, Anzeiger für slavische
Philologie
ASPN, Archivio Storico per le
Province Napoletane
ASPP, Archivio Storico per le
Province Parmensi

ASRSP, Archivio della Società
Romana di Storia Patria
ASSO, Archivio Storico per la Sicilia
Orientale
ASSUL, Annali del Dipartimento di
Scienze Storiche e Sociali
dell'Università di Lecce
AST, Analecta Sacra Tarraconensia
ASt, Austrian Studies
ASTic, Archivio Storico Ticinese
AŞUI, (e), (f), Analele Ştiinţifice ale
Universităţii 'Al. I. Cuza' din Iaşi,
secţ. e, Lingvistică, secţ. f,
Literatură
AT, Athenäums Taschenbücher,
Frankfurt, Athenäum
ATB, Altdeutsche Textbibliothek,
Tübingen, Niemeyer
ATCA, Arxiu de Textos Catalans
Antics, IEC, Barcelona
Ate, Nueva Atenea, Universidad de
Concepción, Chile
ATO, A Trabe de Ouro
ATS, Arbeiten und Texte zur
Slavistik, Munich, Sagner
ATV, Aufbau Taschenbuch Verlag,
Berlin, Aufbau
AtV, Ateneo Veneto
AUBLLR, Analele Universităţii
Bucureşti, Limba şi literatura
română
AUBLLS, Analele Universităţii
Bucureşti, Limbi şi literaturi
străine
AUC, Anales de la Universidad de
Cuenca
AUCP, Acta Universitatis
Carolinae Pragensis
AUL, Acta Universitatis Lodziensis
AUL, Annali della Facoltà di Lettere
e Filosofia dell'Università di
Lecce
AUMCS, Annales Uniwersytetu
Marii Curie-Skłodowskiej, Lublin
AUML, Anales de la Universidad de
Murcia: Letras
AUMLA, Journal of the Australasian
Universities Modern Language
Association
AUN, Annali della Facoltà di Lettere
e Filosofia dell'Università di
Napoli

AUNCFP, Acta Universitatis Nicolai
Copernici. Filologia Polska,
Toruń
AUPO, Acta Universitatis
Palackianae Olomucensis
AUS, American University Studies,
Berne — New York, Lang
AUSP, Annali dell'Università per
Stranieri di Perugia
AUSSSR, Acta Universitatis
Stockholmiensis. Stockholm
Studies in Russian Literature
AUSSS, Acta Universitatis
Stockholmiensis. Stockholm
Slavic Studies
AUTŞF, Analele Universităţii din
Timişoara, Ştiinţe Filologice
AUUSRU, Acta Universitatis
Upsaliensis. Studia Romanica
Upsaliensia
AUUUSH, Acta Universitatis
Umensis, Umeå Studies in the
Humanities, Umeå U.P.
AUW, Acta Universitatis
Wratislaviensis
AVen, Archivio Veneto
AVEP, Assouciacien vareso pèr
l'ensignamen dòu prouvençou,
La Farlède
AvT, L'Avant-Scène Théâtre
AWR, Anglo-Welsh Review

BA, Bollettino d'Arte
BAAA, Bulletin de l'Association des
Amis d'Alain
BAAG, Bulletin des Amis d'André
Gide
BAAJG, Bulletin de l'Association des
Amis de Jean Giono
BAAL, Boletín de la Academia
Argentina de Letras
BaB, Bargfelder Bote
BAC, Biblioteca de Autores
Cristianos
BACol, Boletín de la Academia
Colombiana
BÄDL, Beiträge zur Älteren
Deutschen Literaturgeschichte,.
Berne, Lang
BADLit, Bonner Arbeiten zur
deutschen Literatur, Bonn,
Bouvier

BAE, Biblioteca de Autores
Españoles
BAEO, Boletín de la Asociación
Española de Orientalistas
BAFJ, Bulletin de l'Association
Francis Jammes
BAG, Boletín de la Academia
Gallega
BAIEO, Bulletins de l'Association
Internationale d'Études
Occitanes
BAJR, Bulletin des Amis de Jules
Romains
BAJRAF, Bulletin des Amis de
Jacques Rivière et d'Alain-
Fournier
BALI, Bollettino dell'Atlante
Linguistico Italiano
BALM, Bollettino dell'Atlante
Linguistico Mediterraneo
BAN, Българска Академия на
Науките, София
BAO, Biblioteca Abat Oliva,
Publicacions de l'Abadia de
Montserrat, Barcelona
BAPC, Bulletin de l'Association Paul
Claudel
BAPRLE, Boletín de la Academia
Puertorrigueña de la Lengua
Española
BAR, Biblioteca dell'Archivum
Romanicum
BARLLF, Bulletin de l'Académie
Royale de Langues et de
Littératures Françaises de
Bruxelles
BAWA, Bayerische Akademie der
Wissenschaften. Phil.-hist. Kl.
Abhandlungen, n.F.
BB, Biblioteca Breve, Lisbon
BB, Bulletin of Bibliography
BBAHLM, Boletín Bibliografico de
la Asociación Hispánica de
Literatura Medieval
BBB, Berner Beiträge zur
Barockgermanistik, Berne, Lang
BBGN, Brünner Beiträge zur
Germanistik und Nordistik
BBib, Bulletin du Bibliophile
BBL, Bayreuther Beiträge zur
Literaturwissenschaft, Frankfurt,
Lang
BBMP, Boletín de la Biblioteca de
Menéndez Pelayo

BBN, Bibliotheca Bibliographica Neerlandica, Nieuwkoop, De Graaf

BBNDL, Berliner Beiträge zur neueren deutschen Literaturgeschichte, Berne, Lang

BBSANZ, Bulletin of the Bibliographical Society of Australia and New Zealand

BBSIA, Bulletin Bibliographique de la Société Internationale Arthurienne

BBSMES, Bulletin of the British Society for Middle Eastern Studies

BBUC, Boletim da Biblioteca da Universidade de Coimbra

BC, Bulletin of the 'Comediantes', University of Wisconsin

BCB, Boletín Cultural y Bibliográfico, Bogatá

BCEC, Bwletin Cymdeithas Emynwyr Cymru

BCél, Bulletin Célinien

BCh, Болдинские чтения

BCLSMP, Académie Royale de Belgique: Bulletin de la Classe des Lettres et des Sciences Morales et Politiques

BCMV, Bollettino Civici Musei Veneziani

BCRLT, Bulletin du Centre de Romanistique et de Latinité Tardive

BCS, Bulletin of Canadian Studies

BCSM, Bulletin of the Cantigueiros da Santa Maria

BCSS, Bollettino del Centro di Studi Filologici e Linguistici Siciliani

BCSV, Bollettino del Centro di Studi Vichiani

BCZG, Blätter der Carl Zuckmayer Gesellschaft

BD, Беларуская думка

BDADA, Bulletin de documentation des Archives départementales de l'Aveyron, Rodez

BDB, Börsenblatt für den deutschen Buchhandel

BDBA, Bien Dire et Bien Aprandre

BDP, Beiträge zur Deutschen Philologie, Giessen, Schmitz

BEA, Bulletin des Études Africaines

BEC, Bibliothèque de l'École des Chartes

BelE, Беларуская энцыклапедыя

BelL, Беларуская лінгвістыка

BelS, Беларускі сьвет

BEP, Bulletin des Études Portugaises

BEPar, Bulletin des Études Parnassiennes et Symbolistes

BEzLit, Български език и литература

BF, Boletim de Filologia

BFA, Bulletin of Francophone Africa

BFC, Boletín de Filología, Univ. de Chile

BFE, Boletín de Filología Española

BFF, Bulletin Francophone de Finlande

BFFGL, Boletín de la Fundación Federico García Lorca

BFi, Bollettino Filosofico

BFLS, Bulletin de la Faculté des Lettres de Strasbourg

BFo, Biuletyn Fonograficzny

BFPLUL, Bibliothèque de la Faculté de Philosophie et Lettres de l'Université de Liège

BFR, Bibliothèque Française et Romane, Paris, Klincksieck

BFR, Bulletin de la Fondation C.F. Ramuz

BFr, Börsenblatt Frankfurt

BG, Bibliotheca Germanica, Tübingen, Francke

BGB, Bulletin de l'Association Guillaume Budé

BGDSL, Beiträge zur Geschichte der deutschen Sprache und Literatur, Tübingen

BGKT, Беларускае грамадска-культуральнае таварыства

BGL, Boletin Galego de Literatura

BGLKAJ, Beiträge zur Geschichte der Literatur und Kunst des 18. Jahrhunderts, Heidelberg, Winter

BGP, Bristol German Publications, Bristol U.P

BGREC, Bulletin du Groupe de Recherches et d'Études du Clermontais, Clermont-l'Hérault

BGS, Beiträge zur Geschichte der Sprachwissenschaft

BGS, Beiträge zur germanistischen Sprachwissenschaft, Hamburg, Buske

BGT, Blackwell German Texts, Oxford, Blackwell

BH, Bulletin Hispanique

BHR, Bibliothèque d'Humanisme et Renaissance

BHS(G), Bulletin of Hispanic Studies (Glasgow)

BHS(L), Bulletin of Hispanic Studies (Liverpool)

BI, Bibliographisches Institut, Leipzig

BibAN, Библиотека Академии наук СССР

BIDS, Bulletin of the International Dostoevsky Society, Klagenfurt

BIEA, Boletín del Instituto de Estudios Asturianos

BIHBR, Bulletin de l'Institut Historique Belge de Rome

BIHR, Bulletin of the Institute of Historical Research

BJA, British Journal of Aesthetics

BJCS, British Journal for Canadian Studies

BJECS, The British Journal for Eighteenth-Century Studies

BJHP, British Journal of the History of Philosophy

BJHS, British Journal of the History of Science

BJL, Belgian Journal of Linguistics

BJR, Bulletin of the John Rylands University Library of Manchester

BKF, Beiträge zur Kleist-Forschung

BL, Brain and Language

BLAR, Bulletin of Latin American Research

BLBI, Bulletin des Leo Baeck Instituts

BLe, Börsenblatt Leipzig

BLFCUP, Bibliothèque de Littérature Française Contemporaine de l'Université Paris 7

BLI, Beiträge zur Linguistik und Informationsverarbeitung

BLi, Беларуская літаратура. Міжвузаўскі зборнік.

BLJ, British Library Journal

BLL, Beiträge zur Literatur und Literaturwissenschaft des 20. Jahrhunderts, Berne, Lang

BLM, Bonniers Litterära Magasin

BLR, Bibliothèque Littéraire de la Renaissance, Geneva, Slatkine–Paris, Champion

BLR, Bodleian Library Record

BLVS, Bibliothek des Literarischen Vereins, Stuttgart, Hiersemann

BM, Bibliothek Metzier, Stuttgart

BMBP, Bollettino del Museo Bodoniano di Parma

BMCP, Bollettino del Museo Civico di Padova

BML, Беларуская мова і літаратура ў школе

BMo, Беларуская мова. Міжвузаўкі зборнік

BNE, Beiträge zur neueren Epochenforschung, Berne, Lang

BNF, Beiträge zur Namenforschung

BNL, Beiträge zur neueren Literaturgeschichte, 3rd ser., Heidelberg, Winter

BNP, Beiträge zur nordischen Philologie, Basel, Helbing & Lichtenhahn

BOCES, Boletín del Centro de Estudios del Siglo XVIII, Oviedo

BOP, Bradford Occasional Papers

ВР, Български писател

BP, Lo Bornat dau Perigòrd

BPTJ, Biuletyn Polskiego Towarzystwa Językoznawczego

BR, Болгарская русистика.

BRA, Bonner Romanistische Arbeiten, Berne, Lang

BRABLB, Boletín de la Real Academia de Buenas Letras de Barcelona

BRAC, Boletín de la Real Academia de Córdoba de Ciencias, Bellas Letras, y Nobles Artes

BRAE, Boletín de la Real Academia Española

BRAH, Boletín de la Real Academia de la Historia

BRIES, Bibliothèque Russe de l'Institut d'Études Slaves, Paris, Institut d'Études Slaves

BRJL, Bulletin ruského jazyka a literatury

BrL La Bretagne Linguistique

BRP, Beiträge zur romanischen Philologie

BS, Biuletyn slawistyczny, Łódź

BSAHH, Bulletin de la Société archéologique et historique des hauts cantons de l'Hérault, Bédarieux

BSAHL, Bulletin de la Société archéologique et historique du Limousin, Limoges

BSAHLSG, Bulletin de la Société Archéologique, Historique, Littéraire et Scientifique du Gers

BSAM, Bulletin de la Société des Amis de Montaigne

BSAMPAC, Bulletin de la Société des Amis de Marcel Proust et des Amis de Combray

BSASLB, Bulletin de la Société Archéologique, Scientifique et Littéraire de Béziers

BSATG, Bulletin de la Société Archéologique de Tarn-et-Garonne

BSBS, Bollettino Storico–Bibliografico Subalpino

BSCC, Boletín de la Sociedad Castellonense de Cultura

BSD, Bithell Series of Dissertations — MHRA Texts and Dissertations, London, Modern Humanities Research Association

BSD, Bulletin de la Société de Borda, Dax

BSDL, Bochumer Schriften zur deutschen Literatur, Berne, Lang

BSDSL, Basler Studien zur deutschen Sprache und Literatur, Tübingen, Francke

BSE, Галоўная рэдакцыя Беларускай савеюкай энцыклапедыі

BSEHA, Bulletin de la Société d'Études des Hautes-Alpes, Gap

BSEHTD, Bulletin de la Société d'Études Historiques du texte dialectal

BSELSAL, Bulletin de la Société des Études Littéraires, Scientifiques et Artistiques du Lot

BSF, Bollettino di Storia della Filosofia

BSG, Berliner Studien zur Germanistik, Frankfurt, Lang

BSHAP, Bulletin de la Société Historique et Archéologique du Périgord, Périgueux

BSHPF, Bulletin de la Société de l'Histoire du Protestantisme Français

BSIH, Brill's Studies in Intellectual History, Leiden, Brill

BSIS, Bulletin of the Society for Italian Studies

BSLLW, Bulletin de la Société de Langue et Littérature Wallonnes

BSLP, Bulletin de la Société de Linguistique de Paris

BSLV, Bollettino della Società Letteraria di Verona

BSM, Birmingham Slavonic Monographs, University of Birmingham

BSOAS, Bulletin of the School of Oriental and African Studies

BSP, Bollettino Storico Pisano

BSPC, Bulletin de la Société Paul Claudel

BSPia, Bollettino Storico Piacentino

BSPN, Bollettino Storico per le Province di Novara

BSPSP, Bollettino della Società Pavese di Storia Patria

BsR, Beck'sche Reihe, Munich, Beck

BSRS, Bulletin of the Society for Renaissance Studies

BSSAAPC, Bollettino della Società per gli Studi Storici, Archeologici ed Artistici della Provincia di Cuneo

BSSCLE, Bulletin of the Society for the Study of the Crusades and the Latin East

BSSP, Bullettino Senese di Storia Patria

BSSPHS, Bulletin of the Society for Spanish and Portuguese Historical Studies

BSSV, Bollettino della Società Storica Valtellinese

BSZJPS, Bałtosłowiańskie związki językowe. Prace Slawistyczne

BT, Богословские труды, Moscow

BTe, Biblioteca Teatrale

BTH, Boletim de Trabalhos Historicos
BulEz, Български език
BW, Bibliothek und Wissenschaft
BySt, Byzantine Studies

CA, Cuadernos Americanos
CAAM, Cahiers de l'Association Les Amis de Milosz
CAB, Commentari dell'Ateneo di Brescia
CAC, Les Cahiers de l'Abbaye de Créteil
CadL, Cadernos da Lingua
CAG, Cahiers André Gide
CAIEF, Cahiers de l'Association Internationale des Études Françaises
CalLet, Calabria Letteraria
CAm, Casa de las Américas, Havana
CAm, Casa de las Américas, Havana
CanJL, Canadian Journal of Linguistics
CanL, Canadian Literature
CanSP, Canadian Slavonic Papers
CanSS, Canadian–American Slavic Studies
CARB, Cahiers des Amis de Robert Brasillach
CarQ, Caribbean Quarterly
CAT, Cahiers d'Analyse Textuelle, Liège, Les Belles Lettres
CatR, Catalan Review
CAVL, Cahiers des Amis de Valery Larbaud
CB, Cuadernos Bibliográficos
CC, Comparative Criticism
CCe, Cahiers du Cerf XX
CCend, Continent Cendrars
CCF, Cuadernos de la Cátedra Feijoo
CCMe, Cahiers de Civilisation Médiévale
CCol, Cahiers Colette
CCU, Cuadernos de la Cátedra M. de Unamuno
CD, Cuadernos para el Diálogo
CdA, Camp de l'Arpa
CDA, Christliche deutsche Autoren des 20. Jahrhunderts, Berne, Lang

CDB, Coleção Documentos Brasileiros
CDr, Comparative Drama
ČDS, Čeština doma a ve světě
CDs, Cahiers du Dix-septième, Athens, Georgia
CDU, Centre de Documentation Universitaire
CduC, Cahiers de CERES. Série littéraire, Tunis
CE, Cahiers Élisabéthains
CEA, Cahiers d'Études Africaines
CEAL, Centro Editor de América Latina
CEC, Cahiers d'Études Cathares, Narbonne
CEC, Conselho Estadual de Cultura, Comissão de Literatura, São Paulo
CECAES, Centre d'Études des Cultures d'Aquitaine et d'Europe du Sud, Université de Bordeaux III
CEcr, Corps Écrit
CEDAM, Casa Editrice Dott. A. Milani
CEG, Cuadernos de Estudios Gallegos
CEL, Cadernos de Estudos Lingüísticos, Campinas, Brazil
CEM, Cahiers d'Études Médiévales, Univ. of Montreal
CEMa, Cahiers d'Études Maghrebines, Cologne
CEPL, Centre d'Étude et de Promotion de la Lecture, Paris
CER, Cahiers d'Études Romanes
CERCLiD, Cahiers d'Études Romanes, Centre de Linguistique et de Dialectologie, Toulouse
CERoum, Cahiers d'Études Roumaines
CeS, Cultura e Scuola
CESCM, Centre d'Études Supérieures de Civilisation Médiévale, Poitiers
CET, Centro Editoriale Toscano
CEtGer, Cahiers d'Études Germaniques
CF, Les Cahiers de Fontenay
CFC, Contemporary French Civilization
CFI, Cuadernos de Filologia Italiana

CFLA, Cuadernos de Filología.
Literaturas: Análisis, Valencia
CFM, Cahiers François Mauriac
CFMA, Collection des Classiques
Français du Moyen Âge
CFol, Classical Folia
CFS, Cahiers Ferdinand de Saussure
CFSLH, Cuadernos de Filología:
Studia Linguistica Hispanica
CFTM, Classiques Français des
Temps Modernes, Paris,
Champion
CG, Cahiers de Grammaire
CGD, Cahiers Georges Duhamel
CGFT, Critical Guides to French
Texts, London, Grant & Cutler
CGGT, Critical Guides to German
Texts, London, Grant & Cutler
CGP, Carleton Germanic Papers
CGS, Colloquia Germanica
Stetinensia
CGST, Critical Guides to Spanish
Texts, London, Támesis, Grant &
Cutler
CH, Crítica Hispánica
CHA, Cuadernos Hispano-
Americanos
CHAC, Cuadernos Hispano-
Americanos. Los
complementarios
CHB, Cahiers Henri Bosco
ChC, Chemins Critiques
ChR, The Chesterton Review
ChRev, Chaucer Review
ChrA, Chroniques Allemandes
ChrI, Chroniques Italiennes
ChrL, Christianity and Literature
ChrN, Chronica Nova
ChS, Champs du Signe
CHum, Computers and the
Humanities
CHP, Cahiers Henri Pourrat
CI, Critical Inquiry
CiD, La Ciudad de Dios
CIDO, Centre International de
Documentation Occitane, Béziers
CIF, Cuadernos de Investigación
Filológica
CIH, Cuadernos de Investigación
Historica
CILF, Conseil International de la
Langue Française

CILH, Cuadernos para
Investigación de la Literatura
Hispanica
CILL, Cahiers de l'Institut de
Linguistique de l'Université de
Louvain
CIMAGL, Cahiers de l'Institut du
Moyen Âge Grec et Latin,
Copenhagen
CIn, Cahiers Intersignes
CIRVI, Centro Interuniversitario di
Ricerche sul 'Viaggio in Italia',
Moncalieri
CISAM, Centro Italiano di Studi
sull'Alto Medioevo
CIt, Carte Italiane
CIUS, Canadian Institute of
Ukrainian Studies Edmonton
CivC, Civiltà Cattolica
CJ, Conditio Judaica, Tübingen,
Niemeyer
CJb, Celan-Jahrbuch
CJC, Cahiers Jacques Chardonne
CJG, Cahiers Jean Giraudoux
CJIS, Canadian Journal of Italian
Studies
ČJL, Český jazyk a literatura
CJNS, Canadian Journal of
Netherlandic Studies
CJP, Cahiers Jean Paulhan
CJR, Cahiers Jules Romains
CL, Cuadernos de Leiden
CL, Comparative Literature
ČL, Česká literatura
CLA, Cahiers du LACITO
CLAJ, College Language
Association Journal
CLCC, Cahiers de Littérature
Canadienne Comparée
CLE, Comunicaciones de Literatura
Española, Buenos Aires
CLe, Cahiers de Lexicologie
CLEAM, Coleción de Literatura
Española Aljamiado–Morisca,
Madrid, Gredos
CLESP, Cooperativa Libraria
Editrice degli Studenti
dell'Università di Padova, Padua
CLett, Critica Letteraria
CLF, Cahiers de Linguistique
Française
CLHM, Cahiers de Linguistique
Hispanique Médiévale
CLin, Cercetări de Lingvistica

CLit, Cadernos de Literatura, Coimbra
Cll, La Clau lemosina
CLO, Cahiers Linguistiques d'Ottawa
ClP, Classical Philology
CLS, Comparative Literature Studies
CLSl, Cahiers de Linguistique Slave
CLTA, Cahiers de Linguistique Théorique et Appliquée
CLTL, Cadernos de Lingüística e Teoria da Literatura
CLUEB, Cooperativa Libraria Universitaria Editrice Bologna
CM, Classica et Mediaevalia
CMA, Cahier Marcel Aymé
CMCS, Cambridge Medieval Celtic Studies
CMERSA, Center for Medieval and Early Renaissance Studies, State University of New York at Binghamton. Acta
ČMF (PhP), Časopis pro moderni filologii: Philologica Pragensia
CMHLB, Cahiers du Monde Hispanique et Luso-Brésilien
CMi, Cultura Milano
CML, Classical and Modern Literature
ČMM, Časopis Matice Moravské
CMon, Communication Monographs
CMP, Cahiers Marcel Proust
CMRS, Cahiers du Monde Russe et Soviétique
CN, Cultura Neolatina
CNat, Les Cahiers Naturalistes
CNCDP, Comissão Nacional para a Comemoração dos Descobrimentos Portugueses, Lisbon
CNor, Los Cuadernos del Norte
CNR, Consiglio Nazionale delle Ricerche
CNRS, Centre National de la Recherche Scientifique
CO, Camera Obscura
CoF, Collectanea Franciscana
COK, Centralny Ośrodek Kultury, Warsaw
CoL, Compás de Letras
ColA, Colóquio Artes
ColGer, Colloquia Germanica
ColH, Colloquium Helveticum

ColL, Colóquio Letras
ComB, Communications of the International Brecht Society
ComGer, Comunicaciones Germánicas
CompL, Computational Linguistics
ConL, Contrastive Linguistics
ConLet, Il Confronto Letterario
ConLit, Contemporary Literature
ConS, Condorcet Studies
CP, Castrum Peregrini
CPE, Cahiers Prévost d'Exiles, Grenoble
CPL, Cahiers Paul Léautand
CPr, Cahiers de Praxématique
CPR, Chroniques de Port-Royal
CPUC, Cadernos PUC, São Paulo
CQ, Critical Quarterly
CR, Contemporary Review
CRAC, Cahiers Roucher — André Chénier
CRCL, Canadian Review of Comparative Literature
CREL, Cahiers Roumains d'Études Littéraires
CRev, Centennial Review
CRI, Cuadernos de Ruedo Ibérico
CRIAR, Cahiers du Centre de Recherches Ibériques et Ibéro-Américains de l'Université de Rouen
CRIN, Cahiers de Recherches des Instituts Néerlandais de Langue et Littérature Françaises
CRLN, Comparative Romance Linguistics Newsletter
CRQ, Cahiers Raymond Queneau
CRR, Cincinnati Romance Review
CRRI, Centre de Recherche sur la Renaissance Italienne, Paris
CS, Cornish Studies
ČSAV, Československá akademie věd
CSDI, Centro di Studio per la Dialettologia Italiana
CSem, Caiete de Semiotică
CSFLS, Centro di Studi Filologici e Linguistici Siciliani, Palermo
CSG, Cambridge Studies in German, Cambridge U.P.
CSGLL, Canadian Studies in German Language and Literature, Berne — New York — Frankfurt, Lang

CSH, Cahiers des Sciences
Humaines
CSIC, Consejo Superior de
Investigaciones Científicas,
Madrid
CSJP, Cahiers Saint-John Perse
CSl, Critica Slovia, Florence
CSM, Les Cahiers de Saint-Martin
ČSp, Československý spisovatel
CSS, California Slavic Studies
CSSH, Comparative Studies in
Society and History
CST, Cahiers de Sémiotique
Textuelle
CSt, Critica Storica
CT, Christianity Today
CTC, Cuadernos de Teatro Clásico
CTE, Cuadernos de Traducción e
Interpretación
CTe, Cuadernos de Teología
CTex, Cahiers Textuels
CTH, Cahiers Tristan l'Hermite
CTh, Ciencia Tomista
CTL, Current Trends in Linguistics
CTLin, Commissione per i Testi di
Lingua, Bologna
CUECM, Cooperativa
Universitaria Editrice Catanese
Magistero
CUP, Cambridge University Press
CUUCV, Cultura Universitaria de la
Universidad Central de
Venezuela
CWPL, Catalan Working Papers in
Linguistics
CWPWL, Cardiff Working Papers in
Welsh Linguistics

DAEM, Deutsches Archiv für
Erforschung des Mittelalters
DaF, Deutsch als Fremdsprache
DalR, Dalhousie Review
DanU, Dansk Udsyn
DaSt, Dante Studies
DB, Дзяржаўная бібліятэка
БССР
DB, Doitsu Bungaku
DBl, Driemaandelijkse Bladen
DBO, Deutsche Bibliothek des
Ostens, Berlin, Nicolai
DBR, Les Dialectes Belgo-Romans
DBr, Doitsu Bungakoranko

DCFH, Dicenda. Cuadernos de
Filología Hispánica
DD, Diskussion Deutsch
DDG, Deutsche Dialektgeographie,
Marburg, Elwert
DDJ, Deutsches Dante-Jahrbuch
DegSec, Degré Second
DESB, Delta Epsilon Sigma
Bulletin, Dubuque, Iowa
DeutB, Deutsche Bücher
DeutUB, Deutschungarische
Beiträge
DFC, Durham French Colloquies
DFS, Dalhousie French Studies
DGF, Dokumentation
germanistischer Forschung,
Frankfurt, Lang
DgF, Danmarks gamle Folkeviser
DHA, Diálogos Hispánicos de
Amsterdam, Rodopi
DHR, Duquesne Hispanic Review
DhS, Dix-huitième Siècle
DI, Deutscher Idealismus, Stuttgart,
Klett-Cotta Verlag
DI, Декоративное искусство
DIAS, Dublin Institute for
Advanced Studies
DiL, Dictionnairique et
Lexicographie
DiS, Dickinson Studies
DisA, Dissertation Abstracts
DisSlSHL, Dissertationes Slavicae:
Sectio Historiae Litterarum
DisSlSL, Dissertationes Slavicae:
Sectio Linguistica
DK, Duitse Kroniek
DkJb, Deutschkanadisches Jahrbuch
DKV, Deutscher Klassiker Verlag,
Frankfurt
DL, Детская литература
DLA, Deutsche Literatur von den
Anfängen bis 1700, Berne —
Frankfurt — Paris — New York,
Lang
DLit, Discurso Literario
DLM, Deutsche Literatur des
Mittelalters (Wissenschaftliche
Beiträge der Ernst-Moritz-Arndt-
Universität Greifswald)
DLR, Deutsche Literatur in
Reprints, Munich, Fink
DLRECL, Diálogo de la Lengua.
Revista de Estudio y Creación
Literaria, Cuenca

DM, Dirassat Masrahiyyat
DMRPH, De Montfort Research
 Papers in the Humanities, De
 Montfort University, Leicester
DMTS, Davis Medieval Texts and
 Studies, Leiden, Brill
DN, Дружба народов
DNT, De Nieuwe Taalgids
DOLMA, Documenta Onomastica
 Litteralia Medii Aevi,
 Hildesheim, Olms
DosS, Dostoevsky Studies
DoV, Дошкольное воспитание
DPA, Documents pour servir à
 l'histoire du département des
 Pyrénées-Atlantiques, Pau
DPL, De Proprietatibus Litterarum,
 The Hague, Mouton
DpL, День поэзии, Leningrad
DpM, День поэзии, Moscow
DR, Drama Review
DRev, Downside Review
DRLAV, DRLAV, Revue de
 Linguistique
DS, Diderot Studies
DSEÜ, Deutsche Sprache in
 Europa und Übersee, Stuttgart,
 Steiner
DSL, Det danske Sprog- og
 Litteraturselskab
DSp, Deutsche Sprache
DSRPD, Documenta et Scripta.
 Rubrica Paleographica et
 Diplomatica, Barcelona
DSS, XVIIᵉ Siècle
DSt, Deutsche Studien,
 Meisenheim, Hain
DSt, Danske Studier
DT, Deutsche Texte, Tübingen,
 Niemeyer
DteolT, Dansk teologisk Tidsskrift
DtL, Die deutsche Literatur
DTM, Deutsche Texte des
 Mittelalters, Berlin, Akademie
DTV, Deutscher Taschenbuch
 Verlag, Munich
DUB, Deutschunterricht, East
 Berlin
DUJ, Durham University Journal
 (New Series)
DUS, Der Deutschunterricht,
 Stuttgart
DUSA, Deutschunterricht in
 Südafrika

DV, Дальний Восток
DVA, Deutsche Verlags-Anstalt,
 Stuttgart
DVLG, Deutsche Vierteljahresschrift
 für Literaturwissenschaft und
 Geistesgeschichte

E, Verlag Enzyklopädie, Leipzig
EAL, Early American Literature
EALS, Europäische Aufklärung in
 Literatur und Sprache, Frankfurt,
 Lang
EAS, Europe-Asia Studies
EB, Estudos Brasileiros
EBal, Etudes Balkaniques
EBM, Era Bouts dera mountanho,
 Aurignac
EBTch, Études Balkaniques
 Tchécoslovaques
EC, El Escritor y la Crítica,
 Colección Persiles, Madrid,
 Taurus
EC, Études Celtiques
ECan, Études Canadiennes
ECar, Espace Caraïbe
ECent, The Eighteenth Century,
 Lubbock, Texas
ECentF, Eighteenth-Century Fiction
ECF, Écrits du Canada Français
ECI, Eighteenth-Century Ireland
ECIG, Edizioni Culturali
 Internazionali Genova
ECla, Les Études Classiques
ECon, España Contemporánea
EconH, Économie et Humanisme
ECr, Essays in Criticism
ECS, Eighteenth Century Studies
EdCat, Ediciones Cátedra, Madrid
EDESA, Ediciones Españolas S.A.
EDHS, Études sur le XVIIIᵉ Siècle
EDL, Études de Lettres
EDT, Edizioni di Torino
EE, Erasmus in English
EEM, East European Monographs
EEQ, East European Quarterly
EF, Erträge der Forschung,
 Darmstadt, Wissenschaftliche
 Buchgesellschaft
EF, Études Françaises
EFAA, Échanges Franco-Allemands
 sur l'Afrique
EFE, Estudios de Fonética
 Experimental

EFF, Ergebnisse der Frauenforschung, Stuttgart, Metzler

EFil, Estudios Filológicos, Valdivia, Chile

EFL, Essays in French Literature, Univ. of Western Australia

EFR, Éditeurs Français Réunis

EG, Études Germaniques

EH, Europäische Hochschulschriften, Berne–Frankfurt, Lang

EH, Estudios Humanísticos

EHF, Estudios Humanísticos. Filología

EHN, Estudios de Historia Novohispana

EHQ, European History Quarterly

EHR, English Historical Review

EHS, Estudios de Historia Social

EHT, Exeter Hispanic Texts, Exeter

EIA, Estudos Ibero-Americanos

EIP, Estudos Italianos em Portugal

EL, Esperienze Letterarie

El, Elementa, Würzburg, Königshausen & Neumann –Amsterdam, Rodopi

ELA, Études de Linguistique Appliquée

ELF, Études Littéraires Françaises, Paris, J.-M. Place — Tübingen, Narr

ELH, English Literary History

El'H, Études sur l'Hérault, Pézenas

ELit, Essays in Literature

ELLC, Estudis de Llengua i Literatura Catalanes

ELLF, Études de Langue et Littérature Françaises, Tokyo

ELM, Études littéraires maghrebines

ELR, English Literary Renaissance

EM, English Miscellany, Rome

EMarg, Els Marges

EMus, Early Music

ENC, Els Nostres Clàssics, Barcelona, Barcino

ENSJF, École Nationale Supérieure de Jeunes Filles

EO, Édition Orpheus, Tübingen, Francke

EO, Europa Orientalis

EOc, Estudis Occitans

EP, Études Philosophiques

Ep, Epistemata, Würzburg, Königshausen & Neumann

EPESA, Ediciones y Publicaciones Españolas S.A.

EPoet, Essays in Poetics

ER, Estudis Romànics

ERab, Études Rabelaisiennes

ERB, Études Romanes de Brno

ER(BSRLR), Études Romanes (Bulletin de la Société Roumaine de Linguistique Romane)

ERL, Études Romanes de Lund

ErlF, Erlanger Forschungen

EROPD, Ежегодник рукописного отдела Пушкинского дома

ERR, European Romantic Review

ES, Erlanger Studien, Erlangen, Palm & Enke

ES, Estudios Segovianos

EsC, L'Esprit Créateur

ESGP, Early Studies in Germanic Philology, Amsterdam, Rodopi

ESI, Edizioni Scientifiche Italiane

ESk, Edition Suhrkamp, Frankfurt, Suhrkamp

ESor, Études sorguaises

EspA, Español Actual

ESt, English Studies

EstE, Estudios Escénicos

EstG, Estudi General

EstH, Estudios Hispánicos

EstL, Estudios de Lingüística, Alicante

EstR, Estudios Románticos

EStud, Essays and Studies

ET, L'Écrit du Temps

EtCan, Études Canadiennes

ETF, Espacio, Tiempo y Forma, Revista de la Facultad de Geografía e Historia, UNED

EtF, Etudes francophones

EtH, Études sur l'Hérault, Pézenas

EthS, Ethnologia Slavica

ETJ, Educational Theatre Journal

ETL, Explicación de Textos Literarios

EtLitt, Études Littéraires, Quebec

EUDEBA, Editorial Universitaria de Buenos Aires

EUNSA, Ediciones Universidad de Navarra, Pamplona

EUS, European University Studies, Berne, Lang

ExP, Excerpta Philologica
EzLit, Език и литература

FAL, Forum Academicum
Literaturwissenschaft,
Königstein, Hain
FAPESP, Fundação de Amparo à
Pesquisa do Estado de São Paulo
FAR, French-American Review
FAS, Frankfurter Abhandlungen zur
Slavistik, Giessen, Schmitz
FBAN, Фундаментальная
бібліятэка Акадэміі навук
БССР
FBG, Frankfurter Beiträge zur
Germanistik, Heidelberg, Winter
FBS, Franco-British Studies
FC, Filologia e Critica
FCE, Fondo de Cultura Económica,
Mexico
FCG — CCP, Fondation Calouste
Gulbenkian — Centre Culturel
Portugais, Paris
FCS, Fifteenth Century Studies
FDL, Facetten deutscher Literatur,
Berne, Haupt
FEI, Faites entrer l'infini. Journal de
la Société des Amis de Louis
Aragon et Elsa Triolet
FEK, Forschungen zur
europäischen Kultur, Berne,
Lang
FemSt, Feministische Studien
FF, Forma y Función
FFM, French Forum Monographs,
Lexington, Kentucky
FGÄDL, Forschungen zur
Geschichte der älteren deutschen
Literatur, Munich, Fink
FH, Fundamenta Historica,
Stuttgart-Bad Cannstatt,
Frommann-Holzboog
FH, Frankfurter Hefte
FHL, Forum Homosexualität und
Literatur
FHS, French Historical Studies
FIDS, Forschungsberichte des
Instituts für Deutsche Sprache,
Tübingen, Narr
FilM, Filologia Mediolatina
FilMod, Filologia Moderna, Udine
–Pisa
FilN, Филологические науки

FilR, Filologia Romanza
FilS, Filologické studie
FilZ, Filologija, Zagreb
FiM, Filologia Moderna, Facultad
de Filosofía y Letras, Madrid
FinS, Fin de Siglo
FIRL, Forum at Iowa on Russian
Literature
FL, La France Latine
FLa, Faits de Langues
FLG, Freiburger
literaturpsychologische
Gespräche
FLin, Folia Linguistica
FLinHist, Folia Linguistica Historica
FLK, Forschungen zur Literatur-
und Kulturgeschichte. Beiträge
zur Sprach- und
Literaturwissenschaft, Berne,
Lang
FLS, French Literature Series
FLV, Fontes Linguae Vasconum
FM, Le Français Moderne
FMADIUR, FM: Annali del
Dipartimento di Italianistica,
Università di Roma 'La Sapienza'
FMDA, Forschungen und
Materialen zur deutschen
Aufklärung, Stuttgart — Bad
Cannstatt, Frommann-Holzboog
FMLS, Forum for Modern
Language Studies
FmSt, Frühmittelalterliche Studien
FMT, Forum Modernes Theater
FN, Frühe Neuzeit, Tübingen,
Niemeyer
FNDIR, Fédération nationale des
déportés et internés résistants
FNS, Frühneuzeit-Studien,
Frankfurt, Lang
FNT, Foilseacháin Náisiúnta Tta
FoI, Forum Italicum
FoS, Le Forme e la Storia
FP, Folia Phonetica
FPub, First Publications
FR, French Review
FrA, Le Français Aujourd'hui
FranS, Franciscan Studies
FrCS, French Cultural Studies
FrF, French Forum
FrH, Französisch Heute
FrP Le Français Préclassique
FS, Forum Slavicum, Munich, Fink
FS, French Studies

FSB, French Studies Bulletin
FSlav, Folia Slavica
FSSA, French Studies in Southern Africa
FT, Fischer Taschenbuch, Frankfurt, Fischer
FT, Finsk Tidskrift
FTCG, 'La Talanquere': Folklore, Tradition, Culture Gasconne, Nogano
FUE, Fundación Universitaria Española
FV, Fortuna Vitrea, Tübingen, Niemeyer
FZPT, Freiburger Zeitschrift für Philosophie und Theologie

GA, Germanistische Arbeitshefte, Tübingen, Niemeyer
GAB, Göppinger Akademische Beiträge, Lauterburg, Kümmerle
GAG, Göppinger Arbeiten zur Germanistik, Lauterburg, Kümmerle
GAKS, Gesammelte Aufsätze zur Kulturgeschichte Spaniens
GANDLL, Giessener Arbeiten zur neueren deutschen Literatur und Literaturwissenschaft, Berne, Lang
GAS, German-Australian Studies, Berne, Lang
GASK, Germanistische Arbeiten zu Sprache und Kulturgeschichte, Frankfurt, Lang
GBA, Gazette des Beaux-Arts
GBE, Germanistik in der Blauen Eule
GC, Generalitat de Catalunya
GCFI, Giornale Critico della Filosofia Italiana
GEMP, Groupement d'Ethnomusicologie en Midi-Pyrénées, Gaillac-Cordes
GerAb, Germanistische Abhandlungen, Stuttgart, Metzler
GerLux, Germanistik Luxembourg
GermL, Germanistische Linguistik
GeW, Germanica Wratislaviensia
GF, Giornale di Fisica
GFFNS, Godišnjak Filozofskog fakulteta u Novom Sadu

GG, Geschichte und Gesellschaft
GGF, Göteborger Germanistische Forschungen, University of Gothenburg
GGVD, Grundlagen und Gedanken zum Verständnis des Dramas, Frankfurt, Diesterweg
GGF, Greifswalder Germanistische Forschungen
GGVEL, Grundlagen und Gedanken zum Verständnis erzählender Literatur, Frankfurt, Diesterweg
GIDILOc, Grop d'Iniciativa per un Diccionari Informatizat de la Lenga Occitana, Montpellier
GIF, Giornale Italiano di Filologia
GIGFL, Glasgow Introductory Guides to French Literature
GIGGL, Glasgow Introductory Guides to German Literature
GJ, Gutenberg-Jahrbuch
GJb, Goethe Jahrbuch
GJLL, The Georgetown Journal of Language and Linguistics
GK, Goldmann Klassiker, Munich, Goldmann
GL, Germanistische Lehrbuchsammlung, Berne, Lang
GL, General Linguistics
GLC, German Life and Civilisation, Berne, Lang
GLL, German Life and Letters
GLML, The Garland Library of Medieval Literature, New York –London, Garland
GLR, García Lorca Review
GLS, Grazer Linguistische Studien
Glyph, Glyph: Johns Hopkins Textual Studies, Baltimore
GM, Germanistische Mitteilungen
GML, Gothenburg Monographs in Linguistics
GMon, German Monitor
GN, Germanic Notes and Reviews
GPB, Гос. публичная библиотека им. М. Е. Салтыкова-Щедрина
GPI, Государственный педагогический институт
GPSR, Glossaire des Patois de la Suisse Romande
GQ, German Quarterly
GR, Germanic Review

GREC, Groupe de Recherches et d'Études du Clermontais, Clermont-l'Hérault

GRELCA, Groupe de Recherche sur les Littératures de la Caraïbe, Université Laval

GRLH, Garland Reference Library of the Humanities, New York — London, Garland

GRLM, Grundriss der romanischen Literaturen des Mittelalters

GRM, Germanisch-Romanische Monatsschrift

GrSt, Grundtvig Studier

GS, Lo Gai Saber, Toulouse

GSA, Germanic Studies in America, Berne–Frankfurt, Lang

GSC, German Studies in Canada, Frankfurt, Lang

GSI, German Studies in India

GSl, Germano-Slavica, Ontario

GSLI, Giornale Storico della Letteratura Italiana

GSR, German Studies Review

GSSL, Göttinger Schriften zur Sprach– und Literaturwissenschaft, Göttingen, Herodot

GTN, Gdańskie Towarzystwo Naukowe

GTS, Germanistische Texte und Studien, Hildesheim, Olms

GV, Generalitat Valenciana

GY, Goethe Yearbook

H, Hochschulschriften, Cologne, Pahl-Rugenstein

HAHR, Hispanic American Historical Review

HB, Horváth Blätter

HBA, Historiografía y Bibliografía Americanistas, Seville

HBG, Hamburger Beiträge zur Germanistik, Frankfurt, Lang

HDG, Huis aan de Drie Grachten, Amsterdam

HEI, History of European Ideas

HEL, Histoire, Epistemologie, Language

HES, Histoire, Économie et Société

HeyJ, Heythrop Journal

HF, Heidelberger Forschungen, Heidelberg, Winter

HHS, History of the Human Sciences

HI, Historica Ibérica

HIAR, Hamburger Ibero-Amerikanische Reihe

HICL, Histoire des Idées et Critique Littéraire, Geneva, Droz

HIGL, Holland Institute for Generative Linguistics, Leiden

HisJ, Hispanic Journal, Indiana–Pennsylvania

HisL, Hispanic Linguistics

HistL, Historiographia Linguistica

HistS, History of Science

His(US), Hispania, Los Angeles

HJ, Historical Journal

HJb, Heidelberger Jahrbücher

HJBS, Hispanic Journal of Behavioural Sciences

HKADL, Historisch-kritische Arbeiten zur deutschen Literatur, Frankfurt, Lang

HKZMTLG, Handelingen van de Koninklijke Zuidnederlandse Maatschappij voor Taalen, Letterkunde en Geschiedenis

HL, Hochschulschriften Literaturwissenschaft, Königstein, Hain

HL, Humanistica Lovaniensia

HLB, Harvard Library Bulletin

HLQ, Huntington Library Quarterly

HLS, Historiska och litteraturhistoriska studier

HM, Hommes et Migrations

HMJb, Heinrich Mann Jahrbuch

HP, History of Psychiatry

HPh, Historical Philology

HPos, Hispanica Posnaniensia

HPS, Hamburger Philologische Studien, Hamburg, Buske

HPSl, Heidelberger Publikationen zur Slavistik, Frankfurt, Lang

HPT, History of Political Thought

HR, Hispanic Review

HRel, History of Religions

HRev, Hrvatska revija

HRSHM, Heresis, revue semestrielle d'hérésiologie médiévale

HS, Helfant Studien, Stuttgart, Helfant

HS, Hispania Sacra

ILASLR, Istituto Lombardo. Accademia di Scienze e Lettere. Rendiconti
ILen, Искусство Ленинграда
ILing, Incontri Linguistici
ILTEC, Instituto de Linguistica Teórica e Computacional, Lisbon
IMN, Irisleabhar Mhá Nuad
IMR, International Migration Review
IMU, Italia Medioevale e Umanistica
INCM, Imprensa Nacional, Casa da Moeda, Lisbon
InfD, Informationen und Didaktik
INLF, Institut National de la Langue Française
INIC, Instituto Nacional de Investigação Científica
InL, Иностранная литература
INLE, Instituto Nacional del Libro Español
InstEB, Inst. de Estudos Brasileiros
InstNL, Inst. Nacional do Livro, Brasilia
IO, Italiano e Oltre
IPL, Istituto di Propaganda Libraria
IPZS, Istituto Poligrafico e Zecca dello Stato, Rome
IR, L'Immagine Riflessa
IRAL, International Review of Applied Linguistics
IRIa, Институт русского языка Российской Академии Наук
IrR, The Irish Review
IRSH, International Review of Social History
IRSL, International Review of Slavic Linguistics
ISC, Institut de Sociolingüística Catalana
ISLIa, Известия Академии наук СССР. Серия литературы и языка
ISOAN, Известия сибирского отделения АН СССР, Novosibirsk
ISP, International Studies in Philosophy
ISS, Irish Slavonic Studies
IsS, Islamic Studies, Islamabad
ISSA, Studi d'Italianistica nell'Africa Australe: Italian Studies in Southern Africa

ISt, Italian Studies
IT, Insel Taschenbuch, Frankfurt, Insel
ItC, Italian Culture
ITL, ITL. Review of Applied Linguistics, Instituut voor Toegepaste Linguistiek, Leuven
ItQ, Italian Quarterly
ItStudien, Italienische Studien
IUJF, Internationales Uwe-Johnson-Forum
IUP, Irish University Press
IUR, Irish University Review
IV, Istituto Veneto di Scienze, Lettere ed Arti
IVAS, Indices Verborum zum altdeutschen Schrifttum, Amsterdam, Rodopi
IVN, Internationale Vereniging voor Nederlandistiek

JAAC, Journal of Aesthetics and Art Criticism
JAE, Journal of Aesthetic Education
JAMS, Journal of the American Musicological Society
JAOS, Journal of the American Oriental Society
JanL, Janua Linguarum, The Hague, Mouton
JAPLA, Journal of the Atlantic Provinces Linguistic Association
JARA, Journal of the American Romanian Academy of Arts and Sciences
JAS, The Journal of Algerian Studies
JASI, Jahrbuch des Adalbert-Stifter-Instituts
JATI, Association of Teachers of Italian Journal
JazA, Jazykovědné aktuality
JazŠ, Jazykovedné štúdie
JAZU, Jugoslavenska akademija znanosti i umjetnosti
JBSP, Journal of the British Society for Phenomenology
JČ, Jazykovedný časopis, Bratislava
JCanS, Journal of Canadian Studies
JCHAS, Journal of the Cork Historical and Archaeological Society
JCL, Journal of Child Language

JCLin, Journal of Celtic Linguistics
JCS, Journal of Celtic Studies
JDASD, Deutsche Akademie für Sprache und Dichtung: Jahrbuch
JDF, Jahrbuch Deutsch als Fremdsprache
JDSG, Jahrbuch der Deutschen Schiller-Gesellschaft
JEA, Lou Journalet de l'Escandihado Aubagnenco
JEGP, Journal of English and Germanic Philology
JEH, Journal of Ecclesiastical History
JEL, Journal of English Linguistics
JES, Journal of European Studies
JF, Južnoslovenski filolog
JFDH, Jahrbuch des Freien Deutschen Hochstifts
JFinL, Jahrbuch für finnisch-deutsche Literaturbeziehungen
JFL, Jahrbuch für fränkische Landesforschung
JFLS, Journal of French Language Studies
JFR, Journal of Folklore Research
JG, Jahrbuch für Geschichte, Berlin, Akademie
JGO, Jahrbücher für die Geschichte Osteuropas
JHA, Journal for the History of Astronomy
JHI, Journal of the History of Ideas
JHispP, Journal of Hispanic Philology
JHP, Journal of the History of Philosophy
JHR, Journal of Hispanic Research
JHS, Journal of the History of Sexuality
JIAS, Journal of Inter-American Studies
JIES, Journal of Indo-European Studies
JIG, Jahrbuch für Internationale Germanistik
JIL, Journal of Italian Linguistics
JILS, Journal of Interdisciplinary Literary Studies
JIPA, Journal of the International Phonetic Association
JIRS, Journal of the Institute of Romance Studies
JJQ, James Joyce Quarterly

JJS, Journal of Jewish Studies
JL, Journal of Linguistics
JLAL, Journal of Latin American Lore
JLAS, Journal of Latin American Studies
JLH, Journal of Library History
JLS, Journal of Literary Semantics
JLSP, Journal of Language and Social Psychology
JMemL, Journal of Memory and Language
JMEMS, Journal of Medieval and Early Modern Studies
JMH, Journal of Medieval History
JML, Journal of Modern Literature
JMLat, Journal of Medieval Latin
JMMD, Journal of Multilingual and Multicultural Development
JMMLA, Journal of the Midwest Modern Language Association
JModH, Journal of Modern History
JMP, Journal of Medicine and Philosophy
JMRS, Journal of Medieval and Renaissance Studies
JMS, Journal of Maghrebi Studies
JNT, Journal of Narrative Technique
JONVL, Een Jaarboek:-Overzicht van de Nederlandse en Vlaamse Literatuur
JOWG, Jahrbuch der Oswald von Wolkenstein Gesellschaft
JP, Journal of Pragmatics
JPC, Journal of Popular Culture
JPCL, Journal of Pidgin and Creole Languages
JPh, Journal of Phonetics
JPol, Język Polski
JPR, Journal of Psycholinguistic Research
JQ, Jacques e i suoi Quaderni
JRA, Journal of Religion in Africa
JRG, Jahrbücher der Reineke-Gesellschaft
JRH, Journal of Religious History
JRIC, Journal of the Royal Institution of Cornwall
JŘJR, Jazyk a řeč jihočeského regionu. České Budějovice, Pedagogická fakulta Jihočeské univerzity

JRMA, Journal of the Royal Musical Association
JRMMRA, Journal of the Rocky Mountain Medieval and Renaissance Association
JRS, Journal of Romance Studies
JRUL, Journal of the Rutgers University Libraries
JS, Journal des Savants
JSEES, Japanese Slavic and East European Studies
JSem, Journal of Semantics
JSFWUB, Jahrbuch der Schlesischen Friedrich-Wilhelms-Universität zu Breslau
JSH, Jihočeský sborník historický
JSHR, Journal of Speech and Hearing Research
JSL, Journal of Slavic Linguistics
JSS, Journal of Spanish Studies: Twentieth Century
JTS, Journal of Theological Studies
JU, Judentum und Umwelt, Berne, Lang.
JUS, Journal of Ukrainian Studies
JV, Jahrbuch für Volkskunde
JVF, Jahrbuch für Volksliedforschung
JVLVB, Journal of Verbal Learning and Verbal Behavior
JWBS, Journal of the Welsh Bibliographical Society
JWCI, Journal of the Warburg and Courtauld Institutes
JWGV, Jahrbuch des Wiener Goethe-Vereins, Neue Folge
JWH, Journal of World History
JWIL, Journal of West Indian Literature
JZ, Jazykovedný zborník

KANTL, Koninklijke Akademie voor Nederlandse Taal- en Letterkunde
KASL, Kasseler Arbeiten zur Sprache und Literatur, Frankfurt, Lang
KAW, Krajowa Agencja Wydawnicza
KAWLSK, Koninklijke Academie voor Wetenschappen, Letteren en Schone Kunsten van België, Brussels

KB, Književni barok
KBGL, Kopenhagener Beiträge zur germanistischen Linguistik
Kbl, Korrespondenzblatt des Vereins für niederdeutsche Sprachforschung
KDPM, Kleine deutsche Prosadenkmäler des Mittelalters, Munich, Fink
KGOS, Kultur- und geistesgeschichtliche Ostmitteleuropa-Studien, Marburg, Elwert
KGS, Kölner germanistische Studien, Cologne, Böhlau
KGS, Kairoer germanistische Studien
KH, Komparatistische Hefte
KhL, Художественная литература
KI, Književna istorija
KiW, Książka i Wiedza
KJ, Književnost i jezik
KK, Kirke og Kultur
KJb, Kleist-Jahrbuch
KLWL, Krieg und Literatur: War and Literature
Klage, Klage: Kölner linguistische Arbeiten. Germanistik, Hürth-Efferen, Gabel
KN, Kwartalnik Neofilologiczny
KnK, Kniževna kritika
KO, Университетско издателство 'Климент Охридски'
KO, Книжное обозрение
КР, Книжная палата
KRA, Kölner Romanistische Arbeiten, Geneva, Droz
KS, Kúltura slova
KSDL, Kieler Studien zur deutschen Literaturgeschichte, Neumünster, Wachholtz
KSL, Kölner Studien zur Literaturwissenschaft, Frankfurt, Lang
KSt, Kant Studien
KTA, Kröners Taschenausgabe, Stuttgart, Kröner
KTRM, Klassische Texte des romanischen Mittelalters, Munich, Fink
KU, Konstanzer Universitäts-reden

KUL, Katolicki Uniwersytet Lubelski, Lublin
KuSDL, Kulturwissenschaftliche Studien zur deutschen Literatur, Opladen, Westdeutscher Verlag
KZG, Koreanische Zeitschrift für Germanistik
KZMTLG, Koninklijke Zuidnederlandse Maatschappij voor Taal- en Letterkunde en Geschiedenis, Brussels
KZMTLGH, Koninklijke Zuidnederlandse Maatschaapij voor Taal- en Letterkunde en Geschiedenis. Handelingen

LA, Linguistische Arbeiten, Tübingen, Niemeyer
LA, Linguistic Analysis
LaA, Language Acquisition
LAbs, Linguistics Abstracts
LaF, Langue Française
LAILJ, Latin American Indian Literatures Journal
LaLi, Langues et Linguistique
LALR, Latin-American Literary Review
LaM, Les Langues Modernes
LangH, Le Langage et l'Homme
LArb, Linguistische Arbeitsberichte
LARR, Latin-American Research Review
LaS, Langage et Société
LATR, Latin-American Theatre Review
LatT, Latin Teaching, Shrewsbury
LB, Leuvense Bijdragen
LBer, Linguistische Berichte
LBIYB, Leo Baeck Institute Year Book
LBR, Luso-Brazilian Review
LC, Letture Classensi
LCC, Léachtaí Cholm Cille
LCh, Literatura Chilena
LCP, Language and Cognitive Processes
LCrit, Lavoro Critico
LCUTA, Library Chronicle of the University of Texas at Austin
LD, Libri e Documenti
LDan, Lectura Dantis
LDanN, Lectura Dantis Newberryana

LDGM, Ligam-DiGaM. Quadèrn de lingüística e lexicografía gasconas, Fontenay aux Roses
LE, Language and Education
LEA, Lingüística Española Actual
LebS, Lebende Sprachen
LenP, Ленинградская панорама
LetA, Letterature d'America
LetD, Letras de Deusto
LETHB, Laboratoires d'Études Théâtrales de l'Université de Haute-Bretagne. Études et Documents, Rennes
LetMS, Letopis Matice srpske, Novi Sad
LetP, Il Lettore di Provincia
LetS, Letras Soltas
LevT, Levende Talen
LF, Letras Femeninas
LFil, Listy filologické
LFQ, Literature and Film Quarterly
LFQDLLC, Linguistica e Filologia. Quaderni del Dipartimento di Linguistica e Letterature Comparate, Bergamo, Università degli Studi
LGF, Lunder Germanistische Forschungen, Stockholm, Almqvist & Wiksell
LGGL, Literatur in der Geschichte, Geschichte in der Literatur, Cologne–Vienna, Böhlau
LGL, Langs Germanistische Lehrbuchsammlung, Berne, Lang
LGP, Leicester German Poets, Leicester U.P.
LGW, Literaturwissenschaft — Gesellschaftswissenschaft, Stuttgart, Klett
LH, Lingüística Hispánica
LHum, Litteraria Humanitas, Brno
LI, Linguistic Inquiry
LIÅA, Litteraturvetenskapliga institutionen vid Åbo Akademi, Åbo Akademi U.P.
LiB, Literatur in Bayern
LIC, Letteratura Italiana Contemporanea
LiCC, Lien des chercheurs cévenols
LIE, Lessico Intellettuale Europeo, Rome, Ateneo
LiL, Limbă şi Literatură

LiLi, Zeitschrift für Literaturwissenschaft und Linguistik

LingAk, Linguistik Aktuell, Amsterdam, Benjamins

LingBal, Галканско езикознание – Linguistique Balkanique

LingCon, Lingua e Contesto

LingLett, Linguistica e Letteratura

LíngLit, Língua e Literatura, São Paulo

LinLit, Lingüística y Literatura

LINQ, Linq [Literature in North Queensland]

LInv, Linguisticae Investigationes

LiR, Limba Română

LIT, Literature Interpretation Theory

LIt, Lettera dall'Italia

LitAP, Literární archív Památníku národního písemnictví

LItal, Lettere Italiane

LitB, Literatura, Budapest

LitC, Littératures Classiques

LitG, Литературная газета, Moscow

LitH, Literature and History

LItL, Letteratura Italiana Laterza, Bari, Laterza

LitL, Literatur für Leser

LitLing, Literatura y Lingüística

LitM, Literární měsíčník

LitMis, Литературна мисъл

LitP, Literature and Psychology

LitR, The Literary Review

LittB, Litteraria, Bratislava

LittK, Litterae, Lauterburg, Kümmerle

LittS, Litteratur og Samfund

LittW, Litteraria, Wrocław

LiU, Література Україна

LJb, Literaturwissenschaftliches Jahrbuch der Görres–Gesellschaft

LK, Literatur-Kommentare, Munich, Hanser

LK, Literatur und Kritik

LKol, Loccumer Kolloquium

LL, Langues et Littératures, Rabat

LlA, Lletres Asturianes

LLC, Literary and Linguistic Computing

LlC, Llên Cymru

LlLi, Llengua i Literatura

LLS, Lenguas, Literaturas, Sociedades. Cuadernos Hispánicos

LLSEE, Linguistic and Literary Studies in Eastern Europe, Amsterdam, Benjamins

LM, Le Lingue del Mondo

LN, Lingua Nostra

LNB, Leipziger namenkundliche Beiträge

LNL, Les Langues Néo-Latines

LNouv, Les Lettres Nouvelles

LoP, Loccumer Protokolle

LOS, Literary Onomastic Studies

LP, Le Livre de Poche, Librairie Générale Française

LP, Lingua Posnaniensis

LPen, Letras Peninsulares

LPh, Linguistics and Philosophy

LPLP, Language Problems and Language Planning

LPO, Lenga e Païs d'Oc, Montpellier

LPr, Linguistica Pragensia

LQ, Language Quarterly, University of S. Florida

LR, Linguistische Reihe, Munich, Hueber

LR, Les Lettres Romanes

LRev, Linguistic Review

LRI, Libri e Riviste d'Italia

LS, Literatur als Sprache, Münster, Aschendorff

LS, Lingua e Stile

LSa, Lusitania Sacra

LSc, Language Sciences

LSil, Linguistica Silesiana

LSNS, Lundastudier i Nordisk Språkvetenskap

LSo, Language in Society

LSp, Language and Speech

LSPS, Lou Sourgentin/La Petite Source. Revue culturelle bilingue nissart-français, Nice

LSty, Language and Style

LSW, Ludowa Spółdzielnia Wydawnicza

LTG, Literaturwissenschaft, Theorie und Geschichte, Frankfurt, Lang

ŁTN, Łódzkie Towarzystwo Naukowe

LTP, Laval Théologique et Philosophique

Humanismusforschung,
Weinheim, Acta Humaniora
MKNAWL, Mededelingen der
Koninklijke Nederlandse
Akademie van Wetenschappen,
Afd. Letterkunde, Amsterdam
ML, Mediaevalia Lovaniensia,
Leuven U.P.
ML, Modern Languages
MLAIntBibl, Modern Language
Association International
Bibliography
MLIÅA, Meddelanden utgivna av
Litteraturvetenskapliga
institutionen vid Åbo Akademi,
Åbo Akademi U.P.
MLIGU, Meddelanden utgivna av
Litteraturvetenskapliga vid
Göteborgs universitet,
Gothenburg U.P.
MLit, Мастацкая літаратура
MLit, Miesięcznik Literacki
MLJ, Modern Language Journal
MLN, Modern Language Notes
MLQ, Modern Language Quarterly
MLR, Modern Language Review
MLS, Modern Language Studies
MM, Maal og Minne
MMS, Münstersche Mittelalter-
Schriften, Munich, Fink
MN, Man and Nature. L'Homme et
la Nature
MNGT, Manchester New German
Texts, Manchester U.P.
ModD, Modern Drama
ModS, Modern Schoolman
MoL, Modellanalysen: Literatur,
Paderborn, Schöningh–Munich,
Fink
MON, Ministerstwo Obrony
Narodowej, Warsaw
MosR, Московский рабочий
MoyFr, Le Moyen Français
MP, Modern Philology
MQ, Mississippi Quarterly
MQR, Michigan Quarterly Review
MR, Die Mainzer Reihe, Mainz,
Hase & Koehler
MR, Medioevo e Rinascimento
MRev, Maghreb Review
MRo, Marche Romane
MRS, Medieval and Renaissance
Studies

MRTS, Medieval and Renaissance
Texts and Studies, Binghamton,
NY, Renaissance Society of
America
MS, Marbacher Schriften,
Stuttgart, Cotta
MS, Moderna Språk
MSC, Medjunarodni slavistički
centar, Belgrade
MSG, Marburger Studien zur
Germanistik, Marburg, Hitzeroth
MSISS, Materiali della Socièta
Italiana di Studi sul Secolo XVIII
MSL, Marburger Studien zur
Literatur, Marburg, Hitzeroth
MSLKD, Münchener Studien zur
literarischen Kultur in
Deutschland, Frankfurt, Lang
MSMS, Middeleeuse Studies —
Medieval Studies, Johannesburg
MSNH, Mémoires de la Société
Néophilologique de Helsinki
MSp, Moderne Sprachen
(Zeitschrift des Verbandes der
österreichischen Neuphilologen)
MSSp, Münchener Studien zur
Sprachwissenschaft, Munich
MTCGT, Methuen's Twentieth-
Century German Texts, London,
Methuen
MTG, Mitteilungen zur
Theatergeschichte der
Goethezeit, Bonn, Bouvier
MTNF, Monographien und Texte
zur Nietzsche-Forschung, Berlin,
New York — de Gruyter
MTU, Münchener Texte und
Untersuchungen zur deutschen
Literatur des Mittelalters,
Tübingen, Niemeyer
MTUB, Mitteilungen der T. U.
Braunschweig
MUP, Manchester University Press
MusL, Music and Letters
MusP, Museum Patavinum
MyQ, Mystics Quarterly

NA, Nuova Antologia
NAFMUM, Nuovi Annali della
Facoltà di Magistero
dell'Università di Messina
NArg, Nuovi Argomenti

NAS, Nouveaux Actes Sémiotiques, PULIM, Université de Limoges
NASNCGL, North American Studies in Nineteenth-Century German Literature, Berne, Lang
NASSAB, Nuovi Annali della Scuola Speciale per Archivisti e Bibliotecari
NAWG, Nachrichten der Akademie der Wissenschaften zu Göttingen, phil.-hist. Kl., Göttingen, Vandenhoeck & Ruprecht
NBGF, Neue Beiträge zur George-Forschung
NC, New Criterion
NCA, Nouveaux Cahiers d'Allemand
NCEFRW, Nouvelles du Centre d'études francoprovençales 'René Willien'
NCF, Nineteenth-Century Fiction
NCFS, Nineteenth-Century French Studies
NCo, New Comparison
NCSRLL, North Carolina Studies in the Romance Languages and Literatures, Chapel Hill
ND, Наукова думка
NDH, Neue deutsche Hefte
NdJb, Niederdeutsches Jahrbuch
NDL, Nachdrucke deutscher Literatur des 17. Jahrhunderts, Berne, Lang
NDL, Neue deutsche Literatur
NdS, Niederdeutsche Studien, Cologne, Böhlau
NDSK, Nydanske Studier og almen kommunikationsteori
NdW, Niederdeutsches Wort
NE, Nueva Estafeta
NEL, Nouvelles Éditions Latines, Paris
NFF, Novel: A Forum in Fiction
NFS, Nottingham French Studies
NFT, Német Filológiai Tanulmányok. Arbeiten zur deutschen Philologie
NG, Nordistica Gothoburgensia
NGC, New German Critique
NGFH, Die Neue Gesellschaft/Frankfurter Hefte
NGR, New German Review
NGS, New German Studies, Hull
NH, Nuevo Hispanismo

NHi, Nice Historique
NHLS, North Holland Linguistic Series, Amsterdam
NHVKSG, Neujahrsblatt des Historischen Vereins des Kantons St Gallen
NI, Наука и изкуство
NIMLA, NIMLA. Journal of the Modern Language Association of Northern Ireland
NJ, Naš jezik
NJL, Nordic Journal of Linguistics
NKT, Norske klassiker-tekster, Bergen, Eide
NL, Nouvelles Littéraires
NLÅ, Norsk Litterær Årbok
NLD, Nuove Letture Dantesche
NLH, New Literary History
NLi, Notre Librairie
NLLT, Natural Language and Linguistic Theory
NLN, Neo-Latin News
NLT, Norsk Lingvistisk Tidsskrift
NLWJ, National Library of Wales Journal
NM, Народна младеж
NMi, Neuphilologische Mitteilungen
NMS, Nottingham Medieval Studies
NN, Наше наследие
NNH, Nueva Narrativa Hispano-americana
NOR, New Orleans Review
NORNA, Nordiska samarbetskommittén för namnforskning, Uppsala
NovE, Novos Estudos (CEBRAP)
NovM, Новый мир
NovR, Nova Renascenza
NOWELE, North-Western European Language Evolution. Nowele
NP, Народна просвета
NQ, Notes and Queries
NR, New Review
NŘ, Naše řeč
NRE, Nuova Rivista Europea
NRF, Nouvelle Revue Française
NRFH, Nueva Revista de Filología Hispánica
NRL, Neue russische Literatur. Almanach, Salzburg
NRLett, Nouvelles de la République des Lettres

NRMI, Nuova Rivista Musicale Italiana
NRO, Nouvelle Revue d'Onomastique
NRP, Nouvelle Revue de Psychanalyse
NRS, Nuova Rivista Storica
NRSS, Nouvelle Revue du Seizième Siècle
NRu, Die Neue Rundschau
NS, Die Neueren Sprachen
NSc, New Scholar
NSh, Начальная школа
NSL, Det Norske Språk- og Litteraturselskap
NSlg, Neue Sammlung
NSo, Наш современник . . . Альманах
NSP, Nuovi Studi Politici
NSS, Nysvenska Studier
NSt, Naše stvaranje
NT, Навука і тэхніка
NT, Nordisk Tidskrift
NTBB, Nordisk Tidskrift för Bok- och Biblioteksväsen
NTC, Nuevo Texto Crítico
NTE, Народна творчість та етнографія
NTg, Nieuwe Taalgids
NTQ, New Theatre Quarterly
NTSh, Наукове товариство ім. Шевченка
NTW, News from the Top of the World: Norwegian Literature Today
NU, Narodna umjetnost
NV, Новое время
NVS, New Vico Studies
NWIG, Niewe West-Indische Gids
NyS, Nydanske Studier/Almen Kommunikationsteori
NYSNDL, New Yorker Studien zur neueren deutschen Literaturgeschichte, Berne, Lang
NYUOS, New York University Ottendorfer Series, Berne, Lang
NZh, Новый журнал
NZh (StP), Новый журнал, St Petersburg
NZJFS, New Zealand Journal of French Studies

NZSJ, New Zealand Slavonic Journal

OA, Отечественные архивы
OB, Ord och Bild
OBS, Osnabrücker Beiträge zur Sprachtheorie, Oldenbourg, OBST
OBTUP, Universitetsforlaget Oslo–Bergen–Tromsø
ÖBV, Österreichischer Bundesverlag, Vienna
OC, Œuvres et Critiques
OcL, Oceanic Linguistics
OCP, Orientalia Christiana Periodica, Rome
OCS, Occitan/Catalan Studies
ÖGL, Österreich in Geschichte und Literatur
OGS, Oxford German Studies
OH, Ottawa Hispánica
OIU, Oldenbourg Interpretationen mit Unterrichtshilfen, Munich, Oldenbourg
OL, Orbis Litterarum
OLR, Oxford Literary Review
OLSI, Osservatorio Linguistico della Svizzera italiana
OM, L'Oc Médiéval
ON, Otto/Novecento
OPBS, Occasional Papers in Belarusian Studies
OPEN, Oficyna Polska Encyklopedia Nezależna
OPI, Overseas Publications Interchange, London
OPL, Osservatore Politico Letterario
OPM, 'Ou Païs Mentounasc': Bulletin de la Société d'Art et d'Histoire du Mentonnais, Menton
OPRPNZ, Общество по распространению политических и научных знаний
OPSLL, Occasional Papers in Slavic Languages and Literatures
OR, Odrodzenie i Reformacja w Polsce
ORP, Oriental Research Partners, Cambridge
OS, 'Oc Sulpic': Bulletin de l'Association Occitane du Québec, Montreal

OSP, Oxford Slavonic Papers
OT, Oral Tradition
OTS, Onderzoeksinstituut voor Taal en Spraak, Utrecht
OUP, Oxford University Press
OUSL, Odense University Studies in Literature
OUSSLL, Odense University Studies in Scandinavian Languages and Literatures, Odense U.P.
OWPLC, Odense Working Papers in Language and Communication
OZ, Onomastický zpravodaj

PA, Présence Africaine
PAf, Politique Africaine
PAGS, Proceedings of the Australian Goethe Society
Pal, Palaeobulgarica — Старобългаристика
PAM, Publicacions de l'Abadia de Montserrat, Barcelona
PAN, Polska Akademia Nauk, Warsaw
PaP, Past and Present
PapBSA, Papers of the Bibliographical Society of America
PAPhS, Proceedings of the American Philosophical Society
PapL, Papiere zur Linguistik
ParL, Paragone Letteratura
PartR, Partisan Review
PaS, Pamiętnik Słowiański
PASJ, Pictish Arts Society Journal
PAX, Instytut Wydawniczy PAX, Warsaw
РВ, Д–р Петър Берон
PBA, Proceedings of the British Academy
PBib, Philosophische Bibliothek, Hamburg, Meiner
PBLS, Proceedings of the Annual Meeting of the Berkeley Linguistic Society
PBML, Prague Bulletin of Mathematical Linguistics
PBSA, Publications of the Bibliographical Society of America
PC, Problems of Communism

PCLS, Proceedings of the Chicago Linguistic Society
PCP, Pacific Coast Philology
PD, Probleme der Dichtung, Heidelberg, Winter
PDA, Pagine della Dante
PE, Poesía Española
PEGS(NS), Publications of the English Goethe Society (New Series)
PenP, Il Pensiero Politico
PerM, Perspectives Médiévales
PEs, Lou Prouvençau à l'Escolo
PF, Présences Francophones
PFil, Prace Filologiczne
PFPS, Z problemów frazeologii polskiej i słowiańskiej, ZNiO
PFSCL, Papers on French Seventeenth Century Literature
PG, Païs gascons
PGA, Lo pais gascon/Lou pais gascoun, Anglet
PGIG, Publikationen der Gesellschaft für interkulturelle Germanistik, Munich, Iudicium
PH, La Palabra y El Hombre
PhilosQ, Philosophical Quarterly
PhilP, Philological Papers, West Virginia University
PhilR, Philosophy and Rhetoric
PhilRev, Philosophical Review
PhLC, Phréatique, Langage et Création
PHol, Le Pauvre Holterling
PhonPr, Phonetica Pragensia
PhP, Philologica Pragensia
PhR, Phoenix Review
PHSL, Proceedings of the Huguenot Society of London
PI, педагогическиб институт
PId, Le Parole e le Idee
PIGS, Publications of the Institute of Germanic Studies, University of London
PiH, Il Piccolo Hans
PIMA, Proceedings of the Illinois Medieval Association
PIW, Państwowy Instytut Wydawniczy, Warsaw
PJ, Poradnik Językowy
PLing, Papers in Linguistics
PLit, Philosophy and Literature
PLL, Papers on Language and Literature

PL(L), Pamiętnik Literacki, London
PLRL, Patio de Letras/La Rosa als
Llavis
PLS, Přednášky z běhu Letní školy
slovanských studií
PL(W), Pamiętnik Literacki,
Warsaw
PM, Pleine Marge
PMH, Portugaliae Monumenta
Historica
PMHRS, Papers of the Medieval
Hispanic Research Seminar,
London, Department of Hispanic
Studies, Queen Mary and
Westfield College
PMLA, Publications of the Modern
Language Association of America
PMPA, Publications of the Missouri
Philological Association
PN, Paraulas de novelum, Périgueux
PNCIP, Plurilinguismo. Notizario
del Centro Internazionale sul
Plurilinguismo
PNR, Poetry and Nation Review
PNUS, Prace Naukowe
Uniwersytetu Śląskiego,
Katowice
PoetT, Poetics Today
PolR, Polish Review
PortSt, Portuguese Studies
PP, Prace Polonistyczne
PPNCFL, Proceedings of the Pacific
Northwest Conference on
Foreign Languages
PPr, Papers in Pragmatics
PPU, Promociones y Publicaciones
Universitarias, S.A., Barcelona
PQ, The Philological Quarterly
PR, Podravska Revija
PrA, Prouvenço aro, Marseilles
PraRu, Prace Rusycystyczne
PRF, Publications Romanes et
Françaises, Geneva, Droz
PRH, Pahl-Rugenstein
Hochschulschriften, Cologne,
Pahl–Rugenstein
PrH, Provence Historique
PrHlit, Prace Historycznoliterackie
PrHum, Prace Humanistyczne
PRIA, Proceedings of the Royal
Irish Academy
PrIJP, Prace Instytutu Języka
Polskiego

Prilozi, Prilozi za književnost, jezik,
istoriju i folklor, Belgrade
PrilPJ, Prilozi proučavanju jezika
PrLit, Prace Literackie
PRom, Papers in Romance
PrRu, Przegląd Rusycystyczny
PrzH, Przegląd Humanistyczny
PrzW, Przegląd Wschodni
PS, Проблеми слов'янознавства
PSCL, Papers and Studies in
Contrastive Linguistics
PSE, Prague Studies in English
PSGAS, Politics and Society in
Germany, Austria and
Switzerland
PSLu, Pagine Storiche Luganesi
PSML, Prague Studies in
Mathematical Linguistics
PSQ, Philologische Studien und
Quellen, Berlin, Schmidt
PSRL, Полное собрание русских
летописей
PSS, Z polskich studiów
slawistycznych, Warsaw, PWN
PSSLSAA, Procès-verbaux des
séances de la Société des Lettres,
Sciences et Arts de l'Aveyron
PSV, Polono-Slavica Varsoviensia
PT, Pamiętnik Teatralny
PUC, Pontifícia Universidade
Católica, São Paulo
PUF, Presses Universitaires de
France, Paris
PUMRL, Purdue University
Monographs in Romance
Languages, Amsterdam —
Philadelphia, Benjamins
PUStE, Publications de l'Université
de St Étienne
PW, Poetry Wales
PWN, Państwowe Wydawnictwo
Naukowe, Warsaw, etc

QALT, Quaderni dell'Atlante
Lessicale Toscano
QCFLP, Quaderni del Circolo
Filologico Linguistico Padovano
QDLC, Quaderni del Dipartimento
di Linguistica, Università della
Calabria
QDLF, Quaderni del Dipartimento
di Linguistica, Università degli
Studi, Firenze

QDLLSMG, Quaderni del
Dipartimento di Lingue e
Letterature Straniere Moderne,
Università di Genova
QDSL, Quellen zur deutschen
Sprach- und Literaturgeschichte,
Heidelberg, Winter
QFCC, Quaderni della Fondazione
Camillo Caetani, Rome
QFESM, Quellen und Forschungen
zur Erbauungsliteratur des späten
Mittelalters und der frühen
Neuzeit, Amsterdam, Rodopi
QFGB, Quaderni di Filologia
Germanica della Facoltà di
Lettere e Filosofia dell'Università
di Bologna
QFIAB, Quellen und Forschungen
aus italienischen Archiven und
Bibliotheken
QFLK, Quellen und Forschungen
zur Literatur- und
Kulturgeschichte, Berlin, de
Gruyter
QFLR, Quaderni di Filologia e
Lingua Romanze, Università di
Macerata
QFSK, Quellen und Forschungen
zur Sprach- und Kulturge-
schichte der germanischen
Völker, Berlin, de Gruyter
QI, Quaderni d'Italianistica
QIA, Quaderni Ibero-Americani
QIGC, Quaderni dell'Istituto di
Glottologia, Università degli
Studi 'G. D'Annunzio' di Chieti,
Facoltà di Lettere e Filosofia
QIICM, Quaderni dell'Istituto
Italiano de Cultura, Melbourne
QILLSB, Quaderni dell'Istituto di
Lingue e Letterature Straniere
della Facoltà di Magistero
dell'Università degli Studi di Bari
QILUU, Quaderni dell'Istituto di
Linguistica dell'Università di
Urbino
QINSRM, Quaderni dell'Istituto
Nazionale di Studi sul
Rinascimento Meridionale
QJMFL, A Quarterly Journal in
Modern Foreign Literatures
QJS, Quarterly Journal of Speech,
Speech Association of America

QLII, Quaderni di Letterature
Iberiche e Iberoamericane
QLL, Quaderni di Lingue e
Letterature, Verona
QLLSP, Quaderni di Lingua e
Letteratura Straniere, Facoltà di
Magistero, Università degli Studi
di Palermo
QLO, Quasèrns de Lingüistica
Occitana
QM, Quaderni Milanesi
QMed, Quaderni Medievali
QP, Quaderns de Ponent
QPet, Quaderni Petrarcheschi
QPL, Quaderni Patavini di
Linguistica
QQ, Queen's Quarterly, Kingston,
Ontario
QRCDLIM, Quaderni di Ricerca,
Centro di Dialettologia e
Linguistica Italiana di
Manchester
QRP, Quaderni di Retorica e
Poetica
QS, Quaderni di Semantica
QSF, Quaderni del Seicento
Francese
QSGLL, Queensland Studies in
German Language and
Literature, Berne, Francke
QSt, Quaderni Storici
QStef, Quaderni Stefaniani
QSUP, Quaderni per la Storia
dell'Università di Padova
QT, Quaderni di Teatro
QuF, Québec français
QuS, Quebec Studies
QV, Quaderni del Vittoriale
QVen, Quaderni Veneti
QVer, Quaderni Veronesi di
Filologia, Lingua e Letteratura
Italiana

RA, Romanistische Arbeitshefte,
Tübingen, Niemeyer
RA, Revista Agustiniana
RAA, Rendiconti dell'Accademia di
Archeologia, Lettere e Belle Arti
RABM, Revista de Archivos,
Bibliotecas y Museos
RAct, Regards sur l'Actualité
Rad, Rad Jugoslavenske akademije
znanosti i umjetnosti

RAE, Real Academia Española
RAfL, Research in African
Literatures
RAL, Revista Argentina de
Lingüística
RAN, Regards sur l'Afrique du Nord
RAPL, Revista da Academia
Paulista de Letras, São Paulo
RAR, Renaissance and Reformation
RAS, Rassegna degli Archivi di
Stato
RB, Revue Bénédictine
RBC, Research Bibliographies and
Checklists, London, Grant &
Cutler
RBDSL, Regensburger Beiträge zur
deutschen Sprach- und
Literaturwissenschaft, Frankfurt–
Berne, Lang
RBG, Reclams de Bearn et
Gasconha
RBGd, Rocznik Biblioteki Gdańskiej
PAN (Libri Gedanenses)
RBKr, Rocznik Biblioteki PAN w
Krakowie
RBL, Revista Brasileira de
Lingüística
RBLL, Revista Brasileira de Lingua
e Literatura
RBN, Revista da Biblioteca
Nacional
RBPH, Revue Belge de Philologie et
d'Histoire
RC, Le Ragioni Critiche
RCat, Revista de Catalunya
RČAV, Rozpravy Československé
akademie věd, Prague, ČSAV
RCB, Revista de Cultura Brasileña
RCCM, Rivista di Cultura Classica e
Medioevale
RCEH, Revista Canadiense de
Estudios Hispánicos
RCEN, Revue Canadienne d'Études
Néerlandaises
RCF, Review of Contemporary
Fiction
RCL, Revista Chilena de Literatura
RCLL, Revista de Crítica Literaria
Latino-Americana
RCo, Revue de Comminges
RCSF, Rivista Critica di Storia della
Filosofia
RCVS, Rassegna di Cultura e Vita
Scolastica

RD, Revue drômoise: archéologie,
histoire, géographie
RDE, Recherches sur Diderot et sur
l'Encyclopédie'
RDM, Revue des Deux Mondes
RDsS, Recherches sur le XVIIe
Siècle
RDTP, Revista de Dialectología y
Tradiciones Populares
RE, Revista de Espiritualidad
REC, Revista de Estudios del Caribe
RedLet, Red Letters
REE, Revista de Estudios
Extremeños
REEI, Revista del Instituto Egipcio
de Estudios Islámicos, Madrid
REH, Revista de Estudios
Hispánicos, Washington
University, St Louis
REHisp, Revista de Estudios
Hispánicos, Puerto Rico
REI, Revue des Études Italiennes
REJ, Revista de Estudios de
Juventud
REL, Revue des Études Latines
RELA, Revista Española de
Lingüística Aplicada
RelCL, Religion in Communist
Lands
RELI, Rassegna Europea di
Letteratura Italiana
RELing, Revista Española de
Lingüística, Madrid
RelLit, Religious Literature
ReMS, Renaissance and Modern
Studies
RenD, Renaissance Drama
RenP, Renaissance Papers
RenR, Renaissance and Reformation
RenS, Renaissance Studies
RES, Review of English Studies
RESEE, Revue des Études Sud-Est
Européennes
RESS, Revue Européenne des
Sciences Sociales et Cahiers
Vilfredo Pareto
RevA, Revue d'Allemagne
RevAl, Revista de l'Alguer
RevAR, Revue des Amis de Ronsard
RevAuv, Revue d'Auvergne,
Clermont-Ferrand
RevF, Revista de Filología
RevHA, Revue de la Haute-
Auvergne

RevG, Revista de Girona
RevIb, Revista Iberoamericana
RevL, Revista Lusitana
RevLM, Revista de Literatura Medieval
RevLR, Revista do Livro
RevO, La Revista occitana, Montpellier
RevPF, Revista Portuguesa de Filosofia
RevR, Revue Romane
RF, Romanische Forschungen
RFe, Razón y Fe
RFE, Revista de Filología Española
RFHL, Revue Française d'Histoire du Livre
RFLSJ, Revista de Filosofía y Lingüística de San José, Costa Rica
RFLUL, Revista da Faculdade de Letras da Universidade de Lisboa
RFLUP, Revista da Faculdade de Letras da Universidade do Porto
RFN, Rivisti di Filosofia Neoscolastica
RFo, Ricerca Folklorica
RFP, Recherches sur le Français Parlé
RFR, Revista de Filología Románica
RFr, Revue Frontenac
RG, Recherches Germaniques
RGand, Romanica Gandensia
RGCC, Revue du Gévaudan, des Causses et des Cévennes
RGG, Rivista di Grammatica Generativa
RGI, Revue Germanique Internationale
RGL, Reihe Germanistische Linguistik, Tübingen, Niemeyer
RGo, Romanica Gothoburgensia
RH, Reihe Hanser, Munich, Hanser
RH, Revue Hebdomadaire
RHA, Revista de Historia de America
RHAM, Revue Historique et Archéologique du Maine
RHCS, Rocznik Historii Czasopiśmiennictwa Polskiego
RHDFE, Revue Historique de Droit Français et Étranger
RHE, Revue d'Histoire Ecclésiastique

RHEF, Revue d'Histoire de l'Église de France
RHel, Romanica Helvetica, Tübingen and Basle, Francke
RHFB, Rapports — Het Franse Boek
RHI, Revista da Historia das Ideias
RHis, Revue Historique
RHL, Reihe Hanser Literaturkommentare, Munich, Hanser
RHLF, Revue d'Histoire Littéraire de la France
RHLP, Revista de História Literária de Portugal
RHM, Revista Hispánica Moderna
RHMag, Revue d'Histoire Maghrébine
RHMC, Revue d'Histoire Moderne et Contemporaine
RHPR, Revue d'Histoire et de Philosophie Religieuses
RHR, Réforme, Humanisme, Renaissance
RHRel, Revue de l'Histoire des Religions
RHS, Revue Historique de la Spiritualité
RHSc, Revue d'Histoire des Sciences
RHSt, Ricarda Huch. Studien zu ihrem Leben und Werk
RHT, Revue d'Histoire du Théâtre
RHTe, Revue d'Histoire des Textes
RI, Rassegna Iberistica
RIA, Rivista Italiana di Acustica
RIa, Русский язык
RIAB, Revista Interamericana de Bibliografía
RIaR, Русский язык за рубежом
RICC, Revue Itinéraires et Contacts de Culture
RicSl, Ricerche Slavistiche
RID, Rivista Italiana di Dialettologia
RIE, Revista de Ideas Estéticas
RIEB, Revista do Instituto de Estudos Brasileiros
RIL, Rendiconti dell'Istituto Lombardo
RILA, Rassegna Italiana di Linguistica Applicata
RILCE, Revista del Instituto de Lengua y Cultura Españoles

RILP, Revista Internacional da
Língua Portuguesa
RIM, Rivista Italiana di Musicologia
RIndM, Revista de Indias
RInv, Revista de Investigación
RIO, Revue Internationale
d'Onomastique
RIOn, Rivista Italiana di
Onomastica
RIP, Revue Internationale de
Philosophie
RIS, Revue de l'Institute de
Sociologie, Université Libre,
Brussels
RiS, Ricerche Storiche
RITL, Revista de Istorie şi Teorie
Literară, Bucharest
RivF, Rivista di Filosofia
RivL, Rivista di Linguistica
RJ, Romanistisches Jahrbuch
RKHlit, Rocznik Komisji
Historycznoliterackiej PAN
RKJŁ, Rozprawy Komisji Językowej
Łódzkiego Towarzystwa
Naukowego
RKJW, Rozprawy Komisji
Językowej Wrocławskiego
Towarzystwa Naukowego
RLA, Romance Languages Annual
RLaR, Revue des Langues Romanes
RLB, Recueil Linguistique de
Bratislava
RLC, Revue de Littérature
Comparée
RLD, Revista de Llengua i Dret
RLet, Revista de Letras
RLettI, Rivista di Letteratura
Italiana
RLF, Revista de Literatura
Fantástica
RLFRU, Recherches de Linguistique
Française et Romane d'Utrecht
RLH, Revista de Literatura
Hispanoamericana
RLI, Rassegna della Letteratura
Italiana
RLib, Rivista dei Libri
RLing, Russian Linguistics
RLiR, Revue de Linguistique
Romane
RLit, Revista de Literatura
RLJ, Russian Language Journal

RLLCGV, Revista de Lengua y
Literatura Catalana, Gallega y
Vasca, Madrid
RLLR, Romance Literature and
Linguistics Review
RLM, Revista de Literaturas
Modernas, Cuyo
RLMC, Rivista di Letterature
Moderne e Comparate
RLMed, Revista de Literatura
Medieval
RLMod, Revue des Lettres
Modernes
RLModCB, Revue des Lettres
Modernes. Carnets
Bibliographiques
RLSer, Revista de Literatura Ser,
Puerto Rico
RLSL, Revistă de Lingvistică śi
Ştiinţă Literară
RLT, Russian Literature
Triquarterly
RLTA, Revista de Lingüística
Teórica y Aplicada
RLV, Revue des Langues Vivantes
RM, Romance Monograph Series,
University, Mississippi
RM, Remate de Males
RMAL, Revue du Moyen Âge Latin
RMar, Revue Marivaux
RMH, Recherches sur le Monde
Hispanique au XIXe Siècle
RMM, Revue de Métaphysique et
de Morale
RMRLL, Rocky Mountain Review
of Language and Literature
RMS, Reading Medieval Studies
RNC, Revista Nacional de Cultura,
Carácas
RNDWSPK, Rocznik Naukowo-
Dydaktyczny WSP w Krakowie
RO, Revista de Occidente
RoczH, Roczniki Humanistyczne
Katolickiego Uniw. Lubelskiego
RoczSl, Rocznik Slawistyczny
ROl, Rossica Olomucensia
RoM, Rowohlts Monographien,
Reinbek, Rowohlt
RomGG, Romanistik in Geschichte
und Gegenwart
ROMM, Revue de L'Occident
Musulman et de la Méditerranée
RoN, Romance Notes
RoQ, Romance Quarterly

RORD, Research Opportunities in
  Renaissance Drama
RoS, Romance Studies
RoSl, Роднае слова
RP, Радянський письменник
RP, Revista de Portugal
RPA, Revue de Phonétique
  Appliquée
RPac, Revue du Pacifique
RPC, Revue Pédagogique et
  Culturelle de l'AVEP
RPF, Revista Portuguesa de
  Filologia
RPFE, Revue Philosophique de la
  France et de l'Étranger
RPh, Romance Philology
RPL, Revue Philosophique de
  Louvain
RPl, Río de la Plata
RPLit, Res Publica Litterarum
RPP, Romanticism Past and Present
RPr, Raison Présente
RPS, Revista Paraguaya de
  Sociologia
RPyr, Recherches pyrénéennes,
  Toulouse
RQ, Renaissance Quarterly
RQL, Revue Québécoise de
  Linguistique
RR, Romanic Review
RRe, Русская речь
RRL, Revue Roumaine de
  Linguistique
RRou, Revue du Rouergue
RS, Reihe Siegen, Heidelberg,
  Winter
RS, Revue de Synthèse
RSC, Rivista di Studi Canadesi
RSCI, Rivista di Storia della Chiesa
  in Italia
RSEAV, Revue de la Société des
  enfants et amis de Villeneuve-de-
  Berg
RSF, Rivista di Storia della Filosofia
RSH, Revue des Sciences Humaines
RSh, Радянська школа
RSI, Rivista Storica Italiana
RSJb, Reinhold Schneider Jahrbuch
RSL, Rusycystyczne Studia
  Literaturoznawcze
RSl, Revue des Études Slaves
RSLR, Rivista di Storia e
  Letteratura Religiose

RSPT, Revue des Sciences
  Philosophiques et Théologiques
RSR, Rassegna Storica del
  Risorgimento
RSSR, Rivista di Storia Sociale e
  Religiosa
RST, Rassegna Storica Toscana
RSt, Research Studies
RStI, Rivista di Studi Italiani
RT, Revue du Tarn
RTAM, Recherches de Théologie
  Ancienne et Médiévale
RTLiM, Rocznik Towarzystwa
  Literackiego im. Adama
  Mickiewicza
RTr, Recherches et Travaux,
  Université de Grenoble
RTUG, Recherches et Travaux de
  l'Université de Grenoble III
RUB, Revue de l'Université de
  Bruxelles
RUC, Revista de la Universidad
  Complutense
RuLit, Ruch Literacki
RUM, Revista de la Universidad de
  Madrid
RUMex, Revista de la Universidad
  de México
RUOt, Revue de l'Université
  d'Ottawa
RUS, Rice University Studies
RusH, Russian History
RusL, Русская литература, ПД,
  Leningrad
RusM, Русская мысль
RusMed, Russia Medievalis
RusR, Russian Review
RUW, Rozprawy Uniwersytetu
  Warsawskiego, Warsaw
RVB, Rheinische Vierteljahrsblätter
RVF, Revista Valenciana de
  Filología
RVi, Revue du Vivarais
RVQ, Romanica Vulgaria Quaderni
RVV, Romanische Versuche und
  Vorarbeiten, Bonn U.P.
RVVig, Reihe der Villa Vigoni,
  Tübingen, Niemeyer
RyF, Razón y Fe
RZLG, Romanistische Zeitschrift für
  Literaturgeschichte
RZSF, Radovi Zavoda za slavensku
  filologiju

SA, Studien zum Althochdeutschen, Göttingen, Vandenhoeck & Ruprecht
SAB, South Atlantic Bulletin
Sac, Sacris Erudiri
SAG, Stuttgarter Arbeiten zur Germanistik, Stuttgart, Heinz
SAH, Studies in American Humour
SANU, Srpska akademija nauka i umetnosti
SAOB, Svenska Akademiens Ordbok
SAQ, South Atlantic Quarterly
SAR, South Atlantic Review
SAS, Studia Academica Slovaca
SaS, Slovo a slovesnost
SASc, Studia Anthroponymica Scandinavica
SATF, Société des Anciens Textes Français
SAV, Slovenská akadémia vied
SAVL, Studien zur allgemeinen und vergleichenden Literaturwissenschaft, Stuttgart, Metzler
SB, Slavistische Beiträge, Munich, Sagner
SB, Studies in Bibliography
SBAW, Sitzungsberichte der Bayerischen Akad. der Wissenschaften, phil.-hist. Kl., Munich, Beck
SBL, Saarbrücker Beiträge zur Literaturwissenschaft, St. Ingbert, Röhrig
SBL, Старобългарска литература
SBR, Swedish Book Review
SBVS, Saga-Book of the Viking Society
SC, Studia Celtica, The Bulletin of the Board of Celtic Studies
SCB, Skrifter utgivna av Centrum för barnkulturforskning, Stockholm U.P.
SCC, Studies in Comparative Communism
SCen, The Seventeenth Century
SCES, Sixteenth Century Essays and Studies, Kirksville, Missouri, Sixteenth Century Journal
SCFS, Seventeenth-Century French Studies
SchG, Schriftsteller der Gegenwart, Berlin, Volk & Wissen

SchSch, Schlern-Schriften, Innsbruck, Wagner
SchwM, Schweizer Monatshefte
SCJ, Sixteenth Century Journal
SCL, Studii și Cercetări Lingvistice
SCl, Stendhal Club
ScL, Scottish Language
ScM, Scripta Mediterranea
SCN, Seventeenth Century News
ScO, Scriptoralia, Tübingen, Narr
SCR, Studies in Comparative Religion
ScRev, Scandinavian Review
ScSl, Scando-Slavica
ScSt, Scandinavian Studies
SD, Sprache und Dichtung, n.F., Berne, Haupt
SD, Современная драматургия.
SdA, Storia dell'Arte
SDFU, Skrifter utgivna genom Dialekt- och folkminnesarkivet i Uppsala
SDG, Studien zur deutschen Grammatik, Tübingen, Narr
SDL, Studien zur deutschen Literatur, Tübingen, Niemeyer
SDLNZ, Studien zur deutschen Literatur des 19. und 20. Jahrhunderts, Berne, Lang
SdO, Serra d'Or
SDOFU, Skrifter utgivna av Dialekt-, ortnamns- och folkminnesarkivet i Umeå
SDS, Studien zur Dialektologie in Südwestdeutschland, Marburg, Elwert
SDSp, Studien zur deutschen Sprache, Tübingen, Narr
SDv, Sprache und Datenverarbeitung
SE, Série Esludos Uberaba
SeC, Scrittura e Civiltà
SECC, Studies in Eighteenth-Century Culture
SEDES, Société d'Éditions d'Enseignement Supérieur
SEEA, Slavic and East European Arts
SEEJ, The Slavic and East European Journal
SEER, Slavonic and East European Review
SEES, Slavic and East European Studies

SEI, Società Editrice
Internazionale, Turin
SELA, South Eastern Latin
Americanist
SEN, Società Editrice Napoletana,
Naples
SEP, Secretaría de Educación
Pública, Mexico
SeS, Serbian Studies
SEz, Съпоставително
езикознание
SF, Slavistische Forschungen,
Cologne — Vienna, Böhlau
SFAIEO, Section Française de
l'Association Internationale
d'Études Occitanes, Montpellier
SFI, Studi di Filologia Italiana
SFIS, Stanford French and Italian
Studies
SFKG, Schriftenreihe der
Franz–Kafka–Gesellschaft,
Vienna, Braumüller
SFL, Studies in French Literature,
London, Arnold
SFL, Studi di Filologia e Letteratura
SFPS, Studia z Filologii Polskiej i
Słowiańskiej PAN
SFR, Stanford French Review
SFr, Studi Francesi
SFRS, Studia z Filologii Rosyjskiej i
Slowiańskiej, Warsaw
SFS, Swiss-French Studies
SFUŠ, Sborník Filozofickej Fakulty
Univerzity P. J. Šafárika, Prešov
SG, Sprache der Gegenwart,
Düsseldorf, Schwann
SGAK, Studien zu Germanistik,
Anglistik und Komparatistik,
Bonn, Bouvier
SGECRN, Study Group on
Eighteenth-Century Russia
Newsletter
SGEL, Sociedad General Española
de Librería
SGesch, Sprache und Geschichte,
Stuttgart, Klett-Cotta
SGF, Stockholmer Germanistische
Forschungen, Stockholm,
Almqvist & Wiksell
SGG, Studia Germanica Gandensia
SGI, Studi di Grammatica Italiana
SGLL, Studies in German
Language and Literature,
Lewiston-Queenston-Lampeter

SGLLC, Studies in German
Literature, Linguistics, and
Culture, Columbia, S.C.,
Camden House, Woodbridge,
Boydell & Brewer
SGP, Studia Germanica
Posnaniensia
SGS, Stanford German Studies,
Berne, Lang
SGS, Scottish Gaelic Studies
SGU, Studia Germanistica
Upsaliensia, Stockholm, Almqvist
& Wiksell
SH, Slavica Helvetica, Berne, Lang
SH, Studia Hibernica
SHAW, Sitzungsberichte der
Heidelberger Akademie der
Wissenschaften, phil.-hist. Klasse,
Heidelberg, Winter
SHCT, Studies in the History of
Christian Thought, Leiden, Brill
SHPF, Société de l'Histoire du
Protestantisme Français
SHPS, Studies in History and
Philosophy of Science
SHR, The Scottish Historical
Review
SI, Sprache und Information,
Tübingen, Niemeyer
SIAA, Studi di Italianistica
nell'Africa Australe
SiCh, Слово і час
SIDES, Société Internationale de
Diffusion et d'Édition
Scientifiques, Antony
SIDS, Schriften des Instituts für
deutsche Sprache, Berlin, de
Gruyter
Siglo XX, Siglo XX/20th Century
SILTA, Studi Italiani di Linguistica
Teorica ed Applicata
SiN, Sin Nombre
SINSU, Skrifter utgivna av
institutionen för nordiska språk
vid Uppsala universitet, Uppsala
U.P.
SIR, Stanford Italian Review
SIsp, Studi Ispanici
SISSD, Società Italiana di Studi sul
Secolo XVIII
SJLŠ, Slovenský jazyk a literatúra v
škole
SkSt, Skandinavistische Studien

SKZ, Srpska Književna Zadruga, Belgrade
SL, Sammlung Luchterhand, Darmstadt, Luchterhand
SL, Studia Linguistica
SLÅ, Svensk Lärarföreningens Årsskrift
SlaG, Slavica Gandensia
SlaH, Slavica Helsingensia
SlaL, Slavica Lundensia
SlavFil, Славянска филология, Sofia
SlavH, Slavica Hierosolymitana
SlavLit, Славянските литератури в България
SlavRev, Slavistična revija
SlaW, Slavica Wratislaviensia
SLeg, Studium Legionense
SLeI, Studi di Lessicografia Italiana
SLESPO, Suplemento Literário do Estado de São Paulo
SLF, Studi di Letteratura Francese
SLG, Studia Linguistica Germanica, Berlin, de Gruyter
SLI, Società di Linguistica Italiana
SLI, Studi Linguistici Italiani
SLIGU, Skrifter utgivna av Litteraturvetenskapliga institutionen vid Göteborgs universitet, Gothenburg U.P.
SLit, Schriften zur Literaturwissenschaft, Berlin, Dunckler & Humblot
SLit, Slovenská literatúra
SLitR, Stanford Literature Review
SLIUU, Skrifter utgivna av Litteraturvetenskapliga institutionen vid Uppsala universitet, Uppsala U.P.
SLK, Schwerpunkte Linguistik und Kommunikationswissenschaft
SLL, Skrifter utg. genom Landsmålsarkivet i Lund
SLM, Studien zur Literatur der Moderne, Bonn, Bouvier
SlN, Slovenský národopis
SLO, Slavica Lublinensia et Olomucensia
SlO, Slavia Orientalis
SlOc, Slavia Occidentalis
SlOth, Slavica Othinensia
SlPN, Slovenské pedagogické nakladateľstvo
SlPoh, Slovenské pohľady

SlPr, Slavica Pragensia
SLPS, Studia Linguistica Polono-Slovaca
SLR, Second Language Research
SLS, Studies in the Linguistic Sciences
SlSb, Slezský sborník
SlSl, Slavica Slovaca
SlSp, Slovenský spisovateľ
SLRev, Southern Literary Review
SLu, Studia Lulliana
SLWU, Sprach und Literatur in Wissenschaft und Unterricht
SM, Sammlung Metzler, Stuttgart, Metzler
SM, Studi Medievali
SMC, Studies in Medieval Culture
SME, Schöninghs mediävistische Editionen, Paderborn, Schöningh
SMer, Студенческий меридиан
SMGL, Studies in Modern German Literature, Berne – Frankfurt – New York, Lang
SMLS, Strathclyde Modern Language Studies
SMRT, Studies in Medieval and Reformation Thought, Leiden, Brill
SMS, Sewanee Medieval Studies
SMu, Советский музей
SMV, Studi Mediolatini e Volgari
SN, Studia Neophilologica
SNL, Sveučilišna naklada Liber, Zagreb
SNM, Sborník Národního muzea
SNov, Seara Nova
SNTL, Státní nakladatelství technické literatury
SÖAW, Sitzungsberichte der Österreichischen Akademie der Wissenschaften, phil.-hist. Klasse
SoCR, South Central Review
SOH, Studia Onomastica Helvetica, Arbon, Eurotext: Historisch-Archäologischer Verlag
SoK, Sprog og Kultur
SopL, Sophia Linguistica, Tokyo
SoRA, Southern Review, Adelaide
SoRL, Southern Review, Louisiana
SOU, Skrifter utgivna genom Ortnamnsarkivet i Uppsala
SP, Sammlung Profile, Bonn, Bouvier

SP, Studies in Philology
SPat, Studi Patavini
SpC, Speech Communication
SPCT, Studi e Problemi di Critica Testuale
SPES, Studio per Edizioni Scelte, Florence
SPFB, Sborník Pedagogické fakulty v Brně
SPFFBU, Sborník prací Filosofické fakulty Brněnské Univerzity
SPFHK, Sborník Pedagogické fakulty, Hradec Králové
SPFO, Sborník Pedagogické fakulty, Ostrava
SPFOl, Sborník Pedagogické fakulty, Olomouc
SPFUK, Sborník Pedagogické fakulty Univerzity Karlovy, Prague
SPGS, Scottish Papers in Germanic Studies, Glasgow
SPh, Studia philologica, Olomouc
SPi, Serie Piper, Munich, Piper
SPIEL, Siegener Periodicum zur Internationalen Empirischen Literaturwissenschaft
SPK, Studia nad polszczyzną kresową, Wrocław
SpLit, Sprache und Literatur
SpMod, Spicilegio Moderno, Pisa
SPN, Státní pedagogické nakladatelství
SPol, Studia Polonistyczne
SPR, Slavistic Printings and Reprintings, The Hague, Mouton
SpR, Spunti e Ricerche
SPRF, Société de Publications Romanes et Françaises, Geneva, Droz
SPS, Specimina Philologiae Slavicae, Munich, Otto Sagner
SPS, Studia Philologica Salmanticensia
SPSO, Studia Polono–Slavica–Orientalia. Acta Litteraria
SpSt, Spanish Studies
SPUAM, Studia Polonistyczna Uniwersytetu Adama Mickiewicza, Poznań
SR, Slovenská reč
SRAZ, Studia Romanica et Anglica Zagrabiensia
SRev, Slavic Review

SRF, Studi e Ricerche Francescane
SRL, Studia Romanica et Linguistica, Frankfurt, Lang
SRLF, Saggi e Ricerche di Letteratura Francese
SRo, Studi Romanzi
SRom, Studi Romeni
SRoP, Studia Romanica Posnaniensia
SRP, Studia Rossica Posnaniensia
SRU, Studia Romanica Upsaliensia
SS, Symbolae Slavicae, Frankfurt–Berne–Cirencester, Lang
SS, Syn og Segn
SSBI, Skrifter utgivna av Svenska barnboksinstitutet
SSB, Strenna Storica Bolognese
SSCJ, Southern Speech Communication Journal
SSDSP, Società Savonese di Storia Patria
SSE, Studi di Storia dell'Educazione
SSF, Studies in Short Fiction
SSFin, Studia Slavica Finlandensia
SSGL, Studies in Slavic and General Linguistics, Amsterdam, Rodopi
SSH, Studia Slavica Academiae Scientiarum Hungaricae
SSL, Studi e Saggi Linguistici
SSLP, Studies in Slavic Literature and Poetics, Amsterdam, Rodopi
SSLS, Studi Storici Luigi Simeoni
SSMP, Stockholm Studies in Modern Philology
SSPHS, Society for Spanish and Portuguese Historical Studies, Millersville
SSS, Stanford Slavic Studies
SSSAS, Society of Spanish and Spanish-American Studies, Boulder, Colorado
SSSlg, Sagners Slavistische Sammlung, Munich, Sagner
SSSN, Skrifter utgivna av Svenska språknämnden
SSSP, Stockholm Studies in Scandinavian Philology
SST, Sprache — System und Tätigkeit, Frankfurt, Lang
SSt, Slavic Studies, Hokkaido
ST, Suhrkamp Taschenbuch, Frankfurt, Suhrkamp

StB, Studi sul Boccaccio
STC, Studies in the Twentieth Century
StCJ, Studia Celtica Japonica
STCL, Studies in Twentieth Century Literature
StCL, Studies in Canadian Literature
StCrit, Strumenti Critici
StD, Studi Danteschi
StF, Studie Francescani
StFil, Studia Filozoficzne
STFM, Société des Textes Français Modernes
StG, Studi Germanici
StGol, Studi Goldoniani
StH, Studies in the Humanities
StI, Studi Italici, Kyoto
StIt, Studi Italiani
StL, Studium Linguistik
StLa, Studies in Language, Amsterdam
StLI, Studi di Letteratura Ispano-Americana
StLIt, Studi Latini e Italiani
StLM, Studies in the Literary Imagination
StLo, Studia Logica
StM, Studies in Medievalism
STM, Suhrkamp Taschenbuch Materialien, Frankfurt, Suhrkamp
STML, Studies on Themes and Motifs in Literature, New York, Lang
StMon, Studia Monastica
StMus, Studie Musicali
StMy, Studia Mystica
StN, Studi Novecenteschi
StNF, Studier i Nordisk Filologi
StO, Studium Ovetense
StP, Studi Piemontesi
StPet, Studi Petrarcheschi
StR, Studie o rukopisech
StRLLF, Studi e Ricerche di Letteratura e Linguistica Francese
StRo, Studi Romani
StRom, Studies in Romanticism
StRu, Studia Russica, Budapest
StS, Studi Storici
StSec, Studi Secenteschi
StSk, Studia Skandinavica
StSet, Studi Settecenteschi

STSL, Studien und Texte zur Sozialgeschichte der Literatur, Tübingen, Niemeyer
StT, Studi Tassiani
STUF, Sprachtypologie und Universalienforschung
StV, Studies on Voltaire and the 18th Century
STW, Suhrkamp Taschenbücher Wissenschaft, Frankfurt, Suhrkamp
StZ, Sprache im technischen Zeitalter
SU, Studi Urbinati
SUBBP, Studia Universitatis Babeş-Bolyai, Philologia, Cluj
SUDAM, Editorial Sudamericana, Buenos Aires
SuF, Sinn und Form
SUP, Spisy University J. E. Purkyně, Brno
SupEz, Съпоставително езикознание, Sofia
SV, Studi Veneziani
SZ, Studia Zamorensia

TAL, Travaux d'Archéologie Limousine, Limoges
TAm, The Americas, Bethesda
TB, Tempo Brasileiro
TBL, Tübinger Beiträge zur Linguistik, Tübingen, Narr
TC, Texto Crítico
TCBS, Transactions of the Cambridge Bibliographical Society
TCERFM, Travaux du Centre d'Études et de Recherches sur François Mauriac, Bordeaux
TCL, Twentieth-Century Literature
TCLN, Travaux du Cercle Linguistique de Nice
TCWAAS, Transactions of the Cumberland and Westmorland Antiquarian and Archaeological Society
TD, Teksty Drugie
TDC, Textes et Documents pour la Classe
TEC, Teresiunum Ephemerides Carmeliticae
TECC, Textos i Estudis de Cultura Catalana, Curial — Publicacions

de l'Abadia de Montserrat,
Barcelona
TeK, Text und Kontext
TELK, Trouvaillen — Editionen
zur Literatur- und
Kulturgeschichte, Berne, Lang
TeN, Terminologies Nouvelles
TeSt, Teatro e Storia
TE(XVIII), Textos y Estudios del
Siglo XVIII
TF, Texte zur Forschung,
Darmstadt, Wissenschaftliche
Buchgesellschaft
TFN, Texte der Frühen Neuzeit,
Frankfurt am Main, Keip
TGLSK, Theorie und Geschichte
der Literatur und der Schönen
Künste, Munich, Fink
TGSI, Transactions of the Gaelic
Society of Inverness
THL, Theory and History of
Literature, Manchester U.P.
THM, Textos Hispánicos
Modernos, Barcelona, Labor
THR, Travaux d'Humanisme et
Renaissance, Geneva, Droz
THSC, Transactions of the
Honourable Society of
Cymmrodorion
TI, Le Texte et l'Idée
TidLit, Tidskrift för
Litteraturvetenskap
TILAS, Travaux de l'Institut
d'Études Latino-Américaines de
l'Université de Strasbourg
TILL, Travaux de l'Institut de
Linguistique de Lund
TJ, Theatre Journal
TK, Text und Kritik, Munich
TKS, Търновска книжевна
школа, Sofia
TL, Theoretical Linguistics
TLF, Textes Littéraires Français,
Geneva, Droz
TLit, Travaux de Littérature
TLP, Travaux de Linguistique et de
Philologie
TLQ, Travaux de Linguistique
Québécoise
TLTL, Teaching Language
Through Literature
TM, Les Temps Modernes
TMJb, Thomas Mann-Jahrbuch
TMo, O Tempo e o Modo

TMS, Thomas Mann–Studien,
Berne, Francke
TN, Theatre Notebook
TNA, Tijdschrift voor Nederlands
en Afrikaans
TNT, Towarzystwo Naukowe w
Toruniu
TODL, Труды Отдела
древнерусской литературы
Института русской
литературы АН СССР
TP, Textual Practice
TPa, Torre de Papel
TPS, Transactions of the
Philological Society
TQ, Theatre Quarterly
TR, Телевидение и
радиовещание
TravL, Travaux de Linguistique,
Luxembourg
TRCTL, Texte-Revue de Critique et
de Théorie Littéraire
TRI, Theatre Research
International
TrK, Трезвость и культура
TrL, Travaux de Linguistique
TrLit, Translation and Literature
TRS, The Transactions of the
Radnorshire Society
TS, Theatre Survey
TSC, Treballs de Sociolingüística
Catalana
TSDL, Tübinger Studien zur
deutschen Literatur, Frankfurt,
Lang
TSJ, Tolstoy Studies Journal
TSL, Trierer Studien zur Literatur,
Frankfurt, Lang
TSLL, Texas Studies in Literature
and Language
TSM, Texte des späten Mittelalters
und der frühen Neuzeit, Berlin,
Schmidt
TsNTL, Tijdschrift voor
Nederlandse Taal- en
Letterkunde
TSRLL, Tulane Studies in
Romance Languages and
Literature
TsSk, Tijdschrift voor
Skandinavistiek
TsSV, Tijdschrift voor de Studie van
de Verlichting

TSWL, Tulsa Studies in Women's Literature

TT, Tekst en Tijd, Nijmegen, Alfa

TT, Travail Théâtral

TTAS, Twayne Theatrical Arts Series, Boston–New York

TTG, Texte und Textgeschichte, Tübingen, Niemeyer

TTr, Terminologie et Traduction

TUGS, Texte und Untersuchungen zur Germanistik und Skandinavistik, Frankfurt, Lang

TVS, Theorie und Vermittlung der Sprache, Frankfurt, Lang

TWAS, Twayne's World Authors Series, Boston–New York

TWQ, Third World Quarterly

UAB, Universitat Autònoma de Barcelona

UAC, Universidad de Antioquia, Colombia

UAM, Uniwersytet Adama Mickiewicza, Poznań

UB, Universal-Bibliothek, Stuttgart, Reclam

UBL, Universal-Bibliothek, Leipzig, Reclam

UCPL, University of California Publications in Linguistics

UCPMP, University of California Publications in Modern Philology

UDL, Untersuchungen zur deutschen Literaturgeschichte, Tübingen, Niemeyer

UDR, University of Dayton Review

UFPB, Universidade Federal da Paraíba

UFRGS, Univ. Federal do Rio Grande do Sul (Brazil)

UFRJ, Universidade Federal do Rio de Janeiro

UFSC, Universidade Federal de Santa Catarina

UGE, Union Générale d'Éditions

UGFP, University of Glasgow French and German Publications

UL, Українське літературознавство, Lvov U.P.

UM, Українська мова і література в школі

UMCS, Uniwersytet Marii Curie-Skłodowskiej, Lublin

UMov, Українське мовазнавство

UNAM, Universidad Nacional Autónoma de Mexico

UNC, Univ. of North Carolina

UNCSGL, University of North Carolina Studies in Germanic Languages and Literatures, Chapel Hill

UNED, Universidad Nacional de Enseñanza a Distancia

UNESP, Universidade Estadual de São Paulo

UNMH, University of Nottingham Monographs in the Humanities

UPP, University of Pennsylvania Press, Philadelphia

UQ, Ukrainian Quarterly

UR, Umjetnost riječi

USCFLS, University of South Carolina French Literature Series

USFLQ, University of South Florida Language Quarterly

USH, Umeå Studies in the Humanities, Stockholm, Almqvist & Wiksell International

USLL, Utah Studies in Literature and Linguistics, Berne, Lang

USP, Universidade de São Paulo

UTB, Uni-Taschenbücher

UTET, Unione Tipografico-Editrice Torinese

UTPLF, Università di Torino, Pubblicazioni della Facoltà di Lettere e Filosofia

UTQ, University of Toronto Quarterly

UVAN, Українська Вільна Академія Наук, Winnipeg

UVWPL, University of Venice Working Papers in Linguistics

UWCASWC, The University of Wales Centre for Advanced Studies in Welsh and Celtic

UZLU, Ученые записки Ленинградского университета

VAM, Vergessene Autoren der Moderne, Siegen U.P.

VAS, Vorträge und Abhandlungen zur Slavistik, Giessen, Schmitz

VASSLOI, Veröffentlichungen der Abteilung für Slavische Sprachen und Literaturen des Osteuropa–

Instituts (Slavistiches Seminar) an
der Freien Universität Berlin
VB, Vestigia Bibliae
VBDU, Веснік Беларускага
дзяржаўнага ўніверсітэта імя
У. І. Леніна. Серыя IV
VCT, Les Voies de la Création
Théâtrale
VDASD, Veröffentlichungen der
Deutschen Akademie für Sprache
und Dichtung, Darmstadt,
Luchterhand
VF, Вопросы философии
VGBIL, Всесоюзная
государственная библиотека
иностранной литературы
VH, Vida Hispánica,
Wolverhampton
VHis, Verba Hispanica
VI, Военно издателество
VI, Voix et Images
VIa, Вопросы языкознания
VIN, Veröffentlichungen des
Instituts für niederländische
Philologie, Erftstadt, Lukassen
ViSH, Вища школа
VIst, Вопросы истории
Vit, Вітчизна
VKP, Всесоюзная книжная
палата
VL, Вопросы литературы
VLet, Voz y Letras
VM, Время и мы, New York —
Paris — Jerusalem
VMKA, Verslagen en Mededelingen,
Koninklijke Academie voor
Nederlandse Taal- en
Letterkunde
VMUF, Вестник Московского
университета. Серия IX,
филология
VMUFil, Вестник Московского
университета. Серия VII,
философия
Voz, Возрождение
VP, Встречи с прошлым, Moscow
VPen, Vita e Pensiero
VR, Vox Romanica
VRKhD, Вестник Русского
христианского движения
VRL, Вопросы русской
литературы
VRM, Volkskultur am Rhein und
Maas

VS, Вопросы семантики
VSAV, Vydavateľstvo Slovenskej
akadémie vied
VSh, Вышэйшая школа
VSh, Визвольний шлях
VSPU, Вестник Санкт-
Петербургского университета
VSSH, Вечерняя средняя школа
VV, Византийский временник
VVM, Vlastivědný věstník moravský
VVSh, Вестник высшей школы
VWGÖ, Verband der
wissenschaftlichen Gesellschaften
Österreichs
VySh, Вища школа
VysSh, Высшая школа
VyV, Verdad y Vida
VZ, Vukova zadužbina, Belgrade

WAB, Wolfenbütteler Arbeiten zur
Barockforschung, Wiesbaden,
Harrassowitz
WADL, Wiener Arbeiten zur
deutschen Literatur, Vienna,
Braumüller
WAGAPH, Wiener Arbeiten zur
germanischen Altertumskunde
und Philologie, Vienna, Halosar
WAiF, Wydawnictwa Artystyczne i
Filmowe, Warsaw
WaT, Wagenbachs
Taschenbücherei, Berlin,
Wagenbach
WB, Weimarer Beiträge
WBDP, Würzburger Beiträge zur
deutschen Philologie, Würzburg,
Königshausen & Neumann
WBG, Wissenschaftliche
Buchgesellschaft, Darmstadt
WBN, Wolfenbütteler Barock-
Nachrichten
WF, Wege der Forschung,
Darmstadt, Wissenschaftliche
Buchgesellschaft
WGCR, West Georgia College
Review
WGY, Women in German Yearbook
WHNDL, Würzburger
Hochschulschriften zur neueren
Deutschen Literaturgeschichte,
Frankfurt, Lang
WHR, The Welsh History Review
WIFS, Women in French Studies

WKJb, Wissenschaftskolleg.
Institute for Advanced Study,
Berlin. Jahrbuch
WL, Wydawnictwo Literackie,
Cracow
WŁ, Wydawnictwo Łódzkie
WLub, Wydawnictwo Lubelskie
WLT, World Literature Today
WM, Wissensliteratur im
Mittelalter, Wiesbaden, Reichert
WNB, Wolfenbütteler Notizen zur
Buchgeschichte
WNT, Wydawnictwa Naukowo-
Techniczne
WoB, Wolfenbütteler Beiträge
WP, Wiedza Powszechna, Warsaw
WPEL, Working Papers in
Educational Linguistics
WPFG, Working Papers in
Functional Grammar,
Amsterdam U.P.
WRM, Wolfenbütteler Renaissance
Mitteilungen
WS, Wort und Sinn
WSA, Wolfenbütteler Studien zur
Aufklärung, Tübingen, Niemeyer
WSiP, Wydawnictwa Szkolne i
Pedagogiczne, Warsaw
WSJ, Wiener Slavistisches Jahrbuch
WSl, Die Welt der Slaven
WSlA, Wiener Slawistischer
Almanach
WSP, Wyższa Szkoła Pedagogiczna
WSp, Word and Spirit
WSPRRNDFP, Wyższa Szkoła
Pedagogiczna w Rzeszowie.
Rocznik Naukowo-Dydaktyczny.
Filologia Polska
WuW, Welt und Wort
WUW, Wydawnictwo Uniwersytetu
Wrocławskiego
WW, Wirkendes Wort
WWAG, Woman Writers in the Age
of Goethe
WWE, Welsh Writing in English. A
Yearbook of Critical Essays
WZHUB, Wissenschaftliche
Zeitschrift der Humboldt-
Universität, Berlin: gesellschafts-
und sprachwissenschaftliche
Reihe
WZPHP, Wissenschaftliche
Zeitschrift der pädagogischen
Hochschule Potsdam.

Gesellschafts- und
sprachwissenschaftliche Reihe
WZUG, Wissenschaftliche
Zeitschrift der Ernst-Moritz-
Arndt- Universität Greifswald
WZUH, Wissenschaftliche
Zeitschrift der Martin-Luther-
Universität Halle-Wittenberg:
gesellschafts- und
sprachwissenschaftliche Reihe
WZUJ, Wissenschaftliche
Zeitschrift der Friedrich-Schiller-
Universität Jena/Thüringen:
gesellschafts-und
sprachwissenschaftliche Reihe
WZUL, Wissenschaftliche
Zeitschrift der Karl Marx
Universität Leipzig: gesellschafts-
und sprachwissenschaftliche
Reihe
WZUR, Wissenschaftliche
Zeitschrift der Universität
Rostock: gesellschafts- und
sprachwissenschaftliche Reihe

YaIS, Yale Italian Studies
YB, Ysgrifau Beirniadol
YCC, Yearbook of Comparative
Criticism
YCGL, Yearbook of Comparative
and General Literature
YDAMEIS, Yearbook of the Dutch
Association for Middle Eastern
and Islamic Studies
YEEP, Yale Russian and East
European Publications, New
Haven, Yale Center for
International and Area Studies
YES, Yearbook of English Studies
YFS, Yale French Studies
YIS, Yearbook of Italian Studies
YJC, Yale Journal of Criticism
YM, Yearbook of Morphology
YPL, York Papers in Linguistics
YR, Yale Review
YSGP, Yearbook. Seminar for
Germanic Philology
YSPS, The Yearbook of the Society
of Pirandello Studies
YWMLS, The Year's Work in
Modern Language Studies

ZÄAK, Zeitschrift für Ästhetik und allgemeine Kunstwissenschaft

ZB, Zeitschrift für Balkanologie

ZBL, Zeitschrift für bayerische Landesgeschichte

ZbS, Zbornik za slavistiku

ZCP, Zeitschrift für celtische Philologie

ZD, Zielsprache Deutsch

ZDA, Zeitschrift für deutsches Altertum und deutsche Literatur

ZDL, Zeitschrift für Dialektologie und Linguistik

ZDNÖL, Zirkular. Dokumentationsstelle für neuere österreichische Literatur

ZDP, Zeitschrift für deutsche Philologie

ZFKPhil, Zborník Filozofickej fakulty Univerzity Komenského. Philologica

ZFL, Zbornik za filologiju i lingvistiku

ZFSL, Zeitschrift für französische Sprache und Literatur

ZGB, Zagreber germanistische Beiträge

ZGer, Zeitschrift für Germanistik

ZGKS, Zeitschrift der Gesellschaft für Kanada-Studien

ZGL, Zeitschrift für germanistische Linguistik

ZGS, Zürcher germanistische Studien, Berne, Lang

ZK, Zeitschrift für Katalanistik

ZL, Zeszyty Literackie, Paris

ZMS(FL), Zbornik Matice srpske za filologiju i lingvistiku

ZMS(KJ), Zbornik Matice srpske za književnost i jezik

ZMS(Sl), Zbornik Matice srpske za slavistiku

ZNiO, Zakład Narodowy im. Ossolińskich, Wrocław

ZnS, Знание — сила

ZNTSh, Записки Наукового товариства ім. Шевченка

ZNUG, Zeszyty Naukowe Uniw. Gdańskiego, Gdańsk

ZNUJ, Zeszyty Naukowe Uniw. Jagiellońskiego, Cracow

ZNWHFR, Zeszyty Naukowe Wydziału Humanistycznego. Filologia Rosyjska

ZNWSPO, Zeszyty Naukowe Wyższej Szkoły Pedagogicznej w Opolu

ZO, Zeitschrift für Ostforschung

ZPŠSlav, Zborník Pedagogickej fakulty v Prešove Univerzity Pavla Jozefa Šafárika v Košiciach-Slavistika, Bratislava

ZR, Zadarska revija

ZRAG, Записки русской академической группы в США

ZRBI, Зборник радова бизантолошког института, Belgrade

ZRL, Zagadnienia Rodzajów Literackich

ZRP, Zeitschrift für romanische Philologie

ZS, Zeitschrift für Sprachwissenschaft

ZSJ, Zápisnik slovenského jazykovedca

ZSK, Ze Skarbca Kultury

ZSL, Zeitschrift für siebenbürgische Landeskunde

ZSl, Zeitschrift für Slawistik

ZSP, Zeitschrift für slavische Philologie

ZSVS, Zborník Spolku vojvodinských slovakistov, Novi Sad

ZT, Здесь и теперь

ZV, Zeitschrift für Volkskunde

ZvV, Звезда востока

ZWL, Zeitschrift für württembergische Landesgeschichte

NAME INDEX

Index — Names

Fabbri, M., 603
Fabián, Z., 481
Fabiano, A., 580
Fabra, P., 382
Fabre, H., 176
Fabre, P. A., 122
Fàbrega Escatllar, V., 394
Fàbregas, X., 404
Fabrizi, A., 577, 578
Facio, B., 515, 516
Facó, A., 469
Faguet, G., 138
Fagundo, A. M., 448
Fahlström, Ö., 974
Fahy, C., 513
Faidherbe, L., 259
Failace, J., 469
Falciani, C., 522
Falcó, J. J., 287
Falcomer, E., 578
Falcone, G., 514
Falconer, G., 176
Falconio, A., 556
Faldbakken, K., 957
Falé, I., 411
Faletti, G., 537
Falileyev, A., 636
Falk, J. D., 846
Falkeid, K., 962
Fall, K., 258
Fallaize, E., 221, 229
Falletti, F., 522
Falster Jakobsen, L., 941
Fanciullo, F., 475, 490
Fanfani, M., 483
Fangen, R., 962
Faninger, K., 831
Fanlo, J.-R., 94, 111, 122
Fanning, U., 613
Fantosme, J., 69
Fantuzzi, M., 483
Fara, A., 538
Farasse, G., 212
Farchadi, A., 218
Farel, G., 89
Farenkia, B. M., 694
Fares, G., 457
Faria, I. H., 408, 421, 422
Faria, N. de, 1029
Fariello, A., 566
Farinella, C., 574
Farinelli, G., 603, 608
Farini, R. F., 616
Faris, W., 446
Farnell, A. F., 246
Farnese (*family*), 525
Farnese, F., 551
Farnetti, M., 585, 619
Farone (*Saint*), 8
Farquhar, S. W., 119

Farrant, T., 165
Farré Capdevila, M. J., 394
Farrell, J., 599, 616
Fasani, R., 605
Fasano, G., 168
Fasano, P., 601
Fasbender, C., 756
Fasciati, L., 617
Fasco, F., 484
Fassbind, B., 898
Fassbinder, R. W., 899
Fassel, L, 625, 626, 629
Fatio, O., 483
Fattori, D., 514
Faucher, E., 1026
Faucher, J., 869
Fauchery, A., 179
Fauchon, A., 247
Fauli, J., 405
Faulkner, W., 206, 233, 294
Faulstich, W., 710
Fauser, M., 786
Faustino, M., 466
Fava, E., 15
Favalier, S., 528
Faverau, F., 650, 652
Fávero, L. L., 407, 420
Favre de Vaugelas, C., 121
Fawcett, P., 210
Faye, G., 219
Fazzini, E., 721
Feal, C., 349, 351, 365, 445
Féal, G., 228
Febrer, A., 282
Febvre, L., 93
Fechner, J.-U., 817, 824
Fedele, A., 511
Federhofer, M.-T., 829
Federici, M., 575
Federico, J., 895
Federle, C., 817
Federlin, W.-L., 821
Fedi, R., 498
Feger, H., 816
Fehr, D. von der, 961
Fehrenbach, R. J., 514
Fehrman, C., 969
Fehrs, J. H., 886
Feichter, V., 769
Feifel, W., 849
Feijoo y Montenegro (*padre*), 315, 320
Feijter, A. de, 936
Feik, C., 701
Fein, G., 872
Feine, A., 685, 753
Feinsilber, A., 156
Feistner, E., 727, 747, 749
Feith, R., 936
Feitsma, A., 913, 920

Felberg-Levitt, M., 84
Feld, H., 772
Feld, L., 877
Feldman, M., 535
Feldweg, H., 685
Feliciano, W., 456
Felip de Malla, 394
Felipe, L., 368
Felix, J., 627
Feliz Carbajal, A., 287
Fellini, F., 366
Fellows, J., 1028
Felten, H., 329, 594
Fénelon, F. de S. de la M., 157, 818
Fenelon, I., 109
Fenlon, I., 512
Fennell, S., 849
Fenner, W., 825
Fenoglio, B., 589, 598
Fenoglio, M., 598, 599
Fenollar, B., 394
Fens, K., 931
Fenster, T., 82
Feo, M., 494, 502, 611
Ferchertne, 666
Ferdinand II of Tyrol (*Duke*), 754, 765
Ferguson, A., 800
Ferguson, F., 152
Ferguson, R., 539
Ferguson, R., 959
Ferlampin-Archer, C., 84
Fernán Caballero, 329, 331, 333
Fernandes, M., 466
Fernández, A. M., 386
Fernández, L., 309
Fernández, L. M., 333
Fernández, M., 449
Fernández, P., 331
Fernández Alvarez, M., 286
Fernández Cabezón, R., 324
Fernández Cifuentes, L., 343
Fernández de Híjar, J., 278
Fernández de Lizardi, J. J., 442–43
Fernández de Moratin, L., 315, 320
Fernández de Moratín, N., 321
Fernández Fernández, J., 287
Fernández-Fernández, R., 455
Fernández Insuela, A., 367
Fernández Marcos, N., 287
Fernández Martínez, D., 375
Fernández Molina, M., 456
Fernández Mosquera, S., 288
Fernández Rei, F., 431, 434
Fernández Rodríguez, M. A., 433
Fernández Tejero, E., 287

36*